DON'T THROW THIS CARD AWAY!
THIS MAY BE REQUIRED FOR YOUR COURSE!

THOMSON ONE Business School Edition

Congratulations!

Your purchase of this NEW textbook includes complimentary access to THOMSON ONE – Business School Edition for Accounting. THOMSON ONE – Business School Edition is a Web-based portal product that provides integrated access to Thomson Financial content for the purpose of financial analysis. This is an educational version of the same financial resources used by Wall Street analysts on a daily basis!

For hundreds of companies, this online resource provides seamless access to:

- **Current and Past Company Data:** Worldscope which includes company profiles, financials and accounting results, market per-share data, annual information, and monthly prices going back to 1980.
- **Financial Analyst Data and Forecasts:** I/B/E/S Consensus Estimates which provides consensus estimates, analyst-by-analyst earnings coverage, and analysts' forecasts.
- **SEC Disclosure Statements:** Disclosure SEC Database which includes company profiles, annual and quarterly company financials, pricing information, and earnings.
- **And More!**

ISBN: 0-324-23304-3

THOMSON
SOUTH-WESTERN

THOMSON ONE
Business School Edition

ACCESS CODE

PP6JNS0PPN2DQ3

HOW TO REGISTER YOUR ACCESS CODE

1. Launch a web browser and go to **http://tabseacct.swlearning.com**
2. Click the "Register" button to enter your access code.
3. Enter your access code **exactly** as it appears here and create a unique User ID, or enter an existing User ID if you have previously registered for a different South-Western product via an access code.
4. When prompted, create a password (or enter an existing password, if you have previously registered for a different product via an access code.) Submit the necessary information when prompted. **Record your User ID and password in a secure location.**
5. Once registered, return to the URL above and select the "Enter" button; have your User ID and password handy.

NOTE: The duration of your access to the product begins when registration is complete.

For technical support, contact 1-800-423-0563 or email **tl.support@thomson.com**

Financial Reporting, Financial Statement Analysis, and Valuation

A Strategic Perspective

Sixth Edition

CLYDE P. STICKNEY
The Signal Companies Professor of Management Emeritus
Tuck School of Business
Dartmouth College

PAUL RICHARD BROWN
Dean, College of Business and Economics
Lehigh University

JAMES M. WAHLEN
Professor of Accounting and
Ford Motor Company Teaching Fellow
Kelley School of Business
Indiana University

THOMSON
SOUTH-WESTERN

Australia · Brazil · Canada · Mexico · Singapore · Spain · United Kingdom · United States

THOMSON

SOUTH-WESTERN

Financial Reporting, Financial Statement Analysis, and Valuation: A Strategic Perspective, Sixth Edition

Clyde P. Stickney, Paul R. Brown, James M. Wahlen

VP/Editorial Director:
Jack W. Calhoun

Publisher:
Rob Dewey

Acquisitions Editor:
Matthew Filimonov

Sr. Developmental Editor:
Craig Avery

Marketing Manager:
Chris McNamee

Sr. Content Project Manager:
Heather Mann

Manager of Technology, Editorial:
Vicky True

Technology Project Editor:
Robin Browning

Web Coordinator:
Karen Schaffer

Manufacturing Coordinator:
Doug Wilke

Production House:
Lachina Publishing Services, Inc.

Printer:
Quebecor World
Taunton, MA

Art Director:
Bethany Casey

Internal Designer:
Beckmeyer Design, Inc.

Cover Designer:
Beckmeyer Design, Inc.

Cover Images:
Getty Images

Library of Congress Control Number:
2006923151

Printed in the United States of America
2 3 4 5 09 08 07 06

ISBN-13: 978-0-324-30295-0
ISBN-10: 0-324-30295-9

For more information about our products, contact us at:

Thomson Learning Academic Resource Center

1-800-423-0563

Thomson Higher Education
5191 Natorp Boulevard
Mason, OH 45040
USA

For our students,
with thanks for permitting us to take the journey with you

For our families, with love,
Kathy, Joan, Emma, Debbie, Jessica, and Jaymie

Preface

The usual goal of financial statement analysis is to value a firm. The effective analysis of a set of financial statements begins with an understanding of (1) the economic characteristics and current conditions of a firm's businesses, and (2) the particular strategies the firm selects to compete in each of these businesses. It then moves to (3) assessing how well the firm's financial statements reflect the economic effects of the firm's decisions and actions. This assessment requires an understanding of the generally accepted accounting principles (GAAP), the procedures that underlie the financial statements, and the appropriate adjustments that the analyst should make to improve the quality of the information provided. Next, the analyst (4) assesses the profitability and risk of the firm in the recent past, using financial statements ratios and other analytical tools, and then (5) forecasts its expected future profitability and risk, incorporating information about expected changes in economics of the firm's industry and the firm's strategies. Finally, the analyst (6) values the firm using various valuation methods. This six-step process forms the conceptual and pedagogical flow for this book.

All textbooks in financial statement analysis include step (4), assessing the profitability and risk of a company. Textbooks differ, however, with respect to their emphases on the other five steps. Consider the following depiction of these steps.

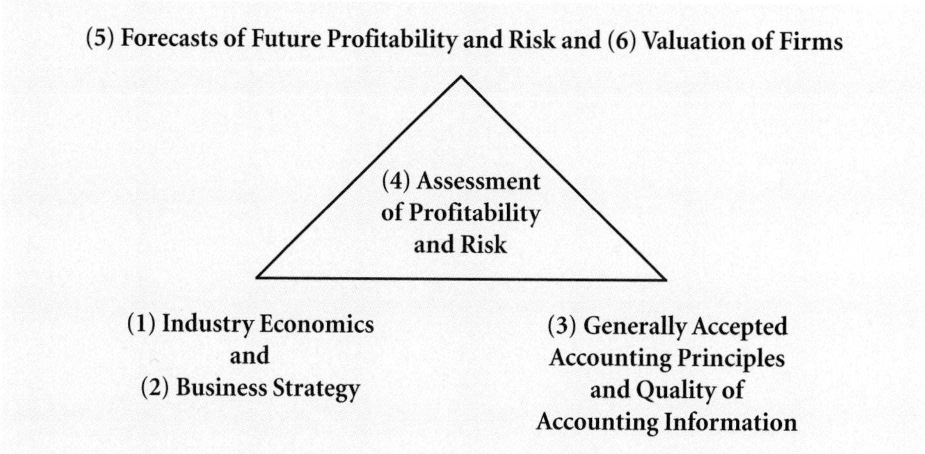

Our view is that these six steps must form an integrated whole for effective and complete financial statement analysis. We have therefore positioned this book so that we provide balanced, integrated coverage of all six elements. We sequence our study by beginning with industry economics and strategy, then moving to consideration of GAAP and the quality of accounting information, and then concluding with forecasting and valuation. We anchor each step in the sequence on the analysis of a firm's profitability and risk, the fundamental drivers of value. We continually relate each part to those preceding and succeeding it to maintain this balanced, integrated perspective.

The premise of this book is that students learn financial statement analysis most effectively by performing the analysis on actual companies. The book's narrative sets forth the important concepts and analytical tools and demonstrates their application using the financial statements of PepsiCo. Each chapter contains a set of questions, exercises, problems and cases based primarily on financial statement data of actual companies. A financial statement analysis package (FSAP) is available to aid in the analytical tasks (discussed later).

MAJOR CHANGES IN THIS EDITION

The next section discusses the content of each chapter and the changes made in this edition. Listed below are the major changes made in this edition that impact all chapters or groups of chapters.

1. The chapters on valuation have been restructured. Chapter 11 contains a discussion of the cost of capital and the dividend-based valuation model. Chapter 12 moves on to valuation using the present values of a firm's cash flows. Chapter 13 focuses on earnings-based valuation models. Chapter 14 considers the use of market multiples of comparable companies.
2. The end of chapter material for each chapter contains portions of an integrative case applying the concepts and tools discussed in that chapter to Starbucks. This series of cases builds on the illustrations in the chapter in which the concepts and tools are applied to PepsiCo.
3. Each chapter now contains approximately ten short questions and exercises. These questions and exercises generally emphasize a single important concept or tool discussed in the chapter.
4. Each chapter contains approximately 25 percent new or substantially revised end-of-chapter material.
5. The Financial Statement Analysis Package (FSAP) available with this book has been substantially revised and made more user friendly.

OVERVIEW OF TEXT

This section describes briefly the content of each chapter, indicating the major changes made since the previous edition.

Chapter 1 Overview of Financial Reporting, Financial Statement Analysis, and Valuation. This chapter introduces the six key interrelated sequential steps in financial statement analysis that serve as an organization structure for this book. It presents several frameworks for understanding the industry economics and business strategy of a firm and applies them to PepsiCo. It also reviews the purpose, underlying concepts, and content of each of the three principal financial statements, including those of non-U.S. companies appearing in a different format. A new section includes key provisions of the Sarbanes-Oxley Act of 2002 that are of particular relevance to the analyst. Another new section discusses the relation between earnings and common share prices and provides the rationale for analyzing financial statements in capital market settings. The appendix presents an extensive discussion to help students do a term project involving the analysis of one or more companies. Our examination of the course syllabi of users of the previous edition indicated that most courses require students to engage in such a project. This appendix should guide students in how to proceed, where to get information, and so on. In addition to the new integrative case involving Starbucks, the chapter includes an updated version of the case from the previous edition involving Nike.

Chapter 2 Asset and Liability Valuation and Income Measurement. This chapter covers three topics we believe our students need to review and reinforce from previous courses before delving into the more complex topics in this book. First, we discuss the link between the valuation of assets and liabilities on the balance sheet and the measurement of income. We believe that students understand topics such as revenue recognition and accounting for marketable securities, derivatives, pensions, and other topics more easily and in greater depth when they examine them from the perspective of both the balance sheet valuation and income measurement. We also examine whether firms should recognize value changes immediately in net income or delay their recognition, sending them temporarily through other comprehensive income. Second, and related to the first, we present a framework for analyzing the dual effects of transactions and other events on the financial statements. This framework relies on the balance sheet equation to trace through these dual effects. Even students that are well grounded in double-entry accounting find this framework helpful in visually identifying the effects of various complex business transactions, such as corporate acquisitions, derivatives, and leases. We use this framework in later chapters as we discuss various GAAP topics. Third, we discuss the measurement of income tax expense, particularly with regard to the treatment of temporary differences between book income and taxable income. Virtually every business transaction has income tax consequences. Delaying consideration of the income tax consequences until later in the text hinders effective coverage of such topics as restructuring charges, asset impairments, depreciation, and leases.

Chapter 3 Income Flows Versus Cash Flows: Key Relationships in the Dynamics of a Business. Chapter 3 reviews the statement of cash flows and presents a model for relating the cash flows from operating, investing, and financing activities to a firm's position in its product life cycle. The chapter demonstrates procedures for preparing the statement of cash flows when a firm provides no cash flow information. A new section discusses EBITDA, earnings before interest, taxes, depreciation, and amortization, and describes the differences between EBITDA and cash flow from operations. A new case (Prime Contractors) illustrates the relation between earnings and cash flows as a firm experiences profitable and unprofitable operations and changes its business strategy.

Chapter 4 Profitability Analysis. This chapter discusses the concepts and tools for analyzing a firm profitability, integrating industry economic and strategic factors that impact the interpretation of financial ratios. It then applies these concepts and tools to the analysis of the profitability of PepsiCo. The analysis of profitability centers on the rate of return on assets and its disaggregated components, the rate of return on common shareholders' equity and its disaggregated components, and earnings per share. The chapter contains a new section on economic value added (EVA) and shows its relation to net income under GAAP. This chapter also considers analytical tools unique to certain industries, such as airlines, service firms, and financial institutions. The integrative case on Starbucks involves analysis of Starbucks in both a time series setting and in a cross section setting in comparison to Panera Bread Company. Another case involves the time series analysis of Wal-Mart Stores and the cross section analysis of its profitability versus Target and Carrefour.

Chapter 5 Risk Analysis. This chapter begins with an expanded discussion of recently required disclosures on the extent to which firms are subject to the risk of changes in commodity prices, exchange rates, and interest rates and how firms manage these risks. This chapter also describes and illustrates the calculation and interpretation of risk ratios and applies them to the financial statements of PepsiCo, focusing on both short-term liquidity risk and long-term solvency risk. We also explore credit risk and bankruptcy risk in greater depth. An important section examines the risk of financial reporting manipulation, illustrating Beneish's multivariate model for identifying potential manipulators. A unique feature of the problems in Chapters 4 and 5 is the linking of the analysis of several companies across the two chapters, including problems involving Hasbro, Abercrombie & Fitch, Coca-Cola, Starbucks, and Wal-Mart. Chapter-end cases involve credit analysis (Massachusetts Stove Company), bankruptcy prediction (Fly-By-Night International Group), and financial reporting manipulation (Millennial Technologies).

Chapter 6 Quality of Accounting Information and Adjustments to Reported Financial Statement Data. This chapter begins with an expanded discussion of the quality of accounting information, emphasizing substantive economic content and earnings persistence as the key characteristics. This discussion sets the stage for the discussion of various GAAP in Chapters 6 to 9. We then consider several financial reporting topics that primarily affect the persistence of earnings, including discontinued operations, extraordinary gains and losses, restructuring charges, and asset impairment charges. New GAAP rules (FASB *Statement No. 154*) for reporting changes in accounting principles are discussed in the chapter. The chapter concludes with a discussion of earnings management, contrasting it with earnings manipulation discussed in Chapter 5. Chapter-end materials include new problems involving GlaxoSmithKline, Parametric Technology, Hewlett Packard, and Wyeth. Chapter-end materials also include an integrative case involving the analysis of profitability and risk of International Paper Company in light of the inclusion of several potentially nonrecurring items in earnings.

Chapter 7 Revenue Recognition and Related Expenses. This chapter discusses various GAAP topics that affect the assessment of a firm's profitability. The chapter begins with an expanded discussion of revenue recognition, incorporating SEC *Staff Accounting Bulletin No. 101,* and applying it to several recent purported reporting abusers, including Hartford Financial Services Group, Wal-Mart, Global Crossing, Quest Communications, and Microstrategy. We then consider GAAP for inventories, fixed assets, and intangible assets. The discussion of intangible assets incorporates FASB *Statement No. 141* and *Statement No. 142.* Several new chapter-end problems explore revenue recognition in greater depth. Cases involve revenue recognition (Arizona Land Development Company), intangibles (Chiron), and changing pricing (ASE Gener S.A.).

Chapter 8 Liability Recognition and Related Expenses. Chapter 8 discusses various GAAP topics that primarily affect the assessment of a firm's risk. The chapter begins with a conceptual discussion of an accounting liability, including an expanded discussion of off-balance sheet financing. We apply the principles for liability recognition to various potential off-balance sheet transactions, including the sale of receivables, product financing, R&D partnerships, and joint ventures. We then explore several GAAP topics in depth, including leases, derivatives, retirement benefits, income taxes, and reserves. The discussion of derivatives incorporates the provisions of FASB *Statement No. 133* and of retirement benefits incorporates the provisions of FASB *Statement No. 132.* Chapter-end materials include updated problems involving Wal-Mart, The GAP, Limited Brands, Ford Motor Credit , Northwest Airlines, Coca-Cola, General Electric, Goodyear, and Boeing, as well as an updated case from the previous edition involving leases and retirement benefits for American Airlines and United Airlines.

Chapter 9 Intercorporate Entities. Chapter 9 examines various GAAP topics that affect many accounts on the financial statements, including corporate acquisitions, investments in securities and consolidated financial statements, and foreign currency translation. The discussion of corporate acquisitions incorporates the provisions of FASB *Statements No. 141* and *142.* The discussion of consolidation policy includes consideration of the treatment of variable interest entities, including special purpose entities and the provisions of FASB *Interpretation No. 46.* A new section in this edition discusses the provisions of FASB *Statement No. 123* and *123 (Revised 2004).* These statements address accounting for stock options and their impact on both financial statement amounts and firm value. New problems relating to stock options involve Eli Lilly & Co, General Electric, and Coca-Cola. The case involving Fisher Corporation illustrates the effects of accounting, tax, and financing decisions on the structure of a corporate acquisition and the related financial statements. The case involving Clark Equipment Company analyzes the effect on the financial statements of various ways of accounting for a joint venture. The case involving Loucks Corporation illustrates the choice of a functional currency and the financial statement impact of alternatives methods of foreign currency translation.

Chapter 10 Forecasting Financial Statements. This chapter describes and illustrates the procedures for preparing forecasted financial statements. This material plays a central role in the valuation of companies, a topic discussed in Chapters 11 to 14. The chapter begins with an overview of forecasting and the importance of creating integrated and articulated financial statement forecasts. It then illustrates the preparation of projected financial statements for PepsiCo. The chapter also demonstrates how to get forecasted balance sheets to balance and how to compute implied statements of cash flows from forecasts of balance sheets and income statements. The chapter also discusses forecast shortcuts analysts sometimes take, and when such forecasts are reliable and when they are not. The Forecast and Forecast Development spreadsheets within FSAP provide templates students can use to develop and build their own financial statement forecasts. Short chapter-end problems illustrate techniques for projecting key accounts for firms like Home Depot, Intel, Hasbro, and Barnes and Noble, determining the cost structure of firms like Nucor Steel and Sony, and dealing with irregular changes in accounts. Longer problems and cases require the preparation of financial statements for cases discussed in earlier chapters involving Wal-Mart and Starbucks. The end-of-chapter material also includes a case involving the projection of financial statements to assist a firm in its strategic decision to add gas stoves to its wood stove line. The problems and cases specify the assumptions students should make to illustrate the preparation procedure. We link and use these longer problems and cases in later chapters that rely on these financial statement forecasts in determining share value estimates for these firms.

Chapter 11 Risk-Adjusted Expected Rates of Return and the Dividends Valuation Approach. Chapters 11 to 14 form a unit in which we explore various approaches to valuing a firm. Chapter 11 is a new chapter that focuses on fundamental issues of valuation that apply to all of the valuation chapters. This chapter provides an extensive discussion of the measurement of the cost of debt and equity capital and the weighted average cost of capital, as well as the dividends-based valuation approach. The chapter also discusses various issues of valuation, including forecasting horizons, projecting long-run continuing dividends, and computing continuing (sometimes called terminal) value. The chapter also describes and illustrates the internal consistency in valuing firms using dividends, free cash flows, or earnings. The chapter also helps students to understand that the different approaches to valuation are simply differences in perspective (dividends capture wealth distribution, free cash flows capture wealth realization in cash, and earning represent wealth creation), and that these approaches should produce internally consistent estimates of value. In this chapter we demonstrate the cost of capital measurements and the dividends-based valuation approach for PepsiCo, using the forecasted amounts from PepsiCo's financial statements discussed in Chapter 10. The chapter also presents techniques for assessing the sensitivity of value estimates, varying key assumptions such as the costs of capital and long-term growth rates. The chapter also discusses and illustrates the cost of capital computations and dividends valuation model computations within the Valuation spreadsheet in FSAP. This spreadsheet takes the forecast amounts from the Forecast spreadsheet and other relevant information and values the firm using the various valuation methods discussed in Chapters 11 to 14. New problem material includes the computation of costs of capital across different industries and companies, including Daimler-Chrysler AG, IBM, and Target Stores, as well as short dividends valuation problems for companies like Exxon-Mobil. Longer problems and cases involve computing costs of capital and dividends-based valuation of Wal-Mart, Starbucks, and Massachusetts Stove Company from financial statement forecasts developed in Chapter 10 problems and cases.

Chapter 12 Valuation: Cash-Flow-Based Approaches. Chapter 12 focuses on valuation using the present value of free cash flows. This chapter distinguishes free cash flows to all debt and equity stakeholders and free cash flows to common equity shareholders and the settings where one or the other measure of free cash flows is appropriate for valuation. The chapter develops and demonstrates valuation using free cash flows for common equity shareholders, and valuation using free cash flows to all debt and equity stakeholders. We also consider and apply techniques for projecting free cash flows and measuring the continuing value after the forecast horizon. We apply both of the discounted free cash flows valuation methods to PepsiCo, demonstrating how to measure the free cash flows to all debt and equity stakeholders, as well as the free cash flows to common equity. The valuations for PepsiCo use the forecasted amounts from PepsiCo's projected financial statements discussed in Chapter 10. The chapter also presents techniques for assessing the sensitivity of value estimates, varying key assumptions such as the costs of capital and long-term growth rates. The chapter also explains and demonstrates the consistency of valuation estimates across different approaches and shows students that the dividends approach in Chapter 11 and the free cash flows approaches in Chapter 12 should and do lead to identical value estimates for PepsiCo. The Valuation spreadsheet in FSAP uses projected amounts from the Forecast spreadsheet and other relevant information and values the firm using both of the free cash flows valuation approaches. New, shorter problem material asks students to compute free cash flows from financial statement data for companies like 3M and Dicks Sporting Goods. Problem material also includes using free cash flows to value firms in LBO transactions. New, longer problem material includes the valuation of Wal-Mart, Coca-Cola, Starbucks, and Massachusetts Stove Company. The chapter also introduces The Holmes Corporation case, which is an integrated case relevant for Chapter 10 to 13 in which students select forecast assumptions, prepare projected financial statements, and value the firm using the various methods discussed in Chapters 10 to 13. This case can be assigned piecemeal with each chapter or as an integrated case after Chapter 13.

Chapter 13 Valuation: Earnings-Based Approaches. Chapter 13 emphasizes the role of accounting earnings in valuation, focusing on valuation methods using the residual income approach. The residual income approach uses the ability of a firm to generate comprehensive income in excess of the cost of capital as the principal driver of a firm's value in excess of its book value. We apply the residual income valuation method to the forecasted amounts for PepsiCo from Chapter 10. The chapter also demonstrates that the dividends valuation methods, the free cash flows valuation methods, and the residual income valuation methods are consistent with a fundamental valuation approach. In the chapter we explain and demonstrate that these approaches yield identical estimates of value for PepsiCo. The Valuation spreadsheet in FSAP includes valuation models that use the residual income valuation method. New chapter-end problems include various problems involving computing residual income across different firms, including DaimlerChrysler AG, IBM, Target Stores, Microsoft, Intel, Dell, Southwest Airlines, Kroger, and Yum! Brands. Short problems also involve the valuation of other firms such as Steak N Shake in which the needed financial statement information is given. New, longer chapter-end problems and cases apply the residual income approach to Coca-Cola as well as to Wal-Mart, Starbucks, and Massachusetts Stove, considered in Chapters 10, 11, and 12.

Chapter 14 Valuation: Market-Based Approaches. Chapter 14 demonstrates how to analyze and use the information in market value. In particular, the chapter describes and applies market-based valuation multiples, including the market-to-book ratio and the price-to-earnings ratio. The chapter describes and illustrates the theoretical and conceptual approaches to market multiples, and contrasts them with the practical approaches to market multiples. The chapter demonstrates how the market-to-book ratio is consistent with residual ROCE valuation and the residual income model discussed in Chapter 13. The chapter also describes the factors that drive market multiples, so analysts can adjust multiples appropriately to reflect differences in profitability, growth, and risk across comparable firms. The chapter also demonstrates how to reverse engineer a firm's stock price to infer the valuation assumptions that the stock market appears to be making. We apply all of these valuation methods to PepsiCo. Chapter-end materials continue problems involving Coca-Cola, Wal-Mart, and Steak N Shake and the integrative case involving Starbucks.

Appendices. Appendix A includes the financial statements and notes for PepsiCo used in the illustrations throughout the book. Appendix B is PepsiCo's management discussion and analysis of operations, which we use when interpreting PepsiCo's financial ratios and in our pro forma projections. Appendix C is a printout of the profitability and risk ratio analyses, forecasts, and valuations for PepsiCo from FSAP. Appendix D is the user manual for FASP.

CHAPTER SEQUENCE AND STRUCTURE

Our own experience and our discussions with other professors suggest that there are various approaches to teaching the financial statement analysis course, each of which works well in particular settings. We have therefore designed this book for flexibility with respect to the sequence of chapter assignments. The following diagram sets forth the overall structure of the book.

<table>
<tr><td colspan="2">Chapter 1: Overview of Financial Reporting, Financial Statement Analysis, and Valuation</td></tr>
<tr><td>Chapter 2: Asset Valuation and Income Measurement</td><td>Chapter 3: Income Flows Versus Cash Flows</td></tr>
<tr><td>Chapter 4: Profitability Analysis</td><td>Chapter 5: Risk Analysis</td></tr>
<tr><td colspan="2">Chapter 6: Quality of Accounting Information and Adjustments to Reported Financial Statement Data</td></tr>
<tr><td>Chapter 7: Revenue Recognition and Related Expenses</td><td>Chapter 8: Liability Recognition and Related Expenses</td></tr>
<tr><td colspan="2">Chapter 9: Intercorporate Entities</td></tr>
<tr><td colspan="2">Chapter 10: Forecasting Financial Statements</td></tr>
<tr><td colspan="2">Chapter 11: Risk-Adjusted Expected Rates of Return and the Dividends Valuation Approach</td></tr>
<tr><td>Chapter 13: Valuation: Earnings-Based Approaches</td><td>Chapter 12: Valuation: Cash-Flow-Based Approaches</td></tr>
<tr><td colspan="2">Chapter 14: Valuation: Market-Based Approaches</td></tr>
</table>

The chapter sequence follows the six steps in financial statement analysis discussed in Chapter 1. Chapters listed in left-side boxes relate primarily to income and balance sheet information and profitability analysis. Chapters listed in right-side boxes relate primarily to cash flow information and risk analysis. Chapters in boxes extending to both sides relate to topics affecting all three financial statements, both profitability and risk analysis, and valuation in general. Chapters 2 and 3 provide the conceptual foundation for the three financial statements. Chapters 4 and 5 present tools for analyzing the financial statements. Chapters 6 to 9 examine the quality of accounting information and various GAAP. Chapters 10 to 14 focus primarily on forecasting financial statements and valuation.

Some schools teach GAAP topics and financial statement analysis in separate courses. Chapters 6 to 9 are an integrated unit and sufficiently rich for the GAAP course. The remaining chapters will then work well in the financial statement analysis course. Some schools leave the topic of valuation to finance courses. Chapters 1 to 9 (or, alternatively, Chapters 1 to 10) will then work well for the accounting prelude to the finance course. Some instructions may wish to begin with valuation (Chapters 11 to 14) and then examine data issues that might impact the numbers used in the valuations (Chapters 6 to 9). This textbook is adaptable to other sequences of the various topics.

OVERVIEW OF THE ANCILLARY PACKAGE

A financial statement analysis package (FSAP) is available on the website for this book (www.thomsonedu.com/accounting/stickney) to all purchasers of the text. The package performs various analytical tasks (common size and trend statements, ratio computations), provides a worksheet template for preparing financial statements forecasts, and applies amounts from the financial statement forecasts to valuing a firm using various valuation methods. In addition to information tabs embedded within FSAP, Appendix D includes a user manual for FSAP.

FSAP

Packaged with this book is Thomson Analytics' Business School Edition for the purpose of supplementary financial research beyond the problems and cases in the book. Thomson Analytics' Business School Edition is an educational version of the same financial data provided by Thomson Financial that experts use on a daily basis. For 500 companies, this online resource provides:

- Worldscope®, which includes company profiles, financials and accounting results, market per-share data, annual information, and monthly prices going back to 1980.
- I/B/E/S Consensus Estimates, which provides consensus estimates, analyst-by-analyst earnings coverage, and analysts' forecasts.
- Disclosure SEC Database, which includes company profiles, annual and quarterly company financials, pricing information and earnings.

An Instructor's Manual is also available to faculty who adopt this book. It contains suggestions for using the textbook, solutions to all problems and cases, and teaching notes to cases.

A Test Bank in ExamView® contains an expanded number and scope of test items, and new downloadable PowerPoint® slides are available to instructors as well.

ACKNOWLEDGMENTS

Many individuals provided invaluable assistance in the preparation of this book and we wish to acknowledge their help in a formal manner here.

The following professional colleagues have assisted in the development of this edition by reviewing or providing helpful comments on the previous edition:

Messod Daniel Beneish, Indiana University
Aaron Hipscher, New York University
Robert Howell, Dartmouth College
Amy Hutton, Dartmouth College
Prem Jain, Georgetown University
Ross Jennings, University of Texas at Austin
April Klein, New York University
Yuri Loktionov, New York University
Craig Nichols, Cornell University
Virginia Soybel, Babson College
Christine Wiedman, University of Western Ontario
Michael Williamson, University of Texas at Austin

The following reviewers provided valuable suggestions for the development of the Sixth Edition, and we thank them for their insights:

Curtis Bernstein, Florida Atlantic University
Allan W. Hanson, St. Edward's University
Mark P. Holtzman, Seton Hall University
Bikki Jaggi, Rutgers University
Krishna R. Kumar, The George Washington University
Zoe-Vonna Palmrose, University of Southern California
Kenton Yee, Columbia University

A number of instructors were kind enough to share their syllabi with the authors, and we are grateful for their contributions as we considered their needs for the Sixth Edition.

We wish to acknowledge the assistance of David M. DeLott, Director of External Financial Reporting, PepsiCo, who not only carefully reviewed textual material related to PepsiCo but provided other helpful comments as well.

We wish to thank the following individuals at Thomson Business & Economics, who provided guidance, encouragement, or assistance in various phases of the revision: Craig Avery, Rob Dewey, Matt Filimonov, and Heather Mann. Katherine Rybowiak did an outstanding job assisting with preparation of the solutions/instructor's manual. We appreciate the effective checking of the solutions to every question, exercise, problem, and case by Jason Fink.

Finally, we wish to acknowledge the role played by former students in our financial statement analysis classes for being challenging partners in our learning endeavors and to our families for being encouraging and patient partners in this work. We dedicate this book to each of you.

Clyde P. Stickney
Paul R. Brown
James M. Wahlen

About the Authors

Clyde P. Stickney is The Signal Companies Professor of Management at the Amos Tuck School at Dartmouth College. He received his doctoral degree from Florida State University and served on the faculties of the University of Chicago and the University of North Carolina at Chapel Hill before joining the faculty of the Tuck School in 1977. He has also taught at the International University of Japan, Swinburne Institute of Technology, and Helsinki School of Economics and Business Administration.

Professor Stickney's teaching and research interests center around the analysis and interpretation of financial statements. Recent research has examined the impact of different accounting principles on U.S. versus Japanese price-earnings rations, the use of financial statement ratios to infer the content, and to evaluate the success of corporate-level strategies. He has authored and co-authored books on financial accounting, managerial accounting and financial statement analysis.

Paul Richard Brown, Ph.D., CPA is Dean at the College of Business and Economics, Lehigh University. Formerly, he was Associate Dean, Executive MBA Programs at the Leonard N. Stern School of Business, New York University. He was also a Professor of Accounting and past Chairman of the Department of Accounting, Taxation and Business Law at New York University. He received his doctoral degree from the University of Texas at Austin and has served on the faculties of the Yale School of Management and INSEAD.

Dean Brown publishes in a wide range of academic and professional publications. He appears on television and is quoted in the press often, providing commentary on such topics as financial statement analysis, earnings management, financial reporting regulation and reform, IASB reporting, and auditor independence. The professional activities of Dean Brown include serving on corporate boards as well as board consulting. Prior to entering academe, he worked as an auditor for Andersen & Co., and as a staff member of the Financial Accounting Standards Board. Dean Brown is a member of the New York State Society of CPAs, American Institute of CPAs, and the American Accounting Association.

James M. Wahlen is the Ford Motor Company Teaching Fellow in accounting at the Kelley School of Business at Indiana University. He received his doctoral degree from the University of Michigan in 1991, and has served on the faculties of the Kenan-Flagler Business School at the University of North Carolina and at Pacific Lutheran University. He has also taught at INSEAD, the University of Washington, and in executive education programs for KPMG, Arthur Andersen & Co., Bank of America, the Amsterdam Institute of Finance, and others.

Professor Wahlen's teaching and research interests focus on financial accounting, financial statement analysis, and the capital markets. He has published extensively in leading research journals in accounting and finance. He has had public accounting experience in both Milwaukee and Seattle. Professor Wahlen is a member of the American Accounting Association.

BRIEF CONTENTS

CONTENTS

Chapter 1

Overview of Financial Reporting, Financial Statement Analysis, and Valuation

Learning Objectives

1. Understand the analytical framework that is the foundation for this book. This framework enables the analyst to link the economic characteristics and strategies of a firm, its financial statements and notes, assessments of its current and forecasted profitability and risk, and its market value.
2. Study and apply three tools for studying the economic characteristics of an industry in which a firm competes.
3. Become familiar with PepsiCo, the firm that we analyze throughout the book, obtaining an overview of its economics, strategy, and financial statements.
4. Review the purpose, underlying concepts, and format of the balance sheet, the income statement, and the statement of cash flows.
5. Examine the provisions of the Sarbanes-Oxley Act of 2002 that relate to financial statement information.
6. Obtain an overview of the tools available to the analyst to analyze a firm's profitability and risk.
7. Obtain an overview of how the analyst might use financial statement information in the valuation of a firm.
8. Understand the role of financial statement analysis in an efficient capital market.
9. Review sources of financial information available for publicly held firms.
10. Obtain helpful hints for conducting a financial statement analysis project (Appendix 1.1).

The principal activity of security analysts is to value firms. Security analysts use financial statements and other information to evaluate a firm's success in the past and to predict its likely future performance. They then use the predicted information to measure the value of the firm's shares. Comparisons of their estimates of the firm's share value with the market's price for the shares provide the basis for making buy, hold, or sell investment recommendations.

This book has three principal purposes:

1. To demonstrate the links between a firm's economics and strategy and analysis of its financial statements, with the objective of gaining insights about the firm's profitability and its risk. Chapters 1 to 5 discuss the principal financial statements and tools for analyzing profitability and risk.
2. To enhance understanding of the accounting principles and methods that firms use to prepare their financial statements and the adjustments that the analyst might make to reported amounts to increase their relevance and reliability. Chapters 6 to 9 explore accounting principles in depth.
3. To illustrate the use of financial statement data to build forecasts of future financial statements and use the forecasted amounts of future earnings, cash flows, and dividends in the valuation of firms. Chapters 10 to 14 focus on forecasting and valuation.

Financial analysis is an exciting and rewarding activity, particularly when the objective is to assess whether the market is pricing fairly a firm's shares. Studying the intrinsic characteristics of a firm—for example, its business model; product and service market share; and operating, investing and financing decisions—and employing this information to make informed judgments can be a very satisfying endeavor. Financial statements play a central role in the study and analysis of a firm.

The tools of effective financial statement analysis adapt to many settings in addition to measuring firm value. Other settings include the following:

- extending credit, either for a short-term period (for example, a bank loan used to finance accounts receivable or inventories) or for a long-term period (for example, a bank loan or public bond issue used to finance the acquisition of property, plant, or equipment);
- assessing the operating performance and financial health of a supplier, customer, competitor, or potential employer;
- managing a firm;
- consulting with a firm and offering helpful strategic advice;
- evaluating firms for potential acquisitions or mergers;
- valuing a firm in the initial public offering of its stock;
- forming a judgment about damages sustained in a lawsuit; and
- assessing the extent of auditing needed to form an opinion on a client's financial statements.

OVERVIEW OF FINANCIAL STATEMENT ANALYSIS

The effective analysis of financial statements involves six interrelated, sequential steps, depicted in Exhibit 1.1:

1. **Identify the economic characteristics of the industry in which a particular firm participates.** For example, does the industry include a large number of firms selling similar products, such as grocery stores, or is the industry characterized by a small number of competitors selling unique products, such as pharmaceutical companies? Does technological change play an important role in maintaining a competitive advantage, as in computer software? Are industry sales growing rapidly or slowly?
2. **Identify the strategies that the firm pursues to gain and sustain a competitive advantage.** Are its products designed to meet the needs of specific market seg-

EXHIBIT 1.1

Interrelated Sequential Steps in Financial Statement Analysis

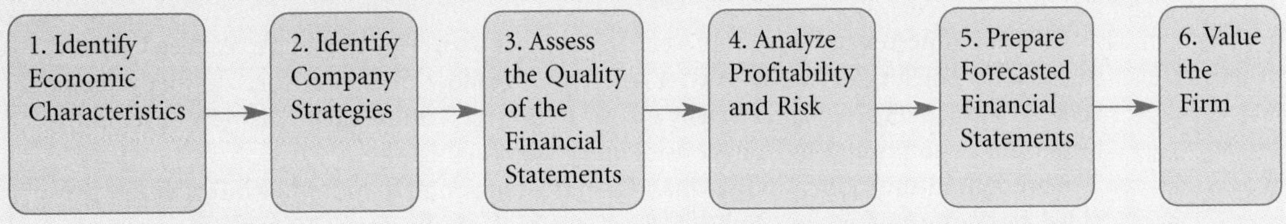

ments, such as ethnic or health foods, or are they intended for a broader consumer market, such as typical grocery stores and family restaurants? Has the firm integrated backward into the growing or manufacture of raw materials for its products, such as a steel company that owns iron ore mines? Has the firm integrated forward into retailing to final consumers, such as an athletic footwear manufacturer that operates retail stores to sell its products? Is the firm diversified across several geographic markets or industries?

3. **Assess the quality of the firm's financial statements and, if necessary, adjust them for such desirable characteristics as sustainability or comparability.** For example, do the firm's financial statements provide a clear and informative representation of the firm's economic performance, financial position, and risk? Has the firm prepared its financial statements in accordance with generally accepted accounting principles of the United States, Japan, Mexico, or some other country, or are they prepared in accordance with principles established by the International Accounting Standards Board (IASB)? Has the firm recognized revenues at the appropriate time, after giving due consideration to uncertainties regarding the collectibility of cash from customers and the accurate measurement of expenses? Do earnings include nonrecurring gains and losses, such as a write-down of an equity investment or goodwill, which the analyst should evaluate differently from recurring components of earnings? Has the firm structured transactions or commercial arrangements and has it selected accounting principles that make it appear more profitable or less risky than economic conditions otherwise suggest?
4. **Analyze the current profitability and risk of the firm using information in the financial statements.** Most financial analysts assess the profitability of a firm relative to the risks involved. Ratios of particular items in the financial statements are the tools used to analyze profitability and risk.
5. **Prepare forecasted financial statements.** Assessments of the recent profitability from step 4 provide the basis for projecting the likely future profitability and, in turn, the likely future returns from investing in the company. Forecasts of a firm's ability to manage risks, particularly those elements of risk with measurable financial consequences, permit the analyst to estimate the likelihood that the firm will experience financial difficulties in the future. Forecasted financial statements that rely on a set of analyst assumptions about the future provide the basis for projecting future profitability and risk.
6. **Value the firm.** Financial statement analysis is most frequently applied to value companies. Financial analysts make recommendations to buy, sell, or hold the equity securities of various firms whose price they think is too low, too high, or

about right. Investment banking firms that underwrite the initial public offering of a firm's common stock must set the initial offering price. Translating information from the financial statements into reliable estimates of firm value, and therefore into intelligent investment decisions, is the principal activity of financial analysts.

These six interrelated steps represent the subject matter of this book. We use these six steps as the analytical framework for analysts to follow in their efforts to analyze and value a company. This chapter briefly explores each step. Subsequent chapters develop the important concepts and tools in considerably more depth.

Throughout this book, we use financial statements, notes, and other information provided by PepsiCo, Inc. and Subsidiaries (PepsiCo) to illustrate the various topics discussed. Appendix A at the end of the book includes recent financial statements and notes for PepsiCo, as well as statements by management and the opinion of the independent accountant regarding these financial statements. Appendix B includes excerpts from a financial review provided by management that discusses the business strategy of PepsiCo, and also offers explanations for changes in its profitability and risk over time. Appendix C presents the output of a financial statement analysis software package called FSAP showing the profitability and risk ratios for PepsiCo for recent years. Appendix C also presents forecasted financial statements and a variety of valuation models applied to the forecasted data for PepsiCo. FSAP is available at www.thomsonedu.com/accounting/stickney. Students can use FSAP for many of the problems and cases in this book to aid their analysis. Appendix D presents a user manual for FSAP.

STEP 1: IDENTIFY THE INDUSTRY ECONOMIC CHARACTERISTICS

The economic characteristics of an industry play a key role in determining the types of financial statement relationships the analyst should expect to observe when analyzing a set of financial statements. Consider, for example, the financial statement data for firms in four different industries in Exhibit 1.2. This exhibit expresses all items on the balance sheet and income statement as a percentage of revenue. Consider how the economic characteristics of these industries affect their financial statement relationships.

Grocery Store Chain

The products of a particular grocery store chain are difficult to differentiate from similar products of other grocery store chains, a trait that results in characterizing such products as *commodities.* In addition, low barriers to entry exist in the grocery store industry; an entrant primarily needs retail space and access to food products distributors. Thus, extensive competition and nondifferentiated products result in a relatively low net income to sales, or profit margin, percentage (3.5 percent in this case). Grocery stores, however, need relatively few assets in order to generate sales (34.2 cents in assets for each dollar of sales in this case). The assets are described as turning over 2.9 times (= 100.0%/34.2%) per year. Each time the assets of this grocery store chain turn over, or generate one dollar of revenue, it generates a profit of 3.5 cents. Thus, during a one-year period, the grocery store earns 10.15 cents (= 3.5% × 2.9) for each dollar invested in assets.

Pharmaceutical Company

The barriers to entry in the pharmaceutical industry are much higher than for grocery stores. Pharmaceutical firms must invest considerable amounts in research and develop-

EXHIBIT 1.2

Common-Size Financial Statement Data for Four Firms

	Grocery Store Chain	Pharmaceutical Company	Electric Utility	Commercial Bank
Balance Sheet at End of Year				
Cash and Marketable Securities	.7%	11.0%	1.5%	261.9%
Accounts and Notes Receivable	.7	18.0	7.8	733.5
Inventories	8.7	17.0	4.5	—
Property, Plant, and Equipment, net	22.2	28.7	159.0	18.1
Other Assets	1.9	72.8	29.2	122.6
Total Assets	34.2%	147.5%	202.0%	1,136.1%
Current Liabilities	7.7%	30.8%	14.9%	936.9%
Long-Term Debt	7.6	12.7	130.8	71.5
Other Noncurrent Liabilities	2.6	24.6	1.8	27.2
Shareholders' Equity	16.3	79.4	54.5	100.5
Total Equities	34.2%	147.5%	202.0%	1,136.1%
Income Statement for Year				
Revenue	100.0%	100.0%	100.0%	100.0%
Cost of Goods Sold	(74.1)	(31.6)	(79.7)	—
Operating Expenses	(19.7)	(37.1)	—	(41.8)
Research and Development	—	(10.1)	—	—
Interest	(.5)	(3.1)	(4.6)	(36.6)
Income Taxes	(2.2)	(6.0)	(5.2)	(8.6)
Net Income	3.5%	12.1%	10.5%	13.0%

ment to create new drugs. If new drugs survive a lengthy government approval process, firms receive patents for these new drugs. These patents give firms exclusive rights to manufacture and sell these drugs for an extended period. These high entry barriers (research and development expenditures, the government approval process, patent protection) permit pharmaceutical firms to realize much higher profit margins on approved, patent-protected products than grocery stores. Exhibit 1.2 indicates that the pharmaceutical firm generated a profit margin of 12.1 percent, more than three times that reported by the grocery store chain. Pharmaceutical firms, however, face product liability risks as well as the risk that competitors will develop superior drugs that make a particular firm's drug offerings obsolete. Because of these business risks, pharmaceutical firms tend to take on relatively small amounts of debt financing.

Electric Utility

The principal assets of an electric utility are its capital-intensive generating plants. Thus, property, plant, and equipment dominate the balance sheet. Because of the large investments required in such assets, electric utility firms in the past have generally demanded a monopoly position in a particular locale. Government regulators permitted this monopoly position but set the rates that utilities charged customers for electric services. Thus, electric utilities have traditionally realized relatively high profit margins (10.5 percent in this case) to offset their relatively low total asset turnovers (.495 = 100.0%/202.0% in this case). The monopoly position and regulatory protection reduced the risk of financial failure and permitted electric utilities to invest large amounts of capital in long-lived assets and take on relatively high proportions of debt in their capital structures. The economic characteristics of electric utilities have changed dramatically in recent years. The gradual elimination of monopoly positions and the setting of rates as market conditions dictate are reducing profit margins considerably.

Commercial Bank

The principal assets of commercial banks are investments in financial securities and loans to businesses and consumers. The principal financing for commercial banks comes from customers' deposits and short-term borrowing. Because customers can generally withdraw deposits at any time, commercial banks invest in securities that they can quickly sell for cash, if necessary. The lending of money is a commodity business: money borrowed from one bank is similar to money borrowed from another bank. Thus, one would expect a commercial bank to realize a small profit margin on the revenue it earns from lending (interest revenue) over the price it pays for its borrowed funds (interest expense). The profit margins on lending are indeed relatively small. The 13.0 percent margin for the commercial bank shown in Exhibit 1.2 reflects the much higher profit margins it generates from offering fee-based financial services, such as arranging mergers and acquisitions, structuring financing packages for businesses, and guaranteeing financial commitments of business customers. Note that the assets of this commercial bank turn over just .09 (=100.0%/1,136.1%) times per year, reflecting the net effect of interest revenues from investments and loans of 6 to 8 percent per year and fee-based revenues, which require relatively few assets.

TOOLS FOR STUDYING INDUSTRY ECONOMICS

Three tools for studying the economic characteristics of an industry are (1) value chain analysis, (2) Porter's five forces classification framework, and (3) an economic attributes framework. The microeconomics literature suggests other analytical frameworks as well.

Value Chain Analysis

The value chain for an industry sets forth the sequence or chain of activities involved in the creation, manufacture, and distribution of its products and services. Exhibit 1.3 portrays a value chain for the pharmaceutical industry. Pharmaceutical companies invest in research and development to discover and develop new drugs. When promising drugs emerge, a lengthy drug approval process begins. Estimates suggest that it takes 8 to 12 years and almost $1 billion to discover and obtain approval of new drugs. To expedite the approval process, reduce costs, and permit their scientists to devote energies to the more creative drug discovery phase, pharmaceutical companies often contract with clinical research firms to conduct the testing and shepherding of new drugs through the approval process.

EXHIBIT 1.3

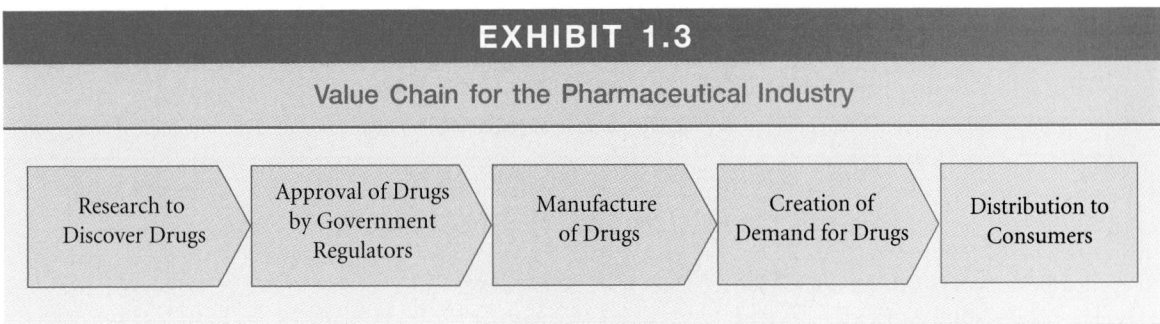

Value Chain for the Pharmaceutical Industry

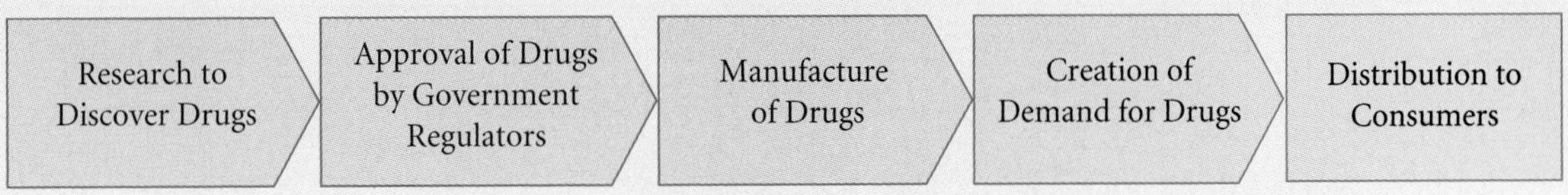

The manufacture of drugs involves combining various chemicals and other elements. For quality control and product purity reasons, pharmaceutical companies use highly automated manufacturing processes.

Pharmaceutical companies employ sales forces to market drugs to doctors, hospitals, and health maintenance organizations. In an effort to create demand, these companies have increasingly advertised new products through multiple advertising media, suggesting that consumers ask their doctors about the drug. Drug distribution typically channels through pharmacies, although bulk mail-order and Internet purchases are increasingly common (and encouraged by health insurers).

To the extent that prices are available for products or services at any stage in the value chain, the analyst can study where value is added within an industry. For example, the analyst can look at the prices paid to acquire firms with promising or newly discovered drugs to ascertain the value of the drug discovery phase. The prices charged by clinical research firms to test and obtain approval of new drugs signal the value added by this activity. The higher the value added from any activity, the higher should be the profitability from engaging in that phase.

The analyst can also use the value chain to identify the strategic positioning of a particular firm within the industry. Pharmaceutical firms have traditionally maintained a presence in the discovery through demand creation phases, leaving distribution to pharmacies and, increasingly, contracting out the drug testing and approval phase.

Refer to Note 1, "Basis of Presentation and Our Divisions" to the financial statements of PepsiCo (Appendix A). PepsiCo operates in four business segments: Frito-Lay North America (branded snacks, chips and other food products), PepsiCo Beverages North America (soft drinks and other beverages), Quaker Foods North America (cereal and related products), and PepsiCo International (products of all three North American divisions but sold outside the United States and Canada). Exhibit 1.4 shows the amounts, taken from Note 1 to PepsiCo's financial statements in Appendix A, and proportions of revenues and operating profit that PepsiCo derived from each of these four segments for Year 4.

Exhibit 1.5 illustrates a value chain for one of PepsiCo's principal businesses, the soft drink/beverage industry.

Although the classic PepsiCo soft drinks (Pepsi, Mountain Dew, Slice, and others) have not changed for many years, the company continually engages in new product development. Once a product appears to have commercial feasibility, PepsiCo combines raw materials into a concentrate or syrup base. The ingredients and their mixes are highly confidential. PepsiCo then ships the concentrate to its franchise bottlers (or, in the case of syrup, to its national fountain accounts), who combine it with water and sweeteners to produce the finished soft drink beverage.

EXHIBIT 1.4

Segment Revenues and Operating Profit for PepsiCo for Year 4 (dollar amounts in millions)

	Revenues		Operating Profit	
Frito-Lay North America	$ 9,560	32.7%	$2,389	39.2%
PepsiCo Beverages North America	8,313	28.4	1,911	31.3
Quaker Foods North America	1,526	5.2	475	7.8
PepsiCo International	9,862	33.7	1,323	21.7
Total	$29,261	100.0%	$6,098	100.0%

EXHIBIT 1.5

Value Chain for the Soft Drink/Beverage Industry

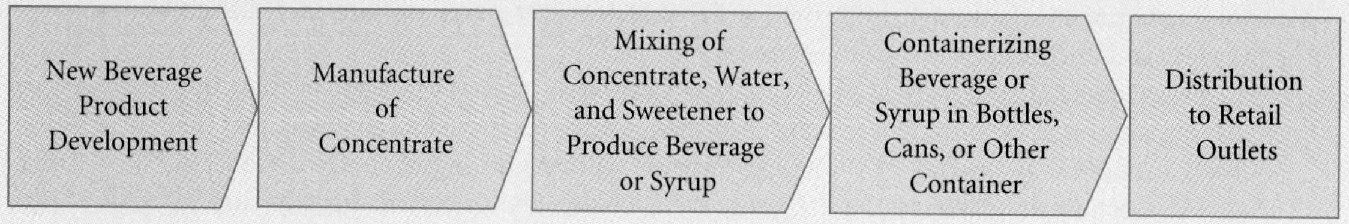

PepsiCo relies on noncontrolled affiliates to bottle and distribute a large percentage of its beverages. That is, PepsiCo contracts out the bottling operation (we discuss the rationale for this arrangement in the strategy section later in this chapter). The bottlers transport the bottled beverages and syrups to independent distributors and retail establishments.

Because the analyst can obtain separate financial statements for PepsiCo and for its bottlers, one can observe where value is added along the value chain. We examine the profitability and risk of PepsiCo and its bottlers in greater depth in Chapters 4, 5, and 9.

Porter's Five Forces Classification Framework

Porter suggests that five forces influence the profitability of firms within an industry.[1]

1. **Buyer Power.** Are consumers sensitive to product prices? If products are similar to those offered by competitors, consumers may switch to the lowest-priced offering. If consumers view a particular firm's products as unique, however, they will likely be less sensitive to price differences. Another dimension of price sensitivity is the relative cost of a product. Consumers are less sensitive to the prices of products that represent a small portion of income, such as beverages, than to higher-priced products, such as automobiles.

[1]Michael E. Porter, *Competitive Strategy: Techniques for Analyzing Industries and Competitors* (New York: Free Press), 1998.

Buyer power relates to the relative number of buyers and sellers in a particular industry. If there are many sellers of a product and a small number of buyers, such as military equipment and weapons systems bought by governments, the buyer can exert significant downward pressure on prices and therefore on the profitability of suppliers. If there are few sellers and many buyers, as with beverages, then the sellers have more bargaining power. Brand loyalty, control of distribution channels, low price, and the small number of suppliers result in relatively low buyer power in the beverage industry. However, certain buyers, such as Wal-Mart Stores and fast-food chains, make such large beverage purchases on a national level that they can exert significant buyer power.

2. **Supplier Power.** A similar set of factors applies on the input side as well. Beverage companies purchase the raw materials that make up their concentrate or syrup. Although PepsiCo does not disclose every ingredient, it is unlikely that PepsiCo is dependent on one or even a few suppliers for any of its raw materials. It is also unlikely that any of these ingredients are sufficiently unique that the suppliers could exert much power over PepsiCo. Given PepsiCo's size, the power more likely resides with PepsiCo than with its suppliers. By contrast, certain suppliers of microchips, operating systems, and software are very powerful suppliers to PC manufacturers.
3. **Rivalry among Existing Firms.** PepsiCo and Coca-Cola dominate the soft drink/beverage industry in the United States. Because some consumers view their products as similar, intense competition based on price could develop. Also, the soft drink market in the United States is mature (that is, not growing rapidly), so price cutting could become a strategy to gain market share.

   While intense rivalries have a tendency to reduce profitability, in this case PepsiCo and Coca-Cola, the two largest players, can tacitly avoid competing based on price and compete instead on brand image, access to key distribution channels (for example, fast-food chains and grocery store shelf space), and other attributes. Growth opportunities do exist in other countries, which these companies pursue aggressively. Thus, we might characterize industry rivalry as low to moderate.
4. **Threat of New Entrants.** How easily can new firms enter a market? Are there entry barriers, such as large capital investment, technological expertise, patents, or regulation that inhibit new entrants? If so, firms in the industry will likely generate higher earnings than if new entrants can easily enter the market and compete away the excess profits.

   Entry barriers in the soft drink industry are high, so the threat of new entrants is low. Brand recognition by PepsiCo and Coca-Cola serves as one entry barrier. Another barrier is domination of the distribution channels by these two firms. Most restaurant chains sign exclusive contracts to serve the beverages of one or the other of these two firms. Also, PepsiCo and Coca-Cola often dominate shelf space in grocery stores.
5. **Threat of Substitutes.** How easily can customers switch to substitute products? How likely are they to switch? When there are close substitutes in a market, profitability is dampened, as often occurs, for example, between restaurants and grocery stores for certain types of prepared foods, and between airlines, driving an automobile, and other means of leisure travel for short distances. Unique products with few substitutes, such as certain prescription medications, enhance profitability. Fruit juices, bottled waters, sports drinks, teas, and coffees serve a similar thirst-quenching function to that of soft drinks, which is why PepsiCo purchased Tropicana and Gatorade. Consumer buying habits, brand loyalty, and channel availability, however, minimize the threat of substitutes in the soft drink industry.

Thus, the soft drink/beverage industry rates low on buyer power, supplier power, threat of new entrants, and threat of substitutes, and moderate on rivalry within the industry. Unless either PepsiCo or Coca-Cola decides to compete on the basis of low price, the analyst might expect these firms to report relatively high profitability.

Economic Attributes Framework

We have found the following framework useful in studying the economic attributes of a business, in part because it ties in with items reported in the financial statements.

1. **Demand**
   - Are customers highly price sensitive, as in the case of automobiles, or are they relatively insensitive, as in the case of soft drinks?
   - Is demand growing rapidly, as in the case of long-term health care, or is the industry relatively mature, as in the case of grocery stores?
   - Does demand move with the economic cycle, as in the case of construction of new homes and offices, or is it insensitive to business cycles, as in the case of food products or medical care?
   - Does demand vary with the seasons of a year, as in the case of summer clothing or ski equipment, or is it relatively stable throughout the year, as in the case of most grocery store products?
2. **Supply**
   - Are many suppliers offering similar products, or are few suppliers offering unique products?
   - Are there high barriers to entry or can new entrants gain easy access?
   - Are there high barriers to exit?
3. **Manufacturing**
   - Is the manufacturing process capital intensive, as in the case of electric power generation; labor intensive, as in the case of advertising and auditing services; or a combination of the two, as in the case of automobile manufacturing and airline transportation?
   - Is the manufacturing process complex with low tolerance for error, as in the case of heart pacemakers or microchips, or relatively simple with ranges of acceptable-quality products, as in the case of apparel and nonmechanized toys?
4. **Marketing**
   - Is the product promoted to other businesses, in which case a sales staff plays a key role, or is it marketed to consumers, so that advertising, location, and coupons serve as the principal promotion mechanisms?
   - Does steady demand pull products through distribution channels, or must firms continually create demand?
5. **Investing and Financing**
   - Are the assets of firms in the industry relatively short term, as in the case of commercial banks, which require short-term sources of funds to finance them? Or are assets relatively long term, as in the case of electric utilities, which require primarily long-term financing?
   - Is there relatively little risk in the assets of firms in the industry, such as from technological obsolescence, so firms can carry high proportions of debt financing? Alternatively, are there high risks resulting from short product life cycles or product liability concerns that dictate low debt and high shareholders' equity financing?

EXHIBIT 1.6

Economic Characteristics of the Soft Drink/Beverage Industry

Demand

- Relatively insensitive to price.
- Low growth in the United States but more rapid growth opportunities in other countries.
- Demand is not cyclical.
- Demand is higher during warmer weather.

Supply

- Two principal suppliers (PepsiCo and Coca-Cola) selling branded products.
- Branded products and domination of distribution channels by two principal suppliers create high barriers to entry.

Manufacturing

- Manufacturing process for concentrate and syrup is not capital intensive.
- Bottling and distribution of final product is capital intensive.
- Manufacturing process is simple (essentially a mixing operation) with some tolerance for quality variation.

Marketing

- Brand recognition and established demand pull products through distribution channels, but advertising can stimulate demand to some extent.

Investing and Financing

- Bottling operations and transportation of products to retailers require long-term financing.
- Profitability is relatively high and growth is slow in the United States, leading to excess cash flow generation. Growth markets in other countries require financing from internal domestic cash flow or from external sources.

- Is the industry relatively profitable and mature, generating more cash flow from operations than is needed for acquisitions of property, plant, and equipment? Alternatively, is the industry growing rapidly and in need of external financing?

Exhibit 1.6 summarizes the economic characteristics of the soft drink/beverage industry.

STEP 2: IDENTIFY THE COMPANY STRATEGIES

Firms establish business strategies in an attempt to differentiate themselves from competitors, but an industry's economic characteristics affect the flexibility that firms have in designing these strategies. In some cases, firms can create sustainable competitive advantages. PepsiCo's size and brand name give it a sustainable competitive advantage, although Coca-Cola can boast similar advantages. The reputation for quality family entertainment provides Disney with a sustainable advantage.

In many industries, however, products and ideas quickly get copied. Consider, for example, computer hardware; chicken, pizza, and hamburger restaurant chains; and financial services. In these cases, firms may achieve competitive advantage by being the first with new concepts or ideas (referred to as *first mover advantage*) or by continually investing in product development to remain on the leading edge of change within an industry.

Framework for Strategy Analysis

The set of strategic choices confronting a particular firm varies across industries. A framework dealing with product and firm characteristics helps in structuring the choice set.

1. **Nature of Product or Service.** Is a firm attempting to create unique products or services for particular market niches and thereby achieving relatively high profit margins (referred to as a *product differentiation strategy*) or it is offering nondifferentiated products at low prices, accepting a lower profit margin in return for a higher market share (referred to as a *low-cost leadership strategy*)? Is it possible to achieve both objectives by creating brand loyalty and maintaining control over costs?
2. **Degree of Integration within Value Chain.** Is the firm pursuing a vertical integration strategy, participating in all phases of the value chain, or selecting just certain phases within the chain? With respect to manufacturing, is the firm conducting all manufacturing operations itself (as usually occurs in steel manufacturing), outsourcing all manufacturing (common in athletic shoes), or outsourcing the manufacturing of components but conducting the assembly operation in-house (common in automobile and computer hardware manufacturing)?

   With respect to distribution, is the firm maintaining control over the distribution function or outsourcing it? Some restaurant chains, for example, own all of their restaurants while other chains operate through independently owned franchises. Computer hardware firms have recently shifted from selling through their own sales staffs to using various indirect sellers, such as value-added resellers and systems integrators, in effect shifting from in-house sourcing to outsourcing of the distribution function.
3. **Degree of Geographical Diversification.** Is the firm targeting its products to its domestic market or integrating horizontally across many countries? Operating in other countries creates opportunities for growth but exposes firms to risks from exchange rate changes, political uncertainties, and additional competitors.
4. **Degree of Industry Diversification.** Is the firm operating in a single industry or diversifying across multiple industries? Operating in multiple industries permits firms to diversify product, cyclical, regulatory, and other risks encountered when operating in a single industry but raises questions about management's ability to understand and manage multiple and different businesses effectively.

Application of Strategy Framework to PepsiCo's Beverage Segment

To apply this strategy framework to PepsiCo's beverage segment, we rely on the description provided by PepsiCo's management, which we reproduce in Appendix B. Most U.S.

firms include this type of management discussion and analysis in their Form 10-K filing with the Securities and Exchange Commission (SEC).

1. **Nature of Product or Service.** PepsiCo competes broadly within the beverage industry, with offerings in soft drinks, fruit juices, bottled waters, sports drinks, teas, and coffees. However, its principal product is soft drinks. Although one might debate whether its products differ from similar products offered by Coca-Cola and other competitors, brand recognition and domination of distribution channels permit it to sell a somewhat differentiated product.
2. **Degree of Integration within Value Chain.** PepsiCo engages in new product development, manufactures concentrates and syrups, and promotes its products, while it allows its bottlers to manufacture and distribute soft drink products. This arrangement exists because PepsiCo realizes that the principal value added comprises the secret formulas that make up the concentrates and syrups, and product and brand promotion to maintain its brand name and brand loyalty. Maintaining product quality and efficient and effective distribution channels are critical to PepsiCo's success, so PepsiCo emphasizes the important role bottlers play and the oversight role PepsiCo plays to ensure its financial strength and efficient operation. Thus, a close operational relationship exists between PepsiCo and its bottlers. However, bottling operations are relatively simple, yet capital intensive; require long-term financing, typically debt; and are not particularly value enhancing. By not owning the bottling and distribution operations, PepsiCo reports greater profitability. It also appears less risky because it keeps the debt of the bottling operations off its balance sheet.

   Because of its heavy influence (seller power) over its bottlers, PepsiCo is able to price its concentrate sales to these bottlers to garner a significant portion of the profit margin for itself. The bottlers are willing to accept a lower margin because of the monopoly power given them by PepsiCo in a particular locale and the strong demand for the PepsiCo products that they produce. (In subsequent chapters, we consider PepsiCo's strategy with respect to its bottlers when we assess its profitability, quality of financial information, and risk.)

   It's interesting to note that PepsiCo's main competitor in the soft drink industry, Coca-Cola, structures its operations similarly. Just as with PepsiCo, Coca-Cola's principal products are the concentrates that it sells to bottlers, who are responsible for bottling and distributing the final Coca-Cola soft drinks.
3. **Degree of Geographical Diversification.** Note 1, "Basis of Presentation and Our Divisions" to PepsiCo's financial statements (Appendix A) and Exhibit 1.4 indicate that the firm generated 28.4 percent of its revenues during Year 4 from beverages in North America. PepsiCo derived 33.7 percent of its revenues during Year 4 from international operations, but PepsiCo does not disclose the proportion of international revenues it derived from beverages alone. Overall, PepsiCo derived about two-thirds of its revenues from within North America and one-third from other countries.
4. **Degree of Industry Diversification.** Exhibit 1.4 indicates that PepsiCo generated 32.7 percent of its Year 4 revenues from the North America snack food segment, 28.4 percent from the North America soft drinks/beverage segment, and 5.2 percent from North American cereals and related products. Because PepsiCo does not disclose the proportions of international sales it derives from snack foods, soft drinks/beverages, and cereal and related products, we cannot measure PepsiCo's worldwide mix of its product sales. Although PepsiCo is more industry diverse

than Coca-Cola, many economic characteristics of the beverage, snack food, and cereal industries are similar in nature (importance of brand recognition and distribution channels, for example).

STEP 3: ASSESS THE QUALITY OF THE FINANCIAL STATEMENTS

Business firms prepare three principal financial statements to report the results of their activities: (1) balance sheet, (2) income statement, and (3) statement of cash flows. Many firms prepare a fourth statement, the statement of shareholders' equity, which provides further detail of the shareholders' equity section of the balance sheet. Firms also include a set of notes that elaborate on items included in these statements. This section presents a brief overview of the purpose and content of each of these three financial statements, using the financial statements and notes for PepsiCo in Appendix A as examples.

Generally accepted accounting principles (GAAP) determine the valuation and measurement methods used in preparing financial statements. Official rule-making bodies set these principles. The Securities and Exchange Commission (SEC), an agency of the federal government, has the legal authority to specify acceptable accounting principles in the United States (www.sec.gov). The SEC has, for the most part, delegated the responsibility for setting GAAP to the Financial Accounting Standards Board (FASB), a private-sector body within the accounting profession (www.fasb.org). The FASB specifies acceptable accounting principles only after receiving extensive comments on proposed accounting standards from various preparers, auditors, and users of financial statements.

The International Accounting Standards Board (IASB) is an independent entity comprising fourteen members and a full-time professional staff (www.iasb.org). The IASB strives to reduce diversity in accounting principles across countries and to encourage greater standardization. Its pronouncements, however, have no enforceability of their own. Rather, the representatives to the IASB pledge their best efforts in establishing the pronouncements of the IASB as GAAP within their countries. Beginning in 2005, the financial statements of firms within the European Community must conform to the pronouncements of the IASB.

The IASB has increased its activity in recent years, and the FASB has worked closely with the IASB to harmonize reporting worldwide. Many still believe, however, that it will be some time before accounting standards conform worldwide.

Balance Sheet—Measuring Financial Position

The balance sheet, or statement of financial position, presents a snapshot of the resources of a firm (assets) and the claims on those resources (liabilities and shareholders' equity) as of a specific date.

The assets portion of the balance sheet reports the effects of a firm's operating decisions (principally those involving current assets) and investing decisions (principally those involving noncurrent assets). Refer to the balance sheet for PepsiCo on December 25 of Year 4 and December 27 of Year 3 in Exhibit 1.7. PepsiCo's principal current assets are accounts and notes receivable, inventories, and prepaid expenses. PepsiCo's principal noncurrent assets are property, plant, and equipment; intangible assets; and investments in the equity securities of noncontrolled bottlers.

The liabilities and shareholders' equity portion of the balance sheet reports the effects of a firm's operating decisions (involving most current liabilities) and financing decisions (involving primarily noncurrent liabilities and shareholders' equity). PepsiCo obtains financing from suppliers of goods and services (reported as accounts payable and other current liabilities), bank and other loans (reported as both short-term obligations and long-term obligations), other long-term liabilities, and shareholders' equity.

The balance sheet derives its name from the fact that it shows the following balance or equality:

$$\text{Assets} = \text{Liabilities} + \text{Shareholders' Equity}$$

That is, a firm's assets or resources are in balance with, or equal to, the claims on those assets by creditors (liabilities) and owners (shareholders' equity). The balance sheet views resources from two perspectives: a list of the specific forms in which a firm holds the resources (cash, inventory, equipment) and a list of the persons or entities that provided the funds to obtain the assets and therefore have claims on them (suppliers, employees, governments, shareholders).

Formats of balance sheets in some countries differ from that in the United States. In Germany and France, for example, property, plant, and equipment and other noncurrent assets often appear first, followed by current assets. On the financing side, shareholders' equity appears first, followed by noncurrent liabilities and then current liabilities. This format maintains the balance sheet equality but presents accounts in the opposite sequence to that common in the United States.

In the United Kingdom, the balance sheet equation takes the following form:

$$\text{Noncurrent Assets} + [\text{Current Assets} - \text{Current Liabilities}] - \text{Noncurrent Liabilities} = \text{Shareholders' Equity}$$

This format takes the perspective of shareholders by reporting the assets available for shareholders after subtracting claims by creditors. Financial analysts can rearrange the components of published balance sheets to whichever format they consider most informative, although ambiguity may exist for some balance sheet categories.

Assets—Recognition, Valuation, and Classification

Which of its resources does a firm recognize as assets? At what amount does the firm report these assets? How does it classify them within the assets portion of the balance sheet? GAAP determines responses to these questions.

Assets are resources that have the potential for providing a firm with future economic benefits: the ability to generate future cash inflows (as with accounts receivable and inventories) or to reduce future cash outflows (as with prepayments). A firm recognizes as assets those resources (1) for which it has acquired rights to future use as a result of a past transaction or event, and (2) for which the firm can measure, or quantify, the future benefits with a reasonable degree of precision.[2] Resources that firms do not normally recognize as assets because they fail to meet one or both of the criteria include purchase orders received from customers, employment contracts with corporate officers, and a quality reputation with employees, customers, or citizens of the community.

Perhaps the most valuable resources of PepsiCo are its brand names (Pepsi, Frito-Lay, Quaker Oats, and others). PepsiCo, or companies it acquired, created these brand names through past expenditures on advertising, event sponsorships, product development, and quality control. Yet ascertaining the portion of these expenditures that creates sustainable

---

[2] Financial Accounting Standards Board, *Statement of Financial Accounting Concepts No. 6*, "Elements of Financial Statements" (1985), par. 25.

EXHIBIT 1.7

PepsiCo, Inc. and Subsidiaries
Consolidated Balance Sheets
December 25, Year 4, and December 27, Year 3
(in millions except per share amounts)

	Year 4	Year 3
ASSETS		
Current Assets		
Cash and cash equivalents	$ 1,280	$ 820
Short-term investments	2,165	1,181
	3,445	2,001
Accounts and notes receivable, net	2,999	2,830
Inventories	1,541	1,412
Prepaid expenses and other assets	654	687
Total Current Assets	8,639	6,930
Property, Plant, and Equipment, net	8,149	7,828
Amortizable Intangible Assets, net	598	718
Goodwill	3,909	3,796
Other nonamortizable intangible assets	933	869
Nonamortizable Intangible Assets	4,842	4,665
Investments in Noncontrolled Affiliates	3,284	2,920
Other Assets	2,475	2,266
Total Assets	$27,987	$25,327

Continued

future benefits and the portion that simply stimulates sales during the current period is too uncertain to justify recognizing an asset. The amounts that PepsiCo does report for goodwill and other intangible assets (see Note 4, "Property, Plant, and Equipment and Intangible Assets," to PepsiCo's financial statements in Appendix A) result from PepsiCo's purchase of other companies, a transaction-based event that provides market evidence of the value of intangibles. PepsiCo's balance sheet reports $598 million of amortizable intangibles and $933 million of nonamortizable intangibles, principally brand names. The remaining $3,909 million of intangibles is goodwill, which represents the portion of the purchase price of other businesses that PepsiCo could not allocate to identifiable assets and liabilities. Chapter 7 discusses the accounting for intangibles.

Most assets on the balance sheet are either *monetary* or *nonmonetary.* Using the definition for these categories as discussed in Chapter 9 (foreign currency translation), monetary assets include cash and claims to a fixed amount of cash receivable in the future. PepsiCo's monetary assets include cash, accounts and notes receivable, and investments in the debt securities of other firms. The balance sheet reports monetary assets at the amount of cash the firm expects to receive in the future. If the date or dates of receipt extend beyond one year, the firm reports the monetary asset at the present value of the future cash flows, using a discount rate that reflects the underlying uncertainty of collecting the cash as assessed at the time the claim initially arose.

EXHIBIT 1.7

continued

	Year 4	Year 3
LIABILITIES AND SHAREHOLDERS' EQUITY		
Current Liabilities		
Short-term obligations	$ 1,054	$ 591
Accounts payable and other current liabilities	5,599	5,213
Income taxes payable	99	611
Total Current Liabilities	6,752	6,415
Long-Term Debt Obligations	2,397	1,702
Other Liabilities	4,099	4,075
Deferred Income Taxes	1,216	1,261
Total Liabilities	14,464	13,453
Preferred Stock, no par value	41	41
Repurchased Preferred Stock	(90)	(63)
Common Shareholders' Equity		
Common stock, par value $1^2/_3$¢ per share (issued 1,782 shares)	30	30
Capital in excess of par value	618	548
Retained earnings	18,730	15,961
Accumulated other comprehensive loss	(886)	(1,267)
	18,492	15,272
Less: repurchased common stock, at cost (103 and 77 shares, respectively)	(4,920)	(3,376)
Total Common Shareholders' Equity	13,572	11,896
Total Liabilities and Shareholders' Equity	$27,987	$25,327

See accompanying notes to consolidated financial statements.

Nonmonetary assets include assets that are *tangible,* such as inventories, buildings, and equipment, and assets that are *intangible,* including brand names, patents, trademarks, licenses, and goodwill. In contrast to monetary assets, nonmonetary assets do not represent claims to fixed amounts of cash. The amount of cash firms receive from using or selling nonmonetary assets depends on market conditions at the time of their use or sale. Firms might report nonmonetary assets at the amounts initially paid to acquire them (acquisition, or historical, cost); the amounts required currently to acquire them (current replacement cost); the amounts for which firms could currently sell the asset (current net realizable value); or the present values of the amounts firms expect to receive in the future from selling or using the assets (present value of future cash flows). GAAP generally requires the reporting of nonmonetary assets on the balance sheet at their acquisition cost amounts because this valuation is usually more objective and verifiable than other possible valuation bases. GAAP in some countries, such as the United Kingdom and the Netherlands, permits periodic revaluation of property, plant, and equipment to current values. Chapter 2 discusses alternative valuation methods and their implications for measuring earnings.

The classification of assets within the balance sheet varies widely in published annual reports. The principal asset categories are as follows:

Current Assets. Current assets include cash and other assets that a firm expects to sell or consume during the normal operating cycle of a business, usually one year. Cash, short-term investments, accounts and notes receivable, inventories, and prepayments appear as current assets for PepsiCo.

Investments. This category includes long-term investments in the debt and equity securities of other entities. If a firm makes such investments for short-term purposes, it classifies them under current assets. A principal asset for PepsiCo is the investments in its bottlers (Pepsi Bottling Group [PBG], PepsiAmericas, and other bottlers). Note 8, "Noncontrolled Bottling Affiliates," to PepsiCo's financial statements (Appendix A) indicates that it owns less than 50 percent of the common stock of these bottlers. PepsiCo therefore does not prepare consolidated financial statements with these bottlers, but instead reports the investments on the balance sheet using the equity method (discussed in Chapter 9).

Property, Plant, and Equipment. This category includes the tangible, long-lived assets that a firm uses in operations over a period of years. Note 4, "Property, Plant, and Equipment and Intangible Assets," to PepsiCo's financial statements (Appendix A) indicates that property, plant, and equipment includes land and improvements, buildings and improvements, machinery and equipment, and construction in progress. It reports property, plant, and equipment at acquisition cost and then subtracts the accumulated depreciation recognized on these assets since acquisition.

Intangibles. Intangibles include the rights established by law or contract to the future use of property. Patents, trademarks, and franchises are intangible assets. The most troublesome asset recognition questions revolve around which rights satisfy the criteria for an asset. As Chapter 7 discusses in more depth, firms generally recognize as assets intangibles acquired in external market transactions with other entities (as is the case for brand names and goodwill included in PepsiCo's balance sheet under the categories of amortizable and nonamortizable intangible assets, which it details in Note 4, "Property, Plant, and Equipment and Intangible Assets," in Appendix A), but do not recognize as assets intangibles developed internally by the firm (the Pepsi brand names, for example). The rationale for the different accounting treatment is that the value of intangibles acquired in external market transactions is more reliable than the value of internally developed intangibles.

Liabilities—Recognition, Valuation, and Classification

A liability represents a firm's obligation to make payments of cash, goods, or services in a reasonably predictable amount at a reasonably predictable future time for benefits or services received in the past.[3] Liabilities for PepsiCo include obligations to suppliers of goods and services (accounts payable and other current liabilities), banks (short-term obligations), governments (income taxes payable), and lenders (long-term debt obligations).

Most troublesome questions regarding liability recognition relate to executory contracts. GAAP does not recognize labor contracts, purchase order commitments, and some lease agreements as liabilities because firms will receive the benefits from these items in the future instead of having received them in the past. Notes to the financial statements disclose material, executory contracts, and other contingent claims. For example, refer to

[3] *Ibid.*, par. 35.

PepsiCo's long-term contractual commitments in Note 9, "Debt Obligations and Commitments" (Appendix A). PepsiCo lists noncancelable operating leases, purchasing commitments, marketing commitments, and debt guarantees among its executory contracts. Chapter 8 discusses these claims more fully.

Most liabilities are monetary, requiring future payments of cash. GAAP reports those due within one year at the amount of cash the firm expects to pay to discharge the obligation. If the payment dates extend beyond one year, then GAAP states the liability at the present value of the required future cash flows (discounted at an interest rate that reflects the underlying uncertainty of paying the cash as assessed at the time the obligation initially arose). Some liabilities, such as warranties, require delivery of goods or services instead of payment of cash. The balance sheet states those liabilities at the expected future cost of providing these goods and services.

Published balance sheets classify liabilities in various ways. Virtually all firms (except banks) use a current liabilities category, which includes obligations that a firm expects to settle within one year. Balance sheets report the remaining liabilities in a section labeled noncurrent liabilities or long-term debt. PepsiCo uses three noncurrent liability categories: long-term debt obligations, other liabilities, and deferred income taxes. Chapters 2 and 8 discuss deferred income taxes.

Shareholders' Equity Valuation and Disclosure

The shareholders' equity in a firm is a residual interest or claim. That is, the owners have a claim on all assets not required to meet the claims of creditors. The valuation of assets and liabilities in the balance sheet therefore determines the valuation of total shareholders' equity.[4]

Balance sheets separate total shareholders' equity into (1) amounts initially contributed by shareholders for an interest in a firm (PepsiCo uses the accounts, common stock, and capital in excess of par value), (2) cumulative net income in excess of dividends declared (PepsiCo's account is retained earnings), (3) shareholders' equity effects of the recognition or valuation of certain assets or liabilities (PepsiCo includes items related to foreign currency translation, derivatives, and pensions in accumulated other comprehensive income), and (4) treasury stock (PepsiCo shares repurchased by PepsiCo).

Assessing the Quality of the Balance Sheet as a Complete Representation of Economic Position

Analysts frequently examine the relation between items in the balance sheet when assessing a firm's financial position and credit risk. For example, an excess of current assets over current liabilities suggests that a firm has sufficient liquid resources to pay short-term creditors. A relatively low percentage of long-term debt to shareholders' equity suggests that a firm likely has sufficient long-term assets to repay the long-term debt at maturity, or at least an ability to take on new debt financing using the long-term assets as collateral to repay debt coming due.

When using the balance sheet for these purposes, however, the analyst must recognize the following:

1. Certain valuable resources of a firm that generate future cash flows, such as a patent for a pharmaceutical firm or a brand name for a consumer products firm

[4]The issuance of bonds with equity characteristics, such as convertible bonds; the issuance of equity claims with debt characteristics, such as redeemable preferred or common stock; and the issuance of obligations to be settled with the issuance of equity shares, such as stock options, cloud the distinction between liabilities and shareholders' equity.

such as PepsiCo, will appear as assets only if they were acquired from another firm and therefore have a measurable acquisition cost.

2. Nonmonetary assets appear at acquisition cost, even though their current market values might exceed their recorded amounts. An example is the market value versus recorded value of land on the balance sheets of railroads and many urban department stores.
3. Certain rights to use resources and commitments to make future payments may not appear as assets and liabilities. We generally do not see on the balance sheet of airlines, for example, their leased aircraft or their commitments to make future lease payments on those aircraft. We also do not see on the balance sheets of steel, tire, and automobile companies the rights to receive labor services or the commitments to make future payments for labor services under labor union contracts.
4. Noncurrent liabilities appear at the present value of expected cash flows discounted at an interest rate determined at the time the liability initially arose, instead of at a current market interest rate.

For certain firms under these circumstances, these factors can result in the balance sheet reporting incomplete measures of the economic position of a firm. When using the balance sheet, the analyst should consider making adjustments for items that impact balance sheet quality. Chapters 7 through 9 discuss these issues more fully.

Income Statement—Measuring Operating Performance

The total assets of a firm change over time because of investing and financing activities. For example, a firm may issue common stock for cash, acquire a building by assuming a mortgage for part of the purchase price, or issue common stock in exchange for convertible bonds. These investing and financing activities affect the amount and structure of a firm's assets, liabilities, and shareholders' equity.

The total assets of a firm also change over time because of operating activities. A firm sells goods or services to customers for a larger amount than the cost to the firm to acquire or produce the goods and services. Creditors and owners provide capital to a firm with the expectation that the firm will use it to generate a profit and provide an adequate return to the suppliers of capital for the level of risk involved.

The second principal financial statement, the income statement, provides information about the profitability of a firm for a period of time. We use the terms *net income, earnings,* and *profit* interchangeably in referring to the bottom-line amount in the income statement. Exhibit 1.8 presents the income statement for PepsiCo for Year 2, Year 3, and Year 4.

Net income equals revenues and gains minus expenses and losses. Revenues measure the inflows of assets from selling goods and providing services. Expenses measure the outflows of assets that a firm uses, or consumes, in the process of generating revenues. As a measure of performance, revenues reflect resources generated by a firm, and expenses indicate the resources consumed. Gains and losses result from selling assets or settling liabilities peripherally related to a firm's central operations for more or less than their book values. For example, the sale of a building by PepsiCo for more than its book value would appear as a gain on the income statement.

PepsiCo generates revenues from selling goods in three principal product lines: Frito-Lay snack foods; various soft drink concentrates, syrups, and bottled beverages; and Quaker Foods cereals and related items. Revenues also include interest income from

EXHIBIT 1.8

PepsiCo, Inc. and Subsidiaries
Consolidated Statements of Income
Fiscal Years Ended December 25, Year 4; December 27, Year 3; and December 28, Year 2
(in millions except per share amounts)

	Year 4	Year 3	Year 2
Net Revenue	$29,261	$26,971	$25,112
Costs of sales	13,406	12,379	11,497
Selling, general, and administrative expenses	10,299	9,460	8,958
Amortization of intangible assets	147	145	138
Impairment and restructuring charges	150	147	—
Merger-related charges	—	59	224
Operating Profit	5,259	4,781	4,295
Bottling equity income	380	323	280
Interest expense	(167)	(163)	(178)
Interest income	74	51	36
Income from Continuing Operations before Income Taxes	5,546	4,992	4,433
Provision for Income Taxes	1,372	1,424	1,433
Income from Continuing Operations	4,174	3,568	3,000
Tax Benefit of Discontinued Operations	38	—	—
Net Income	$ 4,212	$ 3,568	$ 3,000
Net Income per Common Share—Basic			
Continuing operations	$ 2.45	$ 2.07	$ 1.69
Discontinued operations	.02	—	—
Total	$ 2.47	$ 2.07	$ 1.69
Net Income per Common Share—Diluted			
Continuing operations	$ 2.41	$ 2.05	$ 1.68
Discontinued operations	.02	—	—
Total	$ 2.44*	$ 2.05	$ 1.68

*Based on unrounded amounts.
See accompanying notes to consolidated financial statements.

investments in debt instruments and equity method income from investments in affiliated but noncontrolled bottlers.

Costs of sales include the cost of manufacturing snack foods; the cost of producing concentrates, syrups, and bottled beverages; and the cost of manufacturing cereals and related items. Expenses also include selling, general, and administrative expenses (including advertising and other promotion costs) and interest expense on short- and long-term borrowing.

PepsiCo reported two other expenses on its income statement: impairment and restructuring charges in Year 3 and Year 4 and merger-related costs in Year 2 and Year 3. Note 3, "Impairment and Restructuring Charges and Merger-Related Costs," to PepsiCo's financial statements (Appendix A) describes the nature of these charges. The impairment and restructuring charges relate to the closure of manufacturing facilities. The merger-related costs result from the acquisition of Quaker Oats.

When using the income statement to assess a firm's profitability, the analyst is interested not only in its past profitability but in the likely level of sustainable earnings in the future. When projecting future earnings, the analyst must decide whether past levels of revenues and expenses will likely continue. Expenses such as cost of sales and selling, general, and administrative expenses will certainly continue at some level. The analyst must make a judgment about whether expenses such as PepsiCo's impairment and restructuring charges and merger-related costs will likely continue, and if so at what level. Chapters 4 and 6 discuss some of the factors that the analyst should consider in making these judgments. Chapter 10 provides an extensive discussion of building forecasts of future financial statements.

Accrual Basis of Accounting

Exhibit 1.9 depicts the operating, or earnings, cycle for a manufacturing firm. Net income from this series of activities equals the amount of cash received from customers minus the amount of cash paid for raw materials, labor, and the services of production facilities. If the entire operating cycle occurred within one accounting period, few difficulties would arise in measuring operating performance. Net income would equal cash inflows minus cash outflows related to these operating activities. However, firms acquire raw materials in one accounting period and use them in several future accounting periods. They acquire buildings and equipment in one accounting period and use them during many future accounting periods. A firm often sells goods or services in an earlier period than the one in which it receives cash from customers.

Under a cash basis of accounting, a firm recognizes revenue when it receives cash from customers and recognizes expenses when it pays cash to suppliers, employees, and other providers of goods and services. Because a firm's operating cycle usually extends over several accounting periods, the cash basis of accounting provides a poor measure of performance for specific periods of time because it provides a poor matching of resources earned (revenues) with resources used (expenses). To overcome this deficiency of the cash basis, GAAP generally requires that firms use the accrual basis of accounting in measuring performance.

Under the accrual basis of accounting, a firm recognizes revenue when it meets two criteria: (1) it has completed all (or substantially all) of the revenue-generating process by

EXHIBIT 1.9

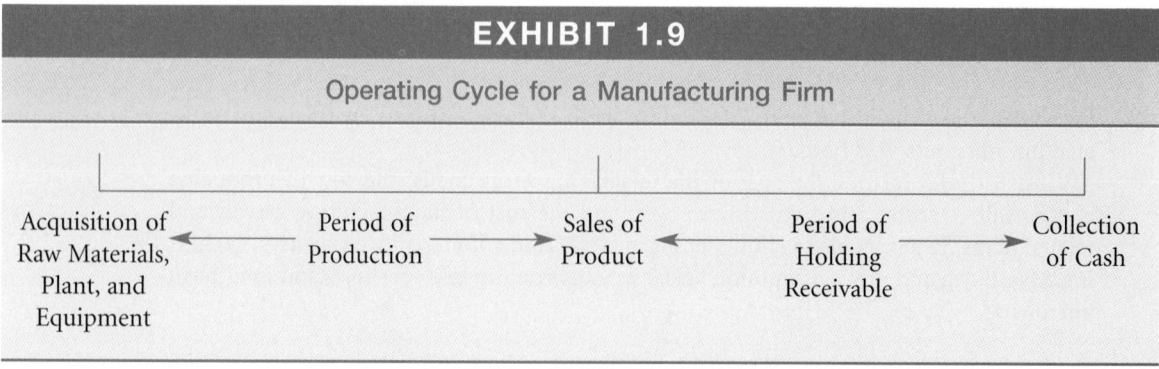

Operating Cycle for a Manufacturing Firm

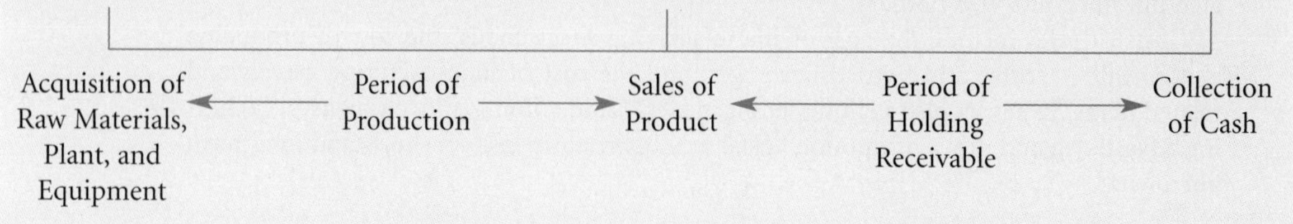

delivering products or services to customers, and (2) it has received cash or is reasonably certain it will collect a receivable whose cash-equivalent amount the firm can measure reliably. Most firms recognize revenue at the time they sell goods or render services. They measure profit by matching expenses with the associated revenues, to the extent such matching is possible. Consider the accrual basis of accounting applied to a manufacturing firm. The cost of manufacturing a product remains on the balance sheet as an asset (inventory) until the time of sale. At the time of sale, the firm recognizes revenue in the amount of cash it expects to collect. It recognizes the cost of manufacturing the product as a matching expense. When a firm cannot clearly match costs to a particular revenue (for example, the salary of the chief executive officer likely influences all revenues recognized during a period), it recognizes an expense in the period when it consumes those resources (that is, matching expenses to a period rather than to a specific revenue).

Note that a firm need not delay revenue recognition until it receives cash from customers as long as the firm can estimate with reasonable precision the amount of cash it will ultimately receive. The amount will appear in accounts receivable prior to the receipt of cash. The accrual basis provides a better measure of operating performance than the cash basis because it matches inputs with outputs more accurately.

Classification and Format within the Income Statement

Investors commonly assess a firm's value based on the firm's expected future sustainable earnings stream. As Chapter 10 discusses more fully, analysts predict the future earnings, or net income, of a firm by studying the past trend of earnings. Inaccurate projections from past data can occur if net income includes unusual or nonrecurring amounts (such as the impairment and restructuring charges and merger-related costs discussed previously for PepsiCo). To provide more useful information for prediction, GAAP requires that the income statement include some or all of the following sections or categories, depending on the nature of the firm's income for a period:

1. Income from continuing operations.
2. Income, gains, and losses from discontinued operations.
3. Extraordinary gains and losses.

Income from Continuing Operations. The first section, Income from Continuing Operations, reports the revenues and expenses of activities in which a firm anticipates an ongoing involvement. If a firm does not have items in the second and third categories of income in a particular year, it will probably not use the continuing-operations label as such.

Firms report their expenses in various ways. Most firms in the United States report expenses by their function: cost of goods sold for manufacturing, selling expenses for marketing, administrative expenses for administrative management, and interest expense for financing. Other firms, particularly those in the European Community, report expenses by their nature: raw materials, compensation, advertising, and research and development.

The continuing-operations section of the income statement frequently appears in two formats. The single-step format lists all revenues and all expenses and then derives net income in a single mathematical step as the difference between the two. The multiple-step format generally lists revenues from selling a firm's goods and services and then shows subtractions for the cost of goods and services sold and the costs of selling and administrative services. The multiple-step format then reports a subtotal for operating income. The income statement then reports nonoperating revenues (interest income, equity income), nonoperating expenses (interest expense), and nonoperating gains and losses. The multiple-step format derives its name from the various subtotals that generally appear before the disclosure of net income. PepsiCo uses this multiple-step format, but many variations in income statement format appear in corporate annual reports.

Income from Discontinued Operations. A firm that intends to remain in a line of business but decides to sell or close down some portion of that line would report any income, gain, or loss from such an action under continuing operations. On the other hand, if a firm decides to terminate its involvement in a line of business, it would report the income, gain, or loss in the second section of the income statement, labeled Income, Gains, and Losses from Discontinued Operations.

During Year 4, PepsiCo reported a $38 million tax benefit related to discontinued operations. PepsiCo discontinued its restaurant business in a year prior to Year 2. At the time of the discontinuance, PepsiCo recognized an estimated amount of taxes on the transaction. Some of this estimated amount must have been subject to disagreement with taxing authorities. During Year 4, it reached final agreement with taxing authorities on the amount of taxes related to this discontinued operation. The final amount was less than the amount initially estimated, resulting in an increase in earnings for Year 4.

Extraordinary Gains and Losses. Extraordinary gains and losses arise from events that are (1) unusual, given the nature of a firm's activities, (2) nonrecurring, and (3) material in amount. Corporate annual reports rarely disclose such items.

Many firms, including PepsiCo, have reported restructuring charges and impairment losses in their income statements in recent years. Such items often reflect the write-down of assets or the recognition of liabilities arising from changes in economic conditions and corporate strategies. Because restructuring charges and impairment losses do not usually satisfy the criteria for discontinued operations or extraordinary items, firms report them in the continuing-operations section of the income statement. If the amounts are material, they appear on a separate line to distinguish them from recurring-income items.

Income, gains, and losses from discontinued operations and extraordinary gains and losses appear in the income statement net of any income tax effects. The majority of published income statements include only the first section because discontinued operations and extraordinary gains and losses occur infrequently.

Comprehensive Income

The recognition and valuation of assets and liabilities usually give rise to an adjustment to some other account. This other account is often a revenue or expense account. For example, a firm might sell inventory for cash. Cash increases by the amount of the selling price, and revenues, a component of retained earnings, increase. Inventory decreases by the amount of the acquisition cost of the inventory item sold, and expenses, a negative component of retained earnings, increases.

Some changes in the recognition and valuation of assets and liabilities do not immediately affect net income and retained earnings but will likely affect them in future periods. Chapter 9 discusses, for example, the effect of exchange rate changes on the valuation of assets and liabilities of a foreign subsidiary of a U.S. company. Any gain or loss from exchange rate changes is unrealized until the foreign unit makes a currency conversion from its currency into U.S. dollars. These unrealized "gains" and "losses" appear in a separate shareholders' equity account titled Accumulated Other Comprehensive Income or Loss.

Review the Consolidated Statement of Common Shareholders' Equity for PepsiCo in Appendix A. It details three items in accumulated other comprehensive loss that relate to the valuation of assets and liabilities: (1) currency translation adjustment, (2) cash flow hedges, net of tax, and (3) minimum pension liability adjustment, net of tax. (Later chapters discuss the accounting for each of these items.)

The FASB is aware that users of financial statements might overlook items of this nature that affect the market value of firms but do not yet appear in net income. It therefore requires firms to report an amount in one of their financial statements that the FASB refers to as comprehensive income.[5]

Comprehensive income equals net income for a period plus or minus the changes in shareholders' equity accounts other than from net income and transactions with owners. Refer to PepsiCo's consolidated statement of common shareholders' equity in Appendix A, which shows the change in accumulated other comprehensive income each year. Comprehensive income for PepsiCo for Year 4 is as follows (in millions):

Net income	$4,212
Currency translation adjustment	401
Cash flow hedges, net of tax	(7)
Minimum pension liability adjustment, net of tax	(19)
Other	6
Comprehensive income	$4,593

Firms have considerable flexibility as to where they report comprehensive income in the financial statements. It may appear in the income statement, in a separate statement of comprehensive income, or as part of the analysis of changes in shareholders' equity accounts. PepsiCo uses this last method of disclosure.

Firms also have flexibility as to how they label disclosures related to comprehensive income. That is, firms need not use the term "comprehensive income" but instead may label the amount, for example, as net income plus or minus changes in other non-owner equity accounts. The balance sheet disclosure might use the term "accumulated other comprehensive income/loss" for the portions of comprehensive income not related to reported earnings, or use a term such as "accumulated non-owner equity account changes."

Appendix A indicates that PepsiCo uses the term "Accumulated Other Comprehensive Loss" in its Consolidated Balance Sheet. In addition, PepsiCo reports the accumulated balances for each component of its comprehensive income in Note 13, "Accumulated Other Comprehensive Loss," to the financial statements.

Assessing the Quality of Earnings as a Complete Representation of Economic Performance

Common stock prices in the capital markets usually react quickly when firms announce new earnings information, indicating that earnings play an important role in the valuation of firms. We provide some striking empirical evidence of the association between earnings and stock returns later in this chapter. In using earnings information for valuation, however, the analyst needs to be alert to the possibility that reported earnings for a particular period represent an incomplete measure of current period profitability, or are a poor predictor of ongoing sustainable profitability. For example, reported net income may exclude certain gains or losses that have not yet been realized in cash. Reported net income may also include amounts that are not likely to recur in the future, such as restructuring or impairment charges; income, gains, and losses from discontinued operations; or extraordinary gains or losses. The analyst may wish to eliminate the effects of nonrecurring items when assessing operating performance for purposes of forecasting future earnings.

Management can also use subtle means to manage earnings. For example, a firm might reduce its estimate of bad-debt expense or warranty expense, cut back on advertising or research and development expenditures, or delay maintenance expenditures as a

[5]Financial Accounting Standards Board, *Statement of Financial Accounting Standards Statement No. 130,* "Reporting Comprehensive Income" (1997).

EXHIBIT 1.10

PepsiCo, Inc. and Subsidiaries
Consolidated Statements of Cash Flows
Fiscal Years Ended December 25, Year 4; December 27, Year 3; and December 28, Year 2
(in millions)

	Year 4	Year 3	Year 2
Operating Activities			
Net income	$4,212	$3,568	$3,000
Adjustments to reconcile net income to net cash provided by operating activities			
Depreciation and amortization	1,264	1,221	1,112
Stock-based compensation expense	368	407	435
Merger-related costs	—	59	224
Impairment and restructuring charges	150	147	—
Cash payments for merger-related costs and restructuring charges	(92)	(109)	(123)
Tax benefit from discontinued operations	(38)	—	—
Pension plan contributions	(458)	(535)	(820)
Bottling equity income, net of dividends	(297)	(276)	(222)
Deferred income taxes	17	(323)	174
Other noncash charges and credits, net	341	415	263
Changes in operating working capital, excluding effects of acquisitions and dispositions:			
Accounts and notes receivable	(130)	(220)	(260)
Inventories	(100)	(49)	(53)
Prepaid expenses and other current assets	(31)	23	(78)
Accounts payable and other current liabilities	216	(11)	426
Income taxes payable	(268)	182	270
Net change in operating working capital	(313)	(75)	305
Other	(100)	(171)	279
Net Cash Provided by Operating Activities	5,054	4,328	4,627

Continued

means of increasing earnings in a particular period. Chapter 6 discusses the concept of the quality of accounting information and illustrates the adjustments that the analyst might make to improve the quality of earnings.

Statement of Cash Flows

The third principal financial statement is the statement of cash flows. This statement reports for a period of time the net cash flows (inflows minus outflows) from three principal business activities: operating, investing, and financing. Exhibit 1.10 presents the statement of cash flows for PepsiCo for Year 2, Year 3, and Year 4.

EXHIBIT 1.10

continued

	Year 4	Year 3	Year 2
Investing Activities			
Capital spending	(1,387)	(1,345)	(1,437)
Sales of property, plant, and equipment	38	49	89
Acquisitions and investments in noncontrolled affiliates	(64)	(71)	(351)
Divestitures	52	46	376
Short-term investments, by original maturity			
More than three months—purchases	(44)	(38)	(62)
More than three months—maturities	38	28	122
Three months or less, net	(963)	(940)	697
Snack Ventures Europe consolidation	—	—	39
Net Cash Used for Investing Activities	(2,330)	(2,271)	(527)
Financing Activities			
Proceeds from issuances of long-term debt	504	52	11
Payments of long-term debt	(512)	(641)	(353)
Short-term borrowings, by original maturity			
More than three months—proceeds	153	88	707
More than three months—payments	(160)	(115)	(809)
Three months or less, net	1,119	40	40
Cash dividends paid	(1,329)	(1,070)	(1,041)
Share repurchases—common	(3,028)	(1,929)	(2,158)
Share repurchases—preferred	(27)	(16)	(32)
Proceeds from exercises of stock options	965	689	456
Net Cash Used for Financing Activities	(2,315)	(2,902)	(3,179)
Effect of exchange rate changes on cash and cash equivalents	51	27	34
Net Increase (Decrease) in Cash and Cash Equivalents	460	(818)	955
Cash and Cash Equivalents, Beginning of Year	820	1,638	683
Cash and Cash Equivalents, End of Year	$1,280	$ 820	$1,638

See accompanying notes to consolidated financial statements.

Rationale for the Statement of Cash Flows

The statement of cash flows provides information on the sources and uses of cash. Even profitable firms, and especially those growing rapidly, sometimes find themselves strapped for cash and unable to pay suppliers, employees, and other creditors. This can occur for two principal reasons:

1. The timing of cash receipts from customers does not necessarily coincide with the recognition of revenue, and the timing of cash expenditures does not necessarily coincide with the recognition of expenses under the accrual basis of accounting. In the usual case, cash expenditures precede the recognition of expenses and cash receipts occur after the recognition of revenue. Thus, a firm might have positive net income for a period but a cash outflow for operations that exceeds the cash inflow.
2. The firm may need to acquire new property, plant, and equipment; retire outstanding debt; or reacquire shares of its common stock when there is insufficient cash available.

In many cases, a profitable firm finding itself short of cash can obtain the needed funds from either short- or long-term creditors or owners. The firm must repay with interest the funds borrowed from creditors. Owners may require that the firm pay periodic dividends as an inducement to invest in the firm. Eventually, the firm must generate sufficient cash from operations if it is to survive.

Cash flows are the connecting link between operating, investing, and financing activities. They permit each of these three principal business activities to continue functioning smoothly and effectively. The statement of cash flows also can be helpful in assessing a firm's past ability to generate free cash flows and for predicting future free cash flows. The concept of free cash flows is first introduced in Chapter 3. As discussed in Chapter 12, free cash flows are central to cash flow-based valuation models.

An examination of the statement of cash flows for PepsiCo reveals that cash flow from operations exceeded the net cash outflow for investing activities in each of the three years. PepsiCo used the excess cash flow to reduce debt, to pay dividends to shareholders, and to repurchase shares of its common stock.

Classification of Cash Flows

The statement of cash flows classifies cash flows as relating to either operating, investing, or financing activities.

Operating. Selling goods and providing services are among the most important ways that a financially healthy company generates cash. Assessing cash flow from operations over several years indicates the extent to which operating activities have provided the necessary cash to maintain operating capabilities, and the extent to which firms have had to rely on other sources of cash.

Investing. The acquisition of long-lived productive assets, particularly property, plant, and equipment, usually represents major ongoing uses of cash. Firms must replace such assets as they wear out and acquire additional long-lived productive assets if they are to grow. Firms obtain a portion of the cash needed to acquire long-lived productive assets from sales of existing assets. However, such cash inflows are seldom sufficient to cover the cost of new acquisitions.

Financing. A firm obtains cash from short- and long-term borrowing and from issuing preferred and common stock. It uses cash to repay short- and long-term borrowing, to pay dividends, and to reacquire shares of outstanding preferred and common stock.

Firms sometimes engage in investing and financing transactions that do not directly involve cash. For example, a firm might acquire a building by assuming a mortgage obligation. It might issue common stock upon conversion of long-term debt. Firms disclose these transactions in a supplementary schedule or note to the statement of cash flows in a way that clearly indicates that they are investing and financing transactions that do not affect cash. PepsiCo reports the portion of its acquisitions in recent years that did not directly involve the use of cash in Note 14 under Supplemental Financial Information.

The statement of cash flows is required under both U.S. and IASB GAAP, but it is not a required financial statement in some countries. Increasingly, however, large international firms are providing the statement on a voluntary basis. Chapter 3 describes and illustrates analytical procedures for preparing a statement of cash flows in situations where firms provide only a balance sheet and income statement.

Independent Auditor's Opinion and the Sarbanes-Oxley Act of 2002

A firm's accounting system records the results of transactions, events, and commercial arrangements and generates the financial statements. The design and operation of the accounting system are the responsibility of a firm's management. The SEC and most stock exchanges, however, require firms with publicly traded common stock to have their accounting records and financial statements audited by independent auditors. The independent auditor's attestation as to the fairness and reliability of a firm's financial statements relative to GAAP is an essential element in the efficiency of the capital markets. Investors and other users of the financial statements can rely on financial statements for essential information about a firm only if they are confident that the independent auditor has examined the accounting records and concluded that the financial statements are fair and reliable according to GAAP.

In response to some managers' misrepresenting their financial statements and audit breakdowns in now infamous cases involving Enron, Global Crossing, Qwest Communications, and other firms, Congress passed the Sarbanes-Oxley Act of 2002 (www.sarbanes-oxley.com). This act defines more clearly the explicit responsibility of managers for financial statements, the relation between the independent auditor and the firm audited, and the kinds of services permitted and not permitted. Exhibit 1.11 summarizes some of the more important provisions of the Sarbanes-Oxley Act as they relate to financial statements.

For many years firms have included with their financial statements a report by management that states its responsibility for the financial statements. The Sarbanes-Oxley Act of 2002 now requires that the management report include a statement that management also assumes responsibility for establishing and maintaining adequate internal control structure and procedures (referred to as the *Management Assessment*). This new requirement now makes explicit management's responsibility not only for the financial statements but also for the underlying accounting and control system that generates the financial statements. The chief executive officer and the chief financial officer must sign this management report. PepsiCo's management report appears in Appendix A.

Also for many years, the independent auditor assessed a firm's internal control system, designed its audit tests in light of the quality of these internal controls, and then formed an opinion about the fairness of the amounts reported in the financial statements based on its audit tests. The independent auditor must now include opinions on both the effectiveness of the internal control system (referred to as the *Assurance Opinion*) and the fairness of the amounts reported in the financial statements. This dual opinion makes explicit the independent audit's responsibility for both testing the effectiveness of the internal control system and then judging the fairness of the amounts reported. The report of PepsiCo's independent auditor appears in Appendix A after Note 14, "Supplemental Financial Information." Note that the last paragraph includes opinions on both the internal control system and the financial statements and reads as follows:

EXHIBIT 1.11

Summary of the Principal Provisions of the Sarbanes-Oxley Act of 2002

1. Violation of the provisions of the Sarbanes-Oxley Act of 2002 is a violation of the Securities Exchange Act of 1934. The Securities Exchange Act of 1934 governs the public trading of securities.
2. The Sarbanes-Oxley Act of 2002 created the Public Company Accounting Oversight Board (PCAOB), which has responsibility for setting generally accepted auditing standards, ethics standards, and quality-control standards for audits.
3. The SEC has oversight and enforcement authority over the PCAOB.
4. The act precludes a registered public accounting firm from performing non-audit services contemporaneously with the audit. Certain services, such as tax work, are allowed if they are preapproved by the firm's audit committee or constitute less than 5 percent of the billing price for audit and other services.
5. The lead audit or coordinating partner and the reviewing partner of the public accounting firm must rotate, or change, every five years.
6. Members of the audit committee of a firm's board of directors will have primary responsibility for appointment, oversight, and compensation of the registered public accounting firm.
7. At least one member of the audit committee of the board of directors must be a "financial expert."
8. The firm's chief executive officer and the chief financial officer must issue a statement along with the audit report stating that the financial statements and notes fairly present the operations and financial position of the firm.
9. Each annual report must contain an "internal control report" that states management's responsibility for establishing and maintaining an adequate internal control structure and procedures (Management Assessment Report). The annual report must also contain an assessment of the effectiveness of the internal control structure and procedures by the firm's auditor (Assurance Opinion). The assurance opinion can be unqualified, qualified, adverse, or a disclaimer, the same as the independent accountant's opinion on the financial statements and notes.

> In our opinion, the consolidated financial statements referred to above present fairly, in all material respects, the financial position of PepsiCo, Inc. and Subsidiaries as of December 25, Year 4 and December 27, Year 3, and the results of their operations and their cash flows for each of the years in the three-year period ended December 25, Year 4, in conformity with the United States generally accepted accounting principles. Also, in our opinion, management's assessment that PepsiCo, Inc. maintained effective internal control over financial reporting as of December 25, Year 4, is fairly stated, in all material respects, based on criteria established in Internal Control-Integrated Framework issued by COSO. Furthermore, in our opinion, PepsiCo, Inc. maintained, in all material respects, effective internal control over financial reporting as of December 25, Year 4, based on criteria established in Internal Control-Integrated Framework issued by COSO.

Summary of Financial Statements, Notes, and Accountant's Opinion

The three principal financial statements report various aspects of a firm's operating, investing, and financing activities. The balance sheet reports the results of firms' decisions to acquire assets and the financing of those assets. Most current assets result from operating decisions (credit policies for customers, control systems for inventories) and most noncurrent assets result from investing decisions (plant capacity, access to patents). Firms typically use current liabilities to finance current assets and therefore link with operating decisions. Firms typically use long-term debt and common stock to finance noncurrent assets.

The income statement primarily reflects the results of operating decisions (product mix and pricing, insourcing or outsourcing of production and marketing). The income statement also reports amounts related to investing decisions (depreciation and amortization expense) and financing decisions (interest expense).

The statement of cash flows classifies the reasons that cash changes during a period into operating, investing, and financing categories.

The independent auditor's opinion includes statements about both the quality and effectiveness of the firm's internal control system and the fairness of its financial statements and notes in reporting a firm's financial position, performance, and cash flows. The independent audit adds credibility to the financial statements and notes prepared by management.

STEP 4: ANALYZE PROFITABILITY AND RISK

Armed with three key building blocks—(1) an understanding of the economics of the industry in which a firm competes, (2) an understanding of the particular strategies that the firm has chosen to compete in its industry, and (3) an assessment of the quality of the financial statements and notes that report the results of a firm's operating, investing, and financing activities—the analyst is ready to conduct a financial statement analysis.

Most financial statement analysis aims to assess a firm's profitability and risk. This twofold focus stems from the emphasis of investment decisions on returns and risk. Investors acquire shares of common stock in a company because of the return they expect from such investments. This return includes any dividends received plus the change in the market price of the shares of stock while the investor holds them. A rational investor will not be indifferent between two investments that are expected to yield, say, 20 percent return, if there are differences in the uncertainty, or risk, of earning 20 percent. The investor will demand a higher expected return from higher-risk investments to compensate for the additional risk assumed.

The income statement reports a firm's net income during the current and prior years. Assessing the profitability of the firm during these periods, after adjusting as appropriate for nonrecurring or unsustainable items, permits the analyst both to evaluate the firm's past profitability and to begin forecasting its likely future profitability. Empirical research has shown an association between earnings and market rates of return on common stock, a point discussed briefly in the next section in this chapter and in greater depth in Chapters 13 and 14 of the book.

Financial statements are also useful for assessing the risk of a firm. Empirical research has shown that volatility in reported earnings over time is correlated with stock market–based measures of firm risk, such as market equity beta. In addition, firms that are unable to generate sufficient cash flow from operations will likely encounter financial difficulties and perhaps even bankruptcy. Firms that have high proportions of debt in their capital structures will experience financial difficulties if they are unable to repay the debt at maturity or replace maturing debt with new debt. Assessing the financial risk of a firm assists the investor in identifying the level of risk incurred when investing in the firm's common stock.

Tools of Profitability and Risk Analysis

Most of this book describes and illustrates tools for analyzing financial statements. Our purpose here is simply to introduce several of these tools as a broad overview.

Common-Size Financial Statements

One analytical tool is common-size financial statements, a tool that is helpful in highlighting financial data relations both within statements and across statements. Common-size statements express all items in a particular financial statement as a percentage of some common base. Common-size balance sheets often use total assets as the base. Sales revenue is a common base in a common-size income statement.

The first two columns of Exhibit 1.12 present common-size balance sheets for PepsiCo for Year 3 and Year 4. Note the stability of the various common-size percentages for PepsiCo over this two-year period. PepsiCo experienced a significant increase in the proportion of assets comprising cash and marketable securities during Year 4. To understand better the reasons for the increased proportion of cash and marketable securities, refer to PepsiCo's statement of cash flows in Exhibit 1.10. We see there that increased net income led to increased cash flow from operations. The cash flow from operations was more than sufficient to finance expenditures on property, plant, and equipment. PepsiCo used the excess cash plus cash from additional short-term borrowing and issuing common stock to pay dividends and repurchase shares of its own stock. PepsiCo invested a portion of the remaining excess cash in marketable securities, leading to the increased common-size percentage for cash and marketable securities.

The proportion of shareholders' equity comprising retained earnings increased, but so did the proportion of treasury stock. Again, we can look at PepsiCo's statement of cash flows in Exhibit 1.10 to see that the retention of earnings increased retained earnings and total shareholders' equity by $2,883 million (= $4,212 − $1,329), whereas treasury stock purchases totaled $3,055 million, thereby reducing total shareholders' equity. These two changes were largely offsetting.

The first two columns of Exhibit 1.13 present common-size income statements for PepsiCo for Year 3 and Year 4. Note that net income as a percentage of sales (also known as the *profit margin*) increased from 13.2 percent in Year 3 to 14.4 percent in Year 4. Most expenses as a percentage of sales revenue remained stable between the two years. The increased profit margin results primarily from a smaller amount of impairment, restructuring, and merger-related expenses as a percentage of sales, a reduction of PepsiCo's tax burden (which we discuss more fully in Chapter 8), and the tax benefit of discontinued operations. Management's discussion and analysis of operations presented in Appendix B explains some of these changes. The task of the financial analyst is to delve into the reasons for such changes, taking into consideration industry economics, company strategies, management's explanations, and the operating results for competitors. We explore the reasons for PepsiCo's increased profit margin in Chapter 4.

The analyst must interpret common-size financial statements carefully. The amount for any one item in these statements is not independent of all other items. The dollar amount for an item might increase between two periods but its relative percentage in the common-size statement would decrease (or remain the same) if the dollar amount increased at a smaller rate than other items. For example, the dollar amounts for accounts and notes receivable, inventories, property, plant and equipment, and intangibles and other assets all increased between Year 3 and Year 4, but their common-size percentages decreased because they did not increase at as fast a rate as cash and marketable securities. Common-size percentages provide a general overview of financial position and operating performance, but the analyst must supplement them with other analytical tools.

EXHIBIT 1.12

Common-Size and Percentage Change Balance Sheets for PepsiCo

	Common Size		Percentage Change	
	Year 4	Year 3	Year 4	Five-Year Compound Annual Growth Rate
Assets				
Cash and Short-Term Investments	12.3%	7.9%	72.2%	20.8%
Accounts and Notes Receivable, net	10.7	11.2	6.0%	8.9%
Inventories	5.5	5.6	9.1%	5.8%
Other Current Assets	2.4	2.7	(4.8%)	(1.5%)
Total Current Assets	30.9%	27.4%	24.7%	10.8%
Investments	11.7	11.5	12.5%	2.9%
Property, Plant, and Equipment, net	29.1	30.9	4.1%	5.0%
Intangible and Other Assets	28.3	30.2	3.5%	7.3%
Total Assets	100.0%	100.0%	10.5%	7.0%
Liabilities and Shareholders' Equity				
Accounts Payable	6.2%	6.5%	5.7%	5.3%
Short-Term Obligations	3.8	2.3	78.3%	22.1%
Other Current Liabilities	14.2	16.5	(5.2%)	5.7%
Total Current Liabilities	24.2%	25.3%	5.3%	7.4%
Long-Term Debt Obligations	8.6	6.7	40.8%	(7.4%)
Deferred Tax	4.3	5.0	(3.6%)	0.1%
Other Noncurrent Liabilities	14.6	16.1	0.6%	3.9%
Total Liabilities	51.7%	53.1%	7.5%	2.4%
Preferred Stock	.1%	.2%	0.0%	12.3%
Common Stock	.1	.1	0.0%	(2.5%)
Additional Paid-In Capital	2.2	2.2	12.8%	2.0%
Retained Earnings	66.9	63.0	17.3%	4.7%
Accumulated Other Comprehensive Income (Loss)	(3.1)	(5.0)	(30.1%)	(7.4%)
Treasury Stock	(17.9)	(13.6)	45.7%	(7.3%)
Total Shareholders' Equity	48.3%	46.9%	13.9%	13.7%
Total Liabilities and Shareholders' Equity	100.0%	100.0%	10.5%	7.0%

Percentage Change Statements

Another analytical tool is percentage change financial statements, a tool that is helpful in highlighting the relative magnitudes of changes in financial statement data from year to year and over longer periods of time. These statements present the percentage change in

EXHIBIT 1.13

Common-Size and Percentage Change Income Statements for PepsiCo

	Common Size		Percentage Change	
	Year 4	Year 3	Year 4	Five-Year Compound Annual Growth Rate
Sales	100.0%	100.0%	8.5%	3.5%
Interest and Other Revenues	1.6	1.4	21.4%	20.5%
Cost of Sales	(45.8)	(45.9)	8.3%	7.0%
Selling, General, and Administrative Expenses	(35.2)	(35.1)	8.9%	(1.9%)
Amortization of Intangibles	(0.5)	(0.5)	1.4%	0.0%
Impairment, Restructuring, and Merger-Related Costs	(0.5)	(0.8)	(27.2%)	(5.0%)
Interest Expense	(0.6)	(0.6)	2.5%	(11.5%)
Income Before Income Taxes	19.0%	18.5%	11.1%	10.2%
Income Tax Expense	(4.7)	(5.3)	(3.7%)	3.0%
Income from Continuing Operations	14.3%	13.2%	17.0%	13.2%
Tax Benefit of Discontinued Operations	0.1	—	—	—
Net Income	14.4%	13.2%	18.0%	13.4%

the amount of an item relative to its amount in the previous period, or the average change over several prior periods.

The third and fourth columns of Exhibit 1.12 present changes in balance sheet items between Year 3 and Year 4 and the compound annual growth rates for the preceding five years for PepsiCo. Note that the percentage change in cash and marketable securities is the largest change between Year 3 and Year 4, consistent with the preceding observations with respect to changes in the common-size balance sheet. Another large percentage change between Year 3 and Year 4 occurred for short-term obligations. PepsiCo does not rely heavily on short-term borrowing. Although it increased its amount of short-term borrowing in Year 4, the amount of such borrowing in Year 3 is sufficiently small that the increase represents a large percentage change. Another large percentage change between Year 3 and Year 4 occurred for long-term debt obligations. PepsiCo's statement of cash flows in Exhibit 1.10 does not show much net change in long-term debt. Note 9, "Debt Obligations and Commitments," to PepsiCo's financial statements (Appendix A) explains why long-term debt increased. The firm reclassified a portion of its short-term borrowing as long-term debt because of the firm's intent and ability to refinance the short-term debt with long-term debt at maturity, a procedure allowed by GAAP. This reclassification affects the amount of long-term debt but does not appear in the statement of cash flows.

An examination of the compound annual growth rates in PepsiCo's balance sheet for the past five years reveals a significant increase in cash and marketable securities and in short-term borrowing. Most of these five-year rates of increase occurred, however, between Year 3 and Year 4.

The analyst must exert particular caution when interpreting percentage change balance sheets for any particular year. If the amount for the preceding year that serves as the base is relatively small, then even a small change in dollar amount can result in a large percentage change. This is the case, for example, with short-term obligations, discussed previously. Note also that the percentage change in accumulated other comprehensive loss for Year 4 was (30.1) percent. This change reflects a decrease in the amount from a negative \$1,267 million in Year 3 to a negative \$886 million in Year 4. However, note that accumulated other comprehensive loss comprises only 5.0 percent of total liabilities plus shareholders' equity at the end of Year 4. A large percentage change in an account that makes up only a small portion of total financing is not as meaningful as a smaller percentage change in an account that makes up a larger portion of total assets or total financing.

The third and fourth columns of Exhibit 1.13 present percentage change income statement amounts for PepsiCo. Note that for the preceding five years, net income for PepsiCo increased significantly faster than sales. Selling, general, and administrative expenses and interest expenses actually decreased, resulting in a significant increase in the growth rate of net income.

Financial Statement Ratios

Perhaps the most useful analytical tools for assessing profitability and risk are financial statement ratios. Financial statement ratios express relationships between various items from the three financial statements. Researchers and practitioners have found that such ratios serve as effective indicators of various dimensions of profitability and risk. Chapters 4 and 5 discuss these financial ratios in depth. This discussion merely introduces several of them.

Profitability Ratios. Perhaps the most commonly encountered financial ratio is earnings per common share (EPS). Basic EPS equals net income available to the common shareholders (that is, net income minus dividends on preferred stock) divided by the weighted average number of common shares outstanding. For Year 4, basic EPS for PepsiCo from continuing operations (see Exhibit 1.8 and Note 11, "Net Income per Common Share from Continuing Operations," to PepsiCo's financial statements in Appendix A) is \$2.45 [(= \$4,174 − \$25)/1,696 shares]. Firms typically report both basic and diluted EPS in their income statements, with per share amounts for continuing operations, discontinued operations, and extraordinary gains and losses shown separately. Chapter 4 discusses the computation of EPS. As Chapter 14 makes clear, financial analysts often use a multiple of EPS to derive what they consider an appropriate price for a firm's common stock.

Another profitability ratio is the rate of return on common shareholders' equity (ROCE). ROCE equals net income available to the common shareholders divided by average common shareholders' equity for the year. ROCE for PepsiCo for Year 4 from continuing operations is 32.6 percent [= (\$4,174 − \$25)/(0.5(\$11,896 + \$13,572))]. This ROCE is large relative to those of many firms. However, we should expect PepsiCo to generate a high rate of return for its shareholders because it has developed an effective and sustainable strategy as one of only two major players in the soft drink industry, which we assessed to have relatively favorable competitive conditions. This example illustrates that it is difficult to interpret ROCE and other financial ratios without a frame of reference. Analysts compare ratios to corresponding ratios of earlier periods (time-series analysis), to corresponding ratios of other firms in similar industries (cross-sectional analysis), and to average industry ratios in order to interpret the ratios. Chapter 4 provides an in-depth analysis of PepsiCo's ROCE and other profitability ratios.

Risk Ratios. To assess the volatility in a firm's earnings over time and to gauge the uncertainty inherent in the firm's future earnings, analysts can calculate the standard deviation in ROCE over time.

To assess the ability of firms to repay short-term obligations, analysts frequently calculate the current ratio, which equals current assets divided by current liabilities. The current ratio for PepsiCo at the end of Year 4 is 1.28 (= $8,639/$6,752). As with profitability ratios, this ratio is meaningful only when the analyst performs a time-series and cross-sectional analysis. Most firms have current ratios that exceed 1.0, so PepsiCo would appear to have minimal short-term risk.

To assess the ability of firms to continue operating for a longer term (that is, to avoid bankruptcy), the analyst looks at the amount of long-term debt in the capital structure. The ratio of long-term debt to shareholders' equity for PepsiCo at the end of Year 4 is 17.7 percent (= $2,397/$13,523). This percentage for PepsiCo declined in the recent years but increased slightly in Year 4. Thus, PepsiCo would appear to have low debt levels. Given PepsiCo's level of profitability and low debt levels, bankruptcy risk is very low. Chapter 5 provides an in-depth analysis of PepsiCo's debt to equity ratio and other risk ratios.

STEP 5: PREPARE FORECASTED FINANCIAL STATEMENTS

The analyst uses financial statement ratios, common-size and percentage change statements, and other analytical tools both to evaluate the profitability and risk of the firm in the recent past and to provide useful information to begin forecasting future financial statements. Forecasted financial statements rely on assumptions that the analyst makes about the future: Will the firm's strategy remain the same or change? Will the firm likely gain or lose market share relative to competitors? Will its costs change? Will it change the mix of debt versus equity financing? Responses to these and other questions provide the basis for preparing forecasted income statements, balance sheets, and statements of cash flows. The analyst can compare financial ratios of forecasted financial statement items with the corresponding ratios from the reported financial statements to judge the reasonableness of the assumptions made. Amounts from the forecasted financial statements serve as the basis for the valuation models in step 6, discussed next. Chapter 10 describes and illustrates the preparation of forecasted financial statements.

STEP 6: VALUE THE FIRM

Capital market participants most commonly use financial statement analysis to value firms. Financial statements and, specifically, key metrics from the statements such as earnings and operating cash flows play a central role in firm valuation. Thus, the emphasis of this book is to arm the analyst with the knowledge necessary to apply sophisticated and comprehensive valuation models.

To develop reliable estimates of firm value, and therefore to make intelligent buy/sell/hold investment decisions, the analyst must rely on well-reasoned and objective forecasts of the firm's future profitability and risk. Forecasts of future dividends, earnings, and cash flows form the basis for the most frequently used valuation models.

In some cases, analysts prefer to assess firm value using the classical dividends-based approach, which takes the perspective of valuing the firm from the standpoint of the cash that investors can expect to receive through dividends (or the sale of their shares). In practice, it is also common for analysts to assess firm value using measures of the firm's expected future free cash flows—cash flows that are available to be paid as dividends, after making necessary payments to reinvest in productive assets and meet required debt payments. A relatively new, state-of-the-art approach to firm value involves computing firm value based on the book value of equity and the earnings of the firm that the analyst expects to exceed the firm's cost of capital (similar in logic to "economic value added" computations). In many circumstances, analysts find it necessary or desirable to estimate firm value quickly using valuation rules of thumb, such as price-earnings ratios. Chapters 11 through 14 describe the theory and demonstrate the practical applications of each of these approaches to valuation using PepsiCo.

THE ASSOCIATION BETWEEN EARNINGS AND SHARE PRICES

As discussed earlier in this chapter, performing financial analysis that relies on analysis, forecasting, and valuation of key accounting measures (such as earnings) from a firm's financial statements can be very rewarding. To illustrate the striking linkage between accounting earnings and stock returns, and to foreshadow the potential to generate positive excess returns through analysis and forecasting, consider the results from empirical research by D. Craig Nichols and James Wahlen.[6] They studied the average cumulative market-adjusted returns generated by firms during the twelve months leading up to and including the month in which each firm announced annual earnings numbers. For a sample of 31,923 firm-years between 1988 and 2001, they found that the average firm that announced an increase in earnings (over the prior year's earnings) experienced stock returns that exceeded market average returns by roughly 19.2 percent. On the other hand, the average firm that announced a decrease in earnings experienced stock returns that were roughly 16.4 percent lower than the market average. Their results suggest that merely the sign of the change in earnings is associated with a 35 percent stock return differential in one year, on average. Exhibit 1.14 presents a graph of their results.

To an analyst, the results of the Nichols-Wahlen study indicate the magnitude of potential returns to be earned by forecasting the changes in earnings one year ahead. Analysts should view the Nichols-Wahlen results as very encouraging and intriguing because they imply that if analysts can forecast earnings changes correctly more often than not, then they should be able to earn some portion of the excess returns documented in this study. To be sure, analysts will not be able to beat the market consistently by 35 percent per year—Nichols and Wahlen's research had the advantage of perfect foresight, which analysts do not have. Using historical earnings data, Nichols and Wahlen knew with certainty which firms would announce earnings increases or decreases one year ahead. Analysts must forecast earnings changes and take positions in stocks on the basis of their earnings expectations.

Note in the graph of the Nichols-Wahlen results in Exhibit 1.14 that their study also examined the relation between changes in cash flows from operations and cumulative market-adjusted stock returns. Using the same firm-years and study period, Nichols and

[6]D. Craig Nichols and James Wahlen, "How Do Earnings Numbers Relate to Stock Returns? A Review of Classic Accounting Research with Updated Evidence," *Accounting Horizons* (December 2004), pp. 263–286. The portion of the Nichols and Wahlen study described here is a replication of path-breaking research in accounting by Ray Ball and Philip Brown, "An Evaluation of Accounting Income Numbers," *Journal of Accounting Research* (Autumn 1968), pp. 159–178.

EXHIBIT 1.14

The Association between Change in Annual Earnings and Cumulative Abnormal Returns

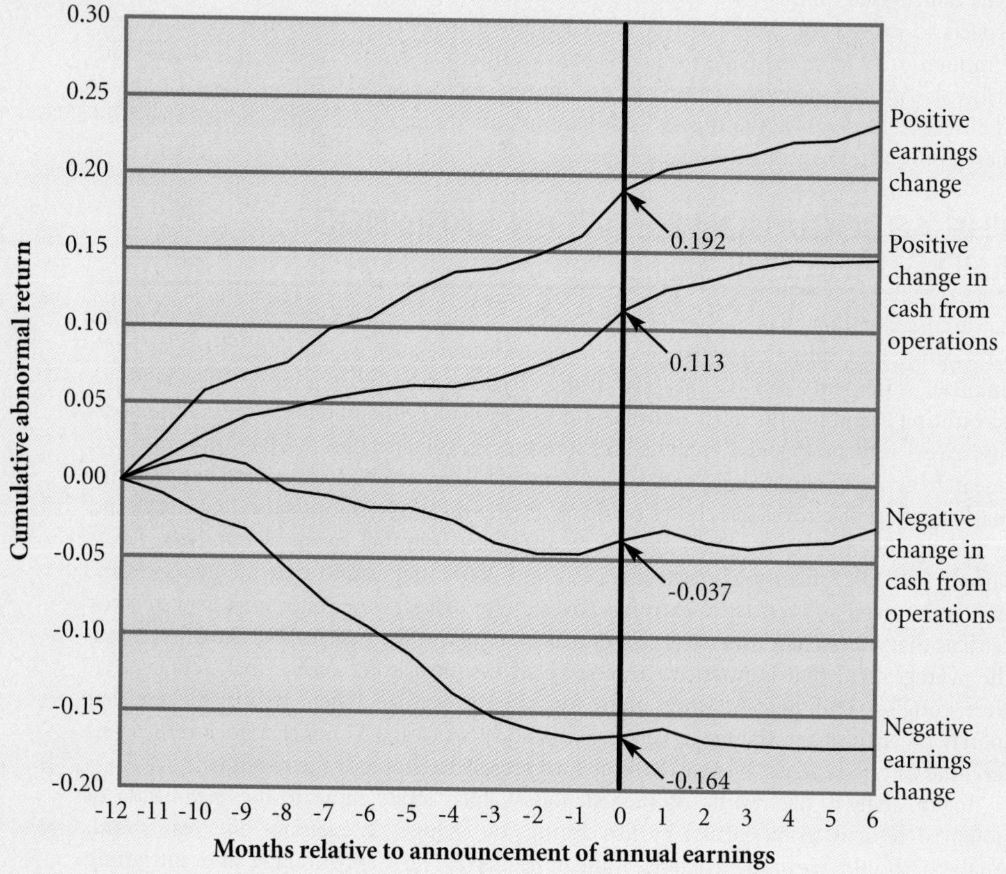

Source: D. Craig Nichols and James Wahlen, "How Do Earnings Numbers Relate to Stock Returns? A Review of Classic Accounting Research with Updated Evidence," *Accounting Horizons*, December 2004, pp. 263–286.

Wahlen documented that firms experiencing positive changes in cash from operations experienced stock returns that beat the market by an average of 11.3 percent, whereas firms experiencing decreases in cash from operations experienced stock returns that were lower than the market by an average of 3.7 percent. These results suggest that the sign of the change in cash from operations is associated with a 15 percent stock return differential in one year, on average. This implies that changes in cash flows are also strongly related to stock returns, but they are not as informative for the capital markets as changes in earnings. This should not be surprising, because changes in cash flow are less indicative of the firm's performance in one period than are changes in earnings. For example, if a firm experiences a negative change in cash from operations, it could be attributable to cash flow difficulties (bad news) or a large investment of cash in growth opportunities (good news). A negative change in earnings, on the other hand, is almost always bad news. This explains, in part, why analysts, firm managers, the financial press, boards of directors, auditors, and therefore financial statement analysis textbook writers focus so much attention on analyzing and forecasting earnings numbers.

Empirical research in accounting has deepened our understanding of the many dimensions of the role of accounting numbers in the capital market by documenting that share prices react strongly to the magnitude of the change in earnings and the persistence of the change in earnings for future periods, and that financial statement ratios are useful for predicting future earnings changes. We will refer to important research results like these throughout this book.

ROLE OF FINANCIAL STATEMENT ANALYSIS IN AN EFFICIENT CAPITAL MARKET

There are differing views as to the benefits of analyzing a set of financial statements. One view is that stock market prices react efficiently to published information about a firm. That is, market participants react intelligently and quickly to information they receive, so that market prices continually reflect underlying economic values. One implication of an efficient capital market is that financial statement users cannot routinely analyze financial statements to find "undervalued" or "overvalued" securities. The market quickly impounds new information into security prices.

Opposing views include the following:

1. Even if markets are perfectly efficient, someone must do the analysis to bring about the appropriate prices. Financial analysts, with their expertise and access to information about firms, do the analysis quickly and engage in the trading necessary to achieve efficient pricing.
2. Research on capital market efficiency aggregates financial data for individual firms and studies the average reaction of the market to earnings and other financial statement information. A finding that the market is efficient on average does not preclude temporary mispricing of individual firms' shares.[7] A principal task of the financial analyst is to identify mispriced securities of particular firms and to act to bring about appropriate pricing.
3. Research has shown that equity markets are not perfectly efficient. Anomalies include the tendency for market prices to adjust with a lag to new information, systematic underreaction to the information contained in earnings announcements, and the ability to use a combination of financial ratios to detect under- and overpriced securities.[8]
4. Management has incentives related to job security and compensation to report as favorable a picture as possible in the financial statements within the constraints of GAAP. These reports may therefore represent biased indicators of the economic performance and financial position of firms. Financial analysts should adjust these

---

[7]For an elaboration on the role of financial statement analysis in an efficient capital market and the insights provided by academic research to this process, see Clyde P. Stickney, "The Academic's Approach to Securities Research: Is It Relevant to the Analyst?" *Journal of Financial Statement Analysis* (Summer 1997), pp. 52–60.

[8]For a summary of the issues and related research, see Ray Ball, "The Theory of Stock Market Efficiency: Accomplishments and Limitations," *Journal of Applied Corporate Finance* (Spring 1995), pp. 4–17.

financial statements to remove such biases if market prices are to reflect underlying economic values.

5. Financial statement analysis is valuable in numerous settings outside equity capital markets (for example, credit analysis by a bank to support corporate lending, competitor analysis to identify competitive advantages, and merger and acquisition analysis to identify buyout candidates).

SOURCES OF FINANCIAL STATEMENT INFORMATION

Firms in the United States whose bonds or capital stock trade in public markets typically make available the following information:

1. **Annual Report to Shareholders.** The "glossy" annual report includes balance sheets for the most recent two years and income statements and statements of cash flows for the most recent three years, along with various notes and supporting schedules. The annual report also includes a letter from the chairperson of the board of directors and chief executive officer summarizing the activities of the most recent year. It also includes a discussion and analysis by management of the firm's operating performance, financial position, and liquidity. Firms vary with respect to the information provided in this Management Discussion and Analysis of operations. Some firms, such as PepsiCo as shown in Appendix B, give helpful information about the firm's strategy and reasons for the changes in profitability, financial position, and risk. Other firms merely repeat amounts presented in the financial statements without providing helpful explanations for operating results.
2. **Form 10-K Annual Report.** The Form 10-K annual report filed with the SEC includes the same financial statements and notes as the corporate annual report plus additional supporting schedules required by the SEC. For example, Form 10-K often includes more detailed information than the corporate annual report on changes in the allowance for uncollectible accounts and other valuation accounts. Large firms must file their annual reports with the SEC within 60 days after the end of their annual accounting period.
3. **Form 10-Q Quarterly Report.** The Form 10-Q quarterly report filed with the SEC includes condensed balance sheet and income statement information for the most recent three months, as well as comparative data for earlier quarters.
4. **Prospectus or Registration Statement.** Firms intending to issue new bonds or capital stock file a prospectus with the SEC that describes the offering (amount, intended uses of proceeds). The prospectus includes much of the financial information found in the Form 10-K annual report.
5. **Form 20-F Annual Report.** Non-U.S. firms whose bonds or capital stock trade in capital markets in the United States must file annual reports with the SEC. The Form 20-F annual report is similar to Form 10-K except that it includes schedules to reconcile net income and shareholders' equity from GAAP of the domicile of the non-U.S. firm to GAAP in the United States.

A large number of firms include all or a portion of their annual reports and SEC filings on a web site. For example, PepsiCo provides all of the financial data and analysis provided in Appendices A and B on the firm's web site (www.pepsico.com). In addition, many firms provide additional financial data at these sites that is not published in the annual reports. For example, Gap, Inc., consisting of The Gap, Banana Republic, and Old Navy clothing store chains, provides monthly sales data for each of these chains. It also provides information on the opening and closing of stores.

Firms are required to file reports electronically with the SEC, with these filings for recent years available at the SEC web site (www.sec.gov). Numerous commercial online and CD-ROM services also provide financial statement information (Thomson Analytics, Bloomberg, Standard & Poor's, Moody's, and others).

Appendix 1.1 discusses sources of financial information more fully.

SUMMARY

The purpose of this chapter is to provide a broad overview of six interconnected activities related to financial statement analysis:

1. Identify the economic characteristics of the industry in which a firm participates.
2. Identify the corporate strategy that a firm pursues to compete within its industry.
3. Assess the quality of a firm's financial statements and adjust them, if necessary, for items lacking sustainability or comparability.
4. Analyze and interpret the profitability and risk of a firm, assessing how well the firm performed and the strength of its financial position.
5. Prepare forecasted financial statements.
6. Value the particular firm.

You should not expect to fully understand these six steps at this stage of your studies. Future chapters discuss each in greater depth. Chapter 2 discusses the important links between the valuation of assets and liabilities on the balance sheet, and revenues and expenses on the income statement. Chapter 3 details the preparation and interpretation of the statement of cash flows for firms in various industries at various stages in their growth. Chapter 4 describes common financial statement ratios for assessing profitability and illustrates their calculation and interpretation for PepsiCo. Chapter 5 parallels the preceding chapter by describing common financial statement ratios for assessing risk. Chapters 6 through 9 examine GAAP for various financial statement items and address concerns that affect the quality of earnings and financial position. Chapters 10 to 14 shift our focus to valuation. Chapter 10 demonstrates the preparation of forecasted financial statements. Chapters 11 through 14 examine various valuation models based on cash flows, earnings, and amounts for comparable firms. With firm valuation the most frequent objective of financial statement analysis, these chapters represent a fitting culmination to the book.

Appendix **1.1**

Preparing a Term Project

Our reading of the course syllabi by various users of previous editions of this book indicates that many instructors require their students to apply the concepts and tools of analysis in this book to the financial statements of one or more companies. This appendix provides helpful hints for you in conducting such a project. Our students find it useful to complete each part of the project as we cover that topic in class. For example, soon after completing Chapter 1, you should select the companies you intend to study and complete the industry economics and company strategy portion of the project. Obtaining financial statement data and performing a first pass on profitability and risk ratios follows coverage of Chapters 4 and 5. Assessments of the quality of the financial statements should coincide with coverage of Chapters 6 to 9. Forecasts of future financial statement amounts follow coverage of Chapter 10. Applying various valuation models must await coverage of Chapters 11 to 14. Based on our experience, we can assure you that if you follow this approach, your learning experience in a project like this will be much richer and rewarding than it will be if you wait until the last few weeks of the course to do the major work on the project. For this reason, we have our students submit progress reports throughout the term. These progress reports both help our students stay on schedule and permit us to provide suggestions that might assist them going forward.

SELECTING COMPANIES FOR THE TERM PROJECT

Some instructors ask their students to analyze a single company over time (a time-series analysis), while other instructors ask students to compare two or more companies over time (a cross-section analysis). We have found that comparing companies in the same industry provides the most interesting insights.

When selecting companies to analyze, select an industry and firms in which you have an interest. You will likely spend considerable time on the project. Selecting firms of interest enhances motivation. Some of our students select firms for which they hope or expect to work. The in-depth analysis of the firm often enhances the job interview and early work experience once hired. Our students find that selecting firms with somewhat different strategies usually provides better insights than selecting firms with similar strategies. Some of our students' richest term projects involve analyzing firms in the same industry but headquartered in different countries. However, such projects involve additional work to learn GAAP, as well as institutional and cultural differences in each country that might affect interpretation of the financial analyses.

Various online databases list firms within the United States and worldwide in various industries. Your library may or may not subscribe to all the databases discussed in this appendix. Packaged with this book is access to the Business & Company Resource Center. This site provides information about particular industries and particular companies. Information provided includes company overviews and histories, newspaper and magazine articles, financial data, and investment reports. A similar online information service is OneSource, published by Global Business Browser (www.onesource.com).

UNDERSTANDING INDUSTRY ECONOMICS AND COMPANY STRATEGIES

Perhaps the best place to start understanding the economics of an industry and the particular strategy that a firm has selected to compete in the industry is the Form 10-K report the firm filed with the SEC (www.sec.gov). The first section of Form 10-K is a narrative entitled "Business." This section usually describes the firm's principal businesses and provides information about suppliers, competitors, regulation, and other items.

Reading this section of Form 10-K for the other firms selected for study will usually turn up sufficient information so that you can summarize the economics of the industry using either a value chain, Porter's five forces framework, or the economics attributes framework discussed in the chapter. These sources will not likely set forth the economics precisely to fit any of these industry economics frameworks, so some interpretation and synthesis on your part will be necessary.

The reading of the Business section of the Form 10-K report should also provide information on the strategy of each firm studied. We find it useful to search the notes to the financial statements to find the segment data by products or services and by geographical location. We convert the reported numbers to mix percentages, as we did for PepsiCo in Exhibit 1.4, to obtain an overview of the firm's principal involvements.

Another source for industry information is Standard & Poor's Industry Surveys. These surveys describe the most important factors affecting the industry, the key firms in the industry, and key financial ratios for each firm. The Business & Company Resource Center and OneSource resources, described previously, also provide helpful information about the industry.

ASSESSING THE QUALITY OF THE FINANCIAL STATEMENTS

Two steps are needed here: (1) creating a data file with the amounts from the financial statements, and (2) adjusting the reported financial statement amounts to improve the quality of the financial statement data.

Creating a Data File

One initial choice in creating a data file is whether to use the accounts and amounts provided by the firm in its Form 10-K or annual report to shareholders or to use amounts from various online sources or databases that format the amounts into a standardized template. One advantage of following the first approach is that you rely on the primary source of the financial statements, not a secondary source for which you may not know all of the reclassifications and adjustments made to conform the reported amounts to the standardized template. Another advantage of following the first approach is that the financial statement data will be classified into accounts consistent with the notes to the financial statements, the main source of information for assessing the quality of the reported amounts, a topic discussed shortly. The principal advantage of using amounts in a standardized template is that the financial statement amounts are reasonably comparable across firms.

FSAP

The next decision to be made is whether to input the financial statement data into FSAP, a financial statement analysis package that accompanies this text, or to create a new spreadsheet file. The principal advantages of FSAP are that it provides spreadsheets with embedded formulas for the various profitability and risk ratios, provides a template to prepare forecasted financial statements using the previously reported actual amounts as a base, and then inputs the forecasted amounts into several valuation models to arrive at equity values. (Appendix C illustrates the use of FSAP to analyze and value PepsiCo and Appendix D contains a user manual for FSAP, explaining how to create a data file.) The disadvantage of using FSAP from a learning perspective is that much of the work is done for you. The advantage of creating a new spreadsheet file is that you must program the spreadsheets to compute the financial ratios, prepare forecasted financial statements, and apply the various valuation models. To enhance learning, many instructors prefer that their students program the spreadsheet themselves.

Downloading financial statement data from online sources means that the data will already be in a standard format. You can program the spreadsheet for this format and then use it for all firms analyzed. Downloading financial statement data from a firm's Form 10-K requires that at least initially the spreadsheet use the firm's specific categories and grouping of accounts. It is unlikely that the other firms analyzed will use precisely the same accounts. Thus, you then must either transform the reported amounts to a standard format or program each firm's spreadsheet to conform to its specific accounts and categories.

It is a good idea to program various mathematical checks into the spreadsheet. For example, the sum of the individual assets must equal the sum of the individual liability and shareholders' equity accounts. The net of individual revenues and expenses must equal net income. The cash flow from operating, investing, and financing activities must equal the change in cash. The latter should agree with the change in cash on the balance sheet from the beginning to the end of the year.

One issue you must face is how many years of financial statement data to obtain. We recommend using at least three years of income statements and statements of cash flows and four years of balance sheets (although this many years of data may not be available for very young firms or for initial public offering firms). The extra year for the balance sheets results from the need for average amounts on certain accounts on the balance sheet in order to calculate particular financial ratios for a year. In most cases, the average amount is the sum of the amounts on the balance sheet at the beginning and end of the year divided by 2. FSAP permits the inputting of five years of income statement and cash flow data and six years of balance sheet data. The longer historical time frame is useful when deciding on appropriate growth rates for forecasting financial statements, particularly if the recent past is unusual for some reason (for example, because of a recession).

Another issue you must face is whether to use the originally reported amounts for each year or to use amounts as retroactively restated for discontinued operations, acquisitions or divestitures, or other factors. The advantage of using restated numbers is that the financial statements report amounts more like those that one might expect going forward. The disadvantage is that firms seldom provide restated data beyond the three income statements and statements of cash flows and two balance sheets commonly found in annual reports. Thus, using restated data is not likely to yield financial statements that are fully consistent over time. Chapter 6 discusses this issue more fully.

Assessing the Quality of the Reported Amounts

One of the most important steps in financial statement analysis is to assess the quality of the reported amounts and make appropriate adjustments before proceeding to the analysis of profitability and risk. The saying "garbage in, garbage out" applies with particular force with respect to financial statements. To assess quality, it is imperative to read the financial statements and notes. Chapters 6 to 9 describe the most important factors to look for in this quality assessment. Material nonrecurring or unusual income items are candidates for adjustment. Significant off-balance sheet assets or liabilities are also candidates. Some adjustments may be needed to increase the comparability of the financial statement amounts for each of the firms analyzed in the term project. It is helpful to keep a log of adjustments made to refer to later when interpreting profitability and risk ratios and forecasting future financial statements.

ANALYZING PROFITABILITY AND RISK

If you use FSAP to create data files, then FSAP automatically calculates the profitability and risk ratios discussed in Chapters 4 and 5. If you create your own spreadsheet file for the financial statement data, you will want to include a separate spreadsheet within that file to compute the financial statement ratios. This spreadsheet should contain the formulas for the financial ratios, referring back to the spreadsheets with the financial statement data to obtain the amounts for the numerator and denominator of each ratio. If you change any of the amounts in the financial statements portion of the spreadsheet later on in the project (for example, from making adjustments to improve the quality of the data), then the financial ratios will automatically update.

When analyzing profitability and risk using the financial statement ratios, we find it helpful to do a time-series analysis for each firm first, and then do cross-section comparisons across firms. As a first pass, look for financial ratios that have changed significantly over time or differ significantly across firms. Then relate the changes and differences to the economics of the industry and strategies of the firms. You will find it helpful to read the Management Discussion and Analysis section of the annual report to shareholders or the Form 10-K to find explanations for the time-series changes. A sequence that we have found useful is as follows:

- Time-series analysis of profitability for each firm using (a) common-size and percentage change financial statements, (b) rate of return on assets and its components, and (c) rate of return on common shareholders' equity and its components.
- Cross-sectional profitability analysis of profitability for all firms using (a) common-size and percentage change financial statements, (b) rate of return on assets and its components, and (c) rate of return on common shareholders' equity and its components.
- Time-series and cross-sectional comparisons of short-term liquidity risk.
- Time-series and cross-sectional comparisons of long-term liquidity risk.

PREPARING FORECASTED FINANCIAL STATEMENTS

Having analyzed the profitability and risk of each firm in the recent past, you are now ready to project the financial statement amounts into the future. As Chapter 10 discusses, you will want to identify any important factors that will likely differ in the future, such as a major divestiture or acquisition, changes in the economic or regulatory environment, or a change in business strategy.

Spreadsheets are particularly powerful tools for preparing forecasted financial statements. It is desirable to link the forecasted financial statements with the financial statement data and related ratios from the recent past. FSAP does this automatically. If you program your own spreadsheet file with the financial statement data, you can simply program additional spreadsheets within this file for the forecasted amounts. We suggest that you build in the same kinds of mathematical data checks into the forecasted amounts that you included for the reported amounts. We also find it useful to include a spreadsheet that computes the same financial ratios for the forecasted amounts as it does for the reported amounts. You can then study the financial ratios to see if the assumptions underlying the forecasted amounts make sense relative to the past and to expected changes going forward.

VALUE THE FIRMS

Chapters 11 to 14 describe and illustrate various models to value firms, including the following:

- Present value of projected dividends (Chapter 11).
- Present value of expected free cash flows to the firm (Chapter 12).
- Residual income valuation (Chapter 13).
- Market-based comparables (Chapter 14).

The first three of these valuation models rely on data from the forecasted financial statements. Your instructor may ask you to follow only one or more than one of these approaches in your valuations.

QUESTIONS, EXERCISES, PROBLEMS, AND CASES

Questions and Exercises

1.1 VALUE CHAIN ANALYSIS APPLIED TO THE TIMBER AND TIMBER PRODUCTS INDUSTRY. Create a value chain for the timber and timber products industry, beginning with the growing of timber and ending with the retailing of timber and paper products. Describe each link in the value chain briefly and list the name of one U.S. company involved in each link. (*Hint: Access Thomson/Gale's Business & Company Resource Center, Global Business Browser, or Standard & Poor's Industry Surveys to obtain the needed information.*)

1.2 PORTER'S FIVE FORCES APPLIED TO THE AIR COURIER INDUSTRY. Apply Porter's five forces to the air courier industry. Industry participants include such firms as FedEx, United Parcel Service, and DHL. (*Hint: Access Thomson/Gale's Business & Company Resource Center, Global Business Browser, or Standard & Poor's Industry Surveys to obtain the needed information.*)

1.3 ECONOMIC ATTRIBUTES FRAMEWORK APPLIED TO THE SPECIALTY RETAILING APPAREL INDUSTRY. Apply the economic attributes framework discussed in the chapter to the specialty retailing apparel industry, which includes such firms as The Gap, Limited Brands, and Abercrombie & Fitch. (*Hint: Access Thomson/Gale's Business & Company Resource Center, Global Business Browser, or Standard & Poor's Industry Surveys to obtain the needed information.*)

1.4 IDENTIFICATION OF COMMODITY BUSINESSES. A recent article of *Fortune* magazine listed the following firms among the top ten most admired companies in the United States: Dell, Southwest Airlines, Microsoft, and Johnson & Johnson. Access the web sites of these four companies or read the Business section of their Form 10-K reports (www.sec.gov) and describe whether you would view their products or services as commodities. Be sure to explain your reasoning.

1.5 IDENTIFICATION OF COMPANY STRATEGIES. Refer to the web sites and the Form 10-K reports of Home Depot (www.homedepot.com) and Lowe's Companies (www.lowes.com). Compare and contrast their business strategies.

1.6 RESEARCHING THE FASB WEB SITE. Go to the web site of the Financial Accounting Standards Board (www.fasb.org). Identify the most recently issued financial reporting standard and summarize briefly (in one paragraph) its principal provisions. Also, search under Project Activities to identify the reporting issue with the most recent update. Describe the issue briefly and the nature of the action taken by the FASB.

1.7 RESEARCHING THE IASB WEB SITE. Go to the web site for the International Accounting Standards Board (www.iasb.org). Search for the International Financial Reporting Standards (IFRS) summaries. Identify the most recently issued international financial reporting standard and summarize briefly (in one paragraph) its principal provisions.

1.8 EFFECT OF INDUSTRY ECONOMICS ON BALANCE SHEET. Access the web sites of American Airlines (www.aa.com), Intel (www.intel.com) and Disney (www.disney.com) and study the business involvements of each firm. Examine the financial ratios below and indicate which firms are likely to be American Airlines, Intel, and Disney. Explain your reasoning.

	Firm A	Firm B	Firm C
Property, Plant and Equipment/Assets	30.6%	32.8%	66.5%
Long-Term Debt/Assets	17.4%	1.8%	47.0%

1.9 EFFECT OF BUSINESS STRATEGY ON COMMON-SIZE INCOME STATEMENT. Access the web sites of Apple Computer (www.apple.com) and Dell (www.dell.com) and study the strategies of each firm. Examine the following common-size income statements and indicate which firm is likely to be Apple Computer and which is likely to be Dell. Explain your reasoning. Indicate any percentages that seem inconsistent with their strategies.

	Firm A	Firm B
Sales	100.0%	100.0%
Cost of Goods Sold	(81.7)	(72.7)
Selling and Administrative	(8.7)	(17.4)
Research and Development	(.9)	(5.9)
Income Taxes	(2.8)	(1.3)
All Other Items	.3	.6
Net Income	6.2%	3.3%

1.10 EFFECT OF BUSINESS STRATEGY ON COMMON-SIZE INCOME STATEMENT. Access the web sites of Dollar General (www.dollargeneral.com) and Federated Department Stores (www.federated-fds.com) and study the strategies of each firm. Examine the following common-size income statements and indicate which firm is likely to be Dollar General and which is likely to be Federated Department Stores. Explain your reasoning. Indicate any percentages that seem inconsistent with their strategies.

	Firm A	Firm B
Sales	100.0%	100.0%
Cost of Goods Sold	(70.6)	(59.5)
Selling and Administrative	(21.8)	(31.6)
Income Taxes	(2.6)	(2.7)
All Other Items	(.6)	(1.8)
Net Income	4.4%	4.4%

Problems and Cases

1.11 EFFECT OF INDUSTRY CHARACTERISTICS ON FINANCIAL STATEMENT RELATIONSHIPS. Effective financial statement analysis requires an understanding of a firm's economic characteristics. The relations between various financial statement items provide evidence of many of these economic characteristics. Exhibit 1.15 presents common-size condensed balance sheets and income statements for twelve firms in different industries. These common-size balance sheets and income statements express various items as a percentage of operating revenues (that is, the statement divides all amounts by operating revenues for the year). Exhibit 1.15 also shows the ratio of cash flow from operations to capital expenditures. A dash for a particular financial statement item does not necessarily mean that the amount is zero. It merely indicates that the amount is not sufficiently large for the firm to disclose it. The twelve companies and a brief description of their activities follow.

1. Amazon.com: Operates web sites to sell a wide variety of products online. The firm operated at a net loss in all years prior to that reported in Exhibit 1.15.
2. Anheuser-Busch: Manufactures and distributes beer and operates theme parks.
3. Carnival Corporation: Owns and operates cruise ships.
4. Cisco Systems: Manufacturers and sells computer networking and communications products. Cisco Systems has made minority ownership investments in other networking and communications firms in recent years.
5. Citigroup: Offers a wide range of financial services in the commercial banking, insurance, and securities business. Operating expenses represent the compensation of employees.
6. eBay: Operates an online trading platform for buyers and sellers to make purchases and sales of a variety of goods. The firm has grown in part by acquiring other companies to enhance or support its online trading platform.
7. Harrah's Entertainment: Owns and operates hotels and casinos.
8. Johnson & Johnson: Develops, manufactures, and sells pharmaceutical products, medical equipment, and branded over-the-counter consumer personal care products.
9. Kellogg: Manufactures and distributes cereal and other food products. The firm acquired other branded food companies in recent years.
10. Merrill Lynch: Offers brokerage and investment banking services. Operating expenses represent the compensation of employees.
11. Verizon Communications: Maintains a telecommunications network and offers telecommunications services. Operating expenses represent the compensation of employees.
12. Yum Brands: Operates chains of restaurants.

EXHIBIT 1.15

Common-Size Financial Statement Data for Firms in 12 Industries (Problem 1.11)

	(1)	(2)	(3)	(4)
Balance Sheet at End of Year				
Cash and Marketable Securities	25.7%	1.3%	1.5%	4.3%
Receivables	—	2.1	4.7	8.1
Inventories	6.9	0.8	4.6	7.1
Property, Plant, and Equipment, at cost	6.2	67.3	116.6	47.1
Accumulated Depreciation	(2.6)	(29.1)	(57.4)	(18.8)
Net	3.6	38.2	59.2	28.3
Intangibles	2.0	10.0	8.0	53.2
Other Assets	8.7	10.8	30.3	11.3
Total Assets	46.9%	63.2%	108.3%	112.3%
Current Liabilities	23.4%	15.3%	13.2%	29.6%
Long-Term Debt	26.7	19.2	55.4	40.5
Other Noncurrent Liabilities	0.1	11.0	21.8	18.7
Shareholders' Equity	(3.3)	17.7	17.9	23.5
Total Equities	46.9%	63.2%	108.3%	112.3%
Income Statement for Year				
Operating Revenues	100.0%	100.0%	100.0%	100.0%
Cost of Sales (excluding depreciation) or Operating Expenses[a]	(76.0)	(71.6)	(55.3)	(52.3)
Depreciation and Amortization	(1.1)	(5.0)	(6.2)	(4.3)
Selling and Administrative	(16.6)	(11.6)	(15.9)	(26.0)
Research and Development	—	—	—	—
Interest	(1.5)	(3.1)	(2.7)	(3.2)
Income Taxes	3.4	(3.2)	(7.8)	(4.9)
All Other Items, net	0.3	2.7	2.9	—
Net Income	8.5%	8.2%	15.0%	9.3%
Cash Flow from Operations/ Capital Expenditures	6.4	1.8	2.7	4.4

[a]See the problem narrative for items included in operating expenses.

Required

Use whatever clues you can to match the companies in Exhibit 1.15 with the firms listed here.

1.12 EFFECT OF INDUSTRY CHARACTERISTICS ON FINANCIAL STATEMENT RELATIONSHIPS. Effective financial statement analysis requires an understanding of a firm's economic characteristics. The relations between various finan-

EXHIBIT 1.15

continued

(5)	(6)	(7)	(8)	(9)	(10)	(11)	(12)
27.2%	39.3%	10.8%	6.4%	66.3%	6.8%	721.2%	1,507.2%
14.4	8.3	2.9	13.7	11.1	4.2	496.5	385.0
7.9	5.5	0.6	2.2	—	2.5	—	—
39.5	34.7	143.3	260.2	34.7	248.6	46.2	23.9
(17.4)	(19.7)	(39.0)	(156.3)	(13.0)	(34.6)	(18.5)	(16.2)
22.1	15.0	104.3	103.9	21.7	214.0	27.7	7.7
25.0	20.5	48.7	66.6	93.9	47.6	43.7	19.0
16.0	72.9	21.5	40.0	51.3	9.0	81.6	77.1
112.6%	161.5%	188.8%	232.8%	244.3%	284.1%	1,370.7%	1,996.0%
29.4%	39.5%	16.6%	32.5%	33.2%	51.8%	1,017.8%	1,531.1%
5.4	—	113.3	50.0	—	64.7	192.0	368.3
10.6	4.4	13.4	62.5	5.3	5.6	60.0	—
67.2	117.6	45.5	87.8	205.8	162.0	100.9	96.6
112.6%	161.5%	188.8%	232.8%	244.3%	284.1%	1,370.7%	1,996.0%
100.0%	100.0%	100.0%	100.0%	100.0%	100.0%	100.0%	100.0%
(26.3)	(28.3)	(52.9)	(32.5)	(16.9)	(56.1)	(31.2)	(32.6)
(4.5)	(6.5)	(7.4)	(19.5)	(7.8)	(8.3)	(1.9)	(1.6)
(31.1)	(22.1)	(22.5)	(29.6)	(35.6)	(13.2)	(24.2)	(15.7)
(11.0)	(14.5)	—	—	(7.4)	—	—	—
(0.4)	—	(6.0)	(3.3)	(0.3)	(2.9)	(20.4)	(32.2)
(9.1)	(9.2)	(4.2)	(4.0)	(10.5)	(0.5)	(6.4)	(4.3)
0.4	3.1	0.2	(0.9)	2.3	0.1	(0.2)	0.1
18.0%	22.5%	7.2%	10.2%	23.8%	19.1%	15.7%	13.7%
5.1	11.6	1.2	1.6	4.4	0.9	18.9	23.2

cial statement items provide evidence of many of these economic characteristics. Exhibit 1.16 presents common-size condensed balance sheets and income statements for 12 firms in different industries. These common-size balance sheets and income statements express various items as a percentage of operating revenues (that is, the statement divides all amounts by operating revenues for the year). Exhibit 1.16 also shows the ratio of cash flow from operations to capital expenditures. A dash for a particular financial statement item does not necessarily mean that the amount is zero. It merely indicates that the amount is

EXHIBIT 1.16

Common-Size Financial Statement Data for Firms in 12 Industries (Problem 1.12)

	(1)	(2)	(3)	(4)
Balance Sheet at End of Year				
Cash and Marketable Securities	1.8%	10.6%	30.5%	16.2%
Receivables	14.6	1.4	0.4	16.5
Inventories	—	10.6	11.8	8.8
Property, Plant, and Equipment, at cost	7.2	14.6	39.6	17.3
Accumulated Depreciation	(3.6)	(5.5)	(13.5)	(9.0)
Net	3.6	9.1	26.1	8.3
Intangibles	1.9	2.1	—	24.9
Other Assets	3.1	1.4	1.4	20.6
Total Assets	25.0%	35.2%	70.2%	95.3%
Current Liabilities	9.7%	18.3%	16.4%	35.8%
Long-Term Debt	—	2.0	—	5.8
Other Noncurrent Liabilities	2.2	1.0	2.8	6.7
Shareholders' Equity	13.1	13.9	51.0	47.0
Total Equities	25.0%	35.2%	70.2%	95.3%
Income Statement for Year				
Operating Revenues	100.0%	100.0%	100.0%	100.0%
Cost of Sales (excluding depreciation) or Operating Expenses[a]	(84.0)	(73.2)	(55.2)	(75.3)
Depreciation and Amortization	(0.9)	(1.6)	(3.9)	(3.0)
Selling and Administrative	(14.4)	(19.9)	(21.5)	(11.8)
Research and Development	—	—	—	(4.4)
Interest	—	—	—	(0.2)
Income Taxes	(0.3)	(2.0)	(7.6)	(0.9)
All Other Items, net	—	—	0.2	—
Net Income	0.4%	3.3%	12.0%	4.4%
Cash Flow from Operations/ Capital Expenditures	1.7	2.6	2.8	2.4

[a]See the problem narrative for items included in operating expenses.

not sufficiently large for the firm to disclose it. The twelve companies and a brief description of their activities follow.

1. Abercrombie & Fitch: Sells retail apparel primarily through stores to the fashion-conscious adult and has established itself as a trendy, popular player in the specialty apparel industry.
2. Allstate Insurance: Sells property and casualty insurance, primarily on buildings and automobiles. Operating revenues include insurance premiums collected or

EXHIBIT 1.16

continued

(5)	(6)	(7)	(8)	(9)	(10)	(11)	(12)
11.5%	12.9%	7.2%	17.8%	30.9%	22.2%	24.9%	321.8%
7.9	17.9	3.9	50.4	15.8	203.9	28.1	13.6
8.6	16.4	0.8	5.5	8.3	—	2.7	—
49.2	87.7	160.0	15.9	99.4	1.3	275.3	4.4
(21.8)	(50.3)	(51.4)	(9.3)	(35.3)	(0.3)	(103.9)	(1.1)
27.4	37.4	108.6	6.6	64.1	1.0	171.4	3.3
46.5	18.0	9.6	66.9	7.7	18.6	—	2.9
9.1	27.7	15.9	17.0	58.8	7.6	82.5	75.7
111.0%	130.3%	146.0%	164.2%	185.6%	253.3%	309.6%	417.3%
43.1%	29.0%	18.5%	89.7%	51.2%	17.6%	61.2%	295.7%
24.4	20.3	43.8	24.2	20.5	192.9	117.0	15.8
9.9	35.3	9.2	6.3	28.0	9.8	49.0	41.8
33.6	45.7	74.5	43.8	85.9	33.0	82.4	64.0
111.0%	130.3%	146.0%	164.2%	185.6%	253.3%	309.6%	417.3%
100.0%	100.0%	100.0%	100.0%	100.0%	100.0%	100.0%	100.0%
(46.7)	(71.1)	(63.4)	(70.2)	(19.1)	(27.1)	(40.6)	(66.6)
(3.4)	(4.9)	(6.3)	(1.8)	(6.3)	(3.0)	(13.5)	—
(30.8)	(10.9)	(11.7)	(15.5)	(28.3)	(32.0)	(25.6)	(22.0)
(1.2)	(4.9)	—	—	(17.5)	—	—	—
—	(1.3)	(1.9)	(0.5)	—	(19.6)	(6.0)	—
(5.6)	(1.5)	(4.8)	(4.1)	(9.4)	(6.2)	(7.6)	(2.6)
0.3	1.1	0.1	(0.5)	5.9	—	0.5	(0.3)
12.6%	6.5%	12.0%	7.4%	25.3%	12.1%	7.2%	8.5%
4.6	2.6	2.8	8.1	5.1	72.5	1.3	133.7

due from customers and revenues earned from investments made with cash received from customers prior to the time that Allstate pays customers' claims. Operating expenses include amounts actually paid or expected to be paid in the future on insurance coverage outstanding during the year.

3. Best Buy: Operates a chain of retail stores selling consumer electronic and entertainment equipment at competitively low prices.
4. E. I. du Pont de Nemours: Manufactures chemical and electronics products.

5. Hewlett-Packard: Develops, manufactures, and sells computer hardware. The firm outsources many of its computer components.
6. HSBC Finance: Lends money to consumers for periods ranging from several months to several years. Operating expenses represent estimated uncollectible loans.
7. Kelly Services: Provides temporary office services to businesses and other firms. Operating revenues represent amounts billed to customers for temporary help services and operating expenses include amounts paid to the temporary help employees of Kelly.
8. McDonald's: Operates fast-food restaurants worldwide. A large percentage of McDonald's restaurants are owned and operated by franchisees. McDonald's frequently owns the restaurant buildings of franchisees and leases them to franchisees under long-term leases.
9. Merck: A leading research-driven pharmaceutical products and services company. Merck discovers, develops, manufactures, and markets a broad range of products (primarily ethical drugs) to improve human and animal health, directly and through its joint ventures.
10. Omnicom Group: Creates advertising copy for clients and is the largest marketing services firm in the world. Omnicom purchases advertising time and space from various media and sells it to clients. Operating revenues represent the commission or fee earned by Omnicom for advertising copy created and media time and space sold. Operating expenses include compensation paid to employees. Omnicom acquired a large number of marketing services firms in recent years.
11. Pacific Gas & Electric: Generates and sells power to customers in the western United States.
12. Procter & Gamble: Manufactures and markets a broad line of branded consumer products.

Required

Use whatever clues you can to match the companies in Exhibit 1.16 with the firms listed here.

1.13 EFFECT OF INDUSTRY CHARACTERISTICS ON FINANCIAL STATEMENT RELATIONSHIPS—GLOBAL PERSPECTIVE. Effective financial statement analysis requires an understanding of a firm's economic characteristics. The relations between various financial statement items provide evidence of many of these economic characteristics. Exhibit 1.17 presents common-size condensed balance sheets and income statements for twelve firms in different industries. These common-size balance sheets and income statements express various items as a percentage of operating revenues (that is, the statement divides all amounts by operating revenues for the year). A dash for a particular financial statement item does not necessarily mean that the amount is zero. It merely indicates that the amount is not sufficiently large for the firm to disclose it. The twelve companies, the country of their headquarters, and a brief description of their activities follow.

1. Accor (France): World's largest hotel group, operating hotels under the names of Sofitel, Novotel, Motel 6, and others. Accor has grown in recent years by acquiring established hotel chains.

2. Arbed-Acier (Luxembourg): Offers flat-rolled steel products, primarily to the European automobile industry.
3. Carrefour (France): Operates grocery supermarkets and hypermarkets in Europe, Latin America, and Asia.
4. Deutsche Telekom (Germany): Europe's largest provider of wired and wireless telecommunication services. The telecommunications industry has experienced increased deregulation in recent years.
5. Fortis (Netherlands): Offers both insurance and banking services. Operating revenues include insurance premiums received, investment income, and interest revenue on loans. Operating expenses include amounts actually paid or amounts it expects to pay in the future on insurance coverage outstanding during the year.
6. Interpublic Group (U.S.): Creates advertising copy for clients. Interpublic purchases advertising time and space from various media and sells it to clients. Operating revenues represent the commission or fee earned by Interpublic for advertising copy created and media time and space sold. Operating expenses include compensation paid to employees. Interpublic acquired other marketing services firms in recent years.
7. Marks & Spencer (U.K.): Operates department stores in England and other retail stores in Europe and the United States. Offers its own credit card for customers' purchases.
8. Nestlé (Switzerland): World's largest food processor, offering prepared foods, coffees, milk-based products, and mineral waters.
9. Roche Holding (Switzerland): Creates, manufactures, and distributes a wide variety of prescription drugs.
10. Sun Microsystems (U.S.): Designs, manufactures, and sells workstations and servers used to maintain integrated computer networks. Sun outsources the manufacture of many of its computer components.
11. Tokyo Electric Power (Japan): Provides electric power services, primarily to the Tokyo community. It maintains almost a monopoly in its service area.
12. Toyota Motor (Japan): Manufactures automobiles and offers financing services to its customers.

Required

Use whatever clues you can to match the companies in Exhibit 1.17 with the firms listed here.

1.14 VALUE CHAIN ANALYSIS AND FINANCIAL STATEMENT RELATIONSHIPS. Exhibit 1.18 presents common-size income statements and balance sheets for seven firms that operate at various stages in the value chain for the pharmaceutical industry. These common-size statements express all amounts as a percentage of sales revenue. Exhibit 1.18 also shows the cash flow from operations to capital expenditures ratios for each firm. A dash for a particular financial statement item does not necessarily mean that the amount is zero. It merely indicates that the amount is not sufficiently large for the firm to disclose it. The seven companies and a brief description of their activities follow.

1. Wyeth: Engages in the development, manufacture, and sale of ethical drugs (that is, drugs requiring a prescription). The drugs of Wyeth primarily represent mixtures

EXHIBIT 1.17

Common-Size Financial Statement Data for Firms in 12 Industries (Problem 1.13)

	(1)	(2)	(3)	(4)
Balance Sheet at End of Year				
Cash and Marketable Securities	4.7%	16.4%	8.9%	8.4%
Receivables	8.5	15.9	16.5	27.6
Inventories	9.9	2.8	9.9	5.8
Property, Plant, and Equipment, at cost	40.8	20.9	59.0	69.6
Accumulated Depreciation	(15.0)	(9.1)	(33.2)	(17.8)
Net	25.8	11.8	25.8	51.8
Intercorporate Investments	4.0	14.3	3.0	.6
Other Assets	15.0	10.9	11.7	3.6
Total Assets	67.9%	72.1%	75.8%	97.8%
Current Liabilities	37.3%	25.5%	29.7%	26.4%
Long-Term Debt	12.0	6.1	6.6	9.1
Other Noncurrent Liabilities	2.1	1.8	5.9	2.3
Shareholders' Equity	16.5	38.7	33.6	60.0
Total Equities	67.9%	72.1%	75.8%	97.8%
Income Statement for Year				
Operating Revenues	100.0%	100.0%	100.0%	100.0%
Other Revenues	1.1	2.7	1.0	.2
Cost of Goods Sold (excluding depreciation) or Operating Expenses[a]	(87.8)	(45.2)	(44.5)	(64.6)
Depreciation and Amortization	(3.0)	(4.9)	(4.1)	(3.2)
Selling and Administrative	(6.3)	(24.8)	(38.9)	(24.3)
Interest	(1.4)	(.4)	(2.0)	(1.3)
Research and Development	—	(9.8)	(1.3)	—
Income Taxes	(1.3)	(5.8)	(3.1)	(2.4)
All Other Items, net	.8	—	(.8)	(.3)
Total Expenses	99.0%	90.9%	94.7%	96.1%
Net Income	2.1%	11.8%	6.3%	4.1%

[a]See the problem narrative for items included in operating expenses.

of chemical compounds. Ethical-drug companies must obtain approval of new drugs from the Food and Drug Administration (FDA). Patents protect such drugs from competition until either other drug companies develop more effective substitutes or the patent expires.

2. Amgen: Engages in the development, manufacture, and sale of drugs based on biotechnology research. Biotechnology drugs must obtain approval from the FDA and enjoy patent protection similar to those for chemical-based drugs. The

EXHIBIT 1.17

continued

(5)	(6)	(7)	(8)	(9)	(10)	(11)	(12)
16.7%	7.4%	16.1%	21.3%	72.0%	8.3%	1.4%	338.8%
35.9	17.7	81.1	29.6	24.0	10.5	5.9	533.4
6.4	25.7	—	1.3	20.0	2.9	—	—
88.3	130.9	23.0	110.3	83.3	278.9	535.4	15.3
(50.5)	(67.7)	(11.8)	(35.5)	(35.2)	(112.5)	(284.9)	(12.9)
37.8	63.2	11.2	74.8	48.1	166.4	250.5	2.4
18.8	10.3	1.3	10.7	7.7	22.4	16.9	41.9
7.1	1.9	63.5	42.1	69.1	56.3	5.4	61.9
122.7%	126.2%	173.2%	179.8%	240.9%	266.8%	280.1%	978.4%
42.7%	34.5%	106.0%	65.1%	48.3%	42.6%	51.3%	820.8%
22.2	23.3	22.7	49.6	56.4	95.8	167.7	76.9
4.2	17.2	10.6	10.9	24.5	27.8	24.7	42.2
53.6	51.2	33.9	54.2	111.7	100.6	36.4	38.5
122.7%	126.2%	173.2%	179.8%	240.9%	266.8%	280.1%	978.4%
100.0%	100.0%	100.0%	100.0%	100.0%	100.0%	100.0%	100.0%
.7	2.3	1.9	.3	13.8	.7	—	—
(68.0)	(81.0)	(55.3)	(74.5)	(27.2)	(45.0)	(57.3)	(32.6)
(5.9)	(5.3)	(2.0)	(7.1)	(9.9)	(23.9)	(19.9)	—
(16.4)	(13.6)	(27.8)	(8.1)	(40.0)	(15.2)	(7.3)	(22.5)
(.4)	(3.5)	(1.9)	(3.0)	(5.2)	(8.6)	(8.6)	(35.4)
(3.7)	—	—	—	(13.8)	—	—	—
(2.5)	(.3)	(5.9)	(3.7)	(4.4)	(3.9)	(2.8)	(2.2)
(.6)	2.1	(.8)	.6	—	(.6)	—	(1.7)
97.5%	101.6%	93.7%	95.8%	100.5%	97.2%	95.9%	94.4%
3.2%	.7%	8.2%	4.5%	13.3%	3.5%	4.1%	5.6%

biotechnology segment is less mature than the ethical-drug industry, with relatively few products having received FDA approval.

3. Mylan Laboratories: Engages in the development, manufacture, and sale of generic drugs. Generic drugs have the same chemical compositions as drugs that had previously benefited from patent protection but for which the patent has now expired. Generic-drug companies have benefited in recent years from the patent expiration of several major ethical drugs. The major ethical-drug companies, however, have

increasingly offered generic versions of their ethical drugs to compete against the generic-drug companies.

4. Johnson & Johnson: Engages in the development, manufacture, and sale of over-the-counter health care products. Such products do not require a prescription and often benefit from brand recognition.
5. Quintiles: Offers laboratory testing services and expedition of the drug approval process through the FDA for ethical-drug companies that have discovered new drugs. Cost of goods sold for this company represents the salaries of personnel conducting the laboratory testing and drug approval services.

EXHIBIT 1.18

Common-Size Financial Statement Data for Seven Firms in the Pharmaceutical Industry (Problem 1.14)

	(1)	(2)	(3)	(4)	(5)	(6)	(7)
Income Statement							
Sales	100.0%	100.0%	100.0%	100.0%	100.0%	100.0%	100.0%
Cost of Goods Sold	(47.0)	(11.0)	(24.0)	(58.4)	(28.9)	(73.3)	(92.5)
Selling and Administrative	(18.8)	(24.2)	(36.7)	(31.0)	(36.3)	(21.0)	(4.2)
Research and Development	(8.0)	(21.5)	(13.2)	—	(10.9)	—	—
Interest	—	(.3)	(1.0)	(2.6)	(1.6)	—	(.3)
Income Taxes	(10.6)	(14.1)	(7.0)	(3.2)	(6.8)	(2.2)	(1.0)
Other	3.5	5.2	(1.5)	1.0	1.4	.1	(.2)
Net Income	19.1%	34.1%	16.6%	5.8%	16.9%	3.6%	1.8%
Balance Sheet							
Cash	33.7%	66.3%	21.4%	34.9%	24.2%	.1%	1.9%
Receivables	27.5	12.3	19.4	26.4	14.0	3.2	5.0
Inventories	19.1	8.9	12.4	—	9.1	14.1	13.1
Other Current	7.6	8.6	15.9	5.4	8.7	.4	2.3
Intercorporate Investments	—	—	—	—	—	—	—
Property, Plant, and Equipment, net	19.9	48.5	44.6	22.4	23.4	17.7	3.8
Other Noncurrent Assets	49.9	15.9	48.9	31.2	37.2	.4	4.4
Total Assets	157.7%	160.5%	162.6%	120.3%	116.6%	35.9%	30.5%
Current Liabilities	34.4%	25.0%	51.4%	28.5%	24.4%	12.2%	13.7%
Long-Term Debt	2.8	5.6	11.4	2.0	6.5	—	3.9
Other Noncurrent Liabilities	2.2	—	23.8	—	12.3	2.6	1.6
Shareholders' Equity	118.3	129.9	76.0	89.8	73.4	21.1	11.3
Total Equities	157.7%	160.5%	162.6%	120.3%	116.6%	35.9%	30.5%
Cash Flow from Operations/ Capital Expenditures	2.2	3.4	2.3	1.3	2.8	.6	1.3

6. Cardinal Health: Distributes drugs as a wholesaler to drugstores, hospitals, and mass merchandisers. Also offers pharmaceutical benefit management services in which it provides customized databases designed to help customers order more efficiently, contain costs, and monitor their purchases. Cost of goods sold for Cardinal Health includes the cost of drugs sold plus the salaries of personnel providing pharmaceutical benefit management services.
7. Walgreen: Operates a chain of drugstores nationwide. The data in Exhibit 1.18 for Walgreen include the recognition of operating lease commitments for retail space.

Required

Use whatever clues you can to match the companies in Exhibit 1.18 with the firms listed here.

1.15 RECASTING THE FINANCIAL STATEMENTS OF A U.K. COMPANY INTO U.S. FORMATS, TERMINOLOGY, AND ACCOUNTING PRINCIPLES. WPP Group, headquartered in the United Kingdom, is one of the largest marketing and communication services firms in the world. It offers advertising, market research, public relations, and other marketing services through a worldwide network of offices. The firm employs over 65,000 individuals and is located in approximately 100 countries. WPP Group, as the parent company, operates through activities of its individual operating companies.

The financial statements of WPP Group for Year 10 and Year 11 appear in Exhibit 1.19 (balance sheet), Exhibit 1.20 (profit and loss account), and Exhibit 1.21 (cash flow statement). These financial statements reflect reporting formats, terminology, and accounting principles employed in the United Kingdom.

Required

Recast the consolidated balance sheet, consolidated profit and loss account, and the consolidated cash flow statement of WPP Group using reporting formats, terminology, and accounting principles customarily used in the United States.

1.16 COMPREHENSIVE INCOME. Refer to the financial statements of the WPP Group reported in Problem 1.15 as Exhibits 1.19, 1.20, and 1.21. You will note that the U.S. requirement of reporting comprehensive income does not exist in the United Kingdom, as the WPP Group does not report comprehensive income anywhere in these statements. However, WPP Group does report several changes in the recognition and valuation of assets and liabilities that are not reported currently in the consolidated profit and loss account, but likely will be in the future. Examples of these types of changes are detailed in the chapter for PepsiCo, which are reported as part of the firm's comprehensive income.

Required

a. Prepare a Statement of Comprehensive Income for WPP Group for Year 11. Use whatever disclosures from WPP Group's financial statements and notes you believe are appropriate to prepare the statement. Clearly label the components reported in the statement.
b. Calculate WPP Group's net income as a percent of turnover (equivalent to revenues in the United States) for Year 11. Recalculate this ratio using comprehensive income instead of net income and assess the effect of the difference between the two calculations.

EXHIBIT 1.19

WPP Group
Consolidated Balance Sheet
(amounts in millions of pounds)
(Problem 1.15)

	December 31	
	Year 11	Year 10
Fixed Assets		
Intangible Assets (Corporate Brands and Goodwill—see Note 1)	£5,389	£4,447
Tangible Assets	432	390
Investments	553	552
Total Fixed Assets	£6,374	£5,389
Current Assets		
Stocks and Work in Progress	£ 237	£ 223
Debtors (Note 2)	2,640	2,414
Investments	77	—
Cash at Bank and in Hand	586	1,086
	£3,540	£3,723
Creditors: Amounts Falling Due within One Year (Note 3)	(4,322)	(4,252)
Net Current Liabilities	£ (782)	£ (529)
Total Assets Less Current Liabilities	£5,592	£4,860
Creditors: Amounts Falling Due after One Year	(1,712)	(1,280)
Provisions for Liabilities and Charges (Note 4)	(105)	(98)
Net Assets Excluding Pension Provision	3,775	3,482
Pension Provision	(135)	(88)
Net Assets	£3,640	£3,394
Capital and Reserves		
Called-Up Share Capital	£ 115	£ 111
Share Premium Account	1,044	1,096
Reserves (Note 5)	2,488	2,374
Profit and Loss Account	(48)	(211)
Share Owners' Funds	£3,599	£3,370
Minority Interests	41	24
Total Capital Employed	£3,640	£3,394

Notes to Exhibit 1.19

Note 1: Intangible Assets represents the portion of the purchase price of marketing services agencies acquired that WPP allocated to the brand names of these agencies. WPP breaks out the £5,389 for Year 11 as Corporate Brands, £950, and Goodwill, £4,439. For Year 10, the breakdown is Corporate Brands, £950, and Goodwill, £3,497.

Note 2: Debtors include the following:

	December 31	
	Year 11	**Year 10**
Trade Debtors	£2,392	£2,181
Other Debtors	248	233
Total	£2,640	£2,414

Note 3: Creditors falling due within one year include the following:

	December 31	
	Year 11	**Year 10**
Bank Loans	£ 319	£ 298
Trade Creditors	2,506	2,575
Taxation	166	164
Other Creditors and Accruals	1,331	1,215
Total	£4,322	£4,252

Note 4: Provisions include the following:

	December 31	
	Year 11	**Year 10**
Deferred Taxation	£ 41	£30
Pensions	18	11
Other	46	57
Total	£105	£98

Note 5: Reserves include the following amounts:

	December 31	
	Year 11	**Year 10**
Cumulative Translation Adjustment	£ 80	£ 133
Retirement Benefit Reserves	45	27
Merger Reserve[a]	2,363	2,214
Total	£2,488	£2,374

[a]WPP Group issued common shares in Year 10 and Year 11 for the acquisition of additional agencies. The increase in the reserve represents the "share premium" (using WPP's terminology) above the "called-up share capital" (again, using WPP's terminology). The equivalent terminology in U.S. GAAP is *additional paid-in capital* for "share premium" and *common stock, par value* for "called-up share capital."

EXHIBIT 1.20

WPP Group
Consolidated Profit and Loss Account
(amounts in millions of pounds)
(Problem 1.15)

	Year 11	Year 10
Turnover	£20,887	£13,949
Gross Profit	£20,655	£13,704
Other Operating Expenses	20,149	13,325
Operating Profit	£ 506	£ 379
Other Income (Expense) Items, net	(24)	38
Interest Payable	(71)	(52)
Profit on Ordinary Activities before Taxation	£ 411	£ 365
Tax on Profit on Ordinary Activities	(126)	(110)
Profit (Loss) on Ordinary Activities after Taxation	£ 285	£ 255
Minority Interest	(14)	(11)
Profit (Loss) for the Financial Year	£ 271	£ 244
Ordinary Dividends	(52)	(38)
Retained Profit (Loss) for the Year	£ 219	£ 206

1.17 RECASTING THE FINANCIAL STATEMENTS OF A GERMAN COMPANY INTO U.S. FORMATS AND TERMINOLOGY. Volkswagen Group AG manufactures passenger cars and commercial vehicles and provides financing for its customers' purchases. The firm also provides financing to dealers that sell its products. Brand names include Volkswagen, Audi, SEAT, Rolls-Royce, and Bentley. Exhibit 1.22 presents a balance sheet at the end of Year 9 and Year 10, and Exhibit 1.23 presents an income statement for Year 9 and Year 10 for Volkswagen.

Required

a. Prepare a balance sheet for Volkswagen on December 31, Year 9 and Year 10, using reporting formats and terminology commonly encountered in the United States.

b. Prepare an income statement for Volkswagen for Year 9 and Year 10, using terminology commonly encountered in the United States. Separate operating revenues and expenses from nonoperating revenues and expenses.

EXHIBIT 1.21

WPP Group
Consolidated Cash Flow Statement
(amounts in millions of pounds)
(Problem 1.15)

	Year 11	Year 10
Operating Activities		
Operating Profit	£ 506	£ 379
Depreciation Charge	125	79
(Increase) Decrease in Stocks	(18)	(15)
(Increase) Decrease in Debtors	(5)	(434)
Increase (Decrease) in Trade Creditors	(473)	539
Increase in Provisions	27	74
Other Adjustments	12	2
Net Cash Flow from Operating Activities	£ 174	£ 624
Returns on Investments and Servicing of Finance		
Interest and Dividends Received	£ 53	£ 25
Interest Paid	(84)	(78)
Dividend Paid	(44)	(26)
Net Cash Flow from Investments and Servicing of Finance	£ (75)	£ (79)
Taxation	£ (78)	£ (81)
Investing Activities		
Purchase of Tangible Fixed Assets	£ (218)	£ (112)
Acquisitions	(696)	(230)
Other Investing Activities	(125)	(51)
Net Cash Outflow from Investing Activities	£(1,039)	£ (393)
Financing Activities		
Proceeds from Issue of Share Capital	£ 69	£ 78
Increase (Decrease) in Bank Loans	439	128
Net Cash Flow from Financing Activities	£ 508	£ 206
Effect of Exchange Rate Changes on Cash and Cash Equivalents	£ 10	£ 35
Cash and Cash Equivalents—Beginning of Year	£ 1,086	£ 774
Cash and Cash Equivalents—End of Year	£ 586	£1,086

EXHIBIT 1.22

Balance Sheet for Volkswagen Group AG
(in millions of euros)
(Problem 1.17)

	December 31	
	Year 10	**Year 9**
Assets		
Fixed Assets		
Intangible Assets (Note 1)	€ 6,596	€ 5,355
Tangible Assets, net	21,735	19,726
Financial Assets	3,999	4,216
Total Fixed Assets	€ 32,330	€29,297
Leasing and Rental Assets (Note 2)	€ 7,284	€ 4,783
Current Assets		
Inventories	€ 9,945	€ 9,335
Receivables	45,166	41,432
Securities	3,610	3,886
Cash on Hand	4,285	2,156
Total Current Assets	€ 63,006	€56,809
Prepaid and Deferred Charges (Note 3)	€ 378	€ 299
Deferred Tax Assets	€ 1,426	€ 1,377
Balance Sheet Total	€104,424	€92,565
Shareholders' Equity and Liabilities		
Shareholders' Equity		
Subscribed Capital:		
Ordinary Shares	€ 815	€ 803
Preferred Shares	272	268
Capital Reserve	4,415	4,296
Revenue Reserves (Note 4)	14,546	13,690
Accumulated Profits	3,947	2,314
Minority Interests (Note 5)	53	49
Total Shareholders' Equity	€ 24,048	€21,420
Deferred Tax Liabilities	2,299	2,095
Provisions (Note 6)	21,782	21,128
Current Borrowings	30,044	26,201
Noncurrent Borrowings	12,750	8,383
Trade Payables	7,055	7,435
Other Payables (Note 7)	6,161	5,699
Deferred Income (Note 8)	285	204
Balance Sheet Total	€104,424	€92,565

EXHIBIT 1.23

Income Statement for Volkswagen Group AG
(in millions of euros)
(Problem 1.17)

	Year 10	Year 9
Sales	€88,540	€83,127
Cost of Sales	(75,586)	(71,130)
Gross Profit—Automotive Division	€12,954	€11,997
Gross Profit—Financial Services Division (Note 9)	1,328	1,213
Selling and Distribution Expenses	(7,554)	(7,080)
General and Administrative Expenses	(2,154)	(2,001)
Other Operating Income (Note 10)	4,118	3,656
Other Operating Expenses (Note 11)	(3,268)	(3,761)
Operating Profit	€ 5,424	€ 4,024
Share of Profit and Losses of Group Companies (Note 12)	289	335
Other Income (Expenses)	(419)	99
Other Financial Results (Note 13)	(885)	(739)
Profit before Tax	€ 4,409	€ 3,719
Taxes on Income	(1,483)	(1,105)
Minority Interest	(11)	(7)
Net Earnings	€ 2,915	€ 2,607

Notes to Exhibits 1.22 and 1.23

Note 1: Intangible Assets consists of license rights, goodwill, and miscellaneous other intangible assets.

Note 2: Leasing and Rental Assets represents vehicles leased to customers. The leases are treated as operating leases, which means that the vehicle remains on the balance sheet of Volkswagen Group AG as vehicle property.

Note 3: Prepaid and Deferred Charges consists of the following:

	December 31	
	Year 10	Year 9
Prepaid Operating Cost	€ 78	€ 63
Other	300	236
Total	€378	€299

Note 4: Revenue Reserves represents earnings not officially designated by the board of directors as available for dividends.

Note 5: Minority Interests represents the ownership interests of shareholders outside Volkswagen Group AG in a consolidated entity within the group. The minority interests at the end of Year 10 consisted primarily of Audi AG shareholders.

Note 6: Provisions include the following:

	December 31	
	Year 10	**Year 9**
Pensions	€ 9,984	€ 9,558
Warranties	3,884	3,704
Restructuring	1,920	2,063
Taxable Payable	1,418	1,424
Other Provisions	4,576	4,379
Total	€21,782	€21,128

Note 7: Other liabilities that are primarily due within one year relate to various aspects of the firm's operations (such as accrued wages and salaries, social security taxes, and other payroll taxes).

Note 8: Consists of up-front payments from operating lease customers and other operating lease-related items.

Note 9: Gross Profit—Financial Services Division consists of the following:

	Year Ended December 31	
	Year 11	**Year 10**
Interest Income—Dealer Financing	€ 499	€ 463
Interest Income—Customer Financing	1,587	1,412
Interest Income—Finance Leases	1,122	1,150
Interest Expense	(1,880)	(1,812)
Gross Profit	€1,328	€1,213

Note 10: Other Operating Income consists primarily of reversing provisions made in prior years and other unspecified operating income.

Note 11: Other Operating Expenses consists of the effects of exchange rate changes and other unspecified operating expenses.

Note 12: Results from participation represent Volkswagen Group AG's share in the earnings of less than majority owned entities.

Note 13: Other Financial Results consists of pension expenses and related provisions.

INTEGRATIVE CASE 1.1

STARBUCKS

The first case at the end of this chapter and each of the remaining chapters in the book is an integrative case involving Starbucks. The series of cases applies the concepts and analytical tools discussed in each chapter to the financial statements and notes of Starbucks. The preparation of responses to the questions in these cases results in an integrated illustration of the six sequential steps in financial statement analysis discussed in this chapter.

Introduction

"They don't just sell coffee, they sell the *Starbucks Experience,*" remarked Deb Mills, while sitting down to enjoy a cup of Starbucks cappuccino with her friend, Kim Shannon. Kim, an investment fund manager for a large insurance firm, reflected on that observation and what it might mean for Starbucks as a potential investment opportunity. Glancing around the store, Kim saw a number of people sitting individually or in groups, lingering over their drinks while chatting, reading, or checking e-mail and surfing the Internet through the store's Wi-Fi network. Kim noted that in addition to the wide selection of hot coffees, French- and Italian-style espressos, teas, and cold coffee-blended drinks, Starbucks also offered some food items and baked goods, packages of roast coffees, coffee-related accessories and equipment, and even a line of its own compact discs. Intrigued, Kim decided to do a full-blown valuation analysis of Starbucks to evaluate whether its business model and common equity shares were as good as their coffee. But first, Kim needed to understand more about the company's business strategy and the economics of its industry and then take an initial look at Starbucks' financial statements.

Recent Growth

Kim's research quickly confirmed her friend's observation that Starbucks is about the experience of enjoying a good cup of coffee, and not just about selling coffee beverages and related products. The Starbucks fiscal Year 4 annual report began with a discussion of "creating new experiences" and repeatedly focused on the *Starbucks Experience.* This approach enabled the firm to grow rapidly from just a single store near Pike's Place Market in Seattle to a global company with 8,569 locations worldwide at the end of fiscal Year 4. Of that total, Starbucks owned and operated 4,293 U.S. stores and 922 international stores, while licensees owned and operated 1,839 U.S. stores and 1,515 international stores. In fiscal Year 4 alone, Starbucks opened 1,344 net new retail locations, of which Starbucks owns 634 stores and licenses the remaining 710 to other owners.

The majority of Starbucks' retail stores (6,132 stores) at the end of fiscal Year 4 are located in the United States, amounting to one Starbucks retail location for approximately every 45,000 U.S. residents! However, Starbucks is clearly not content to simply focus on the U.S. market, as is it extending the reach of its stores globally, with 2,437 stores outside the United States. At the end of fiscal Year 4, Starbucks had 422 company-operated stores in the United Kingdom and another 372 in Canada. In addition, by the end of fiscal Year 4 Starbucks operated more than 1,100 stores in the Asia-Pacific region, and was expanding its already significant presence in the Middle East.

Starbucks' success results in part from its successful development and expansion of a European idea—enjoying a fine coffee-based beverage and sharing that experience with others in a comfortable friendly environment. Starbucks imported the idea of the French and Italian café into the busy North American lifestyle. Ironically, Starbucks now stands poised to attempt to export its brand and style of café to the European continent. On January 16, Year 4, Starbucks opened its first coffeehouse in France, in the heart of Paris, at 26 Avenue de l'Opera. The ultimate test of Starbucks' retail coffeehouse concept, and a major determinant of whether its growth will continue in the future, is the extent to which it can successfully bring its version of a continental European idea back into Europe itself.

Starbucks CEO Howard Schultz states that his vision and ultimate goal for Starbucks is to have 25,000 Starbucks locations worldwide and to have Starbucks recognized among the world's leading brands. Kim Shannon wondered whether Starbucks can ultimately achieve this level of global reach and penetration because she could name only a few such worldwide companies. One that came to mind is McDonald's, with a worldwide brand and 30,000 retail locations in 119 countries.

The growth in the number of its retail stores is one of the primary drivers of Starbucks' remarkable rate of growth in revenues. In fiscal Year 4, total revenues exceeded $5.3 billion, representing a 30 percent growth rate over fiscal Year 3 revenues of $4.1 billion. But Starbucks' revenue growth is not driven only by opening new stores. On a consolidated basis, Starbucks generated 10 percent comparable store sales growth in fiscal Year 4, which marked the 13th consecutive year in which Starbucks' stores achieved comparable store sales growth rates in excess of 5 percent. Comparable store sales growth reflects the increase in sales from stores opened at least two full years.

New Product Development

One element contributing to Starbucks' same store sales growth is the company's continuing focus on new product development. Starbucks regularly introduces new specialty coffee-based drinks and coffee flavors, as well as iced coffee-based drinks, such as the very successful line of Frappuccino drinks and Iced Shaken Refreshment drinks.

In addition, Starbucks is expanding the scope of its business model through new channel development in order to "reach customers where they work, travel, shop, and dine." The most significant area of expansion of the Starbucks model in recent years is the rapid growth in the number of licensed retail stores. As recently as five years ago, Starbucks had 363 licensed stores, but by the end of fiscal Year 4 the number of licensed stores had mushroomed to 3,354.

To further expand the business model, Starbucks entered into a licensing agreement with Kraft Foods to market and distribute Starbucks whole bean and ground coffee to grocery stores and warehouse club stores. By the end of fiscal Year 4, Starbucks whole bean and ground coffees were available throughout the United States in approximately 20,000 grocery and warehouse club stores. Further, Starbucks sells whole bean and ground coffee through institutional foodservice companies that service business, education, office, hotel, restaurant, airline and other foodservice accounts. For example, in fiscal Year 4 Starbucks (and its subsidiary, Seattle's Best Coffee) was the only super premium national brand coffees promoted by SYSCO Corporation to such foodservice accounts. Finally, Starbucks has formed partnerships to produce and distribute bottled Frappuccino and DoubleShot drinks with PepsiCo, and premium ice creams with Dreyer's Grand Ice Cream, Inc.

Product Supply

Starbucks purchases green coffee beans from coffee-producing regions around the world and then custom roasts and blends them to its exacting standards. Although coffee beans in general trade in commodity markets and experience volatile prices, Starbucks purchases higher-quality coffee beans that sell at a premium to commodity coffees. Starbucks purchases its coffee beans under fixed-price purchase contracts with various suppliers, with purchase prices reset annually. Starbucks also purchases significant amounts of dairy products from suppliers located near its retail stores. Starbucks purchases paper and plastic products from several suppliers, the prices of which vary with changes in the prices of commodity paper and plastic resin.

Competition in the Specialty Coffee Industry

After some reflection, Kim realized that one of the aspects that made Starbucks' business so successful thus far was that it faced relatively little direct competition. Kim could think of very few companies implementing a comparable business strategy to that of Starbucks. After some investigation, she uncovered several companies with growing chains of retail coffee shops that could be compared to Starbucks, including firms such as Panera Bread Company, Diedrich Coffee, the New World Restaurant Group Inc., and Caribou Coffee Company Inc. (a privately held firm). However, these firms tended to be much smaller than Starbucks, the largest among them being Panera, with 602 bakery-cafés systemwide (515 franchised and 226 company-owned) and total revenues of $479 million for fiscal Year 4.

Kim reasoned that Starbucks' business likely faced some competition from a broader scope of coffee beverage retailers, including fast-food chains such as McDonald's and doughnut chains such as Krispy Kreme, Dunkin' Donuts, and Tim Hortons, but that these types of outlets offered a very different experience from that which Starbucks offered. In addition, Starbucks faced competition from retail sales of coffee beans, which one could brew into coffee at home or at the office. Of course, Starbucks also encountered competition from teas, waters, juices, and other types of soft drinks and nonalcoholic beverages.

Financial Statements

Exhibit 1.24 presents comparative balance sheets for Starbucks for the four fiscal years ending September, Year 4. Exhibit 1.25 presents comparative income statements and Exhibit 1.26 presents comparative statements of cash flows for the three fiscal years ending September, Year 4.

Required

Respond to the following questions relating to Starbucks.

Industry and Strategy Analysis

a. Apply Porter's five forces framework to the specialty coffee retail industry.

b. How would you characterize the strategy of Starbucks? How does Starbucks create value for its customers? What critical risk and success factors must Starbucks manage?

Balance Sheet

c. Describe how Cash differs from Cash Equivalents.

d. Why do debt and equity securities appear on the balance sheet under both current assets (Marketable Securities) and noncurrent assets (Investments in Securities)?

e. Why do accounts receivable appear net of allowance for uncollectible accounts? Identify the events or transactions that cause the allowance account to increase and decrease.

EXHIBIT 1.24

Starbucks Corporation Comparative Balance Sheet
(amounts in millions)
(Integrative Case 1.1)

September 30:	Year 4	Year 3	Year 2	Year 1
Assets				
Cash and Cash Equivalents	$ 299.1	$ 200.9	$ 99.7	$ 51.3
Marketable Securities	353.9	149.1	227.7	169.2
Accounts Receivable, net	140.2	114.5	97.6	90.4
Inventories	422.7	342.9	263.2	221.3
Prepayments and Deferred Income Taxes	135.0	102.6	84.6	61.7
Total Current Assets	$1,350.9	$ 910.0	$ 772.8	$ 593.9
Investment in Securities	$ 306.9	$ 280.4	$ 102.5	$ 63.1
Property, Plant, and Equipment, at cost	$2,877.7	$2,516.3	$2,116.2	$1,702.3
Accumulated Depreciation	(1,326.3)	(1,068.6)	(814.4)	(605.3)
Net	$1,551.4	$1,447.7	$1,301.8	$1,097.0
Other Noncurrent Assets	$ 181.3	$ 140.4	$ 73.2	$ 53.7
Total Assets	$3,390.5	$2,778.5	$2,250.3	$1,807.7
Liabilities and Shareholders' Equity				
Accounts Payable	$ 199.3	$ 169.0	$ 136.0	$ 127.9
Notes Payable	—	—	—	62.0
Current Portion of Long-Term Debt	.7	.7	.7	.7
Other Current Liabilities	546.2	404.5	325.9	240.1
Total Current Liabilities	$ 746.2	$ 574.2	$ 462.6	$ 430.7
Long-Term Debt	3.6	4.4	5.1	5.8
Deferred Income Taxes	21.8	12.5	22.5	4.5
Other Noncurrent Liabilities	144.7	116.3	46.8	.4
Total Liabilities	$ 916.3	$ 707.4	$ 537.0	$ 441.4
Common Stock	$ .4	$ .4	$ .4	$ .4
Additional Paid-In Capital	995.7	998.1	930.0	791.2
Retained Earnings	1,448.9	1,058.3	791.5	580.1
Accumulated Other Comprehensive Income	29.2	14.3	(8.6)	(5.4)
Total Shareholders' Equity	$2,474.2	$2,071.1	$1,713.3	$1,366.3
Total Liabilities and Shareholders' Equity	$3,390.5	$2,778.5	$2,250.3	$1,807.7

EXHIBIT 1.25

Starbucks Corporation Comparative Income Statement for the Year Ended September 30 (amounts in millions) (Integrative Case 1.1)

	Year 4	Year 3	Year 2
Revenues			
Company-Operated Retail Stores	$4,457.4	$3,449.6	$2,792.9
Specialty:			
Licensing	565.8	409.6	311.9
Foodservice and Other	271.1	216.3	184.1
Total Operating Revenues	$5,294.3	$4,075.5	$3,288.9
Expenses			
Cost of Sales Including Occupancy Costs	$2,191.4	$1,681.4	$1,347.0
Store Operating Expenses	1,790.2	1,379.6	1,109.8
Nonretail Operating Expenses	171.6	141.3	106.1
Depreciation and Amortization	289.2	244.7	210.7
General and Administrative	304.3	244.6	234.6
Total Expenses	$4,746.7	$3,691.6	$3,008.2
Income from Equity Investees	$ 60.7	$ 38.4	$ 33.5
Operating Income	$ 608.3	$ 422.3	$ 314.2
Interest and Other Income	14.4	11.9	9.6
Interest Expense	(.3)	(.3)	(.3)
Gain on Sale of Investments	—	—	13.4
Income before Income Taxes	$ 622.4	$ 433.9	$ 336.9
Income Tax Expense	231.8	167.1	125.5
Net Income	$ 390.6	$ 266.8	$ 211.4

f. How does the account Accumulated Deprecation on the balance sheet differ from Depreciation Expense on the income statement?

g. Deferred income taxes appear among both current assets and noncurrent liabilities on the balance sheet. Under what circumstances will deferred income taxes give rise to an asset? To a liability?

h. Accumulated Other Comprehensive Income includes unrealized gains and losses from marketable securities and investments in securities, as well as unrealized gains and losses from translating the financial statements of foreign subsidiaries into U.S. dollars. Why are these gains and losses not included in net income on the income statement? When, if ever, will these gains and losses appear in net income?

EXHIBIT 1.26

Starbucks Corporation Comparative Statements of Cash Flows for the Year Ended September 30 (amounts in millions) (Integrative Case 1.1)

	Year 4	Year 3	Year 2
Operations			
Net Income	$ 390.6	$ 266.8	$ 211.4
Depreciation and Amortization	314.0	266.3	226.3
Other Adjustments	51.3	20.7	31.1
Changes in Working Capital:			
(Increase) Decrease in Receivables	(25.7)	(16.9)	(7.2)
(Increase) Decrease in Inventories	(77.7)	(64.8)	(41.4)
(Increase) Decrease in Prepayments	9.1	4.0	(5.3)
Increase (Decrease) in Accounts Payable	27.9	25.0	5.5
Increase (Decrease) in Other Current Liabilities	130.5	85.9	76.0
Cash Flow from Operations	$ 820.0	$ 587.0	$ 496.4
Investing			
Marketable Securities and Investments Sold	$ 354.6	$ 269.6	$ 223.1
Acquisition of Property, Plant, and Equipment	(412.5)	(378.0)	(394.3)
Marketable Securities and Investments Purchased	(566.6)	(323.3)	(340.0)
Other Investing	(33.9)	(88.2)	7.0
Net Cash Flow from Investing	$(658.4)	$(519.9)	$(504.2)
Financing			
Issue of Common Stock	$ 137.6	$ 107.2	$ 107.5
Decrease in Short-Term Borrowing	—	—	—
Decrease in Long-Term Borrowing	(.7)	(.7)	(.7)
Acquisition of Common Stock	(203.4)	(75.7)	(52.2)
Other Financing	3.1	3.3	1.6
Net Cash Flow from Financing	$ (63.4)	$ 34.1	$ 56.2
Change in Cash	$ 98.2	$ 101.2	$ 48.4
Cash, Beginning of Year	200.9	99.7	51.3
Cash, End of Year	$ 299.1	$ 200.9	$ 99.7

Income Statement

i. Starbucks reports three principal sources of revenues: company-operated stores, licensing, and foodservice. Using the narrative information provided in this case, describe the nature of each of these three sources of revenue.

j. What types of expenses does Starbucks likely include in (1) Cost of Sales, (2) Occupancy Costs, and (3) Store Operating Expenses?

k. Starbucks reports Income from Equity Investees in its income statement. Using the narrative information provided in this case, describe the nature of this type of income.

Statement of Cash Flows

l. Why does net income differ from the amount of cash flow from operations?
m. Why does Starbucks add the amount of depreciation and amortization expense to net income when computing cash flow from operations?
n. Why does Starbucks show an increase in accounts receivable as a subtraction when computing cash flow from operations?
o. Why does Starbucks show an increase in inventory as a subtraction when computing cash flow from operations?
p. Why does Starbucks show an increase in accounts payable as an addition when computing cash flow from operations?
q. Starbucks includes marketable securities in current assets on the balance sheet, yet it reports purchases and sales of marketable securities as investing activities on the statement of cash flows. Explain why changes in marketable securities are investing activities when changes in most other current assets (accounts receivable, inventories) are operating activities.
r. Starbucks includes changes in Notes Payable (short-term borrowing) as a financing activity on the statement of cash flows. Explain why changes in Notes Payable are a financing activity when most other changes in current liabilities (accounts payable, other current liabilities) are operating activities.

Relations between Financial Statements

s. Prepare an analysis that explains the change in retained earnings from $1,058.3 at the end of fiscal Year 3 to $1,448.9 at the end of fiscal Year 4.
t. Prepare an analysis that explains the change in property, plant, and equipment, at cost, from $2,516.3 at the end of fiscal Year 3 to $2,877.7 at the end of fiscal Year 4.

Interpreting Financial Statement Relations

Exhibit 1.27 presents common-size and percentage change balance sheets and Exhibit 1.28 presents common-size and percentage change income statements for Starbucks for Year 2 to Year 4. Respond to the following questions.

u. The dollar amount shown for property, plant, and equipment net of accumulated depreciation (see Exhibit 1.24) increased between the end of fiscal Year 2 and the end of fiscal Year 4, yet the percentage of total assets comprising these assets declined (see Exhibit 1.27). Explain.
v. The proportion of liabilities plus shareholders' equity comprising liabilities increased between the end of fiscal Year 2 and fiscal Year 4, while the proportion of shareholders' equity declined. What are the likely explanations for these changes?
w. The proportion of total shareholders' equity comprising common stock and additional paid-in capital declined between the end of fiscal Year 2 and fiscal Year 4, while the proportion of retained earnings increased. What are the likely explanations for these changes?
x. How has the revenue mix of Starbucks changed between fiscal Year 2 and fiscal Year 4? Relate these changes to Starbucks' business strategy.
y. Net income as a percentage of total revenues increased from 6.4 percent in fiscal Year 2 to 7.4 percent in fiscal Year 4. Identify the most important reasons for this change.

EXHIBIT 1.27

Starbucks Corporation Common-Size and Percentage Change Balance Sheet (Integrative Case 1.1)

	Common-Size Balance Sheet			Percentage Change Balance Sheet	
September 30:	Year 4	Year 3	Year 2	Year 4	Year 3
Assets					
Cash and Cash Equivalents	8.8%	7.2%	4.4%	48.9%	101.5%
Marketable Securities	10.4	5.4	10.1	137.6%	(34.5%)
Accounts Receivable, net	4.1	4.1	4.3	22.4%	17.3%
Inventories	12.5	12.3	11.7	23.3%	30.3%
Prepayments and Deferred Income Taxes	4.0	3.7	3.8	31.6%	21.3%
Total Current Assets	39.8%	32.7%	34.3%	48.5%	17.8%
Investment in Securities	9.1%	10.1%	4.6%	9.5%	173.6%
Property, Plant, and Equipment, at cost	84.9%	90.6%	94.0%	14.4%	18.9%
Accumulated Depreciation	(39.1)	(38.5)	(36.2)	24.1%	31.2%
Net	45.8	52.1	57.8	7.2%	11.2%
Other Noncurrent Assets	5.3	5.1	3.3	29.1%	91.8%
Total Assets	100.0%	100.0%	100.0%	22.0%	23.5%
Liabilities and Shareholders' Equity					
Accounts Payable	5.9%	6.1%	6.1%	17.9%	24.3%
Notes Payable	—	—	—	—	—
Current Portion of Long-Term Debt	—	—	—	—	—
Other Current Liabilities	16.1	14.6	14.5	35.0%	24.1%
Total Current Liabilities	22.0%	20.7%	20.6%	30.0%	24.1%
Long-Term Debt	.1	.2	.2	(18.2%)	(13.7%)
Deferred Income Taxes	.6	.4	1.0	74.4%	(44.4%)
Other Noncurrent Liabilities	4.3	4.2	2.1	24.4%	148.5%
Total Liabilities	27.0%	25.5%	23.9%	29.5%	31.7%
Common Stock	—	—	—	—	—
Additional Paid-In Capital	29.4%	35.9%	41.3%	(.2)%	7.3%
Retained Earnings	42.7	38.1	35.2	36.9%	33.7%
Accumulated Other Comprehensive Income	.9	.5	(.4)	104.2%	(266.3%)
Total Shareholders' Equity	73.0%	74.5%	76.1%	19.5%	20.9%
Total Liabilities and Shareholders' Equity	100.0%	100.0%	100.0%	22.0%	23.5%

EXHIBIT 1.28

Starbucks Corporation Common-Size and Percentage Change Income Statements for the Year Ended September 30 (Integrative Case 1.1)

	Common-Size Income Statement			Percentage Change Income Statement	
	Year 4	Year 3	Year 2	Year 4	Year 3
Revenues					
Company-Operated Retail Stores	84.2%	84.6%	84.9%	29.2%	23.5%
Specialty:					
Licensing	10.7	10.1	9.5	38.1%	31.3%
Foodservice and Other	5.1	5.3	5.6	25.3%	17.4%
Total Revenues	100.0%	100.0%	100.0%	29.9%	23.9%
Expenses					
Cost of Sales Including Occupancy Costs	41.4%	41.2%	41.0%	30.3%	24.8%
Store Operating Expenses	33.8	33.8	33.7	29.8%	24.9%
Nonretail Operating Expenses	3.2	3.5	3.2	21.4%	33.2%
Depreciation and Amortization	5.5	6.0	6.4	18.2%	16.1%
General and Administrative	5.7	6.0	7.1	24.4%	4.3%
Total Expenses	89.6%	90.5%	91.4%	28.6%	22.7%
Income from Equity Investees	1.1	.9	1.0	58.1%	14.6%
Operating Income	11.5%	10.4%	9.6%	44.0%	34.4%
Interest and Other Income	.3	.3	.2	21.0%	20.8%
Interest Expense	—	—	—	—	—
Gain (Loss) on Investments	—	—	.4	—	—
Income before Income Taxes	11.8%	10.7%	10.2%	43.4%	28.8%
Income Tax Expense	4.4	4.1	3.8	38.7%	33.1%
Net Income	7.4%	6.6%	6.4%	46.4%	26.2%

CASE 1.2

NIKE: SOMEWHERE BETWEEN A SWOOSH AND A SLAM DUNK

Nike's principal business activity involves the design, development, and worldwide marketing of high-quality footwear, apparel, equipment, and accessory products. Almost 25,000 employees work for the firm. Nike boasts the largest worldwide market share in the athletic-footwear industry and a leading market share in sports and athletic apparel.

This case uses the financial statements for Nike and excerpts from its notes to review important concepts underlying the three principal financial statements (balance sheet, income statement, and statement of cash flows) and relationships among them. The case also introduces tools for analyzing financial statements.

Industry Economics

Product Lines

Industry analysts debate whether the athletic-footwear industry is a performance-driven athletic-footwear industry or a fashion-driven sneaker industry. Proponents of the performance view point to Nike's dominant market position, which results in part from continual innovation in product development. Proponents of the fashion view point to the difficulty of protecting technological improvements from competitor imitation, the large portion of total expenses comprising advertising, the role of sports and other personalities in promoting athletic shoes, and the fact that only a small percentage of athletic-footwear consumers use the footwear for its intended purpose (such as basketball or running).

Growth

There are only modest growth opportunities for footwear in the United States. Concern exists with respect to both volume increases (how many pairs of athletic shoes will consumers tolerate in their closets) and price increases (will consumers continue to pay prices for innovative athletic footwear that is often twice as costly as other footwear).

Athletic-footwear companies have diversified their revenue sources in two directions in recent years. One direction involves increased emphasis on international sales. With dress codes becoming more casual in Europe and East Asia and interest in American sports such as basketball and football becoming more widespread, industry analysts view international markets as the major growth markets during the next several years. Increased emphasis on soccer in the United States aids companies such as Adidas with reputations for quality soccer footwear.

The second direction for diversification is sports and athletic apparel. The three leading athletic-footwear companies capitalize on their brand name recognition and distribution channels to create a line of sportswear that coordinates with their footwear. Team uniforms and matching apparel for coaching staffs have become a major growth avenue recently. For example, Bauer/Nike Hockey manufactures and distributes ice skates, skate blades, in-line roller skates, protective gear, hockey sticks, and hockey jerseys and accessories under both the Bauer and Nike brand names.

Production

Essentially all athletic footwear and most apparel come from factories in Asia, primarily China (40 percent), Indonesia (31 percent), Vietnam, South Korea, Taiwan, and Thailand. The footwear companies do not own any of these manufacturing facilities. They typically hire manufacturing representatives to source and oversee the manufacturing process, helping to ensure quality control and serving as a link between the design and the manufacture of products. The manufacturing process is labor intensive, with sewing machines used as the primary equipment. Footwear companies typically price their purchases from these factories in U.S. dollars.

Marketing

Athletic-footwear and sportswear companies sell their products to consumers through various independent department, specialty, and discount stores. Their sales forces educate retailers on new product innovations, store display design, and similar activities. The dominant market shares of Nike and the other major players limit retailers' shelf space, and slower growth in sales makes it increasingly difficult for the remaining athletic footwear companies to gain market share. The slower growth has also led the major players to increase significantly their advertising and payments for celebrity endorsements.

Athletic-footwear and sportswear companies have typically used independent distributors to market their products in other countries. With increasing brand recognition and anticipated growth in international sales, these companies have recently acquired an increasing number of their distributors to capture more of the profits generated in other countries and maintain better control of international marketing.

Finance

Compared to other apparel firms, the athletic-footwear firms generate higher profit margins and rates of return. These firms use cash flow generated from this superior profitability to finance needed working capital investments (receivables and inventories). Long-term debt tends to be minimal, reflecting the absence of significant investments in manufacturing facilities.

Nike

Nike targets the serious athlete with performance-driven footwear. In recent years, the firm has particularly emphasized growth outside the United States. The firm sums up the company's philosophy and driving force behind Nike's success by saying: "We are midway on our journey to becoming a truly global company. We are creating a product that is meaningful beyond the stick-and-ball shores of the United States. Consumers around the world are seeing and embracing Nike."

To maintain its technological edge, Nike engages in extensive research at its research facilities in Beaverton, Oregon. It continually alters its product line to introduce new footwear and evolutionary improvements in existing products.

Nike maintains a reputation for timely delivery of footwear products to its customers, primarily as a result of its "Futures" ordering program. Under this program, retailers book orders five to six months in advance. Nike guarantees 90 percent delivery of the order within a set time period at the agreed price at the time of ordering. Approximately 86 percent of footwear orders received by Nike during Year 4 came though its Futures program. This program allows the company to improve production scheduling, thereby reducing inventory risk. However, the program locks in prices and increases Nike's risk of change in raw materials and labor costs.

Independent contractors manufacture virtually all of Nike's products. Nike sources all of its footwear from other countries and approximately 95 percent of its apparel.

The following exhibits present information for Nike:

Exhibit 1.29: Consolidated balance sheets for Year 3 and Year 4.
Exhibit 1.30: Consolidated income statements for Year 2, Year 3, and Year 4.
Exhibit 1.31: Consolidated statements of cash flows Year 2, Year 3, and Year 4.
Exhibit 1.32: Excerpts from the notes to Nike's financial statements.
Exhibit 1.33: Common-size and percentage change income statements.
Exhibit 1.34: Common-size and percentage change balance sheets.

Required

Study the financial statements and notes for Nike and then respond to the following questions.

EXHIBIT 1.29

Consolidated Balance Sheet for Nike (amounts in millions) (Case 1.2)

May 31:	**Year 4**	**Year 3**
Assets		
Cash and Cash Equivalents	$ 828	$ 634
Short-Term Investments	401	—
Accounts Receivable, less allowance for doubtful accounts of $95 and $82	2,120	2,084
Inventories	1,634	1,515
Deferred Income Taxes	165	222
Prepayments	364	332
Total Current Assets	$5,512	$4,787
Property, Plant, and Equipment, net of accumulated depreciation of $1,545 and $1,368	1,587	1,621
Identifiable Intangible Assets	367	118
Goodwill	135	66
Deferred Income Taxes and Other Assets	291	229
Total Assets	$7,892	$6,821
Liabilities and Shareholders' Equity		
Accounts Payable	$ 764	$ 573
Notes Payable	146	75
Current Portion of Long-Term Debt	7	206
Other Current Liabilities	1,092	1,167
Total Current Liabilities	$2,009	$2,021
Long-Term Debt	683	551
Deferred Income Taxes and Other Liabilities	418	258
Total Liabilities	$3,110	$2,830
Common Stock	$ 3	$ 3
Additional Paid-In Capital	888	589
Accumulated Other Comprehensive Income	(86)	(240)
Retained Earnings	3,977	3,639
Total Shareholders' Equity	$4,782	$3,991
Total Liabilities and Shareholders' Equity	$7,892	$6,821

Income Statement

a. Identify the time at which Nike recognizes revenues. Does this timing of revenue recognition seem appropriate? Explain.

b. Identify the cost-flow assumption(s) that Nike uses to measure cost of goods sold. Does Nike's choice of cost-flow assumption(s) seem appropriate? Explain.

EXHIBIT 1.30

Consolidated Income Statement for Nike
(amounts in millions)
(Case 1.2)

Year Ended May 31:	Year 4	Year 3	Year 2
Sales Revenue	$12,253	$10,697	$ 9,893
Cost of Goods Sold	(7,001)	(6,314)	(6,005)
Selling and Administrative	(3,702)	(3,154)	(2,836)
Interest	(25)	(29)	(34)
Other Income (Expense), net	(75)	(77)	(1)
Income before Income Taxes	$ 1,450	$ 1,123	$ 1,017
Income Taxes	(504)	(383)	(349)
Net Income	$ 946	$ 740	$ 668

c. Nike reports property, plant, and equipment on its balance sheet and discloses the amount of depreciation for each year in its statement of cash flows. Why doesn't depreciation expense appear among its expenses on the income statement?

d. Identify the portion of Nike's income tax expense of $504 million for Year 4 that is currently payable to governmental entities and the portion that is deferred to future years. Why do governmental entities permit firms to defer payment of their income taxes to future years?

Balance Sheet

a. Why do accounts receivable appear net of allowance for doubtful accounts? Identify the events or transactions that cause the allowance account to increase or decrease.

b. Identify the depreciation method(s) that Nike uses for its buildings and equipment. Does Nike's choice of depreciation method(s) seem appropriate?

c. Nike includes identifiable intangible assets on its balance sheet as an asset. Does this account include the value of the Nike name and "swoosh" trademark? Explain.

d. Nike includes deferred income taxes among current assets, noncurrent assets, and noncurrent liabilities. Under what circumstances will deferred income taxes give rise to an asset? To a liability?

e. Nike reports accumulated other comprehensive income of ($86) million at the end of Year 4 and ($240) million at the end of Year 3. Why are these "losses" reported as part of shareholders' equity and not as part of net income in the income statement?

Statement of Cash Flows

a. Why does the amount of net income differ from the amount of cash flow from operations?

b. Why does Nike report depreciation as an addition to net income in calculating cash flow from operations?

c. Why does Nike report deferred income taxes as an addition to net income in calculating cash flow from operations for Year 4 (as well as each of the previous years)?

EXHIBIT 1.31

Consolidated Statement of Cash Flows for Nike
(amounts in millions)
(Case 1.2)

Year Ended May 31:	Year 4	Year 3	Year 2
Operations			
Net Income	$ 946	$ 740	$ 668
Depreciation	252	239	224
Deferred Income Taxes	19	55	16
Other	105	36	62
(Increase) Decrease in Accounts Receivable	83	(136)	(135)
(Increase) Decrease in Inventories	(56)	(103)	55
(Increase) Decrease in Other Current Assets	(104)	61	17
Increase (Decrease) in Accounts Payable and Other Current Liabilities	269	30	175
Cash Flow from Operations	$1,514	$ 922	$1,082
Investing			
Additions to Property, Plant, and Equipment	$ (224)	$(186)	$ (283)
Disposals of Property, Plant, and Equipment	12	15	16
Purchase of Short-Term Investments	(401)	—	—
Acquisition of Subsidiary	(289)	—	—
Additions to Other Assets	(43)	(47)	(29)
Increases (Decrease) in Other Liabilities	(1)	2	(7)
Cash Flow from Investing	$ (946)	$(216)	$ (303)
Financing			
Additions to Long-Term Debt	$ 154	$ 90	$ 330
Reductions in Long-Term Debt	(207)	(56)	(80)
Increase (Decrease) in Notes Payable	—	(351)	(433)
Proceeds from Exercise of Stock Options and Other Stock Issues	254	44	60
Repurchase of Common Stock	(420)	(196)	(227)
Dividends	(179)	(138)	(129)
Other	24	(41)	(28)
Cash Flow from Financing	$ (374)	$(648)	$ (507)
Change in Cash	$ 194	$ 58	$ 272
Cash—Beginning of Year	634	576	304
Cash—End of Year	$ 828	$ 634	$ 576

d. Why does Nike add decreases in accounts receivable to net income when calculating cash flow from operations for Year 4?

e. Why does Nike subtract increases in inventory from net income when calculating cash flow from operations for Year 4?

EXHIBIT 1.32

Excerpts from Notes to Consolidated Financial Statements for Nike (amounts in millions) (Case 1.2)

Summary of Significant Accounting Policies

Recognition of Revenues: Nike recognizes revenue at time of sale to its customers and as it earns fees on sales by licensees. Provisions for sales discounts and returns are made at the time of sale.

Inventory Valuation: Inventories appear at lower of cost or market. Nike determines cost using the first-in, first-out (FIFO) method.

Property, Plant, and Equipment and Depreciation: Property, plant, and equipment appear at acquisition cost. Nike computes depreciation using the straight-line method for buildings and leasehold improvements and a declining-balance method for machinery and equipment, based on estimated useful lives ranging from 3 to 32 years.

Identifiable Intangible Assets and Goodwill: This account represents the excess of the purchase price of acquired businesses over the market values of identifiable net assets, net of amortization to date on assets with limited lives.

Foreign Currency Translation: Adjustments resulting from translating foreign functional currency financial statements into U.S. dollars and gains and losses from derivatives that Nike uses to hedge changes in exchange rate are included in accumulated other comprehensive income.

Income Taxes: Nike provides deferred income taxes for temporary differences between income before taxes for financial reporting and tax reporting. Income tax expense includes the following:

	Year 4	Year 3	Year 2
Currently Payable	$495	$349	$336
Deferred	9	34	3
Income Tax Expense	$504	$383	$349

Stock Repurchases: Nike repurchases outstanding shares of its common stock each year and retires them. Any difference between the price paid and the book value of the shares appears as an adjustment of retained earnings.

f. Why does Nike add increases in accounts payable and other current liabilities to net income when calculating cash flow from operations for Year 4?

g. Given that firms often sell property, plant, and equipment at a gain or loss, why does Nike include the proceeds of disposal of these assets as an investing activity instead of as an operating activity?

h. Given that notes payable appear on the balance sheet as a current liability, why does Nike include changes in this liability as a financing activity instead of as an operating activity?

Relations between Financial Statement Items

a. Compute the amount of cash collected from customers during Year 4.

b. Compute the amount of cash payments made to suppliers of merchandise during Year 4.

EXHIBIT 1.33

Common-Size and Percentage Change Income Statements for Nike (Case 1.2)

	Common-Size Income Statements			Percentage Change Income Statements	
Fiscal Year Ended May 31:	**Year 4**	**Year 3**	**Year 2**	**Year 4**	**Year 3**
Nike					
Sales Revenues	100.0%	100.0%	100.0%	14.5%	8.1%
Cost of Goods Sold	(57.2)	(59.0)	(60.7)	10.9%	5.1%
Selling and Administrative Expenses	(30.2)	(29.5)	(28.7)	17.4%	11.2%
Interest Expense	(.2)	(.3)	(.3)	(13.8%)	(14.7%)
Other Income (Expense)	(.6)	(.7)	—	(2.6%)	—
Income before Taxes	11.8%	10.5%	10.3%	29.1%	10.4%
Income Taxes	(4.1)	(3.6)	(3.5)	31.6%	9.7%
Net Income	7.7%	6.9%	6.8%	27.8%	10.8%

c. Prepare an analysis that accounts for the change in the property, plant, and equipment account and the accumulated depreciation account during Year 4. Calculate the gain or loss that Nike recognized on the disposal of property, plant, and equipment during Year 4.

d. Identify the reasons for the change in retained earnings during Year 4.

Interpreting Financial Statement Relationships

a. Exhibit 1.33 presents common-size and percentage change income statements for Nike for Year 2, Year 3, and Year 4. What are the likely reasons for the higher net income/sales revenue percentages for Nike between Year 2 and Year 4?

b. What are the likely reasons for the decrease in the cost of goods sold to sales percentages between Year 2 and Year 4?

c. What are the likely reasons for the increase in the selling and administrative expenses to sales percentages between Year 2 and Year 4?

d. Exhibit 1.34 presents common-size and percentage change balance sheets for Nike at the end Year 2, Year 3, and Year 4. What is the likely explanation for the relatively small percentages for property, plant, and equipment?

e. What is the likely explanation for the relatively small percentages for long-term debt?

f. What is the likely explanation for the small percentage increase for property, plant, and equipment for Nike for Year 3 and the small decrease in Year 4?

g. Refer to the statement of cash flows for Nike in Exhibit 1.31. Net income increased between Year 2 and Year 3, but cash flow from operations decreased. What is the likely reason for the different direction of these changes?

EXHIBIT 1.34

Common-Size and Percentage Change Balance Sheets for Nike (Case 1.2)

	Common-Size Balance Sheets			Percentage Change Balance Sheets	
	Year 4	Year 3	Year 2	Year 4	Year 3
Assets					
Cash	15.6%	9.3%	8.9%	93.8%	10.1%
Accounts Receivable	26.9	30.6	28.0	1.7%	15.5%
Inventories	20.7	22.2	21.3	7.9%	10.3%
Prepayments	6.7	8.1	6.3	(4.5%)	38.2%
Total Current Assets	69.9%	70.2%	64.5%	15.1%	15.2%
Property, Plant, and Equipment, net	20.1	23.7	25.1	(2.1%)	0.4%
Other Noncurrent Assets	10.0	6.1	10.4	92.0%	(38.5%)
Total Assets	100.0%	100.0%	100.0%	15.7%	5.9%
Liabilities and Shareholders' Equity					
Accounts Payable	9.7%	8.4%	7.8%	33.3%	13.7%
Notes Payable	1.8	1.1	6.6	94.7%	(82.4%)
Current Portion of Long-Term Debt	0.1	3.0	0.9	(96.6%)	274.5%
Other Current Liabilities	13.8	17.1	13.2	(6.4%)	37.6%
Total Current Liabilities	25.4%	29.6%	28.5%	(0.6%)	10.3%
Long-Term Debt	8.7	8.1	9.7	24.0%	(12.0%)
Deferred Income Taxes and Other Liabilities	5.3	3.8	2.2	(62.0%)	81.7%
Total Liabilities	39.4%	41.5%	40.4%	9.9%	8.8%
Minority Interest	—	—	—	—	—
Common Stock	—	—	—	—	—
Additional Paid-In Capital	11.3%	8.6%	8.4%	50.8%	9.3%
Retained Earnings	50.4	53.3	54.2	9.3%	4.3%
Accumulated Other Comprehensive Income	(1.1)	(3.4)	(3.0)	(62.2%)	25.0%
Treasury Stock	—	—	—	—	—
Total Shareholders' Equity	60.6%	58.5%	59.6%	19.8%	3.9%
Total Liabilities and Shareholders' Equity	100.0%	100.0%	100.0%	15.7%	5.9%

h. Cash flow from operations exceeded net income during all three years. Why is this the case?

i. How has Nike primarily financed its acquisitions of property, plant, and equipment during the three years?

j. What are the likely reasons for the repurchases of common stock during the three years?

k. The dividends paid by Nike increased each year ($129 million in Year 2, $138 million in Year 3, and $179 million in Year 4). Given that Nike repurchased its stock each year, what is the likely explanation for the increasing amount of dividends?

Chapter 2

Asset and Liability Valuation and Income Measurement

Learning Objectives

1. **Understand the difference between measuring assets and liabilities using historical values versus current values.**
2. **Understand the relation between the valuation of assets and liabilities on the balance sheet and the measurement of net income on the income statement.**
3. **Measure the income tax effects of various income transactions.**
4. **Use an analytical framework to identify the effects of various business transactions on the balance sheet and the income statement.**

Chapter 1 provided a broad overview of financial statement analysis, introducing the six-step framework for financial statement analysis that we use throughout this text. It also described tools used to analyze industry economics and firm strategies and the effects of economic and strategic factors on profitability and risk. Chapter 1 also described the purpose and content of the three principal financial statements, tools for analyzing them, and links between financial statement information and valuation. The remainder of the text develops all of these ideas more completely and provides tools for each step of the framework. To lay the groundwork for these tools for effective analysis of financial statements, we must first understand three fundamental elements that are part of the foundation of financial statements: (1) the principles that underlie the measurement and reporting of financial position and profitability; (2) the pervasive role of income taxes; and (3) the impact of business transactions on financial statements. This chapter explores these three fundamental elements by demonstrating their effects on the balance sheet and income statement. Specifically, we do the following:

- Examine the critical link between the valuation of assets and liabilities and the measurement of net income and comprehensive income.
- Examine the income tax effects of recognizing changes in the value of assets and liabilities on net income and comprehensive income.
- Provide an analytical framework for identifying the effects of value changes on individual balance sheet and income statement accounts.

Chapter 3 discusses the important concepts and analytical tools for the statement of cash flows in greater depth.

ASSET AND LIABILITY VALUATION

The balance sheet reports the assets of a firm and the claims on those assets by creditors (liabilities) and owners (shareholders' equity) at a moment in time. Assets are economic resources that provide a firm with future services or benefits. Liabilities are obligations to sacrifice economic resources in the future for services or benefits already received. Shareholders' equity is the residual claim on assets not required to satisfy the claims of creditors. Chapter 7 discusses the economic resources that firms recognize as assets (for example, inventories, buildings, and equipment) and those that GAAP does not recognize as assets (for example, internally developed brand names and technologies). Chapter 8 discusses the obligations that firms recognize as liabilities (for example, advances from customers or accounts payable to suppliers) and those not normally recognized (for example, obligations related to unsettled lawsuits or mutually unexecuted contracts). Our concern in this section is the valuation of *recognized* assets and liabilities.

Assets provide economic benefits to a firm in the future, and liabilities require firms to sacrifice economic resources in the future. Although assets and liabilities clearly have a future orientation, their valuation on the balance sheet might reflect historical information, current information, or future information. Historical values use information about the value of an asset when a firm acquired it, and the value of a liability when a firm initially incurred it. Current values use information about the value of an asset and a liability at the date of the balance sheet. Valuation methods that reflect historical values include the following:

1. acquisition cost,
2. adjusted acquisition cost, and
3. present value of cash flows using historical interest rates.

Valuation methods that reflect current values include the following:

1. current replacement cost,
2. net realizable value, and
3. present value of cash flows using current interest rates.

Both present value methods use projected cash flows but discount those cash flows to a present value using either historical interest rates or current interest rates. Thus, we view these two present value methods as reflecting either historical values or current values.

Historical Value: Acquisition Cost

The acquisition cost of an asset is the amount paid initially to acquire the asset. Acquisition cost includes all costs required to prepare the asset for its intended use, but does not include costs to operate, or use, the asset.

Example 1

Red Lobster Restaurants acquired a tract of land for a restaurant site at a cost of $120,000. It paid attorneys $4,500 to conduct a title search and prepare the required legal documents for the purchase. It paid a state real estate transfer tax of $1,200. The acquisition cost of the land is $125,700 (= $120,000 + $4,500 + $1,200).

Example 2

Gallo Wines paid employees $1,040,000 to oversee the growing of grapes in its orchards, to harvest the grapes, and to process the grapes into wine. Depreciation on buildings and equipment related to wine production totaled $220,000. Gallo incurred insurance, taxes, and other operating costs related to wine production of $146,000. The acquisition cost of the wine in inventory prior to commencement of aging totals $1,406,000 (= $1,040,000 + $220,000 + $146,000). Gallo Wines will increase the inventory account in later periods for costs incurred during the aging process. Note that the wine is not ready for sale, its intended use, until aging is complete.

Acquisition cost valuations are relatively reliable in that invoices, cancelled checks, and other documents evidence the amount. One valuation question that often arises concerns the costs to include in the asset amount. Should the acquisition cost of the land in Example 1 include the salaries of Red Lobster personnel engaged in selecting the site? Should the acquisition cost of the wine in Example 2 include interest on funds borrowed to finance the production of the wine? A second valuation question concerns the relevancy of acquisition cost valuations to users of the financial statements. At the time that a firm acquires an asset, acquisition cost valuations are reliably, or objectively, measured, and are the relevant valuation method to users of financial statements desiring to value a firm's assets at that time. As time passes, the acquisition cost valuation is still reliably measured but loses relevance for current users desiring to value the firm. Thus, acquisition cost valuations often require trade-offs between *reliability* and *relevance.*

Historical Value: Adjusted Acquisition Cost

The service potential of some assets, such as land, typically do not decline with usage over time and therefore remain at acquisition cost on the balance sheet. Firms consume the service potential of assets such as inventory all at once at the time of sale. The acquisition cost of the asset becomes an expense (cost of goods sold) at that time. Firms consume the service potential of assets such as buildings, equipment, license fees, and contractual rights gradually over time. Firms initially record these assets on the balance sheet at acquisition cost and then amortize or depreciate them over time in some systematic manner.

Example 3

Citicorp, a financial services firm, acquires a computer from IBM for $5 million. Citicorp expects to use the computer for five years and then to sell it for $1 million. Citicorp depreciates $4 million over the five-year useful life to the bank. It matches the remaining $1 million of book value at the end of five years against the selling price and recognizes a gain or loss for any difference.

Example 4

American Airlines acquires a regional airline in the midwestern United States for $450 million. American Airlines allocates $150 million of the purchase price to landing rights at various airports. The landing rights expire in five years. American Airlines amortizes the $150 million over the five years of usage.

Adjusted acquisition cost valuations share the advantages and disadvantages of acquisition cost valuations discussed previously. In addition, the difficulty of physically observing the consumption of service potential that results from usage makes measuring the amount of depreciation or amortization inevitably subjective. Firms must estimate the expected useful life and salvage value of the assets. Furthermore, GAAP permits firms to select from among several time-series patterns (such as straight line or accelerated) for measuring depreciation and amortization expenses.

Firms use acquisition cost valuations and adjusted acquisition cost valuations for assets that do not have fixed amounts of future cash flows. For example, nonmonetary assets have no fixed amount of cash the firm will receive when it uses or sells these assets. Inventories; land; buildings; equipment; legal rights to use another entities' facilities, name, or distribution channels; and goodwill are examples of nonmonetary assets. When the future economic benefits (future cash flows) of an asset are uncertain, firms use acquisition cost and adjusted acquisition cost as a reliable measure of the asset's value.

Monetary assets and liabilities, on the other hand, represent amounts of cash the firm can expect to receive or pay in the future. Cash and accounts and notes receivable are monetary assets; accounts, notes, and bonds payable are examples of monetary liabilities. Firms typically value monetary assets and liabilities using present values, although GAAP permits firms to ignore the discounting process for monetary assets and liabilities due within one year. Firms might also value nonmonetary assets at the present value of expected future cash flows, as the next section discusses.

Historical Value: Present Value of Cash Flows Using Historical Interest Rates

Selling goods or services on account to customers or lending funds to others creates either an account receivable or note receivable for the selling or lending firm. Purchasing goods or services on account from a supplier or borrowing funds from others creates a liability (for example, accounts payable, notes payable, or bonds payable). Discounting the expected future cash flows under such arrangements to a present value expresses those cash flows in terms of a current cash-equivalent value. The discounting procedure might use (1) the interest rate appropriate to the particular financing arrangement at the time the firm initially enters it, referred to as the *historical interest rate,* or (2) the interest rate appropriate to the particular financing arrangement at the date of the balance sheet, referred to as the *current interest rate.* This section discusses present values based on historical interest rates. A later section on valuation methods reflecting current values discusses present values based on current interest rates.

Example 5

Sun Microsystems sells computer equipment to Sun Trust Banks. Sun Trust Banks agrees to pay Sun Microsystems $250,000 at the end of each of the next five years, pledging the equipment as collateral for the loan. An assessment of the credit standing of Sun Trust Banks at the time of the sale and of the value of the collateral suggests that 8 percent is an appropriate interest rate for this loan. The present value of $250,000 per year for five years when discounted at 8 percent is $998,178. Sun Microsystems records a note receivable and Sun Trust Banks records a note payable in the amount of $998,178. During the first year, interest on the note of $79,854 (= .08 × $998,178) increases the book value of the note, and the cash payment of $250,000 reduces the book value of the note to $828,032 (= $998,178 + $79,854 − $250,000). The book value of the note of $828,032 equals the present value of the four remaining annual cash flows of $250,000 when discounted at the historical interest rate of 8 percent.

Example 6

Sears, a department store chain, sells a refrigerator to a customer on July 1, permitting the customer to delay payment of the $500 selling price until December 31. An assessment of the credit standing of the customer suggests that 6 percent per year is an appropriate interest rate for this extension of credit. The present value of $500 when discounted back for one-half year at 6 percent is $485.44. A strict application of the present value of cash flows valuation method results in reporting sales revenue of $485.44 on July 1 and interest revenue of $14.56 (= .06 × 1/2 × $485.44) for the six-month period from July 1 to December 31. As indicated earlier, GAAP permits firms to ignore the discounting process for monetary assets and liabilities due within one year on the grounds that the financial statement effects of discounting or not discounting are not materially different.

Valuing monetary assets and liabilities at the present value of cash flows using historical interest rates is relatively reliable. The arrangement between the two entities usually specifies the required future cash flows. Some subjectivity might exist in establishing an appropriate interest rate at the time of the transaction. The borrower, for example, might choose to use the interest rate at which it could borrow on similar terms from a bank, whereas the seller might use the interest rate that would discount the preset cash flows to a present value equal to the cash selling price of the good or service sold. These small differences in interest rates usually do not result in material differences in valuation between the entities involved in the transaction.

Current Values: Current Replacement Cost

Current replacement cost is the amount a firm would have to pay currently to acquire an asset it now holds. Current replacement cost should reflect normal purchases and sales between unrelated parties, and not distressed purchases and sales in which one party holds a major advantage in setting prices.

Example 7

Refer to Example 1. Red Lobster Restaurants initially recorded the land on its books for $125,700. The land would remain on the books for this amount under the acquisition cost valuation method. Assume that real estate values in the vicinity of this tract of land increased during the next two years. A study of recent real estate transactions suggests that the current cost of purchasing this land or replacing it with similar land is now $145,700.

Example 8

Refer to Example 4. American Airlines amortizes the landing rights for one year in the amount of $30 million (= $150 million/5 years), resulting in a book value of $120 million. Assume now that a curtailment of air travel results in a decline in the replacement cost of these landing rights. A study of recent sales of landing rights suggests that the current replacement cost of landing rights with a four-year remaining life is $55 million.

Current replacement cost valuations generally reflect somewhat greater subjectivity than acquisition cost valuations. Current replacement cost valuations are least subjective and most reliable when they are based on observable market prices from recent transactions in which similar assets or liabilities have been exchanged in active markets. For example, one could obtain reliable measures of current replacement costs of raw commodities by reference to spot prices in commodities markets. When active markets do not exist, as is often the case for equipment specifically designed for a particular firm's needs, then the degree of subjectivity increases. Yet users of financial statements may find current replacement cost valuations more relevant to their needs than out-of-date acquisition cost valuations. Thus, trade-offs exist between the greater reliability of acquisition cost valuations and the greater relevance of replacement cost valuations.

Current Values: Net Realizable Value

Net realizable value is the net amount a firm would receive if it sold an asset or the net amount it would have to pay to settle a liability. As with current replacement cost valuation, net realizable value should reflect normal, instead of distressed, sales.

Example 9

Microsoft, a computer software firm, holds investments in various marketable securities of other firms. It could use the closing price of each security on the nearest trading day to the date of its balance sheet to value these securities at their net realizable value.

Example 10

Refer to Example 3. Citicorp uses the computer equipment for two years and each year records depreciation of \$.8 million [= (\$5 million − \$1 million)/5 years]. The book value of the computer based on adjusted acquisition cost valuation is \$3.4 million [= \$5 million − (2 × \$.8)]. Assume now that new technologies render the computer equipment partially obsolete. A study of used computer equipment offered for sale in business computer magazines indicates an average offering price for similar equipment of \$2.5 million. IBM offers Citicorp \$2.7 million for the equipment as a trade-in on a new, technologically superior computer. The net realizable value of the used computer likely falls in the range of \$2.5 million to \$2.7 million.

Using net realizable values to value assets encounters the same advantages and disadvantages as using current replacement costs. Net realizable values may provide more relevant information to users of the financial statements but result in greater subjectivity when active markets for the assets do not exist.

Current Values: Present Value of Cash Flows Using Current Interest Rates

The present value of a series of cash flows changes with the passage of time, as Example 5 illustrates. Even though the preset cash flows do not change, the present value of those cash flows will change if the interest, or discount, rate changes. The discount rate might change either because of changes in interest rates in the economy or because of a change in the credit risk of the particular borrower.

Example 11

Refer to Example 5. At the end of the first year, the note receivable on the books of Sun Microsystems and the note payable on the books of Sun Trust Banks has a book value of \$828,032, which equals the present value of the remaining four payments of \$250,000 when discounted at the historical interest rate of 8 percent. Assume now the market interest rate appropriate to this note declines to 6 percent. The present value of these payments at 6 percent is \$866,276. These firms could revalue the receivables and payables to \$866,276 to reflect the change in value caused by the change in the discount rate.

Example 12

Hilton Hotels owns a chain of hotels throughout the world. It reports these hotels at adjusted acquisition cost. Hilton Hotels could forecast the net cash flows it anticipates from each hotel in the future and discount them to a present value using current interest rates to value these hotels on its balance sheet at a current value.

Using the present value of cash flows to value a monetary asset or liability with preset cash flows is relatively reliable. Selecting the appropriate current interest rate to revalue

EXHIBIT 2.1

Summary of Valuation Methods for Various Assets and Liabilities

Historical Values

- Acquisition Cost: Prepayments, Land, Intangibles with Indefinite Lives, Goodwill
- Adjusted Acquisition Cost: Buildings, Equipment and Other Depreciable Assets, Intangibles with Limited Lives
- Present Value of Cash Flows Using Historical Interest Rates: Investments in Bonds Held to Maturity, Long-Term Receivables and Payables. This valuation method in theory applies to current receivables and payables, but GAAP ignores the discounting process on the grounds that discounted and undiscounted cash flows do not result in materially different valuations.

Fair Values (current market price or present value of cash flows using current interest rates)

- Investments in Marketable Equity Securities
- Investments in Debt Securities Classified as either Trading Securities or Securities Available for Sale
- Financial Instruments and Derivative Instruments Subject to Hedging Activities
- Assets and Liabilities of a Business Acquired Using the Purchase Method
- Assets and Liabilities of a Business to Be Discontinued

Combination of Values

- Lower of Cost or Market for Inventories
- Lower of Cost or Fair Value for Assets Experiencing an Asset Impairment

the monetary item each period entails a degree of subjectivity. Valuing nonmonetary assets, such as the hotels of Hilton Hotels in Example 12, entails considerable subjectivity. Unlike the case for a monetary asset, the cash flows for a nonmonetary asset are not preset. The accountant must forecast the timing and amount of the expected cash flows for some number of years into the future. The accountant must also revalue the asset each period for either changes in expected cash flows or changes in the discount (interest) rate.

GAAP Valuations

GAAP does not utilize a single valuation method for all assets and liabilities. Instead, GAAP stipulates that firms use historical values for some assets and liabilities, and current, or fair, values for other assets and liabilities. GAAP uses the term *fair value* instead of current value. When GAAP requires firms to use fair value for an asset or liability, firms can measure fair value using either current replacement cost or net realizable value. If markets are not sufficiently active to provide reliable evidence of fair value, then firms can use present value of cash flows, with current interest rates used as the discount rate, to approximate fair value.[1] GAAP has increasingly required use of fair values in the valuation of certain assets and liabilities in recent years. Exhibit 2.1 summarizes the use of

[1]Financial Accounting Standards Board, *Statement of Financial Accounting Concepts No. 7,* "Using Cash Flow Information and Present Value Accounting Measurement" (February 2000).

these valuations methods for various assets and liabilities, which later chapters discuss more fully.

INCOME RECOGNITION

The income statement reports the earnings from a firm's operating activities for a period of time, as well as any gains or losses realized from investing activities (for example, sale of fixed assets at a gain or loss) and financing activities (for example, retirement of debt before maturity at a gain or loss). Net income equals revenues and gains minus expenses and losses. In an ideal world, net income for a period would equal all changes in economic value during that period. Users of the financial statements would then forecast future value changes, using the current period's value changes as a base to value the shareholders' equity of a firm. Unfortunately, many of the changes in economic value of the assets and liabilities of a firm during the period are unobservable.

GAAP recognizes, therefore, that the measurement of value changes often requires trade-offs between the relevance of value changes to the user and the reliability of those measurements. The preceding section discussed the types of judgments often required to value assets and liabilities using current values. GAAP treats value changes in one of three ways:

Treatment 1: Recognize value changes on the balance sheet and the income statement when they are realized in a market transaction (that is, when a firm sells an asset or pays a liability).

Treatment 2: Recognize value changes on the balance sheet when the value changes occur over time but recognize them in net income when they are realized in a market transaction.

Treatment 3: Recognize value changes on the balance sheet and the income statement when they occur over time, even though they are not yet realized in a market transaction.

Exhibit 2.2 summarizes these three treatments, which the following sections discuss. An important guiding principle in asset/liability valuation and income measurement is as follows:

EXHIBIT 2.2

Treatment of Fair Value Changes

	Recognized in the Indicated Financial Statement When Fair Value Change Is Realized	Recognized in the Indicated Financial Statement When Fair Value Change Occurs
Balance Sheet	Treatment 1	Treatment 2 Treatment 3
Income Statement	Treatment 1 Treatment 2	Treatment 3

Over sufficiently long time periods, net income equals cash inflows minus cash outflows, other than cash flows with owners (for example, issuing or repurchasing common stock, paying dividends). Asset and liability valuation and income measurement merely affect when and how the financial statements report these value changes. All value changes eventually affect net income and retained earnings.

Treatment 1: Value Changes Recognized on the Balance Sheet and Income Statement When Realized

The traditional accounting model rests on the realization convention for the recognition of revenues and gains, and the matching convention for the recognition of expenses and losses. Firms typically recognize revenues when they receive cash, a receivable, or some other asset subject to reasonably reliable measurement from a customer for goods sold or services performed. The receipt of this asset validates the amount of the value change. Accountants characterize the firm as having realized the value change. Accountants match all costs incurred to create and sell the good or service as expenses against this revenue. The objective is to match inputs with outputs and thereby measure the net value change, or incremental value added.

Delaying the recognition of value changes for assets and liabilities until realized means that the balance sheet reports assets and liabilities at historical values. Note that realization of the value change is the driver for recognition on both the balance sheet and the income statement under Treatment 1. The receipt or disbursement of cash is not a requirement for either realization or matching. Because the cash flows may precede, coincide with, or follow the value change, the balance sheet reports various accruals (such as accounts receivable, accounts payable, or prepayments).

Example 13

Refer to Example 2 for Gallo Wines. The firm accumulates various costs of producing the wine in its inventory account while the aging occurs. When Gallo Wines completes the aging and sells the wine, it recognizes the value increase in both its assets and its net income. Assume that Gallo Wines incurs total costs of processing and aging the wine of $1,600,000 (= $1,406,000 for the initial processing and $194,000 for aging) and sells the wine at the completion of the aging for $2,000,000 on account. Gallo Wines reports inventories on its balance sheet each year during aging at the accumulated acquisition cost, even though the current value of the wine likely exceeds the accumulated acquisition cost. At the time of sale to a customer, Gallo Wines receives an account receivable of $2,000,000 and gives inventory with a book value of $1,600,000 in exchange. The firm realizes and recognizes revenues of $2,000,000 and matches the accumulated cost of goods sold of $1,600,000 against the revenue to report the net value increase of $400,000 in net income. Assets on the balance sheet increase by a corresponding $400,000 (= $2,000,000 increase in accounts receivable offset by a $1,600,000 decrease in inventories).

Example 14

Refer to Example 7. Red Lobster reports the land on the balance sheet at $125,700, its acquisition cost, as long as the firm continues to hold it. Suppose that Red Lobster decides to sell the land two years after acquiring it for $145,700 in cash. The firm recognizes the $20,000 value increase in its assets (= $145,700 increase in cash minus the $125,700 decrease in land) and simultaneously reports a gain on sale of the land of $20,000 in net income. Firms typically report the income from sales of assets peripheral to their main business as a net amount, $20,000, instead of showing the selling price of $145,700 as revenue and the cost of the asset sold of $125,700 as an expense. In contrast, income from a firm's principal business activities appears as gross amounts. Gallo Wines in Example 13 reports revenue of $2,000,000 and expense for the cost of goods sold of $1,600,000 because selling wines is its primary business.

Treatment 2: Value Changes Recognized on the Balance Sheet When They Occur but Recognized in Net Income When Realized

The traditional accounting model follows Treatment 1 and delays the recognition of value changes of assets and liabilities until a market transaction validates their amounts (that is, realization occurs). The value changes of some assets and liabilities are of particular interest to users and are measurable with a sufficiently high degree of reliability that GAAP requires firms to revalue them to fair value each period. GAAP recognizes, however, that the value change is *unrealized* until the firm sells the asset or settles the liability. The ultimate *realized* gain or loss will likely differ from the unrealized gain or loss each period. GAAP therefore requires firms to delay including the gain or loss in net income until realization of the gain or loss occurs. In the meantime, the firm must include the unrealized gain or loss arising in each period in Other Comprehensive Income and the cumulative unrealized gain or loss in Accumulated Other Comprehensive Income. Recall from Chapter 1 that Accumulated Other Comprehensive Income is a balance sheet account appearing in shareholders' equity. Accumulated Other Comprehensive Income changes each period by the amount of Other Comprehensive Income for the period. Only at the time of realization of the value change will the firm include the realized gain or loss in net income. The firm must simultaneously remove any amounts in Accumulated Other Comprehensive Income related to the asset or liability. Accumulated Other Comprehensive Income serves as a "holding tank" for value changes recognized for assets and liabilities but not yet for net income.

Example 15

Refer to Example 9. Assume that Microsoft has cash in excess of its near-term needs. Rather than allow the cash to remain in its bank account, Microsoft purchases marketable equity securities costing $4,500,000. The fair value of these securities on December 31 is $4,900,000. Microsoft intends to sell these securities when it needs cash. The current fair value of these securities is likely of more interest to users of the firm's financial statements than acquisition cost. The ready market for these securities provides reliable evidence of their fair value.

GAAP requires Microsoft to revalue the securities to fair value and recognize an unrealized holding gain of $400,000 in Other Comprehensive Income. Thus, assets increase by $400,000 and shareholders' equity increases by $400,000.

Next, suppose that Microsoft sells the securities in early June of the following year for $5,000,000. The firm recognizes a realized gain on sale in net income of $500,000 (= $5,000,000 − $4,500,000). It must also eliminate the $400,000 unrealized gain from Accumulated Other Comprehensive Income. Thus, assets increase by $100,000 (cash increases by $5,000,000 and marketable securities decrease by $4,900,000) and shareholders' equity increases by $100,000 (net income causes retained earnings to increase by $500,000, and Accumulated Other Comprehensive Income decreases by $400,000). Chapter 9 discusses the accounting for marketable securities more fully.

Example 16

Ford Motor Company operates in Europe through its subsidiary, Ford Europe. Ford Europe keeps its accounts in euros each period. Ford Motor Company must translate these euro amounts into their U.S. dollar equivalent amounts each period in order to prepare consolidated financial statements for the two entities. As the exchange rate between the U.S. dollar and the euro changes each period, the U.S. dollar equivalent of the euro-measured assets and liabilities of Ford Europe changes.

GAAP requires firms in most circumstances to use the current exchange rate on the date of the balance sheet to translate the assets and liabilities of foreign entities into U.S. dollars. The U.S. parent will not realize the economic effect of the value change, however, until the foreign unit remits cash to the parent and the parent converts the euro cash into U.S. dollars. GAAP therefore does not permit firms to flow through the unrealized foreign exchange gain or loss to net income immediately. Instead, firms must include the unrealized gain or loss in Other Comprehensive Income for the period. Later, when Ford Motor Company makes a currency conversion with the cash received, it realizes an exchange gain or loss and includes it in net income. It simultaneously reduces Accumulated Other Comprehensive Income for a portion of the unrealized gain or loss recognized in earlier periods. Chapter 9 discusses the accounting for foreign entities more fully.

Treatment 3: Value Changes Recognized on the Balance Sheet and the Income Statement When They Occur

The third possibility is that firms revalue assets and liabilities to fair value each period and recognize the unrealized gains and losses in net income in that same period. GAAP generally does not permit firms to revalue assets upward for value increases and recognize the unrealized gain in net income. Firms must await the validation of the value increase through a market transaction (that is, realization) to justify recognizing the gain.

GAAP, however, is not symmetric with value increases and decreases. Firms must generally write down assets whose fair values decrease below their book values and flow through the value decrease to net income immediately. This asymmetric treatment of gains and losses rests on the conservatism convention. Given the judgments often required in measuring net income, GAAP is more concerned that firms not overstate net income than that they understate it.

Example 17

Refer to Example 8. At the end of the first year after their acquisition, the landing rights of American Airlines have a book value of $120 million and a fair value of $55 million. The decrease in air travel results in an impairment in the value of the landing rights of $65 million (= $120 million − $55 million). American Airlines must write down the value of the landing rights and recognize an asset impairment loss of $65 million on its income statement. Thus, assets and shareholders' equity decrease by $65 million. It must recognize this loss even though the firm has not realized the loss in a market transaction. Chapter 6 discusses asset impairment losses more fully.

Example 18

Refer to Example 10. The book value of the computer equipment on Citicorp's books is $3,400,000. Assume that the fair value of the equipment is $2,600,000 as a result of technological obsolescence. GAAP requires Citicorp to write down the computer to $2,600,000 and recognize an asset impairment loss of $800,000 (= $3,400,000 – $2,600,000). Thus, assets and shareholders' equity decrease by $800,000.

Example 19

Refer to Example 11. Recall that the present value of the note payable on the books of Sun Trust Banks is $828,032 based on the historical interest rate of 8 percent. The decrease in interest rates to 6 percent results in an increase in the fair value of the note to $866,276. GAAP generally does not permit firms to revalue financial instruments to market value to reflect changes in interest rates. However, Sun Trust Banks may wish to repay the note prior to maturity. Sun Microsystems, the holder of the note, will likely set a price for earlier repayment that reflects current market interest rates at the time of repayment. For example, Sun Microsystems would probably require Sun Trust Banks to pay $866,276 to repay the note at this time if interest rates have declined to 6 percent.

Sun Trust Banks may obtain a hedging contract, referred to as a derivative, from another entity that protects the net amount Sun Trust Banks must pay to retire the debt prior to maturity. When firms acquire derivatives to hedge changes in value of a financial instrument, GAAP requires the firms to revalue both the financial instrument and the derivative to fair value each period and recognize unrealized gains and losses in net income immediately. In this example, Sun Trust Banks writes up the note payable from $828,032 to $866,276 and recognizes a loss in net income for the difference, $38,244. It would also revalue the derivative, which in this case is an asset. If the derivative perfectly hedges the change in interest rates, it will increase in value by $38,244 as well. Sun Trust Banks increases the derivative asset and recognizes a gain of $38,244. If the hedge is not perfectly effective, the gain and loss will not precisely offset and net income will increase or decrease for the difference (net of any tax effect). Chapter 8 discusses the accounting for financial instruments and derivatives. The discussion there indicates that not all unrealized gains and losses immediately flow through to net income, but instead may first flow through Other Comprehensive Income.

Summary of Asset and Liability Valuation and Income Recognition

The traditional accounting model relies mostly on historical values for assets and liabilities, and the realization and matching conventions for income recognition (Treatment 1). In this model, asset and liability valuation directly link to income measurement. Standard-setting bodies have increasingly required the use of fair values in the valuation of certain assets and liabilities in recent years. Some of these value changes (generally, declines in asset values) affect net income immediately (Treatment 3). GAAP invokes the conservatism convention to justify recognition of value declines but not value increases. Other value changes affect asset and liability amounts before they affect net income (Treatment 2). In the intervening time, firms park the unrealized gains and losses in Accumulated Other Comprehensive Income. When the firm realizes the value change, it reclassifies the unrealized gains and losses from Accumulated Other Comprehensive Income to net income. GAAP has not yet evolved to the point of providing a sufficient conceptual rationale for these three different approaches to asset and liability valuation and income measurement to permit the user of financial statements to anticipate, apart from prescribed GAAP, how firms account for any particular transaction. Given the trade-offs between reliability and relevance often encountered in setting GAAP for particular assets and liabilities and the different preferences and concerns of the various constituencies involved in the standard-setting process, obtaining agreement on a single valuation approach in the near future seems unlikely.

ACCOUNTING FOR INCOME TAXES

The discussion thus far in this chapter has considered the measurement of revenues, gains, expenses, and losses before considering any income tax effects. Income taxes affect virtually every transaction in which a firm engages. Consider the following examples:

- American Airlines in Example 17 and Citicorp in Example 18 must recognize impairment losses for financial reporting as the fair values of their assets decline. These firms cannot deduct such losses immediately for tax purposes, but instead must continue to depreciate or amortize them over time. Thus, GAAP and the income tax law treat these decreases in value differently.
- Microsoft in Example 15 includes the $400,000 increase in fair value of marketable equity securities in Other Comprehensive Income. The firm will report the effect of any value changes in taxable income only when it sells the securities. Should Microsoft recognize any income tax expense now on the $400,000 of Other Comprehensive Income?
- Ford Motor Company in Example 16 must include unrealized foreign exchange gains and losses in Other Comprehensive Income. The firm will not include such gains and losses in taxable income until the foreign unit remits cash to the parent company. If the foreign unit intends to reinvest its earnings permanently, then it may never pay a dividend to its parent. When and how much income tax expense should Ford Motor Company recognize on the unrealized foreign exchange gain or loss?

Thus, in order to fully understand business transactions, we need to understand their income tax effects. Before discussing various financial reporting topics in Chapters 6 to 9, we need an overview of the required accounting for income taxes under GAAP. Chapter 8 discusses the accounting for income taxes more fully.

Overview of Income Tax Accounting

Income taxes affect the analysis of a firm's profitability (income tax expense is a subtraction in computing net income) and its cash flows (income taxes paid are an operating use of cash). Income tax expense for a period does not necessarily equal income taxes payable for that period. The balance sheet recognizes the difference between the two amounts as a deferred tax asset or a deferred tax liability.

A simple example illustrates the issues in accounting for income taxes. Exhibit 2.3 sets forth information for a firm for its first two years of operations. The first column for each year shows the amounts reported to shareholders (referred to as "book amounts" or "financial reporting"). The second column shows the amounts reported to income tax authorities (referred to as "tax amounts" or "tax reporting"). The third column indicates the effect of each item on cash flows. Assume for this example and those throughout this chapter that the income tax rate is 40 percent. Additional information on each item is as follows:

- Sales Revenue: The firm reports sales of $500 each year for both book and tax reporting. We assume that it collects the full amount each year in cash (that is, the firm has no accounts receivable).

- Interest Revenue on Municipal Bonds: The firm earns $25 of interest on municipal bonds. The firm includes this amount in its book income. The federal government does not subject interest on state and municipal bonds to taxation, so we exclude this amount from the computation of taxable income. We assume that the firm receives the full amount of interest revenue in cash each year.
- Depreciation Expense: The firm has equipment costing $120 with a two-year life. It depreciates the equipment using the straight-line method for financial reporting, recognizing $60 of depreciation expense on its books each year. Income taxing authorities permit the firm to write off a larger portion of the asset's cost in the first year, $80, than the straight-line method. Because total depreciation over the life of an asset cannot exceed acquisition cost, the firm recognizes only $40 of depreciation for tax reporting in the second year.
- Warranty Expense: The firm estimates that the cost of providing warranty services on products sold equals 2 percent of sales. It recognizes warranty expense of $10 (= .02 × $500) each year for financial reporting, which matches the estimated cost of warranties against the revenue from the sale of products subject to warranty. Income tax laws do not permit firms to claim a deduction for warranties in computing taxable income until they make cash expenditures to provide warranty services. We assume that the firm incurs cash costs of $4 in the first year and $12 in the second year.
- Other Expenses: The firm incurs and pays in cash other expenses of $300 each year.
- Income before Taxes and Taxable Income: Income before taxes for financial reporting is $155 each year. Taxable income is $116 in the first year and $148 in the second year.

EXHIBIT 2.3

Illustration of the Effects of Income Taxes on Net Income, Taxable Income, and Cash Flows

	First Year			Second Year		
	Book Amounts	Tax Amounts	Cash Flow Amounts	Book Amounts	Tax Amounts	Cash Flow Amounts
Sales Revenue	$500	$500	$500	$500	$500	$500
Interest on Municipal Bonds	25	—	25	25	—	25
Depreciation Expense	(60)	(80)	—	(60)	(40)	—
Warranty Expense	(10)	(4)	(4)	(10)	(12)	(12)
Other Expenses	(300)	(300)	(300)	(300)	(300)	(300)
Net Income before Taxes or Taxable Income	$155	$116		$155	$148	
Income Tax Expense or Payable	(52)	(46.4)	(46.4)	(52)	(59.2)	(59.2)
Net Income	$103			$103		
Depreciation Addback	60			60		
Change in Warranty Liability	6			(2)		
Change in Deferred Taxes	5.6			(7.2)		
Cash Flow from Operations	$174.6		$174.6	$153.8		$153.8

Income before taxes for financial reporting differs from taxable income for two principal reasons:

1. **Permanent Differences:** Revenues and expenses that firms include in net income to shareholders but that never appear in the income tax return. Interest revenue on the municipal bond is a permanent difference.
2. **Temporary Differences:** Revenues and expenses that firms include in both net income to shareholders and taxable income but in different periods. Depreciation expense is a temporary difference. The firm recognizes total depreciation of $120 over the life of the equipment for both financial and tax reporting but in a different pattern over time. Warranty expense is likewise a temporary difference. The firm recognizes $20 of warranty expense over the two-year period for financial reporting. It recognizes only $16 over the two-year period for tax reporting. If the firm's estimate of total warranty costs turns out to be correct, then the firm will recognize the remaining $4 of warranty expense for tax reporting in future years as it provides warranty services.

A central conceptual question in accounting for income taxes concerns the measurement of income tax expense on the income statement for financial reporting:

1. Should the firm compute income tax expense based on book income before taxes ($155 for each year in Exhibit 2.3)?
2. Should the firm compute income tax expense based on book income before taxes but excluding permanent differences ([$130 = $155 − $25] for each year in Exhibit 2.3)?
3. Should the firm compute income tax expense based on taxable income ($116 in the first year and $148 in the second year in Exhibit 2.3)?

Standard-setting bodies require firms to follow the second approach. Income tax expense is not simply the amount of income taxes currently payable (the third approach). Firms must also recognize the benefit of future tax deductions and the obligations related to future taxable income that arise because of temporary differences. The underlying concept is matching: matching income tax expense with the income reported for financial reporting, even though the associated cash flows for income taxes will not occur until future periods.

Permanent differences do not affect taxable income or income taxes paid in any year. Because total expenses over sufficiently long time periods must equal the related cash outflows, firms never recognize income tax expense or income tax savings on permanent differences (the first approach). Thus, income tax expense is $52 (= .40 × $130) in each year.

The firm makes the following entry to recognize income tax expense in the first year:

Income Tax Expense (.40 × $130)	52.0	
Deferred Tax Asset—Warranty (.40 × $6)	2.4	
Deferred Tax Liability—Depreciation (.40 × $20)		8.0
Income Taxes Payable (.40 × $116)		46.4

The deferred tax asset measures the future tax saving that the firm will realize when it provides warranty services in future years and claims a tax deduction on products sold in the first year. The firm expects to incur $6 (= $10 − $4) of warranty costs in the second and later years. When it incurs these costs, it will reduce its taxable income and reduce income taxes payable for the year. For financial reporting, the firm follows the matching principle and recognizes all of the $10 expected costs of providing warranty services on products sold during the first year.

The deferred tax liability measures the income taxes saved in the first year as a result of recognizing $20 more depreciation for tax purposes than for financial reporting purposes, taxes that the firm must pay in the second year when it recognizes $20 less depreciation for tax reporting than for financial reporting.

Now consider the effect on cash flows. The third column for each year in Exhibit 2.3 shows that the increases and decreases in cash net to $174.6 for the first year. This reporting format follows the direct method of computing cash flow from operations. As Chapter 3 discusses more fully, most firms report cash flow from operations using the *indirect method.* The indirect method begins with net income and then adjusts that amount to compute cash flow from operations.

The lower portion of the book income amounts in the first column of Exhibit 2.3 demonstrates the calculation of cash flow from operations for the indirect method. Depreciation is an expense that does not use cash, so we add back the $60 of depreciation recognized for book purposes to offset its subtraction in measuring net income. The firm recognized warranty expense of $10 in measuring net income but used only $4 of cash in satisfying warranty claims. The firm adds back the $6 difference, which is the credit change in the warranty liability account during the period. The warranty liability account begins with a zero balance and ends the year with a balance of $6 (= $10 − $4). Likewise, the firm recognized $52 of income tax expense in measuring net income but used only $46.4 cash for income taxes. The firm adds back the $5.6 difference, which is the net credit change in the Deferred Tax Asset ($2.4 debit change) and Deferred Tax Liability ($8 credit change) accounts (see the preceding journal entry).

The firm makes the following entry in the second year to recognize income tax expense:

Income Tax Expense (.40 × $130)	52.0	
Deferred Tax Liability—Depreciation (.40 × $20)	8.0	
Deferred Tax Asset—Warranty (.40 × $2)		.8
Income Tax Payable (.40 × $148)		59.2

The temporary difference related to depreciation completely reversed in the second year, so the firm reduces the deferred tax liability to zero, which increases income taxes currently payable by $8. The temporary difference related to the warranty partially reversed during the second year, but the firm created additional temporary differences in that year. For the two years as a whole, warranty expense for financial reporting of $20 (= $10 + $10) exceeds the amount recognized for tax reporting of $16 (= $4 + $12). Thus, the firm will recognize tax savings of $1.6 (= .4 × $4) in future years. The deferred tax asset had a balance of $2.4 at the end of the first year. The entry for the second year reduces the balance in the deferred tax assets by $.8 (= $2.4 − $1.6) for the net tax benefit realized during that year.

Now consider the cash flow effects for the second year. Cash flow from operations is $153.8. The firm again adds back to net income depreciation expense of $60. The firm recognized warranty expense of $10 for financial reporting but used $12 of cash to satisfy warranty claims. It subtracts the additional $2 of cash used in excess of the expense. The $2 subtraction also equals the debit change in the warranty liability accounting during the second year, as the following analysis shows:

Warranty Liability, beginning of second year	$ 6
Warranty Expense, second year	10
Warranty Claims, second year	(12)
Warranty Liability, end of second year	$ 4

The firm recognized $52 of income tax expense but used $59.2 of cash for income taxes. The additional $7.2 of cash used to pay taxes in excess of the tax expense reduced the net deferred tax liability position. The $7.2 subtraction also equals the net debit change in the Deferred Tax Asset ($.8 credit change) and Deferred Tax Liability ($8 debit change) during the second year, as the following analysis shows:

Net Deferred Tax Liability, beginning of second year ($8 − $2.4)	$ 5.6
Income Tax Expense, second year	52.0
Income Taxes Payable, second year	(59.2)
Net Deferred Tax Asset, end of second year	$(1.6)

Measuring Income Tax Expense: A Bit More to the Story

The preceding illustration followed what we might term an *income statement approach* to measuring income tax expense. We compared revenues and expenses recognized for book and tax purposes, eliminated permanent differences, and then computed income tax expense based on book income before taxes excluding permanent differences. *Financial Accounting Standards Board Statement 109,*[2] however, requires firms to follow a *balance sheet approach* when computing income taxes expense. We describe this approach next.

1. Identify at each balance sheet date all differences between the book basis of assets, liabilities, and tax loss carryforwards (that is, the book values for financial reporting) and the tax basis of assets, liabilities, and tax loss carryforwards. Tax loss carryforwards represent net losses incurred in one year that the income tax law allows a firm to carry forward to offset positive taxable income in future years and thereby reduce taxes otherwise payable in those future years. In the preceding illustration, the book basis of the equipment at the end of the first year is $60 (= $120 − $60) and the tax basis is $40 (= $120 − $80). The book and tax basis are zero at the end of the second year. The book basis of the warranty liability at the end of the first year is $6 (= $10 − $4) and the tax basis is zero (that is, the firm recognizes a deduction for tax purposes when it pays warranty claims and therefore has no liability on its tax books). The book basis of the warranty liability at the end of the second year is $4 (= $6 + $10 − $12) and the tax basis is zero.
2. Eliminate differences from step 1 that will not have a future tax consequence (that is, permanent differences). Assume, for example, that the firm in the preceding illustration had not received the $25 of interest on the municipal bond investment by the end of the first year. It would show an Interest Receivable on its financial reporting books of $25, but no receivable would appear on its tax books. Because

[2]Financial Accounting Standards Board, *Statement of Financial Accounting Standards No. 109,* "Accounting for Income Taxes" (1992).

the tax law does not tax such interest, the difference between the book and tax basis is a permanent difference. The firm would eliminate this book/tax difference before moving to the next step.

3. Separate the remaining differences into those that give rise to future tax deductions and those that give rise to future taxable income. Exhibit 2.4 summarizes the possibilities and gives several examples of these temporary differences, as later chapters discuss. The difference between the book basis ($6) and the tax basis ($0) of the warranty liability at the end of the first year gives rise to future tax deductions. The difference between the book basis ($60) and the tax basis ($40) of the equipment at the end of the first year gives rise to future taxable income. Multiply differences that give rise to future tax deductions by the enacted marginal tax rate expected to apply in those future periods. The result is a deferred tax asset. The deferred tax asset related to warranties at the end of the first year is $2.4 [= .4 × ($6 − $0)]. Multiply differences that give rise to future taxable income by the enacted marginal tax rate expected to apply in those future periods. The result is a deferred tax liability. The deferred tax liability related to the equipment at the end of the first year is $8 [= .4 × ($60 − $40)]. A firm may have recognized net losses in its income statement for financial reporting that the firm cannot then recognize for tax reporting. It can carry forward this net loss and offset taxable income of future years, thereby saving taxes. The firm includes the tax effect of tax loss carryforwards (reduce future taxable income) and tax credit carryforwards (reduce future taxes payable) in deferred tax assets at each balance sheet date.

EXHIBIT 2.4

Examples of Temporary Differences

	Assets	Liabilities
Future Tax Deduction *(results in deferred tax assets)*	Tax Basis of Assets Exceeds Financial Reporting Basis[a]	Tax Basis of Liabilities is Less than Financial Reporting Basis[b]
Future Taxable Income *(results in deferred tax liabilities)*	Tax Basis of Assets is Less than Financial Reporting Basis[c]	Tax Basis of Liabilities Exceeds Financial Reporting Basis[d]

Examples

[a]Accounts receivable using the direct charge-off method for uncollectible accounts for tax purposes exceeds accounts receivable (net) using the allowance method for financial reporting.

[b]Tax reporting does not recognize an estimated liability for warranty claims (firms can deduct only actual expenditures on warranty claims), whereas firms must recognize such a liability for financial reporting to match warranty expense with sales revenue in the period of sale.

[c]Depreciation computed using accelerated depreciation for tax purposes and the straight-line method for financial reporting.

[d]Leases recognized by a *lessee*, the user of the leased assets, as a capital lease for tax reporting and an operating lease for financial reporting.

4. Assess the likelihood that the firm will realize the benefits of deferred tax assets in the future. This assessment should consider the nature (whether cyclical or non-cyclical, for example) and characteristics (growing, mature, or declining, for example) of a firm's business and its tax planning strategies for the future. If realization of the benefits of deferred tax assets is "more likely than not" (that is, exceeds 50 percent), then deferred tax assets equal the amounts computed in step 3. If it is more likely than not that the firm will not realize some or all of the deferred tax assets, then the firm must reduce the deferred tax asset for a valuation allowance (similar in concept to the allowance for uncollectible accounts receivable). The valuation allowance reduces the deferred tax assets to the amounts the firm expects to realize by way of reduced taxes in the future. Assume that the firm in the preceding illustration considers it more likely than not that it will realize the tax benefits of the deferred tax assets related to warranties and therefore recognizes no valuation allowance.

The result of this four-step procedure is a deferred tax asset and a deferred tax liability at each balance sheet date. The amounts in the preceding illustration are as follows:

	January 1, First Year	December 31, First Year	December 31, Second Year
Deferred Tax Asset—Warranties	$0	$ 2.4	$1.6
Deferred Tax Liability—Equipment	0	8.0	0.0
Net Deferred Tax Asset (Liability)	$0	$(5.6)	$1.6

Income tax expense for each period equals:

1. income taxes currently payable on taxable income,
2. plus a credit change in the net deferred tax asset and liability, or minus a debit change in the net deferred tax asset and liability.

Income tax expense in the preceding illustration is:

	First Year	Second Year
Income Taxes Currently Payable on Taxable Income	$46.4	$59.2
Plus Credit Change in Net Deferred Tax Asset and Liability	5.6	—
Minus Debit Change in Net Deferred Tax Asset and Liability	—	(7.2)
Income Tax Expense	$52.0	$52.0

The income statement approach illustrated in the first section and the balance sheet approach illustrated in this section yield identical results whenever (1) enacted tax rates applicable to future periods do not change, and (2) the firm recognizes no valuation allowance on deferred tax assets. Legislated changes in tax rates applicable to future periods will cause the tax effects of previously recognized temporary differences to differ from the amounts in the deferred tax asset and deferred tax liability accounts. The firm revalues the deferred tax assets and liabilities for the change in tax rates and flows through the effect of the change to income tax expense in the year of the legislated change. A change in the valuation allowance for deferred tax assets likewise flows through immediately to income tax expense.

Reporting Income Taxes in the Financial Statements

Firms may not include all income taxes for a period on the line for income tax expense in the income statement. Some amounts may appear elsewhere:

1. Discontinued Operations and Extraordinary Items: Firms with either of these categories of income for a particular period report them in separate sections of the income statement, each net of their income tax effects. Thus, income tax expense reflects income taxes on income from continuing operations only.
2. Other Comprehensive Income: Unrealized changes in the market value of marketable equity securities classified as "available for sale," unrealized changes in the market value of hedged financial instruments and derivatives classified as cash flow hedges, unrealized foreign translation adjustments, and changes in the minimum pension liability appear in Other Comprehensive Income, net of their tax effects. These items almost always give rise to deferred tax assets or deferred tax liabilities because the income tax law includes such gains and losses in taxable income when realized in a market transaction. Thus, a portion of the change in deferred tax assets and liabilities on the balance sheet does not flow through income tax expense on the income statement.

PepsiCo's Reporting of Income Taxes

PepsiCo reports information on income taxes in Note 5, "Income Taxes," to its financial statements (Appendix A), excerpts of which appear in Exhibit 2.5. Income tax expense for Year 4 of $1,372 million includes $1,355 million currently payable and $17 million deferred. Thus, excluding permanent differences, PepsiCo's income for financial reporting exceeded its taxable income for Year 4. For Year 3, income taxes currently payable exceeded income tax expense, suggesting that its taxable income exceeded its income for financial reporting.

PepsiCo's deferred tax liabilities exceed its deferred tax assets, for a net deferred tax liability. The change in the net deferred tax liability for Year 4 is $33 million (= $987 − $954). This amount exceeds the $17 million of deferred tax expense for Year 4. Some of the remaining difference of $16 million (= $33 − $17) likely relates to amounts reported in Other Comprehensive Income. PepsiCo's Note 13, "Accumulated Other Comprehensive Income" (Appendix A), indicates that it recognizes income taxes on cash flow hedges and the minimum pension liability adjustment. Some of the difference also likely relates to the tax benefit of discontinued operations.

Note from Exhibit 2.5 that PepsiCo recognized a valuation allowance on its deferred tax assets of $438 million at the end of Year 3 and $564 million at the end of Year 4. The change in the valuation allowance affects the change in the net deferred tax liability and therefore the amount of income tax expense. It is likely that the valuation allowance relates primarily to the deferred tax assets for net operating loss carryforwards, which is one of the items for which PepsiCo recognized a deferred tax asset (see Note 5 to PepsiCo's financial statements in Appendix A).

EXHIBIT 2.5

Excerpts from PepsiCo's Note 5 on Income Taxes
(amounts in millions)

Income Statement for Year:	Year 4	Year 3	Year 2
Provision for income taxes—continuing operations:			
Current	$1,355	$1,747	$1,259
Deferred	17	(323)	174
Total	$1,372	$1,424	$1,433
Balance Sheet at End of Year:			
Deferred tax liabilities (details omitted)	$2,732	$2,592	
Deferred tax assets (details omitted)	$2,309	$2,076	
Valuation allowances.	(564)	(438)	
Deferred tax assets, net	$1,745	$1,638	
Net deferred tax liabilities.	$ 987	$ 954	

We will return to our study of income taxes in Chapter 8 to explore in greater depth the concepts and procedures of accounting for income taxes.

FRAMEWORK FOR ANALYZING THE EFFECTS OF TRANSACTIONS ON THE FINANCIAL STATEMENTS

Each period, firms prepare financial statements that aggregate and summarize the results of numerous transactions. This section presents and illustrates an analytical framework for understanding the effects of various transactions on the financial statements.

One might legitimately ask the question: Why do I need to understand individual transactions when my concern is the analysis of financial statements as a whole? After all, firms engage in millions of transactions during the year, with no single transaction likely having a material effect on the financial statements. The response to this question is twofold.

First, one must understand the effects of the numerous similar, repetitive transactions that dominate balance sheet and income statement amounts in order to make appropriate interpretations about a firm's profitability and risk. Consider the following examples from recent annual reports of several publicly traded corporations.

Example 20

PepsiCo combines various ingredients to produce syrup for its soft drinks. It sells the syrup to its bottlers, who add water and other ingredients to manufacture the finished soft drink and then bottle it. PepsiCo owns approximately 40 percent of the common stock of its bottlers, with individuals and other entities owning the remainder. What is the effect on PepsiCo's net income when it sells syrup to its bottlers? Should it recognize revenue immediately in an amount equal to the selling price of the syrup, the same as it would if it sold the syrup to nonaffiliated bottlers? Or should PepsiCo delay the recognition of revenue until the bottlers manufacture and sell soft drinks to customers? Should PepsiCo include all of the assets and liabilities of the bottlers in its balance sheet, a proportion of the assets and liabilities equal to its ownership percentage, or none of these assets and liabilities? How would the analysis of PepsiCo's profitability and risk differ depending on PepsiCo's accounting method for transactions with its bottlers?

Example 21

Xerox Corporation sells photocopying machines, photographic paper, and after-sale maintenance services in a bundled package to customers on a multiyear installment payment plan. Xerox generates four types of income from this activity: (1) manufacturing income from selling the machines for more than their manufacturing cost, (2) income from selling photographic paper for more than the cost of that paper to Xerox, (3) maintenance income from providing services over the life of the maintenance contract, and (4) interest income from providing financing services over the life of the installment sales contract. What is the impact on total assets and net income each year if Xerox attributes too much of the cash it will receive to the manufacturing activity and too little to the maintenance services? What is the impact on total assets and net income each year if Xerox uses a discount rate of 7 percent instead of 8 percent to discount the cash flows to their present value? What amount, if any, will appear among liabilities related to Xerox's obligation under the maintenance agreement?

Example 22

Enron entered into multiyear contracts to purchase and sell energy products at preset prices. To neutralize the risk of price changes during the term of the contracts, Enron also sold and purchased financial instruments, called derivatives. Enron created variable interest entities (VIEs), to which it transferred some of these energy contracts and derivatives in return for an equity interest. The VIEs also obtained equity capital from other investors. GAAP does not require firms to consolidate the financial statements of the VIEs with their own as long as the investor is not the primary beneficiary of the VIE, as discussed in Chapter 9. What is the effect on Enron's balance sheet if it retains the energy contracts and derivatives versus transferring them to the VIE? What is the effect on the income statement? Will it make a difference if Enron sells the energy contracts and derivatives versus transferring them for an equity interest?

A second response to the question about the need to understand the effects of individual transactions on the financial statements relates to the increased complexity of many nonrecurring transactions in recent years. Consider the following examples.

Example 23

Tyco International engaged in extensive restructuring of its operations, closing down or selling manufacturing facilities and severing employees. GAAP requires firms to recognize restructuring expenses when they commit to a restructuring plan, even though several years may elapse before completing the plan. Will the recognition of restructuring expense result in an immediate decrease in assets, an increase in liabilities, or both? What is the effect on the income statement when the firm actually closes or sells a manufacturing facility or severs employees? What is the effect on subsequent balance sheet and income statement amounts if the firm discovers later that its initial restructuring expense was too small or too large?

Example 24

Nortel Networks made numerous corporate acquisitions totaling $33.5 billion in recent years. It allocated $14.5 billion of the purchase price to identifiable assets, such as accounts receivable, inventories, plant, and equipment, and to identifiable liabilities, such as accounts payable and long-term debt. Nortel allocated the remaining $19 billion to goodwill. What would be the effect on net income of subsequent years if Nortel had allocated more of the purchase price to identifiable assets and liabilities and less to goodwill? Nortel subsequently recognized a $12.3 billion goodwill impairment loss because the fair value of the acquired firms had declined since the acquisitions. What is the impact of the goodwill impairment loss on total assets, total liabilities, and shareholders' equity?

At this point you likely experienced some difficulty in understanding the effects of each of these transactions on the financial statements. This is expected. Later chapters discuss these transactions in greater depth. The purpose of these examples is to illustrate the need for an analytical framework to structure your thinking about business transactions and their effect on the financial statements.

Overview of the Analytical Framework

The analytical framework relies on the balance sheet equation:

Assets = Liabilities + Shareholders' Equity

We can expand the equation as follows:

						Contributed		**Accumulated Other**		**Retained**
Cash	+	**Noncash Assets**	=	**Liabilities**	+	**Capital**	+	**Comprehensive Income**	+	**Earnings**

Using symbols:

C	+	N$A	=	L	+	CC	+	AOCI	+	RE

Firms prepare balance sheets at the beginning and end of a period. Thus:

C	+	N$A	=	L	+	CC	+	AOCI	+	RE
								Other Comprehensive Income		Net Income − Dividends
C	+	N$A	=	L	+	CC	+	AOCI	+	RE

Transactions during a period link balance sheets at the beginning and end of the period. Many value changes affect net income for the period and thereby affect changes in retained earnings for the period. Other value changes affect Other Comprehensive Income for the period and thereby affect changes in Accumulated Other Comprehensive Income for the period.

We illustrate this analytical framework using several of the transactions discussed earlier in this chapter.

Example 25

Refer to Example 13. Gallo Wines (1) sold for \$2,000,000 on account (2) wine costing \$1,600,000 to produce. (3) Gallo Wines recognizes revenues and expenses in the same period for financial and tax reporting and pays income taxes at a rate of 40 percent immediately. We use the following abbreviations throughout the examples:

BS-BOP: Balance Sheet at the Beginning of the Period
IBT: Income before Taxes
OCI: Other Comprehensive Income
NI: Net Income
BS-EOP: Balance Sheet at the End of the Period

	C	+	N\$A	=	L	+	CC	+	AOCI	+	RE
BS-BOP											
(1)			+2,000,000								+2,000,000
(2)			−1,600,000								−1,600,000
IBT											+ 400,000
(3)	−160,000										− 160,000
NI											+ 240,000
BS-EOP	−160,000		+ 400,000								+ 240,000

Net assets increase by \$240,000 (= \$400,000 − \$160,000) and net income and retained earnings increase by \$240,000.

Example 26

Refer to Example 14. (1) Red Lobster Restaurants sells for \$145,700 land with a book value of \$125,700. (2) Red Lobster recognizes the gain at the time of sale for both financial and tax reporting and pays taxes at a rate of 40 percent.

	C	+	N\$A	=	L	+	CC	+	AOCI	+	RE
BS-BOP											
(1)	+145,700		−125,700								+20,000
IBT											+20,000
(2)	− 8,000										− 8,000
NI											+12,000
BS-EOP	+137,700		−125,700								+12,000

Net assets increase by \$12,000 (= \$137,700 − \$125,700) and net income and retained earnings increase by \$12,000.

Example 27

Refer to Example 15. Microsoft (1) purchases marketable securities costing \$4,500,000 for cash, (2) revalues them to their \$4,900,000 market value at the end of the period, (3) recognizes income taxes for the period, and (4) sells them for \$5,000,000 during the next period. (5) The income tax law taxes gains and losses when realized at an income tax rate of 40 percent.

	C	+	N$A	=	L	+	CC	+	AOCI	+	RE
BS-BOP											
(1)	−4,500,000		+4,500,000								
(2)			+ 400,000						+400,000		
IBT									+400,000		
(3)					+160,000				−160,000		
OCI									+240,000		
BS-EOP	−4,500,000		+4,900,000		+160,000				+240,000		
(4)	+5,000,000		−4,900,000						−400,000		+500,000
IBT											+500,000
(5)	− 200,000				−160,000				+160,000		−200,000
NI											+300,000
BS-EOP	+ 300,000		0		0				0		+300,000

During the first year, Microsoft revalues the securities to market value and includes the $400,000 increase in Other Comprehensive Income. It recognizes a liability for future income taxes on the increase in value of $160,000 (= .4 × $400,000). Because Microsoft includes the pretax increase in value in Other Comprehensive Income, it reports the tax effect there as well (matching convention). The income tax law does not tax the unrealized gain immediately, so Microsoft increases its Deferred Tax Liability for $160,000. During the second year, Microsoft includes the realized gain of $500,000 in net income. It must reduce Accumulated Other Comprehensive Income for the $400,000 unrealized gain recognized in the first year. Thus, net income before taxes for the second year increases by $500,000 but shareholders' equity increases by only $100,000 (= $500,000 − $400,000), the value increase during the second year. The firm recognizes and pays $200,000 of income taxes on the realized gain. It must also eliminate the deferred tax liability of $160,000 recognized during the first year and eliminate income taxes of the same amount included in Accumulated Other Comprehensive Income.

Example 28

Refer to Examples 4, 8, and 17. American Airlines (1) purchases landing rights for $150 million, (2) amortizes the landing rights $30 million during the first year for both financial and tax reporting, (3) recognizes an asset impairment loss for the decline in fair value to $55 million at the end of the first year, and (4) recognizes the immediate tax savings from the amortization and the delayed tax savings from the asset impairment loss. The income tax law does not permit the firm to claim a tax deduction for the asset impairment immediately. Instead, it must continue to amortize the landing rights over their original expected life of five years.

	C	+	N$A	=	L	+	CC	+	AOCI	+	RE
BS-BOP											
(1)	−150		+150								
(2)			− 30								−30
(3)			− 65								−65
IBT											−95
(4)	+ 12		+ 26								+38
NI											−57
BS-EOP	−138		+ 81								+57

The income tax effects deserve elaboration. The income tax law requires firms to specify at the outset an expected useful life for the landing rights and to amortize them over this period. American Airlines selects five years as the useful life and amortizes $30 million a year. The firm realizes an immediate tax savings of $12 million for the $30 million of amortization expense recognized for financial and tax reporting. GAAP requires the firm to recognize the $65 million asset impairment loss, but the tax law does not permit American Airlines to claim an immediate tax deduction. Instead, it implicitly includes this amount as part of its amortization deduction over the remaining four years of useful life. Thus, the $65 million asset impairment loss gives rise to a $26 million (= .4 × $65 million) deferred tax asset for the future tax benefits of writing off the landing rights for tax purposes.

Example 29

Refer to Example 5. Sun Trust Banks (1) purchases a computer by giving a note with a present value of $998,178 (= present value of $250,000 a year for five years at 8 percent), (2) recognizes depreciation of $199,636 (= $998,178/5) on the computer for the first year based on a five-year useful life, (3) recognizes interest expense for the first year of $79,854 (= .08 × $998,178), the cash payment of $250,000, and the reduction in principal of $170,146 (= $250,000 − $79,854), and (4) recognizes the tax savings of $111,796 (= .40 × $279,490) from depreciation and interest deductions.

	C	+	N$A	=	L	+	CC	+	AOCI	+	RE
BS-BOP											
(1)			+998,178		+998,178						
(2)			−199,636								−199,636
(3)	−250,000				−170,146						− 79,854
IBT											−279,490
(4)	+111,796										+111,796
NI											−167,694
BS-EOP	−138,204		+798,542		+828,032						−167,694

Summary of Analytical Framework

This analytical framework may seem a bit unfamiliar at this stage in your study. Repeated use in later chapters will not only increase your comfort but demonstrate its richness in understanding the financial statement effects of a variety of complex business transactions. You may find it useful to practice using the framework with several familiar transactions. Several problems at the end of the chapter require the use of this analytical framework.

SUMMARY

This chapter provides the conceptual foundation for understanding the balance sheet and the income statement. Assets and liabilities on the balance sheet may reflect either historical values or current values. The conventional accounting model uses historical, or acquisition, costs to value assets and liabilities, and delays the recognition of value changes until external market transactions validate their amounts. Use of acquisition costs generally results in more reliable financial statements than current values, but such statements might provide less relevant information to users desiring to value the firm.

Recognizing value changes for assets and liabilities still leaves open the question of when the value change should affect net income. Such value changes might affect net income immediately or affect it later, initially lodging in Accumulated Other Comprehensive Income until validated by an external market transaction. Over sufficiently long time periods, net income equals cash inflows minus cash outflows, other than cash transactions with owners. Different approaches to asset and liability valuation and to income measurement affect the pattern of net income over time but not its ultimate amount.

Virtually every transaction affecting net income has an income tax effect. The accounting issue is whether firms should recognize the income tax effect when the related revenue or expense affects net income for financial reporting, or when it affects taxable income. That is, should the income tax match against the book amounts or the tax amounts? GAAP requires firms to measure income tax expense each period based on the pretax income for financial reporting. When income tax expense differs from income taxes currently payable on taxable income, firms recognize deferred tax assets and deferred tax liabilities. Deferred tax assets arise when taxable income exceeds book income. Firms prepay taxes now but reduce taxes paid later when the temporary difference reverses and book income exceeds taxable income. Deferred tax liabilities arise when book income exceeds taxable income. Firms delay paying taxes now but will pay the taxes later when the temporary differences reverse and taxable income exceeds book income.

Later chapters discuss the accounting for various assets, liabilities, revenues, and expenses. The analytical framework discussed in this chapter provides a tool for analyzing business transactions and understanding their effects on the financial statements. The analytical framework uses the balance sheet equation and changes in balance sheet amounts between the beginning and end of a period as its structuring device. You may not yet feel comfortable using this analytical framework, but repeated use in later chapters will demonstrate its richness as a tool of analysis.

QUESTIONS, EXERCISES, PROBLEMS, AND CASES

Questions and Exercises

2.1 ASSET VALUATION AND INCOME MEASUREMENT. "Asset valuation and income measurement closely relate." Explain, including conditions when they do not.

2.2 RELIABILITY VERSUS RELEVANCE. "With respect to asset valuation, reliability and relevance are often on opposite ends of the continuum." Explain.

2.3 INCOME FLOWS VERSUS CASH FLOWS. The text states: "Over sufficiently long time periods, net income equals cash inflows minus cash outflows, other than cash flows with owners." Demonstrate the accuracy of this statement in the following scenario. Two friends contributed $50,000 each to form a new business. The business used the amounts contributed to purchase a machine for $100,000 cash. The business estimated that the useful life of the machine was five years and the salvage value was $20,000. The business rented out the machine to a customer for an annual rental of $25,000 a year for five years. Annual cash operating costs for insurance, taxes, and other items totaled $6,000 annually. At the end of the fifth year, the business sold the equipment for $22,000, instead of the $20,000 salvage value initially estimated. *(Hint: Compute the total net income and the total cash flows other than cash flows with owners for the five-year period as a whole.)*

2.4 MEASUREMENT OF ACQUISITION COST. United Van Lines purchased a truck with a list price of $250,000 and subject to a 6 percent discount if paid within 30 days. United Van Lines paid within the discount period. It paid $4,000 to obtain title to the truck with the state and $800 as the license fee for the first year of operation. It paid $1,500 to paint the firm's name on the truck and $2,500 for property and liability insurance for the first year of operation. What acquisition cost of this truck should United Van Lines record in its accounting records? Indicate the treatment of any amount not included in acquisition cost.

2.5 MEASUREMENT OF A MONETARY ASSET. Boeing sold a 787 aircraft to American Airlines on January 1, Year 4. The sales agreement required American Airlines to pay $10 million immediately and $10 million on December 31 of each year for 20 years, with the first delayed payment to be made on December 31, Year 4. Boeing and American Airlines judge that 8 percent is an appropriate interest rate for this arrangement.

a. Compute the present value of the receivable on Boeing's books on January 1, Year 4, immediately after receiving the $10 million down payment.
b. Compute the present value of the receivable on Boeing's books on December 31, Year 4.
c. Compute the present value of the receivable on Boeing's books on December 31, Year 5.

2.6 COMPUTATION OF INCOME TAX EXPENSE. A firm's income tax return shows taxes currently payable for Year 4 of $50,000. It reports deferred tax assets of $42,900 at the beginning of Year 4 and $38,700 at the end of Year 4. It reports deferred tax liabilities of $28,600 at the beginning of Year 4 and $34,200 at the end of Year 4.

a. Compute the amount of income tax expense for Year 4.
b. Assume for this part that the firm's deferred tax assets are as stated above for Year 4 but that its deferred tax liabilities were $58,600 at the beginning of Year 4 and $47,100 at the end of Year 4. Compute the amount of income tax expense for Year 4.

2.7 COMPUTATION OF INCOME TAX EXPENSE. A firm's income tax return shows taxes currently payable for Year 4 of $35,000. It reports deferred tax assets before any valuation allowance of $24,600 at the beginning of Year 4 and $27,200 at the end of Year 4. It reports deferred tax liabilities of $18,900 at the beginning of Year 4 and $16,300 at the end of Year 4.

a. Assume for this part that the valuation allowance on the deferred tax assets totaled $6,400 at the beginning of Year 4 and $7,200 at the end of Year 4. Compute the amount of income tax expense for Year 4.
b. Assume for this part that the valuation allowance on the deferred tax assets totaled $6,400 at the beginning of Year 4 and $4,800 at the end of Year 4. Compute the amount of income tax expense for Year 4.

Problems and Cases

2.8 EFFECT OF VALUATION METHOD FOR NONMONETARY ASSET ON BALANCE SHEET AND INCOME STATEMENT. Wal-Mart acquires a tract of land on January 1, Year 4, for $100,000 cash. On December 31, Year 4, the current market value of the land is $150,000. On December 31, Year 5, the current market value of the land is $120,000. The firm sells the land on December 31, Year 6, for $180,000 cash.

Required

Ignore income taxes. Using the analytical framework discussed in the chapter, indicate the effect of the preceding information for Year 4, Year 5, and Year 6 under each of the following valuation methods:

a. Valuation of the land at acquisition until sale of the land.
b. Valuation of the land at current market value but including unrealized gains and losses in Accumulated Other Comprehensive Income until sale of the land.
c. Valuation of the land at current market value and including market value changes each year in net income.
d. Why is retained earnings on December 31, Year 6, equal to $80,000 in all three cases despite the reporting of different amounts of net income each year?

2.9 EFFECT OF VALUATION METHOD FOR MONETARY ASSET ON BALANCE SHEET AND INCOME STATEMENT. Refer to Problem 2.8. Assume that Wal-Mart sells the land on December 31, Year 6, for a note receivable with a present value of $180,000 instead of for cash. The note bears interest at 8 percent and requires cash payments of $100,939 on December 31, Year 7 and Year 8. Interest rates for notes of this risk level increase to 10 percent on December 31, Year 7, resulting in a market value for the note on this date of $91,762.

Required

Ignore income taxes. Using the analytical framework discussed in the chapter, indicate the effect of the preceding information for Year 7 and Year 8 under each of the following valuation methods:

a. Valuation of the note at the present value of future cash flows using the historical market interest rate of 8 percent.
b. Valuation of the note at the present value of future cash flows using the current market interest rate of 8 percent for Year 7 and 10 percent for Year 8. Include unrealized holding gains and losses in net income.
c. Why is retained earnings on December 31, Year 8, equal to $101,878 in both cases despite the reporting of different amounts of net income each year?

2.10 EFFECT OF VALUATION METHOD FOR NONMONETARY ASSET ON BALANCE SHEET AND INCOME STATEMENT. General Motors (GM) acquired equipment used in its administrative activities for $100,000 on January 1, Year 4. The equipment had an expected useful life of four years and zero salvage value. GM calculates depreciation using the straight-line method over the remaining expected useful life in all cases. On December 31, Year 4, after recognizing depreciation for the year, GM learns that new equipment now offered on the market makes the equipment that GM purchased partially obsolete. The market value of the equipment on December 31, Year 4, reflecting this obsolescence, is $60,000. The expected useful life does not change. On December 31, Year 5, the market value of the equipment is $48,000. GM sells the equipment on January 1, Year 7, for $26,000.

Required

Ignore income taxes.

a. Assume for this part that GM accounts for the equipment using acquisition cost adjusted for depreciation and impairment losses. Using the analytical framework discussed in the chapter, indicate the effect of the following events on the balance sheet and income statement:

(1) Acquisition of the equipment for cash on January 1, Year 4.
(2) Depreciation for Year 4.
(3) Impairment loss for Year 4.
(4) Depreciation for Year 5.
(5) Depreciation for Year 6.
(6) Sale of the equipment on January 1, Year 7.

b. Assume for this part that GM accounts for the equipment using current market values adjusted for depreciation and impairment losses. Using the analytical framework discussed in the chapter, indicate the effect of the following events on the balance sheet and income statement.

(1) Acquisition of the equipment for cash on January 1, Year 4.
(2) Depreciation for Year 4.
(3) Impairment loss for Year 4.
(4) Depreciation for Year 5.
(5) Recognition of unrealized holding gain or loss for Year 5.
(6) Depreciation for Year 6.
(7) Recognition of unrealized holding gain or loss for Year 6.
(8) Sale of the equipment on January 1, Year 7.

c. After selling the equipment, why is retained earnings on January 1, Year 7, equal to a negative $74,000 in both cases, despite showing a different pattern of expenses, gains, and losses over time?

2.11 EFFECT OF VALUATION METHOD FOR MONETARY ASSET ON BALANCE SHEET AND INCOME STATEMENT. Mercedes Benz (MB) incurs costs of $30,000 in manufacturing an automobile during Year 4. Assume that it incurs all of these costs in cash. MB sells this automobile to you on January 1, Year 5, for $45,000. You pay $5,000 immediately and agree to pay $14,414 on December 31 of Year 5, Year 6, and Year 7. Based on the interest rate appropriate for this note of 4 percent on January 1, Year 5, the present value of the note is $40,000. The interest rate appropriate to this note is 5 percent on December 31, Year 5, resulting in a present value of the remaining cash flows of $26,802. The interest rate appropriate to this note is 8 percent on December 31, Year 6, resulting in a present value of the remaining cash flows of $13,346.

Required

Ignore income taxes.

a. Assume for this part that MB accounts for this note throughout the three years using the historical market interest rate of 4 percent. Using the analytical framework discussed in the chapter, indicate the effect of the following events on the balance sheet and income statement.

(1) Manufacture of the automobile during Year 4.
(2) Sale of the automobile on January 1, Year 5.
(3) Cash received and interest revenue recognized on December 31, Year 5.
(4) Cash received and interest revenue recognized on December 31, Year 6.
(5) Cash received and interest revenue recognized on December 31, Year 7.

b. Assume for this part that MB accounts for this note using the current market interest rate each year. Changes in market interest rates affect the valuation of the note on the balance sheet immediately and the computation of interest revenue for the next year.

(1) Manufacture of the automobile during Year 4.
(2) Sale of the automobile on January 1, Year 5.
(3) Cash received and interest revenue recognized on December 31, Year 5.
(4) Note receivable revalued and an unrealized holding gain or loss recognized on December 31, Year 5.
(5) Cash received and interest revenue recognized on December 31, Year 6.
(6) Note receivable revalued and an unrealized holding gain or loss recognized on December 31, Year 6.
(7) Cash received and interest revenue recognized on December 31, Year 7.

c. Why is retained earnings on December 31, Year 7, equal to $18,242 in both cases, despite showing a different pattern of income over time?

2.12 INTERPRETING INCOME TAX DISCLOSURES. The financial statements of Target Corporation, a retail chain, reveal the information regarding income taxes shown in Exhibit 2.6.

Required

a. Assuming that Target had no significant permanent differences between book income and taxable income, did income before taxes for financial reporting exceed or fall short of taxable income for Year 3? Explain.

b. Did income before taxes for financial reporting exceed or fall short of taxable income for Year 4? Explain.

c. Will the adjustment to net income for deferred taxes to compute cash flow from operations in the statement of cash flows result in an addition or subtraction for Year 3? For Year 4?

d. Target does not contract with an insurance agency for property and liability insurance, but instead self-insures. Target recognizes an expense and a liability each year for financial reporting to reflect its average expected long-term property and liability losses. When it experiences an actual loss, it charges it against the liability. The income tax law permits a deduction for such losses only in the year sustained when firms self-insure. Why are deferred taxes related to self-insurance disclosed as a deferred tax asset instead of a deferred tax liability? Suggest reasons for the direction of the change in amounts for this deferred tax asset between Year 2 and Year 4.

e. Target treats certain storage and other inventory costs as expenses in the year incurred for financial reporting but must include these in inventory for tax reporting. Why are deferred taxes related to inventory disclosed as a deferred tax asset? Suggest reasons for the direction of the change in amounts for this deferred tax asset between Year 2 and Year 4.

f. Firms must recognize expenses related to postretirement health care and pension obligations as employees provide services but claim an income tax deduction only when they make cash payments under the benefit plan. Why are deferred taxes related to health care obligation disclosed as a deferred tax asset? Why are deferred taxes related to pensions disclosed as a deferred tax liability? Suggest reasons for the direction of the change in amounts for these deferred tax items between Year 2 and Year 4.

g. Firms must recognize expenses related to uncollectible accounts when they recognize sales revenues but claim an income tax deduction when they deem a particular customer's accounts uncollectible. Why are deferred taxes related to this item disclosed

EXHIBIT 2.6

Income Tax Disclosures for Target Corporation (amounts in millions) (Problem 2.12)

For the Year Ended January 31:	Year 4	Year 3
Income before Income Taxes		
United States	$3,031	$2,603
Income Tax Expense		
Current:		
Federal	$ 908	$ 669
State and Local	144	107
Total Current	$1,052	$ 776
Deferred:		
Federal	$ 83	$ 184
State and Local	11	24
Total Deferred	$ 94	$ 208
Total	$1,146	$ 984

January 31:	Year 4	Year 3	Year 2
Components of Deferred Tax Assets and Liabilities			
Deferred Tax Assets:			
Self-Insured Benefits	$ 179	$ 143	$ 188
Deferred Compensation	332	297	184
Inventory	47	44	56
Postretirement Health Care Obligation	38	42	41
Uncollectible Accounts	147	133	113
Other	128	53	166
Total Deferred Tax Assets	$ 871	$ 712	$ 748
Deferred Tax Liabilities:			
Depreciation	(1,136)	(945)	(826)
Pensions	(268)	(218)	(190)
Other	(96)	(84)	(59)
Total Deferred Tax Liabilities	$(1,500)	$(1,247)	$(1,075)
Net Deferred Tax Liability	$ (629)	$ (535)	$ (327)

as a deferred tax asset? Suggest reasons for the direction of the change in amounts for this deferred tax asset between Year 2 and Year 4.

h. Target uses the straight-line depreciation method for financial reporting and accelerated depreciation methods for income tax purposes. Why are deferred taxes related to depreciation disclosed as a deferred tax liability? Suggest reasons for the direction of the change in amounts for this deferred tax liability between Year 2 and Year 4.

2.13 INTERPRETING INCOME TAX DISCLOSURES. The financial statements of Nike Corporation reveal the information regarding income taxes shown in Exhibit 2.7.

Required

a. Assuming that Nike had no significant permanent differences between book income and taxable income, did income before taxes for financial reporting exceed or fall short of taxable income for Year 3? Explain.

b. Did book income before taxes for financial reporting exceed or fall short of taxable income for Year 4? Explain.

EXHIBIT 2.7

Income Tax Disclosures for Nike Corporation (amounts in millions) (Problem 2.13)

For the Year Ended December 31:	Year 4	Year 3
Income before Income Taxes	$1,450	$1,123
Income Tax Expense		
Current:		
Federal	$ 185	$ 125
State and Local	43	34
Total Current	$ 495	$ 349
Deferred	9	34
Total	$ 504	$ 383

December 31:	Year 4	Year 3	Year 2
Components of Deferred Tax Assets and Liabilities			
Deferred Tax Assets:			
Sales Returns	$ 31	$ 27	$ 20
Allowance for Doubtful Accounts	14	12	10
Deferred Compensation	82	68	56
Inventory	28	18	16
Foreign Loss Carryforwards	54	36	24
Other	42	68	22
Gross Deferred Tax Assets	$ 251	$ 229	$148
Valuation Allowance	(27)	(13)	(8)
Net Deferred Tax Assets	$ 224	$ 216	$140
Deferred Tax Liabilities:			
Depreciation	(110)	(86)	(60)
Undistributed Earnings of Foreign Subsidiaries	(96)	(90)	(24)
Other	(15)	(28)	(10)
Total Deferred Tax Liabilities	$(221)	$(204)	$(94)
Net Deferred Tax Asset	$ 3	$ 12	$ 46

c. Will the adjustment to net income for deferred taxes to compute cash flow from operations in the statement of cash flows result in an addition or subtraction for Year 3? For Year 4?

d. Nike recognizes provisions for sales returns and doubtful accounts each year in computing income for financial reporting. Nike cannot claim an income tax deduction for these returns and doubtful accounts until customers return goods or accounts become uncollectible. Why do the deferred taxes for returns and doubtful accounts appear as deferred tax assets instead of deferred tax liabilities? Suggest possible reasons why the deferred tax asset for sales returns and doubtful accounts increased between the end of Year 2 and the end of Year 4.

e. Nike recognizes an expense related to deferred compensation as employees render services but cannot claim an income tax deduction until it pays cash to a retirement fund. Why do the deferred taxes for deferred compensation appear as a deferred tax asset? Suggest possible reasons why the deferred tax asset increased between the end of Year 2 and the end of Year 4.

f. Nike recognizes a valuation allowance on its deferred tax assets related to foreign loss carryforwards because the benefits of some of these losses will expire before the firm will realize the benefits. Why might the valuation allowance have increased between Year 2 and Year 4?

g. Nike uses the straight-line depreciation method for financial reporting and accelerated depreciation for income tax reporting. Why do the deferred taxes related to depreciation appear as deferred tax liabilities? Suggest possible reasons why the amount of the deferred tax liability related to fixed assets increased between Year 2 and Year 4.

h. Nike recognizes its share of the earnings from investments in foreign subsidiaries each year for financial reporting but recognizes income from these investments for income tax reporting only when it receives a dividend. Why do the deferred taxes related to these investments appear as a deferred tax liability?

i. Why does Nike recognize both deferred tax assets and deferred tax liabilities related to investments in foreign operations?

2.14 INTERPRETING INCOME TAX DISCLOSURES. The financial statements of Ford Motor Company reveal the information regarding income taxes shown in Exhibit 2.8.

Required

a. Assuming that Ford had no significant permanent differences between book income and taxable income, did income before taxes for financial reporting exceed or fall short of taxable income for Year 10? Explain.

b. Did net loss before taxes for financial reporting exceed or fall short of taxable loss for Year 11? Explain.

c. Will the adjustment to net income for deferred taxes to compute cash flow from operations in the statement of cash flows result in an addition or subtraction for Year 10? For Year 11?

d. Firms must recognize expenses related to employee benefit plans as employees provide services but claim an income tax deduction only when they make cash payments to the benefit plan. Why are deferred taxes related to employee benefit plans disclosed as a deferred tax asset instead of a deferred tax liability? Suggest reasons for the direction of the change in amounts for this deferred tax asset between Year 9 and Year 11.

EXHIBIT 2.8

Income Tax Disclosures for Ford Motor Company
(amounts in millions)
(Problem 2.14)

For the Year Ended December 31:	Year 11	Year 10
Income before Income Taxes		
United States	$(6,015)	$9,559
Non-United States	(1,085)	(1,241)
Total	$(7,100)	$8,318
Income Tax Expense		
Current:		
Federal	$ 22	$ 154
Non-United States	103	760
State and Local	—	116
Total Current	$ 125	$1,030
Deferred:		
Federal	$(2,126)	$2,617
Non-United States	(248)	(1,153)
State and Local	98	211
Total Deferred	$(2,276)	$1,675
Total	$(2,151)	$2,705

December 31:	Year 11	Year 10	Year 9
Components of Deferred Tax Assets and Liabilities			
Deferred Tax Assets:			
Employee Benefit Plans	$ 5,895	$ 5,138	$ 4,195
Dealer and Customer Allowances and Claims	1,919	2,365	2,709
Credit Losses	1,518	1,067	1,006
Other	8,297	4,026	2,068
Total Deferred Tax Assets	$ 17,629	$ 12,596	$ 9,978
Deferred Tax Liabilities:			
Depreciation	(11,784)	(11,753)	(9,902)
Finance Receivables	(2,388)	(2,593)	(1,328)
Other	(5,084)	(2,153)	(976)
Total Deferred Tax Liabilities	$(19,256)	$(16,499)	$(12,206)
Net Deferred Tax Asset (Liability)	$ (1,627)	$ (3,903)	$ (2,228)

e. Firms must recognize expenses related to dealer and customer allowances and claims when they recognize sales revenues but claim an income tax deduction when they make cash payments or provide warranty services. Why are deferred taxes related to this item disclosed as a deferred tax asset? Suggest reasons for the direction of the change in amounts for this deferred tax asset between Year 9 and Year 11.

f. Firms must recognize expenses for credit losses as they recognize sales revenues but claim an income tax deduction when they establish the uncollectibility of a particular customer's account. Why are deferred taxes related to credit losses disclosed as a deferred tax asset? Suggest reasons for the direction of the change in amounts for this deferred tax asset between Year 9 and Year 11.

g. Ford uses the straight-line depreciation method for financial reporting and accelerated depreciation methods for income tax purposes. Why are deferred taxes related to depreciation disclosed as a deferred tax liability? Suggest reasons for the direction of the change in amounts for this deferred tax liability between Year 9 and Year 11.

h. Ford leases automobiles and trucks to customers under multiyear leases. For financial reporting, Ford treats these leases as capital, or financing, leases, with income from the manufacturing activity recognized at the time of delivery of the vehicle to the customer and interest revenue on the finance receivable recognized over time. For tax reporting, Ford treats these arrangements as operating leases, with rent revenue recognized over time as customers make periodic lease payments. Why are deferred taxes related to finance receivables disclosed as a deferred tax liability? Suggest reasons for the direction of the change in amounts for this deferred tax liability between Year 9 and Year 11.

2.15 ANALYZING TRANSACTIONS. Using the analytical framework illustrated in the chapter, indicate the effect of the following related transactions of a firm:

a. January 1: Issued 10,000 shares of common stock for $50,000.

b. January 1: Acquired a building costing $35,000, paying $5,000 in cash and borrowing the remainder from a bank.

c. During the year: Acquired inventory costing $40,000 on account from various suppliers.

d. During the year: Sold inventory costing $30,000 for $65,000 on account.

e. During the year: Paid employees $15,000 as compensation for services rendered during the year.

f. During the year: Collected $45,000 from customers related to sales on account.

g. During the year: Paid merchandise suppliers $28,000 related to purchases on account.

h. December 31: Recognized depreciation on the building of $7,000 for financial reporting. Depreciation expense for income tax purposes was $10,000.

i. December 31: Recognized compensation for services rendered during the last week in December but not paid by year end of $4,000.

j. December 31: Recognized and paid interest on the bank loan in part b of $2,400 for the year.

k. Recognized income taxes on the net effect of the preceding transactions at an income tax rate of 40 percent. Assume that the firm pays cash immediately for any taxes currently due to the government.

2.16 ANALYZING TRANSACTIONS. Using the analytical framework illustrated in the chapter, indicate the effect of each of the three independent sets of transactions described next.

a. (1) January 15, Year 10: Purchased marketable equity securities for $100,000.
   (2) December 31, Year 10: Revalued the marketable securities to their market value of $90,000. Unrealized changes in the market value of marketable equity securities appear in Accumulated Other Comprehensive Income.

(3) December 31, Year 10: Recognized income tax effects of the revaluation in item (2) at an income tax rate of 40 percent. The income tax law includes changes in the market value of equity securities in taxable income only when the investor sells the securities.
(4) January 5, Year 11: Sold the marketable equity securities for $94,000.
(5) January 5, Year 11: Recognized the tax effect of the sale of the securities in item (4). Assume that the tax effect affects cash immediately.

b. (1) During Year 11: Sells inventory on account for $500,000.
(2) During Year 11: The cost of the goods sold in item (1) is $400,000.
(3) During Year 11: Estimated that uncollectible accounts on the goods sold in item (1) will equal 2 percent of the selling price.
(4) During Year 11: Estimated that warranty claims on the goods sold in item (1) will equal 4 percent of the selling price.
(5) During Year 11: Actual accounts written off as uncollectible totaled $3,000.
(6) During Year 11: Actual cash expenditures on warranty claims totaled $8,000.
(7) December 31, Year 11: Recognized income tax effects of the preceding six transactions. The income tax rate is 40 percent. The income tax law permits a deduction for uncollectible accounts when a firm writes off accounts as uncollectible and for warranty claims when a firm makes warranty expenditures. Assume that any tax effect on taxable income affects cash immediately.

c. (1) January 1, Year 11: Purchased $100,000 face value of zero-coupon bonds for $68,058. These bonds mature on December 31, Year 15, and are priced on the market at the time of issuance to yield 8 percent compounded annually. Zero-coupon bonds earn interest as time passes for financial and tax reporting but the issuer does not pay interest until maturity. Assume that any tax effect on taxable income affects cash immediately.
(2) December 31, Year 11: Recognized interest revenue on the bonds for Year 11.
(3) December 31, Year 11: Recognized income tax effect of the interest revenue for Year 11. The income tax law taxes interest on zero-coupon bonds as it accrues each year.
(4) December 31, Year 12: Recognized interest revenue on the bonds for Year 12.
(5) December 31, Year 12: Recognized income tax effect of the interest revenue for Year 12.
(6) January 2, Year 13: Sold the zero-coupon bonds for $83,683.
(7) January 2, Year 13: Recognized the income tax effect of the gain or loss on the sale. The applicable income tax rate is 40 percent and affects cash immediately.

INTEGRATIVE CASE 2.1

STARBUCKS

The financial statements of Starbucks Corporation reveal the information regarding income taxes shown in Exhibit 2.9.

Required

a. Assuming that Starbucks had no significant permanent differences between book income and taxable income, did income before taxes for financial reporting exceed or fall short of taxable income for Year 3? Explain.

b. Did book income before taxes for financial reporting exceed or fall short of taxable income for Year 4? Explain.

EXHIBIT 2.9

Income Tax Disclosures for Starbucks (amounts in millions) (Integrative Case 2.1)

For the Year Ended December 31:	Year 4	Year 3
Income before Income Taxes	$622.4	$433.9
Income Tax Expense		
Current:		
Federal	$188.6	$140.2
Foreign	10.2	8.5
State	36.4	25.4
Total Current	$235.2	$174.1
Deferred	(3.4)	(7.0)
Total	$231.8	$167.1

December 31:	Year 4	Year 3	Year 2
Components of Deferred Tax Assets and Liabilities			
Deferred Tax Assets:			
Equity Investments	$ 10.8	$ 17.6	$ 15.3
Deferred Compensation	31.1	20.5	12.7
Accrued Occupancy Costs	27.0	22.3	14.6
Other	52.0	48.2	39.8
Gross Deferred Tax Assets	$120.9	$108.6	$ 82.4
Valuation Allowance	(8.3)	(13.7)	(6.7)
Net Deferred Tax Assets	$112.6	$ 94.9	$ 75.7
Deferred Tax Liabilities:			
Depreciation	(58.5)	(49.4)	(40.8)
Other	(12.2)	(7.0)	(3.4)
Total Deferred Tax Liabilities	$(70.7)	$(56.4)	$(44.2)
Net Deferred Tax Asset	$ 41.9	$ 38.5	$ 31.5

c. Will the adjustment to net income for deferred taxes to compute cash flow from operations in the statement of cash flows result in an addition or subtraction for Year 3? For Year 4?

d. Starbucks holds investments in the equity securities of several Internet companies for which it recognized impairment losses for financial reporting. Starbucks cannot claim an income tax deduction for these losses until it realizes the loss at the time of sale. Why do the deferred taxes for losses on these investments appear as deferred tax assets instead of deferred tax liabilities?

e. Starbucks recognizes an expense related to retirement benefits as employees rendered services but cannot claim an income tax deduction until it pays cash to a retirement fund. Why do the deferred taxes for deferred compensation appear as a deferred tax asset? Suggest possible reasons why the deferred tax asset increased between the end of Year 2 and the end of Year 4.

f. Starbucks rents retail space for its coffeehouses. It must recognize rent expense as it uses rental facilities but cannot claim an income tax deduction until it pays cash to the landlord. Suggest the scenario that would give rise to a deferred tax asset instead of a deferred tax liability related to occupancy cost.

g. Starbucks recognizes a valuation allowance on its deferred tax assets related to losses on investments because the benefits of some of these losses will expire before the firm will realize the benefits. Why might the valuation allowance have increased between Year 2 and Year 3 and decreased between Year 3 and Year 4?

h. Starbucks uses the straight-line depreciation method for financial reporting and accelerated depreciation for income tax reporting. Why do the deferred taxes related to depreciation appear as deferred tax liabilities? Suggest possible reasons why the amount of the deferred tax liability related to depreciation increased between Year 2 and Year 4.

Chapter **3**

Income Flows versus Cash Flows: Key Relationships in the Dynamics of a Business

Learning Objectives

1. **Understand the relation between net income and cash flow from operations for firms in various industries.**
2. **Understand the relation between cash flows from operating, investing, and financing activities for firms in various stages of their life cycles.**
3. **Prepare a statement of cash flows from balance sheet and income statement data.**

The income statement reports the financial performance of a firm during a period by summarizing the revenues, expenses, gains, and losses of the firm following the principles of the accrual basis of accounting. A primary objective in preparing an income statement is to obtain a measure of operating performance that matches economic resources used, or consumed, as expenses with the associated economic resources earned as revenues. When the accountant cannot directly match economic resources earned and consumed, accrual accounting matches the economic resources consumed with the period when they are consumed. The accrual basis of accounting ignores the timing of cash receipts when recognizing revenues and gains and the timing of cash expenditures when recognizing expenses and losses. The desire to match revenues and expenses either to each other or to the appropriate period in measuring operating performance overrides the desirability of reporting information on an important ingredient for remaining in business: cash flows. This creates the need for firms to provide another financial statement that reports the flows of cash in and out of a firm: the statement of cash flows.

Chapter 1 points out that a firm's cash flows will differ from net income each period because (1) cash receipts from customers do not necessarily occur in the same period in which a firm recognizes revenues, (2) cash expenditures to employees, suppliers, and governments do not necessarily occur in the same period in which a firm recognizes expenses, and (3) cash inflows and outflows occur relating to investing and financing activities that do not immediately flow through the income statement. Thus, to augment information on operating performance in accrual-based income statements, firms prepare a statement of cash flows that reports the relation between net income and cash flow from operations. It also reports the cash flow effects of investing and financing activities.

An understanding of cash flows is helpful in each of the six steps in financial statement analysis discussed in Chapter 1:

- **Identifying the Economic Characteristics of a Business:** The pattern of cash flows from operating, investing, and financing activities differs for various types of businesses and for firms in various stages of their life cycle. High-growth, capital-intensive firms likely experience insufficient cash flow from operations to finance capital expenditures and require external financing to maintain their growth. Mature consumer products companies usually generate more than sufficient cash flow from operations to finance their modest needs for capital expenditures and can use the excess cash flow to repay debt, pay dividends, or repurchase common stock.
- **Identify the Strategy of the Firm:** The analyst should expect a rapidly growing capital-intensive firm to invest heavily in fixed assets. A firm pursuing a strategy of growth by acquiring other firms should report significant cash outflows for corporate acquisitions. A firm divesting itself of noncore businesses should report cash inflows from disposing of these businesses.
- **Adjust the Financial Statements for Nonrecurring, Unusual Items:** An analyst who chooses to eliminate nonrecurring or unusual items from net income to assess ongoing operating performance should also adjust cash flow from operations for those items that affect cash flows.
- **Analyze Profitability and Risk:** Chapter 2 makes clear that, over sufficiently long periods, net income equals the net cash flow from operating, investing, and non-owner financing activities. Thus, a reality check on net income is that it should converge on this net cash flow amount. Also, the ability of a firm to generate sufficient cash flow from operations to finance capital expenditures and repay borrowing is a key signal of the financial health of the firm.
- **Prepare Forecasted Financial Statements:** A statement of cash flows is one of the financial statements that the analysis should prepare when preparing forecasts of future cash flows and earnings for use in valuation. Forecasts of cash flows can provide analysts with key insights into whether operations will generate sufficient cash flow for future investing and financing activities, or whether the firm will face capital constraints and need to borrow with new debt or issue common stock.
- **Value the Firm:** Chapter 12 discusses the use of free cash flow in the valuation of a firm. Free cash flow to all debt and common-equity stakeholders approximately equals cash flow from operations in excess of cash flow from investing. Discounting these cash flows at the appropriate discount rate yields the value of total debt plus equity. Free cash flow to common-equity shareholders equals cash flows from operations in excess of cash flow from investing and cash flow from non-owner (debt) financing. Discounting these cash flows at the appropriate discount rate yields the value of equity.[1]

This chapter explores the statement of cash flows in greater depth than the overview presented in Chapter 1. We look at the relation between net income and cash flow from operations for various types of businesses and at the relation between the cash flows from operating, investing, and financing activities for firms in various stages of their life cycles. We also describe and illustrate procedures for preparing the statement of cash flows using information from the balance sheet and income statement.[2]

---

[1]Chapter 12 defines free cash flows and describes its calculation more precisely.

[2]*Statement No. 95* defines cash flows in terms of their effect on cash and cash equivalents. Cash equivalents include highly liquid investments that are both readily convertible into cash and so near to maturity that changes in interest rates present an insignificant risk to their market value. Cash equivalents usually include Treasury bills, commercial paper, and money market funds. Throughout this book, we use the term *cash* to mean cash and cash equivalents as defined in Financial Accounting Standards Board, *Statement of Financial Accounting Standards No. 95,* "Statement of Cash Flows" (1987).

NET INCOME, CASH FLOWS, AND LIFE CYCLE RELATIONS

Interpreting the statement of cash flows requires an understanding of two relations:

1. The relation between net income and cash flow from operations.
2. The relation among the net cash flows from operating, investing, and financing activities.

Net Income and Cash Flow from Operations

The first section of the statement of cash flows reports the amount of cash flow from operations: the cash received from selling goods and services to customers net of the cash paid to suppliers, employees, governments, and other providers of goods and services. Firms present cash flow from operations in one of two formats: the direct method or the indirect method. Under the *direct method,* firms list the cash inflows from selling goods and services and then subtract the cash outflows to providers of goods and services. The top panel of Exhibit 3.1 shows the direct method of calculating cash flow from operations for Northrop Grumman, a developer and manufacturer of technology-based military defense products and systems.

Under the *indirect method,* firms begin with net income to calculate cash flow from operations. The provisional assumption is that cash increased by the amount of revenues and decreased by the amount of expenses. However, not all revenues result in simultaneous and identical cash receipts and not all expenses result in simultaneous and identical cash expenditures. Firms must then adjust net income to convert revenues and expenses into cash receipts and disbursements to obtain cash flow from operations. The lower panel of Exhibit 3.1 illustrates the indirect method of presentation.

Most firms use the indirect method because it reconciles net income for a period with the net amount of cash received or paid for operations. GAAP in fact requires firms that report cash flow from operations using the direct method to provide a reconciliation between net income and cash flow from operations in a separate schedule or notes to the financial statements.[3] Critics of the indirect method suggest that the rationale for some of the reconciling items is difficult for less sophisticated users to understand, although more seasoned analysts should encounter less difficulty. We use the indirect method throughout this text because of its widespread use by business firms and familiarity to analysts.

The calculation of cash flow from operations under the indirect method involves two types of adjustments:

Type 1—adjustments to net income for revenues, expenses, gains, and losses that are recognized in income and are associated with changes in noncurrent assets, noncurrent liabilities, and shareholders' equity accounts but that do not affect cash by the same amounts that period (for example, adding back depreciation expense to net income).

Type 2—adjustments to net income for revenues, expenses, gains, and losses that are recognized in income and are associated with changes in operating working capital accounts (for example, accounts receivable, inventories, and accounts payable) but that do not affect cash by the same amount that period (for example, the difference between revenues recognized and cash collected from customers).[4]

---

[3] *Ibid.*, par. 29–30.

[4] Working capital means current assets minus current liabilities. Operating working capital accounts generally include all current assets except marketable securities and all current liabilities except short-term loans and the current portion of long-term debt. A later section of this chapter explains the rationale for excluding these items from operating working capital.

EXHIBIT 3.1

Cash Flow from Operations Presented in Direct and Indirect Methods for Northrop Grumman (amounts in millions)

	Year Ended December 31:		
	Year 4	Year 3	Year 2
Direct Method			
Cash Received from Customers	$29,693	$26,507	$17,617
Other Cash Receipts	163	259	397
Cash Paid to Suppliers and Employees	(26,751)	(24,011)	(15,860)
Interest Paid	(443)	(593)	(334)
Income Taxes Paid	(449)	(1,152)	(149)
Other Cash Payments	(267)	(241)	(17)
Cash Flow from Continuing Operations	$ 1,946	$ 769	$ 1,654
Cash Flow from Discontinued Operations	(10)	29	35
Net Cash Flow from Operations	$ 1,936	$ 798	$ 1,689
Indirect Method			
Income from Continuing Operations	$ 1,093	$ 758	$ 455
Depreciation and Amortization	734	682	517
Other Additions and Subtractions	162	110	93
Adjustments for Changes in Working Capital:			
(Increase) Decrease in Accounts and Notes Receivable	(5,674)	(5,385)	(771)
(Increase) Decrease in Inventories	3	(53)	(211)
(Increase) Decrease in Prepayments	3	5	38
Increase (Decrease) in Progress Payments	5,400	5,264	1,109
Increase (Decrease) in Accounts Payable	322	(276)	78
Increase (Decrease) in Other Current Liabilities	(97)	(336)	346
Cash Flow from Continuing Operations	$ 1,946	$ 769	$ 1,654
Cash Flow from Discontinued Operations	(10)	29	35
Net Cash Flow from Operations	$ 1,936	$ 798	$ 1,689

Refer to the statement of cash flows for PepsiCo in Exhibit 3.2. PepsiCo reports cash flow from operations using the indirect method. The cash flow statement begins with net income. PepsiCo then lists a set of "Adjustments to reconcile net income to net cash provided by operating activities." The first set of items listed, beginning with "Depreciation and amortization" and ending with "Other noncash charges and credits, net" represents Type 1 adjustments. PepsiCo then lists "Changes in operating working capital, excluding effects of acquisitions and dispositions." This second set of adjustments represents Type 2 adjustments. We discuss each of these adjustments next.

EXHIBIT 3.2

PepsiCo, Inc. and Subsidiaries
Consolidated Statements of Cash Flows
Fiscal Years Ended December 25, Year 4; December 27, Year 3; and December 28, Year 2
(in millions)

	Year 4	Year 3	Year 2
Operating Activities			
Net income	$ 4,212	$ 3,568	$ 3,000
Adjustments to reconcile net income to net cash provided by operating activities:			
Depreciation and amortization	1,264	1,221	1,112
Stock-based compensation expense	368	407	435
Merger-related costs	—	59	224
Impairment and restructuring charges	150	147	—
Cash payments for merger-related costs and restructuring charges	(92)	(109)	(123)
Tax benefit from discontinued operations	(38)	—	—
Pension plan contributions	(458)	(535)	(820)
Bottling equity income, net of dividends	(297)	(276)	(222)
Deferred income taxes	17	(323)	174
Other noncash charges and credits, net	341	415	263
Changes in operating working capital, excluding effects of acquisitions and dispositions:			
Accounts and notes receivable	(130)	(220)	(260)
Inventories	(100)	(49)	(53)
Prepaid expenses and other current assets	(31)	23	(78)
Accounts payable and other current liabilities	216	(11)	426
Income taxes payable	(268)	182	270
Net change in operating working capital	$ (313)	$ (75)	$ 305
Other	(100)	(171)	279
Net Cash Provided by Operating Activities	$ 5,054	$ 4,328	$ 4,627
Investing Activities			
Capital spending	$(1,387)	$(1,345)	$(1,437)
Sales of property, plant, and equipment	38	49	89
Acquisitions and investments in noncontrolled affiliates	(64)	(71)	(351)
Divestitures	52	46	376
Short-term investments, by original maturity			
More than three months—purchases	(44)	(38)	(62)
More than three months—maturities	38	28	122
Three months or less, net	(963)	(940)	697
Snack Ventures Europe consolidation	—	—	39
Net Cash Used for Investing Activities	$(2,330)	$(2,271)	$ (527)

Continued

EXHIBIT 3.2

continued

	Year 4	Year 3	Year 2
Financing Activities			
Proceeds from issuances of long-term debt	$ 504	$ 52	$ 11
Payments of long-term debt	(512)	(641)	(353)
Short-term borrowings, by original maturity			
More than three months—proceeds	153	88	707
More than three months—payments	(160)	(115)	(809)
Three months or less, net	1,119	40	40
Cash dividends paid	(1,329)	(1,070)	(1,041)
Share repurchases—common	(3,028)	(1,929)	(2,158)
Share repurchases—preferred	(27)	(16)	(32)
Proceeds from exercises of stock options	965	689	456
Net Cash Used for Financing Activities	$(2,315)	$(2,902)	$(3,179)
Effect of exchange rate changes on cash and cash equivalents	$ 51	$ 27	$ 34
Net (Decrease) Increase in Cash and Cash Equivalents	$ 460	$ (818)	$ 955
Cash and Cash Equivalents, Beginning of Year	820	1,638	683
Cash and Cash Equivalents, End of Year	$ 1,280	$ 820	$ 1,638

Type 1 Adjustments for Changes in Noncurrent Assets, Noncurrent Liabilities, and Shareholders' Equity Accounts

Certain revenues and expenses accompany changes in a noncurrent asset, a noncurrent liability, or a shareholders' equity account and affect cash flow differently from net income. Firms must add amounts to, or subtract amounts from, net income to convert net income to cash flow from operations for these items.

Depreciation expense, for example, reduces net property, plant, and equipment and net income. However, depreciation expense does not require an *operating* cash outflow in the period of the expense (on the contrary, firms classify the cash outflow to acquire depreciable assets as an *investing* activity in the year of acquisition; PepsiCo lists such acquisitions as "Capital spending" in the investing section of its statement of cash flows in Exhibit 3.2). The addback of depreciation expense to net income when computing cash flow from operations offsets the effect of the subtraction of depreciation expense when computing net income (that is, the addback nets its effect on cash flow from operations to zero). Note that PepsiCo includes depreciation on buildings and equipment and amortization of intangibles on a single line as an addback to net income in computing cash flow from operations.

Chapter 2 points out that firms recognize on the income statement income tax expense that contains a component for deferred income taxes, and they recognize deferred tax assets and/or deferred tax liabilities on the balance sheet when they use different methods of accounting for financial reporting and income tax reporting. The total amount of income tax expense, both current and deferred, will differ from the amount of income taxes currently payable. Firms add back an excess of income tax expense over income taxes currently payable and subtract an excess of income taxes currently payable over income tax expense when converting net income to cash flow from operations. PepsiCo shows an addback for deferred income taxes of $17 million in Year 4, suggesting that income tax expense exceeds income taxes currently payable for the year. In contrast, PepsiCo shows a subtraction for deferred taxes of $323 million in Year 3, indicating that taxes payable in Year 3 exceeded income tax expense. Note that the adjustments described here for deferred taxes adjust income tax expense to the amount of tax currently payable. In the next section, we describe adjustments to convert taxes currently payable to the actual amount of cash paid for taxes.

Chapter 9 discusses GAAP's required recognition of an expense for the benefit to employees of stock options, which permit employees to purchase shares of the firm's common stock for less than their market value. This expense reduces net income and increases a shareholders' equity account. Because the expense does not use cash, firms add back stock option expense to net income when computing cash flow from operations (in fact, the receipt of cash when employees exercise stock options is a *financing* activity; PepsiCo lists such stock issuances as "Proceeds from exercises of stock options" in the financing section of its statement of cash flows in Exhibit 3.2). PepsiCo lists the addback as "Stock-based compensation expense" in the operating section of its statement of cash flows.

Firms that sell an item of property, plant, or equipment report the full cash proceeds as an investing activity (see the line "Sales of property, plant, and equipment" for PepsiCo in Exhibit 3.2). Because net income includes any gain or loss on the sale (that is, sale proceeds minus the book value of the item sold), the operating section of the statement of cash flows shows an addback for a loss and a subtraction for a gain to offset their inclusion in net income. The amount of any gain or loss for PepsiCo must be sufficiently small that it includes it on the line "Other noncash charges and credits, net."

Chapter 9 points out that a firm holding an investment of 20 to 50 percent in another entity generally uses the equity method to account for the investment (a noncurrent asset). The investor recognizes its share of the investee's earnings each period, increasing the investment account and net income. It reduces the investment account for dividends received. Thus, net income reflects the investor's share of earnings, not the cash received. The statement of cash flows usually shows a subtraction from net income for the excess of the investor's share of the investee's earnings over dividends received. PepsiCo reports "Bottling equity income, net of dividends" as a subtraction when converting net income to cash flow from operations.

Other examples of revenues and expenses that relate to changes in noncurrent asset, noncurrent liability, and shareholders' equity accounts include minority interest in the earnings of consolidated subsidiaries, some asset impairment and restructuring charges, and differences between pension expense and pension funding. Later chapters discuss more fully each of the items described in this section.

Type 2 Adjustments for Changes in Operating Working Capital Accounts

The second type of adjustment to reconcile net income to cash flow from operations involves changes in operating current asset and current liability accounts. Firms must adjust the amounts for revenues and expenses included in net income to the corresponding amounts of cash receipts and disbursements for these items as well as those discussed in the preceding section. For example, an increase in accounts receivable for a period indicates that a firm did not collect as much cash as the amount of revenues included in net income. PepsiCo's statement of cash flows in Exhibit 3.2, for example, shows a subtraction each year for the change in accounts and notes receivable. The subtraction converts the amount of revenues included in net income to the amount of cash received from customers.

PepsiCo also reports a subtraction for the change in inventories, indicating that it used more cash to purchase inventories than the amount of cost of sales included as an expense in computing net income.

An increase in current operating liabilities means that a firm did not use as much cash for operating expenses as the amounts appearing on the income statement. An addition to net income for the increase in current operating liabilities converts operating expenses on an accrual basis to cash paid to suppliers of various goods and services. PepsiCo, for example, shows an addition for "Accounts payable and other current liabilities" for Year 4, indicating that it has not yet paid for some of the expenses on the income statement for the year.

PepsiCo also reports an adjustment for the change in income taxes payable. Recall from the earlier discussion that the addition to or subtraction from net income for the change in deferred income taxes converts income tax expense to income taxes currently payable. The adjustment for the changes in income taxes payable converts income taxes currently payable as indicated on the income tax return for the year to the income taxes actually paid. Firms typically do not pay all taxes due for a particular year during that year. Some taxes that a firm pays within a year relate to taxes due for the preceding year; some taxes due for the current year the firm pays in the following year.

We note two other items with respect to the adjustments for changes in working capital. First, the adjustments in this section are only to *operating* working capital accounts. Some current assets and current liabilities relate to investing or financing activities and not operating activities. Changes in marketable securities, for example, are investing activities. Note that PepsiCo reports cash flows from changes in "Short-term investments, by original maturity" in the investing section of its statement of cash flows. Also, changes in short-term borrowing are financing activities. PepsiCo reports cash flows related to "Short-term borrowings, by original maturity" in the financing section.

Second, the amounts of the adjustments for changes in operating working capital accounts in the statement of cash flows often do not always equal the amounts on the comparative balance sheets at the beginning and end of the year. For example, PepsiCo's subtraction of $130 million for the change in accounts and notes receivable for Year 4 indicates that this account increased during the year. The comparative balance sheet for PepsiCo in Appendix A indicates that accounts and notes receivable increased from $2,830 million at the end of Year 3 to $2,999 million at the end of Year 4, an increase of $169 million. Thus, $130 million of the $169 million increase in accounts and notes receivable relates to operating activities. The remaining $39 million of the increase results from the net change in this account from acquisitions and divestitures during the year.[5] PepsiCo reports the amounts of cash used for acquisitions and the cash received from divestitures in the investing section of its statement of cash flows in Exhibit 3.2. The $64 million shown for acquisitions and investments for Year 4 is the cash used to acquire the

[5]In PepsiCo's case, the $39 million also includes the effects of fluctuations in foreign currencies in which PepsiCo conducts business worldwide.

assets and liabilities of other businesses. One of the assets likely acquired is accounts and notes receivable. GAAP requires firms to report the amount of cash used to acquire other businesses, which implicitly includes the net amount of individual assets and liabilities acquired with that cash, in the investing section. PepsiCo alerts the reader to the reason that changes in working capital in the operating section of the statement of cash flows do not equal changes in the corresponding accounts on the comparative balance sheet by using the terms "Changes in operating working capital, *excluding effects of acquisitions and dispositions.*" Very few firms include this qualifying phrase, although it applies to almost all firms each year.

Relation between Net Income and Cash Flow from Operations

What is the relation between net income and cash flow from operations? Should one generally exceed the other or should they be approximately the same over a long time period, and, if so, how long? The answers to these questions relate in part to the economic characteristics of the industry, the firm, and its rate of growth.

The adjustments to net income for changes in noncurrent assets, noncurrent liabilities, and shareholders' equity accounts (Type 1 adjustments) generally result in net additions to net income instead of net subtractions. Additions for noncash expenses such depreciation, amortization, stock options, and asset impairment and restructuring charges usually exceed subtractions for equity income in excess of dividends received. Thus, one would provisionally expect cash flow from operations to exceed net income. However, the relation between net income and cash flow from operations also depends on changes in operating working capital accounts (Type 2 adjustments).

Firms that are mature and not growing rapidly will report relatively small amounts for changes in operating current asset and current liability accounts. Firms that grow rapidly will report more substantial adjustments for changes in accounts receivable, inventories, and current operating liabilities. If a firm uses current operating liabilities to finance the increases in accounts receivable and inventories, then the adjustments for changes in operating working capital accounts will net to a relatively small amount. Most growing firms, however, expand their accounts receivable and inventories more rapidly than their current operating liabilities and find that the net effect of changes in operating working capital is a subtraction from net income when computing cash flow from operations.

Another factor that may cause cash flow from operations to differ from net income is the length of the operating cycle (see Exhibit 1.9 for a graphic depiction). The operating cycle encompasses the period of time from when a firm commences the manufacture of its products until it receives cash from customers from the sale of the products. Firms such as construction companies and aerospace manufacturers with relatively long operating cycles often experience a lag between when they expend cash for design, development, raw materials, and labor costs and when they receive cash from customers. Unless such firms receive cash advances from their customers prior to completion and delivery of the products or delay payments to their suppliers, the net effect of changes in operating working capital accounts is a subtraction from net income when computing cash flow from operations. (Note in Exhibit 3.1 that cash flow from operations exceeds net income each year for Northrop Grumman primarily because of increases in "progress payments," which represent advances from customers on contracts in process.) The longer the operating cycle and the more rapid the growth of a firm, the larger the difference between net income and cash flow from operations. Firms with short operating cycles, such as restaurants and service firms, experience less of a lag between the creation and delivery of their

EXHIBIT 3.3

Relation between Net Income, Net Income Plus or Minus Type 1 Adjustments, Cash Flow from Operations, and EBITDA for PepsiCo
(amounts in millions)

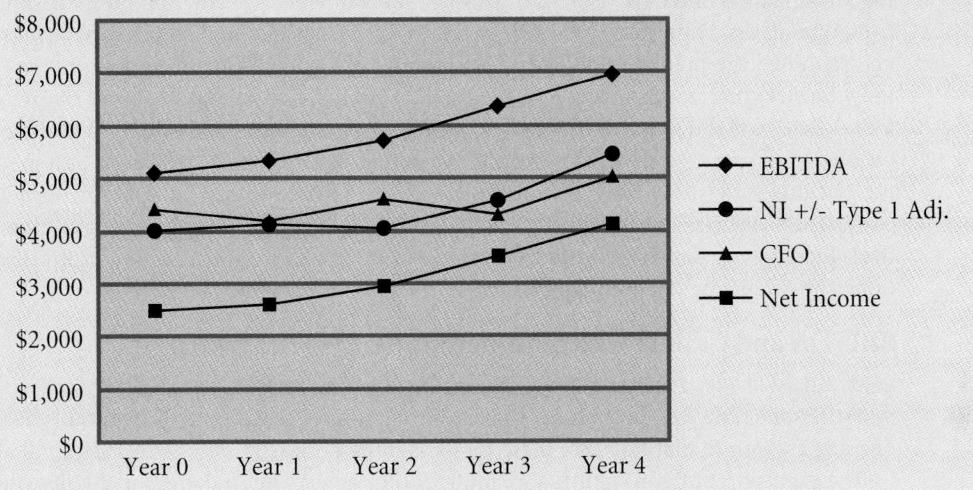

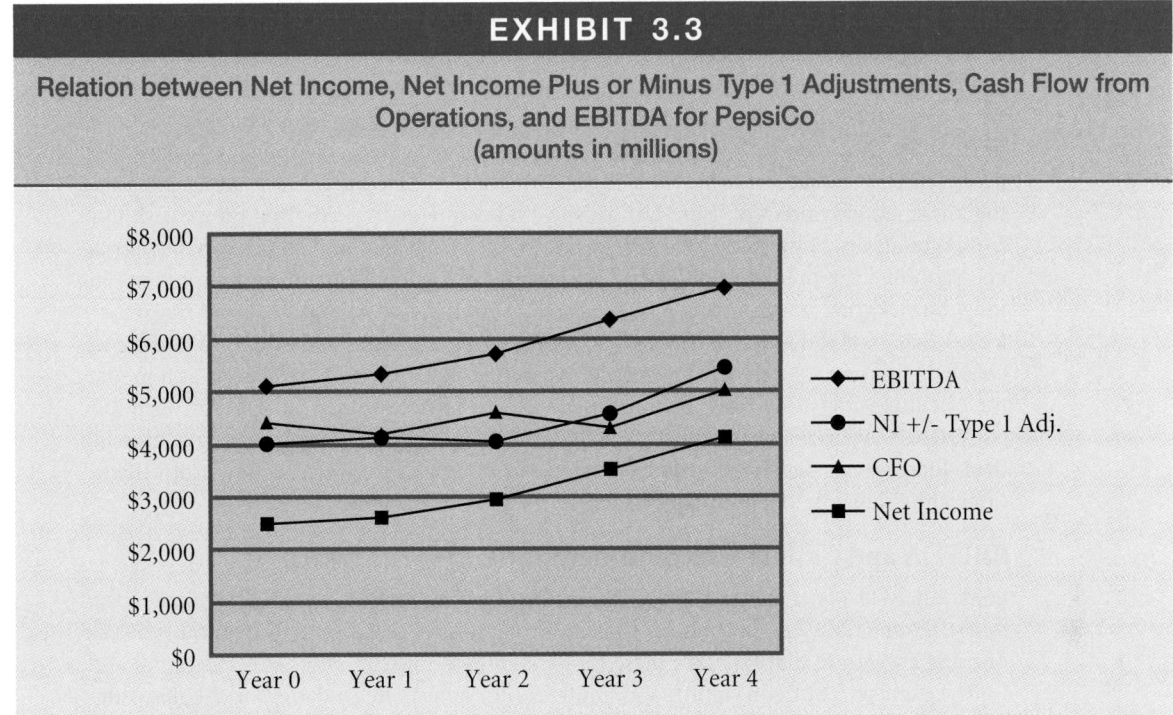

products and the collection of cash from customers. Thus, changes in operating working capital accounts will not cause net income to differ substantially from cash flow from operations.

Exhibit 3.3 shows graphically the relation between net income and cash flow from operations for PepsiCo for Year 0 to Year 4. Cash flow from operations exceeds net income each year, but cash flow from operations shows more variability. To determine whether the variation in cash flow from operations is due to adjustments in noncurrent assets, noncurrent liabilities, and shareholders' accounts (Type 1 adjustments) or to adjustments for operating working capital accounts (Type 2 adjustments), Exhibit 3.3 also graphs net income plus or minus Type 1 adjustments. Note that net income and net income plus or minus Type 1 adjustments portray the same pattern of change over time, suggesting that the variation in cash flow from operations is due primarily to changes in operating working capital accounts. Note also that net income plus or minus Type 1 adjustments and cash flow from operations tend to fluctuate around each other over time, suggesting that net changes in operating working capital accounts net to zero over time. This pattern is not surprising for a relatively mature firm like PepsiCo. We discuss shortly the metric of earnings before interest, taxes, depreciation, and amortization (EBITDA).

A study of the relation between net income, net income plus or minus Type 1 adjustments, and cash flow from operations revealed (1) a high correlation between net income and net income plus or minus Type 1 adjustments, (2) a low correlation between net income and cash flow from operations, and (3) a low correlation between cash flow from operations and net income plus or minus Type 1 adjustments over time.[6] The empirical results suggest that the patterns portrayed in Exhibit 3.3 for PepsiCo are typical.

Other studies have looked at the information content of net income versus cash flow from operations in predicting future cash flow from operations. As Chapter 12 discusses more fully, future cash flow from operations is an important component of free cash flows, which plays an important role in the valuation of firms. One such study examined the information content of Type 1 and Type 2 adjustments in predicting future cash flow from operations.[7] The study, which referred to Type 1 and Type 2 adjustments as *accruals,* examined the predictive ability of net income versus cash flow from operations plus individual accrual items in predicting future cash flow from operations. The researchers found that individual accrual items had information content. Individual accrual items, coupled with past cash flow from operations, outperformed net income alone as a predictor of future cash flow from operations. Increases in accounts receivable, for example, correlated with increase in future cash flow from operations, thus signaling a growing firm. Increases in depreciation likewise signaled increased future cash flow from operations, thus signaling the building of capacity to support growth.

EBITDA and Cash Flow from Operations

Some analysts use a metric known as *earnings before interest, taxes, depreciation, and amortization* (EBITDA) in their analysis and valuation of firms. The theoretical rationale of using a measure that excludes these four expenses is unclear.

The exclusion of depreciation and amortization adjusts net income for the items that for most firms are the largest Type 1 adjustments in computing cash flow from operations. If a firm is not growing rapidly, then adjustments for changes in operating working capital accounts should be relatively small (as is the case for PepsiCo). EBITDA in this case roughly approximates cash flow from operations. However, if a firm is growing rapidly, EBITDA ignores the additional investments in working capital required to sustain that growth. The exclusion of depreciation expense, without a similar exclusion for rent expense, can create inconsistent treatment of expenses for assets that a firm owns and depreciates versus expenses for "assets" that a firm leases, and it can lead to false comparisons between firms that own and those that lease depreciable assets.

The exclusion of interest expense provides a measure of earnings independent of financing costs. The exclusion of interest in computing EBITDA has an element of logic if the analyst is interested in EBITDA as a crude measure of the firm's ability to pay down debt, or if the analyst uses EBITDA for valuation using a discount rate or earnings multiple that incorporates the cost of both debt and equity capital.

The rationale for the exclusion of income taxes is not clear. Firms that generate positive earnings must pay income taxes just as they must pay suppliers, employees, and other providers of goods and services. Unprofitable firms do not incur income taxes, but in such situations net income becomes a less useful metric anyway.

A reading of analyst reports and the financial literature suggests that analysts view EBITDA as an approximation of a cash-based measure of pretax operating earnings. Its ease of calculation adds to its popularity. The analyst can generally compute its amount quickly and easily by using information on the income statement. Exhibit 3.3 indicates

---

[6]Robert M. Bowen, David Burgstahler, and Lane A. Daley, "Evidence on the Relationships between Earnings and Various Measures of Cash Flow," *Accounting Review* (October 1986), pp. 713–725. The authors used the label "working capital from operations" for what we have called "net income plus or minus Type 1 changes."

[7]Mary E. Barth, Donald P. Cram, and Karen K. Nelson, "Accruals and the Prediction of Future Cash Flows," *Accounting Review* (January 2001), pp. 27–58.

for PepsiCo that EBITDA correlates highly with net income and with net income plus or minus Type 1 adjustments, but not with cash flow from operations.

A recent study examined the correlation between market rates of return on common stock and (1) earnings, (2) cash flow from operations, and (3) EBITDA.[8] The study found that stock returns are more highly correlated with earnings than with either cash flow from operations or EBITDA. This finding is not surprising given that earnings are bottom-line measures of profitability. The finding that cash flow from operations has less information content for equity valuation than earnings results from the omission of accruals, which we noted have information content for future cash flows, and from the omission of cash flows related to investing and financing activities. Cash flow from operations is an incomplete measure of cash flows for valuation purposes. EBITDA excludes expenses that are value-relevant for profitable, capital-intensive, leveraged firms.

Given that both net income and cash flow from operations are required disclosures, one wonders why analysts use EBITDA as an approximation of either of these measures. Most fundamentally, EBITDA not only ignores these four expenses discussed previously, but also ignores changes in operating working capital accounts.

Relation between Cash Flows from Operating, Investing, and Financing Activities

A helpful framework for understanding more fully the relation between net income and cash flows is the product life cycle concept from marketing and microeconomics. Individual products (goods or services) move through four more or less identifiable phases: introduction, growth, maturity and decline, as the top panel of Exhibit 3.4 depicts. The length of these phases and the steepness of the revenue curve vary by the type of product. Products subject to rapid technological change, such as semiconductors and computer software, move through these four phases in two to three years. Other products, such as PepsiCo's beverages, can remain in the maturity phase for many years. Although the analyst will experience difficulty pinpointing the precise location of a product on its life cycle curve at any particular time, it is usually possible to identify the phase and whether the product is in the early or later portion of that phase.

The middle panel of Exhibit 3.4 shows the trend of net income over the product life cycle. Net losses usually occur in the introduction and early growth phases because revenues do not cover the cost of designing and launching new products. Net income peaks during the maturity phase and then begins to decline.

The lower panel of Exhibit 3.4 shows the cash flows from operating, investing, and financing activities during the four life cycle phases. During the introduction and early growth phases, negative cash flow from operations results from the cash outflows needed to launch the product. Negative cash flow from investing activities also occurs during these early phases to build productive capacity. The relative size of this negative cash flow for investing activities depends on the degree of capital intensity of the business. Firms must obtain the cash needed for operating and investing activities during these early phases from external sources (lenders and shareholders).

As the growth phase accelerates, operations become profitable and begin to generate cash. However, firms must use the cash generated to finance accounts receivable and build inventories for expected higher sales levels in the future. Thus, net income usually turns positive earlier than cash flow from operations. The extent of the negative cash flow

[8]Jennifer Francis, Katherine Schipper, and Linda Vincent, "The Relative and Incremental Explanatory Power of Earnings and Alternatives (to Earnings) Performances Measures for Returns," *Contemporary Accounting Research* (Spring 2003), pp. 121–164.

EXHIBIT 3.4

Relation of Revenues, Net Income Flows, and Cash Flows from Operations, Investing, and Financing at Various Stages of Product Life Cycle

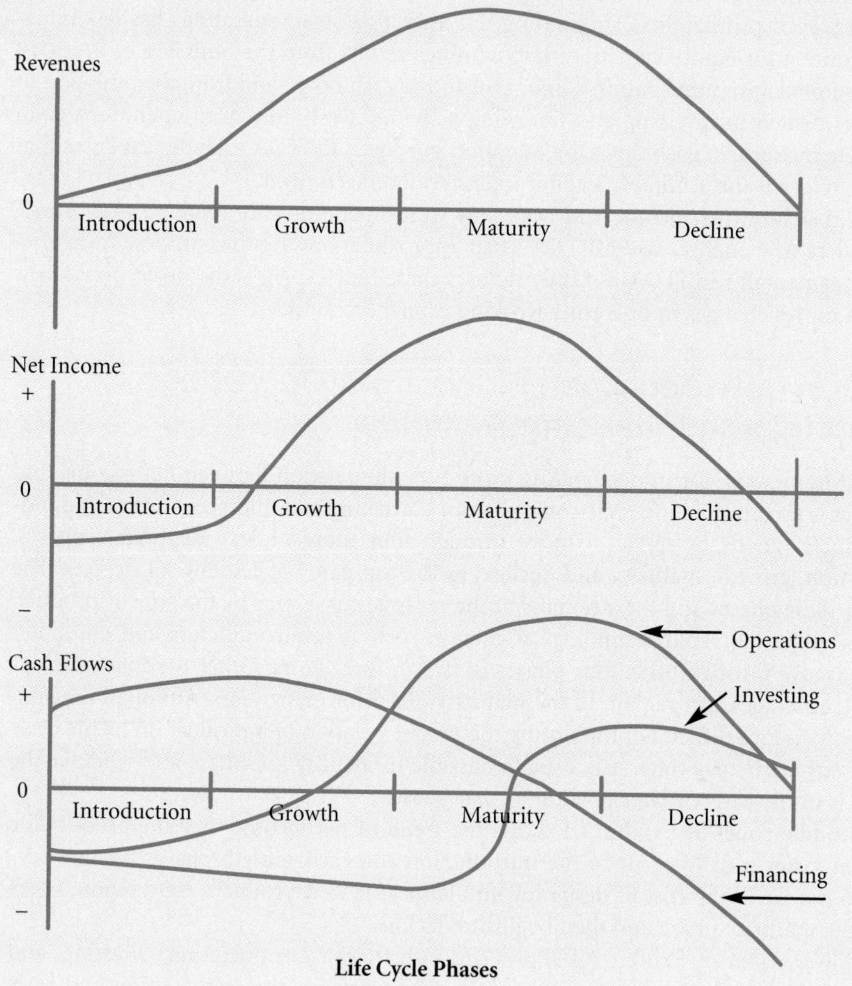

from investing activities depends on the rate of growth and the degree of capital intensity. As in the introduction phase, firms obtain most of the cash needed during the growth phase from external sources (a multiproduct firm can use cash generated from products in the maturity phase of their life cycle to finance products in the introduction and growth phases and therefore not need as much external financing).

As products move through the maturity phase, the cash flow pattern changes dramatically. Operations become a net provider of cash, because of both market acceptance of the product and a leveling off of working capital needs. Also, with revenues leveling off, firms invest to maintain rather than increase productive capacity. During the later stages of the maturity phase, net cash flows from sales of unneeded plant assets sometimes result in a net positive cash flow from investing activities. Firms can use the excess cash flow from operations and, to a lesser extent, from the sale of investments to repay debt incurred during the introduction and growth phases, to pay dividends, and to repurchase their common stock.

During the decline phase, cash flow from operations and investing activities taper off as sales decrease. Firms repay their remaining debt, pay dividends, and repurchase common stock.

The product life cycle model discussed previously provides helpful insights about the relation between sales, net income, and cash flows from operating, investing, and financing activities for a single product. Few business firms, however, rely on a single product; most have a range of products at different stages of their life cycles. Furthermore, the statement of cash flows reports amounts for a firm as a whole and not for each product. If the life cycle concept is to assist in interpreting published statements of cash flows, the analyst needs a multiproduct view.

The analyst obtains such a multiproduct view by aggregating the position of each product in its respective life cycle into a reading on the average life cycle position of the firm. For example, the average position of a firm in technology-driven industries, such as biotechnology, is probably in the growth phase. Although such firms have some products fresh off the drawing board and other products in their decline phase because of the emergence of new technologies, most of these firms' products are in their high-growth phase. Most consumer food companies have an average life cycle position in the maturity phase. Branded consumer food products can remain in their maturity phase for many years with proper product quality control and promotion (consider, for example, PepsiCo's and Coca-Cola's beverages). Such companies continually bring new products to the market and eliminate products that do not meet consumer acceptance, but their average position is probably in the maturity phase. Certain industries in the United States, such as textiles, old-line steel, and automotive, are probably in the early decline phase because of foreign competition and/or outdated technology. Some companies in these industries have built technologically advanced production facilities to compete more effectively on a worldwide basis and have, therefore, essentially reentered the maturity phase. Other firms have diversified into more growth-oriented industries.

Illustrations of Cash Flow Relations

Refer to the statement of cash flows for PepsiCo in Exhibit 3.2. Cash flow from operations exceeds net income each year, primarily as a result of the addback for depreciation and amortization. Changes in operating working capital accounts net to relatively small amounts each year ($305 million in Year 2, $75 million in Year 3, and $313 million in Year 4, for a net change of $83 million (= $305 − $75 − $313) for the three years as a whole. This $83 million net change in working capital is less than 1 percent of total net income or total cash flow from operations for the three years. This small change in working capital is typical of a mature firm.

PepsiCo experienced an excess of cash inflows from operations over cash outflows for investing, a pattern also typical of a mature firm. Thus, PepsiCo did not need external financing for purchases of property, plant, equipment, and corporate acquisitions, but instead used cash from operating activities and excess cash and investments on hand to fund these expenditures. Note that changes in (1) short-term investments and (2) investments with maturities of three months or less appear as investing activities. PepsiCo used the excess cash flow from operations over the cash outflow for investing activities to pay dividends and repurchase shares of its common stock, activities typical of a mature firm.

Exhibits 3.5 to 3.9 present statements of cash flows for firms in five different industries to illustrate the point that a firm's phase in its aggregate product life cycle affects the interpretation of its statement of cash flows. These statements of cash flows also reveal information about the economic characteristics and strategies of these firms.

Overstock.com

Exhibit 3.5 shows a statement of cash flows for Overstock.com (Overstock), an Internet-based retailer of brand-name products purchased from manufacturers and retailers in overstock or liquidation situations. Overstock is in the rapid-growth phase of its life cycle, as indicated by the growth rates in revenue on the last line of Exhibit 3.5. The firm

EXHIBIT 3.5

Overstock.com
Statement of Cash Flows
(amounts in thousands)

	Year 4	Year 3	Year 2
Operations			
Net Income (Loss)	$ (5,002)	$(11,887)	$ (4,560)
Depreciation and Amortization	3,937	2,325	1,873
Other Additions and Subtractions	873	1,022	4,463
Adjustments for Changes in Working Capital:			
(Increase) Decrease in Accounts Receivable	4,468	(3,189)	(5,429)
(Increase) Decrease in Inventories	(24,729)	(17,556)	(7,467)
(Increase) Decrease in Other Current Assets	(1,807)	(666)	(758)
Increase (Decrease) in Accounts Payable	33,697	16,632	10,051
Increase (Decrease) in Other Current Liabilities	13,601	2,907	4,316
Cash Flow from Operations	$ 25,038	$(10,412)	$ 2,489
Investing			
Fixed Assets Acquired	$ (8,714)	$ (6,707)	$ (1,746)
Change in Marketable Securities	(79,106)	10,025	(21,576)
Other Investing Transactions	—	(172)	(5)
Cash Flow from Investing	$ (87,820)	$ 3,146	$(23,327)
Financing			
Increase in Long-Term Borrowing	$116,199	$ —	$ 1,160
Issue of Common Stock	117,352	25,195	32,929
Decrease in Long-Term Borrowing	(959)	(141)	(5,921)
Other Financing Transactions	22	(1)	—
Cash Flow from Financing	$232,614	$ 25,053	$ 28,168
Change in Cash	$169,832	$ 17,787	$ 7,330
Cash—Beginning of Year	28,846	11,059	3,729
Cash—End of Year	$198,678	$ 28,846	$ 11,059
Growth in Revenues from Previous Year	107.0%	160.3%	129.4%

operated at a net loss in all three years and generated a negative cash flow from operations in Year 3. It would have reported negative cash flow from operations in Year 2 and Year 4 as well if it had not stretched out payments to its suppliers and other providers of goods and services. Cash flow from operations exceeds net income or net loss, in part because of the addback for depreciation and amortization. In addition, Overstock recognized substantial stock compensation expense in Year 2, increasing the net loss. The stock compensation expense did not use cash, so the firm added it back to net income when computing cash flow from operations (see Other Addbacks and Subtractions for Year 2).

Cash flow from operations was sufficient to finance expenditures on fixed assets in Year 2 and Year 4, although the firm is not highly capital intensive. Overstock issued common stock each year to finance its growth. It also issued long-term debt in the form of convertible notes in Year 4. Because the firm did not immediately use the cash obtained from these financings, it purchased marketable securities in Year 2 and Year 4. It sold marketable securities in Year 3 when it experienced negative cash flow from operations. Note that the firm did not pay dividends, a typical characteristic of a start-up or high-growth firm.

Target Corporation

Exhibit 3.6 presents a statement of cash flows for Target Corporation (Target), a moderately growing discount store and grocery store chain. Cash flow from operations exceeded net income each year, primarily because of the addback of depreciation and amortization. Target increased its accounts payable each year in amounts approximately matching increases in inventories, indicating that it used supplier financing for inventory growth. Cash flow from operations was just sufficient in each year to finance the acquisition of fixed assets. Note that expenditures on new fixed assets exceeded depreciation and amortization each year, consistent with a growing firm. To provide a capital base for future growth, Target increased its long-term borrowing in Year 2 and Year 3. It used the cash generated from the sale of its discontinued department store businesses in Year 4 to repay long-term debt and to reacquire shares of its common stock. These cash flow patterns are typical of a firm in the late high-growth stage of its life cycle.

Johnson & Johnson

Exhibit 3.7 shows the statement of cash flows for Johnson & Johnson (J&J), a pharmaceutical and medical equipment company. Like Target, J&J experienced moderate growth in revenues during the three years. Net income and cash flow from operations experienced similar growth rates. J&J's investments in fixed assets approximately equal depreciation and amortization each year, suggesting that the firm is not growing its fixed assets appreciably. J&J's growth in revenues likely comes primarily from acquisitions of other firms. J&J's cash flow from operations exceeded its acquisitions of fixed assets and other businesses. J&J used the excess cash flow to pay dividends and repurchase its common stock, while still maintaining large cash balances at the end of each year. J&J's cash flow pattern is typical of a mature company, with the growth rates in revenues coming from acquisitions.

American Airlines

Exhibit 3.8 presents a statement of cash flows for American Airlines (American). American's growth in revenues is highly variable. Cash flow from operations exceeded net income in Year 3 and Year 4, and the negative cash flow from operations in Year 2 was not as large as the net loss for the year because of the large addback of depreciation expense. Reporting cash flow from operations significantly in excess of net income is typical of

EXHIBIT 3.6

Target Corporation
Statement of Cash Flows
(amounts in millions)

	Year 4	Year 3	Year 2
Operations			
Income from Continuing Operations	$ 1,885	$ 1,619	$ 1,376
Depreciation and Amortization	1,259	1,098	967
Deferred Tax Provision	233	208	208
Other Additions and Subtractions	479	437	517
Adjustment for Changes in Working Capital:			
(Increase) Decrease in Accounts Receivable	(209)	(279)	(454)
(Increase) Decrease in Inventories	(853)	(579)	(370)
(Increase) Decrease in Other Current Assets	(37)	(196)	13
Increase (Decrease) in Accounts Payable	823	721	545
Increase (Decrease) in Other Current Liabilities	241	184	(77)
Cash Flow from Continuing Operations	$ 3,821	$ 3,213	$ 2,725
Cash Flow from Discontinued Operations	(626)	292	508
Cash Flow from Operations	$ 3,195	$ 3,505	$ 3,233
Investing			
Fixed Assets Sold	$ 56	$ 67	$ 32
Fixed Assets Acquired	(3,068)	(2,738)	(3,040)
Proceeds from Sale of Discontinued Operations	4,881	—	—
Other Investing Transactions	(690)	(538)	(1,768)
Cash Flow from Investing	$ 1,179	$(3,209)	$(4,776)
Financing			
Increase in Short-Term Borrowing	$ —	$ —	$ —
Increase in Long-Term Borrowing	10	1,200	3,116
Issue of Common Stock	146	36	27
Decrease in Short-Term Borrowing	—	(100)	—
Decrease in Long-Term Borrowing	(1,487)	(1,179)	(1,098)
Acquisition of Common Stock	(1,290)	(48)	(3)
Dividends	(272)	(237)	(218)
Other Financing Transactions	56	(10)	(20)
Cash Flow from Financing	$(2,837)	$ (338)	$ 1,804
Change in Cash	$ 1,537	$ (42)	$ 261
Cash—Beginning of Year	708	750	489
Cash—End of Year	$ 2,245	$ 708	$ 750
Growth in Revenues from Previous Year	11.6%	12.1%	12.0%

EXHIBIT 3.7

Johnson & Johnson
Statement of Cash Flows
(amounts in millions)

	Year 4	Year 3	Year 2
Operations			
Net Income	$ 8,509	$ 7,197	$ 6,597
Depreciation and Amortization	2,124	1,869	1,662
Deferred Income Taxes	(498)	(720)	(74)
Other Additions and Subtractions	21	924	183
Adjustments for Changes in Working Capital:			
(Increase) Decrease in Accounts Receivable	(111)	(691)	(510)
(Increase) Decrease in Inventories	11	39	(109)
(Increase) Decrease in Prepayments	(395)	(746)	(1,429)
Increase (Decrease) in Accounts Payable	607	2,192	1,420
Increase (Decrease) in Other Current Liabilities	863	531	436
Cash Flow from Operations	$11,131	$10,595	$ 8,176
Investing			
Fixed Assets Sold	$ 237	$ 335	$ 156
Fixed Assets Acquired	(2,175)	(2,262)	$(2,099)
Acquisition of Businesses	(580)	(2,812)	(478)
Change in Marketable Securities	444	472	430
Other Investing Transactions	(273)	(259)	(206)
Cash Flow from Investing	$(2,347)	$(4,526)	$(2,197)
Financing			
Increase in Short-Term Borrowing	$ 514	$ 3,062	$ 2,359
Increase in Long-Term Borrowing	17	1,023	22
Issue of Common Stock	642	311	390
Decrease in Short-Term Borrowing	(1,291)	(4,134)	(560)
Decrease in Long-Term Borrowing	(395)	(196)	(245)
Acquisition of Common Stock	(1,384)	(1,183)	(6,538)
Dividends	(3,251)	(2,746)	(2,381)
Other Financing Transactions	190	277	110
Cash Flow from Financing	$(4,958)	$(3,586)	$(6,843)
Change in Cash	$ 3,826	$ 2,483	$ (864)
Cash—Beginning of Year	5,377	2,894	3,758
Cash—End of Year	$ 9,203	$ 5,377	$ 2,894
Growth in Revenues from Previous Year	13.1%	15.3%	12.3%

EXHIBIT 3.8

American Airlines
Statement of Cash Flows
(amounts in millions)

	Year 4	Year 3	Year 2
Operations			
Net Income	$ (761)	$(1,228)	$(3,511)
Depreciation and Amortization	1,292	1,377	1,366
Deferred Income Taxes	—	—	(845)
Other Additions and Subtractions	(115)	(525)	1,895
Adjustments for Changes in Working Capital:			
(Increase) Decrease in Accounts Receivable	(89)	690	(66)
(Increase) Decrease in Inventories	8	56	48
Increase (Decrease) in Accounts Payable	(26)	(198)	(32)
Increase (Decrease) in Other Current Liabilities	408	429	34
Cash Flow from Operations	$ 717	$ 601	$(1,111)
Investing			
Fixed Assets Acquired	$(1,027)	$ (680)	$(1,881)
Change in Marketable Securities	(9)	11	512
Other Investing Transactions	(12)	24	(24)
Cash Flow from Investing	$(1,048)	$ (645)	$(1,393)
Financing			
Increase in Long-Term Borrowing	$ 1,977	$ 945	$ 3,190
Issue of Common Stock	7	1	3
Decrease in Long-Term Borrowing	(1,653)	(886)	(687)
Cash Flow from Financing	$ 331	$ 60	$ 2,506
Change in Cash	$ 0	$ 16	$ 2
Cash—Beginning of Year	120	104	102
Cash—End of Year	$ 120	$ 120	$ 104
Growth in Revenues from Previous Year	6.9%	.1%	−8.2%

capital-intensive firms. Although American experienced a positive cash flow from operations in two of the three years, this cash flow was not sufficient to finance capital expenditures. It used long-term debt to finance these acquisitions. Generally speaking, debt is a less costly source of capital than equity because it is less risky and because interest payments to debtholders are tax-deductible whereas dividends payments to equity shareholders are not. The assets acquired serve as collateral for the borrowing, which reduces the risk to the debtholders. The heavy use of debt financing in the capital structure of airlines adds considerable risk for common-equity shareholders.

Kelly Services

Finally, Exhibit 3.9 presents a statement of cash flows for Kelly Services (Kelly), a provider of temporary help services. Revenues of Kelly vary with economic conditions. Year 2 for Kelly occurred during a recession and Years 3 and 4 are years of exiting the recession. The primary source of variation between net income and cash flow from operations is management of working capital, particularly accounts receivable and accrued payroll. A temporary help agency serves as a conduit between clients, with the services of workers giving rise to an accounts receivable for the agency and employees earning compensation giving

EXHIBIT 3.9

Kelly Services
Statement of Cash Flows
(amounts in thousands)

	Year 4	Year 3	Year 2
Operations			
Net Income	$ 22,130	$ 5,110	$ 18,569
Depreciation and Amortization	44,137	47,795	45,428
Deferred Income Taxes	(9,611)	2,936	6,590
Adjustments for Changes in Working Capital:			
(Increase) Decrease in Accounts Receivable	(48,755)	(63,516)	(9,420)
(Increase) Decrease in Prepayments	(6,833)	(5,930)	7,162
Increase (Decrease) in Accounts Payable	3,285	4,727	(4,040)
Increase (Decrease) in Accrued Payroll	46,933	20,490	17,522
Increase (Decrease) in Other Current Liabilities	8,074	18,981	7,795
Cash Flow from Operations	$ 59,360	$ 30,593	$ 89,606
Investing			
Fixed Assets Acquired	$(35,556)	$(30,222)	$(33,406)
Change in Marketable Securities	105	142	31
Other Investing Transactions	(736)	(2,487)	(3,476)
Cash Flow from Investing	$(36,187)	$(32,567)	$(36,851)
Financing			
Increase in Short-Term Borrowing, net	$ (8,188)	$ 10,280	$(11,723)
Issue of Common Stock	8,422	3,865	991
Acquisition of Common Stock	(3)	(26,149)	(13,216)
Dividends	(14,043)	(14,143)	(14,293)
Other Financing Transactions	1,815	3,563	2,961
Cash Flow from Financing	$(11,997)	$(22,584)	$(35,280)
Change in Cash	$ 11,176	$(24,558)	$ 17,475
Cash—Beginning of Year	76,378	100,936	83,461
Cash—End of Year	$ 87,554	$ 76,378	$100,936
Growth in Revenues from Previous Year	15.2%	6.6%	1.3%

rise to accrued payroll. The variations each year in working capital result from differences in the dates for billing clients versus the payroll-ending dates for employees. Kelly has an unusually large addback for depreciation and amortization for a service firm. The depreciation is primarily on its corporate office building and equipment and the amortization is on certain intangibles from corporate acquisitions. Cash flow from operations was sufficient to finance acquisitions of fixed assets each year, typical of a service firm. Kelly used the excess cash flow to reacquire common stock and pay dividends. Note that Kelly relies more on short-term debt financing than on long-term debt financing. Accounts receivable serve as collateral for short-term borrowing. Service firms have relatively few assets that can serve as collateral for long-term borrowing.

These five statements of cash flows present typical patterns for firms in different types of industries and in different stages of their product life cycles. They also illustrate some of the insights that an analyst can derive about the economic characteristics, strategy, and performance of an entity by studying its statement of cash flows.

PREPARING THE STATEMENT OF CASH FLOWS

U.S. GAAP requires firms to include a statement of cash flows in their published financial statements each period.[9] Other countries generally require a similar statement as well. Smaller, privately held firms often prepare just a balance sheet and an income statement.

This section illustrates a procedure for preparing a statement of cash flows using information from the balance sheet and income statement. The implied statement of cash flows that we prepare merely approximates the amounts that the statement of cash flows would report if the analyst had full access to a firm's accounting records. For example, we assume that all changes in operating working capital accounts are operating transactions, even though some of these changes might arise from a corporate acquisition, an investing activity. As another example, consider a firm that acquires another firm by both paying cash and assuming its liabilities. Only the cash outflow appears in the investing section of the statement of cash flows. Acquiring assets by assuming liabilities is a noncash acquisition of assets (that is, assets increase and liabilities increase). Such noncash exchanges do not appear in the statement of cash flows because they do not affect cash. Firms, however, must report them in a supplemental note to the financial statements.[10] PepsiCo includes the disclosures in Note 14, "Supplemental Financial Information" (Appendix A). Absent information about noncash exchanges, the preparation procedure described in this section assumes that all of the change in each account involves a cash flow that relates to one of the three activities reported in the statement of cash flows. Despite these concerns, the estimated amounts should approximate the actual amounts closely enough for the analyst to make meaningful interpretations.

Algebraic Formulation

We know from the accounting equation that:

$$\text{Assets} = \text{Liabilities} + \text{Shareholders' Equity}$$

This equality holds for balance sheets at the beginning and end of each period. If we subtract the amounts on the balance sheet at the beginning of the period from the corre-

---

[9]Financial Accounting Standards Board, *Statement of Financial Accounting Standards No. 95*, "Statement of Cash Flows" (1987).

[10]*Ibid.*, par. 74.

sponding amounts on the balance sheet at the end of the period, we obtain the following equality for changes (Δ) in balance sheet amounts:

$$\Delta \text{ Assets} = \Delta \text{ Liabilities} + \Delta \text{ Shareholders' Equity}$$

We can now expand the change in assets as follows:

$$\Delta \text{ Cash} + \Delta \text{ Noncash Assets} = \Delta \text{ Liabilities} + \Delta \text{ Shareholders' Equity}$$

Rearranging terms:

$$\Delta \text{ Cash} = \Delta \text{ Liabilities} + \Delta \text{ Shareholders' Equity} - \Delta \text{ Noncash Assets}$$

The statement of cash flows explains the reasons for the change in cash during a period. We can see that the change in cash equals the change in all other (noncash) balance sheet amounts.

Refer to Exhibit 3.10, which shows the comparative balance sheet of Logue Shoe Store for the years ending December 31, Year 4, Year 3, and Year 2. The balance sheets at the end of Year 2 and Year 3 report the following equalities:

	Cash	**+**	**Noncash Assets**	**=**	**Liabilities**	**+**	**Shareholders' Equity**
Year 2	\$13,698	+	\$132,136	=	\$105,394	+	\$40,440
Year 3	\$12,595	+	\$129,511	=	\$ 85,032	+	\$57,074

Subtracting the amounts at the end of Year 2 from the amounts at the end of Year 3, we obtain:

$$\begin{array}{cccc} \Delta \text{ Cash} + & \Delta \text{ Noncash Assets} = & \Delta \text{ Liabilities} + & \Delta \text{ Shareholders' Equity} \\ -\$1{,}103 + & -\$2{,}625 = & -\$20{,}362 + & \$16{,}634 \end{array}$$

Rearranging terms:

$$\begin{array}{ccccc} \Delta \text{ Cash} = & \Delta \text{ Liabilities} + & \Delta \text{ Shareholders' Equity} & - & \Delta \text{ Noncash Assets} \\ -\$1{,}103 = & -\$20{,}362 + & \$16{,}634 & - & -\$2{,}625 \end{array}$$

The decrease in cash of \$1,103 equals the decrease in liabilities plus the increase in shareholders' equity minus the decrease in noncash assets.

Classifying Changes in Balance Sheet Accounts

The statement of cash flows classifies the reasons for the change in cash as being either an operating, investing, or financing activity. The remaining task then is to classify the change in each noncash balance sheet account (right-hand side of the preceding equation) into one of these three categories. Some of the analyst's classifications in this step will necessarily be approximations. Some of the changes in balance sheet accounts clearly fit into one of the three categories (for example, the change in long-term debt is almost always a financing transaction). However, some balance sheet changes (for example, retained earnings) result from the netting of several changes, some of which relate to operations (net income) and some of which relate to investing or financing (dividends)

EXHIBIT 3.10

Logue Shoe Store
Balance Sheet

	December 31, Year 4	December 31, Year 3	December 31, Year 2
Assets			
Cash	$ 5,815	$ 12,595	$ 13,698
Accounts Receivable	1,816	1,978	1,876
Inventories	123,636	106,022	98,824
Other Current Assets	1,560	—	3,591
Total Current Assets	$132,827	$120,595	$117,989
Property, Plant, and Equipment, at cost	$ 64,455	$ 65,285	$ 63,634
Less Accumulated Depreciation	(54,617)	(45,958)	(37,973)
Net Property, Plant, and Equipment	$ 9,838	$ 19,327	$ 25,661
Intangible Assets	2,184	2,184	2,184
Total Assets	$144,849	$142,106	$145,834
Liabilities and Shareholders' Equity			
Accounts Payable	$ 13,954	$ 15,642	$ 21,768
Notes Payable	10,814	—	—
Current Portion of Long-Term Debt	7,288	10,997	18,256
Other Current Liabilities	5,489	6,912	4,353
Total Current Liabilities	$ 37,545	$ 33,551	$ 44,377
Long-Term Debt	43,788	51,481	61,017
Total Liabilities	$ 81,333	$ 85,032	$105,394
Common Stock	$ 1,000	$ 1,000	$ 1,000
Additional Paid-In Capital	124,000	124,000	124,000
Retained Earnings	(61,484)	(67,926)	(84,560)
Total Shareholders' Equity	$ 63,516	$ 57,074	$ 40,440
Total Liabilities and Shareholders' Equity	$144,849	$142,106	$145,834

activities. The analyst should use whatever information the financial statements and notes provide about changes in balance sheet accounts to classify the net change in each account each period.

Exhibit 3.11 classifies the changes in the noncash balance sheet accounts. The next section discusses the classification of each account.

1. Accounts Receivable

Cash collections from customers during a period equal sales for the period plus accounts receivable at the beginning of the period minus accounts receivable at the end of the period. Thus, the change in accounts receivable clearly relates to operations. Line (18) of Exhibit 3.11 shows net income as a source of cash from operations. Net income includes sales revenue. The amount for sales revenue included in the amount on line (18) plus or

EXHIBIT 3.11

Worksheet for Preparation of Statement of Cash Flows

Balance Sheet Accounts	Amount of Balance Sheet Changes	Operations	Investing	Financing
(Increase) Decrease in Assets				
(1) Accounts Receivable		x		
(2) Marketable Securities			x	
(3) Inventories		x		
(4) Other Current Assets		x		
(5) Investments in Securities			x	
(6) Property, Plant, and Equipment Cost			x	
(7) Accumulated Depreciation		x		
(8) Intangible Assets		x	x	
Increase (Decrease) in Liabilities and Shareholders' Equities				
(9) Accounts Payable		x		
(10) Notes Payable				x
(11) Current Portion of Long-Term Debt				x
(12) Other Current Liabilities		x		
(13) Long-Term Debt				x
(14) Deferred Income Taxes		x		
(15) Other Noncurrent Liabilities				x
(16) Common Stock				x
(17) Additional Paid-In Capital				x
(18) Retained Earnings		x (net income)		x (dividends)
(19) Treasury Stock				x
(20) Cash				

minus the change in accounts receivable on line (1) results in the amount of cash received from customers.

2. Marketable Securities

Firms typically acquire marketable securities when they temporarily have excess cash and sell these securities when they need cash. The holding of marketable securities for a relatively short period might make their purchases and sales appear as operating activities. However, the temporarily excess cash could result from selling fixed assets, from issuing bonds or common stock, or from operating activities. Likewise, firms might use the cash inflow from the sale of marketable securities to purchase fixed assets, retire debt, repurchase common or preferred stock, or finance operating activities. GAAP in the United States ignores the reason for the excess cash (with which firms purchase marketable securities) and the use of the cash proceeds (from the sale of marketable securities), and classifies the cash flows associated with purchases and sales of marketable securities as investing activities. (The analyst, however, can feel free to reclassify purchases and sales of marketable securities as operating or financing activities if deemed appropriate for purposes of analysis.) Because net income includes gains or losses on sales of marketable securities, the analyst must subtract gains and add back losses to net income in deriving cash flow from operations if purchases and sales are viewed as investing activities. Failure to offset the gain or loss included in earnings results in reporting too much (sales of marketable securities at a gain) or too little (sales of marketable securities at a loss) cash flow from operations. Cash flow from operations should include none of the cash flows associated with sales of marketable securities if such transactions are viewed as investing activities.

3. Inventories

Purchases of inventory during a period equal cost of goods sold for the period plus inventories at the end of the period minus inventories at the beginning of the period. Line (18) includes cost of goods sold as an expense in measuring net income. The change in inventories on line (3) coupled with cost of goods sold included in the amount on line (18) results in the amount of purchases for the period. The presumption at this point is that the firm made a cash outflow equal to the amount of purchases. If the firm does not pay cash for all of these purchases, then accounts payable changes. We adjust for the change in accounts payable on line (9), discussed later.

4. Other Current Assets

This balance sheet account typically includes prepayments for various operating costs such as insurance and rent. Unless the financial statements and notes present information to the contrary, the presumption is that the change in Other Current Assets relates to operations.

5. Investments in Securities

The Investments in Securities account can change for the following possible reasons:

Source of Change	Classification in Statement of Cash Flows
Acquisition of New Investments	Investing (outflow)
Recognition of Income or Loss Using Equity Method	Operations (subtraction or addition)
Receipt of Dividend from Investee	Operations (inflow)
Sale of Investments	Investing (inflow)

If the balance sheet, income statement, or notes provide information that permits the disaggregation of the net change in Investments in Securities into these components, then the analyst can make appropriate classifications of the components. Absent such information, we classify the change in the account as an investing activity.

6. Property, Plant, and Equipment Cost

GAAP classifies the cash flows related to purchases and sales of fixed assets as investing activities. Because net income includes any gains or losses from sales of fixed assets, we offset their effect on earnings by adding back losses and subtracting gains from net income when computing cash flow from operations. We then include the full amount of the proceeds from sales of fixed assets as an investing activity.

7. Accumulated Depreciation

The amount of depreciation expense recognized each period reduces net income but does not use cash. Thus, we add back depreciation expense as an operating item with a positive sign on line (7). When we add the amount for depreciation expense included under operations on line (7) to depreciation expense included as a negative element in net income on line (18), we eliminate the effect of depreciation expense on the Operations column. This treatment is appropriate because depreciation expense is not a cash flow (ignoring income tax consequences). If a firm sells depreciable assets during a period, the net change in accumulated depreciation includes both the accumulated depreciation removed from the account for assets sold and depreciation expense for the period. Thus, the analyst cannot assume that the change in the accumulated depreciation account relates to depreciation expense only, unless disclosures indicate that the firm did not sell depreciable assets during the year.

8. Intangible Assets

Intangible assets on the balance sheet include patents, copyrights, goodwill, and similar assets. A portion of the change in these accounts represents amortization, which requires an addback to net income when computing cash flow from operations. Unless the financial statements and notes provide contrary information, the presumption is that the remaining change in these accounts is an investing activity.

Many firms include another line item on their balance sheets labeled Other Noncurrent Assets. The analyst should use whatever information firms disclose to determine the appropriate classification of the change in this account.

9. Accounts Payable

The cash outflow for accounts payable equals inventory purchases during the period plus accounts payable at the beginning of the period minus accounts payable at the end of the period. We derived the amount for inventory purchases of the period as part of the calculations in line (3) for inventories. The adjustment on line (9) for the change in accounts payable converts purchases to cash payments on purchases and, like inventories, is an operating activity.

10. Notes Payable

Notes payable is the account generally used when a firm engages in short-term borrowing from a bank or other financial institution. GAAP typically classifies such borrowing as a financing activity on the statement of cash flows, even though the firm might use the proceeds to finance accounts receivable, inventories, or other working capital needs. The presumption underlying the classification of bank borrowing as a financing activity is that firms derive operating cash inflows from their customers, not by borrowing from banks.

11. Current Portion of Long-Term Debt

The change in the current portion of long-term debt during a period equals (a) the reclassification of long-term debt from a noncurrent liability to a current liability (that is, debt that the firm expects to repay within one year as of the end-of-the-period balance sheet) minus (b) the current portion of long-term debt actually repaid during the period. The latter amount represents the cash outflow from this financing transaction. We consider shortly the amount arising from the reclassification in connection with line (13).

12. Other Current Liabilities

Firms generally use this account for obligations related to goods and services used in operations other than purchases of inventories. Thus, changes in Other Current Liabilities appear as operating activities.

13. Long-Term Debt

This account changes for the following reasons:

- Issuance of new long-term debt.
- Reclassification of long-term debt from a noncurrent to a current liability.
- Retirement of long-term debt.
- Conversion of long-term debt to preferred or common stock.

These items are clearly financing transactions but they do not all affect cash. The issuance of new debt and the retirement of old debt do affect cash flows. The reclassification of long-term debt included in the amount on line (13) offsets the corresponding amount included in the change on line (11) and they effectively cancel each other. This is appropriate because the reclassification does not affect cash flow. Likewise, any portion of the change in long-term debt on line (13) due to a conversion of debt into common stock offsets a similar change on lines (16) and (17). The analyst enters reclassifications and conversions of debt, such as those described previously, on the worksheet for the preparation of a statement of cash flows, because such transactions help explain changes in balance sheet accounts. However, these transactions do not appear on the formal statement of cash flows because they do not involve actual cash flows.

14. Deferred Income Taxes

Income taxes currently payable equal income tax expense (included on line (18) as a negative element of net income) plus or minus the change in deferred taxes during the period. Thus, changes in Deferred Income Taxes appear as an operating activity.

15. Other Noncurrent Liabilities

This account includes unfunded pension or retirement benefit obligations, long-term deposits received, and other miscellaneous long-term liabilities. Changes in pension and retirement benefit obligations are operating activities. Absent information to the contrary, however, we classify the change in other noncurrent liability accounts as financing activities.

16 and 17. Common Stock and Additional Paid-In Capital

These accounts change when a firm issues new common stock or repurchases and retires outstanding common stock, and they appear as financing activities. The additional paid-in capital account also changes when firms recognize compensation expense related to stock options (discussed in Chapter 9). This is a noncash expense that, like depreciation, requires an addback to net income when computing cash flow from operations.

18. Retained Earnings

Retained earnings increase by the amount of net income and decrease with the declaration of dividends each period. Net income is an operating activity and dividends are a financing activity.

19. Treasury Stock

Repurchasing a firm's outstanding capital stock is a financing activity.

Illustration of the Preparation Procedure

We illustrate the procedure for preparing the statement of cash flows using the data for Logue Shoe Store in Exhibit 3.10. Net income was $16,634 for Year 3 and $6,442 for Year 4.

Exhibit 3.12 presents the worksheet for Year 3. The first column shows the change in each noncash balance sheet account that nets to the $1,103 decrease in cash for the

EXHIBIT 3.12

Worksheet for Statement of Cash Flows for Logue Shoe Store
Year 3

Balance Sheet Accounts	Amount of Balance Sheet Changes	Operations	Investing	Financing
(Increase) Decrease in Assets				
Accounts Receivable	$ (102)	$ (102)		
Inventories	(7,198)	(7,198)		
Other Current Assets	3,591	3,591		
Property, Plant, and Equipment	(1,651)		$(1,651)	
Accumulated Depreciation	7,985	7,985		
Intangible Assets	—			
Increase (Decrease) in Liabilities and Shareholders' Equities				
Accounts Payable	$(6,126)	$(6,126)		
Notes Payable	—			—
Current Portion of Long-Term Debt	(7,259)			$ (7,259)
Other Current Liabilities	2,559	2,559		
Long-Term Debt	(9,536)			(9,536)
Common Stock	—			—
Additional Paid-In Capital	—		—	—
Retained Earnings	16,634	16,634		
Cash	$(1,103)	$17,343	$(1,651)	$(16,795)

period. One should observe with particular care the direction of the change. Recall from the earlier equation:

Δ Cash	=	Δ Liabilities	+	Δ Shareholders' Equity	−	Δ Noncash Assets
Increase	=	Increase				
Decrease	=	Decrease				
Increase	=			Increase		
Decrease	=			Decrease		
Decrease	=					Increase
Increase	=					Decrease

Thus, changes in liabilities and shareholders' equity have the same directional effect on cash, whereas changes in noncash assets have the opposite directional effect. Bank borrowings increase liabilities and cash; debt repayments decrease liabilities and cash. Issuing common stock increases shareholders' equity and cash; paying dividends or repurchasing outstanding common stock reduces shareholders' equity and cash. Purchasing equipment increases noncash assets and reduces cash; selling equipment reduces noncash assets and increases cash.

We classify the change in each account as an operating, investing, or financing activity, because we have no information that more than one activity caused the change in the account. Observe the following for Year 3:

1. Operating activities were a net source of cash for the period. Cash flow from operations approximately equaled net income. Logue Shoe Store increased its inventories but reduced accounts payable. Most firms attempt to increase accounts payable to finance increases in inventories. The reduced accounts payable suggests either a desire to pay more quickly, perhaps to take advantage of cash discounts, or pressure from suppliers to pay more quickly.
2. Cash flow from operations was more than sufficient to finance the increase in property, plant, and equipment. Note that capital expenditures were small relative to the amount of depreciation for the year, suggesting that the firm was now increasing its capacity.
3. Logue Shoe Store used the cash derived from operations in excess of capital expenditures to repay long-term debt.

Exhibit 3.13 presents a worksheet for Year 4. The preparation procedure is identical to that in Exhibit 3.12. Note in this case that operations were a net user of cash. The increase in accounts payable did not match the substantial increase in inventories. Long-term debt was again redeemed in Year 4, but it appears that the firm used short-term bank borrowing to finance the redemption. The negative cash flow from operations coupled with the use of short-term debt to redeem long-term debt suggests an increase in short-term liquidity risk.

Exhibit 3.14 presents the statement of cash flows for Logue Shoe Store for Year 3 and Year 4 using the amounts taken from the worksheets in Exhibits 3.12 and 3.13.

SUMMARY

As a complement to the balance sheet and the income statement, the statement of cash flows is an informative statement for analysts for the following reasons:

1. Analysts that understand the types of information that this statement presents and the kinds of interpretations that are appropriate find that the statement of cash

EXHIBIT 3.13

Worksheet for Statement of Cash Flows for Logue Shoe Store
Year 4

Balance Sheet Accounts	Amount of Balance Sheet Changes	Operations	Investing	Financing
(Increase) Decrease in Assets				
Accounts Receivable	$ 162	$ 162		
Inventories	(17,614)	(17,614)		
Other Current Assets	(1,560)	(1,560)		
Property, Plant, and Equipment	830		$830	
Accumulated Depreciation	8,659	8,659		
Intangible Assets	—			
Increase (Decrease) in Liabilities and Shareholders' Equities				
Accounts Payable	$(1,688)	$(1,688)		
Notes Payable	10,814			$10,814
Current Portion of Long-Term Debt ...	(3,709)			(3,709)
Other Current Liabilities	(1,423)	(1,423)		
Long-Term Debt	(7,693)			(7,693)
Common Stock	—			—
Additional Paid-In Capital	—		—	—
Retained Earnings	6,442	6,442	—	—
Cash	$(6,780)	$(7,022)	$830	$ (588)

flows reveals information about the economic characteristics of a firm's industry, its strategy, and the stage in its life cycle.

2. The statement of cash flows provides information to assess the financial health of a firm. Analysts increasingly recognize that cash flows do not necessarily track income flows. A firm with a healthy income statement is not necessarily financially healthy. Cash requirements to service debt, for example, may outstrip the ability of operations to generate cash.
3. The statement of cash flows permits the calculation of free cash flows, an important factor in the valuation of firms.

QUESTIONS, EXERCISES, PROBLEMS, AND CASES

Questions and Exercises

3.1 NEED FOR A STATEMENT OF CASH FLOWS. "The accrual basis of accounting creates the need for a statement of cash flows." Explain.

EXHIBIT 3.14

Statement of Cash Flows for Logue Shoe Store

	Year 4	Year 3
Operations		
Net Income	$ 6,442	$ 16,634
Depreciation	8,659	7,985
(Increase) Decrease in Accounts Receivable	162	(102)
(Increase) Decrease in Inventories	(17,614)	(7,198)
(Increase) Decrease in Other Current Assets	(1,560)	3,591
Increase (Decrease) in Accounts Payable	(1,688)	(6,126)
Increase (Decrease) in Other Current Liabilities	(1,423)	2,559
Cash Flow from Operations	$ (7,022)	$ 17,343
Investing		
Sale (Acquisition) of Property, Plant, and Equipment	$ 830	$ (1,651)
Financing		
Increase in Notes Payable	$ 10,814	—
Repayment of Long-Term Debt	$(11,402)	$(16,795)
Cash Flow from Financing	$ (588)	$(16,795)
Net Change in Cash	$ (6,780)	$ (1,103)
Cash at Beginning of Year	12,595	13,698
Cash at End of Year	$ 5,815	$ 12,595

3.2 CLASSIFICATION OF CASH FLOWS RELATED TO BORROWING. The statement of cash flows classifies cash expenditures for interest expense as an operating activity but classifies cash expenditures to redeem debt as a financing activity. Explain this apparent paradox.

3.3 CLASSIFICATION OF CASH FLOWS RELATED TO THE COST OF FINANCING. The statement of cash flows classifies cash expenditures for interest expense on debt as an operating activity but classifies cash expenditures for dividends to shareholders as a financing activity. Explain this apparent paradox.

3.4 CLASSIFICATION OF CHANGES IN SHORT-TERM FINANCING. The statement of cash flows classifies changes in accounts payable as an operating activity but classifies changes in short-term borrowing as a financing activity. Explain this apparent paradox.

3.5 TREATMENT OF NONCASH EXCHANGES. The acquisition of equipment by assuming a mortgage is a transaction that firms cannot report in their statement of cash flows but must report in a supplemental schedule or note. Of what value is information about this type of transaction? What is the reason for its exclusion from the statement of cash flows?

3.6 COMPUTING CASH COLLECTIONS FROM CUSTOMERS. Caterpillar manufactures heavy machinery and equipment and provides financing for purchases by its customers. Caterpillar reported sales and interest revenues of $30,251 million for Year 4. The balance sheet showed current and noncurrent receivables of $18,987 million at the beginning of Year 4 and $23,308 million at the end of Year 4. Compute the amount of cash collected from customers during Year 4.

3.7 COMPUTING CASH PAYMENTS TO SUPPLIERS. Lowe's Companies, a retailer of home improvement products, reported cost of goods sold of $24,165 million for Year 4. It reported merchandise inventories of $4,584 million at the beginning of Year 4 and $5,982 million at the end of Year 4. It reported accounts payable to suppliers of $2,212 million at the beginning of Year 4 and $2,687 million at the end of Year 4. Compute the amount of cash paid to merchandise suppliers during Year 4.

3.8 COMPUTING CASH PAYMENTS FOR INCOME TAXES. Radio Shack, a retailer of electronics products, reported income tax expense for Year 4 of $204.9 million, comprising $166.3 million of current taxes and $38.6 million of deferred taxes. The balance sheet showed income taxes payable of $137.5 million at the beginning of Year 4 and $117.5 million at the end of Year 4. Compute the amount of income taxes paid in cash during Year 4.

3.9 INTERPRETING RELATIONS BETWEEN NET INCOME AND CASH FLOW FROM OPERATIONS. Combined data for three years for two firms appear here (in millions):

	Firm A	Firm B
Net Income	$2,381	$2,825
Cash Flow from Operations	$1,133	$7,728

One of these firms is Amazon.com, a rapidly growing Internet retailer, and the other is Kroger, a retail grocery store chain growing at the growth rate in the population. Indicate which firm is which and explain your reasoning.

3.10 INTERPRETING RELATIONS BETWEEN NET INCOME AND CASH FLOW FROM OPERATIONS. Combined data for three years for two firms appear here (in millions):

	Firm A	Firm B
Net Income	$ 996	$2,846
Cash Flow from Operations	$3,013	$3,401

The two firms experienced similar growth rate in revenues during the three-year period. One of these firms is Accenture, Ltd., a management consulting firm, and the other is Southwest Airlines, a provider of airline transportation services. Indicate which firm is which and explain your reasoning.

3.11 INTERPRETING RELATIONS BETWEEN CASH FLOWS FROM OPERATING, INVESTING, AND FINANCING ACTIVITIES. Combined data for three years of two firms appear here (in millions):

	Firm A	Firm B
Net Income	$ 2,378	$ 2,399
Cash Flow from Operations	$ 7,199	$ 3,400
Cash Flow from Investing	$(6,764)	$ (678)
Cash Flow from Financing	$ 570	$(2,600)

One of these firms is FedEx, a relatively high-growth firm that provides courier services, and the other is Kellogg, a more mature consumer foods processor. Indicate which firm is which and explain your reasoning.

3.12 INTERPRETING RELATIONS BETWEEN CASH FLOWS FROM OPERATING, INVESTING, AND FINANCING ACTIVITIES. Combined data for three years of two firms appear here (in millions):

	Firm A	Firm B
Cash Flow from Operations	$ 2,639	$ 2,759
Cash Flow from Investing	$(3,491)	$(1,281)
Cash Flow from Financing	$ 1,657	$(1,654)

One of these firms is eBay, an online retailer with a three-year growth in sales of 337.3 percent, and the other is TJX Corporation, a specialty retail store with a three-year growth in sales of 39.3 percent. Indicate which firm is which and explain your reasoning.

3.13 RELATION BETWEEN NET INCOME, EBITDA, AND CASH FLOW FROM OPERATIONS. Selected data for The Walt Disney Company appear here (in millions):

	Year 4	Year 3	Year 2	Year 1
Net Income	$2,345	$1,267	$1,236	$1,169
Conversion of Net Income to Cash Flow from Operations:				
Type 1 Adjustments	2,076	1,370	1,077	2,124
Type 2 Adjustments	(51)	264	(27)	(245)
Cash Flow from Operations	$4,370	$2,901	$2,286	$3,048
EBITDA	$5,554	$4,106	$3,919	$3,759
Growth Rate in Revenues	13.6%	6.8%	.6%	(.6%)

Prepare a graph similar to Exhibit 3.3 that shows net income, net income plus Type 1 adjustments, cash flow from operations, and EBITDA. Comment on the relations between these series over time.

Problems and Cases

3.14 INTERPRETING THE STATEMENT OF CASH FLOWS. The Coca-Cola Company (Coca-Cola), like PepsiCo, manufactures and markets a variety of beverages. Exhibit 3.15 presents a statement of cash flows for Coca-Cola for Year 0 to Year 4.

Required

Discuss the relationship between net income and cash flow from operations and between cash flows from operating, investing, and financing activities for the firm over the five-year period. Identify characteristics of Coca Cola's cash flows that one would expect for a mature company.

3.15 INTERPRETING THE STATEMENT OF CASH FLOWS. Texas Instruments primarily develops and manufactures semiconductors for use in technology-based products for various industries. The manufacturing process is capital intensive and subject to cyclical swings in the economy. Because of overcapacity in the industry and a cutback on spending for technology products due to a recession, semiconductor prices collapsed in Year 1 and commenced a steady comeback between Year 2 and Year 4. Exhibit 3.16 presents a statement of cash flows for Texas Instruments for Year 0 to Year 4.

Required

Discuss the relationship between net income and cash flows from operations and between cash flows from operating, investing, and financing activities for the firm over the five-year period.

3.16 INTERPRETING THE STATEMENT OF CASH FLOWS. The Gap operates chains of retail clothing stores under the names of The Gap, Banana Republic, and Old Navy. Exhibit 3.17 presents the statement of cash flows for The Gap for Year 0 to Year 4.

Required

Discuss the relationship between net income and cash flow from operations and between cash flows from operating, investing, and financing activities for the firm over the five-year period.

3.17 INTERPRETING THE STATEMENT OF CASH FLOWS. XM Satellite Radio, which launched its satellite radio service in Year 1, is the leading satellite radio service provider in the United States, with more than 3.2 million subscribers at the end of Year 4. The firm generally receives subscription fees in advance of providing subscription services. Its lineup includes 150 channels, including sixty-five music channels, thirty news and talk show channels, thirty-one sports channels, and twenty-one traffic and weather channels. XM Satellite Radio is the official satellite radio of Major League Baseball and also broadcasts football and basketball games. The firm markets its services to 100 million households and 200 million registered vehicles in the United States. General Motors and Honda, two of the firm's investors, offer XM Satellite Radio service on

EXHIBIT 3.15

The Coca-Cola Company
Statement of Cash Flows
(amounts in millions)
(Problem 3.14)

	Year 4	Year 3	Year 2	Year 1	Year 0
Operations					
Net Income	$ 4,847	$ 4,347	$ 3,976	$ 3,969	$ 3,093
Depreciation and Amortization	893	850	806	803	773
Equity Income, net of dividends	(476)	(294)	(256)	(54)	380
Deferred Income Taxes	162	(188)	40	56	3
Stock Compensation	345	422	365	41	43
Other Additions (Subtractions)	814	487	218	(243)	145
(Increase) Decrease in Accounts Receivable	(5)	80	(83)	(73)	(39)
(Increase) Decrease in Inventories	(57)	111	(49)	(17)	(2)
(Increase) Decrease in Prepayments	(397)	(276)	74	(349)	(618)
Increase (Decrease) in Accounts Payable	45	(164)	(442)	(179)	(84)
Increase (Decrease) in Other Current Liabilities	(203)	81	93	156	(109)
Cash Flow from Operations	$ 5,968	$ 5,456	$ 4,742	$ 4,110	$ 3,585
Investing					
Fixed Assets Sold	$ 341	$ 87	$ 69	$ 91	$ 45
Fixed Assets Acquired	(755)	(812)	(851)	(769)	(733)
Acquisition of Bottlers	(267)	(359)	(544)	(651)	(397)
Change in Marketable Securities	115	(30)	102	(1)	(218)
Other Investing Transactions	63	178	159	142	138
Cash Flow from Investing	$ (503)	$ (936)	$(1,065)	$(1,188)	$(1,165)
Financing					
Increase in Long-Term Borrowing	$ 3,030	$ 1,026	$ 1,622	$ 3,011	$ 3,671
Issue of Common Stock	193	98	107	164	331
Decrease in Long-Term Borrowing	(1,316)	(1,119)	(2,378)	(3,937)	(4,256)
Acquisition of Common Stock	(1,739)	(1,440)	(691)	(277)	(133)
Dividends	(2,429)	(2,166)	(1,987)	(1,791)	(1,685)
Other	141	183	44	(45)	(140)
Cash Flow from Financing	$(2,120)	$(3,418)	$(3,283)	$(2,875)	$(2,212)
Change in Cash	$ 3,345	$ 1,102	$ 394	$ 47	$ 208
Cash—Beginning of Year	3,362	2,260	1,866	1,819	1,611
Cash—End of Year	$ 6,707	$ 3,362	$ 2,260	$ 1,866	$ 1,819
Change in Sales from Previous Year	+4.4%	+7.6%	+11.5%	− 4.4%	+3.5%

EXHIBIT 3.16

Texas Instruments
Statement of Cash Flows
(amounts in millions)
(Problem 3.15)

	Year 4	Year 3	Year 2	Year 1	Year 0
Operations					
Net Income (Loss)	$ 1,861	$1,198	$ (344)	$ (201)	$ 3,087
Depreciation and Amortization	1,549	1,528	1,689	1,828	1,376
Deferred Income Taxes	68	75	13	19	1
Other Additions (Subtractions)	(179)	(469)	709	(68)	(2,141)
(Increase) Decrease in Accounts Receivable	(238)	(197)	(114)	958	(377)
(Increase) Decrease in Inventories	(272)	(194)	(39)	482	(372)
(Increase) Decrease in Prepayments	134	(183)	191	(235)	56
Increase (Decrease) in Accounts Payable	(71)	264	(81)	(687)	246
Increase (Decrease) in Other Current Liabilities	294	129	(32)	(277)	309
Cash Flow from Operations	$ 3,146	$2,151	$ 1,992	$ 1,819	$ 2,185
Investing					
Fixed Assets Acquired	$(1,298)	$ (800)	$ (802)	$(1,790)	$(2,762)
Change in Marketable Securities	145	86	(238)	164	834
Acquisition of Businesses	(8)	(128)	(69)	—	(3)
Other Investing Transactions	—	—	—	—	107
Cash Flow from Investing	$(1,161)	$ (842)	$(1,109)	$(1,626)	$(1,824)
Financing					
Increase in Short-Term Borrowing	$ —	$ —	$ 9	$ —	$ 23
Increase in Long-Term Borrowing	—	—	—	3	250
Issue of Common Stock	192	157	167	183	242
Decrease in Short-Term Borrowing	(6)	(8)	(16)	(3)	(19)
Decrease in Long-Term Borrowing	(429)	(418)	(22)	(132)	(307)
Acquisition of Common Stock	(753)	(284)	(370)	(395)	(155)
Dividends	(154)	(147)	(147)	(147)	(141)
Other Financing Transactions	15	260	14	(16)	(290)
Cash Flow from Financing	$(1,135)	$ (440)	$ (365)	$ (507)	$ (397)
Change in Cash	$ 850	$ 869	$ 518	$ (314)	$ (36)
Cash—Beginning of Year	1,818	949	431	745	781
Cash—End of Year	$ 2,668	$1,818	$ 949	$ 431	$ 745
Change in Sales from Previous Year	+27.9%	+17.3%	+2.2%	−30.9%	−1.9%

EXHIBIT 3.17

The Gap
Statement of Cash Flows
(amounts in millions)
(Problem 3.16)

	Year 4	Year 3	Year 2	Year 1	Year 0
Operations					
Net Income (Loss)	$ 1,150	$ 1,031	$ 478	$ (8)	$ 877
Depreciation	620	675	706	811	590
Other Additions and Subtractions	(28)	180	166	30	92
(Increase) Decrease in Inventories	(90)	385	(258)	213	(455)
(Increase) Decrease in Prepayments	(18)	5	33	(13)	(61)
Increase (Decrease) in Accounts Payable	42	(10)	(47)	42	250
Increase (Decrease) in Other Current Liabilities	(56)	(106)	165	243	(3)
Cash Flow from Operations	$ 1,620	$ 2,160	$1,243	$1,318	$ 1,290
Investing					
Fixed Assets Acquired	$ (442)	$ (261)	(308)	(940)	(1,859)
Changes in Marketable Securities	259	(2,063)	(313)	—	—
Other Investing Transactions	343	6	(8)	(11)	(16)
Cash Flow from Investing	$ 160	$(2,318)	$ (629)	$ (951)	$(1,875)
Financing					
Increase in Short-Term Borrowing	$ —	$ —	$ —	$ —	$ 621
Increase in Long-Term Borrowing	—	85	1,346	1,194	250
Issue of Capital Stock	130	26	153	139	152
Decrease in Short-Term Borrowing	—	0	(42)	(735)	—
Decrease in Long-Term Borrowing	(871)	(668)	—	(250)	—
Acquisition of Capital Stock	(976)	—	—	(1)	(393)
Dividends	(79)	(79)	(78)	(76)	(75)
Other Financing Transactions	—	28	27	(11)	(11)
Cash Flow from Financing	$(1,796)	$ (608)	$1,406	$ 260	$ 544
Change in Cash	$ (16)	$ (766)	$2,020	$ 627	$ (41)
Cash—Beginning of Year	2,261	3,027	1,007	380	421
Cash—End of Year	$ 2,245	$ 2,261	$3,027	$1,007	$ 380
Change in Sales from Previous Year	+2.6%	+9.7%	+4.4%	+1.3%	+17.5%

selected automobiles. Exhibit 3.18 presents a statement of cash flows for XM Satellite Radio for Year 2, Year 3, and Year 4.

Required

Discuss the relation between net loss and cash flow from operations and the pattern of cash flow from operating, investing, and financing activities during the three years.

EXHIBIT 3.18

XM Satellite Radio
Statement of Cash Flows
(amounts in thousands)
(Problem 3.17)

	Year 4	Year 3	Year 2
Operations			
Net Loss	$(650,033)	$(589,759)	$(491,585)
Depreciation and Amortization	145,775	156,927	117,202
Amortization of Deferred Financing Fees	17,676	15,496	4,479
Stock-Based Compensation	2,020	3,003	1,507
Interest on Zero Coupon Bonds	53,222	45,227	—
Deferred Income Taxes	27,317	—	—
Loss on Conversion of Notes	66,279	29,904	—
Impairment of Goodwill	—	—	11,461
Other Additions and Subtractions	3,203	1,414	163
(Increase) Decrease in Accounts Receivable	(8,407)	(11,480)	(3,772)
(Increase) Decrease in Prepayments	(381)	(7,095)	4,189
Increase (Decrease) in Accounts Payable	52,657	80,496	25,940
Increase in Payable to Deferred Revenue	98,463	41,587	11,242
Increase (Decrease) in Other Current Liabilities	85,317	13,009	31,132
Cash Flow from Operations	$(106,892)	$(221,271)	$(288,042)
Investing			
Fixed Assets Acquired	$(142,449)	$ (18,335)	$ (68,437)
Change in Marketable Securities	119	22,750	54,343
Insurance Proceeds	133,924	—	—
Other Investing Transactions	—	2,272	—
Cash Flow from Investing	$ (8,406)	$ 6,687	$ (14,094)
Financing			
Issue of Common Stock	$ 304,846	$ 11,768	$ 249,150
Increase in Long-Term Borrowing	200,000	293,132	—
Decrease in Long-Term Borrowing	(272,430)	(2,722)	(2,440)
Other Financing Transactions	(4,816)	(4,101)	(216)
Cash Flow from Financing	$ 227,600	$ 298,077	$ 246,494
Change in Cash	$ 112,302	$ 83,493	$ (55,642)
Cash—Beginning of Year	90,219	6,726	62,368
Cash—End of Year	$ 202,521	$ 90,219	$ 6,726
Growth in Revenues from Previous Year	+166.7%	354.8%	3,686.3%

3.18 INTERPRETING THE STATEMENT OF CASH FLOWS. Sunbeam Corporation manufactures and sells a variety of small household appliances, including toasters, food processors, and waffle grills. Exhibit 3.19 presents a statement of cash flows for Sunbeam for Year 5, Year 6, and Year 7. After experiencing decreased sales in Year 5,

EXHIBIT 3.19

Sunbeam Corporation
Statement of Cash Flows
(amounts in millions)
(Problem 3.18)

	Year 7	Year 6	Year 5
Operations			
Net Income (Loss)	$109.4	$(228.3)	$ 50.5
Depreciation and Amortization	38.6	47.4	44.2
Restructuring and Asset Impairment Charges	—	283.7	—
Deferred Income Taxes	57.8	(77.8)	25.1
Other Additions	13.7	46.2	10.8
Other Subtractions	(84.6)	(27.1)	(21.7)
(Increase) Decrease in Accounts Receivable	(84.6)	(13.8)	(4.5)
(Increase) Decrease in Inventories	(100.8)	(11.6)	(4.9)
(Increase) Decrease in Prepayments	(9.0)	2.7	(8.8)
Increase (Decrease) in Accounts Payable	(1.6)	14.7	9.2
Increase (Decrease) in Other Current Liabilities	52.8	(21.9)	(18.4)
Cash Flow from Operations	$ (8.3)	$ 14.2	$ 81.5
Investing			
Fixed Assets Acquired	$(58.3)	$ (75.3)	$(140.1)
Sale of Businesses	91.0	—	65.3
Acquisitions of Businesses	—	(.9)	(33.0)
Cash Flow from Investing	$ 32.7	$ (76.2)	$(107.4)
Financing			
Increase (Decrease) in Short-Term Borrowing	$ 5.0	$ 30.0	$ 40.0
Increase in Long-Term Debt	—	11.5	—
Issue of Common Stock	26.6	9.2	9.8
Decrease in Long-Term Debt	(12.2)	(1.8)	(5.4)
Acquisition of Common Stock	—	—	(13.0)
Dividends	(3.4)	(3.3)	(3.3)
Other Financing Transactions	.5	(.4)	(.2)
Cash Flow from Financing	$ 16.5	$ 45.2	$ 27.9
Change in Cash	$ 40.9	$ (16.8)	$ 2.0
Cash—Beginning of Year	11.5	28.3	26.3
Cash—End of Year	$ 52.4	$ 11.5	$ 28.3
Growth in Revenues from Previous Year	18.7%	−3.2%	−2.6%

Sunbeam hired Albert Dunlap in Year 6 try to turn the company around. Albert Dunlap, known in the industry as "Chainsaw Al," had directed restructuring efforts at Scott Paper Company previously. The restructuring effort at Sunbeam generally involved firing employees and cutting costs aggressively. Most of these restructuring efforts took place during Year 6. The market expected significantly improved results in Year 7. Reported sales increased 18.7 percent between Year 6 and Year 7 and net income improved. However, subsequent revelations showed that almost half of the sales increase resulted from recognizing revenues in the fourth quarter of Year 7 that the firm should have recognized in the first quarter of Year 8.

Required

a. Using information in the statement of cash flows for Year 5, identify any signals that Sunbeam was experiencing operating difficulties and in need of restructuring.
b. Using information in the statement of cash flows for Year 6, identify indicators of the turnaround efforts and any relations between cash flows that trouble you.
c. Using information in the statement of cash flows for Year 7, indicate any signals that the firm might have overstated its revenues and had not yet fixed its operating problems.

3.19 INTERPRETING THE STATEMENT OF CASH FLOWS. Montgomery Ward operates a retail department store chain. It filed for bankruptcy during the first quarter of Year 12. Exhibit 3.20 presents a statement of cash flows for Montgomery Ward for Year 7 to Year 11. The firm acquired Lechmere, a discount retailer of sporting goods and electronic products, during Year 9. It acquired Amoco Enterprises, an automobile club, during Year 11. During Year 10, it issued a new series of preferred stock and used the cash proceeds in part to repurchase a series of outstanding preferred stock. The "other subtractions" in the operating section for Year 10 and Year 11 represent reversals of deferred tax liabilities.

Required

Discuss the relationship between net income and cash flow from operations and between cash flows from operating, investing, and financing activities for the firm over the five-year period. Identify signals of Montgomery Ward's difficulties that might have led to its filing for bankruptcy.

3.20 IDENTIFYING INDUSTRY DIFFERENCES IN STATEMENT OF CASH FLOWS. Exhibit 3.21 presents common-size statements of cash flows for eight firms in various industries. All amounts in the common-size statements of cash flows are expressed as a percentage of cash flow from operations. To construct the common-size percentages for each firm, reported amounts for each firm for three consecutive years were summed and the common-size percentages are based on the summed amounts. This procedure reduces the effects of a nonrecurring item in a particular year, such as a major debt or common stock issue. Exhibit 3.21 also shows the compound annual rate of growth in revenues over the three-year period. The eight companies are as follows:

1. Biogen: creates and manufactures biotechnology drugs. Many drugs are still in the development phase in this high-growth, relatively young industry. Research and manufacturing facilities are capital intensive, although the research process requires skilled scientists.
2. ChevronTexaco: explores, extracts, refines, and markets petroleum products. Extraction and refining activities are capital intensive. Petroleum products are in the mature phase of their product life cycles.

EXHIBIT 3.20

Montgomery Ward
Statement of Cash Flows
(amounts in millions)
(Problem 3.19)

	Year 11	Year 10	Year 9	Year 8	Year 7
Operating					
Net Income	$(237)	$ (9)	$ 109	$ 101	$ 100
Depreciation	122	115	109	98	97
Other Addbacks	13	8	24	25	32
Other Subtractions	(197)	(119)	(29)	—	—
(Increase) Decrease in Accounts Receivable	(32)	(54)	(38)	(9)	9
(Increase) Decrease in Inventories	225	(112)	(229)	(204)	(38)
(Increase) Decrease in Prepayments	27	(32)	(39)	(58)	36
Increase (Decrease) in Accounts Payable	(222)	85	291	148	(17)
Increase (Decrease) in Other Current Liabilities	(55)	(64)	(45)	28	(64)
Cash Flow from Operations	$(356)	$(182)	$ 153	$ 129	$ 155
Investing					
Fixed Assets Acquired	$ (75)	$(122)	$(184)	$(142)	$(146)
Change in Marketable Securities	20	(14)	(4)	(27)	137
Other Investing Transactions	(93)	27	(113)	6	9
Cash Flow from Investing	$(148)	$(109)	$(301)	$(163)	$—
Financing					
Increase in Short-Term Borrowing	$ 588	$ 16	$ 144	$ —	$—
Increase in Long-Term Borrowing	—	205	168	100	—
Issue of Capital Stock	3	193	78	1	1
Decrease in Short-Term Borrowing	—	—	—	—	—
Decrease in Long-Term Borrowing	(63)	(17)	(275)	(18)	(403)
Acquisition of Capital Stock	(20)	(98)	(9)	(11)	(97)
Dividends	(9)	(4)	(24)	(23)	(19)
Other	—	—	1	2	2
Cash Flow from Financing	$ 499	$ 295	$ 83	$ 51	$(516)
Change in Cash	$ (5)	$ 4	$ (65)	$ 17	$(361)
Cash—Beginning of Year	37	33	98	81	442
Cash—End of Year	$ 32	$ 37	$ 33	$ 98	$ 81
Change in Sales from Previous Year	−10.0%	−.5%	+17.2%	+3.7%	+2.0%

3. H. J. Heinz: manufactures and markets branded consumer food products. Heinz has acquired several other branded food products companies in recent years.
4. Home Depot: retails home improvement products. Home Depot competes in a new retail category known as "category killer" stores. Such stores offer a wide selection of products in a particular product category (for example, books, pet products, office products). These stores have taken significant market share away from the more diversified department and discount stores in recent years.
5. Inland Steel: manufactures steel products. Although steel plants are capital intensive, they also use unionized workers to process iron into steel products. Demand for steel products follows cyclical trends in the economy. Steel manufacturing in the United States is in the mature phase of its life cycle.
6. Pacific Gas & Electric: provides electric and gas utility services. The electric utility industry in the United States has excess capacity. Increased competition from less regulated, more open markets has forced down prices and led some utilities to reduce their capacity.
7. ServiceMaster: provides home cleaning and restoration services. ServiceMaster has recently acquired firms offering cleaning services for health care facilities and broadened its home services to include termite protection, garden care, and other services. ServiceMaster operates as a partnership. Partnerships do not pay income taxes on their earnings each year. Instead, partners (owners) include their share of the earnings of ServiceMaster in their taxable income.
8. Sun Microsystems: creates, manufactures, and markets computers, primarily to the scientific and engineering markets and to network applications. Sun follows an assembly strategy in manufacturing computers, outsourcing the components from various other firms worldwide. Sun has been rumored to be a takeover target by larger technology companies in recent years.

Required

Use whatever clues you can to match the companies in Exhibit 3.21 with the companies listed here. Discuss the reasoning for your selection in each case.

3.21 PREPARING A STATEMENT OF CASH FLOWS FROM BALANCE SHEETS AND INCOME STATEMENTS. Fuso Pharmaceutical Industries develops, manufactures, and markets pharmaceutical products in Japan. Its main product is a solution used by individuals with artificial kidneys. Most individuals in Japan are covered by a national health insurance system. The Japanese government sets the policies for the proportion of health care costs covered by the government versus the proportion that is the responsibility of the individual. The government also establishes the prices for prescription drugs. The Japanese economy experienced recessionary conditions in recent years. In response to these conditions, the Japanese government increased the proportion of medical costs that is the patient's responsibility and lowered the prices for prescription drugs. Exhibit 3.22 presents the firm's balance sheets on March 31 of Year 1 to Year 4, and Exhibit 3.23 presents the firm's income statements for the years ending March 31, Year 2 to Year 4.

Required

a. Prepare a worksheet for the preparation of a statement of cash flows for Fuso Pharmaceutical Industries for each of the years ending March 31, Year 2 to Year 4.

EXHIBIT 3.21

Common-Size Statements of Cash Flows for Selected Companies (Problem 3.20)

	1	2	3	4	5	6	7	8
Operations								
Net Income	34.9%	38.6%	40.9%	45.4%	61.2%	62.4%	76.5%	97.6%
Depreciation	47.9	55.2	62.9	37.7	46.0	22.3	38.0	23.3
Other	3.1	24.3	5.1	(5.0)	9.4	11.6	2.3	3.9
(Increase) Decrease in Accounts Receivable	6.5	(4.8)	(.6)	(12.4)	(34.2)	(7.8)	(6.8)	(8.5)
(Increase) Decrease in Inventories	1.5	(15.1)	(1.2)	(14.4)	(11.9)	(3.1)	(7.4)	(58.4)
Increase (Decrease) in Accounts Payable	1.5	3.1	(5.6)	12.4	3.0	2.9	12.6	39.9
Increase (Decrease) in Other Current Liabilities	4.6	(1.3)	(1.5)	36.3	26.5	11.7	(15.2)	2.2
Cash Flow from Operations	100.0%	100.0%	100.0%	100.0%	100.0%	100.0%	100.0%	100.0%
Investing								
Fixed Assets Acquired	(37.1%)	(64.0%)	(81.1%)	(165.7%)	(44.7%)	(13.4%)	(39.3%)	(153.4%)
Change in Marketable Securities	—	—	(2.8)	(75.1)	(14.8)	(3.5)	5.9	(17.5)
Other Investing Transactions	(7.7)	8.5	16.4	(28.4)	(15.9)	(17.3)	(40.6)	23.2
Cash Flow from Investing	(44.8%)	(55.5%)	(67.5%)	(269.2%)	(75.4%)	(34.2%)	(74.0%)	(147.7%)
Financing								
Change in Short-Term Debt	(.6%)	—	(7.4%)	—	(2.4%)	—	7.9%	—
Increase in Long-Term Debt	19.5	41.4%	8.4	75.7%	—	33.1%	24.0	46.9%
Issue of Capital Stock	11.2	9.9	—	82.5	17.7	1.7	6.7	13.5
Decrease in Long-Term Debt	(36.0)	(85.0)	(9.1)	(2.7)	(7.0)	(27.6)	(3.1)	(1.2)
Repurchase of Capital Stock	(18.9)	(1.5)	(.1)	—	(50.7)	(21.4)	(26.9)	—
Dividends	(29.5)	(10.9)	(29.9)	—	—	(46.1)	(43.5)	(11.5)
Other Financing Transactions	—	—	(.2)	—	—	.6	9.8	1.9
Cash Flow from Financing	(54.3%)	(46.1%)	(38.3%)	155.5%	(42.4%)	(59.7%)	(25.1%)	49.6%
Net Change in Cash	.9%	(1.6%)	(5.8%)	13.7%	(17.8%)	6.1%	.9%	1.9%
Growth in Revenues	(3.6%)	5.7%	5.7%	23.0%	18.2%	7.7%	8.6%	28.3%

EXHIBIT 3.22

Fuso Pharmaceutical Industries
Balance Sheets
(amounts in millions of yen)
(Problem 3.21)

March 31:	Year 4	Year 3	Year 2	Year 1
Assets				
Cash	¥ 6,233	¥ 4,569	¥ 4,513	¥ 5,008
Accounts and Notes Receivable—Trade	19,003	17,828	19,703	19,457
Inventories	7,693	7,948	8,706	8,607
Deferred Income Taxes	1,355	1,192	948	824
Prepayments	432	325	640	634
Total Current Assets	¥34,716	¥31,862	¥34,510	¥34,530
Investments	3,309	2,356	3,204	4,997
Property, Plant, and Equipment, at cost	71,792	71,510	71,326	71,018
Less Accumulated Depreciation	(40,689)	(38,912)	(36,854)	(35,797)
Deferred Income Taxes	236	1,608	1,481	494
Other Assets	4,551	3,904	3,312	3,463
Total Assets	¥73,915	¥72,328	¥76,979	¥78,705
Liabilities and Shareholders' Equity				
Accounts and Notes Payable—Trade	¥10,087	¥ 9,629	¥10,851	¥10,804
Notes Payable to Banks	10,360	10,328	9,779	10,023
Current Portion of Long-Term Debt	100	200	—	—
Other Current Liabilities	7,200	6,170	9,779	7,565
Total Current Liabilities	¥27,747	¥26,327	¥30,409	¥28,392
Long-Term Debt	8,140	7,889	6,487	8,147
Deferred Income Taxes	3,361	—	—	—
Employee Retirement Benefits	809	905	1,087	1,166
Other Noncurrent Liabilities	175	174	200	216
Total Liabilities	¥40,232	¥35,295	¥38,183	¥37,921
Common Stock	¥10,758	¥10,758	¥10,758	¥10,758
Additional Paid-In Capital	15,012	15,012	15,012	15,012
Retained Earnings	9,179	11,838	13,697	15,014
Accumulated Other Comprehensive Income	(342)	(490)	(659)	—
Treasury Stock	(924)	(85)	(12)	—
Total Shareholders' Equity	¥33,683	¥37,033	¥38,796	¥40,784
Total Liabilities and Shareholders' Equity	¥73,915	¥72,328	¥76,979	¥78,705

Follow the format of Exhibit 3.11 in the text. Notes to the financial statements indicate the following:

(1) The changes in Accumulated Other Comprehensive Income relate to revaluations of Investments in Securities to market value. The remaining changes in

EXHIBIT 3.23

Fuso Pharmaceutical Industries
Income Statements
(amounts in millions of yen)
(Problem 3.21)

Year Ended March 31:	Year 4	Year 3	Year 2
Sales	¥ 41,352	¥ 41,926	¥ 44,226
Cost of Goods Sold	(27,667)	(27,850)	(28,966)
Selling and Administrative Expenses	(13,396)	(15,243)	(15,283)
Interest Expense	(338)	(364)	(368)
Income Tax Expense	(1,823)	443	34
Net Income	¥ (1,872)	¥ (1,088)	¥ (357)

Investments in Securities result from purchases and sales. Assume that the sales occurred at no gain or loss.

(2) There were no sales of property, plant, and equipment during the three-year period.
(3) The changes in Other Noncurrent Assets are investing activities.
(4) The changes in Employee Retirement Benefits relate to provisions made for retirement benefits net of payments made to retired employees, both of which the statement of cash flows classifies as operating activities.
(5) The changes in Other Noncurrent Liabilities are financing activities.

b. Prepare a comparative statement of cash flows for Year 2, Year 3, and Year 4.

c. Discuss the relation between net income and cash flow from operations, and the pattern of cash flows from operating, investing, and financing transactions for Year 2, Year 3, and Year 4.

3.22 PREPARING A STATEMENT OF CASH FLOWS FROM BALANCE SHEETS AND INCOME STATEMENTS. Flight Training Corporation is a privately held firm that provides fighter pilot training under contracts with the U.S. Air Force and the U.S. Navy. The firm owns approximately 100 Lear jets that it equips with radar jammers and other sophisticated electronic devices to mimic enemy aircraft. The company recently experienced cash shortages to pay its bills. The owner and manager of Flight Training Corporation stated: "I was just dumbfounded. I never had an inkling that there was a problem with cash."

Exhibit 3.24 presents comparative balance sheets for Flight Training Corporation on December 31, Year 1 through Year 4, and Exhibit 3.25 presents income statements for Year 2 through Year 4.

Required

a. Prepare a worksheet for the preparation of a statement of cash flows for Flight Training Corporation for each of the years ending December 31, Year 2 through

EXHIBIT 3.24

Flight Training Corporation
Balance Sheets
(amounts in thousands)
(Problem 3.22)

December 31:	Year 4	Year 3	Year 2	Year 1
Current Assets				
Cash	$ 159	$ 583	$ 313	$ 142
Accounts Receivable	6,545	4,874	2,675	2,490
Inventories	5,106	2,514	1,552	602
Prepayments	665	829	469	57
Total Current Assets	$ 12,475	$ 8,800	$ 5,009	$ 3,291
Noncurrent Assets				
Property, Plant, and Equipment	$106,529	$76,975	$24,039	$17,809
Less Accumulated Depreciation	(17,231)	(8,843)	(5,713)	(4,288)
Net	$ 89,298	$68,132	$18,326	$13,521
Other Assets	$ 470	$ 665	$ 641	$ 1,112
Total Assets	$102,243	$77,597	$23,976	$17,924
Current Liabilities				
Accounts Payable	$ 12,428	$ 6,279	$ 993	$ 939
Notes Payable	—	945	140	1,021
Current Portion of Long-Term Debt	60,590	7,018	1,789	1,104
Other Current Liabilities	12,903	12,124	2,423	1,310
Total Current Liabilities	$ 85,921	$26,366	$ 5,345	$ 4,374
Noncurrent Liabilities				
Long-Term Debt	$ —	$41,021	$ 9,804	$ 6,738
Deferred Income Taxes	—	900	803	—
Other Noncurrent Liabilities	—	—	226	—
Total Liabilities	$ 85,921	$68,287	$16,178	$11,112
Shareholders' Equity				
Common Stock	$ 34	$ 22	$ 21	$ 20
Additional Paid-In Capital	16,516	5,685	4,569	4,323
Retained Earnings	(29)	3,802	3,208	2,469
Treasury Stock	(199)	(199)	—	—
Total Shareholders' Equity	$ 16,322	$ 9,310	$ 7,798	$ 6,812
Total Liabilities and Shareholders' Equity	$102,243	$77,597	$23,976	$17,924

EXHIBIT 3.25

Flight Training Corporation
Comparative Income Statement
(amounts in thousands)
(Problem 3.22)

Year Ended December 31:	Year 4	Year 3	Year 2
Continuing Operations			
Sales	$54,988	$36,597	$20,758
Expenses			
Cost of Services	47,997	29,594	14,247
Selling and Administrative	5,881	2,972	3,868
Interest	5,841	3,058	1,101
Income Taxes	(900)	379	803
Total Expenses	$58,819	$36,003	$20,019
Net Income	$ (3,831)	$ 594	$ 739

Year 4. Follow the format of Exhibit 3.11 in the text. Notes to the financial statements indicate the following:

(1) The firm did not sell any aircraft during the three-year period.
(2) Changes in Other Noncurrent Assets are investing transactions.
(3) Changes in Deferred Income Taxes are operating transactions.
(4) Changes in Other Noncurrent Liabilities and Treasury Stock are financing transactions.
(5) The firm violated covenants in its borrowing agreements during Year 4. The lenders can therefore require Flight Training Corporation to repay its long-term debt immediately. Although the banks have not yet demanded payment, the firm reclassified its long-term debt as a current liability.

b. Prepare a comparative statement of cash flows for Flight Training Corporation for each of the years ending December 31, Year 2 through Year 4.

c. Comment on the relation between net income and cash flow from operations and the pattern of cash flows from operating, investing, and financing activities for each of the three years.

d. Describe the likely reasons for the cash flow difficulties of Flight Training Corporation.

3.23 PREPARING A STATEMENT OF CASH FLOWS FROM BALANCE SHEETS AND INCOME STATEMENTS. GTI, Inc. manufactures parts, components, and processing equipment for electronics and semiconductor applications in the communications, computer, automotive, and appliance industries. Its sales tend to vary with changes in the business cycle because the sales of most of its customers are cyclical. Exhibit 3.26 presents balance sheets for GTI as of December 31, Year 7 through Year 9, and Exhibit 3.27 presents income statements for Year 8 and Year 9.

EXHIBIT 3.26

GTI, Inc.
Balance Sheets
(amounts in thousands)
(Problem 3.23)

December 31:	Year 9	Year 8	Year 7
Assets			
Cash	$ 367	$ 475	$ 430
Accounts Receivable	2,545	3,936	3,768
Inventories	2,094	2,966	2,334
Prepayments	122	270	116
Total Current Assets	$5,128	$ 7,647	$ 6,648
Property, Plant, and Equipment, net	4,027	4,598	3,806
Other Assets	456	559	193
Total Assets	$9,611	$12,804	$10,647
Liabilities and Shareholders' Equity			
Accounts Payable	$ 796	$ 809	$ 1,578
Notes Payable to Banks	2,413	231	11
Other Current Liabilities	695	777	1,076
Total Current Liabilities	$3,904	$ 1,817	$ 2,665
Long-Term Debt	2,084	4,692	2,353
Deferred Income Taxes	113	89	126
Total Liabilities	$6,101	$ 6,598	$ 5,144
Preferred Stock	$ 289	$ 289	$ —
Common Stock	85	85	83
Additional Paid-In Capital	4,395	4,392	4,385
Retained Earnings	(1,259)	1,440	1,035
Total Shareholders' Equity	$3,510	$ 6,206	$ 5,503
Total Liabilities and Shareholders' Equity	$9,611	$12,804	$10,647

Required

a. Prepare a worksheet for the preparation of a statement of cash flows for GTI, Inc. for Year 8 and Year 9. Follow the format of Exhibit 3.11 in the text. Notes to the firm's financial statements reveal the following (amounts in thousands):

(1) Depreciation expense was $641 in Year 8 and $625 in Year 9. GTI, Inc. did not sell any fixed assets during Year 8 and Year 9.

(2) Other Assets represents patents. Patent amortization was $25 in Year 8 and $40 in Year 9. GTI, Inc. sold a patent during Year 9 at no gain or loss.

(3) Changes in Deferred Income Taxes are operating transactions.

b. Discuss the relation between net income and cash flow from operations, and the pattern of cash flows from operating, investing, and financing activities.

EXHIBIT 3.27

GTI, Inc.
Income Statements
(amounts in thousands)
(Problem 3.23)

Year Ended December 31:	Year 9	Year 8
Sales	$11,960	$22,833
Cost of Goods Sold	(11,031)	(16,518)
Selling and Administrative Expenses	(3,496)	(4,849)
Interest Expense	(452)	(459)
Income Tax Expense	328	(590)
Net Income	$ (2,691)	$ 417
Dividends on Preferred Stock	(8)	(12)
Net Income Available to Common	$ (2,699)	$ 405

INTEGRATIVE CASE 3.1

STARBUCKS

Exhibit 3.28 presents a statement of cash flows for Starbucks for Year 2, Year 3, and Year 4. This statement is an expanded version of the statement of cash flows for Starbucks in Exhibit 1.26.

Required

a. Explain why equity in income of investees appears as a subtraction when converting net income to cash flow from operations.

b. Compute the amount of cash received from investees as dividends each year. To respond to this question, you will need to refer to the income statement of Starbucks in Exhibit 1.25 in Chapter 1 (Integrative Case 1.1).

c. Explain why stock options appears as an addition to net income when computing cash flow from operations.

d. Discuss the relation between net income and cash flow from operations for each of the three years.

e. Discuss the relation between cash flows from operating, investing, and financing activities for each of the three years.

f. Refer to the income statement for Starbucks in Exhibit 1.25 in Chapter 1 (Integrative Case 1.1). Compute the amount of EBITDA for Year 2, Year 3, and Year 4.

g. Prepare a graph that portrays EBITDA, net income plus Type 1 adjustments, cash flow from operations, and net income. Discuss the relationships between the patterns of these four measures for the three years.

EXHIBIT 3.28

Starbucks Corporation
Comparative Statements of Cash Flows
(amounts in millions)
(Integrative Case 3.1)

Year Ended September 30:	Year 4	Year 3	Year 2
Operations			
Net Income	$ 390.6	$ 266.8	$ 211.4
Depreciation and Amortization	314.0	266.3	226.3
Asset Impairments and Disposals	13.6	7.8	26.9
Deferred Income Taxes	(3.8)	(6.8)	(6.9)
Equity in Income of Investees	(33.4)	(22.8)	(19.6)
Stock Options	63.4	36.6	44.2
Other Adjustments	11.5	5.9	(13.5)
Changes in Operating Working Capital:			
(Increase) Decrease in Receivables	(25.7)	(16.9)	(7.2)
(Increase) Decrease in Inventories	(77.7)	(64.8)	(41.4)
(Increase) Decrease in Prepayments	9.1	4.0	(5.3)
Increase (Decrease) in Accounts Payable	27.9	25.0	5.5
Increase (Decrease) in Other Current Liabilities	130.5	85.9	76.0
Cash Flow from Operations	$ 820.0	$ 587.0	$ 496.4
Investing			
Marketable Securities and Investments Sold	$ 354.6	$ 269.6	$ 223.1
Acquisition of Property, Plant, and Equipment	(412.5)	(378.0)	(394.3)
Marketable Securities and Investments Purchased	(566.6)	(323.3)	(340.0)
Other Investing	(33.9)	(88.2)	7.0
Cash Flow from Investing	$(658.4)	$(519.9)	$(504.2)
Financing			
Issue of Common Stock	$ 137.6	$ 107.2	$ 107.5
Decrease in Long-Term Borrowing	(.7)	(.7)	(.7)
Acquisition of Common Stock	(203.4)	(75.7)	(52.2)
Other Financing	3.1	3.3	1.6
Cash Flow from Financing	$ (63.4)	$ 34.1	$ 56.2
Change in Cash	$ 98.2	$ 101.2	$ 48.4
Cash, Beginning of Year	200.9	99.7	51.3
Cash, End of Year	$ 299.1	$ 200.9	$ 99.7

CASE 3.2

PRIME CONTRACTORS

Prime Contractors (Prime) is a privately owned company that contracts with the U.S. government to provide various services under multiyear (usually five-year) contracts. Its principal services are as follows:

Refuse: Picks up and disposes of refuse from military bases.
Shuttle: Provides parking and shuttle services on government-sponsored research campuses.
Animal Care: Provides feeding and veterinary care for animals used in research at government-sponsored facilities.

Prime's sales mix for the years ending September 30, Year 6 to Year 10, is as follows:

	Refuse Services	Shuttle Services	Animal Care Services
Year 6	59.9%	40.1%	—
Year 7	48.5%	31.2%	20.3%
Year 8	20.7%	22.0%	57.3%
Year 9	11.4%	26.9%	61.7%
Year 10	7.1%	22.5%	70.4%

As the sales mix data indicate, Prime engaged in a strategic shift beginning in Year 7. It began to exit the refuse-services business and geared up its animal-care services business. Exhibit 3.29 presents a statement of cash flows for Prime for Year 6 to Year 10.

Required

a. What evidence do you see in Exhibit 3.29 of Prime's strategic shift from refuse services to animal-care services?

b. Discuss how Prime's net income could decline between Year 6 and Year 8 while its cash flow from operations increased.

c. Discuss how Prime's net income could increase between Year 8 and Year 10 while its cash flow from operations decreased.

d. What is the likely reason that the adjustment for deferred income taxes when converting net income to cash flow from operations was an addition in Year 6 to Year 8 but a subtraction in Year 9 and Year 10?

e. Explain why gains on the disposition of fixed assets appear as a subtraction from net income when computing cash flow from operations.

f. Prime increased its long-term debt net in Year 6 and Year 7 but decreased it net in Year 8 to Year 10. What is the likely reason for this shift in financing?

EXHIBIT 3.29

Prime Contractors
Statement of Cash Flows
(amounts in thousands)
(Case 3.2)

	Year 10	Year 9	Year 8	Year 7	Year 6
Operations					
Net Income	$ 568	$ 474	$ 47	$ 249	$ 261
Depreciation	595	665	827	616	306
Deferred Income Taxes	(139)	(110)	55	180	159
Loss (Gain) on Disposition of Fixed Assets	(82)	(178)	—	—	20
Other Additions and Subtractions	(4)	(19)	(52)	(7)	2
(Increase) Decrease in Accounts Receivable	62	(865)	(263)	(647)	(1,421)
(Increase) Decrease in Other Current Assets	19	(9)	(40)	(26)	(38)
Increase (Decrease) in Accounts Payable	(174)	(272)	(33)	(177)	507
Increase (Decrease) in Other Current Liabilities	(310)	926	423	100	268
Cash Flow from Operations	$ 535	$ 612	$ 964	$ 288	$ 64
Investing					
Fixed Assets Sold	$ 146	$ 118	$ —	$ —	$ 80
Fixed Assets Acquired	(15)	(19)	(56)	(911)	(2,003)
Other Investing Transactions	37	—	—	62	(17)
Cash Flow from Investing	$ 168	$ 99	$ (56)	$(849)	$(1,940)
Financing					
Increase Decrease in Short-Term Borrowing	$ 324	$ 12	$ (127)	$ 276	$ 204
Increase in Long-Term Borrowing	—	—	208	911	1,987
Decrease in Long-Term Borrowing	(960)	(742)	(1,011)	(658)	(423)
Cash Flow from Financing	$(634)	$(730)	$ (930)	$ 529	$ 1,768
Change in Cash	$ 69	$ (19)	$ (22)	$ (32)	$ (108)
Cash—Beginning of Year	6	25	47	79	187
Cash—End of Year	$ 75	$ 6	$ 25	$ 47	$ 79
Change in Sales from Previous Year	+15.5%	+18.0%	+38.5%	+47.1%	+53.5%

CASE 3.3

W. T. GRANT COMPANY[11]

When it filed for bankruptcy in October 1975, W. T. Grant (Grant) was the seventeenth largest retailer in the United States, with almost 1,200 stores, more than 82,000 employees, and sales of $1.7 billion. It had paid dividends consistently since 1906. The collapse of Grant came largely as a surprise to the capital markets, particularly to the banks that provided short-term working capital loans. Grant had altered its business strategy in the mid-1960s to transform itself from an urban discount store chain to a suburban housegoods store chain. Its failure serves as a classic study of poor implementation of what seemed like a sound business strategy. What happened to Grant, and why, are questions that, with some analysis, can be answered. On the other hand, why the symptoms of Grant's prolonged illness were not diagnosed and treated earlier is difficult to understand.

The Strategic Shift

Prior to the mid-1960s, Grant built its reputation on sales of low-priced soft goods (clothing, linens, sewing fabrics). It placed its stores in large, urban locations and appealed primarily to lower-income consumers.

The mid-1960s marked the beginning, however, of urban unrest and a movement to the suburbs. To service the needs of these new homeowners, suburban shopping centers experienced rapid growth. Sears led the way in this movement, establishing itself as the anchor store in many of the more upscale locations. Montgomery Ward and JCPenney followed suit. At this time, Sears held a dominant market share in the middle-income consumer market. It saw an opportunity, however, to move its product line more upscale to compete with the established department stores (Macy's, Marshall Field), which had not yet begun their move to the suburbs. To implement this new strategy, Sears introduced its Sears Best line of products.

The outward population move to the suburbs and increased competition from growing discount chains such as Kmart caused Grant to alter its strategy as well. One aspect of this strategic shift was rapid expansion of new stores into suburban shopping centers. Between 1963 and 1973, Grant opened 612 new stores and expanded ninety-one others. It concentrated most of that expansion in the 1969–1973 period when it opened 369 new stores, fifteen on one particularly busy day. Because Grant's reputation had been built on sales to lower-income consumers, it was often unable to locate its new stores in the choicest shopping centers. Louis C. Lustenberger, president of Grant from 1959 to 1968, started the expansion program, although later, as a director, he became concerned over dimensions of the growth and the problems it generated. After Lustenberger stepped down, the pace of expansion accelerated under the leadership of Chairman Edward Staley and President Richard W. Mayer.

A second aspect of Grant's strategy involved a change in its product line. Grant perceived a vacuum in the middle-income consumer market when Sears moved more upscale. Grant introduced a higher-quality, medium-priced line of products into its new

[11]This case was coauthored with Professor James A. Largay.

shopping center stores to fill this vacuum. In addition, it added furniture and private-brand appliances to its product line and implemented a credit card system. With much of the move to the suburbs representing middle-income consumers, Grant attempted to position itself as a primary supplier to outfit the new homes being constructed.

To implement this new strategy, Grant chose a decentralized organizational structure. Each store manager controlled credit extension and credit terms. At most stores, Grant permitted customers thirty-six months to pay for their purchases; the minimum monthly payment was $1, regardless of total purchases. Bad-debt expenses averaged 1.2 percent of sales each year until fiscal 1975, when a provision of $155.7 million was made. Local store managers also made inventory and pricing decisions. Merchandise was either acquired from regional Grant warehouses or ordered directly from the manufacturer. At this time, Grant did not have an information system in place that permitted one store to check the availability of a needed product from another store. Compensation of employees was considered among the most generous in the industry, with most employees owning shares of Grant's common stock acquired under employee stock option plans. Compensation of store managers included salary plus stated percentages of the store's sales and profits.

To finance the expansion of receivables and inventory, Grant used commercial paper, bank loans, and trade credit. To finance the expansion of store space, Grant entered into leasing arrangements. Because Grant was liquidated before the Financial Accounting Standards Board issued *Statement of Financial Accounting Standards No. 13,* requiring the capitalization of capital leases on the balance sheet and the disclosure of information on operating leases in the notes to the financial statements, it did not disclose its long-term leasing arrangements. Property, plant, and equipment reported on its balance sheet consisted mostly of store fixtures. Grant's long-term debt included debentures totaling $200 million issued in 1971 and 1973. Based on per-square-foot rental rates at the time, Grant's disclosures of total square footage of space, and an 8 percent discount rate, the estimated present values of Grant's leases are as follows (in thousands):

January 31	Present Value of Lease Commitments	January 31	Present Value of Lease Commitments
1966	$394,291	1971	$496,041
1967	$400,090	1972	$626,052
1968	$393,566	1973	$708,666
1969	$457,111	1974	$805,785
1970	$486,837	1975	$821,565

Advance and Retreat—The Attempt to Save Grant

By 1974, it became clear that Grant's problems were not of a short-term operating nature. In the spring of 1974, both Moody's and Standard & Poor's eliminated their credit rating for Grant's commercial paper. Banks entered the picture in a big way in the summer of 1974. To provide financing, a group of 143 banks agreed to offer lines of credit totaling $525 million. Grant obtained a short-term loan of $600 million in September 1974, with three New York money center banks absorbing approximately $230 million of the total. These three banks also loaned $50 million out of a total of $100 million provided to Grant's finance subsidiary.

Support of the banks during the summer of 1974 was accompanied by a top management change. Staley and Mayer stepped down in the spring and were replaced in August 1974 by James G. Kendrick, brought in from Zeller's Ltd., Grant's Canadian subsidiary. As chief executive officer, Kendrick moved to cut Grant's losses. He slashed payroll significantly, closed 126 unprofitable stores and phased out the big-ticket furniture and appliance lines. New store space opened in 1975 was 75 percent less than in 1974.

The positive effects of these moves could not overcome the disastrous events of early 1975. In January, Grant defaulted on about $75 million in interest payments and in February, results of operations for the year ended January 31, 1975, were released. Grant reported a loss of $177 million, with substantial losses from credit operations accounting for 60 percent of the total.

The banks now assumed a more active role in what was becoming a struggle to save Grant. Robert H. Anderson, a vice president of Sears, was offered a lucrative $2.5 million contract. He decided to accept the challenge to turn the company around, and joined Grant as its new president in April 1975. Kendrick remained as chairman of the board. The banks holding 90 percent of Grant's debt extended their loans from June 2, 1975, to March 31, 1976. The balance of about $56 million was repaid on June 2. A major problem confronting Anderson was how to maintain the continued flow of merchandise into Grant stores. Suppliers became skeptical of Grant's ability to pay for merchandise and, in August 1975, the banks agreed to subordinate $300 million of debt to the suppliers' claims for merchandise shipped. With the approach of the Christmas shopping season, the need for merchandise became critical. Despite the banks' subordination of their claims to those of suppliers and the intensive cultivation of suppliers by Anderson, Grant did not receive sufficient quantities of merchandise in the stores.

During this period, Grant reported a $111.3 million net loss for the six months ended on July 31, 1975. Sales had declined 15 percent from the comparable period in 1974. Kendrick observed that a return to profitability before the fourth quarter was unlikely.

On October 2, 1975, Grant filed a Chapter 11 bankruptcy petition. The rehabilitation effort was formally underway and the protection provided by Chapter 11 permitted a continuation of the reorganization and rehabilitation activities for the next four months. On February 6, 1976, after store closings and liquidations of inventories had generated $320 million in cash, the creditors committee overseeing the bankruptcy voted for liquidation, and W. T. Grant ceased to exist.

Financial Statements for Grant

Two changes in accounting principles affect Grant's financial statements. Prior to fiscal 1970, Grant accounted for the investment in its wholly owned finance subsidiary using the equity method. Beginning with the year ending January 31, 1970, Grant consolidated the finance subsidiary. Prior to fiscal 1975, Grant recorded the total finance charge on credit sales as income in the year of the sale. Accounts receivable therefore included the full amount to be received from customers, not the present value of such amount. Beginning with the fiscal year ending January 31, 1975, Grant recognized finance changes on credit sales over the life of the installment contract.

Exhibit 3.30 presents comparative balance sheets and Exhibit 3.31 presents statements of income and retained earnings for Grant, based on the amounts as originally reported for each year. Exhibits 3.32, 3.33, and 3.34 present balance sheets, income statements, and statements of cash flow, respectively, based on revised amounts reflecting retroactive restatement for the two changes in accounting principles described earlier. These latter statements consolidate the finance subsidiary for all years. Grant provided the necessary data to restate for the change in income recognition of finance charges for the 1971 to 1975 fiscal years only. Exhibit 3.35 presents selected other data for Grant, the variety chain store industry, and the aggregate economy.

Required

Using the narrative information and the financial data provided in Exhibits 3.30 through 3.35, your mission is to apply tools of financial analysis to determine the major causes of Grant's financial problems. If you had been performing this analysis contemporaneously with the release of publicly reported information, when would you have become skeptical of the ability of Grant to continue as a viable going concern? To assist in this analysis, Exhibits 3.36 through 3.38 present selected ratio and growth rate information based on the following assumptions:

Exhibit 3.36: Based on the amounts as originally reported for each year (Exhibits 3.30 and 3.31).

Exhibit 3.37: Based on the amounts as retroactively restated for changes in accounting principles (Exhibits 3.32, 3.33, and 3.34).

Exhibit 3.38: Same as Exhibit 3.37, except assets and liabilities reflect the capitalization of leases using the amounts presented in the case.

EXHIBIT 3.30

W. T. Grant Company
Comparative Balance Sheets
(as originally reported in thousands)
(Case 3.3)

January 31:	1966	1967	1968
Assets			
Cash and Marketable Securities	$ 22,559	$ 37,507	$ 25,047
Accounts Receivable[c]	110,943	110,305	133,406
Inventories	151,365	174,631	183,722
Other Current Assets	—	—	—
Total Current Assets	$284,867	$322,443	$342,175
Investments	38,419	40,800	56,609
Property, Plant, and Equipment, net	40,367	48,071	47,572
Other Assets	1,222	1,664	1,980
Total Assets	$364,875	$412,978	$448,336
Liabilities and Shareholders' Equity			
Short-Term Debt	$ —	$ —	$ 300
Accounts Payable—Trade	58,252	75,885	79,673
Current Deferred Taxes	37,590	47,248	57,518
Total Current Liabilities	$ 95,842	$123,133	$137,491
Long-Term Debt	70,000	70,000	62,622
Noncurrent Deferred Taxes	6,269	7,034	7,551
Other Long-Term Liabilities	4,784	4,949	4,858
Total Liabilities	$176,895	$205,116	$212,522
Preferred Stock	$ 15,000	$ 15,000	$ 14,750
Common Stock	15,375	15,636	16,191
Additional Paid-In Capital	25,543	27,977	37,428
Retained Earnings	132,062	149,249	167,445
Total	$187,980	$207,862	$235,814
Less Cost of Treasury Stock	—	—	—
Total Stockholders' Equity	$187,980	$207,862	$235,814
Total Liabilities and Shareholders' Equity	$364,875	$412,978	$448,336

[a]In the year ending January 31, 1970, W. T. Grant changed its consolidation policy and commenced consolidating its wholly owned finance subsidiary.
[b]In the year ending January 31, 1975, W. T. Grant changed its method of recognizing finance income on installment sales. In prior years, Grant recognized all finance income in the year of the sale. Beginning in the 1975 fiscal period, it recognized finance income over the time the installment receivable was outstanding.
[c]Accounts receivable comprises the following:

January 31:	1966	1967	1968
Customer Installment Receivables	$114,470	$114,928	$140,507
Less Allowances for Uncollectible Accounts	(7,065)	(9,383)	(11,307)
Unearned Credit Insurance	—	—	—
Unearned Finance Income	—	—	—
Net	$107,405	$105,545	$129,200
Other Receivables	3,538	4,760	4,206
Total Receivables	$110,943	$110,305	$133,406

EXHIBIT 3.30

continued

1969	1970[a]	1971	1972	1973	1974	1975[b]
$ 28,460	$ 32,977	$ 34,009	$ 49,851	$ 30,943	$ 45,951	$ 79,642
154,829	368,267	419,731	477,324	542,751	598,799	431,201
208,623	222,128	260,492	298,676	399,533	450,637	407,357
—	5,037	5,246	5,378	6,649	7,299	6,581
$391,912	$628,409	$719,478	$831,229	$ 979,876	$1,102,686	$ 924,781
62,854	20,694	23,936	32,367	35,581	44,251	49,764
49,213	55,311	61,832	77,173	91,420	100,984	101,932
2,157	2,381	2,678	3,901	3,821	5,063	5,790
$506,136	$706,795	$807,924	$944,670	$1,110,698	$1,252,984	$1,082,267
$ 180	$182,132	$246,420	$237,741	$ 390,034	$ 453,097	$ 600,695
102,080	104,144	118,091	124,990	112,896	104,883	147,211
64,113	80,443	94,785	112,846	130,137	132,085	2,000
$166,373	$366,719	$459,296	$475,577	$ 633,067	$ 690,065	$ 749,906
43,251	35,402	32,301	128,432	126,672	220,336	216,341
7,941	8,286	8,518	9,664	11,926	14,649	—
5,519	5,700	5,773	5,252	4,694	4,196	2,183
$223,084	$416,107	$505,888	$618,925	$ 776,359	$ 929,246	$ 968,430
$ 13,250	$ 11,450	$ 9,600	$ 9,053	$ 8,600	$ 7,465	$ 7,465
17,318	17,883	18,180	18,529	18,588	18,599	18,599
59,945	71,555	78,116	85,195	86,146	85,909	83,914
192,539	211,679	230,435	244,508	261,154	248,461	37,674
$283,052	$312,567	$336,331	$357,285	$ 374,488	$ 360,434	$ 147,652
—	(21,879)	(34,295)	(31,540)	(40,149)	(36,696)	(33,815)
$283,052	$290,688	$302,036	$325,745	$ 334,339	$ 323,738	$ 113,837
$506,136	$706,795	$807,924	$944,670	$1,110,698	$1,252,984	$1,082,267

1969	1970[a]	1971	1972	1973	1974	1975[b]
$162,219	$381,757	$433,730	$493,859	$ 556,091	$ 602,305	$ 518,387
(13,074)	(15,270)	(15,527)	(15,750)	(15,770)	(18,067)	(79,510)
—	(5,774)	(9,553)	(12,413)	(8,768)	(4,923)	(1,386)
—	—	—	—	—	—	(37,523)
$149,145	$360,713	$408,650	$465,696	$ 531,553	$ 579,315	$ 399,968
5,684	7,554	11,081	11,628	11,198	19,484	31,233
$154,829	$368,267	$419,731	$477,324	$ 542,751	$ 598,799	$ 431,201

EXHIBIT 3.31

W. T. Grant Company
Statements of Income and Retained Earnings
(as originally reported in thousands)
(Case 3.3)

Year Ended January 31:	**1967**	**1968**	**1969**
Sales	$920,797	$979,458	$1,096,152
Concessions	2,249	2,786	3,425
Equity in Earnings	2,072	2,987	3,537
Finance Charges	—	—	—
Other Income	1,049	2,010	2,205
Total Revenues	$926,167	$987,241	$1,105,319
Cost of Goods Sold	$631,585	$669,560	$ 741,181
Selling, General, and Administration	233,134	253,561	287,883
Interest	4,970	4,907	4,360
Taxes:			
Current	13,541	17,530	25,600
Deferred	11,659	9,120	8,400
Total Expenses	$894,889	$954,678	$1,067,424
Net Income	$ 31,278	$ 32,563	$ 37,895
Dividends	(14,091)	(14,367)	(17,686)
Change in Accounting Principles:			
Consolidation of Finance Subsidiary	—	—	4,885
Recognition of Financing Charges	—	—	—
Change in Retained Earnings	$ 17,187	$ 18,196	$ 25,094
Retained Earnings—Beginning of Period	132,062	149,249	167,445
Retained Earnings—End of Period	$149,249	$167,445	$ 192,539

EXHIBIT 3.31

continued

1970	1971	1972	1973	1974	1975
$1,210,918	$1,254,131	$1,374,811	$1,644,747	$1,849,802	$1,761,952
3,748	4,986	3,439	3,753	3,971	4,238
2,084	2,777	2,383	5,116	4,651	3,086
—	—	—	—	—	91,141
2,864	2,874	3,102	1,188	3,063	3,376
$1,219,614	$1,264,768	$1,383,735	$1,654,804	$1,861,487	$1,863,793
$ 817,671	$ 843,192	$ 931,237	$1,125,261	$1,282,945	$1,303,267
307,215	330,325	374,334	444,879	491,287	769,253
14,919	18,874	16,452	21,127	78,040	86,079
24,900	21,140	13,487	9,588	(6,021)	(19,439)
13,100	11,660	13,013	16,162	6,807	(98,027)
$1,177,805	$1,225,191	$1,348,523	$1,617,017	$1,853,058	$2,041,133
$ 41,809	$ 39,577	$ 35,212	$ 37,787	$ 8,429	$ (177,340)
(19,737)	(20,821)	(21,139)	(21,141)	(21,122)	(4,457)
(2,932)	—	—	—	—	—
$ —	$ —	$ —	$ —	$ —	$ (28,990)
$ 19,140	$ 18,756	$ 14,073	$ 16,646	$ (12,693)	$ (210,787)
192,539	211,679	230,435	244,508	261,154	248,461
$ 211,679	$ 230,435	$ 244,508	$ 261,154	$ 248,461	$ 37,674

EXHIBIT 3.32

W. T. Grant Company
Comparative Balance Sheets
(as retroactively reported for changes in accounting principles in thousands)
(Case 3.3)

January 31:	1966	1967	1968
Assets			
Cash and Marketable Securities	$ 22,638	$ 39,040	$ 25,141
Accounts Receivable[c]	172,706	230,427	272,450
Inventories	151,365	174,631	183,722
Other Current Assets	3,630	4,079	3,982
Total Current Assets	$350,339	$448,177	$485,295
Investments	13,405	14,791	16,754
Property, Plant, and Equipment, net	40,372	48,076	47,578
Other Assets	1,222	1,664	1,980
Total Assets	$405,338	$512,708	$551,607
Liabilities and Shareholders' Equity			
Short-Term Debt	$ 37,314	$ 97,647	$ 99,230
Accounts Payable	58,252	75,885	79,673
Current Deferred Taxes	36,574	44,667	56,545
Total Current Liabilities	$132,140	$218,199	$235,448
Long-Term Debt	70,000	70,000	62,622
Noncurrent Deferred Taxes	6,269	7,034	7,551
Other Long-Term Liabilities	4,785	5,159	5,288
Total Liabilities	$213,194	$300,392	$310,909
Preferred Stock	$ 15,000	$ 15,000	$ 14,750
Common Stock	15,375	15,636	16,191
Additional Paid-In Capital	25,543	27,977	37,428
Retained Earnings	136,226	153,703	172,329
Total	$192,144	$212,316	$240,698
Less Cost of Treasury Stock	—	—	—
Total Stockholders' Equity	$192,144	$212,316	$240,698
Total Liabilities and Shareholders' Equity	$405,338	$512,708	$551,607

[a]See Note (a) to Exhibit 3.30.
[b]See Note (b) to Exhibit 3.30.
[c]Accounts receivable comprises the following:

	1966	1967	1968
Customer Installment Receivables			
Less Allowances for Uncollectible Accounts	NOT DISCLOSED ON A FULLY		
Unearned Credit Insurance	CONSOLIDATED BASIS		
Unearned Finance Income			
Net Other Receivables	WITH FINANCE SUBSIDIARY		
Total Receivables	$172,706	$230,427	$272,450

EXHIBIT 3.32

continued

1969	1970[a]	1971	1972	1973	1974	1975[b]
$ 25,639	$ 32,977	$ 34,009	$ 49,851	$ 30,943	$ 45,951	$ 79,642
312,776	368,267	358,428	408,301	468,582	540,802	431,201
208,623	222,128	260,492	298,676	399,533	450,637	407,357
4,402	5,037	5,246	5,378	6,649	7,299	6,581
$551,440	$628,409	$658,175	$762,206	$ 905,707	$1,044,689	$ 924,781
18,581	20,694	23,936	32,367	35,581	44,251	49,764
49,931	55,311	61,832	77,173	91,420	100,984	101,932
2,157	2,381	2,678	3,901	3,821	5,063	5,790
$622,109	$706,795	$746,621	$875,647	$1,036,529	$1,194,987	$1,082,267
$118,125	$182,132	$246,420	$237,741	$ 390,034	$ 453,097	$ 600,695
102,080	104,144	118,091	124,990	112,896	104,883	147,211
65,073	80,443	58,536	72,464	87,431	103,078	2,000
$285,278	$366,719	$423,047	$435,195	$ 590,361	$ 661,058	$ 749,906
43,251	35,402	32,301	128,432	126,672	220,336	216,341
7,941	8,286	8,518	9,664	11,926	14,649	—
5,519	5,700	5,773	5,252	4,694	4,196	2,183
$341,989	$416,107	$469,639	$578,543	$ 733,653	$ 900,239	$ 968,430
$ 13,250	$ 11,450	$ 9,600	$ 9,053	$ 8,600	$ 7,465	$ 7,465
17,318	17,883	18,180	18,529	18,588	18,599	18,599
59,945	71,555	78,116	85,195	86,146	85,909	83,914
189,607	211,679	205,381	215,867	229,691	219,471	37,674
$280,120	$312,567	$311,277	$328,644	$ 343,025	$ 331,444	$ 147,652
—	(21,879)	(34,295)	(31,540)	(40,149)	(36,696)	(33,815)
$280,120	$290,688	$276,982	$297,104	$ 302,876	$ 294,748	$ 113,837
$622,109	$706,795	$746,621	$875,647	$1,036,529	$1,194,987	$1,082,267

1969	1970[a]	1971	1972	1973	1974	1975[b]
	$381,757	$433,730	$493,859	$ 556,091	$ 602,305	$ 518,387
	(15,270)	(15,527)	(15,750)	(15,770)	(18,067)	(79,510)
	(5,774)	(9,553)	(12,413)	(8,768)	(4,923)	(1,386)
	—	(61,303)	(69,023)	(74,169)	(57,997)	(37,523)
	$360,713	$347,347	$396,073	$ 457,384	$ 521,318	$ 399,968
	7,554	11,081	11,628	11,198	19,484	31,233
$312,776	$368,267	$358,428	$408,301	$ 468,582	$ 540,802	$ 431,201

EXHIBIT 3.33

W. T. Grant Company
Statements of Income and Retained Earnings
(as retroactively revised for changes in accounting principles in thousands)
(Case 3.3)

Year Ended January 31:	**1967**	**1968**	**1969**
Sales	$920,797	$979,458	$1,096,152
Concessions	2,249	2,786	3,425
Equity in Earnings	1,073	1,503	1,761
Finance Charges	—	—	—
Other Income	1,315	2,038	2,525
Total Revenues	$925,434	$985,785	$1,103,311
Cost of Goods Sold	$631,585	$669,560	$ 741,181
Selling, General, and Administration	229,130	247,093	278,031
Interest	7,319	8,549	9,636
Taxes:			
Current	14,463	18,470	27,880
Deferred	11,369	9,120	8,400
Total Expenses	$893,866	$952,792	$1,065,128
Net Income	$ 31,568	$ 32,993	$ 38,183
Dividends	(14,091)	(14,367)	(17,686)
Change in Accounting Principles:			
Consolidation of Finance Subsidiary	—	—	(3,219)
Recognition of Financing Charges	—	—	—
Change in Retained Earnings	$ 17,477	$ 18,626	$ 17,278
Retained Earnings—Beginning of Period	136,226	153,703	172,329
Retained Earnings—End of Period	$153,703	$172,329	$ 189,607

EXHIBIT 3.33

continued

	1970	1971	1972	1973	1974	1975
	$1,210,918	$1,254,131	$1,374,812	$1,644,747	$1,849,802	$1,761,952
	3,748	4,986	3,439	3,753	3,971	4,238
	2,084	2,777	2,383	5,116	4,651	3,086
	—	63,194	66,567	84,817	114,920	91,141
	2,864	2,874	3,102	1,188	3,063	3,376
	$1,219,614	$1,327,962	$1,450,303	$1,739,621	$1,976,407	$1,863,793
	$ 817,671	$ 843,192	$ 931,237	$1,125,261	$1,282,945	$1,303,267
	307,215	396,877	445,244	532,604	601,231	769,253
	14,919	18,874	16,452	21,127	78,040	86,079
	24,900	22,866	13,579	11,256	(6,021)	(19,439)
	13,100	9,738	12,166	14,408	9,310	(98,027)
	$1,177,805	$1,291,547	$1,418,678	$1,704,656	$1,965,505	$2,041,133
	$ 41,809	$ 36,415	$ 31,625	$ 34,965	$ 10,902	$ (177,340)
	(19,737)	(20,821)	(21,139)	(21,141)	(21,122)	(4,457)
	—	—	—	—	—	—
	—	(21,892)	—	—	—	—
	$ 22,072	$ (6,298)	$ 10,486	$ 13,824	$ (10,220)	$ (181,797)
	189,607	211,679	205,381	215,867	229,691	219,471
	$ 211,679	$ 205,381	$ 215,867	$ 229,691	$ 219,471	$ 37,674

EXHIBIT 3.34

W. T. Grant Company
Statement of Cash Flows
(as retroactively revised for changes in accounting principles)
(Case 3.3)

Year Ended January 31:	1967	1968	1969
Operations			
Net Income	$ 31,568	$ 32,993	$ 38,183
Depreciation	7,524	8,203	8,388
Other	66	(856)	(1,140)
(Increase) Decrease in Receivables	(57,721)	(42,023)	(40,326)
(Increase) Decrease in Inventories	(23,266)	(9,091)	(24,901)
(Increase) Decrease in Prepayments	(449)	97	(420)
Increase (Decrease) in Accounts Payable	17,633	3,788	22,407
Increase (Decrease) in Other Current Liabilities	8,093	11,878	8,528
Cash Flow from Operations	$(16,552)	$ 4,989	$ 10,719
Investing			
Acquisition of Property, Plant, and Equipment	$(15,257)	$ (7,763)	$(10,626)
Acquisition of Investments	(269)	(418)	(35)
Cash Flow from Investing	$(15,526)	$ (8,181)	$(10,661)
Financing			
Increase (Decrease) in Short-Term Borrowing	$ 60,333	$ 1,583	$ 18,895
Increase (Decrease) in Long-Term Borrowing	—	(1,500)	(1,500)
Increase (Decrease) in Capital Stock	2,695	3,958	844
Dividends	(14,091)	(14,367)	(17,686)
Cash Flow from Financing	$ 48,937	$(10,326)	$ 553
Other	$ (457)	$ (381)	$ (113)
Change in Cash	$ 16,402	$(13,899)	$ 498

EXHIBIT 3.34

continued

1970	1971	1972	1973	1974	1975
$ 41,809	$ 36,415	$ 31,625	$ 34,965	$ 10,902	$(177,340)
8,972	9,619	10,577	12,004	13,579	14,587
(1,559)	(2,470)	(1,758)	(1,699)	(1,345)	(16,993)
(55,491)	(11,981)	(49,873)	(60,281)	(72,220)	109,601
(13,505)	(38,364)	(38,184)	(100,857)	(51,104)	43,280
(635)	(209)	(132)	(1,271)	(650)	718
2,064	13,947	6,899	(12,094)	(8,013)	42,328
15,370	(21,907)	13,928	14,967	15,647	(101,078)
$ (2,975)	$(14,950)	$(26,918)	$(114,266)	$(93,204)	$ (84,897)
$(14,352)	$(16,141)	$(25,918)	$ (26,251)	$(23,143)	$ (15,535)
—	(436)	(5,951)	(2,216)	(5,700)	(5,282)
$(14,352)	$(16,577)	$(31,869)	$ (28,467)	$(28,843)	$ (20,817)
$ 64,007	$ 64,288	$ (8,679)	$ 152,293	$ 63,063	$ 147,598
(1,687)	(1,538)	98,385	(1,584)	93,926	(3,995)
(17,860)	(8,954)	7,407	(8,227)	1,833	886
(19,737)	(20,821)	(21,139)	(21,141)	(21,122)	(4,457)
$ 24,723	$ 32,975	$ 75,974	$ 121,341	$137,700	$ 140,032
$ (58)	$ (416)	$ (1,345)	$ 2,484	$ (645)	$ (627)
$ 7,338	$ 1,032	$ 15,842	$ (18,908)	$ 15,008	$ 33,691

EXHIBIT 3.35

W. T. Grant Company
Other Data
(Case 3.3)

December 31:	1965	1966	1967	1968
W. T. Grant Co.				
Sales (millions of dollars)[a]	$ 839.7	$ 920.8	$ 979.5	$1,096.1
Number of Stores	1,088	1,104	1,086	1,092
Store Area				
(thousands of square feet)[a]	Data Not Available			
Dividends per Share[a]	$ .80	$ 1.10	$ 1.10	$ 1.30
Stock Price—High	31 1/8	35 1/8	37 3/8	45 1/8
—Low	18	20 1/2	20 3/4	30
—Close (12/31)	31 1/8	20 3/4	34 3/8	42 5/8
Variety Chain Store Industry				
Sales (millions of dollars)	$5,320.0	$5,727.0	$6,078.0	$6,152.0
Standard & Poor's Variety				
Chain Stock Price Index—High	31.0	31.2	38.4	53.6
—Low	24.3	22.4	22.3	34.7
—Close (12/31)	31.0	22.4	37.8	50.5
Aggregate Economy				
Gross National Product				
(billions of dollars)	$ 684.9	$ 747.6	$ 789.7	$ 865.7
Average Bank Short-Term				
Lending Rate	4.99%	5.69%	5.99%	6.68%
Standard & Poor's 500				
Stock Price Index—High	92.6	94.1	97.6	108.4
—Low	81.6	73.2	80.4	87.7
—Close (12/31)	92.4	80.3	96.5	103.9

[a]These amounts are for the fiscal year ending January 31 of the year after the year indicated in the column. For example, sales for W. T. Grant of $839.7 in the 1965 column are for the fiscal year ending January 31, 1966.

EXHIBIT 3.35

continued

1969	1970	1971	1972	1973	1974
$1,210.9	$ 1,254.1	$1,374.8	$1,644.7	$ 1,849.8	$1,762.0
1,095	1,116	1,168	1,208	1,189	1,152
—	38,157	44,718	50,619	53,719	54,770
$ 1.40	$ 1.40	$ 1.50	$ 1.50	$ 1.50	$ .30
59	52	70 5/8	48 3/4	44 3/8	12
39 1/4	26 7/8	41 7/8	38 3/4	9 7/8	1 1/2
47	47 1/8	47 3/4	43 7/8	10 7/8	1 7/8
$6,426.0	$ 6,959.0	$6,972.0	$7,498.0	$ 8,212.0	$8,714.0
66.1	61.4	92.2	107.4	107.3	73.7
48.8	40.9	60.2	82.1	60.0	39.0
59.6	60.4	88.0	106.8	66.2	41.9
$ 932.1	$ 1,075.3	$1,107.5	$1,171.1	$ 1,233.4	$1,210.0
8.21%	8.48%	6.32%	5.82%	8.30%	11.28%
106.2	93.5	104.8	119.1	120.2	99.8
89.2	69.3	90.2	101.7	92.2	62.3
92.1	92.2	102.1	118.1	97.6	68.6

EXHIBIT 3.36

W. T. Grant Company
Financial Ratios and Growth Rates for W. T. Grant Based on Amounts as Originally Reported (Case 3.3)

Financial Ratios	1967	1968	1969
Profitability Analysis			
Profit Margin for ROA	3.7%	3.6%	3.7%
Assets Turnover	2.4	2.3	2.3
Return on Assets (ROA)	8.7%	8.2%	8.4%
Return on Common Shareholders' Equity (ROCE)	16.8%	15.5%	15.2%
Operating Performance			
Cost of Goods Sold/Sales	68.6%	68.4%	67.6%
Selling and Administrative Expenses/Sales	25.3%	25.9%	26.3%
Asset Turnovers			
Accounts Receivable	8.3	8.0	7.6
Inventory	3.9	3.7	3.8
Fixed Asset	20.8	20.5	22.7
Short-Term Liquidity Risk			
Current Ratio	2.62	2.49	2.36
Quick Ratio	1.20	1.15	1.10
Days Receivables	44	45	48
Days Inventory	94	98	97
Days Payables	37	42	43
Operating Cash Flow/Current Liabilities	(15.1%)	3.8%	7.1%
Long-Term Liquidity Risk			
Liabilities/Assets	49.7%	47.4%	44.1%
Long-Term Debt/Assets	17.0%	14.0%	8.5%
Operating Cash Flow/Total Liabilities	(8.7%)	2.4%	4.9%
Interest Coverage Ratio	12.4	13.1	17.5

Growth Rates	1968	1969
Accounts Receivable	20.9%	16.1%
Inventories	5.2%	13.6%
Fixed Assets	(1.0%)	3.4%
Total Assets	8.6%	12.9%
Accounts Payable	5.0%	28.1%
Bank Loans	—	(40.0%)
Long-Term Debt	(10.5%)	(30.9%)
Shareholders' Equity	13.4%	20.0%
Sales	6.4%	11.9%
Cost of Goods Sold	6.0%	10.7%
Selling and Administrative Expenses	8.8%	13.5%
Net Income	4.1%	16.4%

EXHIBIT 3.36

continued

1970	1971	1972	1973	1974	1975
4.1%	3.9%	3.2%	3.0%	2.6%	(7.5%)
2.0	1.7	1.6	1.6	1.6	1.5
8.2%	6.5%	5.0%	4.7%	4.1%	(11.4%)
15.1%	13.7%	11.4%	11.7%	2.5%	(84.1%)
67.5%	67.2%	67.7%	68.4%	69.4%	74.0%
25.4%	26.3%	27.2%	27.0%	26.6%	43.7%
4.6	3.2	3.1	3.2	3.2	3.4
3.8	3.5	3.3	3.2	3.0	3.0
23.2	21.4	19.8	19.5	19.2	17.4
1.71	1.57	1.75	1.55	1.60	1.23
1.09	.99	1.11	.91	.93	.68
79	115	119	113	113	107
96	104	110	113	121	120
45	46	46	35	30	37
(1.1%)	(3.6%)	(5.8%)	(20.6%)	(14.1%)	(11.8%)
58.9%	62.6%	65.5%	69.9%	74.2%	85.9%
5.0%	4.0%	13.6%	11.4%	17.6%	20.0%
(.9%)	(3.2%)	(4.8%)	(16.4%)	(10.9%)	(9.0%)
6.4	4.8	4.8	4.0	1.1	(2.4)

1970	1971	1972	1973	1974	1975
137.9%	14.0%	13.7%	13.7%	10.3%	(28.0%)
6.5%	17.3%	14.7%	33.8%	12.8%	(9.6%)
12.4%	11.8%	24.8%	18.5%	10.5%	.9%
39.6%	14.3%	17.0%	17.6%	12.8%	(13.6%)
2.0%	13.4%	5.8%	(9.7%)	(7.1%)	40.4%
N/A	35.3%	(3.5%)	64.1%	16.2%	32.6%
(18.1%)	(8.8%)	297.6%	(1.4%)	73.9%	(1.8%)
2.7%	3.9%	7.8%	2.6%	(3.2%)	(64.8%)
10.5%	3.6%	9.6%	19.6%	12.5%	(4.7%)
10.3%	3.1%	10.4%	20.8%	14.0%	1.6%
6.7%	7.5%	13.3%	18.8%	10.4%	56.6%
10.3%	(5.3%)	(11.0%)	7.3%	(77.7%)	(2,203.9%)

Exhibit 3.37

W. T. Grant Company Financial Ratios and Growth Rates for W. T. Grant Based on Amounts Retroactively Restated for Changes in Accounting Principles (Leases Not Capitalized) (Case 3.3)

Financial Ratios	1967	1968	1969
Profitability Analysis			
Profit Margin for ROA	3.8%	3.8%	3.9%
Assets Turnover	2.0	1.8	1.9
Return on Assets (ROA)	7.7%	7.0%	7.4%
Return on Common Shareholders' Equity (ROCE)	16.6%	15.3%	15.3%
Operating Performance			
Cost of Goods Sold/Sales	68.6%	68.4%	67.6%
Selling and Administrative Expenses/Sales	24.9%	25.2%	25.4%
Asset Turnovers			
Accounts Receivable	4.6	3.9	3.7
Inventory	3.9	3.7	3.8
Fixed Asset	20.8	20.5	22.5
Short-Term Liquidity Risk			
Current Ratio	2.05	2.06	1.93
Quick Ratio	1.23	1.26	1.19
Days Receivables	80	94	97
Days Inventory	94	98	97
Days Payables	37	42	43
Operating Cash Flow/Current Liabilities	(9.4%)	2.2%	4.1%
Long-Term Liquidity Risk			
Liabilities/Assets	58.6%	56.4%	55.0%
Long-Term Debt/Assets	13.7%	11.4%	7.0%
Operating Cash Flow/Liabilities	(6.4%)	1.6%	3.3%
Interest Coverage Ratio	8.8	8.1	8.7

Growth Rates	1968	1969
Accounts Receivable	18.2%	14.8%
Inventories	5.2%	13.6%
Fixed Assets	(1.0%)	4.9%
Total Assets	7.6%	12.8%
Accounts Payable	5.0%	28.1%
Bank Loans	1.6%	19.0%
Long-Term Debt	(10.5%)	(30.9%)
Shareholders' Equity	13.4%	16.4%
Sales	6.4%	11.9%
Cost of Goods Sold	6.0%	10.7%
Selling and Administrative Expenses	7.8%	12.5%
Net Income	4.5%	15.7%

Exhibit 3.37

continued

1970	1971	1972	1973	1974	1975
4.1%	3.7%	2.9%	2.8%	2.8%	(7.5%)
1.8	1.7	1.7	1.7	1.7	1.5
7.5%	6.4%	5.0%	4.8%	4.6%	(11.6%)
15.1%	13.2%	11.3%	11.9%	3.6%	(90.2%)
67.5%	67.2%	67.7%	68.4%	69.4%	74.0%
25.4%	31.6%	32.4%	32.4%	32.5%	43.7%
3.6	3.5	3.6	3.8	3.7	3.6
3.8	3.5	3.3	3.2	3.0	3.0
23.0	21.4	19.8	19.5	19.2	17.4
1.71	1.56	1.75	1.53	1.58	1.23
1.09	.93	1.05	.85	.89	.68
103	106	102	97	100	101
96	104	110	113	121	120
45	46	46	35	30	37
(.9%)	(3.8%)	(6.3%)	(22.3%)	(14.9%)	(12.0%)
58.9%	62.9%	66.1%	70.8%	75.3%	89.5%
5.0%	4.3%	14.7%	12.2%	18.4%	20.0%
(.8%)	(3.4%)	(5.1%)	(17.4%)	(11.4%)	(9.1%)
6.4	4.7	4.5	3.9	1.2	(2.4)

1970	1971	1972	1973	1974	1975
17.7%	(2.7%)	13.9%	14.8%	15.4%	(20.3%)
6.5%	17.3%	14.7%	33.8%	12.8%	(9.6%)
10.8%	11.8%	24.8%	18.5%	10.5%	.9%
13.6%	5.6%	17.3%	18.4%	15.3%	(9.4%)
2.0%	13.4%	5.8%	(9.7%)	(7.1%)	40.4%
54.2%	35.3%	(3.5%)	64.1%	16.2%	32.6%
(18.1%)	(8.8%)	297.6%	(1.4%)	73.9%	(1.8%)
3.8%	(4.7%)	7.3%	1.9%	(2.7%)	(61.4%)
10.5%	3.6%	9.6%	19.6%	12.5%	(4.7%)
10.3%	3.1%	10.4%	20.8%	14.0%	1.6%
10.5%	29.2%	12.2%	19.6%	12.9%	27.9%
9.5%	(12.9%)	(13.2%)	10.6%	(68.8%)	(1,726.7%)

EXHIBIT 3.38

W. T. Grant Company Financial Ratios and Growth Rates for W. T. Grant Based on Amounts Retroactively Restated for Changes in Accounting Principles (Leases Capitalized) (Case 3.3)

Financial Ratios	1967	1968	1969
Profitability Analysis			
Profit Margin for ROA	3.8%	3.8%	3.9%
Assets Turnover	1.1	1.1	1.1
Return on Assets (ROA)	4.1%	4.0%	4.3%
Return on Common Shareholders' Equity (ROCE)	16.6%	15.3%	15.3%
Operating Performance			
Cost of Goods Sold/Sales	68.6%	68.4%	67.6%
Selling and Administrative Expenses/Sales	24.9%	25.2%	25.4%
Asset Turnovers			
Accounts Receivable	4.6	3.9	3.7
Inventory	3.9	3.7	3.8
Fixed Asset	2.1	2.2	2.3
Short-Term Liquidity Risk			
Current Ratio	2.05	2.06	1.93
Quick Ratio	1.23	1.26	1.19
Days Receivables	80	94	97
Days Inventory	94	98	97
Days Payables	37	42	43
Operating Cash Flow/Current Liabilities	(9.4%)	2.2%	4.1%
Long-Term Liquidity Risk			
Liabilities/Assets	76.7%	74.5%	74.0%
Long-Term Debt/Assets	51.5%	48.3%	46.4%
Operating Cash Flow/Liabilities	(2.5%)	.7%	1.4%
Interest Coverage	8.8	8.1	8.7

Growth Rates	1968	1969
Accounts Receivable	18.2%	14.8%
Inventories	5.2%	13.6%
Fixed Assets	1.6%	14.9%
Total Assets	3.5%	14.2%
Accounts Payable	5.0%	28.1%
Bank Loans	1.6%	19.0%
Long-Term Debt	(3.0%)	9.7%
Shareholders' Equity	13.4%	16.4%
Sales	6.4%	11.9%
Cost of Goods Sold	6.0%	10.7%
Selling and Administrative Expenses	7.8%	12.5%
Net Income	4.5%	15.7%

EXHIBIT 3.38

continued

1970	1971	1972	1973	1974	1975
4.1%	3.7%	2.9%	2.8%	2.8%	(7.5%)
1.1	1.0	1.0	1.0	1.0	.9
4.4%	3.8%	2.9%	2.8%	2.7%	(6.8%)
15.1%	13.2%	11.3%	11.9%	3.6%	(90.2%)
67.5%	67.2%	67.7%	68.4%	69.4%	74.0%
25.4%	31.6%	32.4%	32.4%	32.5%	43.7%
3.6	3.5	3.6	3.8	3.7	3.6
3.8	3.5	3.3	3.2	3.0	3.0
2.3	2.3	2.2	2.2	2.2	1.9
1.71	1.56	1.75	1.53	1.58	1.23
1.09	.93	1.05	.85	.89	.68
103	106	102	97	100	101
96	104	110	113	121	120
45	46	46	35	30	37
(.9%)	(3.8%)	(6.3%)	(22.3%)	(14.9%)	(12.0%)
75.6%	77.7%	80.2%	82.6%	85.3%	94.0%
43.8%	42.5%	50.2%	47.9%	51.3%	54.5%
(.3%)	(1.6%)	(2.5%)	(8.6%)	(5.9%)	(4.9%)
6.4	4.7	4.5	3.9	1.2	(2.4)

1970	1971	1972	1973	1974	1975
17.7%	(2.7%)	13.9%	14.8%	15.4%	(20.3%)
6.5%	17.3%	14.7%	33.8%	12.8%	(9.6%)
6.9%	2.9%	26.1%	13.8%	13.3%	1.8%
10.6%	4.1%	20.8%	16.2%	14.6%	(4.8%)
2.0%	13.4%	5.8%	(9.7%)	(7.1%)	40.4%
54.2%	35.3%	(3.5%)	64.1%	16.2%	32.6%
4.4%	1.2%	42.8%	10.7%	22.8%	1.1%
3.8%	(4.7%)	7.3%	1.9%	(2.7%)	(61.4%)
10.5%	3.6%	9.6%	19.6%	12.5%	(4.7%)
10.3%	3.1%	10.4%	20.8%	14.0%	1.6%
10.5%	29.2%	12.2%	19.6%	12.9%	27.9%
9.5%	(12.9%)	(13.2%)	10.6%	(68.8%)	(1,726.7%)

Chapter **4**

Profitability Analysis

Learning Objectives

1. **Analyze and interpret levels of, and changes in, the profitability of a firm using the rate of return on assets and its components, profit margin and total assets turnover.**
2. **Understand the effect of economic and strategic factors on the interpretation of the rate of return on assets and its components.**
3. **Examine other measures of operating performance that supplement the rate of return on assets in assessing profitability.**
4. **Analyze and interpret levels of, and changes in, the rate of return on common shareholders' equity, including the conditions when a firm uses financial leverage successfully to increase the return to the common shareholders.**
5. **Calculate earnings per common share and understand the strengths and weaknesses of this financial ratio as a measure of profitability.**

The primary objective in most financial statement analysis is to value a firm's equity securities. As Chapters 10 to 14 make clear, the value of an equity security relates to the return an investor anticipates relative to the risk involved. Most financial statement analysis examines aspects of a firm's *profitability* and its *risk*. Examining the profitability of a firm in the recent past provides information to help the analyst project its likely future profitability and the expected return from investing in the firm's equity securities. Evaluations of risk involve judgments about a firm's success in managing various dimensions of risk in the past and its ability to manage risks in the future.

This chapter describes several commonly used financial statement ratios for analyzing profitability. Chapter 5 explores the use of financial statements in assessing risk. In these chapters, we illustrate the application of these tools of analysis to the financial statements of PepsiCo, which appear in Appendix A. These financial statements also appear as Exhibits 1.7 (balance sheet), Exhibit 1.8 (income statement) and Exhibit 1.10 (statement of cash flows) in Chapter 1. We recommend that you trace the calculation of each financial ratio discussed in this chapter and in Chapter 5 to these financial statements to ensure that you understand the source of the amounts used. The analytical tools discussed in Chapters 4 and 5 provide the framework for the discussion of alternative accounting principles and other data issues in Chapters 6 to 9 and the valuation of firms in Chapters 10 to 14.

EXHIBIT 4.1

Building Blocks for Financial Statement Analysis

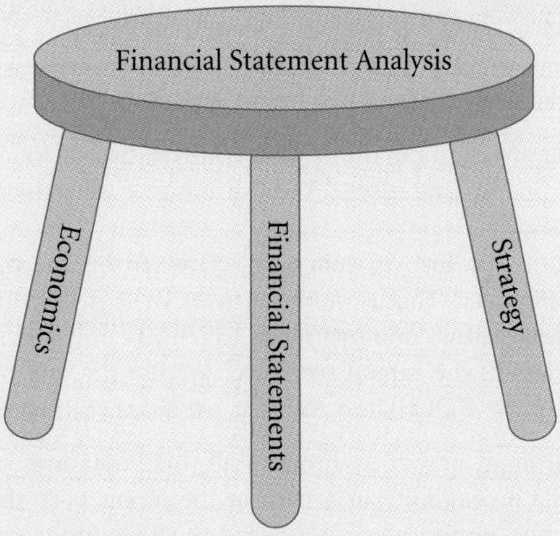

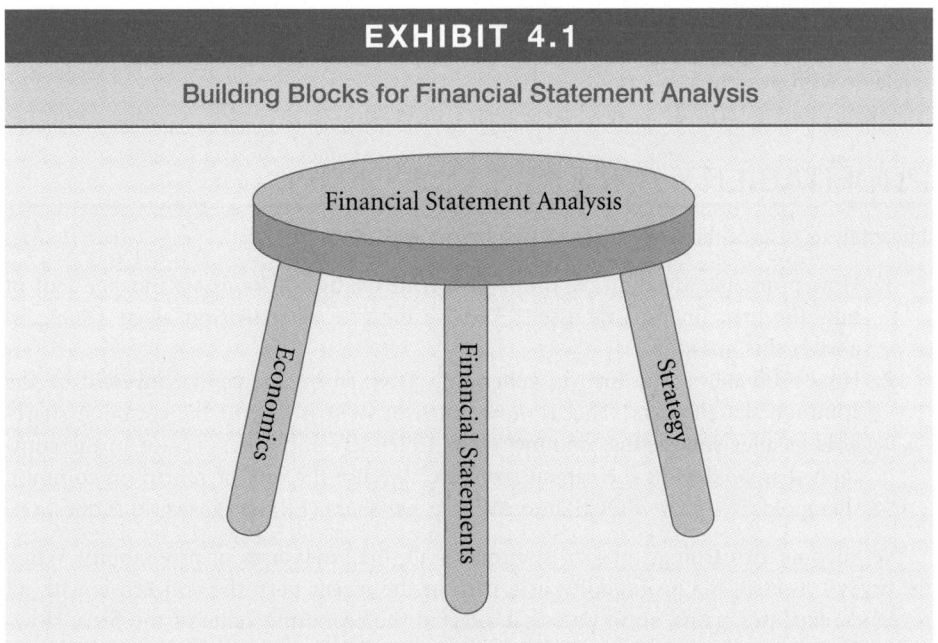

Although we will make some preliminary interpretations of the analytical results for PepsiCo in Chapters 4 and 5, a deeper understanding requires consideration of data issues relating to PepsiCo's financial statements discussed in later chapters.

Our analysis examines changes in the financial ratios for PepsiCo over time, a process referred to as *time-series analysis.* Is PepsiCo becoming more or less profitable over time? Is it becoming more or less risky? Are changes in PepsiCo's strategy, economic conditions, competition, or other factors causing its profitability and risk to change? Time-series analysis attempts to answer these questions.

It is also useful to compare the financial ratios for PepsiCo to those of its competitors, a process referred to as *cross-sectional analysis.* PepsiCo's principal competitor is The Coca-Cola Company (Coca-Cola). We might compare our analysis of PepsiCo to the corresponding financial ratios for Coca-Cola to gain a cross-sectional perspective. We might also compare the results for PepsiCo with average industry ratios, such as those published by Moody's, Robert Morris Associates, Dun & Bradstreet, and others (discussed later in this chapter).

We view effective financial statement analysis as a three-legged stool, as Exhibit 4.1 depicts. Three building blocks for effective analysis are as follows:

1. Understanding the financial statements, including the accounting concepts and methods that underlie them and the quality of the information they provide.
2. Understanding the economic characteristics of the industries in which a firm participates and the relation of those economic characteristics to the various financial statement ratios.
3. Understanding the strategies that a firm pursues to differentiate itself from competitors as a basis for evaluating the sustainability of a firm's earnings and its risks.

Chapter 1 introduced the economic characteristics of the beverage industry and the strategy of PepsiCo to compete in this industry. We incorporate this information and other information provided by PepsiCo in its management discussion and analysis, or

MD&A (Appendix B), into our interpretations of PepsiCo's financial ratios. Appendix C provides a printout for PepsiCo of the Financial Statement Analysis Package, called FSAP, available with this book.

PROFITABILITY ANALYSIS

The analysis of profitability addresses two broad questions:

1. How profitable are the operations of a firm relative to its assets independent of how the firm finances its assets? We use the rate of return on assets (ROA) to answer this question.
2. How profitable is the firm in generating a return on the capital invested by the common shareholders? That is, how much of ROA is left for the common shareholders after subtracting amounts owed to lenders and others senior to the common shareholders in the capital structure? We use the rate of return on common shareholders' equity (ROCE) and earnings per share (EPS) to answer this question.

Net income, or earnings, plays a key role in all three measures of profitability. When the analyst assesses the profitability of a firm in the recent past, the concern is with all revenues, expenses, gains, and losses that affected the economic value of the firm. However, when the analyst uses measures of past profitability to forecast the firm's future profitability, the emphasis is on those revenues, expenses, gains, and losses expected to persist. If net income in the recent past includes nonrecurring gains from sales of assets or unusual asset impairment or restructuring charges, the analyst might decide to eliminate these items from past earnings when using past earnings to forecast future earnings. For purposes of valuation, the analyst strives to forecast the sustainable earnings of a firm. Sustainable earnings is the level of earnings and the growth in the level of earnings expected to persist in the future. Nonrecurring gains and losses may occur in future periods but the analyst cannot anticipate their occurrence, their timing, or their amount with sufficient precision to include them in sustainable earnings. Chapter 6 discusses nonrecurring income items more fully.

RATE OF RETURN ON ASSETS

The rate of return on assets measures a firm's success in using assets to generate earnings independent of the financing of those assets. ROA takes as given the particular set of environmental factors and strategic choices that a firm makes and focuses on how well a firm has used its assets to generate earnings for a particular period. ROA ignores, however, the means and costs of financing the assets (that is, the proportion of debt versus equity financing and the costs of those forms of capital).

The analyst calculates ROA as follows:

$$\text{ROA} = \frac{\text{Net Income} + (1 - \text{Tax Rate})(\text{Interest Expense}) + \text{Minority Interest in Earnings}}{\text{Average Total Assets}}$$

The numerator of ROA is net income excluding the effects of any financing costs. Calculating the numerator is usually accomplished most easily by starting with net income. If a firm has income from discontinued operations or extraordinary gains or losses, the analyst might start with income from continuing operations instead of net income if the objective is to measure a firm's sustainable profitability.

PepsiCo, for example, reports a $38 million tax benefit from discontinued operations for Year 4. Note 5, "Income Taxes" (Appendix A) indicates that the tax benefit relates to PepsiCo's restaurant business, which it discontinued several years previously. PepsiCo recognized income tax expenses related to the discontinued operation in the years before it discontinued this business. One or more aspects of the taxation of this business was apparently not settled with the Internal Revenue Service at the time, requiring PepsiCo to estimate the income tax impact. Subsequent resolution of the issue(s) for less than the amount of income taxes previously recognized resulted in an increase in net income for Year 4. The tax benefit clearly relates to events occurring in an earlier year and not likely to persist. Thus, we exclude the $38 tax benefit from net income and compute ROA using income from continuing operations of $4,174 million for Year 4. Year 4 was the only year in the three-year period in which PepsiCo reported income from discontinued operations or extraordinary gains or losses.

We must eliminate any financing costs included in the computation of net income. Because accountants subtract interest expense in computing net income, the analyst must add it back in computing ROA. However, firms can deduct interest expense in measuring taxable income. The *incremental* effect of interest expense on net income therefore equals one minus the marginal tax rate times interest expense. That is, the analyst adds back the full amount of interest expense to net income and then subtracts, or eliminates, the tax savings from that interest expense.

The tax savings from interest expense depends on the statutory tax rate in the tax jurisdiction where the firm raises its debt. The statutory federal tax rate is currently 35 percent in the United States. Firms must disclose in a note to the financial statements why the average income tax rate (defined as income tax expense divided by net income before income taxes) differs from the federal statutory tax rate of 35 percent. The statutory federal rate will differ from a firm's average tax rate because of (1) state, local, and foreign tax rates that differ from 35 percent and (2) revenues and expenses that firms include in book income but that do not impact taxable income (that is, permanent differences as described in Chapter 2). The analyst can attempt to approximate the combined statutory federal, state, local, and foreign tax rate applicable to tax savings from interest expense using 35 percent plus or minus the amounts disclosed related to item (1) above. Permanent differences in item (2) usually do not relate to interest expense and therefore should not affect the statutory tax rate applicable to interest expense deductions. To simplify the calculations, we will use the statutory federal tax rate of 35 percent in our computations of the tax savings from interest in the numerator of ROA throughout this book. Because accountants do not subtract dividends on preferred and common stocks in measuring net income, calculating the numerator of ROA requires no adjustment for dividends.[1]

The rationale for adding back the minority interest in earnings relates to attaining consistency in the numerator and the denominator of ROA. The denominator of ROA includes all assets of the consolidated entity, not just the parent's share. Net income in the numerator, however, represents the parent's earnings plus the parent's share of the earnings of consolidated subsidiaries. The accountant computes consolidated earnings by combining the earnings of the parent and consolidated subsidiaries and then subtracting the minority interest's claim on the earnings of consolidated subsidiaries. Consistency with the inclusion of all of the assets of the consolidated entity in the denominator of

[1]One could argue that the analyst should exclude returns from short-term investments of excess cash (that is, interest revenue) from the numerator of ROA and the short-term investments from the denominator of ROA under the view that such investments are really negative financings (that is, savings rather than borrowings). We do not make this adjustment when computing ROA, although we consider the effect of such short-term investments in the discussion of valuation in Chapters 10 to 14.

ROA requires that the numerator include all of the earnings of the consolidated entity, not just the parent's share. The addback of the minority interest in earnings accomplishes this objective. Most publicly traded corporations, including PepsiCo, do not disclose the minority interest in earnings because its amount, if any, is usually immaterial. Thus, the analyst makes this adjustment only for significant minority interests.

Because income from operations in the numerator of ROA reports the results for a period of time, the denominator uses a measure of average assets in use during that same period. For a nonseasonal business, an average of assets at the beginning and end of the year is usually satisfactory. For a seasonal business, the analyst should use an average of assets at the end of each quarter.

Refer to the financial statements for PepsiCo in Appendix A or in Chapter 1. The calculation of ROA for Year 4 is as follows:

$$\text{ROA} = \frac{\begin{matrix}\text{Income from} \\ \text{Continuing Operations}\end{matrix} + \begin{matrix}(1 - \text{Tax Rate}) \\ (\text{Interest Expense})\end{matrix} + \begin{matrix}\text{Minority Interest} \\ \text{in Earnings}\end{matrix}}{\text{Average Total Assets}}$$

$$16.1\% = \frac{\$4{,}174 + (1 - .35)(\$167) + \$0}{.5(\$25{,}327 + \$27{,}987)}$$

The analyst should consider whether reported net income includes any unusual or nonrecurring items that might affect assessments of a firm's ongoing profitability. The notes to the financial statements and the MD&A provide information for making these assessments. PepsiCo includes a section in its MD&A (Appendix B) labeled "Items Affecting Comparability." PepsiCo lists several items affecting net income that the analyst might consider unusual or nonrecurring. If the objective is to measure the sustainable profitability of PepsiCo, the analyst might decide to adjust the reported amounts for such items. Chapter 6 discusses and illustrates these adjustments more fully.

We consider adjusting PepsiCo's reported net income for four items for Year 2, Year 3, and Year 4 (in addition to eliminating the tax benefit from discontinued operations in Year 4 as discussed earlier):

1. PepsiCo reports for Year 3 $147 million of pretax impairment and restructuring charges ($100 million after taxes) related to streamlining operations in North America and in PepsiCo International.
2. PepsiCo reports for Year 4 $150 million of pretax impairment and restructuring charges ($96 million after tax) related to the consolidation of manufacturing operations at Frito-Lay North America.
3. PepsiCo reports merger-related costs of $224 million pretax ($190 million after tax) for Year 2 and $59 million pretax ($42 million after tax) for Year 3 arising from the merger with Quaker Oats in Year 1.
4. PepsiCo reports the realization of tax benefits of $109 million in Year 3 and $266 million in Year 4 resulting from the settlement with taxing authorities of taxes due for earlier years.

Impairment and Restructuring Charges. The first two items result from a similar event: PepsiCo is closing manufacturing plants and other facilities, which requires the firm to write off or write down the amounts appearing on the balance sheet for these plants and other facilities and to provide severance payments to employees. PepsiCo recognized such charges in two of the last three years and four of the last five years, having made similar charges in Year 0 and Year 1. When deciding whether to eliminate these charges when assessing sustainable profitability, the analyst will likely consider whether the plant closures are now complete or will likely continue. PepsiCo does not disclose specific information about its plans in this regard, so the analyst must predict based on events of the recent past. Recent history suggests that such charges will likely continue, supporting an analyst's decision to leave them in earnings when assessing profitability.

On the other hand, PepsiCo will not likely continue to close manufacturing facilities indefinitely. Closing such plants is also not central to PepsiCo's ongoing activities, which is manufacturing and distributing foods and beverages. Thus, the analyst could decide in this case to eliminate such charges.

A third approach is to leave the charges in earnings but de-emphasize them when analyzing ongoing profitability.

We follow the second approach and eliminate the charges in Year 3 and Year 4 based on their peripheral nature to PepsiCo's central operations and the assumption that the closing of manufacturing facilities is now complete. (We view the decision whether to eliminate the charges in this case as very close to call and could easily have concluded not to eliminate them based on their recurring nature in the recent past.) We illustrate the elimination procedure later in this section.

Merger-Related Costs. The merger-related costs in Year 2 and Year 3 result from the Quaker Oats merger in Year 1. PepsiCo also recognized merger-related costs in Year 1, resulting in such charges for three years in a row. The absence of such charges in Year 4, the clear link to a major acquisition several years ago, and the absence of another major acquisition since Year 1 also support a decision to eliminate these merger-related costs when assessing sustainable profitability.

Net Tax Benefits—Continuing Operations. In addition to the tax benefits related to PepsiCo's discontinued restaurant segment, PepsiCo also settled taxes for ongoing businesses in Year 3 and Year 4. PepsiCo applied GAAP correctly by reducing income tax expense in the years it settled with taxing authorities, even though the income taxes relate to earnings of prior years. The argument for eliminating the tax benefits for the discontinued restaurant business applies to continuing businesses as well. The tax benefits do not relate to earnings of current years, but to those of earlier years. One difference in this case is that PepsiCo continues to operate these businesses, and similar tax charges or benefits might arise in the future. We eliminate the tax benefits realized in Year 3 and Year 4.

We adjust net income for each of these items, net of their income tax effects. If firms disclose the income tax effect, we use the reported amounts. Otherwise, we assume that the marginal federal tax rate of 35 percent applies. PepsiCo discloses the pretax and after-tax amounts for each of these items in the section of the MD&A labeled "Items Affecting Comparability (Appendix B)." The adjustments to net income appear in Exhibit 4.2.

The adjusted ROA for PepsiCo for Year 4 is:

$$15.4\% = \frac{\$4{,}004 + (1 - .35)(\$167) + \$0}{.5(\$25{,}327 + \$27{,}987)} = \frac{\$4{,}113}{\$26{,}657}$$

We make similar adjustments for impairment and restructuring charges in Year 3, the merger-related costs in Year 2 and Year 3, and the tax benefits in Year 3. The adjusted ROA for PepsiCo is 14.6 percent for Year 2 and 15.2 percent for Year 3. Thus, PepsiCo's ROA based on the adjusted income amounts increased continually during the three-year period.

EXHIBIT 4.2

Adjustments to Reported Net Income for Unusual and Nonrecurring Items for PepsiCo (amounts in millions)

	Year 4	Year 3	Year 2
Reported Income from Continuing Operations before Income Taxes	$5,546	$4,992	$4,433
Impairment and Restructuring Charges:			
Year 4	150		
Year 3		147	
Merger-Related Costs:			
Year 3		59	
Year 2			224
Adjusted Income from Continuing Operations before Income Taxes	$5,696	$5,198	$4,657
Reported Income Tax Expense	$1,372	$1,424	$1,433
Impairment and Restructuring Charges:			
Year 4: $150 − $96	54		
Year 3: $147 − $100		47	
Merger-Related Costs:			
Year 3: $59 − $42		17	
Year 2: $224 − $190			34
Tax Benefits from Settlements with Taxing Authorities:			
Year 3		109	
Year 4	266		
Adjusted Income Tax Expense	$1,692	$1,597	$1,467
Adjusted Net Income	$4,004	$3,601	$3,190

A Note on the Calculation of ROA

Some financial economists subtract average noninterest-bearing liabilities (such as accounts payable and salaries payable) from average total assets in the denominator of ROA. Economists realize that when liabilities do not provide for explicit interest charges, the creditor charges implicit interest by adjusting the terms of the contract, such as setting a higher selling price or lower discount, for those who do not pay cash immediately. ROA requires in the numerator the income amount before a firm accrues any charges to suppliers of funds. We cannot measure the interest charges implicit in the noninterest-bearing liabilities; items such as cost of goods sold and salary expense are somewhat larger because of these charges. Thus, implicit interest charges reduce the measure of operating income in the numerator. Subtracting average noninterest-bearing liabilities from average total assets likewise reduces the denominator for assets financed with such liabilities. Despite the logic of reducing assets for noninterest-bearing liabilities, the examples and problems in this book follow the conventional practice of using average total assets in the denominator of ROA, making no adjustment for noninterest-bearing liabilities.

EXHIBIT 4.3

ROA, Profit Margin, and Assets Turnover for PepsiCo—Year 2 to Year 4

	Year 2	Year 3	Year 4
ROA	14.6%	15.2%	15.4%
Profit Margin for ROA	13.2%	13.7%	14.1%
Assets Turnover	1.1	1.1	1.1

Disaggregating ROA

The analyst obtains further insight into the behavior of ROA by disaggregating it into profit margin for ROA and total assets turnover (hereafter referred to as assets turnover) components as follows:

$$\textbf{ROA} = \textbf{Profit Margin for ROA} \times \textbf{Assets Turnover}$$

$$\frac{\text{Net Income + Interest Expense (net of taxes) + Minority Interest in Earnings}}{\text{Average Total Assets}} = \frac{\text{Net Income + Interest Expense (net of taxes) + Minority Interest in Earnings}}{\text{Sales}} \times \frac{\text{Sales}}{\text{Average Total Assets}}$$

The profit margin for ROA indicates the ability of a firm to generate earnings for a particular level of sales.[2] The assets turnover indicates the ability to manage the level of investment in assets for a particular level of sales or, to put it another way, the ability to generate sales from a particular investment in assets.

The disaggregation of ROA for PepsiCo for Year 4, after adjusting for nonrecurring items, is as follows:

$$\textbf{ROA} = \textbf{Profit Margin for ROA} \times \textbf{Assets Turnover}$$

$$\frac{\$\ 4{,}113}{\$26{,}657} = \frac{\$\ 4{,}113}{\$29{,}261} \times \frac{\$29{,}261}{\$26{,}657}$$

$$15.4\% = 14.1\% \times 1.1$$

Exhibit 4.3 summarizes ROA, profit margin for ROA, and assets turnover for PepsiCo for Year 2, Year 3, and Year 4. PepsiCo's profit margin for ROA steadily increased, while its assets turnover remained stable. After exploring economic and strategic factors underlying ROA and its components in the next section, we return to analyzing the profit margin for ROA and assets turnover of PepsiCo in greater depth.

Economic and Strategic Factors in the Interpretation of ROA[3]

ROA and its components differ across industries depending on their economic characteristics, and across firms within an industry depending on the design and implementation

[2]One might argue that the analyst should use total revenues, not just sales, in the denominator because assets generate returns in forms other than sales (for example, interest revenue, equity in earnings of affiliates). However, interpretations of various expense ratios (discussed later in this chapter) are usually easier when we use sales in the denominator.

[3]The material in this section draws heavily from Thomas I. Selling and Clyde P. Stickney, "The Effects of Business Environments and Strategy on a Firm's Rate of Return on Assets," *Financial Analysts Journal* (January/February 1989), pp. 43–52.

EXHIBIT 4.4

Average Median ROA, Profit Margin for ROA, and Assets Turnover for 23 Industries for 1990 to 2004

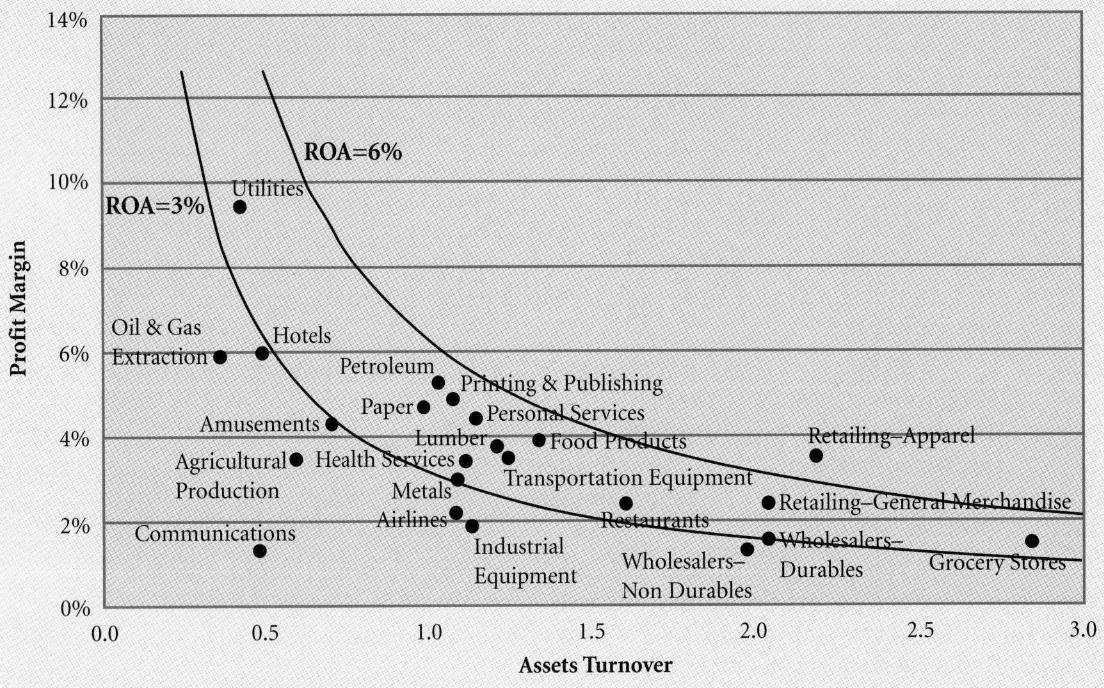

of their strategies. This section explores economic and strategic factors that impact the interpretation of ROA and its components.

Exhibit 4.4 depicts graphically the 15-year average of the median annual ROAs, profit margins for ROA, and assets turnovers of 23 industries for the years 1990 to 2004. The two isoquants reflect ROAs of 3 percent and 6 percent. The isoquants show the various combinations of profit margin for ROA and assets turnover that yield an ROA of 3 percent and 6 percent. For instance, an ROA of 6 percent results from any of the following profit margin for ROA × assets turnover combinations: 6% × 1.0, 3% × 2.0, 2% × 3.0, 1% × 6.0.

The data for ROA, profit margin for ROA, and assets turnover underlying the plots in Exhibit 4.4 reflect aggregated amounts across firms and across years. The focus of financial statement analysis is on the ROAs of specific firms, or even segments of specific firms, for particular years (or even quarters). We can obtain useful insights about the behavior of ROA at the segment or firm level, however, by examining the average industry-level data. In particular,

1. What factors explain the consistently high or consistently low ROAs of some industries relative to the average of all industries (that is, what are the reasons for differences in the distribution of industries in the bottom left versus the top right in Exhibit 4.4)?

2. What factors explain the fact that certain industries have high profit margins and low assets turnovers, while other industries experience low profit margins and high assets turnovers (that is, what are the reasons for differences in the distribution of industries in the upper left versus the lower right in Exhibit 4.4)?

The microeconomics and business strategy literature provides useful background for interpreting the behavior of ROA, profit margin, and assets turnover.

Differences or Changes in ROA

Economic theory suggests that higher levels of perceived risk in any activity should lead to higher levels of expected return if that activity is to attract capital. The extra return compensates for the extra risk assumed. Realized rates of return (ROAs) derived from financial statement data for any particular period will not necessarily correlate perfectly with expected returns or with the level of risk involved in an activity as economic theory suggests if:

1. Faulty assumptions were used in deriving expected ROAs.
2. Changes in the environment after forming expectations (such as an unexpected recession) cause realized ROAs to deviate from expectations.
3. ROA is an incomplete measure of economic rates of return (that is, rates of return that include all changes in economic value) because GAAP relies on acquisition costs for reliable measurement of assets and conservatism in measuring income.

Despite these potential weaknesses, ROAs based on reported financial statement data provide useful information for tracking the past periodic performance of a firm and its segments, and for developing expectations about future earnings potential. Three elements of risk help in understanding differences across firms and changes over time in ROAs: (1) operating leverage, (2) cyclicality of sales, and (3) product life cycles.

Operating Leverage. Firms operate with different mixtures of fixed and variable costs in their cost structures. Firms in the utilities, communications, hotel, petroleum, and chemical industries are capital intensive. Depreciation and many operating costs are more or less fixed for any given period. Most retailers and wholesalers, on the other hand, have high proportions of variable costs in their cost structures. Firms with high proportions of fixed costs experience significant increases in operating income as sales increase, a phenomenon known as *economies of scale.* The increased income occurs because the firms spread fixed costs over a larger number of units sold, resulting in a decrease in average unit cost. Likewise, when sales decrease, these firms experience sharp decreases in operating income, the result of *diseconomies of scale.* Economists refer to this process of operating with high proportions of fixed costs as *operating leverage.* Firms with high levels of operating leverage experience greater variability in their ROAs than firms with low levels of operating leverage. All else being equal (see the discussion of cyclicality of sales in the next section), firms with high levels of operating leverage incur more risk in their operations and should earn higher rates of return.

Measuring the degree of operating leverage of a firm or its segments requires information about the fixed and variable cost structure. The top panel of Exhibit 4.5 shows the total revenue and total cost functions of two firms, A and B. The graphs assume that the two firms are the same size and have the same total revenue functions and break-even points. These assumptions simplify the discussion of operating leverage but are not necessary when comparing actual companies.

Firm B has a higher level of fixed costs than Firm A, as measured by the intersection of the vertical axis at zero sales in the top panel of Exhibit 4.5. Firm A has a higher level of

EXHIBIT 4.5

Cost Structure and Operating Leverage

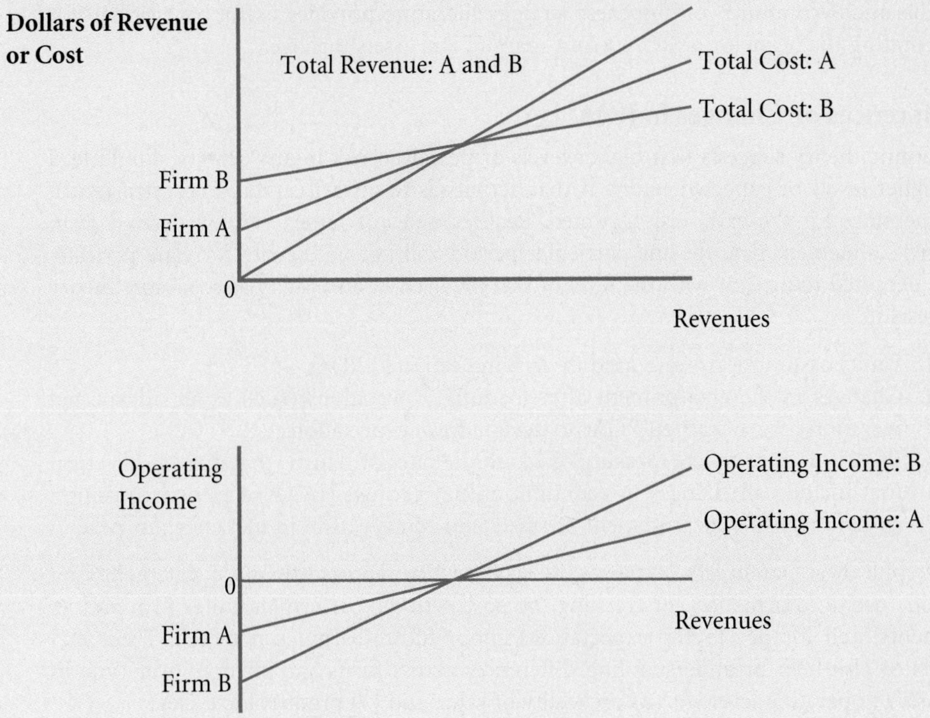

variable costs than Firm B, as measured by the slope of its total cost functions as revenues increase above zero. The lower panel nets the total revenue and total cost functions to derive the operating income function. Operating income is negative in an amount equal to fixed costs when revenues are zero and operating income is zero at break-even revenues. We use the slope of the operating income line as a measure of the extent of operating leverage. Firm B, with its higher fixed-cost and lower variable-cost mix, has more operating leverage. As revenues increase, its operating income increases more sharply than that of Firm A. On the downside, however, income decreases more sharply for Firm B as revenues decrease.

Unfortunately, firms do not publicly disclose information about their fixed and variable cost structures. To examine the influence of operating leverage on the behavior of ROA for a particular firm or its segments, the analyst must estimate the fixed/variable cost structure. One approach to such estimation is to study the various cost items of a firm and attempt to identify items that are likely to behave as fixed costs. Firms incur some costs in particular amounts, referred to as *committed fixed costs,* regardless of the actual level of activity during the period. Examples include depreciation, amortization, and rent. Firms can alter the amount of other costs, referred to as *discretionary fixed costs,* in the short run in response to operating conditions but, in general, these costs do not vary directly with the level of activity. Examples include research and development, maintenance, advertising, and central corporate staff expenses. Whether the analyst should classify these latter costs as fixed costs or as variable costs in measuring operating leverage depends on their behavior in a particular firm.

Cyclicality of Sales. The sales of certain goods and services are sensitive to conditions in the economy. Examples include construction services, industrial equipment, computers, automobiles, and other durable goods. When the economy is in an upswing (healthy GNP growth, low unemployment, low interest rates), customers purchase these relatively high-priced items and sales of these firms grow accordingly. When the economy enters a recession, customers curtail their purchases and the sales of these firms decrease significantly. Contrast these cyclical sales patterns with those of grocery stores, food processors, nonfashion clothing, and electric utilities. These latter industries sell products that most consumers consider necessities. Their products also tend to carry lower per-unit costs, reducing the benefits of delaying purchases in order to realize cost savings. Firms with cyclical sales patterns incur more risk than firms with noncyclical sales.

One means of reducing the risk inherent in cyclical sales is to strive for a high proportion of variable cost in the cost structure. Examples of variable-cost strategies include paying employees an hourly wage instead of a fixed salary and renting buildings and equipment under short-term cancelable leases instead of purchasing them. Cost levels should change proportionally with sales, thereby maintaining profit margin percentages and reducing risk.

The nature of the activities of some firms is such that they must carry high levels of fixed costs (that is, operating leverage). Examples include capital-intensive service firms such as airlines and railroads. Firms in these industries may attempt to transform the cost of their physical capacity from a fixed cost to a variable cost by engaging in short-term leases. However, lessors will then bear the risk of cyclical sales and demand higher returns (that is, rental fees). Thus, some firms bear a combination of operating leverage and cyclical sales risks.

A noncyclical sales pattern can compensate for high operating leverage and effectively neutralize this latter element of risk. Electric utilities, for example, carry high levels of fixed costs. Their dominant positions in most service areas, however, reduce their operating risks and permit them to achieve stable profitability.

Product Life Cycle. A third element of risk that affects ROA relates to the stage and length of a firm's product life cycle, a concept discussed in Chapter 3 with regard to relations between cash flows from operating, investing, and financing activities. Products move through four identifiable phases: introduction, growth, maturity, and decline. During the introduction and growth phases, a firm focuses on product development (product R&D spending) and capacity enlargement (capital spending). The objective is to gain market acceptance and market share. Considerable uncertainty may exist during these phases regarding the market viability of a firm's products. Products that have survived into the maturity phase have gained market acceptance. Also, firms have probably been able to cut back capital expenditures on new operating capacity. During the maturity phase, however, competition becomes more intense, and the emphasis shifts to reducing costs through improved capacity utilization (economies of scale) and more efficient production (process R&D spending aimed at reducing manufacturing costs through better utilization of labor and materials). During the decline phase, firms exit the industry as sales decline and profit opportunities diminish.

Exhibit 4.6 depicts the behavior of revenues, operating income, investment, and ROA that corresponds to the four phases of the product life cycle. During the introduction and early-growth phases, expenditures on product development and marketing, coupled with relatively low sales levels, lead to operating losses and negative ROAs. As sales accelerate during the high-growth phase, operating income and ROAs turn positive. Extensive

EXHIBIT 4.6

Relation between Sales, Operating Income, Investment, and ROA during Product Life Cycle

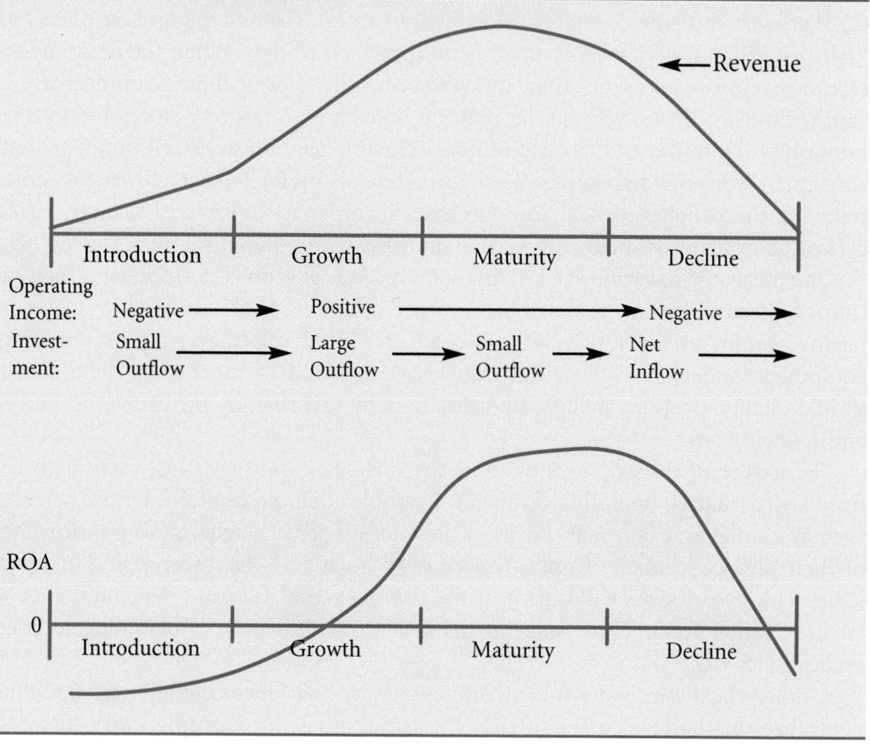

product development, marketing, and depreciation expenses during this phase moderate operating income, while heavy capital expenditures to build capacity for expected higher future sales increase the denominator of ROA. Thus, ROA does not grow as rapidly as sales. ROA increases significantly during the maturity phase due to benefits of economies of scale and learning curve phenomena, and to curtailments of capital expenditures. ROA deteriorates during the decline phase as operating income decreases, but may remain positive or even increase for some time into this phase. Thus, as products move through their life cycles, their ROAs should move to the upper right area in Exhibit 4.4, peak during the maturity stage, and then move to the lower left area as the decline phase sets in. This movement in ROA appears negatively correlated with the level of risk. Risks are probably highest in the introduction and growth stages, when ROA is low or negative, and least in the maturity phase, when ROA is high. Recall, though, that ROA measures realized accounting returns in a given period, whereas the usual risk-return trade-off metric refers to expected returns. Taking a weighted average of ROAs over several years will reflect more accurately the economic returns generated by high-growth firms.

Note that the product life cycle theory focuses on individual products. We can extend the theory to an industry level by examining the average stage in the product life cycle of all products within that industry. For instance, products in the computer industry range from the introduction to the decline phases, but the overall industry is probably in the latter part of the high-growth phase. The beverage and food-processing industries, the primary involvements of PepsiCo, are mature, although PepsiCo and its competitors continually introduce new products. We might view the steel industry, at least in the United States, as in the early-decline phase, although some companies have modernized production sufficiently to stave off the decline.[4]

In addition to the stage in the product life cycle, the length of the product life cycle is also an element of risk. Products with short product life cycles require more frequent expenditures to develop replacement or new products and thereby increase risks. The product life cycles of most computer products run one to two years. Most pharmaceutical products experience product life cycles of approximately seven years. In contrast, the life cycles of PepsiCo's soft drinks, branded food products, and some toys (for example, Barbie dolls) are much longer.

Refer again to the average industry ROAs in Exhibit 4.4. The location of several industries is consistent with their incurring one or more of these elements of risk. The relatively high ROAs of the utilities and petroleum industries are consistent with high operating leverage. Paper, petroleum, and transportation equipment experience cyclical sales. Apparel retailers face the risk of fashion obsolescence of their products.

Some of the industry locations in Exhibit 4.4 appear inconsistent with these elements of risk. Oil and gas extraction, agricultural production, and communications are capital intensive, yet their ROAs are the lowest of the twenty-three industries. One might view these positions as disequilibrium situations. Generating such low ROAs will not likely attract capital over the longer term.

The ROA locations of several industries appear to be affected by GAAP. A principal resource of food products firms, such as General Mills or Kellogg, is the value of their brand names. Yet GAAP requires these firms to expense immediately advertising and other costs incurred to develop these brand names. Thus, their asset bases are understated and their ROAs are overstated.[5] Likewise, the publishing industry does not recognize the value of copyrights or authors' contracts as assets, resulting in an overstatement of ROAs. A similar overstatement problem occurs for service firms, for which the value of their employees does not appear as an asset.

Differences in the Profit Margin/Assets Turnover Mix

In addition to the differences in ROA depicted in Exhibit 4.4, we must also examine reasons for differences in the relative mix of profit margin and assets turnover. Explanations come from both the microeconomics and business strategy literature.

Microeconomic Theory. Exhibit 4.7 sets out some important economic factors that constrain certain firms and industries to operate with particular combinations of profit margins and assets turnovers. Firms and industries characterized by heavy fixed capacity costs and lengthy periods required to add new capacity operate under a capacity constraint. There is an upper limit on the size of assets turnover achievable. In order to attract sufficient capital, these firms must generate a relatively high profit margin. Such firms will therefore operate in the area of Exhibit 4.7 marked (A). The firms usually achieve the high profit margin through some form of entry barrier. The entry barrier may take the form of large required capital outlays, high risks, or regulation. Such factors help explain the profit margin/assets turnover mix of utilities, oil and gas extraction, communications, hotels, and amusements in Exhibit 4.4.

---

[4]Empirical support for a link between life cycle stage, sales growth, capital expenditure growth, and stock market reaction appears in Joseph H. Anthony and K. Ramesh, "Association between Accounting Performance Measures and Stock Prices: A Test of the Life Cycle Hypothesis," *Journal of Accounting and Economics* 15 (1992), pp. 203–227.

[5]The immediate expensing of advertising costs understates net income as well, but the difference between the amount expensed and amortization of amounts from the current and prior periods that perhaps should have been capitalized will result in less distortion of net income than of total assets.

EXHIBIT 4.7

Economic Factors Affecting the Profit Margin/Assets Turnover Mix

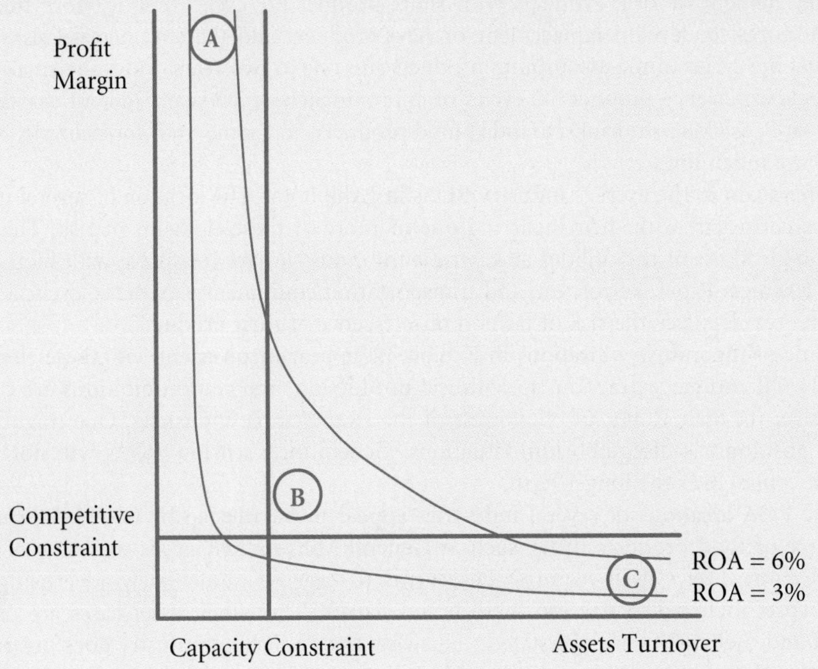

Firms whose products are commodity-like in nature, where there are few entry barriers, and where competition is intense operate under a competitive constraint. There is an upper limit on the achievable level of profit margin for ROA. In order to attract sufficient capital, these firms must strive for high assets turnovers. Such firms will therefore operate in the area of Exhibit 4.7 marked (C). Firms achieve the high assets turnovers by keeping costs as low as possible (for example, minimizing fixed overhead costs, purchasing in sufficient quantities to realize discounts, and integrating vertically or horizontally to obtain cost savings). These firms match such actions to control costs with aggressively low prices to gain market share and drive out marginal firms. Most retailers and wholesalers operate in the low profit margin for ROA/high assets turnover area of Exhibit 4.4.

Firms that operate in the area of Exhibit 4.7 marked (B) are not as subject to either capacity or competitive constraints as severe as those that operate in the tails of the ROA curves. Therefore, they have more flexibility to take actions that will increase profit margin for ROA, assets turnover, or both, to achieve a higher ROA.

The notion of flexibility in trading off profit margin for assets turnover (or vice versa) is important when a firm considers strategic alternatives. The underlying economic concept is the marginal rate of substitution.

Consider first a firm with a profit margin for ROA/assets turnover combination that puts it in area (A) of Exhibit 4.7. Such a firm will have to give up a significant amount of profit margin for ROA to obtain a meaningful increase in assets turnover. To increase ROA, this firm should emphasize actions that increase profit margin for ROA; it might, for example, increase selling prices or reduce variable costs. Likewise, a firm in area (C) of

Exhibit 4.7 will have to give up considerable assets turnover to achieve a higher profit margin for ROA. To increase ROA, such a firm should emphasize actions that increase assets turnover. For firms operating in the tails of the ROA curves, the poor marginal rates of substitution do not favor trading off one variable for the other. Such firms must generally emphasize only one of these factors.

For firms operating in area (B) of Exhibit 4.7, the marginal rates of substitution of profit margin for assets turnover are more equal. Such firms, therefore, have more flexibility to design strategies that promote profit margin for ROA, assets turnover, or some combination, when striving to increase ROA. Unless the economic characteristics of a business constrain it to operate in area (A) or (C), firms should strive to position themselves in area (B). Such positioning provides greater potential to adapt to changing economic and business conditions.

Firms operating in area (A) might attempt to reposition the capacity constraint to the right by outsourcing some of their production. Such an action reduces the amount of fixed assets needed per dollar of sales (that is, increases the fixed asset turnover), but will likely reduce the profit margin for ROA (because of the need to share some of the margin with the outsourcing company). Firms operating in area (C) might add products with a higher profit margin for ROA. Grocery stores, for example, have added fresh flowers, salad bars, fresh bakery products, and pharmaceutical prescription services to their product offerings in recent years in an effort to increase their profit margin for ROA and advance beyond the competitive constraint common for grocery products.

In summary, the economic concepts underlying the profit margin for ROA/assets turnover mix are the following:

Area in Exhibit 4.7	Capital Intensity	Competition	Likely Strategic Focus
(A)	High	Monopoly	Profit Margin for ROA
(B)	Medium	Oligopolistic or Monopolistic Competition	Profit Margin for ROA, Assets Turnover, or Some Combination
(C)	Low	Pure Competition	Assets Turnover

Business Strategy. Hall[6] and Porter[7] suggest that firms have two generic, alternative strategies for any particular product: product differentiation and low-cost leadership. The thrust of the product differentiation strategy is to differentiate a product in such a way as to obtain market power over revenues and, therefore, profit margins. The differentiation could relate to product capabilities, product quality, service, channels of distribution, or some other factor. The thrust of the low-cost leadership strategy is to become the lowest-cost producer, thereby enabling the firm to charge the lowest prices and to achieve higher volumes. Such firms can achieve the low-cost position through economies of scale, production efficiencies, outsourcing, or similar factors, or by asset parsimony (maintaining strict controls on investments in receivables, inventories, and capital expenditures).[8]

[6]W. K. Hall, "Survival Strategies in a Hostile Environment," *Harvard Business Review* (September–October 1980), pp. 78–85.

[7]M. E. Porter, *Competitive Strategy: Techniques for Analyzing Industries and Competitors* (New York: Free Press, 1998). Porter suggests that firms might also pursue a niche strategy. Because a niche strategy essentially represents differentiation within a market segment, we include it here under product differentiation strategy.

[8]Research in business strategy suggests that firms can simultaneously pursue product differentiation and low-cost leadership because product differentiation is revenue (output) oriented and low-cost leadership is more expense (input) oriented.

In terms of Exhibit 4.7, movements in the direction of area (A) from any point along the ROA curves focus on product differentiation. Likewise, movements in the direction of area (C) from any point along the ROA curves focus on low-cost leadership. To illustrate, let us look at the average profit margins for ROA and assets turnovers for three types of retailers during the period from 1990 to 2004:

	Profit Margin for ROA	Assets Turnover
Specialty Retailers	2.97%	2.21
General Merchandise Stores	2.38%	2.02
Grocery Stores	1.43%	2.82

Within the retailing industry, specialty retailers have differentiated themselves by following a niche strategy and achieved a higher profit margin for ROA than the other two segments. Competition severely constrains the profit margin for ROA of grocery stores and they must pursue more low-cost leadership strategies. Thus, a firm does not have to be in the tails of the ROA curves to be described as a product differentiator or low-cost leader. The appropriate basis of comparison is not other industries but other firms in the same industry. Remember, however, that the relative location along the ROA curve affects a firm's flexibility to trade off profit margin for ROA (product differentiation) for assets turnover (low-cost leadership).

Summarizing, differences in the profit margin for ROA/assets turnover mix relate to economic factors external to a firm (such as degree of competition, extent of regulation, entry barriers, and similar factors) and to internal strategic choices (such as product differentiation and low-cost leadership). The external and internal factors are, of course, interdependent and dynamic.

PepsiCo's Positioning Relative to the Consumer Foods Industry

PepsiCo is part of the consumer foods industry. The average of the median ROA, profit margin for ROA, and assets turnover for the consumer foods industry for Year 2, Year 3, and Year 4, and the average amounts for PepsiCo for the three years, are as follows:

	Consumer Foods Industry	PepsiCo
ROA	5.1%	15.3%
Profit Margin for ROA	4.5%	14.1%
Total Assets Turnover	1.2	1.1

Note that the average ROA of PepsiCo significantly exceeds that for the food products industry because of higher profit margins for ROA earned by PepsiCo. Possible economic or strategic explanations for the higher profit margin for ROA include (1) more value to PepsiCo's brand names than other food products companies, (2) greater pricing power because of domination of the beverage industry by PepsiCo and Coca-Cola, (3) greater pricing power because of PepsiCo's influence over its bottlers, and (4) greater efficiencies due to its size or quality of management. The next section explores this higher profit margin for ROA more fully.

Analyzing the Profit Margin for ROA

The ROA of PepsiCo increased continually between Year 2 and Year 4. The disaggregation of ROA into the profit margin for ROA and assets turnover components in Exhibit 4.3

reveals that the increased ROA results from an increased profit margin for ROA. The assets turnover did not change. One might liken this disaggregation to peeling an onion. ROA is the outer layer (Level 1). Peeling away that layer reveals the profit margin for ROA and assets turnover (Level 2). We can peel the onion an additional layer by examining the components of the profit margin for ROA and the components of total assets turnover (Level 3).

We express each revenue and expense amount as a percentage of sales to identify reasons for changes in the profit margin for ROA. Exhibit 4.8 presents these revenue and expense percentages for PepsiCo. We should note that these percentages can change because of (a) changes in revenues and expenses in the numerator independent of changes in sales (for example, an increase in employee compensation levels), (b) changes in sales independent of changes in expenses (for example, because the expense is fixed for the period), (c) interaction effects between numerator and denominator (an increase in advertising expenses leads to an increase in sales), or (d) coincident but independent changes in the numerator and denominator (that is, combinations of the other three possibilities).

Note from Exhibit 4.8 that PepsiCo's profit margin for ROA increases because of the following:

- Increases in the interest revenues percentage.
- Increases in the bottling equity income percentage.
- Decreases in the selling and administrative expense percentage.

The task for the financial analyst is to identify reasons for the changes in these revenue and expense percentages. The MD&A provides information for interpreting the changes in these profitability percentages. Firms vary with respect to the informativeness of these discussions. Some firms give specific reasons for changes in various financial ratios. Other firms simply indicate the amount or rate of increase or decrease without providing explanations for the changes. Even when firms provide explanations, the analyst should assess their reasonableness in light of conditions in the economy and in the industry, as well as the firm's stated strategy and the results for the firms' competitors.

We use information provided by PepsiCo in its MD&A (Appendix B) to identify reasons for changes in the profit margin for ROA.

EXHIBIT 4.8

Analysis of the Profit Margin for PepsiCo—Year 2 to Year 4

	Year 2	Year 3	Year 4
Sales	100.0%	100.0%	100.0%
Interest Revenues	0.1	0.2	0.3
Bottling Equity Income	1.1	1.2	1.3
Cost of Goods Sold	(45.8)	(45.9)	(45.8)
Selling, General, and Administrative	(35.7)	(35.1)	(35.2)
Amortization of Intangibles	(0.5)	(0.5)	(0.5)
Income Taxes	(6.1)	(6.1)	(6.0)
Profit Margin for ROA	13.2%	13.7%	14.1%

Interest Revenue

PepsiCo earns interest on cash balances and short-term investments. Interest revenue as a percentage of the average balance in cash and short-term investments during Year 2, Year 3, and Year 4 are as follows (in millions):

Year 2: \$36/\$1,747 = 2.1%
Year 3: \$51/\$1,923 = 2.7%
Year 4: \$74/\$2,723 = 2.7%

Thus, the increased interest revenue to sales percentage results from larger average balances in cash and short-term investments and, during Year 3, an increase in the yield.

Firms with temporarily excess cash should invest the cash in income-yielding securities, as PepsiCo has done, instead of allowing the cash to remain idle. However, analysts generally do not view interest revenue as an important source of profitability for most manufacturing and retailing firms (except retailing firms that offer their own credit cards). To have the greatest impact on share value, firms should derive most of the increases in profitability from their core operations, which in PepsiCo's case is manufacturing and selling consumer foods and beverages. A buildup of excess cash and marketable securities may suggest that a firm has few opportunities to invest in its core operations. The proportion of assets comprising cash and short-term investments for PepsiCo averaged approximately 10 percent of total assets during the most recent three years, which does not suggest an excessive buildup at the end of any of the three years.

Bottling Equity Income

Chapter 1 indicated that PepsiCo owns approximately 40 percent of the common stock of some of its bottlers. Because PepsiCo does not own more than 50 percent of the common stock of these bottlers, it cannot consolidate its financial statements with those of the bottlers. Instead, PepsiCo accounts for these investments using the equity method, which Chapter 9 discusses more fully. Firms using the equity method recognize as income each period their share of the net income or net loss of the investees. Thus, bottling equity income for PepsiCo represents its share of the net income of its noncontrolled bottling companies. PepsiCo discloses in its MD&A (Appendix B) that bottling equity income also includes gains and losses from selling shares of its bottlers. Bottling equity income as a percent of sales increased from 1.1 percent to 1.3 percent between Year 2 and Year 4. Bottling equity income as a percentage of the average balance in Investments in Noncontrolled Affiliates is as follows (in millions):

Year 2: \$280/\$2,741 = 10.2%
Year 3: \$323/\$2,766 = 11.7%
Year 4: \$380/\$3,102 = 12.3%

Thus, the increase in bottling equity income as a percentage of sales results from a combination of increased profitability of bottlers, gains on PepsiCo's sales of its common stock in the bottlers, and a larger investment base. PepsiCo does not provide sufficient information to determine how much of the bottling equity income is its share of the income of the bottlers and how much represents gains on sales of common stock in the bottlers.

In contrast to interest revenue, bottling equity income is more central to PepsiCo's core operations. The analyst should evaluate the increases in profitability of these bottlers cautiously. These bottlers derive most of their income by purchasing concentrate or syrup from PepsiCo, processing it into consumable beverages, placing it in a bottle or other container, and then selling it. A principal cost to these bottlers is the amount it pays PepsiCo for the concentrate or syrup. Thus, PepsiCo's pricing policies in selling to the bottlers impacts the profitability of the bottlers. Also affecting the income of the bottlers is their control over other manufacturing, selling, and administrative costs. Firms seldom provide the necessary information for the analyst to identify how much of any changes in profitability results from pricing actions by the investor company and how much results from better management of other costs.

Cost of Goods Sold

Interpreting changes in the cost of goods sold to sales percentage are often difficult because explanations might relate to sales revenue only, to cost of goods sold only, or to common factors affecting both the numerator and the denominator. Consider, for example, the following possible explanations for a decrease in the cost of goods sold to sales percentage for a firm:

1. An increase in demand for products in excess of available capacity in an industry will likely result in an increase in selling prices. Even though the cost of manufacturing the product does not change, the cost of goods sold percentage will decrease.
2. As a result of product improvements or effective advertising, a firm's market share for its product increases. The firm allocates the fixed cost of manufacturing the product over a larger volume of production, thereby lowering its per-unit cost. Even though selling prices do not change, the cost of goods sold to sales percentage will decrease.
3. A firm lowers the price for its product in order to gain a larger market share. It lowers its manufacturing cost per unit by purchasing raw materials in larger quantities to take advantage of quantity discounts. Cost of goods sold per unit declines more than selling price per unit, causing the cost of goods sold to sales percentage to decline.
4. A firm sells multiple products with different cost of goods sold to sales percentages. The product mix shifts toward higher-profit-margin products, thereby lowering the overall cost of goods sold to sales percentage.

Thus, the analyst must consider changes in selling prices, manufacturing costs, and product mix when interpreting changes in the cost of goods sold percentage.

Exhibit 4.8 indicates that PepsiCo's cost of goods sold to sales percentage was relatively stable during the three-year period. Management's discussion of the results of operations (Appendix B) indicates that PepsiCo encountered higher commodity costs, particularly for corn oil and natural gas, in Year 3, accounting for the slight increase in the cost of goods sold to sales percentage in that year.

Selling, General, and Administrative Expenses

Most firms combine selling, general, and administrative expenses on the income statement. Combining these expense items is unfortunate from an analysis perspective because different factors tend to drive these two expenses. Selling expenses include sales commissions, advertising, and promotion materials, and usually vary with the level of sales. General and administrative expenses include top management's salaries and the cost of operating staff departments, such as information systems, legal services, and research and development. These costs tend not to vary with the level of sales.

PepsiCo's selling, general, and administrative expenses to sales percentage decreased significantly between Year 2 and Year 3 and then increased slightly in Year 4. Management's discussion of operations (Appendix B) does not give sufficient information to understand the reason for the decreased percentage between Year 2 and Year 3. Sales increased 7.4 percent between Year 2 and Year 3, so the spreading of relatively fixed administrative costs over a larger sales base might explain the decrease. However, sales increased 8.5 percent between Year 3 and Year 4 but the selling, general, and administrative expense to sales percentage increased slightly, casting doubt on the preceding explanation regarding the spreading of fixed costs.

Segment Data

GAAP requires firms in the United States to provide financial data for their product and geographical segments.[9] Firms typically report segment sales, operating income, assets, capital expenditures, and depreciation and amortization for their product segments. They typically report sales for their geographical segments. Note 1, "Basis of Presentation and Our Divisions," to PepsiCo's financial statements (Appendix A) presents these segment data for Year 2, Year 3, and Year 4. PepsiCo reports product segment data for Frito-Lay North America, PepsiCo Beverages North America, Quaker Foods North America, and PepsiCo International. It reports geographical segment sales data for the United States, Mexico, the United Kingdom, Canada, and all other countries combined.

The segment disclosures permit the analyst to examine ROA, profit margin, and assets turnover at an additional level (Level 4) of depth, in effect peeling the onion one more layer. Unfortunately, firms do not report cost of goods sold and selling, general, and administrative expenses for each segment, so we cannot reconcile changes in segment profit margins to changes in the overall levels of these two expense percentages. Firms also report segment data pretax, so the segment ROAs and profit margins exceed those for the overall company to a considerable extent.

Exhibit 4.9 presents sales mix data for PepsiCo. PepsiCo's sales mix has shifted during the three years from its North American segments to PepsiCo International, with most of the international growth in the United Kingdom and the All Other Countries segments. Exhibit 4.10 presents ROAs, profit margins, and assets turnovers for each of PepsiCo's product segments. We compute segment ROAs and asset turnover using assets at the end of the period, instead of the average of the period as we do for the firm as a whole, to ease calculations.[10] Note that with the minor exception of the profit margin for Quaker Foods North America in Year 4, the ROA and the profit margin increased for each segment in each year. The assets turnovers remained relatively steady.

The improvement in segment profit margins between Year 2 and Year 3 likely relates to the decrease in the selling, general, and administrative expense to sales percentage between those years. As indicated earlier, PepsiCo does not disclose the reasons for the decreased percentage, but the benefits appear to favorably affect all of PepsiCo operating segments.

---

[9]Financial Accounting Standards Board, *Statement of Financial Accounting Standards No. 131*, "Disclosures about Segments of an Enterprise and Related Information" (1997).

[10]The difficulty that the analyst often encounters with using average segment assets is that firms frequently change their definition of segments over time. Firms report the three most recent years of segment asset data in their current annual report. The analyst would need to access asset data for the fourth year back in order to compute average assets for the three years. Firms that have changed their segment definitions within the last year will not show assets on a consistent basis with current segment definitions. For a stable, mature company like PepsiCo, the use of assets at the end of the period instead of the average for the period will affect the level of the ROAs and the asset turnover ratios but will not likely have a material effect on the trend of these segment ratios over time unless the firm made a significant corporate acquisition during one of the years.

EXHIBIT 4.9

Sales Mix Data for PepsiCo

	Year 2	Year 3	Year 4
Product Segments			
Frito-Lay North America	34.3%	33.7%	32.7%
PepsiCo Beverages North America	28.8	28.7	28.4
Quaker Foods North America	5.9	5.4	5.2
PepsiCo International	31.0	32.2	33.7
Total	100.0%	100.0%	100.0%
Geographical Segments			
United States	66.1%	64.4%	62.6%
Mexico	10.7	9.8	9.3
United Kingdom	4.4	5.6	5.8
Canada	3.8	4.3	4.5
All Other Countries	15.0	15.9	17.8
Total	100.0%	100.0%	100.0%

EXHIBIT 4.10

Product Segment Pretax Profitability Analysis for PepsiCo

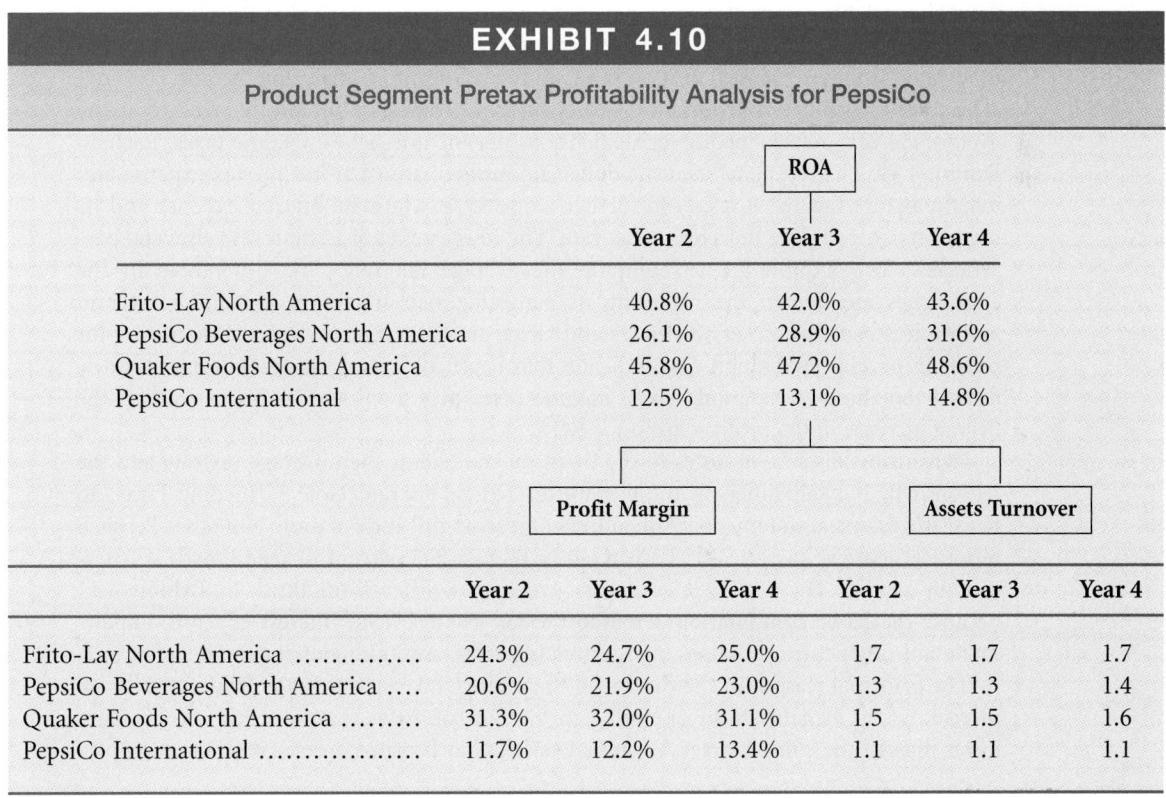

ROA

	Year 2	Year 3	Year 4
Frito-Lay North America	40.8%	42.0%	43.6%
PepsiCo Beverages North America	26.1%	28.9%	31.6%
Quaker Foods North America	45.8%	47.2%	48.6%
PepsiCo International	12.5%	13.1%	14.8%

	Profit Margin			Assets Turnover		
	Year 2	Year 3	Year 4	Year 2	Year 3	Year 4
Frito-Lay North America	24.3%	24.7%	25.0%	1.7	1.7	1.7
PepsiCo Beverages North America	20.6%	21.9%	23.0%	1.3	1.3	1.4
Quaker Foods North America	31.3%	32.0%	31.1%	1.5	1.5	1.6
PepsiCo International	11.7%	12.2%	13.4%	1.1	1.1	1.1

The improved segment profit margins between Year 3 and Year 4 would not seem to relate to a decrease in the selling, general, and administrative expense to sales percentage because this ratio actually increased between Year 3 and Year 4. PepsiCo provides the likely explanation under the heading "Net Revenue and Operating Profit and Corporate Unallocated Expenses" in its MD&A, which appears in Appendix B. PepsiCo's unallocated corporate expenses increased 14 percent between Year 2 and Year 3, while its sales increased 7.4 percent. PepsiCo's unallocated corporate expenses increased 38 percent between Year 3 and Year 4, while its sales increased 8.5 percent. PepsiCo includes these expenses in selling, general, and administrative expenses in its income statement but does not allocate them to its operating segments when disclosing segment data. Corporate unallocated expenses as a percentage of sales were as follows for the three years:

Year 2: $438/$25,112 = 1.7%
Year 3: $502/$26,971 = 1.9%
Year 4: $689/$29,261 = 2.4%

The analyst must exert caution when interpreting segment profit margins and ROAs. Changes in the amount of expenses allocated versus not allocated to segments, a choice made by management, affect these ratios. PepsiCo discloses that the increases in corporate unallocated expenses relate to higher employee-related costs, including deferred compensation, higher costs related to an initiative to improve process efficiencies, and, in Year 4, the settlement of a contract dispute with a former business partner. Most of the increase in Year 4 relates to higher employee-related costs.

Income Taxes

Exhibit 4.8 indicates that income taxes as a percentage of sales were relatively stable each year. These stable income tax percentages do not necessarily mean that PepsiCo's income tax burden is not changing. Governmental entities impose income taxes on income (that is, revenues minus expenses), not on sales. So that rather than analyzing income taxes relative to sales, a more appropriate measure of the income tax burden, referred to as the *average tax rate,* relates income tax expense to net income before income taxes. Refer to Exhibit 4.11. The top panel uses the dollar amounts of adjusted income tax expense and income before income taxes, both further adjusted to eliminate interest expense and its tax effects, to compute the average tax rate. The lower panel of Exhibit 4.11 uses the percentages from Exhibit 4.8 to compute the average tax rate. The differences in the approaches are due to the rounding of percentages in the lower panel. The second approach is usually quicker and easier and yields amounts that are sufficiently precise for purposes of analysis. Exhibit 4.11 indicates that PepsiCo's average tax rate declined slowly during the three-year period. Thus, income taxes play a minor role in explaining the overall increase in the profit margin for ROA.

Firms must disclose in notes to the financial statements their average tax rate and the reasons why this rate differs from the statutory federal tax rate. Note 5, "Income Taxes," to PepsiCo's financial statements (Appendix A) presents this information. Note that PepsiCo reports an average tax rate of 32.3 percent in Year 2, 28.5 percent in Year 3, and 24.7 percent in Year 4. These average tax rate percentages differ from those in Exhibit 4.11 because the latter computations exclude the tax savings from interest expense, impairment and restructuring charges, merger-related costs, and nonrecurring tax benefits.

The principal reason for the decline in the average tax rate shown in Exhibit 4.11 is an increase in tax benefits from operating in foreign countries that have income tax rates lower than in the United States. We noted earlier that PepsiCo derived an increasing per-

EXHIBIT 4.11

Calculation of Effective Tax Rate on Profit Margin for ROA (amounts for top panel taken from Exhibit 4.2 and for lower panel taken from Exhibit 4.8)

	Year 2	Year 3	Year 4
Calculation using Dollar Amounts			
(1) Adjusted Income Tax Expense	$1,467	$ 1,597	$1,692
(2) Tax Effect of Interest Expense at 35%	62	57	58
(3) Adjusted Income Tax Expense excluding Tax Effects of Interest Expense	$1,529	$1,654	$1,750
(4) Adjusted Income before Income Taxes	$4,657	$5,198	$5,696
(5) Interest Expense	178	163	167
(6) Adjusted Income before Income Taxes and Interest Expense	$4,835	$5,361	$5,863
(7) Effective Tax Rate (3) ÷ (6)	31.6%	30.9%	29.8%
Calculation using Percentages of Sales			
Numerator			
(8) Income Taxes Expense	6.1%	6.1%	6.0%
Denominator			
(9) Profit Margin for ROA	13.2%	13.7%	14.1%
(10) Income Taxes	6.1	6.1	6.0
(11) Profit Margin before Income Taxes	19.3%	19.8%	20.1%
(12) Effective Tax Rate (8) ÷ (11)	31.6%	30.8%	29.9%

centage of its revenues from PepsiCo International, consistent with increased tax savings from other countries.

Summary of Profit Margin Analysis

We noted at the beginning of this section that PepsiCo's profit margin for ROA increased steadily between Year 2 and Year 4. The increased profit margin for ROA results from increased interest and bottling equity income, a decreased selling and administrative expense to sales percentage in Year 3, and a decline in the effective tax rate. The increased interest revenues result from larger amounts of cash and short-term investments in all three years and a higher yield in Year 3. The increased bottling equity income results from larger investments in affiliates and a higher yield, the latter due to increased profitability of the bottlers and/or larger gains on sales of their common stock by PepsiCo. The reason for decline in the selling and administrative expense to sales percentage in Year 3 is not clear. The product segment data indicate an increased profit margin in virtually all segments for all years. Offsetting this improved segment profitability is an increase in unallocated corporate expenses, the result of larger employee-related costs, expenditures on improving process efficiencies, and costs of settling a contract dispute. The effective tax rate declined slightly as a result of deriving a higher proportion of income from lower-tax-rate countries.

Analyzing Total Assets Turnover

We noted earlier that PepsiCo's total assets turnover remained steady at 1.1 between Year 2 and Year 4. We can gain greater insight into changes in the total assets turnover by examining turnover ratios for particular assets. Analysts frequently calculate three turnover ratios: accounts receivable turnover, inventory turnover, and fixed asset turnover. Management's discussion and analysis of operations usually does not include explanations for changes in asset turnovers, so the analyst will need to search for possible clues.

Accounts Receivable Turnover

The rate at which accounts receivable turn over indicates how soon firms will collect them in cash. The analyst calculates the accounts receivable turnover by dividing net sales on account by average accounts receivable. Most sales transactions between businesses are on account instead of for cash. Except for retailers and restaurants that deal directly with consumers, the assumption that all sales are on account is usually reasonable. The calculation of the accounts receivable turnover for Year 4 for PepsiCo, assuming that it makes all sales on account, is as follows:

$$\text{Accounts Receivable Turnover} = \frac{\text{Net Sales on Account}}{\text{Average Accounts Receivable}}$$

$$10.0 = \frac{\$29{,}261}{.5\ (\$2{,}830 + \$2{,}999)}$$

PepsiCo's accounts receivable turnover was 10.7 in Year 2 and 10.1 in Year 3.

The analyst often expresses the accounts receivable turnover in terms of the average number of days receivables are outstanding before firms will collect them in cash. The calculation divides 365 days by the accounts receivable turnover. The average number of days that accounts receivable were outstanding is 34.1 days (= 365/10.7) for Year 2, 36.1 days (= 365/10.1) for Year 3, and 36.5 days (= 365/10.0) for Year 4.

The interpretation of the average collection period depends on the terms of sale. If customers must pay within forty-five days, then it appears that most of PepsiCo's customers pay within the required period. If the terms of sale are, say, fifteen days, then PepsiCo does not collect on average within the required period. Many firms transact business with terms of thirty days.

The interpretation of changes in the accounts receivable turnover and average collection period also relates to a firm's credit extension policies. Firms often use credit terms as a means of stimulating sales. For example, firms might permit customers to delay making payments on purchases of lawn mowers until after the summer and on snowmobiles until after the winter in an effort to stimulate sales. Such actions would lead to a decrease in the accounts receivable turnover and an increase in the days receivables are outstanding. The changes in these accounts receivable ratios would not necessarily signal negative news if the increase in net income from the additional sales exceeded the cost of carrying accounts receivable for the extra time.

Retailing firms, particularly department store chains such as Sears and JCPenney, offer their own credit cards to customers. They use credit cards both to stimulate sales and to earn interest revenue from delayed payments by customers. Interpreting an increase in the number of days accounts receivable are outstanding involves two conflicting signals. The increase might suggest greater risk of uncollectibility but it also provides additional interest revenues. Some firms price their products to obtain a relatively low gross margin from the sale and depend on interest revenues as a principal source of earnings. Thus, the analyst must consider a firm's credit strategy and policies when interpreting the accounts receivable turnover and days receivable outstanding ratios.

PepsiCo does not explain the slower accounts receivable turnover. A significant proportion of PepsiCo's accounts receivable likely relates to amounts owed PepsiCo by its bottlers and grocery retailers. PepsiCo might have intentionally granted its bottlers and grocery retailers more favorable repayment terms. Another possibility is that repayment terms in other countries may differ from those in the United States. The increased percentage of sales from countries with longer repayment times might account for the slower accounts receivable turnover. In any case, the increase in the number of days it takes to collect accounts receivable from 34.1 days in Year 2 to 36.5 days in Year 4 would not seem to be a major concern. Assuming that PepsiCo borrowed short-term at 4 percent interest to finance the greater number of days receivables were outstanding, it would have cost PepsiCo approximately \$.766 million [= ((36.5 − 34.1)/365) × (.04) × .5(\$2,830 + \$2,999)] during Year 4. PepsiCo's interest expense for Year 4 was \$167 million. Thus, the delayed collections increased interest expense approximately .5 percent (= \$.766/\$167). Even though the amounts for PepsiCo do not appear material, management should monitor the decreased accounts receivable turnover to ensure that a larger problem does not ensue in the future.

Inventory Turnover

The rate at which inventories turn over indicates the length of time needed to produce, hold, and sell inventories. The analyst calculates the inventory turnover by dividing cost of goods sold by the average inventory during the period. The calculation of inventory turnover for PepsiCo for Year 4 is as follows:

$$\text{Inventory Turnover} = \frac{\text{Cost of Goods Sold}}{\text{Average Inventories}}$$

$$9.1 = \frac{\$13{,}406}{.5(\$1{,}412 + \$1{,}541)}$$

Thus, PepsiCo's inventory was on hand for 40.1 days (= 365/9.1) on average during Year 4. Pepsi's inventory turnover was 8.7 (42.0 days) in Year 2 and 9.0 (40.6 days) in Year 3. Thus, the inventory turnover increased during the three-year period, with most of the increase between Year 2 and Year 3.

PepsiCo does not explain the increased inventory turnover. One possibility is improved inventory control systems. As discussed previously, PepsiCo invested in an initiative to improve process efficiencies. This program might have led to purchasing raw materials just in time for production (thereby reducing raw-material inventory) or producing just in time for customer needs (thereby reducing finished-goods inventory). Another possibility is that PepsiCo experienced a sales mix shift to snack foods that likely have a shorter shelf life than beverages. The analyst cannot assess this possibility without a breakout of the various products of PepsiCo International.

The interpretation of the inventory turnover figure involves two opposing considerations. A firm would like to sell as many goods as possible with a minimum of capital tied up in inventories. An increase in the rate of inventory turnover between periods would seem to indicate more profitable use of the investment in inventory. On the other hand, a firm does not want to have so little inventory on hand that shortages result and the firm might miss sales opportunities. An increase in the rate of inventory turnover in this case may mean a loss of sales opportunities and thereby offset any advantage gained by a decreased investment in inventory. Firms must make trade-offs in deciding the optimum level of inventory and thus the desirable rate of inventory turnover.

The analyst often gains insights into changes in the inventory turnover by examining changes in both the inventory turnover and the cost of goods sold to sales percentage simultaneously. Consider the following scenarios and possible interpretations:

1. **Increasing cost of goods sold to sales percentage, coupled with an increasing inventory turnover.** The firm lowers prices to sell inventory more quickly. The firm shifts its product mix toward lower-margin, faster-moving products. The firm outsources the production of a higher proportion of its products, requiring it to share profit margin with the outsourcer but reducing the amount of raw materials and work-in-process inventories.
2. **Decreasing cost of goods sold to sales percentage, coupled with a decreasing inventory turnover.** The firm raises prices to increase its gross margin but inventory sells more slowly. The firm shifts its product mix toward higher-margin, slower-moving products. The firm produces a higher proportion of its products instead of outsourcing, thereby capturing more of the gross margin but requiring the firm to carry raw materials and work-in-process inventories.
3. **Increasing cost of goods sold to sales percentage, coupled with a decreasing inventory turnover.** Weak economic conditions lead to reduced demand for the firm's products, necessitating price reductions to move goods. Despite price reductions, inventory builds up.
4. **Decreasing cost of goods sold to sales percentage, coupled with an increasing inventory turnover.** Strong economic conditions lead to increased demand for the firm's products, allowing price increases. An inability to replace inventory as fast as the firm sells it leads to an increased inventory turnover. The firm implements a just-in-time inventory system, reducing storage costs, product obsolescence, and the amount of inventory held.

Some analysts calculate the inventory turnover ratio by dividing sales, rather than cost of goods sold, by the average inventory. As long as there is a reasonably constant relation between selling prices and cost of goods sold, the analyst can identify changes in the trend of the inventory turnover with either measure. It is inappropriate to use sales in the numerator if the analyst desires to use the inventory turnover ratio to calculate the average number of days inventory is on hand until sale.

The cost-flow assumption (FIFO, LIFO, weighted average) for inventories and cost of goods sold can significantly affect both the inventory turnover ratio and the cost of goods sold to sales percentage. Chapter 7 discusses the impact of the cost-flow assumption and illustrates adjustments the analyst might make to deal with these effects.

Fixed Asset Turnover

The fixed asset turnover ratio measures the relation between sales and the investment in property, plant, and equipment. The analyst calculates the fixed asset turnover by dividing sales by average fixed assets (net of accumulated depreciation) during the year. The fixed assets turnover ratio for PepsiCo for Year 4 is as follows:

$$\text{Fixed Asset Turnover} = \frac{\text{Sales}}{\text{Average Fixed Assets}}$$

$$3.7 = \frac{\$29{,}261}{.5(\$7{,}828 + \$8{,}149)}$$

The fixed asset turnover for PepsiCo was 3.5 in Year 2 and in Year 3. The small increase in the fixed asset turnover in Year 4 results from a slight decrease in the rate of growth in expenditures on fixed assets in Year 3 and in Year 4, relative to Year 2.

The analyst must interpret changes in the fixed asset turnover ratio carefully. Firms invest in fixed assets in anticipation of higher sales in future periods. Thus, a low or decreasing rate of fixed asset turnover may indicate an expanding firm preparing for future growth. On the other hand, a firm may reduce its capital expenditures if the near-term outlook for its products is poor. Such an action could lead to an increase in the fixed asset turnover ratio.

In recent years, many firms have increased the proportion of production outsourced to other manufacturers. This action allows firms to achieve the same (or increasing) sales levels with less fixed assets, thereby increasing the fixed asset turnover.

Summary of Assets Turnover Analysis

To summarize, PepsiCo's assets turnover was steady between Year 2 and Year 4. The accounts receivable turnover decreased while the inventory and fixed asset turnovers increased. Accounts receivable make up approximately 11 percent of total assets, whereas inventories and fixed assets comprise approximately 35 percent of total assets (see the common-size balance sheet percentages in Exhibit 1.12). Thus, one would expect that the increasing inventory and fixed asset turnovers would dominate the decreasing accounts receivable turnover and result in an increasing total assets turnover. However, other assets beside receivables, inventories, and fixed assets affect the total assets turnover. Exhibit 1.12 indicates that the proportion of total assets comprising cash and short-term investments increased during the last three years, slowing down the total assets turnover and offsetting the advantage of an increased inventory and fixed asset turnover.

Summary of ROA Analysis

Our analysis of operating profitability involves four levels of depth:

Level 1: ROA for the firm as a whole.
Level 2: Disaggregation of ROA into profit margin for ROA and assets turnover for the firm as a whole.
Level 3a: Disaggregation of profit margin into expense ratios for various cost items.
Level 3b: Disaggregation of assets turnover into turnovers for individual assets.
Level 4: Analysis of profit margins and asset turnovers for the segments of a firm.

Exhibit 4.12 summarizes this analysis in a format we use throughout the remainder of this book.

Supplementing ROA in Profitability Analysis

ROA uses average total assets as a base for assessing a firm's effectiveness in using resources to generate earnings. For some firms and industries, total assets may not serve an informative role for this purpose because GAAP (1) excludes certain valuable resources from assets (brand names, technological knowledge, human capital), and (2) reports assets at their acquisition costs instead of current market values (forests for forest products companies, land and buildings for department stores). Analysts often supplement ROA by relating sales, expenses, and earnings to nonfinancial bases when evaluating profitability. This section discusses techniques for assessing profitability unique to certain industries. The discussion is not intended to be exhaustive of all industries but to provide a flavor for the types of supplemental measures used.

EXHIBIT 4.12

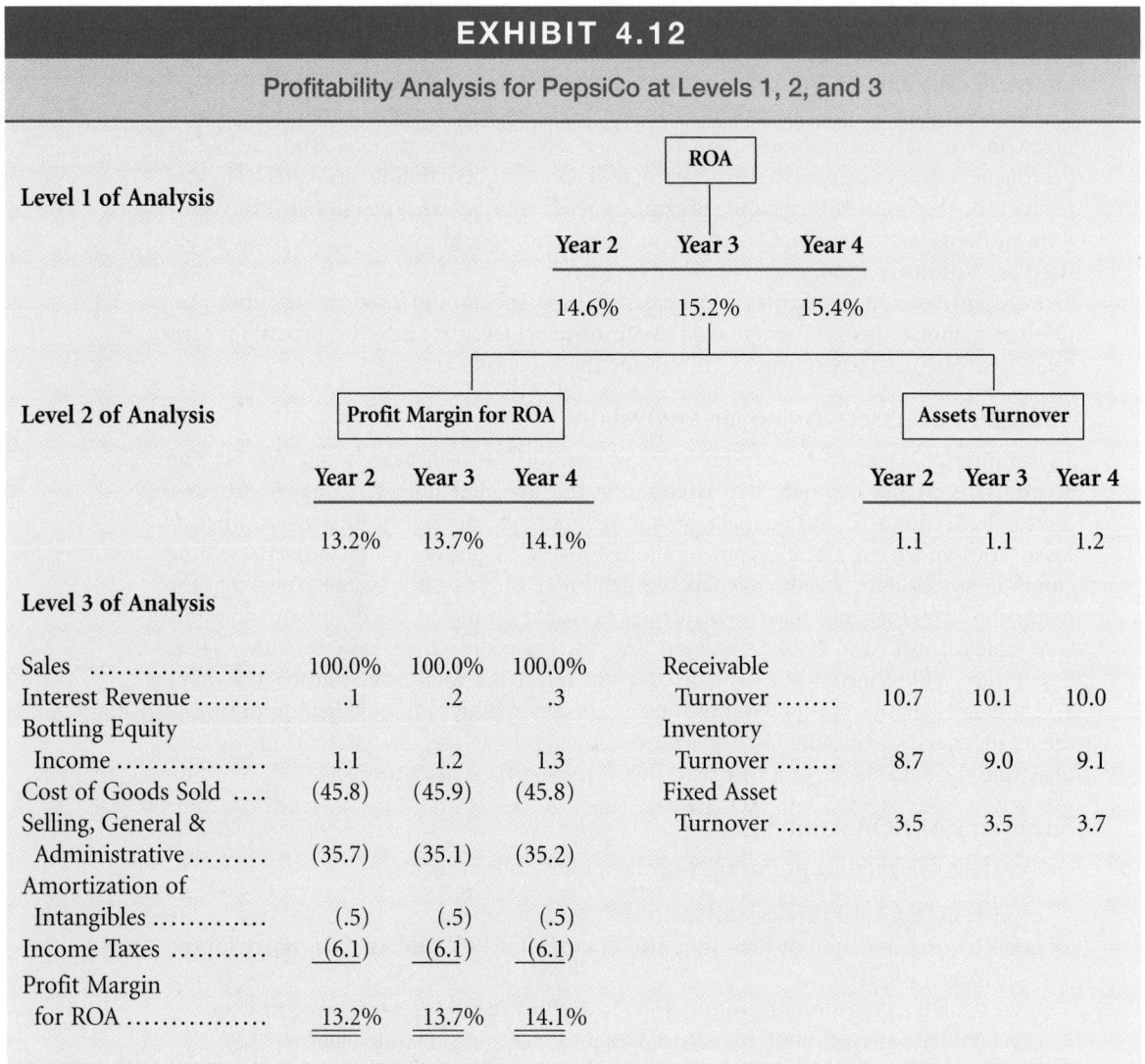

Profitability Analysis for PepsiCo at Levels 1, 2, and 3

Level 1 of Analysis

ROA

Year 2	Year 3	Year 4
14.6%	15.2%	15.4%

Level 2 of Analysis

Profit Margin for ROA

Year 2	Year 3	Year 4
13.2%	13.7%	14.1%

Assets Turnover

Year 2	Year 3	Year 4
1.1	1.1	1.2

Level 3 of Analysis

	Year 2	Year 3	Year 4
Sales	100.0%	100.0%	100.0%
Interest Revenue	.1	.2	.3
Bottling Equity Income	1.1	1.2	1.3
Cost of Goods Sold	(45.8)	(45.9)	(45.8)
Selling, General & Administrative	(35.7)	(35.1)	(35.2)
Amortization of Intangibles	(.5)	(.5)	(.5)
Income Taxes	(6.1)	(6.1)	(6.1)
Profit Margin for ROA	13.2%	13.7%	14.1%

	Year 2	Year 3	Year 4
Receivable Turnover	10.7	10.1	10.0
Inventory Turnover	8.7	9.0	9.1
Fixed Asset Turnover	3.5	3.5	3.7

Analyzing Retailers

A key resource of retailers is their retail space. Some retailers own their stores while others lease their space. The analyst can capitalize the present value of operating lease commitments to ensure that total assets include store buildings under operating leases (Chapter 8 discusses this adjustment). An alternative approach when analyzing retailers is to express sales, operating expenses, and operating income on a per-store basis or per square foot of retail selling space. This supplemental base for evaluating profitability circumvents the issue of whether firms own or lease their space. It also eliminates the effects on the denominator of ROA of using different depreciation methods and depreciable lives, and having fixed assets with different ages. It does not, however, eliminate the effect of different depreciation methods or depreciable lives on income in the numerator.

EXHIBIT 4.13

Profitability Ratios for Target and Wal-Mart

Per Square Foot:	Target	Wal-Mart
Sales	$275	$ 430
Cost of Goods Sold	(189)	(331)
Selling and Administrative	(71)	(77)
Operating Income	$ 15	$ 22
Profit Margin for ROA	4.9%	3.9%
Assets Turnover	1.4	2.4
ROA	6.8%	9.4%

Exhibit 4.13 presents per-square-foot data for Target Corporation (Target) and Wal-Mart Stores (Wal-Mart) for a recent year, as well as profit margin for ROA, assets turnover, and ROA. The superior ROA of Wal-Mart results from a much higher sales and operating income per square foot. Although its expenses per square foot are higher than those of Target, its ability to obtain higher sales from its space largely accounts for its superior profitability in the year analyzed.

Analyzing Airlines

Aircraft provide airlines with a fixed amount of capacity during any particular period. The total number of seats available to carry passengers times the number of miles flown equals the available capacity. The number of seats occupied times the number of miles flown equals the amount of capacity used (referred to as revenue passenger miles). Common practice in the airline industry is to compute the revenues and expenses per available seat mile and per revenue passenger mile flown to judge pricing, cost structure, and profitability.

Exhibit 4.14 presents selected profitability data for American Airlines, Southwest Airlines, and United Airlines for a year when the three airlines were profitable. American and United operate both domestic and international routes, while Southwest provides primarily domestic services. The employees of American and United are unionized while those of Southwest are not. All three airlines are publicly owned. The first three columns present revenues, expenses, and operating income before income taxes per available seat mile, and the last three columns present the same income items per revenue passenger mile flown.

The costs of an airline (such as depreciation and compensation) are largely fixed for any particular year. Thus, the operating expenses per available seat mile indicate the costs of operating each airline. The operating costs of Southwest are lower than those of American and United. The advantage of Southwest relates to lower compensation costs and lower other operating expenses. The income data per revenue passenger mile indicates the usage of the available capacity. American generates the highest revenues per revenue passenger mile but also has the highest costs. Its compensation costs and other operating expenses are the highest of the three airlines. Southwest realizes lower revenues per revenue passenger mile than American but its lower cost structure permits it to generate almost the same operating income before income taxes. United falls between American

EXHIBIT 4.14

Profitability Ratios for American Airlines, Southwest Airlines, and United Airlines

	Per Available Seat Mile			Per Revenue Passenger Mile		
	American	Southwest	United	American	Southwest	United
Operating Revenues	10.60¢	8.36¢	10.05¢	15.48¢	12.58¢	14.02¢
Compensation	(3.56)	(2.45)	(3.31)	(5.20)	(3.69)	(4.63)
Fuel	(1.16)	(1.19)	(1.28)	(1.69)	(1.79)	(1.78)
Other Operating Expenses	(4.94)	(3.86)	(4.77)	(7.21)	(5.80)	(6.65)
Operating Income	.94¢	.86¢	.69¢	1.38¢	1.30¢	.96¢
Profit Margin for ROA				6.2%	6.8%	4.5%
Assets Turnover				.61	.65	.65
ROA				3.8%	4.4%	2.9%

and Southwest on both revenues and operating expenses per revenue passenger mile but has the lowest operating income before income taxes. The ROA data are consistent with the per-seat-mile data, except that the profit margin of Southwest reflects higher interest revenues from investments of excess cash relative to American and United.

The analyst can apply similar metrics to other firms with fixed capacity. The analysis of hospitals focuses on income data per available bed or per patient day. The analysis of hotels uses income data per room. The analysis of cable or telecommunications companies examines income data per subscriber or customer.

Analyzing Advertising Firms

Using ROA to analyze the profitability of firms that provide services can result in misleading conclusions because their most important resource, their employees, does not appear on the balance sheet as assets under GAAP. One approach to deal with this omission is to express income data on a per-employee basis. The analyst must use this data cautiously because of differences among firms in their use of full- versus part-time employees, and their mix of direct service providers versus support personnel.

Exhibit 4.15 presents profitability data for three advertising agencies. Grey Advertising has the highest revenue per employee but also the highest compensation per employee. Its administrative expenses are similar to those of Interpublic but its higher compensation leads to the lowest operating income before income taxes per employee and the lowest profit margin and ROA. Interpublic and Omnicom have similar operating revenues per employee but Omnicom's higher compensation, offset by its lower administrative expenses, yields it lower operating income per employee and a lower profit margin. Omnicom has a faster assets turnover than Interpublic, so it has the highest ROA.

Other service industries for which per-employee data might usefully supplement traditional financial ratios include investment banking, management consulting, temporary help services, and engineering services. The use of per-employee data might also supplement the analysis of firms that use fixed assets in the provision of services, such as airlines, health care providers, and hotels.

EXHIBIT 4.15

Profitability Data for Grey Advertising, Interpublic Group, and Omnicom Group

Per Employee:	Grey Advertising	Interpublic Group	Omnicom Group
Operating Revenues	$121,508	$116,936	$116,373
Compensation	(75,347)	(61,946)	(68,527)
Administrative Expenses	(36,870)	(36,653)	(33,460)
Operating Income before Income Taxes	$ 9,291	$ 18,337	$ 14,386
Profit Margin for ROA	4.6%	9.7%	9.2%
Assets Turnover	.75	.56	.70
ROA	3.4%	5.4%	6.4%

Analyzing Technology-Based Firms

ROA can be an even more misleading ratio for analyzing technology-based firms than for analyzing service firms because the two most important resources of technology firms do not appear in their assets: (1) their people, and (2) their technologies. Employees contribute to the creation of technologies but the most important resource not recognized is the value of the technologies. GAAP requires firms to expense R&D costs in the year incurred. Thus, both assets and net income are understated during periods in which firms invest heavily in R&D. Subsequently, after that R&D has led to the introduction of successful, profitable new products, assets are understated but income is overstated because the firms has already expensed investments in R&D.

Research by Lev and Sougiannis[11] documents the value of technologies that might provide a basis for recognizing a technology asset on the balance sheet and recomputing net income each year. The authors propose a methodology that involves studying the relationship between R&D expenditures in a particular year and revenues of subsequent years. The technology "asset" equals the present value of the future revenue stream net of the R&D expenditure during the year. The analyst would then amortize this "asset" over the future periods of benefit based on the projected stream of revenues.

The research previously described is in an early development stage and not yet used widely by analysts of technology companies. Traditional financial ratio analysis works reasonably well for established technology firms that have products in all stages of their life cycles. Traditional financial ratio analysis does not work as well for start-up firms and firms with most of their products in the early, high-growth stages of their life cycles.

RATE OF RETURN ON COMMON SHAREHOLDERS' EQUITY

The rate of return on assets measures the profitability of operations before considering the effects of financing. That is, ROA ignores the proportion of debt versus equity financing that a firm uses to finance the assets and the cost of debt financing. The rate of return

[11]Baruch Lev and Theodore Sougiannis, "The Capitalization, Amortization and Value-Relevance of R&D," *Journal of Accounting and Economics* (1996), pp. 107–138.

on common shareholders' equity (ROCE) measures the return to common shareholders after subtracting from revenues not only operating expenses (such as cost of goods sold, selling and administration expenses, and income taxes) but also the costs of financing debt and preferred stock that are senior to the common stock. The latter includes interest expense on debt and dividends on preferred stock (if any). Thus, ROCE incorporates the results of a firm's operating, investing, and financing decisions.

The analyst calculates ROCE as follows:

$$\text{ROCE} = \frac{\text{Net Income} - \text{Preferred Stock Dividends}}{\text{Average Common Shareholders' Equity}}$$

The numerator measures the amount of income for the period allocable to the common shareholders after subtracting all amounts allocable to senior claimants. The accountant subtracts interest expense on debt in measuring net income, so the calculation of the numerator of ROCE requires no adjustment for creditors' claims on earnings. The analyst must subtract dividends paid or payable on preferred stock from net income to obtain income attributable to the common shareholders.[12]

The denominator of ROCE measures the average amount of common shareholders' equity in use during the period. An average of the total common shareholders' equity at the beginning and end of the year is appropriate unless a firm made a significant new common stock issue or buyback during the year. If the latter occurred, the analyst should use an average of the common shareholders' equity at the end of each quarter.

Common shareholders' equity equals total shareholders' equity minus the minority interest in the net assets of consolidated subsidiaries and minus the par value of preferred stock. Because net income to common shareholders in the numerator reflects a subtraction for the minority interest in earnings of consolidated subsidiaries, the denominator should exclude the minority interest in net assets (if any). Chapter 9 discusses consolidated financial statements more fully. Firms seldom issue preferred stock significantly above par value, so the analyst can assume that the amount in the Additional Paid-In Capital account relates to common stock.[13]

PepsiCo reports no minority interest in either its income statement or balance sheet. It does have preferred stock outstanding. The calculation of the ROCE of PepsiCo for Year 4, using the adjusted amounts of net income discussed previously, is as follows:[14]

$$\text{ROCE} = \frac{\text{Net Income} - \text{Preferred Stock Dividends}}{\text{Average Common Shareholders' Equity}}$$

---

[12]Chapter 13 indicates that for purposes of valuation, the analyst might compute ROCE using comprehensive income available to common shareholders, not net income available to common shareholders. Recall from Chapter 2 that comprehensive income equals net income plus or minus changes in the value of certain assets and liabilities that GAAP requires firms to include in Other Comprehensive Income until realized.

[13]Some analysts use the acronym ROCE to refer to "return on capital employed." The numerator of this ratio is net income before interest expense (net of tax savings) on long-term debt. The denominator is the average amount of long-term debt and shareholders' equity during the year. The rate of return on capital employed generally falls between ROA and ROCE as we have defined the latter ratios. We do not use return on capital employed in this book.

[14]The $25 million amount for preferred dividends in the numerator is actually a preferred dividend of $3 million and a redemption premium on preferred stock of $22 million. The SEC requires firms that redeem preferred stock for more than its book, or carrying, value to subtract the excess from net income when computing net income available to common shareholders in the computation of earnings per share. See Securities and Exchange Commission, *EITF Abstracts,* Topic No. D 42, "The Effect on the Calculation of Earnings per Share for the Redemption or Induced Conversion of Preferred Stock" (1994). To maintain consistency in the calculation of ROCE and earnings per share, we subtract the redemption premium in the numerator of both ratios. Analysts will likely encounter such redemption premiums infrequently.

$$31.2\% = \frac{\$4,004 - \$25}{.5\ (\$11,896 + \$13,572)}$$

The amount for the preferred stock appears in Note 11, "Net Income per Common Share from Continuing Operations" (Appendix A). The ROCE of PepsiCo was 34.8 percent in Year 2 and 33.5 percent in Year 3, reflecting a decrease over the three-year period.

A Note on Residual Income and Economic Value Added

Chapter 13 describes a measure known as *residual income* (also called *abnormal earnings*). The principal difference between net income available to common shareholders, the numerator of ROCE, and residual income is that residual income includes a subtraction for the cost of common shareholders' equity capital. The analyst might view residual income as a measure of the wealth a firm generates for its common shareholders in a period beyond the required return on their investment in the firm. Chapter 13 describes and demonstrates the use of residual income in equity valuation.

In recent years the financial press and some corporate managers have given considerable attention to a measure called *economic value added* (EVA). Stern Stewart & Co., a management consulting firm, has taken the leadership in promoting this measure. Similar to but not identical to residual income, EVA likewise includes a subtraction for the cost of common shareholders' equity capital.[15] The concept behind EVA is that a firm does not create value unless it earns more than the cost of all of its capital, including common shareholders' equity capital.

Accountants do not treat the cost of common shareholders' equity capital as an expense when computing net income. On the other hand, a firm that earns less than the cost of common equity capital destroys value. ROCE measures the return to the common shareholders but does not indicate whether this rate of return exceeds or falls short of the cost of common equity capital.

To illustrate, PepsiCo's ROCE for Year 4 as computed earlier is 31.2 percent. If the cost of common equity capital of PepsiCo is, say, 8 percent, then PepsiCo generated an excess return of 23.2 percent (= 31.2% − 8.0%). If the cost of common equity capital is, say, 40 percent, then PepsiCo did not generate a return sufficient to equal the cost of common equity capital.[16] Measures such as residual income and EVA take the computation of return to the common shareholders one step further than ROCE by incorporating a measure of the required rate of return to the common shareholders.

Conceptually, the cost of common equity capital is the rate of return the common shareholders demand as compensation for forging consumption and bearing the risk of investing in a firm. Measuring the cost of common equity capital is more difficult than measuring the cost of debt because debt instruments typically specify an interest rate. The dividend on common stock is not an accurate measure of the cost of common equity capital because managers determine dividend payout policies, whereas equity investors determine the cost of equity capital. Chapter 11 discusses the computation of the cost of equity capital and Chapters 11 to 14 incorporate it into various valuation methods. We do not explicitly use EVA in our illustrations in this book.

---

[15]The precise computation of EVA involves other adjustments to net income that we do not consider here. See G. Bennett Stewart, III, *The Quest for Value* (New York: HarperCollins Publishers, 1999).

[16]PepsiCo's cost of common equity capital is likely closer to 8 percent than to 40 percent. Chapter 11 discusses PepsiCo's cost of equity capital more fully.

Relating ROA to ROCE

ROA measures operating performance independent of financing while ROCE explicitly considers the cost of debt and preferred stock financing. The relation between ROA and ROCE is as follows:[17]

Return on Assets	→	**Return to Creditors**	**Return to Preferred Shareholders**	**Return to Common Shareholders**
$\frac{\text{Net Income + Interest Expense Net of Taxes}}{\text{Average Total Assets}}$	→	$\frac{\text{Interest Expense Net of Taxes}}{\text{Average Total Liabilities}}$	$\frac{\text{Preferred Dividends}}{\text{Average Preferred Shareholders' Equity}}$	$\frac{\text{Net Income to Common}}{\text{Average Common Shareholders' Equity}}$

The analyst allocates each dollar of return generated from using assets to the various providers of capital. Creditors receive their return in the form of interest. The cost of this capital is interest expense net of the income tax benefit derived from deducting interest in calculating taxable income. Many liabilities, such as accounts payable and salaries payable, carry no explicit interest cost.

The preferred stock carries a cost equal to the preferred dividend amount. Firms historically could not deduct preferred dividends in calculating taxable income. Firms in recent years have been successful in structuring preferred stock issues so that they qualify for tax deductibility of dividends paid. In those cases, the analyst should adjust preferred dividends for the related tax savings.

The income from operations (that is, the numerator of ROA) that is not allocated to creditors or preferred shareholders belongs to the common shareholders as the residual claimants. Likewise, the portion of a firm's assets not financed with capital provided by creditors or preferred shareholders represents the capital provided by the common shareholders.[18]

Consider now the relation between ROA and ROCE. Under what circumstances will ROCE exceed ROA? Under what circumstances will ROCE be less than ROA?

ROCE will exceed ROA whenever ROA exceeds the cost of capital provided by creditors and preferred shareholders. If a firm can generate a higher return on capital provided by creditors and preferred shareholders than the cost of that capital, the excess return belongs to the common shareholders.

To illustrate, recall that PepsiCo generated an ROA of 15.4 percent during Year 4. The after-tax cost of capital provided by creditors during Year 4 was .8 percent [= (1−.35)($167)/.5($13,453 + $14,464)].[19] The difference between the .8 percent cost of creditor capital and the 15.4 percent ROA generated on assets financed with debt capital belongs to the common shareholders. The preferred shareholders received a dividend of $3 million and PepsiCo paid a redemption premium of $22 million when it redeemed preferred stock during Year 4. PepsiCo paid this dividend on the $41 million of outstanding preferred stock. PepsiCo, however, repurchased preferred stock for more than it initially issued it, resulting in a negative net amount for preferred stock in the balance sheet.

---

[17]Note that the relation does not appear as an equation. We use an arrow instead of an equal sign to indicate that the return on assets gets allocated to the various suppliers of capital. To express the relation as an equality requires that we weight each rate by the proportion of each type of capital in the capital structure.

[18]If a firm does not own 100 percent of the common stock of a consolidated subsidiary, the accountant must allocate a portion of the ROA to the minority shareholders. Thus, a fourth term would appear on the right-hand side of the arrow: minority interest in earnings/average minority interest in net assets.

[19]The amounts in the denominator for PepsiCo equal total assets minus total shareholders' equity, or total liabilities. The after-tax cost of creditor capital seems low, but recall that many liabilities do not carry an explicit interest cost.

The average amount of preferred stock equity is a negative \$35.5 million [= .5 (\$41 − \$64 + \$41 − \$90). The cost of preferred equity capital is therefore a negative 70.4 percent (= \$25/−\$35.5).[20] The common shareholders also have a full claim on the 15.4 percent ROA generated on the assets financed with the equity capital that they provided. Thus, the ROCE of PepsiCo for Year 4 comprises the following (calculations use rates taken to more decimal points than the three decimal points shown):

Excess Return on Capital Provided by Creditors:	
[.154 − .008][.5(\$13,453 + \$14,464)]	\$2,045
Deficient Return on Negative Capital Provided by Preferred Shareholders:	
[.154 − .704][.5(\$41 − \$63 + \$41 − \$90)]	(30)
Return on Capital Provided by Common Shareholders:	
[.154][.5(\$11,896 + \$13,572)]	1,964
Total Return to Common Shareholders	\$3,979
ROCE: \$3,979/[.5(\$11,896 +\$13,572)]	31.2%

Common business terminology refers to the practice of using lower-cost creditor and preferred stock capital to increase the return to common shareholders as *financial leverage.* With respect to debt and preferred shareholders' equity combined, financial leverage worked to the advantage of PepsiCo's common shareholders in Year 2, Year 3, and Year 4 because its ROCE exceeds its ROA.

We can measure the incremental effect of financial leverage beyond ROA by computing the ratio of ROCE divided by ROA. The ratios for PepsiCo are as follows:

Year 2: 34.8%/14.6% = 2.38
Year 3: 33.5%/15.2% = 2.20
Year 4: 31.2%/15.4% = 2.03

Thus, financial leverage worked less effectively each succeeding year for PepsiCo. We explore next the possible reasons for this decreased effectiveness.

Disaggregating ROCE

We can disaggregate ROCE into several components to aid in its interpretation, much as we did earlier with ROA. The disaggregated components of ROCE are profit margin for ROCE, total assets turnover, and capital structure leverage:

ROCE	=	**Profit Margin for ROCE**	×	**Assets Turnover**	×	**Capital Structure Leverage**
$\frac{\text{Net Income to Common}}{\text{Average Common Shareholders' Equity}}$	=	$\frac{\text{Net Income to Common}}{\text{Sales}}$	×	$\frac{\text{Sales}}{\text{Average Total Assets}}$	×	$\frac{\text{Average Total Assets}}{\text{Average Common Shareholders' Equity}}$

The profit margin for ROCE indicates the earnings allocable to the common shareholders after subtracting from revenues all operating expenses and all financing costs of

[20] Although showing a negative preferred shareholders' equity is mathematically correct, it is not conceptually sound. The excess in an economic sense reduces common shareholders' equity. We follow PepsiCo's treatment of the repurchased preferred stock as an element of preferred stock equity and not common stock equity.

EXHIBIT 4.16

Disaggregation of ROCE of PepsiCo—Year 2 to Year 4

	ROCE	=	Profit Margin for ROCE	×	Total Assets Turnover	×	Capital Structure Leverage
Year 2	34.8%	=	12.6%	×	1.1	×	2.5
Year 3	33.5%	=	13.3%	×	1.1	×	2.3
Year 4	31.2%	=	13.6%	×	1.1	×	2.1

capital senior to the common shareholders. Note that the profit margin for ROA, used in the disaggregation of ROA, is before financing costs. The profit margin for ROCE is after financing costs for debt and preferred stock capital. The total assets turnover is identical to that used to disaggregate ROA. The capital structure leverage (CSL) ratio measures the degree to which a firm uses common shareholders' funds to finance assets. The difference between the numerator and denominator of the CSL ratio is the amount of liabilities and preferred shareholders' equity in the capital structure. The larger is the amount of capital obtained from these senior sources; the smaller will be the amount of capital obtained from common shareholders and the larger will therefore be the CSL ratio.

The disaggregation of ROCE for PepsiCo for Year 4 appears as follows:

$$\text{ROCE} = \text{Profit Margin for ROCE} \times \text{Assets Turnover} \times \text{Capital Structure Leverage}$$

$$\frac{\$4{,}004 - \$25}{.5(\$11{,}896+\$13{,}572)} = \frac{\$4{,}004 - \$25}{\$29{,}261} \times \frac{\$29{,}261}{.5(\$25{,}327+\$27{,}987)} \times \frac{.5(\$25{,}327+\$27{,}987)}{.5(\$11{,}896 + \$13{,}572)}$$

$$31.2\% = 13.6\% \times 1.1 \times 2.1$$

Exhibit 4.16 presents the disaggregation of ROCE of PepsiCo for Year 2 to Year 4. The decreasing ROCE of PepsiCo results from the net effect of an increasing profit margin for ROCE and a decreasing CSL ratio during the three-year period. The increasing profit margin for ROCE results from an increasing profit margin for ROA and reduced interest expense. PepsiCo had net repayments of debt during Year 2 and Year 3 (see PepsiCo's statement of cash flows in Appendix A). Also, the retention of earnings and new stock issuances exceeded dividends and stock repurchases, resulting in an increase in common shareholders' equity and a reduction in the CSL ratio. Although financial leverage worked to the benefit of the common shareholders in all three years, the decreasing CSL ratio moderated the positive effects of the increasing profit margin for ROCE.

EARNINGS PER COMMON SHARE

A second financial statement ratio besides ROCE that common equity investors frequently use to assess profitability is earnings per common share (EPS). As Chapter 14 discusses more fully, analysts and investors frequently use multiples of EPS, referred to as *price-earnings ratios,* to value firms. EPS is the only financial ratio that GAAP requires firms to disclose on the face of the income statement and is covered explicitly by the opinion of the independent auditor.[21] This section briefly describes the calculation of EPS and discusses some of its uses and limitations.

Calculating EPS

Simple Capital Structure

Firms that do not have (1) outstanding convertible bonds or convertible preferred stock that holders can exchange for shares of common stock, or (2) options or warrants that holders can use to acquire common stock, have simple capital structures. For such firms, the accountant calculates basic EPS as follows:

$$\begin{matrix}\text{Basic EPS} \\ \text{(Simple Capital Structure)}\end{matrix} = \frac{\text{Net Income} - \text{Preferred Stock Dividends}}{\begin{matrix}\text{Weighted Average Number of} \\ \text{Common Shares Outstanding}\end{matrix}}$$

The numerator of basic EPS for a simple capital structure is the same as the numerator of ROCE. The denominator is a daily weighted average of common shares outstanding during the period, reflecting new stock issues, treasury stock acquisitions, and similar transactions.

Example 1. Brown Corporation had the following capital structure during its most recent year.

	January 1	December 31
Preferred Stock, $20 Par Value, 500 Shares Issued and Outstanding	$ 10,000	$ 10,000
Common Stock, $10 Par Value, 4,000 Shares Issued	40,000	40,000
Additional Paid-In Capital	50,000	50,000
Retained Earnings	80,000	85,600
Treasury Shares—Common (1,000 shares)	—	(30,000)
Total Shareholders' Equity	$180,000	$155,600

Retained earnings changed during the year as follows:

Retained Earnings, January 1	$80,000
Plus Net Income	7,500
Less Dividends:	
Preferred Stock	(500)
Common Stock	(1,400)
Retained Earnings, December 31	$85,600

[21]Financial Accounting Standards Board, *Statement of Financial Accounting Standards No. 128,* "Earnings per Share" (1997).

The preferred stock is not convertible into common stock. The firm acquired the treasury stock on July 1. No stock options or warrants are outstanding. The calculation of basic earnings per share for Brown Corporation follows:

$$\text{Basic EPS} = \frac{\$7{,}500 - \$500}{(.5 \times 4{,}000) + (.5 \times 3{,}000)} = \frac{\$7{,}000}{3{,}500} = \$2.00 \text{ per share}$$

Complex Capital Structure

Firms that have either convertible securities or stock options or warrants outstanding have complex capital structures. Such firms must present two EPS amounts: basic EPS and diluted EPS. Diluted EPS reflects the dilution potential of convertible securities, options, and warrants. Dilution refers to the reduction in basic EPS that would result if holders of convertible securities exchanged them for shares of common stock, or holders of stock options or warrants exercised them. Firms include in diluted EPS calculations only those securities, options, and warrants that would reduce EPS. The accountant excludes such equity instruments if their conversion would increase EPS (such securities would be referred to as "out of the money"). This section describes the calculation of diluted EPS in general terms.

$$\begin{array}{c}\text{Diluted EPS}\\ \text{(Complex Capital Structure)}\end{array} = \frac{\begin{array}{c}\text{Net Income—Preferred}\\ \text{Stock Dividends}\end{array} + \begin{array}{c}\text{Adjustments for}\\ \text{Dilutive Securities}\end{array}}{\begin{array}{c}\text{Weighted Average}\\ \text{Number of Common}\\ \text{Shares Outstanding}\end{array} + \begin{array}{c}\text{Weighted Average Number}\\ \text{of Shares Issuable from}\\ \text{Dilutive Securities}\end{array}}$$

To calculate diluted EPS, the accountant assumes the conversion of convertible bonds and convertible preferred stock and the exercise of stock options and warrants if their effect would be dilutive. The accountant adds back any interest expense (net of taxes) on convertible bonds and dividends on convertible preferred stock that the firm subtracted in computing net income to common shareholders. Consistency would seem to suggest that the accountant add back to net income any compensation expense recognized on the employee stock options. GAAP, however, does not stipulate such an addback, but instead requires firms to incorporate any unamortized compensation expense on those options into the calculation of the denominator of diluted EPS,[22] as discussed next.

The additional common shares issuable on conversion of bonds and preferred stock, and exercise of stock options and warrants, are added to the denominator. The computation of the additional shares to be issued on the exercise of stock options assumes that the firm would use an amount equal to the sum of (1) any cash proceeds from such exercise, (2) any unamortized compensation expense on those options,[23] and (3) any tax benefits that would be credited to additional paid-in capital, assuming exercise of the options to repurchase common shares on the open market. Only the net incremental shares

---

[22] *Ibid.*, par. 21.

[23] Understanding the rationale for including unamortized compensation expense in the computation of the incremental shares issuable requires an understanding of the accounting for stock options, which Chapter 9 discusses. In general terms, GAAP views the value of stock options as a substitute for cash compensation. Firms amortize this value over the expected period of benefit, which usually begins in the year firms grant the options and terminates when employees exercise the options. The assumption underlying diluted EPS is that employees have exercised the options and the firm realizes a pseudo cash savings equal to the value of options not yet recognized, or amortized.

issued (shares issued under options minus assumed shares repurchased) enter the computation of diluted EPS.

Example 2. Assume the preferred stock of Brown Corporation is convertible into 1,000 shares of common stock. Also assume that Brown Corporation has stock options outstanding that holders can currently exchange for 300 incremental shares of common stock. The calculation of diluted EPS is as follows:

$$\text{Diluted EPS} = \frac{\$7{,}500 - \$500 + \$500}{(.5 \times 4{,}000) + (.5 \times 3{,}000) + (1.0 \times 1{,}000) + (1.0 \times 300)} = \frac{\$7{,}500}{4{,}800}$$

$$= \$1.56$$

The calculation assumes the conversion of the convertible preferred stock into common stock as of January 1. If conversion had taken place, the firm would not have paid preferred dividends during the year. Thus, the analyst adds back to the numerator of fully diluted earnings per share the $500 of preferred dividends, which the accountant subtracted in computing net income available to common stock when calculating basic earnings per share. The weighted average number of shares in the denominator increases for the 1,000 common shares that the firm would issue on conversion of the preferred stock. The weighted average number of shares in the denominator also increases for the incremental shares issuable under stock option plans.

Refer to the income statement of PepsiCo in Appendix A. PepsiCo reports both basic and diluted EPS, disclosing separate EPS amounts for continuing and discontinued operations. PepsiCo's Note 11, "Net Income per Common Share from Continuing Operations" (Appendix A), shows the calculation of its EPS amounts. Basic EPS shows a subtraction from net income for preferred dividends. It also shows a subtraction for the redemption premium that PepsiCo paid when it redeemed some of its preferred stock. The treatment of redemption premiums in calculating EPS occurs infrequently and is beyond the scope of this book (see footnote 14).

The numerator of diluted EPS shows an addition for the portion of the preferred dividend and redemption premium that relates to convertible preferred stock. The minor differences between the amounts subtracted for preferred stock in computing basic EPS and the amounts added back in computing diluted EPS likely result from a portion of the convertible preferred stock being antidilutive. PepsiCo also reports the additional common shares issuable under stock option plans, from convertible preferred stock, and for stock awards.

Criticisms of EPS

Critics of EPS as a measure of profitability point out that it does not consider the amount of assets or capital required to generate a particular level of earnings. Two firms with the same earnings and EPS are not equally profitable if one firm requires twice the amount of assets or capital to generate those earnings as does the other firm. Also, the number of shares of common stock outstanding serves as a poor measure of the amount of capital in use. The number of shares outstanding usually relates to a firm's attempts to achieve a desirable trading range for its common stock. For example, suppose a firm has an aggregate market value for its common shares of $10 million. If the firm has 500,000 shares outstanding, the shares will sell for $20 per share. If the firm has 1,000,000 shares outstanding, the shares will sell for $10 per share. The amount of capital in place is the same in both instances but the number of shares outstanding, and therefore EPS, are different.

For similar reasons, analysts cannot compare EPS amounts across firms. Two firms can have identical earnings, common shareholders' equities, and ROCEs, but their EPSs will differ if they have different numbers of shares outstanding.

EPS is also an ambiguous measure of profitability because it reflects (1) operating performance in the numerator, and (2) capital structure decisions in the denominator. For example, a firm can experience reduced earnings during the year but report a higher EPS than the previous year if it has repurchased sufficient shares during the period. When assessing earnings performance, the analyst must separate the impact of these two factors on EPS.

Despite these criticisms of EPS as a measure of profitability, analysts frequently use it in valuing firms. Chapter 14 discusses the use of EPS in valuation.

INTERPRETING FINANCIAL STATEMENT RATIOS

The analyst can compare financial ratios for a particular firm with similar ratios for the same firm for earlier periods (time-series analysis), as we have done in this chapter for PepsiCo, or with those of other firms for the same period (cross-sectional analysis). This section discusses some of the issues involved in making such comparisons.

Comparisons with Corresponding Ratios of Earlier Periods

A time-series analysis of a particular firm's financial statement ratios permits a historical tracking of the trends and variability in the ratios over time. A firm's financial ratios in the past serve as a benchmark for interpreting its financial ratios during the current period. The analyst can draw useful insights from comparing a firm with itself over time. The analyst can study the impact of economic conditions (recession, inflation), industry conditions (shift in regulatory status, new technology), and firm-specific conditions (shift in corporate strategy, new management) on the time-series pattern of these ratios.

Some questions that the analyst should raise before using ratios of past financial statement data as a basis for interpreting ratios for the current period are as follows:

1. Has the firm made a significant change in its product, geographical, or customer mix that affects the comparability of financial statement ratios over time?
2. Has the firm made a major acquisition or divestiture?
3. Has the firm changed its methods of accounting over time? For example, does the firm now consolidate a previously unconsolidated entity?

Analysts should not simply use past performance as a basis for comparison without considering the level of past and current performance. For example, prior performance might have been at an unsatisfactory level. Any improvement during the current year may still leave the firm at an undesirable level. An improved profitability ratio may mean little if a firm still ranks last in its industry in terms of profitability in all years. Similarly, if the firm's prior performance was exceptional, but declined in the current period, it may still mean the firm performed well in the current period. An analyst may be less concerned about a decline in profitability if the firm ranks as the most profitable firm in its industry.

Another concern involves interpreting the rate of change in a ratio over time. The analyst's interpretation of a 10 percent increase in profit margin for ROA differs depending on whether other firms in the industry experienced a 15 percent versus a 5 percent increase. Comparing a particular firm's ratios with those of similar firms lessens the concerns discussed here.

Comparisons with Corresponding Ratios of Other Firms

The major task confronting the analyst in performing a cross-sectional analysis is identifying the other firms to use for comparison. The objective is to select firms with similar products and strategies and similar size and age. Few firms may meet these criteria. Coca-Cola, for example, is a logical comparison firm for PepsiCo. Coca-Cola, however, derives virtually all of its revenues from beverages, whereas PepsiCo derives revenues from beverages and food products.

An alternative approach uses average industry ratios, such as those published by Moody's, Dun & Bradstreet, and Robert Morris Associates, or as derived from computerized databases. These average industry ratios provide an overview of the performance of an industry.

The analyst should consider the following issues when using industry ratios:

1. **Definition of the industry:** Publishers of average industry ratios generally classify diversified firms into the industry of their major product. PepsiCo, for example, appears as a "beverage" company, even though it generates a large percentage of its revenues from consumer foods. The "industry" also excludes privately held and foreign firms. If these types of firms are significant for a particular industry, the analyst should recognize the possible impact of their absence from the published data.
2. **Calculation of industry average:** Is the published ratio a simple (unweighted) average of the ratios of the included firms or is it weighted by size of firm? Is the weighting based on sales, assets, market value, or some other factor? Is the median of the distribution used instead of the mean?
3. **Distribution of ratios around the mean:** To interpret a deviation of a particular firm's ratio from the industry average requires information on the distribution around the mean. The analyst interprets a ratio that is 10 percent larger than the industry mean differently depending on whether the standard deviation is 5 percent versus 15 percent greater or less than the mean. The published sources of industry ratios give either the quartiles or the range of the distribution.
4. **Definition of financial statement ratios:** The analyst should examine the definition of each published ratio to ensure that it is consistent with that calculated by the analyst. For instance, is the rate of return on common shareholders' equity based on average or beginning-of-the-period common shareholders' equity?

Average industry ratios serve as a useful basis of comparison as long as the analyst recognizes their possible limitations.

SUMMARY

This chapter presents various financial statement ratios for assessing profitability. The large number of financial ratios discussed is probably overwhelming at this point. Enhanced understanding of these financial ratios results from using and interpreting the ratios, not from memorizing them. The FSAP software package available with this book facilitates calculation of the ratios and permits the analyst to devote more time to interpretations.

EXHIBIT 4.17

Summary of Profitability Ratios

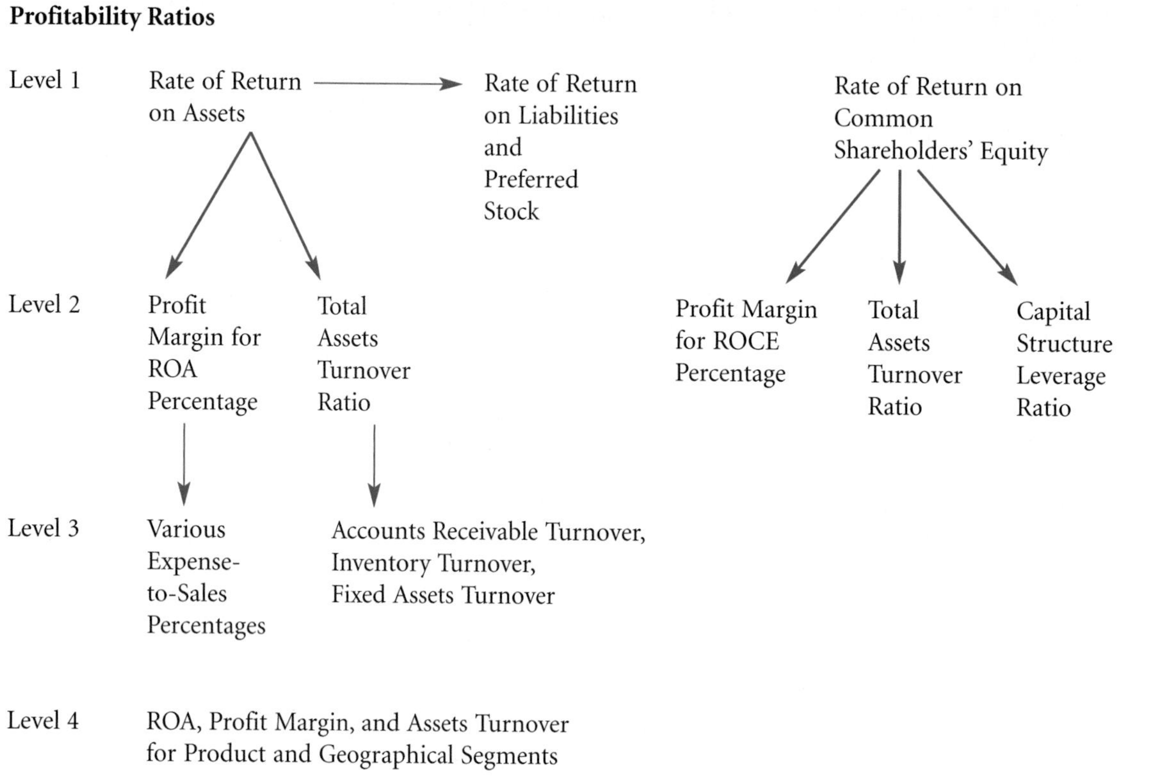

Exhibit 4.17 summarizes the financial ratios discussed in this chapter. Profitability analysis proceeds through four levels of depth. Level 1 involves measures of profitability for a firm as a whole: the rate of return on assets and the rate of return on common shareholders' equity. Level 2 disaggregates ROA and ROCE into important components. ROA disaggregates into profit margin for ROA and assets turnover. ROCE disaggregates into profit margin for ROCE, assets turnover, and capital structure leverage components. Level 3 disaggregates the profit margin into various expense-to-sales percentages and disaggregates the total assets turnover into individual asset turnovers. Level 4 uses product and geographical segment data to study ROA, profit margin, and assets turnover more fully.

QUESTIONS, EXERCISES, PROBLEMS, AND CASES

Questions and Exercises

4.1 PROFIT MARGIN FOR ROA VERSUS ROCE.

Describe the difference between the profit margin for ROA and the profit margin for ROCE. Indicate why the numerator of each profit margin measure is appropriate for measuring the rate of return on assets and the rate of return on common shareholders' equity, respectively.

4.2 CONCEPT AND MEASUREMENT OF FINANCIAL LEVERAGE. Define financial leverage. Explain why financial leverage works to the benefit of the common shareholders whenever the ROCE exceeds the ROA.

4.3 ADVANTAGES OF FINANCIAL LEVERAGE. A company president remarked: "The operations of our company are such that we can take advantage of only a minor amount of financial leverage." Explain the likely reasoning the company president had in mind to support this statement.

4.4 CONCEPTS OF RESIDUAL INCOME AND ECONOMIC VALUE ADDED. Distinguish between net income available to the common shareholders and measures such as residual income and economic value added (EVA).

4.5 RATE OF RETURN ON COMMON SHAREHOLDERS' EQUITY VERSUS BASIC EARNINGS PER COMMON SHARE. Analysts can compare ROCEs across companies but should not compare basic EPSs, despite the fact that both ratios use net income to the common shareholders in the numerator. Explain.

4.6 CALCULATING ROA AND ITS COMPONENTS. Nucor, a steel manufacturer, reported net income for Year 4 of $1,121 million on sales of $11,377 million. Interest expense for Year 4 was $29 million. The income tax rate is 35 percent. Nucor has no minority interests in its equity. Total assets were $4,492 million at the beginning of Year 4 and $6,133 million at the end of Year 4. Compute the rate of return on assets for Year 4 and disaggregate ROA into profit margin for ROA and assets turnover components.

4.7 CALCULATING ROCE AND ITS COMPONENTS. Phillips–Van Heusen, an apparel manufacturer, reported net income (amounts in thousands) for Year 4 of $58,615 on sales of $1,460,235. It declared preferred dividends of $21,122. Preferred shareholders' equity totaled $264,746 at both the beginning and end of Year 4. Common shareholders' equity totaled $296,157 at the beginning of Year 4 and $364,026 at the end of Year 4. Phillips–Van Heusen had no minority interest in its equity. Total assets were $1,439,283 at the beginning of Year 4 and $1,549,582 at the end of Year 4. Compute the rate of return on common shareholders' equity for Year 4 and disaggregate it into profit margin for ROCE, assets turnover, and capital structure leverage ratio components.

4.8 CALCULATING BASIC AND DILUTED EPS. TJX, Inc., an apparel retailer, reported net income (amounts in thousands) of $609,699 for Year 4. The weighted average of common shares outstanding during Year 4 was 488,809 shares. TJX, Inc. subtracted interest expense net of tax saving on convertible debt of $4,482. If the convertible debt had been converted into common stock, it would have increased the weighted average common shares outstanding by 16,905 shares. TJX, Inc. has outstanding stock options that, if exercised, would increase the weighted average of common shares outstanding by 6,935 shares. Compute basic and diluted earnings per share for Year 4, showing supporting computations.

4.9 RELATING ROA AND ROCE. Boston Scientific, a medical device manufacturer, reported net income (amounts in millions) of $1,062 on sales of $5,624 during Year 4.

Interest expense totaled $64. The income tax rate was 35 percent. Average total assets were $6,934.5 and average common shareholders' equity was $3,443.5. The firm did not have preferred stock outstanding or minority interest in its equity.

a. Compute the rate of return on assets. Disaggregate ROA into profit margin for ROA and assets turnover components.

b. Compute the rate of return on common shareholders' equity. Disaggregate ROCE into profit margin for ROCE, assets turnover, and capital structure leverage ratio components.

c. Calculate the amount of net income to common shareholders derived from the excess return on creditors' capital and the amount from the return on common shareholders' capital respectively.

4.10 RELATING ROA AND ROCE. Valero Energy, a petroleum company, reported net income of $1,803.8 on revenues of $54,618.6 for Year 4. Interest expense totaled $359.7 and preferred dividends totaled $12.5. Average total assets for Year 4 were $17,527.9. The income tax rate is 35 percent. Average preferred shareholders' equity totaled $204.3 and average common shareholders' equity totaled $6,562.3. All amounts are in millions.

a. Compute the rate of return on assets. Disaggregate ROA into profit margin for ROA and assets turnover components.

b. Compute the rate of return on common shareholders' equity. Disaggregate ROCE into profit margin for ROCE, assets turnover, and capital leverage ratio components.

c. Calculate the amount of net income to common shareholders derived from the excess return on creditors' capital, the excess return on preferred shareholders' capital, and the return on common shareholders' capital, respectively.

Problems and Cases

4.11 ANALYZING OPERATING PROFITABILITY. Exhibit 4.18 presents selected operating data for three retailers for a recent year. Albertsons sells grocery products. Home Depot sells a wide range of home improvement products, which includes products ranging from riding lawnmowers to lighting fixtures to kitchen countertops. Federated Department Stores operates several department store chains selling products ranging from brand-name clothing to china, cosmetics, and bedding.

Required

a. Compute the rate of return on assets for each firm. Disaggregate the rate of return on assets into profit margin for ROA and assets turnover components. The income tax rate is 35 percent.

b. Describe the likely reasons for the differences in the profit margins for ROA and assets turnovers of the three companies.

4.12 CALCULATING AND INTERPRETING ACCOUNTS RECEIVABLE TURNOVER RATIOS. Microsoft Corporation (Microsoft) and Oracle Corporation (Oracle) engage in the design, manufacture, and sale of computer software. Microsoft sells and licenses a wide range of systems and application software to businesses, computer hardware manufacturers, and consumer retailers. Oracle sells software for informa-

EXHIBIT 4.18

Selected Data for Three Retailers
(amounts in millions)
(Problem 4.11)

	Albertsons	Home Depot	Federated Department Stores
Sales	$39,897	$73,094	$15,630
Cost of Goods Sold	28,711	48,664	9,297
Interest Expense	493	70	299
Net Income	474	5,001	689
Average Inventory	3,077	10,691	3,168
Average Fixed Assets	9,936	22,879	6,096
Average Total Assets	16,989	40,432	14,718

EXHIBIT 4.19

Selected Data for Microsoft and Oracle
(amounts in millions)
(Problem 4.12)

	Year 4	Year 3	Year 2
Microsoft			
Sales	$36,835	$32,187	$28,365
Average Accounts Receivable	5,543	5,163	4,400
Change in Sales from Previous Year	+14.4%	+13.5%	+12.1%
Oracle			
Sales	$10,156	$ 9,475	$ 9,623
Average Accounts Receivable	1,965	1,978	2,234
Change in Sales from Previous Year	+7.2%	−1.5%	−11.8%

tion management almost exclusively to businesses. Exhibit 4.19 presents selected data for the two firms for Year 2, Year 3, and Year 4.

Required

a. Calculate the accounts receivable turnover ratio for Microsoft and Oracle for Year 2, Year 3, and Year 4.

b. Suggest possible reasons for the differences in the accounts receivable turnovers of Microsoft and Oracle during the three-year period.

c. Suggest possible reasons for the changes in the accounts receivable turnover for the two firms over the three-year period.

4.13 CALCULATING AND INTERPRETING INVENTORY TURNOVER RATIOS. Dell produces computers and related equipment on a made-to-order basis for consumers. It has recently expanded this manufacturing strategy to sell to businesses as well. Sun Microsystems designs and manufacturers higher-end computers that function as servers and for use in computer-aided design. Sun Microsystems sells primarily to businesses. It has shifted its strategy in recent years to provide services to business customers in addition to product sales of computers. Selected data for each firm for Year 2, Year 3, and Year 4 appear in Exhibit 4.20.

Required

a. Calculate the inventory turnover ratio for each firm for Year 2, Year 3, and Year 4.

b. Suggest reasons for the differences in the inventory turnover ratios of these two firms.

c. Suggest reasons for the changes in the inventory turnover ratios during the three-year period.

4.14 CALCULATING AND INTERPRETING ACCOUNTS RECEIVABLE AND INVENTORY TURNOVER RATIOS. AK Steel and Nucor are steel manufacturers. AK Steel is an integrated steel producer, transforming ferrous metals into rolled steel and then into various steel products for the automobile, appliance, construction, and other industries. Its steel falls on the higher end in terms of quality (strength and durability). Nucor produces steel in mini-mills. Mini-mills transform scrap ferrous metals into standard sizes of rolled steel, which Nucor then sells to steel service centers and distributors. Its steel falls on the lower end in terms of quality. Exhibit 4.21 sets forth various data for these two companies for Year 3 and Year 4.

Required

a. Calculate the accounts receivable turnovers for AK Steel and Nucor for Year 3 and Year 4.

EXHIBIT 4.20

Selected Data for Dell and Sun Microsystems
(amounts in millions)
(Problem 4.13)

	Year 4	Year 3	Year 2
Dell			
Cost of Goods Sold	$40,190	$33,892	$20,055
Average Inventories	393	317	292
Change in Sales from Previous Year	+18.7%	+17.1%	+13.6%
Sun Microsystems			
Cost of Goods Sold	$ 4,290	$ 4,342	$ 5,506
Average Inventories	440	504	819
Change in Sales from Previous Year	−5.6%	−14.3%	−39.4%

EXHIBIT 4.21

Selected Data for AK Steel and Nucor
(amounts in millions)
(Problem 4.14)

	Year 4	Year 3
AK Steel		
Sales	$ 5,217	$4,042
Cost of Goods Sold	4,554	3,887
Average Accounts Receivable	516	393
Average Inventories	707	790
Change in Sales from Previous Year	+12.9%	−2.8%
Nucor		
Sales	$11,377	$6,266
Cost of Goods Sold	9,129	5,997
Average Accounts Receivable	768	528
Average Inventories	900	575
Change in Sales from Previous Year	+81.6%	+30.5%

b. Describe the likely reasons for the differences in the accounts receivable turnovers for these two firms.
c. Describe the likely reasons for the trend in the accounts receivable turnovers of these two firms during the two-year period.
d. Calculate the inventory turnovers for AK Steel and Nucor for Year 3 and Year 4.
e. Describe the likely reasons for the differences in the inventory turnovers of these two firms.
f. Describe the likely reasons for the trend in the inventory turnovers of these two firms during the two-year period.

4.15 CALCULATING AND INTERPRETING FIXED ASSET TURNOVER RATIOS. Texas Instruments (TI) designs and manufactures semiconductor products for use in computers, telecommunications equipment, automobiles, and other electronics-based products. The manufacturing of semiconductors is highly capital intensive. Hewlett-Packard Corporation (HP) manufactures computer hardware and various imaging products, such as printers and fax machines. HP outsources the manufacture of a portion of the components for its products. HP acquired Compaq Computer in May, Year 2, halfway through its Year 2 fiscal year. Exhibit 4.22 presents selected data for TI and HP for Year 2, Year 3, and Year 4.

Required

a. Compute the fixed asset turnover for each firm for Year 2, Year 3, and Year 4.
b. Suggest reasons for the differences in the fixed asset turnovers of TI and HP.
c. Suggest reasons for the changes in the fixed asset turnovers of TI and HP during the three-year period.

EXHIBIT 4.22

Selected Data for Texas Instruments and Hewlett-Packard
(amounts in millions)
(Problem 4.15)

	Year 4	Year 3	Year 2
Texas Instruments			
Sales	$12,580	$ 9,834	$ 8,383
Cost of Goods Sold	6,902	5,728	5,313
Capital Expenditures	1,298	800	802
Average Fixed Assets	4,025	4,463	5,192
Percentage Fixed Assets Depreciated	59.1%	56.7%	49.6%
Percentage Change in Sales	+27.9%	+17.3%	−17.8%
Hewlett-Packard			
Sales	$79,905	$73,061	$56,588
Cost of Goods Sold	60,340	53,858	41,793
Capital Expenditures	2,126	1,995	1,710
Average Fixed Assets	6,894	6,703	5,661
Percentage Fixed Assets Depreciated	51.9%	51.3%	44.8%
Percentage Change in Sales	+9.4%	+29.1%	+25.1%

4.16 CALCULATING AND INTERPRETING THE RATE OF RETURN ON COMMON SHAREHOLDERS' EQUITY AND ITS COMPONENTS.

JCPenney operates a chain of retail department stores, selling apparel, shoes, jewelry, and home furnishings. It also offers most of its products through catalog distribution. During fiscal Year 5 it sold Eckerd Drugs, a chain of retail drugstores, and used the cash proceeds in part to repurchase shares of its common stock. Exhibit 4.23 presents selected data for JCPenney for fiscal Year 3, Year 4, and Year 5.

Required

a. Calculate the rate of return on assets for fiscal Year 3, Year 4, and Year 5. Disaggregate ROA into the profit margin for ROA and total assets turnover components. The income tax rate is 35 percent.

b. Calculate the rate of return on common shareholders' equity for fiscal Year 3, Year 4, and Year 5. Disaggregate ROCE into the profit margin for ROCE, total assets turnover, and capital structure leverage components.

c. Suggest reasons for the changes in ROCE over the three years.

d. Compute the ratio of ROCE to ROA for each year.

e. Calculate the amount of net income available to common stockholders derived from the use of financial leverage with respect to creditors' capital, the amount derived from the use of preferred shareholders' capital, and the amount derived from common shareholders' capital for each year.

f. Did financial leverage work to the advantage of the common shareholders in each of the three years? Explain.

EXHIBIT 4.23

Selected Data for JCPenney
(amounts in millions)
(Problem 4.16)

	Year Ended January 31:			
	Year 5	Year 4	Year 3	
Sales	$18,424	$17,786	$17,633	
Net Income (Loss)	524	(928)	405	
Interest Expense	279	271	245	
Preferred Stock Dividend	12	25	27	
Income Tax Rate	35%	35%	35%	
January 31:	**Year 5**	**Year 4**	**Year 3**	**Year 2**
Total Assets	$14,127	$18,300	$17,787	$18,048
Preferred Stock	0	304	333	363
Total Common Shareholders' Equity	4,856	5,121	6,037	5,766

4.17 INTERPRETING THE RATE OF RETURN ON COMMON SHAREHOLDERS' EQUITY AND ITS COMPONENTS. Selected financial data for Georgia-Pacific Corporation, a forest products firm, appear in Exhibit 4.24.

Required

a. In which years did financial leverage work to the advantage of the common shareholders and in which years did it work to their disadvantage? Explain.

b. Identify possible reasons for the changes in the capital structure leverage ratio during the five-year period.

EXHIBIT 4.24

Selected Data for Georgia-Pacific Corporation
(Problem 4.17)

	Year 4	Year 3	Year 2	Year 1	Year 0
Rate of Return on Common Shareholders' Equity	10.8%	6.5%	(4.2%)	(9.1%)	7.4%
Rate of Return on Assets	4.8%	3.7%	1.5%	.8%	3.3%
Profit Margin for ROA	5.8%	4.6%	1.7%	.9%	3.3%
Profit Margin for ROCE	3.2%	1.6%	(.9%)	(1.9%)	1.6%
Total Assets Turnover	.8	.8	.9	.9	1.0
Capital Structure Leverage Ratio	4.1	4.9	5.4	5.3	4.8
Growth Rate in Sales	0.0%	(13.5%)	(9.2%)	13.4%	24.1%

4.18 CALCULATING AND INTERPRETING THE RATE OF RETURN ON COMMON SHAREHOLDERS' EQUITY AND EARNINGS PER COMMON SHARE. Selected data for General Mills for Year 2, Year 3, and Year 4 appear below (amounts in millions):

	Year 4	Year 3	Year 2
Net Income	$ 506.1	$ 505.6	$472.7
Weighted Average Number of Common Shares Outstanding	163.1	165.7	164.5
Average Common Shareholders' Equity	$1,294.7	$1,242.2	$961.6

Required

a. Compute the rate of return on common shareholders' equity (ROCE) for Year 2, Year 3, and Year 4.

b. Compute basic earnings per common share (EPS) for Year 2, Year 3, and Year 4.

c. Interpret the changes in ROCE versus EPS over the three-year period.

FSAP

4.19 CALCULATING AND INTERPRETING PROFITABILITY RATIOS. Hasbro is a leading firm in the toy, game, and amusement industry. Its promoted brands group includes products from Playskool, Tonka, Milton Bradley, Parker Brothers, Tiger, and Wizards of the Coast. Sales of toys and games are highly variable from year to year, depending on whether the latest products meet consumer interests. Hasbro also faces increasing competition from electronic games and Internet online games. Hasbro develops and promotes its core brands and also manufactures and distributes products created by others under license arrangements. Hasbro pays a royalty to the creator of such products. In recent years, Hasbro has attempted to reduce its reliance on license arrangements and place more emphasis on its core brands. Hasbro has also embarked on a strategy of reducing fixed selling and administrative costs in an effort to offset the negative effects on earnings of highly variable sales. Exhibit 4.25 presents the balance sheets for Hasbro for the years ended December 31, Year 1 through Year 4. Exhibit 4.26 presents the income statement and Exhibit 4.27 presents the statement of cash flows for Year 2 through Year 4.

Required

a. Exhibit 4.28 presents profitability ratios for Hasbro for Year 2 and Year 3. Calculate each of these financial ratios for Year 4. The income tax rate is 35 percent.

b. Analyze the changes in ROA and its components for Hasbro over the three-year period, suggesting reasons for the changes observed.

c. Analyze the changes in ROCE and its components for Hasbro over the three-year period, suggesting reasons for the changes observed.

EXHIBIT 4.25

Hasbro
Balance Sheets
(amounts in millions)
(Problem 4.19)

	December 31:			
	Year 4	Year 3	Year 2	Year 1
Assets				
Cash	$ 725	$ 521	$ 496	$ 233
Accounts Receivable	579	607	555	572
Inventories	195	169	190	217
Prepayments	219	212	191	346
Total Current Assets	$1,718	$1,509	$1,432	$1,368
Property, Plant, and Equipment, net	207	200	213	236
Other Assets	1,316	1,454	1,498	1,765
Total Assets	$3,241	$3,163	$3,143	$3,369
Liabilities and Shareholders' Equity				
Accounts Payable	$ 168	$ 159	$ 166	$ 123
Short-Term Borrowing	342	24	223	36
Other Current Liabilities	639	747	578	599
Total Current Liabilities	$1,149	$ 930	$ 967	$ 758
Long-Term Debt	303	687	857	1,166
Other Noncurrent Liabilities	149	141	128	92
Total Liabilities	$1,601	$1,758	$1,952	$2,016
Common Stock	$ 105	$ 105	$ 105	$ 105
Additional Paid-In Capital	381	398	458	455
Retained Earnings	1,721	1,567	1,430	1,622
Accumulated Other Comprehensive Income	82	30	(47)	(68)
Treasury Stock	(649)	(695)	(755)	(761)
Total Shareholders' Equity	$1,640	$1,405	$1,191	$1,353
Total Liabilities and Shareholders' Equity	$3,241	$3,163	$3,143	$3,369

EXHIBIT 4.26

Hasbro
Income Statements
(amounts in millions)
(Problem 4.19)

	For the Year Ended December 31:		
	Year 4	Year 3	Year 2
Sales	$2,998	$3,139	$2,816
Cost of Goods Sold	(1,252)	(1,288)	(1,099)
Selling and Administrative Expenses:			
Advertising	(387)	(364)	(297)
Research and Development	(157)	(143)	(154)
Royalty Expense	(223)	(248)	(296)
Other Selling and Administrative	(687)	(799)	(788)
Interest Expense	(32)	(53)	(78)
Income Tax Expense	(64)	(69)	(29)
Net Income	$ 196	$ 175	$ 75

EXHIBIT 4.27

Hasbro
Statements of Cash Flows
(amounts in millions)
(Problem 4.19)

	For the Year Ended December 31:		
	Year 4	Year 3	Year 2
Operations			
Net Income	$196	$175	$ 75
Depreciation and Amortization	146	164	184
Addbacks and Subtractions, net	17	68	(67)
(Increase) Decrease in Accounts Receivable	76	(13)	34
(Increase) Decrease in Inventories	(16)	35	39
(Increase) Decrease in Prepayments	29	8	185
Increase (Decrease) in Accounts Payable and Other Current Liabilities	(90)	17	23
Cash Flow from Operations	$358	$454	$473

Continued

Exhibit 4.27 continued	For the Year Ended December 31: Year 4	Year 3	Year 2
Investing			
Property, Plant, and Equipment Acquired	$(79)	$ (63)	$ (59)
Other Investing Transactions	(6)	(2)	(3)
Cash Flow from Investing	$(85)	$ (65)	$ (62)
Financing			
Increase in Common Stock	$ 26	$ 40	$ 3
Decrease in Short-Term Borrowing	(7)	0	(15)
Decrease in Long-Term Borrowing	(58)	(389)	(127)
Acquisition of Common Stock	0	(3)	0
Dividends	(37)	(21)	(21)
Other Financing Transactions	7	9	12
Cash Flow from Financing	$(69)	$(364)	$(148)
Change in Cash	$204	$ 25	$ 263
Cash—Beginning of Year	521	496	233
Cash—End of Year	$725	$ 521	$ 496

EXHIBIT 4.28

Hasbro
Financial Statement Ratio Analysis
(Problem 4.19)

	Year 4	Year 3	Year 2
Profit Margin for ROA		6.7%	4.5%
Assets Turnover		1.0	.9
Rate of Return on Assets		6.6	3.9
Profit Margin for ROCE		5.6	2.7
Capital Structure Leverage Ratio		2.4	2.6
Rate of Return on Common Shareholders' Equity		13.5	5.9
Cost of Goods Sold/Sales		41.0	39.0
Advertising Expense/Sales		11.6	10.5
Research and Development/Sales		4.6	5.5
Royalty Expense/Sales		7.9	10.5
Other Selling and Administrative Expense/Sales		25.4	28.0
Income Tax Expense (excluding tax effects of interest expense)/Sales		2.8%	2.0%
Accounts Receivable Turnover		5.4	5.0
Inventory Turnover		7.2	5.4
Fixed Asset Turnover		15.2	12.5

FSAP

4.20 CALCULATING AND INTERPRETING PROFITABILITY RATIOS. Abercrombie & Fitch sells casual apparel and personal-care products for men, women, and children through retail stores located primarily in shopping malls. Its fiscal year ends January 31 of each year. Financial statements for Abercrombie & Fitch for fiscal years ending January 31, Year 3, Year 4, and Year 5 appear in Exhibit 4.29 (balance sheet), Exhibit 4.30 (income statement), and Exhibit 4.31 (statement of cash flows). These financial statements reflect the capitalization of operating leases in property, plant, and equipment and long-term debt, a topic discussed in Chapter 8. Exhibit 4.32 presents financial statement ratios

EXHIBIT 4.29

Abercrombie & Fitch
Balance Sheets
(amounts in millions)
(Problem 4.20)

	January 31:			
	Year 5	**Year 4**	**Year 3**	**Year 2**
Assets				
Cash	$ 350	$ 56	$ 43	$ 188
Marketable Securities	0	465	387	51
Accounts Receivable	26	7	10	21
Inventories	248	201	169	130
Prepayments	28	24	20	15
Total Current Assets	$ 652	$ 753	$ 629	$ 405
Property, Plant, and Equipment, net	1,560	1,342	1,172	947
Other Assets	8	1	1	0
Total Assets	$2,220	$2,096	$1,802	$1,352
Liabilities and Shareholders' Equity				
Accounts Payable	$ 84	$ 58	$ 79	$ 32
Short-Term Borrowing	54	33	0	0
Other Current Liabilities	276	220	193	132
Total Current Liabilities	$ 414	$ 311	$ 272	$ 164
Long-Term Debt	872	713	629	581
Other Noncurrent Liabilities	265	214	165	12
Total Liabilities	$1,551	$1,238	$1,066	$ 757
Common Stock	$ 1	$ 1	$ 1	$ 1
Additional Paid-In Capital	140	139	143	141
Retained Earnings	1,076	906	701	520
Treasury Stock	(548)	(188)	(109)	(67)
Total Shareholders' Equity	$ 669	$ 858	$ 736	$ 595
Total Liabilities and Shareholders' Equity	$2,220	$2,096	$1,802	$1,352

EXHIBIT 4.30

Abercrombie & Fitch
Income Statements
(amounts in millions)
(Problem 4.20)

	For the Year Ended January 31:		
	Year 5	Year 4	Year 3
Sales	$ 2,021	$1,708	$1,596
Cost of Goods Sold	(1,048)	(936)	(893)
Selling and Administrative Expenses	(562)	(386)	(343)
Interest Expense	(63)	(54)	(48)
Interest Income	5	4	4
Income Tax Expense	(137)	(131)	(121)
Net Income	$ 216	$ 205	$ 195

EXHIBIT 4.31

Abercrombie & Fitch
Statements of Cash Flows
(amounts in millions)
(Problem 4.20)

	For the Year Ended January 31:		
	Year 5	Year 4	Year 3
Operations			
Net Income	$ 216	$ 205	$ 195
Depreciation and Amortization	106	90	76
Addbacks and Subtractions, net	13	56	49
(Increase) Decrease in Inventories	(34)	(27)	(34)
Increase (Decrease) in Current Liabilities	125	19	60
Cash Flow from Operations	$ 426	$ 343	$ 346
Investing			
Property, Plant, and Equipment Acquired	$ (185)	$ (160)	$ (146)
Marketable Securities Sold	4,779	3,771	2,419
Marketable Securities Purchased	(4,314)	(3,849)	(2,729)
Other Investing Transactions	0	0	5
Cash Flow from Investing	$ 280	$ (238)	$ (451)

Continued

Exhibit 4.31 continued	For the Year Ended January 31: Year 5	Year 4	Year 3
Financing			
Increase in Short-Term Borrowing	$ 20	$ 4	$ 4
Increase in Common Stock	49	20	0
Acquisition of Common Stock	(435)	(116)	(43)
Dividends	(46)	0	0
Cash Flow from Financing	$ (412)	$ (92)	$ (39)
Change in Cash	$ 294	$ 13	$ (144)
Cash—Beginning of Year	56	43	188
Cash—End of Year	$ 350	$ 56	$ 43

EXHIBIT 4.32

Abercrombie & Fitch
Financial Statement Ratio Analysis
(Problem 4.20)

	Year 5	Year 4	Year 3
Profit Margin for ROA		14.1%	14.2%
Assets Turnover		.9	1.0
Rate of Return on Assets		12.3%	14.3%
Profit Margin for ROCE		12.0%	12.2%
Capital Structure Leverage Ratio		2.4	2.4
Rate of Return on Common Shareholders' Equity		25.7%	29.3%
Cost of Goods Sold/Sales		54.8%	56.0%
Selling and Administrative Expense/Sales		22.6%	21.5%
Interest Revenue/Sales		.2%	.3%
Income Tax Expense (excluding tax effects of interest expense)/Sales		8.8%	8.6%
Accounts Receivable Turnover		200.9	103.0
Inventory Turnover		5.1	6.0
Fixed Asset Turnover		1.4	1.5
Sales per Store		$2,440,000	$2,673,367
Sales per Square Foot		$ 340.51	$ 366.22
Sales per Employee		$ 56,556	$ 72,545

for Abercrombie & Fitch for Year 3 and Year 4. Selected data for Abercrombie & Fitch appear here:

	Year 5	Year 4	Year 3
Number of Stores	788	700	597
Square Feet of Retail Space (in thousands)	5,590	5,016	4,358
Number of Employees	48,500	30,200	22,000
Growth Rate in Sales	18.3%	7.0%	16.9%
Comparable Store Sales Increase	2.0%	(9.0%)	5.0%

Required

a. Calculate the ratios in Exhibit 4.32 for Year 5. The income tax rate is 35 percent.

b. Analyze the changes in ROA for Abercrombie & Fitch during the three-year period, suggesting possible reasons for the changes observed.

c. Analyze the changes in ROCE for Abercrombie & Fitch during the three-year period, suggesting possible reasons for the changes observed.

4.21 INTERPRETING PROFITABILITY RATIOS IN A CROSS-SECTIONAL SETTING. Coca-Cola Company is the principal competitor of PepsiCo in the soft drink beverage business. Coca-Cola engages almost exclusively in beverages, whereas PepsiCo also engages in the manufacture and distribution of packaged foods, such as chips, salsas, and cereals.

The value chain for beverages involves the following:

1. Manufacturing concentrate and syrup to be used in the beverages.
2. Mixing syrup, water, and other ingredients and then placing the finished beverage in a container (can or bottle). This process is relatively capital intensive.
3. Distributing packaged beverages to food distributors and retail establishments. This activity is also capital intensive.

Coca-Cola and PepsiCo are primarily engaged in the manufacture of concentrate and syrup (step 1). They both rely heavily on other entities to perform steps 2 and 3.

The value chain for packaged foods involves the following:

1. Combining ingredients, cooking as appropriate, and then packaging the finished food products.
2. Distributing packaged food products to food distributors and retail establisments.

Exhibit 4.33 presents ROA and its disaggregated components for Coca-Cola and PepsiCo for Year 2 to Year 4. Exhibit 4.34 presents ROCE and its disaggregated components, and Exhibit 4.35 presents segment data for these two companies. The ratio amounts for PepsiCo correspond to those discussed in the chapter but appear next to those for Coca-Cola to ease interpretation. The segment computations of ROA and asset turnover use asset amounts at the end of the year, instead of average assets during the year, to ease computations (see footnote 10 in the chapter for an explanation of the use of end-of-year assets). The segment profit margins and ROA are based on operating income before interest and income taxes. Thus, the profit margins and ROAs for the segments exceed those for the companies as a whole. Coca-Cola includes operations in the United

EXHIBIT 4.33

ROA and Its Disaggregated Components for Coca-Cola and PepsiCo (Problem 4.21)

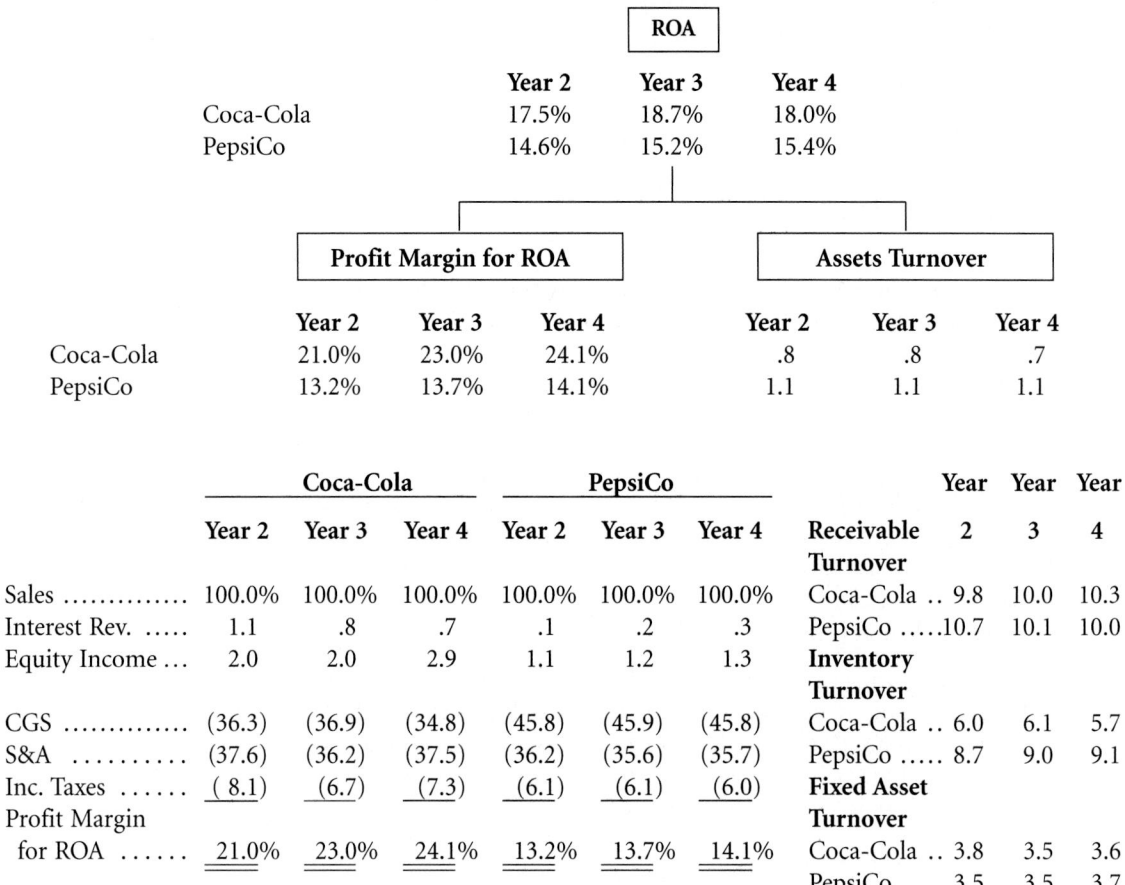

ROA

	Year 2	Year 3	Year 4
Coca-Cola	17.5%	18.7%	18.0%
PepsiCo	14.6%	15.2%	15.4%

	Profit Margin for ROA			Assets Turnover		
	Year 2	**Year 3**	**Year 4**	**Year 2**	**Year 3**	**Year 4**
Coca-Cola	21.0%	23.0%	24.1%	.8	.8	.7
PepsiCo	13.2%	13.7%	14.1%	1.1	1.1	1.1

	Coca-Cola			PepsiCo		
	Year 2	**Year 3**	**Year 4**	**Year 2**	**Year 3**	**Year 4**
Sales	100.0%	100.0%	100.0%	100.0%	100.0%	100.0%
Interest Rev.	1.1	.8	.7	.1	.2	.3
Equity Income	2.0	2.0	2.9	1.1	1.2	1.3
CGS	(36.3)	(36.9)	(34.8)	(45.8)	(45.9)	(45.8)
S&A	(37.6)	(36.2)	(37.5)	(36.2)	(35.6)	(35.7)
Inc. Taxes	(8.1)	(6.7)	(7.3)	(6.1)	(6.1)	(6.0)
Profit Margin for ROA	21.0%	23.0%	24.1%	13.2%	13.7%	14.1%

	Year 2	Year 3	Year 4
Receivable Turnover			
Coca-Cola	9.8	10.0	10.3
PepsiCo	10.7	10.1	10.0
Inventory Turnover			
Coca-Cola	6.0	6.1	5.7
PepsiCo	8.7	9.0	9.1
Fixed Asset Turnover			
Coca-Cola	3.8	3.5	3.6
PepsiCo	3.5	3.5	3.7

States, Canada, and Puerto Rico in its North American segment, whereas PepsiCo includes operations for the United States and Canada only.

Required

a. What are the likely reasons that the cost of goods sold to sales percentage for Coca-Cola is lower than that for PepsiCo?

b. What are the likely reasons that PepsiCo's inventory turnover ratio exceeds that for Coca-Cola?

c. Compute the average income tax rate for Coca-Cola for each year using amounts that exclude interest expense and related tax savings (see the lower panel of Exhibit 4.11 for the corresponding average income tax rate calculation for PepsiCo). Suggest reasons for Coca-Cola's lower average income tax rate.

d. For which firm is financial leverage helping the common shareholders more? Explain in such a way as to demonstrate your understanding of financial leverage.

EXHIBIT 4.34

ROCE and Its Disaggregated Components for Coca-Cola and PepsiCo (Problem 4.21)

ROCE

	Year 2	Year 3	Year 4
Coca-Cola	34.3%	36.5%	34.4%
PepsiCo	34.8%	33.5%	31.2%

	Profit Margin for ROCE			Asset Turnover			Capital Structure Leverage Ratio		
	Year 2	**Year 3**	**Year 4**	**Year 2**	**Year 3**	**Year 4**	**Year 2**	**Year 3**	**Year 4**
Coca-Cola	20.3%	22.4%	23.5%	.8	.8	.7	2.0	2.0	2.0
PepsiCo	12.6%	13.3%	13.6%	1.1	1.1	1.1	2.5	2.3	2.1

EXHIBIT 4.35

Segment Data for Coca-Cola and PepsiCo (Problem 4.21)

	Coca-Cola			PepsiCo		
	Year 2	**Year 3**	**Year 4**	**Year 2**	**Year 3**	**Year 4**
Geographical Segment Data Sales Mix						
North America	32.4%	30.5%	30.6%	69.9%	68.9%	67.1%
Other Countries	67.6	69.5	69.4	30.1	31.1	32.9
Profitability North America						
Profit Margin	24.4%	20.2%	24.2%	23.4%	24.1%	24.6%
Asset Turnover	1.25	1.28	1.40	1.46	1.50	1.55
ROA	30.6%	25.9%	33.9%	34.1%	36.1%	38.2%
Other Countries						
Profit Margin	35.8%	33.3%	33.6%	11.7%	12.2%	13.4%
Asset Turnover	1.52	1.56	1.62	1.07	1.07	1.10
ROA	54.4%	51.8%	54.5%	12.5%	13.1%	14.8%

4.22 ANALYZING THE PROFITABILITY OF A SERVICE FIRM. Kelly Services (Kelly) places employees at clients' businesses on a temporary basis. It segments its services into (1) commercial, (2) professional and technical, and (3) international. Kelly recognizes revenues for the amount billed to clients. Kelly includes the amount it pays to temporary employees in cost of services sold. It includes the compensation paid to permanent employees that administer its offices in selling and administrative expenses. The latter expense also includes data processing costs relating to payroll records for all employees, rent, taxes, and insurance on office space. Amounts receivable from clients appear in accounts receivable, and amounts payable to permanent and temporary employees appear in current liabilities.

The temporary personnel business offers clients flexibility in adjusting their number of workers to meet changing capacity needs. Temporary employees are typically less costly than permanent workers because they have fewer fringe benefits. Temporary workers, however, generally are not as well trained as permanent workers and have less loyalty to clients.

Barriers to entry in the personnel supply business are low. This business does not require capital for physical facilities (most space is rented), does not need specialized assets (most temporary employees do not possess unique skills; needed data processing technology is readily available), and operates with little government regulation. Thus, competition is intense and margins tend to be thin.

Exhibit 4.36 presents selected profitability ratios and other data for Kelly Services, the largest temporary personnel supply firm in the United States. The data in Exhibit 4.36 reflect the capitalization of operating leases in property, plant, and equipment and long-term debt, a topic discussed in Chapter 8.

Required

Analyze the changes in the profitability of Kelly Services during the three-year period in as much depth as permitted by the data provided.

4.23 ANALYZING THE PROFITABILITY OF TWO HOTELS. La Quinta Inns (La Quinta) operates a chain of midpriced hotels aimed at the cost-conscious business traveler. Its targeted guests desire quality rooms in convenient locations at attractive prices but do not require banquet and convention facilities, in-house restaurants, cocktail lounges, or room service. Exhibit 4.37 presents selected profitability ratios and other data for La Quinta.

Prime Hospitality Corporation (Prime) operates several hotel chains with different targeted customers from those of La Quinta. Its AmeriSuites and Wellesley Inns offer hotel suites in primarily suburban commercial centers and corporate office parks. These hotels are located with easy access to shopping, food, and entertainment amenities. Prime also operates full-service hotels under national brand names (Marriott, Sheraton, Crowne Plaza) that offer banquet and convention facilities. Exhibit 4.38 presents selected profitability and other data for Prime.

Required

Analyze the changes and the differences in the profitability of these two hotel chains to the maximum depth permitted by the given data.

EXHIBIT 4.36

Profitability Ratios and Other Data for Kelly Services (Problem 4.22)

	Year 4	Year 3	Year 2
Profit Margin for ROA	.6%	.3%	.6%
Assets Turnover	3.8	3.5	3.5
Rate of Return on Assets	2.2%	.9%	2.1%
Profit Margin for ROCE	.4%	.1%	.4%
Capital Structure Leverage Ratio	2.1	2.0	1.9
Rate of Return on Common Shareholders' Equity	3.3%	.8%	2.9%
Revenues	100.0%	100.0%	100.0%
Compensation of Temporary Employees/Revenues	84.0%	83.9%	82.9%
Selling and Administrative Expense/Revenues	15.1%	15.7%	16.1%
Income Tax Expense/Revenues	.3%	.2%	.4%
Accounts Receivable Turnover	7.2	7.1	7.3
Fixed Asset Turnover	16.0	14.0	12.9
Sales Mix Data:			
Commercial	46.7%	49.3%	51.9%
Professional and Technical	20.7	20.7	21.4
International	32.6	30.0	26.7
Total	100.0%	100.0%	100.0%
Segment Profit Margin:			
Commercial	5.1%	4.4%	5.6%
Professional and Technical	6.0%	5.9%	5.8%
International	.8%	0%	.5%
Number of Offices	2,600	2,500	2,400
Number of Permanent Employees	8,400	7,900	8,200
Number of Temporary Employees, approximate	700,000	700,000	700,000
Growth Rate in Revenues	15.2%	6.9%	−4.7%
Per-Office Data:			
Revenues	$1,916,923	$1,730,000	$1,690,417
Net Income	$ 8,077	$ 2,000	$ 7,500
Permanent Employees	3.2	3.2	3.4
Temporary Employees	269	280	292
Per-Permanent-Employee Data:			
Revenues	$ 593,333	$ 547,468	$ 494,756
Net Income	$ 2,500	$ 633	$ 2,195
Temporary Employees	83.3	88.6	85.4
Per-Temporary-Employee Data:			
Revenues	$ 7,120	$ 6,177	$ 5,796
Net Income	30	7	26

EXHIBIT 4.37

Profitability Ratios and Other Data for La Quinta Inns (Problem 4.23)

	Year 9	Year 8	Year 7
Profit Margin for ROA	19.9%	18.8%	17.4%
Assets Turnover	.43	.46	.45
Rate of Return on Assets	8.6%	8.6%	7.9%
Profit Margin for ROCE	13.5%	12.2%	10.6%
Capital Structure Leverage Ratio	3.0	3.5	4.7
Rate of Return on Common Shareholders' Equity	17.4%	19.7%	22.4%
Number of Hotels	248	237	228
Number of Rooms	32,728	31,363	29,712
Rooms/Hotel	132	132	130
Occupancy Rate	68.9%	70.8%	70.1%
Revenue/Available Room Night	$ 37.09	$ 36.16	$ 33.40
Operating Income/Available Room Night	$ 7.39	$ 6.78	$ 5.82
Revenue/Occupied Room Night	$ 53.83	$ 51.07	$ 47.65
Operating Income/Occupied Room Night	$ 10.73	$ 9.58	$ 8.30
Revenue/Hotel	$1,786,528	$1,746,494	$1,588,781
Operating Income/Hotel	$ 356,141	$ 327,629	$ 276,640

4.24 ANALYZING THE PROFITABILITY OF TWO RESTAURANT CHAINS. Analyzing the profitability of restaurants requires consideration of their strategies with respect to ownership of restaurants versus franchising. Firms that own and operate their restaurants report the assets and financing of those restaurants on their balance sheets, and the revenues and operating expenses of the restaurants on their income statements. Firms that franchise their restaurants to others (that is, franchisees) often own the land and buildings of franchised restaurants and lease them to the franchisees. The income statement includes fees received from franchisees in the form of license fees for using the franchiser's name; rent for facilities and equipment; and various fees for advertising, menu planning, and food and paper products used by the franchisee. The revenues and operating expenses of the franchised restaurants appear on the financial statements of the franchisees.

Exhibit 4.39 presents profitability ratios and other data for Brinker International, and Exhibit 4.40 presents similar data for McDonald's. Brinker operates chains of specialty sit-down restaurants in the United States under the names of Chili's, Romano's Macaroni Grill, On the Border, Maggiano's Little Italy, and Corner Bakery Cafe. Its restaurants average approximately 7,000 square feet. Brinker owns and operates approximately 81 percent of its restaurants. McDonald's operates chains of fast-food restaurants in the United States and other countries under the names of McDonald's, Boston Market, Chipotle Mexican Grill, and Donatos Pizza. Its restaurants average approximately 2,800 square feet. McDonald's owns and operates approximately 29 percent of its restaurants. It also owns approximately 25 percent of the restaurant land and buildings of franchisees. The financial ratios and other data in Exhibits 4.39 and 4.40 reflect the capitalization of oper-

EXHIBIT 4.38

Profitability Ratios and Other Data for Prime Hospitality Corporation (Problem 4.23)

	Year 9	Year 8	Year 7
Profit Margin for ROA	13.8%	15.3%	20.4%
Assets Turnover	.38	.41	.32
Rate of Return on Assets	5.2%	6.3%	6.5%
Profit Margin for ROCE	8.5%	8.5%	13.2%
Capital Structure Leverage Ratio	2.1	2.3	2.3
Rate of Return on Common Shareholders' Equity	6.8%	8.0%	9.7%
Number of Hotels	108	95	86
Number of Rooms	16,232	11,110	8,965
Rooms/Hotel	150	117	104
Occupancy Rate	69.0%	69.2%	68.0%
Revenue/Available Room Night	$ 43.09	$ 50.71	$ 41.04
Operating Income/Available Room Night	$ 5.96	$ 7.77	$ 8.36
Revenue/Occupied Room Night	$ 62.45	$ 73.28	$ 60.36
Operating Income/Occupied Room Night	$ 8.64	$ 11.23	$ 12.30
Revenue/Hotel	$2,363,944	$2,164,505	$1,561,663
Operating Income/Hotel	$ 208,620	$ 331,653	$ 318,058

ating leases in property, plant, and equipment and long-term debt, a topic discussed in Chapter 8.

Required

a. Suggest reasons for the changes in the profitability of Brinker during the three-year period.

b. Suggest reasons for the changes in the profitability of McDonald's during the three-year period.

c. Suggest reasons for differences in the profitability of Brinker and McDonald's during the three-year period.

4.25 ANALYZING TWO COMMERCIAL BANKS. Commercial banks generate their revenues from three principal sources: (1) lending, (2) investing, and (3) fee-based services. Commercial banks obtain the majority of their funds from deposits by customers and short-term borrowing. They invest a portion of the funds in relatively liquid government and high-grade corporate debt securities and lend most of the remainder to businesses and consumers. Some banks conduct trading activities in various securities both to help establish an active market and to trade on their own account for profit.

Competition among banks and from other financial institutions has reduced the net interest margin banks generate from the spread between the rate paid for funds and the return generated from lending. As a consequence, commercial banks have increasingly turned to fee-based revenues to increase their profitability, including service charges for

EXHIBIT 4.39

Profitability Ratios and Other Data for Brinker International (Problem 4.24)

	Year 4	Year 3	Year 2
Profit Margin for ROA	5.1%	6.2%	6.5%
Assets Turnover	1.4	1.3	1.3
Rate of Return on Assets	7.1%	8.4%	8.8%
Profit Margin for ROCE	4.1%	5.1%	5.2%
Capital Structure Leverage Ratio	2.5	2.3	2.3
Rate of Return on Common Shareholders' Equity	14.1%	15.8%	16.1%
Cost of Goods Sold/Revenues	81.2%	80.9%	81.0%
Selling and Administrative Expenses/Revenues	10.9%	9.8%	9.1%
Income Tax Expense (excluding tax effects of interest expense)/ Revenues	2.8%	3.1%	3.4%
Accounts Receivable Turnover	100.2	106.0	101.3
Inventory Turnover	97.1	115.5	95.5
Fixed Asset Turnover	1.7	1.6	1.6
Revenues per Restaurant (000's)	$ 2,516	$ 2,343	$ 2,277
Operating Income per Restaurant (000's)	$ 129	$ 145	$ 148
Fixed Assets per Restaurant (000's)	$ 1,476	$ 1,493	$ 1,506
Percentage of Restaurants Owned and Operated	80.1%	81.7%	81.9%
Growth in Revenues	12.8%	13.8%	16.7%
Growth in Number of Restaurants	5.3%	10.6%	10.9%

bank services (checking accounts, trust services, and investment advisory and management services) and fees for structuring new financing, mergers and acquisitions, and other advisory services for businesses. The principal expenses of commercial banks, besides interest, are compensation of employees, occupancy costs, information systems cost, and uncollectible accounts.

The commercial banking industry has experienced major consolidation during the last decade, the result of (1) reduced restrictions on interstate banking, (2) the desirability of building a national, and even international, presence to serve customers more effectively, and (3) perceived benefits of economies of scale in information processing and one-stop customer shopping for financial services. Mergers between commercial banks and investment banks are currently occurring at a rapid pace with the relaxation of restrictions previously imposed by the Glass-Steagall Act of 1933.

Analyzing the profitability of a commercial bank uses rate of return on assets and on common shareholders' equity and their disaggregated components: profit margin, assets turnover, and capital structure leverage ratio. One difference in the calculation of these ratios is that the analyst makes no adjustment to ROA and profit margin for interest expense, because interest expense for a commercial bank is similar to cost of goods sold for a manufacturing or retailing firm. Commercial banks provide sufficient information to compute the return from loans, investments in securities, and trading securities, and the cost of deposits and other borrowing. Because most balance sheet accounts experience significant increases and decreases each day, commercial banks provide the average

EXHIBIT 4.40

Profitability Ratios and Other Data for McDonald's (Problem 4.24)

	Year 4	Year 3	Year 2
Profit Margin for ROA	15.1%	12.2%	10.0%
Assets Turnover	.6	.5	.5
Rate of Return on Assets	8.5%	6.7%	5.3%
Profit Margin for ROCE	12.0%	8.8%	6.4%
Capital Structure Leverage Ratio	2.6	2.8	2.9
Rate of Return on Common Shareholders' Equity	17.4%	13.5%	9.8%
Cost of Goods Sold/Revenues	65.8%	66.7%	66.7%
Selling and Administrative Expenses/Revenues	12.6%	14.4%	17.0%
Income Tax Expense (excluding tax effects of interest expense)/ Revenues	6.5%	6.7%	6.3%
Accounts Receivable Turnover	25.7	21.6	17.7
Inventory Turnover	90.9	94.8	94.2
Fixed Asset Turnover	.7	.6	.6
Revenues per Restaurant (000's)	$605	$551	$495
Operating Income per Restaurant (000's)	$ 91	$ 67	$ 50
Fixed Assets per Restaurant (000's)	$881	$856	$795
Percentage of Restaurants Owned and Operated	29.2%	28.8%	28.9%
Growth in Revenues	11.2%	11.3%	3.6%
Growth in Number of Restaurants	1.4%	.1%	3.4%

daily balances in various accounts to serve as the basis for computing various rates of return.

The principal sources of risk for commercial banks include (1) credit risk from lending, (2) interest rate risk from borrowing and lending at fixed interest rates, and (3) liquidity risk. Analysis of credit risk utilizes the following ratios:

1. Loan Loss Reserve Ratio = Loan Loss Reserve/Loans Receivable.
2. Net Charge-Offs Ratio = Net Charge-Offs/Average Loans Receivable during the Year. Net charge-offs equal loans charged off minus recoveries of loans charged off in a previous year.
3. Nonperforming Loan Percentage = Nonperforming Loans/Total Loans Receivable. Nonperforming loans are loans that are more than ninety days overdue on principal and interest payments. Some of these loans no longer accrue interest and some have been restructured.

Commercial banks have become quite sophisticated in managing their interest rate risk. They use computer software to ensure that the level and term structure of their interest-sensitive assets match their interest-sensitive liabilities on a daily basis. Commercial banks disclose their interest-sensitive position by maturity date.

The analyst assesses liquidity risk by examining the proportion of long-term debt and shareholders' equity in the capital structure. The higher this proportion, the more cushion banks have to cover deposits by customers and repay short-term borrowing. The Federal

Reserve Board establishes minimum capital requirements that are a stated percentage of risk-adjusted assets. Tier 1 capital primarily includes common and preferred stock. Tier 2 capital includes certain long-term debt. Risk-adjusted assets include most assets reported on the balance sheet plus various off-balance sheet commitments. Commercial banks apply various risk-adjustment factors to these assets to form the denominator of the capital ratios. Tier 1 capital as a percentage of risk-adjusted assets must reach a minimum of 4 percent. Tier 1 plus Tier 2 capital must reach at least 8 percent of risk-adjusted assets.

Exhibit 4.41 presents various profitability and risk ratios and Exhibit 4.42 presents a common-size balance sheet for Wells Fargo for Year 6 through Year 8. Exhibits 4.43 and

EXHIBIT 4.41

Profitability and Risk Ratios for Wells Fargo (Problem 4.25)

	Year 8	Year 7	Year 6
Company-Level Profitability Analysis			
Profit Margin for Rate of Return on Assets	12.28%	21.92%	16.94%
Assets Turnover	.09	.11	.10
Rate of Return on Assets	1.15%	2.44%	1.62%
Capital Structure Leverage Ratio	8.21	14.93	14.57
Rate of Return on Shareholders' Equity	8.78%	35.21%	22.68%
Operating Performance Analysis			
Gross Yield on Earning Assets	8.80%	9.14%	8.01%
Rate Paid on Funds	2.70	3.20	2.46
Net Interest Margin	6.10	5.94	5.55
Non-Interest Revenue Percentage	25.22	26.36	24.17
Non-Interest Expense Percentage	69.84	60.60	65.12
Loan Loss Provision Percentage	1.61%	0.0%	5.31%
Segment Profitability Analysis			
Return on Bank Deposits	3.04%	3.05%	2.88%
Return on Domestic Loans	9.40	9.86	8.86
Return on Foreign Loans	6.90	8.70	6.45
Return on Investment Securities	6.40	6.75	5.85
Cost of Domestic Deposits	3.23	3.19	2.62
Cost of Foreign Deposits	5.06	5.93	4.76
Cost of Other Borrowing	6.09%	6.18%	5.11%
Risk Analysis			
Loan Loss Reserve Ratio	2.99%	5.04%	5.73%
Net Charge-Off Ratio	1.06	.83	.71
Non-Performing Loan Percentage	1.06	1.51	1.56
Risk-Adjusted Capital Ratio—Tier 1	7.68	8.81	9.09
Risk-Adjusted Capital Ratio—Tier 1 and 2	11.70%	12.46%	13.16%

EXHIBIT 4.42

Common-Size Balance Sheets for Wells Fargo (Problem 4.25)

	Year 8	Year 7	Year 6
Assets			
Interest-Bearing Deposits	1.1%	.3%	.5%
Investment Securities	13.5	20.2	24.5
Domestic Loans	64.7	69.3	65.6
Foreign Loans	.2	.1	.1
Total Earning Assets	79.5	89.9	90.7%
Other Assets	20.5	10.1	9.3
	100.0	100.0	100.0%
Liabilities and Shareholders' Equity			
Domestic Interest-Bearing Deposits	52.0	55.0	59.6%
Foreign Interest-Bearing Deposits	.4	3.5	1.8
Non-Interest-Bearing Deposits	24.3	17.9	17.4
Short-Term Borrowing	2.3	7.8	4.7
Long-Term Borrowing	5.0	6.1	6.6
Other Non-Interest-Bearing Liabilities	3.0	2.2	2.0
Total Liabilities	87.0	92.5	92.1%
Preferred Stock Equity	.8	1.0	1.0%
Common Stock Equity	12.2	6.5	6.9
Total Shareholders' Equity	13.0	7.5	7.9%
Total Liabilities and Shareholders' Equity	100.0	100.0	100.0%

4.44 present similar information for J. P. Morgan. Wells Fargo maintains its principal presence in the west and southwest portion of the United States. It maintains a network of branch banks to obtain deposits from customers and to lend to businesses and consumers. It emphasizes the traditional borrowing and lending activities of commercial banks. Wells Fargo acquired First Interstate Bancorp during the second quarter of Year 8 through an exchange of common stock in a transaction accounted for using the purchase method. J. P. Morgan maintains a minor presence in traditional borrowing and lending. Instead, it emphasizes investing and trading activities and the offering of fee-based financial advisory services.

Required

a. Analyze the changes in the profitability and risk of Wells Fargo during the three-year period.

b. Analyze the changes in the profitability and risk of J. P. Morgan during the three-year period.

c. Analyze the differences in the profitability and risk of Wells Fargo and J. P. Morgan, indicating how differences in their strategies affect their operating performance and risk.

EXHIBIT 4.43

Profitability and Risk Ratios for J. P. Morgan (Problem 4.25)

	Year 8	Year 7	Year 6
Company-Level Profitability Analysis			
Profit Margin for Rate of Return on Assets.	9.92%	9.37%	10.20%
Assets Turnover	.73	.08	.07
Rate of Return on Assets	.35%	.73%	.70%
Capital Structure Leverage Ratio	20.68	19.06	18.63
Rate of Return on Shareholders' Equity	15.14%	13.58%	12.90%
Operating Performance Analysis			
Gross Yield on Earning Assets	6.24%	7.30%	6.24%
Rate Paid on Funds	5.25	5.83	4.76
Net Interest Margin	.99	1.47	1.47
Non-Interest Revenue Percentage	32.48	28.19	29.68
Non-Interest Expense Percentage	33.42	33.51	36.59
Loan Loss Provision Percentage	0.00%	0.00%	0.00%
Segment Profitability Analysis			
Return on Bank Deposits	2.76%	3.64%	5.17%
Return on Resale Agreements	5.17	6.00	4.63
Return on Domestic Loans	6.66	7.21	5.58
Return on Foreign Loans	6.24	6.97	6.02
Return on Trading Account Securities	12.44	11.50	9.84
Return on Investment Securities	17.95	16.33	13.90
Cost of Domestic Deposits	5.15	4.79	4.64
Cost of Foreign Deposits	5.18	5.80	4.89
Cost of Other Borrowing	5.67%	6.27%	5.06%
Risk Analysis			
Loan Loss Reserve Ratio	4.06%	5.06%	6.06%
Net Charge-Off Ratio	.05	0.00	.11
Non-Performing Loan Percentage	.44	.52	1.01
Risk-Adjusted Capital Ratio—Tier 1	8.8	8.8	9.6
Risk-Adjusted Capital Ratio—Tier 1 and 2	12.2%	13.0%	14.2%

FSAP

INTEGRATIVE CASE 4.1

STARBUCKS

Part A

Integrative Case 1.1 introduced the industry economics of coffee shops and the business strategy of Starbucks to compete in this industry. Exhibit 1.24 presents balance sheets for

EXHIBIT 4.44

Common-Size Balance Sheets for J. P. Morgan (Problem 4.25)

	Year 6	Year 7	Year 8
Assets			
Interest-Bearing Deposits	1.9%	2.6%	2.2%
Resale Agreements	31.8	26.3	27.7
Investment Securities	11.6	12.3	11.6
Trading Account Securities	21.6	21.5	22.4
Domestic Loans	2.9	3.7	4.5
Foreign Loans	10.1	9.8	9.4
Total Earning Assets	79.8%	76.2%	77.8%
Other Assets	20.2	23.8	22.2
Total Assets	100.0%	100.0%	100.0%
Liabilities and Shareholders' Equity			
Domestic Interest-Bearing Deposits	1.8%	1.2%	1.3%
Foreign Interest-Bearing Deposits	21.0	23.4	21.9
Non-Interest-Bearing Deposits	1.4	2.6	3.0
Short-Term Borrowing	48.1	43.5	47.6
Long-Term Borrowing	5.0	4.9	3.4
Other Non-Interest-Bearing Liabilities	17.6	18.9	17.1
Total Liabilities	94.9%	94.5%	94.3%
Preferred Stock Equity	.3%	.3%	.3%
Common Stock Equity	4.8	5.2	5.4
Total Shareholders' Equity	5.1%	5.5%	5.7%
Total Liabilities and Shareholders' Equity	100.0%	100.0%	100.0%

Starbucks for the year ending September 30, Year 1 to Year 4. Exhibit 1.25 presents its income statements and Exhibit 1.26 presents the statement of cash flows for fiscal Year 2, Year 3, and Year 4. Exhibit 1.27 presents common-size and percentage change balance sheets and Exhibit 1.28 presents common-size and percentage change income statements for Starbucks. Before beginning preparation of Integrative Case 4.1, we recommend that you familiarize yourself again with Integrative Case 1.1 in Chapter 1.

Part A of Integrative Case 4.1 analyzes changes in the profitability of Starbucks for fiscal Year 2 to fiscal Year 4.

Required

a. Exhibit 4.45 presents profitability ratios for Starbucks for fiscal Year 2 and fiscal Year 3. Using the financial statement data in Exhibits 1.24 and 1.25, compute the values of these ratios for fiscal Year 4. The income tax rate is 35 percent. Use cost of sales including occupancy costs for the numerator of the inventory turnover, because Starbucks does not disclose separately the cost of products sold (the appropriate numerator) and occupancy costs.

b. What are the most important reasons that Starbucks' ROA increased during the three-year period? Analyze the financial ratios to the maximum depth possible with the given information. Exhibit 4.45 provides information to analyze profitability at Level 1, Level 2, and Level 3. Exhibit 4.46 presents additional information for Starbucks at a business segment level to permit analysis at Level 4. Corporate-level expenses not allocated to either domestic or international operations, which include depreciation, amortization, general, and administrative expenses, as a percentage of total revenues were 5.9 percent for fiscal Year 2, 4.6 percent for fiscal Year 3, and 3.9 percent for fiscal Year 4.

c. What are the most important reasons that Starbucks' ROCE increased during the three-year period?

EXHIBIT 4.45

Starbucks
Financial Statement Ratio Analysis
(Integrative Case 4.1, Part A)

	Year 4	Year 3	Year 2
Profit Margin for ROA		6.6%	6.4%
Assets Turnover		1.6	1.6
Rate of Return on Assets		10.6%	10.4%
Profit Margin for ROCE		6.5%	6.4%
Capital Structure Leverage Ratio		1.3	1.3
Rate of Return on Common Shareholders' Equity		14.1%	13.7%
Cost of Sales/Operating Revenues		41.3%	41.0%
Store Operating Expenses/Operating Revenues		33.8%	33.8%
Nonretail Operating Expenses/Operating Revenues		3.5%	3.2%
Depreciation and Amortization Expense/Operating Revenues		6.0%	6.4%
General and Administrative Expense/Operating Revenues		6.0%	7.1%
Income from Equity Investees/Operating Revenues		.9%	1.0%
Interest Revenue/Operating Revenues		.3%	.3%
Gain on Sale of Investments/Operating Revenues		—	.4%
Income Tax Expense (excluding tax effects of interest expense)/Operating Revenues		4.1%	3.8%
Accounts Receivable Turnover		38.4	35.0
Inventory Turnover		5.5	5.6
Fixed Asset Turnover		3.0	2.7

EXHIBIT 4.46

Starbucks
Segment Profitability Data
(Integrative Case 4.1, Parts A and B)

	Domestic			International		
	Year 4	Year 3	Year 2	Year 4	Year 3	Year 2
Total Revenue Mix	84.8%	85.2%	86.0%	15.2%	14.8%	14.0%
Operating Revenues:						
Company Retail Stores	84.6%	85.4%	85.7%	81.8%	80.3%	79.8%
Licensing	9.7	8.7	8.1	16.0	18.0	18.3
Foodservice and Other	5.6	5.9	6.2	2.2	1.8	1.9
Total Operating Revenues	100.0%	100.0%	100.0%	100.0%	100.0%	100.0%
Operating Expenses:						
Cost of Sales, including occupancy costs	(39.7)	(39.1)	(39.3)	(50.9)	(53.5)	(51.1)
Store Operating Expenses	(34.4)	(34.5)	(34.0)	(30.3)	(29.9)	(32.2)
Nonretail Operating Expenses	(3.2)	(3.5)	(3.1)	(3.3)	(3.5)	(4.0)
Depreciation and Amortization	(4.7)	(5.0)	(5.2)	(5.8)	(6.4)	(7.4)
General and Administrative	(1.8)	(1.3)	(1.2)	(6.0)	(7.4)	(7.6)
Income from Equity Investees	.8	.8	.7	2.9	1.6	3.1
Segment Operating Income	17.0%	17.4%	17.8%	6.6%	.9%	.8%
Segment Asset Turnover	3.3	2.8	2.8	1.7	1.6	1.4
Segment ROA	56.5%	49.5%	50.4%	10.9%	1.4%	1.1%
Stores Owned	4,293	3,779	3,209	922	802	703
Stores Licensed	1,839	1,422	1,033	1,515	1,222	941
Total Stores	6,142	5,201	4,242	2,437	2,024	1,644
Revenues[a]/Stores Owned	$885,247	$784,763	$755,738	$712,593	$603,499	$523,102
Revenues[b]/Stores Licensed	$237,619	$211,797	$220,437	$ 85,028	$ 88,687	$ 89,502
Total Revenues/Total Stores	$732,363	$667,651	$666,726	$329,666	$297,960	$280,204
Operating Income/Total Stores	$124,482	$116,202	$119,006	$ 21,851	$ 2,606	$ 2,306
Assets/Total Stores	$220,134	$234,908	$236,007	$200,228	$190,669	$203,477
Total Revenues Increase	29%	23%	23%	36%	32%	32%
Comparable Stores Sales Increase[c]	11%	9%	7%	6%	7%	1%

[a] Revenues represent sales from company-operated retail stores.
[b] Revenues represent fees and other revenues from licensees.
[c] Comparable stores represent stores open at least two full years.

Part B

Part B of Integrative Case 4.1 compares the profitability of Starbucks with Panera Bread Company. Although Starbucks and Panera Bread Company are not direct competitors in terms of the principal food products offered, they compete in the sense of offering a relaxed café experience. Whereas the products of Starbucks center on coffee and related beverages, Panera Bread Company emphasizes freshly baked bread and pastries. Panera Bread Company sells sandwiches, soups, and similar lunch and light dinner products that build on their bread offerings, as well as coffee and other beverages. The average size of a Panera Bread Company retail outlet is larger than that of Starbucks. Both Starbucks and Panera Bread Company own some of their retail stores and franchise rights to use their names and products to franchisees, which own and operate other retail stores. Panera Bread Company prepares fresh dough daily in various regional facilities to use in company-owned stores and to sell to franchisees. Unlike Starbucks, it has not expanded beyond the United States.

Exhibit 4.47 presents profitability ratios for Panera Bread Company for Year 2, Year 3, and Year 4 and Exhibit 4.48 presents segment profitability and other data. The format of these two exhibits is similar to Exhibits 4.45 and 4.46, the corresponding exhibits for Starbucks. The proportions of general and administrative expenses not allocated to divisions for Panera Bread Company are similar to the corresponding percentages for Starbucks.

EXHIBIT 4.47

Panera Bread Company
Financial Statement Ratio Analysis
(Case 4.1, Part B)

	Year 4	Year 3	Year 2
Profit Margin for ROA	8.1%	8.5%	7.6%
Assets Turnover	1.6	1.6	1.7
Rate of Return on Assets	13.4%	14.0%	13.1%
Profit Margin for ROCE	8.1%	8.4%	7.5%
Capital Structure Leverage Ratio	1.3	1.3	1.2
Rate of Return on Common Shareholders' Equity	17.6%	17.8%	15.9%
Cost of Sales/Operating Revenues	26.8%	25.5%	27.9%
Store Operating Expenses/Operating Revenues	33.8%	32.5%	32.3%
Nonretail Operating Expenses/Operating Revenues	13.7%	15.1%	13.6%
Depreciation and Amortization Expense/Operating Revenues	5.3%	5.0%	4.9%
General and Administrative Expense/Operating Revenues	7.7%	8.5%	9.3%
Income Tax Expense (excluding tax effects of interest expense)/Operating Revenues	4.6%	4.9%	4.3%
Accounts Receivable Turnover	32.3	33.1	38.4
Inventory Turnover	39.8	31.0	27.1
Fixed Asset Turnover	2.8	3.0	3.2

EXHIBIT 4.48

Panera Bread Company
Segment Profitability Data
(Case 4.1, Part B)

	Domestic		
	Year 4	Year 3	Year 2
Total Revenue Mix	100.0%	100.0%	100.0%
Operating Revenues:			
Company Retail Stores	75.6%	73.1%	75.3%
Licensing	9.3	10.0	9.9
Fresh Dough Sales to Franchisees	15.1	16.9	14.8
Total Operating Revenues	100.0%	100.0%	100.0%
Operating Expenses:			
Cost of Sales, including occupancy expenses	(26.8)	(25.5)	(27.9)
Store Operating Expenses	(33.8)	(32.5)	(32.3)
Nonretail Operating Expenses	(13.7)	(15.1)	(13.6)
Depreciation and Amortization	(4.6)	(4.3)	(4.1)
General and Administrative	(2.2)	(2.2)	(2.6)
Segment Operating Income	18.9%	20.4%	19.5%
Segment Asset Turnover	2.0	2.0	2.3
Segment ROA	37.5%	40.6%	45.3%
Stores Owned	226	173	132
Stores Licensed	515	429	346
Total Stores	741	602	478
Revenues[a]/Stores Owned	$1,602,305	$1,537,185	$1,610,947
Revenues[b]/Stores Licensed	$ 227,219	$ 227,900	$ 201,098
Total Revenues/Total Stores	$ 646,611	$ 604,156	$ 590,428
Operating Income/Total Stores	$ 52,523	$ 51,603	$ 44,981
Assets/Total Stores	$ 325,655	$ 303,121	$ 255,086
Total Revenues Increase	32%	29%	40%
Comparable Stores Sales Increase[c]	3%	0%	6%

[a] Revenues represent sales from company-operated retail stores.
[b] Revenues represent fees and other revenues from licensees.
[c] Comparable stores represent stores open at least two full years.

Required

a. What are the likely reasons that the ROAs of Panera Bread Company exceed those of Starbucks? Analyze the data to the maximum depth permitted by the given information.

b. What are the likely reasons that the ROCEs of Panera Bread Company exceed those of Starbucks?

CASE 4.2

PROFITABILITY AND RISK ANALYSIS OF WAL-MART STORES

Part A

Wal-Mart Stores (Wal-Mart) is the world's largest retailer. It employs an "everyday low price" strategy and operates stores through five principal concepts:

1. **Wal-Mart Stores:** Discount department stores that offer clothing, housewares, electronic equipment, pharmaceuticals, health and beauty products, sporting goods, and similar items. The number of Wal-Mart Stores decreased 17.9 percent and square footage decreased 14.1 percent during the last three years. The average size of a Wal-Mart Store was 100,134 square feet at the end of fiscal Year 4.[24]
2. **Wal-Mart Supercenters:** A full-line supermarket combined with a discount department store. Supercenters represent for Wal-Mart a move to grocery products. Combining grocery products with Wal-Mart's traditional discount department store offerings attempts to capitalize on one-stop shopping by consumers and to gain efficiencies in product distribution, stocking, and advertising. Growth rates during the last three years for Wal-Mart Supercenters are 60.7 percent in the number of stores and 62.1 percent in square footage. A portion of the growth in Wal-Mart Supercenters represents conversions of previous Wal-Mart Stores. The average size of a Wal-Mart Supercenter was 186,839 square feet at the end of fiscal Year 4.
3. **Neighborhood Markets:** Smaller grocery stores located in residential neighborhoods. Growth rates during the last three years are 62.1 percent in number of stores and 155.4 percent in square footage. The average size of a Neighborhood Market was 42,600 square feet at the end of fiscal Year 4.
4. **Sam's Clubs:** Members-only warehouse stores that offer large quantities of food and household products as well as automotive supplies, electronics, sporting goods, and similar products at wholesale prices. Compound annual growth rates during the last three years for Sam's Clubs are 10.2 percent in the number of stores and 14.4 percent in square footage. The average size of a Sam's Club store was 128,270 square feet at the end of fiscal Year 4.
5. **International:** Wal-Mart expanded its international operations significantly in recent years and now conducts operations (number of stores in parentheses) in Canada (262), Mexico (679), Puerto Rico (54), Brazil (149), Argentina (11), the United Kingdom (282), China (43), Korea (16), and Germany (91). Wal-Mart operates internationally through discount stores, supercenters, and some specialty stores and restaurants. It grew its international operations 37.5 percent in number of stores and 36.7 percent in square footage during the last three years. The average size of a store in the international segment was 84,047 square feet at the end of fiscal Year 4.

Wal-Mart uses centralized purchasing through its home office for substantially all of its merchandise. It distributes products to its stores through regional distribution centers.

[24]Wal-Mart's fiscal year ends at the end of January of each year. We refer to its year ending January 31, Year 5, as its fiscal Year 4, because eleven of the twelve months fall within Year 4.

During fiscal Year 4, the proportion of merchandise channeled through its regional distribution centers was as follows:

Wal-Mart Stores, Supercenters, and Neighborhood Markets	81%
Sam's Club	62%
International	76%

Exhibit 4.49 sets out various operating data for Wal-Mart for its most recent three years. Exhibit 4.50 presents segment data. Exhibit 4.51 presents comparative balance sheets, Exhibit 4.52 presents comparative income statements, and Exhibit 4.53 presents comparative statements of cash flows for Wal-Mart for its Year 2, Year 3, and Year 4 fiscal years. Exhibit 4.54 presents selected financial statement ratios for Wal-Mart for its Year 2, Year 3 and Year 4 fiscal years. The income tax rate is 35 percent.

Required

a. What are the likely reasons for the changes in Wal-Mart's rate of return on assets during the three-year period? Analyze the financial ratios to the maximum depth possible.

EXHIBIT 4.49

Operating Data for Wal-Mart Stores (Case 4.2, Part A)

	Fiscal Year:		
	Year 4	Year 3	Year 2
Wal-Mart Stores, Supercenters, and Neighborhood Markets (Domestic)			
Number	3,151	3,013	2,875
Square Footage (millions)	459.2	422.9	388.7
Sales per Square Foot	$ 417.74	$ 411.97	$ 404.22
Operating Income per Square Foot	$ 30.84	$ 30.54	$ 30.46
Sam's Club (Domestic)			
Number	551	538	525
Square Footage (millions)	70.7	68.1	65.7
Sales per Square Foot	$ 525.02	$ 507.15	$ 482.53
Operating Income per Square Foot	$ 18.10	$ 16.53	$ 15.57
International			
Number	1,587	1,355	1,272
Square Footage (millions)	133.4	115.4	106.5
Sales per Square Foot	$ 421.87	$ 412.24	$ 383.04
Operating Income per Square Foot	$ 22.40	$ 20.54	$ 18.76
Domestic Comparable Store Sales Increase	3%	4%	5%
Sales per Employee	$209,722	$213,607	$212,305

EXHIBIT 4.50

Segment Profitability Analysis for Wal-Mart Stores (Case 4.2, Part A)

	Fiscal Year:		
	Year 4	**Year 3**	**Year 2**
Sales Mix			
Wal-Mart Discount Stores, Supercenters, and Neighborhood Markets	67.3%	68.0%	68.4%
Sam's Club	13.0	13.5	13.8
International	19.7	18.5	17.8
	100.0%	100.0%	100.0%
Wal-Mart Discount Stores, Supercenters, and Neighborhood Markets			
Profit Margin	7.4%	7.4%	7.5%
Total Assets Turnover	6.5	6.4	6.3
Rate of Return on Assets	48.0%	47.8%	47.6%
Sam's Club			
Profit Margin	3.4%	3.3%	3.2%
Total Assets Turnover	6.5	7.3	7.2
Rate of Return on Assets	22.5%	23.7%	23.2%
International			
Profit Margin	5.3%	5.0%	4.9%
Total Assets Turnover	1.4	1.3	1.3
Rate of Return on Assets	7.3%	6.7%	6.5%

b. What are the likely reasons for the changes in Wal-Mart's rate of return on common shareholders' equity during the three-year period?

NOTE: Parts c. and d. require coverage of material from Chapter 5.

c. How has the short-term liquidity risk of Wal-Mart changed during the three-year period?

d. How has the long-term solvency risk of Wal-Mart changed during the three-year period?

Part B

Part A of Case 4.2 analyzed the profitability and risk of Wal-Mart Stores for its fiscal Year 2, Year 3, and Year 4. Part B of this case compares the profitability and risk ratios of Wal-Mart and two other leading discount retailers, Carrefour and Target, for their Year 2 to Year 4 fiscal years.

EXHIBIT 4.51

Wal-Mart Stores
Balance Sheets
(amounts in millions)
(Case 4.2, Part A)

	End of Fiscal Year:			
	Year 4	**Year 3**	**Year 2**	**Year 1**
Assets				
Cash	$ 5,488	$ 5,199	$ 2,758	$ 2,161
Accounts Receivable	1,715	1,254	2,108	2,000
Inventories	29,447	26,612	24,401	22,614
Prepayments	1,841	1,356	726	1,471
Total Current Assets	$ 38,491	$ 34,421	$29,993	$28,246
Property, Plant, and Equipment, net	73,745	63,969	56,492	50,529
Other Assets	13,165	11,961	12,422	9,545
Total Assets	$125,401	$110,351	$98,907	$88,320
Liabilities and Shareholders' Equity				
Accounts Payable	$ 21,671	$ 19,425	$17,140	$15,617
Notes Payable	3,812	3,267	1,079	743
Current Portion of Long-Term Debt	3,969	3,100	4,714	2,405
Other Current Liabilities	13,436	12,048	9,194	8,517
Total Current Liabilities	$ 42,888	$ 37,840	$32,127	$27,282
Long-Term Debt	28,847	25,045	24,196	23,511
Other Noncurrent Liabilities	4,270	3,843	3,123	2,335
Total Liabilities	$ 76,005	$ 66,728	$59,446	$53,128
Common Stock	$ 423	$ 431	$ 440	$ 445
Additional Paid-In Capital	2,425	2,135	1,954	1,838
Accumulated Other Comprehensive Income	2,694	851	(509)	(1,268)
Retained Earnings	43,854	40,206	37,576	34,177
Total Shareholders' Equity	$ 49,396	$ 43,623	$39,461	$35,192
Total Liabilities and Shareholders' Equity	$125,401	$110,351	$98,907	$88,320

Carrefour

Carrefour, headquartered in France, is Europe's largest retailer and the second largest retailer in the world. Sales in Year 4 totaled €72,668 million ($90,281 million). It segments its activities into four groups (Year 4 sales mix percentages in parentheses):

> **Hypermarkets (58%):** Offer a wide variety of household and food products at competitively low prices under the Carrefour store brand.
>
> **Supermarkets (18%):** Sell traditional grocery products under the Champion, Norte, GS and GB supermarkets, and other store brands.

EXHIBIT 4.52

Wal-Mart Stores
Income Statements
(amounts in millions)
(Case 4.2, Part A)

	Fiscal Year:		
	Year 4	Year 3	Year 2
Sales Revenue	$285,222	$256,329	$229,616
Other Revenues	2,968	2,516	2,093
Total Revenues	$288,190	$258,845	$231,709
Expenses:			
Cost of Goods Sold	$219,793	$198,747	$178,299
Selling and Administrative	51,354	45,123	40,176
Interest	1,187	996	1,059
Income Taxes	5,589	5,118	4,357
Total Expenses	$277,923	$249,984	$223,891
Net Income	$ 10,267	$ 8,861	$ 7,818

EXHIBIT 4.53

Wal-Mart Stores
Statements of Cash Flows
(amounts in millions)
(Case 4.2, Part A)

	Fiscal Year:		
	Year 4	Year 3	Year 2
Operations			
Net Income	$ 10,267	$ 8,861	$ 7,818
Depreciation	4,405	3,852	3,364
Other Additions	641	350	1,159
(Increase) Decrease in Accounts Receivable	(304)	373	(159)
(Increase) Decrease in Inventories	(2,635)	(1,973)	(2,219)
Increase in Accounts Payable	1,694	2,587	1,748
Increase in Other Current Liabilities	976	1,946	1,294
Cash Flow from Operations	$ 15,044	$ 16,996	$13,005
Investing			
Sale of Property, Plant, and Equipment	$ 953	$ 481	$ 311
Acquisition of Property, Plant, and Equipment	(12,893)	(10,308)	(9,245)
Acquisition of Investments	(315)	(38)	(749)
Other	(96)	1,553	(156)
Cash Flow from Investing	$(12,351)	$ (8,312)	$ (9,839)
Financing			
Increase (Decrease) in Short-Term Borrowing	$ 544	$ 688	$ 1,836
Increase in Long-Term Borrowing	5,832	4,099	2,044
Decrease in Long-Term Borrowing	(2,335)	(3,846)	(1,477)
Acquisition of Common Stock	(4,549)	(5,046)	(3,383)
Dividends	(2,214)	(1,569)	(1,328)
Other	318	431	(261)
Cash Flow from Financing	$ (2,404)	$ (5,243)	$ (2,569)
Change in Cash	$ 289	$ 2,441	$ 597
Cash—Beginning of Year	5,199	2,758	2,161
Cash—End of Year	$ 5,488	$ 5,199	$ 2,758

EXHIBIT 4.54

Wal-Mart Stores
Financial Ratio Analysis
(Case 4.2, Part A)

	Fiscal Year:		
	Year 4	**Year 3**	**Year 2**
Profitability Ratios			
Rate of Return on Assets	9.4%	9.1%	9.1%
Profit Margin for ROA	3.9%	3.7%	3.7%
Total Assets Turnover	2.41	2.45	2.45
Cost of Goods Sold/Sales	77.1%	77.5%	77.7%
Selling and Administrative Expense/Sales	18.0%	17.6%	17.5%
Interest Expense (net of taxes)/Sales	.3%	.3%	.3%
Income Tax Expense (excluding tax effects of interest expense)/Sales	2.1%	2.1%	2.1%
Accounts Receivable Turnover Ratio	192.1	152.5	111.8
Inventory Turnover Ratio	7.8	7.8	7.6
Fixed Assets Turnover Ratio	4.1	4.4	4.4
Rate of Return on Common Shareholders' Equity	22.1%	21.3%	20.9%
Profit Margin for ROCE	3.6%	3.5%	3.4%
Capital Structure Leverage Ratio	2.53	2.52	2.51
Risk Ratios			
Current Ratio	.90	.91	.93
Quick Ratio	.17	.17	.15
Accounts Payable Turnover	10.8	11.0	11.0
Cash Flow from Operations to Current Liabilities Ratio	37.3%	45.7%	43.8%
Long-Term Debt Ratio	36.9%	36.5%	38.0%
Total Liabilities/Total Assets Ratio	60.6%	60.5%	60.1%
Cash Flow from Operations to Total Liabilities Ratio	21.1%	25.4%	23.1%
Interest Coverage Ratio	14.4	15.0	12.5

Hard Discount (8%): Offer a limited variety of food products in smaller stores than those of hypermarkets and supermarkets at aggressively low prices under the Dia, Ed, and Minipreco store brands.

Other (16%): Includes convenience stores and wholesale stores, the latter targeted at business customers, under the SHOPI, Marche Plus, 8 A Huit, express, Contact, and Proxi store brands.

Carrefour derived approximately 49 percent of its Year 4 sales within France, 37 percent within Europe excluding France, 7 percent in Latin America, and 7 percent in Asia.

Target

Target Corporation, headquartered in the United States, generated sales of $45,682 million in fiscal Year 4. It operates retail chains under two related store concepts: Target Discount Stores and Target Superstores. Target stores offer a wide variety of clothing, household, electronics, sports, toys, and entertainment products at discount prices. Target stores attempt to differentiate themselves from Wal-Mart's discount stores by pushing trend merchandising with more brand-name products. Target emphasizes customer service, referring to its customers as "guests" and focusing on the theme of "Expect More, Pay Less." Target Corporation attempts to differentiate itself from competitors by providing wider aisles and a less cluttered store appearance. The recent addition of Target Superstores represents Target Corporation's effort to compete directly with Wal-Mart's superstores. At the end of fiscal Year 4, Target Corporation operated 1,172 discount stores and 136 superstores. Target Corporation's offers its own credit card to customers.

Exhibits 4.55 and 4.56 present profitability ratios for Carrefour, Target, and Wal-Mart for their Year 2 to Year 4 fiscal years. Exhibit 4.57 presents risk ratios for the three firms. Exhibit 4.58 presents selected other data for these firms. The financial statements include in property, plant, and equipment and in long-term debt the present value of commitments under all leases.

Required

a. Wal-Mart and Target follow somewhat different strategies. Wal-Mart consistently has a higher ROA than Target. Using information in Exhibits 4.55 and 4.58, suggest reasons for these differences in operating profitability.

b. Wal-Mart and Carrefour follow similar strategies. Wal-Mart consistently outperforms Carrefour on ROA. Using information in Exhibits 4.55 and 4.58, suggest reasons for these differences in operating profitability.

c. Refer to Exhibit 4.56. Which firm appears to have used financial leverage most effectively in enhancing the rate of return on common shareholders' equity (ROCE)? Explain your reasoning.

NOTE: Parts d and e require coverage of material from Chapter 5.

d. Refer to Exhibit 4.57. Rank-order these firms in terms of their short-term liquidity risk. Do any of these firms appear unduly risky as of the end of fiscal Year 4?

e. Refer to Exhibit 4.57. Rank-order these firms in terms of their long-term liquidity risk. Do any of these firms appear unduly risky as of the end of fiscal Year 4?

EXHIBIT 4.55

Cross-Section ROA Profitability Analysis for Carrefour, Target, and Wal-Mart (Case 4.2, Part B)

ROA

	Year 2	Year 3	Year 4
Carrefour	4.7%	5.1%	4.5%
Target	7.6%	6.8%	6.8%
Wal-Mart	9.1%	9.1%	9.4%

	Profit Margin for ROA			Total Assets Turnover		
	Year 2	Year 3	Year 4	Year 2	Year 3	Year 4
Carrefour	3.2%	3.2%	2.8%	1.5	1.6	1.6
Target	4.8%	4.8%	4.9%	1.6	1.4	1.4
Wal-Mart	3.7%	3.7%	3.9%	2.5	2.5	2.4

	Carrefour			Target			Wal-Mart		
	Year 2	Year 3	Year 4	Year 2	Year 3	Year 4	Year 2	Year 3	Year 4
Sales	100.0%	100.0%	100.0%	100.0%	100.0%	100.0%	100.0%	100.0%	100.0%
Other Revenues	1.6	1.4	1.6	2.4	2.7	2.5	1.0	.9	1.1
Cost of Goods Sold	(77.4)	(77.5)	(77.8)	(69.8)	(69.4)	(68.8)	(77.7)	(77.5)	(77.1)
Selling and Administrative	(19.5)	(19.0)	(19.4)	(24.9)	(25.6)	(25.8)	(17.5)	(17.6)	(18.0)
Income Taxes	(1.6)	(1.6)	(1.6)	(2.9)	(2.9)	(3.0)	(2.1)	(2.1)	(2.1)
Profit Margin for ROA	3.2%	3.2%	2.8%	4.8%	4.8%	4.9%	3.7%	3.7%	3.9%
Receivable Turnover	31.0	22.2	23.3	8.9	9.1	9.4	111.8	152.5	192.1
Inventory Turnover	9.1	9.6	9.5	6.8	6.7	6.3	7.6	7.8	7.8
Fixed Asset Turnover	3.8	4.0	4.0	2.9	2.7	2.7	4.3	4.3	4.1

EXHIBIT 4.56

Cross-Section ROCE Profitability Analysis for Carrefour, Target, and Wal-Mart (Case 4.2, Part B)

ROCE

	Year 2	Year 3	Year 4
Carrefour	19.3%	24.4%	20.4%
Target	15.8%	15.7%	15.6%
Wal-Mart	20.9%	21.3%	22.1%

	Profit Margin for ROCE			Total Assets Turnover			Capital Structure Leverage		
	Year 2	Year 3	Year 4	Year 2	Year 3	Year 4	Year 2	Year 3	Year 4
Carrefour	2.0%	2.3%	1.9%	1.5	1.6	1.6	6.6	6.7	6.7
Target	3.8%	4.0%	4.1%	1.6	1.4	1.4	2.6	2.8	2.7
Wal-Mart	3.4%	3.5%	3.6%	2.5	2.5	2.4	2.5	2.5	2.5

EXHIBIT 4.57

Cross-Section Risk Analysis for Carrefour, Target, and Wal-Mart (Case 4.2, Part B)

	Carrefour			Target			Wal-Mart		
	Year 2	Year 3	Year 4	Year 2	Year 3	Year 4	Year 2	Year 3	Year 4
Short-Term Liquidity									
Current Ratio	.64	.65	.60	1.30	1.56	1.69	.93	.91	.90
Quick Ratio	.28	.27	.26	.67	.64	.78	.15	.17	.17
Cash Flow from Operations/ Average Current Liabilities	12.2%	16.9%	18.6%	37.3%	40.5%	46.2%	43.8%	45.7%	37.3%
Days Receivable	12	16	16	41	40	39	3	2	2
Days Inventory	40	38	39	54	55	58	48	47	47
Days Payable	90	90	90	56	58	61	33	33	34
Long-Term Solvency									
Long-Term Debt Ratio	63.2%	64.1%	62.0%	53.8%	50.0%	43.9%	38.0%	36.5%	36.9%
Total Liabilities/ Total Assets Ratio	82.9%	83.5%	83.1%	78.7%	65.7%	61.1%	60.1%	60.5%	60.6%
Cash Flow from Operations/ Average Total Liabilities	7.5%	10.2%	11.4%	14.7%	15.6%	18.3%	23.1%	25.4%	21.1%
Interest Coverage Ratio	3.4	4.0	3.8	4.8	5.7	6.3	12.5	15.0	14.4

EXHIBIT 4.58

Selected Other Financial Data for Carrefour, Target, and Wal-Mart (Case 4.2, Part B)

	Year 2	Year 3	Year 4
Growth Rate in Sales			
Carrefour	(1.1%)	2.6%	3.1%
Target	12.0%	12.1%	11.6%
Wal-Mart	12.6%	11.6%	11.3%
Number of Stores			
Carrefour	5,531	6,067	6,546
Target	1,147	1,225	1,308
Wal-Mart	4,672	4,906	5,289
Square Footage (000's)			
Carrefour	105,132	108,103	118,867
Target	140,294	152,563	166,015
Wal-Mart	560,900	606,480	663,217
Sales per Square Foot			
Carrefour	$601	$741	$759
Target	$260	$268	$275
Wal-Mart	$409	$423	$430
Sales per Store			
Carrefour	$11,420,177	$13,197,132	$13,791,781
Target	$31,838,710	$33,410,612	$34,925,076
Wal-Mart	$49,147,260	$52,248,060	$53,927,400
Square Feet per Store			
Carrefour	19,008	19,545	18,159
Target	122,314	124,541	126,923
Wal-Mart	120,056	123,620	125,396
Fixed Assets per Square Foot			
Carrefour	$154	$187	$196
Target	$104	$106	$109
Wal-Mart	$100	$105	$111
Sales per Employee			
Carrefour	$205,478	$238,838	$262,022
Target	$171,422	$178,281	$174,093
Wal-Mart	$212,305	$213,607	$209,722
Exchange Rate:			
U.S. Dollars per Euro	$.91906	$1.13591	$1.24238

Chapter 5

Risk Analysis

Learning Objectives

1. **Understand the types of information that GAAP requires firms to disclose about their risk exposures and risk management activities.**
2. **Understand the importance of effective working capital management and apply analytical tools for assessing short-term liquidity risk.**
3. **Understand the benefits and risks of financial leverage and apply analytical tools for assessing long-term solvency risk.**
4. **Use risk analysis tools in assessing credit risk.**
5. **Use risk analysis tools in assessing bankruptcy risk.**
6. **Understand the distinction between firm-specific risks, as measured by various financial statement ratios, and systematic risk, as measured by market equity beta, and relationships between these types of risks.**
7. **Examine factors that might lead firms to manipulate reported financial statement amounts and apply tools for analyzing the risk of fraudulent reporting.**

Individuals make equity investment decisions based on the return expected from investments relative to the risks of realizing those returns. Lenders make lending decisions based on the return expected in the form of interest revenue relative to the risks of default. The analysis of risk is central to any decision to commit economic resources. This chapter (1) describes disclosures required by GAAP to inform financial statement users about how certain risks can affect a firm and how the firm manages those risks, and (2) explores the analysis of various types of risk using financial statement ratios and other analytical tools.

DISCLOSURES REGARDING RISK AND RISK MANAGEMENT

The sources and types of risk that a firm faces are numerous and often interrelated. They include the following:

Source	Type or Nature
International	Exchange rate changes
	Host government regulations and attitudes
	Political unrest
	Expropriation of assets
Domestic	Recession
	Inflation or deflation
	Interest rate changes
	Demographic changes
	Political changes
Industry	Technology
	Competition
	Regulation
	Availability and price of raw materials
	Labor and other input price changes
	Unionization
Firm-Specific	Management competence
	Strategic direction
	Lawsuits

Although a firm should continually monitor each of these and other types of risk, we focus our attention on the financial consequences of these elements of risk using data and disclosures from the financial statements. Various financial reporting standards require firms to discuss in notes to the financial statements how important elements of risk affect a particular firm and the actions the firm takes to manage these risks. We introduce some of the more important disclosures here. Later chapters discuss the accounting more fully. We use the disclosures of PepsiCo in Note 10, "Risk Management" (Appendix A), and the discussion under the heading "Market Risks" in its MD&A (Appendix B), to illustrate information that firms provide about risk.

Commodity Prices

Firms purchase raw materials to use in manufacturing products. Changes in the prices of those raw materials will affect future profitability, unless the firm can pass along price increases to customers, engage in fixed-price contractual arrangements with suppliers, or purchase commodity futures contracts. For example, some firms manage this risk by engaging in a purchase commitment with suppliers to purchase certain quantities at a specified price over a particular period of time. Alternatively, the firm might acquire a futures contract or other hedging instrument to neutralize the risk of changes in prices. Chapter 8 discusses the accounting for such hedging instruments, called derivatives.

PepsiCo discloses the following with respect to commodity price risk in Note 10:

> We are subject to commodity price risk because our ability to recover increased costs through higher pricing may be limited in the competitive environment in

> which we operate. This risk is managed through the use of fixed-price purchase orders, pricing agreements, geographic diversity and cash flow hedges. We use cash flow hedges, with terms of no more than two years, to hedge price fluctuations related to a portion of our anticipated commodity purchases, primarily for corn, heating oil and natural gas. Any ineffectiveness is recorded immediately. However, our commodity hedges have not had any significant ineffectiveness.

In the MD&A, PepsiCo provides information about the extent of hedging on commodity prices and the effect on pretax earnings if commodity prices declined:

> Our open commodity derivative contracts designated as hedges had a face value of $155 million at December 25, Year 4 and $43 million at December 27, Year 3. These derivatives resulted in a net unrealized loss of $1 million at December 25, Year 4 and $4 million at December 27, Year 3. We estimate that a 10% decline in commodity prices would have resulted in an unrealized loss of $16 million in Year 4 and $1 million in Year 3.

It is unclear whether the $155 million of open derivative contracts at the end of Year 4 relate to accounts payable and other current liabilities on the balance sheet of $5,599 million or to purchase commitments of $4,386 million (see Note 9, "Debt Obligations and Commitments," in Appendix A), but regardless, the amount of open contracts is small compared to either base. PepsiCo uses a 10 percent decline in commodity prices to illustrate the sensitivity of earnings to hedged commodity price changes. The $16 million loss that would result from a 10 percent decline in commodity prices is .3 percent of income before income taxes for Year 4 (= $16/$5,546), certainly an immaterial amount.

Foreign Exchange

Changes in foreign exchange rates can affect a firm in multiple ways:

- The prices that a firm pays to acquire raw materials from suppliers abroad.
- The prices that a firm charges for products sold to customers abroad.
- The amount of cash a firm will receive when it collects an account receivable, loan receivable, or other receivable denominated in a currency other than its own.
- The amount of cash a firm will pay when it settles an account payable, loan payable, or other payable denominated in a currency other than its own.
- The amount of cash a firm will collect when it receives remittances from a foreign branch or dividends from a foreign subsidiary.
- The cash-equivalent value of assets invested abroad in the event the firm decides to liquidate the foreign unit.

Firms often use foreign-exchange contracts to hedge some or all of these risks. Chapter 8 discusses forward contracts and Chapter 9 discusses the effect of exchange rate changes on reporting the operations of foreign units.

PepsiCo states in Note 10:

> Our operations outside of the U.S. generate over a third of our net revenue of which Mexico, the United Kingdom, and Canada comprise nearly 20%. As a result, we are exposed to foreign currency risks from unforeseen economic changes and political unrest. On occasion, we enter into hedges, primarily forward contracts with terms of no more than two years, to reduce the effect of foreign exchange rates. Ineffectiveness of these hedges has not been material.

PepsiCo discloses in its MD&A that foreign currency derivatives had a face value of $908 million at the end of Year 4, considerably more than the amount of commodity derivatives. A 10 percent unfavorable change in exchange rates would have resulted in a pretax loss of $123 million for Year 4. This amount is 2.2 percent of income before income taxes (= $123/$5,546), a larger amount than for commodity derivatives and a larger amount than that for Year 3.

Interest Rates

Changes in interest rates can affect firms in various ways:

- The value of investments in bonds or other investment securities with fixed interest rates.
- The value of liabilities with fixed interest rates.
- The returns a firm generates from pension fund investments.

Firms often use interest rate swaps to hedge, or neutralize, the risk of interest rate changes. As Chapter 8 discusses, interest rate swaps effectively change fixed interest rate debt, for which the principal amount of the debt is at risk to interest rate change, to variable interest rate debt, for which the principal amount is not at risk. Chapter 8 illustrates interest rate swaps. Firms, particularly financial institutions, also hedge some interest rate risk by matching investments in fixed-interest-rate assets with fixed-rate liabilities of equivalent duration.

PepsiCo discloses in Note 10:

> We centrally manage our debt and investment portfolios considering investment opportunities and risks, tax consequences and overall financing strategies. We may use interest rate and cross currency interest rate swaps to manage our overall interest expense and foreign exchange risk. These instruments effectively change the interest rate and currency of specific debt issuances. These swaps are entered into concurrently with the issuance of the debt that they are intended to modify. The notional amount, interest payment and maturity date of the swaps match the principal, interest payment and maturity date of the related debt. These swaps are entered into only with strong creditworthy counterparties, are settled on a net basis and are of relatively short duration.

The MD&A indicates that a 1-percentage-point increase in interest rates would have decreased net interest expense by $11 million for Year 4, suggesting that PepsiCo sufficiently hedged its interest rate risk.

Other Risk-Related Disclosures

The particular elements of risk that firms include in their risk management disclosures depend on the types of risks each firm encounters. PepsiCo discloses in Note 7, "Pension, Retiree Medical and Savings Plans" (Appendix A), the effect that a 1-percentage-point change in the assumed health care trend rate would have on health care expense and the health care liability. In its MD&A under Stock-Based Compensation Expense, PepsiCo indicates the effect on stock-based compensation expense of a 1-percentage-point change in assumptions underlying the valuation of stock options.

Firms now disclose considerably more information for the analyst to assess the effect of various risks on a firm than in the past. Standard setters have increasingly required firms to disclose the sensitivity of reported amounts to changes in various variables and assumptions. One would expect the information value of these disclosures to increase even more in the future as analysts and other users of financial statements become more familiar with them.

FINANCIAL STATEMENT ANALYSIS OF RISK

In addition to using information about risk disclosed in the notes to the financial statements and in the MD&A, analysts typically assess other dimensions of risk using ratios of various items in the financial statements. The statement of cash flows (discussed in Chapter 3), which reports the net amount of cash generated or used by operating, investing, and financing activities, is an important source of information for studying risk.

Exhibit 5.1 relates the factors affecting a firm's ability to generate cash with its need to use cash. Most financial statement-based risk analysis focuses on a comparison of the supply of cash and demand for cash. Risk analysis using financial statement data typically examines (1) *short-term liquidity risk,* the near-term ability to generate cash to service working capital needs and debt service requirements, and (2) *long-term solvency risk,* the longer-term ability to generate cash internally or from external sources to satisfy plant capacity and debt repayment needs. We structure our discussion of the analytical tools for assessing risk around short-term liquidity risk and long-term solvency risk.

The field of finance identifies two types of firm-specific risk: *credit risk* and *bankruptcy risk.* Credit risk concerns a firm's ability to make interest and principal payments on borrowings as they come due. Bankruptcy risk relates to the likelihood that a firm will file for bankruptcy and perhaps subsequently liquidate. The analyst might view these two types of risk as states of financial distress that fall along a continuum of increasing gravity from (1) failing to make a required interest payment on time, to (2) restructuring debt, to (3) defaulting on a principal payment on debt, to (4) filing for bankruptcy, to (5) liquidating a firm. Analysts concerned with the economic loss of a portion or the entire amount lent to or invested in a firm would examine a firm's position on this financial distress continuum. We demonstrate how analysts can use tools of short-term liquidity and long-term solvency risk in assessing credit risk and bankruptcy risk.

Less than 5 percent of publicly traded firms experience financial distress as defined by one of the five states listed above. Moreover, these types of risk do not encompass the full range of risks that equity investors must consider as the residual risk bearers of firms. Therefore, to value firms, investors rely on a broader definition of risk that encompasses elements of risk inherent in investing in common shares of a firm, relative to the risks that are common to all firms. One research stream that strives for a broader definition of risk attempts to measure systematic (nondiversifiable) risk and use it to explain differences in market rates of return on common stocks. Economic theory teaches that

EXHIBIT 5.1

Framework for Financial Statement Analysis of Risk

Activity	Ability to Generate Cash	Need to Use Cash	Financial Statement Analysis Performed
Operations	Profitability of goods and services sold	Working capital requirements	Short-term liquidity risk
Investing	Sales of existing plant assets or investments	Plant capacity requirements	Long-term solvency risk
Financing	Borrowing capacity	Debt service requirements	

differences in market returns relate to differences in risk. Studies of this risk/return relation use market equity beta as one measure of *market equity risk.* Market equity beta measures the covariability of a firm's returns with an index of returns of all securities in the equity capital market. Because only a small percentage of publicly traded firms experience significant risk from financial distress, additional factors besides short-term liquidity risk, long-term solvency risk, credit risk, and bankruptcy risk must explain market beta. We discuss the research relating financial statement data and market equity beta later in this chapter, and then elaborate on it more fully in Chapters 11 to 14.

This chapter examines various tools of financial statement analysis for identifying and measuring the five types of risk highlighted and described earlier (short-term liquidity, long-term solvency, credit, bankruptcy, and market equity). The presumption is that a firm follows GAAP in preparing its financial statements so that the analyst can use the reported amounts to assess each type of risk. In some cases, however, firms intentionally report amounts outside, or beyond the limits of, GAAP in an effort to portray a more profitable or less risky profile than is appropriate. In these cases, the analyst cannot rely on reported amounts as meaningful indicators of risk. Assessing *financial reporting manipulation risk* is an important element of risk analysis.

Thus, the discussion of risk analysis in the remainder of this chapter considers analysis of the following types of risk:

1. Short-term liquidity risk.
2. Long-term solvency risk.
3. Credit risk.
4. Bankruptcy risk.
5. Market equity risk.
6. Financial reporting manipulation risk.

As will become clear, these elements of risk are interrelated. Analysts use short-term liquidity and long-term solvency risk ratios in assessing both credit risk and bankruptcy risk. Some of the factors affecting long-term solvency risk affect market equity risk.

We illustrate the analyses of various dimensions of risk using the financial statements of PepsiCo in Appendix A. As we did in Chapter 4, we compare financial ratios for PepsiCo for Year 4 with the corresponding ratios for Year 2 and Year 3 in a time-series setting. We can also compare the ratios for PepsiCo with average industry ratios or with those of PepsiCo's competitors.

ANALYZING SHORT-TERM LIQUIDITY RISK

The analysis of short-term liquidity risk requires an understanding of the operating cycle of a firm, introduced in Chapter 1. Consider a typical manufacturing firm. It acquires raw materials on account, promising to pay suppliers within thirty to sixty days. The firm then combines the raw materials, labor services, and other inputs to produce a product. It pays for some of these costs at the time of incurrence and delays payment of other costs. At some point, the firm sells the product to a customer, probably on account. It then collects the customer's account and pays suppliers and others for purchases on account.

If a firm (1) can delay all cash outflows to suppliers, employees, and others until it receives cash from customers, and (2) receives more cash than it must disburse, then the firm will not likely encounter short-term liquidity problems. Most firms, however, cannot time their cash inflows and outflows precisely. Employees may require weekly or semimonthly payments, whereas customers may delay payments for thirty days or more. Firms may experience rapid growth and need to produce more units of product than they sell during a period. Even if perfectly timed, the cash outflows to support the higher level of production in this period can exceed the cash inflows from customers in this period from the lower level of sales of prior periods. Firms that operate at a net loss for a period often find that the completion of the operating cycle results in a net cash outflow instead of a net cash inflow.

Short-term liquidity problems also arise from longer-term solvency difficulties. For example, a firm may assume a relatively high percentage of debt in its capital structure. This level of debt usually requires periodic interest payments and may require repayments of principal as well. For some firms, interest expense is their largest single cost. The operating cycle must not only generate sufficient cash to supply operating working capital needs, it must generate sufficient cash to service debt as well.

Financially healthy firms frequently close any cash flow gap in their operating cycles with short-term borrowing. Such firms may issue commercial paper on the market or obtain three- to six-month bank loans. Most firms maintain a line of credit with their banks so they can obtain cash quickly for working capital needs. The notes to the financial statements usually disclose the amount of the line of credit and the level of borrowing used on that line during the year. PepsiCo, for example, discloses the following in Note 9, "Debt Obligations and Commitments" (Appendix A):

> At year-end Year 4, we maintained $1.5 billion in corporate lines of credit subject to normal banking terms and conditions. These credit facilities support short-term debt issuances and remained unused as of December 25, Year 4. Of the $1.5 billion, $750 million expires in June Year 5 with the remaining $750 million expiring in June Year 9. Upon consent of PepsiCo and the lenders, these facilities can be extended an additional year. In addition, $267 million of our debt was outstanding on various lines of credit maintained for our international divisions. These lines of credit are subject to normal banking terms and conditions and are committed to the extent of our borrowings.

Note 9 indicates that PepsiCo's outstanding short-term debt totaled $1,054 million and its long-term debt totaled $2,397 million at the end of Year 4. Thus, PepsiCo has the ability to increase borrowing approximately 43.5 percent [= $1,500/($1,054 + $2,397)] at the end of Year 4 with existing loan commitments.

We discuss seven financial statement ratios for assessing short-term liquidity risk: (1) current ratio, (2) quick ratio, (3) operating cash flow to current liabilities ratio, (4) accounts receivable turnover, (5) inventory turnover, (6) accounts payable turnover, and (7) revenues to cash ratio.

Current Ratio

The current ratio equals current assets divided by current liabilities. It indicates the amount of cash available at the balance sheet date plus the amount of other current assets that the firm expects to turn into cash within one year of the balance sheet date (from collection of receivables and sale of inventory) relative to obligations coming due during that period. The current ratio for PepsiCo at the end of Year 4 is as follows:

$$\text{Current Ratio} = \frac{\text{Current Assets}}{\text{Current Liabilities}}$$

$$1.28 = \frac{\$8{,}639}{\$6{,}752}$$

The current ratio for PepsiCo was 1.06 at the end of Year 2 and 1.08 at the end of Year 3. Thus, PepsiCo experienced an increasing current ratio during the three years.

Banks, suppliers, and others that extend short-term credit to a firm generally prefer a current ratio in excess of 1.0. They typically evaluate the appropriate level of a firm's current ratio based on the length of the firm's operating cycle, the extent to which the firm has noncurrent assets that could be used for liquidity if necessary, and similar factors. Large current ratios indicate the availability of cash and near-cash assets to repay obligations coming due within the next year. Prior to the 1980s, the average current ratios for most industries exceeded 2.0. As interest rates increased in the early 1980s, firms attempted to stretch their accounts payable and use suppliers to finance a greater portion of their working capital needs (that is, receivables and inventories). Also, firms increasingly instituted just-in-time inventory systems that reduced the amount of raw materials and finished-goods inventories. As a consequence of these two factors, current ratios began moving in the direction of 1.0. Current ratios hovering around this level, or even just below 1.0, are now common. Although this directional movement suggests an increase in short-term liquidity risk, the level of risk is tolerable. Recall that accountants report inventories, a major component of current assets for many firms, at acquisition cost. The cash that firms expect to generate from selling inventories is larger than the amount used in calculating the current ratio. PepsiCo, for example, has a cost of goods sold to sales percentage of approximately 45 percent. Thus, inventories have selling prices of 2.2 (= 1.00/.45) times the amount appearing on the balance sheet. Thus, a current ratio just slightly greater than 1.0 at the end of Year 2 and Year 3 is not a major concern for PepsiCo.

Analysts should consider several additional interpretive issues when evaluating the current ratio:

1. An increase of equal amounts in both current assets and current liabilities (for example, purchasing inventory on account) results in a decrease in the current ratio when the ratio is greater than 1.0 before the transaction but an increase in the current ratio if it is less than 1.0 before the transaction. Similar interpretive difficulties arise when current assets and current liabilities decrease by an equal amount. With current ratios for many firms now in the neighborhood of 1.0, this concern with the current ratio gains greater significance.
2. A very high current ratio may accompany unsatisfactory business conditions, whereas a falling ratio may accompany profitable operations. During a recession, firms may encounter difficulties in selling inventories or collecting receivables, causing the current ratio to increase to very high levels. In a boom period, just the reverse can occur.
3. The current ratio is susceptible to "window dressing"; that is, management can take deliberate steps leading up to the balance sheet date to produce a better current ratio than is the normal or average ratio for the period. For instance, toward the end of the period a firm may accelerate normal purchases on account (if the current ratio is less than 1.0) or delay such purchases (if the current ratio is greater than 1.0) in an effort to improve the current ratio. Alternatively, a firm may collect loans previously made to officers, classified as noncurrent assets, and use the proceeds to reduce current liabilities.

Despite these interpretive problems with the current ratio, the analyst will find widespread use of the current ratio as a measure of short-term liquidity risk. Empirical studies of bond default, bankruptcy, and other conditions of financial distress have found that the current ratio has strong predictive power. A later section of this chapter discusses this empirical research more fully.

Quick Ratio

A variation of the current ratio is the quick, or acid test, ratio. The analyst computes the quick ratio by including in the numerator only those current assets that the firm could convert quickly into cash. The numerator customarily includes cash, marketable securities, and receivables. However, the analyst should study the facts in each case before deciding whether to include receivables and exclude inventories. Some businesses can convert their inventory of merchandise into cash more quickly (for example, a retail chain like Wal-Mart) than other businesses can collect their receivables (for example, an equipment manufacturer like John Deere that provides financing for its customers' purchases).

Assuming that we include accounts receivable but exclude inventories, the quick ratio of PepsiCo at the end of Year 4 is:

$$\text{Quick Ratio} = \frac{\text{Cash} + \text{Marketable Securities} + \text{Accounts Receivable}}{\text{Current Liabilities}}$$

$$.95 = \frac{\$1{,}280 + \$2{,}165 + \$2{,}999}{\$6{,}752}$$

The quick ratio for PepsiCo was .72 at the end of Year 2 and .75 at the end of Year 3. Unless inventory turnovers have changed dramatically, the trends in the quick ratio and the current ratio correlate highly. That is, the analyst obtains the same information about improving or deteriorating short-term liquidity risk by examining either ratio. Note that the current and quick ratios for PepsiCo follow the same upward trends. With current ratios recently trending toward 1.0, quick ratios have trended toward .5.

The quick ratio is subject to some of the same interpretive issues as the current ratio. With quick ratios typically less than 1.0, equal increases in the numerator and denominator increase the ratio and equal decreases decrease the ratio. The quick ratio is also susceptible to year-end window dressing.

Operating Cash Flow to Current Liabilities Ratio

The analyst can overcome the deficiencies discussed previously in using current assets measured at a point in time as an indicator of a firm's ability to generate cash in the near term by using cash flow from operations instead. Cash flow from operations, reported on the statement of cash flows, indicates the amount of cash that the firm derived from (or used in) operations after funding working capital needs. Because the numerator of this ratio uses amounts for a period of time, the denominator uses an average of current liabilities for the same period. This ratio for PepsiCo for Year 4 is as follows:

$$\text{Operating Cash Flow to Current Liabilities Ratio} = \frac{\text{Cash Flow from Operations}}{\text{Average Current Liabilities}}$$

$$76.8\% = \frac{\$5{,}054}{.5(\$6{,}415 + \$6{,}752)}$$

The ratio was 83.7 percent for Year 2 and 69.4 percent for Year 3. An empirical study utilizing the operating cash flow to current liabilities ratio found that a ratio of 40 percent or more was common for a typical healthy manufacturing or retailing firm.[1] PepsiCo consistently has an operating cash flow to current liabilities ratio in excess of 40 percent. Thus, PepsiCo does not display much short-term liquidity risk.

---

[1]Cornelius Casey and Norman Bartczak, "Cash Flow—It's Not the Bottom Line," *Harvard Business Review* (July–August 1984), pp. 61–66.

Working Capital Turnover Ratios

The analyst uses three measures of the rate of activity in working capital accounts to study the cash-generating ability of operations and the short-term liquidity risk of a firm:

$$\text{Accounts Receivable Turnover} = \frac{\text{Sales}}{\text{Average Accounts Receivable}}$$

$$\text{Inventory Turnover} = \frac{\text{Cost of Goods Sold}}{\text{Average Inventories}}$$

$$\text{Accounts Payable Turnover} = \frac{\text{Purchases}}{\text{Average Accounts Payable}}$$

Chapter 4 discussed the accounts receivable and inventory turnovers, components of the total assets turnover, as measures of profitability. We use these ratios here as measures of the speed with which firms turn accounts receivable into cash and sell inventories. The accounts payable turnover indicates the speed at which a manufacturing or retailing firm pays for purchases of inventories on account. Purchases is not an amount that the financial statements typically disclose. The analyst can approximate purchases as follows:[2]

$$\text{Purchases} = \text{Cost of Goods Sold} + \text{Ending Inventory} - \text{Beginning Inventory}.$$

The analyst often expresses these three ratios in terms of the number of days each balance sheet item (that is, receivables, inventories, accounts payable) is outstanding. To do so, divide 365 days by the three turnover amounts.

Exhibit 5.2 presents the calculation of these three turnover ratios and the related number of days for PepsiCo for Year 4. PepsiCo combines accounts payable and other current

EXHIBIT 5.2

Working Capital Activity Ratios for PepsiCo for Year 4

Accounts Receivable Turnover

$$\frac{\$29,261}{.5(\$2,830 + \$2,999)} = 10.3 \text{ times per year}$$

Days Receivables Outstanding

$$\frac{365}{10.3} = 36 \text{ days}$$

Inventory Turnover

$$\frac{\$13,406}{.5(\$1,412 + \$1,541)} = 9.1 \text{ times per year}$$

Days Inventory Held

$$\frac{365}{9.1} = 40 \text{ days}$$

Accounts Payable Turnover

$$\frac{(\$13,406 + \$1,541 - \$1,412)}{.5(\$1,638 + \$1,731)} = 8.0 \text{ times per year}$$

Days Accounts Payable Outstanding

$$\frac{365}{8.0} = 45 \text{ days}$$

[2]The accounts payable turnover ratio will be skewed upward if cost of goods sold includes a high proportion of costs (such as depreciation and labor) that do not flow through accounts payable. This skewness is more of a concern for manufacturing firms than for retailing firms. The skewness is more of an issue in cross-sectional comparisons than in time-series analyses.

liabilities on its balance sheet. Note 14, "Supplemental Financial Information" (Appendix A), disaggregates this combined amount into its various elements and reports the amounts for accounts payable separately. We use the amounts for accounts payable from Note 14 to compute the accounts payable turnover.

The number of days that firms hold inventory until sale plus the number of days that firms hold accounts receivable until collection indicates the total number of days from the production or purchase of inventory until collection of cash from the sale of inventory to customers. This combined number of days indicates the length of time for which the firm must obtain financing for its primary working capital assets. The number of days that accounts payable is outstanding indicates the portion of the number of days of needed working capital financing that the firm obtained from suppliers. The difference between the total number of days for which the firm requires financing for its working capital and the number of days for which it obtained financing from suppliers of inventory indicates the additional days for which it must obtain financing. We depict these relations here:

Days of Working Capital Financing Required:

Days Inventory Held	Days Accounts Receivable Outstanding

Days of Working Capital Financing Provided:

Days Account Payable Outstanding	Days of Working Capital Financing Needed from Other Sources

Exhibit 5.3 shows the net number of days of financing needed from other sources for PepsiCo for Year 2, Year 3, and Year 4. PepsiCo's days accounts payable approximately equals its days inventory, indicating that suppliers provided the financing for PepsiCo's inventory. The net days financed from other sources approximately equal the days accounts receivable were outstanding. PepsiCo used short-term borrowing to finance part of the net days of needed financing.

In general, the shorter the number of days of needed financing, the larger the cash flow from operations to average current liabilities ratio. A small number of net days indicates either relatively little need to finance accounts receivable and inventories (that

EXHIBIT 5.3

Net Number of Days of Working Capital Financing Needed from Other Sources for PepsiCo

Year	Days Accounts Receivable Outstanding	Days Inventory Held	Days Accounts Payable Outstanding	Days Other Financing Required
Year 2	34	42	(44)	32
Year 3	36	41	(47)	30
Year 4	36	40	(45)	31

is, the firm sells inventory quickly and receives cash from customers soon after sale) or aggressive use of suppliers to finance these current assets (that is, the firm delays paying cash to suppliers). Both scenarios enhance cash flow from operations in the numerator of this ratio. Furthermore, firms with a shorter number of days of financing required from other sources need not engage in as much short-term borrowing from banks and other financing institutions. Such borrowing increases current liabilities in the denominator of the operating cash flow to current liabilities ratio and, therefore, lowers this ratio.

Revenues to Cash Ratio

Firms ultimately collect revenues in cash and pay operating costs and current liabilities with cash. The amount of cash on the balance sheet reflects the net effect of operating, investing, and financing activities on cash, as well as management's judgments about the desired level of cash. A ratio that incorporates the amount of cash on the balance sheet helps the analyst evaluate short-term liquidity. To aid comparability across time and across firms, we must relate the amount of cash to some measure of operating activity. Either revenues or cash operating expenses might serve as the measure of activity. We use revenues. The revenues to cash ratio for PepsiCo for Year 4 is as follows:

$$\text{Revenues to Cash Ratio} = \frac{\text{Revenues}}{\text{Average Cash Balance}}$$

$$27.9 = \frac{\$29{,}261}{.5(\$820 + 1{,}280)}$$

The revenues to cash flow ratio was 21.6 for Year 2, and 21.9 for Year 3.

One can view the revenues to cash ratio as a cash turnover ratio, analogous to the accounts receivable turnover ratio described previously. We can express the revenues to cash ratio in terms of the number of days of revenue held in cash by dividing 365 days by the revenues to cash ratio. That ratio for PepsiCo is as follows:

Days Revenues Held in Cash

Year 2: 365/21.6 = 16.9 days
Year 3: 365/21.9 = 16.7 days
Year 4: 365/27.9 = 13.1 days

Interpreting the revenues to cash ratio requires caution. From the viewpoint of short-term liquidity risk, lenders prefer a smaller revenues to cash ratio (that is, more cash in the denominator) and a larger number of days revenue held as cash. Management, however, prefers not to tie up too much in idle cash.

One variation in this ratio is to include not only the amount of cash but also the amount of marketable securities. Firms typically invest in marketable securities when they have temporarily excess cash. The classification of marketable securities as a current asset suggests that firms could easily sell the securities if they needed cash. Including cash and marketable securities in the denominator results in a revenues to cash and marketable securities ratio of 10.7 [= $29,261/.5($820 + $1,181 + $1,280 + $2,165)] for Year 4 and a days revenues held in cash and marketable securities of 34.1 days (= 365/10.7).

Another variation of this ratio uses cash operating expenses in the numerator instead of revenues. The rationale is that firms generally need cash to pay operating expenses. The analyst can approximate cash operating expenses by summing cost of goods sold and selling and administrative expenses and subtracting depreciation and amortization. Refer to the income statement of PepsiCo in Appendix A. PepsiCo reports amortization expense separately. However, it includes depreciation expense in cost of sales and selling, general, and administrative expenses. Note 4, "Property, Plant, and Equipment and Intangible Assets" (Appendix A), indicates that depreciation expense for Year 4 is $1,062 million. Thus, cash operating expenses, excluding impairment and restructuring charges, total $22,643 million (= $13,406 + $10,299 – $1,062). The ratio of cash operating expenses to average cash for Year 4 is 21.6 [= $22,643/ (.5[$820 + $1,280])] and the days of cash held for paying operating expenses is 16.9 days (= 365/21.6). This ratio is a variant of the *defensive interval*[3] or *run rate,* which indicates the number of days a firm could continue operating without injections of additional cash.

We use the ratio of revenues to cash in this book instead of these variations in the ratio.

Summary of Short-Term Liquidity Risk

The short-term liquidity risk ratios suggest that PepsiCo has relatively little short-term liquidity risk. Although the current ratio is slightly more than 1, the quick ratio is nearly equal to 1 and the operating cash flow to current liabilities ratio exceeds 40 percent in all years. PepsiCo has an established brand name and dominates (along with Coca-Cola) the soft drink beverage industry. Chapter 4 discussed PepsiCo's healthy profitability picture, suggesting that it could obtain short-term financing if needed. Its established line of credit of $1.5 billion provides a cushion if short-term liquidity becomes a problem.

ANALYZING LONG-TERM SOLVENCY RISK

Chapter 4 discussed the concept of financial leverage. When firms obtain funds from borrowing and invest those funds in assets that generate a higher return than the after-tax cost of the borrowing, the common shareholders benefit. Common shareholders continue to benefit with increasing proportions of debt in the capital structure as long as the firm maintains an excess of ROA over the after-tax cost of the debt. Financial leverage therefore enhances the return to the common shareholders. Increasing the proportion of debt in the capital structure, however, increases the risk that the firm cannot pay interest and repay the principal on the amount borrowed. That is, credit and bankruptcy risk increases and the incremental cost of borrowing likely also increases. When the excess of ROA over the after-tax cost of borrowing declines, additional financial leverage begins to reduce the return to the common shareholders. Analysts use measures of long-term solvency risk to examine a firm's ability to make interest and principal payments on long-term debt and similar obligations as they come due.

Perhaps the best indicator for assessing long-term solvency risk is a firm's ability to generate earnings over a period of years. Profitable firms either generate sufficient cash from operations or obtain needed cash from creditors or owners. The measures of profitability discussed in Chapter 4 therefore apply for this purpose as well. Also, firms must survive in the short term if they are to survive in the long term. Thus, analysis of long-term solvency risk must begin with an analysis of short-term liquidity risk. Three measures used in examining long-term solvency risk are (1) debt ratios, (2) interest coverage ratio, and (3) operating cash flow to total liabilities ratio.

---

[3]See George H. Sorter and George Benston, "Appraising the Defensive Position of a Firm: The Interval Measure," *Accounting Review* 35 (October 1960), pp. 633–640. The denominator of their defensive interval measure included marketable securities and accounts receivable in additional to cash. See the discussion of bankruptcy risk later in this chapter.

Debt Ratios

Analysts use debt ratios to measure the amount of liabilities, particularly long-term debt, in a firm's capital structure. The higher this proportion, the greater the long-term solvency risk. The capital structure leverage ratio discussed in Chapter 4, one of the disaggregated components of ROCE, is one version of a debt ratio. Several additional variations in debt ratios exist. Four commonly encountered measures are as follows:

$$\text{Liabilities to Assets Ratio} = \frac{\text{Total Liabilities}}{\text{Total Assets}}$$

$$\text{Liabilities to Shareholders' Equity Ratio} = \frac{\text{Total Liabilities}}{\text{Total Shareholders' Equity}}$$

$$\begin{array}{c}\text{Long-Term Debt to}\\ \text{Long-Term Capital Ratio}\end{array} = \frac{\text{Long-Term Debt}}{\text{Long-Term Debt} + \text{Shareholders' Equity}}$$

$$\text{Long-Term Debt to Shareholders' Equity Ratio} = \frac{\text{Long-Term Debt}}{\text{Shareholders' Equity}}$$

The debt ratios for PepsiCo at the end of Year 4 are as follows:

$$\text{Liabilities to Assets Ratio} = \frac{\$14{,}464}{\$27{,}979} = 51.7\%$$

$$\text{Liabilities to Shareholders' Equity Ratio} = \frac{\$14{,}464}{\$13{,}523} = 107.0\%$$

$$\text{Long-Term Debt to Long-Term Capital Ratio} = \frac{\$2{,}397}{\$2{,}397 + \$13{,}523} = 15.1\%$$

$$\text{Long-Term Debt to Shareholders' Equity Ratio} = \frac{\$2{,}397}{\$13{,}523} = 17.7\%$$

Exhibit 5.4 shows the debt ratios for PepsiCo at the end of Year 2, Year 3, and Year 4. The debt ratios involving total liabilities declined during the three-year period. The long-term debt ratios declined between Year 2 and Year 3 and increased slightly in Year 4.

Note the high correlations between changes in the two debt ratios involving total liabilities over time and in the two debt ratios involving long-term debt over time. These results are not surprising because they use the same financial statement data. The analyst can generally select one of these ratios and use it consistently over time. Because different

EXHIBIT 5.4

Debt Ratios for PepsiCo at the End of Year 2 to Year 4

	Year 2	Year 3	Year 4
Liabilities to Assets Ratio	59.4%	53.1%	51.7%
Liabilities to Shareholders' Equity Ratio	146.5%	113.3%	107.0%
Long-Term Debt to Long-Term Capital Ratio	18.7%	12.5%	15.1%
Long-Term Debt to Shareholders' Equity Ratio	23.0%	14.3%	17.7%

debt ratios exist, the analyst should use caution when reading financial periodicals and discussing debt ratios with others to be sure of the particular version of the debt ratio used. A liabilities to shareholders' equity ratio greater than 1.0 (that is, more liabilities than shareholders' equity) is not unusual, but a liabilities to assets ratio or a long-term debt to long-term capital ratio greater than 1.0 is highly unusual (requires a negative shareholders' equity).

In addition to computing debt ratios, the analyst should study the note to the financial statements on long-term debt. The note includes information on the types of debt that a firm has issued and the interest rates and maturity dates of the debt. The analyst should also examine the debt contract for each debt issue to assess whether the firm is nearing violation of any debt covenants.

Refer to Note 9, "Debt Obligations and Commitments" (Appendix A), for PepsiCo. PepsiCo indicates that it classifies a portion of its short-term borrowing as a noncurrent liability, even though the amounts are due within the next year. PepsiCo states:

> Short-term borrowings are reclassified to long-term when we have the intent and ability, through the existence of the unused lines of credit, to refinance these borrowings on a long-term basis.

GAAP permits PepsiCo and other firms to reclassify short-term debt in this way. PepsiCo's reclassification of $375 million in additional short-term borrowing as long-term borrowing accounts for almost all of the increase in the long-term debt ratios between the end of Year 3 and the end of Year 4.

In an effort to appear less risky and lower their cost of financing or perhaps to avoid violating debt covenants in existing borrowing arrangements, firms often attempt to structure financing in a manner that keeps debt off the balance sheet. Chapter 8 discusses some of the avenues available under GAAP (for example, accounting for leases as operating leases instead of capital leases) to minimize reported long-term debt. The analyst should recognize the possibility of such actions when interpreting debt ratios and perhaps adjust the reported amounts.

Interest Coverage Ratio

The interest coverage ratio indicates the number of times that net income before interest expense and income taxes exceeds interest expense. The interest coverage ratio for PepsiCo, using the adjusted amounts of net income and income tax expense from Exhibit 4.2, for Year 4 is as follows:[4]

$$\text{Interest Coverage Ratio} = \frac{\begin{array}{c}\text{Net Income} + \text{Interest Expense}\\ + \text{Income Tax Expense} + \text{Minority Interest in Earnings}\end{array}}{\text{Interest Expense}}$$

$$35.1 = \frac{\$4{,}004 + \$167 + \$1{,}692 + \$0}{\$167}$$

The interest coverage ratio for PepsiCo was 27.2 in Year 2 and 32.9 in Year 3. PepsiCo's profitability increased during the three-year period (see the discussion in Chapter 4)

[4]Increased precision suggests that the denominator include total interest cost for the year, not just the amount recognized as interest expense. If a firm self-constructs fixed assets, it must capitalize a portion of its interest cost each year and add it to the cost of the self-constructed assets. The analyst should probably apply this refinement of the interest coverage ratio only to electric utilities, which engage in heavy borrowing to construct their capital-intensive plants.

while its debt levels decreased, resulting in an increasing interest coverage ratio. Analysts typically view coverage ratios of less than approximately 2.0 as risky situations. Thus, PepsiCo exhibits low long-term solvency risk by this measure.

If a firm must make other required periodic payments (such as pensions or leases), the analyst could include these amounts in the calculation as well. If so, the analyst refers to the ratio as the *fixed charges coverage ratio.*

One criticism of the interest and the fixed charges coverage ratios as measures of long-term solvency risk is that they use earnings rather than cash flows in the numerator. Firms pay interest and other fixed charges with cash, not with earnings. The analyst can create cash-flow-based variations of these coverage ratios by using cash flow from operations (before interest and income taxes) in the numerator. When the value of the ratio based on earnings in the numerator is relatively low (that is, less than approximately 2.0), the analyst should use cash flow from operations before interest and income taxes in the numerator to calculate coverage ratios.

To illustrate, cash flow from operations for PepsiCo for Year 4 was $5,054 million. Note 14, "Supplemental Financial Information" (Appendix A), indicates that PepsiCo paid $137 million for interest and $1,833 million for income taxes during Year 4. The calculation of the interest coverage ratio using cash flows is as follows:

$$\text{Interest Coverage Ratio} = \frac{\begin{array}{c}\text{Cash Flow from Operations} \\ \text{Payments for Interest and Income Taxes}\end{array}}{\text{Cash Payments for Interest}}$$

$$43.5 = \frac{\$5{,}054 + \$137 + \$1{,}833}{\$137}$$

Operating Cash Flow to Total Liabilities Ratio

The debt ratios give no recognition to the ability of a firm to generate cash flow from operations to service debt. The ratio of cash flow from operations to average total liabilities overcomes this deficiency. This cash flow ratio is similar to the one used in assessing short-term liquidity, but here the denominator includes all liabilities (current and noncurrent).

The operating cash flow to total liabilities ratio for Year 4 for PepsiCo is as follows:

$$\begin{array}{c}\text{Operating Cash Flow to} \\ \text{Total Liabilities Ratio}\end{array} = \frac{\text{Cash Flow from Operations}}{\text{Average Total Liabilities}}$$

$$36.2\% = \frac{\$5{,}054}{.5(\$13{,}453 + \$14{,}464)}$$

The ratio for PepsiCo was 34.3 percent in Year 2 and 31.6 percent in Year 3. A ratio of 20 percent or more[5] is common for a financially healthy company. Thus, PepsiCo appears to have low long-term solvency risk by this measure.

Summary of Long-Term Solvency Risk

The debt, interest coverage, and cash flow ratios indicate that PepsiCo has low long-term solvency risk. PepsiCo is profitable and generates the needed cash flow to service its debt.

---

[5]Casey and Bartczak, op. cit.

ANALYZING CREDIT RISK

Potential lenders to a firm, whether short- or long-term, assess the likelihood that the firm will pay periodic interest and repay the principal amount lent. Lenders use the short-term liquidity and long-term solvency ratios discussed thus far in this chapter to assess credit risk. Lenders also consider other factors when extending credit. Common practice uses a set of terms that begin with the letter C to characterize factors to consider in lending decisions. This section discusses a number of such C terms. The list is not an exhaustive catalog of the factors that lenders consider in assessing credit risk.

1. Circumstances Leading to Need for the Loan

The reason that a firm needs to borrow affects the riskiness of the loan and the likelihood of repayment. Consider the following examples.

Example 1. W. T. Grant Company, a discount retail chain, filed for bankruptcy in 1975. Its bankruptcy has become a classic example of how poorly designed and implemented controls can lead a firm into financial distress (see Case 3.3 in Chapter 3). Between 1968 and 1975, Grant experienced increasing difficulty collecting its accounts receivable from credit card customers. To finance the buildup of its accounts receivable, Grant borrowed short-term funds from commercial banks. Grant, however, failed to fix the credit extension and cash collection problems with its receivables. The bank loans simply kept Grant in business in an ever-worsening credit situation. Lending to satisfy cash-flow needs related to an unsolved problem or difficulty can be highly risky.

Example 2. Toys "R" Us purchases toys, games, and other entertainment products in September and October in anticipation of heavy demand during the end-of-the-year holiday season. It typically pays its suppliers within thirty days for these purchases but doesn't collect cash from customers until December, January, or later. To finance its inventory, Toys "R" Us borrows short term from its banks. It repays these loans with cash collected from customers. Lending to satisfy cash-flow needs related to ongoing seasonal business operations is generally relatively low risk. Toys "R" Us has an established brand name and predictable demand. Although some risk exists that the products offered will not meet customer preferences in a particular year, Toys "R" Us offers a sufficiently diverse product line that failure to collect sufficient cash to repay the bank loan is low.

Example 3. Wal-Mart Stores has grown the number of its stores at a rate of approximately 12 percent per year during the last five years (see Case 4.2 in Chapter 4). The fastest growth is in its superstores, which represent a combination of its traditional discount store and a grocery store. Wal-Mart borrows a large portion of the funds needed to construct new stores using twenty- to twenty-five-year loans. (Wal-Mart also enters into leases for a portion of the space needed for its new stores.) Such loans are relatively low risk, given the operating success of Wal-Mart in the past and the existence of land and buildings that serve as collateral for the loans.

Example 4. National Semiconductor designs and manufactures semiconductors for use in computers and other electronic products. Its principal competitor, Intel, maintains the dominant market share for semiconductors. National Semiconductor has increasingly lost market share to Intel in recent years. Assume now that National Semiconductor desires to develop new semiconductors and needs to borrow funds to finance the design and development effort. Such a loan would likely be relatively high risk. Technological change occurs rapidly in semiconductors, which could make obsolete any semiconductors developed by

National Semiconductor. In addition, expenditures on design and development of semiconductors would not likely result in assets that can serve as collateral for the loan.

Thus, lending to established firms for ongoing operating needs presents the lowest credit risk. Lending to firms experiencing operating problems, lending to emerging businesses, and lending to support investments in intangible assets typically carry higher risks. Lenders should be wary of borrowers that are unclear as to how they intend to use the proceeds of a loan.

2. Credit History

A second C term is *credit.* Lenders like to see that a firm has borrowed in the past and successfully repaid the loans. Young firms sometimes shy away from borrowing to avoid constraints that such borrowing may impose. Such firms often find, however, that an inadequate credit history precludes them from borrowing later when they need to do so. On the other hand, developing a poor credit history early on can doom a firm to failure because of the difficulty of overcoming initial impressions.

3. Cash Flows

A third C term is *cash flows.* Lenders prefer that firms generate sufficient cash flows to pay interest and repay principal (collectively referred to as *debt service)* on a loan rather than having to rely on selling the collateral. Tools for studying the cash-generating ability of a firm include examining the statement of cash flows for recent years, computing various cash flow financial ratios, and studying cash flows in projected financial statements.

Statement of Cash Flows. An examination of a firm's statement of cash flows for the most recent three or four years will indicate whether certain relations expected for a particular business occurred. Some of the indicators of potential cash flow problems, if observed for several years in a row, include the following:

1. Growth in accounts receivable or inventories that exceeds the growth rate in sales.
2. Increases in accounts payable that exceed the increase in inventories.
3. Other operating current liabilities that grow at a faster rate than sales.
4. Persistent negative cash flow from operations, because of either net losses or substantial increases in net working capital (current assets minus current liabilities).
5. Capital expenditures that substantially exceed cash flow from operations. Although the analyst should expect such an excess for a rapidly growing, capital-intensive firm, the negative excess cash flow (cash flow from operations minus capital expenditures) indicates a firm's continuing need for external financing to sustain that growth.
6. Reductions in capital expenditures over time. Although such reductions conserve cash in the near term, they might signal that the firm expects declines in future sales, earnings, and operating cash flows.
7. Sales of marketable securities in excess of purchases of marketable securities. Such sales provide cash immediately but might signal the inability of a firm's operations to provide adequate cash flow to finance working capital and long-term investments. Firms sell the marketable securities to obtain the cash needed for these purposes. Such sales, however, may not indicate cash flow problems if the firm invested temporarily excess cash that it now plans to use to make a corporate acquisition or to acquire fixed assets.
8. A substantial shift from long-term borrowing to short-term borrowing. The increase in short-term borrowing may signal a firm's inability to obtain long-term loans because lenders are uncertain about a firm's future.
9. A reduction or elimination of dividend payments. Although such actions conserve cash in the near term, dividend changes can provide a negative signal about a firm's future prospects.

Although none of these indicators by themselves represents conclusive evidence of cash flow problems, they signal the need to obtain explanations from management to see whether an emerging cash flow problem may exist.

Cash Flow Financial Ratios. Previous sections of this chapter discussed two cash flow ratios that might signal a cash flow problem: (1) operating cash flow to current liabilities ratio, and (2) operating cash flow to total liabilities ratio.

Cash Flows in Projected Financial Statements. Projected financial statements represent forecasted income statements, balance sheets, and statements of cash flows for some number of years in the future. Lenders may require potential borrowers to prepare such statements to demonstrate the borrower's ability to repay the loan with interest as it comes due. The credit analyst should question each of the important assumptions (such as sales growth, cost structure, or capital expenditures plans) underlying these projected financial statements. The credit analyst should also assess the sensitivity of the projected cash flows to changes in key assumptions. Suppose, for example, that sales grow by 4 percent instead of the 6 percent projected. Suppose that raw materials costs increase 5 percent instead of the 3 percent projected. Suppose that additional plant expenditures are necessary because a firm reaches capacity limits with a higher-than-expected sales increase. What impact will each of these changed assumptions have on cash flow from operations? Chapter 10 illustrates the preparation of projected, or forecasted, financial statements.

4. Collateral

A fourth consideration when assessing credit risk is the availability and value of collateral for a loan. If cash flows are insufficient to pay interest and repay the principal on a loan, the lender has the right to take possession of any collateral pledged in support of the loan. Depending on the nature of the collateral pledged, the analyst might examine the following:

1. Marketable Securities. Chapter 9 discusses the accounting for marketable securities. Marketable equity securities representing less than a 20 percent ownership appear on the balance sheet at market value. The analyst can assess whether the market value of securities pledged as collateral exceeds the unpaid balance of a loan. Marketable securities representing 20 percent or more of another entity generally appear on the balance sheet using the equity method. Determining whether the market value of such securities adequately covers the unpaid balance of a loan is more difficult. The analyst might examine the amount reported as equity in earnings of affiliates in recent years to assess the level and changes in profitability of the investee.

2. Accounts Receivable. A lender should assess whether the current value of accounts receivable is sufficient to cover the unpaid portion of a loan collateralized by accounts receivable. Determining whether the book value of accounts receivable accurately reflects their market value involves an examination of changes in the provision for uncollectible accounts relative to sales, the balance in allowance for uncollectible accounts relative to gross accounts receivable, the amount of accounts written off as uncollectible relative to gross accounts receivable, and the number of days receivables are outstanding.

3. Inventories. The analyst should examine changes in the inventory turnover ratio, in the cost of goods sold to sales percentage, and in the mix of raw-materials, work-in-process, and finished-goods inventories to identify possible inventory obsolescence problems. The analyst should remember that the market value of inventories would likely differ more from their book value for a firm using LIFO than for a firm using FIFO. Firms using LIFO must report the excess of market or FIFO value over LIFO cost, permitting the analyst to assess the adequacy of LIFO inventories to cover the unpaid balance on a loan collateralized by inventories. (See the discussion of inventories in Chapter 7.)

Property, Plant, and Equipment. Firms often pledge fixed assets as collateral for long-term borrowing. Determining the market values of such assets is difficult using reported financial statement information because of the use of acquisition cost valuations. Market values of unique, firm-specific assets are particularly difficult to ascertain. Clues indicating market value declines include restructuring charges, asset impairment charges, or recent sales of such assets at a loss. (See the discussion of property, plant, and equipment in Chapter 7.)

Intangibles. Intangibles generally do not serve well as collateral for borrowing because lenders cannot easily repossess the intangible (that is, sever it from all the other assets or capabilities of the firm) in the event of a loan default. For example, the value of a customer list of a newspaper or magazine publisher is closely tied to its writers and reporters and its production and distribution capability. The value of a brand name of a consumer foods product is closely tied to the firm's manufacturing quality control and marketing expertise. On the other hand, some intangibles can serve as collateral for borrowing. Rights owned by airlines to landing and gate slots at airports can be transferred to lenders in the event of loan default and resold to cover unpaid balances on a loan.

Some lending occurs on a nonsecured basis (that is, the borrower pledges no specific collateral in support of the loan). In these cases, the lender should study the notes to the financial statements to ascertain how much, if any, of the borrower's assets are not already pledged or otherwise restricted. The liquidation value of such assets represents the available resources of a firm to repay unsecured creditors. For smaller, family-owned businesses, an additional source of collateral may be the personal assets of management or major shareholders. Has management or the shareholders pledged their personal residence, debt or equity securities owned, or other assets to serve as additional collateral for a business loan?

5. Capacity for Debt

Closely related to a firm's cash-generating ability and available collateral is a firm's capacity to assume additional debt. The cash flows and the collateral represent the means to repay the debt. Most firms do not borrow up to the limit of their debt capacity. Lenders want to be sure that a margin of safety exists. Although no precise methodology exists to measure debt capacity, the analyst can study various financial statement ratios when assessing debt capacity.

1. Debt Ratios. An earlier section described several ratios that relate the amount of long-term debt or total liabilities to shareholders' equity or total assets as measures of the proportion of liabilities in the capital structure. In general, the higher the debt ratios, the higher the credit risk and the lower the unused debt capacity of the firm. When measuring debt ratios, the analyst must be careful to consider possible off-balance-sheet obligations (such as operating lease commitments or underfunded pension or health care benefit obligations). The analyst can compare a particular firm's debt ratios with those of similar firms in the same industry.

2. Interest Coverage Ratio. The number of times that interest payments are covered by operating income before interest and income taxes serves as a gauge of the margin of safety provided by operations to service debt. When firms make heavy use of operating leases for their fixed assets, as is common for airlines and retail stores, the analyst might convert the operating leases to capital leases for the purpose of computing the interest coverage ratio (see the discussion of leases in Chapter 8). The analyst adds back the lease payments (that is, rent expense) to net income when computing cash flows from operations in the numerator of this ratio and includes the lease payments in the denominator. When the interest coverage ratio falls below approximately 2, the credit risk is generally considered high. Interest coverage ratios that exceed 4 or 5 usually suggest a capacity to carry additional debt.

6. Contingencies

The credit standing of a firm could change abruptly in the future if current uncertainties turn out negatively for the firm. Questions that the analyst might ask include the following:

1. Is the firm a defendant in a major lawsuit involving its principal products, its technological advantages, its income tax returns, or other core endeavors that could change its profitability and cash flows in the future? Consider, for example, the uncertainty currently confronting the tobacco and asbestos industries with the unsettled status of lawsuits in the United States. Most large firms are continually engaged in lawsuits as a normal part of their business. Most of their losses are insured. Negative legal judgments will likely have a more pronounced effect on smaller firms, however, because they have less of a resource base with which to defend themselves and sustain such losses and may not carry adequate insurance.
2. Has the firm sold receivables with recourse or served as guarantor on a loan by a subsidiary, joint venture, special-purpose entity, or corporate officer that, if payment is required, will consume cash flows otherwise available to service other debt obligations?
3. Has the firm committed itself to making payments related to derivative financial instruments that could adversely affect future cash flows if interest rates, exchange rates, or other prices change significantly in an unexpected direction (see the discussion of derivatives in Chapter 8)?
4. Is the firm dependent on one or a few key employees, contracts or license agreements, or technologies, the loss of which could substantially affect the viability of the business?

Obtaining answers to such questions will require the analyst to read the notes to the financial statement carefully and to ask astute questions of management, attorneys, and others.

7. Character of Management

An intangible that can offset to some extent otherwise weak signals about the creditworthiness of a firm is the character of its management. Has the management team successively weathered previous operating problems and challenges that could have bankrupted most firms? Has the management team delivered in the past on projections regarding sales levels, cost reductions, new product development, and similar operating targets? Does the firm have a reputation for honest and fair dealings with suppliers, customers, bankers, and others? Lenders are also more comfortable lending to firms in which management has a substantial portion of its personal wealth invested in the firm's common equity. Managers desiring to increase the value of their equity holdings have incentives to operate the firm profitably and avoid defaulting on debt.

8. Communication

Developing relations with lenders requires effective communication both initially and on an ongoing basis. If lenders are unfamiliar with either the business or its managers, efforts must be directed at communicating the nature of the firm's products and services and the strategies the firm pursues to gain competitive advantage. The firm's managers must demonstrate their knowledge of the business, including principal competitors, role of technological change, extent of government regulation, and similar factors. Inviting lenders to an office or plant visit provides visual evidence of an ongoing business.

Throughout the term of a loan, the borrowing firm should communicate regularly with lenders. If lenders required projected financial statements at the outset, communicating the extent to which the firm meets its projections is desirable. Alerting lenders to unexpected problems that may arise demonstrates that the firm's managers are on top of the problem and dealing with it. Lenders don't like surprises and need to be brought along throughout the term of the loan.

9. Conditions or Covenants

Lenders often place restrictions, or constraints, on a firm to protect their interests. Such restrictions might include minimum or maximum levels of certain financial ratios (for example, the current ratio cannot decline below 1.2; the long-term debt to shareholders' equity ratio cannot exceed 75 percent). Firms may also be precluded from paying dividends, repurchasing common stock, or taking on new financing with rights senior to existing lenders in the event of bankruptcy. Violation of these debt constraints, or covenants, could result in the need to repay borrowing immediately. Although these covenants can protect the interest of senior, collateralized lenders, they can place less senior lenders in jeopardy if the firm must quickly liquidate assets to repay debt. Thus, debt covenants are a double-edged sword from the viewpoint of credit risk. They provide protection against undue deterioration in the financial condition of a firm but increase the likelihood of default or bankruptcy if the constraints are too tight.

Summary of Credit Risk Analysis

The analysis of credit risk is a multifaceted endeavor. The financial statements and notes provide evidence on a firm's cash-generating ability, extent of collateralized assets, amount of unused debt capacity, and constraints imposed by existing borrowing agreements. Although the financial statements might provide some clues, the credit analyst must search beyond the financial statements for information on the credit history of the borrower, the market value of collateral, contingencies confronting the firm, and the character of management. Existing lenders should monitor a firm's credit risk on an ongoing basis, maintaining communications throughout the process. New lenders should assess how their loan will incrementally affect the firm's credit risk.

ANALYZING BANKRUPTCY RISK

This section discusses the analysis of bankruptcy risk using information in the financial statements.

The Bankruptcy Process

Most firms in the United States that file for bankruptcy file under Chapter 11 of the National Bankruptcy Code. Under Chapter 11, firms have six months in which to present a plan of reorganization to the court. After that period elapses, creditors, employees, and others can file their plans of reorganization. One such plan might include immediately selling the assets of the business and paying creditors the amounts due. The court decides which plan provides the fairest treatment for all parties concerned. While the firm is in bankruptcy, creditors cannot demand payment of their claims. The court oversees the execution of the reorganization. When the court determines that the firm has executed the plan of reorganization successfully and appears to be a viable entity, the firm is released from bankruptcy.

A Chapter 7 filing entails an immediate sale, or liquidation, of the firm's assets and a distribution of the proceeds to the various claimants in the order of their priority.

Firms typically file for bankruptcy when they have insufficient cash to pay creditors' claims coming due. If such firms did not file for bankruptcy, creditors could exercise their right to take possession of any collateral pledged to secure their lending and effectively begin liquidation of the firm. In an effort to keep assets intact and allow time for the firm to reorganize, the firm files for bankruptcy. In recent years, some firms have filed for bankruptcy for reasons other than insufficient liquid resources to pay creditors. Some firms have filed for bankruptcy to avoid labor contracts or retirement obligations that they consider too costly. Other firms facing potentially costly litigation have filed for bankruptcy as a means of forcing the contending party to negotiate a settlement.

Models of Bankruptcy Prediction

Empirical studies of bankruptcy attempt to distinguish the financial characteristics of firms that file for bankruptcy from those that do not, a dichotomous outcome. The objective is to develop a model that predicts which firms will likely file for bankruptcy one or more years before the filing. These models use financial statement ratios and other data.

Univariate Bankruptcy Prediction Models

Early research on bankruptcy prediction in the mid-1960s used univariate analysis. Univariate models examine the relation between a particular financial statement ratio and bankruptcy. Multivariate models, discussed next, combine several financial statement ratios to determine whether the set of ratios together can improve bankruptcy prediction. Beaver[6] studied twenty-nine financial statement ratios for the five years preceding bankruptcy for a sample of seventy-nine bankrupt and seventy-nine nonbankrupt firms. The objective was to identify the ratios that distinguished best between these two groups of firms and to determine how many years prior to bankruptcy the differences in the ratios emerged. The six ratios with the best discriminating power (and the nature of the risk each ratio measures) were as follows:

1. Net Income plus Depreciation, Depletion, and Amortization/Total Liabilities (long-term solvency risk).[7]
2. Net Income/Total Assets (profitability).
3. Total Debt/Total Assets (long-term solvency risk).
4. Net Working Capital/Total Assets (short-term liquidity risk).
5. Current Assets/Current Liabilities (short-term liquidity risk).
6. Cash, Marketable Securities, Accounts Receivable/Operating Expenses Excluding Depreciation, Depletion, and Amortization (short-term liquidity risk).[8]

Note that this list includes profitability, short-term liquidity risk, and long-term solvency risk ratios. Beaver's best predictor was net income before depreciation, depletion, and amortization divided by total liabilities. Exhibit 5.5 summarizes the success of this ratio in correctly classifying sample firms as bankrupt or not for each of the five years

[6]William Beaver, "Financial Ratios as Predictors of Failure," *Empirical Research in Accounting: Selected Studies, 1966*, supplement to *Journal of Accounting Research* (1966), pp. 71–102.

[7]This ratio is similar to the operating cash flow to total liabilities ratio discussed earlier in this chapter except that the numerator of Beaver's ratio does not include changes in working capital accounts. Published "funds flow" statements at the time of Beaver's study defined funds as working capital (instead of cash).

[8]This ratio, referred to as the *defensive interval*, indicates the proportion of a year that a firm could continue to operate by paying cash operating expenses with cash and near-cash assets. See the discussion earlier in this chapter in the section on the revenues to cash ratio.

EXHIBIT 5.5

Classification Accuracy and Error Rates for Net Income before Depreciation, Depletion, and Amortization/Total Liabilities

Years Prior to Bankruptcy	Proportion Correctly Classified	Error Rate	
		Type I	Type II
5	78%	42%	4%
4	76%	47%	3%
3	77%	37%	8%
2	79%	34%	8%
1	87%	22%	5%

Source: William Beaver, "Financial Ratios as Predictors of Failure," *Empirical Research in Accounting: Selected Studies, 1966*, supplement to *Journal of Accounting Research* (1966), p. 90.

preceding bankruptcy. The classification accuracy increased as bankruptcy approached, but was close to 80 percent for as early as five years preceding bankruptcy.

The error rates deserve particular attention, however. A Type I error is classifying a firm as nonbankrupt when it ultimately goes bankrupt. A Type II error occurs when a firm is classified as bankrupt and ultimately survives. A Type I error is more costly to an investor because of the likelihood of losing the full amount invested. A Type II error costs the investor the opportunity cost of funds invested. Note in Exhibit 5.5 that the Type I error rates are much higher than the Type II error rates in Beaver's study. In using the net income before depreciation, depletion, and amortization to total liabilities ratio to predict bankruptcy four years prior to bankruptcy, 47 percent of the predictions that firms would be nonbankrupt turned out to be incorrect, whereas only 3 percent of the predictions that firms would be bankrupt turned out to be incorrect.

Univariate analysis helps identify factors related to bankruptcy and is therefore a useful step in the initial development of predictors of bankruptcy risk. However, univariate analysis does not provide a means of measuring the relative importance of individual financial statement ratios or of combining them when assessing risk. For example, does a firm with a high current ratio and a high debt-to-assets ratio have more bankruptcy risk than a firm with a low current ratio and a low debt-to-assets ratio? The analyst must also judge subjectively the level of each financial ratio that signals a high probability of bankruptcy.

Multivariate Bankruptcy Prediction Models Using Multiple Discriminant Analysis

Deficiencies of univariate analysis led researchers during the late 1960s and throughout the 1970s to use multiple discriminant analysis (MDA), a multivariate statistical technique, to develop bankruptcy prediction models. Researchers typically selected a sample of bankrupt firms and matched these firms with healthy firms of approximately the same size and in the same industry. This matching procedure attempts to control for size and industry factors so the researcher can examine the impact of other factors that might explain bankruptcy. The researcher then calculates a large number of financial statement ratios expected a priori to explain bankruptcy. Using these financial ratios as inputs, the

MDA model selects the subset (usually four to six ratios) that best discriminates between bankrupt and nonbankrupt firms. The resulting MDA model includes a set of coefficients that, when multiplied by the particular financial statement ratios and then summed, yields a multivariate score. The researcher then examines the pattern of Type I and Type II errors and chooses a cutoff that distinguishes firms with a high probability of bankruptcy from those with a low probability. Researchers usually develop the MDA model on an estimation sample and then apply the resulting model to a separate holdout, or prediction, sample to check on the general applicability and predictability of the model.

Perhaps the best-known MDA bankruptcy prediction model is Altman's Z-score.[9] Altman used data for manufacturing firms to develop the model. The calculation of the Z-score appears here:

$$\text{Z-score} = 1.2\left[\frac{\text{Net Working Capital}}{\text{Total Assets}}\right] + 1.4\left[\frac{\text{Retained Earnings}}{\text{Total Assets}}\right]$$
$$+ 3.3\left[\frac{\text{Earning before Interest and Taxes}}{\text{Total Assets}}\right] + .6\left[\frac{\text{Market Value of Equity}}{\text{Book Value of Liabilities}}\right]$$
$$+ 1.0\left[\frac{\text{Sales}}{\text{Total Assets}}\right]$$

Each ratio captures a different dimension of profitability or risk:

1. Net Working Capital/Total Assets: The proportion of total assets comprising relatively liquid net current assets (current assets minus current liabilities). This ratio serves as a measure of short-term liquidity risk.
2. Retained Earnings/Total Assets: Accumulated profitability and relative age of a firm.
3. Earnings before Interest and Taxes/Total Assets: A variant of ROA. This ratio measures current profitability.
4. Market Value of Equity/Book Value of Liabilities: This is a form of the debt/equity ratio, but it incorporates the market's assessment of the value of the firm's shareholders' equity. This ratio therefore measures long-term solvency risk and the market's overall assessment of the profitability and risk of the firm.
5. Sales/Total Assets: This ratio is similar to the total assets turnover ratio discussed in Chapter 4 and indicates the ability of a firm to use assets to generate sales.

In applying this model, Altman found that Z-scores of less than 1.81 indicated a high probability of bankruptcy, while Z-scores higher than 3.00 indicated a low probability of bankruptcy. Scores between 1.81 and 3.00 were in the gray area.

We can convert the Z-score into a probability of bankruptcy using the normal density function within Excel.[10] A Z-score of 3.00 translates into a probability of bankruptcy of 2.75 percent. A Z-score of 1.81 translates into a probability of bankruptcy of 20.90 percent. Thus, Z-scores that correspond to probabilities of less than 2.75 percent indicate low probability of bankruptcy, probabilities between 2.75 percent and 20.90 percent are in the gray area, and probabilities above 20.90 percent are in the high probability area.

---

[9]Edward Altman, "Financial Ratios, Discriminant Analysis, and the Prediction of Corporate Bankruptcy," *Journal of Finance* (September 1968), pp. 589–609.

[10]The formula within Excel is: =NORMSDIST(1–Z score). Altman developed his model so that higher positive Z-scores mean lower probability of bankruptcy, so computing the probability of bankruptcy requires that the normal density function be applied to 1 minus the Z-score. The web site for this book (www.thomsonedu.com/accounting/stickney) contains an Excel spreadsheet for computing Altman's Z-score and the probability of bankruptcy. FSAP also computes these values.

One cannot interpret these probabilities levels in the usual way. Altman had to trade off Type I and Type II errors when specifying the cutoff points for low-, gray-area, and high-probability ranges.

Altman obtained 95 percent correct classification accuracy rate one year prior to bankruptcy, with a Type I error rate of 6 percent and a Type II error rate of 3 percent. The correct classification rate two years before bankruptcy was 83 percent, with a Type I error rate of 28 percent and a Type II error rate of 6 percent. As with Beaver's study, the more costly Type I error rate is larger than the Type II error rate.

Exhibit 5.6 shows the calculation of Altman's Z-score for PepsiCo for Year 4. We use the originally reported amounts for PepsiCo instead of the adjusted amounts that eliminate nonrecurring items because Altman developed his model using originally reported amounts. If Altman had adjusted the earnings numbers to eliminate nonrecurring items, the coefficients would likely have been different and the financial ratios with the most discriminating power might also have been different. PepsiCo's Z-score of 6.3545 clearly indicates a low probability of bankruptcy. The probability of bankruptcy is 0.00000001.

The principal strengths of MDA are as follows:

1. It incorporates multiple financial ratios simultaneously.
2. It provides the appropriate coefficients for combining the independent variables.
3. It is easy to apply once the initial model has been developed.

The principal criticisms of MDA are as follows:

1. As in univariate applications, the researcher cannot be sure that the MDA model includes all relevant discriminating financial ratios. Most early studies, for example, used only accrual-basis income statement and balance sheet data and did not augment those data with cash flow data. MDA selects the best ratios from those provided to it, but that set does not necessarily provide the best explanatory power.
2. As in univariate applications, the researcher must judge subjectively the value of the cutoff score that best distinguishes bankrupt from nonbankrupt firms, taking into consideration the levels and costs of Type I and Type II errors.

EXHIBIT 5.6

Altman's Z-Score for PepsiCo

Net Working Capital/Total Assets	
1.2[($8,639 − $6,752)/$27,987]	.0809
Retained Earnings/Total Assets	
1.4[$18,730/$27,987]	.9369
Earnings before Interest and Taxes/Total Assets	
3.3[($4,212 − $38 + $167 + $1,372)/$27,987]	.6736
Market Value of Equity/Book Value of Liabilities	
.6[($51.94 × 1,679)/$14,464]	3.6176
Sales/Total Assets	
1.0[$29,261/$27,987]	1.0455
Z-Score	6.3545

3. The development and application of the MDA model requires firms to disclose the necessary information to compute each financial ratio. Firms excluded because they do not provide the necessary data may bias the MDA model.
4. MDA assumes that each of the financial ratios for bankrupt and nonbankrupt firms is normally distributed. Firms experiencing financial distress often display unusually large or small ratios that can skew the distribution away from normal. In addition, the researcher cannot include dummy variables (for example, 0 if financial statements are audited, 1 if they are not audited). Dummy variables are not normally distributed.
5. MDA requires that the variance-covariance matrix of the explanatory variables be the same for bankrupt and nonbankrupt firms.[11]

Multivariate Bankruptcy Prediction Models Using Logit Analysis

A third stage in the methodological development of bankruptcy prediction research was the move during the 1980s and early 1990s to using logit analysis instead of MDA. Logit does not require that the data display the underlying statistical properties described previously for MDA.

The use of logit analysis to develop a bankruptcy prediction model follows a similar procedure to MDA: (1) initial calculation of a large set of financial ratios, (2) reduction of the set of financial ratios to a subset that best discriminates bankrupt and nonbankrupt firms, and (3) estimation of coefficients for each included variable.

The logit model defines the probability of bankruptcy as follows:

$$\text{Probability of Bankruptcy for a Firm} = \frac{1}{1 + e^{-y}}$$

where e equals approximately 2.718282. The exponent y is a multivariate function that includes a constant and coefficients for a set of explanatory variables (that is, financial statement ratios).

Ohlson[12] and Zavgren[13] used logit analysis to develop bankruptcy prediction models. Their models use different financial statement ratios than Altman's model and are somewhat more complex to apply. We do not discuss their models in depth here, but interested readers can consult the research cited. Despite the shortcomings of discriminant models, Altman's Z-score model is still the most widely referenced and the one we emphasize in this chapter.

Application of Altman's Bankruptcy Prediction Model to W. T. Grant Company

W. T. Grant Company (Grant), one of the largest retailers in the United States at the time, filed for bankruptcy in October 1975. Case 3.3 in Chapter 3 includes financial statement data for Grant for its fiscal years ended January 31, 1968 through 1975. Exhibit 5.7 shows the calculation of Altman's Z-score for each of these fiscal years using amounts from Exhibits 3.30 and 3.31 of Case 3.3.[14]

---

[11] For an elaboration of these criticisms, see James A. Ohlson, "Financial Ratios and the Probabilistic Prediction of Bankruptcy," *Journal of Accounting Research* (Spring 1980), pp. 109–131, and Mark E. Zmijewski, "Methodological Issues Related to the Estimation of Financial Distress Prediction Models," *Journal of Accounting Research-Supplement* (1984), pp. 59–82.

[12] Ohlson, op. cit.

[13] Christine V. Zavgren, "Assessing the Vulnerability to Failure of American Industrial Firms: A Logistic Analysis," *Journal of Business Finance and Accounting* (Spring 1985), pp. 19–45.

[14] FSAP includes Altman's Z-score and the corresponding probability of bankruptcy.

Altman's model shows a low probability of bankruptcy prior to the 1973 fiscal year, a move into the gray area in 1973 and 1974, and a high probability of bankruptcy in 1975. The absolute levels of these Z-scores are inflated because Grant is a retailer, whereas Altman developed the model using manufacturing firms. Retailing firms typically have a faster assets turnover than manufacturing firms. In this case, the trend of the Z-score is more meaningful than its absolute level. Note that the Z-score declined steadily beginning in the 1970 fiscal year. With a few exceptions in individual years, each of the five components also declined steadily.[15]

Other Methodological Issues in Bankruptcy Prediction Research

Bankruptcy prediction research has addressed several other methodological issues.

1. **Equal Sample Sizes of Bankrupt and Nonbankrupt Firms.** The proportion of bankrupt firms in the economy is substantially smaller than the proportion of nonbankrupt firms. The matched-pairs research design common in most studies results in overfitting the MDA and logit models toward the characteristics of bankrupt firms. This overfitting is not necessarily a problem if the objective is to identify characteristics of bankrupt firms. However, it will likely result in classifying too many nonbankrupt firms as bankrupt (a Type II error) when the model is applied to the broader population of firms. Researchers (such as Ohlson in the study cited previously) have addressed this criticism by using a proportion of nonbankrupt firms that more closely reflects the population of firms.
2. **Matching Bankrupt and Nonbankrupt Firms on Size and Industry Characteristics.** This matching precludes consideration of either of these factors as possible explanatory variables for bankruptcy. Yet small firms may experience greater difficulty obtaining funds when needed than larger firms. Industry membership, particularly for cyclical industries, may be an important factor explaining bankruptcy. Some researchers select a random sample of nonbankrupt firms. Another approach is to develop the MDA or logit models for each industry. Platt,[16] for example, developed models for sixteen two-digit SIC industries. The explanatory variables and their coefficients varied across the various industries. Platt and Platt[17] normalized the financial ratios of each firm by relating them to the corresponding average industry ratio of the firm's industry. They found that normalized financial ratios increased the classification accuracy of their sample to 90 percent, versus 78 percent based on a model of non-normalized ratios.
3. **Use of Accrual versus Cash Flow Variables.** Until the mid-1980s, most bankruptcy research used accrual-basis balance sheet and income statement ratios or ratios from the "funds flow" statement, which defined funds as working capital. The transition to a cash definition of funds in the statement of cash flows led researchers to add cash flow variables to bankruptcy prediction models. Casey and Bartczak,[18] among others, found that adding cash flow from operations/current liabilities and cash flow from operations/total liabilities did not significantly add

[15]The solution to the Grant case indicates that, prior to its 1975 fiscal year, Grant failed to provide adequately for uncollectible accounts. The effect of this action was to overstate the net working capital/assets, retained earnings/assets, and EBIT/assets components of the Z-score; understate the sales/assets component; and probably overstate the overall Z-score.

[16]Harlan D. Platt, "The Determinants of Interindustry Failure," *Journal of Economics and Business* (1989), pp. 107–126.

[17]Harlan D. Platt and Marjorie B. Platt, "Development of a Class of Stable Predictive Variables: The Case of Bankruptcy Prediction," *Journal of Business, Finance, and Accounting* (Spring 1990), pp. 31–51.

[18]Casey and Bartczak, op. cit.

EXHIBIT 5.7

Application of Altman's Bankruptcy Prediction Models to W. T. Grant

Fiscal Year:	1968	1969
Altman's Z-Score Model		
Net Working Capital/Assets	.54353	.51341
Retained Earnings/Assets	.43738	.42669
EBIT/Assets	.41358	.44611
Market Value Equity/Book Value Liabilities	.86643	1.01740
Sales/Assets	1.77564	1.76199
Z-Score	4.03656	4.16560
Probability of Bankruptcy Range	Low	Low
Probability of Bankruptcy	.12%	.07%

explanatory power to models based on accrual basis amounts. Other researchers have found contrary results.[19]

4. **Stability in Bankruptcy Prediction Models over Time.** A final methodological issue in bankruptcy prediction research concerns the stability of the bankruptcy prediction models over time, with regard to both the explanatory variables included and their coefficients. Bankruptcy laws and their judicial interpretation change over time. The frequency of bankruptcy filings changes as economic conditions change. New financing vehicles emerge (for example, redeemable preferred stock or debt and equity securities with various option rights) that previous MDA or logit models did not consider in their formulation. To apply these models in practical settings, the analyst should periodically update them.

Begley, Ming, and Watts[20] applied Altman's MDA model and Ohlson's logit model to a sample of bankrupt and nonbankrupt firms in the 1980s, a later period than those used by Altman and Ohlson. They found that the Type I and Type II error rates increased substantially relative to those in the original studies. They then re-estimated the coefficients for each model using data for a portion of their 1980s sample. The coefficients on the liquidity ratios increased and the coefficients on the debt ratio decreased relative to those in the original studies. When they applied the original and re-estimated coefficients to the 1980s sample, they observed a reduction in Type II errors but no improvement in Type I errors for the Altman model. For the Ohlson model, they found that a reduction in Type II errors was offset by an equal increase in Type I errors. Thus, the revised coefficients result in fewer errors in classifying nonbankrupt firms as bankrupt, but similar or worse errors occur in classifying bankrupt firms as nonbankrupt.

---

[19]For a summary of this research, see M. F. Gombola, M. E. Haskins, J. E. Ketz, and D. D. Williams, "Cash Flow in Bankruptcy Prediction," *Financial Management* (Winter 1987), pp. 55–65.

[20]Joy Begley, Jin Ming, and Susan Watts, "Bankruptcy Classification Errors in the 1980s: An Empirical Analysis of Altman's and Ohlson's Models," *Review of Accounting Studies* 1, no. 4 (1996), pp. 267–284.

EXHIBIT 5.7

continued

1970	1971	1972	1973	1974	1975
.44430	.37791	.44814	.36508	.38524	.19390
.41929	.38511	.34513	.31023	.25712	.04873
.44228	.38848	.27820	.26029	.25470	−.63644
.95543	.89539	.69788	.50578	.10211	.01730
1.71325	1.67974	1.57005	1.58678	1.54797	1.62802
3.97455	3.72663	3.33940	3.02816	2.54714	1.25151
Low	Low	Low	Gray	Gray	High
.15%	.32%	.97%	2.13%	6.09%	40.07%

Synthesis of Bankruptcy Prediction Research

The preceding sections of this chapter discussed bankruptcy prediction models. Similar streams of research relate to commercial bank lending,[21] bond ratings,[22] corporate restructurings,[23] corporate liquidations,[24] and earnings management.[25] Although the statistical models used and the relevant financial statement ratios vary across the numerous studies, certain commonalities appear as well. This section attempts to summarize the factors that seem to explain bankruptcy most consistently across various studies.

Investment Factors

Two factors relate to the asset side of the balance sheet:

1. Relative Liquidity of a Firm's Assets. The probability of financial distress decreases as the relative liquidity of a firm's assets increases. Firms with relatively large proportions of current assets tend to experience less financial distress than firms with fixed assets or intangible assets as the dominant assets. Greater asset liquidity means that the firm either has or will soon generate the necessary cash to meet creditors' claims. It is of interest to note that the expected return from more liquid assets, such as cash, marketable securities, and accounts receivable, is usually less (reflecting lower risk) than the expected return from fixed and intangible assets. Thus, firms must balance their mix of assets to obtain the desired return/risk profile. Researchers typically use the following ratios to measure relative liquidity—cash/total assets, current assets/total assets, and net working capital/total assets; they use fixed assets/total assets to measure relative illiquidity.

---

[21]Edward Altman, *Corporate Financial Distress and Bankruptcy,* 2nd ed., (New York: John Wiley & Sons, 1993), pp. 245–266.

[22]G. E. Pinches and K. A. Mingo, "A Multivariate Analysis of Industrial Bond Ratings," *Journal of Finance* (March 1973), pp. 1–18.

[23]James E. Seward, "Corporate Restructuring and Reorganization," in *Handbook of Modern Finance,* ed. Dennis Logue, (New York: Warren, Gorham & Lamont, 1993), pp. E8–1 to E8–36.

[24]Cornelius J. Casey, Victor McGee, and Clyde P. Stickney, "Discriminating between Reorganized and Liquidated Firms in Bankruptcy," *Accounting Review* (April 1986), pp. 249–262.

[25]Messod D. Beneish, "Detecting GAAP Violation: Implications for Assessing Earnings Management among Firms with Extreme Financial Performance," *Journal of Accounting and Public Policy* (1997), pp. 271–309.

2. Rate of Asset Turnover. The returns from investment of funds in any asset are ultimately realized in cash. Firms acquire fixed assets or create intangibles to produce a salable product (inventory) or create a desired service. Goods or services are often sold on account (accounts receivable) and later collected in cash. The faster assets turn over, the more quickly funds work their way toward cash on the balance sheet. Thus, a retailer may have the same proportion of fixed assets to total assets as a manufacturing firm. The other assets of the retailer (that is, accounts receivable and inventories) likely turn over more quickly and are thus more liquid. Commonly used financial ratios for this factor are total assets turnover, accounts receivable turnover, and inventory turnover. The working capital turnover ratio [= sales/(current assets minus current liabilities)] and fixed asset turnover ratios have not generally showed statistical significance in studies of financial distress.

Financing Factors

Two factors relate to the liability side of the balance sheet:

1. Relative Proportion of Debt in the Capital Structure. Firms experience bankruptcy because they are unable to pay liabilities as they come due. The higher the proportion of liabilities in the capital structure, the higher the probability that firms will experience bankruptcy. Firms with lower proportions of debt tend to have unused borrowing capacity that they can use in times of difficulty. Some measure of the proportion of debt in the capital structure appears in virtually all bankruptcy prediction models. Commonly used ratios include total liabilities/total assets and total liabilities/shareholders' equity.

2. Relative Proportion of Short-Term Debt in the Capital Structure. This factor has a similar rationale to that described previously except that the earlier maturity of short-term debt increases the risk of bankruptcy. Thus, considering only the financing side of the balance sheet, a retailer using extensive short-term bank and creditor financing will likely have greater risk of bankruptcy than a manufacturer with a similar proportion of total liabilities but whose liabilities are primarily long-term debt. A commonly used ratio for this factor is current liabilities/total assets.

Operating Factors

Two factors relate to the operating activities of a firm:

1. Relative Level of Profitability. Profitable firms ultimately turn their earnings into cash. Profitable firms are also usually able to borrow funds more easily than unprofitable firms. Firms with low or negative profitability must often rely on available cash or additional borrowing to meet financial commitments as they come due. Research has demonstrated that most bankruptcies initiate with one or several years of poor operating performance. Firms with unused debt capacity can often borrow for a year or two until the operating difficulties reverse. A combination of weak profitability and high debt ratios usually spells "financial distress." Commonly used financial ratios for profitability are net income/assets, income before interest and taxes/assets, net income/sales, and cash flow from operations/assets. The second profitability measure identifies profitability problems in the core input/output markets of a firm before considering debt service costs and income taxes. The third measure appears in bankruptcy distress prediction models because profit margin, rather than assets turnover, is usually the driving force behind return on assets. The fourth measure substitutes cash flow from operations for net income in measuring profitability on the premise that cash pays the bills, not earnings.

2. Variability of Operations. Firms that experience variability in their operations, such as from cyclical sales patterns, exhibit a greater likelihood of bankruptcy than do firms with low variability. During the down times in the cycle, such firms must obtain financing to meet financial commitments and maintain operating levels. The risk of bankruptcy in these cases relates to the unknown length of the down portion of the cycle. For how many years can a firm hold on until the cycle reverses? Researchers typically use the change in sales or the change in net income from the previous year to measure variability, although a longer period would seem more reasonable.

Other Possible Explanatory Variables

Three other factors examined in bankruptcy research warrant discussion.

1. Size. Studies of bankruptcy, particularly since the early 1980s, have increasingly identified size as an important explanatory variable. Larger firms generally have access to a wider range of financing sources and more flexibility to redeploy assets than smaller firms. Larger firms therefore experience a lower probability of bankruptcy than smaller firms. Most studies measure size using total assets.

2. Growth. Studies of bankruptcy often include some measure of growth (for example, growth in sales, assets, or net income) as a possible explanatory variable. The statistical significance of growth as an independent variable has varied considerably across studies. It is therefore difficult to conclude much about its relative importance. The mixed results may relate in part to ambiguity as to how growth relates to bankruptcy. Rapidly growing firms often need external financing to cover cash shortfalls from operations and permit acquisitions of fixed assets. These firms often display financial ratios typical of a firm in financial difficulty (that is, high debt ratios and weak profitability). Yet their growth potential provides access to capital that permits them to survive. Firms in the late maturity or early decline phase of their life cycles may display healthy financial ratios but prospects are sufficiently poor that the probability of future financial difficulty is high.

3. Qualified Audit Opinion. Several studies have examined the information value of a qualified audit opinion in predicting bankruptcy. Hopwood, McKeown, and Mutchler compared the predictive accuracy of a qualified audit opinion versus models that include only financial ratios in predicting bankruptcy.[26] They found that the qualified audit opinion had similar predictive accuracy to that of the models based on financial ratios. This result is not surprising if auditors use bankruptcy prediction models in deciding whether to issue a qualified opinion. Chen and Church found that the negative stock price reaction at the time of a bankruptcy filing was less for firms that had previously had a qualified audit opinion than firms that had only clean audit opinions, suggesting that the audit opinion had information content.[27]

Some Final Thoughts

Bankruptcy prediction research represents an effort to integrate traditional financial statement analysis with statistical modeling. This area of research evolved between the mid-1960s and mid-1980s from relatively simple univariate models to multivariate models. Despite the importance of predicting bankruptcy, this area of research has provided few new insights since the mid-1980s. The models developed by Altman, Ohlson, and Zavgren rely on data that are decades old and based on business activities and bankruptcy laws that differ from those currently encountered. Yet the models continue to be used by security analysts and academic researchers.[28]

---

[26]William Hopwood, James C. McKeown, and Jane F. Mutchler, "A Reexamination of Auditor versus Model Accuracy within the Context of the Going-Concern Opinion Decision," *Contemporary Accounting Research* (Spring 1994), pp. 409–431.

[27]Kevin C. W. Chen and Bryan K. Church, "Going Concern Opinions and the Market's Reaction to Bankruptcy Filings," *Accounting Review* (January 1996), pp. 117–128.

[28]A recent study models bankruptcy prediction as an option pricing valuation using market values. The authors compare the prediction accuracy of this market-based model with the Altman and Ohlson models and find that their model has better prediction accuracy. However, using either the Altman or Ohlson model in addition to the option pricing model adds to the prediction accuracy. See Stephen A. Hillegeist, Donald P. Cram, Elizabeth K. Keating, and Kyle G. Lundstedt, "Assessing the Probability of Bankruptcy," *Review of Accounting Studies* (March 2004), pp. 5–34.

MARKET EQUITY BETA RISK

Firms face additional risks besides credit and bankruptcy risk. Recessions, inflation, changes in interest rates, rising unemployment, and similar economic factors affect all firms but in varying degrees, depending on the nature of their operations. The investor in a firm's common stock must consider these dimensions of risk when making investment decisions. Economic theory teaches that differences in expected rates of return between investment alternatives should relate to differences in risk. Thus, we can turn to equity markets to obtain a broader measure of risk. We will then relate this market measure of risk to financial statement information.

Studies of market rates of return have traditionally used the capital asset pricing model (CAPM). The research typically regresses the rate of returns on a particular firm's common shares [dividends plus (minus) capital gains (losses)/beginning of period share price] over some period of time on the excess of the returns of all common stocks over the risk-free rate. The regression takes the following form:

$$\begin{array}{c}\text{Returns on Common Stock}\\\text{of a Particular Firm}\end{array} = \begin{array}{c}\text{Risk-Free}\\\text{Interest Rate}\end{array} + \begin{array}{c}\text{Market}\\\text{Beta}\end{array}\left[\begin{array}{c}\text{Market}\\\text{Return}\end{array} - \begin{array}{c}\text{Risk-Free}\\\text{Interest Rate}\end{array}\right]$$

The beta coefficient measures the covariability of a firm's returns with the returns of a diversified portfolio of all shares traded on the market (in excess of the risk-free interest rate). Firms with a market beta of 1.0 experience covariability in returns equal to the average covariability of the stock market as a whole. Firms with a beta greater than 1.0 experience greater covariability than the average. Firms with a beta less than 1.0 experience less covariability than the average firm. A beta of 1.20 suggests 20 percent greater covariability. A beta of .80 suggests 20 percent less covariability.

Beta is a measure of the *systematic* (or *nondiversifiable*) *risk* of the firm. The market, through the pricing of a firm's shares, rewards shareholders for bearing systematic risk. Elements of risk that do not contribute to systematic risk are referred to as nonsystematic risk. By constructing a diversified portfolio of securities, the investor can eliminate the effects of nonsystematic risk on the returns to the portfolio as a whole. Thus, market pricing should provide no returns for the assumption of nonsystematic risk.

Studies of the determinants of market beta have identified three principal explanatory variables:[29]

1. Degree of operating leverage.
2. Degree of financial leverage.
3. Variability of sales.

Each of these factors causes the earnings of a particular firm to vary over time.

Operating leverage refers to the extent of fixed operating costs in the cost structure. Costs such as depreciation and amortization do not vary with the level of sales. Other costs, such as insurance and executive and administrative salaries and benefits, may vary somewhat with the level of sales but remain relatively fixed for any particular period. The presence of fixed operating costs leads to variations in operating earnings as sales increase and decrease. Likewise, the presence of debt in the capital structure adds a fixed cost for interest and creates the potential for causing earnings to increase or decrease as sales vary.

---

[29]Robert S. Hamada, "The Effect of a Firm's Capital Structure on the Systematic Risk of Common Stocks," *Journal of Finance* (May 1972), pp. 435–452; Barr Rosenberg and Walt McKibben, "The Prediction of Systematic and Specific Risk in Common Stocks," *Journal of Financial and Quantitative Analysis* (March 1973), pp. 317–333; James M. Gahlon and James A. Gentry, "On the Relationship between Systematic Risk and Degrees of Operating and Financial Leverage," *Financial Management* (Summer 1982), pp. 15–23.

The presence of these fixed costs does not necessarily lead to earnings fluctuations over time. A firm with stable or growing sales may be able to adjust the level of fixed assets and related financing (for example, through leasing) to the level of sales, in effect converting fixed costs into variable costs. Firms such as electric utilities with high fixed costs from operating and financial leverage have historically had a regulated form of monopoly power to price their services to cover costs regardless of demand. Such firms likewise have not experienced wide variations in earnings. Operating and financial leverage create variations in earnings when sales vary and firms cannot alter their level of fixed costs. Thus, we would expect capital-intensive firms in cyclical industries to experience wide variations in earnings over the business cycle.

Research has shown a link between changes in earnings and changes in stock prices.[30] Thus, operating leverage, financial leverage, and variability of sales should result in fluctuations in the market returns for a particular firm's common shares. The average returns for all firms in the market should reflect the average level of operating leverage, financial leverage, and sales variability of these firms. Therefore, the market beta for a particular firm reflects its degree of variability relative to the average firm. Chapters 11 and 14 discuss the relation between financial statement information and market beta more fully and the use of market beta in the valuation of firms.

FINANCIAL REPORTING MANIPULATION RISK

Enron, WorldCom, Global Crossing, Sunbeam, AIG, Fannie Mae, and others have been the subject of SEC investigations and negative media coverage in recent years for allegedly preparing financial statements outside the limits of GAAP in an effort to portray the firm in a more favorable light than is appropriate. Analysts cannot rely on intentionally misleading financial statements when assessing profitability and risk. This section explores the characteristics of firms accused of falsifying their financial statements and describes tools for assessing this type of risk.

At the outset, we need to recognize the distinction between earnings manipulation and earnings management. *Earnings manipulation* refers to reporting amounts outside the limits of GAAP and is the subject of this section. *Earnings management* refers to choices made within the limits of GAAP and is a topic discussed in Chapter 6. Regulations of the SEC and rules of various stock exchanges require the preparation of financial reports according to, or within the bounds of, GAAP. Thus, firms that intentionally report outside the limits of GAAP in an effort to mislead financial statement users are potentially subject to legal and regulatory actions for fraudulent reporting.

Motivations for Earnings Manipulation

Reasons that a firm might manipulate earnings include the following:

1. Obtain debt financing at a lower cost by appearing more profitable or less risky.
2. Positively influence stock prices, or delay inevitable stock price declines, by meeting or beating the market's expectations for earnings.
3. Increase management bonuses that are based on earnings or stock prices.
4. Avoid violation of debt covenants, or influence the effects of other binding constraints from accounting-based contracts.

---

[30]Ray Ball and Philip Brown, "An Empirical Evaluation of Accounting Income Numbers," *Journal of Accounting Research* (Autumn 1968), pp. 159–178.

5. Influence the outcomes of transactions that affect corporate control, such as proxy fights, takeovers, initial public offerings, seasoned equity offerings, or share repurchases.
6. Avoid regulatory intervention or adverse political consequences.

Empirical Research on Earnings Manipulation

Dechow, Sloan, and Sweeney[31] examined the governance characteristics of firms subject to accounting and auditing enforcement actions by the SEC. They found that such firms have weak corporate governance structures, including the absence of an audit committee within their board of directors, the appointment of the founder of the company as the chief executive officer (CEO), the appointment of the CEO as the chairperson of the board, and the domination of the board by insiders (employees, consultants, or individuals otherwise closely associated with the firm). The SEC enforcement action led to a 9 percent reduction in stock price on average, an increase in the bid-ask spread, less analyst consensus on earnings forecasts, and increased short interest, each of which likely increases the firm's cost of capital.

Beneish developed a probit model to identify the financial characteristics of firms likely to engage in earnings manipulation. Beneish developed both a twelve-factor model[32] and an eight-factor model.[33] The twelve-factor model relies on a combination of financial statement items and changes in stock prices for a firm's shares. The eight-factor model uses only financial statement items. Beneish developed the models using data for firms subject to SEC enforcement actions.

Developing these models involves identifying characteristics of firms likely to manipulate earnings, selecting financial statement ratios or other measures of these characteristics, and then using probit regressions to select the significant factors and the appropriate coefficient for each factor (similar to the MDA and logit approaches for identifying predictors of bankruptcy, described earlier in this chapter). Applying the coefficient to the value of each factor for a particular firm yields a score that becomes the value of y.

Unlike logit models, which convert the value of y into a probability based on a logistical distribution using $\frac{1}{1 + e^{-y}}$, probit converts y into a probability using a standardized normal distribution and a specified prior probability of earnings manipulation. The command NORMSDIST within Excel, when applied to a particular value of y, converts it to the appropriate probability value.[34] Positive coefficients increase the probability of earnings manipulation.

Beneish's eight factors and the rationale for their inclusion are as follows:

1. Days Sales in Receivables Index (DSRI). This index relates the ratio of accounts receivable at the end of the current year as a percentage of sales for the current year to

---

[31]Patricia M. Dechow, Richard G. Sloan, and Amy P. Sweeney, "Causes and Consequences of Earnings Manipulation: An Analysis of Firms Subject to Enforcement Actions by the SEC," *Contemporary Accounting Research* (Spring 1996), pp. 1–36.

[32]Beneish, op. cit. For an instructional case applying this model to an actual company, see Christine I. Wiedman, "Instructional Case: Detecting Earnings Manipulation," *Issues in Accounting Education* (February 1999), pp. 145–176. Also see Messod D. Beneish, "A Note on Wiedman's (1999) Instructional Case: Detecting Earnings Manipulation," *Issues in Accounting Education* (May 1999), pp. 369–370.

[33]Messod D. Beneish, "The Detection of Earnings Manipulation," *Financial Analyst Journal* (September/October 1999), pp. 24–36.

[34]In contrast to Altman's Z-score model, Beneish set up his model so that larger positive values increase the probability of earnings manipulation. Thus, one can simply apply the normal density function directly to the value of y to compute the probability of earnings manipulation.

the corresponding amounts for the preceding year. A large increase in accounts receivable as a percentage of sales might indicate an overstatement of accounts receivable and sales during the current year to boost earnings. Such an increase might also result from a change in the firm's credit policy (for example, liberalizing credit terms).

2. Gross Margin Index (GMI). This index relates gross margin (that is, sales minus cost of goods sold) as a percentage of sales last year to the gross margin as a percentage of sales for the current year. A decline in the gross margin percentage will result in an index greater than 1.0. Firms with weaker profitability this year are more likely to engage in earnings manipulation.

3. Asset Quality Index (AQI). Asset quality refers to the proportion of total assets comprising assets other than (1) current assets, (2) property, plant, and equipment, and (3) investments in securities. The remaining assets include intangibles for which future benefits are less certain than for current assets and property, plant, and equipment. The asset quality index equals the proportion of these lower-quality assets during the current year relative to the preceding year. An increase in the proportion suggests an increased effort to capitalize and defer costs that the firm should have expensed.

4. Sales Growth Index (SGI). This index equals sales of the current year relative to sales of the preceding year. Growth does not necessarily imply manipulation. Growing companies, however, usually rely on external financing more than mature companies. The need for low-cost external financing might motivate managers to manipulate sales and earnings. Young, growing companies also often have less developed governance practices to monitor managers' manipulation efforts.

5. Depreciation Index (DEPI). This index equals depreciation expense as a percentage of net property, plant, and equipment before depreciation for the preceding year relative to the corresponding percentage for the current year. A ratio greater than 1.0 indicates that the firm has slowed the rate of depreciation, perhaps by lengthening depreciable lives, and thereby increased earnings.

6. Selling and Administrative Expense Index (SAI). This index equals selling and administrative expenses as a percentage of sales for the current year to the corresponding percentage for the preceding year. An index greater than 1.0 might suggest increased marketing expenditures that would lead to increased sales in future periods. Firms not able to sustain the sales growth would then more likely engage in earnings manipulation. An alternative interpretation is that an index greater than 1.0 suggests that the firm has not taken advantage of capitalizing various costs but instead has expensed them. Firms attempting to manipulate earnings would defer costs and the index value would be less than 1.0. If this latter explanation is descriptive, then the coefficient on this variable will be negative.

7. Leverage Index (LVGI). This index equals the proportion of total financing comprising current liabilities and long-term debt for the current year relative to the proportion for the preceding year. An increase in the proportion of debt likely subjects a firm to a greater risk of violating debt covenants and the need to manipulate earnings to avoid the violation.

8. Total Accruals to Total Assets (TATA). Total accruals equals the difference between income from continuing operations and cash flow from operations. Dividing total accruals by total assets at the end of the year scales total accruals across firms and across time. Beneish used this variable as an indicator of the extent to which earnings result from accruals instead of from cash flows. A large excess of income from continuing operations over cash flow from operations indicates that accruals play a large part in measuring income. Accruals can serve as a means of manipulating earnings.

Beneish developed both a weighted probit model that takes the proportion of earnings manipulations into account and an unweighted probit model. We illustrate the unweighted model in this section. The unweighted model tends to classify more nonmanipulating firms as manipulators (higher Type II error), but lowers the most costly Type I error rate. The value of y is as follows:

$$y = -4.840 + .920\,(\text{DRRI}) + .528\,(\text{GMI}) + .404\,(\text{AQI}) + .892\,(\text{SGI}) + .115\,(\text{DEPI}) - .172\,(\text{SAI}) - .327\,(\text{LVGI}) + 4.670\,(\text{TATA})$$

The coefficient on SAI is negative, suggesting that a lower selling and administrative expense to sales percentage in the current year relative to the preceding year increases the likelihood that the firm engaged in earnings manipulation to boost earnings. The coefficient on the leverage variable is also negative. A decrease in the proportion of debt in the capital structure may suggest decreased ability to obtain funds from borrowing and the need to engage in earnings manipulation to portray a healthier firm. The coefficients on the SAI and LVGI variables were not statistically significant. However, one cannot interpret the sign or statistical significance of a coefficient in a multivariate model independent of the other variables in the model.

Application of Beneish's Model to Sunbeam Corporation

We illustrate the application of Beneish's probit model to the financial statements of Sunbeam Corporation (Sunbeam). Sunbeam manufactures countertop kitchen appliances and barbecue grills. Its sales growth and profitability slowed considerably in the mid-1990s and the firm experienced market price declines for its common stock. The firm hired Al Dunlap in mid-1996 as CEO. Known as "Chainsaw Al," he had developed a reputation for dispassionately cutting costs and strategically redirecting troubled companies. Dunlap laid off half of the workforce, closed or consolidated more than half of Sunbeam's factories, and divested several businesses in 1996 and 1997. He also announced major growth initiatives centering on new products and corporate acquisitions.

The reported results for 1997 showed significant improvement over 1996. Sales increased 18.7 percent while gross margin increased to 28.3 percent from 8.5 percent. The stock price more than doubled between the announcement of Dunlap's hiring in mid-1996 and the end of 1997.

The turnaround appeared to proceed according to plan until the firm announced earnings for the first quarter of 1998, seven quarters into the turnaround effort. To the surprise of analysts and the stock market, Sunbeam reported a net loss for the quarter. Close scrutiny by analysts and the media suggested that Sunbeam might have manipulated earnings in 1997. The SEC instituted a formal investigation into this possibility in mid-1997. Sunbeam responded in October 1998 by restating its financial statements from the fourth quarter of 1996 to the first quarter of 1998. The restatements revealed that Sunbeam had engaged in various actions that boosted earnings for 1997. The actions included the following:

1. Sunbeam instituted "early buy" and "bill and hold" programs in 1997 to encourage retailers to purchase inventory from Sunbeam during the last few months of 1997. Sunbeam did not adequately provide for returns and cancelled transactions, resulting in an overstatement of sales and net income for 1997.
2. Sunbeam overstated a restructuring charge in the fourth quarter of 1996 for expenses that should have appeared in the income statement for 1997.
3. Sunbeam understated bad debt expense for 1997.

EXHIBIT 5.8

Application of Beneish's Earnings Manipulation Model to Sunbeam Corporation

	Originally Reported		Restated	
Value of Variable before Applying Coefficient	**1996**	**1997**	**1996**	**1997**
Days in Receivables Index	1.020	1.167	1.020	.982
Gross Margin Index	2.403	.300	2.303	.393
Asset Quality Index	.912	.928	.912	.919
Sales Growth Index	.968	1.187	.968	1.090
Depreciation Index	.752	1.284	.752	1.290
Selling and Administrative Expense Index	1.608	.516	1.665	.632
Leverage Index	1.457	.795	1.457	.917
Total Accruals/Total Assets	−.196	.117	−.208	.055
Beneish's Manipulation *y* Value	−2.983	−1.827	−3.101	−2.388
Probability of Manipulation	.143%	3.386%	.096%	.848%

Note: The amounts in this table are rounded to three decimal places.

Exhibit 5.8 shows the application of Beneish's earnings manipulation model to the originally reported financial statement amounts and the restated amounts for 1996 and 1997.[35]

Selecting the cutoff probability that signals earnings manipulation involves trade-offs between Type I and Type II errors, in a similar manner to that of Beaver's bankruptcy prediction tests discussed earlier. A Type I error involves failing to identify a firm as an income manipulator when it turns out to be one. A Type II error involves identifying a firm as an income manipulator when it turns out not to be one. The Type I error is more costly to the investor than a Type II error. The cutoff probability depends on the analyst's view of the relative cost of the Type I error compared to a Type II error. That is, how much more costly is it to classify an actual earnings manipulator as a nonmanipulator than to classify an actual nonmanipulator as a manipulator? A Type I error can result in an investor losing all of the investment in a firm when the manipulation comes to light. Misclassifying an actual nonmanipulator results in the investor losing the return that would have been earned on that investment. The investor, however, presumably invested the funds in another firm. Thus, as with bankruptcy prediction, the Type I error is more costly. If a particular investment makes up a small proportion of an investor's diversified portfolio of investments, then a Type I error is less costly than if the investment comprises a more significant proportion of a less diversified portfolio of investments. The cutoff probabilities for various relative mixtures of Type I and Type II error costs are as follows:

---

[35]The web site for this book (www.thomsonedu.com/accounting/stickney) contains an Excel spreadsheet, called Beneish's Manipulation Index, for use in calculating the probability of earnings manipulation using Beneish's probit model. This spreadsheet is adapted from one prepared by Professor Christine I. Wiedman (see footnote 32). FSAP also computes Beneish's Manipulation Index and the corresponding probability of earnings manipulation.

Cost of Type I Error Relative to Type II Error	Cutoff Probability
10:1	6.85%
20:1	3.76%
30:1	3.76%
40:1 or higher	2.94%

Exhibit 5.8 indicates that the probability of manipulation for Sunbeam for 1996 is .143% based on its originally reported amounts. This probability level falls below the cutoff probabilities listed previously for all mixtures of Type I and Type II errors and therefore does not suggest earnings manipulation. On the other hand, the probability for 1997 of 3.386% (see Exhibit 5.8) suggests that manipulation for Type I error costs forty or more times as much as Type II error costs. An examination of changes in the individual variables between 1996 and 1997 signals the nature of the manipulation that might have occurred. Total accruals to total assets increased significantly. Sunbeam reported a significant increase in income from continuing operations from a net loss of $196.7 million in 1996 to a net profit of $123.1 million 1997, but cash flow from operations turned from $13.3 million in 1996 to a negative $8.2 million in 1997. Buildups of accounts receivable and inventories are the major reasons for the negative cash flow from operations in 1997. The days receivable index increased between these two years, consistent with the buildup of receivables related to the early buy and bill and hold programs. The sales growth index also increased, consistent with the aggressive recognition of revenues. The depreciation index variable increased between the two years, but there is no obvious explanation from the firm's financial statements and notes to suggest manipulation. The gross margin improved significantly between the two years, moderating the increased probability of earnings manipulation. This improvement is misleading, however, because of failure to provide adequately for returns and cancelled transactions.

Exhibit 5.8 indicates that the probabilities of manipulation based on the restated data are below the cutoff points for both 1996 and 1997. The most important difference between the reported and restated probabilities arises for 1997. The downward restatement of income from continuing operations results in fewer accruals, moderating the influence of this variable on the manipulation index. It is interesting to note that the model would not indicate that Sunbeam was an income manipulator if it had reported accurately to begin with (that is, reported the restated data). Initially reporting the restated data, however, would likely have decreased Sunbeam's stock price, which Dunlap tried to avoid.

Summary of Income Manipulation Risk

The recent revelations of corporate reporting abuses add to the importance of assessing whether firms have intentionally manipulated earnings. Academic research on earnings manipulation is at an early stage of development. The data in the studies discussed previously deal with reporting violations prior to the mid-1990s. The business environment since that time has changed dramatically, particularly for technology-based companies. One might expect additional research in this area in coming years.

SUMMARY

An effective analysis of risk requires the analyst to consider a wide range of factors (government regulatory status, technological change, management's health, competitors' actions). This chapter examines those dimensions of risk that have financial consequences and impact the financial statements.

This chapter examined the analysis of financial risk along four dimensions:

1. *With respect to time frame:* First, we examined the analysis of a firm's ability to pay liabilities coming due within the next year (short-term liquidity risk analysis) and its ability to pay liabilities coming due over a longer term (long-term solvency risk analysis). The financial ratios examined a firm's need for cash and other liquid resources relative to amounts coming due within various time frames.
2. *With respect to the degree of financial distress:* We emphasized the need to consider risk as falling along a continuum from low risk to high risk of financial distress. Most credit analysis occurs on the low- to medium-risk side of this continuum. Most bankruptcy risk analysis occurs on the medium- to high-risk side of this continuum.
3. *With respect to covariability of returns with other securities in the market:* We introduced the use of market equity beta as an indicator of systematic risk with the market, a topic discussed more fully in Chapters 11 and 14.
4. *With respect to financial reporting:* We described various motives that induce managers to manipulate and report earnings numbers and other accounting data outside the bounds of GAAP, and illustrated models to estimate the likelihood of financial reporting manipulation.

Analysts and academic researchers refer to the first two dimensions of risk as nonsystematic, or firm-specific, risk. They refer to the third dimension of risk as systematic risk. They sometimes refer to the fourth dimension of risk as *information risk.* Common factors come into play in all four settings for risk analysis. Fixed costs related either to operations or to financing constrain the flexibility of a firm to adapt to changing economic, business, and firm-specific conditions. The profitability and cash-generating ability of a firm permit it to operate within its constraints or to change the constraints in some desirable direction. If the constraints are too high or the capabilities to adapt are too low, then a firm faces the risk of financial distress. Firms facing potential financial distress are more likely to manipulate earnings and accounting information.

Chapter 6 explores a related element of risk, the risk of managing earnings within the bounds of GAAP.

QUESTIONS, EXERCISES, PROBLEMS, AND CASES

Questions and Exercises

5.1 RELATION BETWEEN CURRENT RATIO AND OPERATING CASH FLOW TO CURRENT LIABILITIES RATIO. A firm has experienced an increasing current ratio but a decreasing operating cash flow to current liabilities ratio during the last three years. What is the likely explanation for these results?

5.2 RELATION BETWEEN CURRENT RATIO AND QUICK RATIO. A firm has experienced a decrease in its current ratio but an increase in its quick ratio during the last three years. What is the likely explanation for these results?

5.3 RELATION BETWEEN WORKING CAPITAL TURNOVER RATIOS AND CASH FLOW FROM OPERATIONS. While sales and net income have been steady during the last three years, a firm has experienced a decrease in its accounts receivable and inventory turnovers and an increase in its accounts payable turnover. What is the likely direction of change in cash flow from operations? How would your answer be different if sales and net income were increasing?

5.4 EFFECT OF TRANSACTIONS ON DEBT RATIOS. A firm had the following values for the four debt ratios discussed in the chapter:

Liabilities to Assets Ratio: less than 1.0.
Liabilities to Shareholders' Equity Ratio: equal to 1.0.
Long-Term Debt to Long-Term Capital Ratio: less than 1.0.
Long-Term Debt to Shareholders' Equity Ratio: less than 1.0.

a. Indicate whether each of the following independent transactions increases, decreases, or has no effect on each of the four debt ratios:
(1) The firm issued long-term debt for cash.
(2) The firm issued short-term debt and used the cash proceeds to redeem long-term debt (treat as a unified transaction).
(3) The firm redeemed short-term debt with cash.
(4) The firm issued long-term debt and used the cash proceeds to repurchase shares of its common stock (treat as a unified transaction).

b. The text states that analyst need not compute all four debt ratios each year because the debt ratios are highly correlated. Does your analysis in part a support this statement? Explain.

5.5 INTEREST COVERAGE RATIO AS A MEASURE OF LONG-TERM SOLVENCY RISK. Identify the assumptions underlying the interest coverage ratio needed to make it an appropriate measure for analyzing long-term solvency risk.

5.6 INTEREST COVERAGE RATIO AS A MEASURE OF SHORT-TERM LIQUIDITY RISK. In what sense is the interest coverage ratio more a measure for assessing short-term liquidity risk than it is a measure for assessing long-term solvency risk?

5.7 INTERPRETING OPERATING CASH FLOW TO CURRENT AND TOTAL LIABILITIES RATIOS. Empirical research cited in the text indicates that firms with an operating cash flow to current liabilities ratio exceeding 40 percent portray low short-term liquidity risk. Similarly, firms with an operating cash flow to total liabilities ratio exceeding 20 percent portray low long-term solvency risk. What do these empirical results suggest about the mix of current and noncurrent liabilities for a financially healthy firm? What do they suggest about the mix of liabilities versus shareholders' equity financing?

5.8 INTERPRETING ALTMAN'S Z-SCORE BANKRUPTCY PREDICTION MODEL. Altman's bankruptcy prediction model places a coefficient of 3.3 on the earnings before interest and taxes divided by total assets variable but a coefficient of only 1.0 on the sales to total assets variable. Does this mean that the earnings variable is 3.3 times as important in predicting bankruptcy as the asset turnover variable?

5.9 MARKET EQUITY BETA IN RELATION TO SYSTEMATIC AND NONSYSTEMATIC RISK. Market equity beta measures the covariability of a firm's returns with all shares traded on the market (in excess of the risk-free interest rate). We refer to the degree of covariability as systematic risk. The market prices securities so that the investor is compensated for the systematic risk of a particular stock. Stocks carrying a market equity beta of 1.20 should generate a higher return than stocks carrying a market equity beta of .90. Nonsystematic risk is any source of risk that does not affect the covariability of a firm's returns with the market. Some writers refer to nonsystematic risk as firm-specific risk. Why is the characterization of nonsystematic risk as firm-specific risk a misnomer?

5.10 COMPARISON OF ALTMAN'S BANKRUPTCY PREDICTION MODEL AND BENEISH'S EARNINGS MANIPULATION RISK MODEL. Altman's bankruptcy risk model measures the values of the variables at a particular point in time (balance sheet variables) or for a period of time (income statement values). Beneish's earnings manipulations model for the most part measures changes in variables from one period to the next. Why might the levels of values in Altman's model be more appropriate for bankruptcy prediction and changes in values in Beneish's model be more appropriate for identifying earnings manipulation?

Problems and Cases

5.11 CALCULATING AND INTERPRETING RISK RATIOS. Refer to the financial statement data for Hasbro in Problem 4.19 in Chapter 4. Exhibit 5.9 presents risk ratios for Hasbro for Year 2 and Year 3.

FSAP

EXHIBIT 5.9

Risk Ratios for Hasbro
(Problem 5.11)

	Year 4	Year 3	Year 2
Revenues to Cash Ratio		6.2	7.7
Days Revenues Held in Cash		59	47
Current Ratio		1.6	1.5
Quick Ratio		1.2	1.1
Operating Cash Flow to Average Current Liabilities Ratio		47.9%	54.8%
Days Accounts Receivable		68	73
Days Inventory		51	68
Days Accounts Payable		47	49
Net Days Working Capital		72	91
Liabilities to Assets Ratio		55.6%	62.1%
Liabilities to Shareholders' Equity Ratio		125.1%	163.9%
Long-Term Debt to Long-Term Capital Ratio		32.8%	41.8%
Long-Term Debt to Shareholders' Equity Ratio		48.9%	72.0%
Operating Cash Flow to Total Liabilities Ratio		24.5%	23.8%
Interest Coverage Ratio		5.6	2.3

EXHIBIT 5.10

Risk Ratios for Abercrombie & Fitch (Problem 5.12)

	Year 5	Year 4	Year 3
Revenues to Cash Ratio		34.5	13.8
Days Revenues in Cash		11	26
Current Ratio		2.4	2.3
Quick Ratio		1.7	1.6
Operating Cash Flow to Current Liabilities Ratio		117.7%	158.7%
Days Accounts Receivable		2	4
Days Inventory		72	61
Days Accounts Payable		26	22
Net Days Working Capital		48	43
Liabilities to Assets Ratio		59.1%	59.2%
Liabilities to Shareholders' Equity Ratio		144.3%	144.8%
Long-Term Debt to Long-Term Capital Ratio		45.4%	46.1%
Long-Term Debt to Shareholders' Equity Ratio		83.1%	85.5%
Operating Cash Flow to Total Liabilities Ratio		29.8%	38.0%
Interest Coverage Ratio		7.2	7.6

Required

a. Calculate the amounts of these ratios for Year 4.

b. Assess the changes in the short-term liquidity risk of Hasbro between Year 2 and Year 4 and the level of that risk at the end of Year 4.

c. Assess the changes in the long-term solvency risk of Hasbro between Year 2 and Year 4 and the level of that risk at the end of Year 4.

FSAP

5.12 CALCULATING AND INTERPRETING RISK RATIOS. Refer to the financial statement data for Abercrombie & Fitch in Problem 4.20 in Chapter 4. Exhibit 5.10 presents risk ratios for Abercrombie & Fitch for fiscal Year 3 and Year 4.

Required

a. Compute the amounts of these ratios for fiscal Year 5.

b. Assess the changes in the short-term liquidity risk of Abercrombie & Fitch between fiscal Year 3 and fiscal Year 5 and the level of that risk at the end of fiscal Year 5.

c. Assess the changes in the long-term solvency risk of Abercrombie & Fitch between fiscal Year 3 and fiscal Year 5 and the level of that risk at the end of fiscal Year 5.

EXHIBIT 5.11

Risk Ratios for Coca-Cola
(Problem 5.13)

	Year 4	Year 3	Year 2
Revenues to Cash Ratio	4.4	7.5	9.5
Days Revenues in Cash	84	49	38
Current Ratio	1.1	1.1	1.0
Quick Ratio	.8	.7	.6
Operating Cash Flow to Average Current Liabilities Ratio	63.3%	71.7%	60.1%
Days Accounts Receivable	35	36	37
Days Inventory	64	60	60
Days Accounts Payable	99	94	99
Net Days Working Capital	0	2	(2)
Liabilities to Assets Ratio	49.1%	48.5%	51.7%
Liabilities to Shareholders' Equity Ratio	96.6%	94.1%	106.8%
Long-Term Debt to Long-Term Capital Ratio	6.8%	15.2%	18.6%
Long-Term Debt to Shareholders' Equity Ratio	7.3%	17.9%	22.9%
Operating Cash Flow to Average Total Liabilities Ratio	41.7%	42.2%	40.1%
Interest Coverage Ratio	35.2	35.1	28.6

5.13 INTERPRETING RISK RATIOS. Refer to the profitability ratios of Coca-Cola in Problem 4.21 in Chapter 4. Exhibit 5.11 presents risk ratios for Coca-Cola for Year 2, Year 3, and Year 4.

Required

a. Assess the changes in the short-term liquidity risk of Coca-Cola between Year 2 and Year 4.

b. Assess the changes in the long-term solvency risk of Coca-Cola between Year 2 and Year 4.

c. Compare the short-term liquidity ratios of Coca-Cola with those of PepsiCo discussed in the chapter. Which firm appears to have more short-term liquidity risk? Explain.

d. Compare the long-term solvency ratios of Coca-Cola with those of PepsiCo discussed in the chapter. Which firm appears to have more long-term solvency risk? Explain.

5.14 COMPUTING AND INTERPRETING RISK AND BANKRUPTCY PREDICTION RATIOS. Delta Air Lines is one of the largest airlines in the United States. It has operated on the verge of bankruptcy for several years. Exhibit 5.12 presents selected financial data for Delta Air Lines for each of the five years ending December 31,

EXHIBIT 5.12

Financial Data for Delta Air Lines
(amounts in millions)
(Problem 5.14)

Year Ended December 31:	Year 4	Year 3	Year 2	Year 1	Year 0
Sales	$15,002	$14,087	$13,866	$13,879	$15,657
Net Income (Loss) before Interest and Taxes	$(3,168)	$ (432)	$(1,337)	$(1,365)	$ 1,829
Interest Expense	$ 824	$ 757	$ 665	$ 499	$ 380
Net Income (Loss)	$(5,198)	$ (773)	$(1,272)	$(1,216)	$ 828
Current Assets	$ 3,606	$ 4,550	$ 3,902	$ 3,567	$ 3,205
Total Assets	$21,801	$25,939	$24,720	$23,605	$21,931
Current Liabilities	$ 5,941	$ 6,157	$ 6,455	$ 6,403	$ 5,245
Long-Term Debt	$12,507	$11,040	$ 9,576	$ 7,781	$ 5,797
Total Liabilities	$27,320	$26,323	$23,563	$19,581	$16,354
Retained Earnings (Deficit)	$(4,373)	$ 844	$ 1,639	$ 2,930	$ 4,176
Shareholders' Equity	$(5,519)	$ (384)	$ 1,157	$ 4,024	$ 5,577
Cash Flow Provided by Operations	$(1,123)	$ 142	$ 225	$ 236	$ 2,898
Common Shares Outstanding	139.8	123.5	123.4	123.2	123.0
Market Price per Share	$ 7.48	$ 11.81	$ 12.10	$ 29.26	$50.185

Year 0, to December 31, Year 4. We recommend that you create an Excel spreadsheet to compute the values of the ratios and Altman's Z-score in parts a and b.

Required

a. Compute the value of each the following risk ratios.
 (1) Current Ratio (at the end of Year 0 to Year 4).
 (2) Operating Cash Flow to Current Liabilities Ratio (for Year 1 to Year 4).
 (3) Liabilities to Assets Ratio (at the end of Year 0 to Year 4).
 (4) Long-Term Debt to Long-Term Capital (at the end of Year 0 to Year 4).
 (5) Operating Cash Flow to Total Liabilities Ratio (for Year 1 to Year 4).
 (6) Interest Coverage Ratio (for Year 0 to Year 4).

b. Compute the value of Altman's Z-score for Delta Air Lines for each year from Year 0 to Year 4.

c. Using the analyses in parts a and b, discuss the most important factors that signal the likelihood of bankruptcy of Delta Air Lines in Year 5.

5.15 COMPUTING AND INTERPRETING RISK AND BANKRUPTCY PREDICTION RATIOS. Sun Microsystems develops, manufactures, and sells computers for network systems. Exhibit 5.13 presents selected financial data for Sun Microsystems for each of the five years ending December 31, Year 0, to December 31, Year

EXHIBIT 5.13

Financial Data for Sun Microsystems
(amounts in millions)
(Problem 5.15)

December 31:	Year 4	Year 3	Year 2	Year 1	Year 0
Sales	$11,185	$11,434	$12,496	$18,250	$15,721
Net Income (Loss) before Interest and Taxes	$ 474	$(2,610)	$ (990)	$ 1,684	$ 2,855
Interest Expense	$ 37	$ 43	$ 58	$ 100	$ 84
Net Income (Loss)	$ (388)	$(3,429)	$ (587)	$ 927	$ 1,854
Current Assets	$ 7,303	$ 6,779	$ 7,777	$ 7,934	$ 6,877
Total Assets	$14,503	$12,985	$16,522	$18,181	$14,152
Current Liabilities	$ 5,113	$ 4,129	$ 4,593	$ 5,146	$ 4,546
Long-Term Debt	$ 1,175	$ 1,531	$ 1,449	$ 1,565	$ 1,720
Total Liabilities	$ 8,065	$ 6,494	$ 6,721	$ 7,595	$ 6,843
Retained Earnings	$ 2,481	$ 2,869	$ 6,298	$ 6,885	$ 5,959
Shareholders' Equity	$ 6,438	$ 6,491	$ 9,801	$10,586	$ 7,309
Cash Flow Provided by Operations	$ 2,226	$ 1,037	$ 880	$ 2,089	$ 3,754
Common Shares Outstanding	3,336	3,236	3,234	3,248	3,194
Market Price per Share	$ 4.33	$ 4.65	$ 5.01	$ 15.92	$ 90.94

4. We recommend that you create an Excel spreadsheet to compute the values of the ratios and Altman's Z-score in parts a and b of this question.

Required

a. Compute the value of each of the following risk ratios.
 (1) Current Ratio (at the end of Year 0 to Year 4).
 (2) Operating Cash Flow to Current Liabilities Ratio (for Year 1 to Year 4).
 (3) Liabilities to Assets Ratio (at the end of Year 0 to Year 4).
 (4) Long-Term Debt to Long-Term Capital (at the end of Year 0 to Year 4).
 (5) Operating Cash Flow to Total Liabilities Ratio (for Year 1 to Year 4).
 (6) Interest Coverage Ratio (for Year 0 to Year 4).

b. Compute the value of Altman's Z-score for Sun Microsystems for each year from Year 0 to Year 4.

c. Using the analyses in parts a and b, discuss the most important factors that signal the likelihood of bankruptcy of Sun Microsystems in Year 5.

5.16 COMPUTING AND INTERPRETING BANKRUPTCY PREDICTION RATIOS. Payless Cashways operates a chain of retail stores that offers home improvement products for professional craftspeople (carpenters, plumbers, painters) as well as do-it-yourself homeowners. The firm filed for Chapter 11 bankruptcy protection on July 21, Year 7. Exhibit 5.14 presents selected financial data for Payless Cashways for each of the four fiscal years ending November 30, Year 3, Year 4, Year 5, and Year 6, that

EXHIBIT 5.14

Financial Data for Payless Cashways
(amounts in thousands)
(Problem 5.16)

Year Ended November 30:	Year 6	Year 5	Year 4	Year 3
Sales	$2,642,829	$2,680,186	$2,722,539	$2,601,003
Net Income (Loss) before Interest and Taxes	$ 10,458	$ (60,562)	$ 161,792	$ 151,086
Interest Expense	$ 60,488	$ 61,067	$ 65,571	$ 125,247
Net Income (Loss)	$ (19,078)	$ (128,549)	$ 44,889	$ (36,159)
Current Assets	$ 450,497	$ 442,679	$ 449,870	$ 427,702
Total Assets	$1,293,118	$1,344,436	$1,495,882	$1,458,481
Current Liabilities	$ 319,593	$ 344,279	$ 310,742	$ 345,560
Long-Term Debt	$ 618,667	$ 608,627	$ 654,131	$ 640,127
Total Liabilities	$1,003,387	$1,036,273	$1,060,017	$1,071,170
Retained Earnings	$ (238,997)	$ (219,919)	$ (91,370)	$ (136,259)
Cash Flow Provided by Operations	$ 32,447	$ 108,428	$ 117,330	$ 109,027
Common Shares Outstanding	39,959	39,914	39,874	39,537
Market Price per Share	$ 1.125	$ 3.625	$ 8.25	$ 11.00

preceded its bankruptcy filing. We recommend that you create an Excel spreadsheet to compute the values of the ratios and Altman's Z-score in parts a and b of this question.

Required

a. Compute the value of each the following risk ratios for Year 4, Year 5, and Year 6.
  (1) Current Ratio (at year end).
  (2) Operating Cash Flow to Current Liabilities Ratio.
  (3) Long-Term Debt to Long-Term Capital Ratio (at year end).
  (4) Total Liabilities to Total Assets Ratio (at year end).
  (5) Operating Cash Flow to Total Liabilities Ratio.
  (6) Interest Coverage Ratio.

b. Compute the value of Altman's Z-score for Payless Cashways for Year 3, Year 4, Year 5, and Year 6.

c. Using the analyses in parts a and b, discuss the most important factors that signal the bankruptcy of Payless Cashways in Year 7.

5.17 APPLYING AND INTERPRETING BANKRUPTCY PREDICTION MODELS. Exhibit 5.15 presents selected financial data for Harvard Industries and Marvel Entertainment for fiscal Year 5 and Year 6. Harvard Industries manufactures automobile components that it sells to automobile manufacturers. Competitive conditions in the automobile industry in recent years have led automobile manufacturers to put pressure on suppliers like Harvard Industries to reduce costs and selling prices. Marvel Entertainment creates and sells comic books, trading cards, and other youth entertainment

EXHIBIT 5.15

Financial Data for Harvard Industries and Marvel Entertainment
(amounts in thousands)
(Problem 5.17)

	Harvard Industries		Marvel Entertainment	
	Year 6	Year 5	Year 6	Year 5
Sales	$ 824,835	$ 631,832	$ 745,400	$ 828,900
Net Income (Loss) before Interest and Taxes	$ (11,012)	$ 40,258	$(370,200)	$ 25,100
Net Income (Loss)	$ (68,712)	$ 6,921	$(464,400)	$ (48,400)
Current Assets	$ 156,226	$ 195,417	$ 399,500	$ 490,600
Total Assets	$ 617,705	$ 662,262	$ 844,000	$1,226,310
Current Liabilities	$ 163,384	$ 176,000	$ 345,800	$ 318,100
Total Liabilities	$ 648,934	$ 624,817	$ 999,700	$ 948,100
Retained Earnings	$(184,308)	$(115,596)	$(350,300)	$ 114,100
Common Shares Outstanding	7,014	6,995	101,810	101,703
Market Price per Share	$ 85.00	$ 100.50	$ 1.625	$ 10.625

products, and licenses others to use fictional characters created by Marvel Entertainment in their products. Youth readership of comic books and interest in trading cards have been in steady decline in recent years. Marvel Entertainment recognized a significant asset impairment charge in fiscal Year 6.

Required

a. Compute Altman's Z-score for Harvard Industries and Marvel Entertainment for fiscal Year 5 and Year 6.

b. How did the bankruptcy risk of Harvard Industries change between fiscal Year 5 and Year 6? Explain.

c. How did the bankruptcy risk of Marvel Entertainment change between Year 5 and Year 6? Explain.

d. Which firm do you think is more likely to file for bankruptcy during fiscal Year 7? Explain, using the analyses from part b.

5.18 APPLYING AND INTERPRETING BANKRUPTCY PREDICTION MODELS. Exhibit 5.16 presents selected financial data for Old America Stores and Levitz Furniture for fiscal Year 6 and Year 7. Old America Stores operates a chain of retail stores that sells craft supplies, framing services, artificial flowers and flower-arranging services, baskets, and knickknacks. Levitz Furniture operates a chain of retail stores offering furniture in a warehouse-showroom format. The firm switched to a value pricing strategy beginning in fiscal Year 6.

EXHIBIT 5.16

Financial Data for Old America Stores and Levitz Furniture
(amounts in thousands)
(Problem 5.18)

	Old America Stores Year Ended January:		Levitz Furniture Year Ended March:	
	Year 7	**Year 6**	**Year 7**	**Year 6**
Sales	$134,605	$117,943	$ 965,855	$ 986,622
Net Income (Loss) before Interest and Taxes	$ 7,560	$ 7,986	$ 43,859	$ 42,208
Net Income (Loss)	$ 3,911	$ 4,154	$ (27,586)	$ (23,753)
Current Assets	$ 56,753	$ 48,944	$ 222,859	$ 198,046
Total Assets	$ 87,991	$ 76,059	$ 934,368	$ 606,867
Current Liabilities	$ 19,002	$ 19,779	$ 271,276	$ 217,915
Total Liabilities	$ 36,150	$ 28,323	$1,028,440	$ 674,539
Retained Earnings (Deficit)	$ 9,537	$ 5,627	$ (305,951)	$(278,365)
Common Shares Outstanding	4,515	4,483	30,321	30,321
Market Price Per Share	$ 7.50	$ 8.137	$ 2.125	$ 2.50

Required

a. Compute Altman's Z-score for Old America Stores and Levitz Furniture for fiscal Year 6 and Year 7.

b. How did the bankruptcy risk of Old America Stores change between fiscal Year 6 and Year 7? Explain.

c. How did the bankruptcy risk of Levitz Furniture change between fiscal Year 6 and Year 7? Explain.

d. Which firm do you think is more likely to file for bankruptcy during fiscal Year 8? Explain, using the analyses from part a.

FSAP

5.19 APPLYING AND INTERPRETING THE EARNINGS MANIPULATION MODEL. Exhibit 5.17 presents selected financial statement data for Enron Corporation for Year 7, Year 8, Year 9, and Year 10. These data reflect amounts from the financial statements as originally reported for each year. In Year 11, Enron restated its financial statements for earlier years because it reported several items beyond the limits of GAAP.

Required

a. Compute the probability that Enron engaged in earnings manipulation for Year 8, Year 9, and Year 10 using Beneish's probit model.

b. Identify the major reasons for the changes in the probability of earnings manipulation during the three-year period.

EXHIBIT 5.17

Financial Statement Data for Enron Corporation
(amounts in millions)
(Problem 5.19)

	Year 10	Year 9	Year 8	Year 7
Accounts Receivable	$ 10,396	$ 3,030	$ 2,060	$ 1,697
Current Assets	30,381	7,255	5,933	4,669
Property, Plant, and Equipment, net	11,743	10,681	10,657	9,170
Total Assets	65,503	33,381	29,350	23,422
Current Liabilities	28,406	6,759	6,107	4,412
Long-Term Debt	8,550	7,151	7,357	6,254
Sales	100,789	40,112	31,260	20,273
Cost of Goods Sold	94,517	34,761	26,381	17,311
Selling and Administrative Expenses	3,184	3,045	2,473	1,406
Income from Continuing Operations	979	1,024	703	105
Cash Flow from Operations	4,779	1,228	1,640	501
Depreciation Expense	485	565	563	480

INTEGRATIVE CASE 5.1

FSAP

STARBUCKS

Exhibit 5.18 presents risk ratios for Starbucks for Year 2 and Year 3. Exhibits 1.24, 1.25, and 1.26 in Chapter 1 present the financial statements for Starbucks.

Required

a. Compute the values of each of the ratios in Exhibit 5.18 for Starbucks for Year 4. Starbucks had 397.4 million common shares outstanding at the end of Year 4 and the market price per share was $28.80. Use cost of sales including occupancy costs in the numerator of the gross margin index in the Beneish earnings manipulation model.

b. Interpret the changes in Starbucks risk ratios during the three-year period, indicating areas of concern.

CASE 5.2

FSAP

MASSACHUSETTS STOVE COMPANY—BANK LENDING DECISION

Massachusetts Stove Company manufactures wood-burning stoves for the heating of homes and businesses. The company has approached you, as chief lending officer for the Massachusetts Regional Bank, seeking to increase its loan from the current level of $93,091 as of January 15, Year 12, to $143,091. Jane O'Neil, chief executive officer and majority stockholder of the company, indicates that the company needs the loan to finance the working capital

EXHIBIT 5.18

Risk Ratios for Starbucks (Integrative Case 5.1)

	Year 4	Year 3	Year 2
Revenues to Cash Ratio		27.1	43.6
Days Revenues Held in Cash		14	8
Current Ratio		1.6	1.7
Quick Ratio		.8	.9
Operating Cash Flow to Average Current Liabilities Ratio		113.2%	111.1%
Days Accounts Receivable		9	10
Days Inventory		66	66
Days Accounts Payable		32	35
Net Days Working Capital		44	41
Liabilities to Assets Ratio		25.5%	23.9%
Liabilities to Shareholders' Equity Ratio		34.2%	31.3%
Long-Term Debt to Long-Term Capital Ratio		.2%	.3%
Long-Term Debt to Shareholders' Equity Ratio		.2%	.3%
Operating Cash Flow to Average Total Liabilities Ratio		94.3%	101.5%
Interest Coverage Ratio		1,447.3	1,124.0
Altman's Z-Score		12.278	11.592
Probability of Bankruptcy		0.0%	0.0%
Beneish's Earnings Manipulation Score		−2.630	−2.915
Probability of Earnings Manipulation		.4%	.2%

required for an expected 25 percent annual increase in sales during the next two years, to repay suppliers, and to provide funds for expected nonrecurring legal and retooling costs.

The company's woodstoves have two distinguishing characteristics: (1) the metal frame of the stoves includes inlaid soapstone, which increases the intensity and duration of the heat provided by the stoves and enhances their appearance as an attractive piece of furniture, and (2) a catalytic combuster, which adds heating potential to the stoves and reduces air pollution.

The company manufactures wood-burning stoves in a single plant in Greenfield, Massachusetts. It purchases metal castings for the stoves from foundries in Germany and Belgium. The soapstone comes from a supplier in Canada. These purchases are denominated in U.S. dollars. The catalytic combuster is purchased from a supplier in the United States. The manufacturing process is essentially an assembly operation. The plant employs an average of eight workers. The two keys to quality control are structural airtightness and effective operation of the catalytic combuster.

The company rents approximately 60 percent of the 25,000-square-foot building that it uses for manufacturing and administrative activities. This building also houses the company's factory showroom. The remaining 40 percent of the building is not currently rented.

The company's marketing of woodstoves follows three channels:

1. Wholesaling of stoves to retail hardware stores. This channel represents approximately 20 percent of the company's sales in units.
2. Retail direct marketing to individuals in all fifty states. This channel utilizes (a) national advertising in construction and design magazines and (b) the sending of brochures to potential customers identified from personal inquiries. This channel represents approximately 70 percent of the company's sales in units. The company is the only firm in the industry with a strategic emphasis on retail direct marketing.
3. Retailing from the company's showroom. This channel represents approximately 10 percent of the company's sales in units.

The company offers three payment options to retail purchasers of its stoves:

1. Full payment: Check, money order, or charge to a third-party credit card.
2. Layaway plan: Monthly payments over a period not exceeding one year. The company ships the stove after receiving the final payment.
3. Installment financing plan: The company has a financing arrangement with a local bank to finance the purchase of stoves by credit-approved customers. The company is liable if customers fail to repay their installment bank loans.

The imposition of strict air emission standards by the Environmental Protection Agency (EPA) has resulted in a major change in the woodstove industry. By December 31, Year 9, firms were required by EPA regulations to demonstrate that their woodstoves met or surpassed specified air emission standards. Not only were these standards stricter than industry practices at the time, but firms had to engage in numerous company-sponsored and independent testing of their stoves to satisfy EPA regulators. As a consequence, the number of firms in the woodstove industry decreased from more than 200 in the years prior to Year 10 to approximately 35 by December 31, Year 11.

The company received approval for its Soapstone Stove I in Year 11, after incurring retooling and testing costs of $63,001. It capitalized these costs in the Property, Plant, and Equipment account. It depreciates these costs over the five-year EPA approval period. A second stove, Soapstone Stove II, is currently undergoing retooling and testing. The company incurred costs of $19,311 in Year 10 and $8,548 in Year 11 on this stove and has received preliminary EPA approval. It anticipates additional design, tooling, and testing costs of approximately $55,000 in Year 12 and $33,000 in Year 13 in order to obtain final EPA approval.

The company holds an option to purchase the building in which it is located for $608,400. The option also permits the company to assume the unpaid balance on a low-interest-rate loan on the building from the New England Regional Industrial Development Authority. The interest rate on this loan is adjusted annually and equals 80 percent of the bank prime interest rate. The unpaid balance on the loan exceeds the option price and will result in a cash transfer to the company from the owner of the building at the time of transfer. The company exercised its option in Year 9, but the owner of the building refused to comply with the option provisions. The company sued the owner. The case has gone through the lower court system in Massachusetts and is currently under review by the Massachusetts Supreme Court. The company incurred legal costs totaling $68,465 through Year 11 and anticipates additional costs of approximately $45,000 in Year 12. The lower courts have ruled in favor of the company's position on all of the major issues in the case. The company expects the Massachusetts Supreme Court to concur with the decisions of the lower courts when it renders its final decision in the spring of Year 12. The company has held discussions with two prospective tenants for the 10,000 square feet of the building that it does not use in its operations.

Jane O'Neil owns 51 percent of the company's common stock. The remaining stockholders include John O'Neil (chief financial officer and father of Jane O'Neil), Mark Forest (vice president for manufacturing), and four independent local investors.

To assist in the loan decision, the company provides you with financial statements (see the first three columns of Exhibits 5.19 to 5.21) and notes for the three years ending December 31, Year 9, Year 10, and Year 11. These financial statements were prepared by John O'Neil, chief financial officer, and are not audited. The company also provides you with projected financial statements for Year 12 and Year 13 (see the last two columns of Exhibits 5.19 to 5.21) to demonstrate both its need for the loan and its ability to repay. The loan requested involves an increase in the current loan amount from $93,091 to $143,091. The company will pay interest monthly and repay the $50,000 additional amount borrowed by December 31, Year 13. Exhibit 5.22 presents financial statement ratios for the company.

The assumptions underlying the projected financial statements are as follows:

Sales: Projected to increase 25 percent annually during the next two years, after increasing 17.7 percent in Year 10 and 21.9 percent in Year 11. The increase reflects continuing market opportunities related to the company's strategic emphasis on retail direct marketing and to the expected continuing contraction in the number of competitors in the industry.

Cost of Goods Sold: Most manufacturing costs vary with sales. The company projects cost of goods sold to equal 51 percent of sales in Year 12 and 49 percent of sales in Year 13, having declined from 69.2 percent of sales in Year 9 to 53.9 percent of sales in Year 11. The reductions resulted from a higher proportion of retail sales in the sales mix (which have a higher gross margin than wholesale sales), a more favorable pricing environment in the industry (fewer competitors), switching to lower-cost suppliers, and more efficient production.

Selling and Administrative Expenses: The company projects these costs to equal 41 percent of sales, having increased from 26.7 percent of sales in Year 9 to 40.9 percent of

EXHIBIT 5.19

Massachusetts Stove Company
Income Statements
(Case 5.2)

	Actual			Projected	
	Year 9	Year 10	Year 11	Year 12	Year 13
Sales	$ 665,771	$ 783,754	$ 955,629	$1,194,535	$1,493,170
Cost of Goods Sold	(460,797)	(474,156)	(514,907)	(609,213)	(731,653)
Selling and Administrative	(177,631)	(290,719)	(390,503)	(489,760)	(612,200)
Legal (Note 1)	(28,577)	(30,092)	(9,796)	(45,000)	—
Interest	(25,948)	(24,122)	(23,974)	(26,510)	(26,510)
Income Tax (Note 2)	—	—	—	—	—
Net Income (Loss)	$ (27,182)	$ (35,335)	$ 16,449	$ 24,052	$ 122,807

EXHIBIT 5.20

Massachusetts Stove Company
Balance Sheets
(Case 5.2)

	Actual				Projected	
December 31:	**Year 8**	**Year 9**	**Year 10**	**Year 11**	**Year 12**	**Year 13**
Assets						
Cash	$ 3,925	$ 11,707	$ 8,344	$ 37,726	$ 11,289	$ 6,512
Accounts Receivable	94,606	54,772	44,397	31,964	40,035	49,964
Inventories	239,458	208,260	209,004	225,490	291,924	329,480
Total Current Assets	$ 337,989	$ 274,739	$ 261,745	$ 295,180	$ 343,248	$ 385,956
Property, Plant, and Equipment, at cost	$ 258,870	$ 316,854	$ 362,399	$ 377,784	$ 440,284	$ 487,784
Accumulated Depreciation	(205,338)	(228,985)	(250,189)	(274,347)	(302,502)	(333,694)
Property, Plant, and Equipment, Net	$ 53,532	$ 87,869	$ 112,210	$ 103,437	$ 137,782	$ 154,090
Other Assets	$ 17,888	$ 17,888	$ 17,594	$ 17,006	$ 17,006	$ 17,006
Total Assets	$ 409,409	$ 380,496	$ 391,549	$ 415,623	$ 498,036	$ 557,052
Liabilities and Shareholders' Equity						
Accounts Payable	$ 148,579	$ 139,879	$ 189,889	$ 160,905	$ 198,206	$ 176,915
Notes Payable—Banks (Note 3)	152,985	140,854	125,256	93,091	143,091	93,091
Other Current Liabilities (Note 4)	13,340	11,440	23,466	62,440	33,500	41,000
Total Current Liabilities	$ 314,904	$ 292,173	$ 338,611	$ 316,436	$ 374,797	$ 311,006
Long-Term Debt (Note 3)	248,000	269,000	268,950	298,750	298,750	298,750
Total Liabilities	$ 562,904	$ 561,173	$ 607,561	$ 615,186	$ 673,547	$ 609,756
Common Stock	$ 2,000	$ 2,000	$ 2,000	$ 2,000	$ 2,000	$ 2,000
Additional Paid-In Capital	435,630	435,630	435,630	435,630	435,630	435,630
Accumulated Deficit	(591,125)	(618,307)	(653,642)	(637,193)	(613,141)	(490,334)
Total Shareholders' Equity	$(153,495)	$(180,677)	$(216,012)	$(199,563)	$(175,511)	$ (52,704)
Total Liabilities and Shareholders' Equity	$ 409,409	$ 380,496	$ 391,549	$ 415,623	$ 498,036	$ 557,052

EXHIBIT 5.21

Massachusetts Stove Company
Statements of Cash Flows
(Case 5.2)

	Actual			Projected	
	Year 9	Year 10	Year 11	Year 12	Year 13
Operations					
Net Income (Loss)	$(27,182)	$(35,335)	$ 16,449	$ 24,052	$122,807
Depreciation and Amortization	23,647	21,204	24,158	28,155	31,192
(Increase) Decrease in Accounts Receivable	39,834	10,375	12,433	(8,071)	(9,929)
(Increase) Decrease in Inventories	31,198	(744)	(16,486)	(66,434)	(37,556)
Increase (Decrease) in Accounts Payable	(8,700)	50,010	(28,984)	37,301	(21,291)
Increase (Decrease) in Other Current Liabilities	(1,900)	12,026	38,974	(28,940)	7,500
Cash Flow from Operations	$ 56,897	$ 57,536	$ 46,544	$(13,937)	$ 92,723
Investing					
Fixed Assets Acquired	$(57,984)	$(45,545)	$(15,385)	$(62,500)	$(47,500)
Other Investing	—	294	588	—	—
Cash Flow from Investing	$(57,984)	$(45,251)	$(14,797)	$(62,500)	$(47,500)
Financing					
Increase (Decrease) in Short-Term Borrowing	$(12,131)	$(15,598)	$(32,165)	$ 50,000	$(50,000)
Increase (Decrease) in Long-Term Borrowing	21,000	(50)	29,800	—	—
Cash Flow from Financing	$ 8,869	$(15,648)	$ (2,365)	$ 50,000	$(50,000)
Change in Cash	$ 7,782	$ (3,363)	$ 29,382	$(26,437)	$ (4,777)
Cash—Beginning of Year	3,925	11,707	8,344	37,726	11,289
Cash—End of Year	$ 11,707	$ 8,344	$ 37,726	$ 11,289	$ 6,512

sales in Year 11. The increases resulted from a heavier emphasis on retail sales, which require more aggressive marketing than wholesale sales.

Legal Expenses: The additional $45,000 of legal costs represents the best estimate by the company's attorneys.

Interest Expense: Interest expense has averaged approximately 6 percent of short- and long-term borrowing during the last three years. The projected income statement assumes a continuation of the 6 percent average rate.

Exhibit 5.22

Massachusetts Stove Company
Profitability and Risk Ratios
(Case 5.2)

	Actual			Projected	
	Year 9	Year 10	Year 11	Year 12	Year 13
Profit Margin for ROA	(.2%)	(1.4%)	4.2%	4.2%	10.0%
Assets Turnover	1.7	2.0	2.4	2.6	2.8
Return on Assets	(.3%)	(2.9%)	10.0%	11.1%	28.3%
Cost of Goods Sold/Sales	69.2%	60.5%	53.9%	51.0%	49.0%
Selling and Administrative/Sales	26.7%	37.1%	40.9%	41.0%	41.0%
Legal Expense/Sales	4.3%	3.8%	1.0%	3.8%	—
Interest Expense/Sales	3.9%	3.1%	2.5%	2.2%	1.8%
Days Accounts Receivable	41	23	15	11	11
Days Inventory	177	161	154	155	155
Days Accounts Payable	122	127	122	96	89
Fixed Asset Turnover	9.4	7.8	8.9	9.9	10.2
Current Ratio	.9	.8	.9	.9	1.2
Quick Ratio	.2	.2	.2	.1	.2
Operating Cash Flow to Current Liabilities Ratio	18.7%	18.2%	14.2%	(4.0%)	27.0%
Liabilities to Assets Ratio	147.5%	155.2%	148.0%	135.2%	109.5%
Long-Term Debt to Total Assets Ratio	70.7%	68.7%	71.9%	60.0%	53.6%
Operating Cash Flow to Total Liabilities Ratio	10.1%	9.8%	7.6%	(2.2%)	14.5%
Interest Coverage Ratio	.0	(.5)	1.7	1.9	5.6

Income Tax Expense: The company has elected to be taxed as a Subchapter S corporation, which means that the net income of the firm is taxed at the level of the individual shareholders and not at the corporate level. Thus, the pro forma financial statements include no income tax expense. The firm has operated at a net loss for tax purposes for several years prior to Year 11, primarily because of losses of a lawn products business that it acquired ten years ago. The company discontinued the lawn products business in Year 10.

Cash: The projected amounts for cash represent a plug to equate projected assets with projected liabilities and shareholders' equity. Projected liabilities include the requested loan during Year 12 and its repayment at the end of Year 13.

Accounts Receivable: Days accounts receivable outstanding, calculated on the average accounts receivable balances, will be 11 days in Year 12 and Year 13.

Inventories: Days inventory held, calculated on the average inventory balances, will be 155 days in Year 12 and Year 13.

Property, Plant, and Equipment: Capital expenditures for Year 12 include a $55,000 cost for retooling the Soapstone Stove II and $7,500 for other equipment, and for Year 13 include $33,000 for retooling the Soapstone Stove II and $14,500 for other equipment. The projected balance excludes the cost of acquiring the building, its related debt, the cash to be received at the time of transfer, and rental revenues from leasing the unused 40 percent of the building to other businesses.

Accumulated Depreciation: Continuation of the historical relation between depreciation expense and the cost of property, plant, and equipment.

Other Assets: A new financial reporting standard no longer requires amortization of intangibles after Year 11.

Accounts Payable: Days accounts payable outstanding, based on the average accounts payable balances, will be 97 days in Year 12 and 89 days in Year 13. The decrease in days payable reflects the ability to pay suppliers more quickly with the proceeds of the increased bank loan.

Notes Payable: Projected to increase by the amount of the bank loan in Year 12 and to decrease by the loan repayment at the end of Year 13.

Other Current Liabilities: The large increase at the end of Year 11 resulted from a major promotional offer in the fall of Year 11, which increased the amount of deposits by customers. The projected amounts for Year 12 and Year 13 represent more normal expected levels of deposits.

Long-Term Debt: Long-term borrowing represents loans from shareholders to the company. The company does not plan to repay any of these loans in the near future.

Retained Earnings: The change each year represents net income or net loss from operations. The company does not pay dividends.

Statement of Cash Flows: Amounts are taken from the changes in various accounts on the actual and projected balance sheets.

Notes to Financial Statements

Note 1: The company has incurred legal costs to enforce its option to purchase the building used in its manufacturing and administrative activities. The case is under review by the Massachusetts Supreme Court, with a decision expected in the spring of Year 12.

Note 2: The company is not subject to income tax because it has elected Subchapter S tax status.

Note 3: The notes payable to banks are secured by machinery and equipment, shares of common stock of companies traded on the New York Stock Exchange owned by two shareholders, and personal guarantees of three of the shareholders. The long-term debt consists of unsecured loans from three shareholders.

Note 4: Other current liabilities include the following:

	Year 8	Year 9	Year 10	Year 11
Customer Deposits	$11,278	$ 9,132	$20,236	$59,072
Employee Taxes Withheld	2,062	2,308	3,230	3,368
	$13,340	$11,440	$23,466	$62,440

Required (Excel spreadsheet available at www.thomsonedu.com/accounting/stickney for this case.)

Would you make the loan to the company in accordance with the stated terms? In responding, consider the reasonableness of the company's projections, positive and negative factors affecting the industry and the company, and the likely ability of the company to repay the loan.

CASE 5.3

FLY-BY-NIGHT INTERNATIONAL GROUP: CAN THIS COMPANY BE SAVED?

Douglas C. Mather, founder, chairman, and chief executive of Fly-by-Night International Group (FBN), lived the fast-paced, risk-seeking life that he tried to inject into his company. Flying the company's Learjets, he logged twenty-eight world speed records. Once he throttled a company plane to the top of Mount Everest in three and a half minutes.

These activities seemed perfectly appropriate at the time. Mather was a Navy fighter pilot in Vietnam and then flew commercial airlines. In the mid-1970s, he started FBN as a pilot training school. With the defense buildup beginning in the early 1980s, Mather branched out into government contracting. He equipped the company's Learjets with radar jammers and other sophisticated electronic devices to mimic enemy aircraft. He then contracted his "rent-an-enemy" fleet to the Navy and Air Force for use in fighter pilot training. The Pentagon liked the idea and FBN's revenues grew to $55 million in the fiscal year ending April 30, Year 14. Its common stock, issued to the public in Year 9 at $8.50 a share, reached a high of $16.50 in mid-Year 13. Mather and FBN received glowing write-ups in *Business Week* and *Fortune.*

In mid-Year 14, however, FBN began a rapid descent. Although still growing rapidly, its cash flow was inadequate to service its debt. According to Mather, he was "just dumbfounded. There was never an inkling of a problem with cash."

In the fall of Year 14, the board of directors withdrew the company's financial statements for the year ending April 30, Year 14, stating that there appeared to be material misstatements that needed investigation. In December of Year 14, Mather was asked to step aside as manager and director of the company pending completion of an investigation of certain transactions between Mather and the company. On December 29, Year 14, NASDAQ (over-the-counter stock market) discontinued quoting the company's common shares. In February, Year 15, the board of directors, following its investigation, terminated Mather's employment and membership on the board.

Exhibits 5.23 to 5.25 present the financial statements and related notes of FBN for the five years ending April, Year 10, through April, Year 14. The financial statements for Year 10 to Year 12 use the amounts as originally reported for each year. The amounts reported on the statement of cash flows for Year 10 (for example, the change in accounts receivable) do not precisely reconcile to the amounts on the balance sheet at the beginning and end of the year because certain items classified as relating to continuing operations on the balance sheet at the end of Year 9 were reclassified as relating to discontinued operations on the balance sheet at the end of Year 10. The financial statements for Year 13 and Year 14 represent the restated financial statements for those years after the board of directors completed its investigation of suspected material misstatements that caused it to withdraw the originally issued financial statements for fiscal Year 14. Exhibit 5.26 lists the members of the board of directors. Exhibit 5.27 presents profitability and risk ratios for FBN.

Required

Study these financial statements and notes and respond to the following questions:

a. What evidence can you observe from analyzing the financial statements that might signal the cash flow problems experienced in mid-Year 14?

b. Can FBN avoid bankruptcy during Year 15? What changes in either the design or implementation of FBN's strategy would you recommend? To compute Altman's

Exhibit 5.23

Fly-by-Night International Group
Comparative Balance Sheets
(amounts in thousands)
(Case 5.3)

April 30:	Year 14	Year 13	Year 12	Year 11	Year 10	Year 9
Assets						
Cash	$ 159	$ 583	$ 313	$ 142	$ 753	$ 192
Notes Receivable	—	—	—	1,000	—	—
Accounts Receivable	6,545	4,874	2,675	1,490	1,083	2,036
Inventories	5,106	2,514	1,552	602	642	686
Prepayments	665	829	469	57	303	387
Net Assets of Discontinued Businesses	—	—	—	—	1,926	—
Total Current Assets	$ 12,475	$ 8,800	$ 5,009	$ 3,291	$ 4,707	$ 3,301
Property, Plant, and Equipment	$106,529	$76,975	$24,039	$17,809	$37,250	$17,471
Less Accumulated Depreciation	(17,231)	(8,843)	(5,713)	(4,288)	(4,462)	(2,593)
Net	$ 89,298	$68,132	$18,326	$13,521	$32,788	$14,878
Other Assets	$ 470	$ 665	$ 641	$ 1,112	$ 1,566	$ 1,278
Total Assets	$102,243	$77,597	$23,976	$17,924	$39,061	$19,457
Liabilities and Shareholders' Equity						
Accounts Payable	$ 12,428	$ 6,279	$ 993	$ 939	$ 2,285	$ 1,436
Notes Payable	—	945	140	1,021	4,766	—
Current Portion of Long-Term Debt	60,590	7,018	1,789	1,104	2,774	1,239
Other Current Liabilities	12,903	12,124	2,423	1,310	1,845	435
Total Current Liabilities	$ 85,921	$26,366	$ 5,345	$ 4,374	$11,670	$ 3,110
Long-Term Debt	—	41,021	9,804	6,738	20,041	9,060
Deferred Income Taxes	—	900	803	—	1,322	1,412
Other Noncurrent Liabilities	—	—	226	—	248	—
Total Liabilities	$ 85,921	$68,287	$16,178	$11,112	$33,281	$13,582
Common Stock	$ 34	$ 22	$ 21	$ 20	$ 20	$ 20
Additional Paid-In Capital	16,516	5,685	4,569	4,323	3,611	3,611
Retained Earnings	(29)	3,802	3,208	2,469	2,149	2,244
Treasury Stock	(199)	(199)	—	—	—	—
Total Shareholders' Equity	$ 16,322	$ 9,310	$ 7,798	$ 6,812	$ 5,780	$ 5,875
Total Liabilities and Shareholders' Equity	$102,243	$77,597	$23,976	$17,924	$39,061	$19,457

Exhibit 5.24

Fly-by-Night International Group
Comparative Income Statements
(amounts in thousands)
(Case 5.3)

For the Year Ended April 30:	Year 14	Year 13	Year 12	Year 11	Year 10
Continuing Operations					
Sales	$54,988	$36,597	$20,758	$19,266	$31,992
Expenses					
Cost of Services	$38,187	$26,444	$12,544	$ 9,087	$22,003
Selling and Administrative	5,880	3,020	3,467	2,989	4,236
Depreciation	9,810	3,150	1,703	2,798	3,003
Interest	5,841	3,058	1,101	2,743	2,600
Income Taxes	(900)	379	803	671	74
Total Expenses	$58,818	$36,051	$19,618	$18,288	$31,916
Income—Continuing Operations	$(3,830)	$ 546	$ 1,140	$ 978	$ 76
Income—Discontinued Operations	—	47	(400)	(659)	(171)
Net Income	$(3,830)	$ 593	$ 740	$ 319	$ (95)

Z-score, use the low-bid market price for the year to determine the market value of common shareholders' equity.

Notes to Financial Statements

1. Summary of Significant Accounting Policies

Consolidation. The consolidated financial statements include the accounts of the company and its wholly owned subsidiaries. The company uses the equity method for subsidiaries not majority owned (50 percent or less) and eliminates significant intercompany transactions and balances.

Inventories. Inventories, which consist of aircraft fuel, spare parts, and supplies, appear at lower of FIFO cost or market.

Property and Equipment. Property and equipment appear at acquisition cost. The company capitalizes major inspections, renewals, and improvements, while it expenses replacements, maintenance, and repairs that do not improve or extend the life of the respective assets. The company computes depreciation of property and equipment using the straight-line method.

Contract Income Recognition. Contractual specifications (such as revenue rates, reimbursement terms, and functional considerations) vary among contracts; accordingly, the company recognizes guaranteed contract income (guaranteed revenue less related direct costs) either as it logs flight hours or on a straight-line monthly basis over the contract year, whichever method better reflects the economics of the contract. The company recognizes income from discretionary hours flown in excess of the minimum guaranteed amount each month as it logs such discretionary hours.

Exhibit 5.25

Fly-by-Night International Group
Comparative Statements of Cash Flows
(amounts in thousands)
(Case 5.3)

For the Year ended April 30:	Year 14	Year 13	Year 12	Year 11	Year 10
Operations					
Income—Continuing Operations	$ (3,830)	$ 546	$ 1,140	$ 978	$ 76
Depreciation	9,810	3,150	1,703	2,798	3,003
Other Adjustments	1,074	1,817	1,119	671	74
Working Capital from Operations	$ 7,054	$ 5,513	$ 3,962	$ 4,447	$ 3,153
Changes in Working Capital:					
(Increase) Decrease in Receivables	(1,671)	(2,199)	(1,185)	(407)	403
(Increase) Decrease in Inventories	(2,592)	(962)	(950)	40	19
(Increase) Decrease in Prepayments	164	(360)	(412)	246	36
Increase (Decrease) in Accounts Payable	6,149	5,286	54	(1,346)	359
Increase (Decrease) in Other Current Liabilities	779	9,701	1,113	(535)	596
Cash Flow from Continuing Operations	$ 9,883	$ 16,979	$ 2,582	$ 2,445	$ 4,566
Cash Flow from Discontinued Operations	—	(77)	(472)	(752)	(335)
Net Cash Flow from Operations	$ 9,883	$ 16,902	$ 2,110	$ 1,693	$ 4,231
Investing					
Sale of Property, Plant, and Equipment	$ 259	$ 3	$ 119	$18,387	$ 12
Acquisition of Property, Plant, and Equipment	(33,035)	(52,960)	(6,573)	(2,424)	(20,953)
Other	(1,484)	78	1,017	(679)	30
Net Cash Flow from Investing	$(34,260)	$(52,879)	$(5,437)	$15,284	$(20,911)

Continued

Exhibit 5.25

continued

	Year 14	Year 13	Year 12	Year 11	Year 10
Financing					
Increase in Short-Term Borrowing	$ —	$ 805	$ —	$ —	$ 4,766
Increase in Long-Term Borrowing	43,279	42,152	5,397	5,869	14,739
Issue of Common Stock	12,266	191	428	—	—
Decrease in Short-Term Borrowing	(945)	—	(881)	(3,745)	—
Decrease in Long-Term Borrowing	(30,522)	(7,024)	(1,647)	(19,712)	(2,264)
Acquisition of Common Stock	—	(198)	—	—	—
Other	(125)	321	201	—	—
Net Cash Flow from Financing	$ 23,953	$36,247	$ 3,498	$(17,588)	$17,241
Change in Cash	$ (424)	$ 270	$ 171	$ (611)	$ 561
Cash—Beginning of Year	583	313	142	753	192
Cash—End of Year	$ (159)	$ 583	$ 313	$ 142	$ 753

Exhibit 5.26

Fly-by-Night International Group
Members of the Board of Directors
(Case 5.3)

Charles A. Barry, USAF (Ret.), Executive Vice President of Wicks and Associates, Inc., a management consulting firm

Thomas P. Gilkey, Vice President, Marketing

Lawrence G. Hicks, Secretary and General Counsel

Michael S. Holt, Vice President, Finance, and Chief Financial Officer

Gordon K. John, Executive Vice President and Chief Operating Officer

Douglas C. Mather, Chairman of the Board, President and Chief Executive Officer

Edward F. O'Hara, President of the O'Hara Companies, which manufactures aircraft products

E. William Shapiro, Professor of Law, Emory University

Exhibit 5.27

Profitability and Risk Ratios for FBN (Case 5.3)

	Year 14	Year 13	Year 12	Year 11	Year 10
Profit Margin for ROA	(.1%)	6.9%	9.0%	14.5	5.6%
Assets Turnover	.6	.7	1.0	.7	1.1
Return on Assets	0.0%	5.0%	8.9%	9.8%	6.1%
Cost of Goods and Services/Sales	69.4%	72.3%	60.4%	47.2%	68.8%
Selling and Administrative/Sales	10.7%	8.3%	16.7%	15.5%	13.2%
Depreciation Expense/Sales	17.8%	8.6%	8.2%	14.5%	9.4%
Income Tax Expense (excluding tax effects of interest)/Sales	2.1%	4.0%	5.7%	8.3%	3.0%
Interest Expense/Sales	10.6%	8.4%	5.3%	14.2%	8.1%
Days Accounts Receivable	38	38	37	24	18
Days Accounts Payable	84	48	26	65	31
Fixed Asset Turnover	.7	.8	1.3	.8	1.3
Profit Margin for ROCE	(7.0%)	1.5%	5.5%	5.1%	.2%
Capital Structure Leverage Ratio	7.0	5.9	2.9	4.5	5.0
Rate of Return on Common Equity	(29.9%)	6.4%	15.6%	15.5%	1.3%
Current Ratio	.2	.3	.9	.8	.4
Quick Ratio	.1	.2	.6	.6	.2
Operating Cash Flow to Current Liabilities Ratio	17.6%	107.1%	53.1%	30.5%	61.8%
Liabilities to Assets Ratio	84.0%	88.0%	67.5%	62.0%	85.2%
Long-Term Debt to Long-Term Capital Ratio	0.0%	81.5%	55.7%	49.7%	77.6%
Operating Cash Flow to Total Liabilities Ratio	12.8%	40.2%	18.9%	11.2%	19.5%
Interest Coverage Ratio	.2	1.3	2.8	1.6	1.1

Income Taxes. The company recognizes deferred income taxes for temporary differences between financial and tax reporting amounts.

2. Transactions with Major Customers

The company provides contract flight services to three major customers: the U.S. Air Force, the U.S. Navy, and the Federal Reserve Bank System. These contracts have termination dates in Year 16 or Year 17. Revenues from all government contracts as a percentage of total revenues were as follows: Year 14, 62 percent; Year 13, 72 percent; Year 12, 73 percent; Year 11, 68 percent; Year 10, 31 percent.

3. Segment Data

During Year 10, the company operated in five business segments as follows:

Flight Operations—Business. Provides combat readiness training to the military and nightly transfer of negotiable instruments for the Federal Reserve Bank System, both under multiyear contracts.

Flight Operations—Transport. Provides charter transport services to a variety of customers.

Fixed-Base Operations. Provides ground support operations (fuel, maintenance) to commercial airlines at several major airports.

Education and Training. Provides training for nonmilitary pilots.

Aircraft Sales and Leasing. Acquires aircraft that the company then either resells or leases to various firms.

The company discontinued the Flight Operations—Transport and Education and Training segments in Year 11. It sold most of the assets of the Aircraft Sales and Leasing segment in Year 11.

Segment revenue, operating profit, and asset data for the various segments appear here (amounts in thousands):

April 30:	**Year 14**	**Year 13**	**Year 12**	**Year 11**	**Year 10**
Revenues					
Flight Operations—Business	$ 44,062	$31,297	$16,026	$11,236	$10,803
Flight Operations—Transport	—	—	—	—	13,805
Fixed-Base Operations	9,597	4,832	4,651	3,911	3,647
Education and Training	—	—	—	—	542
Aircraft Sales and Leasing	1,329	468	81	4,119	3,195
Total	$ 54,988	$36,597	$20,758	$19,266	$31,992
Operating Profit					
Flight Operations—Business	$ 5,707	$ 4,863	$ 3,455	$ 2,463	$ 849
Flight Operations—Transport	—	—	—	—	(994)
Fixed-Base Operations	(2,041)	1,362	1,038	174	332
Education and Training	—	—	—	—	12
Aircraft Sales and Leasing	1,175	378	(15)	1,217[b]	2,726[a]
Total	$ 4,841	$ 6,603	$ 4,478	$ 3,854	$ 2,925
Assets					
Flight Operations—Business	$ 85,263	$64,162	$17,738	$11,130	$13,684
Flight Operations—Transport	—	—	—	—	1,771
Fixed-Base Operations	16,544	13,209	5,754	5,011	4,784
Education and Training	—	—	—	—	1,789
Aircraft Sales and Leasing	436	226	438	1,262	18,524
Total	$102,243	$77,597	$23,930	$17,403	$40,552

[a] Includes a gain of $2.6 million on the sale of aircraft.

[b] Includes a gain of $1.2 million on the sale of aircraft.

4. **Discontinued Operations.** Income from discontinued operations consists of the following (amounts in thousands):

Year 13	
Income from operations of Flight Operations—Transport ($78), net of income taxes of $31	$ 47
Year 12	
Loss from write-off of airline operations certificates in Flight Operations—Transport business	$(400)
Year 11	
Loss from operations of Flight Operations—Transport ($1,261) and Education and Training ($172) segments, net of income tax benefits of $685	$(748)
Gain on disposal of Education and Training business, net of income taxes of $85	89
Total	$(659)
Year 10	
Loss from operations of Charter Tour business, net of income tax benefits of $164	$(171)

5. Related-Party Transactions

On April 30, Year 11, the company sold most of the net assets of the Aircraft Sales and Leasing segment to Interlease, Inc., a Georgia corporation wholly owned by the company's majority stockholder, whose personal holdings represented at that time approximately 75 percent of the company.

Under the terms of the sale, the sales price was $1,368,000, of which the buyer paid $368,000 in cash and gave a promissory note for the remaining $1,000,000. The company treated the proceeds received in excess of the book value of the net assets sold of $712,367 as a capital contribution due to the related-party nature of the transaction. FBN originally acquired the assets of the Aircraft Sales and Leasing segment during Year 10.

On September 29, Year 14, the company's board of directors established a Transaction Committee to examine certain transactions between the company and Douglas Mather, its chairman, president, and majority stockholder. These transactions appear here:

Certain Loans to Mather. In early September, Year 13, the board of directors authorized a $1,000,000 loan to Mather at the company's cost of borrowing plus 1/8 percent. On September 19, Year 13, Mather tendered a $1,000,000 check to the company in repayment of the loan. On September 22, Year 13, at Mather's direction, the company made an additional $1,000,000 loan to him, the proceeds of which Mather apparently used to cover his check in repayment of the first $1,000,000 loan. The Transaction Committee concluded that the board of directors did not authorize the September 22, Year 13, loan to Mather, nor was any director aware of the loan at the time other than Mather. The company's Year 13 Proxy Statement, dated September 27, Year 13, incorrectly stated that "as of September 19, Year 13, Mather had repaid the principal amount of his indebtedness to the company." Mather's $1,000,000 loan remained outstanding until it was cancelled in connection with the ESOP transaction discussed next.

ESOP Transaction. On February 28, Year 14, the company's employee stock ownership plan (ESOP) acquired 100,000 shares of the company's common stock from Mather at $14.25 per share. FBN financed the purchase. The ESOP gave the company a $1,425,000 unsecured demand note. To complete the transaction, the company cancelled a $1,000,000 promissory note from Mather and paid the remaining $425,000 in cash. The

Transaction Committee determined that the board of directors did not authorize the $1,425,000 loan to the ESOP, the cancellation of Mather's $1,000,000 note, or the payment of $425,000 in cash.

Eastwind Transaction. On April 27, Year 14, the company acquired four Eastwind aircraft from a German company. FBN subsequently sold these aircraft to Transreco, a corporation owned by Douglas Mather, for a profit of $1,600,000. In late September and early October, Transreco sold these four aircraft at a profit of $780,000 to unaffiliated third parties. The Transactions Committee determined that none of the officers or directors of the company were aware of the Eastwind transaction until late September, Year 14.

On December 12, Year 14, the company announced that Mather had agreed to step aside as chairman and director and take no part in the management of the company pending resolution of the matters presented to the board by the Transactions Committee. On February 13, Year 15, the company announced that it had entered into a settlement agreement with Mather and Transreco resolving certain of the issues addressed by the Transactions Committee. Pursuant to the agreement, the company will receive $211,000, the bonus paid to Mather for fiscal Year 14, and $780,000, the gain recognized by Transreco on the sale of the Eastwind aircraft. Also pursuant to the settlement, Mather will resign all positions with the company and waive his rights under his employment agreement to any future compensation or benefits to which he might otherwise have a claim.

6. Long-Term Debt

Long-term debt consists of the following (amounts in thousands):

April 30:	Year 14	Year 13	Year 12	Year 11	Year 10
Notes Payable to Banks:					
Variable Rate	$44,702	$30,495	$ 2,086	$2,504	$ 3,497
Fixed Rate	13,555	14,679	6,292	3,562	1,228
Notes Payable to Finance Companies:					
Variable Rate	—	—	1,320	1,667	10,808
Fixed Rate	—	—	—	—	325
Capitalized Lease Obligations	2,333	2,865	1,295	70	5,297
Other	—	—	600	39	1,660
Total	$60,590	$48,039	$11,593	$7,842	$22,815
Less Current Portion	(60,590)	(7,018)	(1,789)	(1,104)	(2,774)
Net	$ —	$41,021	$ 9,804	$6,738	$20,041

Substantially all of the company's property, plant, and equipment serve as collateral for this debt. The borrowings from bank and finance companies contain restrictive covenants, the most restrictive of which appear in the following table:

	Year 14	Year 13	Year 12	Year 11	Year 10
Liabilities/Tangible Net Worth	<2.5	<3.0	<4.2	<5.5	<6.7
Tangible Net Worth	>20,000	>5,800	>5,400	>5,300	>5,100
Working Capital	>5,000	—	—	—	—
Interest Coverage Ratio	>1.15	—	—	—	—

As of April 30, Year 14, the company is in default of its debt covenants. It is also in default with respect to covenants underlying its capitalized lease obligations. As a result, lenders have the right to accelerate repayment of their loans. Accordingly, the company has classified all of its long-term debt as a current liability.

The company has entered into operating leases for aircraft and other equipment. The estimated present value of the minimum lease payments under these operating leases as of April 30 of each year is as follows:

Year 14:	$2,706
Year 13:	3,142
Year 12:	3,594
Year 11:	3,971
Year 10:	4,083

7. Income Taxes

Income tax expense consists of the following:

	Year Ended April 30				
	Year 14	Year 13	Year 12	Year 11	Year 10
Current					
Federal	$ —	$—	$—	$—	$—
State	—	—	—	—	—
Deferred					
Federal	$(845)	$380	$685	$67	$(85)
State	(55)	30	118	4	(5)
Total	$(900)	$410	$803	$71	$(90)

The cumulative tax loss and tax credit carryovers as of April 30 of each year are as follows:

April 30:	Tax Loss	Tax Credit
Year 14	$10,300	$250
Year 13	5,200	280
Year 12	1,400	300
Year 11	2,100	450
Year 10	4,500	750

The deferred tax provision results from temporary differences in the recognition of revenues and expenses for income tax and financial reporting. The sources and amounts of these differences for each year are as follows:

	Year 14	Year 13	Year 12	Year 11	Year 10
Depreciation	$ —	$ 503	$336	$(770)	$ 778
Aircraft Modification Costs	—	1,218	382	982	703
Net Operating Losses	(900)	$(1,384)	290	—	$(1,729)
Other	—	73	(205)	(141)	158
Total	$(900)	$ 410	$803	$ 71	$ (90)

A reconciliation of the effective tax rate with the statutory tax rate is as follows:

	Year 14	Year 13	Year 12	Year 11	Year 10
Federal Taxes at Statutory Rate	(35.0)%	35.0%	34.0%	34.0%	(34.0)%
State Income Taxes	(2.5)	3.0	3.0	3.0	(3.0)
Effect of Net Operating Loss and Investment Credits	16.5	—	(7.2)	(29.9)	—
Other	2.0	2.9	22.2	11.1	(12.0)
	(19.0)%	40.9%	52.0%	18.2%	(49.0)%

8. **Market Price Information.** The company's common stock trades on the NASDAQ National Market System under the symbol FBN. Trading in the company common stock commenced on January 10, Year 10. High- and low-bid prices during each fiscal year are as follows:

Fiscal Year	High Bid	Low Bid
Year 14	$16.50	$9.50
Year 13	$14.63	$6.25
Year 12	$11.25	$3.25
Year 11	$ 4.63	$3.00
Year 10	$ 5.25	$3.25

On December 29, Year 14, the company announced that NASDAQ had decided to discontinue quoting the company's common stock because of the company's failure to comply with NASDAQ's filing requirements.

Ownership of the company's stock at various dates appears here:

April 30:	Year 14	Year 13	Year 12	Year 11	Year 10
Douglas Mather	42%	68%	72%	75%	75%
Public	48	23	24	25	25
Company ESOP	10	9	4	—	—
	100%	100%	100%	100%	100%
Common Shares Outstanding (000's)	3,357.5	2,222.8	2,095.0	2,000.0	2,000.0

CASE 5.4

MILLENNIAL TECHNOLOGIES: APOCALYPSE NOW

Millennial Technologies, a designer, manufacturer, and marketer of PC cards for portable computers, printers, telecommunications equipment, and equipment diagnostic systems, was the darling of Wall Street during Year 6. Its common stock price was the leading gainer for the year on the New York Stock Exchange. Its bubble burst during the third quarter of Year 7 when revelations about seriously misstated financial statements for prior years became known. This case seeks to identify signals of the financial shenanigans and to assess the likelihood of the firm's future survival.

Industry and Products

Digital computing and processing have expanded beyond desktop computing systems in recent years to include a broad array of more mobile applications, including portable computers, cellular telephones, digital cameras, and medical and automobile diagnostic equipment. A PC card is a rugged, lightweight, credit-card-sized device inserted into a dedicated slot in these products that provides programming, processing, and storage capabilities normally provided on hard drives and floppy disks in conventional desktop computers. The PC card has high shock and vibration tolerance, low power consumption, small size, and high access speed. The market for PC cards is one of the fastest growing segments of the electronics industry.

Millennial Technologies designs PC cards for four principal industries: (1) communications (routers, cellular telephones, and local-area networks), (2) transportation (vehicle diagnostics, navigation), (3) mobile computing (handheld data collection terminals, notebook computers), and (4) medical (blood gas analysis systems, defibrillators). The firm targets its engineering and product development, all of which it conducts in-house, to these four industry groups. It works closely with original equipment manufacturers (OEMs) to design PC cards that meet specific needs of products aimed at these four industries. Its customers include Lucent Technologies, Philips Electronics, 3Com Corporation, and Bay Networks. Millennial Technologies also conducts its manufacturing in-house, which allows it to respond quickly to changing requirements and schedules of these OEMs. The firm markets its products using its own sales force.

Millennial Technologies was incorporated in Year 4 in Delaware as the successor of M. Millennial, a Massachusetts corporation. The firm made its initial public offering of common stock (1,000,000 shares) on April 19, Year 4, at a price of $5.625 per share. Each common share issued included a redeemable common stock purchase warrant that permitted the holder to purchase one share of the firm's common stock for $7.20. Prior to its initial public offering, Millennial Technologies obtained a $550,000 bridge loan during Year 4, which it repaid with proceeds from the initial public offering. Holders of the stock purchase warrants exercised their options during Year 5 and Year 6. The firm obtained equity capital during Year 5 as a result of a private placement of its common stock at $5.83 a share. It issued additional shares to the public during Year 6 at $18 a share. Its stock price was $5.25 on June 30, Year 4; $22.625 on June 30, Year 5; $29.875 on June 30, Year 6; and $52 on December 31, Year 7.

Millennial Technologies maintained a line of credit throughout Year 4 to Year 6 with a major Boston bank to finance its accounts receivables and inventories. The borrowing is at the bank's prime lending rate. Substantially all of the assets of the firm collateralize this borrowing.

The firm's chief executive officer, Manuel Pinoza, is also its major shareholder. The firm maintains an employment agreement with Pinoza under which it pays his compensation to a Swiss executive search firm, which then pays Pinoza.

Beginning in Year 6, Millennial Technologies made minority investments in five corporations engaged in technology development, four of which the firm accounts for using the cost method and one of which it accounts for using the equity method. Products developed by these companies could conceivably use PC cards. Millennial Technologies also advanced amounts to some of these companies using interest-bearing notes.

Exhibits 5.28 to 5.30 present the financial statements for the fiscal years ended June 30, Year 4, Year 5, and Year 6 for Millennial Technologies based on the amounts originally reported for each year. Exhibit 5.31 presents selected financial statement ratios based on these reported amounts.

Financial Statement Irregularities

On February 10, Year 7, after receiving information regarding various accounting and reporting irregularities, the board of directors fired Pinoza and relieved the chief financial officer of his duties. The Board formed a special committee of outside directors to investigate the purported irregularities, obtaining the assistance of legal counsel and

Exhibit 5.28

Balance Sheets for Millennial Technologies
As Originally Reported
(amounts in thousands)
(Case 5.4)

June 30:	Year 6	Year 5	Year 4	Year 3
Assets				
Cash	$ 6,182	$ 970	$ 981	$ —
Marketable Securities	4,932	—	—	—
Accounts Receivable	12,592	3,932	1,662	730
Inventories	18,229	8,609	3,371	2,257
Other Current Assets	6,256	1,932	306	234
Total Current Assets	$48,191	$15,443	$6,320	$3,221
Investments in Securities	2,472	—	—	—
Property, Plant, and Equipment, net	4,698	1,323	669	208
Other Assets	421	1,433	601	666
Total Assets	$55,782	$18,199	$7,590	$4,095
Liabilities and Shareholders' Equity				
Accounts Payable	$ 3,494	$ 3,571	$ 616	$1,590
Notes Payable	4,684	1,153	—	980
Current Portion of Long-Term Debt	336	103	—	—
Other Current Liabilities	614	765	516	457
Total Current Liabilities	$ 9,128	$ 5,592	$1,132	$3,027
Long-Term Debt	367	162	—	—
Deferred Tax Liability	242	—	39	24
Total Liabilities	$ 9,737	$ 5,754	$1,171	$3,051
Common Stock	$ 165	$ 110	$ 90	$ 60
Additional Paid-In Capital	38,802	10,159	5,027	146
Retained Earnings	7,078	2,176	1,302	838
Total Shareholders' Equity	$46,045	$12,445	$6,419	$1,044
Total Liabilities and Shareholders' Equity	$55,782	$18,199	$7,590	$4,095

Exhibit 5.29

Income Statements for Millennial Technologies
As Originally Reported
(amounts in thousands)
(Case 5.4)

For the Year Ended June 30:	Year 6	Year 5	Year 4
Sales	$ 37,848	$12,445	$ 8,213
Other Revenues	353	10	9
Cost of Goods Sold	(23,636)	(6,833)	(4,523)
Selling and Administrative	(4,591)	(3,366)	(1,889)
Research and Development	(1,434)	(752)	(567)
Interest	(370)	(74)	(495)[a]
Income Taxes	(3,268)	(556)	(284)
Net Income	$ 4,902	$ 874	$ 464

[a]Includes the cost of selling receivables to a factor and interest on bridge financing obtained and repaid during the year.

the firm's independent accountants. On February 21, Year 7, the New York Stock Exchange announced the suspension of trading in the firm's common stock. The stock was delisted on April 25, Year 7. On February 14, Year 7, the major Boston bank providing working capital financing notified the firm that the firm had defaulted on its line of credit agreement. Although this bank subsequently extended the line of credit through July 31, Year 7, it increased the interest rate significantly above prime. Millennial Technologies decided to seek a new lender.

The investigation by the board's special committee revealed the following accounting and reporting irregularities:

1. Recording of invalid sales transactions: The firm created fictitious purchase orders from regular customers using their purchase order forms from legitimate purchase transactions. The firm then shipped empty PC card housings purportedly to these customers at bogus addresses. Pinoza then apparently paid the accounts receivable underlying these sales with his personal funds.
2. Recording of revenues from bill and hold transactions: The firm kept its books open beyond June 30 each year and recorded as sales of each year products that were shipped in July and should have been recorded as revenues of the next fiscal year.
3. Manipulation of physical counts of inventory balances and inclusion of empty PC card housings in finished-goods inventories.
4. Failure to write down inventories adequately for product obsolescence.
5. Inclusion of certain costs in property, plant, and equipment that the firm should have expensed in the period incurred.

EXHIBIT 5.30

Statements of Cash Flows for Millennial Technologies
As Originally Reported
(amounts in thousands)
(Case 5.4)

For the Year Ended June 30:	Year 6	Year 5	Year 4
Operations			
Net Income	$ 4,902	$ 874	$ 464
Depreciation	645	337	193
Other Addbacks and Subtractions, net	1,159	(5)	219
Working Capital Provided by Operations	$ 6,706	$ 1,206	$ 876
(Increase) Decrease in Accounts Receivables	(8,940)	(2,433)	(981)
(Increase) Decrease in Inventories	(9,620)	(5,238)	(1,115)
(Increase) Decrease in Other Current Assets	(836)	(2,406)	(71)
Increase (Decrease) in Accounts Payable	(76)	2,955	(974)
Increase (Decrease) in Other Current Liabilities	(152)	251	87
Cash Flow from Operations	$(12,918)	$(5,665)	$(2,178)
Investing			
Sale of Investments	$ 3,981	$ —	$ —
Acquisition of Fixed Assets	(3,899)	(862)	(525)
Acquisitions of Investments	(11,186)	—	—
Other Investing Transactions	(2,800)	—	—
Cash Flow from Investing	$(13,904)	$ (862)	$ (525)
Financing			
Increase in Short-Term Borrowing	$ 3,531	$ 1,153	$ 550
Increase in Long-Term Borrowing	691	320	—
Increase in Common Stock	28,064	5,099	4,663
Decrease in Short-Term Borrowing	—	—	(1,529)
Decrease in Long-Term Borrowing	(252)	(56)	—
Cash Flow from Financing	$ 32,034	$ 6,516	$ 3,684
Net Change in Cash	$ 5,212	$ (11)	$ 981
Cash—Beginning of Year	970	981	—
Cash—End of Year	$ 6,182	$ 970	$ 981

EXHIBIT 5.31

Financial Ratios for Millennial Technologies Based on Originally Reported Amounts (Case 5.4)

	Year 6	Year 5	Year 4
Profit Margin for ROA	13.6%	7.4%	9.6%
Assets Turnover	1.0	1.0	1.4
Rate of Return on Assets	13.9%	7.2%	13.5%
Profit Margin for ROCE	13.0%	7.0%	5.6%
Capital Structure Leverage	1.3	1.4	1.6
Rate of Return on Common Shareholders' Equity	16.8%	9.3%	12.4%
Cost of Goods Sold/Sales	62.4%	54.9%	55.1%
Selling and Administrative/Sales	12.1%	27.0%	23.0%
Research and Development/Sales	3.8%	6.0%	6.9%
Income Tax Expense (excluding tax effects of interest expense)/Sales	9.0%	4.7%	5.5%
Accounts Receivable Turnover	4.6	4.4	6.9
Inventory Turnover	1.8	1.1	1.6
Fixed Asset Turnover	12.6	12.5	18.7
Current Ratio	5.3	2.8	5.6
Quick Ratio	2.6	.9	2.3
Days Accounts Payable	39	63	71
Operating Cash Flow to Current Liabilities Ratio	(175.5%)	(168.5%)	(104.7%)
Long-Term Debt to Long-Term Capital Ratio	.8%	1.3%	—
Liabilities/Assets	17.5%	31.6%	15.4%
Operating Cash Flow toTotal Liabilities Ratio	(166.8%)	(163.6%)	(103.2%)
Interest Coverage Ratio	23.1	20.3	2.5

6. Inclusion in advances to other technology companies of amounts that represent prepaid license fees. The firm should have amortized these fees over the license period.
7. Failure to provide adequately for uncollectible amounts related to advances to other technology companies.
8. Failure to write down or write off investments in other technology companies when their market value was less than the cost of the investment.

Exhibits 5.32 to 5.34 present the restated financial statements for Millennial Technologies for the fiscal years ending June 30, Year 4, Year 5, and Year 6 after correcting for the irregularities described previously. These exhibits also present the financial statements for the nine months ended March 30, Year 7. The firm decided during February of Year 7 to change its fiscal year to a March year end. Exhibit 5.35 presents selected financial ratios based on the restated financial statements.

EXHIBIT 5.32

Balance Sheets for Millennial Technologies
Using Restated Data
(amounts in thousands)
(Case 5.4)

	March 31:	June 30:			
	Year 7	Year 6	Year 5	Year 4	Year 3
Assets					
Cash	$ 57	$ 6,182	$ 970	$ 981	$ —
Marketable Securities	—	4,932	—	—	—
Accounts Receivable	5,571	11,260	2,802	1,280	730
Inventories	7,356	8,248	2,181	1,581	2,257
Other Current Assets	14,229	6,395	2,284	839	669
Total Current Assets	$ 27,213	$ 37,017	$ 8,237	$4,681	$3,656
Investments in Securities	20,332	1,783	—	—	—
Property, Plant, and Equipment, net	3,087	2,033	923	399	243
Other Assets	566	299	390	123	172
Total Assets	$ 51,198	$ 41,132	$ 9,550	$5,203	$4,071
Liabilities and Shareholders' Equity					
Accounts Payable	$ 4,766	$ 3,025	$ 3,303	$ 772	$1,590
Notes Payable	10,090	4,684	1,153	—	980
Current Portion of Long-Term Debt	671	336	103	—	—
Other Current Liabilities	7,117	811	562	116	457
Total Current Liabilities	$ 22,644	$ 8,856	$ 5,121	$ 888	$3,027
Long-Term Debt	—	367	162	—	—
Total Liabilities	$ 22,644	$ 9,223	$ 5,283	$ 888	$3,027
Common Stock	$ 177	$ 165	$ 110	$ 90	$ 60
Additional Paid-In Capital	82,240	42,712	10,843	5,059	146
Retained Earnings	(53,630)	(10,968)	(6,686)	(834)	838
Foreign Currency Adjustment	(233)	—	—	—	—
Total Shareholders' Equity	$ 28,554	$ 31,909	$ 4,267	$4,315	$1,044
Total Liabilities and Shareholders' Equity	$ 51,198	$ 41,132	$ 9,550	$5,203	$4,071

EXHIBIT 5.33

Income Statements for Millennial Technologies Using Restated Data (amounts in thousands) (Case 5.4)

	Nine Months Ended March 31:	Year Ended June 30:		
	Year 7	Year 6	Year 5	Year 4
Sales	$ 28,263	$ 33,412	$ 8,982	$ 7,801
Other Revenues	67	353	10	9
Cost of Goods Sold	(24,453)	(29,778)	(11,575)	(6,508)
Selling and Administrative	(7,318)	(3,803)	(2,442)	(2,083)
Research and Development	(1,061)	(1,434)	(753)	(567)
Loss on Investments	(14,096)[a]	(2,662)[a]	—	—
Investigation Costs	(3,673)[b]	—	—	—
Provision for Settlement of Shareholder Litigation	(20,000)[c]	—	—	
Interest	(391)	(370)	(74)	(495)
Income Taxes	—[d]	—[d]	—[d]	171
Net Income (Loss)	$(42,662)	$ (4,282)	$ (5,852)	$(1,672)

[a] Write-offs of advances, and write-downs or write-offs of investments, in technology companies.

[b] Legal, accounting, and related costs of investigating misstatements of financial statements.

[c] Estimated cost of class-action lawsuits arising from misstatements of financial statements. Millennial Technologies reached an agreement on June 18, Year 7, to pay the plaintiffs $1,475,000 in cash (included in Accounts Payable on March 31, Year 7, balance sheet) and common stock of $18,525,000 (included in Additional Paid-In Capital on March 31, Year 7, balance sheet). The common stock portion of the settlement represents 37 percent of the common stock of Millennial Technologies.

[d] Millennial Technologies incurred net losses for income tax purposes and maintains a valuation allowance equal to the balance in deferred tax assets.

Required

a. Using information in the financial statements as originally reported in Exhibits 5.28 to 5.30, compute the value of Beneish's manipulation index for fiscal Year 5 and Year 6.

b. Using information from part a. and the financial ratios in Exhibit 5.31, indicate possible signals that Millennial Technologies might have been manipulating its financial statements.

c. Describe the effect of each of the eight accounting irregularities on the balance sheet, income statement, and statement of cash flows.

d. Using information in the restated financial statements in Exhibits 5.32 to 5.34, the financial ratios in Exhibit 5.35, and the information provided in this case, would you as a commercial banker be willing to offer Millennial Technologies a line of credit as of July 31, Year 7? State the conditions that would induce you to offer such a line of credit.

EXHIBIT 5.34

Statements of Cash Flows for Millennial Technologies
Using Restated Data
(amounts in thousands)
(Case 5.4)

	Nine Months Ended March 31:	Year Ended June 30:		
	Year 7	Year 6	Year 5	Year 4
Operations				
Net Loss	$(42,662)	$ (4,282)	$(5,852)	$(1,672)
Depreciation and Amortization	831	471	281	176
Other Addbacks and Subtractions, net	28,812	2,005	224	352
Working Capital Provided by Operations	$(13,019)	$ (1,806)	$(5,347)	$(1,144)
(Increase) Decrease in Accounts Receivable	5,289	(8,883)	(1,693)	(599)
Increase (Decrease) in Inventories	454	(6,067)	(600)	676
(Increase) Decrease in Other Current Assets	(8,092)	(5,213)	(1,932)	(176)
Increase (Decrease) in Accounts Payable	6,572	(9)	3,072	(818)
Increase (Decrease) in Other Current Liabilities	—	(20)	(96)	(340)
Cash Flow from Operations	$ (8,796)	$(21,998)	$(6,596)	$(2,401)
Investing				
Sale of Investments	$ 32,182	$ 3,981	$ —	$ —
Acquisition of Fixed Assets	(2,074)	(1,459)	(583)	(332)
Acquisition of Investments	(38,892)	(11,186)	—	—
Cash Flow from Investing	$ (8,784)	$ (8,664)	$ (583)	$ (332)
Financing				
Increase in Short-Term Borrowing	$ 5,406	$ 3,531	$ 1,153	$ 550
Increase in Long-Term Borrowing	250	691	320	—
Increase in Capital Stock	4,060	28,813	5,099	4,663
Decrease in Short-Term Borrowing	—	—	—	(1,529)
Decrease in Long-Term Borrowing	(282)	(252)	(56)	—
Proceeds from Related-Party Transaction	2,021	3,091	652	30
Cash Flow from Financing	$ 11,455	$ 35,874	$ 7,168	$ 3,714
Change in Cash	$ (6,125)	$ 5,212	$ (11)	$ 981
Cash—Beginning of Year	6,182	970	981	—
Cash—End of Year	$ 57	$ 6,182	$ 970	$ 981

e. Exhibit 5.36 presents the values of Altman's Z-score for fiscal Year 4, Year 5, and Year 6 based on both the originally reported amounts and the restated amounts. Compute the value of Altman's Z-score for the fiscal year ended March 31, Year 7. Although not technically correct, use the income amounts for the nine-month period ending March 31, Year 7. Based on the amounts in the proposed settlement of the class-action lawsuits, the value of the common equity on March 31, Year 7, is $50,068,568.

f. Can Millennial Technologies avoid bankruptcy as of mid-Year 7? Why doesn't the Altman model signal the financial difficulties earlier than it does?

EXHIBIT 5.35

Financial Ratios for Millennial Technologies
Based on Restated Data
(Case 5.4)

	Year 7[a]	Year 6	Year 5	Year 4
Profit Margin for ROA	(150.0%)	(12.1%)	(64.6%)	(17.2%)
Assets Turnover	.6	1.3	1.2	1.7
Rate of Return on Assets	(91.9%)	(15.9%)	(78.7%)	(29.0%)
Profit Margin for ROCE	(150.9%)	(12.8%)	(65.2%)	(21.4%)
Capital Structure Leverage	1.5	1.4	1.7	1.7
Rate of Return on Common Shareholders' Equity	(141.1%)	(23.7%)	(136.4%)	(62.4%)
Cost of Goods Sold/Sales	86.5%	89.1%	128.9%	83.4%
Selling and Administrative/Sales	25.9%	11.4%	27.2%	26.7%
Research and Development/Sales	3.8%	4.3%	8.4%	7.3%
Special Provisions/Sales	133.6%	8.0%	—	—
Accounts Receivable Turnover	3.4	4.8	4.4	7.8
Inventory Turnover	3.1	5.7	6.2	3.4
Fixed Asset Turnover	11.0	22.6	13.6	24.3
Current Ratio	1.2	4.2	1.6	5.3
Quick Ratio	.3	2.5	.7	2.6
Days Accounts Payable	60	32	61	74
Operating Cash Flow to Current Liabilities Ratio	(55.8%)	(314.8%)	(219.5%)	(122.7%)
Long-Term Debt to Long-Term Capital Ratio	—	1.1%	3.7%	—
Liabilities to Assets Ratio	44.2%	22.4%	55.3%	17.1%
Operating Cash Flow to Total Liabilities Ratio	(55.2%)	(303.3%)	(213.8%)	(122.7%)
Interest Coverage Ratio	(108.1)	(10.6)	(78.1)	(2.7)

[a]Amounts based on a nine-month fiscal year.

EXHIBIT 5.36

Altman's Z-Score for Millennial Technologies (Case 5.4)

	Originally Reported Data			Restated Data		
	Year 6	Year 5	Year 4	Year 6	Year 5	Year 4
Net Working Capital/Total Assets	.8403	.6496	.8203	.8216	.3915	.8748
Retained Earnings/Total Assets	.1776	.1674	.2402	−.3733	−.9801	−.2244
Income Before Interest and Taxes/ Total Assets	.5052	.2727	.5404	−.3139	−1.9966	−.8550
Market Value of Equity/Book Value of Liabilities	15.3089	13.1911	8.0700	16.1620	14.3672	10.6419
Sales/Total Assets	.6785	.6838	1.0821	.8123	.9405	1.4993
Z-Score	17.5105	14.9646	10.7530	17.1088	12.7225	11.9366

Chapter 6

Quality of Accounting Information and Adjustments to Reported Financial Statement Data

Learning Objectives

1. **Understand the concept of quality of accounting information, including the attributes of economic content and earnings sustainability.**
2. **Review GAAP reporting for various items that occur infrequently and yet can have a large impact on the reported financial data, including gains and losses from discontinued operations, extraordinary gains and losses, changes in accounting principles, other comprehensive income items, impairment losses, restructuring charges, changes in estimates, and gains and losses from peripheral activities.**
3. **Develop the skills to know when and how to adjust the current period's earnings for income items not expected to persist.**
4. **Understand how to deal with and analyze restated financial statements, account classification differences, and differences in accounting principles across firms.**
5. **Review the definition of earnings management, and understand the conditions under which managers might more likely engage in earnings management.**

The third step of the six-step financial analysis process introduced in Chapter 1 (Exhibit 1.1) stresses assessing the quality of a firm's financial statements prior to performing profitability and risk analysis, forecasting, and firm valuation. We begin the discussion of accounting quality analysis in this chapter, and continue the discussion in Chapters 7 through 9, in which we describe in greater depth how to analyze accounting quality in various generally accepted accounting principles (GAAP).

Chapters 4 and 5 provided a framework and tools for analyzing the profitability and risk of a firm using financial statement data. The presumption in using reported financial statement data is that they portray accurately the economic effects of a firm's decisions and actions during the current period, appropriately characterize the firm's financial position at the end of the period, and are informative about the firm's likely future profitability and risk. However, to make insightful decisions about profitability and risk based on relations among accounting data (such as ratios and time-series trends), we must first assess whether the unadjusted, reported data are the appropriate inputs in the profitability and risk measures used. In this chapter, we develop the concept of accounting quality as the basis for assessing the information content of reported financial statement data, and discuss whether the analyst needs to adjust that data before analyzing a firm's profitability and risk, forecasting its future financial statements, and valuing the firm.

This chapter illustrates financial reporting for a wide array of items, primarily income statement related, that typically occur infrequently and yet can have a large impact on the financial statements. Specifically, the chapter discusses reporting for discontinued operations, extraordinary gains and losses, changes in accounting principles, other comprehensive income items, impairment losses, restructuring charges, changes in estimates, and gains and losses from peripheral activities. The important objectives in analyzing these items are to assess (1) their economic effect on the current period's performance and (2) the likelihood that they will persist in the future. This distinction, as you will see, is important for identifying when to consider making adjustments to the reported financial data.

This chapter also discusses additional accounting and reporting items that may require adjustment. These include retroactively restated financial statements, account classification differences, and different accounting principles across countries.

The chapter concludes with a discussion of the definition of earnings management, and the conditions that might trigger earnings management. Chapter 5 defines earnings manipulation and fraud as the reporting of accounting data outside the limits of GAAP. This chapter discusses earnings management, defined as reporting accounting data based on rules within the limits of GAAP but probably not the best economic characterization of the firm. The chapter concludes with a discussion of earnings management because the concepts of accounting quality and earnings management often are linked when discussing the need to adjust financial data to better reflect the economic performance and position of a firm.

ACCOUNTING QUALITY

Financial reporting abuses by companies such as HealthSouth, AIG, Adelphia, Enron, WorldCom, Global Crossing, and others have raised questions about the quality of accounting information. Terms such as *earnings quality* and, less frequently, *balance sheet quality* appear in the financial press, but often are defined poorly and used loosely to capture a myriad of reporting and accountability concerns.

We prefer to use the broader concept of quality of accounting information. We define *accounting quality* to encompass the economic information content of the income statement, the balance sheet, the statement of cash flows, notes to the financial statements, and management's discussion and analysis (MD&A). We define accounting quality broadly because each of these elements of the financial statements integrates and articulates with the others; thus, a firm's accounting quality depends on the quality of all of these elements. We intend to analyze broadly the firm's accounting quality so that our analysis can fully inform our assessment of the firm's reported financial position, performance, and risk.

Our view of accounting quality is also broader than, and should not be confused with, accounting conservatism, which is sometimes construed as an attribute of reporting quality. Conservative accounting numbers in their own right are not high quality for purposes of financial statement analysis and valuation, but conservatism is a prudent response by accountants when faced with uncertainty in measuring the economic effects of transactions, events, and commercial arrangements.

Although accounting quality has many dimensions, we focus on two that are central to analysis and valuation:

1. Accounting information should be a fair and complete representation of the firm's economic performance, financial position, and risk.
2. Accounting information should provide relevant information to forecast the firm's expected future earnings and cash flows.

Next, we explore each of these two elements more fully.

High Quality Reflects Economic Information Content

Quality accounting information portrays fairly and completely the economic effects of a firm's decisions and actions. Quality accounting information paints an accurate economic portrait of the firm's financial position, performance, and risk.

A high-quality balance sheet portrays the economic resources under a firm's control that can be reasonably expected to generate future economic benefits, and the claims on those resources, at a point in time. The assets on the balance sheet should reflect resources that the firm controls—cash and investment securities, collectible receivables, sellable inventory, plant and equipment, intangible rights—and that the firm expects to use to generate future economic benefits. If measurement of the expected future economic benefits is highly uncertain (as in the case of the benefits from certain research and development, advertising, or brand management expenditures) or outside the firm's control (for example, human capital), or if the expected future economic benefits have expired, then a high-quality balance sheet should exclude these items. A high-quality balance sheet provides a complete and fair portrayal of all of the firm's obligations at a point in time, including the present value of long-term liabilities for future payments, such as for pensions, leases, and other commitments. Shareholders' equity on a high-quality balance sheet represents the net asset position of the firm at that point in time—the residual value of the assets of the firm, after deducting the obligations of the firm.

A high-quality income statement summarizes completely and fairly the firm's income or loss from operations, as well as any other gains or losses from other transactions or events during a period. A high-quality income statement includes all of the revenues that the firm earned during the period and can reasonably expect to collect. A high-quality income statement includes the costs of all of the resources consumed, including resources consumed in the production process to generate revenues (that is, costs that can be matched to revenues such as costs of sales), as well as resources consumed during the period as a function of time that might not match directly with revenues (such as fixed administrative costs and interest expenses). A high-quality income statement also includes the effects of any gains or losses from other transactions and events of that period. Accounting quality is low if net income includes revenues that the firm did not earn during the period or may not be able to collect; if it fails to include expenses or losses of the period; if it includes expenses or losses that are attributable to other periods; or if it misclassifies or disguises key income items.

A high-quality statement of cash flows summarizes the cash flow implications of the firm's performance and changes in the firm's financial position over a period. All noncash exchanges appear in the notes and are not reported in the statement of cash flows. A high-quality statement of cash flows appropriately classifies cash flows into operating, investing, and financing activities in sufficient detail for the analyst to understand why cash flows change each period.

Notes to the financial statements should disclose additional information that enhances the users' understanding of the judgments and estimates the firm's managers made in measuring and reporting accounting amounts and changes in those amounts. Firms often provide informative disclosures in the notes to the financial statements and enhance these disclosures with qualitative discussions of operations and risks in the MD&A section of the annual report and Form 10-K (see Appendix B for PepsiCo's MD&A discussions of key assumptions, critical accounting policies, and estimates made by the firm). High-quality notes and MD&A discussions provide an in-depth qualitative context to the quantitative data reported in the financial statements.

Standard setters establish GAAP to provide firms with guidance and rules on measuring the economic effects of firms' activities, performance, and financial position. Standard setters also establish GAAP to provide auditors with a common basis for auditing the fairness of firms' reporting, and to provide users of financial statements with a comparable and understandable set of principles for firms' accounting. Standard setters recognize, however, that measuring the economic effects of firms' activities, performance, and financial position often requires subjectivity. Managers must estimate, for example, the rate at which a long-lived asset such as a building or machine loses service potential; the point when a particular customer's account becomes uncollectible; and the point when a firm has earned revenues. As the degree of subjectivity in measuring economic effects increases, it also increases the potential for firms to report accounting information that includes unintentional measurement error, or intentional bias to portray the firm in a light most favorable to the firm or its managers. Standard setters often react to this potential for intentional bias or unintentional estimation error when establishing GAAP by making trade-offs between accurately reflecting economic reality and obtaining reliable accounting information. Thus, quality accounting information seeks to maximize relevance and economic faithfulness, subject to the constraints of the reliability of the measurements.

Standard setters recognize that a single accounting method may not always portray the economic effects of a particular transaction for all firms. Firms' choices and estimates within GAAP should be determined by firms' underlying economic circumstances, including conditions in their industry, competitive strategy, and technology. For example, firms use up the services of buildings and equipment at different rates over time, so GAAP allows firms to select from among straight-line or accelerated depreciation methods. Firms structure leasing arrangements so that the lessor bears most of the economic risk in some cases (such as very short-term leases), whereas the lessee bears most of the economic risk in other cases (such as leases that extend for most of an asset's useful life). GAAP allows two methods of accounting for leases—the operating lease method and the capital lease method—to reflect differences in the economics of these leasing arrangements. Thus, to obtain quality accounting information, firms should select the accounting principles that best portray the economics of their activities from the set permitted by GAAP.

Even when firms select the accounting principles, or methods, that best portray the economics of their activities, firms must still make estimates in applying those accounting principles. Virtually all accounting amounts require some degree of estimation. Firms must estimate the period of time during which buildings and equipment will provide benefits. Firms must estimate the amount of cash they will ultimately receive from customers from credit sales. Firms must estimate the expected future cost of warranty plans on products sold during the period. Thus, obtaining quality accounting information requires firms' judgments and estimates in applying GAAP.

Given that firms have discretion in choosing their accounting principles in some cases and must make estimates in applying those accounting principles in most cases, firms should disclose sufficient information in the financial statements and notes to permit users to assess the economic appropriateness of those choices. Thus, informative disclosures are an essential element of quality accounting information.

In summary, users of financial statements should consider the following when evaluating the quality of accounting information:

1. Economic faithfulness of accounting measurements and classifications.
2. Reliability of the measurements.
3. Fit of GAAP selections to the activities of a firm.
4. Reasonableness of the estimates made in applying GAAP.
5. Adequacy of disclosures.

The analyst may conclude that the reported financial statements for a particular firm fall short of the desired level of accounting quality. In these cases, the analyst might adjust reported amounts to enhance the accounting quality before using them to assess operating performance, financial position, or risk. For example, the analyst might judge that an accelerated depreciation method reflects more accurately than the straight-line method the economic decline in service potential of a building or machine. Converting the reported amounts from straight-line to accelerated depreciation enhances accounting quality. Or the analyst might judge that a bad-debt provision of 3 percent of sales, instead of the 2 percent rate used by the firm, reflects more accurately the likely uncollectible accounts. Adjusting the reported amounts enhances accounting quality. Chapters 7 to 9 discuss various GAAP and the choices and estimates firms must make in applying them. These chapters discuss the types of adjustments that the analyst might make to reported amounts to enhance the quality of accounting information.

The analyst can use the adjusted financial statement amounts for the current period to evaluate the firm's managers, to assess risk, and to test for earnings management or fraud. The analyst can also use the adjusted financial statement amounts to evaluate a second element of quality accounting information: persistence over time.

High Quality Signals Earnings Persistence over Time

When using financial statements to value firms, the analyst should ask: What do the reported or restated amounts for the current period suggest about the long-run persistence of income, and therefore the economic value of a firm? This question points out the importance of judging the economic content of current-period earnings in order to assess historical earnings persistence and to project future earnings persistence.

Recall that we use a two-pronged definition of accounting quality. Quality accounting information should be informative as to both the economic value implications of the current period's earnings and the long-run sustainability of profits. For accounting to be deemed of high quality, both components—fair and complete representation of current economic performance, and information about expected future earnings and cash flows—are necessary. Consider the following four possibilities.

1. Earnings could be very informative about current performance, and tell you that current performance is sustainable. This constitutes high quality on both counts (for example, a big jump in sales and earnings this period because of new products that will continue to be successful for a long time).

2. Earnings could be very informative about current performance and tell you that the current level of earnings performance is not sustainable. Again, this constitutes high quality on both counts (for example, the firm realizes an unexpected gain (or loss) this year, but clearly classifies and reports it as nonrecurring; there is no ambiguity, because the gain is informative in that it will not likely affect future earnings).
3. Earnings could be informative about current performance but not informative (that is, does not reduce uncertainty) about the future. In this case, we have high current-period information quality, but low information quality for the future. For example, a firm recognizes a fair value gain on a financial asset as a result of a favorable move in interest rates and the asset is marked to observable market value. The measure is relevant and reliable, but this year's gain does not help the analyst forecast whether interest rates will move up or down next year, so it is not informative about sustainable earnings.
4. Earnings are not informative about current-period performance but are informative about sustainability of future earnings. Here we have low current-period information quality, but high information quality for the long run (for example, earnings this period include expenses for pre-opening costs for new stores; the new stores are operational and are expected to be profitable in the future).

Chapters 1, 4, 5, and 11 point out that the value of an equity security is a function of the returns expected from investing in the equity security relative to the level of risk. Chapters 10 to 14 discuss and illustrate how the analyst forecasts future financial statement amounts and uses them to derive appropriate equity values. Our concern in this section is with understanding the different signals that quality accounting information might provide about economic values. To link our discussion so far about current period earnings and expected future earnings to the value implications of earnings, consider the following four scenarios. In each case, we assume that the analyst has adjusted or restated reported earnings amounts to achieve the desired level of economic information content as discussed in the previous section.

Scenario 1: Earnings for the current period are high quality, are in line with previous expectations, and do not suggest any changes in expected future earnings. The analyst should not expect to observe a change in the market price of the equity securities. Market prices likely already reflect the expected earnings levels. Earnings are informative in the sense that they signal the market that its prior expectations have been met and there are no surprises that trigger a change in expectations for the future.

Scenario 2: Earnings for the current period differ from expectations and the new earnings level is expected to persist. A firm may have introduced a successful new product during the period, and the market had not previously fully anticipated the success of the new product in pricing the equity security. The new product should enhance earnings for some number of years in the future. The market price of the security should increase for the realized additional earnings of the current period and for the present value of the expected additional earnings in the future. Earnings are informative if they signal the portion of the current period's earnings due to the new product and the additional earnings in the future as a result of the persistence of this new earnings stream. Consider a second example. A firm unexpectedly loses a patent infringement lawsuit. As a consequence, the firm is enjoined from selling a key line of products and is required to pay immediate damages. The market value of the firm's equity securities should decline in the amount of the damages paid. In addition, the level of expected earnings for the future will decline relative to those previously anticipated, so the market value of the firm's equity securities should decline for the present value of the lower expected future earnings. Earnings are informative if they signal the amount of the immediate economic loss and the persistent negative effect on future earnings.

Scenario 3: Earnings for the current period differ from expectations but expected future earnings do not change. A firm receives an unexpected rebate on property taxes previously paid because the local government corrects a processing error. The market value of the firm's equity securities should increase in the amount of the rebate. Because expected future earnings do not change, there should be no further market price reaction for the equity securities. Earnings are informative if they disclose the amount of the rebate and signal its one-time nature.

Scenario 4: Earnings for the current period do not differ from expectations but expected future earnings do change. At the end of the current period, a manufacturing firm replaces a piece of equipment with a new piece of equipment that has an identical cost but is more efficient. The new piece of equipment adds to the firm's productive capacity and will reduce manufacturing costs, increasing expected earnings for future periods. The acquisition of the equipment itself should not materially affect the market value of the firm's equity securities; however, the market value should increase for the present value of the higher expected future earnings. Earnings are informative if they disclose sufficient information for the analyst to forecast the increase in expected future earnings.

The topics we discuss are as follows:

1. Discontinued operations.
2. Extraordinary gains and losses.
3. Changes in accounting principles.[1]
4. Other comprehensive income items.
5. Impairment losses on long-lived assets.
6. Restructuring and other charges.
7. Changes in estimates.
8. Gains and losses from peripheral activities.

Of these eight categories, financial disclosures related to the first five are the most comprehensive and consistent across firms because the FASB has issued specific pronouncements on the topics. Exhibit 6.1 presents an income statement that separates the income effects of the first four items from income from continuing operations.

DISCONTINUED OPERATIONS

When a firm decides to exit a particular component of its business, it classifies that business as a discontinued business for purposes of reporting the balance sheet, income statement, and statement of cash flows. The purpose behind this reporting requirement is to provide analysts and other financial statements users with information to distinguish the effects of continuing versus discontinuing operations on current-period performance, and to provide a basis for forecasting future income from the continuing operations of the firm. GAAP stipulates that a discontinued business is either a separable business or a component of the firm with clearly distinguishable operations and cash flows.[2] The

---

[1]Currently, most firms do not report changes in accounting principles on the income statement because of rule changes that took effect beginning in 2006. However, as discussed in a later section, analysts still see changes in accounting principles reported on the income statement for those changes that took place in (and were reported for) years prior to 2006.

[2]Accounting Principles Board, *Opinion No. 30,* "Reporting the Results of Operations" (1973); Financial Accounting Standards Board, *Statement of Financial Accounting Standards No. 144,* "Accounting for the Impairment or Disposal of Long-Lived Assets" (2001).

EXHIBIT 6.1

Statement of Comprehensive Income for a Hypothetical Company
Year 3

Income from Continuing Operations:	
Sales Revenue	X
Cost of Goods Sold	(X)
Selling and Administrative Expenses	(X)
Operating Income	X
Gain on Sale of Equipment	X
Interest Income	X
Interest Expense	(X)
Income before Income Taxes	X
Income Tax Expense	(X)
Income from Continuing Operations	X
Income from Discontinued Operations, net of taxes	X
Extraordinary Gains and Losses, net of taxes	X
Adjustments for Changes in Accounting Principles, net of taxes[a]	X
Net Income	X
Other Comprehensive Income Items, net of taxes	X
Comprehensive Income	X

[a]See footnote 1.

most recent ruling on discontinued operations, *Statement No. 144,* maintained the basic provisions of *Opinion No. 30* for presenting discontinued operations, but broadened the presentation to include more disposal transactions.

The degree to which a particular divested component operationally integrates with ongoing businesses will likely vary across firms depending on their organizational structures and operating policies. Thus, the gain or loss from the sale of a business might appear in income from continuing operations for one firm (that is, the divested business is operationally integrated) and in discontinued operations for another firm (that is, the divested business is not operationally integrated).

Two dates are important in measuring the income effects of discontinued operations. The measurement date is the date on which a firm commits itself to a formal plan to dispose of a segment. The disposal date is the date of closing the sale, if the firm intends to sell the segment, or the date operations cease, if the firm intends to abandon the segment.

A firm reports the net income or loss from operating the discontinued business prior to the disposal date as a separate item in the discontinued operations section of the income statement. Firms also report the gain or loss on disposal (net of tax effects) in this same section of the income statement, often labeled "Income, Gains, and Loss from Discontinued Operations." Most U.S. firms include three years of income statement information in their income statements. A firm that decides during the current year to divest a business includes the net income or loss of this business in discontinued operations not only for the current year but in comparative income statements for the preceding two years as well, even though the firm had previously reported the latter income in continuing operations in the income statements originally prepared for those two years.

At the measurement date, the firm estimates (1) the net income or loss it expects the discontinued business to generate between the measurement date and the disposal date, and (2) the gain or loss it expects from the sale or abandonment of the segment. The firm then nets these two amounts. If the net amount is an estimated loss, the firm recognizes the loss in the year that includes the measurement date. It simultaneously increases an account, Estimated Losses from Discontinued Operations, that appears among liabilities on the balance sheet. Realized losses (or gains) subsequent to the measurement date from either item (1) or (2) reduce (increase) this account instead of appearing in the income statements of those years. Only when cumulative losses exceed the amount initially established in the Estimated Losses from Discontinued Operations account will additional losses appear in the income statement.

If the net amount from netting items (1) and (2) is a gain, the firm recognizes the income and gains only when realized in subsequent years. These provisions rest on the conservatism convention of recognizing losses as soon as they become evident but postponing the recognition of gains until realization occurs.

Example 1

Bowne & Co. is one of the largest printers of financial documents in the United States, specializing in the creation and distribution of regulatory and compliance documents. Bowne prints and distributes Form 10-K filings and proxy reports to shareholders, as well as a wide range of other compliance filings required of U.S. firms. During Year 4, Bowne decided to sell its document-related outsourcing business to Williams Lea, Inc. and focus on its core competency of creation and distribution of regulatory documents. Exhibit 6.2 presents selected data from the financial statements related to discontinued operations.

Note that Bowne sets forth the net income from operating discontinued businesses separately from the gain on disposal, each net of their tax effects. Bowne reports a gain on disposal that exceeds the net income from operating the discontinued unit. Thus, it is likely that Bowne estimated the net effect on earnings from both operating and selling these units and concluded that a net gain would ultimately result. The firm therefore recognized the income and gain as they were realized in each year.

Bowne reports the amount of assets and liabilities related to discontinued operations on its balance sheet each year. Consistency with ignoring income from discontinued operations suggests that the analyst exclude these amounts from assets on the balance sheet. To keep the balance sheet in balance, the analyst must either increase some other asset or decrease shareholders' equity. The firm will ultimately sell these assets for cash. However, increasing cash at this point is inappropriate because the firm does not yet have the cash, nor does it know how much cash it will ultimately realize. Decreasing shareholders' equity implies that the firm will realize no cash on the disposal of these assets and therefore will report a loss equal to the book value of the net assets. Neither adjustment seems appropriate. The best approach is to leave the assets of the discontinued operations on the balance sheet but to exclude them from the calculation of any financial ratios that relate an income statement item to a balance sheet item. For example, excluding income from discontinued operations from the numerator of the rate of return on assets suggests excluding the related assets from the denominator of this ratio as well. Excluding sales of discontinued operations from the numerator of the total assets turnover suggests excluding the net assets of discontinued operations from the denominator of this ratio.

Exhibit 6.2 indicates that Bowne eliminated the effect of discontinued operations from the calculation of cash flow from operations and classified all of the cash flows related to discontinued operations in a separate section of the statement of cash flows after financing activities. Because cash flow from operations contains no amounts related to discontinued operations, the analyst can use it when computing cash flow ratios (for example, cash flow from operations to average current liabilities) without making additional adjustments. If the firm had not excluded the cash flow effects of discontinued operations from cash flow from operations, the analyst would want to do so.

In general, the overriding task for the analyst is to judge firms' strategies regarding the purchase and sale of businesses. For some firms, income from discontinued operations is an ongoing source of profitability and the analyst might decide to include this income in forecasts of future earnings. For most firms, however, income from discontinued operations represents a source of earnings that cannot persist. Recall that the definition of a discontinued operation envisions a firm's exit from a major area of business as opposed to divestment of a portion of an ongoing business, such as a plant or a geographical division. Most firms do not change the major areas of business in which they are involved on a sufficiently regular basis to justify considering income from discontinued operations as a recurring source of profitability.

A second argument for excluding income from discontinued operations from forecasts of future earnings relates to its measurement. Recall that at the measurement date, the firm estimates (1) the net income or loss it expects the discontinued business to generate between the measurement date and the disposal date, and (2) the gain or loss it expects from the sale or abandonment of the segment. The amount reported as income from discontinued operations for a particular year may represent (a) an estimated amount applicable to the current and future years, if the netting of items (1) and (2) at the measurement date is an estimated loss; or (b) an actual, or realized, amount applicable to the current year only if the netting of items (1) and (2) at the measurement date is an estimated gain. These measurement and reporting procedures cloud the interpretation of the time-series behavior of income from discontinued operations.

Thus, in most cases, the analyst should exclude income from discontinued operations from forecasts of future earnings and focus instead on income from continuing operations.[3]

EXTRAORDINARY GAINS AND LOSSES

The income statement can include extraordinary gains and losses. An income item classified as extraordinary must meet all three of the following criteria:[4]

1. Unusual in nature.
2. Infrequent in occurrence.
3. Material in amount.

---

[3]Note that during Year 4, PepsiCo reported a $38 million tax benefit related to businesses discontinued in previous years. PepsiCo discontinued its restaurant business in a year prior to Year 2. At the time of the discontinuance, PepsiCo recognized an estimated amount of taxes on the transaction. Some of this estimated amount appears to have been subject to disagreement with taxing authorities. During Year 4, it reached final agreement with taxing authorities on the amount of taxes related to these discontinued operations. The final amount was less than the amount initially estimated, resulting in an increase in earnings for Year 4. We eliminated this $38 million tax benefit in assessing PepsiCo's Year 4 profitability in Chapter 4.

[4]*Opinion No. 30* (1973); *Statement of Financial Accounting Standards No. 144* (2001).

EXHIBIT 6.2

Bowne & Co.
Selected Information Related to Discontinued Operations
(amounts in thousands)

Year Ended December 31:	Year 4	Year 3
Income Statement		
Revenue	$899,011	$847,636
Expenses:		
Cost of Revenue	(574,264)	(536,166)
Selling and Administrative	(266,034)	(247,977)
Depreciation	(32,121)	(35,466)
Amortization	(2,713)	(2,478)
Gain on Sale of Building	896	—
Restructuring, Integration, and Asset Impairment Charges	(14,644)	(23,076)
Operating (Loss) Income	$ 10,131	$ 2,473
Interest Expense	(10,709)	(11,389)
Loss on Extinguishment of Debt	(8,815)	—
Other Expense, net	(118)	(1,367)
Loss from Continuing Operations before Income Taxes	$ (9,511)	$(10,283)
Income Tax Benefit (Expense)	1,313	729
Loss from Continuing Operations	$ (8,198)	$ (9,554)
Discontinued Operations:		
Income from Discontinued Operations, net of tax	$ 4,150	$ 1,805
Gain on Sale of Discontinued Operations, net of tax	31,552	—
Net Income from Discontinued Operations	$ 35,702	$ 1,805
Net Income (Loss)	$ 27,504	$ (7,749)

December 31:	Year 4	Year 3
Condensed Consolidated Balance Sheets		
Assets Held for Sale, noncurrent	—	$106,898
Other Assets (details not provided)	—	620,927
Total Assets	$648,811	$727,825
Liabilities Held for Sale, noncurrent	—	3,882
Other Liabilities and Shareholders' Equity	—	723,943
Total Liabilities and Shareholders' Equity	$648,811	$727,825

Continued

A firm applies these criteria in the context of its own operations and to similar firms in the same industry, taking into consideration the environment in which the entities operate. Thus, an item might be extraordinary for some firms but not for others. Income items that meet all three of these criteria are rarely found in corporate annual reports in the United States.

EXHIBIT 6.2

continued

Year Ended December 31:	Year 4	Year 3
Condensed Consolidated Statements of Cash Flows		
Cash Flows from Operating Activities:		
Loss from Continuing Operations	$ (8,198)	$ (9,554)
Depreciation and Amortization	34,834	37,944
Asset Impairment Charges	518	2,198
Gain on Sale of Building	(896)	—
Loss on Extinguishment of Debt	8,815	—
Changes in Other Assets and Liabilities, net of noncash transactions	(2,404)	(10,339)
Net Cash Provided by Operating Activities	$ 32,669	$ 20,249
Cash Flows from Investing Activities (details omitted)	148,200	(21,117)
Cash Used in Financing Activities (details omitted)	(97,784)	(10,872)
Net Cash Used in Discontinued Operations	(20,123)	(4,131)
Net Increase (Decrease) in Cash and Cash Equivalents	$ 62,962	$(15,871)
Cash and Cash Equivalents—Beginning of Period	17,010	32,881
Cash and Cash Equivalents—End of Period	$ 79,972	$ 17,010

Example 2

DIMON Inc. is an international dealer of leaf tobacco, with operations in more than thirty countries. It is headquartered in Virginia, and its major customers include the U.S. cigarette manufacturers. In Year 3, DIMON recognized an extraordinary gain of $1.7 million resulting from a claim resolution with the United Nations Compensation Commission. The claim was based on an uncollected trade receivable due from the Iraqi Tobacco Monopoly, generated from transactions that took place with the organization prior to the Iraqi/Kuwait war of 1991.

The income statement for the company reveals the following (amounts in thousands):

	Year 3
Earnings from Continuing Operations before Extraordinary Items	$3,427.6
Gain on Settlement of Lawsuit (net of $957 in income taxes)	1,777.0
Net Earnings	$1,650.6
Basic Earnings per Share	
Continuing Operations	$ 0.36
Gain from Lawsuit	0.04
	$ 0.40

Using the analytical framework described and illustrated in Chapter 2, the effect of (1) the lawsuit and (2) related taxes are as follows:

	C	+	N$A	=	L	+	CC	+	AOCI	+	RE
BS-BOP											
(1)	+2,734.0										+2,734.0
IBT											+2,734.0
(2)	−957.0										−957.0
NI											+1,777.0
BS-EOP	**+1,777.0**										**+1,777.0**

This analysis assumes that the firm received cash at the time of settlement of the lawsuit and paid income taxes immediately.

The question for the analyst is whether to include or exclude extraordinary gains and losses in current-period earnings when using current earnings to forecast expected future earnings.[5] The response depends on the persistence of these gains and losses for a particular firm. By definition, the analyst can assume that they are infrequent in occurrence and in most cases will exclude them from forecasts of future profitability, focusing instead on income from continuing operations. As with discontinued operations, the income statement reports the amounts net of any tax effects.

In the case of DIMON, the analyst probably should not consider the extraordinary gain on the UN settlement as an ongoing source of earnings because Year 3 is the only year in the last three that DIMON reported such a gain or loss. Furthermore, the claim settlement relates to an event that occurred more than ten years earlier than the period in which the gain is reported.

DIMON includes the cash provided by the settlement in cash flow from operations in the statement of cash flows (not reported here). Consistent with excluding this extraordinary gain from earnings when using it to assess future profitability, the analyst should exclude the cash provided by the settlement when forecasting future cash flow from ongoing operations. Eliminating the amount entirely from the statement of cash flows, however, results in the change in cash on the cash flow statement not reconciling to the change in cash on the balance sheet. This would be inappropriate. If the company has not done so, as is the case with DIMON, the analyst might create a separate section of operating cash flows for unusual or extraordinary items and reclassify the cash provided by the settlement there. This was the approach followed by Bowne with respect to its discontinued operations in Example 1 (Exhibit 6.2). When calculating financial ratios that use cash flow from operations, the analyst should use cash flow from ongoing operations only.

CHANGES IN ACCOUNTING PRINCIPLES

For various reasons firms occasionally change the accounting principles employed to generate the financial statements. Sometimes standard setters mandate the changes, while in other cases firms voluntarily change from one acceptable principle to another. Until recently, GAAP required firms to recognize the cumulative effect of changing to an alterna-

[5]Note that for DIMON, regardless of the decision to adjust for the extraordinary gain for assessing persistent earnings, the gain has real economic content for Year 3. That is, the gain positively affects current period performance, regardless of whether it recurs.

tive accounting principle on net income of the period of the change. The firm reported this cumulative difference (net of taxes) in a separate section of the income statement.[6] Reporting the effects of the change in accounting method in the income statement raised the visibility of the change and increased the likelihood that statement users would not overlook it. However, this reporting resulted in amounts for net income that did not provide sufficient information for forecasting future earnings. Under this cumulative reporting approach, net income of periods prior to the current period was not formally restated to reflect the new method (although pro forma disclosures of the effect on earnings were required when practicable). Also, net income of the current period included the cumulative effect of the change even though it applied to prior periods.

Beginning in 2006, firms must generally report amounts for the current and prior years as if the new accounting principle had been applied all along. The rationale for this reporting is that it results in net income amounts for the current and prior periods measured using the same accounting principles that the firm intends to use in future periods, thereby enhancing the information content of reported earnings in forecasting future earnings.

Firms need not restate prior-year earnings retrospectively if it is impracticable to determine either the period-specific effects of the change or the cumulative effect of the change.[7] In this case, *Statement No. 154* requires firms to apply the new accounting policy to the balances of assets and liabilities as of the earliest period for which retrospective application is practicable and to make a corresponding adjustment to retained earnings for that period. When it is impracticable for an entity to determine the cumulative effect of applying a change in accounting principle to *all* prior periods to which it relates, *Statement No. 154* requires firms to apply the new accounting principle as if it were made prospectively from the start of the year of the change.

For example, if a firm switches from the FIFO cost-flow assumption to the LIFO cost-flow assumption for inventories and cost of goods sold, typically it is impracticable to reconstruct the effects of the accounting change on prior years. In this case, the change to the LIFO cost-flow assumption will be applied prospectively at the start of the year in which the accounting change takes place.

Note that any cumulative effect of accounting changes that occurred before 2006 will continue to be reported by firms on their income statement. In other words, some firms will still report the cumulative effect of changes in accounting principles on their income statements because the changes were made in years prior to the effective date of *Statement No. 154*. Because *Statement No. 154* will not have been implemented by firms before this book goes to press, we cannot show examples of actual companies' reporting under the new standard. However, the following example illustrates both the old and new reporting of accounting changes.

Example 3

Occidental Petroleum Corporation operates in two industry segments. The oil and gas segment explores for, produces, and markets crude oil and natural gas. The chemical segment manufacturers and markets basic chemicals, vinyls, and performance chemicals. Both segments require large expenditures on property, plant, and equipment to support their operations. Related to these expenditures, Occidental recognizes a liability for any

---

[6]Accounting Principles Board, *Opinion No. 20*, "Accounting Changes" (1971).

[7]Financial Accounting Standards Board, *Statement of Financial Accounting Standards No. 154*, "Accounting Changes and Error Corrections—A Replacement of APB Opinion No. 20 and FASB Statement No. 3" (2005).

costs it might have to occur to retire the assets, such as costs to dismantle assets or remediate properties at the end of their useful lives.[8]

In its Form 10-K filing for Year 3, Occidental states: "The initial adoption of SFAS No. 143 on January 1, Year 3 resulted in an after-tax charge of $50 million, which was recorded as a cumulative effect of a change in accounting principles." Occidental discloses the pro forma effects of the accounting change on previously reported income, indicating that net income for Year 2 would have been reduced by approximately $21 million, net of tax, and net income for Year 1 would have been reduced by approximately $29 million, net of tax.

The top portion of Exhibit 6.3 illustrates how the change to the new accounting principle required by *Statement No. 143* was reported by Occidental Petroleum following the cumulative-effect technique prescribed by *Opinion No. 20.* The bottom portion of the exhibit illustrates how the firm would have reported the accounting change if the retrospective technique had been applied as required currently under *Statement No. 154.* Note that *Statement No. 154* would require an adjustment to income from continuing operations and retained earnings for each year the effect of the change is known. In addition, Occidental would apply the accounting change to the balances of assets and liabilities of each year that the effect of the change in known (not reported in Exhibit 6.3). Retained earnings as of the end of Year 3 is the same under both approaches because at that point the total effect of the change has been captured in income.

EXHIBIT 6.3

Occidental Petroleum Company
Reporting Approaches: *Opinion No. 20* and *Statement No. 154*
(amounts in millions)

	Year 3	Year 2	Year 1
***Opinion No. 20* Approach**			
Income from Continuing Operations	$1,595.0	$1,163.0	$1,179.0
Cumulative Effect of Change in Accounting Principle:			
Adoption of *Statement No. 143*	(50.0)	—	—
Income from Continuing Operations after Accounting Change	$1,545.0	$1,163.0	$1,179.0
Retained Earnings, beginning of year	$2,303.0	$1,788.0	$1,007.0
Retained Earnings, end of year	3,530.0	2,303.0	1,788.0
***Statement No. 154* Approach**			
Pro Forma Restatement of:			
Income from Continuing Operations	$1,595.0	$1,142.0	$1,150.0
Retained Earnings, beginning of year	$2,253.0	$1,759.0	$1,007.0
Retained Earnings, end of year	$3,530.0	$2,253.0	$1,759.0

[8]Financial Accounting Standards Board, *Statement of Financial Accounting Standards No. 143,* "Accounting for Asset Retirement Obligations" (2001).

The FASB continues to issue new reporting standards. In most cases, the accounting change will be reported retrospectively, which enhances comparability across reporting periods. Firms periodically change reporting principles on a voluntary basis as well. Analysts should examine carefully any voluntary changes in accounting principles made by firms. Such changes may have some bearing on assessing management's attempts to manage earnings upward or downward. We discuss earnings management at the conclusion of the chapter.

OTHER COMPREHENSIVE INCOME ITEMS

GAAP often requires firms to restate certain assets and liabilities to market value each period even though firms have not yet realized the value change in a market transaction. As discussed in Chapter 2, the recognition and valuation of these assets and liabilities do not immediately affect net income and retained earnings but will likely affect them only in future periods. For this reason, standard setters do not require the change in value to be reported as part of income. These unrealized "gains" and "losses" appear in a separate shareholders' equity account titled Accumulated Other Comprehensive Income or Loss.

Under current GAAP, four balance sheet items receive this accounting treatment: investment securities deemed available for sale, derivatives held as cash flow hedges, minimum pension obligations, and investments in certain foreign operations. Later chapters discuss the accounting for each of these items more fully.

Example 4

Refer to Note 13, "Accumulated Other Comprehensive Loss" (Appendix A), in which PepsiCo details three items that comprise "other comprehensive loss" for Year 4: (1) currency translation adjustment; (2) derivatives held as cash flow hedges; and (3) minimum pension liability adjustment. (Chapters 8 and 9 discuss the accounting for these three items.) PepsiCo's Statement of Common Shareholders' Equity (also reported in Appendix A) details the changes in these items for Year 4.

Example 5

Cisco Systems Inc., the world's leading manufacturer of computer and telecommunications networking equipment, invested a large amount of its excess cash in publicly traded equity securities during the technology bubble. Cisco states in a note to its financial statements: "At end of Year 10 and Year 9, substantially all of the Company's investments were classified as available for sale. Unrealized gains and losses on these investments are included as a separate component of accumulated other comprehensive income (loss), net of any related tax effect."

Chapter 9 provides a discussion of accounting for investments in securities. Among other requirements, the rules require Cisco to report at the balance sheet date its equity investments at their fair values as reported in actively traded markets. The change in their values between balance sheet dates is reported as part of other comprehensive income. For fiscal Year 9, Cisco reports a net positive change in unrealized gain on investments of $3.2 billion in the subsection of the Consolidated Statement of Shareholders' Equity labeled "Accumulated Other Comprehensive Income (Loss)." Comprehensive income for the year was $5.9 billion, which comprises net income for the year ($2.7 billion) and the unrealized gain on holding marketable equity securities ($3.2 billion).

Dramatic changes occurred in both the information technology industry and the economy in general between Year 9 and Year 10. For fiscal Year 10, Cisco reports a net negative change in unrealized gains on investments of $3.8 billion in the same section of the statement of shareholders' equity referred to previously. Comprehensive loss for the year was $4.8 billion, consisting of a net loss for the year ($1.0 billion) and the unrealized losses on holding marketable equity securities ($3.8 billion).

The analyst must decide whether to include the unrealized gains and losses when assessing earnings persistence and predicting future profitability. The case for considering these gains and losses as part of sustainable earnings is as follows: (1) Such gains and losses closely relate to ongoing operating activities and will likely recur, and (2) measuring the amount of the gain or loss on certain assets is relatively objective when active markets exist to indicate the amount of the value changes. The case against including the value changes in assessments of persistent profitability is as follows: (1) The amount of gain or loss that firms ultimately realize when they sell the assets or settle the liabilities will differ from the amount reported each period, (2) the gains and losses could easily reverse in future years prior to disposal or settlement, and (3) measuring the amount of the gain or loss on certain types of assets can be subjective if they are not traded in active markets.

IMPAIRMENT LOSSES ON LONG-LIVED ASSETS

When a firm acquires assets such as property, plant, equipment, and intangible assets, it assumes that it will generate future benefits through their use. This does not always turn out to be the case, however. The development of new technologies by competitors, changes in government regulations, changes in demographic trends, and other factors external to a firm may reduce the future benefits originally anticipated from the assets. GAAP requires firms to assess whether the carrying amounts of long-lived assets are recoverable and, if they are not, to write down the assets to their fair values and recognize an impairment loss in income from continuing operations.[9]

It is impractical to expect firms to evaluate every asset each reporting period, so GAAP requires testing for asset impairment only when events or circumstances indicate that their carrying amounts may be not recovered. Nurnberg and Dittmar suggest the following events or circumstances as examples that may signal recoverability problems:

1. A significant decrease in the market value of an asset.
2. A significant change in the extent or manner in which an asset is used, or a significant physical change in an asset.
3. A significant adverse change in legal factors or in the business climate that affects the value of an asset, or an adverse action or assessment by a regulator.
4. An accumulation of costs significantly in excess of the amount originally anticipated to acquire or construct an asset.
5. A current-period operating or cash flow loss combined with a history of operating or cash flow losses, or a projection or forecast that demonstrates continuing losses associated with an asset used for the purpose of producing revenue.
6. Insufficient rental demand for a rental project currently under construction.
7. Write-downs by competitors and other industry leaders.[10]

---

[9]*Statement of Financial Accounting Standards No. 144* (2001). *Statement No. 144* superseded *Statement No. 121,* "Accounting for the Impairment of Long-Lived Assets and for Long-Lived Assets to Be Disposed of" (1995). *Statement No. 144* retains the fundamental provisions of *Statement No. 121* for recognizing and measuring impairment losses on long-lived assets held for use and long-lived assets to be disposed of by sale, while also resolving significant implementation issues associated with *Statement No. 121.*

[10]Hugo Nurnberg and Nelson Dittmar, "Reporting Impairments of Long-Lived Assets: New Rules and Disclosures," *Journal of Financial Statement Analysis* (Winter 1997), pp. 37–50. The article includes examples of how these impairment indicators are applied by firms in the oil and gas, restaurant, retail food, and service-related industries.

What is particularly noteworthy about this list is that a firm, in effect, must disclose when it anticipates that assets previously acquired will no longer provide the future benefits initially anticipated. This is a valuable disclosure for the analyst attempting to assess a past strategic decision by a firm. GAAP does require the testing of goodwill and other intangibles not requiring amortization for asset impairment annually, independent of the triggering events listed earlier. Chapter 7 discusses the nature of the impairment test for various types of long-lived assets.

Example 6

Consider PepsiCo's disclosures related to impairment of its long-lived assets with *definite* lives. In Note 3, "Impairment and Restructuring Charges and Merger-Related Costs" (Appendix A), PepsiCo provides details on impairment and restructuring charges taken by the firm in Year 3 ($147 million) and Year 4 ($150 million). (Restructuring charges are discussed in the next section, but firms often combine impairment and restructuring charges in one line item on the income statement.) For each year, the portion of the charge for impairment of long-lived assets relates to the closure of manufacturing plants, specifically $93 million for Year 4 and $81 million for Year 3. Note that PepsiCo reports the pretax effect of the asset impairment and restructuring charges *combined*, rather than disclosing the amounts related to each item.

Statement No. 144 requires that firms include impairment losses in income before taxes from continuing operations. Although asset impairments do not warrant disclosure in a separate section of the income statement, such as that given for discontinued operations or extraordinary gains or losses discussed earlier, alternative methods for disclosing the losses include a separate line item on the income statement or a detailed note that describes what line item on the income statement includes the impairment losses. In fact, PepsiCo provides both a separate line item on the income statement and a detailed note discussing the losses.

Example 7

Consider PepsiCo's impairment tests for intangible assets with *indefinite* lives. In Note 4, "Property, Plant, and Equipment and Intangible Assets" (Appendix A), PepsiCo reports perpetual brands and goodwill as intangible assets that have indefinite lives and are thus nonamortizable. However, as discussed in Chapter 7, firms must assess these assets annually for impairment, or more frequently if events and circumstances indicate that the asset may be impaired. In Note 4, PepsiCo states: "Perpetual brands and goodwill are assessed for impairment at least annually to ensure that discounted future cash flows continue to exceed the related book value. A perpetual brand is impaired if its book value exceeds its fair value. Goodwill is evaluated for impairment if the book value of its reporting units exceeds their fair value." The note concludes by stating that the impairments test results indicated that no impairment charges were necessary in Year 4.

Example 8

Exhibit 6.2 presents a partial income statement for Bowne & Co. Recall from Example 1 that Bowne is a large financial printer that specializes in producing regulatory and compliance documents. The firm reports "restructuring, integration, and asset impairment charges" of $14.6 million for Year 4 and $23.1 million for Year 3. Bowne's business model is heavily influenced by capital market activity, and the low number of mergers and acquisitions in the Year 2 to Year 4 period necessitated business realignment and asset write-downs by the firm. Exhibit 6.4 describes the components of the restructuring, integration and impairment charges reported by Bowne during this period.

EXHIBIT 6.4

Bowne & Co.
Selected Excerpt from Note 10—Accrued Restructuring and Integration Charges
(amounts in thousands)

During Year 3, the Company continued implementation of the cost reduction efforts announced in the fourth quarter of Year 2, and initiated further cost reductions as it responded to the continued lower levels of capital market activity during the first half of Year 3. These cost reductions included additional workforce reductions in all business segments and in certain corporate departments, the closing of its London manufacturing facility and a portion of the London financial printing customer service center, closing two other offices in the financial print segment, as well as adjustments related to changes in assumptions in some previous office closings in the financial print segment. There was also an asset impairment charge for a technology system which no longer had value to the Company. The integration of GlobalNet's operations with the existing BGS operation continued which resulted in additional headcount reductions, office closings and integration-related expenses. These actions resulted in restructuring, integration and asset impairment charges totaling $23,076 during the year ended December 31, Year 3.

During the year ended December 31, Year 4 the Company initiated further cost reductions aimed at increasing operational efficiencies. These restructuring charges included additional workforce reductions in all business segments, the consolidation of the Company's fulfillment operations with the digital print facility within the financial print segment, further consolidation of the globalization segment's operations in Italy, as well as adjustments related to changes in assumptions in some previous office closings in the financial print and globalization segments. These actions resulted in restructuring, integration and asset impairment charges totaling $14,644 for the year ended December 31, Year 4.

Example 9

Exhibit 6.5 contains impairment charge details for JDS Uniphase. The firm employs fiber-optics technology to design and manufacture products used in data communications, telecommunications, and cable television, as well as subsystem components in the aerospace and defense industries. The company was founded in the early 1990s and is the product of several large mergers and acquisitions, including JDS FITEL, OCLI, E-TEK Dynamics, and SDL, Inc.

The downturn in the telecommunications industry was devastating to JDS Uniphase, and demonstrates the dramatic affect of asset impairments on the income statement. The magnitude of the asset impairment charge by JDS Uniphase—more than $50 billion as detailed in Exhibit 6.5—is record breaking and the result of a collapse in the telecommunications industry. JDS Uniphase attributed the downturn to a precipitous decrease in network deployment and capital spending by telecommunications carriers.

The majority of the $50 billion asset impairment charge relates to goodwill associated with the acquisitions of E-TEK Dynamics, SDL, Inc., and OCLI. Note (a) to Exhibit 6.5 explains how JDS Uniphase determined the fair value of the asset impairment, with management acknowledging that the process entails a large amount of estimation. The firm also points out, both in its statement of cash flows and in its notes to the financial statements, that all of the $50 billion asset impairment is a noncash charge.

The analyst must assess whether to exclude a portion or all of impairment losses from reported earnings when using the current period's earnings to forecast future earnings. For example, JDS Uniphase indicates that it anticipates additional impairment charges in the future, suggesting a recurring pattern. However, it is unlikely that a charge as large as that in Year 1 will recur. Because firms report asset impairment losses pretax, a decision to eliminate a particular asset impairment loss requires the analyst to adjust for the income tax effect as well. In some cases, firms disclose the tax effect in notes to the financial statements. In other cases, firms do not disclose tax effects directly. In such cases, the analyst should study the note on income taxes to see whether the firm discloses any information related to the impairment charge. If the firm can claim a deduction later, then it will recognize a deferred tax asset. If the firm cannot take a tax deduction at any time, as is often the case for goodwill, then the analysis of the firm's effective tax rate will show an increase because of the nondeductibility of the impairment charge.

JDS Uniphase reports an increase in its effective tax rate reconciliation for Year 1 of $17.5 billion because of asset impairments. This amount equals the 35 percent statutory tax rate times the $50.1 billion asset impairment change. Thus, the charge does not give rise to a tax deduction. If no information appears in the notes, then one should assume that the asset impairment charge gives rise to an immediate tax deduction in an amount equal to the statutory tax rate times the asset impairment change.

EXHIBIT 6.5

JDS Uniphase Corporation
Note 12—Special Charges
(amounts in millions)

	Year Ended June 30, Year 1
Reduction of Goodwill and Other Long-Lived Assets[a]	$50,085.0
Restructuring Activities:	
Worldwide Workforce Reduction[b]	$ 79.1
Facilities and Equipment[c]	122.2
Lease Commitments[d]	63.0
Total Restructuring Charges[e]	$ 264.3
Total Special Charges	$50,349.3

[a] Fair value was determined based on discounted cash flows for the operating entities that had separately identifiable cash flows. The cash flow periods used were five years using annual growth rates of 15 percent to 60 percent, the discount rate used was 13.0 percent in the third quarter of Year 1 and 14.5 percent in the fourth quarter of Year 1, and the terminal values were estimated based upon terminal growth rates of 7 percent. The assumptions supporting the estimated future cash flows, including the discount rate and estimated terminal values, reflect management's best estimates. The discount rate was based upon the Company's weighted average cost of capital as adjusted for the risks associated with its operations.

[b] Primarily relates to severance and fringe benefits associated with the reduction of 9,000 employees.

[c] Property and equipment that was disposed of or removed from operations during Year 1.

[d] Primarily relates to exiting and terminating leases for excess or closed facilities with planned exit dates.

[e] Write-downs of facilities and equipment totaled $122.2 million in Year 1 and $2.7 million in Year 2. Cash payments to severed employees and lessors totaled $25.8 million in Year 1 and $50.7 million in Year 2. The firm adjusted its restructuring liability by $4.7 million pretax in Year 2 because it appeared that actual costs would be less than originally expected.

RESTRUCTURING AND OTHER CHARGES

Assessing the quality of earnings as related to the five topics discussed to this point—discontinued operations, extraordinary gains and losses, changes in accounting principles, other comprehensive income items, and impairment losses on long-lived assets—benefits from the fact that the FASB has issued specific pronouncements on each topic. Disclosures for restructuring and other charges and the remaining topics presented in this section—changes in estimates and gains and losses from peripheral activities—are not as comprehensive and consistent across firms because rulings on the topic are more general in nature.

Firms may decide to remain in a segment of their business, but elect to make major changes in the strategic direction or level of operations of that business.[11] In many of these cases, firms record a restructuring charge against earnings for the estimated cost of implementing the decision. The treatment of restructuring charges in analyzing profitability and assessing earnings persistence is important for the following reasons:

1. Recessionary conditions often induce firms to include restructuring charges in their reported earnings for the current period. Whether the recessionary conditions are expected to persist will have a bearing on forecasting earnings in the future.
2. The FASB has not issued a specific pronouncement regarding how firms should measure restructuring charges and when firms should include such charges in income. Because of this, the analyst must judge whether to include the charges in forecasts of future earnings, or whether they relate only to the current and past periods.

Interpreting a particular firm's restructuring charge is difficult because firms vary in their treatment of these items:

1. Some firms apply their accounting principles conservatively (for example, use relatively short lives for depreciable assets, expense immediately expenditures for repairs of equipment, or use relatively short amortization lives for intangible assets). Such firms have smaller amounts to write off as restructuring charges than if they had applied their accounting principles less conservatively.
2. Some firms attempt to minimize the amount of the restructuring charge each year so as not to penalize reported earnings too much. Such firms often must take restructuring charges for several years in order to provide adequately for restructuring costs.
3. Some firms attempt to maximize the amount of the restructuring charge in a particular year. This approach communicates the "bad news" all at once (referred to as the "big bath" approach) and reduces or eliminates the need for additional restructuring charges in the future. If the restructuring charge later turns out to have been too large, income from continuing operations in a later period includes a restructuring credit that increases reported earnings (such as with Iomega in Examples 10 and 13).

Firms also report "other charges" on the income statement using a variety of different account titles. These other charges have characteristics similar to restructuring charges, but often are not directly related to any strategic decision by the firm or to the level or direction of its operations. The following examples provide three illustrations of restructuring and other similar charges.

---

[11]If the firm decides to abandon a business segment or component altogether, the reporting policies discussed earlier for discontinued operations apply. In many cases, however, firms are not abandoning current areas of business, but "restructuring" them to improve profitability.

Example 10

Iomega Corporation sells data storage products to both consumer and corporate customers. Iomega is a leading manufacturer of portable data storage solutions, including drives and disks, which are used for sharing, transporting, sorting, and backing up critical information. In press releases and at trade shows, the firm defines its role as helping people "protect, secure, capture and share their digital lives."

Employee compensation and associated costs represent one of the largest expenses for Iomega. The cost of leased space and depreciation of furniture and fixtures represent other significant expenses. In a recent annual filing, Iomega provided an extensive note on the composition of its restructuring charges for Year 3 and Year 4, including amounts for employee severance packages, lease termination fees, and furniture write-offs. An excerpt from Note 5, "Restructuring Charges/Reversals," states:

> *Year 4 Restructuring Actions.* During Year 4, the Company recorded $3.7 million of restructuring charges for the Year 4 restructuring actions, including $2.6 million of cash charges for severance and benefits for 108 regular and temporary personnel worldwide (approximately 19% of the Company's worldwide workforce) who were notified by September 26, Year 4 that their positions were being eliminated, $0.7 million of cash charges for lease termination costs and $0.4 million of non-cash charges related to excess furniture. All of the $3.7 million of restructuring charges recorded during Year 4 are being shown as restructuring expenses as a component of operating expenses. None of these restructuring charges were allocated to any of the business segments.
>
> *Year 3 Restructuring Actions.* The $14.5 million of charges for the Year 3 restructuring actions included $6.5 million for severance and benefits for 198 regular and temporary personnel worldwide, or approximately 25% of the Company's worldwide workforce, $3.0 million to exit contractual obligations, $2.6 million to reimburse a strategic supplier for its restructuring expenses, $1.8 million for lease termination costs and $0.6 million related to excess furniture.

Note that Iomega does not disclose the tax savings resulting from the charges for either year. Also note that the firm discloses the cash component of the charges for Year 4, but not for Year 3.

Example 11

As described in Example 9, JDS Uniphase recorded both restructuring and asset impairment charges in Year 1. Exhibit 6.5 reports a restructuring charge totaling $264.3 million, comprising laying off employees, closing facilities, disposing of equipment, and terminating leases. Similar to Iomega in Example 10, these items typify the activities often captured in restructuring charges. They also exemplify the consequences of the collapse in the telecommunications industry after almost a decade of growth.

JDS Uniphase makes no mention of tax savings related to the restructuring charge. However, its income tax note shows an increase in deferred tax assets related to net operating losses. Firms generally cannot claim income tax deductions for restructuring charges until the firm makes severance payments to employees, terminates leases, and closes down or disposes of facilities and equipment. The restructuring charge likely created a net operating loss, which will give rise to future tax deductions. Thus, the recognition of the $264.3 million restructuring charge in Year 1 likely increased deferred tax assets by $92.5 million ($= .35 \times \$264.3$).

The following analysis summarizes the effects on the balance sheets and income statements of JDS Uniphase from the following:

(1) restructuring charge during Year 1.
(2) tax effect of the restructuring charge.
(3) disposal or removal of facilities and equipment during Year 1.
(4) tax effect of the disposals in item (3).
(5) cash payments to severed employees and lessors for lease terminations in Year 1.
(6) tax effect of item (5).
(7) disposal or removal of facilities and equipment during Year 2.
(8) tax effect of the disposals in item (7).
(9) cash payments to severed employees and lessors for lease terminations in Year 2.
(10) tax effect of item (9).
(11) adjustment to change the estimated amount of the restructuring liability account.
(12) tax effect of item (11).

	C	+	N$A	=	L	+	CC	+	AOCI	+	RE
BS-BOP											
(1)					+264.3						−264.3
IBT											−264.3
(2)			+92.5								+ 92.5
NI											−171.8
(3)			−122.1		−122.1						
(4)	+42.8		−42.8								
(5)	−25.8				−25.8						
(6)	+9.0		−9.0								
BS-EOP	**+26.0**		**−81.5**		**+116.3**						**−171.8**
(7)			−2.7		−2.7						
(8)	+.9		−.9								
(9)	−50.7				−50.7						
(10)	+17.7		−17.7								
(11)					−4.7						+4.7
IBT											+4.7
(12)			−1.7								−1.7
NI											+3.0
BS-EOP	**−6.1**		**−104.5**		**+58.2**						**−168.8**

Note several aspects of the accounting for the restructuring charge. JDS Uniphase establishes the restructuring charge and the related liability in Year 1 and then charges actual costs against the liability in Year 1, Year 2, and later years. Except for the adjustment for the change in estimate in Year 2, net income in subsequent years will not be affected by these restructuring charges. The remaining liability at the end of Year 12 is $58.2 million. The remaining deferred tax asset is $20.4 million (=.35 × $58.2).

Example 12

Refer to Note 3, "Impairment and Restructuring Charges and Merger-Related Costs," of PepsiCo's annual report (Appendix A). During Year 2, PepsiCo reported a $224 million charge associated with its merger with Quaker Foods in the previous year. PepsiCo reported in Year 3 an additional $59 million charge associated with the merger. The firm classified the charges as a separate line on the Consolidated Statement of Income ("Merger-Related Costs" as detailed in Appendix A), reducing operating profit for the year. (Chapter 4 includes a discussion of these charges when assessing PepsiCo's profitability for Years 2 and 3.)

PepsiCo disclosed the tax savings resulting from the charges. It appears that the vast majority of the merger-related costs did not qualify as tax deductions. For example, Note 3 reports an after-tax amount of $190 million for Year 2, representing a tax savings of only $34 million (= $224 − $190). The analyst would use this actual tax savings reported by PepsiCo, rather than multiplying the statutory rate times the charge, if a decision is made to adjust PepsiCo's income statement for the charge. Using actual amounts reported by firms is preferable to hypothetical calculations.

The analyst must assess in each of these three examples (1) whether similar restructuring and unusual charges are likely to recur and therefore represent an ongoing drain on earnings, and (2) whether the restructuring and other charges adequately provide for the costs encompassed by the charges. If not, estimates of future earnings must take this into account.

With respect to restructuring charges, the assessment is difficult because firms follow different reporting strategies with respect to the charges. As stated earlier, some firms make restructuring charges for several years in a row, attempting perhaps to minimize the negative news by making smaller charges than are appropriate. Also as stated earlier, other firms make a single, presumably larger, restructuring charge as an opportunity to get the bad news behind them.

Let's now consider the analyst's treatment of the three restructuring charges described previously.

JDS Uniphase

JDS Uniphase reported restructuring charges of $264.3 million in fiscal Year 1, as discussed earlier, and $260.0 million in fiscal Year 2. It also reported an additional $8,285.0 million asset impairment charge related to goodwill and other long-lived assets in fiscal Year 2. Thus, it would not appear that the charge in Year 1 was a one-time event. Conditions in the telecommunications industry did not improve to the point where additional charges would be a surprise. Thus, the analyst could easily justify not eliminating the restructuring charges in Year 1 and Year 2 when forecasting future earnings. On the other hand, the $8,285.0 goodwill impairment charge for Year 2 is extremely large and unlikely to recur. The analyst will eliminate it, net of any tax effect, when forecasting future earnings.

Iomega Corporation

The restructuring charges for Iomega also appear to be recurring in nature. Although not reported here, Iomega reported a restructuring charge in Year 2 as well. Thus, the analyst appears justified in including them (and related estimated tax effects) in income from continuing operations when forecasting future profitability.

PepsiCo

The merger-related costs incurred by PepsiCo occur in Year 2 and Year 3 only. In addition, although PepsiCo acquires companies each year, acquisition and related charges of this magnitude for PepsiCo are unusual. Thus, eliminating the charges and related tax effects from income from continuing operations when forecasting future earnings seems appropriate. We eliminated the charges when assessing PepsiCo's Year 2 and Year 3 profitability in Chapter 4.

CHANGES IN ESTIMATES

As discussed earlier in this chapter, application of GAAP requires firms to make many estimates. Examples include the amount of uncollectible accounts receivable; the depreciable lives for fixed assets; the percentage of completion rate for a long-term project; the return rate for warranties; and interest, compensation, and inflation rates for pensions, health care, and other retirement benefits.

Firms periodically change these estimates. The amounts reported in prior years for various revenues and expenses will differ from the amount suggested by the new estimates. Firms might conceivably (1) retroactively restate prior years' revenues and expenses to reflect the new estimates, (2) include the effect of the change in estimate as an adjustment to beginning retained earnings, or (3) spread the effect of the new estimate over the current and future years.

GAAP generally requires firms to follow the third procedure for changes in estimates. Standard setters view making and revising estimates as an integral and ongoing part of applying accounting principles. They are concerned about the credibility of financial statements if firms revise their financial statements each time they change an accounting estimate. Standard setters are also concerned that users of the financial statements will overlook a change in an estimate if its effect does not appear in the income statement of the current and future years.

Example 13

Example 10 illustrates restructuring charges recorded by Iomega Corporation, a leading manufacturer of portable data storage drives and disks. As discussed in that example, Iomega provided extensive restructuring disclosures related to its ongoing downsizing of the firm. The earlier discussion on restructuring charges points out that if the firm subsequently deems the charge too high, income from continuing operations in a later period includes a restructuring credit—in effect, increasing reported earnings in the later period. This describes Iomega's situation in Year 4, with the firm reporting a reversal of a portion of previous years' restructuring charges. The company states:

Year 4 Activity/Changes in Year 3 Restructuring Reserves

The total separation payments or liability for the 198 employees notified under the Year 3 restructuring actions was $6.7 million. During Year 4, the Company recorded an additional $0.5 million of expense related to the ratable recognition of the severance and benefits costs to be paid to the employees who remained in transition into Year 4. However, during the first quarter of Year 4, *the Company also released $0.3 million of outplacement reserves as employee usage of outplacement resources was less than originally estimated (emphasis added).*

Year 3 Activity/Changes in Third Quarter Year 1 Restructuring Reserves

During Year 3, severance and benefit reserves of $0.1 million were reversed due to the original estimates being higher than what was utilized (emphasis added). During Year 3, the Company recorded an additional $0.9 million for Europe lease termination costs as a result of the Company not being able to locate a tenant for the Ireland facility. The Company also recorded an additional $1.2 million for North American lease termination costs as a result of the Company not being able to locate a tenant for a Utah facility.

Given the difficulty in estimating the cost of restructuring programs prior to their implementation, this type of disclosure is not surprising. Unless the magnitude of the reversal is large relative to the original estimate, most analysts are not wary of this type of disclosure.

Example 14

DriveTime is the largest chain of car dealerships in the United States that both sells used cars and provides financing for the purchase of the cars. The firm sells used vehicles and provides financing for customers within what is referred to as the "subprime" segment of the used car market. The subprime market comprises customers who typically have limited credit histories, low income, or past credit problems.

Exhibit 6.6 provides an excerpt from a quarterly filing by DriveTime. In the excerpt taken from the notes to the quarterly financial statements, DriveTime describes its accounting policy for credit losses on loans. The judgments necessary to assess credit losses depend heavily on estimates of uncertain amounts. In the exhibit, DriveTime identifies five factors that it considers in evaluating whether the allowance and the provision for credit losses are adequate. Moreover, it makes clear that this list is not exhaustive.

With the demographics of DriveTime's typical customers, the judgments necessary by management for calculating the effect of these items on reported earnings are extremely subjective and subject to change fairly quickly. Exhibit 6.7 illustrates a change made by DriveTime in Year 2 for estimating the provision for credit losses. The magnitude of the change is dramatic. The firm attributes the need to adjust the provision upward to a decrease in new loans originated and the effects of the recession experienced in Year 2 and Year 1.

EXHIBIT 6.6

DriveTime
Excerpt from Notes to Consolidated Quarterly Financial Statements

Revenue Recognition

Direct loan origination costs related to loans originated at Company dealerships are deferred and charged against finance income over the life of the related installment sales loan using the interest method. The accrual of interest for accounting purposes is suspended if collection becomes doubtful, generally 90 days past due, and is resumed when the loan becomes current. Interest income also includes income on the Company's residual interests from its securitization program.

Allowance for Credit Losses

An allowance for credit losses (allowance) is established by charging the provision for credit losses. To the extent that the allowance is considered insufficient to absorb anticipated credit losses over the next 12 months, additions to the allowance are established through a charge to the provision for credit losses. The evaluation of the allowance considers such factors as (1) the performance of each dealership's loan portfolio, (2) the Company's historical credit losses, (3) the overall portfolio quality and delinquency status, (4) the value of underlying collateral, and (5) the current economic conditions that may affect the borrower's ability to pay.

EXHIBIT 6.7

DriveTime
Excerpt from Form 10-K Notes—Provision for Credit Losses

	Year 2	Year 1	Percent Change
Provision for Credit Losses (000's)	$151,071	$141,971	6.4%
Provision per Loan Originated	$ 3,183	$ 2,513	26.7%
Provision as a Percentage of Principal Balances Originated	35.4%	30.1%	

Provision for Credit Losses ("Provision") is the amount we charge to current operations on each car sold to establish an Allowance for Credit Losses ("Allowance"). The Provision in total, per loan originated, and as a percent of principal balances originated, increased in both Year 2 and Year 1.

The Provision for Year 2 increased to 35.4% of the amount financed versus 30.1% in Year 1. The Company's policy is to maintain an Allowance for all loans in its portfolio to cover estimated net charge-offs for the next twelve months. Our loans have experienced lifetime net losses in the 31% to 34% range for the past few years. With growth in portfolio originations over this time, we have been able to maintain an adequate Allowance in accordance with GAAP and Company policy by providing between 27% and 31% of the amount financed. However, in Year 2 the volume of portfolio originations decreased from Year 1 due to the implementation of higher credit standards and the effects of the recession. Due to the decreased volume of originations, an increase in the Provision as a percentage of loan originations was needed in order to maintain an adequate Allowance.

The Company has begun to improve the underlying credit quality mix of its originations due to improved credit standards and the introduction of loan grading. As a result, Year 2 originations are performing better to date than prior year originations. Offsetting these improvements are the effects of the recession and the performance of loans originated prior to Year 2 that do not have the benefit of the new higher credit standards and are emerging at loss levels higher than previously estimated. As a result, the Provision for Credit Losses increased to $151 million in Year 2 compared to $142 million in Year 1. The Allowance as a percentage of loan principal is 19.8% at December 31, Year 2, up from 19.4% at December 31, Year 1.

The analyst needs to address a set of issues when evaluating changes in estimates. How reasonable are management's stated explanations for the change? For example, DriveTime changed estimates because of a strategic business decision (reduce loan originations to generate higher-quality loans) and a deterioration in economic conditions. Is this reasonable and consistent with the firm's strategy? Have other firms in the same industry made similar changes? Often an extensive set of factors needs to be considered. Has technology changed, necessitating shorter useful lives for depreciable assets to incorporate obsolescence? Has a firm improved quality control on products manufactured, necessitating lower warranty liability levels? Are the firm's new estimates in line with those of its competitors?

GAINS AND LOSSES FROM PERIPHERAL ACTIVITIES

Firms often enter into transactions that are peripheral to their core operations but generate gains and losses that must be reported on the income statement. For example, to create, manufacture, and market products, firms generally need to invest in assets such as buildings and equipment. The sale of such peripheral assets usually results in a gain or loss. Similar to restructuring charges, gains and losses from activities peripheral to the primary activities of a firm are included in income from continuing operations. The analyst should search for such items and decide whether to exclude them when assessing current profitability and forecasting future earnings.

Example 14

Bowne & Co., first discussed in Example 1, is one of the largest financial printers in the United States. Note that Bowne's income statement, reported in Exhibit 6.2, includes a "gain on sale of building" for $896,000 for Year 4. Bowne provides the following information on the sale in Note 9 of its annual report:

> In May Year 4, the Company sold its financial printing facility in Dominguez Hills, California for net proceeds of $6,731,000 recognizing a gain on the sale of $896,000 during the quarter ended June 30, Year 4. The Company moved to a new leased facility in Southern California in September of Year 4.

Exhibit 6.2 includes excerpts from Bowne's consolidated statement of cash flows as well. The $896,000 gain is eliminated from cash flows from operations (reported as a subtraction from operating cash flows in the exhibit), with the $6,731,000 proceeds reported as part of cash flows from investing activities (included in the total cash flows provided by investing activity of $148,200,000 reported in Exhibit 6.2).

Example 15

Delta Air Lines reported net losses of $773 million in Year 3 and $1,272 million in Year 2. The loss in Year 3 was reduced by a gain of $279 million on the sale of the firm's investment in Worldspan, LP. Worldspan operates and markets a computer reservation system for the travel industry, and is also used by Delta Air Lines for its reservation needs. Note 17 to the Delta's Year 3 annual report states:

> On June 30, Year 3, we sold our 40% equity investment in Worldspan, which operates and markets a computer reservation system for the travel industry. In exchange for the sale of our equity interest, we received (1) $285 million in cash and (2) a $45 million subordinated promissory note, which bears interest at 10% per annum and matures in Year 12. As a result of this transaction, we recorded a gain of $279 million ($176 million net of tax) in other income (expense) on our Year 3 Consolidated Statement of Operations. In addition, we will receive credits totaling approximately $125 million, which will be recognized ratably as a reduction of costs through Year 12, for future Worldspan-provided services.

Given Delta Air Lines' difficult operating environment, the firm decided to divest itself of its reservation system in order to generate additional cash necessary to maintain operations. Note that Delta also negotiated to receive future Worldspan services in return for the sale of the investment.

Example 16

Refer to PepsiCo's consolidated financial statements (Appendix A). Income from Continuing Operations before Income Taxes includes the following category (amounts in millions):

	Year 4	Year 3	Year 2
Bottling equity income	$380	$323	$280

PepsiCo describes its bottling equity income as "our share of the net income or loss of our noncontrolled bottling affiliates" (Appendix A). In the past PepsiCo also reported (1) gains on issuance of stock by noncontrolled affiliates and (2) gains on the sale of bottlers as part of "bottling equity income."[12] The reporting for PepsiCo's noncontrolled bottling affiliates is discussed in Chapter 9. Although PepsiCo's business model currently involves partial ownership in key bottlers, this has not always been the case. In the MD&A (Appendix B), the firm addresses the large percentage change for each year. The firm attributed the bottling equity income increase of 18 percent for Year 4 over Year 3 to increased earnings of the bottlers and favorable comparisons from international bottling investments, primarily as a result of the nationwide strike in Venezuela in early Year 3. The equity income increase of 16 percent for Year 3 over Year 2 resulted from increased earnings of the bottlers and a favorable comparison to Year 2 when an impairment charge was taken on a Latin American bottling investment.

The analyst in each of these examples must assess whether the gains and losses are sustainable, even though peripheral to the firm's operations, and thus include them in income from continuing operations. In many cases, even though the gains and losses do not relate to the sale of the firm's principal products and services, such gains and losses recur and should enter into estimates of future earnings. Of course, firms that rely heavily on such gains and losses for their earnings will not likely survive for long. Thus, a large percentage of reported earnings comprising gains and losses from peripheral activities might signal the need to revise downward the estimates of sustainable earnings.

Similar to impairment and restructuring charges, firms report peripheral gains and losses on a *pretax* basis. Income tax expense includes any tax effects of the gain or loss. If the analyst decides to eliminate the gain or loss from income from continuing operations, the analyst must also eliminate the related tax effect from income tax expense using either specific information disclosed about the tax effects or the statutory rate as described previously for restructuring charges if the firm does not disclose specific information about the tax effects.

Summary of Accounting Data Adjustments

This section discussed the reporting of various types of disclosures related to earnings. A large set of factors were identified that may affect the quality of the accounting information as a predictor of future sustainable earnings. The nature and extent of adjustments made to current earnings in order to use it as a predictor requires knowledge of the industry, the firm and its strategy, and the required financial reporting. The process is more art than science and requires considerable judgment on the part of the analyst.

RESTATED FINANCIAL STATEMENT DATA

A notion embedded in the concept of high-quality financial statement data is the ability to compare financial statement data across years for any particular firm. Comparability of data is crucial for effective time-series analysis, a technique used by analysts to judge trends over time. Standard setters also recognize the importance of comparability, and on implementation of *Statement No. 154* as discussed earlier in the chapter, firms will retroactively apply new accounting principles unless it is impracticable to determine either the cumulative effect or the period-specific effects of the change.[13]

[12]For example, several years ago PepsiCo reported a $1.0 billion gain on the sale of its PBG and Whitman bottlers in the income statement category "bottling equity income and transaction gains."

[13]*Statement of Financial Accounting Standards No. 154* (2005).

Firms also restate the financial statements of prior years when they decide to discontinue a particular line of business, even though the firm had included this income in continuing operations in income statements originally prepared for these years. The firm may also reclassify the net assets of the discontinued business as of the end of the preceding year to a single line, Net Assets of Discontinued Business, even though these net assets appeared among individual assets and liabilities in the balance sheet originally prepared for the preceding year.

The analyst must decide whether to use the financial statement data as originally reported for each year or as restated to reflect the new conditions. Because the objective of most financial statement analysis is to evaluate the past as a guide for projecting the future, the logical response is to use the restated data.

The analyst encounters difficulties, however, in using restated data. Most companies include balance sheets for two years and income statements and statements of cash flows for three years in their annual reports. Analysts can calculate ratios and perform other analyses based on balance sheet data (such as current assets/current liabilities or long-term debt to shareholders' equity) on a consistent basis for only two years. Analysts can calculate ratios based on data from the income statement (for example, cost of goods sold/sales) or from the statement of cash flows (for example, cash flow from operations/capital expenditures) for three years at most on a consistent basis. However, many important ratios and other analyses rely on data from the balance sheet and either the income statement or the statement of cash flows. For example, the rate of return on common shareholders' equity equals net income to common stock divided by average common shareholders' equity. The denominator of this ratio requires two years of balance sheet data. Thus, it is possible to calculate ratios based on average data from the balance sheet and one of the other two financial statements for only one year under the new conditions. The analysts could obtain balance sheet amounts for prior years from earlier annual reports, but this results in comparing restated income statement or statement of cash flow data with nonrestated balance sheet data for those earlier years.

Example 17

Refer to the financial statements of General Mills (Mills) in Exhibits 6.8 (income statement) and 6.9 (balance sheet). The notes to Mills' financial statements indicate that Mills decided in Year 5 to dispose of its toy and fashion segments and the nonapparel retailing businesses within its specialty retailing segment. It reported a loss of $188.3 million from these discontinued operations in its income statement for Year 5 (see the first column of Exhibit 6.9). In its comparative income statements for Year 4 and Year 3 (second and third columns), the income from these discontinued operations appears in Discontinued Operations After Tax. Exhibit 6.8 also shows the amounts as originally reported for Year 4 and Year 3 (fourth and fifth columns) in which Mills included the revenues and expenses from these operations in continuing operations. Exhibit 6.9 shows the comparative balance sheets for Year 5 and Year 4. Note that the net assets of these discontinued businesses appear on a separate line in the Year 5 balance sheet. However, individual asset and liability accounts include the amounts for these discontinued activities in the Year 4 balance sheet. Thus, Mills provides three years of income statements with the operations of these discontinued businesses set out separately, but only one balance sheet. The analyst cannot even calculate ratios using income statement and average balance sheet data for one year on a consistent basis in this case.

When a firm provides sufficient information to restate prior years' financial statements without injecting an intolerable number of assumptions, the analyst should use retroactively restated financial statement data. When the firm does not provide sufficient

EXHIBIT 6.8

General Mills, Inc., and Subsidiaries
Consolidated Statement of Earnings
(amounts in millions, except per-share data)

	Year Ended:			As Originally Reported:	
	May 26, Year 5 (52 weeks)	May 27, Year 4 (52 weeks)	May 29, Year 3 (52 weeks)	May 27, Year 4 (52 weeks)	May 29, Year 3 (52 weeks)
Continuing Operations:					
Sales	$4,285.2	$4,118.4	$4,082.3	$5,600.8	$5,550.8
Costs and Expenses: Cost of sales, exclusive of items that follow	2,474.8	2,432.8	2,394.8	3,165.9	3,123.3
Selling, general, and administrative expenses	1,368.1	1,251.5	1,288.3	1,849.4	1,831.6
Depreciation and amortization expenses	110.4	99.0	94.2	133.1	127.5
Interest expense	60.2	31.5	39.5	61.4	58.7
Total Costs and Expenses	4,013.5	3,814.8	3,816.8	5,209.8	5,141.1
Earnings from Continuing Operations, pretax	271.7	303.6	265.5	391.0	409.7
Gain (Loss) from Redeployments	(75.8)	53.0	2.7	7.7	—
Earnings from Continuing Operations after Redeployments, pretax	195.9	356.6	268.2	398.7	409.7
Income Taxes	80.5	153.9	106.1	165.3	164.6
Earnings from Continuing Operations after Redeployments	115.4	202.7	162.1	233.4	245.1
Earnings per Share—Continuing Operations after Redeployments	$ 2.58	$ 4.32	$ 3.24	$ 4.98	$ 4.89

Continued

information to do the restatements, the analyst should use the amounts as originally reported for each year. Then to interpret the resulting ratios, the analyst attempts to assess how much of the change in the ratios results from the new reporting condition and how much relates to other factors.

EXHIBIT 6.8

continued

	Year Ended: May 26, Year 5 (52 weeks)	May 27, Year 4 (52 weeks)	May 29, Year 3 (52 weeks)	As Originally Reported: May 27, Year 4 (52 weeks)	May 29, Year 3 (52 weeks)
Discontinued Operations after Taxes	(188.3)	30.7	83.0	—	—
Net Earnings (Loss)	$(72.9)	$233.4	$245.1	$233.4	$245.1
Net Earnings (Loss) per Share	$ (1.63)	$ 4.98	$ 4.89	$ 4.98	$ 4.89
Average Number of Common Shares	44.7	46.9	50.1	46.9	50.1

ACCOUNTING CLASSIFICATION DIFFERENCES

Accounting classification differences across firms also affect comparability analysis. Firms frequently classify items in their financial statements in different ways. When comparing two or more companies, it is important to obtain comparable data sets. If that is not possible, then it is critical that the analyst understand the significant differences in accounting classifications across firms. A scan of the financial statements should permit the analyst to identify significant differences that might affect the analysis and interpretations.

Example 18

Exhibit 6.10 shows the disclosure of operating expenses for three leading manufacturers of cellular phones: Ericsson (Sweden), Motorola (United States), and Nokia (Finland). Ericsson and Motorola report depreciation separately, whereas Nokia includes it in cost of goods sold and selling and administrative expenses. Nokia reports research and development (R&D) expense separately, whereas Ericsson and Motorola include it in selling and administrative expenses. The analyst must be aware of these classification differences when comparing financial statement ratios directly across these three firms.

To deal with the depreciation differences, the analyst must either allocate the depreciation amount for Ericsson and Motorola to cost of goods sold and selling and administrative expenses, or extract from cost of goods sold and selling and administrative expenses the depreciation amount of Nokia (Nokia reports total depreciation expense as an addback to net income in computing cash flow from operations). Both of these approaches require the analyst to make assumptions about the proportion of depreciation applicable to cost of goods sold versus selling and administrative expenses.

The classification differences for R&D expense are easier to fix. Ericsson and Motorola report the amount of R&D expense in their notes. Thus, the analyst can subtract the amounts from selling and administrative expenses.

When the analyst can easily and unambiguously reclassify accounts, the reclassified data should serve as the basis for analysis. If the reclassifications require numerous assumptions, then it is necessary to make them as precisely as possible. If the assumptions cannot be reasonably precise, then it may be best to avoid making them. The analyst should note the differences in account classification for further reference when interpreting the financial statement analysis.

EXHIBIT 6.9

General Mills, Inc., and Subsidiaries
Consolidated Balance Sheets
(amounts in millions)

		Year Ended: May 26, Year 5	Year Ended: May 27, Year 4
Assets			
Current Assets:	Cash and short-term investments	$ 66.8	$ 66.0
	Receivables, less allowance for doubtful accounts of $4.0 in Year 5 and $18.8 in Year 4	284.5	550.6
	Inventories	377.7	661.7
	Investments in tax leases	—	49.6
	Prepaid expenses	40.1	43.6
	Net assets of discontinued operations and redeployments	517.5	18.4
	Total Current Assets	1,286.6	1,389.9
Land, Buildings, and Equipment, at cost:	Land	93.3	125.9
	Buildings	524.4	668.6
	Equipment	788.1	904.7
	Construction in progress	80.2	130.0
	Total Land, Buildings, and Equipment	1,486.0	1,829.2
	Less accumulated depreciation	(530.0)	(599.8)
	Net Land, Buildings, and Equipment	956.0	1,229.4
Other Assets:	Net noncurrent assets of businesses to be spun off	$ 206.5	$ —
	Intangible assets, principally goodwill	50.8	146.0
	Investments and miscellaneous assets	162.7	92.8
	Total Other Assets	420.0	238.8
Total Assets		$2,662.6	$2,858.1
Liabilities and Stockholders' Equity			
Current Liabilities:	Accounts payable	$ 360.8	$ 477.8
	Current portion of long-term debt	59.4	60.3
	Notes payable	379.8	251.0
	Accrued taxes	1.4	74.3
	Accrued payroll	91.8	119.1
	Other current liabilities	164.0	162.9
	Total Current Liabilities	1,057.2	1,145.4
Long-Term Debt		$ 449.5	$ 362.6

Continued

EXHIBIT 6.9

continued

		Year Ended: May 26, Year 5	Year Ended: May 27, Year 4
Deferred Income Taxes		$ 29.8	$ 76.5
Deferred Income Taxes—Tax Leases		60.8	—
Other Liabilities and Deferred Credits		42.0	49.0
	Total Liabilities	1,639.3	1,633.5
Stockholders' Equity:	Common stock	$ 213.7	$ 215.4
	Retained earnings	1,201.7	1,375.0
	Less common stock in treasury, at cost	(333.9)	(291.8)
	Cumulative foreign currency adjustment	(58.2)	(74.0)
	Total Stockholders' Equity	1,023.3	1,224.6
Total Liabilities and Stockholders' Equity		$2,662.6	$2,858.1

EXHIBIT 6.10

Disclosure of Operating Expenses by Cellular Phone Companies (amounts in millions)

	Ericsson	Motorola	Nokia
Sales	SEK 124,266	$ 27,973	FIM 39,321
Cost of Goods Sold	(70,106)	(18,990)	(28,029)
Selling and Administrative	(40,803)	(4,715)	(3,512)
Depreciation	(4,216)	(2,308)	—
Research and Development	—	—	(3,514)
Operating Income	SEK 9,141	$ 1,960	FIM 4,266

FINANCIAL REPORTING WORLDWIDE

Thus far, we have identified many accounting quality and comparability issues. The concerns discussed in the chapter to this point equally apply to firms that follow reporting systems employed outside the United States, such as the International Financial Reporting

Standards of the IASB. However, important additional concerns also exist when comparing financial data for firms that operate in different countries.

Cross-national analysis of firms entails a two-step approach:

1. Achieve comparability of the reporting methods and accounting principles employed by the firms under scrutiny.
2. Understand corporate strategies, institutional structures, and cultural practices unique to the countries in which the firms operate.

Ideally, financial reporting would be the same worldwide. That has not happened to date, however, and differences in accounting principles worldwide may affect both time-series and cross-sectional comparisons of data reported by multinational firms. The analyst needs to thoroughly understand the reporting system employed by the firms under scrutiny in order to decide what data adjustments are necessary.[14]

When will financial reporting conform worldwide? As discussed in Chapter 1, an objective of the International Accounting Standards Board (IASB) is convergence of financial reporting standards and establishing a global set of generally accepted accounting standards, referred to by the IASB as Global GAAP. The IASB issues International Financial Reporting Standards (IFRS) and has an active and comprehensive agenda. Beginning in 2005, the financial statements of firms within the European Community must confirm to IFRS pronouncements.

Convergence of IASB Global GAAP and U.S. GAAP will be central to achieving worldwide conformity of financial reporting. The IASB and FASB pledged to use their best efforts to make existing U.S. and IASB standards fully compatible as soon as is practicable and to coordinate their future work programs to ensure that once achieved, compatibility is maintained. *Statement No. 154,* for example, is the result of close collaboration between the IASB and FASB.

Firms headquartered outside the United States that have debt or equity securities traded in U.S. capital markets must either file a Form 10-K using U.S. GAAP or file a Form 20-F report with the SEC each year. The Form 20-F report must include a reconciliation of shareholders' equity and net income as reported under GAAP of the firm's local country with GAAP in the United States. With this information, the analyst can convert the financial statements of a non-U.S. firm to achieve comparable accounting principles with U.S. firms.

Preparation of the reconciliation—essentially requiring a U.S. foreign filer to maintain two sets of financial records—is a costly endeavor. However, to date the SEC has not relaxed the reporting requirements of foreign filers to accept financial reports prepared in accordance with the GAAP of their country and/or Global GAAP prepared following IFRS legislated by the IASB.

Example 19

Exhibit 6.11 presents the reconciliations for Year 1 through Year 3 for Ericsson, a Swedish manufacturer of cellular phones. (We study the particular accounting principles requiring adjustment in later chapters and will therefore not discuss them at this time.) Ericsson provides extensive discussion of each reconciling item in its Form 20-F filing in Note 32, "Reconciliation to Accounting Principles Generally Accepted in the United States." In fact, the note is more than five pages long.

---

[14]A study of international accounting standards is beyond the scope of this book. The largest public accounting firms prepare comprehensive guides of financial reporting practices worldwide that are readily available to anyone on request.

EXHIBIT 6.11

Form 20-F Reconciliations for Ericsson (amounts in millions)

	Year 3	Year 2	Year 1
Adjustments to Shareholders' Equity			
Reported Shareholders' Equity	SEK 60,481	SEK 73,607	SEK 68,587
Capitalization of Software	6,409	11,652	16,502
Capitalization of Interest Expense	133	172	211
Pensions	(299)	440	99
Goodwill	2,700	1,064	—
Hedging	3,509	2,744	(2,196)
Restructuring Costs	1,442	217	1,458
Sale-Leaseback	(1,381)	(2,063)	(2,176)
Deferred Taxes	(3,347)	(4,021)	(4,487)
Other	316	(609)	(197)
Stockholders' Equity According to U.S. GAAP	SEK 69,963	SEK 83,203	SEK 77,801
Adjustments to Net Income			
Reported Net Loss	SEK (10,844)	SEK (19,013)	SEK (21,264)
Restructuring Costs	1,225	(1,240)	(1,642)
Capitalization of Software Development Costs	(5,153)	(4,940)	(2,135)
Goodwill Amortization	1,636	1,064	—
Pensions	(840)	459	1,006
Hedging	1,603	2,884	(2,233)
Sale-Leaseback	682	113	(815)
Deferred Income Taxes	533	966	2,042
Other	561	(211)	638
Net Income According to U.S. GAAP	SEK (10,597)	SEK (19,918)	SEK (24,403)

Achieving comparability in reporting is important to the analysis of multinational firms, but the data needs to be carefully interpreted. Analysis of multinational firms is complicated by the fact that the environments in which the firms operate may vary extensively across countries. Operational strategies may exist in one firm's home country that are not common in another. Institutional arrangements, such as significant alliances with banks and extensive intercorporate holdings, may be common in one country and not in another. Cultural characteristics may exist in one country that affect how firms do business in that country—with those same characteristics foreign to other business settings.

For example, in a study addressing comparability of Japanese and U.S. financial reporting, Herrmann, Inoue, and Thomas identify the following environmental characteristics that may influence interpretation of the data:

1. Profitability ratios often are more conservative in Japan, attributable in part to the close link between tax and financial reporting systems.

2. Japanese companies often have higher debt ratios. High debt ratios are sometimes considered a sign of financial strength because debt is the primary source of capital.
3. The corporate group is different in Japan in that Japanese grouping is often based on bank dependence, intercompany loans, mutual shareholding, preferred business transactions, and multiple personal ties.[15]

Herrmann, Inoue, and Thomas stress that environmental factors unique to Japan may influence the financial data reported by Japanese firms in such a way that the data, although comparable to data reported by U.S. firms once the necessary adjustments are made, can be effectively interpreted only when taking these unique factors into consideration.

Other countries have their own unique environmental and business practices. When analyzing multinational firms, the analyst needs to incorporate these factors into the interpretation of the data and understand that, although the data may be comparable from a measurement perspective, they may not be comparable on other dimensions.

EARNINGS MANAGEMENT

We conclude the chapter with a discussion of earnings management because the concepts of accounting quality and earnings management often are linked when discussing the need to adjust financial data to better reflect the economic information content of financial data.

As with other concepts discussed in this chapter, earnings management connotes different things to different users of the term.[16] Healy and Wahlen provide the following definition of earnings management:

> Earnings management occurs when managers use judgment in financial reporting and in structuring transactions to alter financial reports to either mislead some stakeholders about the underlying economic performance of the company or to influence contractual outcomes that depend on reporting accounting numbers.[17]

In the chapter we established that choices, judgments, and estimates are an inevitable consequence of the reporting process. Healy and Wahlen recognize this and define earnings management as the use of these inherent aspects of the reporting model to mask the underlying economic performance of a firm. Any judgments employed by management that result in lower economic information content of the financial reports, and provide a skewed basis for making decisions, are probably the result of a firm practicing earnings management.

Detecting earnings management is difficult because there are so many ways that managers can exercise judgment in financial reporting. One of our objectives in Chapters 7 through 9 is to illustrate the judgments that firms must make to apply the accounting principles under investigation in those chapters so that the analyst can discern whether a firm practices earnings management.

---

[15]Don Herrmann, Tatsuo Inoue, and Wayne Thomas, "Are There Benefits to Restating Japanese Financial Statements According to U.S. GAAP?" *Journal of Financial Statement Analysis* (Fall 1996), pp. 61–73.

[16]As Chapter 5 notes, earnings management also is linked at times with earnings manipulation, a topic discussed in that chapter and defined as preparing financial reports based on reporting techniques outside the limits of GAAP.

[17]Paul M. Healy and James M. Wahlen, "A Review of the Earnings Management Literature and Its Implications for Standard Setting," *Accounting Horizons* (December 1999), pp. 365–383.

Motives to Practice Earnings Management[18]

Possible reasons *for* earnings management by a firm and its managers include the following:

1. Firms manage earnings to create optimal manager compensation payments under compensation contracts.
2. Firms manage earnings to create optimal job security for senior management.
3. Firms manage earnings to create optimal lending environments and to mitigate potential violation of debt covenants.
4. Firms use earnings management in an attempt to influence short-term stock price performance and wealth resource allocation over time.
5. Firms have incentives to minimize/manage reported earnings to thwart industry-specific actions and antitrust actions against the firm.

Disincentives to Practice Earnings Management

Suggested reasons *against* earnings management by a firm and its managers include the following:

1. Earnings and cash flows over the life of the firm agree, so firms cannot manage earnings forever. Eventually, earnings aggressively reported in early years must be offset by lower earnings or even losses in later years to compensate.
2. Capital markets and regulators such as the Securities and Exchange Commission penalize firms identified as flagrant earnings managers.
3. Firms and managers that are perceived as practicing aggressive earnings management will lose reputation for being honest and trustworthy among capital market participants and stakeholders.
4. Legal consequences can result from aggressive earnings management, as well as from earnings management that reverts to earnings manipulations and fraud.[19]

The questions as to whether analysts of financial reports can detect earnings management and make appropriate adjustments to reported amounts in making investment decisions has been the subject of extensive but inconclusive research in recent years.[20]

Boundaries of Earnings Management

It is important to note that earnings management has boundaries. Securities regulations and stock exchanges require annual audits by independent accountants. Auditors can monitor particularly aggressive actions taken by management to influence earnings, although their power to thwart actions taken within the bounds of generally accepted accounting principles is limited. In addition, the ongoing scrutiny of financial analysts and investors serves as a check on earnings management. Security analysts typically follow several firms within an industry and have a sense of the corporate reporting "personalities" of various firms. The frequency, timeliness, and quality of management's communications

---

[18]Often the motivations for practicing earnings management and earnings manipulation (discussed in Chapter 5) are similar; however, the legal consequences of earnings manipulation are generally more severe.

[19]Messod D. Beneish, "Detecting GAAP Violation: Implications for Assessing Earnings Management among Firms with Extreme Financial Performance," *Journal of Accounting and Public Policy* (1997), pp. 271–309; "The Detection of Earnings Management," *Financial Analyst Journal* (September/October 1999), pp. 24–36.

[20]See "The Detection of Earnings Management" (1999) for an extensive list of research related to earnings management provided in the reference list at the end of the article.

with shareholders and analysts signal the forthrightness of management and the likelihood of earnings being highly managed.[21]

The task for the analyst is to identify situations in which earnings management is possible and the avenues management might pursue in those situations to carry out earnings management. Understanding when GAAP provides flexibility to manage earnings should permit the analyst to distinguish high economic information content from what some call "cosmetic" (that is, earnings-managed) content of the reported data. As stated earlier, a close study of the selected accounting principles presented in Chapters 7 to 9 will aid in this task.

SUMMARY

The financial analysis framework discussed in Chapters 1 to 5 and the discussion of forecasting and valuation presented in Chapters 10 to 14 assume that a firm's reported financial statement data reflect accurately the economic effects of a firm's decisions. The assumption also is that the financial data are informative about the firm's likely future profitability and risk. This chapter develops the concept of accounting quality as the basis for assessing the information content of reported financial statement data, and for adjusting that data before assessing a firm's profitability and risk or forecasting or valuing the firm.

The illustrations in this chapter identify items that are part of the current period's performance but may not recur in future years. The chapter indicates adjustments the analyst might make to eliminate the effect of such items from forecasts of future earnings. The chapter also identifies adjustments that the analyst might make to enhance comparability of a particular firm's reported amounts over time.

Analyzing accounting quality and adjusting financial data are themes that continue in Chapters 7 through 9. In this regard, Chapters 6 through 9 represent a unit that together addresses the relevant financial data for analysis. Chapter 7 focuses on revenue recognition and related expenses. Chapter 8 examines the recognition and valuation of liabilities, together with related expenses. Chapter 9 explores topics that have pervasive effects on all three principal financial statements, including corporate acquisitions, intercorporate investments, and foreign currency translation.

The chapter concludes with a discussion of earnings management and the conditions that might trigger earnings management. The concepts of accounting quality and earnings management often are linked when discussing the need to adjust financial data to better reflect the economic information content of financial data.

QUESTIONS, EXERCISES, PROBLEMS, AND CASES

Questions and Exercises

6.1 CONCEPT OF EARNINGS QUALITY. The concept of earnings quality has several dimensions, but two characteristics often dominate: The accounting information should be a fair representation of performance for the reporting period, and it should provide relevant information to forecast expected future earnings. Provide a specific example of poor earnings quality that would hinder forecasting expected future earnings.

[21] See Mark H. Lang and Russell J. Lundholm, "Corporate Disclosure Policy and Analyst Behavior," *Accounting Review* (October 1996), pp. 467–492.

6.2 RESTATING EARNINGS FOR LITIGATION LOSS. Rock of Ages, Inc. is the largest integrated granite quarrier, manufacturer, and retailer of finished granite memorials and granite blocks for memorial use in North America. The firm reported a net loss for Year 4 of $3.2 million. In Year 4, the firm reported a pretax litigation settlement loss of $6.5 million, and management stated that, in its opinion, the litigation settlement loss did not reflect the current year's operations because it was the first year in five years that the firm reported such a loss. Calculate pro forma earnings for Year 4 excluding the settlement costs and speculate on management's reasoning as to why it might believe that pro forma earnings is a better measure of performance for Rock of Ages. State any assumptions you are making in your calculations.

6.3 CONCEPT OF EARNINGS MANAGEMENT. The concept of earnings management connotes different things to different users of the term. Define earnings management and discuss why it is difficult to discern whether, in fact, a firm practices earnings management.

6.4 CRITERIA TO IDENTIFY NONRECURRING ITEMS. The chapter discusses eight accounting and disclosure topics that typically occur infrequently but can have a large impact on financial statements. What criteria should an analyst employ to assess whether to choose to include or eliminate items from the financial statements related to these eight topics?

6.5 EFFECT OF ALTERNATIVE GAAP ON FINANCIAL STATEMENT ANALYSIS. Nestlé Group, a multinational food products firm based in Switzerland, recently issued its financial statements. The auditor's opinion attached to the financial statements stated: "In our opinion, the Consolidated Accounts give a true and fair view of the financial position, the net profit and cash flows in accordance with International Financial Reporting Standards (IFRS) and comply with Swiss law." Note that Nestlé's financial reports are prepared using IFRS standards. One of Nestlé's main competitors is PepsiCo, which prepares financial reports following U.S. GAAP. Describe the necessary steps an analyst should consider to develop comparable accounting data in conducting a profitability and risk analysis of these two firms.

6.6 REPORTING IMPAIRMENT AND RESTRUCTURING CHARGES. Checkpoint Systems is a manufacturer and marketer of integrated systems solutions for retail security, labeling, and merchandising. The firm is a leading provider of source tagging, handheld labeling systems, retail merchandising systems, and bar-code labeling systems. In a press release, Checkpoint stated: "GAAP reported net loss for the fourth quarter of Year 4 was $29.3 million, or $0.78 per diluted share, compared to net earnings of $4.5 million, or $0.13 per diluted share, for the fourth quarter Year 3. Excluding impairment and restructuring charges, net of tax, the Company's net income for the fourth quarter Year 4 was $0.30 per diluted share, compared to $0.27 per diluted share in the fourth quarter Year 3." Calculate the amount of the impairment and restructuring charges reported by Checkpoint in Year 4 and Year 3, and discuss why the firm reported earnings both including and excluding impairment and restructuring charges.

6.7 CONCEPT OF A PERIPHERAL ACTIVITY. Firms often enter into transactions that are peripheral to their core operations but generate gains and losses that must be reported on the income statement. A gain labeled "peripheral" by one firm may not be labeled as such for another firm. Provide an example in which a gain generated from the sale of an equity security may be labeled a peripheral activity by one firm, but considered a core activity for another firm.

6.8 CONCEPT OF AN ASSET IMPAIRMENT CHARGE. Example 9 in the chapter discusses JDS Uniphase's record-breaking asset impairment charge of approximately \$50 billion for Year 1. Explain how the charge of this record-breaking magnitude was generated, and how much cash was lost as a result of the charge.

6.9 REPORTING IMPAIRMENT CHARGES. *Statement No. 144* requires firms to assess whether they will recover carrying amounts of long-lived assets and, if not, to write down the assets to their fair values and recognize an impairment loss in income from continuing operations. Impairment charges often appear as a separate line item on the income statement of companies that experience reductions in the future benefits originally anticipated from the long-lived assets. Conduct a search to identify a firm (other than the examples given in this chapter) that has recently reported an impairment charge and discuss how the firm (a) reported the charge on the income statement, (b) determined the amount of the charge, and (c) used cash related to the charge.

Problems and Cases

6.10 ADJUSTING FOR UNUSUAL INCOME STATEMENT AND CLASSIFICATION ITEMS. H. J. Heinz is one of the world's leading marketers of branded foods to retail and foodservice channels. According to the firm, Heinz holds the number one or two branded products in more than fifty world product markets. Among the company's well-known brands are Heinz, StarKist, Kibbles 'n Bits, and 9Lives. Exhibit 6.12 presents an income statement for Heinz for Year 10, Year 11, and Year 12. Notes to the financial statements reveal the following information:

1. **Gain on sale of Weight Watchers.** In Year 10, Heinz completed the sale of the Weight Watchers classroom business for \$735 million. The transaction resulted in a pretax gain of \$464.5 million. The sale did not include Weight Watchers frozen meals, desserts, and breakfast items. Heinz did not disclose the tax effect of the gain reported in Exhibit 6.12.
2. **Accounting change for revenue recognition.** In Year 11, Heinz changed its method of accounting for revenue recognition to recognizing revenue upon the passage of title, ownership, and risk of loss to the customer. The change was driven by a new ruling of the Securities and Exchange Commission on revenue recognition. The cumulative effect of the change on prior years resulted in a charge to income of \$17 million, net of income taxes of \$10 million. Heinz indicated that the effect on Year 11 and prior years was not material.
3. **Sale and promotion costs.** In Year 11, Heinz changed the classification of certain sale and promotion incentives provided to customers and consumers. In the past, Heinz classified these incentives as selling and administrative expenses (see Exhibit 6.12), with the gross amount of the revenue associated with the incentives reported in sales. Beginning in Year 11, Heinz changed to reporting the incentives as a reduction of revenues. As a result of this change, the firm reported lower revenues of \$693 million in Year 12, \$610 million in Year 11, and \$469 million in Year 10. The firm stated that selling and administrative expenses were "correspondingly reduced such that net earnings were not affected." Exhibit 6.12 already reflects the

adjustments to sales revenues and selling and administrative expenses for Years 10 through 12.

4. **Tax rate.** The U.S. federal statutory income tax rate was 35 percent for each of the years presented in Exhibit 6.12.

Required

a. Discuss whether you would adjust for each of the following items when using earnings to forecast the future profitability of Heinz:
   (1) Gain on sale of Weight Watchers classroom business
   (2) Accounting change for revenue recognition

b. Indicate the adjustment you would make to Heinz's net income for each item in part a.

c. Discuss whether you believe that the reclassification adjustments made by Heinz for the sale and promotion incentive costs (item 3) are appropriate.

d. Prepare a common-size income statement for Year 10, Year 11, and Year 12 using the amounts in Exhibit 6.12. Set sales equal to 100 percent.

e. Repeat part d after making the income statement adjustments in part b.

f. Assess the changes in the profitability of Heinz during the three-year period.

EXHIBIT 6.12

Income Statement
H. J. Heinz Company
(amounts in millions)
(Problem 6.10)

	Year 12	Year 11	Year 10
Sales	$9,431	$8,821	$8,939
Gain on Sale of Weight Watchers	—	—	465
Cost of Goods Sold	(6,094)	(5,884)	(5,789)
Selling and Administrative Expenses	(1,746)	(1,955)	(1,882)
Interest Income	27	23	25
Interest Expense	(294)	(333)	(270)
Other Income (Expense)	(45)	1	(25)
Income before Income Taxes and Cumulative Effect of Accounting Changes	$1,279	$ 673	$1,463
Income Tax Expense	(445)	(178)	(573)
Income before Cumulative Effect of Accounting Change	$ 834	$ 495	$ 890
Cumulative Effect of Accounting Change	—	(17)	—
Net Income	$ 834	$ 478	$ 890

EXHIBIT 6.13

Parametric Technology Corporation
Consolidated Statements of Operations
(amounts in thousands)
(Problem 6.11)

	Year Ended September 30:		
	Year 4	**Year 3**	**Year 2**
Revenue:			
License	$198,860	$205,301	$242,906
Service	461,169	466,639	499,051
Total Revenue	$660,029	$671,940	$741,957
Costs and expenses:			
Cost of License Revenue	$ 8,234	$ 10,990	$ 16,714
Cost of Service Revenue	173,941	207,496	200,244
Sales and Marketing	226,054	298,479	333,249
Research and Development	107,992	128,425	136,073
General and Administrative	58,264	69,418	67,256
Amortization of Goodwill and Other Intangible Assets	5,195	5,861	35,757
Restructuring and Other Charges	42,933	30,896	31,150
Total Costs and Expenses	$622,613	$751,565	$820,443
Operating Income (Loss)	$ 37,416	$(79,625)	$(78,486)
Interest Income	3,484	3,260	4,075
Other Expense	(3,861)	(6,064)	(8,616)
Gain on Sale of a Business	—	—	8,688
Income (Loss) Before Income Taxes	$ 37,039	$(82,429)	$(74,339)
Provision for Income Taxes	2,226	15,851	19,282
Net Income (Loss)	$ 34,813	$(98,280)	$(93,621)

6.11 ADJUSTING FOR UNUSUAL INCOME STATEMENT ITEMS.

Parametric Technology Corporation (PTC) was founded almost twenty-five years ago. It develops, markets, and supports software that helps manufacturers improve the competitiveness of their products. PTC offers a suite of computer-aided design tools and a range of Internet-based software technologies. The firm employed approximately 3,000 people and operated in thirty countries at the end of Year 4. Exhibit 6.13 shows the income statement for PTC for Year 2 through Year 4.

1. **Amortization of goodwill and other intangible assets.** Prior to Year 3, PTC amortized goodwill over five to seven years and trademarks over seven years. It amortized other intangible assets, such as developed technology (software), over seven years. Beginning in Year 3, GAAP no longer requires firms to amortize

goodwill and other intangibles with indefinite lives, such as trademarks. However, intangible assets with finite lives, including software, continue to be amortized. PTC's software amortization was $5.9 million for Year 2, $5.2 million for Year 3, and $5.2 million for Year 4.

2. **Restructuring and other charges.** In Year 2 through Year 4, PTC reorganized its sales force, wrote down some impaired assets, provided severance and termination packages to employees, and implemented several cost reduction programs. PTC did not disclose the tax effects of the charges reported in Exhibit 6.13.
3. **Gain on the sale of a business.** In Year 2, PTC completed the sale of the ICEM surfacing business for $10.2 million in cash, resulting in a pretax gain of $8.7 million.
4. **Other expenses.** In Year 2, Year 3, and Year 4, PTC recorded noncash write-downs on equity investments in "other expense." PTC did not disclose the tax effects of the write-downs reported in Exhibit 6.13.
5. **Tax rate.** The U.S. federal statutory income tax rate was 35 percent for each of the years presented in Exhibit 6.13.

Required

a. Discuss the appropriate treatment of the (1) goodwill and other intangible asset amortization, (2) restructuring and other charges, (3) gain on the sale of a business, and (4) write-down of investments reported as other expenses when using earnings to forecast the future profitability of PTC.

b. Indicate the adjustments to net income of PTC to eliminate each item listed in part a. For item (1), assume that only the goodwill amortization for Year 2 is eliminated.

6.12 ADJUSTING FOR NONRECURRING ITEMS. Ruby Tuesday, Inc. owns and operates Ruby Tuesday casual dining restaurants. The firm also franchises the Ruby Tuesday concept in selected domestic and international markets. As of the end of Year 12, it owned and operated almost 400 restaurants, and had more than 200 franchised restaurants. Exhibit 6.14 presents an income statement for Ruby Tuesday, Inc. for Year 12, Year 11, and Year 10. The notes to the financial statements reveal the following additional information:

1. **Peripheral losses.** In Years 12 and 10, Ruby Tuesday recorded pretax losses on restaurants it sold. For Year 10, the firm recognized the sale of a set of restaurants—American Café, L&N Seafood, and Tia's Tex-Mex restaurants—to Specialty Restaurant Group and recorded a pretax and after-tax loss of $10.0 million. Ruby Tuesday received a note payable of $28.9 million from the Specialty Restaurant Group as partial payment for the restaurants. In Year 12, Ruby Tuesday recorded an additional loss on the sale by writing off the note due to the firm from the Specialty Restaurant Group. Ruby Tuesday indicated that the write-off generated a $11.4 million tax benefit.
2. **Accounting change.** Ruby Tuesday adopted *Statement No. 133* in Year 12. *Statement No. 133* addresses accounting for derivative instruments. The firm reports the cumulative effect of the accounting change net of tax affects. Note that the firm uses the cumulative-effect method for reporting the change because *Statement No. 154* was not effective for Year 12.

EXHIBIT 6.14

Ruby Tuesday, Inc.
Income Statement
(amounts in millions)
(Problem 6.12)

	Year 12	Year 11	Year 10
Restaurant Sales and Operating Revenue	$ 819	$ 770	$ 785
Franchise Revenues	14	12	8
Total Revenues	$ 833	$ 782	$ 793
Payroll and Related Costs	(268)	(248)	(251)
Cost of Merchandise	(221)	(213)	(214)
Other Restaurant Operating Costs	(155)	(148)	(159)
Depreciation and Amortization	(34)	(34)	(42)
Loss on Specialty Restaurant Group, LLC	(29)	—	—
Loss on Sale of Various Restaurants	—	—	(10)
Selling and Administrative Expenses	(45)	(50)	(53)
Interest Income (Expense)	6	4	(1)
Income before Income Taxes and Cumulative Effect of Accounting Change	$ 87	$ 93	$ 63
Provision for Income Taxes	(30)	(33)	(26)
Income before Cumulative Effect of Change in Accounting Principle	$ 57	$ 60	$ 37
Cumulative Effect of Change in Accounting Principle	$ (1)	—	—
Net Income	$ 56	$ 60	$ 37

Required

a. Discuss the appropriate treatment of items 1 and 2 when using earnings to forecast the future profitability of Ruby Tuesday.

b. Indicate the adjustments to the income statement to eliminate the items in part a.

c. Ruby Tuesday's statement of cash flows shows an addback to net income for the losses on the restaurant sales for both Year 12 ($28.9 million) and Year 10 ($10.0 million). What is the interpretation of this addback?

6.13 ADJUSTMENTS FOR PERIPHERAL GAINS, CHARGES, AND OTHER UNUSUAL ITEMS. Wyeth (formerly American Home Products) is a global leader in prescription pharmaceuticals, nonprescription medicines, and animal health care products. Wyeth's products are sold in more than 140 countries, with a product portfolio that includes treatments across a wide range of therapeutic areas. Exhibit 6.15 presents a recent income statement for Wyeth. A set of transactions and activities during Year 1 through Year 3 led to a number of nonrecurring items on the income statement.

1. **Diet drug litigation charges.** Wyeth was named as a defendant in numerous legal actions related to the diet drugs Redux and Pondimin. The drugs were used in the United States by approximately 5.8 million people until their voluntary market withdrawal several years ago. The legal actions alleged that the use of the diet drugs caused certain serious conditions, including valvular heart disease. Extensive class-actions lawsuit and court-administered settlements took place after removal of the drugs from the market. Wyeth recorded the following litigation charges related to these drugs: Year 3, $2,000 million ($1,300 million after taxes); Year 2, $1,400 million ($910 million after taxes); and Year 1, $950 million ($615 million after taxes).
2. **Gains related to Immunex/Amgen stock.** In Year 2, Wyeth recorded gains totaling $4,082.2 ($2,628.1 million after taxes) related to the acquisition of Immunex by Amgen and then the subsequent sale of Amgen common stock by Wyeth. Wyeth sold its remaining shares of Amgen stock in Year 3, generating a gain of $860.6 million ($558.7 million after taxes).
3. **Special charges.** In Year 2, Wyeth recorded a special charge for restructuring and related asset impairments of $340.8 million ($233.5 million after taxes). The charges were recorded to recognize the costs of closing manufacturing facilities and two research facilities. In Year 3, Wyeth recorded a special charge of manufacturing restructuring, asset impairments, and the cost of debt extinguishment of $639.9 million ($466.4 million after taxes). The charges are broken out in its financial reports by personnel costs, asset impairments, contract settlement costs, and other closure/exit costs.

Required

a. Discuss whether you would adjust for each of the three items when using earnings to forecast the future profitability of Wyeth. Discuss each item separately.
b. Indicate the adjustments to the income statement of Wyeth to eliminate each item in part a.
c. Determine the percentage change in income for Year 1 through Year 3 based on (1) reported income as revealed in Exhibit 6.15 and (2) pro forma income calculated in part b, and comment on the different trends. Pro forma income for Year 0 was $2,513 million, with a reported loss for the year of $902 million.
d. The statement of cash flows shows an addback to net income for items 1 and 3, and a subtraction for item 2. Why is this the case?

6.14 ADJUSTING FOR UNUSUAL ITEMS. Prior to Year 14, Borden, Inc. derived approximately 75 percent of its revenues from branded food products and 25 percent from packaging and industrial products. The geographical sales mix comprised approximately 67 percent in the United States and 33 percent from other countries, although, interestingly, the firm's manufacturing and processing facilities were equally split between the United States and other countries. In Year 14 and Year 15, Borden was acquired by a firm that specialized in takeovers and buyouts of established firms. As a result, the firm experienced substantial business realignments and financial restructuring during this period. Exhibit 6.16 presents an income statement and Exhibit 6.17 presents a

EXHIBIT 6.15

Wyeth Corporation
Income Statement
(amount in thousands)
(Problem 6.13)

	Year 3	Year 2	Year 1
Net Revenue	$15,850,632	$14,584,035	$13,983,745
Cost of Goods Sold	4,377,086	3,918,387	3,388,776
Selling, General, and Administrative Expenses	5,468,174	5,010,507	5,034,516
Research and Development Expenses	2,093,533	2,080,191	1,869,679
Interest Expense, net	103,140	202,052	146,358
Other Income, net	(332,264)	(382,931)	(274,331)
Gains Related to Immunex/Amgen Stock	(860,554)	(4,082,216)	—
Diet Drug Litigation Charges	2,000,000	1,400,000	950,000
Special Charges	639,905	340,800	—
Income before Federal and Foreign Taxes	$ 2,361,612	$ 6,097,245	$ 2,868,747
Provision for Federal and Foreign Taxes	310,420	1,650,040	583,453
Net Income	$ 2,051,192	$ 4,447,205	$ 2,285,294

statement of cash flows for Borden for Year 14, Year 15, and Year 16. The notes to the financial statements reveal the following additional information.

1. **Restructuring charges and discontinued operations.** For years, Borden reported continually increasing sales while maintaining a profit margin of approximately 4 percent. Borden regularly purchased branded food products companies and other businesses with the cash flows generated by its mature food products business. Sales and earnings started declining in Year 10, however, brought on by deteriorating market positions in certain branded food products segments and difficulties in managing the diverse set of businesses in which Borden competed. As a result, Borden embarked on a major restructuring program in Year 10. The restructuring program involved both organizational changes and divestiture of its North American snacks, seafood, jams and jellies, and other businesses. Four years later, Borden embarked on another restructuring brought on by factors similar to those identified in Year 10. (The firm reported no restructuring charges in Year 11, Year 12, or Year 13.) The restructuring charges/credits in Year 14, Year 15, and Year 16 related to streamlining operations and the charges involved employee severances and relocations and plant closings, part of which Borden included in continuing operations and part of which it included in income from discontinued operations. The loss on disposal recognized in Year 14 represented a pretax charge of $637 million ($490 million after taxes) to provide for the expected future disposal of the North American businesses described previously. The charges and credits in Year 15 and Year 16 were related to these businesses as well.
2. **Loss/gain on divestitures.** In Year 16, the firm redesigned its operating structure and decided to divest additional businesses. The firm recorded a $245 million

charge related to the estimated losses on the disposal or consolidation of these businesses. The firm indicated that a large portion of the charge was related to the excess of net book values over expected proceeds.

3. **Impairment losses.** In Year 15, Borden wrote down goodwill, plant, and equipment totaling $293 million. The firm concluded that ongoing and projected operating losses reported by the businesses represented by these assets indicated that the carrying values of the assets were not expected to be recovered by their future cash flows. The firm stated that the future cash flow projections were measured at the business level, which is the level at which the business is managed. A similar write-down of $8 million was recorded in Year 16.

Required

a. Why do the amounts for restructuring charges in the income statement in Exhibit 6.16 differ from the amounts for restructuring charges reported in the operations section of the statement of cash flows in Exhibit 6.17?

EXHIBIT 6.16

Borden, Inc.
Income Statement
(amounts in millions)
(Problem 6.14)

	Year 16	Year 15	Year 14
Continuing Operations			
Sales	$5,944	$6,261	$6,226
Other Income (Expense), net	(18)	(138)	35
Cost of Goods Sold	(4,136)	(4,240)	(4,083)
Selling and Administrative	(1,811)	(1,963)	(2,045)
Restructuring Expense	11	(15)	(115)
(Loss) Gain on Divestitures	(245)	59	15
Impairment Losses	(8)	(293)	0
Interest	(140)	(143)	(140)
Minority Interest	(15)	(41)	(41)
Income Taxes	(24)	(53)	51
Income (Loss) from Continuing Operations	$ (442)	$ (566)	$ (97)
Discontinued Operations, net of tax effects			
Income (Loss) from Operations	$ 9	$ 27	$ (26)
Gain (Loss) on Disposal	67	(59)	(490)
Income (Loss) from Discontinued Operations	$ 76	$ (32)	$ (516)
Accounting Changes, net of taxes			
Postretirement Benefits Other than Pensions	—	—	(18)
Net Income (Loss)	$ (366)	$ (598)	$ (631)

EXHIBIT 6.17

Borden, Inc.
Statement of Cash Flows
(amounts in millions)
(Problem 6.14)

	Year 16	Year 15	Year 14
Operations			
Net Income (Loss)	$(366)	$(598)	$(631)
Depreciation and Amortization	157	193	224
Loss on Disposal—Discontinued Operations	245	95	637
Restructuring	(53)	(57)	53
Impairment Losses	8	293	—
(Increase) Decrease in Accounts Receivable	7	(41)	61
(Increase) Decrease in Inventories	10	(44)	30
Increase (Decrease) in Accounts Payable	(27)	50	3
Increase (Decrease) in Current and Deferred Taxes	9	24	(242)
Other Changes in Working Capital Accounts	92	(7)	17
Cash Flow from Operations	$ 82	$ (92)	$ 152
Investing			
Capital Expenditures	$(203)	$(150)	$(177)
Divestiture of Businesses and Sale of Securities	289	409	53
Purchase of Businesses	(6)	—	(9)
Cash Flow from Investing	$ 80	$ 259	$(133)
Financing			
Increase (Decrease) in Short-Term Debt	$(192)	$ (85)	$(536)
Increase in Long-Term Debt	3	616	275
Issuance of Capital Stock	998	6	12
Reduction in Long-Term Debt	(436)	(493)	(129)
Dividends	(43)	(36)	(127)
Other	(472)	(150)	400
Cash Flow from Financing	$(142)	$(142)	$(105)
Change in Cash	$ 20	$ 25	$ (86)
Cash—Beginning of Year	125	100	186
Cash—End of Year	$ 145	$ 125	$ 100

b. Why does the amount for loss on disposal of discontinued operations in the income statement in Exhibit 6.16 in Year 14 differ from the amount reported in the operations section of the statement of cash flows in Exhibit 6.17?

c. Discuss whether you would eliminate each of the following items when using earnings to forecast the future profitability of Borden: (1) restructuring charges,

(2) discontinued operations, (3) loss or gain on divestitures, and (4) impairment losses.

d. Assume for this part that you have decided to eliminate each of the four items in part c plus the adjustment for the accounting change. Indicate the change in net income as a result of such eliminations. The income tax rate is 35 percent for Year 14, Year 15, and Year 16.

e. Prepare a common-size income statement for Borden after eliminating the items in part d. Set sales equal to 100 percent.

f. Assess the changes in the profitability of Borden during the three-year period.

6.15 RESTRUCTURING CHARGES AND IMPAIRMENT OF GOODWILL. Sapient Corporation is a technology consultancy firm. It focuses on helping clients achieve business outcomes through the rapid application and support of advanced information technology. Most of its contracts are fixed-price, fixed-time agreements. After a decade of success, the firm experienced a significant decline in the demand for its services. Exhibit 6.18 presents a recent income statement for Sapient Corporation. A note to the financial statements stated that (a) "restructuring and other charges" were related to the firm's downsizing of its workforce and operations due to a slowdown in product and service demand, and (b) "impairment of goodwill" was related to the firm's conclusion that the carrying amount of the reporting units represented by the goodwill exceeded their fair values and thus, were written off during Year 2. The firm indicated that the impairment of goodwill did not generate a tax deduction.

Required

a. Discuss whether you would eliminate the restructuring charge from the income statement of Sapient Corporation when using earnings to forecast future profitability.

b. The statement of cash flows for Sapient Corporation (not included here) includes an addback for "restructuring costs" in Year 2 of $7.3 million, but no addback in Year 3. Speculate why in Year 2 the addback differs from the $66.885 million reported on the income statement for restructuring charges in that year.

c. The statement of cash flows (not reported here) includes an addback of $107.43 million for "goodwill impairment" for Year 2. This same amount is reported in Exhibit 6.18 as an expense for Year 2. Explain why the amounts are the same.

d. Restructuring charges often cover a wide range of different cost categories. Identify the categories of costs often included in restructuring charges, and identify those categories that usually entail the use of cash and those that do not.

6.16 USING ORIGINALLY REPORTED VERSUS RESTATED DATA. Prior to Year 8, General Dynamics Corporation engaged in a wide variety of industries, including weapons manufacturing under government contracts, information technologies, commercial aircraft manufacturing, missile systems, coal mining, material service, ship management, and ship financing. During Year 8, General Dynamics sold its information technologies business. During Year 9, General Dynamics sold its commercial aircraft manufacturing business. During Year 9, it also announced its intention to sell its missile systems, coal mining, material service, ship management, and ship financing businesses. These strategic moves left General Dynamics with only its weapons manufacturing business. Financial statements for General

EXHIBIT 6.18

Sapient Corporation
Partial Income Statement
(amounts in thousands)
(Problem 6.15)

	Year 3	Year 2
Revenues:		
Service Revenues	$184,795	$ 173,811
Reimbursable Expenses	9,574	8,562
Total Gross Revenues	$194,369	$ 182,373
Operating Expenses:		
Project Personnel Costs	$111,967	$ 133,275
Reimbursable Expenses	9,574	8,562
Total Project Personnel Costs	$121,541	$ 141,837
Selling and Marketing Costs	18,501	26,192
General and Administrative Costs	57,523	79,338
Restructuring and Other Related Charges	2,135	66,885
Impairment of Goodwill	—	107,430
Amortization of Intangible Assets	1,772	4,328
Stock-based Compensation	1,089	3,161
Total Operating Expenses	$202,561	$ 429,171
Loss from Continuing Operations	$ (8,192)	$(246,798)
Interest Income	1,902	4,312
Loss Before Income Taxes	$ (6,290)	$(242,486)
Income Tax Provision (Benefit)	1,337	(18,585)
Loss From Continuing Operations	$ (7,627)	$(223,901)
Loss From Discontinued Operations	—	(6,741)
Net Loss	$ (7,627)	$(230,642)

Dynamics for Year 9 as reported, Year 8 as restated in the Year 9 annual report for discontinued operations, and Year 8 as originally reported appear in Exhibit 6.19 (balance sheet), Exhibit 6.20 (income statement), and Exhibit 6.21 (statement of cash flows).

Required

a. Refer to the balance sheets of General Dynamics in Exhibit 6.19. Why does the restated amount for total assets for Year 8 of $4,672 million differ from the originally reported amount of $6,207 million?

b. Refer to the income statement for General Dynamics in Exhibit 6.20. Why are the originally reported and restated net income amounts for Year 8 the same (that is, $505 million) when each of the individual revenues and expenses decreased on restatement?

c. Refer to the statement of cash flows for General Dynamics in Exhibit 6.21. Why is the restated amount of cash flow from operations for Year 8 of $609 million less than the originally reported amount of $673 million?

d. If the analyst wished to analyze changes in the structure of assets and equities between Year 8 and Year 9, which columns and amounts in Exhibit 6.19 would the analyst use? Explain.

e. If the analyst wished to analyze changes in the operating profitability between Year 8 and Year 9, which columns and amounts in Exhibit 6.20 would the analyst use? Explain.

f. If the analyst wished to use cash flow ratios to assess short-term liquidity and long-term solvency risk, which columns and amounts in Exhibit 6.21 would the analyst use? Explain.

EXHIBIT 6.19

General Dynamics Corporation
Balance Sheet
(amounts in millions)
(Problem 6.16)

	Year 9 as Reported	Year 8 as Restated in Year 9 Annual Report	Year 8 as Originally Reported
Assets			
Cash and Cash Equivalents	$ 513	$ 507	$ 513
Marketable Securities	432	307	307
Accounts Receivable	64	99	444
Contracts in Process	1,550	1,474	2,606
Net Assets of Discontinued Businesses	767	1,468	—
Other Current Assets	329	145	449
Total Current Assets	$3,655	$4,000	$4,319
Property, Plant, and Equipment, net	322	372	1,029
Other Assets	245	300	859
Total Assets	$4,222	$4,672	$6,207
Liabilities and Shareholders' Equity			
Accounts Payable and Accruals	$ 553	$ 642	$2,593
Current Portion of Long-Term Debt	145	450	516
Other Current Liabilities	1,250	1,174	—
Total Current Liabilities	$1,948	$2,266	$3,109
Long-Term Debt	38	163	365
Other Noncurrent Liabilities	362	263	753
Total Liabilities	$2,348	$2,692	$4,227
Common Stock	$ 42	$ 55	$ 55
Additional Paid-In Capital	—	25	25
Retained Earnings	2,474	2,651	2,651
Treasury Stock	(642)	(751)	(751)
Total Shareholders' Equity	$1,874	$1,980	$1,980
Total Liabilities and Shareholders' Equity	$4,222	$4,672	$6,207

EXHIBIT 6.20

General Dynamics Corporation
Income Statement
(amounts in millions)
(Problem 6.16)

	Year 9 as Reported	Year 8 as Restated in Year 9 Annual Report	Year 8 as Originally Reported
Continuing Operations			
Sales	$ 3,472	$ 3,322	$ 8,751
Operating Costs and Expenses	(3,297)	(3,207)	(8,359)
Interest Income (Expense), net	25	4	(34)
Other Expense, net	27	(27)	(27)
Earnings before Income Taxes	$ 227	$ 92	$ 331
Income Tax Credit	21	114	43
Income from Continuing Operations	$ 248	$ 206	$ 374
Discontinued Operations			
Earnings from Operations	$ 193	$ 299	$ 131
Gain on Disposal	374	—	—
Net Income	$ 815	$ 505	$ 505

6.17 USING ORIGINALLY REPORTED VERSUS RESTATED DATA. INTERCO is a manufacturer and retailer of a broad line of consumer products, including London Fog, Florsheim Shoes, Converse, Ethan Allen Furniture, and Lane Furniture. During Year 9, INTERCO became the target of an unfriendly takeover attempt. In an effort to defend itself against the takeover, INTERCO declared a special dividend of $1.4 billion. It financed the dividend by issuing long-term debt and preferred stock. INTERCO planned to dispose of certain businesses to repay a portion of this debt. Exhibits 6.22, 6.23, and 6.24 present balance sheets, income statements, and statements of cash flows, respectively, for INTERCO. The first column of each exhibit shows the amounts as reported for Year 9. The second column shows the restated amounts for Year 8 to reflect the decision to dispose of certain businesses that the company had previously included in continuing operations. The third column shows the amounts originally reported for Year 8. The income tax rate is 35 percent.

Required

a. Refer to the balance sheets of INTERCO in Exhibit 6.22. Why is the restated amount for total assets for Year 8 of $1,830,400 different from the originally reported amount for total assets of $1,985,586?

b. Refer to the income statement of INTERCO in Exhibit 6.23. Why is the originally reported and restated net income the same ($145,003) when each of the company's individual revenues and expenses decreased on restatement?

EXHIBIT 6.21

General Dynamics Corporation
Statement of Cash Flows
(amounts in millions)
(Problem 6.16)

	Year 9 as Reported	Year 8 as Restated in Year 9 Annual Report	Year 8 as Originally Reported
Operations			
Income from Continuing Operations	$ 248	$ 206	$ 374
Depreciation and Amortization	56	140	303
(Increase) Decrease in Accounts Receivable	35	4	(91)
(Increase) Decrease in Contracts in Process	(76)	(83)	237
(Increase) Decrease in Other Current Assets	(6)	8	13
Increase (Decrease) in Accounts Payable and Accruals	(66)	51	262
Increase (Decrease) in Other Current Liabilities	11	(41)	(469)
Cash Flow from Continuing Operations	$ 202	$ 285	$ 629
Cash Flow from Discontinued Operations	288	324	44
Cash Flow from Operations	$ 490	$ 609	$ 673
Investing			
Proceeds from Sale of Discontinued Operations	$ 1,039	$ 184	$ 184
Capital Expenditures	(18)	(29)	(82)
Purchase of Marketable Securities	(125)	(307)	(307)
Other	32	3	56
Cash Flow from Investing	$ 928	$(149)	$(149)
Financing			
Issue of Common Stock	$ 57	$ —	$ —
Repayment of Debt	(454)	(11)	(61)
Purchase of Common Stock	(960)	—	—
Dividends	(55)	(42)	(42)
Other	—	—	(17)
Cash Flow from Financing	$(1,412)	$ (53)	$(120)
Change in Cash	$ 6	$ 407	$ 404
Cash—Beginning of Year	507	100	109
Cash—End of Year	$ 513	$ 507	$ 513

c. Refer to the statement of cash flows for INTERCO in Exhibit 6.24. Why is the restated amount of cash flow from operations for Year 8 of $94,447 less than the originally reported amount of $117,774?

d. If the analyst wished to analyze changes in the structure of assets and equities between Year 8 and Year 9, which columns and which amounts in Exhibit 6.22 would the analyst use? Explain.

e. If the analyst wished to compare the change in operating performance between Year 8 and Year 9, which columns and which amounts in Exhibit 6.23 would the analyst use? Explain.

f. Describe briefly how INTERCO's actions during Year 9 might thwart an unfriendly takeover attempt.

EXHIBIT 6.22

INTERCO
Balance Sheet
(amounts in thousands)
(Problem 6.17)

	Year 9 as Reported	Year 8 as Restated in Year 9 Annual Report	Year 8 as Originally Reported
Cash and Marketable Securities	$ 77,625	$ 23,299	$ 31,882
Receivables	329,299	310,053	486,657
Inventories	490,967	514,193	805,095
Prepayments	41,625	24,984	35,665
Net Assets of Discontinued Businesses	346,372	521,644	—
Total Current Assets	$ 1,285,888	$1,394,173	$1,359,299
Property, Plant, and Equipment, net	327,070	317,238	479,499
Other Assets	162,344	118,989	146,788
Total Assets	$ 1,775,302	$1,830,400	$1,985,586
Current Liabilities	$ 736,268	$ 269,315	$ 373,343
Long-Term Debt	1,986,837	266,191	299,140
Other Noncurrent Liabilities	57,947	43,557	61,766
Total Liabilities	$ 2,781,052	$ 579,063	$ 734,249
Contributed Capital	$ 339,656	$ 256,740	$ 256,740
Retained Earnings	(1,208,250)	1,179,964	1,179,964
Treasury Stock	(137,156)	(185,367)	(185,367)
Total Shareholders' Equity	$(1,005,750)	$1,251,337	$1,251,337
Total Liabilities and Shareholders' Equity	$ 1,775,302	$1,830,400	$1,985,586

EXHIBIT 6.23

INTERCO
Income Statement
(amounts in thousands)
(Problem 6.17)

	Year 9 as Reported	Year 8 as Restated in Year 9 Annual Report	Year 8 as Originally Reported
Sales	$2,011,962	$1,995,974	$3,341,423
Other Income	18,943	13,714	29,237
Total Revenues	$2,030,905	$2,009,688	$3,370,660
Cost of Goods Sold	$1,335,678	$1,288,748	$2,284,640
Selling and Administrative	537,797	493,015	799,025
Interest	141,735	29,188	33,535
Income Taxes	19,977	85,303	108,457
Total Expenses	$2,035,187	$1,896,254	$3,225,657
Income from Continuing Operations	$ (4,282)	$ 113,434	$ 145,003
Income from Discontinued Operations	74,432	31,569	—
Net Income	$ 70,150	$ 145,003	$ 145,003

6.18 ADJUSTING FINANCIAL STATEMENTS FOR DIFFERENT ACCOUNTING PRINCIPLES. GlaxoSmithKline (GSK) is the largest pharmaceutical company in the United Kingdom and the second-largest pharmaceutical company in the world. In a recent Form 20-F filing, the firm estimates that it has captured approximately 7 percent of the world pharmaceutical market. GSK prepares financial statements in accordance with generally accepted accounting principles in the United Kingdom (U.K. GAAP). The statements appear in Exhibit 6.25 (balance sheet) and Exhibit 6.26 (income statement). Exhibit 6.27 presents a reconciliation of shareholders' equity and net income from U.K. accounting principles to U.S. accounting principles. A description of the reconciling items appears next.

Deferred taxation. U.K. GAAP requires the recognition of deferred taxes only when it is probable that deferred tax benefits or liabilities will crystallize. U.S. GAAP requires the recognition of deferred taxes for all temporary differences between financial and tax reporting.

Postretirement benefits other than pensions. U.K. GAAP allows recognition of postretirement benefits other than pensions on a cash basis. U.S. GAAP requires recognition of this benefit obligation on an accrual basis.

Goodwill. The combination of Glaxo Wellcome and SmithKline Beecham was accounted for as a pooling of interests in accordance with U.K. GAAP. Under U.S. GAAP, this business combination did not quality for pooling-of-interests accounting (although it was an acceptable technique at the time) and Glaxo Wellcome was determined to be the acquirer in a business combination accounted for using the purchase method. (The pooling-of-interests and purchase methods are discussed in

EXHIBIT 6.24

INTERCO
Statement of Cash Flows
(amounts in thousands)
(Problem 6.17)

	Year 9 as Reported	Year 8 as Restated in Year 9 Annual Report	Year 8 as Originally Reported
Operations			
Income (Loss) from Continuing Operations	$ (4,282)	$113,434	$ 145,003
Depreciation	40,037	40,570	62,772
Other Addbacks (Subtractions)	(24,230)	8,750	13,957
Change in Operating Working Capital Accounts	29,015	(96,271)	(103,958)
Cash Flow from Continuing Operations	$ 40,540	$ 66,483	$ 117,774
Cash Flow from Discontinued Operations	249,704	27,964	—
Cash Flow from Operations	$ 290,244	$ 94,447	$ 117,774
Investing			
Sale of Fixed Assets	$ 4,134	$ 1,145	$ 8,102
Acquisition of Fixed Assets	(50,966)	(45,925)	(65,880)
Cash Flow from Investing	$ (46,832)	$ (44,780)	$ (57,778)
Financing			
Increase in Short-Term Borrowing	$ —	$ 1,677	$ 1,677
Increase in Long-Term Borrowing	1,967,500	205,533	205,673
Decrease in Long-Term Borrowing	(617,401)	(85,570)	(95,841)
Increase in Capital Stock	19,994	4,606	4,606
Decrease in Capital Stock	(102,341)	(160,442)	(160,442)
Dividends	(1,456,162)	(64,219)	(64,219)
Other	(676)	252	54
Cash Flow from Financing	$ (189,086)	$ (98,163)	$ (108,492)
Net Change in Cash	$ 54,326	$ (48,496)	$ (48,496)

Chapter 9). The difference between the cost of acquisition and the fair value of the assets and liabilities of SmithKline Beecham has been recorded as goodwill under U.S. GAAP. GSK tested the goodwill for impairment and concluded that none of it was impaired at the end of Year 4.

Specifically identifiable intangibles. As noted previously, the combination of Glaxo Wellcome and SmithKline Beecham for U.S. GAAP purposes was accounted for using the purchase method. As a result, U.S. GAAP required GSK to record specifically identifiable intangibles, primarily patents and trademarks, as assets on the balance sheet.

Dividends. U.K. GAAP provides for the recognition of a liability when the board of directors recommends a dividend to shareholders for their approval. U.S. GAAP does not recognize a dividend until declared by the board of directors, which occurs in the U.K. after shareholders' approval.

Required

a. Recast GSK's balance sheet to the format more commonly employed by firms employing U.S. GAAP to prepare their financial statements.

b. Indicate the adjustments to the balance sheet and income statement to convert GSK's financial statements from U.K. GAAP to U.S. GAAP. GSK includes the dividend recommended to shareholders in other current liabilities.

c. Compute the rate of return on assets (ROA) and the rate of return on common shareholders' equity (ROCE) using the reported amounts (U.K. GAAP) and the adjusted amounts (U.S. GAAP).

d. Why are ROCE and ROA larger using the reported amounts (U.K. GAAP) than using the adjusted amounts (U.S. GAAP)?

EXHIBIT 6.25

GlaxoSmithKline
Selected Balance Statement Data
(amounts in millions)
(Problem 6.18)

Year Ended June 30:	Year 4	Year 3
Fixed Assets	£ 8,945	£ 8,575
Current Assets	£13,633	£12,625
Creditors: Amounts Due Within One Year	(8,722)	(8,471)
Net Current Assets	£ 4,911	£ 4,154
Total Assets Less Current Liabilities	£13,856	£12,729
Creditors: Amounts Due After One Year	(4,625)	(3,883)
Provisions for Liabilities and Charges	(3,029)	(3,042)
Net Assets	£ 6,202	£ 5,804
Capital and Reserves		
Equity Shareholders' Funds	£ 5,925	£ 5,059
Minority Interests	£ 277	£ 745
Capital Employed	£ 6,202	£ 5,804

EXHIBIT 6.26

GlaxoSmithKline
Selected Income Statement Data
(amounts in millions)
(Problem 6.18)

	Year 4	Year 3
Turnover		
Pharmaceuticals	£17,146	£18,181
Consumer Health Care	3,213	3,260
Total Turnover	£20,359	£21,441
Cost of Sales	(4,309)	(4,544)
Selling, General, and Administrative Expenditure	(7,061)	(7,597)
Research and Development Expenditure	(2,839)	(2,791)
Operating Profit	£(6,150)	£ 6,509
Other Operating Income (Expense)	(60)	(133)
Disposal of Interests in Equity Affiliates	138	—
Profits of Joint Ventures and Affiliates	95	93
(Loss) Profit on Disposal of Products and Businesses	(1)	5
Net Interest Payable	(203)	(161)
Profit Before Taxation	£ 6,119	£ 6,313
Taxation	(1,701)	(1,729)
Profit After Taxation	£ 4,418	£ 4,584
Minority Interests	(116)	(104)
Net Earnings	£ 4,302	£ 4,480

INTEGRATIVE CASE 6.1

STARBUCKS

Exhibit 1.25 of Integrative Case 1.1 (Chapter 1) presents the income statement for Starbucks for Year 2, Year 3 and Year 4. Two components of the firm's income statement raise questions about the quality of its revenues:

1. For each year, a large majority—averaging approximately 85 percent—of the revenues reported by Starbucks are generated from specialty coffees and other products sold in *company-operated* stores. (The firm generates additional revenues from (a) licensing fees charged to stores that it does not own or manage, and (b) the sale of Starbucks products to grocery stores, warehouse clubs, and foodservice distributors.) As discussed in Integrative Case 1.1, Starbucks opened a large number of new stores in each of these years, representing one of the primary drivers of Starbucks' remarkable rate of growth in revenues. But Starbucks' revenue growth is not just driven by opening new stores. On a consolidated basis, Starbucks generated comparable store sales growth (that is, sales from stores in existence for at least two years) as follows: 10 percent in Year 4; 9 percent in Year 3; and 8 percent in Year 2. For Year 1 (not reported in Exhibit 1.25), Starbucks reported total

EXHIBIT 6.27

GlaxoSmithKline
Reconciliation of U.K. and U.S. GAAP
(amounts in millions)
(Problem 6.18)

	June 30:	
	Year 4	**Year 3**
Shareholders' Equity, U.K. GAAP	£ 5,925	£ 5,059
Deferred Taxation	(4,204)	(5,071)
Specifically Identifiable Intangibles	13,994	15,652
Postretirement Benefits Other Than Pensions	(1,287)	(1,702)
Goodwill	17,982	17,986
Dividends	683	808
Other	949	1,384
Shareholders' Equity, U.S. GAAP	£34,042	£34,116

	Year Ended June 30:	
	Year 4	**Year 3**
Net Income, U.K. GAAP	£4,302	£4,478
Stock-Based Compensation	(296)	(372)
Acquisition and Disposition of Product Rights	(210)	(105)
Deferred Taxation	661	787
Postretirement Benefits Other Than Pensions	(162)	(122)
Amortization and Impairment of Intangible Assets	(1,426)	(2,292)
Other	(137)	46
Net Income, U.S. GAAP	£2,732	£2,420

sales from company-operated stores of \$2,229.6 million, which included a 5 percent comparable store sales growth over the previous year's total company-operated store sales of \$1,823.6 million.

2. Starbucks reported a peripheral gain in Year 2, specifically a \$13.4 million "gain on sale of investment" (see Exhibit 1.25). The gain was related to Starbucks' sale of 30,000 shares of Starbucks Japan common stock.

Required

a. In judging the quality of revenues for growth-oriented firms such as Starbucks, the analyst is especially interested in knowing the revenues generated through *new* store openings versus those generated by *existing* stores. Are both revenue streams increasing at the same rate, for example, or is one increasing but at a decreasing rate? Is one increasing while the other is decreasing? Calculate (1) company-operated comparable store sales for Starbucks for Year 1, Year 2, Year 3, and Year 4, and (2) new store sales for the same four-year period. Describe the trend of the sales breakdown over the four-year period and discuss which revenue stream—new store revenues, or revenues from existing stores—is the higher-quality revenue stream for Starbucks going forward.

b. Starbucks reports a "gain on sale of investment" in Year 2, but doesn't report similar gains or losses in Year 3 or Year 4. Discuss (1) whether you would eliminate it when using earnings to forecast the future profitability of Starbucks and, if so, (2) the adjustment you would make to the income statement, balance sheet and statement of cash flows. Note that Starbucks' financial statements are presented in Integrative Case 1.1.

CASE 6.2

HEWLETT-PACKARD: A PACK ARD (OF) MESS

Hewlett-Packard Corporation (HP) designs, manufactures, and distributes computer systems and imaging and printing products and offers information technology services. The company's offerings span IT infrastructure, global services, business and home computing, and imaging and printing. HP is headquartered in Palo Alto, California, and serves customers throughout the world. It has approximately 150,000 employees worldwide and ranked among the top twenty Fortune 500 firms. HP dedicates significant amounts to research and development of products, solutions, and new technologies. For decades, it has been considered a leader in the IT industry. However, recent years have been turbulent ones for the firm, with effective leadership and the appropriate portfolio of products and services the most hotly debated topics within both the firm and the media.

Financial statements for HP are presented in Exhibits 6.28 (income statement), Exhibit 6.29 (balance sheet), and Exhibit 6.30 (statement of cash flows). Before performing any analysis of these statements, however, it is appropriate to adjust for items considered unusual or nonrecurring and therefore unlikely to affect ongoing assessments of the firm. Selected notes to the financial statements reveal the following information:

1. **Revenue recognition.** HP recognizes revenue at the time of delivery of products to customers, at the same time providing for estimated returns. HP recognizes revenues from services when it performs the services. HP adopted Securities and Exchange Commission *Staff Accounting Bulletin No. 101*, "Revenue Recognition in Financial Statements," in fiscal Year 1. Prior to adoption, HP had recognized revenues at the time of shipment to customers. The cumulative effect of changing the method of revenue recognition was $272 million, net of $108 million of income taxes, and is recognized in earnings for Year 1. The cumulative-effect technique for reporting the accounting change was employed by HP because *Statement No. 154* was not in effect in Year 1.
2. **Corporate acquisition.** HP acquired Compaq Computer Company (Compaq) on May 3, Year 2, for $24,170 million. HP gave shares of its common stock in exchange for the outstanding common stock of Compaq and accounted for the acquisition using the purchase method. In addition to allocating the purchase price to the tangible assets acquired and the liabilities assumed, HP allocated $793 million to in-process technologies, $3,517 million to intangibles with a limited life (such as customer lists, distribution agreements, developed technologies, and patents), $1,422 million to intangibles with an indefinite life (primarily the Compaq brand name), and $14,450 million to goodwill. GAAP requires firms to expense amounts allocated to in-process technologies in the year acquired. Charges related to in-process technologies acquired do not give rise to tax benefits in any year.

EXHIBIT 6.28

Hewlett-Packard Company and Subsidiaries
Statement of Income
(amounts in millions)
(Case 6.2)

	Year Ended October 31:			
	Year 4	Year 3	Year 2	Year 1
Revenues	$79,905	$73,061	$56,588	$45,226
Costs and Expenses:				
Cost of Products	60,150	53,650	41,390	33,512
Financing Interest	190	208	189	236
Research and Development	3,506	3,651	3,368	2,753
Selling, General, and Administrative	11,024	11,012	8,763	6,668
Amortization of Purchased Intangible Assets	603	563	402	174
Restructuring Charges	114	800	1,780	384
Acquisition-related Charges	54	280	701	25
In-process Research and Development Charges	37	1	793	35
Other Expenses	(35)	(21)	(52)	(171)
Total Costs and Expenses	75,643	70,144	57,334	43,616
Earnings (Loss) From Operations	$ 4,262	$ 2,917	$ (746)	$ 1,610
Gains (Losses) on Investments and Early Extinguishment of Debt	4	(29)	56	(419)
Litigation Dispute Settlement	(70)	—	14	(400)
Earnings (Loss) Before Taxes	$ 4,196	$ 2,888	$ (676)	$ 791
Provision for (Benefit From) Taxes	699	349	(118)	111
Cumulative Effect of Change in Accounting Principles	—	—	—	(272)
Net Earnings (Loss)	$ 3,497	$ 2,539	$ (558)	$ 408

During fiscal Year 2 and prior years, GAAP required firms to amortize all intangibles acquired in corporate acquisitions over their expected useful lives. Such amortization did not give rise to a tax benefit. Beginning with fiscal Year 3, GAAP no longer requires firms to amortize goodwill and other intangibles with indefinite lives. However, GAAP does require firms to test such assets annually for possible impairment and to recognize impairment losses if they arise. Firms must continue to amortize intangibles with limited lives.

To consummate the acquisition of Compaq, HP incurred acquisition-related charges in Year 2 totaling $701 million ($529 million after taxes) for professional services, advertising, and proxy solicitation costs. HP incurred additional acquisition-related charges of $280 million ($212 million after taxes) in Year 3.

3. **Restructuring charge.** HP's management approved restructuring actions in fiscal Year 1 "to respond to the global economic downturn and to improve HP's cost structure by streamlining operations and prioritizing resources in strategic areas of HP's business." HP recorded a restructuring charge of $384 million to

EXHIBIT 6.29

Hewlett-Packard Company and Subsidiaries
Balance Sheet
(amounts in millions)
(Case 6.2)

	October 31:		
	Year 4	**Year 3**	**Year 2**
Assets			
Current assets:			
Cash and Cash Equivalents	$12,663	$14,188	$ 4,197
Short-Term Investments	311	403	139
Accounts Receivable	10,226	8,921	4,488
Financing Receivables	2,945	3,026	2,183
Inventory	7,071	6,065	5,204
Other Current Assets	9,685	8,351	5,094
Total Current Assets	$42,901	$40,954	$21,305
Property, Plant, and Equipment	6,649	6,482	4,397
Long-Term Financing Receivables and Other Assets	6,657	8,030	6,882
Goodwill	15,828	14,894	—
Purchased Intangible Assets	4,103	4,356	—
Total Assets	$76,138	$74,716	$32,584
Liabilities and Stockholders' Equity			
Current Liabilities:			
Notes Payable and Short-term Borrowings	$ 2,511	$ 1,080	$ 1,722
Accounts Payable	9,377	9,285	3,791
Employee Compensation and Benefits	2,208	1,755	1,477
Taxes on Earnings	1,709	1,599	1,818
Deferred Revenue	2,958	2,496	—
Accrued Restructuring	193	709	—
Other Accrued Liabilities	9,632	8,545	3,289
Total Current Liabilities	$28,588	$25,469	$13,964
Long-term Debt	$ 4,623	$ 6,494	$ 3,729
Other Liabilities	$ 5,363	$ 5,007	$ 1,201
Commitments and Contingencies			
Stockholders' Equity:			
Common Stock	$ 29	$ 30	$ 19
Additional Paid-in Capital	22,129	24,587	200
Retained Earnings	15,649	13,332	13,953
Accumulated Other Comprehensive Loss	(243)	(203)	41
Total Stockholders' Equity	$37,564	$37,746	$13,953
Total Liabilities and Stockholders' Equity	$76,138	$74,716	$32,584

EXHIBIT 6.30

Hewlett-Packard Company and Subsidiaries
Statement of Cash Flows
(amounts in millions)
(Case 6.2)

	Year Ended October 31:			
	Year 4	Year 3	Year 2	Year 1
Cash Flows from Operating Activities:				
Net Earnings (Loss)	$ 3,497	$ 2,539	$ (903)	$ 408
Adjustments to Reconcile Net Earnings (Loss) to Net Cash Provided by Operating Activities:				
Depreciation and Amortization	2,395	2,527	2,119	1,369
Cumulative Effect of Change in Accounting Principle, Net of Taxes	—	—	—	272
Provision for Doubtful Accounts—Accounts and Financing Receivables	98	102	299	438
Provision for Inventory	367	391	280	539
Restructuring Charges	114	800	1,780	384
Acquisition-related Charges, Including Process Research and Development	91	281	1,494	60
Deferred Taxes on Earnings	26	(279)	(351)	(954)
Other, Net	89	141	234	415
Changes in Assets and Liabilities:				
Accounts and Financing Receivables	(696)	88	899	566
Inventory	(1,341)	(638)	844	677
Accounts Payable	3	2,257	395	(1,249)
Taxes on Earnings	(32)	53	(357)	(162)
Other Assets and Liabilities	477	(2,205)	(1,289)	(190)
Net Cash Provided by Operating Activities	$ 5,088	$ 6,057	$ 5,444	$ 2,573
Cash Flows from Investing Activities:				
Investment in Property, Plant, and Equipment	$(2,126)	$ (1,995)	$(1,710)	$(1,527)
Proceeds from Sale of Property, Plant, and Equipment	447	353	362	435
Purchases of Investments	(715)	(596)	(351)	(434)
Maturities and Sales of Investments	1,064	875	381	742
(Payments Made) Net Cash Acquired in Connection with Business Acquisitions, Net of Acquisition Costs	(1,124)	(149)	3,557	223
Dissolution of an Equity Investee	—	—	879	—
Net Cash (Used in) Provided by Investing Activities	$(2,454)	$ (1,512)	$ 3,118	$ (561)

Continued

EXHIBIT 6.30

continued

	Year Ended October 31:			
	Year 4	Year 3	Year 2	Year 1
Cash flows from financing activities:				
Repayment of Commercial Paper and Notes Payable, Net	$ (172)	$ (223)	$(2,402)	$ 303
Issuance of Debt	9	749	2,529	904
Payment of Long-term Debt	(285)	(829)	(472)	(290)
Repurchase of Zero-coupon Subordinated Convertible Notes	—	—	(127)	(640)
Issuance of Common Stock Under Employee Stock Plans	570	482	377	354
Repurchase of Common Stock	(3,309)	(751)	(671)	(1,240)
Dividends	(972)	(977)	(801)	(621)
Net Cash Used in Financing Activities	$(4,159)	$(1,549)	$(1,567)	$(1,230)
(Decrease) Increase in Cash and Cash Equivalents	$(1,525)	$ 2,996	$ 6,995	$ 782
Cash and Cash Equivalents at Beginning of Period	14,188	11,192	4,197	3,415
Cash and Cash Equivalents at End of Period	$12,663	$14,188	$11,192	$ 4,197

reflect these actions. This charge consisted of severance and other employee benefits related to the planned termination of approximately 7,500 employees, as well as costs related to the consolidation of excess facilities. As of the end of fiscal Year 1, HP had made payments of $264 million related to the restructuring and expected to pay the remainder of the accrual in fiscal Year 2. In fiscal Year 2, HP recognized another restructuring charge ($1,780 million) prior to its acquisition of Compaq. The charge included employee severance and early-retirement benefits, costs of vacating duplicate facilities, and asset impairment losses related to HP's activities. By the end of fiscal Year 2, HP had made payments of $502 million and incurred noncash charges from asset write-downs of $650 million related to this restructuring. During both Year 3 and Year 4, HP recorded additional restructuring "with the intent of better managing HP's cost structure and aligning certain of its operations more effectively with current businesses conditions." Of the $800 million charge for Year 3, HP had paid out $233 million by the end of the year and reported asset write-downs of $180 million. Of the $114 million charge for Year 4, HP reports no payments or asset write-downs.

4. **Gains/losses on investments and early extinguishment of debt.** HP's investments include debt and equity securities in public and privately held emerging-technology companies. HP realized gains and losses on sales of these investments during Years 1 through 4. However, in Year 1 the firm recorded impairment losses of $471 million, which is included in the $419 million loss reported for the year. It recognized impairment losses of $106 million in fiscal Year 2 (included in the $56 million

gain for the year). This line item also includes small gains recorded by HP for early extinguishment of debt in Year 2 and Year 3.

5. **Litigation dispute settlement.** On June 4, Year 1, HP and Pitney Bowes announced that they had entered into agreements that resolved all pending patent litigation between the parties without admission of infringement; accordingly, HP paid Pitney Bowes $400 million in cash on June 7, Year 1. On May 14, Year 4, HP announced that it had resolved a dispute regarding certain contracts with the government of Canada. HP Canada, a wholly owned subsidiary of HP, made payments to the government of Canada resulting in a charge of $70 million in the second quarter of Year 4.

Required

a. For each of the five categories of income items described previously for Year 1 through Year 4, discuss whether you would eliminate it when using earnings to forecast future profitability of HP. Discuss the logic for your decision.
b. Prepare a pro forma income statement for Year 1 through Year 4, assuming that you make an adjustment for each of the five categories of income statement items.
c. Refer to Exhibit 6.30, which reports HP's statement of cash flows for Year 1 through Year 4. Note that cash flows from operations, under "adjustments to reconcile net earnings (loss) to net cash provided by operating activities," includes addbacks for income items (1) through (3), but not for income items (4) and (5). Does this mean that no cash was used or received related to items (1) through (3), but cash was used or received related to items (4) and (5)? Explain your answer.
d. The majority of the goodwill reported at the end of Year 4 relates to the acquisition of Compaq by HP in Year 2. HP must test the Compaq goodwill for impairment every filing year. Refer to the HP web site (www.hp.com) and recap the firm's most recent disclosures for testing the goodwill generated by the Compaq acquisition in Year 2.

CASE 6.3

INTERNATIONAL PAPER: A RECURRING DILEMMA

International Paper Company is the largest forest products company in the world. It operates in five segments of the forest products industry:

1. **Printing paper.** Uncoated and coated papers used for reprographics and printing, envelopes, writing tablets, file folders, and magazines.
2. **Packaging.** Liner board used for corrugated boxes and bleached packaging board used for food, pharmaceutical, cosmetic, and other consumer products.
3. **Distribution.** Sale of printing, graphics, packaging, and similar products through wholesale and retail outlets. Sales of these outlets comprise approximately 20 percent of International Paper's products and 80 percent of other manufacturers' products.
4. **Specialty products.** Film, door facings, wood siding, fabrics, and chemicals used for adhesives and paints.
5. **Forest products.** Logs, lumber, plywood, and wood panels. International Paper has the largest timber holdings of any private-sector entity in the United States.

Exhibit 6.31 presents product segment data for International Paper for Year 7 through Year 10. The proportion of sales generated from within the United States decreased from 79 percent in Year 7 to 71 percent in Year 10. The proportion generated from within Europe fluctuated between 17 and 19 percent during the four-year period. The proportion from the rest of the world, primarily East Asia, increased from 3 percent in Year 7 to 12 percent in Year 10.

EXHIBIT 6.31

International Paper
Product Line Segment Profitability Analysis
(Case 6.3)

	Year 10	Year 9	Year 8	Year 7
Sales Mix				
Printing Papers	26%	29%	28%	27%
Packaging	23	21	22	22
Distribution	22	24	22	22
Specialty Products	16	16	17	17
Forest Products	13	10	11	12
	100%	100%	100%	100%
Rate of Return on Assets				
Printing Papers	2.1%	15.3%	.3%	(1.9%)
Packaging	6.9	17.9	9.5	6.2
Distribution	8.1	7.3	6.1	5.3
Specialty Products	(1.4)	5.7	9.6	10.1
Forest Products	17.2%	8.7%	27.3%	30.4%
Profit Margin				
Printing Papers	3.3%	17.7%	.5%	(3.1%)
Packaging	8.5	16.8	8.7	6.1
Distribution	2.3	2.1	2.1	1.8
Specialty Products	(1.5)	6.3	10.3	10.7
Forest Products	34.7%	18.5%	24.4%	28.7%
Assets Turnover				
Printing Papers	.65	.87	.66	.60
Packaging	.81	1.07	1.09	1.03
Distribution	3.47	3.46	2.86	2.89
Specialty Products	.96	.91	.93	.94
Forest Products	.50	.47	1.12	1.06

The financial statements for International Paper for Year 7 through Year 10 appear in Exhibit 6.32 (income statement), Exhibit 6.33 (balance sheet), and Exhibit 6.34 (statement of cash flows). Exhibit 6.35 presents financial ratios for International Paper based on the reported amounts.

The notes to the financial statements reveal the following information:

1. **Change in accounting principle.** Effective January 1, Year 8, International Paper changed its method of accounting for start-up costs on major projects to expensing these costs as incurred. Prior to Year 8, the firm capitalized these costs as part of property, plant, and equipment and amortized them over a five-year period. The firm made the change to increase the focus on controlling costs associated with

facility start-ups. International Paper recorded a pretax charge of $125 million ($75 million after taxes) as the cumulative effect of an accounting change in Year 8.

2. **Gain on sale of partnership interest.** On March 29, Year 10, International Paper sold its general partnership interest in a partnership that owned 300,000 acres of forestlands located in Oregon and Washington. Included in the partnership were forestlands, roads, and $750 million of long-term debt. As a result of this transaction, International Paper recognized a pretax gain of $592 million ($336 million after taxes). International Paper maintains general partnership interests in several partnerships created by the firm as a means of raising capital from outside investors. International Paper consolidates the financial statements of these partnerships with its own financial statements and shows the interest of the remaining partners (limited partners) as a minority interest.
3. **Restructuring and asset impairment charges.** During the first quarter of Year 10, the firm's board of directors authorized a series of management actions to restructure and strengthen existing businesses that resulted in a pretax charge of $515 million ($362 million after taxes). The charge included $305 million for the write-off of certain assets, $100 million for asset impairments, $80 million in associated severance costs, and $30 million in other expenses, including the cancellation of leases.

   During the fourth quarter of Year 10, International Paper recorded a $165 million pretax charge ($105 million after taxes) for the write-down of its investments in a company that markets digital communications products and to record its share of a restructuring charge announced by that investee.

These restructuring charges were the first recognized by International Paper since Year 6. In November, Year 6, the firm recorded a pretax charge of $398 million ($263 million after taxes) to establish a productivity improvement reserve. More than 80 percent of this charge represented asset write-downs for facility closings or realignments and related severance and relocation costs. The balance covers one-time costs of environmental cleanup, remediation, and legal costs. In December, Year 5, the firm recorded a $60 million ($37 million after taxes) reduction in workforce charge to cover severance costs associated with the elimination of more than 1,000 positions from its worldwide workforce. In December, Year 4, International Paper completed a review of operations in the context of its ongoing programs to emphasize value-added products in growing markets and improve the efficiency of its facilities. As a result, the firm recorded a pretax charge of $212 million ($137 million after taxes), principally related to the planned sale or closure of certain wood products and converting facilities, the estimated costs of environmental remediation, and severance and other personnel expenses associated with the business improvement program.

On July 9, Year 11, International Paper announced a plan to restructure or eliminate certain production operations and cut 9,000 jobs, more than 10 percent of its workforce. It recognized a restructuring charge of $385 million pretax. It also recognized a $93 million charge related to pending litigation.

Required

a. For each of the three categories of income items described earlier for Year 7 through Year 10, discuss (1) whether you would eliminate it when using earnings to forecast the future profitability of International Paper and, if so, (2) the adjustments you would make to the income statement, balance sheet, and statement of cash flows.

b. Taking into consideration the adjustments from part a, analyze and interpret the changes in the profitability and risk of International Paper during this four-year period. The statutory tax rate is 35 percent in each year.

EXHIBIT 6.32

International Paper
Income Statement
(amounts in millions)
(Case 6.3)

	Year Ended December 31:			
	Year 10	Year 9	Year 8	Year 7
Sales	$ 20,143	$ 19,797	$ 14,966	$ 13,685
Gain on Sale of Partnership Interest	592	—	—	—
Cost of Goods Sold	(16,095)	(14,927)	(11,977)	(11,051)
Selling and Administrative Expenses	(2,628)	(2,349)	(1,925)	(1,786)
Restructuring and Asset Impairment Charges	(680)	—	—	—
Interest Expense	(530)	(493)	(349)	(310)
Income Taxes	(330)	(719)	(236)	(213)
Minority Interest in Earnings	(169)	(156)	(47)	(36)
Income from Continuing Operations	$ 303	$ 1,153	$ 432	$ 289
Changes in Accounting Principles	—	—	(75)	—
Net Income	$ 303	$ 1,153	$ 357	$ 289

EXHIBIT 6.33

International Paper
Balance Sheet
(amounts in millions)
(Case 6.3)

	December 31:				
	Year 10	Year 9	Year 8	Year 7	Year 6
Assets					
Cash	$ 352	$ 312	$ 270	$ 242	$ 225
Accounts Receivable	2,553	2,571	2,241	1,856	1,861
Inventories	2,840	2,784	2,075	2,024	1,938
Prepayments	253	206	244	279	342
Total Current Assets	$ 5,998	$ 5,873	$ 4,830	$ 4,401	$ 4,366
Investments in Securities	1,178	1,420	1,032	631	599
Property, Plant, and Equipment, net	16,559	13,800	9,941	9,658	9,643
Other Assets	4,517	2,884	2,033	1,941	1,851
Total Assets	$28,252	$23,977	$17,836	$16,631	$16,459
Liabilities and Shareholders' Equity					
Accounts Payable	$ 1,426	$ 1,464	$ 1,204	$ 1,089	$ 1,259
Notes Payable	3,296	2,283	2,083	2,089	2,356
Other Current Liabilities	1,172	1,116	747	831	916
Total Current Liabilities	$ 5,894	$ 4,863	$ 4,034	$ 4,009	$ 4,531
Long-Term Debt	7,141	6,396	4,464	3,601	3,096
Deferred Income Taxes	2,768	1,974	1,612	1,614	1,417
Other Noncurrent Liabilities	1,240	980	870	1,182	1,226
Total Liabilities	$17,043	$14,213	$10,980	$10,406	$10,270
Minority Interest in Subsidiaries	$ 1,865	$ 1,967	$ 342	$ —	$ —
Common Stock	301	263	256	127	127
Additional Paid-In Capital	3,426	1,963	1,658	1,704	1,792
Retained Earnings	5,639	5,627	4,711	4,553	4,472
Treasury Stock	(22)	(56)	(111)	(159)	(202)
Total Shareholders' Equity	$11,209	$ 9,764	$ 6,856	$ 6,225	$ 6,189
Total Liabilities and Shareholders' Equity	$28,252	$23,977	$17,836	$16,631	$16,459

EXHIBIT 6.34

International Paper
Statement of Cash Flows
(amounts in millions)
(Case 6.3)

	Year Ended December 31:			
	Year 10	**Year 9**	**Year 8**	**Year 7**
Operations				
Net Income	$ 303	$ 1,153	$ 357	$ 289
Depreciation	1,194	1,031	885	898
Restructuring and Asset Impairment Charges	680	—	—	—
Changes in Accounting Principles	—	—	75	—
Gain on Sale of Partnership Interest	(592)	—	—	—
Other Addbacks and Subtractions	240	54	8	32
	$ 1,825	$ 2,238	$ 1,325	$ 1,219
(Increase) Decrease in Accounts Receivable	192	45	(339)	78
(Increase) Decrease in Inventories	174	(320)	8	(93)
(Increase) Decrease in Prepayments	(47)	38	(35)	63
Increase (Decrease) in Accounts Payable	(38)	260	115	(170)
Increase (Decrease) in Other Current Liabilities	(367)	(13)	169	(168)
Cash Flow from Operations	$ 1,739	$ 2,248	$ 1,243	$ 929
Investing				
Capital Expenditures	$(1,394)	$(1,518)	$(1,114)	$ (971)
Investments Acquired, net	(1,586)	(1,038)	(396)	(151)
Cash Flow from Investing	$(2,980)	$(2,556)	$(1,510)	$(1,122)
Financing				
Increase in Short-Term Borrowing	$ —	$ 57	$ —	$ —
Decrease in Short-Term Borrowing	(23)	—	(115)	—
Increase in Long-Term Borrowing	1,909	1,505	1,059	1,276
Decrease in Long-Term Borrowing	(375)	(950)	(275)	(1,016)
Issue of Common Stock	100	66	67	225
Dividends	(291)	(237)	(210)	(208)
Other Financing Transactions	(39)	(91)	(231)	(67)
Cash Flow from Financing	$ 1,281	$ 350	$ 295	$ 210
Change in Cash	$ 40	$ 42	$ 28	$ 17
Cash—Beginning of Year	312	270	242	225
Cash—End of Year	$ 352	$ 312	$ 270	$ 242

EXHIBIT 6.35

International Paper
Financial Statement Ratios
(Case 6.3)

	Year 10	Year 9	Year 8	Year 7
Profit Margin for ROA	4.1%	8.2%	4.2%	3.8%
Assets Turnover	.8	.9	.9	.8
Rate of Return on Assets	3.1%	7.8%	3.7%	3.2%
Profit Margin for ROCE	1.5%	5.8%	2.4%	2.1%
Capital Structure Leverage Ratio	3.0	2.9	2.9	2.7
Rate of Return on Common Shareholders' Equity	3.5%	16.1%	5.6%	4.7%
Equity				
Cost of Goods Sold/Sales	79.9%	75.4%	80.0%	80.8%
Selling and Administrative Expense/Sales	13.0%	11.9%	12.9%	13.1%
Interest Expense/Sales	2.6%	2.5%	2.3%	2.3%
Income Tax Expense/Sales	1.7%	3.6%	1.6%	1.5%
Accounts Receivable Turnover	7.9	8.2	7.3	7.4
Inventory Turnover	5.7	6.1	5.8	5.6
Fixed Asset Turnover	1.3	1.7	1.5	1.4
Current Ratio	1.0	1.2	1.2	1.1
Quick Ratio	.5	.6	.6	.5
Cash Flow from Operations/Average	32.3%	50.5%	30.9%	21.8%
Current Liabilities				
Days Accounts Receivable	46	44	50	50
Days Inventory	64	59	62	65
Days Accounts Payable	33	31	35	38
Liabilities/Assets	60.3%	59.3%	61.6%	62.6%
Long-Term Debt/Shareholders' Equity	76.4%	82.0%	68.5%	57.8%
Cash Flow from Operations/Average	9.9%	16.3%	11.4%	9.0%
Total Liabilities				
Interest Coverage Ratio	2.5	5.1	3.1	2.7
Cash Flow from Operations/Capital Expenditures	1.3	1.5	1.1	1.0

Chapter 7

Revenue Recognition and Related Expenses

Learning Objectives

1. Review the criteria for recognizing revenue and expenses under the accrual basis of accounting and apply these criteria to various types of businesses.
2. Calculate the income statement, balance sheet, and statement of cash flow effects of recognizing income prior to the point of sale, at the time of sale, and subsequent to sale.
3. Analyze and interpret the effects of FIFO versus LIFO on financial statements and convert the statements of a firm from a LIFO to a FIFO basis.
4. Use financial statement disclosures for depreciable assets to calculate average depreciable lives and ages of such assets, and convert the financial statements of a firm from a straight-line to an accelerated depreciation basis.
5. Understand the alternative ways that firms account for intangible assets (highlighting research and development expenditures, software development expenditures, and goodwill) and the difficulties that these alternatives present when analyzing technology firms.
6. Review the rules for evaluating the impairment of long-lived assets, including goodwill, and analyze how to apply the rules to different categories of long-lived assets.
7. Understand the distinction between changes in the general purchasing power of the monetary unit and changes in the prices of specific assets and liabilities, and the accounting methods designed to adjust financial statements for these two types of changing prices. (Appendix 7.1)

This chapter and the next two describe the selection and application of alternative methods of accounting for assets, liabilities, revenues, and expenses commonly encountered in corporate annual reports. These chapters emphasize those methods that have the greatest effects on the income statement and balance sheet. We continue our focus on how a firm's selection of accounting methods and the way it implements them affect its *accounting quality,* its *earnings quality,* and its *balance sheet quality,* topics introduced in Chapter 6.

The assessment of accounting quality begins with understanding GAAP. In this chapter, we examine accounting for revenue recognition, inventory cost flow assumptions, depreciation of tangible assets, amortization of intangible assets, and impairment of long-lived assets. For firms operating in countries that experience high inflation, Appendix 7.1 is especially relevant as it illustrates how changing prices, both in general and for specific assets and liabilities, affect performance, risk analysis and firm valuation.

As Chapter 6 discusses, high quality accounting information should portray fairly and completely the economic effects of a firm's decisions and actions. That is, quality accounting information should paint the most accurate economic portrait of the firm's financial position, performance, and risk that is possible given the complexity of today's business environment. In this chapter (and Chapters 8 and 9), we explain the various reporting principles under investigation, describe the choices firms make in applying them, and discuss the adjustments analysts may make to the reported amounts to enhance the quality of accounting information. In this regard, Chapters 6 through 9 represent a unit that addresses understanding both the *reported* corporate financial data and determining the relevant *adjusted* financial data for analyzing the profitability and risk of a firm.

INCOME RECOGNITION

Earnings from any operating activity undertaken by a firm are ultimately the difference between the economic resources received from customers and the economic resources paid to suppliers, employees, and other providers of goods and services. The ultimate benefit to the firm for undertaking operating activity is the difference between the present value of these inflows and outflows.

Although the incremental flows measure the *amount* of added value, a timing problem often arises because the cash received from a particular operating activity may occur in a different period from the period in which a firm expends cash for that activity. The accrual basis of accounting addresses this problem by developing criteria for recognizing revenues and expenses that are driven not by the immediate period's cash flows, but rather by the economic resources earned and consumed by the firm during the period. The net change in economic resources affects both income for the period and changes in the valuation of assets and liabilities on the balance sheet, an important relation discussed in Chapter 2. The difficulty at times is developing criteria that accurately and reliably capture the net change in economic resources.

Under the accrual basis of accounting, firms apply a set of criteria for revenue recognition that is designed to capture the point when a firm has substantially completed its value-adding activities. And after calculating revenue based on those recognition criteria, firms attempt to match against this revenue the expenses that measure all the costs incurred to generate that revenue. Following this process, earnings match inputs with outputs, aiming to provide an accurate measure of income during the period. We discuss the criteria for revenue and expense recognition in more depth shortly.

Accepting the accrual basis of accounting, however, does not settle the question of *when* firms recognize revenues and matching expenses. Options for recognizing revenues are (1) during the period of production, (2) at the completion of production, (3) at the time of sale, (4) during the period while receivables are outstanding, and (5) at the time of cash collection. Subsequent sections of this chapter provide examples of applying the accrual basis of accounting at various revenue recognition points.

Criteria for Revenue Recognition

Revenue recognition is primarily a question of timing. One of the most important financial reporting decisions firms must make is *when* to recognize revenue. The SEC, for example, has identified revenue recognition as a key reporting decision that often warrants detailed discussion in interim and annual filings of firms. The reason for its importance is straightforward: A firm needs to generate and report revenues in order to generate and report profit. For the analyst, then, no other reporting decision deserves more scrutiny than this one. The analyst needs to be confident that the revenues (net of related expenses) reported represent true economic resources to the firm.

Standard setters recognize the importance of revenue recognition to the reporting model and spend considerable time attempting to refine the criteria for recognizing revenues. As stated in the previous paragraph, financial reporting policymakers at the SEC have given the topic high priority and have issued numerous rulings on revenue recognition in recent years.[1] In addition, both the FASB and IASB have identified revenue recognition as a key topic in their future agendas.

GAAP requires firms to identify the significant accounting policies employed for recognizing revenues in notes to the financial statements. Exhibit 7.1 illustrates a recent disclosure by United Technologies describing how it recognizes revenues on long-term construction contracts, a technique discussed later in the chapter. United Technologies provides technology products and services to the building systems and aerospace industries worldwide. United Technologies' operating units include Otis, Carrier, and Chubb in the commercial and residential property sectors. The Pratt & Whitney, Hamilton Sundstrand, and Sikorsky Aircraft operating units primarily serve commercial and government customers in the aerospace sector.

PepsiCo discloses its revenue recognition policy in both Note 2 to the financial statements, "Our Significant Accounting Policies—Revenue Recognition" (Appendix A), and

EXHIBIT 7.1

United Technologies
Excerpt from Notes to the Consolidated Financial Statements

Revenue Recognition

Sales under elevator and escalator installation and modernization contracts are accounted for under the percentage-of-completion method.

Losses, if any, on contracts are provided for when anticipated. Loss provisions on original equipment contracts are recognized to the extent that estimated inventoriable manufacturing, engineering, estimated product warranty and product performance guarantee costs exceed the projected revenue from the products contemplated under the contractual arrangement. Products contemplated under the contractual arrangement include products purchased under the contract and, in the aerospace business, required replacement parts that are purchased separately and subsequently for incorporation into the original equipment. Revenue projections used in determining contract loss provisions are based upon estimates of the quantity, pricing and timing of future product deliveries. Losses are recognized on shipment to the extent that inventoriable manufacturing costs, estimated warranty costs and product performance guarantee costs exceed revenue realized. Contract accounting requires estimates of future costs over the performance period of the contract as well as estimates of award fees and other sources of revenue. These estimates are subject to change and result in adjustments to margins on contracts in progress.

[1]The SEC issued *Staff Accounting Bulletin No. 101,* "Revenue Recognition in Financial Statements," in December 1999. *SAB 101,* as it is commonly known, is one of the more important documents issued by the SEC in recent years and summarizes in one location all existing guidance on revenue recognition. *SAB 101* and related documents issued subsequently by the SEC significantly impact the choices made by many publicly held companies for recognizing revenue.

the first section of MD&A, "Our Critical Accounting Policies—Revenue Recognition" (Appendix B). Generally, the firm recognizes revenue when it ships its products or delivers them to the customer.

Revenue Recognition Principles

Financial reporting permits the recognition of revenue under the accrual basis of accounting when a firm has done both of the following:

1. Provided all, or a substantial portion, of the services to be performed.
2. Received either cash, a receivable that it is reasonably certain it will collect, or some other asset with a cash-equivalent amount the firm can measure with reasonable precision.

Most firms recognize revenue at the time of sale (delivery) of goods or services. At this point, a firm has completed production of the goods or creation of the services, satisfying the first criterion. The benefit that a firm obtains from providing goods or services is the cash or other consideration that the firm expects to receive. If the customer promises to pay cash in the future, the firm examines the credit standing of the customer and assesses the likelihood of receiving the cash. The second criterion is satisfied so long as the firm can reasonably predict the amount of cash it will collect.

The complexity of today's business environment has heightened the importance of understanding a firm's business model and its relation to the revenue recognition principles chosen for reporting. Although in many cases it is relatively easy to determine when to recognize revenue (such as at the point of retail sales), in many other cases it is not. Businesses with sales that include future performance obligations, sales that involve a barter exchange of services between firms, and sales that bundle several products and services are just a few examples in which the selection and application of revenue recognition principles can have a dramatic effect on the amount and timing of reported revenue.

Revenue Recognition and Reported Earnings

The recognition of revenue at the time of sale (delivery) is so common that analysts may neglect to assess whether this timing is appropriate for a particular firm. Firms may attempt to increase reported earnings numbers by accelerating the timing of revenues or estimating the collectible amounts too aggressively. If so, the quality of accounting information suffers because it does not represent a reliable measure of the economic resources the firm earned that period, and is probably not sustainable.

Consider the following three conditions, each of which is a signal that revenue recognition at the time of sale may be too early: (1) large and volatile amounts of uncollectible accounts receivable, (2) unusually large amounts of returned goods, and (3) excessive warranty expenditures. Each of these sales-related expenses should bear a reasonably stable relationship to revenues over time. Either large percentages of these expenses as a percentage of sales, or widely varying percentages from year to year, should raise questions about the appropriateness of revenue recognition at the time of sale.

Another possible signal about potential deterioration in the quality of a firm's revenue recognition arises when a firm experiences a substantial increase in the number of days accounts receivable are outstanding. (Chapter 4 provides a discussion of how to calculate receivable days outstanding.) Customers taking longer to pay for their purchases may suggest an overstatement of revenues and earnings. Note that the analyst should assess the receivable days outstanding and the stability of bad-debt expense to revenue in tandem because either ratio by itself may provide an incomplete signal about the quality of the firm's revenues. A firm that adequately recognizes bad-debt expense for an increasing proportion of uncollectible sales will likely show a stable accounts receivable turnover, because providing for estimated uncollectible accounts has the same effect on accounts receivable (that is, reduction) as collecting the accounts in cash. Thus, examining just the accounts receivable turnover does not signal the collection problem. The analyst must examine the ratio of bad-debt expense to sales to observe the increasing proportion of uncollectible sales. A firm that does not adequately recognize bad-debt expense for an increasing proportion of uncollectible sales will experience a buildup of accounts receivable relative to sales and therefore higher accounts receivable days outstanding. Examining just the ratio of bad-debt expense to sales will not signal the slow rate at which customers pay.

Recognizing revenues at the time of sale suffers from an even more fundamental problem at times: To accelerate revenue recognition, some firms may alter their definition of *sale.* Does the receipt of firm customer orders for goods held in inventory constitute a sale or is physical delivery of the product to the customer necessary? Is completion of the production of custom-ordered goods sufficient to recognize revenue or is physical delivery necessary? In an effort to achieve sales targets for a period, firms sometimes record sales earlier than physical delivery. Under U.S. GAAP, revenues can be recognized when the earnings process is substantially complete, which would suggest revenues should not be recognized until the firm has delivered legal title of the products to customers.

Some firms, hungry for sales revenue, violate GAAP to the point of recording sales based on merely an indication of possible interest in a product by a customer. Inevitably in these situations the pressure placed on sales personnel, either by themselves or by senior management, leads to this violation of the revenue recognition criteria. A related ploy is to accelerate the recognition of revenues and then hide sales returns by customers. Firms store the returned goods in a remote or independently owned warehouse, hoping that the independent auditor will not detect them.

Chapter 5 points out that the distinction between earnings management and management fraud is often a thin line. In these ploys, however, it is clear that management crosses the line. The actions are fraudulent in nature because they are outside the bounds of GAAP, and management acts to intentionally mislead statement users.[2]

As stated earlier, the analyst should be vigilant in assessing whether firms are managing their revenues. Revenues are at the core of a firm's ability to generate and report profits, and to grow and prosper. A firm experiencing declining sales growth, particularly relative to other firms in its industry, is the type most likely to be tempted to manage earnings by "stretching" the revenue recognition rules. Although this type of earnings management eventually catches up with the firm, it is precisely in these situations when a firm's sustainable earnings are likely to be declining. The analyst needs to take this into account when forecasting future earnings.

Criteria for Expense Recognition

Financial reporting requires the recognition of expenses under the accrual basis of accounting as follows:

1. Costs directly associated with revenues must be recognized as expenses in the period when a firm recognizes the revenues.

[2]A summary of celebrated cases in which management abused the reporting system for recognizing revenue appears in Chapter 6 of Martin S. Fridson and Fernando Alvarez, *Financial Statement Analysis: A Practitioner's Guide*, 3rd ed. (New York: John Wiley & Sons, 2002).

2. Costs not directly associated with revenues must be recognized as expenses in the period when a firm consumes the services or benefits of the costs in operations.

Most of the costs of manufacturing a product closely relate to particular revenues. The firm matches expense recognition with revenue recognition for such costs, referred to as *product* costs. Other costs, such as insurance and property taxes on administrative facilities, salaries of corporate officers, and depreciation on property, plant, and equipment that are not part of the manufacturing process, bear only an indirect relation to revenues generated during the period. Such costs become expenses in the period in which the firm consumes the benefits of these types of insurance, governmental, administrative, and asset services. Accountants refer to such costs as *period* expenses.

Because a large proportion of the expenses that firms report in the income statement associate directly with revenue recognized, assessing the true net economic resources and manageability of expenses and revenues are closely related. However, certain period expenses are more susceptible to management than others. The analyst should carefully monitor advertising, research and development, and maintenance expenditures, as examples, in order to discern whether substantive reasons exist for changes in the levels of these expenditures, or whether the changes are the result of managed earnings. Expenditures that are somewhat discretionary in nature and reported on the income statement as period costs are prime candidates for managing earnings.

Similar to revenue recognition, GAAP requires firms to identify in notes to the financial statements the significant policies employed for recognizing expenses. Exhibit 7.2 illustrates a recent quarterly disclosure by DriveTime for recognition of expenses for credit losses on loans (DriveTime is also discussed in Chapter 6). DriveTime's primary line of business is to sell and finance used vehicles to customers in the "subprime" segment of the used-car market. The subprime market comprises customers who typically have limited credit histories, low income, or past credit problems. The judgment necessary for calculating the effect of credit losses is particularly strewn with estimates and uncertainties. DriveTime identifies five factors in Exhibit 7.2 that it considers in evaluating whether the allowance and the provision for credit losses is adequate. Moreover, it makes clear that this list is not an exhaustive one.

EXHIBIT 7.2

DriveTime
Excerpt from Notes to Consolidated Quarterly Financial Statements

Allowance for Credit Losses

An allowance for credit losses (allowance) is established by charging the provision for credit losses. To the extent that the allowance is considered insufficient to absorb anticipated credit losses over the next 12 months, additions to the allowance are established through a charge to the provision for credit losses. The evaluation of the allowance considers such factors as (1) the performance of each dealership's loan portfolio, (2) the Company's historical credit losses, (3) the overall portfolio quality and delinquency status, (4) the value of underlying collateral, and (5) the current economic conditions that may affect the borrower's ability to pay.

Application of Revenue and Expense Recognition Criteria

Applying the revenue recognition and matching principles to actual business settings is not always as straightforward as the criteria might appear. The common expression "the devil is in the details" aptly describes the problem of assessing whether the principles are correctly applied in particular circumstances. The reporting system currently employed in the United States commonly requires firms to make subjective measurements, estimates, and judgments. Coupling this problem with the complexities of businesses today, it is not surprising that appropriate application of revenue and expense recognition criteria is not always obvious.

To obtain a flavor for the complexities often involved in applying these principles, consider the six examples that follow.

Example 1

Xerox Corporation typically manufactures copiers and leases them to customers under multiyear leases. The length of the leases often approximates the useful life of the copiers. Thus, the arrangement is equivalent to a sale of the copier, with Xerox providing financing to the customer signing the lease. (Chapter 8 describes and illustrates the accounting for leases by both the lessor and lessee.) The accounting is complex, however, because the lease contract usually entails a bundled monthly payment that covers not just use of the copier by the customer over the life of the lease, but also maintenance services, photocopying paper up to certain minimum usage, and financing costs. The revenue recognition question is when Xerox should recognize revenue from the four services covered in the lease: (1) copier use, (2) maintenance services, (3) photocopying paper, and (4) financing.

The question is most easily answered by first considering how Xerox accounts for outright sales of copiers. If Xerox sells a copier to a creditworthy customer, it recognizes revenue from the sale of the copier at the time of delivery. For items (2) through (4), Xerox meets the substantial performance criterion for revenue recognition over time as it provides these goods and services.

In the typical situation, however, the copier is *not* an outright sale, but rather a lease arrangement that involves a bundled periodic lease payment. Xerox must unbundle the monthly payment to ascertain the proportion of revenue related to each component of this bundled transaction. If the leasing arrangement is equivalent in economic substance to a sale, then Xerox must determine (1) how much revenue the firm should recognize up front for manufacturing the copier and providing its use to the customer over its entire life, and (2) how much the firm should allocate to the remaining three categories of the arrangement and recognize later. In fact, Xerox does make these allocations, but the SEC accused Xerox of allocating too much of the monthly payment to the sale of the copiers and too little to maintenance, paper, and financing. The result was an acceleration of revenues and earnings that authorities contended was too aggressive. Xerox accordingly restated its earnings.

Example 2

Founded in 1810, the Hartford Financial Services Group is one of the largest investment and insurance companies in the United States. Hartford is a leading provider of (1) life insurance and group and employee benefits, (2) automobile and homeowners insurance, and (3) business insurance. The company is the largest seller of individual insurance annuities in the United States.

Hartford's life insurance unit receives cash from premiums and from investments each period. It invests in readily marketable securities for the most part, so it can measure objectively the changes in the market value of its investments. Measuring the amount of revenue each period while the life insurance policy is outstanding presents few difficulties. The only issue on the revenue side is whether these firms should recognize as revenue the unrealized gains and losses from changes in the market value of investments. Common practice in the insurance industry is to recognize such gains and losses each year in computing net income.[3]

There is usually little question about the total expense associated with selling and underwriting a life insurance policy. Other than selling commissions and administrative costs, the only expense is the cash value of the policy. The income recognition issue is how much of this total cost life insurance companies should recognize as an expense each year to match against premium and investment revenues. The objective is to spread these costs over the life of the insured. Determining the length of this period and the pattern of expense recognition requires actuarial calculations of expected life, investment returns, and similar factors. Note that allocating an equal portion of the total cost to each year of expected life will not necessarily provide an appropriate matching of revenues and expenses. Although insurance premiums typically remain level over the contract period, investment revenues increase over time as premiums and investment returns accumulate. Life insurance companies increase a liability each period, often called Policyholder Reserves, for the amount of expense recognized. They reduce this account when they pay insurance claims. An analyst examining the financial statements of a life insurance company should study carefully the amount shown for Policyholder Reserves and the change in this account each year. Such an assessment provides information about both the adequacy of assets to cover potential claims and the amount of net income each period.

Example 3

MicroStrategy, Inc. is a software and consulting firm in the information technology sector. The firm specializes in tailoring proprietary software to analyze large databases of clients. Clients often sign two- or three-year contracts with the firm that cover tailoring the software to the specific needs of the client and then licensing (as opposed to selling) the use of software for the length of the contract. The contracts often require MicroStrategy to train the client's personnel to use the software in mining large databases and to assist the client in designing reports and analyses based on this data mining. The contracts establish key deliverables, together with a schedule for the payment of fees over the life of the contract.

Assuming reasonable assurance of the collectibility of fees from the client, the revenue recognition issue is when MicroStrategy meets the substantial performance criterion for revenue recognition. The situation is complicated because MicroStrategy provides both (1) use of its proprietary software tailored to the client's needs and (2) a consulting service to ensure that client personnel produce value-added reports and analyses. What proportion of the contract relates to the software and what proportion to the consulting services? How precise are the deliverables, and what happens if MicroStrategy misses a contract deadline?

In the past, MicroStrategy recognized approximately 50 percent of the amount of the total contract as revenue at the time of signing the contract. The firm, in other words, concluded that it had substantially performed about half of what it promised to the

---

[3] Chapter 9 provides a discussion of how firms other than life insurance companies account for investments in readily marketable debt and equity securities.

customer at the contract signing date. The SEC disagreed with this assessment, however, and concluded that 50 percent was far too aggressive and represented an inappropriate acceleration of revenue. MicroStrategy scaled back the amount of revenue it recognized at the contract signing date to approximately 10 percent and restated past financial statements. The news of the need to restate previously reported earnings led to a substantial drop in MicroStrategy's stock price.

Example 4

AOL, the Internet services division of AOL Time Warner, generates subscription revenues from subscribers to its online services, as well as advertising revenues for advertisements it places on various web sites.

In the past, AOL entered into one such arrangement with eBay. Under the arrangement, AOL located firms that wished to advertise on the eBay web site. AOL sold the advertising space to various companies and then remitted a portion of this amount to eBay. AOL bore no credit risk if the firms failed to pay for the advertising space. AOL guaranteed the sale of a certain minimum amount of advertising space each month. Failure to sell the minimum space required AOL to make payments to eBay. AOL booked the amount to be received from the various companies as revenues and the amount paid to eBay as an expense. In turn, eBay booked the net amount received from AOL as revenue.

The issue is whether AOL is a principal or an agent in purchasing and selling advertising space. The accounting described here considers AOL a principal, because it entails booking the full revenue and expense. GAAP requires a firm to assume substantial product risk if it is to be considered a principal, which does not appear to be the case here because AOL probably can sell sufficient advertising space each month to cover the minimum obligation to eBay. In this case, AOL bears little risk of unsold advertising space and should have accounted for its services as an agent and recognized only the net amount as revenue. The distinction is an important one because, although there is no effect on net income, the magnitude of revenues reported as a principal is substantially higher than that reported as an agent. Revenues often are a driver for assessing firms, particularly technology and Internet firms such as AOL.

Example 5

Global Crossing, Qwest Communications, and other telecommunications companies have created worldwide fiber-optics networks in recent years. Companies in the industry typically enter into long-term leases for the use of the networks developed by other companies in the industry. For example, Global Crossing might create a fiber-optics network in India, Qwest Communications might create a similar network in China, and each in turn might lease part of the capacity of the networks to each other. The leases often give the lessee an indefeasible right of use to the capacity, essentially a legal transfer of title to the capacity. Each company books the "sale" of the legal rights to the capacity as revenue in the year they sign the leases. They treat the "purchase" of the legal rights to the capacity as a capital expenditure, much like the purchase of a long-lived asset.

The issue is whether these firms satisfy the revenue recognition criterion that requires receipt of an asset with a measurable cash-equivalent value when they swap legal rights to capacity. Recognize that, as opposed to the manufacture and sale of physical equipment, these situations simply involve the sale of legal rights to use capacity. If the capacity is already in place, then the "manufacturing" activity is complete. As long as there are no significant restrictions on the ability of the buyer to use the capacity purchased, then the purchaser of the capacity receives an asset: the right to use capacity of the other firm in the future.

The analyst must consider at least two other issues, however. First, is it likely that the seller of the capacity will exist for the full period of the contract and be in a position to provide the services? The free fall of the telecommunications industry in recent years makes this an important consideration. Second, how should the firms establish the value of the contract? Given that contracts often entail the swapping of promises to provide capacity in the future with no cash changing hands, it is difficult to determine their true value. What is the appropriate value to attach to the revenue for the seller at the signing of the contract? What is the appropriate value to attach to the expense recorded by the buyer during the course of the contract? GAAP has not definitively answered how to account for these types of transactions.

Example 6

Wal-Mart is one of the most recognized retail store chains in the world, with total sales of more than $280 billion reported in a recent year. Wal-Mart often receives rebates from its suppliers when its purchases during any given year reach established minimum levels.[4] In some cases, formal agreements exist that state the minimum purchases required for the rebate. In other cases, the arrangement is less formal. Although the supplier decides the amount of rebates to pay as the reporting year progresses, it is fairly predictable from year to year. The issue is how Wal-Mart should recognize supplier rebates in its quarterly reports issued during the course of any reporting year.

The key issue is whether realization of the rebate is necessary to justify recognition of the benefit, or whether estimates of its amounts are sufficient to justify recognition. If the probability of realizing the rebate is high and its amount is predictable, the matching principle supports recognition in each quarter. In this way, Wal-Mart matches cost of goods sold net of the rebates against the revenues earned in the quarter. In fact, reporting the entire rebate credit in one quarter (the quarter when it is received, for example) would be inappropriate because it provides a poor matching of revenues and expenses. However, if the probability of receiving the rebate is low or its amount difficult to predict, then delaying recognition until it is received seems appropriate. Having a contract in place enhances the predictability, but it is not necessary if customary practice is for the suppliers to make rebates. The key is being able to make reasonably solid estimates of the rebate's amount.

Firms in the retail discount industry handle rebates differently. The firm's first note to the financial statements often provides an explanation of its policy on accounting for rebates.

These six examples illustrate the difficulty of applying general principles for recognizing revenues and expenses to business practices specific to particular industries. The analyst needs to ratchet up the usual degree of healthy skepticism practiced in analyzing reported financial data when the activities of the firms or industries under scrutiny involve the level of uncertainty and subjectivity represented by these six illustrations.

The next section explores more fully the impact on financial statements of recognizing income either earlier than the time of sale (a common practice among long-term contractors) or later than the time of sale (a common practice when firms sell goods on an installment payment basis and experience high uncertainty regarding the collectibility of cash).

---

[4]Note that PepsiCo is a large supplier to Wal-Mart. In Note 2, "Significant Accounting Policies—Revenue Recognition" (Appendix A), PepsiCo states: "Wal-Mart represents approximately 11 percent of our net revenue."

Income Recognition for Long-Term Contractors

The operating cycle for a long-term contractor (such as a building contractor, aerospace manufacturer, or ship builder) differs from that of a manufacturing firm in three important respects:

1. The period of construction (production) may span many accounting periods.
2. Contractors identify customers and agree on a contract price in advance (or at least in the early stages of construction).
3. Customers often make periodic payments of the contract price as work progresses.

The operating activities of long-term contractors often satisfy the criteria for the recognition of revenue during the period of construction. Exhibit 7.1 describes this form of revenue recognition for United Technologies, a provider of technology products to the construction and aerospace industries. The existence of a contract indicates that the contractor has identified a buyer and agreed on a price. The contractor either collects cash in advance or concludes, based on an assessment of the customer's credit standing, that it will receive cash equal to the contract price after completion of construction. Although the contract may obligate the contractor to perform substantial future services, the contractor should be able to estimate the cost of these services with reasonable precision. In agreeing to a contract price, the firm must have some confidence in the estimates of the total costs it will incur on the contract.

Percentage-of-Completion Method

When contractors meet the criteria for revenue recognition as construction progresses, they usually recognize revenue during the period of construction using the percentage-of-completion method. Under the percentage-of-completion method, contractors recognize a portion of the total contract price, based on the degree of completion of the work during the period, as revenue for the period. They base this proportion either on engineers' or architects' estimates of the degree of completion or on the ratio of costs incurred to date to the total expected costs for the contract. The actual schedule of cash collections is *not* a determining factor in measuring the amount of revenue recognized each period under the percentage-of-completion method. Even if a contractor expects to collect the entire contract price at the completion of construction, it would still use the percentage-of-completion method as long as it can make reasonable estimates as construction progresses of the amount of cash it will collect and of the costs it will incur.

As contractors recognize portions of the contract price as revenues, they recognize corresponding proportions of the total estimated costs of the contract as expenses. The percentage-of-completion method, following the principles of the accrual basis of accounting, matches expenses with related revenues.

Example 7

To illustrate the percentage-of-completion method, assume that a firm agrees to construct a bridge for $5,000,000. Estimated costs are as follows: Year 1, $1,500,000; Year 2, $2,000,000; Year 3, $500,000. Thus, the expected gross margin from the contract is $1,000,000 (= $5,000,000 − $1,500,000 − $2,000,000 − $500,000).

Assuming that the contractor bases the degree of completion on the percentage of total costs incurred to date and that it incurs actual costs as anticipated, revenue and expense from the contract are as follows:

Year	Degree of Completion	Revenue	Expense	Gross Margin
1	\$1,500,000/\$4,000,000 = 37.5%	\$1,875,000	\$1,500,000	\$ 375,000
2	\$2,000,000/\$4,000,000 = 50.0%	2,500,000	2,000,000	500,000
3	\$500,000/\$4,000,000 = 12.5%	625,000	500,000	125,000
		\$5,000,000	\$4,000,000	\$1,000,000

Actual costs on contracts seldom coincide precisely with expectations. As new information on expected total costs becomes available, contractors must adjust reported income on the contract. They adjust reported income for this change in estimated total costs during the current and future periods rather than retroactively restating income of prior periods.

Example 8

Look at Example 7 again. Assume now that actual costs incurred in Year 2 for the contract were \$2,200,000 instead of \$2,000,000 and that total expected costs on the contract are now \$4,200,000. Revenue, expense, and gross margin from the contract are as follows:

Year	Cumulative Degree of Completion	Revenue	Expense	Margin
1	\$1,500,000/\$4,000,000 = 37.5%	\$1,875,000	\$1,500,000	\$375,000
2	\$3,700,000/\$4,200,000 = 88.1%	2,530,000[a]	2,200,000	330,000
3	\$4,200,000/\$4,200,000 = 100%	595,000[b]	500,000	95,000
		\$5,000,000	\$4,200,000	\$800,000

[a](.881 × \$5,000,000) – \$1,875,000 = \$2,530,000
[b]\$5,000,000 – \$1,875,000 – \$2,530,000 = \$595,000

Example 9

If it appears that the contractor will ultimately realize a loss on completion of a contract, the contractor must recognize the loss in full as soon as it becomes evident. For example, if at the end of Year 2 the contractor expects to realize a loss of \$200,000 on the contract, it must recognize a loss of \$575,000 in Year 2. The \$575,000 amount offsets the income of \$375,000 recognized in Year 1 plus a loss of \$200,000 anticipated on the overall contract.

Contractors report actual contract costs on the balance sheet in a Contracts in Process account. This account includes not only accumulated costs to date but any income or loss recognized on the contract. Assume that the firm in Example 7 pays cash for all costs incurred each year and receives cash from the customer on completion of the contract. Using the analytical framework from Chapter 2, the effect on the financial statements of incurring costs on the contract each year (transactions (1), (3), and (5)), recognizing revenue and expense each year (transactions (2), (4), and

(6)), and completing the contract (transaction (7)) are as follows (ignoring income taxes):

	C +	N$A	= L	+ CC	+ AOCI +	RE
BS-BOP						
(1)	−1,500,000	+1,500,000				
(2)		+1,875,000				+1,875,000
		−1,500,000				−1,500,000
IBT						+ 375,000
BS-EOP	**−1,500,000**	**+1,875,000**				**+ 375,000**
(3)	−2,000,000	+2,000,000				
(4)		+2,500,000				+2,500,000
		−2,000,000				−2,000,000
IBT						+ 500,000
BS-EOP	**−3,500,000**	**+4,375,000**				**+ 875,000**
(5)	− 500,000	+ 500,000				
(6)		+ 625,000				+ 625,000
		− 500,000				− 500,000
IBT						+ 125,000
(7)	+5,000,000	−5,000,000				
BS-EOP	**+1,000,000**	—				**+1,000,000**

Exhibit 7.3 shows the Contracts in Process account for Examples 7 through 9. If the contractor periodically billed the customer for portions of the contract price, it would report the amount billed in Accounts Receivable and as a subtraction from the amount in the Contracts in Process account.

Completed-Contract Method

Some long-term contractors postpone the recognition of revenue until they complete the construction project. Such firms use the completed-contract method of recognizing revenue, which, in effect, is the "time of sale" method of recognizing revenue. If the firm in Example 8 had used the completed-contract method, it would have recognized no revenue or expense from the contract during Year 1 or Year 2. It would recognize contract revenue of $5,000,000 and contract expenses of $4,200,000 in Year 3. Note that total gross margin is $800,000 under both the percentage-of-completion and completed-contract methods, equal to cash inflows of $5,000,000 less cash outflows of $4,200,000. If the contractor anticipates a loss on a contract, it recognizes the loss as soon as the loss becomes evident, even if the contract is incomplete.

The Contracts in Process account under the completed-contract method shows a balance of $1,500,000 on December 31, Year 1—the accumulated costs to date. This account shows a balance on December 31, Year 2, of $3,500,000 under Example 7, $3,700,000 under Example 8, and $3,500,000 under Example 9. These amounts reflect accumulated costs to date minus, in Example 9, the estimated loss on the contract.

These amounts are less than the amounts shown in the Contracts in Process account for Examples 7 and 8 under the percentage-of-completion method (see Exhibit 7.3) by the amount of accumulated income recognized under the latter method. Accelerating the recognition of income under the percentage-of-completion method increases both assets and net income (part of retained earnings). Thus, as Chapter 2 discussed, income recognition and asset valuation closely interrelate.

EXHIBIT 7.3

Calculation of Balance in Contracts in Process Account
Using the Percentage-of-Completion Method

	Accumulated Costs	Accumulated Income	Amount in Contracts in Process Account
Example 7 (Profit = $1,000,000)			
During Year 1	$ 1,500,000	$ 375,000	$ 1,875,000
Balance, December 31, Year 1	$ 1,500,000	$ 375,000	$ 1,875,000
During Year 2	2,000,000	500,000	2,500,000
Balance, December 31, Year 2	$ 3,500,000	$ 875,000	$ 4,375,000
During Year 3	500,000	125,000	625,000
Completion of Contract during Year 3	(4,000,000)	(1,000,000)	(5,000,000)
Balance, December 31, Year 3	$ 0	$ 0	$ 0
Example 8 (Profit = $800,000)			
During Year 1	$ 1,500,000	$ 375,000	$ 1,875,000
Balance, December 31, Year 1	$ 1,500,000	$ 375,000	$ 1,875,000
During Year 2	2,200,000	330,000	2,530,000
Balance, December 31, Year 2	$ 3,700,000	$ 705,000	$ 4,405,000
During Year 3	500,000	95,000	595,000
Completion of Contract during Year 3	(4,200,000)	(800,000)	(5,000,000)
Balance, December 31, Year 3	$ 0	$ 0	$ 0
Example 9 (Loss = $200,000)			
During Year 1	$ 1,500,000	$ 375,000	$ 1,875,000
Balance, December 31, Year 1	$ 1,500,000	$ 375,000	$ 1,875,000
During Year 2	2,200,000	(575,000)	1,625,000
Balance, December 31, Year 2	$ 3,700,000	$ (200,000)	$ 3,500,000
During Year 3	1,500,000	—	1,500,000
Completion of Contract during Year 3	(5,200,000)	200,000	(5,000,000)
Balance, December 31, Year 3	$ 0	$ 0	$ 0

Choice of Reporting Method by Long-Term Contractors

A contractor should not use the percentage-of-completion method when there is substantial uncertainty regarding the total costs it will incur to complete the project. If the contractor cannot estimate the total costs, it cannot estimate the percentage of total costs incurred as of a given date and thereby the percentage of services already rendered. It will also be unable to estimate the total income from the contract prior to its completion.

In some cases, contractors use the completed-contract method because the contracts are of such short duration (such as a few months) that earnings reported with the percentage-of-completion method and the completed-contract method are not significantly different. In these cases, the lower costs of implementing the completed-contract method explain its use. Contractors also use the completed-contract method when they have not obtained a specific buyer during the construction phase, as is sometimes the case in the construction of residential housing. These cases require future selling efforts. Substantial uncertainty may exist regarding the ultimate contract price and the amount of cash that the contractor will receive.

Contractors must use the percentage-of-completion method for income tax purposes. Although most firms would prefer to use the completed-contract method for tax purposes, thereby delaying the recognition of income and payment of income taxes, the Internal Revenue Code does not permit it.

Examples 7 through 9 dramatically illustrate the level of estimation and uncertainty involved with income recognition for long-term contractors. Sometimes a project can take a number of years to complete. In some cases, contractors work with hundreds of subcontractors. Renegotiating contracts several times during the course of a large contract is commonplace. Analysts estimating persistent earnings using historical data for firms that construct (and sell) long-term products must consider these and other firm factors, including the volume of projects underway currently, the success in completing projects on time and within budget, the length of typical projects, and the types of projects undertaken. Long-term construction firms usually address many of these factors in the analysis of operations found in the annual report and Form 10-K filing. (Again, see Exhibit 7.1 for an excerpt from United Technologies' annual report.) Because both (1) the time period between cash inflows and outflows for these firms is so long and (2) a large degree of estimation is needed to measure revenues and expenses, the potential for earnings management is high. The analyst evaluating firms in the construction, aircraft, and defense-related industries, for example, must be particularly sensitive to this fact.

Revenue Recognition When Cash Collectibility Is Uncertain

Occasionally, estimating the amount of cash or cash-equivalent value of other assets that a firm will receive from customers is difficult. This may occur because the future financial condition of the customer is highly uncertain or because the customer may have the right to return the items purchased, thereby avoiding the obligation to make cash payments. This uncertainty regarding future cash inflows may prevent the selling firm from measuring—at the time of sale—the present value of the cash it expects to receive. The firm will therefore recognize revenue at the time it collects cash using either the installment method or the cost-recovery-first method.

The installment and cost-recovery-first methods exist as prudent and conservative approaches to the problem of revenue recognition when cash collection is uncertain. Given the difficulty in estimating cash inflows in these situations, the opportunity to manage earnings may cloud even management's best intentions to measure earnings accurately. The uncertainty of future cash flows also affects assessments of earnings persistence. The task for the analyst is to judge whether a firm recognizing revenue using the time-of-sale method should be using one of these two more conservative methods because the level of uncertainty is high.

Installment Method

Under the installment method, a firm recognizes revenue as it collects portions of the selling price in cash. At the same time, it recognizes corresponding portions of the cost of the good or service sold as an expense. For example, assume that a firm sells for $100 merchandise costing $60. The buyer agrees to pay (ignoring interest) $20 each month for five months. The firm recognizes revenue of $20 each month as it receives cash. Likewise, it recognizes cost of goods sold of $12 (= $20/$100 × $60) each month. By the end of five months, the firm recognizes total income of $40 [= 5 × ($20 – $12)].

Land development companies, which typically sell undeveloped land and promise to develop it over several future years, sometimes use the installment method. The buyer makes a nominal down payment and agrees to pay the remainder of the purchase price in installments over ten, twenty, or more years. In these cases, future development of the land is a significant aspect of the earnings process. Also, substantial uncertainty often exists as to the ultimate collectibility of the installment notes, particularly those not due until many years in the future. The customer can always elect to stop making payments, losing the right to own the land.

Cost-Recovery-First Method

When firms experience substantial uncertainty about cash collection, they can also use the cost-recovery-first method of income recognition. The cost-recovery-first method matches the costs of generating revenues dollar for dollar with cash receipts until the firm recovers all such costs. Revenues equal expenses in each period until full cost recovery occurs. Only when cumulative cash receipts exceed total costs will a firm show profit (that is, revenue without any matching expenses) in the income statement.

To illustrate the cost-recovery-first method, refer to the previous example relating to the sale of merchandise for $100. During the first three months, the firm would recognize revenue of $20 and expense of $20. By the end of the third month, cumulative cash receipts of $60 exactly equal the cost of the merchandise sold. During the fourth and fifth months, the firm would recognize revenue of $20 each month but without an offsetting expense. For the five months as a whole, total income is again $40 (equal to cash inflow of $100 less cash outflow of $60) but the income recognition pattern differs from that of the installment method.

Comprehensive Illustration of Income Recognition Methods for Installment Sales

Technor Computer Corporation (TCC) sold a computer costing $16,000,000 to the City of Boston for $20,000,000 on January 1, Year 1. The City of Boston agreed to make annual payments of $5,548,195 on December 31, Year 1, to December 31, Year 4 (five payments in total). The top panel of Exhibit 7.4 shows an amortization table for the note receivable underlying this transaction. The five payments of $5,548,195 each when discounted at 12 percent have a present value equal to the $20,000,000 selling price. Thus, 12 percent is the interest rate implicit in the note. Column (2) shows the interest revenue that TCC recognizes each year from providing financing services to the City of Boston (that is, permitting the city to delay payment of the $20,000,000 selling price).

The middle panel shows the revenue and expense that TCC recognizes under three income recognition methods. Columns (6) and (7) assume TCC recognizes income from the sale of the computer at the time of sale. Such immediate recognition rests on the premise that the City of Boston will pay the amounts due under the note with a high probability.

If substantial uncertainty exists regarding cash collectibility of the notes, then TCC should use either the installment or cost-recovery-first methods. Columns (8) and (9) show the amounts for the installment method. Revenues in column (8) represent collections of the $20,000,000 principal amount of the note (that is, the portion of each cash payment made by the city that does not represent interest). Column (9) shows the expense each year, which represents 80 percent (= $16,000,000/$20,000,000) of the revenue recognized. Columns (10) and (11) show the amounts for the cost-recovery-first method. Note that TCC recognizes no income until Year 5, when cumulative cash receipts exceed the $16,000,000 cost of manufacturing the computer.

Note that total cash inflows of $27,740,973 (column 3) equal total revenue, sales revenue (columns 6, 8, and 10) plus interest revenue (column 12), and total cash outflows of $16,000,000 equal total expense (columns 7, 9, and 11).

The last panel of Exhibit 7.4 shows the amounts that TCC reports on its balance sheet for each of the three income recognition methods. Note that at the end of five

EXHIBIT 7.4

Illustration of Income Recognition Methods from Installment Sales

Amortization Schedule for Note Receivable

Year	Note Receivable, January 1: (1)	Interest Revenue at 12 Percent (2)	Cash Payment Received (3)	Repayment of Principal (4)	Note Receivable, December 31: (5)
1	$20,000,000	$2,400,000	$ 5,548,195	$ 3,148,195	$16,851,805
2	16,851,805	2,022,217	5,548,195	3,525,978	13,325,827
3	13,325,827	1,599,099	5,548,195	3,949,096	9,376,731
4	9,376,731	1,125,208	5,548,195	4,422,987	4,953,744
5	4,953,744	594,449	5,548,193	4,953,744	0
		$7,740,973	$27,740,973	$20,000,000	

Column (2) = .12 × Column (1)
Column (3) = Given
Column (4) = Column (3) − Column (2)
Column (5) = Column (1) − Column (4)

Income Recognition from Sale of Computer

	Time-of-Sale Method		Installment Method		Cost-Recovery-First Method		All Three Methods
Year	Revenue (6)	Expense (7)	Revenue (8)	Expense (9)	Revenue (10)	Expense (11)	Interest Revenue (12)
1	$20,000,000	$16,000,000	$ 3,148,195	$ 2,518,556	$ 3,148,195	$ 3,148,195	$2,400,000
2	—	—	3,525,978	2,820,782	3,525,978	3,525,978	2,022,217
3	—	—	3,949,096	3,159,277	3,949,096	3,949,096	1,599,099
4	—	—	4,422,987	3,538,390	4,422,987	4,422,987	1,125,208
5	—	—	4,953,744	3,962,995	4,953,744	953,744	594,449
	$20,000,000	$16,000,000	$20,000,000	$16,000,000	$20,000,000	$16,000,000	$7,740,973

Column (8) = Column (4)
Column (9) = .80 × Column (8)
Column (10) = Column (4)
Column (11) = Column (10) until Cumulative Revenues = $16,000,000
Column (12) = Column (2)

Continued

EXHIBIT 7.4

continued

Notes Receivable—Net Reported on Balance Sheet

	Time-of-Sale Method		Installment Method		Cost-Recovery-First Method		
	Notes Receivable (13)	Notes Receivable (14)	Less Deferred Gross Margin (15)	Notes Receivable Net (16)	Notes Receivable (17)	Less Deferred Gross Margin (18)	Notes Receivable Net (19)
January 1, Year 1	$20,000,000	$20,000,000	$4,000,000	$16,000,000	$20,000,000	$4,000,000	$16,000,000
December 31, Year 1	16,851,805	16,851,805	3,370,361	13,481,444	16,851,805	4,000,000	12,851,805
December 31, Year 2	13,325,827	13,325,827	2,665,165	10,660,662	13,325,827	4,000,000	9,325,827
December 31, Year 3	9,376,731	9,376,731	1,875,346	7,501,385	9,376,731	4,000,000	5,376,731
December 31, Year 4	4,953,744	4,953,744	990,749	3,962,995	4,953,744	4,000,000	953,744
December 31, Year 5	—	—	—	—	—	—	—

Column (13), Column (14), Column (17) = Column (1)
Column (15) = $4,000,000 minus cumulative income recognized = Column (8) − Column (9) for the current and prior years. For example, $3,370,361 = $4,000,000 − ($3,148,195 − $2,518,556).
Column (16) = Column (14) − Column (15)
Column (18) = $4,000,000 minus cumulative income recognized = Column (10) − Column (11) for the current and prior years.
Column (19) = Column (17) − Column (18)

years, cumulative income and assets are identical for all three income recognition methods. However, recognizing income at the time of sale results in the largest cumulative income through the first four years and the largest assets. Recognizing income using the installment method results in the next-largest cumulative income and the next-largest assets. The cost-recovery-first method results in the smallest cumulative income and the smallest assets. The differences in assets equal the differences in cumulative income recognized. Thus, we see again that asset valuation closely relates to income recognition.

Choice of Installment and Cost-Recovery-First Methods

Financial reporting permits firms to use the installment method and the cost-recovery-first method only when substantial uncertainty exists about cash collection. For most sales of goods and services, past experience and an assessment of the credit standing of customers provide a sufficient basis for estimating the amount of cash firms will receive. In these cases, firms must generally recognize revenue at the time of sale, and do not use the installment method or the cost-recovery-first method.

Income tax laws allow the installment method for income tax reporting under some circumstances, even when no uncertainty exists regarding cash collections. Manufacturing firms selling on extended payment plans often use the installment method for income tax reporting (while recognizing revenue at the time of sale for financial reporting). Firms seldom use the cost-recovery-first method for tax reporting.

INVENTORY COST-FLOW ASSUMPTION

Firms selling relatively high dollar-valued items, such as automobiles, airplanes, and real estate, can ascertain from the accounting records the specific cost of each item sold. They recognize this amount as an expense, cost of goods sold, and match it against sales revenue in measuring net income.

In most cases, firms cannot identify the cost of the specific items sold. Inventory items are sufficiently similar and their unit costs sufficiently small that firms cannot justify economically the cost of designing an accounting system to keep track of specific unit costs. To measure cost of goods sold in these cases, firms must make some assumption about the *flow of costs* (but not the flow of units, because firms usually sell the oldest goods first). With the introduction of cost-flow assumptions into the reporting system, however, comes the possibility of earnings management and varying degrees of earnings quality. Analyzing earnings quality in the context of inventory accounting first requires understanding the reporting options available to management.

Financial reporting permits three cost-flow assumptions:

1. First-in, first-out (FIFO).
2. Last-in, first-out (LIFO).
3. Weighted average.

FIFO assigns the cost of the earliest purchases to the units sold and the cost of the most recent purchases to ending inventory. LIFO assigns the cost of the most recent purchases to the cost of goods sold and the earliest purchases to inventory. Weighted average assigns the average cost of all units available for sale during the period (units in beginning inventory plus units purchased) to both units sold and units in ending inventory. Note that these methods make assumptions about cost flows and do not necessarily reflect the physical flows of units. Exhibit 7.5 depicts these relationships graphically assuming that a firm purchases units evenly over the year.

EXHIBIT 7.5

Cost-Flow Assumptions

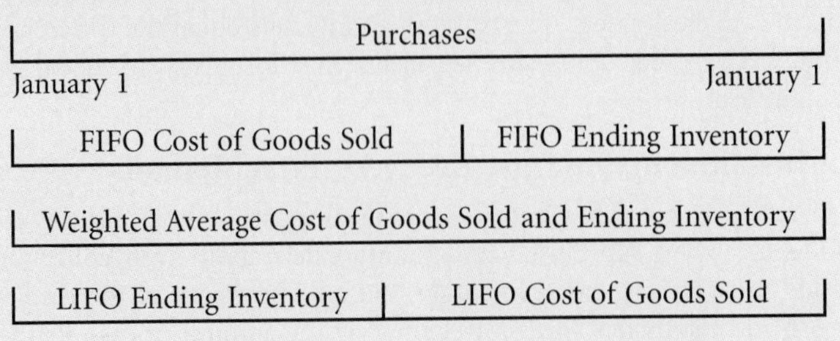

FIFO

FIFO results in balance sheet amounts for ending inventory that are closest to current replacement cost. The cost of goods sold can be somewhat out of date, however, because FIFO recognizes costs of goods sold based on the earlier prices of beginning inventory and the earliest purchases during the year. When inventory costs are rising, FIFO leads to the highest reported net income (lowest cost of goods sold) of the three methods, and when inventory costs fall it leads to the smallest net income.

LIFO

LIFO results in amounts for cost of goods sold that closely approximate current replacement costs. Balance sheet amounts, however, can contain the cost of inventory acquisitions made many years previously. Consider the diagram in Exhibit 7.6 that shows purchases, LIFO ending inventory, and LIFO cost of goods sold over several periods for a firm.

During each of the first four periods, the firm purchases more units than it sells. Thus, the number of physical units in ending inventory grows each year. The firm assigns costs to the units in inventory at the end of Year 1 based on the earliest purchases in Year 1. We refer to the costs assigned to these units as the base LIFO layer (denoted with the letter *a* in Exhibit 7.6).

LIFO prices the units in inventory at the end of Year 2 in two layers. Units equal to those on hand at the end of Year 1 carry unit costs based on purchase prices paid at the beginning of Year 1. Units added to ending inventory during Year 2 carry unit costs based on purchase prices paid at the beginning of Year 2 (denoted with the letter *b* in Exhibit 7.6). The balance sheet at the end of Year 2 states the inventory at the sum of the costs assigned to these two layers. Note that LIFO does not assume that the actual physical flow of units sold will track a LIFO assumption. LIFO is a cost-flow, or cost-assignment, method and not a means of tracking the physical movement of goods.

As the quantity of units in ending inventory continues to increase in Year 3 and Year 4, the firm adds new LIFO layers. At the end of Year 4, LIFO assigns costs to ending inventory

EXHIBIT 7.6

Illustration of LIFO Ending Inventory Layers
Purchases

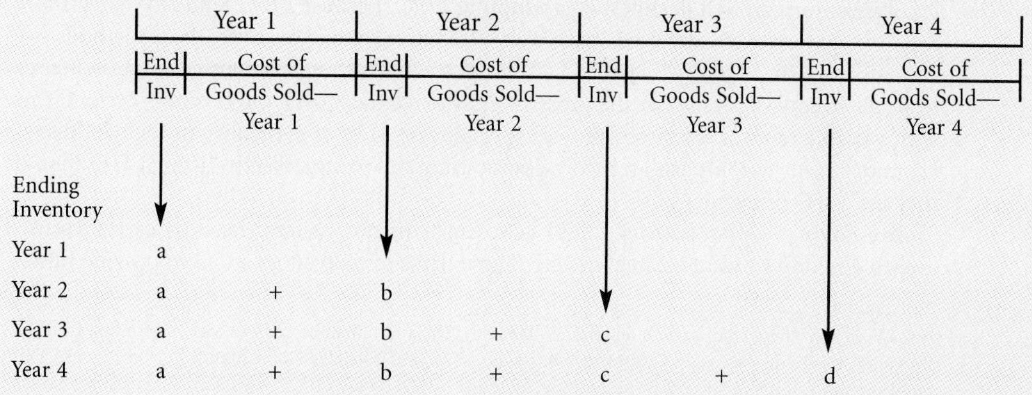

based on purchases made at the beginning of Year 1, Year 2, Year 3, and Year 4. Thus, the longer a firm remains on LIFO, the more its ending inventory valuation will differ from current replacement costs.

During periods of rising inventory costs, LIFO generally results in the highest cost of goods sold and the lowest net income of the three cost-flow assumptions. For this reason, firms usually prefer LIFO for income tax purposes. If a firm chooses a LIFO cost-flow assumption for tax purposes, the income tax law requires the firm to use LIFO for financial reporting to shareholders.

LIFO Liquidation

One exception to the generalization that LIFO produces the lowest net income during periods of rising prices occurs when a firm sells more units during a period than it purchases (referred to as a LIFO layer liquidation). In this case, LIFO assigns the cost of all of the current period's purchases plus the costs assigned to the most recent LIFO layers to the cost of goods sold. For example, assume that sales exceeded purchases in Year 5 in the preceding example. The firm assigns the cost of all of Year 5's purchases to the units sold. LIFO then assigns the cost of Year 4's LIFO layer (reflecting purchase prices at the beginning of Year 4) to the excess units sold, then assigns Year 3's LIFO layer (reflecting purchase prices at the beginning of Year 3) to any remaining excess units, and so on until it has assigned a cost to all units sold. Because LIFO assigns older, lower costs to a portion of the units sold, LIFO cost of goods sold might be less than FIFO cost of goods sold, despite experiencing rising inventory costs during the current period.

When firms experience LIFO liquidations, two cash flow effects likely occur. First, firms delay purchasing inventory items, thereby delaying a cash outflow. Second, firms increase taxable income and the required cash outflow for taxes.

Characteristics of LIFO Adopters

Researchers have examined the characteristics of firms that do and do not adopt LIFO. Although these research studies do not always show consistent results, the following factors appear related to the decision to adopt LIFO:[5]

Direction and Rate of Factor Price Changes for Inventory Items. Firms experiencing rapidly increasing factor prices for raw materials, labor, or other product costs obtain greater tax benefits from LIFO than firms that experience smaller factor price increases or that experience price decreases.

Variability in the Rate of Inventory Growth. LIFO adopters show more variable rates of inventory growth before adopting LIFO than firms that remain on FIFO. The variability of inventory growth declines after adopting LIFO. Because LIFO tends to match more recent inventory costs with sales than does FIFO or weighted average (these methods use costs that are six to fifteen months old relative to current replacement costs), LIFO tends to result in less variability in the gross margin percentage over the business cycle. Firms with variable rates of inventory growth (perhaps because of cyclicality in their industry) can more easily accomplish an income-smoothing reporting objective using LIFO than if they use FIFO or average cost.

Tax Savings Opportunities. LIFO adopters tend not to have tax loss carryforwards available to offset future taxable income. These firms instead adopt LIFO to provide future

---

[5]For a review of these studies, see Frederick W. Lindahl, "Dynamic Analysis of Inventory Accounting Choice," *Journal of Accounting Research* (Autumn 1989), pp. 201–226, and Nicholas Dopuch and Morton Pincus, "Evidence on the Choice of Inventory Accounting Methods: LIFO versus FIFO," *Journal of Accounting Research* (Spring 1988), pp. 28–59.

tax savings. LIFO adopters also realize larger tax savings in the year of adoption than in the surrounding years, suggesting that the decision is in part motivated by tax rather than financial reporting considerations.

Industry Membership. Firms in certain industries are more likely to adopt LIFO than firms in other industries. Because firms in an industry face similar factor price changes and variability in their inventory growth rates, one would expect similar choices of cost-flow assumptions.

Asset Size. Larger firms are more likely to adopt LIFO than smaller firms. LIFO increases record-keeping costs relative to FIFO, both in the year of adoption and in subsequent years. Larger firms realize larger amounts of tax savings than smaller firms to absorb the adoption and ongoing record-keeping costs of LIFO.

One hypothesis examined in this research is the relation between LIFO adoption and managerial compensation. Because LIFO usually results in lower earnings, one would expect that managerial compensation of LIFO adopters would either be less than compensation of non-LIFO adopters or else include a lower component of compensation based on earnings. Studies have found no difference in managerial compensation of LIFO and non-LIFO adopters, although adopters had a smaller earnings component to their compensation.

Weighted Average

The weighted average cost-flow assumption falls between the other two in its effect on the balance sheet and the income statement. It is, however, much more like FIFO than like LIFO in its effects on the balance sheet. When inventory turns over rapidly, purchases during the current period receive a heavy weight in the weighted average unit cost. The weighted average assumption therefore reflects current prices almost as much as FIFO.

Conversion from LIFO to FIFO

No cost-flow assumption based on historical cost can simultaneously report current-cost data in both the income statement and the balance sheet. If a firm reports current costs in the income statement under LIFO, its balance sheet amount for ending inventory might contain some very old costs. If LIFO inventory valuation results in low, out-of-date inventory values, then the balance sheet amounts for inventory reflect poor accounting information quality and provide potentially misleading information to users of financial statements (although costs of goods sold under LIFO may more closely reflect replacement cost and reflect high accounting quality). The Securities and Exchange Commission requires firms using LIFO to disclose in notes to the financial statements the amounts by which LIFO inventories differ from the amounts the firm would recognize for inventories under FIFO or current cost. Analysts sometimes refer to the difference in ending inventory valuation between LIFO and FIFO or current cost as the *LIFO reserve.* From this disclosure, it is possible to restate a LIFO firm's income to a FIFO basis. In this way, the analyst can place firms using LIFO on a basis more comparable to that of firms using FIFO.

Example 10

Note 14, "Supplemental Financial Information" (Appendix A), indicates that PepsiCo uses a combination of average, FIFO, and LIFO for inventories and costs of goods sold. The firm indicates that the differences between the FIFO and LIFO methods for valuing inventories are immaterial for both Year 3 and Year 4. The firm reports inventories on the balance sheet (Appendix A) of $1,541 million at the end of Year 4 and $1,412 at the end of Year 3.

Because reporting standards do not require the disclosure of the excess of current cost over average cost of inventories, it is not possible to restate inventories and cost of goods sold fully on a FIFO basis. It appears that PepsiCo's use of a combination of FIFO, LIFO, and average costs has no material effect on measures of its operating profitability.

Example 11

Belden CDT Inc. is a manufacturer of high-speed electronic cables and focuses on products for the specialty electronics and data networking sectors. Belden CDT was formed through a merger of Cable Design Technologies and Belden, Inc., and reported combined sales of $1.2 billion for Year 4.

After the merger, Belden CDT changed the method of accounting for the inventory of its former Belden operations in the United States from the LIFO method to the FIFO method. This decision, affecting approximately 17 percent of the firm's worldwide inventory, conform the company's inventory accounting policies across all operations. In a recent annual report, Belden CDT states: "The change increased total inventory on the balance sheet by $21.1 million. Prior-period results have been restated as if the FIFO method were used in all periods."

Example 12

The Great Atlantic & Pacific Tea Company Inc. (A&P) was one of the first supermarket chains in the United States. During a recent quarter, A&P changed its method accounting for certain inventories from LIFO to FIFO. The firm stated: "The change from LIFO to FIFO accounting for certain inventories was made so that all inventory accounting in the Company is on a FIFO basis. Previously, two divisions acquired over a decade ago had inventories valued on a LIFO basis. The Company has restated its Year 3 results for the effects of this change."

Example 13

Bethlehem Steel, an integrated steel manufacturer, operated in the eastern half of the United States, primarily Pennsylvania and Maryland, for most of the twentieth century. After almost two decades of downsizing and sustained losses, Bethlehem Steel recently sold its remaining assets to International Steel Group for $805 million. Prior to the sale, however, and because of its ongoing deteriorating conditions, the firm changed its method of valuing inventories from LIFO to FIFO. Annual report data on the firm's inventory prior to the change is provided in Exhibit 7.7. Exhibit 7.8 shows the conversion from LIFO to FIFO for Bethlehem Steel.

The gross margin percentage under LIFO is 16.2 percent [= ($5,250.9 – $4,399.1)/$5,250.9] and under FIFO is 16.8 percent [= ($5,250.9 – $4,366.7)/$5,250.9]. The lower gross margin value under LIFO suggests that the manufacturing costs of steel increased during Year 9.

The calculation of the inventory turnover ratio, a measure that indicates the efficiency with which a firm manages its inventory, is as follows:

$$\text{LIFO: } \$4{,}399.1 \div .5(\$369.0 + \$410.3) = 11.3$$
$$\text{FIFO: } \$4{,}366.7 \div .5(\$899.1 + \$972.8) = 4.7$$

The dramatic difference in the inventory turnover ratio under LIFO and FIFO reflects the many years that have elapsed since Bethlehem Steel adopted LIFO. The current (FIFO) cost of its inventory is more than twice as large as its book (LIFO) value. The inventory turnover ratio based on LIFO amounts gives a poor indication of the actual physical

EXHIBIT 7.7

Bethlehem Steel Company
Annual Report Excerpts
(amounts in millions)

December 31:	Year 8	Year 9
Inventories at FIFO Cost	$ 899.1	$ 972.8
Excess of FIFO Cost over LIFO Cost	(530.1)	(562.5)
Inventories at LIFO Cost	$ 369.0	$ 410.3
Current Assets (LIFO)	$1,439.8	$1,435.2
Current Liabilities	870.1	838.0

	Year 9
Sales	$5,250.9
Cost of Goods Sold (LIFO)	4,399.1
Net Income	245.7
Income Tax Rate	35%

EXHIBIT 7.8

Conversion of Bethlehem Steel Company from LIFO to FIFO
(amounts in millions)

	LIFO	Excess of FIFO Cost over LIFO Cost	FIFO
Beginning Inventory	$ 369.0	$ 530.1	$ 899.1
Purchases	4,440.4	—	4,440.4
Available	$4,809.4	$ 530.1	$5,339.5
Less Ending Inventory	(410.3)	(562.5)	(972.8)
Cost of Goods Sold	$4,399.1	$ (32.4)	$4,366.7

turnover of inventory items because it divides a cost of goods sold amount reflecting current costs by an average inventory amount reflecting very old costs. The inventory turnover ratio under FIFO provides a better indication of the physical turnover of inventory items because it divides a cost of goods sold reflecting only slightly out-of-date costs by an average inventory reflecting relatively recent costs. Although the trend in the inventory turnover ratio for a particular firm is likely to be similar under LIFO and FIFO, cross-sectional comparisons are inappropriate if one firm uses LIFO that recognizes very old costs on the balance sheet and another uses FIFO and recognizes more current costs on the balance sheet. Also, the LIFO measure of the inventory turnover ratio does not accurately portray the number of days inventories are held if LIFO costs are very old.

The inventory cost-flow assumption also affects the current ratio, a measure commonly used to assess short-term liquidity risk that is introduced in Chapter 5. For Bethlehem Steel, the conversion from LIFO to FIFO increases inventories at the end of Year 9 by $562.5 million, increasing the current ratio. However, cumulative pretax income and taxable income would have been $562.5 million higher under FIFO. Income tax laws do not permit a firm to use LIFO for taxes if it uses FIFO for financial reporting. Thus, Bethlehem Steel would have paid $196.9 million (= .35 × $562.5) more in income taxes under FIFO than under LIFO. (We assume that the income taxes saved by adopting LIFO are now partly in cash and partly in other assets.) If the $196.9 million reduces cash on the December 31, Year 9, balance sheet, the current ratios under LIFO and FIFO are:

LIFO:	$1,435.2 ÷ $838.0	1.71
FIFO:	[$1,435.2 + (1 – .35)($562.5)] ÷ $838.0	2.15

Thus, the current ratios differ significantly. The assumption that the extra income taxes paid under FIFO reduce cash only and not other assets moderates the differences in the current ratios. The current ratio on December 31, Year 9, under FIFO would likely exceed 2.15.

Conversion of the financial statements of Bethlehem Steel from LIFO to FIFO requires the following adjustments:

	December 31:	
Balance Sheet	**Year 8**	**Year 9**
Cash: .35 × $530.1; .35 × $562.5	$−185.5	$−196.9
Inventories	$+530.1	$+562.5
Retained Earnings: .65 × $530.1; .65 × $562.5	$+344.6	$+365.6
Income Statement	**For Year 9**	
Reduction in Cost of Goods Sold	$−32.4	
Increase in Income Tax Expense: .35 × $32.4	$+11.3	
Statement of Cash Flows	**For Year 9**	
Net Income	$ +21.1	
Increase in Inventories:		
($410.3 – $369.0) – ($972.8 – $899.1)	$(+32.4)	
Cash Flow from Operations	$ −11.3	

Cash flow from operations decreases for the extra income taxes paid under FIFO.

Users of financial statements find the conversion procedure illustrated in Exhibit 7.8 especially useful when comparing U.S. and non-U.S. firms. Most industrialized countries do not permit the use of LIFO for financial reporting. One important exception is Japan, but even in Japan most firms use specific identification or average costs rather than LIFO. Thus, the analyst should restate inventories and cost of goods sold for U.S. firms using LIFO to make them more comparable to cost-flow assumptions used outside the United States.

Stock Price Reaction to Changes in Inventory Cost-Flow Assumption

The required conformity of tax and financial reporting for firms choosing a LIFO cost-flow assumption provides fertile ground for researchers studying the efficiency of capital markets. LIFO saves taxes when inventory costs are rising. A switch to LIFO could result in a positive stock price reaction if the capital markets react to the future tax savings expected to arise from the switch. The switch also signals that the firm expects future inventory costs to rise, which could trigger a negative stock price reaction. The switch to LIFO also results in lower reported earnings to shareholders and could trigger a negative stock price reaction if capital markets fixate on reported earnings rather than the underlying economic effects driving the firm's accounting method choices.

Persistent Earnings and the Cost-Flow Assumption

For most manufacturing and retail firms, cost of goods sold represents the largest expense on the income statement. Inventory represents one of the most active accounts on the balance sheet because the creation and selling of goods and services is such a central activity for so many firms. Thus, monitoring the effects of cost of goods sold and inventory on the quality of accounting information is critical. To do this, the analyst considers the following:

1. The inventory cost-flow assumption chosen by management.
2. Price variation and the speed at which inventory turns over.
3. Any liquidation of LIFO inventory layers.
4. Any physical deterioration or obsolescence of inventory.
5. The financing of inventory acquisitions.

Choice of Cost-Flow Assumption

Because LIFO generally matches the most recent acquisition costs against revenues in measuring earnings, LIFO-based earnings generally provide the best measure of sustainable earnings. A firm must replace goods sold if it is to continue operating, and the most recent cost of the items purchased serves as the best predictor of their replacement costs. A FIFO cost-flow assumption matches older acquisition costs with current revenues, and a weighted average cost-flow assumption provides results between LIFO and FIFO. Researchers examining the relation between market returns on equity securities and earnings based on LIFO versus FIFO cost of goods sold found that earnings numbers based on LIFO explain more of the cross-sectional returns than do earnings numbers based on FIFO.[6]

Although LIFO generally provides higher-quality earnings measures, FIFO generally provides higher-quality financial position measures. This is because the inventory values under LIFO can be considerably less than replacement or current costs, which FIFO values often approximate. (Exceptions are discussed shortly.) A firm cannot use LIFO for measuring cost of goods sold on the income statement, and FIFO for measuring inventory on the balance sheet, however. All is not lost because, as Example 13 reveals, firms using LIFO must disclose the difference between the FIFO cost and LIFO cost of

[6]Ross Jennings, Paul J. Simko, and Robert B. Thompson II, "Does LIFO Inventory Accounting Improve the Income Statement at the Expense of the Balance Sheet?" *Journal of Accounting Research* (Spring 1996), pp. 85–109.

inventories. With this information, the analyst can convert inventory on the balance sheet to an amount more closely approximating current economic value.

Rapid Inventory Turnover and Price Stability

The preference for LIFO is tempered significantly when (1) inventory turns over quickly or (2) acquisition costs of inventory items do not vary much. LIFO, FIFO, and weighted average cost-flow assumptions all yield approximately the same amounts for cost of goods sold if inventory turns over roughly four or more times each year, or if inventory does not turn over quickly but prices are so stable that the choice of the cost-flow assumption is of little consequence.

Liquidation of LIFO Inventory Layers

When firms dip into LIFO layers, they must report the amount by which cost of goods sold was reduced (the usual case) and earnings were increased. This is a classic example of lower quality of earnings despite higher reported profits. When using earnings of the current period to estimate sustainable earnings, the analyst should eliminate the effect of the dip into old LIFO layers from the current period's earnings. The analyst should also ascertain from management the reason why inventory levels were depleted.

Obsolete or Damaged Inventory

When the current value of inventories declines below acquisition cost because of obsolescence or physical deterioration, firms must write down their inventories to reflect the decline. The analyst needs to rely on management and the auditors to determine when inventory is overvalued, but a good gauge is whether competitors are taking write-downs. Another signal comes from industry-wide publications addressing the demand for the firm's products. In certain cases, it is reasonable for the analyst to estimate independently the economic value of inventory and adjust the reported values accordingly.

Inventory Financing Arrangements

Firms often need substantial amounts of cash early in their operating cycle to finance the purchase of raw materials. Firms may finance these purchases through short-term borrowing agreements with suppliers that appear on the balance sheet as accounts payable. However, firms sometimes obtain financing for their inventories in a manner that avoids reporting a liability on the balance sheet. For example, a firm might create a legal trust with the sole purpose of purchasing raw materials that the firm needs in its operations. The trust purchases the raw materials on account from various suppliers. The firm later purchases the needed raw materials from the trust at agreed-on prices and reimburses the trust for the cost of carrying the raw materials until needed by the firm. The supplier is willing to sell to the trust on account because of the firm's purchase commitment.

The economic substance of this arrangement is that the firm has purchased raw material on account, and yet no accounts payable appear in the financial statements of the firm. Current financial reporting rules sometimes allow the firm to leave both the implicit inventory and the accounts payable off the balance sheet, thereby lowering its debt levels and increasing its inventory and accounts payable turnover ratios. The analyst should examine the notes to the financial statements for significant purchase commitments and consider adding them to inventories and accounts payable. Chapter 8 discusses these arrangements more fully.

ACCOUNTING FOR FIXED ASSETS

Virtually all firms report some amount of property, plant, and equipment (sometimes collectively referred to as long-lived fixed assets) on their balance sheets. The higher the degree of capital intensity of a firm, the higher will be the proportion of total assets represented by property, plant, and equipment. Among the questions analysts should raise about property, plant, and equipment are the following:

1. At what amount does the balance sheet report gross property, plant, and equipment?
2. Over what useful lives does the firm depreciate its property, plant, and equipment?
3. How old is the property, plant, and equipment, particularly when compared to its current replacement cost?
4. What depreciation method does the firm use for property, plant, and equipment?
5. Are the carrying amounts of the fixed assets recoverable through productive use of the assets?
6. How much of the firm's productive property, plant, and equipment is reported on the balance sheet, and how much is off the balance sheet through the use of operating lease financing arrangements (a topic discussed in Chapter 8)?

Fixed-Asset Valuation

GAAP in the United States and virtually all other countries requires the valuation of fixed assets at acquisition costs. An exception is the Netherlands, where financial reporting permits periodic revaluations to current replacement cost. (Appendix 7.1 discusses the accounting for such revaluations.) Accounting's use of acquisition-cost valuations rests on the presumption that such amounts are more objectively measurable than the current market values of fixed assets.

Difficulties encountered in determining current market values include (1) the absence of active markets for many used fixed assets, particularly those specific to a particular firm's needs; (2) the need to identify comparable assets currently available in the market to value assets in place; and (3) the need to make assumptions about the effect of technological and other improvements when using the prices of new assets currently available on the market in the valuation process.

The disclosures of property, plant, and equipment on the balance sheet or in the notes permit the analyst to estimate the relative age of depreciable assets and get some sense of the extent to which acquisition costs reflect outdated valuations. Note 4, "Property, Plant, and Equipment and Intangible Assets," to PepsiCo's financial statements (Appendix A) discloses the following information as of the end of Year 4 (amounts in millions):

	PepsiCo
Depreciable Assets[7] (excluding land and construction in progress)	$14,555
Accumulated Depreciation	(7,781)
Net Depreciable Assets	$ 6,774
Depreciation Expense	$ 1,062

PepsiCo also discloses in Note 4 that it primarily uses the straight-line depreciation method (discussed later in this section). At the end of Year 4, PepsiCo's depreciable assets

[7]PepsiCo also depreciates land improvements, as disclosed in Note 4, but we assume that they are immaterial for the purposes of this analysis.

were approximately 7.3 years old on average (= $7,781/$1,062). Given relatively low inflation rates in the United States in recent years, the historical cost values shown on PepsiCo's balance sheet are probably not significantly out of date.

A second issue related to the gross amount of long-lived assets is the treatment of expenditures to add to or improve existing plant and equipment. GAAP stipulates that firms should capitalize (that is, add to the asset's cost) expenditures that increase the service potential (either in quantity or quality) of an asset beyond that originally anticipated. Firms should expense immediately expenditures that merely maintain the originally expected service potential. A firm's capitalization-versus-expense policy with respect to such expenditures affects its reported earnings and provides management with some flexibility to manage earnings. Unfortunately, firms do not provide sufficient information to permit the analyst to assess the quality of earnings with respect to such expenditures.

Example 14

American Airlines, one of the largest airlines in the world, follows a rigorous maintenance program for all of its aircraft. In its Year 4 annual report, the firm provides the following information about its maintenance and repair costs:

> **Maintenance and Repair Costs** Maintenance and repair costs for owned and leased flight equipment are charged to operating expense as incurred, except costs incurred for maintenance and repair under flight hour maintenance contract agreements, which are accrued based on contractual terms when an obligation exists.

Depreciable Life

Depreciation is a process of allocating the historical cost of depreciable assets to the periods of their use in a reasonably systematic manner. One factor in this depreciation process is the expected useful life. Both physical wear and tear and technological obsolescence affect this life. Firms make estimates of this expected total life, a process that again offers management an opportunity to convey information to the firm's stakeholders about managers' expectations of the future usefulness of fixed assets. However, because useful-life assumptions are managers' estimates, they also provide an opportunity to manage reported earnings.

The disclosures firms make about depreciable lives are usually not very helpful to the analyst in assessing a firm's aggressiveness in lengthening depreciable lives to manage earnings. The problem often is the aggregated nature of the disclosures.

Example 15

American, Delta, and United Airlines are dominant players in the airline industry worldwide and account for a large percentage of domestic travel in the United States. These firms depreciate leased and owned aircraft, along with other fixed assets integral to operating airlines, following the policies detailed in Exhibit 7.9. The range of depreciable lives chosen by the three airlines is large. In addition, note that depreciable lives for *leased* aircraft equipment are often determined by the length of the leases, which are not necessarily the same as the useful lives of the aircraft. (Chapter 8 discusses accounting for capital leases by the lessee.)

Because most firms in the United States use the straight-line depreciation method for financial reporting purposes, the analyst can estimate the average useful life of depreciable assets by dividing average depreciable assets (gross, assuming zero salvage value) by depreciation expense for the year.[8] The calculations for PepsiCo follow (amounts in millions):

	PepsiCo
Depreciable Assets[9] (Gross):	
December 31, Year 3	$14,555.0
December 31, Year 4	13,585.0
Average Depreciable Assets (Gross) for Year 4	$14,070.0
Depreciation Expense, Year 4	$ 1,062.0
Average Total Depreciable Life ($14,070.0/$1,062.0)	13.3 years

Analysts should compare the average useful life of depreciable assets across firms. Firms with similar asset composition should have similar useful lives and, if not, the analyst should assess why they differ. Analysts also need to question firms that report dramatic changes in the useful lives of depreciable assets over time. Is the change because of assumption changes in the useful lives of the assets, or has the composition of firm's assets changed over time? Firms choosing useful lives that accurately represent the period of time they expect to be able to use the assets report the highest-quality accounting data for depreciable assets.

Depreciation Method

The third factor in the calculation of depreciation (in addition to the acquisition cost and expected useful life of depreciable assets) is the depreciation method. Financial reporting permits firms to write off assets evenly over their useful lives (straight-line method) or to write off larger amounts during the early years and smaller amounts in later years (accelerated depreciation methods). Note that total depreciation over an asset's life cannot exceed acquisition costs unless firms revalue such assets to current market values. Thus, straight-line and accelerated depreciation methods differ only in the timing of depreciation expense, not in its total amount over time.

Virtually all firms in the United States use the straight-line method for financial reporting. They use accelerated depreciation methods for tax reporting based on depreciable lives specified in the income tax law, which are usually shorter than the depreciable lives firms use for financial reporting purposes.

Financial reporting in most countries other than the United States also permits both accelerated and straight-line depreciation methods. In countries where tax laws heavily influence financial reporting (such as Germany, France, and Japan), most firms use accelerated depreciation methods for both financial and tax reporting. Thus, comparisons of U.S. firms with those of some other countries require the analyst to assess the effect of different depreciation methods. The analyst must either restate reported U.S. amounts to an accelerated basis or convert reported amounts for other countries to a straight-line basis.

The analyst can place U.S. firms on an accelerated depreciation basis using information in the income tax note. *Statement No. 109*[10] requires firms to report in notes to the financial statements the portion of the deferred tax liability that is attributable to book versus tax

[8]Note that all three of the airlines in Example 15 used the straight-line method for calculating depreciation expense.

[9]See footnote 7.

[10]Financial Accounting Standards Board, *Statement No. 109*, "Accounting for Income Taxes" (1992). Chapter 2 provides an initial discussion of this statement, with the discussion continuing in Chapter 8.

EXHIBIT 7.9

American, Delta, and United Airlines
Note Disclosure Policies—Depreciable Lives

American Airlines

Equipment and Property

The provision for depreciation of operating equipment and property is computed on the straight-line method applied to each unit of property, except that rotable parts, avionics, and assemblies are depreciated on a group basis. The depreciable lives and residual values used for the principal depreciable asset classifications are:

	Depreciable Life	Residual Value
American jet aircraft	20–30 years	5–10%
Major rotable parts, avionics, and assemblies	Life of equipment to which applicable	5–10%
Improvements to leased flight equipment	Term of lease	None
Buildings and improvements (principally on leased land)	10–30 years or term of lease	None
Furniture, fixtures, and equipment	3–20 years	None
Capitalized software	3–10 years	None

Delta Air Lines

Long-Lived Assets

We record our property and equipment at cost and depreciate or amortize these assets on a straight-line basis to their estimated residual values over their respective estimated useful lives. Residual values for flight equipment range from 5 percent to 40 percent of cost. We also capitalize certain internal and external costs incurred to develop internal-use software; these assets are included in ground property and equipment, net on our Consolidated Balance Sheets. The estimated useful lives for major asset classifications are as follows:

Asset Classification	Estimated Useful Life
Owned flight equipment	15–25 years
Flight and ground equipment under capital lease	—
Ground property and equipment	3–10 years

United Airlines

Operating Property and Equipment

Owned operating property and equipment are stated at cost. Property under capital leases, and the related obligation for future lease payments, is recorded at an amount equal to the initial present value of those lease payments.

Depreciation and amortization of owned depreciable assets is based on the straight-line method over their estimated service lives. Leasehold improvements are amortized over the remaining period of the lease

Continued

EXHIBIT 7.9

continued

or the estimated service life of the related asset, whichever is less. Aircraft are depreciated to estimated salvage values, generally over lives of 25 to 30 years; buildings are depreciated over lives of 25 to 45 years; and other property and equipment are depreciated over lives of 3 to 15 years.

Properties under capital leases are amortized on the straight-line method over the life of the lease or, in the case of certain aircraft, over their estimated service lives. Lease terms are 10 to 22 years for aircraft and 29 years for buildings. Amortization of capital leases is included in depreciation and amortization expense.

depreciation timing differences at the beginning and end of the year. For example, PepsiCo reports in Note 5, "Income Taxes" (Appendix A), that the portion of its deferred tax liability that is attributable to property, plant, and equipment was $806.0 million on December 31, Year 3, and $857.0 million on December 31, Year 4. These deferred taxes indicate that PepsiCo depreciated fixed assets faster for tax purposes than for book purposes, because of differences in both depreciable lives and depreciation methods. Converting PepsiCo's financial statements to amounts reported for tax purposes requires the following adjustments (using a 35 percent income tax rate, a rate PepsiCo discloses in the same note):

	December 31:	
Balance Sheet	**Year 3**	**Year 4**
Property, Plant, and Equipment, net:		
$806.0 ÷ .35; $857.0 ÷ .35	$−2,302.9	$−2,448.6
Deferred Tax Liability	− 806.0	− 857.0
Retained Earnings	$−1,496.9	$−1,591.6
Income Statement		**Year 4**
Increase in Depreciation Expense:		
($857.0 – $806.0) ÷ .35		$+ 145.7
Decrease in Income Tax Expense: .35 × $145.7		− 51.0
Decrease in Net Income: .65 × $145.7		$− 94.7
Statement of Cash Flows		**Year 4**
Decrease in Net Income		$− 94.7
Increase in Depreciation Expense		+ 145.7
Change in the Deferred Tax Liability for Depreciation Timing Difference ($857.0 – $806.0)		− 51.0
Cash Flow from Operations		$ 0

Note that PepsiCo's Deferred Tax Liability related to property, plant, and equipment increased during the year by approximately 6.3 percent. This increase accounts for the increase in Year 4's depreciation expense reported for tax purposes.

Impairment of Fixed Assets (Long-Lived Assets)

Chapter 6 addresses how income statement losses for the impairment of fixed assets affect forecasts of future earnings. The development of new technologies by competitors, changes in government regulations, changes in demographic trends, and other factors external to a firm may reduce the future benefits originally anticipated from the assets. Financial reporting requires firms to assess whether the carrying amounts of fixed assets are recoverable and, if they are not, to write down the assets to their fair values and recognize impairment losses in income from continuing operations.[11]

Chapter 6 provides examples involving impairment losses, including a description of PepsiCo's disclosures in this area. Firms recognize an impairment loss when the carrying amount of a tangible, fixed asset (or asset group) is deemed "not recoverable" as specified by standard setters. *Statement No. 144* defines a carrying amount as not recoverable if it is greater than the sum of the *undiscounted* cash flows expected from the asset's use and disposal. The actual impairment charge recorded is the amount by which the carrying value exceeds an asset's fair value. Fair value is defined as market value or present (*discounted*) value of expected cash flows from the fixed asset.

In requiring firms to use undiscounted cash flows to test for impairment of long-lived tangible assets, standard setters reasoned that a loss has not occurred if the firm can recover in future cash flows an amount equal to or larger than the current book value. Accounting theorists questioned the logic of using undiscounted, instead of discounted, cash flows in testing for impairment. In some cases, the economic value of the long-lived asset may decline below its carrying value but the firm would recognize no impairment because the undiscounted future cash flows from the asset exceed its carrying value.

For example, consider the following situation involving a change in real estate value over time. A real estate company owns an apartment building that originally cost $20 million, with a current carrying amount of $15 million. The company originally expected to collect rents of $1.67 million each year for thirty years before selling the apartment complex for $8 million. Deteriorating neighborhood conditions, however, have caused the company to reassess the future rentals, especially given a recent appraisal that set a fair value for the apartment building of $10 million. The company now estimates that it will receive rentals of $1.35 million per year for fifteen years and then sell the building for $5 million. Because total undiscounted future cash flows of $25.25 million (= ($1.35 × 15) + $5) exceed the carrying value of $15 million, no impairment loss is reported by the real estate company. In essence, the firm has suffered an economic loss but will not report any loss for financial reporting.[12]

Firms do not have to judge impairment for every asset every reporting period. However, GAAP requires that firms test for impairment when circumstances change, indicating the

---

[11]Financial Accounting Standards Board, *Statement of Financial Accounting Standards No. 144*, "Accounting for the Impairment or Disposal of Long-Lived Assets" (2001). *Statement No. 144* superseded *Statement No. 121*, "Accounting for the Impairment of Long-Lived Assets and for Long-Lived Assets to Be Disposed Of" (1995). *Statement No. 144* retains the fundamental provisions of *Statement No. 121* for recognizing and measuring impairment losses on long-lived tangible assets held for use and long-lived tangible assets to be disposed of by sale, while also resolving significant implementation issues associated with *Statement No. 121*.

[12]If the total undiscounted future cash flows in this illustration were estimated to fall below the carrying value of $15 million, then the real estate company would record an impairment loss for the difference between the carrying value and the fair market value of the apartment building, in this case $10 million. The company would report an impairment loss of $5 million in income from continuing operations, and the apartment building would be recorded at the "new" carrying value of $10 million. Recognize in this situation that although the firm uses undiscounted future cash flows to decide *whether an* impairment charge is necessary, fair value is used to measure the *actual* charge.

possibility of a significant change in carrying amounts. Chapter 6 provides examples of changing circumstances that might warrant the need for impairment testing.

Financial reporting does not require separate disclosure of impaired assets, although firms often voluntarily provide this information. Also, *Statement No. 144* requires that firms include impairment losses in income from continuing operations.

Persistent Earnings and Fixed-Asset Reporting

For many firms, but particularly for those operating in such capital-intensive industries as freight transportation (trucking and rail), defense, and utilities, expenditures for fixed assets are a large and recurring outflow of cash. The beverage and snack food industry in which PepsiCo operates is moderately capital intensive. In PepsiCo's discussion on "Our Liquidity, Capital Resources, and Financial Position" (Appendix B), the firm reports capital expenditures of $1.4 billion for Year 4 and $1.3 billion for Year 3. These same amounts are reported on the firm's Consolidated Statement of Cash Flows as an investing activity (Appendix A), and represent approximately 30 percent of cash generated by operations.

Analyzing valuation and depreciation of fixed assets for their effects on the quality of accounting information is an important task of the analyst. As discussed at the beginning of this section, the analyst needs to consider (a) the disparity between amounts reported for fixed assets and their current economic values, (b) the depreciable lives established by management, and (c) the depreciation method employed to match fixed-asset costs to reported revenues.

Fixed Assets and Current Economic Values

The valuation most consistent with economic high-quality accounting information is the current cost of replacing fixed assets. But it is difficult to measure objectively current replacement cost. For example, the absence of active, secondhand markets for many used fixed assets means that the analyst must estimate replacement cost by referring to the cost of a similar new asset and then adjusting that replacement cost for the used condition, and perhaps lower productivity, of the asset owned. Adjusting to replacement costs is even more difficult because firms do not provide sufficient detailed information about the nature, location, condition, and age of their fixed assets. The most disaggregated information usually provided in dollar form is the book value of land, buildings, machinery, and equipment. (PepsiCo reports an additional category in Note 4, "Property, Plant, and Equipment and Intangible Assets" (Appendix A), labeled "Construction in Progress." PepsiCo will transfer the expenditures represented by this category to either buildings and improvements or machinery and equipment once construction is complete.)

As demonstrated earlier for PepsiCo, analysts can estimate the average age of depreciable assets by dividing the balance in the accumulated depreciation account at the end of the most recent year by the amount of depreciation expense for the current year, and the average remaining useful life by dividing the net book value of property, plant, and equipment by the current year's depreciation expense. The analyst can use the remaining useful life in concert with data on subsequent price increases to estimate current value, but this involves a high degree of estimation error. Unless firms operate in an industry in which fixed assets are at the core of their activities (for example, real estate firms), probably the analyst should work with the unadjusted numbers and take this into consideration when interpreting the financial analysis.[13]

---

[13]The underlying assumption in this discussion is that fixed assets are *undervalued* on the balance sheet when compared to current economic values. If firms experience fixed-asset value impairments, the analyst benefits from the reporting rules of *Statement No. 144*, discussed earlier, which requires firms to write down fixed assets to their fair values.

Choice of Depreciable Lives

Choosing the number of years during which firms receive benefits from fixed assets can be difficult. Furthermore, firms report any change in depreciable lives as a "change in estimates" (discussed in Chapter 6) and account for its effect prospectively. These two facts make choosing depreciable lives a fruitful avenue for practicing earnings management. The analyst should compare the depreciable lives (a calculation illustrated earlier for PepsiCo) across firms in the same industry to assess whether the firm has assumed a longer or shorter useful life than its peer firms. If the analyst observes differences in useful-life assumptions across firms, the analyst must then interpret the difference—does it reflect a real underlying difference in the fixed-asset portfolio and the expected usefulness of the assets, or is the firm being aggressive (longer lives) or conservative (shorter lives) to manage reported earnings?

Choice of Depreciation Method

Most publicly traded firms in the United States use the straight-line method of depreciation. Although the straight-line method may not accurately reflect the actual deterioration in the usefulness of the fixed assets to help generate revenues, it does not appear that firms use their choice of depreciation method to manage reported earnings. However, there is still an accounting quality issue because many analysts consider earnings based on accelerated depreciation methods to be of higher quality than those based on straight-line depreciation. This is because both (1) the biases caused by using acquisition costs instead of replacement cost to calculate depreciation, and (2) the opportunities to manage earnings through the choice of depreciable lives, are tempered by the fact that more conservative measures of earnings result from the use of accelerated depreciation methods. In many cases, accelerated depreciation of acquisition costs also produces depreciation amounts closer to replacement cost than straight-line depreciation during the early years of assets' lives, thereby providing an enhanced measure of value added. Just the opposite effect occurs during the later years of assets' lives, however.

The preference for accelerated depreciation methods by analysts is not universal. Some analysts judge earnings quality by its comparability to that of competitor firms. Analysts favoring the straight-line method from an earnings quality perspective observe that at least firms are using the method favored by most publicly traded firms.

ACCOUNTING FOR INTANGIBLE ASSETS

Intangible assets include trade and brand names, trademarks, patents, copyrights, franchise rights, customer lists, and goodwill. Two characteristics distinguish intangible assets: their intangibility (that is, lack of physical attributes) and their multiple-period useful life. Financial reporting in the United States accounts for intangible assets as follows:

1. Firms expense the cost of developing intangibles in the period incurred.[14] The rationale for immediate expensing of such costs is the difficulty and uncertainty in ascertaining whether a particular expenditure results in a future benefit (that is, an asset) or not (an expense). Accountants provide more conservative measures of

[14]An exception to this policy is made for certain software development costs discussed later in this section.

earnings by expensing such costs immediately. Thus, although PepsiCo spends millions of dollars each year promoting its products, and the brand names Pepsi and Frito-Lay represent some of the more valuable "assets" of the firm, financial reporting does not permit the firm to recognize an asset for the expenditures made to develop and maintain its brand names. PepsiCo's balance sheet reported in Appendix A does not include an asset labeled "Trade Name—Pepsi," or "Brand Name—Frito-Lay," although these brand names are undoubtedly worth hundreds of millions of dollars to the firm.

2. Firms capitalize as an asset the costs to acquire intangible assets from others.[15] In this case, the firm makes an expenditure on a specifically identifiable intangible asset. The existence of an external market transaction provides evidence of the value of the intangible asset. The acquiring firm must consider the future benefits of the intangible to at least equal the price paid.[16]
3. Specifically identifiable intangible assets acquired from others may have (a) a finite useful life, such as a patent, or (b) an indefinite useful life, such as a brand name. Firms amortize intangibles with a finite useful life over their expected useful lives, taking into consideration the legal, regulatory, economic, competitive, and contractual provisions that may limit the useful life. Common practice uses straight-line amortization if the actual pattern in which the economic benefits are consumed or used up cannot be reliably determined. Firms do not amortize assets with an indefinite useful life.
4. The intangible asset, goodwill, may be recorded by a firm when acquiring another firm in a business combination. Chapter 9 discusses the measurement and recording of goodwill by the acquiring firm. Standard setters concluded that goodwill has an indefinite useful life and is not amortized.
5. Firms periodically test intangible assets *requiring* amortization (that is, intangible assets with a finite useful life such as patents) for impairment following a similar procedure to that described in the previous section, "Impairment of Fixed Assets (Long-Lived Assets)."
6. For intangibles *not requiring* amortization (that is, intangible assets with an indefinite life such as goodwill) firms must test annually for asset impairment, or more frequently if events and circumstances indicate that the asset may be impaired. The test compares the carrying value to the fair value of the intangibles and

---

[15]An exception to this policy is made for "purchased in-process research and development costs." Firms immediately expense any in-process, but unproven, technology purchased in a corporate acquisition, a requirement stipulated by Financial Accounting Standards Board, *Interpretation No. 4,* "Applicability of FASB Statement No. 2 to Business Combinations Accounted for by the Purchase Method" (1975). However, as this book goes to press, FASB is considering revising *Statement No. 141* (discussed in Chapter 9) that addresses accounting for corporate acquisitions. Under the proposal, purchased in-process research and development costs would be capitalized on the date of the acquisition. It is possible that FASB will change its position and/or effective date prior to issuance of a final standard.

[16]Some financial statement preparers and users have criticized the differing treatment of internally developed versus externally purchased intangibles. They point out that internally developed intangibles also result from external market exchanges (such as payments to advertising agencies for promotion services or payments to employees for research and development services). Supporters of the current rules point out that the market exchange in the case of externally acquired intangibles validates the existence of a "completed asset," whereas the market exchange in the case of internally developed intangibles validates only that the firm has made an expenditure. It does not validate the existence and value of future benefits.

requires recognition of an impairment loss whenever the carrying value exceeds the fair value.[17] Determining the fair value of nonamortizable intangibles such as goodwill often is a difficult task. For goodwill, for example, it entails estimating the fair value of the reporting unit that resulted from a previously acquired company in which the acquiring firm allocated a portion of the purchase price to goodwill. Usually the resulting reporting unit does not have shares separately trading in the marketplace, which makes measuring fair value a challenge. Firms often employ valuation consultants that use comparables, industry metrics, and general market conditions to estimate fair values.

Chapter 6 provides impairment charge examples, including PepsiCo's disclosures in this area.

Accounting for Research and Development Costs

Controversy surrounds application of the general principles of intangible-asset accounting to research and development (R&D) costs. Financial reporting requires firms to expense immediately all R&D costs incurred internally because of the inherent uncertainty in determining whether research and development activities will produce sufficient future economic benefits to warrant being capitalized as an asset. The nature of most research and development activities involves uncertain outcomes.[18] For industries with high R&D expenditures, the requirement to expense rather than capitalize research and development expenditures is especially troublesome because financial reporting requires firms to assume that the economic value of all R&D expenditures is zero. Thus, a major asset never appears on the balance sheet.

Consider the three examples that follow from financial reports of biotechnology firms. Firms in the research-intensive biotechnology industry cannot survive without making significant R&D expenditures that will generate future revenues and profits. GAAP requires firms to expense these expenditures when incurred because R&D firms face so much uncertainty about whether R&D activities today will successfully generate future revenues and profits.

Example 16

Biogen Idec, Inc. (formerly Biogen) describes itself as "the world's third largest biotech company with leading products and capabilities in oncology and immunology." Biogen Idec principally develops drug-related products *internally* in its research laboratories and is engaged in discovering and developing drugs for human health care through genetic engineering. Total revenues for Year 4 exceeded $2.2 billion.

As required by *Statement No. 2,* Biogen Idec states in a recent annual report that "research and development expenses are comprised of costs incurred in performing research and development activities including salaries and benefits, facilities costs, overhead costs, clinical trial and related clinical manufacturing costs, contract services, and

---

[17]The test for asset impairment for an intangible not requiring amortization differs from that for fixed and intangible assets requiring amortization. Recall that the asset impairment test for assets requiring amortization (such as buildings and manufacturing equipment) compares the undiscounted cash flows from the asset to the asset's carrying value. Intangibles not requiring amortization have an indefinite life, and thus no defined period over which to estimate undiscounted cash flows.

[18]Financial Accounting Standards Board, *Statement of Financial Accounting Standards No. 2,* "Accounting for Research and Development Costs" (1974).

other outside costs. Research and development costs, including upfront fees and milestones paid to collaborators, are expensed as incurred."

The firm's R&D expense/sales percentage averaged 30 percent in three recent years, and the firm showed no asset on its balance sheet related to this research activity.

Example 17

Genzyme Corporation is a biotechnology and health care products firm engaged in the development of medical products and services. For Year 4, revenues totaled $2.2 billion, with the firm's top products including Cerezyme (Gaucher disease), Renagel (end-stage renal disease), and Fabrazyme (Fabry disease). It follows a strategy of both internal development of technology and acquisition of other companies involved in biotechnology research. Genzyme expenses the portion of the acquisition price of companies related to *in-process* technology, but it capitalizes and subsequently amortizes any portion of the price related to *completed* technologies.

Several years ago Genzyme made a large acquisition and, as a result, expensed a large amount of in-process technology related to the acquisition. The R&D expense/sales percentage for internal R&D costs for the year was slightly more than 20 percent. However, because of the acquisition, it also expensed the portion of the purchase price related to in-process technology. As a result, the total R&D expense/sales percentage for the year was almost 50 percent. A year later, the total R&D expense/sales percentage was less than 25 percent because only a small portion of in-process technology was purchased (and expensed).

Example 18

Amgen's two top-selling products, Epogen and Aranesp, accounted for approximately 50 percent of the firm's product sales in Year 4. Epogen (Epoetin Alfa) is a recombinant version of a human protein that stimulates the production of red blood cells. Aranesp also stimulates red blood cell production; it is used to treat anemia associated with chronic renal failure, including patients on dialysis and patients not on dialysis. The firm follows a strategy of both internal development of biotechnology and external development through a series of joint ventures and partnerships. Amgen contributes preliminary research findings for its interest in these joint ventures and partnerships. The other participants provide funding to continue development of this preliminary research.

In some cases, Amgen contracts with the joint venture or partnership to perform the continued development in its own laboratories. In this case, Amgen receives a fee each period in an amount approximately equal to the R&D costs incurred in conducting the research. In other cases, the joint venture or partnership entity conducts the research, in which case Amgen may show no R&D expense on its books. Amgen generally maintains a right of first refusal for any products developed, in which case it must pay the owners of the joint venture a periodic royalty. (Chapters 8 and 9 discuss the accounting for investments in these joint ventures and partnerships.)

Amgen's Year 4 Form 10-K describes the firm's R&D reporting policies: "R&D costs, which are expensed as incurred, are primarily comprised of the following types of costs incurred in performing R&D activities: salaries and benefits, overhead and occupancy costs, clinical trial and related clinical manufacturing costs, contract services, and other outside costs. R&D expenses also include such costs related to activities performed on behalf of corporate partners."

Amgen's R&D expense/sales percentage for Year 4 was 19.7 percent, the lowest of the three firms for the most recent year. It shows only minor amounts on its balance sheet for investments in joint ventures and partnerships, relating to cash advances. Because Amgen must expense initial development costs when incurred, its contribution of preliminary research findings for an interest in these joint ventures and partnerships does not result in increasing an asset.

Examples 16 through 18 illustrate three different strategies firms pursue in developing biotechnologies and highlight the problem with current R&D reporting rules. The different strategies firms follow, especially when combined with the required accounting for R&D costs, complicate any cross-sectional analysis of firms' financial data. To the extent that the economic substance of these arrangements differ, different accounting treatments may be appropriate. If, on the other hand, the economic substance is similar and the principal aim is to keep R&D costs out of the income statement, then the differing accounting treatments seem unwarranted.

The economic characteristics of R&D arrangements suggest a twofold approach to dealing with these different reporting standards:

1. Capitalize and subsequently amortize all expenditures on R&D that have future service potential, whether a firm incurs the R&D cost internally or purchases in-process or completed technology externally. Expense immediately all R&D costs that have no future service potential.
2. Consolidate the firm's share of the assets, liabilities, revenues, and expenses of R&D joint ventures or partnerships with its own financial statements.

Unfortunately, current financial statement disclosures do not permit the analyst to implement the twofold approach. Without these disclosures, the analyst must proceed with caution when analyzing R&D-intensive firms. The analyst especially benefits from scientific and other disclosures provided by these firms that are outside the financial reporting model.

Accounting for Software Development Costs

Financial reporting treats the cost of developing computer software somewhat differently from R&D costs. Firms must expense when incurred all costs incurred internally in developing computer software until such development proceeds to the point at which the firm establishes the technological feasibility of a product. Thereafter, the firm must capitalize and subsequently amortize additional development costs.[19] The FASB defines technological feasibility as completion of a detailed program design or, in its absence, completion of a working model. A key issue in applying this reporting standard is the treatment of costs to improve an existing product.

---

[19]Financial Accounting Standards Board, *Statement of Financial Accounting Standards No. 86*, "Accounting for the Costs of Computer Software to Be Sold, Leased, or Otherwise Marketed" (1985). *Statement No. 86* applies to software developed for sale, and not software developed or obtained for internal use. Georgia-Pacific describes its implementation of current reporting practice for internal-use software in a recent annual report by stating the following:

> The firm capitalizes incremental costs that are directly associated with the development of software for internal use and implementation of the related systems. Amounts are amortized over five years beginning when the assets are placed in service. Capitalized costs were $121 million at December 31, Year 6, and $65 million at December 31, Year 5. Amounts are included as property, plant, and equipment in the firm's balance sheet.

Example 19

IBM is a world leader in providing software and consultancy services. The firm includes the following note on its accounting for software development costs in its Year 4 Form 10-K filing:

> **Software Costs.** Costs that are related to the conceptual formulation and design of licensed programs are expensed as incurred to R&D expense. Also for licensed programs, the company capitalizes costs that are incurred to produce the finished product after technological feasibility has been established. Capitalized amounts are amortized using the straight-line method, which is applied over periods ranging up to three years. The company performs periodic reviews to ensure that unamortized program costs remain recoverable from future revenue. Costs to support or service licensed programs are charged to software cost as incurred.

As indicated here, IBM's R&D expense includes costs for conceptual formulation of software products as well as amortization of software costs previously capitalized because the product had reached the technological feasibility stage.

Example 20

Microsoft Corporation introduced its first version of Word, the firm's word-processing system, in 1983. Microsoft also continually revises this software to enhance its capabilities. Microsoft expenses all software development costs as incurred. It reports software development expense of $7,779.0 million (21.1 percent of sales) for the year ended June 30, Year 4, and shows no asset on its balance sheet for capitalized software development costs.

Example 21

Adobe Systems is a leading developer of graphics software. Its Acrobat and Reader products are well known because of their extensive use in the financial community. In addition, the SEC allows firms to file annual and quarterly filings using Acrobat-based technology. Adobe develops new software internally and through aggressive external acquisitions of other software companies. Adobe expenses initial software development costs incurred internally as research and development, which represents 18.6 percent of revenue in Year 4 ($311.1 million R&D costs/$1,666.6 million revenues). Adobe capitalizes software development costs once a graphics software program reaches the technological feasibility stage of development. It also capitalizes the cost of software acquired in corporate acquisitions to the extent that the software has achieved technological feasibility. In both scenarios, however, Adobe indicates that the amount of software costs capitalized is immaterial to the financial statements. The firm states in its Year 4 Form 10-K filing:

> Capitalization of software development costs begins upon the establishment of technological feasibility, which is generally the completion of a working prototype that has been certified as having no critical bugs and is a release candidate or when alternative future use exists. To date, software development costs incurred between completion of a working prototype and general availability of the related product have not been material and have not been capitalized.

Examples 19 through 21 illustrate the current diversity in practice. Software development firms interpret *Statement No. 86* so differently that it is debatable whether the standard serves a purpose any longer. Furthermore, the Software Publishers Association, a trade association for firms in the software development industry, advocates expensing all software development costs when incurred. In a position paper submitted to the FASB, the association requests rescission of *Statement No. 86,* suggesting that expensing these costs eliminates the concerns of extremely shortened software product cycles and uncertainty over realization of software assets.

Why would the Software Publishers Association advocate immediate expensing of all software development costs when current reporting offers the best of all worlds to software producers: capitalize or immediately expense the costs depending on their desires? A study[20] addressing this intriguing position of the association shows that in recent years, enhancing reported earnings through software capitalization schemes has diminished. The researchers conclude that because software capitalization no longer provides an opportunity for earnings management, nothing is lost by restricting software producers to only one allowable reporting technique. In addition, the study addresses the more substantive issue of whether software capitalization is "value-relevant" to investors. For firms that capitalize software development costs (that is, report a cumulative software intangible asset on the balance sheet), the researchers find a significant association between these costs and future earnings, concluding that this finding supports continuation of *Statement No. 86.*

The flexibility firms enjoy in applying *Statement No. 86* currently should cause the analyst to proceed cautiously when analyzing computer software development companies. An added concern in this regard is the small size of many such companies and the rapid pace of technological change in this industry. The information technology industry, and particularly the software subsegment of the industry, experienced even a greater rate of change recently due to the surge of interest in the Internet and Internet-related services. The crash of the information technology industry several years ago is further reason to practice a high degree of skepticism when analyzing firms in the industry.

Accounting for Goodwill

The most common setting in which intangibles arise is in corporate acquisitions. As Chapter 9 discusses more fully, acquiring firms must allocate the purchase price to the assets acquired and liabilities assumed when purchasing another entity. Acquiring firms usually allocate the purchase price to identifiable, tangible assets (inventories, land, equipment) and liabilities first. They then allocate any excess purchase price to specifically identifiable intangible assets such as patents, customer lists, and trade names, with the remainder allocated to goodwill. Goodwill is a residual and effectively represents all

---

[20]David Aboody and Baruch Lev, "The Value-Relevance of Intangibles: The Case of Software Capitalization," *Journal of Accounting Research,* supplement (1998), pp. 161–191.

intangibles that are not specifically identifiable. Finally, as discussed at the beginning of this section, specifically identifiable, intangible assets may or may not be amortized, depending on whether they have a finite or indefinite useful life. Goodwill, on the other hand, has an indefinite useful life and is therefore not amortized but tested for impairment.[21]

The disclosures for intangible assets, including goodwill, vary significantly across firms. For example, PepsiCo reports in Note 4, "Property, Plant, and Equipment and Intangible Assets" (Appendix A), three categories of intangibles on its balance sheet at the end of Year 4 (amounts in millions):

Amortizable Intangible Assets, net	\$ 598
Goodwill	\$3,909
Other Nonamortizable Intangible Assets	\$ 933

PepsiCo reports the amortization policy for the amortizable (that is, the specifically identifiable) intangible assets, indicating that the firm records a periodic charge calculated on a straight-line basis over the asset's estimated useful life. The note also confirms that PepsiCo does not amortize goodwill and other nonamortizable intangible assets but does test them for impairment at least annually.

How should an analyst treat goodwill that appears on a firm's balance sheet? One approach is to follow financial reporting rules, leaving goodwill among total assets. The justification for this approach is that the initial valuation of goodwill arose from an exchange between an independent buyer and seller of another corporate entity and simply represents valuable resources that accountants cannot separately identify. These valuable resources enable the firm to generate profits. The analyst should include these resources in the asset base on which management should be expected to generate a reasonable return. If these valuable resources are not likely to last forever, amortization of their cost over some period of years is appropriate.

Another approach eliminates goodwill from assets and subtracts its amount from retained earnings or other common shareholders' equity accounts. The justification for this approach is twofold:

1. The amount allocated to goodwill from a corporate acquisition may occur simply because the firm paid too much and may not necessarily indicate the presence of resources with future service potential. Subtracting the amount allocated to goodwill from retained earnings suggests that the excess purchase price is a loss for the firm.
2. Immediate subtraction of goodwill from retained earnings treats goodwill arising from an acquisition similar to goodwill developed internally. In the latter case, firms expense advertising, training, and other costs when incurred, so no asset appears on the balance sheet.

[21]Financial Accounting Standards Board, *Statement of Financial Accounting Standards No. 142,* "Goodwill and Other Intangible Assets" (2001). Recall from the earlier discussion that testing for impairment of long-lived assets other than goodwill is also required and is addressed in *Statement No. 144.*

Persistent Earnings and Intangible-Asset Reporting

As we discussed in a previous section, the quality of accounting information for *tangible* assets is low when substantial adjustments for changes in economic values are necessary, but at least the analyst knows the acquisition cost of tangible assets to use as a starting point for such revaluations. For *intangible* assets such as the three highlighted previously, the difficulty is more acute because firms seldom report such resources on the balance sheet. If such resources do appear on the balance sheet, usually because they arose from a corporate acquisition, they appear at some mixture of historical and amortized cost. Estimating the economic value of intangibles usually entails a high level of estimation and subjectivity.

The arguments for immediately expensing intangibles, from the perspective of quality of accounting information, include the following:

1. Intangible assets, by definition, involve an inherently high degree of uncertainty regarding future economic benefits. The expense occurs in the same period as the cash outflow, the latter being the economic resource sacrificed.
2. Firms must replace intangibles consumed if they are to continue operating profitably. The best measure of the replacement cost of intangibles consumed in generating revenue in a reporting period is the cost of expenditures made in the same period on such intangibles. Depreciating fixed assets using an accelerated depreciation method argued for earlier in this chapter is similar to this line of reasoning for intangibles consumed.
3. Managers may be optimistically biased when estimating the values of intangible assets they have acquired or are developing internally. Conservatism in accounting exists, in part, to counter managers' optimistic bias and thus protect financial statement users from potentially misleading information. Immediate expensing reduces the opportunities for earnings management that arise when firms must decide on the amortization period and pattern for capitalized intangibles.[22]
4. For a stable or moderate-growth firm, the expense each year from immediate expensing is approximately the same as the expense from capitalizing expenditures and subsequently amortizing them.

Most analysts tend to prefer immediate expensing of all intangible assets.[23] Analysts often remove from the balance sheet any R&D costs, software development costs, and goodwill reported as assets before performing a financial analysis. By doing so, they argue that (1) quality of earnings information improves because the ability to manage earnings is reduced, and (2) quality of balance sheet information improves because the balance

[22]Note, however, that opportunities for earnings management still exist under the immediate expensing option. Firms with a poor earnings year can eliminate or delay expenditures, thereby increasing reporting earnings. Accelerating expenditures reduces current earnings.

Chapter 6 addresses whether it is good business practice to manage earnings in this way. For example, firms that cut back on research and development costs to manage earnings may suffer a poor quality of accounting assessment by analysts. Similarly, firms that cut back on advertising expenditures or delay maintenance expenditures as a means of increasing earnings in a reporting period may suffer the same fate.

[23]Although advocating immediate expending of these costs, few analysts suggest that they are of no value. However, analysts are most concerned with how to value the economic assets represented by these costs, and the potential for earnings management, given the subjectivity involved in any valuation model employed.

sheet is cleansed of "soft" assets lacking physical substance. Analysts eliminate the assets by subtracting them from retained earnings. The financial analysis must be interpreted carefully, however, because the analyst may understate a firm's asset base by eliminating these assets—as is the case with PepsiCo's asset base because PepsiCo's balance sheet does not recognize brand names such as Pepsi and Frito-Lay (among other important intangibles owned by the firm).

SUMMARY

The unifying concept for the various financial reporting rules discussed in this chapter (revenue recognition, inventory cost-flow assumptions, depreciable asset accounting, and intangible-asset accounting) are the links among revenue and expense recognition and asset and liability valuation. The recognition of revenue usually coincides with an increase in assets (usually cash or a receivable). The recognition of expense usually coincides with a decrease in assets (cash, inventories, depreciable or intangible assets) or an increase in liabilities (which will require a decrease in assets in a later period). Thus, the income statement and balance sheet closely interrelate.

The next chapter discusses the financial reporting rules linking expenses to liability recognition and valuation. As with asset valuation issues, liability recognition and valuation issues demonstrate the link between expenses reported on the income statement and liabilities reported on the balance sheet—and the fact that any discussion of income leads inevitably to a consideration of liabilities and their measurement and valuation as well. Similar to this chapter, Chapter 8 explains the various reporting principles under investigation, describes the choices firms make in applying them, and debates whether adjustments are needed to the reported amounts to enhance the quality of accounting information.

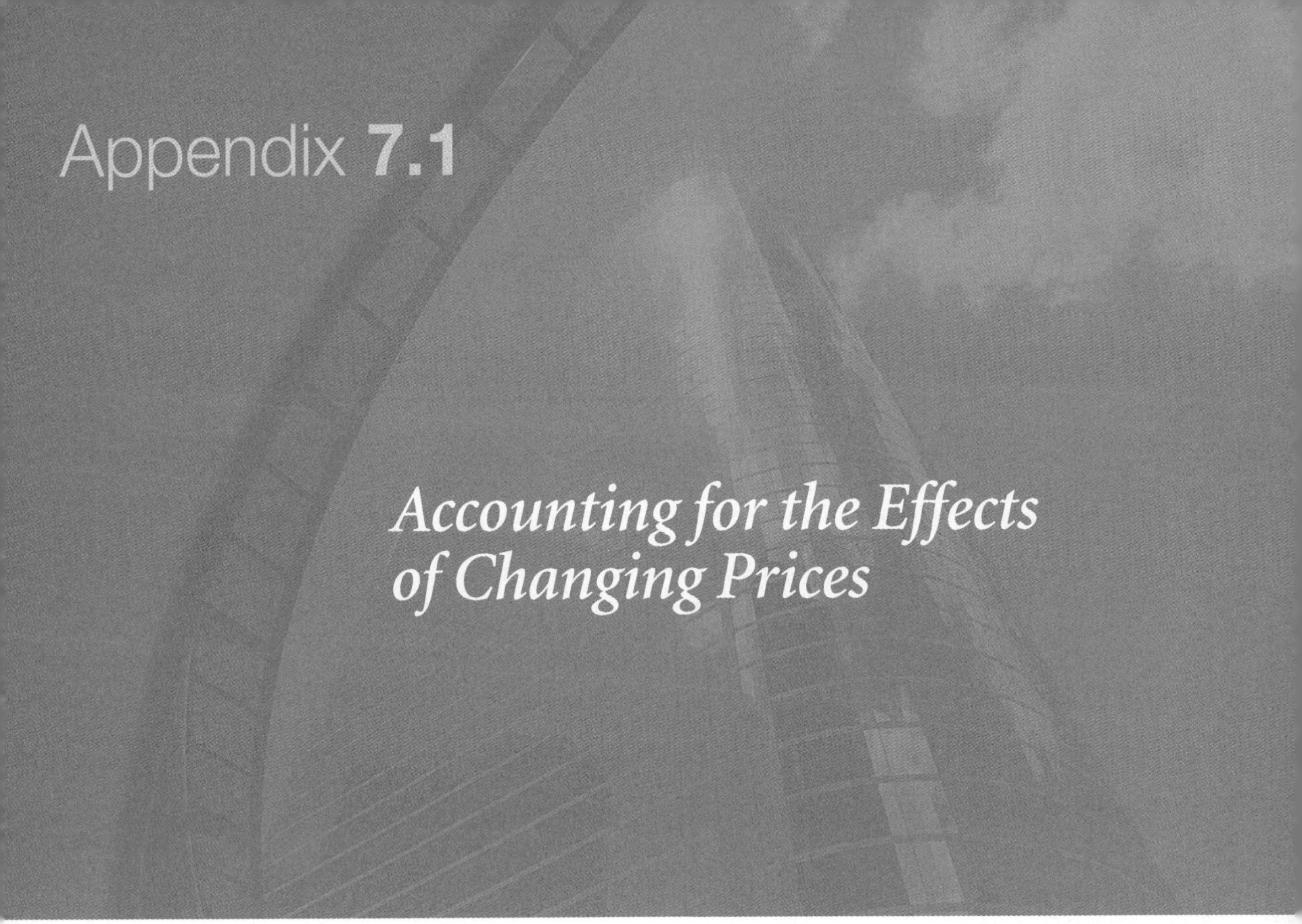

Appendix 7.1

Accounting for the Effects of Changing Prices

Changing prices affect financial reports in two principal ways:

- **Measuring Unit Problem**

  Changes in the *general* level of prices in an economy (as measured by the prices of a broad basket of goods and services) affect the purchasing power of the monetary unit (for example, the U.S. dollar). During periods of inflation (deflation), the measuring unit loses (gains) purchasing power. Because the measuring unit does not reflect a constant amount of purchasing power over time, accounting measurements of assets, liabilities, revenues, and expenses made with this measuring unit are not comparable. Adding the acquisition cost of land acquired ten years ago for $10 million to the acquisition cost of land acquired this year for $10 million is as inappropriate as adding the cost of land acquired in the United States for $10 million to the cost of land acquired by a subsidiary in the United Kingdom for £10 million. We refer to the accounting issues created by changes in the general level of prices as a *measuring unit problem.*

- **Valuation Problem**

  Changes in the *specific* prices of individual assets and liabilities (such as inventories and fixed assets) affect the measurement of revenues and expenses on the income statement and the valuation of assets and liabilities on the balance sheet. Land acquired last year for $10 million may now have a market value of $14 million. Should the accountant report this land on the balance sheet at its acquisition cost of $10 million or at its current market value of $14 million? Should net income include an unrealized holding gain of $4 million? We refer to the accounting issues created by changes in the prices of specific assets and liabilities as a *valuation problem.*

In summary:

1. Financial reporting can use either a *nominal* measuring unit (that is, one that gives no recognition to the changing value of the measuring unit) or a *constant* measuring unit (that is, one that restates measurements made over time to reflect a constant measuring unit).
2. Financial reporting can use either *acquisition*-cost valuations or current- (*replacement*) cost valuations for assets and liabilities; changes in current-cost valuations over time affect the measurement of net income and shareholders' equity.

The combination of alternative measuring units and valuation methods presents four possible treatments of the effects of changing prices:

1. Acquisition cost/nominal dollar accounting.
2. Acquisition cost/constant dollar accounting.
3. Current cost/nominal dollar accounting.
4. Current cost/constant dollar accounting.

We illustrate each of these four combinations using a simple example. Exhibit 7.10 summarizes the data used in the illustration. A firm begins its first year of operations, Year 1, with $400 in cash and contributed capital. On January 1, Year 1, the consumer price index (CPI) is 200. The firm immediately acquires two widgets for $100 each and a piece of equipment for $100. During the first six months of Year 1, general price inflation is 5 percent. Thus, the CPI increases from 200 to 210. On June 30, Year 1, the firm sells one widget for $240 and replaces it at the new higher replacement cost of $115. The firm also pays other expenses totaling $100 on June 30, Year 1. During the second six months

EXHIBIT 7.10

Data for Inflation Accounting Illustration

Balance Sheet as of January 1, Year 1

Cash: $400	**Contributed Capital: $400**

Date:	**January 1, Year 1**	**June 30, Year 1**	**December 31, Year 1**
CPI	200	210 (5% increase)	231 (10% increase)
Cost of One Widget	$100	$115	$140
Cost of Equipment	$100	$110	$120
Transactions	1. Buy 2 widgets at $100 each, $200 2. Purchase equipment (5-year life) for $100	1. Sell 1 widget for $240; replace widget at $115 2. Pay other expenses of $100	Close books and prepare statements

of the year, general price inflation is 10 percent (the CPI increases from 210 to 231). On December 31, Year 1, the replacement cost of the widget is $140 and the replacement cost of the equipment in new condition is $120.

Financial statements prepared under each of the four combinations of measuring units and valuation methods appear in Exhibit 7.11. The following sections discuss each approach to accounting for changing prices.

ACQUISITION COST/NOMINAL DOLLAR ACCOUNTING

Column 1 of Exhibit 7.11 shows the results for Year 1 as they would appear in conventional financial statements prepared in the United States. These financial statements give no explicit consideration to the effects of changing prices, either in general or for specific assets and liabilities.

Sales appear at the nominal dollars received when the firm sold the widget on June 30. Other expenses appear at the nominal dollars expended on June 30. Cost of goods sold, depreciation, and equipment reflect the nominal dollars expended on January 1. Inventories on the balance sheet reflect the nominal dollars expended on January 1 and June 30. Thus, the financial statements use a measuring unit of unequal size (purchasing power).

Likewise, the financial statements do not reflect the increase in the replacement cost of the inventory and the equipment during Year 1. Is the firm better off by the $20 of net income if it must replace the widget for a higher current cost? Is $20 of depreciation a sufficient measure of the cost of the equipment used during Year 1? Might the firm be better off by more than the $20 of net income because it held inventories and equipment while their replacement cost increased?

Nominal dollars as the measuring unit can be justified when the rate of general price inflation is relatively low (for example, less than 5 percent per year). For most businesses, rapid turnover of assets will not result in serious distortions in financial statement

EXHIBIT 7.11

Illustration of Financial Statements Reflecting Inflation Accounting

	(1) Acquisition Cost/ Nominal Dollars		(2) Acquisition Cost/ Constant Dollars		(3) Current Cost/ Nominal Dollars		(4) Current Cost/ Constant Dollars	
Income Statement								
Sales		$240		$264.0[a]		$240		$264.0
Cost of Goods Sold	$100		$115.5[b]		$115		$126.5[n]	
Depreciation	20		23.1[c]		22[i]		24.2[o]	
Other Expenses	100	220	110.0[d]	248.6	100	237	110.0[d]	260.7
Operating Income		$ 20		$ 15.4		$ 3		$ 3.3
Realized Holding Gains:								
Goods Sold		—		—		15[j]		11.0[p]
Depreciation Assets Used		—		—		2[k]		1.1[q]
Unrealized Holding Gains:								
Inventory		—		—		65[l]		38.0[r]
Depreciation Assets		—		—		16[m]		3.6[s]
Purchasing Power Loss		—		(18.0)[e]		—		(18.0)[e]
Net Income (Loss)		$ 20		$ (2.6)		$101		$ 39.0
Balance Sheet								
Cash		$125		$125.0		$125		$125
Inventory		215		242.0[f]		280		280
Equipment	$100		$115.5[g]		$120		$120	
Accumulated Depreciation	(20)	80	(23.1)	92.4	(24)	96	(24)	96
Total Assets		$420		$459.4		$501		$501
Contributed Capital		$400		$462.0[h]		$400		$462[h]
Retained Earnings		20		(2.6)		101		39
Total Equity		$420		$459.4		$501		$501

[a] $240 × (231/210) = $264.0
[b] $100 × (231/200) = $115.5
[c] $100 × (231/200) = $115.5; $115.5/5 = $23.1
[d] $100 × (231/210) = $110
[e] [$100 × (10/200) × (231/210)] + $125 × (21/210) = $5.50 + $12.50 = $18
[f] $100 × (231/200) + $115 × (231/210) = $242
[g] $100 × (231/200) = $115.5
[h] $400 × (231/200) = $462
[i] $110/5 = $22
[j] $115 − $100 = $15
[k] $22 − $20 = $2
[l] $280 − $215 = $65
[m] $96 − $80 = $16
[n] $115 × (231/210) = $126.5
[o] $22 × (231/210) = $24.2
[p] $126.5 − $115.5 = $11
[q] $24.2 − $23.1 = $1.1
[r] $280 − $242 = $38
[s] $96 − $92.4 = $3.6

measurements. Likewise, the use of a last-in, first-out (LIFO) cost-flow assumption for cost of goods sold and accelerated depreciation for fixed assets provides at least a partial solution to the problems created by changes in specific prices (these accounting principles provide measures of expenses that approximate current replacement costs but result in balance sheet valuations for assets that can deviate widely from current costs).

ACQUISITION COST/CONSTANT DOLLAR ACCOUNTING

Column 2 of Exhibit 7.11 shows financial statements restated to dollars of constant general purchasing power. Acquisition-cost valuations still underlie the measurement of revenues, expenses, assets, and liabilities. However, the nominal dollars underlying these measurements are restated to dollars of constant purchasing power at the end of Year 1. Other constant-dollar measuring units are also possible (for example, January 1, Year 1, constant dollars or June 30, Year 1, constant dollars).

Sales revenue was originally measured in dollars of June 30, Year 1, purchasing power. The restatement expresses the $240 of sales revenue in terms of dollars of December 31, Year 1, purchasing power. Likewise, inventories and equipment reflect restatements of nominal-dollar, acquisition-cost valuations to dollars of constant December 31, Year 1, purchasing power. Thus, an equivalent measuring unit underlies the amounts in column 2. Note that these restated amounts do not represent the current replacement costs of the specific assets and liabilities. The specific prices of assets and liabilities could have changed in an entirely different direction and pattern from prices in general.

One new element in column 2 of Exhibit 7.11 is the *purchasing power gain or loss on monetary items.* A firm that holds cash and claims to a fixed amount of cash (such as accounts receivable or marketable debt securities) during a period of inflation loses general purchasing power. The dollars held or received later have less general purchasing power after the period of inflation than they had before. A firm that borrows from others, promising to pay a fixed amount in cash at a later time (for example, accounts payable, income taxes payable, or bonds payable) gains general purchasing power during a period of inflation. The dollars paid later have less general purchasing power after the period of inflation than they had before. The purchasing power gain or loss is a measure of the increase or decrease in general purchasing power during a period due to being in a net lending position (purchasing power loss) or net borrowing position (purchasing power gain). The accountant calculates the purchasing power gain or loss on *monetary items.* Monetary items include cash and claims receivable or payable in a fixed amount of cash regardless of changes in the general price level.

In the illustration, the firm held $100 of cash during the first six months of the year while the general purchasing power of the dollar decreased 5 percent. It therefore lost $5 of general purchasing power. This $5 loss is measured in terms of dollars of June 30, Year 1, purchasing power. Measured in dollars of December 31, Year 1, constant dollars, the purchasing power loss for the first six months of Year 1 is $5.50. The firm held $125 of cash during the second six months of the year. With 10 percent inflation during this six-month period, an additional loss in purchasing power of $12.50 occurs. Note (e) of Exhibit 7.11 shows the calculations. This illustration is simplified in that the firm has no receivables or payables. In more typical settings, firms that engage in long-term borrowing will often be in a net monetary liability position (that is, monetary liabilities exceed monetary assets). During periods of inflation, these firms experience purchasing power gains.

Constant-dollar accounting, in contrast to current-cost accounting (discussed next), carries a higher level of objectivity. Independent accountants can examine canceled checks, invoices, and other documents to verify acquisition-cost valuations. The restatements to constant dollars use general price indexes published by governmental bodies.

Users of constant-dollar financial statements must remember, however, that the amounts reported for individual assets and liabilities do not reflect the current costs of these items. Also, the firm is not necessarily better or worse off in an amount equal to the purchasing power gain or loss on monetary items. Lenders and borrowers incorporate the expected rate of inflation into the interest rate charged for delayed payments. Conceptually, purchasing power gains should offset interest expense and purchasing power losses should offset interest revenue. Whether a firm is better or worse off depends on the actual rate of inflation relative to the expected rate incorporated into the interest rate.

CURRENT COST/NOMINAL DOLLAR ACCOUNTING

Column 3 of Exhibit 7.11 reports amounts in terms of the current replacement cost of specific assets and liabilities. Matched against sales are the current costs of replacing the widget sold and the services of the equipment used. Operating income (sales minus expenses measured at current replacement cost) reports the firm's ability to maintain its operating capacity. If sales revenue is not large enough to cover the cost of replacing goods and services used up, the firm will have to cut back its level of operations (unless it secures outside financing).

Current-cost income also includes *realized and unrealized holding gains and losses.* A holding gain or loss arises from holding an asset (or liability) while its replacement cost changes. The widget purchased on January 1, Year 1, for $100 was held during the first six months of the year while its replacement cost increased to $115. When the firm sold the widget on June 30, it realized a holding gain of $15 (= $115 – $100). Likewise, the two widgets in ending inventory give rise to unrealized holding gains of $65: $40 (= $140 – $100) on the other widget acquired on January 1 and $25 (= $140 – $115) on the widget acquired on June 30.

Controversy surrounds whether holding gains constitute an increase in the value of a firm. Proponents argue that firms that purchase assets early in anticipation of increases in replacement costs are better off than firms that delay purchases and must pay the higher replacement costs. Opponents argue that firms cannot use such holding gains as the basis for dividend payments without impairing the ability to replace those assets used or sold.

Current cost/nominal dollar accounting is subject to two other criticisms. First, current-replacement-cost valuations are not as easy to verify or audit as acquisition-cost valuations. Different appraisers will likely provide different replacement-cost valuations for various assets. The variation in appraisal values will be particularly wide in the case of assets specific to a firm for which active secondhand markets do not exist. Second, the use of nominal dollars means that the measuring unit underlying current-replacement-cost valuations is not constant across time. Revenues and expenses reflect the purchasing power of the monetary unit during the year, whereas assets and liabilities reflect year-end purchasing power. Distortions caused by changes in the general purchasing power of the measuring unit are less severe in current cost/nominal dollar accounting than in acquisition cost/nominal dollar accounting because current replacement costs reflect more recent measurements.

CURRENT COST/CONSTANT DOLLAR ACCOUNTING

Column 4 of Exhibit 7.11 shows the results of accounting for changes in both general and specific prices. Sales, cost of goods sold, and other expenses measured in terms of replacement costs on June 30, Year 1 (column 3 amounts), are restated from dollars of June 30 purchasing power to dollars of December 31 purchasing power in column 4. Balance sheet amounts for assets reflect current-replacement-cost valuations and constant dollars on December 31, Year 1.

Perhaps the most interesting disclosures in column 4 are the holding gains. The reported amounts indicate the extent to which changes in prices of the firm's specific assets exceed (or fall short of) the change in the general price level. Economists refer to such holding gains (or losses) as *real holding gains and losses.* Column 4 also includes the purchasing power gain on monetary items.

Current cost/constant dollar accounting deals with both accounting problems caused by changing prices—the measuring unit problem and the valuation problem. Although current cost/constant dollar accounting provides a comprehensive solution to these problems, users of financial statements based on this approach should keep in mind the concerns discussed previously: (1) current-cost valuations are less objective than acquisition-cost valuations, (2) the firm is not necessarily better or worse off in an amount equal to the purchasing power gain or loss on monetary items, and (3) the firm cannot distribute to shareholders an amount equal to the holding gains on non-monetary items (such as inventories and equipment) if it is to maintain its operating capacity.

QUESTIONS, EXERCISES, PROBLEMS, AND CASES

Questions and Exercises

7.1 REVENUE RECOGNITION. Revenues are at the core of a firm's ability to grow and prosper, and thus are central to the analysis of a firm's profitability. Although the time-of-sale method is the most common technique employed to recognize revenues, in some instances a strong argument can be made for recognizing revenue before the product has been completed. Discuss circumstances in which this scenario might be appropriate.

7.2 ACCOUNTING FOR CUSTOMER SALES INCENTIVES. PepsiCo offers sales incentives to its customers, as discussed in Note 2, "Our Significant Accounting Policies" (Appendix A). Review the note and discuss the percentage effects of the incentives on total revenues reported by the firm for Year 2 through Year 4. Explain why PepsiCo reports the customer sales incentives as a direct adjustment to sales revenues rather than as an increase in marketing and promotion expenses on the firm's income statement.

7.3 LIFO AND FIFO COST-FLOW ASSUMPTIONS FOR INVENTORY. A large manufacturer of truck and car tires recently changed its cost-flow assumption method for inventories at the beginning of Year 4. The manufacturer has been in operation for almost forty years, and for the last decade has reported moderate growth in revenues. The firm changed from the LIFO method to the FIFO method and reported the following information:

December 31:	Year 3	Year 4
	(amounts in millions)	
Inventories at FIFO cost	$ 788.1	$ 861.7
Excess of FIFO cost over LIFO cost	(429.0)	(452.4)
Cost of goods sold (FIFO)		$4,150.8
Cost of goods sold (LIFO)		$4,417.1

Calculate the inventory turnover ratio for Year 4 using both the LIFO and FIFO cost-flow assumption methods, and explain why the costs assigned to inventory under LIFO at the end of Year 3 and Year 4 are so much less than under FIFO.

7.4 EFFECT OF WEIGHTED AVERAGE COST-FLOW ASSUMPTION ON INVENTORY. The weighted average cost-flow assumption is a commonly used technique to value inventory and determine cost of goods sold. It falls between LIFO and FIFO as to the differential effect on inventory and cost of goods sold values, although normally it is much more like FIFO than like LIFO in its effect on the balance sheet. Why is this?

7.5 EARNINGS MANAGEMENT AND DEPRECIATION MEASUREMENT. Earnings management, a concept discussed in Chapter 6, entails managers' using judgment and reporting estimates in such a way to alter reported earnings to their favor. Discuss (a) the three factors that must be estimated in measuring depreciation and (b) illustrate how one or more of these factors can be employed to manage earnings.

7.6 RESEARCH AND DEVELOPMENT COSTS. Financial reporting requires firms to expense immediately all research and development costs (R&D) costs. Alternatively, GAAP could require firms to capitalize and subsequently amortize all expenditures on R&D that have future potential. As a third alternative, GAAP could require firms to take a "successful efforts" approach to R&D, capitalizing all R&D expenditures as assets and then writing these costs off when it is apparent the efforts are unsuccessful. Speculate why standard setters have chosen not to allow the two latter reporting options and discuss whether analysts would be better served if GAAP required capitalization of R&D costs.

7.7 CAPITALIZATION OF SOFTWARE DEVELOPMENT COSTS. In practice, very few firms capitalize costs of developing computer software. However, *Statement No. 86* requires that firms capitalize (and subsequently amortize) development costs when the "technological feasibility" stage of a product is reached. Review the Adobe Systems illustration in the chapter (Example 21) and discuss why the firm does not capitalize any software development costs.

7.8 TESTING FOR GOODWILL IMPAIRMENT. Goodwill is an intangible asset that firms report on their balance sheets as a result of acquiring other firms. GAAP states that goodwill has an indefinite life and should not be amortized but should be tested for impairment at least annually. Describe the procedures followed by firms to test for goodwill impairment. How does this procedure differ from that followed for testing the impairment of a patent, an intangible asset with a definite life?

Problems and Cases

7.9 INCOME RECOGNITION FOR VARIOUS TYPES OF BUSINESSES.

Discuss when each of the following types of businesses is likely to recognize revenues and expenses.

a. A savings and loan association lending money for home mortgages.
b. A travel agency that books hotels, transportation, and similar services for customers and earns a commission from the providers of these services.
c. A Major League Baseball team that sells season tickets before the season begins and signs multi-year contracts with players. These contracts typically defer the payment of a significant portion of the compensation provided by the contract until the player retires.
d. A producer of fine whiskey that ages twelve years before sale.
e. A timber-growing firm that contracts to sell all timber in a particular tract when it reaches twenty years of age. Each year, it harvests another tract. The price per board foot of timber equals the market price when the customer signs the purchase contract plus 10 percent for each year until harvest.
f. An airline that provides transportation services to customers. Each flight grants frequent-flier miles to customers. Customers earn a free flight when they accumulate sufficient frequent-flier miles.

7.10 MEASURING INCOME FOR A SOFTWARE MANUFACTURER.

Parametric Technology Corporation (PTC) is a software manufacturer discussed in Problem 6.11 (Chapter 6) in relation to unusual charges reported for Year 2 though Year 4. It develops, markets, and supports software that helps manufacturers improve the competitiveness of their products. PTC provides a detailed description of its revenue streams in a recent SEC filing, excerpts of which are provided in Exhibit 7.12.

Required

a. PTC generates revenues from software licenses as detailed in Exhibit 7.12. Discuss the appropriateness of revenue recognition techniques employed by the firm for software licenses in relation to the two general criteria for revenue recognition presented in the chapter.
b. PTC recognizes maintenance service revenue ratably over the term of the maintenance contract unless a specific software upgrade is promised to the customer as part of the maintenance contract. Describe the revenue recognition policy of PTC for maintenance contracts that include a specific upgrade and justify the logic for the policy.
c. PTC provides educational services to its clients, such as onsite training and assessment, and recognizes revenue when the services are provided. Speculate on the criteria employed by PTC to justify when the services have been provided by the firm.
d. PTC states in Exhibit 7.12 that the firm must "exercise judgment and use estimates in connection with the determination of the amounts of software license and services revenues to be recognized in each accounting period." Provide several

EXHIBIT 7.12

Parametric Technology Corporation
Excerpts from Form 10-K Filing, Note A, "Description of Business and Summary of Significant Accounting Policies—Revenue Recognition" (Problem 7.10)

We derive revenues from three primary sources: (1) software licenses, (2) maintenance services and (3) other services, which include consulting and education services.

While we apply the guidance of Statement of Position (SOP) No. 97-2, *Software Revenue Recognition*, and Statement of Position No. 98-9, *Modification of SOP 97-2, Software Revenue Recognition with Respect to Certain Transactions*, both issued by the American Institute of Certified Public Accountants, as well as SEC Staff Accounting Bulletin 104, *Revenue Recognition in Financial Statements*, we exercise judgment and use estimates in connection with the determination of the amounts of software license and services revenues to be recognized in each accounting period.

For software license arrangements that do not require significant modification or customization of the underlying software, we recognize revenue when: (1) persuasive evidence of an arrangement exists, (2) delivery has occurred (generally, FOB shipping point or electronic distribution), (3) the fee is fixed or determinable, and (4) collection is probable. Substantially all of our license revenues are recognized in this manner.

Our software is distributed primarily through our direct sales force. However, our indirect distribution channel continues to expand through alliances with resellers. Revenue arrangements with resellers are recognized on a sell-through basis; that is, when we receive persuasive evidence that the reseller has sold the products to an end-user customer. We do not offer contractual rights of return, stock balancing, or price protection to our resellers, and actual product returns from them have been insignificant to date. As a result, we do not maintain reserves for product returns and related allowances.

At the time of each sale transaction, we must make an assessment of the collectibility of the amount due from the customer. Revenue is only recognized at that time if management deems that collection is probable. In making this assessment, we consider customer creditworthiness and historical payment experience. At that same time, we assess whether fees are fixed or determinable and free of contingencies or significant uncertainties. If the fee is not fixed or determinable, revenue is recognized only as payments become due from the customer, provided that all other revenue recognition criteria are met. In assessing whether the fee is fixed or determinable, we consider the payment terms of the transaction and our collection experience in similar transactions without making concessions, among other factors. Our software license arrangements generally do not include customer acceptance provisions. However, if an arrangement includes an acceptance provision, we record revenue only upon the earlier of (1) receipt of written acceptance from the customer or (2) expiration of the acceptance period.

Our software arrangements often include implementation and consulting services that are sold separately under consulting engagement contracts or as part of the software license arrangement. When we determine that such services are not essential to the functionality of the licensed software and qualify as "service transactions" under SOP 97-2, we record revenue separately for the license and service elements of these arrangements.

Maintenance services generally include rights to unspecified upgrades (when and if available), telephone and Internet-based support, updates and bug fixes. Maintenance revenue is recognized ratably over the term of the maintenance contract on a straight-line basis. It is uncommon for us to offer a specified upgrade to an existing product; however, in such instances, all revenue of the arrangement is deferred until the future upgrade is delivered.

When consulting qualifies for separate accounting, consulting revenues under time and materials billing arrangements are recognized as the services are performed.

Education services include on-site training, classroom training, and computer-based training and assessment. Education revenues are recognized as the related training services are provided.

illustrations of judgments or estimates that PTC must employ for determining the amount of software license and service revenues to report each accounting period.

7.11 MEASURING INCOME FOR A CONSULTANCY FIRM. Sapient Corporation is a technology consultancy firm discussed in Problem 6.15 (Chapter 6) in relation to unusual charges reported for Year 2 and Year 3. For Year 3, the firm's Form 10-K filing provided an extensive discussion of its revenue recognition policies, excerpts of which follow:

> We recognize revenue from the provision of professional services under written service contracts with our clients. We derive a significant portion of our revenue from fixed-price, fixed-time contracts. Revenue generated from fixed-price contracts, with the exception of support and maintenance contracts, is recognized based on the ratio of labor hours incurred to estimated total labor hours. This method is used because reasonably dependable estimates of the revenues and costs applicable to various stages of a contract can be made, based on historical experience and milestones set in the contract.
>
> Revenue generated from fixed-price support and maintenance contracts is recognized ratably over the contract term.
>
> Certain contracts provide for revenue to be generated based upon the achievement of certain performance standards. Revenue is recognized when such performance standards are achieved, including $956,000 of revenue recognized in Year 3.
>
> Revenue from multiple element arrangements is accounted for under EITF Issue No. 00–21 (EITF 00–21), "Revenue Arrangements with Multiple Deliverables." For these arrangements, we evaluate all deliverables in the contract to determine whether they represent separate units of accounting. If the deliverables represent separate units of accounting, we then measure and allocate the consideration from the arrangement to the separate units, based on reliable evidence of the fair value of each deliverable. This evaluation is performed at the inception of the arrangement and as each item in the arrangement is delivered, and involves significant judgments regarding the nature of the services and deliverables being provided and whether these services and deliverables can reasonably be divided into the separate units of accounting.

Required

a. Sapient recognizes revenues based on the provisions of the written service contracts generated for each client. The primary types of contracts are (1) fixed-price, fixed-time contracts; (2) support and maintenance contracts; and (3) performance standards contracts. Discuss the criteria used to recognize revenue for each type of contract and the difficulties in applying the criteria.

b. Discuss the appropriateness of the revenue recognition techniques employed by Sapient in relation to the general revenue recognition criterion of "substantial portion of services has been provided" as discussed in the text of this chapter.

c. As detailed earlier, some contracts have multiple-element arrangements with separate deliverable components. Discuss the criteria used to distinguish among multiple components of the contract. Also, speculate on how the firm recognizes revenue when the contract cannot be separated into distinct deliverable components.

7.12 MEASURING INCOME FOR A LONG-HAUL TRANSPORT FIRM. Canadian National Railway Company (CN) spans Canada and mid-America and provides freight transport services from the Atlantic Ocean to the Pacific Ocean and to the Gulf of Mexico. It is currently the largest private rail system in Canada and was privatized by the Canadian government at a time when it was considered one of the worst rail transport companies in North America. CN has been a success story since its privatization, and is now considered one of the strongest and most efficient rail freight transport companies. Its success is partly due to a fundamental change in the way it offers freight services to customers. CN runs what the firm refers to as a "scheduled railroad." Similar to rail passenger service, CN as much as possible maintains a fixed operating schedule and a fixed freight-car fleet movement across the continent. Thus, customers know exactly what shipment options are available to them and know with a high degree of accuracy when shipments will arrive at designated locations.

Typically, a customer contracts a fixed fee with CN to ship its freight from the point of origination (for example, the Port of Halifax) to the point of destination (for example, the Port of Vancouver). CN provides the entire transport (that is, CN does not contract out a portion of the shipment to other rail transport companies), and the length of time taken to deliver the freight depends on the distance and the type of service (fast delivery versus normal delivery, for example) purchased by the customer. In a recent annual report, CN succinctly states its policy on recognizing revenue: "Freight revenues are recognized on services performed by the Company, based on the percentage of complete service method. Costs associated with movements are recognized as the service is performed."

Required

Discuss the appropriateness of the revenue recognition techniques employed by CN for recognizing freight revenues.

7.13 MEASURING INCOME FROM LONG-TERM CONTRACTS. Turner Construction Company agreed on January 1, Year 1, to construct an observatory for Dartmouth College for $120 million. Dartmouth College must pay $30 million on signing and $30 million at the end of Year 1, Year 2, and Year 3. Expected constructed costs are $10 million for Year 1, $60 million for Year 2, and $30 million for Year 3. Assume that these cash flows occur at the end of each year. Also assume that an appropriate interest rate for this contract is 10 percent. Amortization schedules for the deferred cash flows follow:

Amortization Schedule for Cash Received

Year	Balance Jan. 1	Interest Revenue	Payment	Reduction in Principal	Balance Dec. 31
1	$74,606	$7,460	$30,000	$22,540	$52,066
2	52,066	5,207	30,000	24,793	27,273
3	27,273	2,727	30,000	27,273	0

Amortization Schedule for Cash Disbursed

Year	Balance Jan. 1	Interest Expense	Payment	Reduction in Principal	Balance Dec. 31
1	$81,217	$8,122	$10,000	$ 1,878	$79,339
2	79,339	7,934	60,000	52,066	27,273
3	27,273	2,727	30,000	27,273	0

Required

a. Indicate the amount and nature of income (revenue and expense) that Turner would recognize during Year 1, Year 2, and Year 3 if it uses the completed-contract method. Ignore income taxes.

b. Repeat part a using the percentage-of-completion method.

c. Repeat part a using the installment method.

d. Indicate the balance in the Construction in Process account on December 31, Year 1, Year 2, and Year 3 (just prior to completion of the contract) under the completed-contract and the percentage-of-completion methods.

7.14 FINANCIAL STATEMENT DISCLOSURES REGARDING INVENTORIES AND FIXED ASSETS. U. S. Steel Corporation derives most revenues from manufacturing a wide variety of steel products. The steel industry in the United States has experienced intense foreign competition in the past decade, which has caused many U.S. manufacturers, including U. S. Steel, to re-evaluate their product mix and cost structures.

U. S. Steel uses a LIFO cost-flow assumption for inventories, straight-line depreciation for financial reporting, and accelerated depreciation for tax reporting. Exhibit 7.13 presents selected data for U. S. Steel for Year 3 and Year 4. Year 3 was a difficult year for the firm, reporting a net loss of $479 million for the year. Sales rebounded dramatically in Year 4 (approximately a 50 percent increase over Year 3) and the firm reported net income for the year of $1.1 billion.

The income tax rate is 35 percent for Year 2 through Year 4.

Required

a. The excess of FIFO over LIFO inventories was $310 million on December 31, Year 2; $270 million on December 31, Year 3; and $770 million on December 31, Year 4. Compute the cost of goods sold for U. S. Steel for Year 3 and Year 4, assuming that it had used a FIFO cost-flow assumption.

b. Compute the inventory turnover ratio for U. S. Steel for Year 3 and Year 4 using (1) a LIFO cost-flow assumption and (2) a FIFO cost-flow assumption.

c. Compute the amount of depreciation expense that U. S. Steel recognized for income tax purposes for Year 3 and Year 4. Note that the amount reported as the deferred tax liability relating to temporary depreciation differences represents the cumulative income taxes delayed as of each balance sheet date because U. S. Steel uses accelerated depreciation for tax purposes and straight-line depreciation for financial reporting.

EXHIBIT 7.13

U. S. Steel
Financial Statement Data
(amounts in millions)
(Problem 7.14)

	Year Ended December 31:		
	Year 4	Year 3	Year 2
Inventories (LIFO)	$ 1,197	$1,283	$1,030
Property, Plant, and Equipment, net	3,627	3,414	2,978
Total Assets	10,956	7,837	7,977
Deferred Tax Liability Relating to Temporary Depreciation Differences	495	455	365
Common Shareholders' Equity	3,726	865	2,027

	Year Ended December 31:	
	Year 4	Year 3
Sales	$13,969	$9,328
Cost of Goods Sold	11,407	8,469
Depreciation Expense	382	363
Interest Expense	119	130
Net Income (Loss)	1,073	(479)

d. Compute the fixed-asset turnover ratio for Year 3 and Year 4 assuming use of (1) straight-line depreciation and (2) accelerated (tax) depreciation.

e. Compute the rate of return on assets for Year 3 and Year 4 based on the reported amounts (that is, LIFO for inventories and straight-line depreciation). Disaggregate ROA into profit margin and assets turnover components.

f. Repeat part e using FIFO for inventories and accelerated (tax) depreciation. Assume U. S. Steel uses FIFO for both financial and tax reporting. Any tax effects reduce or increase cash. Disaggregate ROA into profit margin and assets turnover components.

g. Compute the rate of return on common shareholders' equity for Year 3 and Year 4 based on the reported amounts. Disaggregate ROCE into two components: (1) Net Income (Loss)/Average Total Assets, and (2) Average Total Assets/Average Common Shareholders' Equity.

h. Repeat part g using FIFO for inventories and accelerated (tax) depreciation.

i. Interpret the changes in the profitability and risk of U. S. Steel between Year 3 and Year 4 in light of the preceding analyses.

7.15 ANALYZING DISCLOSURES REGARDING FIXED ASSETS. Exhibit 7.14 presents selected financial statement data for three chemical companies: NewMarket Corporation (recently formed from a merger of Ethyl Corporation and Afton Chemical Corporation), Monsanto Company, and Olin Corporation.

Required

a. Compute the average total depreciable life of assets in use for each firm during Year 4.

b. Compute the average age to date of depreciable assets in use for each firm at the end of Year 4.

c. Compute the amount of depreciation expense recognized for tax purposes for each firm for Year 4, using the amount of the deferred taxes liability related to depreciation timing differences.

d. Compute the amount of net income for Year 4 for each firm, assuming that depreciation expense for financial reporting equals the amount computed in part c for tax reporting.

e. Compute the amount each company would report for property, plant, and equipment (net) at the end of Year 4 if it had used accelerated (tax reporting) depreciation instead of straight-line depreciation.

f. What factors might explain the difference in average total life of NewMarket Corporation and Olin Corporation relative to Monsanto Company?

g. What factors might explain the older average age for depreciable assets of NewMarket Corporation and Olin Corporation relative to Monsanto Company?

EXHIBIT 7.14

Three Chemical Companies
Selected Financial Statement Data on Depreciable Assets
(amounts in millions)
(Problem 7.15)

	NewMarket Corporation	Monsanto Company	Olin Corporation
Depreciable Assets, at cost:			
Year End, Year 3	$752	$4,611	$1,796
Year End, Year 4	777	4,604	1,826
Accumulated Depreciation:			
Year End, Year 3	578	2,331	1,301
Year End, Year 4	611	2,517	1,348
Net Income, Year 4	33	267	55
Depreciation Expense, Year 4	27	328	72
Deferred Tax Liability Relating to Depreciable Assets			
Year End, Year 3	13	267	83
Year End, Year 4	9	256	96
Income Tax Rate	35%	35%	35%
Depreciation Method for Financial Reporting	Straight-Line	Straight-Line	Straight-Line
Depreciation Method for Tax Reporting	Accelerated	Accelerated	Accelerated

7.16 INTERPRETING FINANCIAL STATEMENT DISCLOSURES RELATING TO INCOME RECOGNITION. Deere & Company manufactures agricultural and industrial equipment and provides financing services for its independent dealers and their retail customers. Exhibit 7.15 presents an income statement and Exhibit 7.16 presents a balance sheet for Deere for Year 3 and Year 4. The notes to these financial statements follow:

Note 1: Deere recognizes income from equipment sales for financial reporting at the time of shipment to dealers. Provisions for sales incentives to dealers, returns and allowances, and uncollectible accounts are made at the time of sale. There is a time lag, which varies based on the timing and level of retail demand, between when Deere records sales to dealers and when dealers sell equipment to retail customers. Deere recognizes income from equipment sales using the installment method for tax reporting.

Note 2: Deere provides financing to independent dealers and retail customers for Deere products. Accounts and notes receivable appear net of unearned finance income. Deere recognizes the unearned finance income as finance revenue over the period that dealer and customer notes are outstanding.

Note 3: Deere uses a LIFO cost flow assumption for inventories and cost of goods sold. The excess of FIFO over LIFO cost of inventories was $950 million on October 31, Year 3 and $1,002 on October 31, Year 4.

EXHIBIT 7.15

Deere & Company
Income Statement
(amounts in millions)
(Problem 7.16)

	Year Ended October 31:	
	Year 4	Year 3
Revenues		
Equipment Sales Revenue (Note 1)	$17,673	$13,349
Finance Revenue (Note 2)	1,196	1,276
Investment Revenue	12	11
Other Income	1,105	899
Total Revenues	$19,986	$15,535
Expenses		
Cost of Goods Sold	$13,568	$10,753
Research and Development Expenses	612	577
Selling, Administrative, and Other Expenses	3,099	2,596
Interest Expense	592	629
Income Tax Expense	709	337
Total Expenses	$18,580	$14,892
Net Income (Loss)	$ 1,406	$ 643

EXHIBIT 7.16

Deere & Company
Balance Sheet
(amounts in millions)
(Problem 7.16)

	October 31:	
	Year 4	Year 3
Assets		
Cash	$ 3,181	$ 4,385
Marketable Securities	247	232
Accounts and Notes Receivable (Note 2)	16,417	14,707
Inventories (Note 3)	1,999	1,366
Property, Plant, and Equipment (Note 4)	2,162	2,076
Intangible assets, net	995	1,125
Other Assets	3,753	2,367
Total Assets	$28,754	$26,258
Liabilities and Shareholders' Equity		
Short-Term Borrowing	$ 3,457	$ 4,347
Accounts Payable and Accrued Expenses	4,431	3,514
Long-Term Borrowing	11,090	10,404
Deferred Income Taxes	63	31
Pension Liability	3,320	3,960
Total Liabilities	$22,361	$22,256
Common Stock	$ 991	$ 841
Accumulated Other Comprehensive Loss	(43)	(1,168)
Retained Earnings	5,445	4,329
Total Shareholders' Equity	$ 6,393	$ 4,002
Total Liabilities and Shareholders' Equity	$28,754	$26,258

Note 4: Property, plant, and equipment include the following:

	October 31:	
	Year 4	Year 3
Land	$ 79	$ 68
Buildings	1,464	1,366
Machinery and Equipment	2,870	2,705
Dies, Patterns, and Tools	987	932
Other	782	763
Total	$6,182	$5,834
Less Accumulated Depreciation	(4,020)	(3,758)
	$2,162	$2,076

Deere depreciates fixed assets using the straight line method for financial reporting. Depreciation expense was $319 million in Year 3 and $342 in Year 4. Deere uses accelerated depreciation for tax reporting.

Required

a. Using the criteria for revenue recognition, justify Deere's timing of revenue recognition for its equipment sales. Consider why recognition of revenue either earlier or later than the time of shipment to dealers would not be more appropriate.
b. Describe briefly how the balance sheet accounts of Deere & Company listed here would change if it recognized revenues during the period of production using the percentage-of-completion method. You need not give amounts but indicate the likely direction of the change and describe the computation of its amount.

   Accounts and Notes Receivable
   Inventories
   Retained Earnings

c. Respond to part b, assuming that Deere & Company recognized revenue using the installment method.

   Accounts and Notes Receivable
   Inventories
   Retained Earnings

d. Compute the amount of cost of goods sold for Year 4, assuming that Deere & Company had used a FIFO instead of a LIFO cost-flow assumption.
e. Did the quantities and costs of inventory items likely increase or decrease during Year 4? Explain.
f. Compute the average age of Deere's depreciable assets at the end of Year 4.

7.17 INTERPRETING DISCLOSURES REGARDING CHANGING PRICES. AES Gener S.A. (formerly Chilgener S.A.) is a large provider of electric transmission services in Chile. The firm also provides electricity to selected regions in Argentina. Exhibit 7.17 presents the balance sheet for Gener on December 31, Year 2 and Year 3. Exhibit 7.18 presents the income statement for Gener for Year 2 and Year 3. Excerpts from the notes to its financial statements follow:

Summary of Significant Accounting Principles

General. The consolidated financial statements have been prepared in conformity with generally accepted accounting principles in Chile and with the regulations issued by the Chilean Superintendence of Securities and Insurance.

Price Level Restatement. These consolidated financial statements have been restated through the application of an adjustment based on the change in the consumer price index in order to reflect the effect of fluctuations in the purchasing power of the Chilean peso. Restatements have been based on the official index published by the Chilean National Institute of Statistics which amounts to a 2.8 percent increase for Year 2 and a 1.1 percent increase for Year 3. Moreover, income and expenses were also restated so as to express them at year-end purchasing power. The Year 2 financial statements and their relevant notes have been adjusted (without being reflected in the accounting records) by 1.1 percent with the only purpose of allowing their comparison with the Year 3 financial statements in constant pesos of December 31, Year 3.

Inventories. Inventories consist of raw materials, parts and accessories valued at their corresponding acquisition cost. The values shown do not exceed their estimated net realizable values and are reflected in income on the basis of weighted-average cost in accordance with generally accepted accounting principles.

EXHIBIT 7.17

AES Gener S.A.
Balance Sheet
(amounts in millions of constant December 31, Year 3, Chilean pesos)
(Problem 7.17)

	December 31:	
	Year 2	Year 3
Assets		
Cash	P 3,090,891	P 5,386,499
Accounts Receivable	33,197,862	206,277,965
Inventories	13,896,635	8,983,858
Other Current Assets	9,662,300	16,920,882
Total Current Assets	P 59,847,688	P 237,569,204
Fixed Assets, at cost	P 753,177,265	P 748,890,960
Technical Revaluation of Fixed Assets	42,213,625	42,213,625
Accumulated Depreciation	(392,117,207)	(407,599,397)
Net Fixed Assets	P 403,273,683	P 383,505,188
Other Assets	P 997,859,522	P 772,719,898
Total Assets	P1,460,980,893	P1,393,794,290
Liabilities and Shareholders' Equity		
Short-Term Borrowing	P 12,025,863	P 9,438,167
Accounts Payable	52,763,494	53,635,673
Other Current Liabilities	6,082,839	7,019,521
Total Current Liabilities	P 70,872,196	P 70,093,361
Long-Term Debt	P 546,684,433	P 481,708,646
Other Noncurrent Liabilities	58,646,512	33,388,399
Total Noncurrent Liabilities	P 605,330,945	P 515,097,045
Paid-In Capital	P 690,150,712	P 690,150,712
Technical Revaluation of Fixed Assets	42,213,625	42,213,625
Retained Earnings	52,413,415	76,239,547
Total Shareholders' Equity	P 784,777,752	P 808,603,884
Total Liabilities and Shareholders' Equity	P1,460,980,893	P1,393,794,290

Fixed Assets. Fixed assets are valued at cost plus price-level restatement. The value of fixed assets was last adjusted 17 years before Year 3 in accordance with the regulations of the Chilean Superintendence of Securities and Insurance. Depreciation has been calculated on a straight-line basis on the adjusted value of assets, in accordance with their remaining useful life. Depreciation amounted to P50,070,542 for Year 2 and P45,980,590 for Year 3. It is included in operating costs and includes additional depreciation for technical reappraisal of fixed assets amounting to P1,687,514 in Year 2 and P1,312,755 in Year 3.

Bonds. Bonds payable are shown at their nominal year-end value plus accrued interest and price-level restatement.

Required

a. Does Gener's reporting most closely resemble (1) acquisition cost/constant peso reporting, (2) current cost/nominal peso reporting, or (3) current cost/constant peso reporting? Explain.

b. Why does Gener restate the financial statements to reflect the changes in the purchasing power of the Chilean peso when the consumer price indices for Year 3 and Year 2 (2.8 percent increase for Year 2 and a 1.1 percent increase for Year 3) increased at relatively low levels?

EXHIBIT 7.18

AES Gener S.A.
Income Statement
(amounts in millions of constant December 31, Year 3, Chilean pesos)
(Problem 7.17)

	December 31:	
	Year 2	Year 3
Operating Revenues	P241,399,880	P229,590,527
Operating Costs	(191,239,032)	(194,445,116)
Operating Margin	P 50,160,848	P 35,145,411
Selling and Administrative Expense	(9,955,170)	(8,883,575)
Operating Profit	P 40,205,678	P 26,261,836
Financial Income	P 33,412,263	P 20,199,229
Share of Profits of Investees	31,454,883	118,593,310
Other Non-Operating Income	3,705,245	1,513,011
Financing Expenses	(31,684,693)	(28,346,815)
Other Non-Operating Expenses	(35,381,913)	(88,737,247)
Price Level Restatement	(416,243)	(686,496)
Non-Operating Income	P 1,089,542	P 22,534,992
Income before Tax	P 41,295,220	P 48,796,828
Income Tax	(5,719,770)	4,881,635
Net Income	P 35,575,450	P 53,678,463

c. Interpret the last sentence in the note on price level restatement.
d. What is the likely reason that Gener reported a price level restatement loss on its income statement for Year 2 and Year 3?
e. Assume that sales and price level changes occurred evenly during Year 2 and Year 3. Compute the *nominal* peso change in sales between Year 2 and Year 3.
f. Have the current replacement costs of Gener's fixed assets increased at a faster or slower rate than the general price level? Explain your reasoning. If you do not think that the disclosures permit an answer to this question, explain your reasoning.
g. Why does the amount in the Technical Revaluation of Fixed Assets account remain at P42,213,625 during Year 3 if the note on fixed assets indicates that Gener recognized depreciation on the revalued fixed-asset amount?

INTEGRATIVE CASE 7.1

STARBUCKS

The first note to Starbucks' Year 4 Form 10-K filing provides a description of the significant accounting policies employed by the firm for preparing its financial statements. Excerpts from five of the policies discussed in the note are provided next. Review the excerpts and answer the set of questions listed at the end of this case.

Inventories

Inventories are stated at the lower of cost (primarily moving average cost) or market. The Company records inventory reserves for obsolete and slow-moving items and for estimated shrinkage between physical inventory counts. Inventory reserves are based on inventory turnover trends, historical experience, and application of the specific identification method.

Property, Plant, and Equipment

Property, plant, and equipment are carried at cost less accumulated depreciation. Depreciation of property, plant, and equipment, which includes assets under capital leases, is provided on the straight-line method over estimated useful lives, generally ranging from two to seven years for equipment and 30 to 40 years for buildings. Leasehold improvements are amortized over the shorter of their estimated useful lives or the related lease life, generally 10 years. For leases with renewal periods at the Company's option, Starbucks generally uses the original lease term, excluding renewal option periods to determine estimated useful lives; if failure to exercise a renewal option imposes an economic penalty to Starbucks, management may determine at the inception of the lease that renewal is reasonably assured and include the renewal option period in the determination of appropriate estimated useful lives. The portion of depreciation expense related to production and distribution facilities is included in "Cost of sales including occupancy costs" on the accompanying consolidated statements of earnings. The costs of repairs and maintenance are expensed when incurred, while expenditures for refurbishments and improvements that significantly add to the productive capacity or extend the useful life of an asset are capitalized. When assets are retired or sold, the asset cost and related accumulated depreciation are eliminated with any remaining gain or loss reflected in net earnings.

Goodwill and Other Intangible Assets

At the beginning of fiscal Year 3, Starbucks adopted *Statement No. 142,* "Goodwill and Other Intangible Assets." As a result, the Company discontinued amortization of its goodwill and indefinite-lived trademarks and determined that provisions for impairment were unnecessary. Impairment tests are performed annually in June and more frequently if facts and circumstances indicate goodwill carrying values exceed estimated reporting unit fair values and if indefinite useful lives are no longer appropriate for the Company's trademarks. If the nonamortization provision of SFAS 142 had been applied to fiscal Year 2, net earnings would have been $213.4 million, as compared to actual net earnings of $211.4 million. Basic earnings per share for fiscal Year 2 would have remained unchanged, while diluted earnings per share would have increased to $0.54 per share from $0.53 per share. Definite-lived intangibles, which mainly consist of contract-based patents and copyrights, are amortized over their estimated useful lives.

Long-Lived Assets

When facts and circumstances indicate that the carrying values of long-lived assets may be impaired, an evaluation of recoverability is performed by comparing the carrying values of the assets to projected future cash flows in addition to other quantitative and qualitative analyses. Upon indication that the carrying values of such assets may not be recoverable, the Company recognizes an impairment loss by a charge against current operations. Property, plant and equipment assets are grouped at the lowest level for which there are identifiable cash flows when assessing impairment. Cash flows for retail assets are identified at the individual store level.

Revenue Recognition

Company-operated retail store revenues are recognized when payment is tendered at the point of sale. Revenues from stored value cards are recognized upon redemption. Until the redemption of stored value cards, outstanding customer balances on such cards are included in "Deferred revenue" on the accompanying consolidated balance sheets. Specialty revenues consist primarily of product sales to customers other than through Company-operated retail stores, as well as royalties and other fees generated from licensing operations. Sales of coffee, tea, and related products are generally recognized upon shipment to customers, depending on contract terms. Initial nonrefundable development fees required under licensing agreements are recognized upon substantial performance of services for new market business development activities, such as initial business, real estate, and store development planning, as well as providing operational materials and functional training courses for opening new licensed retail markets. Additional store licensing fees are recognized when new licensed stores are opened. Royalty revenues based upon a percentage of reported sales and other continuing fees, such as marketing and service fees, are recognized on a monthly basis when earned. Arrangements involving multiple elements and deliverables are individually evaluated for revenue recognition. Cash payments received in advance of product or service delivery are recorded as deferred revenue. Consolidated revenues are net of all intercompany eliminations for wholly owned subsidiaries and for licensees accounted for under the equity method based on the Company's percentage ownership. All revenues are recognized net of any discounts.

Required

a. Starbucks uses the average cost-flow assumption to measure inventory and cost of goods sold. The company also charges cost of goods sold and accrues a liability for obsolete and slow-moving inventory items. Discuss factors specific to Starbucks that the firm would consider in estimating the charges for inventory that is slow moving and/or obsolete.

b. Leasehold improvements are recorded as assets by Starbucks. Refer to Starbucks' financial statements, provided in Integrative Case 1.1, to determine what line item on the balance sheet includes the leasehold improvements reported by the firm at the end of Year 4 and Year 3. Provide several examples of typical leasehold improvements that would be capitalized by Starbucks.

c. Starbucks discontinued amortization of goodwill in Year 3 as required by *Statement No. 142,* but tests it for impairment as required by the statement. Describe the procedures employed by the firm to test for impairment of its goodwill. A review of the notes to Starbucks' financial statements (not provided here) reveals that the firm discloses the effect on earnings and earnings per share for Year 2 assuming that *Statement No. 142* applied to that year as well. Why does the firm provide this disclosure?

d. Starbucks judges its long-lived assets for impairment as discussed in the preceding note excerpt labeled "Long-Lived Assets." How often does Starbucks test its long-lived assets for impairment and what techniques does it use to judge impairment?

e. Starbucks recognizes revenues from stored-value cards on redemption. Until that point, outstanding customer balances on such cards are included in "deferred revenue" on the balance sheet as a liability. Sales of these cards—often referred to as gift cards—are particularly popular during the December holiday season. Those receiving the gift cards often wait until January or substantially beyond to use the gift cards. Is Starbucks correct in recognizing revenue only when those receiving the gift cards use them to make purchases? Explain your reasoning.

CASE 7.2

ARIZONA LAND DEVELOPMENT COMPANY

Joan Locker and Bill Dasher organized the Arizona Land Development Company (ALDC) on January 2, Year 1. They contributed land with a market value of $300,000 and cash of $100,000 for all of the common stock of the corporation. The land served as the initial inventory of property sold to customers.

ALDC sells undeveloped land, primarily to individuals approaching retirement. Within nine years from the date of sale, ALDC promises to develop the land so that it is suitable for the construction of residential housing. ALDC makes all sales on an installment basis. Customers pay 10 percent of the selling price at the time of sale, and remit the remainder in equal installments over the next nine years.

ALDC estimates that development costs will equal 50 percent of the selling price of the land and that development work will take nine years to complete from the date of sale. Actual development costs have coincided with expectations. The firm incurs 10 percent of the development costs at the time of sale, and incurs the remainder evenly over the next nine years.

ALDC remained a privately held firm for its first six years. Exhibits 7.19 to 7.21 present the firm's income statement, balance sheet, and statement of cash flows, respectively, for Year 1 to Year 6. ALDC recognizes income from sales of undeveloped land at the time of

EXHIBIT 7.19

Arizona Land Development Company
Income Statements
Income Recognition at Time of Sale—No Discounting of Cash Flows
(Case 7.2)

	Year 1	Year 2	Year 3	Year 4	Year 5	Year 6
Sales	$650,000	$900,000	$1,500,000	$2,500,000	$1,200,000	$400,000
Less:						
Cost of Land Inventory Sold	(65,000)	(90,000)	(150,000)	(250,000)	(120,000)	(40,000)
Estimated Development Costs	(325,000)	(450,000)	(750,000)	(1,250,000)	(600,000)	(200,000)
Gross Profit	$260,000	$360,000	$ 600,000	$1,000,000	$ 480,000	$160,000
Selling Expenses	(65,000)	(90,000)	(150,000)	(250,000)	(120,000)	(40,000)
Net Income before Taxes	$195,000	$270,000	$ 450,000	$ 750,000	$ 360,000	$120,000
Income Taxes:						
Current	—	—	(9,778)	(26,091)	(73,009)	(94,902)
Deferred	(66,300)	(91,800)	(143,222)	(228,909)	(49,391)	54,102
Net Income	$128,700	$178,200	$ 297,000	$ 495,000	$ 237,600	$ 79,200

EXHIBIT 7.20

Arizona Land Development Company
Balance Sheets
Income Recognition at Time of Sale—No Discounting of Cash Flows
(Case 7.2)

	Year 1	Year 2	Year 3	Year 4	Year 5	Year 6
Assets						
Cash	$100,000	$ 132,500	$ 100,222	$ 126,631	$ 131,122	$ 273,720
Notes Receivable	520,000	1,175,000	2,220,000	3,915,000	4,320,000	3,965,000
Land Inventory	235,000	145,000	95,000	45,000	125,000	185,000
Total Assets	$855,000	$1,452,500	$2,415,222	$4,086,631	$4,576,122	$4,423,720
Liabilities and Shareholders' Equity						
Estimated Development Cost Liability	$260,000	$ 587,500	$1,110,000	$1,957,500	$2,160,000	$1,982,500
Deferred Income Taxes	66,300	158,100	301,322	530,231	579,622	525,520
Common Stock	400,000	400,000	400,000	500,000	500,000	500,000
Retained Earnings	128,700	306,900	603,900	1,098,900	1,336,500	1,415,700
Total Liabilities and Shareholders' Equity	$855,000	$1,452,500	$2,415,222	$4,086,631	$4,576,122	$4,423,720

EXHIBIT 7.21

Arizona Land Development Company
Statements of Cash Flows
Income Recognition at Time of Sale—No Discounting of Cash Flows
(Case 7.2)

	Year 1	Year 2	Year 3	Year 4	Year 5	Year 6
Operations						
Net Income	$ 128,700	$ 178,200	$ 297,000	$ 495,000	$ 237,600	$ 79,200
(Increase) Decrease in Notes Receivable	(520,000)	(655,000)	(1,045,000)	(1,695,000)	(405,000)	355,000
(Increase) Decrease in Land Inventory	65,000	90,000	50,000	50,000	(80,000)	(60,000)
Increase (Decrease) in Estimated Development Cost Liability	260,000	327,500	522,500	847,500	202,500	(177,500)
Increase (Decrease) in Deferred Income Taxes	66,300	91,800	143,222	228,909	49,391	(54,102)
Cash Flow from Operations	$ 0	$ 32,500	$ (32,278)	$ (73,591)	$ 4,491	$ 142,598
Financing						
Common Stock Issued	—	—	—	100,000	—	—
Change in Cash	$ 0	$ 32,500	$ (32,278)	$ 26,409	$ 4,491	$ 142,598

sale. The amount shown for sales each year in Exhibit 7.19 represents the gross amount ALDC ultimately expects to collect from customers for land sold in that year. The amount shown for estimated development costs each year is the gross amount ALDC expects ultimately to disburse to develop land sold in that year. The firm treats selling expenses as a period expense. It is subject to a 34 percent income tax rate. ALDC uses the installment method of income recognition for income tax purposes.

ALDC contemplates making its initial public offering of common stock early in Year 7. The firm asks you to assess whether its income recognition method, as reflected in Exhibits 7.19 to 7.21, accurately reflects its operating performance and financial position. To assist you, the firm has prepared financial statements following three other income recognition methods as described next.

Income Recognition at Time of Sale but with Discounting of Future Cash Flows to Present Value

Exhibits 7.22 to 7.24 present the financial statements following this income recognition method. This method discounts future cash inflows from customers and future cash outflows for development work to their present values. The gross profit recognized at the time of sale equals the present value of cash inflows net of the present value of cash outflows. One might view this gross profit as the current cash-equivalent value of the gross profit that the firm will ultimately realize over the nine-year period. This method reports the increase in the present value of cash inflows as time passes as interest revenue each year and the increase in the present value of cash outflows as interest expense. Thus, this income recognition method results in reporting two types of income: a gross profit from the selling of land and interest from delayed cash flows. The computations of present values underlying the financial statements in Exhibits 7.22 to 7.24 rest on the following assumptions:

1. ALDC makes all sales on January 1 of each year. It receives 10 percent of the gross selling price at the time of sale and also pays 10 percent of the gross development costs immediately.
2. The firm receives 10 percent of the gross selling price from customers and pays 10 percent of the gross development costs on December 31 of each year, beginning with the year of sale.
3. The interest rates used in discounting are as follows:

Sales In:	Interest Rate
Year 1	12%
Year 2	12%
Year 3	15%
Year 4	15%
Year 5	12%
Year 6	12%

Income Recognition Using the Installment Method—With Discounting of Cash Flows

Exhibits 7.25 to 7.27 present the financial statements following this income recognition method. ALDC uses this income recognition method for tax reporting.

EXHIBIT 7.22

Arizona Land Development Company
Income Statements
Income Recognition at Time of Sale—With Discounting of Cash Flows
(Case 7.2)

	Year 1	Year 2	Year 3	Year 4	Year 5	Year 6
Sales	$ 411,336[a]	$ 569,543	$ 865,737	$1,442,895	$ 759,390	$ 253,130
Less:						
Cost of Land Inventory Sold	(65,000)	(90,000)	(150,000)	(250,000)	(120,000)	(40,000)
Estimated Development Costs	(205,668)[b]	(284,771)	(432,869)	(721,448)	(379,695)	(126,565)
Gross Profit	$ 140,668	$ 194,772	$ 282,868	$ 471,447	$ 259,695	$ 86,565
Selling Expenses	(65,000)	(90,000)	(150,000)	(250,000)	(120,000)	(40,000)
Interest Revenue	41,560[c]	96,293	196,609	361,257	411,130	400,899
Interest Expense	(20,780)[d]	(48,147)	(98,304)	(180,628)	(205,566)	(200,449)
Net Income before Taxes	$ 96,448	$ 152,918	$ 231,173	$ 402,076	$ 345,259	$ 247,015
Income Taxes:						
Current	—	—	(9,778)	(26,091)	(73,009)	(94,902)
Deferred	(32,792)	(51,992)	(68,821)	(110,615)	(44,379)	10,917
Net Income	$ 63,656	$ 100,926	$ 152,574	$ 265,370	$ 227,871	$ 163,030

[a]Represents the present value of $65,000 received on January 1, Year 1, plus the present value of a series of $65,000 cash inflows on December 31, Year 1 to Year 9, discounted at 12 percent.

[b]Represents the present value of $32,500 paid on January 1, Year 1, plus the present value of a series of $32,500 cash outflows on December 31, Year 1 to Year 9, discounted at 12 percent.

[c]12($411,336 − $65,000) = $41,560.

[d]12($205,668 − $32,500) = $20,780.

EXHIBIT 7.23

Arizona Land Development Company
Balance Sheets
Income Recognition at Time of Sale—With Discounting of Cash Flows
(Case 7.2)

	Year 1	Year 2	Year 3	Year 4	Year 5	Year 6
Assets						
Cash	$100,000	$ 132,500	$ 100,222	$ 126,631	$ 131,122	$ 273,720
Notes Receivable	322,896[a]	743,732	1,351,078	2,350,230	2,725,750	2,624,779
Land Inventory	235,000	145,000	95,000	45,000	125,000	185,000
Total Assets	$657,896	$1,021,232	$1,546,300	$2,521,861	$2,981,872	$3,083,499
Liabilities and Shareholders' Equity						
Estimated Development Cost Liability	$161,448[b]	$ 371,866	$ 675,539	$1,175,115	$1,362,876	$1,312,390
Deferred Income Taxes	32,792	84,784	153,605	264,220	308,599	297,682
Common Stock	400,000	400,000	400,000	500,000	500,000	500,000
Retained Earnings	63,656	164,582	317,156	582,526	810,397	973,427
Total Liabilities and Shareholders' Equity	$657,896	$1,021,232	$1,546,300	$2,521,861	$2,981,872	$3,083,499

[a] $411,336 − $65,000 + $41,560 − $65,000 = $322,896 (see Notes (a) and (c) to Exhibit 7.22).
[b] $205,668 − $32,500 + $20,780 − $32,500 = $161,448 (see Notes (b) and (d) to Exhibit 7.22).

EXHIBIT 7.24

Arizona Land Development Company
Statements of Cash Flows
Income Recognition at Time of Sale—With Discounting of Cash Flows
(Case 7.2)

	Year 1	Year 2	Year 3	Year 4	Year 5	Year 6
Operations						
Net Income	$ 63,656	$ 100,926	$ 152,574	$ 265,370	$ 227,871	$163,030
(Increase) Decrease in Notes Receivable	(322,896)	(420,836)	(607,346)	(999,152)	(375,520)	100,971
(Increase) Decrease in Land Inventory	65,000	90,000	50,000	50,000	(80,000)	(60,000)
Increase (Decrease) in Estimated Development Cost Liability	161,448	210,418	303,673	499,576	187,761	(50,486)
Increase (Decrease) in Deferred Income Taxes	32,792	51,992	68,821	110,615	44,379	(10,917)
Cash Flow from Operations	$ 0	$ 32,500	$ (32,278)	$ (73,591)	$ 4,491	$142,598
Financing						
Common Stock Issued	—	—	—	100,000	—	—
Change in Cash	$ 0	$ 32,500	$ (32,278)	$ 26,409	$ 4,491	$142,598

EXHIBIT 7.25

Arizona Land Development Company
Income Statements
Income Recognition Using Installment Method—With Discounting of Cash Flows
(Case 7.2)

	Year 1	Year 2	Year 3	Year 4	Year 5	Year 6
Sales Revenue	$ 88,440[a]	$148,707	$ 258,391	$ 443,744	$ 383,868	$ 354,101
Cost of Goods Sold	(58,195)[a]	(97,852)	(172,963)	(297,634)	(254,699)	(235,427)
Gross Profit	$ 30,245[a]	$ 50,855	$ 85,428	$ 146,110	$ 129,169	$ 118,674
Selling Expenses	(65,000)	(90,000)	(150,000)	(250,000)	(120,000)	(40,000)
Interest Revenue	41,560[b]	96,293	196,609	361,257	411,130	400,899
Interest Expense	(20,780)[c]	(48,147)	(98,304)	(180,628)	(205,566)	(200,449)
Net Income before Taxes	$(13,975)	$ 9,001	$ 33,733	$ 76,739	$ 214,733	$ 279,124
Income Taxes:						
Current	—[d]	—[d]	(9,778)[d]	(26,091)	(73,009)	(94,902)
Deferred	4,751	(3,060)	(1,691)	—	—	—
Net Income	$ (9,224)	$ 5,941	$ 22,264	$ 50,648	$141,724	$ 184,222

[a]Exhibit 7.22 indicates that the total gross profit from land sold in Year 1 is $140,668. The present value of the amounts that ALDC will receive from customers is $411,336 (see Exhibit 7.22). Thus, for each dollar of the $411,336 collected, the firm recognizes 34.2 cents (= $140,668/$411,336) of gross profit. During Year 1, ALDC collects $130,000 from sales of land made in Year 1 ($65,000 on January 1 and $65,000 on December 31). However, only $23,440 (= $65,000 − $41,560) of the December 31 payment represents payment of a portion of the $411,336 selling price. The remainder ($41,560) represents interest. Thus, the gross profit recognized in Year 1 is $30,245 [= .342($65,000 + $23,440)].

[b]See Note (c) to Exhibit 7.22.

[c]See Note (d) to Exhibit 7.22.

[d]ALDC carries forward the $13,975 loss in Year 1 to offset taxable income in future years ($9,001 in Year 2 and $4,974 in Year 3).

EXHIBIT 7.26

Arizona Land Development Company
Balance Sheets
Income Recognition Using Installment Method—With Discounting of Cash Flows
(Case 7.2)

	Year 1	Year 2	Year 3	Year 4	Year 5	Year 6
Assets						
Cash	$100,000	$132,500	$ 100,222	$ 126,631	$ 131,122	$ 273,720
Notes Receivable	212,473[a]	489,392	899,298	1,573,113	1,818,107	1,749,245
Land Inventory	235,000	145,000	95,000	45,000	125,000	185,000
Deferred Tax Asset	4,751	1,691	—	—	—	—
Total Assets	$552,224	$768,583	$1,094,520	$1,744,744	$2,074,229	$2,207,965
Liabilities and Shareholders' Equity						
Estimated Development Cost Liability	$161,448[b]	$371,866	$ 675,539	$1,175,115	$1,362,876	$1,312,390
Deferred Income Taxes	—	—	—	—	—	—
Common Stock	400,000	400,000	400,000	500,000	500,000	500,000
Retained Earnings	(9,224)	(3,283)	18,981	69,629	211,353	395,575
Total Liabilities and Shareholders' Equity	$552,224	$768,583	$1,094,520	$1,744,744	$2,074,229	$2,207,965

[a]The derivation of this amount is as follows:

	Notes Receivable—Gross	Deferred Gross Profit	Notes Receivable—Net
January 1, Year 1	$411,336	$140,668	$270,668
Less Cash Received, January 1, Year 1	(65,000)	—	(65,000)
Plus Interest Revenue, Year 1	41,560	—	41,560
Less Cash Received, December 31, Year 1	(65,000)	—	(65,000)
Gross Profit Recognized, Year 1	—	(30,245)	30,245
Totals	$322,896	$110,423	$212,473

[b]See Note (b) to Exhibit 7.23.

EXHIBIT 7.27

Arizona Land Development Company
Statements of Cash Flows
Income Recognition Using Installment Method—With Discounting of Cash Flows
(Case 7.2)

	Year 1	Year 2	Year 3	Year 4	Year 5	Year 6
Operations						
Net Income (Loss)	$ (9,224)	$ 5,941	$ 22,264	$ 50,648	$ 141,724	$184,222
(Increase) Decrease in Notes Receivable	(212,473)	(276,919)	(409,906)	(673,815)	(244,994)	68,862
(Increase) Decrease in Land Inventory	65,000	90,000	50,000	50,000	(80,000)	(60,000)
(Increase) Decrease in Deferred Tax Asset	(4,751)	3,060	1,691	—	—	—
(Increase) Decrease in Estimated Development Cost Liability	161,448	210,418	303,673	499,576	187,761	(50,486)
Cash Flow from Operations	$ 0	$ 32,500	$ (32,278)	$ (73,591)	$ 4,491	$142,598
Financing						
Common Stock Issued	—	—	—	100,000	—	—
Change in Cash	$ 0	$ 32,500	$ (32,278)	$ 26,409	$ 4,491	$142,598

Income Recognition Using the Percentage-of-Completion Method

Exhibits 7.28 to 7.30 present the financial statements following this income recognition method. The presumption underlying this method is that ALDC is primarily a developer of real estate and that its income should reflect its development activity, not its sales activity. The difference between the contract price and the total estimated costs of the land and development work represents the total income from development of the land. The percentage-of-completion method uses actual costs incurred to date as a percentage of estimated total costs to determine the degree of completion each period. Multiplying this percentage times the contract price yields sales revenue each year. Multiplying this percentage times the total expected costs yields cost of goods sold.

Required

a. For each of the four income recognition methods illustrated in Exhibits 7.19 through 7.30, show the supporting calculations for each of the following items for Year 2:

(1) Sales Revenue for Year 2.
(2) Cost of Goods Sold for Year 2.
(3) Gross Profit for Year 2.
(4) Notes Receivable on December 31, Year 2, under the first three income recognition methods and the Contracts in Process account on December 31, Year 2, under the fourth income recognition method.
(5) Estimated Development Costs Liability on December 31, Year 2, under the first three income recognition methods and the Progress Billings account on December 31, Year 2, under the fourth income recognition method.

b. Evaluate each of the four income recognition methods described in the case relative to the criteria for revenue and expense recognition. Which method do you think best portrays the operating performance and financial position of ALDC? Discuss your reasoning.

c. Which income recognition method is ALDC likely to prefer in reporting to shareholders?

d. Why did ALDC choose the installment method for tax reporting?

e. With respect to maximizing cumulative reported earnings, the four income recognition methods rank-order as follows:

1. Income Recognition at Time of Sale—No Discounting of Cash Flows.
2. Income Recognition at Time of Sale—With Discounting of Cash Flows.
3. Income Recognition Using the Percentage-of-Completion Method.
4. Income Recognition Using the Installment Method—With Discounting of Cash Flows.

What is the reason behind this rank ordering?

f. The difference in cumulative reported earnings between any two income recognition methods equals (1) the difference in Notes Receivable or Contracts in Process (net) minus (2) the difference in the Estimated Development Cost Liability minus (3) the difference in the Deferred Income Taxes Liability. What is the rationale behind this relation?

g. Why is the amount shown on the income statement for "current" income taxes the same in each year for all four income recognition methods but the amount of

EXHIBIT 7.28

Arizona Land Development Company
Income Statements
Income Recognition Using Percentage-of-Completion Method
(Case 7.2)

	Year 1	Year 2	Year 3	Year 4	Year 5	Year 6
Sales	$ 216,667[a]	$ 354,167	$ 629,167	$1,087,500	$ 862,500	$ 695,833
Cost of Goods Sold	(130,000)[a]	(212,500)	(377,500)	(652,500)	(517,500)	(417,500)
Gross Profit	$ 86,667[a]	$ 141,667	$ 251,667	$ 435,000	$ 345,000	$ 278,333
Selling Expenses	(65,000)	(90,000)	(150,000)	(250,000)	(120,000)	(40,000)
Net Income before Taxes	$ 21,667	$ 51,667	$ 101,667	$ 185,000	$ 225,000	$ 238,333
Income Taxes:						
Current	—	—	(9,778)	(26,091)	(73,009)	(94,902)
Deferred	(7,367)	(17,567)	(24,789)	(36,809)	(3,491)	13,869
Net Income	$ 14,300	$ 34,100	$ 67,100	$ 122,100	$ 148,500	$ 157,300

[a]Land sold under contract in Year 1 had a contract price of $650,000 and estimated contract cost of $390,000 (= $65,000 + $325,000) (see Exhibit 7.19). ALDC incurred development costs of $130,000 (= $65,000 for land + $32,500 on January 1, Year 1 + $32,500 on December 31, Year 1) during Year 1. Thus, the percentage of completion as of the end of Year 1 is 33.3 percent (= $130,000/$390,000). Sales are 33.3 percent of $650,000 and cost of goods sold is 33.3 percent of $390,000.

EXHIBIT 7.29

Arizona Land Development Company
Balance Sheets
Income Recognition Using Percentage-of-Completion Method
(Case 7.2)

	Year 1	Year 2	Year 3	Year 4	Year 5	Year 6
Assets						
Cash	$ 100,000	$ 132,500	$ 100,222	$ 126,631	$ 131,122	$ 273,720
Contracts in Process	216,667[a]	570,834	1,200,001	2,287,501	3,150,001	3,845,834
Less Progress Billings	(130,000)[b]	(375,000)	(830,000)	(1,635,000)	(2,430,000)	(3,185,000)
Contracts in Process, net	$ 86,667	$ 195,834	$ 370,001	$ 652,501	$ 720,001	$ 660,834
Land Inventory	235,000	145,000	95,000	45,000	125,000	185,000
Total Assets	$ 421,667	$ 473,334	$ 565,223	$ 824,132	$ 976,123	$ 1,119,554
Liabilities and Shareholders' Equity						
Deferred Income Taxes	$ 7,367	$ 24,934	$ 49,723	$ 86,532	$ 90,023	$ 76,154
Common Stock	400,000	400,000	400,000	500,000	500,000	500,000
Retained Earnings	14,300	48,400	115,500	237,600	386,100	543,400
Total Liabilities and Shareholders' Equity	$ 421,667	$ 473,334	$ 565,223	$ 824,132	$ 976,123	$ 1,119,554

[a]Accumulated costs of $130,000 + gross profit recognized in Year 1 of $86,667 (see Note (a) to Exhibit 7.28).

[b]Down payment of $65,000 received on January 1, Year 1, plus $65,000 installment payment received on December 31, Year 1.

EXHIBIT 7.30

Arizona Land Development Company
Statements of Cash Flows
Income Recognition Using Percentage-of-Completion Method
(Case 7.2)

	Year 1	Year 2	Year 3	Year 4	Year 5	Year 6
Operations						
Net Income	$ 14,300	$ 34,100	$ 67,100	$ 122,100	$ 148,500	$ 157,300
(Increase) Decrease in Contracts in Process	(216,667)	(354,167)	(629,167)	(1,087,500)	(862,500)	(695,833)
Increase (Decrease) in Progress Billings	130,000	245,000	455,000	805,000	795,000	755,000
(Increase) Decrease in Land Inventory	65,000	90,000	50,000	50,000	(80,000)	(60,000)
Increase (Decrease) in Deferred Income Taxes	7,367	17,567	24,789	36,809	3,491	(13,869)
Cash Flow from Operations	$ 0	$ 32,500	$ (32,278)	$ (73,591)	$ 4,491	$ 142,598
Financing						
Common Stock Issued	—	—	—	100,000	—	—
Change in Cash	$ 0	$ 32,500	$ (32,278)	$ 26,409	$ 4,491	$ 142,598

total income tax expenses (current plus deferred) in each year different across income recognition methods?

h. Given that net income each year differs across the four income recognition methods, why is the amount of cash provided by operations the same? Under what conditions would a firm report different amounts of cash flow from operations for different income recognition methods?

CASE 7.3

CHIRON CORPORATION—AN R&D PUZZLE

Chiron Corporation is in the human health care industry, applying genetic engineering and other tools of biotechnology to develop products that diagnose, prevent, and treat human diseases. Exhibit 7.31 presents an income statement for Chiron for Year 4, Year 3, and Year 2. Total revenues increased from $1,276 million in Year 2 to $1,723 million in Year 4, a 16.2 percent compound annual growth rate. Income from continuing operations increased from $181.1 million in Year 2 to $220.3 million in Year 3 and then decreased to $54.1 million in Year 4. The analyst encounters difficulties understanding the reasons for such fluctuations in profitability because of the following:

1. The company has grown both internally and through corporate acquisitions.
2. The company uses joint ventures and collaborative research agreements to develop and market new products.
3. Sales to related parties are included in total revenues for each one of the three years: $35.8 million in Year 4, $37.4 million in Year 3, and $32.1 million in Year 2.

The following sectors elaborate on these complicating factors.

Chiron operates in three major product markets:

1. **Blood testing.** This segment is dedicated to preventing the spread of infectious diseases through the development and sale of novel blood-screening assays and equipment.
2. **Biopharmaceuticals.** This segment focuses on discovering, developing, manufacturing, and marketing a range of therapeutic products for cancer and infectious and pulmonary diseases.
3. **Vaccines.** This segment offers immunizations for adult and pediatric diseases.

Blood Testing

The company's involvement in blood testing is mainly through a joint venture with Ortho-Clinical Diagnostics, a subsidiary of Johnson & Johnson. Chiron conducts research, development, and manufacturing for the Chiron/Ortho joint venture. The joint venture reimburses Chiron at cost for these services, which were as follows:

	Research and Development	Manufacturing
Year 4	$8.0	$27.8
Year 3	$9.0	$28.4
Year 2	$9.4	$22.7

Chiron's 50 percent share of the earnings of this joint venture totaled $118.2 million in Year 4, $108.3 million in Year 3, and $104.6 million in Year 2.

Biopharmaceuticals

On February 20, Year 2, Chiron acquired all of the outstanding shares of common stock of Matrix Pharmaceutical Inc. (Matrix) for $67 million. On July 2, Year 4, Chiron acquired Sagres Discovery (Sagres), a privately held company, for $12 million. Chiron accounted for both acquisitions using the purchase method. Chiron restated the assets

EXHIBIT 7.31

Partial Income Statement
Chiron Corporation
(amounts in thousands)
(Case 7.3)

	Year 4	Year 3	Year 2
Revenues			
Product Sales:			
Related Parties	$ 27,800	$ 28,400	$ 22,700
Unrelated Parties	1,240,503	1,317,433	891,421
	$1,268,303	$1,345,833	$ 914,121
Research Revenues:			
Related Parties	$ 8,000	$ 9,000	$ 9,400
Unrelated Parties	10,044	9,562	12,742
	$ 18,044	$ 18,562	$ 22,142
License Fees—Unrelated Parties	289,561	250,142	198,816
Equity in Earnings of Joint Ventures	118,246	108,298	104,576
Other Revenues	29,201	43,526	36,625
Total Revenues	$1,723,355	$1,766,361	$1,276,280
Expenses			
Research and Development	$ 431,128	$ 409,806	$ 325,792
Cost of Goods Sold	669,667	571,897	341,808
Selling and Administrative Expenses	465,779	380,388	283,712
Write-Off of In-Process Technologies	9,629	45,300	45,181
Other Operating Expenses	97,347	67,897	46,809
Total Operating Expenses	$1,673,550	$1,475,288	$1,043,302
Operating Income	$ 49,805	$ 291,073	$ 232,978
Interest Income	56,797	38,892	46,616
Other Income (Expense)	(31,308)	(21,081)	(14,739)
Income before Income Taxes	$ 75,294	$ 308,884	$ 264,855
Income Tax Expense	21,231	88,546	83,710
Income from Continuing Operations	$ 54,063	$ 220,338	$ 181,145

and liabilities of both companies to their market values and allocated the differences of $45.2 million and $9.6 million, respectively, between the purchase price and the market value of identifiable assets and liabilities to in-process technologies. The full amounts of the in-process technologies are included as separate items in operating expenses in Exhibit 7.31. The amounts allocated to in-process research and development are not deductible for tax purposes. Chiron recognizes the earnings of Matrix and Sagres subsequent to the date of acquisition.

Vaccines

On July 8, Year 3, Chiron acquired all of the outstanding shares of common stock of PowderJect for $938.6 million. Chiron accounted for the acquisition using the purchase method. Chiron restated the assets and liabilities of PowderJect to their market values and allocated the difference of $45.3 million between the purchase price and the market value of identifiable assets and liabilities to in-process technologies. The full amount of the in-process technologies is included as a separate item in operating expenses in Exhibit 7.31. The amount allocated to in-process research and development is not deductible for tax purposes. Chiron recognizes the earnings of PowderJect subsequent to the date of acquisition.

Chiron amortizes its developed-product technologies using a variety of methods. The weighted average amortization period for these intangible assets is eleven years and is included in other operating expenses in Exhibit 7.31.

Required

a. Recast the income statement of Chiron Corporation for Year 4, Year 3, and Year 2 into a format that enhances understanding of the changes in its profitability during the three-year period. Give particular consideration to the presentation of each of the following items:
1. The appropriate measure of total revenues and the classification of its components.
2. The measurement of research and development expense, particularly with respect to the treatment of cost-reimbursed research and development services and the cost of in-process purchased technologies.

b. Identify the principal reasons for the changes in the profitability of Chiron during the three-year period.

CASE 7.4

CORPORÃCION INDUSTRIAL SANLUIS: COPING WITH CHANGING PRICES

Corporãcion Industrial Sanluis (Sanluis) is a leading conglomerate firm in Mexico. The firm's main activity is the manufacture and distribution of auto parts such as leaf-springs, coil-springs, torsion bars, discs, and brake drums. The auto parts group accounts for approximately 88 percent of revenues. The remaining 12 percent of revenues results from the mining of precious metals, primarily gold and silver.

Sanluis was the first Mexican company to have its shares traded in the United States through American Depository Receipts (ADR). The financial information included in

EXHIBIT 7.32

Corporãcion Industrial Sanluis, S.A. DE C.V. and Subsidiaries
Consolidated Balance Sheet
(amounts in thousands of constant December 31, Year 8, Mexican pesos)
(Case 7.4)

	December 31:	
	Year 8	**Year 7**
Assets		
Cash and Short-Term Investment	P 219,490	P 177,670
Accounts Receivable	79,866	82,017
Inventories	64,075	68,027
Prepayments	9,856	2,282
Total Current Assets	P 373,287	P 329,996
Property, Plant, and Equipment	P 810,026	P 854,628
Accumulated Depreciation	(240,632)	(294,622)
Total Property, Plant, and Equipment	P 569,394	P 560,006
Other Assets	P 28,395	P 27,193
Total Assets	P 971,076	P 917,195
Liabilities and Shareholders' Equity		
Bank Loans	P 308,323	P 195,090
Accounts Payable	56,639	37,115
Accrued Liabilities	38,960	27,275
Total Current Liabilities	P 403,922	P 259,480
Long-Term Debt	125,957	184,993
Total Liabilities	P 529,879	P 444,473
Preferred Stock—Nominal Value	P 59,796	P 59,796
Restatement Increase	7,134	7,134
	P 66,930	P 66,930
Common Stock—Nominal Value	P 15,000	P 15,000
Restatement Increase	188,902	188,902
	P 203,902	P 203,902
Other Equity Accounts—Nominal Value	P 17,301	P 27,702
Restatement Increase	62,725	58,729
	P 80,026	P 86,431
Retained Earnings—Nominal Value	P 317,505	P 278,492
Restatement Increase	830,050	851,497
	P 1,147,555	P 1,129,989
Deficit in the Restatement of Capital	P(1,057,216)	P(1,014,530)
Total Shareholders' Equity	P 441,197	P 472,722
Total Liabilities and Shareholders' Equity	P 971,076	P 917,195

this case was provided by Sanluis during its early years as an ADR registrant. Sanluis follows generally accepted accounting principles in Mexico to prepare its financial statements. Its Year 8 financial statements and notes are attached as Exhibit 7.32 (balance sheet), Exhibit 7.33 (statement of income), and Exhibit 7.34 (statement of changes in financial position). Excerpts from the notes to its financial statements appear next. This case examines financial disclosures in Mexico with respect to changing prices and assesses Sanluis' success in coping with inflation.

EXHIBIT 7.33

Corporãcion Industrial Sanluis, S.A. DE C.V. and Subsidiaries
Consolidated Statement of Income
(amounts in thousands of constant December 31, Year 8, Mexican pesos)
(Case 7.4)

	Year 8	Year 7
Sales	P 429,471	P 411,213
Cost of Goods Sold	(334,198)	(327,489)
Depreciation and Depletion	(21,032)	(17,924)
Gross Profit	P 74,241	P 65,800
Distribution and Selling Expenses	(11,806)	(13,470)
General and Administrative Expenses	(29,100)	(36,355)
Exploration and Development Expenses	(1,320)	(2,364)
Operating Profit	P 32,015	P 13,611
Interest Expense, net	(19,536)	(18,733)
Exchange Loss, net	(7,514)	(16,540)
Gain on Net Monetary Position	19,481	29,263
Other Income, net	3,463	8,390
Income from Continuing Operations before Tax and Statutory Employee Profit Sharing	P 27,909	P 15,991
Taxes and Statutory Employee Profit Sharing	(10,343)	(8,656)
Income from Continuing Operations	P 17,566	P 7,335

EXHIBIT 7.34

Corporãcion Industrial Sanluis, S.A. DE C.V. and Subsidiaries
Consolidated Statement of Changes in Financial Position
(amounts in thousands of constant December 31, Year 8, Mexican pesos)
(Case 7.4)

	Year 8	Year 7
Operations		
Income from Continuing Operations	P 17,566	P 7,335
Depreciation and Depletion	21,032	17,925
Variation in Current Assets	17,631	3,642
Resources Provided by Operations	P 56,229	P 28,902
Financing		
Increase in Capital Stock	P —	P 66,930
Bank Loans, net	53,104	(15,643)
Resources Provided by Financing	P 53,104	P 51,287
Investing		
(Acquisition) Sale of Subsidiaries	P (9,963)	P 16,590
Acquisition of Property, Plant, and Equipment, net	(57,550)	(63,965)
Resources Used for Investing	P(67,513)	P(47,375)
Increase in Cash and Short-Term Investments	P 41,820	P 32,814
Cash and Short-Term Investments at Beginning of Year	177,670	144,856
Cash and Short-Term Investments at End of Year	P219,490	P177,670

Excerpts from Notes to the Financial Statements

Note 1: Accounting Policies

1. The consolidated financial statements have been prepared in conformity with generally accepted accounting principles in Mexico and are stated in pesos of December 31, Year 8, purchasing power.
2. Marketable Securities and other investments in shares are stated at market value.
3. Inventories are stated at estimated replacement cost. Cost of goods sold is determined by the last-in, first-out (LIFO) method.
4. Property, plant, and equipment are recorded at net replacement cost determined on the basis of appraisals made by independent experts registered at the National Securities Commission. Depreciation, amortization, and depletion are calculated by the straight-line method based on the estimated useful lives of the assets determined by the appraisers.
5. The restatement of capital stock represents the amount necessary to maintain the shareholders' investment in terms of purchasing power at the balance sheet date, and is determined by applying to the historical amounts factors derived from the National Consumer Price Index (NCPI).

6. Retained Earnings is expressed in pesos of purchasing power as of the latest balance sheet date and is determined by applying to the historical amounts factors derived from the NCPI.
7. The gain on net monetary position represents the effect of inflation, as measured by NCPI, on the company's monthly net monetary assets and liabilities during the year, restated in pesos of purchasing power as of the end of the most recent period.
8. The gain or loss from holding nonmonetary assets represents the amount by which the increases in the values of nonmonetary assets exceeds or falls short of the inflation rate measured in terms of the NCPI, and is included in the deficit in the restatement of capital.

Required

a. Which of the methods of accounting for changing prices discussed in Appendix 7.1 does Sanluis apparently use? Indicate the clues supporting your conclusion.

b. Prepare a balance sheet for Sanluis as of December 31, Year 8, under each of the three methodologies indicated in the columns of the following table. Aggregate individual assets in preparing this analysis. You should begin with liabilities and shareholders' equity and work backward toward total assets.

	Historical Cost/ Nominal Pesos	Historical Cost/ Constant Pesos	Current Cost/ Constant Pesos
Assets			
Liabilities			
Preferred Stock			
Common Stock			
Other Equity Accounts. . .			
Retained Earnings			
Deficit in Restatement of Capital			
Total Equities			

c. What is the likely explanation for Sanluis' recognition of a purchasing power gain on its monetary items during Year 8?

d. Did Sanluis experience a holding gain or a holding loss on its nonmonetary items (that is, inventories and fixed assets) during Year 8? What is the interpretation of this gain or loss?

e. How well has Sanluis coped with changing prices during Year 7 and Year 8? NOTE: Mexico's consumer price index increased 18.8 percent in Year 7 and 11.9 percent in Year 8.

Chapter **8**

Liability Recognition and Related Expenses

Learning Objectives

1. **Examine the criteria for the recognition of an obligation as an accounting liability and apply these criteria to various obligations of a firm, including financing arrangements structured to keep debt off the balance sheet.**
2. **Understand the effects of the accounting methods for operating and capital leases on the financial statements and the adjustments required to convert operating leases to capital leases.**
3. **Understand the use of derivative financial instruments for hedging risks and the effects of fair value hedges and cash flow hedges on the financial statements.**
4. **Understand the relation between the accounting records of the sponsoring employer of a pension or other retirement plan and the accounting records of the plan itself, and the reasons for differences between the two sets of records. Adjust the financial statements of the sponsoring employer to incorporate information from the accounting records of the retirement plan with respect to any unrecognized obligation.**
5. **Review the reasons for differences between the book values of assets and liabilities for financial reporting and their tax bases and the effect of such differences on the measurement of income tax expense.**
6. **Use information in the financial statement note on income taxes to identify reasons for changes in the income tax burden of a firm.**
7. **Understand the various uses of reserve accounts, the information they convey, and their potential for managing earnings over time.**

This chapter discusses the accounting for liabilities and related expenses commonly encountered in annual reports. The recognition and valuation of liabilities affect the analysis of financial statements in two important ways:

1. Risk Analysis

The amount shown on the balance sheet for liabilities typically indicates the present value of the cash or other assets that the firm will need to satisfy obligations coming due within the next year (current liabilities) and after one year (noncurrent liabilities). A firm with inadequate resources to satisfy these obligations runs the risk of insolvency or even bankruptcy. Effective analysis of risk requires the analyst to assess whether the firm has recognized and measured all of its economic obligations as liabilities. Recognition issues are particularly important because many firms engage in transactions that create financial risk but do not recognize a liability on the balance sheet for such risks. In fact, GAAP stipulates that the firm not recognize a liability in some cases.

This chapter discusses the concept of an accounting liability and the application of GAAP to various obligations commonly encountered in corporate financial statements, including (1) leases, (2) derivatives, (3) pension and other retirement benefits, and (4) income taxes. We continue our focus on how a firm's choice of accounting methods and the way it implements them affect its *accounting quality*, its *earnings quality*, and its *balance sheet quality*, topics introduced in Chapter 6. A starting point for assessing accounting quality is to understand GAAP's required accounting for a particular transaction. This chapter describes and illustrates GAAP for each of the preceding topics. When the reported amounts for liabilities do not adequately include the economic obligations of a firm, the analyst should adjust the reported amounts to enhance the economic information content of the financial statements.

2. Profitability Analysis

Firms use, or consume, various goods (such as inventories) and services (such as employees' labor services) during a period in generating revenues for which they may not make cash payments until future periods. Also, firms promise to provide goods or perform services in the future related to revenues recognized during the current period (for example, under warranty plans). The costs of these goods and services that the firm has consumed in the current period are expenses of the current period. Effective analysis of profitability requires that the analyst assess whether the firm has measured these expenses properly.

PRINCIPLES OF LIABILITY RECOGNITION

Financial reporting recognizes an obligation as a liability if it satisfies three criteria:[1]

1. The obligation involves a probable future sacrifice of resources—a future transfer of cash, goods, or services, or the forgoing of a future cash receipt—at a specified or determinable date. The firm can measure with reasonable precision the cash-equivalent value of the resources needed to satisfy the obligation.
2. The firm has little or no discretion to avoid the transfer.
3. The transaction or event that gave rise to the obligation has already occurred.

PRINCIPLES OF LIABILITY VALUATION

The general principles underlying the valuation of liabilities are as follows:

1. Liabilities requiring future cash payments (such as bonds payable) appear at the present value of the required future cash flows discounted at an interest rate that reflects the uncertainty that the firm will be able to make these cash payments. The firm establishes the discount rate at the time it initially records a liability in the accounts (often referred to as the *historical interest rate*) and uses this interest rate in accounting for the liability in all future periods.

---

[1]Financial Accounting Standards Board, *Statement of Financial Accounting Standards No. 6*, "Elements of Financial Statements" (1985).

An exception to using the historical interest rate involves liabilities for which firms have hedged interest or foreign-exchange risk. A later section of this chapter indicates that firms in these cases report the liability and the related hedge instrument at the present value of the cash flows using the current market interest rate. For some liabilities due within the next year (such as accounts payable, income taxes payable, and salaries payable), the difference between the amount of the future cash flows and their present value is sufficiently small that accounting ignores the discounting process and reports the liabilities at the amounts ultimately payable.

2. Liabilities requiring the future delivery of goods or services (such as warranties payable) appear at the estimated cost of those goods and services.
3. Liabilities representing advances from customers (such as Rental Fees Received in Advance or Subscription Fees Received in Advance) appear at the amount of the cash advance.

The fair value of a liability may differ from the amount appearing on the balance sheet, particularly for long-term debt. The fair value will reflect current interest rates and assessments of the firm's ability to make the required payments. U.S. GAAP requires firms to disclose the fair values of financial instruments, whether or not these financial instruments appear as liabilities (or assets) on the balance sheet.[2] For example, PepsiCo's Note 10, "Risk Management" (Appendix A), reports both the book value and fair value of a range of financial instruments held by the firm at the end of Year 4 and Year 3.

APPLICATION OF CRITERIA FOR LIABILITY RECOGNITION

The criteria for liability recognition may appear straightforward and subject to unambiguous interpretation. Unfortunately, this is not so. Various obligations of an enterprise fall along a continuum with respect to how well they satisfy these criteria. Exhibit 8.1 classifies obligations into six groups. The following sections discuss each of these groups.

Obligations with Fixed Payment Dates and Amounts

The obligations that most clearly satisfy the liability recognition criteria are those with fixed payment dates and amounts (typically set by contract). Most obligations arising from borrowing arrangements fall into this category. A firm receives the benefit of having funds available for its use. The borrowing agreement specifies the timing and amount of interest and principal payments.

Obligations with Fixed Payment Amounts but Estimated Payment Dates

Most current liabilities fall into this category. Either oral agreements, written agreements, or legal statutes fix the amounts payable to suppliers, employees, and government agencies. Firms normally settle these obligations within a few months after incurring them. The firm can estimate the settlement date with sufficient accuracy to warrant recognizing a liability.

Obligations with Estimated Payment Dates and Amounts

Obligations in this group require estimation because the firm cannot identify the specific future recipients of cash, goods, or services at the time the obligation becomes a liability.

[2]Financial Accounting Standards Board, *Statement of Financial Accounting Standards No. 107*, "Disclosures about Fair Value of Financial Instruments" (1991).

EXHIBIT 8.1

Classification of Accounting Liabilities by Degree of Uncertainty

Obligations with Fixed Payment Dates and Amounts	Obligations with Fixed Payment Amounts but Estimated Payment Dates	Obligations for Which the Firm Must Estimate Both Timing and Amount of Payment	Obligations Arising from Advances from Customers on Unexecuted Contracts and Agreements	Obligations under Mutually Unexecuted Contracts	Contingent Obligations[a]
Notes Payable Interest Payable Bonds Payable	Accounts Payable Salaries Payable Taxes Payable	Warranties Payable Insurance claims	Rental Fees Received in Advance Subscription Fees Received in Advance	Purchase Commitments Employment Commitments	Unsettled Lawsuits Financial Instruments with Off-Balance-Sheet Risk Loan Guarantees

Most Certain ←——→ Least Certain

←—— Recognized as Accounting Liabilities ——→ ←—— Not Generally Recognized as Accounting Liabilities ——→

[a]If an obligation meets certain criteria for a loss contingency, firms must recognize this obligation as a liability. See the discussion later in this chapter.

In addition, the firm cannot compute precisely the amount of resources it will transfer in the future. For example, when a firm sells products under a warranty agreement, it promises to replace defective parts or perform certain repair services for a specified period of time. At the time of sale, the firm can neither identify the specific customers who will receive warranty benefits nor ascertain the amounts of their claims. Past experience, however, often provides the necessary information for estimating the likely proportion of customers who will make claims and the probable average amount of their claims. As long as the firm can estimate the probable amount of the obligation, it satisfies the first criterion for a liability. The selling price of goods sold under warranty includes an explicit or implicit charge for the warranty services. Thus, the receipt of cash or the right to receive cash in the sales transaction benefits the firm and creates the warranty liability.

Obligations Arising from Advances from Customers on Unexecuted Contracts and Agreements

A firm sometimes receives cash from customers in advance for goods or services it will provide in a future period. For example, a rental firm may receive cash in advance of the rental period on rental property. A magazine publisher may receive subscription fees in advance of the subscription period. Organizations and associations may receive membership dues prior to the membership period. Airlines may receive cash for tickets prior to travel by the passengers. These firms could recognize revenue on receipt of cash, as with the sale of products under warranty plans. In the case of advances from customers, however, all of the required transfer of resources (goods or services) will occur in the future. Revenue recognition generally requires that the firm deliver the goods or provide the services. Thus, the receipt of cash in advance creates a liability equal to the cash received. The firm might conceivably recognize a liability equal to the expected cost of delivering the promised goods or services, but doing so would result in recognizing the profit from the transaction before substantial performance had occurred.

Obligations under Mutually Unexecuted Contracts

Mutually unexecuted contracts arise when two entities agree to transfer resources but *neither* entity has yet made a transfer. For example, a firm may agree to purchase from its suppliers specified amounts of merchandise over the next two years. A baseball organization may agree to pay its "franchise" player a certain sum as compensation for services the player will render over the next five years. A bank may agree to provide lines of credit to its business customers in the event that these firms need funds in the future. Both parties have exchanged promises but neither party has transferred resources. Thus, no accounting liability arises at the time of the exchange of promises. A liability arises only when one party or the other transfers resources in the future. This category of obligation, called executory contracts, differs from the preceding two, in which the contracts or agreements are partially executed. With warranty agreements, a firm receives cash but has not fulfilled its warranty obligation. With rental, subscription, and membership fees, a firm receives cash but has not provided the required goods or services.

GAAP generally does not require firms to recognize obligations under mutually unexecuted contracts as accounting liabilities (exceptions occur for some leasing arrangements and for derivatives, discussed later in this chapter). If the amounts involved are material, the firm must disclose the nature of the obligation and its amount in notes to the financial statements. The analyst might conclude, however, that these obligations create sufficient risk for the firm to justify adjusting the reported financial statements to include such obligations.

Contingent Obligations

An event whose outcome today is unknown may create an obligation for the future transfer of resources. For example, a firm may be a defendant in a lawsuit, the outcome of which depends on the results of legal proceedings. Or a firm may guarantee loans of a subsidiary. The obligation is *contingent* on future events.

Contingent obligations may or may not give rise to accounting liabilities. Financial reporting requires firms to recognize an estimated loss from a contingency (called a *loss contingency*) and a related liability only if both of the following conditions are met:

1. Information available prior to the issuance of the financial statements indicates that it is probable that an asset has been impaired or that a liability has been incurred.
2. The firm can estimate the amount of the loss with reasonable precision.[3]

The first criterion for recognition of a loss contingency rests on the probability, or likelihood, that an asset has been impaired or a liability has been incurred. Financial reporting does not provide clear guidance as to what probability cutoff defines *likely* or

---

[3]Financial Accounting Standards Board, *Statement of Financial Accounting Standards No. 5*, "Accounting for Contingencies" (1975).

probable. The FASB has stated that "probable is used with its usual general meaning, rather than in a specific accounting or technical sense, and refers to that which can be expected or believed on the basis of available evidence or logic but is neither certain or proved."[4]

The second criterion requires reasonable estimation of the amount of the loss. Again, financial reporting does not define *reasonably estimated* in precise terms. Instead, if the firm can narrow the amount of the loss to a reasonable range, however large, financial reporting presumes that the firm has achieved sufficient precision to justify recognition of a liability. The amount of the loss is the most likely estimate within the range. If no amount within the range is more likely than any other, then the firm should use the amount at the lower end of the range.

Financial reporting refers to obligations meeting both of these two criteria as loss contingencies. One example suggested by the FASB relates to a toy manufacturer that sold toys later found to present a safety hazard. The toy manufacturer concludes that the likelihood of having to pay damages is high. The firm meets the second criterion if experience or other information enables the manufacturer to make a reasonable estimate of the loss. The toy manufacturer recognizes a loss and a liability in this case. As another example, firms in the tobacco industry and environmentally sensitive industries grapple with measuring loss contingencies related to litigation, and draw on lawyers and others to facilitate quantifying the loss.

Closely related to the concept of a loss contingency is a *guarantee*. For example, one firm may guarantee the repayment of another entity's borrowing in the event the other entity cannot repay the loan at maturity. As another example, a firm may sell a portion of its accounts receivable to another entity, promising to reimburse the other entity if uncollectible accounts exceed a specified amount. The need to make a future cash payment is contingent on future events. GAAP requires firms to recognize the market value of the guarantee as a liability.[5] Measuring this market value involves estimating the likelihood, timing, and amount that might become payable. However, a guarantee can have a market value even when the likelihood of making a future payment is low. A guarantee by a financially strong firm of a financially weaker firm's debt will reduce the weaker firm's cost of borrowing. The guarantor recognizes a receivable and a liability for the market value of the benefit granted to the borrower by the grantor. The obligation to reimburse a purchaser of accounts receivable for excess uncollectibles likely increases the amount the buyer pays the seller for the receivables. Recognizing the market value of this guarantee as a liability affects the amount of gain or loss the seller recognizes on the sale of the receivables. In addition to recognizing the market value of guarantees as liabilities, firms must disclose the maximum amount that could become payable and any available collateral that the guarantor could recover in the event it must execute the guarantee.

Note 10, "Risk Management," of PepsiCo's financial statements (Appendix A) states the following:

> We have guaranteed $2.3 billion of Bottling Group, LLC's long-term debt through Year 12. The guarantee had a fair value of $46 million at December 25, Year 4 and $35 million at December 27, Year 3, based on an external estimate of the cost to us of transferring the liability to an independent financial institution.

---

[4]*Statement of Financial Accounting Concepts No. 6* (1985). Although the FASB has not defined *probable*, practice demands that firms and auditors define it. Currently, most firms and auditors appear to use *probable* to mean 80 to 85 percent or larger.

[5]Financial Accounting Standards Board, *Interpretation No. 45*, "Guarantor's Accounting and Disclosure Requirements for Guarantees, Including Indirect Indebtedness of Others" (2002).

PepsiCo discusses these guarantees further in its Management's Discussion and Analysis (MD&A) (Appendix B):

> It is not our business practice to enter into off-balance sheet arrangements, other than in the normal course of business, nor is it our policy to issue guarantees to our bottlers, noncontrolled affiliates or third parties. However, certain guarantees were necessary to facilitate the separation of our bottling and restaurant operations from us. As of year-end 4, we believe it is remote that these guarantees would require any cash payment.

The financial statements and notes have high accounting quality if they disclose sufficient information for the analyst to judge whether a particular firm's contingencies and guarantees warrant recognition as a liability on the balance sheet and, if so, the appropriate amount. However, firms seldom disclose sufficient information for the analyst to make these judgments.

CONTROVERSIAL ISSUES IN LIABILITY RECOGNITION

Most obligations discussed in the preceding sections clearly either were liabilities or were not liabilities. However, firms sometimes structure innovative financing arrangements in ways that may not satisfy the criteria for the recognition of a liability. That is, firms have structured financing in such a way that GAAP treats any obligation as either an executory contract or a contingency. The principal aim of such arrangements is to reduce the amount shown as liabilities on the balance sheet. Investors and lenders often use the proportion of debt in a firm's capital structure as a measure of risk and therefore as a factor in establishing the cost of funds. (Chapter 5 discusses various ratios for measuring risk, and Chapter 11 describes techniques for using a firm's capital structure to compute the weighted average cost of capital.) Other things being equal, firms prefer to obtain funds without showing a liability on the balance sheet in the hope that future lenders will ignore the risks associated with such financing in setting interest rates. Although there is little empirical evidence to support the notion that lenders ignore such financing in assessing a firm's risk, some firms act as if lenders do overlook such borrowing.

Issuance of Hybrid Securities

One means of reducing the amount shown as liabilities is to issue securities that have both debt and equity characteristics (referred to as *hybrid securities* or *compound financing instruments*) but classify them as equity on the balance sheet. Some firms have issued preferred stock that is subject to mandatory redemption after some period of time by the issuing firm. For example, in the past Sears, Roebuck and Co. borrowed funds through the issuance of "Series A Mandatory Exchangeable Preferred Shares." The preferred stock paid an annual cumulative dividend of $3.75 per share before it was retired. Stock of this nature often has economic characteristics that are more like debt than equity. Firms have also issued preferred stock that is subject to a call option by the issuing firm. The firm sets out provisions in the preferred-stock agreement that make exercise of the call option highly probable. This preferred stock also has more debt than equity characteristics.

GAAP requires firms to report most types of hybrid securities as liabilities.[6] For example, standard setters require that firms classify preferred stock subject to mandatory

---

[6]Financial Accounting Standards Board, Statement No. *150*, "Accounting for Certain Financial Instruments with Characteristics of Both Liabilities and Equity" (2003).

redemption as a liability. Although financial reporting attempts to classify all financial instruments as either a liability or a shareholders' equity account, the securities of most firms fall along a continuum from pure debt to pure equity.

Off-Balance-Sheet Financing Arrangements

Another means of reducing the amount shown as liabilities on the balance sheet is to structure a borrowing arrangement so that the firm does not recognize a liability (referred to as *off-balance-sheet financing*). Firms usually accomplish off-balance-sheet financing using one or a combination of two approaches: (1) sale of an existing asset and (2) use of another entity to obtain the financing.

Sale of an Existing Asset

A firm may use accounts receivable, inventories, property, plant, equipment, and other assets as collateral for a loan. If the firm borrowed funds, using the assets as collateral, it would increase cash and increase a liability. The notes to its financial statements would disclose that certain assets were serving as collateral for the loan. Structuring the transaction in this way places debt on the balance sheet.

If, on the other hand, the firm sold the same asset to the provider of the funds, it would increase cash, reduce the asset transferred, and recognize a gain or loss for the difference. It would have the cash but would not show a liability on the balance sheet. This is appropriate as long as the sale did not expose the selling firm to the risk of having to make payments to the purchaser in the future (for example, if the selling firm had to guarantee that the purchaser could resell the asset for a certain minimum amount).

Use of Another Entity to Obtain Financing

The general theme of this approach to accomplishing off-balance-sheet financing is that the firm obtains access to the asset that the funds finance, but neither the asset nor its financing appears on the firm's balance sheet. Instead, they appear on the balance sheet of another entity.

Suppose, for example, that a firm needs additional manufacturing capacity but does not want to borrow funds to build the extra plant assets. Instead, it commits to purchase a certain amount of output from an unaffiliated company at a specified cost that covers operating and debt-service costs. The unaffiliated company takes the purchase commitment to a financial institution and obtains a loan. The unaffiliated company uses the loan proceeds to construct the needed capacity. The new plant assets and the loan appear on the balance sheet of the unaffiliated company. The purchase commitment is a mutually unexecuted contract of the firm initially needing the additional manufacturing capacity. Recall from the earlier discussion and Exhibit 8.1 that firms do not recognize mutually unexecuted contracts as liabilities.

Alternatively, the firm can accomplish the same result using an affiliated company, one over which it has a greater degree of influence than an unaffiliated one. The key to keeping debt off the balance sheet in this case is to ensure that GAAP does not require the firm to prepare consolidated financial statements with the affiliated company. Consolidated statements aggregate the separate financial statements of two or more entities under the control of one of the entities. The debt will appear on the consolidated balance sheet as long as it appears on the balance sheet of any one entity in the consolidated group. (Chapter 9 discusses consolidated financial statements more fully.) To avoid consolidation, the firm needing the financing must not effectively *control* the entity obtaining the financing.

One means of avoiding consolidation is to set up a joint venture with another entity, with each entity owning 50 percent of the common stock. In this case, neither firm controls the joint venture. GAAP currently does not require either firm to prepare consolidated financial statements with the joint venture.

Another means of avoiding consolidation is to set up a *special-purpose entity (SPE).* The SPE obtains financing and either (1) constructs or acquires the asset desired by the firm attempting to keep debt off its balance sheet or (2) purchases the particular asset from this firm. In both cases, the asset held by the SPE serves as collateral for the loan. The lender to the SPE will likely require some commitment from the firm that sets up the SPE to ensure repayment of the loan. The commitment may take the form of a noncancelable purchase commitment or a loan guarantee. The key to avoiding consolidation is that effective control of the SPE must not reside primarily with the firm setting it up. The SPE must have economic substance of its own and other parties, either the lender or other equity owners, must be the primary beneficiary of the SPE.

Central to the bankruptcy of Enron was the misuse of SPEs to hold off-balance-sheet derivative instruments and securities initially acquired by Enron and keep the related financing for these instruments and securities off the balance sheet. Enron did not consolidate these SPEs, maintaining that it did not control them. Later revelations showed that Enron had effective control, requiring Enron to restate its previously issued financial statements. The restatements increased assets and liabilities on the balance sheet and eliminated gains that Enron recognized on the "sale" of the assets to the SPEs. Chapter 9 discusses the accounting for SPEs.

The following sections describe several off-balance-sheet financing arrangements. In several cases, the FASB has issued an accounting standard that specifies how firms should treat such transactions for financial reporting purposes. In other cases, the FASB has not issued a specific financial reporting standard and the accountant must apply the general criteria for liability recognition when deciding whether to recognize a liability.

Sale of Receivables

Firms sometimes sell their accounts receivable as a means of obtaining financing. If collections from customers are not sufficient to repay the amount borrowed plus interest, then the firm may have to pay the difference (that is, the lender has recourse against the borrowing firm).

The question arises as to whether the recourse provision creates an accounting liability. Some argue that the arrangement is similar to a collateralized loan. The firm should leave the receivables on its books and recognize a liability in the amount of the cash received. Others argue that the firm has sold an asset; it should recognize a liability only if it is *probable* that collections from customers will be insufficient and the firm will be required to repay some portion of the amount received.

The FASB requires that firms recognize transfers of receivables as sales only if the transferor surrenders control of the receivables. Firms surrender control only if all of the following conditions are met:

1. The assets transferred (that is, receivables) have been isolated from the selling ("transferor") firm (that is, neither the transferor nor a creditor of the selling firm could access the receivables in the event of the seller's bankruptcy).
2. The buying ("transferee") firm obtains the right to pledge or exchange the transferred assets, and no condition both constrains the transferee from taking advantage of its right and provides more than a trivial benefit to the transferor.

3. The selling firm does not maintain effective control over the assets transferred through either (a) an agreement that both entitles and obligates it to repurchase the assets or (b) the ability to unilaterally cause the transferee to return specific assets.[7]

The principal refinement to the concept of an accounting liability brought out by *Statement No. 140* relates to identifying the party involved in the transaction that controls the determination of which party enjoys the economic benefits and sustains the economic risk of the assets (receivables in this case). If the selling (borrowing) firm controls the economic benefits/risks, then the transaction is a collateralized loan. If the arrangement transfers these benefits/risks to the buying (lending) firm, then the transaction is a sale.

Example 1

A large retail department store chain reports credit card receivables on its balance sheet on December 31, Year 4. The firm decides to sell some of its credit card receivables to an SPE. The SPE securitizes these receivables by selling debt and equity interests in the SPE to various lenders and investors, with the firm retaining a residual interest. The residual interest serves as a credit enhancement to the SPE. Lenders and investors in the SPE receive cash as customers repay the receivables. The firm does not guarantee the debt of the SPE. Lenders to the SPE have no claim on the firm's assets. However, the firm must contribute additional credit card receivables to the SPE if uncollectible accounts held in the SPE exceed certain amounts. In this case, the firm has a continuing involvement with the receivables by bearing the risk of uncollectible accounts. The SPE apparently cannot maintain its credit ratings over time unless the firm assumes the ongoing risk of changes in the amount of uncollectible accounts. This continuing involvement raises questions as to whether the transferred receivables have been isolated from the firm or whether creditors could lay claim to them in bankruptcy proceedings. The firm treats the transfer of receivables as a collateralized loan, concluding that the ongoing obligation to maintain the credit rating of the SPE constitutes a continuing involvement with the receivables that violates the first condition to qualify as a sale.

Example 2

General Motors Corporation (GM) reported finance receivables on its balance sheet of \$99.8 billion on December 31, Year 11. GM states that it sold automobile loans and other receivables totaling \$132.9 billion to SPEs. The SPEs securitize these receivables by selling debt and equity interests to various investors, with GM retaining a residual equity interest as a credit enhancement to the SPE. GM's residual equity interest is at risk if cash flows from customers are insufficient to repay amounts borrowed. However, GM does not guarantee the debt of the SPEs nor guarantee a return to other equity investors, nor remain liable for excess uncollectibles. The SPEs in this case appear able to maintain their credit ratings on an ongoing basis and do not need a continuing involvement from GM to deal with excess uncollectibles. GM accounts for these receivables as a sale, not a collateralized loan. The lenders and investors bear the risk of any losses from uncollectible accounts beyond GM's residual equity interest.

---

[7]Financial Accounting Standards Board, *Statement of Financial Accounting Standards No. 140*, "Accounting for Transfers and Servicing of Financial Assets and Extinguishments of Liabilities" (2000).

Product Financing Arrangements

Product financing arrangements occur when a firm (sponsor) does either of the following:

1. Sells inventory to another entity and, in a related transaction, agrees to repurchase the inventory at specified prices over specified times.
2. Arranges for another entity to purchase inventory items on the firm's behalf and, in a related transaction, agrees to purchase the inventory items from the other entity.

The first arrangement is similar to the sale of receivables with recourse except that greater certainty exists that the inventory transaction will require a future cash outflow. The second arrangement is structured to appear as a purchase commitment. In this case, however, the sponsoring firm usually creates an SPE for the sole purpose of acquiring the inventory. The sponsoring firm usually guarantees the debt incurred by the SPE in acquiring the inventory.

Financial reporting requires that firms recognize product financing arrangements as liabilities if they meet two conditions:

1. The arrangement requires the sponsoring firm to purchase the inventory, substantially identical inventory, or processed goods of which the inventory is a component at specified prices.
2. The payments made to the other entity cover all acquisition, holding, and financing costs.[8]

The second criterion requires that the sponsoring firm recognize a liability whenever it incurs the economic risks (such as changing costs or interest rates) of purchasing and holding inventory, even though it may not physically control the inventory or have a legal obligation to the supplier of the inventory. Thus, as with sales of receivables with recourse, a firm recognizes a liability when it controls the determination of which party enjoys the economic benefits and incurs the economic risks of the asset involved. It also recognizes an asset of equal amount, usually inventory.

Research and Development Financing Arrangements

When a firm borrows funds to conduct research and development, it recognizes a liability at the time of borrowing and recognizes expenses as it incurs research and development costs.

Firms have engaged in innovative means of financing aimed at both keeping liabilities off the balance sheet and effectively excluding research and development expenses from the income statement.

Example 3

Merck, a pharmaceutical company, forms joint ventures with other pharmaceutical companies to develop, manufacture, and market new products. The joint venture between Merck and Schering-Plough focuses on cholesterol management and respiratory therapeutic products. The joint venture of Merck and Johnson & Johnson (Johnson & Johnson/Merck Pharmaceuticals, Inc.) involves nonprescription (primarily over-the-counter) medicines. Merck's joint venture with Aventis works in animal care products. Merck's joint venture with Aventis Pasteur focuses on vaccines. Thus, Merck conducts a significant amount

---

[8]Financial Accounting Standards Board, *Statement of Financial Accounting Standards No. 49*, "Accounting for Product Financing Arrangements" (1981).

of pharmaceutical research through joint ventures. Because the joint ventures are owned equally by the two entities in each case, Merck does not consolidate the financial statements of the joint ventures with its own financial statements. Any liabilities of the joint ventures appear on the financial statements of the joint ventures, not on Merck's balance sheet. Likewise, the research and development expense of the joint ventures appears on the income statement issued by the joint ventures, not on Merck's income statement.

Firms use other arrangements besides joint ventures. Although the structures vary somewhat across firms, they generally operate as follows:

1. The sponsoring firm contributes either preliminary development work or rights to future products to a partnership in exchange for a general interest in the partnership. It obtains limited partners (often corporate directors or officers) who contribute cash for their partnership interests.
2. The sponsoring firm conducts research and development work for the partnership for a fee. The sponsoring firm usually performs the research and development on a best-efforts basis, with no guarantee of success. The sponsoring firm recognizes amounts received from the partnership for research and development services as revenues. The amount of revenue generally equals or exceeds the research and development costs it incurs.
3. The rights to any resulting products usually reside in the partnership. However, the partnership agreement usually constrains the returns and risks of the limited partners. The sponsoring firm can often acquire the limited partners' interests in the partnership if valuable products emerge. On the other hand, the sponsoring firm may have to guarantee certain minimum royalty payments to the partnership or agree to purchase the partnership's rights to the product.

In arrangements like these, a primary objective of the sponsoring firm involves obtaining financing for its research and development work without having to recognize a liability.

Criteria exist for when firms must recognize such financing arrangements as liabilities.[9] The sponsoring firm recognizes a liability under the following conditions:

1. If the contractual agreement requires the sponsoring firm to repay any of the funds provided by the other parties regardless of the outcome of the research and development.
2. If surrounding conditions indicate that the sponsoring firm bears the risk of failure of the research and development work, even though the contractual agreement does not obligate it to repay the other parties. For example, if a sponsoring firm guarantees the debt of the partnership, must make minimum royalty payments to the partnership, or must acquire the partnership's interest in any product, then the sponsoring firm bears the risk of the research and development work.

The criteria require that, as with the off-balance-sheet financing arrangements involving receivables and inventories discussed previously, firms recognize liabilities when they bear the risk associated with the asset or product involved in the financing of a joint venture for research and development.[10]

---

[9]Financial Accounting Standards Board, *Statement of Financial Accounting Standards No. 68*, "Research and Development Arrangements" (1982).

[10]A study of firms that conduct their research and development through limited partnerships found that the stock market appears to consider the call option that firms have on research findings in the valuation of the firm. The author calls for improved disclosure of these arrangements instead of recognition of a liability in the balance sheet. See Terry Shevlin, "The Valuation of R&D Firms with R&D Limited Partnerships," *Accounting Review* (January 1991), pp. 1–21.

The joint ventures formed by Merck and the other pharmaceutical companies operate as independent entities, with broad oversight by the two joint owners. The joint ventures retain the rights to products developed. Neither joint owner guarantees any debt of the joint ventures. Neither joint owner must pay the other joint owner any amounts if the research effort is nonproductive. Although the two joint owners ultimately bear the risk of failure of the joint venture, GAAP accounting for the Merck joint ventures requires only that the joint owners recognize their equity investment in the joint venture on the balance sheet.

Take-or-Pay or Throughput Contracts

A take-or-pay contract is an agreement in which a purchaser agrees to pay specified amounts periodically to a seller for products or services. A throughput contract is similar to a take-or-pay contract except that the "product" purchased is transportation or processing services.

To understand the rationale for such arrangements, consider the following case. Suppose that two petroleum companies need additional refining capacity. If either company builds a refinery, it will record an asset and any related financing on its balance sheet. Suppose instead that the two companies form a joint venture to construct a refinery. The joint venture, an entity separate from the two petroleum companies, obtains financing and constructs the refinery. In order to secure financing for the joint venture, the two petroleum companies sign take-or-pay contracts agreeing to make certain payments to the joint venture each period for refining services. The payments are sufficient to cover all operating and financing costs of the refinery. The joint owners must make the payments even if they acquire no refinery services.

The economic substance of this arrangement is that each petroleum company owns half of the refinery and is obligated to the extent of half of the financing. The legal status of the arrangement is that the two firms have simply signed noncancelable purchase commitments (that is, executory contracts). Accounting likewise treats these arrangements as executory contracts. At the time of signing the contract, the firms are not viewed as yet having received any benefits that obligate them to pay. As they receive benefits or incur obligations over time, a liability arises. If one or the other entity guarantees the debt of the partnership, the guarantee is a contingent obligation, which GAAP does not recognize as a liability until future events indicate that payment is probable.

Financial reporting requires firms to disclose take-or-pay and throughput commitments in the notes.[11] The analyst should examine disclosures of these commitments in notes to the financial statements to assess whether the firm incurs the risks and rewards of the arrangement and should therefore recognize a liability.

Summary of Off-Balance-Sheet Financing

The conventional accounting model based on historical cost is exchange oriented or transaction oriented. Accounting recognizes events when an exchange takes place. The criteria for liability recognition discussed earlier in this chapter and in Exhibit 8.1 illustrate this exchange orientation. Accounting recognizes liabilities when a firm incurs an obligation to sacrifice resources in the future for benefits already received. Financial reporting has typically not recognized mutually unexecuted contracts as liabilities because the parties have merely exchanged promises to perform in the future. Financial reporting also does not generally require the recognition of contingent obligations as liabilities because some future event must occur to establish the existence of a liability.

[11]Financial Accounting Standards Board, *Statement of Financial Accounting Standards No. 47*, "Disclosure of Long-Term Obligations," 1981.

The evolving concept of an accounting liability recognizes that exchanges of promises can have economic substance even though a legal obligation to pay does not immediately arise. When a firm controls the determination of which party enjoys the economic benefits and/or incurs the economic risks from an asset, then the firm should recognize the asset and its related financing.

The FASB closely monitors reporting issues related to off-balance-sheet commitments of firms, but it continues to be challenged because of the ever-changing nature of business financing arrangements and the flexible and fluid organizational arrangements that firms create.

LEASES

Many firms acquire rights to use assets through long-term leases. A company might, for example, agree to lease an office suite for five years or an entire building for forty years, promising to pay a fixed periodic fee for the duration of the lease. Leasing provides benefits to lessees, the users of the leased assets, such as the following:

1. Ability to shift the tax benefits of depreciation and other deductions from a lessee that has little or no taxable income (such as an airline) to a lessor, or owner of the asset, that has substantial taxable income. The lessee expects the lessor to share some of the benefits of these tax deductions by allowing lower lease payments.
2. Flexibility to change capacity as needed without having to purchase or sell assets.
3. Ability to reduce the risk of technological obsolescence, relative to outright ownership, by maintaining the flexibility to shift to technologically more advanced assets.
4. Ability to finance the "acquisition" of an asset using lessor financing when alternative sources of financing are unavailable or more costly.

These potential benefits of leasing to lessees do not come without a cost. When the lessor assumes the risks of ownership, it will require the lessee to make larger lease payments than if the lessee faces these risks. Which party bears the risks is a matter of negotiation between lessor and lessee.

Promising to make an irrevocable series of lease payments commits the firm just as surely as a bond indenture or mortgage, and the accounting is similar in many cases.[12] This section examines two methods of accounting for long-term leases: the operating lease method and the capital lease method. The illustrations show the accounting by the lessee, the user of the leased asset. A later section illustrates the accounting for the lessor, the owner of the asset.

To illustrate these two methods, suppose that Myers Company wants to acquire a computer that has a three-year life and could be purchased for $45,000. Assume also that Myers Company must pay 10 percent per year to borrow money for three years. The computer manufacturer is willing to sell the equipment for $45,000 or to lease it for three years. Myers Company is responsible for property taxes, maintenance, and repairs of the computer whether it leases or purchases the computer.

Assume that Myers Company signs a lease on January 1, Year 1, and must make payments on the lease on December 31, Year 1, Year 2, and Year 3. (In practice, lessees usually make lease payments in advance, but the assumption of year-end payments simplifies the computations.) Compound interest computations show that each lease payment must be $18,095. (The present value of an annuity of $1 paid at the end of this year and each of the next two years is $2.48685 when the interest rate is 10 percent per year. Because the

[12]Lease disclosures often use the term *noncancelable leases* to capture the contractual lease commitments of the lessee. Under noncancelable leases, the lessee typically can cancel the lease only after incurring a severe penalty.

lease payments must have a present value equal to the current cash purchase price of $45,000 if the computer manufacturer is to be indifferent between selling and leasing the computer, each payment must be $45,000/2.48685 = $18,095.)

Operating Lease Method

In an *operating lease,* the owner, or lessor, transfers only the rights to use the property to the lessee for specified periods of time. At the end of the lease period, the lessee returns the property to the lessor. For example, car rental companies lease cars by the day or week on an operating basis. In leasing arrangements in which the lessee neither assumes the risks nor enjoys the rewards of ownership, GAAP requires the lessee to treat the lease as an operating lease. Accounting gives no recognition to the signing of an operating lease (that is, the lessee reports neither the leased asset nor a lease liability on its balance sheet; the lease is simply a mutually unexecuted contract). The lessee recognizes rent expense in measuring net income each year. The effect on the financial statements of Myers Company each year (ignoring income taxes) if it treats the lease as an operating lease is as follows:

	C	+	N$A	=	L	+	CC	+	AOCI	+	RE
BS-BOP											
(1)	−18,095										−18,095
IBT											−18,095
BS-EOP	**−18,095**										**−18,095**

Myers Company makes the following journal entry on its books on December 31, Year 1, Year 2, and Year 3, under the operating lease method:

Rent Expense	18,095	
Cash		18,095
To recognize annual expense of leasing computer.		

Capital Lease Method

In leasing arrangements in which the lessee assumes the risks and enjoys the rewards of ownership, the arrangement is a form of borrowing and GAAP treats such leases as *capital leases.* This treatment recognizes the signing of the lease as the simultaneous acquisition of a long-term asset and the incurring of a long-term liability for lease payments. The effect on the financial statements of Myers Company at the time it signs the lease and the related journal entry that it makes in its accounting records are as follows:

	C	+	N$A	=	L	+	CC	+	AOCI	+	RE
BS-BOP											
(1)			+45,000		+45,000						

Leased Asset	45,000	
Lease Liability		45,000
To recognize acquisition of leased asset and the related liability.		

Lessees recognize two expense items each year on capital leases. First, the lessee must depreciate the leased asset over its useful life (that is, the term of the lease). Assuming that Myers Company uses straight-line depreciation (see Chapter 7 for a discussion of depreciation methods), it recognizes depreciation expense of $15,000 (= $45,000/3) each year. Second, the lease payment made each year is part interest expense on the lease liability and part reduction in the liability itself. For Year 1, interest expense is $4,500 (= .10 × $45,000) and the repayment of the lease liability is $13,595 (= $18,095 − $4,500). The effects of (1) the signing of the capital lease on January 1, Year 1, and the recognition of (2) depreciation and (3) interest during Year 1 are as follows:

	C	+	N$A	=	L	+	CC	+	AOCI	+	RE
BS-BOP											
(1)		+	45,000		+45,000						
(2)		−	15,000							−	15,000
(3)	−18,095				−13,595					−	4,500
IBT										−	19,500
BS-EOP	**−18,095**	**+**	**30,000**	**=**	**+31,405**					**−**	**19,500**

The journal entries on the books of Myers Company for depreciation and interest are as follows:

December 31, Year 1:

Depreciation Expense	15,000	
Accumulated Depreciation		15,000
To record depreciation of leased asset.		

December 31, Year 1:

Interest Expense	4,500	
Lease Liability	13,595	
Cash		18,095
To recognize lease payment, interest on liability for Year 1 (.10 × $45,000 = $4,500), and the plug for reduction in the liability. The present value of the liability after this entry is $31,405 = $45,000 − $13,595.		

Exhibit 8.2 shows the amortization schedule for this liability. Column (3) shows the amount of interest expense. The entries made for interest expense and the payment of $18,095 at the end of Year 2 and Year 3 are as follows:

December 31, Year 2:

Interest Expense	3,141	
Lease Liability	14,954	
Cash		18,095
To recognize lease payment, interest on liability for Year 2 (.10 × $31,405 = $3,141), and the plug for reduction in the liability. The present value of the liability after this entry is $16,451 = $31,405 − $14,954.		

EXHIBIT 8.2

Amortization Schedule for $45,000 Lease Liability Repaid in Three Annual Installments of $18,095, Interest Rate 10 Percent, Compounded Annually

Year (1)	Lease Liability, Start of Year (2)	Interest Expense for Year (3)	Payment (4)	Portion of Payment Reducing Lease Liability (5)	Lease Liability, End of Year (6)
1	$45,000	$4,500	$18,095	$13,595	$31,405
2	31,405	3,141	18,095	14,954	16,451
3	16,451	1,644[a]	18,095	16,451	0

Column (2) = column (6), previous period.
Column (3) = .10 × column (2).
Column (4) is given.
Column (5) = column (4) − column (3).
Column (6) = column (2) − column (5).
[a]Does not equal .10 × $16,451 due to rounding.

December 31, Year 3:

Interest Expense	1,644	
Lease Liability	16,451	
Cash		18,095

To recognize lease payment, interest on liability for Year 3 (.10 × $16,451 = $1,644), and the plug for reduction in the liability. The present value of the liability after this entry is zero (= $16,451 − $16,451).

Notice that in the capital lease method, the total expense over the three years is $54,285, comprising $45,000 (= $15,000 + $15,000 + $15,000) for depreciation expense and $9,285 (= $4,500 + $3,141 + $1,644) for interest expense. This total expense is exactly the same as that recognized under the operating lease method described previously ($18,095 × 3 = $54,285). The capital lease method recognizes expenses sooner than does the operating lease method, as Exhibit 8.3 summarizes. But over sufficiently long time periods, total expense equals the cash expenditure. One difference between the operating lease method and the capital lease method is the *timing* of the expense recognition. The other difference is that the capital lease method recognizes both the asset and the liability on the balance sheet.

Choosing the Accounting Method

When a lessee treats a lease as a capital lease, it recognizes both an asset and a liability, thereby increasing total liabilities and making the company appear more risky. Given a choice, most lessees prefer not to show the asset and a related liability on the balance sheet. Lessees prefer an operating lease to either an installment purchase or a capital lease, for which both the asset and liability appear on the balance sheet. Lessees also prefer to recognize expenses later rather than sooner for financial reporting. These preferences have led lessees to structure asset acquisitions so that the financing takes the form of an operating lease, thereby achieving off-balance-sheet financing.

EXHIBIT 8.3

Comparison of Expense Recognized under Operating and Capital Lease Methods

	Expense Recognized Each Year Under:	
Year	Operating Lease Method	Capital Lease Method
1	$18,095	$19,500 (= $15,000 + $4,500)
2	18,095	18,141 (= 15,000 + 3,141)
3	18,095	16,644 (= 15,000 + 1,644)
Total	$54,285[a]	$54,285 (= $45,000[b] + $9,285[c])

[a]Rent expense.
[b]Depreciation expense.
[c]Interest expense.

Conditions Requiring Capital Lease Accounting

GAAP provides detailed rules of accounting for long-term leases. The lessor and lessee must account for a lease as a capital lease if the lease meets any one of four conditions.[13] These conditions attempt to identify which party, the lessor or the lessee, bears most of the risk related to the asset under lease. When the lessor bears most of the risk, the lease is an operating lease. If the lessee bears most of the risk, the lease is a capital lease.

A lease is a capital lease if it meets any one of the following conditions:

1. If it extends for at least 75 percent of the asset's total expected useful life (the lessee uses the asset for most of its life).
2. If it transfers ownership to the lessee at the end of the lease term (the lessee bears the risk of changes in the residual value of the asset at the end of the lease term).
3. If it seems likely that the lessor will transfer ownership to the lessee because of a "bargain purchase" option (the lessee again bears the residual value risk; a bargain purchase option gives the lessee the right to purchase the asset for a price less than the expected fair market value of the asset when the lessee exercises its option).
4. The present value of the contractual minimum lease payments equals or exceeds 90 percent of the fair market value of the asset at the time of signing.

The first three conditions are relatively easy to avoid in lease contracts if lessors and lessees prefer to treat a lease as an operating lease instead of a capital lease. The most difficult of the four conditions to avoid is the fourth. When the contractual minimum lease payments equal or exceed 90 percent of the fair market value of the asset at the time of signing, the lessor has less than or equal to 10 percent of the asset's value at risk to an uncertain residual value at the end of the lease term. The lease therefore transfers the major risks and rewards of ownership from the lessor (landlord) to the lessee. In economic substance, the lessee has acquired an asset and has agreed to pay for it under a long-term contract, which the lessee recognizes as a liability. When the present value of the minimum lease payments is less than 90 percent of the fair market value of the asset

[13]Financial Accounting Standards Board, *Statement of Financial Accounting Standards No. 13*, "Accounting for Leases" (1976).

at the time of signing, the lessor bears the major risks and rewards of ownership and the lease is an operating lease.

Firms often report both operating and capital leases because certain lease agreements meet one or more of these conditions, while others meet none of the conditions.

Example 4

Delta Air Lines leases many of its aircraft and ground facilities. In the notes to its financial statements, Delta provides a schedule of capital and operating lease commitments for Year 5 and beyond, as reported in Exhibit 8.4. The firm also reports the present value of its capital lease commitments ($448 million on December 31, Year 4, as reported in Exhibit 8.4). The capital leases reported by Delta on the balance sheet as long-term debt represent approximately 3 percent of Delta's total long-term debt at the end of Year 4. Delta's commitments under operating leases are much more substantial, representing an important off-balance-sheet cash flow commitment of the firm that we will analyze further later in this section.

Most countries outside the United States also set criteria for distinguishing operating and capital leases (sometimes referred to as "financing" leases in other countries). The particular criteria differ somewhat from those described previously but attempt to identify the party enjoying the rewards and bearing the risks of ownership.

Effects on Lessor

The lessor (landlord) generally uses the same criteria as the lessee (tenant) for classifying a lease as an operating lease or a capital lease. Under the operating lease method, the lessor recognizes rent revenue in the same amounts as the lessee recognizes rent expense (note that the lessor recognizes depreciation on the asset). At the time of the signing of a capital lease, the lessor recognizes an asset, Lease Receivable, and revenue in an amount

EXHIBIT 8.4

Delta Air Lines
Lease Commitments
(amounts in millions)

Minimum lease obligations, excluding taxes, insurance, and other expenses payable directly by the company for leases in effect as of December 31, Year 4, were as follows:

	Capital Leases	Operating Leases
Year 5	$ 158	$1,091
Year 6	162	1,017
Year 7	134	915
Year 8	112	980
Year 9	146	836
After Year 9	410	4,823
Minimum Payments	$1,122	$9,662
Imputed Interest	(674)	
Present Value of Minimum Lease Payments, Principally Long-Term	$ 448	

equal to the present value of all future cash flows ($45,000 in the Myers Company lease) and recognizes expense (analogous to cost of goods sold) in an amount equal to the book value of the leased asset. Assume that Myers Company manufactured the computer at a cost of $39,000. The difference between the revenue and expense is the lessor's gross margin from the "sale" of the asset. The effects on the financial statements of Myers Company of (1) manufacturing the leased asset and then (2) signing a capital lease are as follows:

	C	+	N$A	=	L	+	CC	+	AOCI	+	RE
BS-BOP											
(1)	−39,000	+	39,000								
(2)		+	45,000							+	45,000
		−	39,000							−	39,000
IBT										+	6,000

The lessor records the lease receivable like any other long-term receivable at the present value of the future cash flows. It recognizes interest revenue over the term of the lease in amounts that closely mirror interest expense by the lessee. The effects on the financial statements of accounting for the lease as a capital lease by the lessor for Year 1 (we repeat the effects of manufacturing the asset and signing the lease) are as follows:

	C	+	N$A	=	L	+	CC	+	AOCI	+	RE
BS-BOP											
(1)	−39,000	+	39,000								
(2)		+	45,000							+	45,000
		−	39,000							−	39,000
(3)	+18,095	−	13,595							+	4,500
IBT										+	10,500
BS-EOP	**−20,905**	**+**	**31,405**	**=**							**10,500**

The lessor's entries under the operating and capital lease methods, assuming that it manufactured the computer for $39,000, are as follows:

Operating Lease Method
December 31 of Each Year:

Cash	18,095	
Rent Revenue		18,095

To recognize annual revenue from renting computer to lessee.

Depreciation Expense	13,000	
Accumulated Depreciation		13,000

To recognize depreciation on computer rented to lessee ($13,000 = $39,000/3).

Capital Lease Method
January 1, Year 1:

Lease Receivable	45,000	
Sales Revenue		45,000

To recognize the "sale" of a computer for a series of future cash flows with a present value of $45,000.

Cost of Goods Sold	39,000	
Inventory		39,000
To record the cost of the computer "sold" as an expense.		

December 31, Year 1:

Cash	18,095	
Interest Revenue		4,500
Lease Receivable		13,595
To recognize lease receipt, interest on receivable, and reduction in receivable for Year 1. See supporting calculations in the lessee's journal entries.		

December 31, Year 2:

Cash	18,095	
Interest Revenue		3,141
Lease Receivable		14,954
To recognize lease amounts for Year 2.		

December 31, Year 3:

Cash	18,095	
Interest Revenue		1,644
Lease Receivable		16,451
To recognize lease amounts for Year 3.		

Lease Accounting for Tax Purposes

An earlier section indicates that one of the benefits of leasing is that it permits the user of the property (the lessee) to shift the tax benefits of depreciation, interest, and other deductions to the lessor in the expectation of lowering the required lease payments. To achieve this benefit, the lease must satisfy the criteria for an operating lease for tax purposes. These criteria differ somewhat from those GAAP uses to classify leases for financial reporting. The five criteria for operating leases for tax reporting are as follows:

1. Use of the property at the end of the lease term by someone other than the lessee is commercially feasible.
2. The lease does not have a bargain purchase option.
3. The lessor has a minimum 20 percent of its capital at risk.
4. The lessor has a positive cash flow and profit from the lease independent of tax benefits.
5. The lessee does not have an investment in the lease and has not lent any of the purchase price to the lessor.

These criteria attempt to identify the party to the lease that enjoys the rewards and bears the risks of ownership. Because the financial and tax reporting criteria for leases differ, lessors and lessees may treat particular leases one way for financial reporting and another way for tax reporting.

Converting Operating Leases to Capital Leases

The analyst must address accounting quality issues for lessor and lessee firms that enter into substantial lease agreements, given the preference particularly by lessees to structure leases as operating leases. A slight change in the amount or pattern of cash flows can cause the present value of the minimum lease payments to fall just above or just below the 90 percent threshold. Lease commitments by lessees accounted for as operating leases do not appear as liabilities on the balance sheet and can cause the analyst to understate the short-term liquidity or long-term solvency risk of the firm. For these reasons, the analyst may wish to restate the financial statements of lessees to convert all operating leases into capital leases. Such a restatement provides a more conservative measure of total liabilities.

To illustrate the procedure, refer to PepsiCo's noncancelable operating lease disclosures in Note 9, "Debt Obligations and Commitments" (Appendix A). Exhibit 8.5 summarizes PepsiCo's information on operating lease commitments. Column (2) shows PepsiCo's commitments on noncancelable operating leases net of sublease revenues at the end of Year 4. The analyst must express the lease commitments in present value terms. The discount rate that the analyst should use is the lessee's incremental borrowing rate for secured debt with similar risk to that of the leasing arrangement. PepsiCo's interest expense as a percentage of average short- and long-term borrowing for Year 4 is 5.8 percent [= $167/(.5[$591 + $1,702 + $1,054 + $2,397])]. We assume a 6 percent rate in this case to compute the present value of operating lease commitments. To select a present value factor for payments after Year 9, we need to know the years and amounts in which PepsiCo will pay the $198 million. If we presume that payments after Year 9 will

EXHIBIT 8.5

PepsiCo., Inc.
Operating Lease Disclosures
(amounts in millions)

Operating Lease Commitments at the End of Year 4

Year (1)	Reported Operating Lease Commitments (2)	Present Value Factor at 6%	Present Value
5	$155.0	.94340	$146.2
6	96.5	.89000	85.9
7	96.5	.83962	81.0
8	60.0	.79209	47.5
9	60.0	.74726	44.8
After Year 9	$198.0	*	130.7
			$536.1

*Present value of an annuity of $60 million for 3.30 periods (= $198/$60) at 6 percent, then that present value discounted back 5 periods at 6 percent.

continue at the same amount as the $60 million payment in Year 9, then PepsiCo will pay $60 million a year for 3.30 periods (= $198/$60). The present value of an annuity of $120 million for 3.30 periods at 6.0 percent is $174.9 million. This amount represents the present value at the beginning of Year 10. The present value at the end of Year 4 requires that we discount $174.9 million for five periods at 6 percent to obtain a present value of $130.7 million. Lease commitments usually decline over time as existing leases terminate, so assuming a level of $120 million provides a more conservative measure of the obligation from the viewpoint of the analyst.

The analyst adds the $536.1 million lease to property, plant, and equipment and to long-term debt on the December 25, Year 4, balance sheet. For time-series analysis of PepsiCo, similar calculations would be necessary for at least two previous years. The long-term debt to long-term capital ratio of PepsiCo on December 25, Year 4, based on reported amounts, is 15.1 percent (= $2,397/($2,397 − $49 + $13,572)). Capitalizing the operating lease commitments increases the ratio to 17.8 percent (= ($2,397 + $536.1)/($2,397 + $536.1 − $49 + $13,572)).

Assuming that the analyst views the economic substance of this lease more as a means of financing the acquisition of long-term assets (that is, as a capital lease) than as a right to use such assets for a short period of time, the analyst could also convert the income statement from the operating to the capital lease method. In general, if the average lease is in the first half of its life, total expenses under the capital lease method tend to exceed total expenses under the operating lease method, so adjusted income will tend to be less than reported income. If the average lease is in the last half of its life, total expenses under the capital lease method tend to be less than under the operating lease method, and so adjusted income tends to be greater than reported income. The two expense amounts are approximately equal at the midlife point (see Exhibit 8.3).

Often balance sheet restatements are more significant than income statement restatements. Consequently, the analyst can usually ignore restatements of the income statement, particularly if the analyst's emphasis is assessment of a firm's credit risk as discussed in Chapter 5. However, note that even for firms with leases at the midlife point, where the income statement effect may be immaterial, the effect on the balance sheet can be substantial.[14]

The analyst could restate the statement of cash flows for the capitalization of operating leases. Under the operating lease method, the lease payment for the year is an operating use of cash. Its inclusion as a subtraction in computing net income results in reporting its negative effect on the operating section of the statement of cash flows. Under the capital lease method, a portion of the cash payment represents a repayment of the lease liability, a financing use of cash instead of an operating use of cash. The analyst should reclassify this portion of the cash payment from the operating section to the financing section of the statement of cash flows. The analyst could also reduce net income for depreciation expense on the capitalized lease assets, but this same amount appears as an addback to net income for a noncash expense. Thus, the net effect of depreciation expense on operating cash flows is zero.

[14]For an alternative procedure for converting operating leases into capital leases, see Eugene A. Imhoff, Jr., Robert C. Lipe, and David W. Wright, "Operating Leases: Impact of Constructive Capitalization," *Accounting Horizons* (March 1991), pp. 51–63. In this study, the authors found that capitalizing operating leases decreased the rate of return on assets 34 percent for high-lease firms and 10 percent for low-lease firms, and increased the debt-to-equity ratio 191 percent for high-lease firms and 47 percent for low-lease firms.

Impact of Accounting for Operating Leases as Capital Leases

Virtually all firms have some amount of commitments under operating leases. The change in debt ratios for some firms is relatively minor, as is the case for PepsiCo. For other firms, particularly airlines and retail stores, the effect can be significant. Refer again to the lease commitments for Delta Air Lines in Exhibit 8.4. The present value of Delta's lease commitments on December 31, Year 4, at a 6 percent discount rate, based on the same procedure as Exhibit 8.5 illustrates for PepsiCo, is $6,597 million. Delta's long-term debt represents 59.9 percent of the firm's total assets, without recognizing its commitments under operating leases. When the firm includes the present value of operating lease commitments in property, plant, and equipment and long-term debt, the restated long-term debt represents 69.0 percent of the firm's restated total assets. Even for firms for which the effect is relatively small, adding the effect of capitalizing operating leases to the effect of other off-balance-sheet obligations can result in a combined material effect. Thus, the analyst should examine the effect of leases when assessing the risk and accounting quality of a firm's financial statements.

DERIVATIVE INSTRUMENTS

Firms incur various risks when carrying out their business operations. A fire may destroy a warehouse of a retail chain and disrupt the flow of merchandise to stores. An automobile accident involving a member of the sales staff may injure the employee or others and damage the firm's automobile. A firm's products may injure customers and subject the firm to lawsuits. Most firms purchase property, medical, or liability insurance against such risks. The insurance shifts the risk of the loss, at least up to the limits in the insurance policy, to the insurance company. The firm pays insurance premiums for the right to shift the risk of these losses.

Firms engage in numerous other transactions that subject them to risks. Derivative instruments can help a firm mitigate (or take) certain risks. Consider the following scenarios.

Example 5

Firm A, a U.S. firm, orders a machine on June 30, Year 1, for delivery on June 30, Year 2, from a British supplier for £10,000 (Great Britain pounds, also referred to as GBP throughout this section). The exchange rate between the U.S. dollar and the GBP is currently $1.60 per GBP, indicating a purchase price of $16,000. Firm A worries that the value of the U.S. dollar will decline between June 30, Year 1, and June 30, Year 2, when it must convert U.S. dollars into GBP, requiring it to pay more than $16,000 to purchase the machine.

Example 6

Firm B gives a note payable to a supplier on January 1, Year 1, to acquire manufacturing equipment. The note has a face value of $100,000 and bears a fixed interest rate of 8 percent per year. Interest is payable annually on December 31 and the note matures on December 31, Year 3. Firm B has the option of repaying the note prior to maturity. It knows, though, that the equipment supplier will value the note at any time prior to maturity based on existing market interest rates at the time. Firm B worries that the value of the note will increase if interest rates decrease and require it to pay more than $100,000 if it decides to repay the note early.

Example 7

Firm C gives a note payable to a supplier on January 1, Year 1, to acquire manufacturing equipment. The note has a face value of $100,000 and bears interest at the prime lending rate. The prime lending rate is 8 percent on January 1, Year 1. The supplier resets the interest rate each December 31 to establish the interest charge for the next calendar year. Interest is payable on December 31 of each year and the note matures on December 31, Year 3. Firm C worries that interest rates will increase to more than 8 percent during the term of the note and negatively affect its cash flows.

Example 8

Firm D holds 10,000 gallons of whiskey in inventory on October 31, Year 1. Firm D expects to finish aging this whiskey by March 31, Year 2, at which time it intends to sell the whiskey. Uncertainties about the quality of the aged whiskey and economic conditions at the time, however, make predicting the selling price of whiskey on March 31, Year 2, difficult.

Many firms face risks of economic losses from changes in interest rate, foreign-exchange rates, or commodity prices. For example, PepsiCo states in Note 10, "Risk Management" (Appendix A):

> We are exposed to the risk of loss arising from adverse changes in:
>
> - Commodity prices, affecting the cost of our raw materials and energy;
> - Foreign exchange risks;
> - Interest rates;
> - Stock prices; and
> - Discount rates, affecting the measurement of our pension and retiree medical liabilities.

Firms can purchase financial instruments to mitigate these business risks. The general term used for the financial instrument is *derivative.* This section discusses the nature, use, accounting, and reporting of derivative instruments. Financial Accounting Standards Board *Statement of Financial Accounting Standards No. 133*[15] and *Statement of Financial Accounting Standards No. 138*[16] set forth the required accounting for derivative instruments.

Nature and Use of Derivative Instruments

A derivative is a financial instrument that derives its value from some other financial instrument. An option to purchase a share of stock derives its value from the market price of the stock. A commitment to purchase a certain amount of foreign currency in the future derives its value from changes in the exchange rate for that currency. Firms typically use derivative instruments to hedge the risk of losses from changes in interest rates, foreign-exchange rates, and commodity prices. The general idea is that changes in the value of the derivative instrument offset changes in the value of an asset or liability or changes in future cash flows, thereby neutralizing the economic loss. Reconsider the four examples discussed previously.

---

[15]Financial Accounting Standards Board, *Statement of Financial Accounting Standards No. 133*, "Accounting for Derivative Instruments and Hedging Activities" (1998).

[16]Financial Accounting Standards Board, *Statement of Financial Accounting Standards No. 138*, "Accounting for Certain Derivative Instruments and Certain Hedging Activities, an Amendment to FASB Statement No. 133" (2000).

Example 9

Refer to Example 5. Firm A desires to minimize the effect of changes in the exchange rate between the U.S. dollar and the Great Britain pound while it awaits delivery of the equipment. It purchases a forward foreign-exchange contract from a bank on June 30, Year 1, in which it promises to pay a fixed U.S. dollar amount on June 30, Year 2, in exchange for £10,000. The forward foreign-exchange rate between U.S. dollars and British pounds on June 30, Year 1, for settlement on June 30, Year 2, establishes the number of U.S. dollars it must deliver. Assume that the forward rate on June 30, Year 1, for settlement of the forward contract on June 30, Year 2, is $1.64 per GBP. By purchasing the forward contract, Firm A locks in the cost of the equipment at $16,400 (= 10,000 pounds × $1.64 per GBP).

Example 10

Refer to Example 6. Firm B wants to neutralize the effect of changes in the market value of the note payable caused by changes in market interest rates. It engages in a swap contract with its bank. The swap in effect allows Firm B to swap its fixed-interest-rate obligation for a variable-interest-rate obligation. The market value of the note remains at $100,000 as long as the variable interest rate in the swap is the same as the variable rate used by the supplier to revalue the note while it is outstanding.

Example 11

Refer to Example 7. Firm C wants to protect itself against increases in the variable interest rate to more than the initial 8 percent rate. It also engages in a swap contract with its bank. The swap in effect allows Firm C to swap its variable-interest-rate obligation for a fixed-interest-rate obligation. The swap fixes its annual interest expense and cash expenditure to 8 percent of the $100,000 note. By engaging in the swap, Firm C cannot take advantage of decreases in interest rates to less than 8 percent, which it could have done with its variable-rate note.

Example 12

Refer to Example 8. Firm D would like to fix the price at which it can sell the whiskey in its inventory on March 31, Year 2. It acquires a forward commodity contract in which it promises to sell 10,000 gallons of whiskey on March 31, Year 2, at a fixed price. The forward price of whiskey on October 31, Year 1, for delivery on March 31, Year 2, is $320 per gallon. Thus, Firm D locks in a total cash inflow from selling the whiskey of $3,200,000.

Forward contracts and swap contracts are only two of many types of derivative instruments. Banks and other financial intermediaries structure derivatives for a fee to suit the particular needs of their customers. Thus, the nature and complexity of derivatives vary widely. We confine our discussion to forward and swap contracts to illustrate the accounting and reporting of derivatives.

With these examples of derivatives, consider the following elements of a derivative:

1. A derivative has one or more *underlyings*. An underlying is generally a price of a specified item to which the derivative applies, such as an interest rate, commodity price, foreign-exchange rate, or other variable. The underlying in Example 9 is the foreign-exchange rate; in Examples 10 and 11, it is an interest rate; and in Example 12, it is the price of whiskey.
2. A derivative has one or more *notional amounts*. A notional amount is a number of currency units, bushels, shares, or other units specified in the contract. The notional amount in Example 9 is £10,000; in Examples 10 and 11, is the $100,000 face value of the note; and in Example 12, is 10,000 gallons of whiskey.

3. A derivative may or may not require an initial investment. The firm usually acquires a derivative by exchanging promises with a counterparty, such as a commercial or investment bank. The acquisition of a derivative is usually an exchange of promises, a mutually unexecuted contract.
4. Derivatives typically require, or permit, *net settlement.* Firm A in Example 9 will not deliver $16,400 to the counterparty and receive in exchange £10,000. Firm A will actually purchase £10,000 on the market on June 30, Year 2, at the exchange rate on that date, when it needs the British pounds to purchase the equipment. Firm A will receive cash from the counterparty to the extent that the exchange rate on June 30, Year 2, exceeds $1.64 per GBP and must pay the counterparty on this date to the extent that the exchange rate is less than $1.64 per GBP. Firm B in Example 10 will pay the supplier the 8 percent interest established in the fixed-rate note. If the variable interest rate used in the swap contract decreases to 6 percent, the counterparty will pay Firm B an amount equal to 2 percent (= .08 − .06) of the notional amount of the note, $100,000. Paying interest of 8 percent to the supplier and receiving cash of 2 percent from the counterparty results in net interest cost of 6 percent. If the variable interest rate increases to 10 percent, Firm B still pays the supplier interest of 8 percent as specified in the original note. It would then pay the counterparty an additional 2 percent (= .10 − .08), resulting in total interest expense equal to the variable rate of 10 percent.

Accounting for Derivatives

Firms must recognize derivatives in the balance sheet. PepsiCo states in Note 10, "Risk Management" (Appendix A):

> All derivative instruments are recognized in our Consolidated Balance Sheet at fair value. The fair value of our derivative instruments is generally based on quoted market prices.

Derivatives are reported as either assets or liabilities depending on the rights and obligations under the contract. The forward contract in Example 9 is either an asset or a liability, depending on the exchange rate. The swap contracts in Examples 10 and 11 may be assets or liabilities, depending on the level of interest rates. The forward contract in Example 12 may be an asset or liability, depending on the price of whiskey. A later section discusses the initial valuation of these assets and liabilities.

Firms must revalue the derivatives to market value each period. Common terminology refers to this as *marking to market,* or *mark to market.* The revaluation amount, in addition to increasing or decreasing the derivative asset or liability, also affects either (1) net income immediately or (2) other comprehensive income immediately and net income later, depending on GAAP requirements discussed shortly. Recall that Other Comprehensive Income is a temporary shareholders' equity account that reports changes during an accounting period in the recorded amounts of certain assets and liabilities, such as derivatives. Firms transfer the amount of other comprehensive income at the end of the period to the Accumulated Other Comprehensive Income account, a permanent shareholders' equity account. The income effect (that is, item (1) or (2) listed above) depends on the nature of the hedge for which a firm acquires a derivative. GAAP classifies derivatives as (1) speculative investments, (2) fair value hedges, or (3) cash flow hedges. Firms typically classify derivatives as either fair value hedges or cash flow hedges. Firms must choose to designate each derivative as one or the other, depending on their general hedging strategy and purpose in acquiring the particular derivative instrument. If a firm chooses not to designate a particular derivative as either a fair value hedge or a cash flow hedge, GAAP requires that the firm account for the derivative as a speculative investment.

Speculative Investment

Firms that acquire derivatives for reasons other than hedging a specific risk classify the derivative as a speculative investment. Firms must revalue derivatives held as speculative investments to market value each period and recognize the resulting gain or loss in net income.

Fair Value Hedges

Derivative instruments acquired to hedge exposure to changes in the fair value of an asset or liability are *fair value hedges.* Fair value hedges are of two general types: (1) hedges of a *recognized* asset or liability and (2) hedges of an *unrecognized* firm commitment. Firm B in Examples 6 and 10 entered into the interest swap agreement to neutralize the effect of changes in interest rates on the market value of its notes payable, a hedge of a recognized liability. Firm A in Examples 5 and 9 acquired the forward foreign-exchange contract to neutralize the effect of changes in exchange rates on its commitment to purchase the equipment, a hedge of an unrecognized firm commitment. These derivative instruments are therefore fair value hedges.

Cash Flow Hedges

Derivative instruments acquired to hedge exposure to variability in expected future cash flows are *cash flow hedges.* Cash flow hedges are of two general types: (1) hedges of cash flows of an *existing* asset or liability and (2) hedges of cash flows of *forecasted* transactions. Firm C in Examples 7 and 11 entered into the interest swap agreement to neutralize changes in cash flows for interest payments on its variable-rate notes payable, a hedge of an existing liability. Firm D in Examples 8 and 12 acquired the forward contract on whiskey to protect itself from changes in the selling price of whiskey between October 31, Year 1, and March 31, Year 2, a hedge involving a forecasted transaction. These derivative instruments are therefore cash flow hedges.

A particular derivative could be either a fair value hedge or a cash flow hedge, depending on the firm's reason for engaging in the hedge. Both the forward foreign-exchange contract in Example 9 and the forward whiskey contract in Example 12 protect the firms' cash flows. The firms could conceivably classify both derivative instruments as cash flow hedges. Firm B in Example 9 acquires the derivative to protect the value of equipment acquired and therefore classifies it as a fair value hedge. Firm D in Example 12 acquires the derivative to protect its cash flows from changes in the price of whiskey and therefore classifies it as a cash flow hedge. One suspects that the FASB views the firm commitment to purchase the equipment by Firm A as having the economic substance of an asset and a liability, even though accounting treats it as a mutually unexecuted contract, whereas it views the anticipated transaction by Firm D to sell whiskey in the future as too uncertain to have the economic attributes of an asset at this point.

The four examples described thus far in this section illustrate the accounting for four possible scenarios:

Examples	**Type of Hedge**	**Derivative Instrument Used**
5 and 9	Fair Value—Firm Commitment	Forward Foreign Exchange Contract
6 and 10	Fair Value—Liability	Swap Contract—Variable for Fixed Rate
7 and 11	Cash Flow—Interest Payments	Swap Contract—Fixed for Variable Rate
8 and 12	Cash Flow—Forecasted Transaction	Forward Commodity Contract

Treatment of Hedging Gains and Losses

GAAP requires firms to recognize gains and losses from changes in the market value of financial instruments classified as fair value hedges in net income each period while the firm holds the financial instrument. GAAP also requires firms to revalue the asset or liability that is hedged and recognize a corresponding loss or gain. If the hedge is fully effective, the gain (loss) on the financial instrument will precisely offset the loss (gain) on the asset or liability hedged. The net effect on earnings is zero. If the hedge is not fully in effect, the net gain or loss increases or decreases net income.

GAAP requires firms to include gains and losses from changes in the market values of financial instruments classified as cash flow hedges in other comprehensive income each period to the extent that the financial instrument is "highly effective" in neutralizing the risk. Firms must include the ineffective portion in net income currently. FASB *Statement No. 133* gives general guidelines but leaves to professional judgment the meaning of "highly effective." The firm removes the accumulated amount in other comprehensive income related to a particular derivative instrument and transfers it to net income either periodically during the life of the derivative instrument or at the time of settlement, depending on the type of derivative instrument used.

The logic for the FASB's different treatment of gains and losses from changes in fair value of financial instruments results from applying the matching principle. In a fair value hedge of a recognized asset or liability, both the hedged asset (or liability) and its related derivative generally appear on the balance sheet. The firm revalues both the hedged asset (or liability) and its derivative to fair value each period and reports the gain or loss on the hedged asset (or liability) and the loss or gain on the derivative in net income. The net gain or loss indicates the effectiveness of the hedge in neutralizing the risk. In a cash flow hedge of an anticipated transaction, the hedged cash flow commitment does not appear on the balance sheet but the derivative instrument does appear. Recognizing a gain or loss on the derivative instrument in net income each period but recognizing the loss or gain on the anticipated transaction at the time an actual transaction occurs results in poor matching. Thus, the firm classifies the gain or loss on the derivative instrument in other comprehensive income and then, later, reclassifies it to net income when it records the actual transaction.

The logic for the FASB's different treatment would seem to break down for fair value hedges related to a firm commitment. GAAP usually does not recognize the firm commitment as an asset or a liability. Firms must recognize changes in the market value of the firm commitment as an asset and a liability, even though the initial commitment does not give rise to a recognized asset or liability.

Illustrations of Accounting for Derivatives

This section illustrates the accounting for the derivatives using the two examples involving interest rate swaps. (Problems 8.17 and 8.18 examine the accounting for the forward foreign-exchange contract in Example 9 and the forward commodity contract in Example 12, respectively.) We use journal entries to illustrate the accounting for derivatives instead of the analytical framework described in Chapter 2. Exhibits 8.6 and 8.7 summarize the accounting in a format similar to the analytical framework.

Fair Value Hedge: Interest Rate Swap to Convert Fixed-Rate Debt to Variable-Rate Debt

Refer to Examples 6 and 10. Firm B desires to maintain the market value of its note payable in the event that it wishes to repay it prior to maturity. Changes in interest rates

EXHIBIT 8.6

Effects on Various Accounts of $100,000 Fixed-Rate Note and Related Interest Rate Swap Accounted For as a Fair Value Hedge

	Cash	Equipment (at Cost)	Notes Payable	Swap Contract	Income Statement
Year 1					
Issue Note for Equipment	$ —	$100,000	$(100,000)	$ —	$ —
Enter Swap Contract	—	—	—	—	—
Record Interest on Note	(8,000)	—	—	—	8,000
Revalue Note Payable	—	—	(3,667)	—	3,667
Revalue Swap Contract	—	—	—	3,667	(3,667)
December 31, Year 1	$ (8,000)	$100,000	$(103,667)	$ 3,667	$ 8,000
Year 2					
Record Interest on Note	$ (8,000)	—	$ 1,780	—	$ 6,220
Record Interest on Swap Contract	—	—	—	220	(220)
Record Swap Interest Received	2,000	—	—	(2,000)	—
Revalue Note Payable	—	—	3,705	—	(3,705)
Revalue Swap Contract	—	—	—	(3,705)	3,705
December 31, Year 2	$ (14,000)	$100,000	$ (98,182)	$(1,818)	$ 6,000
Year 3					
Record Interest on Note	$ (8,000)	—	$ (1,818)	—	$ 9,818
Record Interest on Swap Contract	—	—	—	(182)	182
Record Swap Interest Paid	(2,000)	—	—	2,000	—
Repay Note Payable	(100,000)	—	100,000	—	—
December 31, Year 3	$(124,000)	$100,000	$ —	$ —	$10,000

Amounts in parentheses are credits to the various accounts.

will change the market value of its fixed-rate note. It enters into a swap contract to convert the fixed-rate debt to variable-rate debt. The market value of the debt will remain at $100,000 as long as the interest rate incorporated into the swap contract is the same as the rate used by the equipment supplier to value the note payable. Firm B designates the swap contract as a fair value hedge.

Firm B issues the note to the supplier on January 1, Year 1, and makes the following entry:

January 1, Year 1:

Equipment	100,000	
Note Payable		100,000

The swap contract is a mutually unexecuted contract on January 1, Year 1. The variable interest rate on this date is 8 percent, the same as the fixed rate for the note to the equipment supplier. The swap contract has a market value of zero on this date. Thus, Firm B makes no entry to record the swap contract.

On December 31, Year 1, Firm B makes the required interest payment on the note for Year 1:

December 31, Year 1:		
Interest Expense (.08 × $100,000)	8,000	
Cash		8,000

Interest rates declined during Year 1. On December 31, the counterparty with whom Firm B entered into the swap contract resets the interest rate for Year 2 to 6 percent. Firm B must restate the note payable to market value and record the change in the market value of the swap contract caused by the decline in the interest rate.

The present value of the remaining cash flows on the note payable when discounted at 6 percent is as follows:

Present Value of Interest Payments: $8,000 × 1.83339	$ 14,667
Present Value of Principal: $100,000 × .89000	89,000
Total Present Value	$103,667

Firm B makes the following entry to record the change in market value:

December 31, Year 1:		
Loss on Revaluation of Note Payable (Inc. State.)	3,667	
Note Payable (= $103,667 − $100,000)		3,667

Firms typically do not revalue financial instruments, such as this note payable, to market value when interest rates change. They continue to account for the financial instruments using the interest rate at the time of the initial recording of the financial instrument in the accounts. When a firm hedges a financial instrument, however, it must recognize changes in market values. It must likewise recognize changes in the market value of the swap contract.

The decline in interest rates to 6 percent means that Firm B will save $2,000 each year in interest payments. The present value of a $2,000 annuity for two periods at 6 percent is $3,667 (= $2,000 × 1.83339). Thus, the value of the swap contract increased from zero at the beginning of Year 1 to $3,667 at the end of the year. Firm B makes the following entry:

December 31, Year 1:		
Swap Contract (Asset)	3,667	
Gain on Revaluation of Swap Contract (Income Statement)		3,667

The loss from the revaluation of the note payable exactly offsets the gain from the revaluation of the swap contract, indicating that the swap contract was fully effective (that is, the Loss on Revaluation of Note Payable is 100 percent offset by the Gain on Revaluation of Swap Contract) in hedging the interest rate risk.

Firm B follows a similar process at the end of Year 2. First, it records interest expense on the note payable:

December 31, Year 2:		
Interest Expense (.06 × $103,667)	6,220	
Note Payable (plug)	1,780	
Cash (.08 × $100,000)		8,000

Firm B uses the effective-interest method to compute interest expense for the year. The effective interest rate for Year 2 is 6 percent and the book value of the note payable at the beginning of the year is $103,667. The cash payment of $8,000 is the amount set forth in the original borrowing arrangement with the equipment supplier.

Second, the firm records interest revenue for the change in the present value of the swap contract for the year:

December 31, Year 2:		
Swap Contract (Asset)	220	
Interest Revenue (.06 × $3,667)		220

Interest expense (net) as a result of the two entries is $6,000 (= $6,220 − $220), which is the variable rate for Year 2 of 6 percent times the face value of the note.

Third, Firm B receives $2,000 under the swap contract with its counterparty because the interest rate decreased from 8 percent to 6 percent.

December 31, Year 2:		
Cash [$100,000 × (.08 − .06)]	2,000	
Swap Contract (Asset)		2,000

The $2,000 cash received from the counterparty in a sense reimburses Firm B for paying interest at 8 percent on the note, whereas the swap contract provides that the firm benefits when interest rates decline, in this case to 6 percent.

Fourth, Firm B must revalue the note payable and the swap contract for changes in market value. Interest rates increased during Year 2, so the bank resets the interest rate in the swap agreement to 10 percent for Year 3. The present value of the remaining payments on the note at 10 percent is as follows:

Present Value of Interest Payment: $8,000 × .90909	$ 7,273
Present Value of Principal: $100,000 × .90909	90,909
Total Present Value	$98,182

The book value of the note payable before revaluation is $101,887 (= $103,667 − $1,780). The entry to revalue the note payable is as follows:

Note Payable ($101,887 − $98,182)	3,705	
Gain on Revaluation of Note Payable (Income Statement)		3,705

The market value of the swap contract decreases. Firm A must now pay an additional $2,000 in interest in Year 3 because of the swap contract. Thus, the swap contract becomes a liability instead of an asset. The present value of $2,000 when discounted at

10 percent is $1,818 (= $2,000 × .90909). The book value of the swap contract before revaluation is an asset of $1,887 (= $3,667 + $220 − $2,000). The entry to revalue the swap contract is as follows:

Loss on Revaluation of Swap Contract (Income Statement)	3,705	
Swap Contract (Asset)		1,887
Swap Contract (Liability)		1,818

The gain on revaluation of the note exactly offsets the loss on revaluation of the swap contract, so the swap contract hedges the change in interest rates.

The entries for Year 3 are as follows:

December 31, Year 3:

Interest Expense (.10 × $98,182)	9,818	
Note Payable (plug)		1,818
Cash (.08 × $100,000)		8,000
Interest Expense (.10 × $1,818)	182	
Swap Contract (Liability)		182

Interest expense (net) after these two entries is $10,000 (= $9,818 + $182), which equals the variable interest rate of 10 percent times the face value of the note.

Firm B must pay the counterparty an extra 2 percent because the variable interest rate of 10 percent exceeds the fixed interest rate of 8 percent.

December 31, Year 3:

Swap Contract (Liability) [$100,000 × (.10 − .08)]	2,000	
Cash		2,000

Firm B must repay the note and close out the Swap Contract.

December 31, Year 3:

Note Payable ($98,182 + $1,181)	100,000	
Cash		100,000

The Swap Contract account has a zero balance on December 31, Year 3, after making the preceding entries (= $1,818 + $182 − $2,000), so the firm need make no additional entries to close out this account.

Exhibit 8.6 summarizes the effects of these entries on various accounts (credit entries in parentheses). Note that net income reflects the variable interest rate each year: 8 percent for Year 1, 6 percent for Year 2, and 10 percent for Year 3. The note payable and the swap contract net to $100,000 at the end of each year.

Summary of the Accounting for a Fair Value Hedge of an Existing Asset or Liability

The following summarizes the accounting for a fair value hedge of an existing asset or liability:

1. The hedged asset or liability already appears on the books. Its valuation depends on GAAP's required accounting for the particular asset or liability (for example,

lower of cost or market for inventories, present value of future cash flows for long-term receivables and payables).

2. The firm recognizes the derivative as an asset on the date of acquisition to the extent it makes an initial investment. Otherwise, no amount appears on the balance sheet for the derivative.
3. At the end of each period, revalue the hedged asset or liability to fair value and include the resulting gain or loss in net income.
4. At the end of each period, revalue the derivative instrument to fair value and include the resulting loss or gain in net income.
5. Show the hedged asset and liability and its related derivative separately on the balance sheet.
6. Remove the hedged asset or liability and its related derivative from the accounts at the time of settlement (for example, at the time of interest payments).

Cash Flow Hedge: Interest Rate Swap to Convert Variable-Rate Debt to Fixed-Rate Debt

Refer to Examples 7 and 11. Firm C desires to hedge the risk of changes in interest rates on its cash payments for interest. It enters into a swap contract with a counterparty to convert its variable-rate note payable to a fixed-rate note. Firm C designates the swap contract as a cash flow hedge. The facts for the case are similar to those for Firm B. The note has a $100,000 face value and an initial variable interest rate of 8 percent, which the counterparty resets to 6 percent for Year 2 and 10 percent for Year 3. The note matures on December 31, Year 3.

The entry to record the note payable is as follows:

January 1, Year 1:

Equipment	100,000	
Note Payable		100,000

Firm C records interest on the note for Year 1.

December 31, Year 1:

Interest Expense (.08 × $100,000)	8,000	
Cash		8,000

The market value of the note in this case, unlike that for Firm B, will not change as interest rates change because the note carries a variable interest rate. The market value of the swap contract does change. The market value on December 31, Year 1, after the counterparty resets the interest rate to 6 percent, is $3,667. This amount is the present value of the $2,000 that Firm C will pay the counterparty on December 31 of Year 2 and Year 3 if the interest rate remains at 6 percent. The entry is as follows:

December 31, Year 1:

Other Comprehensive Income (Swap Contract)	3,667	
Swap Contract (Liability)		3,667

The loss from the revaluation of the swap contract does not affect net income immediately on a cash flow hedge. Instead, it reduces other comprehensive income. Other comprehensive income is an element of accumulated other comprehensive income, a shareholders' equity account.

EXHIBIT 8.7

Effects on Various Accounts of $100,000 Variable-Rate Note and Related Interest Rate Swap Accounted for as a Cash Flow Hedge

	Cash	Equipment (at Cost)	Notes Payable	Swap Contract	Income Statement	Other Comp. Income
Year 1						
Issue Note for Equipment	$ —	$100,000	$(100,000)	$ —	$ —	$ —
Enter Swap Contract	—	—	—	—	—	—
Record Interest on Note	(8,000)	—	—	—	8,000	—
Revalue Swap Contract	—	—	—	(3,667)		3,667
December 31, Year 1	$ (8,000)	$100,000	$(100,000)	$(3,667)	$ 8,000	$ 3,667
Record Interest on Note	(6,000)	—	—	—	6,000	
Record Interest on Swap Contract	—	—	—	(220)	—	220
Record Swap Interest Paid	(2,000)	—	—	2,000	—	—
Reclassify Portion of Other Comprehensive Income	—	—	—	—	2,000	(2,000)
Revalue Swap Contract	—	—	—	3,705	—	(3,705)
December 31, Year 2	$ (16,000)	$100,000	$(100,000)	$ 1,818	$ 8,000	$(1,818)
Record Interest on Note	(10,000)	—	—	—	10,000	
Record Interest on Swap Contract	—	—	—	182		(182)
Record Swap Interest Received	2,000	—		(2,000)	—	—
Reclassify Portion of Other Comprehensive Income	—	—	—		(2,000)	2,000
Repay Note Payable	(100,000)	—	100,000	—	—	
Close Out Swap Contract	—	—	—	—	—	—
December 31, Year 3	$(124,000)	$100,000	$ —	$ —	$ 8,000	$ —

Amounts in parentheses are credits to the various accounts.

Note that the book value of the note payable of \$100,000 plus the book value of the swap contract of \$3,667 is \$103,667. This amount is the present value of the expected cash flows under the fixed-rate note and swap contract combined, discounted at 6 percent.

The entry on December 31, Year 2, to recognize and pay interest on the variable-rate note is as follows:

December 31, Year 2:		
Interest Expense (.06 × \$100,000)	6,000	
Cash		6,000

Firm C must also increase the book value of the swap contract for the passage of time.

December 31, Year 2:		
Other Comprehensive Income (Swap Contract) (.06 × \$3,667)	220	
Swap Contract (Liability)		220

Note that the interest charge does not affect net income immediately but instead decreases other comprehensive income.

Firm C pays the counterparty the \$2,000 [= \$100,000 × (.08 − .06)] required by the swap contract. The entry is as follows:

December 31, Year 2:		
Swap Contract (Liability)	2,000	
Cash		2,000

Because the swap contract hedged cash flows related to interest rate risk during Year 2, Firm C reclassifies a portion of other comprehensive income to net income. The entry is as follows:

December 31, Year 2:		
Interest Expense [= \$100,000 × (.08 − .06)]	2,000	
Other Comprehensive Income (Swap Contract)		2,000

At this point the swap contract account has a credit balance of \$1,887 (= \$3,667 + \$220 − \$2,000). Other comprehensive income related to this transaction likewise has a debit balance of \$1,887. Interest expense on the income statement is \$8,000 (= \$6,000 + \$2,000).

Restating the interest rate on December 31, Year 2, to 10 percent changes the value of the swap contract from a liability to an asset. The present value of the \$2,000 that Firm C will receive from the counterparty at the end of Year 3 when discounted at 10 percent is \$1,818. The entry to revalue the swap contract is as follows:

December 31, Year 2:		
Swap Contract (Liability)	1,887	
Swap Contract (Asset)	1,818	
Other Comprehensive Income (Swap Contract)		3,705

Other comprehensive income has a credit balance of \$1,818, which equals the debit balance in the Swap Contract account.

The entry during Year 3 to recognize and pay interest on the variable rate note is as follows:

December 31, Year 3:		
Interest Expense (.10 × $100,000)	10,000	
Cash		10,000

Firm C also increases the book value of the swap contract for the passage of time.

December 31, Year 3:		
Swap Contract (Asset) (.10 × $1,818)	182	
Other Comprehensive Income (Swap Contract)		182

The swap contract requires the counterparty to pay the firm $2,000 under the swap contract.

December 31, Year 3:		
Cash [$100,000 × (.10 − .08)]	2,000	
Swap Contract (Asset)		2,000

Because the swap contract hedged cash flows related to interest rate risk during Year 3, Firm C reclassifies a portion of other comprehensive income to net income. The entry is as follows:

December 31, Year 3:		
Other Comprehensive Income (Swap Contract)	2,000	
Interest Expense		2,000

Thus, interest expense (net) for Year 3 is $8,000 (= $10,000 − $2,000).

Firm C repays the note on December 31, Year 3:

December 31, Year 3:		
Notes Payable	100,000	
Cash		100,000

It must also close out the swap contract account. This account has a balance of zero on December 31, Year 3 (= $1,818 + $182 − $2,000). Thus, Firm C need make no entry. If the swap contract had been highly, but not perfectly, effective in neutralizing the interest rate risk, then accumulated other comprehensive income would have a balance related to the swap contract, which Firm C would reclassify to net income at this point.

Exhibit 8.7 summarizes the effect of these entries on various accounts (credit entries in parentheses). Note that interest expense is $8,000 each year, the fixed rate of 8 percent that Firm C accomplished by entering into the swap contract. The amounts in other comprehensive income reflect changes in the market value of the swap contract. The swap contract begins and ends with a zero value.

Summary of Accounting for a Cash Flow Hedge of an Existing Asset or Liability

The following summarizes the accounting for a cash flow hedge of an existing asset or liability:

1. The hedged asset or liability already appears on the books. Its valuation depends on GAAP's required accounting for the particular asset or liability (for example, lower of cost or market for inventories, present value of future cash flows for long-term receivables and payables).
2. The firm recognizes the derivative as an asset on the date of acquisition to the extent that it makes an initial investment. Otherwise, no amount appears on the balance sheet for the derivative.
3. At the end of each period, revalue the hedged asset or liability to fair value and include the resulting gain or loss in other comprehensive income.
4. At the end of each period, revalue the derivative instrument to fair value and include the resulting loss or gain in other comprehensive income.
5. Reclassify gains and losses from other comprehensive income to net income when the gain or loss on the hedged item affects net income. If the derivative is not highly effective in neutralizing the gain or loss on the hedged item, then the firm must reclassify the ineffective portion to net income immediately and not wait until the gain or loss on the hedged items affects net income.
6. Show the hedged asset and liability and its related derivative separately on the balance sheet. Also show the cumulative amount of net value changes for the hedged items and its related derivative in accumulated other comprehensive income.
7. Remove the hedged asset or liability and its related derivative from the accounts at the time of settlement (for example, at the time of interest payments).

Summary of Derivative Examples

Firms record changes in the market value of all derivatives each reporting period. Changes in the value of derivatives and the related asset, liability, or commitment for fair value hedges flow through to net income immediately. Changes in the value of derivatives related to cash flow hedges initially increase or decrease other comprehensive income. They affect net income at the same time that the cash flows that they hedge affect net income. Although this section does not illustrate the accounting for derivatives held as speculative investments because of their infrequency, the accounting is the same as for fair value hedges.

Disclosures Related to Derivative Instruments

Several FASB pronouncements address disclosures for derivatives. FASB *Statement No. 107*[17] requires firms to disclose the book value and the fair value of financial instruments. Financial instruments impose on one entity a right to receive cash and an obligation on another entity to pay cash. Financial instruments include accounts receivable, notes receivable, notes payable, bonds payable, forward contracts, swap contracts, and most derivatives. Fair value is the current amount at which two willing parties would exchange the instrument for cash.

---

[17] *Statement of Financial Accounting Standards Statement No. 107* (1991).

FASB *Statement No. 133* requires the following disclosures (among others) with respect to derivatives.

1. Firms must describe their risk management strategy and how particular derivatives help accomplish their hedging objectives. The description should distinguish between derivative instruments designated as fair value hedges, cash flow hedges, and all other derivatives.
2. For fair value and cash flow hedges, firms must disclose the net gain or loss recognized in earnings resulting from the hedges' ineffectiveness (that is, not offsetting the risk hedged) and the line item on the income statement that includes this net gain or loss.
3. For cash flow hedges, firms must describe the transactions or events that will result in reclassifying gains and losses from other comprehensive income to net income and the estimated amount of such reclassifications during the next twelve months.
4. Firms must disclose the net amount of gains and losses recognized in earnings because a hedged firm commitment no longer qualifies as a fair value hedge, or a hedged forecasted transaction no longer qualifies as a cash flow hedge.

As discussed at the beginning of this section, PepsiCo uses derivatives to hedge commodity prices, foreign-exchange rates, interest rates, stock prices, and discount rates used in measuring pension and medical benefits provided to retirees. All hedges are either fair value or cash flow hedges (that is, PepsiCo does not use derivatives for speculative investment purposes). Note 9, "Debt Obligations and Commitments," and Note 10, "Risk Management" (Appendix A), describe the types of derivatives PepsiCo uses (futures, options, swaps) for each type of risk and how each derivative serves to hedge the specified risk. Note 9 details PepsiCo's use of interest-rate and cross-currency swaps to hedge risk. Note 10 details PepsiCo's use of hedges to manage commodity and stock price risk. In both notes, PepsiCo discloses whether the hedge resulted in any net gain or loss for Year 4, and if so, where the amounts are reported in the financial statements. In addition, the firm states that it expected to reclassify gains of less than $1 million from accumulated other comprehensive loss into earnings during the next 12 months.

PepsiCo's Statement of Shareholders' Equity (Appendix A) shows the change in accumulated other comprehensive income for Year 4. The firm discloses that it incurred net derivative losses of $7 million during Year 4 from cash flow hedges (net of tax). This amount is small when compared to reported net income for Year 4 of $4,212 million. The gain or loss for previous years is also immaterial to the firm's net income for the year.

Firms must report the impact on earnings of certain changes in each of the major risk factors to which they are subject. Firms typically disclose this information in their management discussion and analysis of operations. PepsiCo discloses (Appendix B) the effect on earnings of changes in commodity prices, foreign-exchange rates, interest rates, and its stock price (used in measuring deferred compensation expense). This information permits the analyst to assess the extent and effectiveness of hedging activities on each of these risks. The following summarizes PepsiCo's disclosures for Year 4:

Change	Nature of Effect	Effect on Unrealized Earnings
Commodity Prices	10% Decrease	$16 Million Decrease
Foreign-Exchange Rates	10% Unfavorable	$123 Million Decrease
Interest Rates	1-Percentage-Point Increase	$11 Million Increase

Recall that PepsiCo reported earnings of $4,212 million for Year 4. Thus, none of these changes would have a material effect on net income, suggesting that PepsiCo's derivatives would be effective in hedging even larger changes than actually occurred.

Many firms use a value-at-risk simulation model to estimate the impact of adverse price movements. The value-at-risk model develops a distribution of the changes in relevant interest rates, exchange rates, commodity prices, or other underlying for a particular period of prior years (for example, ten years). Using the distribution of prior adverse changes and the average net position in various financial instruments for the current year, the model simulates with a 95 percent or other confidence level the minimum, maximum, or average amount of loss that a firm would incur.

Accounting Quality Issues and Derivatives

Firms must mark derivatives to market value each period. When active, established markets exist for derivatives, as is the case for many forward contracts and interest and currency swaps, market values are usually reliable and easy to obtain. When firms engage in derivative transactions for which active markets do not exist, questions arise about the reliability of the market valuations. Enron, for example, purchased and sold derivatives on the price and availability of broadband services. Broadband services were an emerging market at the time, with Enron one of only a few firms engaging in this type of derivative trading. Another set of Enron activities entailed valuing forward exchange derivative transactions for oil, natural gas and electricity, with some as far as twenty-five years in the future.

A second accounting quality concern involves the classification of derivatives as fair value hedges versus cash flow hedges. Recall that the firms in Examples 9 and 12 could have classified the exchange and commodity contracts as either fair value or cash flow hedges. Gains and losses on cash flow hedges affect earnings later than those on fair value hedges. When gains and losses on cash flow hedges, which GAAP includes in accumulated other comprehensive income, substantially exceed the gains and losses on fair value hedges included in earnings, then the analyst must at least question the firm's classification of its hedges.

When firms use derivatives effectively to manage risks, the net gain or loss each period should be relatively small. Large and varying amounts of gains or losses usually signal ineffective use of derivatives.

RETIREMENT BENEFITS

Employers typically provide two types of benefits to retired employees: (1) pension benefits and (2) health care and life insurance coverage.[18] The matching principle for income measurement and financial reporting, both in the United States and in most other countries, requires that the employer recognize the cost of these benefits as an expense while the employees work and generate revenues rather than when they receive the benefits during retirement. Estimating the expected cost of the benefits requires assumptions

[18]Some retired employees receive a third benefit from employers in the form of severance and similar benefits following active service but prior to retirement. The FASB addresses the reporting for these benefits in *Statement of Financial Accounting Standard No. 112*, "Employer's Accounting for Postemployment Benefits" (1992). The standard requires employers to accrue the cost of these benefits if they can be reasonably estimated and the employees have the unconditional right to the benefits. The statement only peripherally relates to the retiree benefits discussed in this section, however, because applying *Statement No. 112* is not conditional on retirement of the employee.

about employee turnover, future compensation and health care costs, interest rates, and other factors. Because the employer will not know the actual costs of these benefits until many years elapse, measuring their costs while the employees work requires estimation and judgments.

This section describes GAAP accounting and reporting for pensions, health care, and life insurance benefits, and discusses issues that the analyst should consider when interpreting disclosures related to retirement benefits.

Pensions

Pension plans work as follows:

1. Employers agree to provide certain pension benefits to employees. The arrangement may take the form of either a defined contribution plan or a defined benefit plan. Under a defined contribution plan, the employer agrees to contribute a certain amount to a pension fund each period (usually based on a percentage of employees' compensation), without specifying the benefits employees will receive during retirement. The amount employees eventually receive depends on the performance of the pension fund. Under a defined benefit plan, the employer agrees to make pension payments to employees during retirement using a benefits formula based on wages earned and number of years of employment. A typical defined benefit plan might provide an annual pension benefit during retirement equal to 2 percent times the number of years worked times an average of the highest five years of compensation during working years. An employee who worked 30 years at an average highest five years of compensation of \$50,000 would receive an annual pension of \$30,000 ($= .02 \times 30 \times$ \$50,000). The plan does not specify the amount the employer will contribute to the pension fund. The employer must make contributions to the fund such that those amounts plus earnings from pension investments are sufficient to make the promised payments.
2. Employers periodically contribute cash to a pension fund. The trustee, or administrator, of the fund invests the cash received from the employer in stocks, bonds, and other investments. The assets in the pension fund accumulate each period from both employer contributions and income from investments. These assets appear on the balance sheet of the pension plan and not on the employer's balance sheet.
3. The employer satisfies its obligation to employees under a defined contribution plan once it makes periodic contributions to the pension fund. The employer's obligation under a defined benefit plan increases each period from two factors. First, employees earn increased benefits each period as they work an additional period, usually at a higher compensation level. Second, the employer's obligation increases each period because time passes and the remaining time until employees begin receiving their pensions decreases. Thus, the present value of the pension obligation increases. This obligation appears as a liability on the balance sheet of the pension plan and not on the employer's balance sheet. As discussed shortly, GAAP requires firms to report the assets and liabilities of defined benefit plans in notes to the financial statements.
4. The pension fund makes pension payments to retired employees under both defined contribution and defined benefit plans. Both the assets and the liabilities of the pension plan decrease in the amount of the payments.

Accounting Records of the Pension Plan

The balance sheet of a typical defined benefit pension plan lists the assets in the pension fund and the liability for benefits earned but not yet paid to employees. Exhibit 8.8 indicates how the balance sheet changes each period. Assets increase from earnings on investments and from contributions received from the employer, and decrease from losses on investments and payments to retirees. Liabilities increase (1) because the remaining time until working employees will receive their pension decreases and (2) when employees work an additional year and earn rights to a larger pension. Liabilities decrease when the pension plan makes payments to retirees. Liabilities also increase or decrease if firms change the actuarial assumptions (discount rate, employee turnover rate, mortality rate) or the pension benefit formula underlying the defined benefit pension plan.

Pension disclosures permit the analyst to assess the degree to which a firm has an overfunded or underfunded defined benefit pension plan. These disclosures also permit an assessment of the performance of the pension fund during an accounting period.[19]

Defined Benefit Plan Obligations

GAAP requires firms to disclose the funded status of their pension plans at the end of each year. Refer to PepsiCo's Note 7, "Pension, Retiree Medical and Saving Plans" (Appendix A). Exhibit 8.9 reports the status of PepsiCo's pension plan at the end of Year 3 and Year 4. The top portion of Exhibit 8.9 shows the assets and liabilities of the pension plan. The last line shows the amounts that PepsiCo records on its books related to the pension plan. The unrecognized items (middle three lines of the exhibit) represent amounts reflected in assets and liabilities of the pension plan but not yet recognized on the employer's books. We discuss the accounting entries on the employer's books later in this section.

EXHIBIT 8.8

Activity Affecting a Defined Benefit Pension Plan

Pension Fund Assets	Pension Fund Liabilities
Assets at Beginning of Period	Liabilities at Beginning of Period
± Actual Earnings on Investments	+ Increase in Liabilities Due to Passage of Time
+ Contributions Received from the Employer	+ Increase in Liabilities from Employee Services
	± Actuarial Gains and Losses Due to Changes in Assumptions
− Payments to Retirees	− Payments to Retirees
= Assets at End of Period	= Liabilities at End of Period

[19]The accounting and disclosures for pension plans follow two FASB pronouncements: Financial Accounting Standards Board, *Statement of Financial Accounting Standards Statement No. 87*, "Employer's Accounting for Pensions" (1985) and Financial Accounting Standards Board, *Statement of Financial Accounting Standards Statement No. 132*, "Employer's Disclosures about Pensions and Other Retirement Benefits" (1998).

EXHIBIT 8.9

Funded Status of PepsiCo's Pension Plan (amounts in millions)

	Year 4	Year 3
Accounting Records of Pension Plan		
Actuarial Present Value of Projected Benefit Obligation	$(5,920)	$(5,214)
Plan Assets at Fair Value	4,990	4,245
Projected Benefit Obligation (in Excess of) Less Than Plan Assets	$ (930)	$ (969)
Items That Reconcile the Two Sets of Records		
Unrecognized Prior Service	22	44
Unrecognized Experience Loss[a]	2,393	2,207
Other[b]	12	6
Accounting Records of Employer		
Net Amounts Recognized (Accrued Pension Asset on Balance Sheet)	$ 1,497	$ 1,288

[a]Note 7, "Pension, Retiree Medical and Savings Plans," explains the difference between the beginning and ending balance of $186 ($2,393 − $2,207) for Year 4 under the caption "Components of increase in unrecognized experience loss" (Appendix A).

[b]Represents fourth-quarter benefit payments ($12 in Year 4 and $6 in Year 3).

Interpreting these disclosures requires several definitions:

Accumulated Benefit Obligation. The present value of amounts the employer expects to pay to retired employees (taking into consideration actuarial assumptions concerning employee turnover and mortality) based on employees' service to date and current-year compensation levels. The accumulated benefit obligation indicates the present value of the benefits earned to date, excluding any future salary increases that will serve as the base for computing the pension payment and excluding future years of service prior to retirement.

Projected Benefit Obligation. The actuarial present value of amounts the employer expects to pay to retired employees based on employees' service to date but using the expected future salaries that will serve as the base for computing the pension payment. The difference between the accumulated and projected benefit obligation is the effect of future salary increases. Consequently, the projected benefit obligation exceeds the accumulated benefit obligation. The projected benefit obligation is also closer in amount to what one might view as an economic measure of the pension obligation: the present value of amounts the employer expects to pay to employees during retirement based on total expected years of service (past and future) and expected future salaries.

The required disclosures show the relationship between the market value of pension fund assets and the projected benefit obligation at each valuation date. The amounts on the books of the pension plan reflect current market values of both assets and liabilities at each valuation date. A pension plan can be overfunded or underfunded at any point in time.

At the end of Year 3, the assets in PepsiCo's pension plans of $4,245 million were less than the benefit obligation of $5,214 million by $969 million. Thus, the pension plan was *underfunded* at the end of Year 3. At the end of Year 4, the assets in PepsiCo's pension plan of $4,990 million were less than the benefit obligation of $5,920 million. Thus, the pension plan was underfunded at the end of Year 4 as well by $930 million.[20] One might view an excess of the projected benefit obligation over pension fund assets as a liability that firms should report on the balance sheet. The FASB, responding to criticisms that the measurement of the projected benefit obligation requires subjective projections of future salary increases, stipulates instead that firms show an excess of the *accumulated* benefit obligation over pension fund assets on the balance sheet as a liability (included in what *Statement No. 87* labels the *minimum liability*). Because the accumulated benefit obligation is usually smaller than the projected benefit obligation, relatively few firms report a liability for underfunded benefits by this measure. We discuss this minimum liability in a later section.

GAAP also requires firms to show the reasons why their pension assets and pension liabilities changed during the year. Exhibit 8.10 summarizes PepsiCo's disclosures from Note 7. Although PepsiCo's pension plan was slightly underfunded for both Year 3 and Year 4 by similar amounts, as detailed in the previous paragraph, offsetting changes in the components accounted for the similar amounts. For example, note that the actual return on assets increased significantly between Year 3 and Year 4 (decreasing net underfunded status of the plan), but at the same time the contributions to the plan by PepsiCo decreased between Year 3 and Year 4 (increasing the underfunded status of the plan). Also, note that service and interest costs increased between Year 3 and Year 4 (increasing

EXHIBIT 8.10

Changes in the Funded Status of PepsiCo's Pension Plan (amounts in millions)

Accounting Records of Pension Plan	Year 4	Year 3
Assets at Beginning of Year	$4,245	$3,537
Actual Return on Plan Assets	469	281
Plus Contribution from PepsiCo	453	552
Less Payments to Retirees	(234)	(208)
Other Changes, Primarily Foreign Currency Adjustments	57	83
Assets at End of Year	$4,990	$4,245
Benefit Obligation at Beginning of Year	$5,214	$4,324
Plus Service Cost	220	178
Plus Interest Cost	318	284
Less Payments to Retirees	(234)	(208)
Plus Experience Loss	334	541
Other Changes, Primarily Foreign Currency Adjustments	68	95
Benefit Obligation at End of Year	$5,920	$5,214

[20]If the plan is overfunded, one might argue that an excess of pension fund assets over the projected benefit obligation represents an asset of the employer. However, *Statement No. 87* does not permit firms to recognize this resource on the balance sheet.

the underfunded status of the plan), while at the same time the experience loss decreased significantly between Year 3 and Year 4 (decreasing the underfunded status of the plan).

Next, we explore more fully each of these three contributing explanations for a change in the net funded status of a pension plan.

Accounting Records of the Employer

The last line of Exhibit 8.9 shows the net pension assets recorded on the books of PepsiCo. PepsiCo reports a net pension asset of $1,288 million at the end of Year 3 and a slightly larger net pension asset of $1,497 million at the end of Year 4. PepsiCo indicates in Note 7 the particular accounts on the balance sheet that comprise these net amounts. The amounts that appear on the balance sheet of the employer generally result from three entries each period:

1. Recognition of pension expense.
2. Recognition of pension contribution.
3. Recognition of minimum underfunded pension liability.

We discuss each of these three entries next.

Employer's Entry 1: Recognition of Pension Expense

Firms must calculate net pension expense each year based on the projected benefit cost method, which means that actuarial calculations use accumulated service to date and projected future salaries. PepsiCo reports in Note 7 that its pension expense for Year 4 is $245 million.[21] PepsiCo's recognition of net pension expense had the following effects on the financial statements (ignoring income taxes):

	C	+	N$A	=	L	+	CC	+	AOCI	+	RE
BS-BOP											
(1)					+245						−245
IBT											−245

PepsiCo's entry in its accounting records to recognize net pension expense (excluding curtailments and special termination benefits) is as follows:

Pension Expense	245	
Pension Liability		245

Exhibit 8.11 summarizes the five elements that constitute net pension expense and shows the amounts from PepsiCo's Note 7.[22] We discuss each of these elements next.

---

[21]PepsiCo also recognized separate charges to curtail or settle existing pension plans or provide special termination benefits. We do not consider these charges in this discussion of pensions.

[22]Some companies report a sixth element of net pension expense that relates to the adoption of *Statement No. 87*, typically labeled amortization of net pension asset or net pension liability (see Case 8.2 for the reporting of this element of net pension expense for American Airlines and United Airlines). Most firms adopted *Statement No. 87* between 1986 and 1988. At the time of adoption, firms typically had either more assets in the pension fund than the pension obligation or a larger pension obligation than pension fund assets. Instead of immediately reporting the difference as a gain or loss in measuring pension expense, GAAP requires employers to amortize the difference over the remaining working years of employees. Companies are increasingly *not* reporting this element (as is the case with PepsiCo) because either the amortization period has expired or the amortization amount is not material relative to the total amount of the net pension expense.

EXHIBIT 8.11

Components of Pension Expense for PepsiCo

	Debit (Increase)	Credit (Decrease)
1. Service Cost—the increase in the projected benefit obligation because employees worked an additional year	220	
2. Interest Cost—the increase in the projected benefit obligation because of the passage of time	318	
3. Expected Return on Plan Assets—the expected change in the market value of plan assets due to interest, dividends, and changes in the market value of investments		390
4. Amortization of increases in the projected benefit obligation that arise because the firm sweetens the pension benefit formula and gives employees credit for their prior service under the sweetened benefit arrangement. The amortization period is generally the average remaining service life of employees, although a shorter period may be required if an employer regularly sweetens its pension plan	7	
5. Amortization of gains and losses because actual experience differs from actuarial assumptions (e.g., salary interest rate, employee turnover, mortality, asset returns).		
Actuarial Loss	90	
Actuarial Gain		N/A
Net pension expense	**245**	

Element 1: Service Cost. The present value of the projected benefit obligation on the books of the pension plan increases each year because employees work an additional year. GAAP refers to the increase as the service cost. The employer includes the service cost in pension expense each year (PepsiCo's service cost for Year 4 is $220 million).

Element 2: Interest Cost. The present value of the projected benefit obligation on the books of the pension plan also increases each year because pension payments are one year nearer to being made. GAAP refers to this increase as the interest cost. The employer includes this amount in pension expense on its books each year (PepsiCo's interest cost for Year 4 is $318 million). PepsiCo discloses in Note 7 and its Management's Discussion and Analysis (MD&A), "Our Critical Accounting Policies—Pension and Retiree Medical Plans" (Appendix B) that it used an interest rate of 6.1 percent at the end of Year 4 to value the pension fund obligation. Multiplying the pension obligation of $5,214 million on January 1, Year 4, by this interest rate approximately equals the $318 million amount recognized as interest cost for the year.

Element 3: Expected Return on Pension Investments. Pension plans must have sufficient assets to pay retirement benefits. Pension plans obtain the needed assets from employer contributions and from investment income. The higher the return on pension investments, the less cash the employer needs to contribute to the pension plan. GAAP requires firms to reduce their pension expense for the return on pension fund investments. Recall that pension expense and the pension liability increase each year for service and interest costs. The sum of these two amounts is the additional assets needed in the pension fund to fund the increase in the pension obligation for the period. To the extent that earnings on pension fund investments fund this additional liability, the employer can contribute less to the pension fund. Thus, earnings on pension investment reduce the employer's pension expense.

GAAP requires firms to reduce pension expense each period by the *expected,* not the *actual,* return on investments. When deciding on a funding level for employer contributions, firms make an assumption as to the long-term expected return on pension fund investments. Note 7 and PepsiCo's MD&A discussion state that the firm assumed a long-term return on pension assets of 7.8 percent as of the end of Year 4. Actual returns over time will vary around this amount but should average 7.8 percent over the long term. GAAP encourages firms to take a long-term view of their pension plan by reducing pension expense for the long-term expected return on investments. As we discuss later with respect to element 5 of pension expense, GAAP requires firms to amortize into pension expense over time any difference between expected and actual returns on investments. Note that PepsiCo's assets measured at fair value at the beginning of Year 4 totaled $4,245 million. The expected return on these assets for Year 4 at 7.8 percent would be $331 million, which is lower than the reduction in pension expense that PepsiCo recognized for Year 4 of $390 million. Although reconciliation between the two amounts is not possible, it is important to note that the $390 million reported as a reduction in pension expense is the expected, not actual, return on investments.

Recognizing the Effects of Unexpected Changes in Pension Plan Assets and Liabilities

If the assets in a pension fund equal the liabilities of the pension plan at the beginning of the year and the rate of return earned on pension assets exactly equals the discount rate used to compute the pension liability, then pension expense each year will equal the service cost. The return on pension investments will exactly offset the interest cost. This precise matching seldom occurs for the following reasons:

1. Pension funds generate actual earnings on investments at a rate that differs from the long-term rate of return that actuaries assume in deciding on the appropriate level of employer contributions to the pension fund. GAAP does not permit firms to immediately increase pension expense for any investment returns shortfall or reduce pension expense for any excess investment returns.
2. Firms change the pension benefit formula and give employees credit under the new formula for the years of service prior to the change (referred to as a *prior service cost*). The change immediately increases the projected benefit obligation of the pension fund. GAAP does not permit the employer, however, to immediately increase pension expense for the increase in the pension obligation.
3. Actuarial experience with respect to employee turnover, mortality, compensation levels, and the discount rate may differ from that assumed or used at the beginning of the year. The employer may change its actuarial assumptions with respect to any of these factors, which immediately changes the amount of the projected benefit obligation of the pension fund (referred to as an *actuarial gain or loss*). GAAP again does not permit the employer to adjust pension expense immediately for the actuarial gain or loss.

Although these three items change either the assets or liabilities of the pension plan, GAAP does not require that firms recognize, or flow through, their full effect into the measurement of pension expense and earnings immediately when they occur. Instead, GAAP requires firms to defer their effects and amortize them over the remaining expected period of benefit, usually the remaining average working life of employees. The amortization smooths the effect on pension expense and earnings. Items (4) and (5) in Exhibit 8.11 include the items subject to deferral and amortization.

Element 4: Amortization of Prior Service Cost. Firms likewise defer and then amortize increases in the pension benefit obligation that arise from sweetening of the benefit formula. This amortization is the fourth component of pension expense in Exhibit 8.11. PepsiCo amortized $7 million as an addition to pension expense for Year 4.

Element 5: Amortization of Actuarial Gains and Losses. Actuarial gains and losses arise when actual returns on investments differ from expectations and when the actuarial assumptions underlying the pension plan change. GAAP likewise requires firms to defer and then amortize the gain or loss. PepsiCo amortized $90 million of its unrecognized experience loss during Year 4, reporting the amount as an increase in pension expense for the year. PepsiCo reported a total accumulated but unamortized experience loss at the beginning of Year 4 of $2,207 million, which increased to $2,393 million at the end of Year 7. Note 7 provides an analysis of the increase in the total accumulated but unamortized experience loss in a subsection titled "Components of increase in unrecognized experience loss." Three items dominate the increase: (1) changes in employee-related assumptions (turnover); (2) changes in liability-related experience (payment commitments); and (3) actual asset returns differing from expected returns. PepsiCo will amortize the $2,393 million currently unrecognized experience loss over future periods.

We noted earlier that if (1) pension assets equal pension liabilities, (2) the rate of return on pension assets equals the interest rate used to compute the present value of the pension liability, and (3) actuarial assumptions turn out as expected, then the employer's pension expense will equal the current employee service cost (item (1) in Exhibit 8.11). Items (2) and (3) will net to zero, and items (4) and (5) will be zero. The lack of equality of pension assets and liabilities and the realization of a different rate of return on assets than the interest rate used to compute the pension liability result in unequal offsetting of items (2) and (3). This inequality plus changes in the pension benefit formula and an inability to realize actuarial assumptions create the need for larger or smaller employer contributions to the pension fund in the future. Because the employer's total expenses must ultimately equal the cash contributed to the pension fund, pension expense must increase or decrease as well. *Statement No. 87* requires firms to smooth the effect of these excess or deficient amounts (items (4) and (5)), rather than including them in the calculation of pension expense immediately.

Pension expense each period is the net of these five elements. The five elements may result in a net pension expense or a net pension credit. If a pension plan is not significantly overfunded or underfunded, the five items typically net to a pension expense. This is the case for PepsiCo in Year 2, Year 3, and Year 4. During the late 1990s, stock market prices increased significantly and many firms found that the market value of pension investments far exceeded their pension obligations. The credit, or reduction, in pension expense for the expected return on pension assets exceeded the service and interest cost and resulted in a net pension credit instead of a net pension expense.

Employer's Entry 2: Recognition of Pension Contribution

The second entry that the employer will make on its books each year (the first entry is to recognize pension expense, as just described) records its contribution of cash to the pension fund. Exhibit 8.10 and Note 7 indicate that PepsiCo contributed $453 million to its pension fund during Year 4. The effects of (1) the recognition of pension expense of $245 million and (2) the pension contribution of $453 million on the financial statements are as follows:

BS-BOP	C	+	N$A	=	L	+	CC	+	AOCI	+	RE
(1)					+245						−245
(2)	−453				−453						
IBT											−245

PepsiCo's entry to record the pension contribution is as follows:

Pension Liability	453	
Cash		453

The amount that a firm recognizes as pension expense each period typically will not equal the amount the firm contributes to its pension fund. The firm measures the amount for pension expense in accordance with the provisions of *Statement No. 87.* The amount the firm contributes to its pension fund relies on actuaries' recommendations concerning the needed level of funding, minimum required funding dictated by government regulations, tax effects of contribution, and decisions by the firm regarding investments of its financial resources. For example, a firm with a significantly overfunded pension plan might delay additional contributions for a few years and use the cash for other corporate purposes. In this case, the firm recognizes pension expense each year but does not contribute cash to the pension fund. Alternatively, a firm might contribute more than the amount of pension expense. Earnings on pension investments are not subject to income taxation, whereas earnings on cash left within a firm are subject to taxation. Within prescribed limits, firms can make excess pension contributions and delay or avoid taxes on investment earnings.

When a firm contributes more to the pension fund than it recognizes as pension expense, a net pension asset appears on the balance sheet. PepsiCo, for example, recognizes a net pension asset of $1,288 million on its balance sheet at the end of Year 3 and an even larger net pension asset of $1,497 at the end of Year 4. Note that this pension asset (or pension liability) on the balance sheet bears no necessary relation to the more important measure of the status of a pension plan: the difference between the total assets in the pension fund and the projected benefit obligation. Refer again to Exhibit 8.9, showing the status of PepsiCo's pension plan. The assets in PepsiCo's pension plans at the end of Year 3 were *less than* the projected benefit obligation by $969 million. Yet PepsiCo reports a net pension asset on its balance sheet of $1,288 million at the end of Year 3 because its cumulative pension contributions exceed cumulative pension expense. At the end of Year 4, the same relationship exists. PepsiCo reports a net pension asset of $1,497 million on its balance sheet because cumulative pension contributions continue to exceed cumulative pension expense. The primary reason for the differences is that the pension plan has experienced losses that PepsiCo has not yet recognized in measuring pension expense.

Employer's Entry 3: Recognition of Minimum Underfunded Pension Liability

If a firm has any pension plan (most firms maintain separate pension plans for each of the various groups of employees) for which the accumulated benefit obligation exceeds the assets in that pension plan, then the firm must report as a minimum a liability equal to this underfunded accumulated benefit obligation on its balance sheet. (In Note 7 PepsiCo uses the term "Liability at end of year for service to date" for accumulated benefit obligation.) The entry to recognize the minimum liability adjusts any pension liability already on the employer's books resulting from a difference between pension expenses and pension contributions from the first two entries listed earlier. The entry to recognize the minimum liability is as follows:

Intangible Asset	X	
Accumulated Other Comprehensive Income/Loss	Y	
Pension Liability		Z

The firm increases an intangible asset up to the amount of any unrecognized prior service cost on plans with underfunded accumulated benefit obligations. The increase in intangible assets reflects the expected benefits of future productivity of employees that should result from sweetening plan benefits and making those benefits retroactive. The remaining amount of any incremental liability recognized decreases Accumulated Other Comprehensive Income. The amounts debited to Accumulated Other Comprehensive Income primarily represent unamortized actuarial gains and losses. PepsiCo reports in Note 7 for Year 4 that plans with an accumulated benefit obligation in excess of plan assets have assets of $172 million and an accumulated benefit obligation of $511 million, for a net liability of $339 million. PepsiCo includes this $339 million underfunded accumulated benefit obligation for some of its pension plans in the accrued benefit liability account, which at the end of Year 4 totals $424 million (this amount appears under the caption "Net amounts as recognized in the Consolidated Balance Sheet" in Note 7).

Analysts' Treatment of Pensions

The analyst should consider several items when evaluating accounting quality with respect to pensions and analyzing profitability and risk.

Funded Status of Pension Plan

One question that the analyst might ask is: Should I adjust the balance sheet of the employer to recognize an overfunded pension plan as an asset and an underfunded pension plan as a liability? Possible responses include the following:

1. Make no adjustment to the employer's balance sheet for an underfunded or overfunded pension plan. The rationale for this approach is that the under- or overfunding is a temporary condition that will work itself out over a longer time period.
2. Recognize an underfunded projected benefit obligation as a liability. The employer may have to contribute an amount to the pension fund in the future equal to the underfunding. Including the obligation among liabilities provides a better measure for assessing financial structure risk. PepsiCo's underfunded projected benefit obligation is $930 million at the end of Year 4. The books of PepsiCo show a net pension asset of $1,497 million on this date, and thus the analyst's adjustment to eliminate the net pension asset of $1,497 and to recognize a liability of $930 million, assuming an income tax rate of 35 percent, is as follows:

Year 4		
Accumulated Other Comprehensive Loss		
[(1 − .35) × ($1,497 + $930)]	1,578	
Deferred Tax Assets [.35 × ($1,497 + $930)]	849	
Pension Assets (net)		1,497
Pension Liability		930

The debit to Accumulated Other Comprehensive Loss represents unrecognized prior service costs and actuarial gains and losses (net of taxes), which the firm will amortize as an adjustment of pension expense in future periods. When the firm contributes cash to the pension fund to make up for the deficiency in pension assets, it will realize tax benefits. In the meantime, the analyst recognizes a deferred tax asset. The credit of $1,497 million to net pension assets adjusts for the amounts now appearing on the books of PepsiCo that gave rise to this net asset. The credit of $930 million to pension liability recognizes the underfunded status of the pension plan.

3. Recognize an overfunded projected benefit obligation as an asset and an underfunded projected benefit obligation as a liability. This approach shows the potential benefit of not having to contribute as much to the pension fund in the future because of its overfunding (pension asset) and the need to contribute more to the pension fund in the future because of its underfunding (pension liability). At the end of Year 4, PepsiCo did not have any overfunded pension plans, and the adjustment for the underfunded plans at the end of Year 4 is the same as in item 2 above.
4. Include both the assets and liabilities of the pension fund on the employer's balance sheet. Include the return on pension assets as interest and dividend revenue, and the interest cost component of pension expense as interest expense on the employer's income statement. This approach consolidates the financial statements of the pension fund with those of the employer, much like those for a parent company and majority-owned subsidiaries (a topic discussed in Chapter 9). The case for consolidation rests on the employer's right to access pension assets and obligation to provide for pension liabilities. The counterargument for consolidation is that federal pension law significantly constrains the operational relation between the employer and its pension fund as compared to most parent/subsidiary relationships.

Impact of Actuarial Assumptions

Firms must disclose in notes to the financial statements the assumptions made with respect to (1) the discount rate used to compute the pension benefit obligation, (2) the expected rate of return on pension investments (including the pension plan investment guidelines that form the basis for establishing the expected rate of return), and (3) the rate of compensation increase, which affects the amount of the projected benefit obligation.

The amount of the pension benefit obligation is inversely related to the discount rate. *Statement No. 87* specifies that firms should use a long-term government bond rate as the discount rate. Thus, firms should not vary significantly with respect to the discount rate used. One must recognize, however, that even small differences in the discount rate can materially affect the size of the pension benefit obligation.

Firms use different expected rates of return on pension investments, in part because of different mixtures of investments in their pension portfolios. For example, a firm with equal proportions of debt and equity should have a lower expected return than a firm that invests fully in equities. PepsiCo discloses in Note 7 that the target allocation for Year 5 is 60 percent equity securities and 40 percent debt securities. In fact, the actual allocation for Year 4 was 60 percent equity securities, 39 percent debt securities and 1 percent cash, disclosed in Note 7. Recall from earlier discussions that PepsiCo's expected rate of return on plan assets is 7.8 percent for Year 4. In the MD&A section "Our Critical Accounting Policies, Pension and Retiree Medical Plans" (Appendix B), PepsiCo states:

> Our current assumed rate of return on plan assets is 7.8 percent, reflecting an estimated long-term return of 9.3 percent from equity securities and an estimated 5.8 percent from fixed income securities.

Firms may also use different expected rates of return in an effort to manage earnings. The assumed long-term rate of return on pension assets impacts the analysis of pensions in several ways. First, if the firm cannot generate returns on average equal to this rate, then the firm will need to contribute additional assets in the future. Second, the expected return on pension investments reduces pension expense each period and increases earnings. GAAP requires firms to amortize any difference between expected and actual returns, so a deficiency in returns because of assuming too high a level of expected returns shows up slowly in pension expense. Recent decreases in the market values of equity securities have led firms to decrease their expected rates of return on pension assets. Note, for example, that PepsiCo reduced its expected return rate from 9.1 percent to 7.8 percent between Year 2 and Year 4.

The amount of the pension benefit obligation is directly related to the assumed rate of compensation increases. Firms have incentives to use a lower rather than a higher assumed rate of compensation increases, both to lower their projected benefit obligation and to create lower expectations among employees about future compensation increases.

The analyst should compare a firm's assumptions over time and with other firms to evaluate the firm's level of aggressiveness in making assumptions.

Signals about Earnings Persistence

Sharp swings in the market values of investments, as occurred in 1998 to early 2000 with the buildup of Internet technology businesses and in early 2000 to late 2002 with the downturn in technology company stock prices, can impact pension expense and earnings significantly. Although firms use long-term expected returns on investments to compute the expected return on assets each period, they apply this rate to the market value of assets in the pension portfolio. When market values increase, as they did in the early to late 1990s, many firms found that their pension expenses became pension credits. For some firms during this period, a substantial portion of their increased earnings resulted from a swing from pension expense to pension credit. During the stock market downturn that followed, the pension credits became pension expenses, exacerbating the downward pressure on earnings already experienced from weakened economic conditions. When using earnings of the current period to forecast earnings in the future, the analyst should recognize the impact of changing stock prices on the measurement of pension expense.

Postretirement Benefits Other Than Pensions

In addition to pensions, most employers provide health care and life insurance benefits to retired employees. This benefit may take the form of a fixed dollar amount to cover part or all of the cost of health and life insurance (analogous to the defined contribution type of pension plan) or the benefit may specify the level of health care or life insurance provided (analogous to the defined benefit type of pension plan).

The accounting issues related to these postretirement obligations are similar to those discussed previously for pensions. The employer must recognize the cost of the postretirement benefits during the employees' years of service. The employer may or may not set aside funds to cover the cost of these benefits. Health and life insurance expense each period includes an amount for current service plus interest on the health care or life insurance benefits obligation for the period. Expected earnings on investments in a postretirement benefits fund, if any, reduce these expenses. The employer defers and then amortizes actuarial gains and losses due to changes in employee turnover, health care costs, interest rates, and similar factors.

The major difference between the accounting for pensions and the accounting for other postretirement benefits is that firms need not report an excess of the accumulated benefits obligation over assets in a postretirement benefits fund as a liability on the balance sheet.[23] Firms must report this amount in the notes to the financial statements. During the deliberation process on the reporting standard for postretirement benefits, business firms exerted pressure on the FASB not to require recognition of the underfunded accumulated benefits obligation, particularly for health care benefits. These business firms argued that the amount of this obligation was both large, relative to other liabilities and shareholders' equity, and uncertain, because of uncertainties regarding future health care inflation rates. Some firms indicated that they would eliminate health care retirement benefits if the FASB required recognition of the liability. As a compromise, the FASB allows firms to recognize the obligation either in full upon adoption of *Statement No. 106* or piecemeal over employees' working years.[24]

Once again refer to Note 7, "Pension, Retiree Medical and Savings Plans," to PepsiCo's financial statements (Appendix A). When PepsiCo adopted *Statement No. 106*, it elected to recognize the full obligation for health care and life insurance benefits. By the end of Year 3, its balance sheet includes a liability of $894 million (this amount appears under the caption "Funded status as recognized in the Consolidated Balance Sheet" in Note 7). The recognized liability grew to $943 million by the end of Year 4. At the end of Year 3, the total benefit obligation exceeded plan assets (which are zero, because PepsiCo does not fund its retiree medical obligation) by $1,264 million, and at the end of Year 4, the total benefit obligation exceeds plan assets by $1,319 million. Thus, the obligation for postretirement benefits at the end of both Year 3 and Year 4 exceed the liability that PepsiCo reports on its balance sheet. The difference between the two results from two factors:

1. PepsiCo apparently increased the level of benefits for employees since adoption of *Statement No. 106* but has not yet fully recognized the reduction in cost for these benefits on its books. PepsiCo reports these unrecognized benefits as a prior service cost in Note 7.
2. PepsiCo has unrecognized experience losses of $434 million at the end of Year 3 and $473 million at the end of Year 4. PepsiCo does not set aside cash for these benefits, but contributes sufficient cash each year to fund required payments under its plans. PepsiCo contributed $70 in Year 3 and $76 million in Year 4 to cover benefit payments for each of these years (reported in Note 7). Thus, the

---

[23]The accumulated benefits obligation for health care incorporates health care costs expected when employees receive benefits and is therefore more similar to the projected benefit pension obligation than the accumulated benefit pension obligation. See Financial Accounting Standards Board, *Statement of Financial Accounting Standards No. 106*, "Employer's Accounting for Postretirement Benefits Other Than Pensions" (1990).

[24]The implications of the differences between the two methods allowed for adopting *Statement No. 106* are discussed in Eli Amir and Joshua Livnat, "Adoption Choices of SFAS No. 106: Implications for Financial Analysis," *Journal of Financial Statement Analysis* (Winter 1997), pp. 51–60.

unrecognized loss must result from measuring the benefit obligation. The loss could result from providing increased benefits to employees or from increasing the assumed rate of health care cost increases.

Analysts' concerns with postretirement benefits other than pensions are similar to those for pensions. The magnitude of the postretirement benefit obligations, particularly related to health care, can be large because many firms, like PepsiCo, do not fund the plans. In addition, in recent years health care costs have escalated and many firms are reticent to curtail benefits promised to retirees. Should the analyst add the underfunded postretirement benefit obligation to liabilities in assessing risk? How reasonable are the firm's assumptions regarding health care cost increases, discount rates, and amortization periods? Is the postretirement benefit fund, if any, generating returns consistent with the expected rate of return?

INCOME TAXES

Income taxes affect the analysis of a firm's profitability (income tax expense is a subtraction when computing net income) and its cash flows (income tax payments require cash). Deferred tax assets and deferred tax liabilities on the balance sheet affect future cash flows. The note to the financial statements on income taxes contains useful information for assessing a firm's income tax position. This section reviews the required accounting for income taxes[25] and discusses how the analyst might use income tax disclosures when analyzing a firm's financial statements.

Review of Income Tax Accounting

Chapter 2 discussed the required accounting for income taxes. Review these important concepts:

1. Firms often use different methods of accounting for financial reporting and income tax reporting, which means that income before taxes will likely differ from taxable income.
2. Differences between income before taxes and taxable income are either permanent or temporary. Permanent differences arise from revenues and expenses that GAAP requires firms to include in income before taxes but that the income tax law excludes from taxable income. Interest earned on state and municipal bonds is an example of a permanent difference. Temporary differences result from including revenues and expenses in income before taxes in a different period than those items affect taxable income. Depreciation expense computed for financial reporting using the straight-line method and for tax reporting using an accelerated depreciation method is an example of a temporary difference.
3. GAAP requires firms to measure income tax expense each period based on income before taxes excluding permanent differences, not on taxable income. The objective is to match income tax expense against the pretax income recognized for financial reporting.
4. The amount of income tax expense for a period will often differ from the amount of income taxes currently payable because of temporary differences between income for financial reporting and tax reporting. Temporary differences give rise to either deferred tax assets or deferred tax liabilities. Deferred tax assets result in

[25]Financial Accounting Standards Board, *Statement of Financial Accounting Standards No. 109*, "Accounting for Income Taxes" (1992).

future tax savings when temporary differences reverse. Deferred tax liabilities require future tax payments when temporary differences reverse.

The preceding description sets forth the accounting for income taxes from an income statement perspective. Computing income tax expense and income taxes payable involves applying a tax rate to income before taxes excluding permanent differences and to taxable income, respectively. *Statement No. 109,* however, requires firms to follow a balance sheet approach when computing income tax expense. The results are similar in most instances. The following description summarizes the balance sheet approach:

1. Identify at each balance sheet date all differences between the *book basis* (that is, the book value for financial reporting) of assets, liabilities, and tax loss carryforwards, and the *tax basis* of assets, liabilities, and tax loss carryforwards.
2. Eliminate from step 1 items that will not have a future tax consequence (that is, permanent differences).
3. Separate the remaining differences after the first two steps into those that give rise to future tax deductions and those that give rise to future taxable income. Financial reporting refers to these differences as *temporary differences.* Multiply differences between the book and tax basis of assets and liabilities that give rise to future tax deductions by the enacted statutory tax rate expected to apply in those future periods. The result is a *deferred tax asset.* Multiply differences between the book and tax basis of assets and liabilities that give rise to future taxable income by the enacted statutory tax rate expected to apply in those future periods. The result is a *deferred tax liability.*

   Firms may have unused net operating loss and tax credit carryforwards as of a balance sheet date. These items have the potential to reduce future taxable income (operating loss carryforwards) or future taxes payable (tax credit carryforwards). The firm includes the tax effect of these carryforwards in deferred tax assets at each balance sheet date.
4. Assess the likelihood that the firm will realize the benefits of deferred tax assets in the future. This assessment should consider the nature (for example, cyclical or noncyclical) and characteristics (for example, growing, mature, or declining) of the firm's business and its tax planning strategies for the future. If realization of the benefits of deferred tax assets is "more likely than not" (that is, the likelihood exceeds 50 percent), then deferred tax assets equal the amounts computed in step 3. However, if it is more likely than not that a firm will not realize some or all of the deferred tax assets, then the firm must reduce the deferred tax assets for a *valuation allowance* (similar in concept to the allowance for uncollectible accounts). The valuation allowance reduces the deferred tax assets to the amounts the firm expects to realize by way of reduced taxes in the future.

The result of following this four-step procedure is a deferred tax asset and a deferred tax liability at each balance sheet date. Income tax expense each period equals:

1. Income taxes currently payable on taxable income.
2. Plus a net credit change in the deferred tax asset or liability and minus a net debit change in the deferred tax asset or liability between the beginning and the end of the period.

Exhibit 8.12 compares the components of income tax expense using the income statement approach and the balance sheet approach. The principal difference between these two approaches relates to item (2) versus item (5). Item (2) includes only temporary dif-

EXHIBIT 8.12

Comparison of Income Statement and Balance Approaches for Measuring Income Tax Expense

Income Statement Approach	Balance Sheet Approach
(1) Taxes currently payable on taxable income	(4) Taxes currently payable on taxable income
(2) Taxes potentially saved or payable in the future from temporary differences between current period's income for financial and tax reporting	(5) Change in deferred tax assets and deferred tax liabilities during the current period
(3) Income tax expense = (1) + (2)	(6) Income tax expense = (4) + (5)

ferences for the current year between financial and tax reporting incomes, whereas item (5) includes temporary differences, enacted changes during a period in future income tax rates, and changes in the valuation allowance as a result of new information regarding the realizability of deferred tax assets. When tax rates do not change and a firm recognizes no valuation allowance, the income statement and balance sheet approaches yield identical amounts for income tax expense.

Required Income Tax Disclosures

The note to the financial statements on income taxes is a rich source of information not only for understanding a firm's income tax position but for understanding much about its operations as well. This section describes four specific GAAP disclosures, using amounts for a hypothetical firm:

1. Components of income tax expense.
2. Components of income before taxes.
3. Reconciliation of income taxes at statutory rate with income tax expense.
4. Components of deferred tax assets and liabilities.

1. Components of Income Tax Expense

Firms must disclose the amount of income taxes currently payable and the amount deferred, broken down by governmental entity (federal, foreign, state, and local).

Components of Income Tax Expense

	Year 3	Year 2	Year 1
Current —Federal	$191	$105	$123
—Foreign	128	75	61
—State and Local	18	12	13
Total Current	$337	$192	$197
Deferred —Federal	$ 35	$ 40	$ 70
—Foreign	38	30	19
Total Deferred	$ 73	$ 70	$ 89
Total Income Tax Expense	$410	$262	$286

The journal entries made to record income taxes each year follow:

	Year 3		Year 2		Year 1	
Income Tax Expense	410		262		286	
Income Tax Payable		337		192		197
Deferred Tax Asset or Deferred Tax Liability		73		70		89

2. Components of Income before Taxes

Assessing a firm's tax position over time or relative to other firms requires some base for scaling the amount of income tax expense. Income before taxes serves this purpose.

Components of Income before Taxes

	Year 3	Year 2	Year 1
United States	$ 700	$450	$600
Foreign	350	250	200
Total	$1,050	$700	$800

The average, or effective,[26] tax rates for the three years on total income before taxes are as follows:

Year 1: $286/$800 = 35.7%
Year 2: $262/$700 = 37.4%
Year 3: $410/$1,050 = 39.0%

Thus, the average tax rate increased over the three-year period.

3. Reconciliation of Income Taxes at Statutory Rate with Income Tax Expense

The third required disclosure explains why the average tax rates shown previously differ from the statutory federal tax rate on income before taxes. Firms can express reconciling items in either dollar amounts or percentage terms.

Reconciliation of Income Taxes at Statutory Rate with Income Tax Expense

	Year 3	Year 2	Year 1
(1) Income Taxes on Income before Taxes at Statutory Rate	35.0%	35.0%	35.0%
(2) Foreign Tax Rates Greater (Less) Than Statutory Federal Rate	4.1	2.5	1.3
(3) State and Local Taxes	1.1	1.1	1.1
(4) Dividend Deduction	(0.6)	(0.5)	(0.7)
(5) Tax-Exempt Income	(0.4)	(0.4)	(0.5)

[26]The terms *effective tax rate* and *average tax rate* are used interchangeably. Although analysts more commonly use the term *effective tax rate,* we prefer use of the term *average tax rate.*

(6) Restructuring and Impairment Charges	0.6	0.4	0.2
(7) Percentage Depletion in Excess of Cost	(0.8)	(0.7)	(0.7)
Income Tax Expense	39.0%	37.4%	35.7%

The statutory federal tax rate was 35 percent in each year. The average tax rates were greater than the statutory rates. The reconciliation includes two types of reconciling items: (1) tax rate differences and (2) permanent differences. The sections that follow discuss each of these reconciling items more fully.

Foreign Rates Greater (Less) Than the Statutory Federal Rate. The denominator of the average tax rate computation combines both U.S.-source and foreign-source income for financial reporting. The initial assumption on line (1) is that all of this income is subject to taxes at a rate equal to the U.S. federal statutory rate. Foreign tax rates are usually different from the U.S. federal rate, however. This line indicates how much the overall average tax rate increased or decreased because of these foreign rate differences.

Refer to the first two types of income tax disclosures discussed earlier. Foreign tax expense for Year 3 totaled $166 (= $128 + $38). Pretax book income from foreign sources was $350. If this income were subject to tax at the federal rate of 35 percent, foreign income tax expense would have been $123 (= .35 × $350). Foreign tax expense of $166 exceeded the amount at the federal statutory rate by $43 (= $166 − $123). The excess tax as a percentage of total pretax book income, the denominator of the average tax rate, is 4.1 percent (= $43/$1,050). Foreign-source income was taxed at a rate of 47.4 percent (= $166/$350).

It would be desirable to have a breakdown of total foreign income and foreign taxes by individual countries, but firms rarely disclose such information.

State and Local Taxes. The statutory tax rate on line (1) reflects federal taxes only. The reconciliation adds state and local taxes on income for financial reporting because such taxes are part of income tax expense. The amount of the reconciling item is state and local taxes net of their federal tax benefit. State and local taxes are deductible in determining taxable income for federal purposes, so the incremental effect of state and local taxes beyond the federal statutory rate appears on line (3).

Refer to the disclosure of the components of income tax expense discussed previously. State and local taxes for Year 3 were $18. Net of the federal tax benefit of 35 percent, state and local taxes are $12 [(1 − .35)($18)]. This $12 amount increases the average tax rate by 1.1 percent (= $12/$1,050) for Year 3.

As with foreign taxes, the income tax note to the financial statements does not give any further detail on the income and taxes by jurisdictional unit within the United States.

Dividends Received Deduction. Depending on the investor's ownership percentage, only 20 or 30 percent of dividends received from unconsolidated domestic subsidiaries and affiliates is subject to federal taxation. The dividend deduction is intended to reduce the effect of triple taxation of the corporate organization form. The full dividend received is included in income for financial reporting. The calculation on line (1) presumes that the dividend is subject to tax at the statutory rate. The reduction on line (4) indicates the tax savings due to the 70 or 80 percent dividends received deduction.

Tax-Exempt Income. Income for financial reporting includes interest revenue on state and municipal obligations. Such interest revenue, however, is never included in taxable income. The income tax savings from this permanent difference appears on line (5).

Restructuring and Impairment Charges. A firm that acquires another firm must record the assets of the acquired firm at fair market value in the consolidated financial statements. (Chapter 9 addresses accounting for business acquisitions.) Any subsequent write-down of the acquired assets, as either a separate impairment charge or impairments embedded in a restructuring charge, typically cannot be deducted for tax purposes. Because the assets were not revalued to fair market value for tax purposes at the time of the acquisitions (assuming that the purchase was accounted for as a nontaxable reorganization as discussed in Chapter 9), the possibility of an impairment charge for tax purposes does not exist.

Percentage Depletion in Excess of Cost. The Internal Revenue Code permits firms involved in mineral extraction to claim a depletion deduction equal to a specified percentage times the gross income from the property each year. Over the life of a mineral property, total percentage depletion will likely exceed the acquisition cost of the property. For financial reporting purposes, total depletion cannot exceed acquisition cost under GAAP. The excess of percentage depletion over book depletion represents a permanent difference that reduces the average tax rate.

The foregoing discussion illustrates the reconciling items most commonly encountered in corporate annual reports. Other items reported have characteristics similar to those previously discussed.

4. Components of Deferred Tax Assets and Liabilities

The fourth disclosure item in the income tax note is a listing of the components of the deferred tax asset and the deferred tax liability at the beginning and the end of each year. Exhibit 8.13 presents the required disclosures. The change in deferred tax asset and deferred tax liability each year represents deferred income tax expense for that year. Note that Deferred Tax Assets experienced a net credit change of $34 (= $240 − $274) between Year 2 and Year 3, and Deferred Tax Liabilities experienced a net credit change of $39 (= $819 − $780). The total credit change in these accounts of $73 (= $34 + $39) equals the deferred component of income tax expense for Year 3 (see the first income tax disclosure item). The following sections discuss the components of deferred taxes.

Uncollectible Accounts Receivable. Firms provide for estimated uncollectible accounts in the year of sale for financial reporting but cannot recognize bad-debt expense for tax purposes until an actual customer's account becomes uncollectible. Thus, the book value of accounts receivable will be less than its tax basis. The difference represents the future tax deductions for bad-debt expense. These future tax benefits times the tax rate give rise to a deferred tax asset. The deferred tax asset relating to uncollectible accounts increased between Year 0 and Year 2, suggesting that bad-debt expense for financial reporting continued to exceed bad-debt expense for tax reporting. Such a relation characterizes a firm with increasing sales. The decrease in the deferred tax asset during Year 3 suggests that sales declined, causing bad-debt expense for tax reporting to exceed the amount for financial reporting.

Warranties. Firms expense estimated warranty costs in the year of sale for financial reporting but cannot deduct warranty expense for tax reporting until the firm makes actual expenditures to provide warranty services. Thus, the book value of the warranty liability (a positive amount) will exceed the tax basis of the warranty liability (zero, because the income tax law does not permit recognition of a warranty liability). The difference represents the future tax deductions for warranty expense. The increase in the deferred tax asset relating to warranties between Year 0 and Year 2 is consistent with a

EXHIBIT 8.13

Disclosures Related to Deferred Taxes—Components of Deferred Tax Assets and Liabilities

	December 31:			
	Year 3	Year 2	Year 1	Year 0
Deferred Tax Asset				
(8) Uncollectible Accounts Receivable	$ 16	$ 19	$ 17	$ 15
(9) Warranties	91	105	89	76
(10) Pensions	71	83	67	53
(11) Leases	62	54	42	32
(12) Net Operating Losses	—	13	—	—
Total Deferred Tax Asset	$240	$274	$215	$176
Deferred Tax Liability				
(13) Depreciable Assets	$476	$421	$355	$275
(14) Inventories	59	58	49	41
(15) Installment Receivables	193	205	171	149
(16) Intangible Drilling and Development Costs	91	96	76	58
Total Deferred Tax Liability	$819	$780	$651	$523

growing firm, whereas the decrease in Year 3 indicates a firm whose sales of product under warranty plans probably declined.

Pensions. Firms recognize pension expense each year as employees render services for financial reporting and when the firm contributes cash to the pension fund for tax reporting. As discussed in the previous section on pensions in this chapter, the income tax law limits a firm's ability to claim tax deductions when a pension fund is overfunded. Thus, firms may curtail making pension fund contributions even though they must recognize pension expense each year. The book basis of the pension liability (a positive amount) will exceed the tax basis (not recognized). The future tax deductions for pension expense result in a deferred tax asset. For our illustrative firm, pension expense for financial reporting exceeded the amount for tax reporting during Year 1 and Year 2, and the deferred tax asset relating to pensions increased. The deferred tax asset decreased in Year 3, indicating a larger expense for tax reporting than for financial reporting (that is, the book basis of the pension liability decreased during the year). Several explanations might account for such a decrease. First, the firm resumed funding the pension obligation and made a multiyear contribution. Second, the firm curtailed employment during Year 3 in light of the decrease in sales, reducing pension expense, but made a pension contribution sufficient to reduce the pension liability. Third, the firm experienced a negative pension expense (that is, a pension credit) during Year 3 because of an overfunded pension plan. The negative pension expense reduces the pension liability and thereby the amount of future tax deductions previously considered available.

Leases. Our illustrative firm leases equipment from other entities (lessors). As discussed in the section on leases in this chapter, firms may treat leases as either operating leases or capital leases for financial and tax reporting. If the leases qualify as operating leases, the lessor recognizes rent revenue and depreciation expense and the lessee recognizes rent expense. If leases qualify as capital leases, the lessor recognizes a gain on the "sale" of the leased property at the inception of the lease and recognizes interest revenue each year from financing the lessee's "purchase" of the property. The lessee depreciates the assets each period and recognizes interest expense on its borrowing from the lessor.

Leasing arose as an industry in part to shift tax deductions on property from firms that needed the use of property but did not have sufficient taxable income to take advantage of the tax deductions to other entities with higher tax rates that could take advantage of the deductions. If a lease qualifies as an operating lease for tax purposes, the lessor gets the tax deductions for depreciation and can possibly pass through some of these benefits to the lessee in the form of lower lease payments.

The earlier section of this chapter on leases indicates that the criteria for an operating lease and a capital lease for financial reporting are not identical to those for tax reporting. It is possible to structure leases that are operating leases for tax reporting, even though they qualify as capital leases for financial reporting. Our illustrative firm shows a deferred tax asset relating to leases. The likely scenario is that this firm treats leases as capital leases for financial reporting and as operating leases for tax reporting. Thus, the book basis of the leased asset and lease liability (a positive amount) exceeds the tax basis of the asset and liability (not recognized). Depreciation and interest expense recognized for financial reporting exceed rent expense recognized for tax reporting. In later years, rent expense for tax reporting will exceed depreciation and interest expense. These future tax deductions give rise to a deferred tax asset. The deferred tax asset increased each year, suggesting that this firm increased its involvement in leasing during the three-year period (that is, the firm has more leased assets in the early years of the lease period when the book expenses exceed the tax deduction than in the later years when the tax deduction exceeds the book expenses).

Net Operating Losses. A firm may operate for both financial and tax reporting at a net loss for the year. The firm can carry back this net loss to offset taxable income of the three preceding years and receive a refund for income taxes paid in those years. The firm recognizes the refund as an income tax credit in the year of the net loss.

If either the firm has no positive taxable income in the three preceding years against which to carry back the net loss or if the net loss exceeds the taxable income of those three preceding years, the firm must carry forward the net loss. This carryforward provides future tax benefits in that it can offset positive taxable incomes and thereby reduce income taxes otherwise payable. The benefits of the net operating loss carryforward give rise to a deferred tax asset.

Our illustrative firm recognized a deferred tax asset during Year 2 and realized the benefits of the net operating loss carryforward during Year 3. Referring back to the disclosure of the components of income tax expense, we see that this firm paid taxes to all three governmental units during Year 2. Thus, the firm must have been unable to offset the net operating loss incurred by some subunit during the year against the taxable income of the overall entity. One possibility is that the firm owns a majority interest in a subsidiary and therefore consolidates it for financial reporting. Its ownership percentage, however, is less than the 80 percent required to include the subsidiary in a consolidated tax return. Thus, the net loss of the subsidiary can only offset net income of that subsidiary in a later year. The firm recognizes this future benefit as a deferred tax asset. This firm shows no valuation allowance related to the deferred tax asset, indicating a greater than 50 percent probability of realizing the tax benefits in the future.

Depreciable Assets. Firms claim depreciation on their tax returns using accelerated methods over periods shorter than the expected useful lives of depreciable assets. Most firms depreciate assets for financial reporting using the straight-line method over the expected useful lives of such assets. Thus, the book value of depreciable assets will likely exceed their tax basis. Depreciation expense for tax reporting in future years will be less than the amounts for financial reporting, giving rise to a liability for future tax payments. The deferred tax liability relating to depreciable assets increased each year, suggesting that this firm has more assets in their early years when tax depreciation exceeds book depreciation. The deferred tax liability increased, however, at a decreasing rate, suggesting a slowdown in the growth rate of capital expenditures.

Inventories. The book value of inventories for our illustrative firm exceeds their tax basis, giving rise to future tax liabilities. Perhaps this firm includes certain elements of cost as part of manufacturing overhead for financial reporting but deducts them when incurred for tax reporting.

Installment Receivables. Firms that sell assets on account and permit customers to pay over two or more future years often recognize revenue at the time of sale for financial reporting and when they collect cash using the installment method for tax reporting. The book basis of these receivables exceeds their tax basis and gives rise to deferred tax liabilities. The deferred tax liability relating to installment sales increased between Year 0 and Year 2, characteristic of a growing firm (that is, revenues from sales during the current period exceed collections this period from sales made in prior periods). The deferred tax liability on installment sales decreased during Year 3, consistent with the decline in sales noted previously in the discussion of deferred taxes related to uncollectible accounts and warranties.

Intangible Drilling and Development Costs. Firms can deduct in the year of the cash expenditure for tax purposes certain costs of acquiring rights to drill and for drilling a property to ascertain the existence of mineral resources. These firms must capitalize and amortize such costs for financial reporting. The book basis of the property will exceed the tax basis and give rise to a deferred tax liability. The deferred tax liability for this item increased between Year 0 and Year 2, indicating a growth in drilling and development activity. The decrease in the liability during Year 3 suggests a cutback in such expenditures.

Assessing a Firm's Tax Position

The note to the financial statements on income taxes defines the average tax rate as follows:

$$\text{Average Tax Rate} = \text{Income Tax Expense} / \text{Book Income before Income Taxes}$$

Exhibit 8.14 presents an analysis of average tax rates. This analysis separates the amounts for each year into domestic and foreign components. The combined average tax rate based on income tax expense increased each year. The average tax rate on the domestic portion remained relatively steady at a rate close to the 35 percent federal statutory tax rate. Differences in the domestic tax position due to rate differences and permanent differences offset each other. On the other hand, the average tax rate on the foreign portion exceeded 35 percent and that rate increased each year. The analyst should explore the reasons for this increase in the foreign average tax rate more fully with management.

EXHIBIT 8.14

Analysis of Average Tax Rates

	Year 3		Year 2		Year 1	
	Domestic	Foreign	Domestic	Foreign	Domestic	Foreign
(1) Net Income before Income Taxes	$700	$350	$450	$250	$600	$200
Income Taxes at 35% Statutory Federal Rate	$245	$123	$157	$ 87	$210	$ 70
Foreign Tax Rates Greater than 35%	—	43	—	18	—	10
State and Local Taxes	11	—	8	—	9	—
Dividends Deduction	(6)	—	(3)	—	(4)	—
Tax-Exempt Income	(4)	—	(3)	—	(4)	—
Goodwill Amortization	6	—	3	—	1	—
Percentage Depletion	(8)	—	(5)	—	(6)	—
(2) Income Tax Expense	$244	$166	$157	$105	$206	$ 80
Average Tax Rates: (2)÷(1)	34.9%	47.4%	34.9%	42.0%	34.3%	40.0%
Combined Average Tax Rates	39.0%		37.4%		35.7%	

Perhaps the portions of the firm's foreign operations in higher-tax-rate countries grew more rapidly than foreign operations in lower-tax-rate countries. The firm may need to search for more tax-effective ways of operating abroad. For example, the firm might do the following:

1. Shift some operations (manufacturing, marketing) to the United States, where the average tax rate is lower.
2. Assess whether transfer prices or cost allocations can be adjusted to shift income from high-tax-rate to low-tax-rate jurisdictions.
3. Shift from domestic to foreign borrowing to increase deductions for interest against foreign-source income.
4. Shift from equity to debt financing of foreign operations to increase interest deductions against foreign-source income.

The increasing tax rates abroad and an increasing proportion of income derived from abroad suggest a continuing increase in the combined average tax rate that could hurt future profitability unless the firm takes counteractions.

Analyzing PepsiCo's Income Tax Disclosures

Refer to PepsiCo's income tax disclosures in Note 5, "Income Taxes," to its financial statements (Appendix A). PepsiCo's average tax rate was 32.3 percent in Year 2, 28.5 percent in Year 3, and 24.7 percent in Year 4. In each year the average tax rate was less than the

35 percent federal statutory tax rate also disclosed in the note, with the rates for Year 3 and Year 4 significantly lower than the rate for Year 2.

PepsiCo's relatively low and falling average tax rates during this three-year period is primarily a result of lower tax rates on PepsiCo's income from foreign operations. Recall that the denominator of the average tax rate computation combines both U.S.-source and foreign-source income for financial reporting. The initial assumption is that all of this income is subject to taxes at a rate equal to the U.S. federal statutory rate. Foreign tax rates are usually different from the U.S. federal rate, however, and in the case of PepsiCo, the overall average tax rate decreased because of these foreign rate differences.

State and local income taxes generally trigger increases in firms' average tax rates. The statutory tax rate of 35 percent reflects federal taxes only. State taxes are part of income tax expense, so the incremental effect of state taxes is beyond the federal statutory rate. For Year 4, for example, state and local taxes increased the average tax rate for PepsiCo by .8 percent.

For Year 3 and 4, PepsiCo's average tax rate is lower as a result of resolving open tax issues. PepsiCo reached a settlement with regulatory authorities after concluding tax audits related to prior years that resulted in a tax benefit for both Year 3 and Year 4. The percentage reduction in the average tax rate for each year is large (2.2 percent in Year 3 and 4.8 percent in Year 4). PepsiCo provides a discussion of the tax benefits (Appendix B) as part of the firm's MD&A, "Our Financial Results, Items Affecting Comparability." We eliminated the effect of the tax benefits in assessing PepsiCo's Year 3 and Year 4 profitability in Chapter 4.

PepsiCo's tax reconciliation also shows that merger-related costs, impairment charges, and restructuring charges affected the average tax rate in Year 2 and Year 3, although the effect is small for Year 3 (1.0 percent in Year 2 and .1 percent in Year 3). The items relate to merger-related costs incurred in connection with the merger with Quaker Foods and actions taken to streamline North American divisions and PepsiCo International. The increase in the average tax rate in Year 2 and Year 3 for merger-related costs suggests that PepsiCo incurred some costs that are never deductible for tax purposes. The source of the increase in the average tax rate, at least as to the amount, appears to be nonrecurring and is not likely to persist. We eliminated the effect of the items in assessing PepsiCo's profitability. PepsiCo's average tax rate, after eliminating the effect of the settlement of prior years' audits and merger-related and impairment and restructuring charges, is 31.3 percent in Year 2, 30.6 percent in Year 3, and 29.5 percent in Year 3. Thus, the average tax rate after eliminating the tax effects of unusual items declined more slowly than the reported amounts.

The disclosures of current and deferred taxes by PepsiCo indicate that a large amount of the firm's tax expense each year is also currently payable. We can gain additional insights about the operations of PepsiCo by examining the components of its deferred tax assets and liabilities.

Investment in Unconsolidated Affiliates. PepsiCo owns less than a controlling interest in its bottlers and uses the equity method to account for its investments in these bottlers. As Chapter 9 explains more fully, PepsiCo recognizes its share of the earnings of these bottlers each year and includes it in "bottling equity income" on its income statement. Income before taxes for Year 4 includes $380 million of bottling equity income. The income tax law taxes this income only when PepsiCo receives a dividend from the bottlers. Deferred tax liabilities for these investments, as well as other non-bottler-related investments, totaled $792 million at the end of Year 3 and $850 million at the end of Year 4, indicating that PepsiCo has deferred a significant amount of income tax payments because of this temporary difference.

Property, Plant, and Equipment. PepsiCo indicates in Note 4, "Property, Plant, and Equipment and Intangible Assets" (Appendix A), that it principally uses the straight-line depreciation method for financial reporting. Income tax laws provide for accelerated depreciation. PepsiCo has deferred taxes of $857 million as of the end of Year 4 due to depreciating assets faster for tax than for financial reporting. The deferred tax liability increased during Year 4, indicating that PepsiCo has more depreciable assets in the early years of their lives, when accelerated depreciation exceeds straight-line depreciation, than they have depreciable assets in the later years, when straight-line depreciation exceeds accelerated depreciation.

Postretirement Benefits—Pension Benefits and Retiree Medical Benefits. PepsiCo recognizes a deferred tax liability related to pension benefits, and a deferred tax asset related to retiree medical benefits for both Year 3 and Year 4. Both amounts increased during Year 4. For pension benefits, PepsiCo recorded greater pension expense for tax reporting than for financial reporting for Year 4, generating an increase in the deferred tax liability for the year. For retiree medical benefits, PepsiCo reported greater expense for financial reporting than for tax reporting for Year 4, generated an increase in the deferred tax asset for the year.

Intangible Assets Other Than Nondeductible Goodwill. PepsiCo indicates in its MD&A section, "Our Critical Accounting Policies" (Appendix B), that it amortizes intangibles other than goodwill over periods ranging from five to twenty years. The reporting of a deferred tax liability for these items suggests that PepsiCo writes off these intangibles more quickly for tax purposes.

Safe Harbor Leases. PepsiCo does not disclose any additional information about these leases to understand why they give rise to deferred tax liabilities. One possibility is that PepsiCo is the lessee on leases that it accounts for as operating leases for financial reporting and capital leases for tax reporting. Expenses for interest and depreciation on capital leases usually exceed rent expense on operating leases during the early years of the life of a leased asset. The additional expenses for the capital leases permit the firm to delay paying income taxes, which results in a deferred tax liability. The decrease in the amount of deferred tax liabilities for safe harbor leases during Year 4 suggests that the leases are now in the later years of their lives and PepsiCo is beginning to pay the deferred taxes.

Zero Coupon Notes. PepsiCo indicates in Note 9, "Debt Obligations and Commitments" (Appendix A), that it has issued zero coupon notes as a liability. The recognition of a deferred tax liability suggests that the firm has recognized more interest expense on these notes for tax reporting than for financial reporting and thereby deferred the payment of income taxes. PepsiCo likewise does not disclose sufficient information to understand why this item gives rise to a deferred tax liability. One possible explanation is that PepsiCo uses the effective-interest method to amortize the discount on these notes for tax reporting and the straight-line method for financial reporting.

Net Carryforwards. PepsiCo recognizes deferred tax assets for the future saving in taxes when it can offset net operating losses previously incurred against the positive income of future periods. PepsiCo indicates in Note 5, "Income Taxes" (Appendix A), that it has $4.3 billion of net operating loss carryforwards and $49.3 million of tax credit carryforwards as of the end of Year 4. The deferred tax asset of $666 million related to carryforwards at the end of Year 4 includes $49.3 million of tax credit carryforwards and potential tax saving on net operating loss carryforwards of $616.7 (= $666 − $49.3). The average tax rate on the net operating loss carryforwards is 14.3 percent (=$616.7/$4,300). The valuation allowance on deferred tax assets likely relates primarily to carryforwards, and increased significantly during Year 4, indicating that the firm was unable to realize some of the benefits of these loss carryforwards.

Stock-Based Compensation. For financial reporting, PepsiCo records its stock-based compensation expense on the date of the grant of stock options (Note 6, "Stock-Based Compensation," in Appendix A). For tax reporting, the expense is recognized later, most often when the stock options are exercised by employees. PepsiCo has deferred tax assets of $402 million at the end of Year 4, an increase of $70 million during Year 4. PepsiCo's Statement of Common Shareholders' Equity (Appendix A) indicates that the firm received tax deductions for stock-based compensation in both Year 3 and Year 4, but in lesser amounts than the stock-based compensation recorded for financial reporting for each year. This partially explains the increase in the deferred tax asset.

Deferred Tax Asset Valuation Allowances. Recall that firms must recognize a valuation allowance if it is more likely than not that they will not realize the tax benefits of deferred tax assets. PepsiCo's valuation allowance is similar in amount to the deferred tax asset for net carryforwards each year, suggesting that the valuation allowance likely relates to these items. The increase in the valuation allowance for Year 4 is similar in amount to the increase in the deferred tax asset for carryforwards.

Summary of Income Taxes

Income taxes affect each of the principal financial statements.

1. The income statement reports the amount of income tax expense. The analyst can compute the relation between income tax expense and income before taxes, a relation referred to as a firm's average tax rate. The average tax rate affects analysis of a firm's profitability. The income tax note explains the major reasons why the average tax rate differs from the statutory federal tax rate.
2. The statement of cash flows usually shows an adjustment to net income for the change in deferred taxes (for PepsiCo, $17 million for Year 4 and $(323) million for Year 3), which converts tax expense to tax payable when computing cash flow from operations. The income tax note indicates the mix of current and deferred taxes and the extent to which a firm has delayed or accelerated the payment of income taxes. It also indicates the components of deferred tax assets and liabilities, which the analyst can tie to analysis of various other transactions of the firm (such as intercorporate investments and pension and retiree medical obligations).
3. The balance sheet shows the amount of deferred tax assets and deferred tax liabilities. The income tax note indicates the line items on the balance sheet that include deferred taxes. These amounts affect assessments of a firm's financial position (such as the current ratio and debt ratios).

UNDERSTANDING RESERVES IN THE FINANCIAL STATEMENTS

This chapter and the previous one emphasize two important concepts underlying the financial statements:

1. Income over sufficiently long time periods equals cash inflows minus cash outflows from operating, investing, and financing activities (except dividends and capital transactions with shareholders).
2. Because accountants prepare financial statements for discrete periods of time shorter than the life of a firm, under accrual accounting the recognition of revenues does not necessarily coincide with the receipt of cash, and the recognition of expenses does not necessarily coincide with the disbursement of cash.

Assets such as inventories, investments, property, plant, equipment, and intangibles result from past cash outflows. The costs of these assets become expenses in future periods when the firm uses the services of these assets in operations or through sales. Liabilities, such as salaries payable, interest payable, taxes payable, and pensions payable, reflect the cost of services already received by a firm. They generally require a future cash outflow. Thus, most asset and liability accounts result from efforts to match revenues with expenses for discrete periods of time.

Because revenues must ultimately equal the total cash inflows, and expenses must ultimately equal the total cash outflows (except for dividends and capital transactions), firms in the long run cannot alter the total amount of revenues and expenses. In the short run, however, firms can only estimate ultimate cash flows. In addition, accounting allocates benefits received in the form of revenues, and services consumed in the form of expenses, to discrete accounting periods with some imprecision. As Chapter 6 discusses, management may have incentives to shift revenues or expenses between accounting periods to accomplish certain reporting objectives. Audits by the firm's independent accountants, taxing authorities, and government regulators serve as control mechanisms on management's behavior.

The analyst should develop a heightened sensitivity to financial reporting areas in which firms enjoy flexibility in measuring revenues, expenses, assets, and liabilities. This chapter and the previous one discuss reporting areas that allow management to select from acceptable alternatives to influence reported earnings (for example, percentage-of-completion versus completed contract method for revenue recognition, FIFO versus LIFO cost-flow assumptions, or depreciation methods). These chapters also discuss reporting areas that require firms to make estimates in applying accounting principles (for example, useful lives for depreciable assets, assumed investment return on pension fund assets, or future salary increases for pensions). Management's latitude for influencing reported earnings correlates directly with the role or significance of estimates in applying accounting principles.

In the United States, major revenues, gains, expenses, and losses flow through the income statement. In some countries outside the United States, certain income items do not flow through the income statement but instead increase or decrease a shareholders' equity account directly. In addition, common practice in certain countries permits liberal shifting of income between accounting periods either to minimize income taxes or to smooth earnings, especially in countries where financial reporting and tax reporting follow similar rules. The accounting mechanism used to accomplish these reporting results is called a reserve. This section briefly discusses the nature and use of reserves.

Nature of a Reserve Account

As the following sections discuss, reserve accounts may appear on the balance sheet as a deduction from an asset, as a liability, or as a component of shareholders' equity. (Thus, reserve accounts always carry a credit balance.) They may appear for a limited period of time or represent a permanent account. Firms may use reserve accounts to shift earnings between periods, or the accounts may not affect earnings in any period. These multiple uses of reserve accounts and the implication that firms have set aside assets equal to the reserve result in considerable confusion among financial statement users and even some professional analysts.

Using the term *reserve* in the title of an account in the United States is generally unacceptable. When firms use an account that functions similar to a reserve, U.S. firms generally use more descriptive terminology. Reserve accounts—and use of this terminology in an account title—commonly appear in the financial statements of non-U.S. firms. The next section illustrates some of the ways firms both inside and outside the United States use reserve accounts and the issues they raise for analysts.

Use of Reserve Accounts

Matching Expenses with Associated Revenues

The recognition of an expense during the current period could result in an increase in a reserve account. The reserve account might appear on the balance sheet as a reduction in an asset. For example, firms provide for bad-debt expense and increase the account Reserve for Bad Debts (U.S. firms use the account Allowance for Uncollectible Accounts). This reserve account appears as a subtraction from Accounts Receivable on the balance sheet. Likewise, firms recognize depreciation expense and increase the account Reserve for Depreciation (U.S. firms use the account Accumulated Depreciation). The reserve account appears as a reduction from fixed assets on the balance sheet. Alternatively, the reserve account might appear as a liability on the balance sheet. For example, a firm might provide for warranty expense or pension expense and increase the account Reserve for Warranties (Estimated Warranty Liability in the United States) or Reserve for Retirement Benefits (Accrued Retirement Liability in the United States).

When used properly, reserve accounts serve the same functions as the corresponding accounts that U.S. firms use: to permit appropriate matching of revenues and expenses and appropriate valuation of assets and liabilities. Of course, firms in both the United States and abroad can misuse these accounts (that is, by understating or overstating the provisions each year) to manage earnings, as discussed in Chapter 6. In addition to searching for situations in which such management occurs, the analyst's main concern with these reserves is understanding the nature of the reserve account in each case. There is usually an analogous account used in the United States that helps the analyst in this interpretation.

Keeping Expenses out of the Income Statement

A practice in some countries is to create a reserve account by reducing the Retained Earnings account. For example, a firm might decrease Retained Earnings and increase Reserve for Price Increases or Reserve for Contingencies. These accounts appear among the shareholders' equity accounts and may carry a title such as Retained Earnings Appropriated for Price Increases or Retained Earnings Appropriated for Contingencies. When firms later experience the price increase or contingency, they charge the cost against the reserve account rather than include it in expenses. These costs therefore bypass the income statement and usually result in an overstatement of earnings. Note that this use of reserves does not misstate total shareholders' equity because all of the affected accounts (retained earnings, reserve accounts, expense accounts) are components of shareholders' equity. Thus, the analyst's primary concern with these reserves is assessing whether the reported net income that excludes these items is an appropriate base for estimating future earnings. The analyst can study the shareholders' equity portion of the balance sheet to ascertain whether firms have used reserve accounts to avoid sending legitimate expenses through the income statement. Reserves of this type have been particularly common in the German reporting system.

Revaluing Assets but Delaying the Income Recognition Effect

Firms might use reserves in situations in which they revalue assets but do not desire the income effect of the revaluation to affect income of the current period. The next chapter points out that firms in the United States account for investments in marketable equity securities using the market value method. When market value differs from acquisition costs, U.S. firms write up or write down the investment account. Financial reporting in the United States does not generally permit the immediate recognition of this increase or decrease in market value in measuring income (except for securities held for "trading" purposes, as defined in the next chapter). Instead, these firms increase or decrease Accumulated Other Comprehensive Income, a shareholders' equity account. When the firm sells the securities, it eliminates the unrealized gain or loss account and recognizes a realized gain or loss in measuring net income.

Another example of this use of the reserve account relates to foreign currency translation (also discussed in the next chapter). U.S. firms with foreign operations usually translate the financial statements of their foreign entities into U.S. dollars each period using the exchange rate at the end of the period. Changes in the exchange rate cause an unrealized foreign currency gain or loss. Firms do not recognize this gain or loss in measuring income each period but instead increase or decrease Accumulated Other Comprehensive Income. When the firm disposes of the foreign unit, it eliminates the unrealized foreign currency adjustment from Accumulated Other Comprehensive Income and recognizes a gain or loss on disposal.

Financial reporting in the United Kingdom permits periodic revaluations of fixed assets and intangible assets to their current market value. The increased valuation of assets that usually occurs leads to an increase in a revaluation reserve account included in the shareholders' equity section of the balance sheet. Depreciation or amortization of the revalued assets may appear fully on the income statement each period as an expense, or split between the income statement (depreciation or amortization based on acquisition cost) and a reduction in the revaluation reserve (depreciation or amortization based on the excess of current market value over acquisition cost).

The analyst's concern with this type of reserve is the appropriateness of revaluing the asset and delaying recognition of its income effect. Note that total shareholders' equity is the same regardless of whether the unrealized gain or loss immediately affects net income or whether it affects another shareholders' equity account and later affects net income. This use of reserves does affect net income of the current period. The analyst may wish to restate reported net income of the current period to incorporate changes in these reserves.

Permanently Reclassifying Retained Earnings

Local laws or practices may dictate that firms transfer an amount from retained earnings, which is available for dividends, to a more permanent account that is not available for dividends. U.S. firms typically "capitalize" a portion of retained earnings when they issue a stock dividend. Several other countries require firms to report a certain amount of legal capital on the balance sheet. Such firms reduce retained earnings and increase an account titled Legal Capital or Legal Reserve. The implication of such disclosures is that assets equal to the amount of this legal capital are not available for dividends. This use of reserves has no effect on net income of the current period or future periods.

Summary of Reserves

The quality of disclosures regarding reserves varies considerably across countries. Analysts often encounter difficulties attempting to understand, much less adjust for, the effect of changes in reserves. An awareness of the ways that firms might use reserve accounts should help the analyst know what kinds of questions to raise when studying the financial statements. Until greater standardization occurs across countries in the use of reserves, the analyst must recognize the lack of comparability of net income and balance sheet amounts, and perhaps the increased importance of a statement of cash flows.

SUMMARY

This chapter explores various reporting areas in which expense measurement and liability recognition interact. These reporting areas therefore affect both profitability analysis and risk analysis. Managers' desire to keep debt off the balance sheet, with the hope of lowering the cost of financing, should put the analyst on guard for the existence of unreported liabilities and potential for lowering the quality of the measures of financial position reported by firms. The lack of physical existence of liabilities (unlike most assets) increases the difficulty experienced by both the independent auditor and the analyst in identifying the existence of unreported liabilities. This chapter described some of the areas that the analyst should consider when engaging in this search.

QUESTIONS, EXERCISES, PROBLEMS, AND CASES

Questions and Exercises

8.1 ACCOUNTING FOR LOSS CONTINGENCIES. The text states that loss contingencies may or may not give rise to accounting liabilities. Financial reporting requires firms to recognize a loss contingency when two criteria are met. Describe the two criteria and provide an example in which applying the criteria would trigger booking the loss contingency as an accounting liability.

8.2 SECURITIZATION OF RECEIVABLES. Firms such as Deere & Company and Macy's Department Store often sell their receivables as a means of obtaining financing. The question arises as to whether firms selling receivables can remove the receivables from the balance sheet, or whether the receivables should remain on the balance sheet and the firms should recognize a liability in the amount of the cash received for the receivables. Describe the applicable criteria to be applied to determine whether the transfer of receivables can be recorded as a sale.

8.3 LEASE-VERSUS-BUY DECISION. Abercrombie & Fitch, a large specialty apparel chain that caters to young adults, leases essentially all its retail stores. Often the leases are for four to six years, and often Abercrombie spends a considerable amount on leasehold improvements for each store—special shelving, dressing rooms, lighting and sound equipment, and wiring. Suppose, as an alternative, Abercrombie & Fitch could buy the retail stores. Discuss why the firm would choose to lease rather than buy the retail space.

8.4 EFFECT OF CAPITAL AND OPERATING LEASES ON THE FINANCIAL STATEMENTS. All leases for financial reporting purposes are treated as either capital leases or operating leases. The effects of the two reporting techniques on the financial statements differ substantially. From the perspective of the *lessee*, prepare a chart that lists the line items that are reported on the (a) income statement, (b) balance sheet, and (c) statement of cash flows under each reporting technique.

8.5 VALUATION OF DERIVATIVES. GAAP classifies derivatives as (a) speculative investments, (b) fair value hedges, or (c) cash flow hedges. However, firms revalue all derivatives to market value each period regardless of the firm's reason for acquiring the derivatives. The revaluation amount, in addition to increasing or decreasing the derivative asset or liability, affects either net income immediately, or other comprehensive income immediately and net income later. For each type of derivative, describe where firms report the revaluation amount on the financial statements.

8.6 COMPONENTS OF PENSION EXPENSE. Pension expense typically consists of five components. Review Exhibit 8.11, which lists the components, and answer the following questions related to each component:

1. Service cost—Is it possible for the service cost component to *reduce* pension expense for the year? Explain your answer.
2. Interest cost—Is it possible for the interest cost component to *reduce* pension expense for the year? Explain your answer.
3. Expected return on plan assets—GAAP requires firms to reduce pension expense each year by the expected, not the actual, return on investments. Discuss the logic employed by policymakers in reaching this decision.
4. Amortization of prior service cost—Define prior service cost, including providing an example of a plan change that would generate an amount labeled prior service cost.
5. Amortization of actuarial gains and losses—Describe the circumstances that give rise to actuarial gains and losses.

8.7 POSTRETIREMENT BENEFITS OTHER THAN PENSIONS. The notes to a firm's financial statements reveal that the obligations for postretirement health care benefits at the end of Year 4 total $2.1 billion. The fair value of plan assets for these benefits at the end of Year 4 is reported at zero, with an unrecognized net actuarial loss of $310 million reported for the same year. Calculate the amount of the postretirement health care benefit obligation reported by the firm for Year 4, and discuss what classification category (or categories) on the balance sheet would appropriately include the obligation.

8.8 NATURE OF RESERVE ACCOUNTS. The use of the term *reserve* in the title of a financial statement account is not acceptable in the United States, primarily because often its purpose is too vague. However, informal use of the term by chief financial officers, analysts, and the media is common when discussing various aspects of *acceptable* accrual accounting techniques employed by U.S. firms. Provide several examples of financial statement accounts that are often loosely referred to as reserves. What is typically common about all financial statement accounts that are informally referred to as reserves?

8.9 AVERAGE AND STATUTORY TAX RATES. A firm's note to its financial statement reports income before income taxes for Year 4 of $70,000. It reports income tax expense of $26,245 for Year 4. In addition, the note reports the following amounts to facilitate reconciliation between the federal tax rate of 35 percent and the firm's average tax rate: state and local taxes of $775; tax-exempt income of $(610); patent amortization of $690; and restructuring charge of $890.

a. Compute the average tax rate for Year 4.

b. Prepare a schedule that reconciles the average tax rate to the statutory tax rate. Include in the chart the percentage that each of the reconciling items either increases or decreases the statutory rate when compared to the average tax rate.

NOTE: See Exercises 2.6 and 2.7 in Chapter 2 for additional questions on income taxes.

Problems and Cases

8.10 ACHIEVING OFF-BALANCE-SHEET FINANCING (Adapted from Materials by R. Dieter, D. Landsittel, J. Stewart, and A. Wyatt). Patrick Company wishes to raise $50 million cash but, for various reasons, does not wish to do so in a way that results in a newly recorded liability. The firm is sufficiently solvent and profitable that its bank is willing to lend up to $50 million at the prime interest rate. Patrick Company's financial executives have devised six different plans, described in the following sections.

Transfer of Receivables with Recourse

Patrick Company will transfer to Credit Company its long-term accounts receivable, which call for payments over the next two years. Credit Company will pay an amount equal to the present value of the receivables, less an allowance for uncollectibles, as well as a discount, because it is paying now but will collect cash later. Patrick Company must repurchase from Credit Company at face value any receivables that become uncollectible in excess of the allowance. In addition, Patrick Company may repurchase any of the receivables not yet due at face value less a discount specified by formula and based on the prime rate at the time of the initial transfer. (This option permits Patrick Company to benefit if an unexpected drop in interest rates occurs after the transfer.) The accounting issue is whether the transfer is a sale (in which Patrick Company increases Cash, reduces Accounts Receivable, and recognizes expense or loss on transfer) or merely a loan collateralized by the receivables (in which Patrick Company increases Cash and increases Notes Payable at the time of transfer).

Product Financing Arrangement

Patrick Company will transfer inventory to Credit Company, which will store the inventory in a public warehouse. Credit Company may use the inventory as collateral for its own borrowings, whose proceeds will be used to pay Patrick Company. Patrick Company will pay storage costs and will repurchase all of the inventory within the next four years at contractually fixed prices plus interest accrued for the time elapsed between the transfer and later repurchase. The accounting issue is whether the inventory is sold to Credit Company, with later repurchases treated as new acquisitions for Patrick's inventory, or whether the transaction is merely a loan, with the inventory remaining on Patrick's balance sheet.

Throughput Contract

Patrick Company wants a branch line of a railroad built from the main rail line to carry raw material directly to its own plant. It could, of course, borrow the funds and build the branch line itself. Instead, it will sign an agreement with the railroad to ship specified amounts of material each month for ten years. Even if it does not ship the specified amounts of material, it will pay the agreed shipping costs. The railroad will take the contract to its bank and, using it as collateral, borrow the funds to build the branch line. The accounting issue is whether Patrick Company would increase an asset for future rail services and increase a liability for payments to the railroad. The alternative is to make no accounting entry except when Patrick makes payments to the railroad.

Construction Partnership

Patrick Company and Mission Company will jointly build a plant to manufacture chemicals both need in their own production processes. Each will contribute $5 million to the project, called Chemical. Chemical will borrow another $40 million from a bank, with Patrick the only guarantor of the debt. Patrick and Mission are each to contribute equally to future operating expenses and debt service payments of Chemical, but, in return for its guaranteeing the debt, Patrick will have an option to purchase Mission's interest for $20 million four years hence. The accounting issue is whether Patrick Company should recognize a liability for the funds borrowed by Chemical. Because of the debt guarantee, debt service payments will ultimately be Patrick Company's responsibility. Alternatively, the debt guarantee is a commitment merely to be disclosed in notes to Patrick Company's financial statements.

Research and Development Partnership

Patrick Company will contribute a laboratory and preliminary findings about a potentially profitable gene-splicing discovery to a partnership, called Venture. Venture will raise funds by selling the remaining interest in the partnership to outside investors for $2 million and borrowing $48 million from a bank, with Patrick Company guaranteeing the debt. Although Venture will operate under the management of Patrick Company, it will be free to sell the results of its further discoveries and development efforts to anyone, including Patrick Company. Patrick Company is not obligated to purchase any of Venture's output. The accounting issue is whether Patrick Company would recognize the liability.

Hotel Financing

Patrick Company owns and operates a profitable hotel. It could use the hotel as collateral for a conventional mortgage loan. Instead, it considers selling the hotel to a partnership for $50 million cash. The partnership will sell ownership interests to outside investors for $5 million and borrow $45 million from a bank on a conventional mortgage loan, using the hotel as collateral. Patrick Company guarantees the debt. The accounting issue is whether Patrick Company would record the liability for the guaranteed debt of the partnership.

Required

Discuss the appropriate treatment of each of these proposed arrangements from the viewpoint of the auditor, who must apply GAAP in deciding whether the transaction will result in a liability to be recorded or whether footnote disclosure will suffice. Does the GAAP reporting result in accurately portraying the economics of the arrangement in each case?

8.11 ACCOUNTING FOR SECURITIZATION OF RECEIVABLES. Ford Motor Credit Company discloses the following information with respect to finance receivables (amounts in millions):

December 31:	Year 4	Year 3
Finance Receivables	$146,451	$152,276
Securitized Receivables Sold	(35,600)	(46,900)
Finance Receivables on Balance Sheet	$110,851	$105,376
Retained Interest in Securitized Receivables Sold	$ 9,166	$ 12,569

Notes to Financial Statements

The Company periodically sells finance receivables in securitization transactions to fund operations and to maintain liquidity. The securitization process involves the sale of interest-bearing securities to investors, the payment of which is secured by a pool of receivables. In many securitization transactions, the Company surrenders control over certain of its finance receivables by selling these assets to special purpose entities (SPEs). SPEs then securitize the receivables by issuing certificates representing undivided interests in the SPEs' assets to both outside investors and to the Company (retained interest). These certificates entitle the holder to a series of scheduled cash flows under present terms and conditions, the receipt of which is dependent upon cash flows generated by the related SPEs' assets. The cash flows on the underlying receivables are used to pay principal and interest on the debt securities as well as transaction expenses.

In each securitization transaction, the Company retains certain subordinated interests in the SPE, which are the first to absorb credit losses on the sold receivables. As a result, the credit quality of certificates held by outside investors is enhanced. However, the investors and the trusts have no recourse against the Company beyond the trust assets. The Company also retains the servicing rights to the sold receivables and receives a servicing fee. While servicing the sold receivables for the SPE, the Company applies the same servicing policies and procedures that it applies to its own receivables and maintains a normal relationship with its financing customers.

Required

a. Applying the criteria for the sale of receivables from FASB *Statement No. 140,* justify Ford Motor Credit's treatment of the securitization of finance receivables on December 31, Year 3 and Year 4, as a sale instead of as a collateralized loan.

b. Assume that the receivables disclosed as securitized on December 31, Year 3, had been initially securitized on that day. Give the journal entry that Ford Motor Credit would have made to securitize these receivables, assuming that it securitized the receivables at no gain or loss.

c. Assume that Ford Motor Credit decided to consolidate its receivables securitization structure in Year 4 and to start accounting for it as secured borrowings. Give the journal entry that the company would make on December 31, Year 4 to account for this change, assuming that it recognized no gain or loss on this event.

d. Most firms prefer to report the securitization of receivables as a sale. The alternative is to view the arrangement as a collateralized loan with the receivables remaining on the firm's balance sheet. Speculate on why firms prefer to report the securitization of receivables as a sale.

8.12 ACCOUNTING FOR ATTEMPTED OFF-BALANCE-SHEET FINANCING ARRANGEMENTS.

Part A

International Paper Company (IP) needs $100 million of additional financing but, because of restrictions in existing debt covenants, cannot place any more debt on its balance sheet. To obtain the needed funds, it plans to transfer cutting rights to a mature timber tract to a newly created trust as of January 1, Year 8. The trust will use the cutting rights to obtain a $100 million, five-year, 10 percent interest rate bank loan due in five equal installments with interest on December 31 of each year.

The timber will be harvested each year and sold to obtain funds to service the loan and pay operating costs. Based on current prices, there is 10 percent more standing wood available for cutting than should be needed to service the loan and pay ongoing operating costs of the tract (including wind, fire, and erosion insurance). If the selling price of timber decreases in the future, the volume of timber harvested will be increased sufficiently to service the debt. If the selling price of timber increases in the future, the volume harvested will remain as originally anticipated, but any cash left over after debt service and coverage of operating costs will be invested by the trust to provide a cushion for possible future price decreases. The value of any cash or uncut timber at the end of five years will revert to IP.

IP will not guarantee the debt. The bank, however, has the right to inspect the tract at any time and to replace IP's forest management personnel with managers of its own choosing if it feels the tract is being mismanaged.

Required (Part A)

Discuss the appropriate accounting for this transaction by IP in light of other FASB pronouncements on off-balance-sheet financing.

Part B

On June 24, Year 4, Delta Air Lines entered into a revolving accounts receivable facility (Facility) providing for the sale of $489 million of a defined pool of accounts receivable (Receivables) through a wholly owned subsidiary to a trust in exchange for a senior certificate in the principal amount of $300 million (Senior Certificate) and a subordinate certificate in the principal amount of $189 million (Subordinate Certificate). The subsidiary retained the Subordinate Certificate and the company received $300 million in cash from the sale of the Senior Certificate to a third party. The principal amount of the Subordinate Certificate fluctuates daily, depending on the volume of Receivables sold, and is payable to the subsidiary only to the extent that the collections received on the Receivables exceed amounts due on the Senior Certificate. The full amount of the allowance for doubtful accounts related to the Receivables sold has been retained, as the company has substantially the same credit risk as if the Receivables had not been sold. Under the terms of the Facility, the company is obligated to pay fees that approximate the purchaser's cost of issuing a like amount of commercial paper plus certain administrative costs.

Required (Part B)

Delta requests your advice on the appropriate accounting for this transaction. How would you respond?

Part C

In Year 2, a wholly owned subsidiary of Sun Company became a one-third partner in Belvieu Environmental Fuels (BEF), a joint venture formed for the purpose of constructing, owning, and operating a $220 million methyl tertiary butyl ether (MTBE) production facility in Mont Belvieu, Texas. As of December 31, Year 3, BEF had borrowed $128 million against a construction loan facility of which the company guarantees one-third, or $43 million. The plant, which has a designed daily capacity of 12,600 barrels of MTBE, is expected to begin production in mid-Year 4. When production commences, the construction loan will be converted into a five-year, nonrecourse term loan with a first priority lien on all project assets.

In order to obtain a secure supply of oxygenates for the manufacture of reformulated fuels, Sun has entered into a ten-year take-or-pay agreement with BEF, which commences when the plant becomes operational. Pursuant to this agreement, Sun will purchase all of the MTBE production from the plant. The minimum per-unit price to be paid for the MTBE production while the nonrecourse term loan is outstanding will equal BEF's annual raw material and operating costs and debt service payments divided by the plant's annual designed capacity. Notwithstanding this minimum price, Sun has agreed to pay BEF a price during the first three years of the off-take agreement, which approximates prices included in current MTBE long-term sales agreements in the marketplace. This price is expected to exceed the minimum price required by the loan agreement. Sun will negotiate a new pricing arrangement with BEF for the remaining years that the take-or-pay agreement is in effect, which will be based on the expected market conditions existing at such time.

Required (Part C)

How should Sun account for this transaction?

8.13 ACCOUNTING FOR A LEASE BY THE LESSOR AND THE LESSEE.

Ford Motor Company (Ford) needs to acquire computer equipment from IBM as of January 1, Year 4. Ford can borrow the necessary funds to purchase the computer for $10,000,000. Ford, however, desires to keep debt off its balance sheet and to structure an operating lease with IBM. The computer has an estimated life to IBM of five years. Ford will lease the computer for three years, at which time the computer reverts back to IBM. The cost to IBM to manufacture the computer is $8,000,000. Ford's borrowing rate for three-year secured financing is 8 percent.

Required

a. Assume that Ford must make rental payments on December 31 of Year 4 through December 31 of Year 6. What is the maximum annual rental (to the nearest dollar) that Ford can make and still permit this lease to qualify as an operating lease?

b. Assume that Ford must make rental payments on January 1, Year 4, through January 1, Year 6. What is the maximum annual rental (to the nearest dollar) that Ford can make and still permit this lease to qualify as an operating lease?

c. Assume for the remaining parts of this problem that Ford will make annual payments of $3,880,335 on December 31, Year 4, through December 31, Year 6. Indicate the nature and amount of revenues and expenses (excluding income taxes) each company would report for each of the Years 4 through 6, assuming that they accounted for the lease as an operating lease.

d. Repeat part c, assuming that each company accounted for the lease as a capital lease.

e. Assume that these firms treat the lease as a capital lease for financial reporting and an operating lease for tax reporting. Compute the amount of deferred tax asset or deferred tax liability each firm would report related to the lease on December 31, Year 4, through December 31, Year 6. The income tax rate is 35 percent.

8.14 ACCOUNTING FOR CAPITAL LEASES. Wal-Mart Stores leases most of its office, warehouse, and retail space under a combination of capital and operating leases. The disclosures related to *capital leases* for its fiscal year ending January 31, Year 5 follow (amounts in millions):

	January 31:	
	Year 5	**Year 4**
Property, Plant, and Equipment under Capital Leases	$4,997	$4,286
Less Accumulated Depreciation	(1,838)	(1,673)
Net Property, Plant, and Equipment under Capital Leases	$3,159	$2,613
Capitalized Lease Obligation	$3,792	$3,193

The weighted average discount rate used to compute the present value of the capitalized lease obligation was 7.25 percent. Assume that new leases capitalized and lease payments occur evenly throughout the year.

Required

a. Prepare an analysis that explains the change in the following accounts during Year 5.
   (1) Property, Plant, and Equipment under Capital Leases
   (2) Accumulated Depreciation
   (3) Capitalized Lease Obligation
b. Assume that Wal-Mart treats these capitalized leases as operating leases for income tax purposes. The income tax rate is 35 percent. Compute the total amount of pre-tax expenses related to these leased assets for financial and tax reporting for Year 5.
c. Compute the amount of deferred tax asset and/or deferred tax liability that Wal-Mart would report on its January 31, Year 5, balance sheet related to these leases.

8.15 EFFECT OF CAPITALIZING OPERATING LEASES ON BALANCE SHEET RATIOS. Some retailing companies own their own stores or acquire their premises under capital leases. Other retailing companies acquire the use of store facilities under operating leases, contracting to make future payments. An analyst comparing the capital structure risks of retailing companies may wish to adjust reported financial statement data to put all firms on a comparable basis.

Certain data from the financial statements of The Gap and Limited Brands follow (amounts in millions):

	The Gap	**Limited Brands**
Balance Sheet as of End of Year 5		
Current Liabilities	$ 2,242	$1,451
Long-Term Debt	1,886	1,646
Other Noncurrent Liabilities	984	657
Shareholders' Equity	4,936	2,335
Total	$10,048	$6,089

Minimum Payments under Operating Leases		
Year 6	$ 945	$ 547
Year 7	823	495
Year 8	689	424
Year 9	605	361
Year 10	502	331
After Year 10	1,767	1,095
Total	$ 5,331	$3,253

Required

a. Compute the present value of operating lease obligations using an 8 percent discount rate for The Gap and Limited Brands at the end of Year 5. Assume that all cash flows occur at the end of each year. Also assume that the minimum lease payment each year after Year 10 equals the amount for Year 10 and continues until the aggregate payments after Year 10 have been made (that is, $1,767 million for The Gap and $1,095 million for Limited Brands).

b. Compute each of the following ratios for The Gap and Limited Brands as of the end of Year 5 using the amounts as originally reported in their balance sheets for the year.

(1) Liabilities to Assets Ratio = Total Liabilities/Total Assets

(2) Long-Term Debt to Long-Term Capital Ratio = Long-Term Debt/(Long-Term Debt + Shareholders' Equity)

c. Repeat part b but assume that these firms capitalize operating leases.

d. Comment on the results from parts b and c.

8.16 FINANCIAL STATEMENT EFFECTS OF CAPITAL AND OPERATING LEASES. Northwest Airlines leases aircraft used in its operations. Information taken from its financial statements and notes for Year 3 and Year 4 follows (amounts in millions):

Balance Sheet	December 31, Year 4	December 31, Year 3
Property Rights under Capital Leases (net of accumulated depreciation)	$146	$250
Capitalized Lease Obligation	$361	$419

Notes to the Financial Statements

Leases: The present value of minimum lease payments under *capital leases* as of December 31, Year 3 and Year 4, when discounted at 8 percent, are as follows:

	Year 4	Year 3
Lease Payments on December 31:		
Year 4	$ —	$ 93
Year 5	79	66
Year 6	53	52

(*Continued*)

	Year 4	Year 3
Year 7	59	53
Year 8	47	44
After Year 8		470
Total		$ 778
Year 9	36	
After Year 9	421	
Total	$ 695	
Less Imputed Interest	(334)	(359)
Present Value	$ 361	$ 419

Minimum lease payments under *operating leases* as of December 31, Year 3 and Year 4, follow:

	Year 4	Year 3
Lease Payments on December 31:		
Year 4	—	$ 771
Year 5	$ 788	752
Year 6	794	747
Year 7	803	740
Year 8	767	689
After Year 8	—	5,813
Year 9	744	—
After Year 9	5,857	—
Total	$9,753	$9,512

Required

a. Complete the following analyses relating to capital leases for Year 4. Assume that all cash flows occur at the end of the year and new capital leases were signed at the end of the year.

Property Rights under Capital Leases, December 31, Year 3	
New Capital Leases Entered Into during Year 4	
Amortization of Property Rights for Year 4	______
Property Rights under Capital Leases, December 31, Year 4	______
Capitalized Lease Obligation, December 31, Year 3	
Increase in Capitalized Lease Obligation for Interest during Year 4	
New Capitalized Lease Obligations Entered Into During Year 4	
Cash Payments under Capital Leases during Year 4	______
Capitalized Lease Obligation, December 31, Year 4	______

b. Determine the amount that Northwest would have reported as rent expense for Year 4 if it had treated all capital leases as operating leases.

c. Determine the amount reported as rent expense for Year 4 for all operating leases.

d. Compute the present value of commitments under operating leases on December 31, Year 3 and Year 4, assuming that 8 percent is an appropriate discount rate and that all cash flows occur at the end of each period. Cash flows after Year 5 occur in the same amount as those in Year 5 ($689 million when computing the present value at the end of Year 3 and $744 million when computing the present value at the end of Year 4) until the aggregate payments ($5,813 million and $5,857 million, respectively) have been made.

e. Assume that Northwest had capitalized all operating leases using the amounts computed in part d. Complete the following analysis for Year 4:

Capitalized Value of Operating Leases, December 31, Year 3	
Increase in Capitalized Value for Interest during Year 4	
New Operating Leases Capitalized during Year 4	
Cash Payments under Capitalized Operating Leases during Year 4	
Capitalized Value of Operating Leases, December 31, Year 4	

f. Northwest Airlines treats *all* of its leases as operating leases for tax purposes. The income tax rate is 35 percent and Northwest expects this rate to continue into the foreseeable future. Compute the amount of deferred tax asset or deferred tax liability that Northwest Airlines will recognize at the end of Year 3 and the end of Year 4. Indicate whether the change in the deferred tax asset or liability during Year 4 will increase or decrease income tax expense for the year.

8.17 ACCOUNTING FOR FORWARD FOREIGN-EXCHANGE CONTRACT AS A FAIR VALUE HEDGE. Refer to Examples 5 and 9 in the chapter. Firm A places its firm order for the equipment on June 30, Year 1. It simultaneously signs a forward foreign-exchange contract for 10,000 GBP. The forward rate on June 30, Year 1, for settlement on June 30, Year 2, is $1.64 per GBP. Firm A designates the forward foreign-exchange contract as a fair value hedge of the firm commitment.

Required

a. GAAP does not require Firm A to record either the purchase commitment or the forward foreign-exchange contract on the balance sheet as a liability and an asset on June 30, Year 1. What is the GAAP logic for this accounting?

b. On December 31, Year 1, the forward foreign-exchange rate for settlement on June 30, Year 2, is $1.73 per GBP. Give the journal entries to record the change in the value of the purchase commitment and the change in the value of the forward contract for Year 1. Assume an 8 percent per year interest rate for discounting cash flows to their present values on December 31, Year 1.

c. Give the journal entries on June 30, Year 2, to record the change in the present value of the purchase commitment and the forward foreign-exchange contract for the passage of time.

d. On June 30, Year 2, the spot foreign-exchange rate is $1.75 per GBP. Give the journal entries to record the change in the value of the purchase commitment and the change in the value of the forward contract due to changes in the exchange rate during the first six months of Year 2.

e. Give the journal entry on June 30, Year 2, to purchase 10,000 GBP with U.S. dollars and acquire the equipment.

f. Give the journal entry on June 30, Year 2, to settle the forward foreign-exchange contract.

g. How would the entries in parts b through f differ if Firm A had chosen to designate the forward foreign-exchange contract as a cash flow hedge instead of a fair value hedge?

h. Suggest a scenario that would justify Firm A treating the forward foreign-exchange contract as a fair value hedge, and a scenario that would justify the firm treating the contract as a cash flow hedge.

8.18 ACCOUNTING FOR FORWARD COMMODITY PRICE CONTRACT AS A CASH FLOW HEDGE. Refer to Examples 8 and 12 in the chapter. Firm D holds 10,000 gallons of whiskey in inventory on October 31, Year 1, that costs \$225 per gallon. Firm D contemplates selling the whiskey on March 31, Year 2, when it completes the aging process. Uncertainty about the selling price of whiskey on March 31, Year 2, leads Firm D to acquire a forward contract on whiskey. The forward contract does not require an initial investment of funds. Firm D designates the forward commodity contract as a cash flow hedge of an anticipated transaction. The forward price on October 31, Year 1, for delivery on March 31, Year 2, is \$320 per gallon.

Required

a. Give the journal entry, if any, that Firm D would make on October 31, Year 1, when it acquires the forward commodity price contract.

b. On December 31, Year 1, the end of the accounting period for Firm D, the forward price of whiskey for March 31, Year 2, delivery is \$310 per gallon. Give the journal entry to record the change in the value of the forward commodity price contract. Ignore the discounting of cash flows in this part and for the remainder of the problem.

c. Give the journal entry that Firm D must make on December 31, Year 1, for the decline in value of the whiskey inventory.

d. On March 31, Year 2, the price of whiskey declines to \$270 per gallon. Give the journal entry that Firm D must make to revalue the forward contract.

e. Give the entry that Firm D must make on March 31, Year 2, to reflect the decline in value of the inventory.

f. Give the journal entry that Firm D would make on March 31, Year 2, to settle the forward contract.

g. Assume that Firm D sells the whiskey on March 31, Year 2, for \$270 a gallon. Give the journal entries to record the sale and recognize the cost of goods sold.

h. How would the entries in parts b through g differ if Firm D had chosen to designate the forward commodity price contract as a fair value hedge instead of a cash flow hedge?

i. Suggest a scenario that would justify treating the forward commodity price contract as a fair value hedge, and a scenario that would justify treating it as a cash flow hedge.

8.19 INTERPRETING DERIVATIVES DISCLOSURES. Excerpts from the disclosures on derivatives by the Coca-Cola Company (Coke) follow.

> Our Company uses derivative financial instruments primarily to reduce our exposure to adverse fluctuations in interest rates and foreign exchange rates, and, to a

lesser extent, in commodity prices and other market risks. When entered into, the Company formally designates and documents the financial instrument as a hedge of a specific underlying exposure, as well as the risk management objectives and strategies for undertaking the hedge transaction. The Company formally assesses, both at the inception and at least quarterly thereafter, whether the financial instruments that are used in hedging transactions are effective at offsetting changes in either the fair value or cash flows of the related underlying exposures. Our Company does not enter into derivative financial instruments for trading purposes.

Our Company monitors our mix of fixed rate and variable rate debt. This monitoring includes a review of business and other financial risks. We also enter into interest rate swap agreements to manage these risks. These contracts had maturities of less than one year of December 31, Year 4. The fair value of our Company's interest rate swap agreements was approximately \$6 million at December 31, Year 4. The Company estimates the fair value of its interest rate management derivatives based on quoted market prices. Interest rate swap agreements are accounted for as fair value hedges. During Year 4, there has been no ineffectiveness related to fair value hedges.

We enter into forward exchange contracts to hedge certain portions of forecasted cash flows denominated in foreign currencies. These contracts had maturities up to one year on December 31, Year 4. The purpose of our foreign currency hedging activities is to reduce the risk that our eventual U.S. dollar net cash inflows resulting from sales outside the U.S. will be adversely affected by changes in exchange rates. We designate these derivatives as cash flow hedges. During Year 4, we decreased accumulated other comprehensive income by \$76 million (\$46 million after tax) for changes in the fair value of cash flow hedges. The amount recorded in earnings for the ineffective portion of cash flow hedges during Year 4 was not significant. We also reclassified net losses of \$86 million (\$52 million after tax) from accumulated other comprehensive income to earnings. The accumulated net loss on cash flow derivatives on December 31, Year 4 is \$56 million (\$34 million after tax). The carrying and fair value of foreign exchange contracts on December 31, Year 4 is \$39 million.

We monitor our exposure to financial market risks using value-at-risk models. Our value-at-risk calculations use a historical simulation model to estimate potential future losses in the fair value of our derivatives and other financial instruments that could occur as a result of adverse movements in foreign currency and interest rates. We examined historical weekly returns over the previous 10 years to calculate our value at risk. The average value at risk represents the simple average of quarterly amounts over the past year. According to our interest rate value-at-risk calculations, we estimate with 95 percent confidence that an adverse move in interest rates over a one-week period would not have a material impact on our consolidated financial statements for Year 4. Similar calculations for adverse movements in foreign exchange rates indicate a maximum impact on earnings over a one-week period of \$17 million. Net income for Year 4 was \$4,847 million.

Required

a. Coke indicates that it "formally specifies the risk management objectives and strategies for undertaking the hedge transactions." Identify the risk management objective and describe how the particular derivative accomplishes this objective with respect to interest rate swap agreements.

b. Repeat part a for forward exchange contracts.

c. What is the rationale for Coke's designation of the interest rate swaps as fair value hedges and the forward exchange contracts as cash flow hedges?

d. Why does Coke assess both initially and at least quarterly the effectiveness of these hedging instruments?

e. Compute the amount that Coke initially recorded on its books for foreign-exchange contracts outstanding on December 31, Year 4. What events will cause the carrying value of these contracts at any later date to differ from the amounts initially recorded?

f. Coke reports a net loss from changes in the value of cash flow hedges of $76 million for Year 4. What does the disclosure that Coke recognized a net loss instead of a net gain suggest about the direction of changes in exchange rates between the U.S. dollar and the foreign currencies underlying the foreign-exchange contracts? Will the forward exchange contracts likely appear on Coke's balance sheet as assets or as liabilities? Explain.

g. Justify Coke's treatment of the $76 million net loss from changes in the value of cash flow hedges during Year 4 as a decrease in accumulated other comprehensive income instead of as an ineffective cash flow hedge that should be included in earnings.

h. The income tax law taxes gains and losses from changes in the fair value of foreign-exchange contracts at the time of settlement. Will the tax effects of the $76 million pretax loss for Year 4 affect current taxes payable or deferred taxes? If the answer to the previous question is deferred taxes, then will it affect deferred tax assets or deferred tax liabilities? Explain.

i. Describe the likely event that will cause Coke to reclassify amounts from accumulated other comprehensive to earnings.

j. Assess the effectiveness of Coke's management of risk changes from interest and foreign-exchange rates for Year 4.

8.20 INTERPRETING RETIREMENT BENEFIT PLAN DISCLOSURES. Ford Motor Company (Ford) provides pension, health care, and life insurance benefits for retired employees. Exhibit 8.15 presents the components of pension expense and health care and life insurance expense for Year 3 and Year 4. Exhibit 8.16 presents the funded status and changes in the funded status of pension plans and health care and life insurance plans for Year 3 and Year 4. Exhibit 8.16 also indicates the assumptions that Ford used for these various plans each year. In addition, Ford discloses that the average rate of return on pension fund investments has exceeded 8.75 percent for the last ten years (U.S. plans).

Required

a. Why is the net expense for the health care and life insurance plans so much larger than the income or expense for pension plans?

b. Why does the net funded asset or liability of these retirement plans differ from the net asset or net liability recognized in Ford's balance sheet?

c. Why does Ford recognize both assets and liabilities on its books for pension plans?

d. Why is the recognized liability for health care and life insurance plans so much larger than the asset or liability recognized for pension plans?

e. Prepare the entry to recognize the underfunded benefit obligation for non-U.S. plans at the end of Year 3 and Year 4 that is not already recognized on Ford's balance sheet. Assume that the amounts now recognized in Ford's records appear in a single net pension asset or net pension liability account instead of the multiple accounts shown in Exhibit 8.16. Assume an income tax rate of 35 percent. The income tax law does not permit a deduction for pensions until a firm funds its obligation.

f. Give the entry to recognize the underfunded health care and life insurance obligation at the end of Year 3 and Year 4 that is not already recognized on Ford's balance sheet.

EXHIBIT 8.15

Ford Motor Company
Elements of Pension, Health Care, and Life Insurance Expenses
(amounts in millions)
(Problem 8.20)

	Pensions				Health Care and Life Insurance	
	U.S. Plans		Non-U.S. Plans			
	Year 4	Year 3	Year 4	Year 3	Year 4	Year 3
Service Cost	$ 636	$ 600	$ 554	$ 492	$ 542	$ 521
Interest Cost	2,445	2,442	1,332	1,170	1,964	2,004
Expected Return on Assets	(3,219)	(3,202)	(1,651)	(1,382)	(289)	(37)
Amortization of Prior Service Cost	502	472	106	135	(220)	(179)
Amortization of (Gains) Losses	23	33	204	148	610	532
Other	(106)	(88)	78	128	(228)	1,332
Total Expense (Income)	$ 281	$ 257	$ 623	$ 691	$2,379	$4,173

Assume an income tax rate of 35 percent. The income tax law does not permit a deduction for health care and life insurance benefits until a firm funds its obligation.

g. Provide several examples of benefit changes that might increase or decrease the prior service costs for pension and health care and life insurance plans.

h. Calculate the investment performance of the pension fund and the health care and life insurance fund during Year 3 and Year 4, and compare actual returns to expected returns for these years.

8.21 INTERPRETING RETIREMENT BENEFIT PLAN DISCLOSURES.

General Electric Company (GE) provides pension, health care, and life insurance benefits to its retired employees. Exhibit 8.17 presents the components of pension expense (GE's "principal pension plan") and health care and life insurance expense for Year 2 to Year 4. Exhibit 8.18 presents the funded status of the plan on December 31, Year 3 and Year 4.

Required

a. Why do GE's pension plans give rise to a net income for Year 2 through Year 4, whereas its health care and life insurance plans give rise to a net expense for each of these years?

b. Why does the net funded asset or liability of GE's retirement plans at the end of Year 3 and Year 4 differ from the net asset or liability recognized on GE's balance sheet?

c. Why does GE recognize both assets and liabilities on its balance sheet for retirement plans?

EXHIBIT 8.16

Ford Motor Company
Funded Status of Retirement Plans
(amounts in millions)
(Problem 8.20)

	Pensions				Health Care and Life Insurance	
	U.S. Plans		Non-U.S. Plans			
	Year 4	Year 3	Year 4	Year 3	Year 4	Year 3
Benefit Obligation, January 1	$40,463	$37,153	$24,790	$20,698	$ 32,362	$ 30,263
Service Cost	636	600	554	492	542	521
Interest Cost	2,445	2,442	1,332	1,170	1,965	2,004
Amendments	—	1,282	118	5	2	(372)
Actuarial (Gains) Losses	2,249	1,644	1,652	(40)	5,667	1,325
Benefits Paid	(2,832)	(2,697)	(1,160)	(1,018)	(1,540)	(1,419)
Other	116	39	2,166	3,483	117	40
Benefit Obligation, December 31	$43,077	$40,463	$29,452	$24,790	$ 39,115	$ 32,362
Fair Value of Plan Assets, January 1	$37,016	$29,877	$16,548	$12,363	$ 3,565	$ 2,834
Actual Return on Assets	4,568	7,687	1,936	2,070	397	10
Contributions	914	2,207	1,919	1,163	2,800	3,500
Benefits Paid	(2,832)	(2,697)	(1,160)	(1,018)	—	(877)
Other	(38)	(58)	1,352	1,970	—	(1,902)
Fair Value of Plan Assets, December 31	$39,628	$37,016	$20,595	$16,548	$ 6,762	$ 3,565
Net Funded Asset (Liability)	$ (3,449)	$ (3,447)	$ (8,857)	$ (8,242)	$(32,353)	$(28,797)
Unamortized Prior Service Costs	3,146	3,640	853	790	(1,128)	(1,352)
Unamortized Actuarial (Gains) Losses	4,838	3,917	8,794	7,122	16,054	11,075
Net Asset (Liability) Recognized	$ 4,535	$ 4,110	$ 790	$ (330)	$(17,427)	$(19,074)

EXHIBIT 8.16

Continued

	Pensions				Health Care and Life Insurance	
	U.S. Plans		Non-U.S. Plans			
	Year 4	Year 3	Year 4	Year 3	Year 4	Year 3
Recognized In:						
Prepaid Assets	$ 2,460	$ 2,567	$ 1,566	$ 182	$ —	$ —
Accrued Liabilities	(2,643)	(3,144)	(5,364)	(5,250)	(17,427)	(19,074)
Intangible Assets	2,517	2,916	526	874	—	—
Accumulated Other Comprehensive Income	2,201	1,771	4,062	3,864	—	—
Net Amount Recognized	$ 4,535	$ 4,110	$ 790	$ (330)	$(17,427)	$(19,074)
Pension Plans with Underfunded Accumulated Benefit Obligations	$ 2,643	$ 2,956	$ 5,435	$ 5,313	$ —	$ —
Weighted Average Assumptions:						
Discount Rate	5.75%	6.25%	5.18%	5.61%	5.75%	6.25%
Expected Return on Assets	8.75%	8.75%	7.76%	8.38%	7.93%	6.20%
Rate of Compensation Increase	4.50%	4.50%	4.00%	3.98%	—	—
Initial Health Care Cost Trend Rate	—	—	—	—	9.00%	9.00%
Ultimate Health Care Cost Trend Rate	—	—	—	—	5.00%	5.00%
Number of Years to Ultimate Trend Rate	—	—	—	—	7	6

EXHIBIT 8.17

General Electric
Elements of Pension (Principal Plans), Health Care, and Life Insurance Expenses
(amounts in millions)
(Problem 8.21)

	Principal Pension Plans			Health Care and Life Insurance		
	Year 4	Year 3	Year 2	Year 4	Year 3	Year 2
Service Cost	$ 1,178	$ 1,213	$ 1,107	$ 210	$ 307	$ 277
Interest Cost	2,199	2,180	2,116	518	535	469
Expected Return on Assets	(3,958)	(4,072)	(4,084)	(149)	(159)	(170)
Prior Service Cost	311	248	217	298	191	96
Actuarial (Gain) Loss	146	(609)	(912)	60	127	78
Net Expense (Income)	$ (124)	$(1,040)	$(1,556)	$ 937	$1,001	$ 750

d. Give the entry that the analyst would make to recognize GE's underfunded health care and life insurance benefits obligation at the end of Year 3 and Year 4 that is not already recognized by GE on its balance sheet. Assume an income tax rate of 35 percent. The income tax law does not permit a firm to take a tax deduction for health care and life insurance benefits until it funds the obligation.

e. What is the most likely reason that GE reports an actuarial loss for Year 4 and Year 3 in measuring its pension obligation?

f. What is the likely reason that plan amendments related to health care and life insurance were so large in Year 3 ($2,527)?

g. Evaluate the investment performance of the pension, health care, and life insurance funds during Year 3 and Year 4, and compare actual returns to expected returns for these years.

8.22 INTERPRETING RETIREMENT BENEFIT PLAN DISCLOSURES. Goodyear Tire and Rubber Company (Goodyear) provides pension, health care, and life insurance benefits to its retired employees. Exhibit 8.19 presents the components of pension and healthcare and life insurance expense for Year 2 to Year 4. Exhibit 8.20 presents the funded status of the plans on December 31, Year 3 and Year 4.

Required

a. Why does the net liability of Goodyear's pension plans and of its health care and life insurance plans differ from the amounts reported for these plans on Goodyear's balance sheet?

b. Give the entry that the analyst would make to recognize Goodyear's underfunded pension obligation at the end of Year 3 and Year 4 that is not already recognized on the balance sheet. Assume that the amounts now recognized on Goodyear's books appear in a single net liability instead of the separate net asset and net liability accounts shown in Exhibit 8.20. Assume an income tax rate of 35 percent.

EXHIBIT 8.18

General Electric
Funded Status of Pension (Principal Plans), Health Care, and Life Insurance Plans
(amounts in millions)
(Problem 8.21)

	Principal Pension Plans		Health Care and Life Insurance	
	Year 4	Year 3	Year 4	Year 3
Benefit Obligation, January 1	$37,827	$33,266	$ 9,701	$ 7,435
Service Cost	1,178	1,213	210	307
Interest Cost	2,199	2,180	518	535
Plan Amendments	—	654	90	2,527
Actuarial Loss (Gain)	969	2,754	(509)	(416)
Participant Contributions	163	160	37	33
Benefits Paid	(2,367)	(2,409)	(797)	(720)
Benefit Obligation, December 31	$39,969	$37,827	$ 9,250	$ 9,701
Fair Value of Plan Assets, January 1	$43,879	$37,811	$ 1,626	$ 1,426
Actual Return on Assets	4,888	8,203	160	309
Employer Contributions	102	105	626	565
Participant Contributions	163	169	37	33
Benefits Paid	(2,367)	(2,409)	(797)	(707)
Fair Value of Plan Assets, December 31	$46,665	$43,879	$ 1,652	$ 1,626
Net Funded Asset (Liability)	$ 6,696	$ 6,052	$(7,598)	$(8,075)
Unrecognized Prior Service Cost	1,260	1,571	2,747	3,045
Unrecognized Net Actuarial (Gain) Loss	7,481	7,588	1,004	1,584
Net Asset (Liability) Recognized	$15,437	$15,211	$(3,847)	$(3,446)
Recognized In:				
Prepaid Assets	$17,629	$17,038	$ 38	$ 81
Accrued Liabilities	(2,192)	(1,827)	(3,885)	(3,527)
Net Asset (Liability) Recognized	$15,437	$15,211	$(3,847)	$(3,446)
Actuarial Assumptions:				
Discount Rate	5.75%	6.0%	5.75%	6.0%
Expected Return on Assets	8.5%	8.5%	8.5%	8.5%
Rate of Compensation Increase	5.0%	5.0%	—	—
Initial Health Care Cost Trend Rate	—	—	10.3%	10.5%
Ultimate Health Care Cost Trend Rate	—	—	5.0%	5.0%
Number of Years to Ultimate Trend Rate	—	—	9	9

EXHIBIT 8.19

Goodyear Tire and Rubber Company
Elements of Pension, Health Care, and Life Insurance Expenses
(amounts in millions)
(Problem 8.22)

	Pensions			Health Care and Life Insurance		
	Year 4	Year 3	Year 2	Year 4	Year 3	Year 2
Service Cost	$ 85.8	$ 122.6	$ 116.7	$ 24.7	$ 24.1	$ 19.5
Interest Cost	421.0	399.8	385.0	188.1	174.0	186.9
Expected Return on Assets	(350.3)	(310.6)	(391.1)	—	—	—
Amortization Of:						
Prior Service Cost	75.2	74.2	81.6	44.5	17.0	19.4
Actuarial (Gain) Loss	118.0	125.9	36.7	35.2	32.0	26.2
Transition Gain	1.3	1.1	0.6	—	—	—
Other Items	11.0	88.2	1.1	12.8	43.6	—
Net Expense (Income)	$ 362.0	$ 501.2	$ 230.6	$305.3	$290.7	$252.0

The income tax law does not permit a firm to take a tax deduction of pension benefits until it funds the obligation.

c. Repeat part b for Goodyear's underfunded health care and life insurance obligation.

d. Compute the amount by which the actual return on pension investments exceeded or fell short of expectations for Year 4.

e. What is the likely reason that the unrecognized net actuarial loss related to Goodyear's pension plans increased between Year 3 and Year 4 despite the fact that the actual return exceeded expectations by $128.4 million in Year 4 (from part d)?

8.23 INTERPRETING RETIREMENT BENEFIT PLAN DISCLOSURES. The Boeing Company (Boeing) provides pension, health care, and life insurance benefits to retired employees. Exhibit 8.21 presents the components of pension and health care and life insurance expense for Year 2 to Year 4. Exhibit 8.22 presents the funded status of the plans on December 31, Year 3 and Year 4.

Required

a. Why does Boeing report net benefit income for its pension plans but net benefit expense for its health care and life insurance plans in Year 2 and Year 3?

b. Why does Boeing recognize the net funded asset on its balance sheet while the records of its pension plans reveal the net funded liability?

c. Why does the net funded liability for Boeing's health care and life insurance plans differ from the liability recognized on Boeing's balance sheet?

d. Why does Boeing show a net asset on its balance sheet with respect to its pension plans but a net liability with respect to its health care and life insurance plans?

EXHIBIT 8.20

Goodyear Tire and Rubber Company
Funded Status of Pension, Health Care, and Life Insurance Plans
(amounts in millions)
(Problem 8.22)

	Pensions		Health Care and Life Insurance	
	Year 4	Year 3	Year 4	Year 3
Benefit Obligation, January 1	$ 6,883.5	$ 6,070.2	$ 3,078.6	$ 2,723.1
Service Cost	85.8	122.6	24.7	24.1
Interest Cost	421.0	399.8	188.1	174.0
Plan Amendments	85.9	112.4	(3.5)	275.8
Actuarial (Gains) Losses	532.2	348.9	165.4	88.9
Participant Contributions	19.2	18.8	8.8	6.6
Benefits Paid	(484.9)	(473.4)	(257.6)	(273.1)
Other Items	177.6	284.2	13.8	59.2
Benefit Obligation, December 31	$ 7,720.3	$ 6,883.5	$ 3,218.3	$ 3,078.6
Fair Value of Plan Assets, January 1	$ 4,129.1	$ 3,602.4	—	—
Actual Return on Assets	478.7	707.4	—	—
Employer Contributions	264.6	115.7	—	—
Participant Contributions	19.2	18.8	—	—
Benefits Paid	(484.9)	(473.4)	—	—
Other Items	191.6	158.2	—	—
Fair Value of Plan Assets, December 31	$ 4,598.3	$ 4,129.1	$ —	$ —
Net Funded Asset (Liability)	$(3,122.0)	$(2,754.4)	$(3,218.3)	$(3,078.6)
Unrecognized Prior Service Cost	418.1	503.4	420.1	480.9
Unrecognized Net Actuarial (Gain) Loss	2,548.5	2,194.1	895.4	763.1
Unrecognized Transition Obligations	2.8	3.9	—	—
Net Asset (Liability) Recognized	$ (152.6)	$ (53.0)	$(1,902.8)	$(1,834.6)
Recognized In:				
Prepaid Assets	$ 844.9	$ 943.9	$ —	$ —
Accrued Liabilities	(3,304.8)	(2,941.6)	(1,902.8)	(1,834.6)
Accumulated Other Comprehensive Income	1,829.0	1,545.2		
Other Accounts	478.3	399.5	—	—
Net Asset (Liability) Recognized	$ (152.6)	$ (53.0)	$(1,902.8)	$(1,834.6)
Actuarial Assumptions:				
Discount Rate	6.25%	6.75%	6.25%	6.75%
Expected Return on Assets	8.50%	8.50%	—	—
Rate of Compensation Increase	4.00%	4.00%	4.00%	4.00%
Initial Health Care Cost Trend Rate	—	—	12.0%	12.5%
Ultimate Health Care Cost Trend Rate	—	—	5.0%	5.0%
Number of Years to Ultimate Trend Rate	—	—	9	10

EXHIBIT 8.21

Boeing Company
Elements of Pension, Health Care, and Life Insurance Expenses
(amounts in millions)
(Problem 8.23)

	Pensions			Health Care and Life Insurance		
	Year 4	Year 3	Year 2	Year 4	Year 3	Year 2
Service Cost	$ 831	$ 753	$ 703	$ 162	$162	$133
Interest Cost	2,378	2,319	2,261	492	533	472
Expected Return on Assets	(3,378)	(3,403)	(3,558)	(6)	(5)	(4)
Amortization Of:						
Transition Asset	—	(1)	(3)	—	—	—
Prior Service Cost	180	169	160	(102)	(61)	(57)
Actuarial (Gain) Loss	379	83	(35)	188	175	82
Other Items	61	13	68	—	2	(27)
Net Expense (Income)	$ 451	$ (67)	$ (404)	$ 734	$806	$599

e. When assessing the financial position and risk of Boeing, would you restate Boeing's assets from the reported net asset for its pension plans to the net funded liability for these plans? Explain your reasoning.

f. Give the adjustment that the analyst would make to restate Boeing's balance sheet for the difference between its reported net asset for pension plans and the funded net liability. Assume that the amounts now appearing on Boeing's balance sheet are in a single net pension asset account. Also assume an income tax rate of 35 percent. The income tax law does not permit a firm to claim an income tax deduction for pension plans until it contributes cash to its pension plans.

g. When assessing the financial position and risk of Boeing, would you restate Boeing's liabilities from the reported net liability for health care and life insurance benefits to the net funded liability for these plans? Explain your reasoning.

h. Give the adjustment that the analyst would make to restate Boeing's balance sheet for the difference between its reported net liability for health care and life insurance benefits and the funded net liability. Assume an income tax rate of 35 percent. The income tax law does not permit a firm to claim an income tax deduction for health care and life insurance benefits until it contributes cash to its health care and life insurance benefits plans.

i. What is the likely reason for the actuarial loss related to the pension benefit obligation for Year 4?

j. Prepare an analysis that explains the change in the *unrecognized* net actuarial loss for Boeing's pension plans from $13,430 million at the end of Year 3 to $13,756 million at the end of Year 4.

EXHIBIT 8.22

Boeing Company
Funded Status of Pension, Health Care, and Life Insurance Plans
(amounts in millions)
(Problem 8.23)

	Pensions		Health Care and Life Insurance	
	Year 4	Year 3	Year 4	Year 3
Benefit Obligation, January 1	$39,931	$35,971	$ 8,617	$ 8,308
Service Cost	831	753	162	162
Interest Cost	2,378	2,319	492	533
Plan Amendments	190	114	(558)	(470)
Actuarial (Gains) Losses	1,656	2,937	(57)	583
Participant Contributions	13	12	—	—
Benefits Paid	(2,204)	(2,139)	(513)	(490)
Other Items	(14)	(36)	(8)	(9)
Benefit Obligation, December 31	$42,781	$39,931	$ 8,135	$ 8,617
Fair Value of Plan Assets, January 1	$33,209	$28,834	$ 58	$ 48
Actual Return on Assets	4,296	4,728	6	5
Employer Contributions	3,645	1,728	16	16
Participant Contributions	13	12	1	—
Benefits Paid	(2,163)	(2,100)	(9)	(11)
Other Items	(23)	7	—	—
Fair Value of Plan Assets, December 31	$38,977	$33,209	$ 72	$ 58
Net Funded Asset (Liability)	$ (3,804)	$ (6,722)	$(8,063)	$(8,559)
Unrecognized Net Actuarial (Gain) Loss	13,756	13,430	2,676	3,373
Unrecognized Prior Service Cost (Benefit)	1,365	1,376	(762)	(745)
Other Items	752	12	135	126
Net Asset (Liability) Recognized	$12,069	$ 8,096	$(6,014)	$(5,805)
Recognized In:				
Prepaid Assets	$12,813	$ 9,234	$ —	$ —
Accrued Liabilities	(3,913)	(7,767)	(6,014)	(5,805)
Accumulated Other Comprehensive Income	3,169	6,629	—	—
Net Asset (Liability) Recognized	$12,069	$ 8,096	$(6,014)	$(5,805)
Actuarial Assumptions:				
Discount Rate	5.75%	6.00%	5.75%	6.00%
Expected Return on Assets	8.50%	8.75%	8.50%	8.75%
Rate of Compensation Increase	5.50%	5.50%	—	—
Initial Health Care Cost Trend Rate	—	—	9.00%	10.0%
Ultimate Health Care Cost Trend Rate	—	—	5.00%	5.00%
Number of Years to Ultimate Trend Rate	—	—	5	6

k. Prepare an analysis that explains the change in the *unrecognized* prior service cost for Boeing's pension plans from $1,376 million at the end of Year 3 to $1,365 million at the end of Year 4.

8.24 INTERPRETING INCOME TAX DISCLOSURES. Disclosures related to income taxes for Sun Microsystems for its fiscal years ending June 30, Year 2 to Year 4, appear in Exhibits 8.23 and 8.24 (amounts in millions).

Required

a. Compute the pretax profit margin percentage (that is, income before taxes divided by revenues) for each year for domestic operations, foreign operations, and combined domestic and foreign operations.

b. Compute the after-tax profit margin percentage (that is, net income after taxes divided by revenues) for each year for domestic operations, foreign operations, and combined domestic and foreign operations.

EXHIBIT 8.23

Sun Microsystems
Components of Income Tax Expense
(amounts in millions)
(Problem 8.24)

	Year 4	Year 3	Year 2
Revenues			
Domestic	$ 4,768	$ 5,048	$ 5,935
Foreign	6,417	6,386	6,561
Total	$11,185	$11,434	$12,496
Income before Income Taxes			
Domestic	$ 448	$(2,705)	$(1,078)
Foreign	(11)	52	30
Total	$ 437	$(2,653)	$(1,048)
Income Tax Expense			
Current			
U.S. Federal	$ 82	$ —	$ 81
State	7	24	5
Foreign	97	46	126
Total Current	$ 186	$ 70	$ 212
Deferred			
U.S. Federal	$ 284	$ 536	$ (529)
State	286	168	(137)
Foreign	69	2	(7)
Total Deferred	639	706	(673)
Total Income Tax Expense	$ 825	$ 776	$ (461)

EXHIBIT 8.24

Sun Microsystems
Income Tax Reconciliation and Components of Deferred Taxes
(amounts in millions)
(Problem 8.24)

	Year 4	Year 3	Year 2
Income Tax Reconciliation			
Expected Taxes at 35 percent	$153	$(929)	$(366)
State Taxes, net of federal tax benefit	190	125	(87)
Foreign Earnings Permanently Reinvested	135	30	39
Goodwill Amortization	3	693	—
Acquired In-Process R&D	25	1	—
R&D Credit	(33)	(24)	(53)
Valuation Allowance	339	911	—
Other	13	(31)	6
Total Income Tax Expense	$825	$ 776	$(461)
Tax Benefit of Employee Stock Options for the Year	$ 4	$ 9	$ 98

Components of Deferred Taxes on June 30	Year 4	Year 3
Deferred Tax Assets		
Inventory Valuation	$ 65	$ 80
Reserves and Accrued Expenses	231	280
Compensation Not Currently Deductible	78	78
Net Operating Loss Carryforwards	118	226
Deferred Revenue	236	106
Tax Credit Carryforward	620	535
Investment Impairments	118	95
Restructuring Reserves	114	105
Acquisition-Related Intangibles	122	144
Tax Credits on Undistributed Profits	921	844
Other	251	214
Deferred Tax Assets, gross	2,874	2,707
Valuation Allowance	(1,750)	(1,090)
Deferred Tax Assets, net	$ 1,124	$ 1,617
Deferred Tax Liabilities		
Undistributed Profits of Subsidiaries	$(1,128)	$ (989)
Acquisition-Related Intangibles	(45)	(38)
Unrealized Gains on Investments	(50)	(8)
Total Deferred Tax Liabilities	(1,223)	(1,035)
Net Deferred Tax Assets (Liabilities)	$ (99)	$ 582

c. Compute the average tax rate (that is, income tax expense divided by income before income taxes) for each year for domestic operations, foreign operations, and combined domestic and foreign operations.

d. Prepare an income tax reconciliation for Sun Microsystems in a form similar to that in Exhibit 8.24, but separate the amounts for the firm as a whole into the portions attributable to domestic operations and to foreign operations. The reconciliation should explain the reasons for the differences in the average tax rates computed in part c. Assume that the reconciling items for goodwill amortization, acquired in-process R&D, R&D credit, and valuation allowance relate to domestic operations. The line for Other will be the plug required to reconcile to income tax expense in each case, but the net of the domestic and foreign plug must equal $13 for Year 4, ($31) for Year 2, and $6 for Year 2 as shown in the income tax reconciliation.

e. Suggest reasons why the amount for deferred income tax expense for Year 4 of $639 does not equal the decrease in the net deferred tax asset between Year 3 and Year 4.

f. Approximate the amount of income taxes payable in cash each year, assuming only an immaterial change in the Income Taxes Payable account on the balance sheet.

g. Indicate the adjustments to net income required to compute cash flow from operations each year to the extent permitted by the given information.

8.25 INTERPRETING INCOME TAX DISCLOSURES. Disclosures related to income taxes for the Coca-Cola Company (Coke) for Year 2 to Year 4 appear in Exhibits 8.25 and 8.26.

Required

a. Compute the pretax profit margin percentage (that is, income before taxes divided by revenues) for each year for domestic operations, foreign operations, and combined domestic and foreign operations.

b. Compute the after-tax profit margin percentage (that is, net income after taxes divided by revenues) for each year for domestic operations, foreign operations, and combined domestic and foreign operations.

c. Compute the average tax rate (that is, income tax expense divided by income before income taxes) for each year for domestic operations, foreign operations, and combined domestic and foreign operations.

d. What role do income taxes play in understanding changes in the profit margin of Coke over this three-year period?

e. Is it likely that Coke has recognized a net asset or a net liability on its balance sheet for pension and other postretirement benefit plans? Explain your reasoning.

f. Coke discloses that the valuation allowance on deferred tax assets relates primarily to net operating loss carryforwards. Assume for purposes of this question that Coke had recognized a valuation allowance each year exactly equal to the deferred tax assets recognized for net operating loss carryforwards. Indicate the effect on income tax expense and income tax payable in the year when Coke initially recognizes the net operating loss carryforwards.

g. Refer to part f. Indicate the effect on income tax expense and income tax payable in the year when Coke benefits from the net operating loss carryforwards.

h. Interpret Coke's recognition of net deferred tax liabilities, instead of deferred tax assets, for equity investments in Year 4.

i. Why does Coke report tax effects of equity income and investments in both the income tax reconciliation and in deferred tax liabilities?

EXHIBIT 8.25

Coca-Cola Company
Components of Income Tax Expense
(amounts in millions)
(Problem 8.25)

	Year 4	Year 3	Year 2
Revenues			
Domestic	$ 6,633	$ 6,334	$ 6,260
Foreign	15,329	14,710	13,304
Total	$21,962	$21,044	$19,564
Income before Income Taxes			
Domestic	$ 2,535	$ 2,029	$ 2,062
Foreign	3,687	3,466	3,437
Total	$ 6,222	$ 5,495	$ 5,499
Income Tax Expense			
Current			
U.S. Federal	$ 350	$ 426	$ 455
State	64	84	55
Foreign	799	826	973
Total Current	$ 1,213	$ 1,336	$ 1,483
Deferred			
U.S. Federal	$ 209	$ (145)	$ 2
State	29	(11)	23
Foreign	(76)	(32)	15
Total Deferred	162	(188)	40
Total Income Tax Expense	$ 1,375	$ 1,148	$ 1,523

j. Interpret Coke's recognition of deferred tax liabilities, instead of deferred tax assets, for intangible assets.

8.26 ANALYZING INCOME TAX DISCLOSURES. Exhibit 8.27 presents information from the income tax notes of TRW Automotive, Inc. (TRW) for Year 1 to Year 3.

Required

a. Calculate TRW's average tax rate for Year 1, Year 2, and Year 3.
b. TRW provides a reconciliation between the U.S. federal statutory rate and the average tax rate using absolute dollar amounts. Convert this portion of Exhibit 8.27 to a percentage reconciliation for Year 4.
c. What is the likely reason for the change in deferred taxes related to postretirement benefits from a net deferred tax liability at the end of Year 2 to a net deferred tax asset at the end of Year 3?

EXHIBIT 8.26

Coca-Cola Company
Income Tax Reconciliation and Components of Deferred Taxes
(amounts in millions)
(Problem 8.25)

	Year 4	Year 3	Year 2
Income Tax Reconciliation			
U.S. Statutory Tax Rate	35.0%	35.0%	35.0%
State Taxes, net of federal tax benefit	1.0	0.9	0.9
Foreign Earnings Taxes at Lower Rates	(9.4)	(10.6)	(6.0)
Equity Income or Loss	(3.1)	(2.4)	(2.0)
Other Operating Charges	(0.9)	(1.1)	—
Other	(0.5)	(0.9)	(0.2)
Average Tax Rate	22.1%	20.9%	27.7%

Components of Deferred Taxes on December 31:	Year 4	Year 3
Deferred Tax Assets		
Property, Plant, and Equipment	$ 71	$ 87
Trademarks and Other Intangible Assets	65	68
Equity Method Investments	530	485
Other Liabilities	149	242
Benefit Plans	594	669
Net Operating Loss Carryforwards	856	711
Other	257	195
Total Deferred Tax Assets, gross	2,522	2,457
Valuation Allowance	(854)	(630)
Total Deferred Tax Assets, net	$ 1,668	$1,827
Deferred Tax Liabilities		
Property, Plant, and Equipment	$ (684)	$ (737)
Trademarks and Other Intangible Assets	(247)	(247)
Equity Method Investments	(612)	(468)
Other Liabilities	(71)	(55)
Other	(180)	(211)
Total Deferred Tax Liabilities	(1,794)	(1,718)
Net Deferred Tax Assets (Liability)	$ (126)	$ 109

d. What is the likely reason for the valuation allowance related to deferred tax assets?

e. What is the likely explanation for the behavior of the deferred tax liability related to depreciation and amortization?

NOTE: See Problems 2.12 (Target Corporation), 2.13 (Nike), and 2.14 (Ford Motor Company) in Chapter 2 for additional problems on income taxes.

EXHIBIT 8.27

TRW Automotive, Inc.
Income Tax Disclosures
(amounts in millions)
(Problem 8.26)

	Year 3	Year 2	Year 1
Earnings before Income Taxes			
U.S.	(58)	(120)	(447)
Non-U.S.	140	422	381
	$ 82	$ 302	$ (66)
Provision for Income Taxes			
Current: U.S.	$ 13	$(213)	$(125)
Non-U.S.	117	81	56
Deferred: U.S.	(3)	260	16
Non-U.S.	(10)	10	23
	$117	$ 138	$ (30)
Income Tax Reconciliation			
Expected Taxes at 35 Percent	$ 29	$ 105	$ (24)
State Taxes, net of federal tax benefit	5	—	(5)
Foreign Taxes	16	21	13
Acquired In-Process R&D	29	—	—
Valuation Allowance	35	—	—
Other	3	12	(14)
Total Income Tax Expense	$117	$ 138	$ (30)

Components of Deferred Taxes	Year 3	Year 2
Deferred Tax Assets		
Postretirement Benefits	$ 639	$ 622
State Taxes	—	8
Inventory	29	22
Reserves and Accruals	204	139
Net Operating Loss Carryforwards	321	57
Other	9	123
Total Deferred Tax Assets, gross	1,202	971
Valuation Allowance	(223)	(57)
Total Deferred Tax Assets, net	$ 979	$ 914
Deferred Tax Liabilities		
Postretirement Benefits	$(135)	$(1,308)
Depreciation and Amortization	(336)	(146)
Undistributed Profits of Subsidiaries	(189)	—
Foreign Currency Exchange	(55)	(14)
Other	(149)	(33)
Total Deferred Tax Liabilities	(864)	(1,501)
Net Deferred Tax Assets (Liabilities)	$ 115	$ (587)

INTEGRATIVE CASE 8.1

STARBUCKS

A common practice of fast-food and retail coffee shop chains such as Starbucks is to lease some or all of their retail space. The first note to Starbucks' Year 4 Form 10-K filing states that the firm "leases retail store, roasting and distribution facilities and office space under operating leases."

A subsequent financial statement note provides the following future operating lease commitments of Starbucks as of the end of Year 4 (amounts in thousands):

Fiscal Year Ending:	
Year 5	$ 355,079
Year 6	340,360
Year 7	321,047
Year 8	299,601
Year 9	272,806
Thereafter	1,202,143
Total Lease Payments	$2,609,036

Required

a. Compute the present value of operating lease obligations using an 8 percent discount rate for Starbucks at the end of Year 4. Assume that all cash flows occur at the end of each year. Also assume that the minimum lease payment each year after Year 9 equals the amount for Year 9 and continues until the aggregate payments after Year 9 have been made in total.

b. Refer to Exhibit 1.24 (Chapter 1), which reports the comparative balance sheet for Starbucks as of the end of Year 4. Compute each of the following ratios for Starbucks as of the end of Year 4 using the amounts as originally reported in their balance sheets for the year.

(1) Liabilities to Assets Ratio = Total Liabilities/Total Assets

(2) Long-Term Debt to Long-Term Capital Ratio = Long-Term Debt/(Long-Term Debt + Shareholders' Equity)

c. Repeat part b but assume that Starbucks capitalizes operating leases and reports them as part of long-term debt.

d. Comment on the results from parts b and c. To what extent does the capitalization of operating lease obligations affect your assessment of Starbucks' risk?

e. Refer to Exhibit 1.25 (Chapter 1), which reports the comparative income statement for Starbucks for Year 4. Note that the firm reports an expense labeled "Cost of Sales including Occupancy Costs." Speculate why Starbucks reports cost of sales and occupancy (operating lease payments) costs as a combined amount on the income statement.

NOTE: See Integrative Case 2.1 (Chapter 2), which addresses Starbucks' accounting for income taxes.

CASE 8.2

AMERICAN AIRLINES AND UNITED AIRLINES: A PENSION FOR DEBT

American Airlines and United Airlines[27] maintain dominant market positions in the airline market in the United States. Airlines carry heavy investments in fixed assets. Their high proportions of fixed operating costs provide potential benefits and risks of economies and diseconomies of scale.

Airlines rely heavily on debt financing for their fixed asset investments. The financing may take the form of borrowing to purchase fixed assets or leasing under a capital lease arrangement. Airlines have turned increasingly in recent years to operating leases as a means to keep debt off their balance sheets. The fixed costs of servicing on-balance-sheet debt and off-balance-sheet leasing commitments add to the potential scale economies and diseconomies.

Most airlines are unionized and provide pension, health care, and other postretirement benefits to employees. The obligations under various benefit plans are not fully reflected in liabilities on the balance sheet.

An effective analysis of the risk of airlines requires consideration of the effects of commitments under operating leases and underfunded retirement benefit obligations. This case analyzes the disclosures of American and United with respect to leases, pensions, and health care benefits. Data for American and United appear in the following exhibits:

Exhibit 8.28: Balance sheet data.
Exhibit 8.29: Income and cash flow data.
Exhibit 8.30: Capital and operating lease data.
Exhibit 8.31: Pension, health care, and other retirement data for American Airlines.
Exhibit 8.32: Pension, health care, and other retirement data for United Airlines.

Required

Capital Leases

a. Complete the following analysis of changes in the capitalized lease assets and capitalized lease obligation of American for Year 4.

Capitalized Lease Assets (gross), December 31, Year 3	
Plus New Leases Signed during Year 4	
Less Capitalized Cost of Leases Terminated (plug)	______
Capitalized Lease Asset (gross), December 31, Year 4	======

(Continued)

[27]United Airlines filed Chapter 11 bankruptcy on December 9, Year 2. However, the airline continues to operate as an ongoing business and release a Form 10-K annual filing. The Bankruptcy Court overseeing its operations precludes the firm from engaging in any transactions outside the ordinary course of business without prior approval of the court. The financial statements of United Airlines have undergone several reclassifications to facilitate comparison with the financial statements of American Airlines.

Accumulated Depreciation on Capitalized Lease Assets, December 31, Year 3	
Less Accumulated Depreciation on Leases Terminated	
Plus Depreciation Recognized for Year 3 (plug)	______
Accumulated Depreciation on Capitalized Lease Assets, December 31, Year 4	______
Capitalized Lease Liability, December 31, Year 3[a]	
Plus Interest on Lease Liability for Year 4 (plug)	
Plus New Leases Capitalized during Year 4	
Less Cash Payments on Capital Leases during Year 4	______
Capitalized Lease Liability, December 31, Year 4[a]	______

[a]Be sure to include current and noncurrent portions.

b. Repeat part a for United for Year 4.

Operating Leases

c. Assume for this part that 9 percent is the appropriate interest rate to capitalize the operating lease commitments of American and United and that all lease payments occur at the end of each year. Also assume that each firm pays the aggregate amount of payments after the fifth year in an amount each year beginning in the sixth year equal to the minimum lease payment in the fifth year until the aggregate amount is fully paid. Compute the present value of the operating lease commitments of each airline as of December 31, Year 3 and Year 4.

d. Compare the total expenses for operating leases for Year 4, assuming that American and United accounted for these leases as operating leases (that is, as reported) versus as capital leases.

e. Compute the long-term debt to total assets ratio (long-term debt/total assets) as of December 31, Year 4, based on the reported amounts for American and United. Include in long-term debt the amounts reported on the balance sheet as long-term debt, capital leases, and pension, health care, and other retirement obligations.

f. Repeat part e, but now include the present value of operating lease commitments as computed in part c. Assume no change in retained earnings as a result of capitalizing operating leases.

Pension, Health Care, and Other Retirement Obligations

g. Why does the amount that each firm reports on its balance sheet as the net asset or net liability recognized for pension benefits and for health care and other retirement benefits differ from the net funded asset or liability of the benefit plans?

h. Give the entry that the analyst would make on the balance sheet on December 31, Year 4, to recognize any difference between the net liability now recognized on the balance sheet of each firm (including the minimum liability adjustment) and the net funded liability for pension benefits. Assume an income tax rate of 35 percent. The income tax law does not permit a deduction for pension and other retirement benefits until the firm contributes amounts to retirement plans.

i. Repeat part h for health care and other retirement benefits.

j. Refer to parts e and f under Operating Leases. Compute the long-term debt to total assets ratio at the end of Year 4 for each firm by including in the numerator

EXHIBIT 8.28

American Airlines and United Airlines
Balance Sheet Data
(amounts in millions)
(Case 8.2)

	American Airlines		United Airlines	
	December 31:		December 31:	
	Year 4	Year 3	Year 4	Year 3
Assets				
Current Assets	$ 4,886	$ 4,586	$ 3,066	$ 3,420
Property, Plant, and Equipment:				
At Cost	$23,735	$23,210	$17,698	$17,953
Accumulated Depreciation	(8,789)	(7,786)	(5,602)	(5,108)
Net	$14,946	$15,424	$12,096	$12,845
Property, Plant, and Equipment under Capital Leases:				
At Cost	$ 2,082	$ 2,451	$ 2,707	$ 2,721
Accumulated Depreciation	(984)	(1,086)	(652)	(555)
Net	$ 1,098	$ 1,365	$ 2,055	$ 2,166
Other Assets	$ 4,532	$ 5,096	$ 2,456	$ 2,754
Total Assets	$25,462	$26,471	$19,673	$21,185
Liabilities and Shareholders' Equity				
Current Operating Liabilities	$ 6,340	$ 5,702	$ 5,802	$ 5,588
Current Maturities of Long-Term Debt	475	465	875	663
Current Maturities of Capital Leases	104	170	28	26
Total Current Liabilities	$ 6,919	$ 6,337	$ 6,705	$ 6,277
Long-Term Debt	8,787	9,073	7,318	7,598
Capital Leases	1,061	1,156	1,125	1,097
Pension, Health Care, and Other Retirement Obligations	4,743	4,803	6,731	6,671
Other Noncurrent Liabilities	4,057	4,757	4,375	4,080
Total Liabilities	$25,567	$26,126	$26,254	$25,723
Common Stock	$ 3,273	$ 3,023	$ 5,591	$ 5,591
Retained Deficit	(2,606)	(1,785)	(8,841)	(6,839)
Accumulated Other Comprehensive Loss	(772)	(893)	(3,331)	(3,290)
Total Shareholders' Equity	$ (105)	$ 345	$(6,581)	$(4,538)
Total Liabilities and Shareholders' Equity	$25,462	$26,471	$19,673	$21,185

EXHIBIT 8.29

American Airlines and United Airlines
Income and Cash Flow Data
(amounts in millions)
(Case 8.2)

	American Airlines		United Airlines	
	Year 4	**Year 3**	**Year 4**	**Year 3**
Operating Revenues	$ 18,608	$ 17,403	$ 16,027	$ 14,602
Operating Expenses	(19,029)	(18,532)	(17,193)	(16,214)
Operating Loss	$ (421)	$ (1,129)	$ (1,166)	$ (1,612)
Interest Expense	(650)	(524)	(462)	(542)
Other Income (Expense)	250	244	(374)	(931)
Loss before Taxes	$ (821)	$ (1,409)	$ (2,002)	$ (3,085)
Income Tax Benefit	—	91	—	—
Net Loss	$ (821)	$ (1,318)	$ (2,002)	$ (3,085)
Cash Flow From:				
Operations	$ 420	$ 209	$ (368)	$ 559
Investing	(434)	(304)	(216)	243
Financing	13	113	(67)	(357)
Change in Cash	$ (1)	$ 18	$ (651)	$ 445
Capital Lease Obligations Incurred	$ 13	$ 140	$ —	$ 191
Rent Expense	$ 1,300	$ 1,400	$ 1,100	$ 1,200

long-term debt; capital leases; pension, health care, and other retirement benefit obligations reported on the balance sheet; the present value of operating lease commitments from part c; and the incremental amounts of pension, health care, and other retirement benefits from parts h and i.

k. Evaluate the investment performance of each firm's pension plan during Year 3 and Year 4.

l. Did either firm sweeten its pension benefit formula during Year 4 and make the benefits retroactive for employees? How can you tell?

m. What is the likely reason for the actuarial loss in the pension benefit obligation for each firm during Year 4?

n. Analyze the changes in the unrecognized net actuarial loss for each firm in their pension plans between Year 3 and Year 4. What are the likely reasons for these changes?

EXHIBIT 8.30

American Airlines and United Airlines
Capital and Operating Lease Data
(amounts in millions)
(Case 8.2)

	American Airlines		United Airlines	
	Year 4	Year 3	Year 4	Year 3
Commitments under Capital Leases				
Payable In:				
Year 4	$ —	$ 286	$ —	$ 256
Year 5	211	209	157	262
Year 6	233	231	169	262
Year 7	187	184	249	288
Year 8	225	224	207	206
After Year 8	—	1,111	—	214
Year 9	174	—	197	—
After Year 9	950	—	756	—
Total	$ 1,980	$ 2,245	$ 1,735	$ 1,488
Less Imputed Interest	(815)	(919)	(582)	(365)
Total Present Value	$ 1,165	$ 1,326	$ 1,153	$ 1,123
Current Portion	(104)	(170)	(28)	(26)
Long-Term Portion	$ 1,061	$ 1,156	$ 1,125	$ 1,097
Commitments under Operating Leases				
Payable In:				
Year 4	$ —	$ 1,093	$ —	$ 1,258
Year 5	1,066	1,037	1,428	1,314
Year 6	999	972	1,269	1,169
Year 7	982	956	1,227	1,126
Year 8	931	912	1,218	1,106
After Year 8	—	8,387	—	8,256
Year 9	838	—	1,175	—
After Year 9	7,525	—	8,205	—
Total	$12,341	$13,357	$14,522	$14,229

EXHIBIT 8.31

American Airlines
Pension, Health Care, and Other Retirement Data
(amounts in millions)
(Case 8.2)

Elements of Pension, Health Care, and Other Retirement Benefits Expense

	Pensions			Health Care and Other Retirement Benefits		
	Year 4	Year 3	Year 2	Year 4	Year 3	Year 2
Service Cost	$358	$370	$352	$ 75	$ 85	$ 77
Interest Cost	567	569	569	202	218	207
Expected Return on Assets	(569)	(473)	(501)	(11)	(9)	(9)
Amortization Of:						
Transition Asset	(1)	(1)	(1)	—	—	—
Prior Service Cost	14	18	21	(10)	(9)	(6)
Actuarial (Gain) Loss	58	106	49	8	20	—
Other Items	—	46	33	—	—	—
Net Expense (Income)	$427	$635	$522	$264	$305	$269

Funded Status of Pension, Health Care, and Other Retirement Benefit Plans

	Pensions		Health Care and Other Retirement Benefits	
	Year 4	Year 3	Year 4	Year 3
Benefit Obligation, January 1	$ 8,894	$8,757	$3,263	$3,299
Service Cost	358	370	75	85
Interest Cost	567	569	202	218
Plan Amendments	27	(90)	—	(58)
Actuarial (Gains) Losses	647	(96)	(81)	(138)
Benefits Paid	(471)	(554)	(156)	(143)
Other Items	—	(62)	—	—
Benefit Obligation, December 31	$10,022	$8,894	$3,303	$3,263
Fair Value of Plan Assets, January 1	$ 6,230	$5,323	$ 120	$ 100
Actual Return on Assets	1,109	1,268	18	25
Employer Contributions	467	195	169	138
Benefits Paid	(471)	(554)	(156)	(143)
Other Items	—	(2)	—	—
Fair Value of Plan Assets, December 31	$ 7,335	$6,230	$ 151	$ 120

Funded Status of Pension, Health Care, and Other Retirement Benefit Plans

Exhibit 8.31—continued	**Pensions**		**Health Care and Other Benefits**	
	Year 4	**Year 3**	**Year 4**	**Year 3**
Net Funded Asset (Liability)	$(2,687)	$(2,664)	$(3,152)	$(3,143)
Unrecognized Net Actuarial (Gain) Loss	1,698	1,649	311	407
Unrecognized Prior Service Cost (Benefit)	186	173	(71)	(81)
Unrecognized Transition Asset	(2)	(3)	—	—
Net Asset (Liability) Recognized	$ (805)	$ (845)	$(2,912)	$(2,817)
Recognized In:				
Prepaid Assets	$ 5	$ 3	$ —	$ —
Accrued Liabilities	(810)	(848)	(2,912)	(2,817)
Additional Minimum Liability	(1,021)	(1,138)	—	—
Intangible Asset	194	182	—	—
Accumulated Other Comprehensive Loss	827	956	—	—
Net Asset (Liability) Recognized	$ (805)	$ (845)	$(2,912)	$(2,817)
Actuarial Assumptions:				
Discount Rate (on December 31)	6.00%	6.25%	6.00%	6.25%
Expected Return on Assets	9.00%	9.00%	9.00%	9.00%
Rate of Compensation Increase	3.78%	3.78%	—	—
Initial Health Care Cost Trend Rate	—	—	4.5–10.0%	5.0–11.0%
Ultimate Health Care Cost Trend Rate	—	—	4.5%	4.5%
Number of Years to Ultimate Trend Rate	—	—	1–6	2–7

EXHIBIT 8.32

United Airlines
Pension, Health Care, and Other Retirement Data
(amounts in millions)
(Case 8.2)

Elements of Pension, Health Care, and Other Retirement Benefits Expense

	Pensions			Health Care and Other Retirement Benefits		
	Year 4	Year 3	Year 2	Year 4	Year 3	Year 2
Service Cost	$241	$295	$399	$ 42	$ 86	$100
Interest Cost	787	815	809	151	225	211
Expected Return on Assets	(706)	(718)	(822)	(9)	(9)	(9)
Amortization Of:						
Transition Asset	3	3	3	—	—	—
Prior Service Cost	82	90	86	(125)	(57)	10
Actuarial (Gain) Loss	93	73	26	89	102	27
Other Items	152	135	—	—	17	—
Net Expense (Income)	$652	$693	$501	$148	$364	$339

Funded Status of Pension, Health Care, and Other Retirement Benefit Plans

	Pensions		Health Care and Other Retirement Benefits	
	Year 4	Year 3	Year 4	Year 3
Benefit Obligation, January 1	$13,117	$12,673	$ 3,186	$ 3,965
Service Cost	241	295	42	86
Interest Cost	787	815	151	225
Participant Contributions	1	2	36	23
Plan Amendments	—	(66)	(674)	(1,382)
Actuarial (Gains) Losses	437	279	(98)	583
Benefits Paid	(855)	(829)	(242)	(205)
Other Items	(151)	(52)	—	(109)
Benefit Obligation, December 31	$13,577	$13,117	$ 2,401	$ 3,186
Fair Value of Plan Assets, January 1	$ 6,961	$ 6,298	$ 117	$ 119
Actual Return on Assets	843	1,400	5	6
Employer Contributions	200	86	201	175
Participant Contributions	1	2	36	22
Benefits Paid	(856)	(829)	(242)	(205)
Other Items	3	4	—	—
Fair Value of Plan Assets, December 31	$ 7,152	$ 6,961	$ 117	$ 117

Funded Status of Pension, Health Care, and Other Retirement Benefit Plans

	Pensions		Health Care and Other Benefits	
Exhibit 8.32—continued	**Year 4**	**Year 3**	**Year 4**	**Year 3**
Net Funded Asset (Liability)	$ (6,425)	$ (6,156)	$ (2,284)	$(3,069)
Unrecognized Net Actuarial (Gain) Loss	3,953	3,903	1,865	2,048
Unrecognized Prior Service Cost (Benefit)	636	870	(1,677)	(1,128)
Unrecognized Transition Asset	8	11	—	—
Net Asset (Liability) Recognized	$ (1,828)	$ (1,372)	$ (2,096)	$(2,149)
Recognized In:				
Accrued Liabilities	$ (1,828)	$ (1,372)	$ (2,096)	$(2,149)
Additional Minimum Liability	(4,133)	(4,327)	—	—
Intangible Asset	665	904	—	—
Accumulated Other Comprehensive Loss	3,468	3,423	—	—
Net Asset (Liability) Recognized	$ (1,828)	$ (1,372)	$ (2,096)	$(2,149)
Actuarial Assumptions:				
Discount Rate (on December 31)	5.84%	6.25%	5.83%	6.25%
Expected Return on Assets	9.00%	9.00%	8.00%	8.00%
Rate of Compensation Increase	3.45%	3.44%	—	—
Initial Health Care Cost Trend Rate	—	—	9.00%	9.00%
Ultimate Health Care Cost Trend Rate	—	—	4.50%	4.50%
Number of Years to Ultimate Trend Rate	—	—	6	6

Chapter 9

Intercorporate Entities

Learning Objectives

1. **Review the effect on the financial statements of the purchase method of accounting for a corporate acquisition, both at the time of the acquisition and in subsequent years.**
2. **Analyze the financial statement effects of the market value, equity, proportionate consolidation, and full consolidation methods.**
3. **Understand the accounting for variable-interest entities, commonly referred to as special-purpose entities, including the requirement to consolidate them with the firm identified as the primary beneficiary.**
4. **Prepare a set of translated financial statements using the all-current method and the monetary/nonmonetary method and understand the conditions under which each method best portrays the operating relationship between a U.S. parent firm and its foreign subsidiary.**
5. **Understand the accounting for the options given to employees to acquire shares of common stock at a price that is less than the market price of the shares.**

This chapter concludes the four-chapter unit (Chapters 6 through 9) that focuses on how a firm's selection and implementation of accounting methods affect its *accounting information quality:* its *earnings quality* and its *balance sheet quality.* Similar to the previous three chapters, this chapter emphasizes the transactions and reporting techniques that have the greatest interpretive impact on financial statements issued by a firm. Recall that the overall objective of this unit of the text is to understand both the *reported* corporate financial data released by a firm and the relevant *adjusted* financial data for analyzing the profitability and risk of the firm, with forecasting and valuation of the firm often the culminating goal. Chapters 10 through 14 address forecasting and valuation, drawing on many of the issues discussed in this unit.

This chapter addresses three reporting topics related to intercorporate investments:

1. Corporate acquisitions.
2. Investments in securities, including investments in variable-interest entities.
3. Translating and consolidating a foreign subsidiary's financial statements denominated in a foreign currency.

The chapter concludes with a discussion of accounting for share-based compensation, a topic that straddles themes of this chapter and Chapter 8. Historically, the most popular form of share-based compensation has been grants of stock options to employees, most commonly senior management. Stock options permit employees to purchase shares of common stock for an amount less than the market price at the time of exercise, providing a benefit to employees. Firms must now amortize the fair value of stock options as an expense over the expected period of benefit, a change from the accounting previously used by most firms. When employees subsequently exercise the stock options, the firm often issues shares to the employees out of treasury shares, which represent past repurchases the firm has made in its own securities.[1]

CORPORATE ACQUISITIONS

Corporate acquisitions occur when one corporation acquires a controlling interest in another corporation. Since the issuance in 2001 of *Statement No. 141*,[2] U.S. GAAP requires firms to account for all corporate acquisitions using the purchase method. For many years prior to the issuance of *Statement No. 141*, GAAP required firms to use one of two methods to account for corporate acquisitions: a version of the purchase method now required, or the pooling-of-interests method.[3]

Purchase Method

The purchase method views a corporate acquisition as conceptually similar to the purchase of any single asset (such as inventory or a machine). The purchaser records the intercorporate investment in the common stock of the acquired company at the *market value of the consideration given*. When the purchaser prepares consolidated financial statements for the two entities, it then allocates the purchase price of the investment to the fair value of the assets (net of liabilities) acquired in the acquisition. If the purchase price exceeds the fair value of the net assets acquired, the purchaser allocates the excess to all other identifiable assets and liabilities to revalue them to market values. The purchaser allocates any remaining excess to goodwill. This allocation occurs as part of the worksheet entry to eliminate the investment account when preparing consolidated financial statements for the two entities (a topic also discussed later in this chapter). The purchaser must write off the excess purchase price allocated to individual assets with definite lives over the expected service lives of the assets. Prior to the issuance of *Statement No. 142*,[4] firms also amortized any amount allocated to goodwill and other intangibles with

[1]Treasury stock is reported as a reduction in a firm's shareholders' equity. Note that PepsiCo reports (Appendix A) that it holds 103 million shares of its common stock on December 25, Year 4, with a historical cost of $4,920 million. PepsiCo uses the term *repurchased common stock* for its shares held in treasury.

[2]Financial Accounting Standards Board, *Statement of Financial Accounting Standards No. 141*, "Business Combinations" (2001). As this book goes to press, the FASB is considering revisions *to Statement No. 141*. The proposed revisions would retain the requirement that the purchase method, as discussed in this chapter, be employed for all corporate acquisitions, but would require, among other changes, that (1) all assets and liabilities of the acquired firm be recorded at fair market value (including contingent assets and liabilities) on the acquisition date; (2) acquired in-process research and development costs be capitalized; and (3) acquisition-related transaction and restructuring costs be expensed in the year incurred. However, the FASB may change its position and/or the effective date before issuing a final standard.

[3]The pooling-of-interests method viewed a corporate acquisition as a uniting of the ownership interests of two entities that, while legally combined, continued to operate as they did as separate entities prior to the acquisition. To qualify for the pooling-of-interests method under the rules when it was an allowable reporting technique, the "acquiring" firm had to exchange shares of its common stock for the common stock of the "acquired" company. Most firms preferred to account for corporate acquisitions as pooling of interests rather than as purchases because of the positive effect on earnings subsequent to the acquisition.

[4]Financial Accounting Standards Board, *Statement of Financial Accounting Standards No. 142*, "Goodwill and Other Intangible Assets" (2001).

EXHIBIT 9.1

Consolidated Financial Statements for P and S Using the Purchase Method

	Historical Cost P (1)	Historical Cost S (2)	S Shown at Current Market Values (3)	Consolidated at Date of Acquisition under Purchase Method (4)
Balance Sheets				
Assets:				
Current Assets	$1,900,000	$450,000	$ 450,000	$2,350,000
Depreciable Assets less Accumulated Depreciation	1,300,000	450,000	850,000	2,150,000
Goodwill	—	—	1,138,000	1,138,000
Total Assets	$3,200,000	$900,000	$2,438,000	$5,638,000
Equities:				
Liabilities	$1,300,000	$450,000	$ 450,000	$1,750,000
Deferred Income Tax Liability	—	—	140,000	140,000
Shareholders' Equity	1,900,000	450,000	1,848,000	3,748,000
Total Equities	$3,200,000	$900,000	$2,438,000	$5,638,000
Income Statements				
Precombination Income before Income Taxes	$ 300,000	$160,000		$ 460,000
From Combination:				
Extra Depreciation Expense	—	—		(80,000)
Net Income before Taxes	$ 300,000	$160,000		$ 380,000
Income Tax Expense	(105,000)	(56,000)		(133,000)
Net Income	$ 195,000	$104,000		$ 247,000

indefinite lives, but as Chapter 7 discussed in detail, firms no longer amortize goodwill and other intangibles with indefinite lives. However, as Chapters 6 and 7 discuss, firms must test goodwill and other intangibles not requiring amortization for impairment at least annually.

Exhibit 9.1 shows financial information for Company P and Company S. Columns (1) and (2) show the book values of P's and S's assets, liabilities, and shareholders' equity on the date of the acquisition. Column (3) shows the corresponding market values on this date for S. Assume that Company P pays $1,848,000 for 100 percent of the outstanding shares of Company S on the first day of the fiscal year. Company P makes the following entry on its books at the time of the acquisition:

Investment in Stock of Company S	1,848,000	
Cash		1,848,000

The market value of S's shareholders' equity of $1,848,000 exceeds its book value of $450,000 by $1,398,000. There are three reasons for this difference:

1. Long-term depreciable assets have a market value of $850,000 but a book value of only $450,000. The lower book value of depreciable assets results from accounting's use of historical cost valuations for assets. Company S initially recorded its depreciable assets at acquisition cost. Over time, Company S recognized a portion of this acquisition cost as depreciation expense. GAAP does not permit the firm to recognize increases in the market values of these assets. The market value of Company S common stock reflects the market values, not book values, of its net assets.
2. Deferred income taxes of $140,000 arise because the acquiring firm cannot deduct the $400,000 excess of the market value over the book value of depreciable assets as depreciation expense for income tax purposes in future years (although the acquiring firm must depreciate the $400,000 excess for book purposes). Although this $400,000 appears to be a permanent difference between book and taxable income, GAAP requires the firm to recognize deferred taxes of $140,000 (=.35 × $400,000) for it. The $140,000 amount represents the extra income taxes that the firm will pay in future years because taxable income will exceed book income before income taxes. Stated another way, the $140,000 represents the loss in future tax benefits because the company cannot base depreciation on the $850,000 market value of depreciable assets. We might show the $140,000 as a reduction in the market value of depreciable assets ($850,000 − $140,000 = $710,000) on the premise that the market value of these assets to P is only $710,000, not $850,000. As discussed later, GAAP includes the $140,000 in the Deferred Income Tax Liability account.
3. Goodwill of $1,138,000 exists. The $1,138,000 amount for goodwill equals the difference between the acquisition cost ($1,848,000) and the market value of identifiable assets and liabilities ($450,000 + $850,000 − $450,000 − $140,000 = $710,000). As discussed earlier, goodwill includes intangible attributes that a firm cannot separately identify, as well as any merger premium that the acquirer had to pay to consummate the corporate acquisition. Goodwill generates no Deferred Income Tax Liability account because the firms structured the merger in such a way that the firm does not amortize goodwill for either book or tax purposes.

Consolidation on the Date of Acquisition

Column (4) of Exhibit 9.1 shows the consolidated balance sheet on the date of the acquisition. The following worksheet entry eliminates the investment account on Company P's books and the shareholders' equity accounts of Company S, revalues the depreciable assets of Company S, and recognizes the goodwill.

Shareholders' Equity (S)	450,000	
Depreciable Assets (individual assets would be debited) ...	400,000	
Goodwill	1,138,000	
Deferred Tax Liability		140,000
Investment in Stock of Company S (P)		1,848,000

Note that the revaluation of depreciable assets and the recognition of goodwill do not appear on the separate books of either company. These accounts and amounts emerge on the consolidation worksheet as part of the entry to eliminate the investment account.

Net Income Subsequent to the Acquisition

The lower portion of Exhibit 9.1 shows the effect of the purchase method on net income for the first year after the acquisition. The two firms anticipated pretax net income of $300,000 and $160,000, respectively, for the year assuming the acquisition had not occurred. The consolidated financial statements must recognize depreciation on the excess purchase price allocated to depreciable assets. The extra depreciation, assuming a five-year remaining life using the straight-line method, is $80,000 (= $400,000/5). The extra depreciation reduces the Deferred Tax Liability and income tax expense by $28,000 (= .35 × $80,000). Consolidated net income is less than the combined income of the two companies because of the need to amortize the excess purchase price allocated to assets with finite lives.

A quality-of-accounting issue related to corporate acquisitions is the allocation of any excess purchase price. To enhance future earnings, firms have an incentive to allocate as much of the excess purchase price as possible to goodwill and other intangibles with indefinite lives. In this way, they avoid future amortization charges. To counter this tendency, *Statement No. 141* relaxes the usual criterion for asset recognition (resource with reliably measured future benefits) in favor of a new scheme. Firms must allocate a portion of the purchase price to intangibles with finite lives if either of the following is true:

1. They arise from contractual or other legal rights (regardless of whether those rights are transferable or separable from the firm).
2. They are separable (capable of being sold, transferred, licensed, rented, or exchanged), regardless of whether the firm intends to do so.

Examples of contractual or other legal rights are airport landing slots, management contracts, patents, and order backlog. Customer lists and unpatented technology are examples of separable intangibles. However, such items as a well-trained labor force or an efficient product distribution network would not qualify as an intangible with either a finite or infinite life. And recall from Chapter 7 that firms amortize intangibles with a finite useful life over their expected useful lives, taking into consideration the legal, regulatory, economic, competitive, or contractual provisions that may limit or enhance the useful life.

To counter firms' efforts to allocate as much of the purchase price as possible to goodwill and other intangibles with indefinite lives, again as discussed in Chapter 7, firms must test such assets at least annually for impairment and recognize an impairment loss if the book values exceed fair values.

Consolidation Subsequent to the Acquisition

Each year subsequent to the acquisition, Company P applies the equity method to account for its investment in Company S, a technique that the next section discusses. During the first year after the acquisition, S generates net income of $104,000. P recognizes this income on its books with the following entry:

Investment in Stock of Company S	104,000	
Equity in Earnings of Company S		104,000

The investment account shows a balance of $1,952,000 (= $1,848,000 + $104,000) at the end of the first year on P's books. The entry on the consolidation worksheet to eliminate the shareholders' equity of S and the investment account on P's books, and recognize the excess purchase price, is as follows:

Shareholders' Equity (S)	450,000	
Depreciable Assets ($400,000 – $80,000)	320,000	
Depreciation Expense	80,000	
Equity in Earnings of Company S	104,000	
Goodwill	1,138,000	
Deferred Tax Liability ($140,000 − $28,000)		112,000
Income Tax Expense		28,000
Investment in Stock of Company S		1,952,000

These entries adjust the separate income amounts of P and S to produce the amounts in the lower panel of Exhibit 9.1 labeled Net Income.

Acquisition Reserves

Often the purchase method entails establishing "acquisition reserves" at the time one company acquires another company because the acquiring company may not know the potential losses inherent in the acquired assets or the potential liabilities of the acquired company.[5] Acquisition reserve accounts always have credit balances. The acquiring company allocates a portion of the purchase price to various types of acquisition reserves (such as estimated losses on long-term contracts or estimated liabilities for unsettled lawsuits). An acquiring company has up to one year after the date of acquisition to revalue these acquisition reserves as new information becomes available. After that, the acquisition reserve amounts remain in the accounts and absorb losses as they occur. That is, the acquiring firm charges actual losses against the acquisition reserves instead of against income for the period of the loss.

To illustrate, assume in the preceding example that S Company has an unsettled lawsuit in which P Company anticipates a $10 million pretax loss will ultimately result. It allocates $10 million to an acquisition reserve (liability account) and debits Deferred Tax Assets for the $3.5 million (= .35 × $10 million) tax effect. The acquiring firm would presumably pay less for this company because of this potential liability. Assume that settlement of the lawsuit occurs three years after the date of the acquisition for $8 million (pretax). The accountant charges the $8 million loss against the $10 million reserve instead of against net income for the year and reduces Deferred Tax Assets by $2.8 million (= .35 × $8 million). Furthermore, the accountant eliminates the $2 million remaining in the acquisition reserve and the $.7 million remaining in Deferred Tax Assets, increasing net income by $1.3 million (= $2 million − $.7 million) in the year of the settlement. The benefit of this scenario to the acquiring firm is twofold: (1) no charges for the settlement reduce net income, and (2) the "cleaning up" *credit* increases net income in the year of the settlement.

Acquisition reserves can affect assessments of the quality of accounting information, and regulators carefully monitor their use (and abuse). When used properly, acquisition reserves are an accounting mechanism that helps ensure that the assets and liabilities of an acquired company reflect market values. However, given the estimates required in

[5]Chapter 8 discusses the various types of reserve accounts that appear in financial statements. The term *reserve* in the title of an account in the United States is generally unacceptable unless it includes a descriptor as to its purpose. U.S. firms generally use more precise titles for reserve accounts, such as Allowance for Uncollectible Accounts or Estimated Warranty Liability.

establishing such reserves, management has some latitude in managing earnings under the purchase method.

Corporate Acquisitions and Income Taxes

Most corporate acquisitions involve a transaction between the acquiring corporation and the *shareholders* of the acquired corporation. Although the board of directors and management of the acquired company closely monitor the discussions and negotiations, the acquisition usually takes place with the acquiring corporation giving some type of consideration to the shareholders of the acquired corporation in exchange for their stock. From a legal viewpoint, the acquired corporation remains a legally separate entity that has simply had a change in the make-up of its shareholder group.

The income tax treatment of corporate acquisitions follows these legal entity notions. In most acquisitions, the acquired company does not restate its assets and liabilities for tax purposes to reflect the amount that the acquired corporation paid for the shares of common stock. Instead, the tax basis of assets and liabilities of the acquired company before the acquisition carries over after the acquisition.[6] In this sense, the tax treatment of a corporate acquisition is analogous in concept to a pooling of interests as described in the beginning of this chapter. Thus, even if the combining entities use the purchase method for financial reporting, they treat the transaction like a pooling of interests for tax purposes (termed a *nontaxable reorganization* by the Internal Revenue Code).

Corporate Disclosures on Acquisitions

Example 1

PepsiCo has made many corporate acquisitions over the years. The firm acquired Quaker Foods in Year 1, its largest acquisition in the last ten years. In Year 1's annual report, the firms stated:

> Under the Quaker merger agreement dated December 2, Year 1, Quaker shareholders received 2.3 shares of PepsiCo common stock in exchange for each share of Quaker common stock, including a cash payment for fractional shares. We issued approximately 306 million shares of our common stock in exchange for all the outstanding common stock of Quaker.

Subsequently, PepsiCo continues to report Quaker Foods as a distinct segment of its operations. Note 1, "Basis of Presentations–Our Divisions" (Appendix A), reports net revenue and operating profits for the Quaker Foods North America division for Year 2, Year 3, and Year 4. Note that Quaker Foods North America is the smallest of the firm's four divisions.

Example 2

Cingular Wireless purchased AT&T Wireless in Year 4 as part of the ongoing consolidation of the wireless communication industry. Prior to the acquisition, AT&T Wireless was

---

[6]An acquiring company can elect Section 338 of the Internal Revenue Code and thereby record assets and liabilities at their market values for tax purposes. However, the acquired company must pay taxes immediately on differences between these market values and the tax basis of assets and liabilities.

Any goodwill resulting from the restatement of assets and liabilities that qualifies as a Section 197 intangible is amortized over a fifteen-year period as specified in the Revenue Recognition Act of 1993. To qualify for the amortization deduction, the goodwill had to be acquired after August 10, 1993. Goodwill amortization usually is not deducted for tax purposes, however, because few acquired firms restate their assets and liabilities.

one of the largest wireless communications service providers in the United States and operated one of the largest digital wireless networks. In its effort to compete effectively prior to its acquisition by Cingular Wireless, AT&T Wireless acquired TeleCorp Wireless several years earlier. At the time of the acquisition, TeleCorp Wireless provided digital wireless personal communications services to the large customer base of AT&T Wireless. In fact, the AT&T Wireless acquisition of TeleCorp was one of the reasons AT&T Wireless was appealing to Cingular Wireless as an acquisition.

AT&T Wireless provided several key disclosures related to the TeleCorp transaction in its quarterly and annual filings with the SEC:

> ***Accounting Treatment.*** In accordance with *Statement of Financial Accounting Standards No. 141,* "Business Combinations," and *Statement of Financial Accounting Standards No. 142,* "Goodwill and Other Intangible Assets," AT&T Wireless will use the purchase method of accounting for a business combination to account for the merger, as well as new accounting and reporting regulations for goodwill and other intangibles.
>
> ***Tax Consequences.*** We have structured the merger to be a tax-free reorganization for U.S. federal income tax purposes. Holders of TeleCorp class A voting common stock will not recognize gain or loss for U.S. federal income tax purposes in the merger, except for gain or loss recognized because of cash received instead of fractional shares of AT&T Wireless common stock.
>
> ***Goodwill Consequences for Financial and Tax Reporting.*** In accordance with SFAS No. 142, goodwill and licensing costs related to TeleCorp Wireless will not be amortized. Instead, AT&T Wireless Services will test these items for impairment as part of its periodic impairment test of total consolidated goodwill and total consolidated licensing costs. None of the goodwill recorded is deductible for tax purposes. In addition to these disclosures, AT&T Wireless provides selected pro forma information assuming the two firms had been combined in Year 10.

INVESTMENTS IN SECURITIES

Firms invest in the securities (debt, preferred stock, common stock) of other entities (governments, corporations, variable-interest entities, joint ventures, partnerships) for a variety of reasons, such as the following:

1. Short-term investments of temporarily excess cash.
2. Long-term investments to:
   a. Lock in high yields on debt securities.
   b. Exert significant influence on an important raw-materials supplier, customer, technological innovator, or other valued entity.
   c. Gain voting control of another entity whose operations mesh well strategically with those of the investing firm.
3. Short- or long-term investments designed to meet specific operational goals, such as commercial real estate leasing, research and development programs, or reinsurance.

Accounting for investments in other entities has been under heightened scrutiny in recent years because of both what Robert Swieringa, former FASB board member, refers to as the "flexible and fluid organizations" formed to meet the needs of firms[7] (see the

[7]Robert J. Swieringa, "Should Accounting be 'Green and Smooth and Inviting'?" *Journal of Financial Statement Analysis* (Winter 1997), pp. 75–87.

discussion on intangibles in Chapter 7), and the spate of reporting scandals in the early part of this decade, with the most notable case being Enron's abuse of special-purpose entities as investment vehicles.

Accounting for Investments

Various rulings address accounting for investments in one entity by another.[8] In general, firms must consider two paths for deciding the appropriate accounting for its investments:

1. Percentage of ownership that one firm has in another entity.
2. Whether the reporting firm is deemed the primary beneficiary of the investment it has made in a variable-interest entity (VIE), as defined in FASB *Interpretation No. 46*.[9]

The goal of each path is to assess the level of "controlling financial interest" by the firm making the investment, with the first path the more common situation for determining the appropriate accounting for investments.[10] However, it is important to note that the appropriate reporting is determined only after considering both paths. Each path, in turn, will be discussed next.

Percentage of Voting Stock

Exhibit 9.2 identifies three types of investments.

1. Minority, Passive Investments

Firms view debt securities or shares of capital stock of another corporation as a good investment and acquire them for their anticipated interest or dividends and capital gains

EXHIBIT 9.2

Types of Intercorporate Investments in Capital Stock

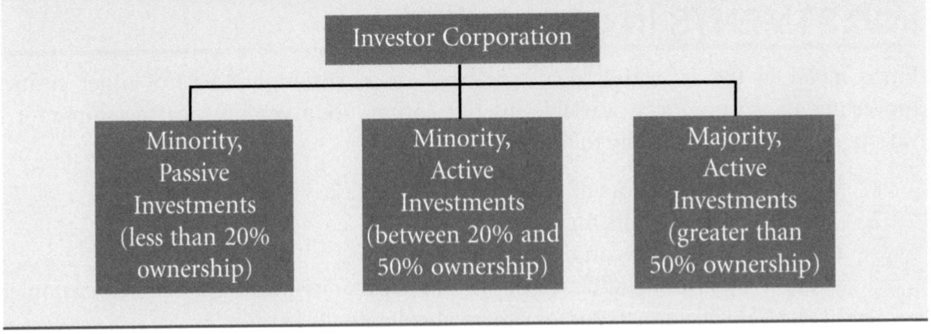

[8]Committee on Accounting Procedure, *Accounting Research Bulletin No. 51*, "Consolidated Financial Statements," as amended by *Statement of Financial Accounting Standards No. 94*, "Consolidation of Majority-Owned Subsidiaries" (1987) (referred to as *ARB No. 51* and *Statement No. 94*); *Statement of Financial Accounting Standards No. 115*, "Accounting for Certain Investments in Debt and Equity Securities" (1993) (referred to *Statement No. 115*); and *FASB Interpretation No. 46*, "Consolidation of Variable Interest Entities: An Interpretation of ARB No. 51" (2003) (referred to as *Interpretation No. 46*).

[9]*Statement No. 140*, discussed in Chapter 8, addresses the accounting for the sale of receivables. Entities formed by the transferor for the sale of receivables, often referred to as qualifying special-purpose entities, are excluded from the scope of *Interpretation No. 46* and thus are never classified as variable-interest entities.

[10]*ARB No. 51*, which addresses when consolidation accounting is appropriate, states that the most common condition for determining "controlling financial interest" is percentage of voting interest held by the investing firm of another firm.

(increases in the market prices of the securities). The percentage owned of another corporation's voting shares is not so large that the acquiring company can control or exert significant influence over the other company, and the investing firm is not deemed the VIE primary beneficiary as defined by *Interpretation No. 46* (discussed in a later section). Financial reporting views investments in debt securities, preferred stock, or common stock when the firm holds less than 20 percent of the voting stock as a minority, passive investment.

2. Minority, Active Investments

Firms acquire shares of another corporation so that the acquiring corporation can exert significant influence over the other company's activities. This significant influence is usually at a broad policymaking level through representation on the other corporation's board of directors. Because of the wide dispersion of ownership of most publicly held corporations, many of whose shareholders do not vote their shares, firms can exert significant influence over another corporation with ownership of less than a majority of the voting stock. Financial reporting views investments of between 20 and 50 percent of the voting stock of another company as a minority, active investment unless evidence indicates that the acquiring firm cannot exert significant influence or the investing firm is deemed the VIE primary beneficiary as defined by *Interpretation No. 46* (discussed in a later section).

3. Majority, Active Investments

Firms acquire shares of another corporation so that the acquiring corporation can control the other company. This control is typically at both the broad policymaking level and the day-to-day operational level. Ownership of more than 50 percent of the voting stock of another company implies an ability to control, unless available evidence indicates to the contrary.

The accounting for these three types of investments attempts to reflect the different purpose of each. Exhibit 9.3 summarizes the accounting for each type of investment in the financial statements.

Minority, Passive Investments

If a firm does not own a sufficient percentage of the voting stock of another corporation to control or significantly influence it, the management of the investment involves two activities: awaiting the receipt of interest or dividends and deciding when to sell the investment for a capital gain or loss. Financial reporting requires firms to account for minority, passive investments using either amortized acquisition cost or the market value method.[11]

Example 15 in Chapter 2 details the accounting for an available-for-sale investment (item 3(c) in the following list) by Microsoft, labeled investments in "marketable securities" in that chapter. Exhibit 2.1 in that chapter summarizes the various valuation techniques employed for all assets and liabilities, including investments in marketable debt and equity securities. A review of the example and exhibit at this point is helpful. A summary of the accounting for minority, passive investments follows:

1. Firms initially record investments at acquisition cost.
2. Revenues each period equal interest and dividends received or receivable.

---

[11] *Statement of Financial Accounting Standards No. 115* (1993).

EXHIBIT 9.3

Reporting Investments in Securities in the Financial Statements

Financial Statement	Minority, Passive Investments[a]	Minority, Active Investments[a]	Majority, Active Investments
Income Statement	Interest and dividend revenue Unrealized increases and decreases in the market value of securities classified as trading securities Realized gains and losses on sales of securities	Investor's share of investee's net income	Individual revenues and expenses of investee minus the minority interest's share of investee's net income included in consolidated net income
Balance Sheet	Marketable securities and investments in securities reported at market value (except that debt securities held to maturity reported at amortized acquisition cost) Unrealized increases and decreases in the market value of securities classified as available for sale included in Accumulated Other Comprehensive Income in the shareholders' equity section of the balance sheet	Investments reported at acquisition cost plus investor's cumulative share of investee's net income minus dividends received from investee since acquisition	Investment in securities account eliminated and replaced by investee's individual assets and liabilities in preparing consolidated balance sheet Minority interest's claim on investee's net assets shown in the shareholders' equity section of the consolidated balance sheet
Statement of Cash Flows	Cash received from interest and dividends included in cash flow from operations; cash flows associated with purchases and sales included in cash flows from investing	Cash received from interest and dividends included in cash flow from operations. Cash flows associated with purchases and sales included in cash flows from investing	Individual cash flows from operating, investing, and financing activities of investee included in consolidated statement of cash flows

[a]The accounting for minority, passive and minority, active investments illustrated in the exhibit assumes that the investing firm is not a VIE primary beneficiary as defined by FASB *Interpretation No. 46*. If the investing firm is a VIE primary beneficiary, the firm must follow the reporting for investments in securities categorized as majority, active investments.

3. The accounting at the end of each period depends on the type of security and the firm's ability and intent to hold it. *Statement No. 115* requires firms to classify securities into three categories:
   a. Debt securities for which a firm has a positive intent and ability to hold to maturity.
   b. Debt and equity securities held as *trading* securities.
   c. Debt and equity securities held as *available for sale.*
4. Firms must account for debt securities that they expect to hold until maturity at amortized acquisition cost. That is, the firm must amortize any difference between the acquisition cost and maturity value of these debt securities as an adjustment to interest revenue over the life of the debt. Firms report all other debt and equity securities at fair (or market) value at the end of each period. The reporting of any unrealized holding gain or loss depends on the purpose of holding the securities. If a firm actively buys and sells securities to take advantage of short-term differences or changes in market values, then the firm classifies the securities as trading securities, a current asset on the balance sheet. Commercial banks, for example, often trade securities in different capital markets worldwide to take advantage of temporary differences in market prices. Manufacturers, retailers, and other nonfinancial firms occasionally invest funds for trading purposes, but such situations are unusual. Firms include unrealized holding gains and losses on trading securities in net income each period.[12] Firms classify debt and equity securities that do not fit one of these first two categories (debt securities held to maturity, trading securities) as securities available for sale, including them as either current assets or noncurrent assets depending on the expected holding period. Unrealized holding "gains" or "losses" on securities available for sale are not included in net income each period but instead appear as a component of comprehensive income, labeled Unrealized Holding Gain or Loss on Securities Available for Sale. The cumulative unrealized holding gain or loss on securities available for sale appears in the shareholders' equity section of the balance sheet as part of Accumulated Other Comprehensive Income.
5. When a firm sells a trading security, it recognizes the difference between the selling price and the book value (that is, the market value at the end of the most recent accounting period prior to sale) as a gain or loss in measuring net income. When a firm sells a security classified as available for sale, it recognizes the difference between the selling price and the acquisition cost of the security as a realized gain or loss. The firm must eliminate at the time of sale any amount in the shareholders' equity account, Accumulated Other Comprehensive Income, for the unrealized holding gain or loss related to that security.

Example 3

PepsiCo reports $2,165 million of "short-term investments" on December 25, Year 4 (Appendix A). PepsiCo provides minimal additional disclosures related to its minority, passive investments. In the MD&A discussion titled "Our Liquidity, Capital Resources and Financial Position" (Appendix B), PepsiCo reports that short-term investments of approximately $1.0 billion were made in both Year 4 and Year 3. Also, PepsiCo's

---

[12]As Chapter 8 discusses, if a firm chooses not to designate a particular derivative as either a fair value hedge or a cash flow hedge, GAAP requires that the firm account for the derivative as a speculative investment. The accounting for trading securities and derivatives classified as a speculative investment is similar in that firms must revalue the derivatives to market value each period and recognize the resulting unrealized gain or loss in earnings.

Statement of Cash Flows (Appendix A) confirms this disclosure by reporting short-term investment activities of three months or less of $963 million for Year 4.

Example 4

Qualcomm, Inc. develops, manufactures, and markets digital wireless telecommunications products and services. The company generates revenues by licensing its proprietary digital technology and through ongoing royalty payments received on the sale of equipment by domestic and international wireless telecommunications equipment suppliers.

Qualcomm provides the following disclosures in the first two notes of a recent annual report, with the second note labeled "Marketable Securities":

> Management determines the appropriate classification of marketable securities at the time of purchase and reevaluates such designation as of each balance sheet date. Held-to-maturity securities are carried at amortized cost, which approximates fair value. Available-for-sale securities are stated at fair value as determined by the most recently traded price of each security at the balance sheet date. The net unrealized gains or losses on available-for-sale securities are reported as a component of comprehensive income (loss), net of tax. The specific identification method is used to compute the realized gains and losses on debt and equity securities.
>
> Available-for-sale securities were as follows on September 30, Year 4 (amounts in millions):

		Unrealized	Unrealized	
	Cost	Gains	Losses	Fair Value
Year 4				
Equity Securities	$1,003	$ 77	$(19)	$1,061
Debt Securities	5,208	27	(15)	5,220
Total	$6,211	$104	$(34)	$6,281
Year 3				
Equity Securities	$ 104	$ 37	$ (1)	$ 140
Debt Securities	2,758	69	(7)	2,820
Total	$2,862	$106	$ (8)	$2,960

> Components of Accumulated Other Comprehensive Income consisted of the following (amounts in millions):

	September 30:	
	Year 4	Year 3
Foreign Currency Translation	$56	$(3)
Unrealized Gain on Marketable Securities, net of income taxes	29	69
	$85	$66

In assessing the quality of accounting information, analysts must decide whether to include any change in the holding gain or loss on securities classified as available for sale in earnings for the period. The principal argument for excluding it is that the unrealized "gain" or "loss" may well reverse and perhaps will not be realized for many years, if ever. The principal argument for including the change relates to the fact that regardless of whether it is realized, the gain or loss has economic significance and therefore has a bearing on evaluating the investment performance of the firm.

Because firms invest in marketable securities with temporarily excess cash, the analyst can generally presume that firms could sell these securities for an amount at least equal to the amount shown on the balance sheet. This is a reasonable presumption for firms located in countries that require the mark-to-market accounting method, such as France and Great Britain. Certain countries, such as Canada, Japan, and Germany, require the valuation of marketable securities at acquisition cost unless firms consider a price decline to be permanent. Firms in the latter countries seldom disclose the market value of their marketable securities. If interest rates have increased or stock prices have declined materially in one of these countries during the last several months of the accounting period, the analyst should interpret the reported amounts for these securities cautiously.

Minority, Active Investments

When a firm owns less than a majority of the voting stock of another corporation, the accountant must exercise judgment in ascertaining whether the firm can exert significant influence. For the sake of uniformity, GAAP presumes that one company can significantly influence another company when it owns 20 percent or more of the voting stock of the other company. Ownership of less than 20 percent may permit a firm to exert significant influence, but in these cases management must demonstrate to the independent accountant that it is possible (for example, by placing individuals on the investee's board of directors).

GAAP requires firms to account for minority, active investments, generally those for which ownership is between 20 and 50 percent, using the *equity method.*[13] Under the equity method, the firm owning shares in another firm recognizes as income (loss) each period its share of the net income (loss) of the other firm. See, for example, the income statement of PepsiCo (Appendix A). The line "Bottling equity income" includes PepsiCo's share of the earnings from 20-percent- to 50-percent-owned bottling affiliates. The investor treats dividends received from the investee as a return of investment and not as income. In the discussion that follows, we designate the firm owning shares as P and the firm whose shares P owns as S.

The rationale for using the equity method when significant influence is present is best understood by considering the financial statement effects of using the market value method for securities classified as available for sale in these circumstances. Under the market value method, P recognizes income or loss on the income statement only when it receives a dividend or sells all or part of the investment. Suppose, as often happens, that S follows a policy of financing its own growing operations through retention of earnings and consistently declares dividends significantly less than its net income. The market price of S's shares will probably increase to reflect the retention of assets generated by earnings. Under the market value method, P's only reported income from the investment will be the modest dividends received.

P, because of its ownership percentage, can influence the dividend policy of S and thereby the amount of income recognized under the market value method. Under these

[13]Accounting Principles Board, *Opinion No. 18,* "The Equity Method of Accounting for Investments in Common Stock" (1971).

conditions, the market value method may not reasonably reflect the earnings of S generated under P's influence. The equity method provides a better measure of a firm's earnings and of its investment when, because of its ownership interest, it can significantly influence the operations and dividend policy of another firm.

Under the equity method, P reports its investment in S on the balance sheet at acquisition cost plus (minus) P's share of S's net income (loss) each period. In deriving cash flow from operations on the statement of cash flows, P subtracts its share of S's earnings from net income and adds any cash dividends received from S. Many firms net these two adjustments on the statement of cash flows, in which P would subtract its share of S's *undistributed* earnings (equity income minus dividends).

The analyst should address three questions in particular when examining the financial statements of firms with significant equity method intercorporate investments:

1. What is the relation between equity method income and cash flows received from the investees?
2. Are assets and liabilities essential to a firm's operations submerged in the intercorporate investment account?
3. Are the fair values of the firm's investments in these affiliates substantially different from the book values?

The analyst answers the first question by comparing equity method income on the income statement with the adjustment to net income for undistributed earnings of investees in the statement of cash flows. PepsiCo reports "Bottling equity income" of $380 million on its income statement for Year 4 (Appendix A). Its statement of cash flows shows a subtraction from net income to compute cash flow from operations of $297 million for "Bottling equity income, net of dividends," suggesting that PepsiCo received dividends from these intercorporate investments during Year 4 of $83 million. PepsiCo derived less than 10 percent of its pretax earnings during Years 4 and 3 from equity method investees.

The analyst answers the second and third questions by studying the notes on intercorporate investments. Firms must disclose partial balance sheet and income statement information for significant intercorporate investments, as well as the fair value of the investments. PepsiCo maintains less than a controlling interest in its major bottling operations for the strategic reasons, which we discussed in Chapter 1 and which PepsiCo discusses throughout Appendix B. The assets and liabilities of these bottlers do not appear on PepsiCo's balance sheet. A later section demonstrates the procedure an analyst might follow to incorporate amounts for such investments on the balance sheet.

The analyst should also exert caution when examining the financial statements of firms in other countries. Firms commonly use the equity method for minority, active investments in Canada, France, and Great Britain and in certain filings with the Ministry of Finance in Japan. Countries that follow a strict legal definition of the entity, such as Germany, tend to report these intercorporate investments at acquisition cost, even when significant influence is present.

Majority, Active Investments

When one firm, P, owns more than 50 percent of the voting stock of another company, S, P can usually control the activities of S. This control may occur at both a broad policy-making level and a day-to-day operational level. The majority investor in this case is the *parent* and the majority-owned company is the *subsidiary*. Financial reporting requires the combining or *consolidating* of the financial statements of majority-owned companies with those of the parent (unless the parent cannot for legal or other reasons exercise control).[14]

Reasons for Legally Separate Corporations

There are many reasons why a business firm prefers to operate as a group of legally separate corporations rather than as a single legal entity. From the viewpoint of the parent company, the more important reasons for maintaining legally separate subsidiary companies include the following:

1. To reduce financial risk. Separate corporations may mine raw materials, transport them to a manufacturing plant, produce the product, and sell the finished product to the public. If any one part of the total process proves to be unprofitable or inefficient, losses from insolvency fall only on the owners and creditors of the one subsidiary corporation. Furthermore, creditors have a claim on the assets of the subsidiary corporation only, not on the assets of the parent company. For corporations with potential environmental and product liabilities, legal separation through the use of subsidiaries can be especially advantageous.
2. To meet more effectively the requirements of corporation laws and tax legislation in different states and countries. If a firm does business in many states and countries, it must often contend with overlapping and inconsistent taxation, regulations, and requirements. Organizing separate corporations to conduct the operations in the various states may reduce administrative costs.
3. To expand or diversify with a minimum of capital investment. A firm may absorb another company by acquiring a controlling interest in its voting stock. It may accomplish this result with a substantially smaller capital investment, as well as with less difficulty, inconvenience, and risk, than if it had constructed a new plant or geared up for a new line of business.

Purpose of Consolidated Statements

For a variety of reasons, then, a parent and several legally separate subsidiaries may exist as a single economic entity. A consolidation of the financial statements of the parent and each of its subsidiaries presents the results of operations, financial position, and changes in cash flows of an affiliated group of companies under the control of a parent, essentially as if the group of companies were a single entity. The parent and each subsidiary are legally separate entities, but they operate as one centrally controlled economic entity. Consolidated financial statements generally provide more useful information to the shareholders of the parent corporation than would separate financial statements of the parent and each subsidiary.

Consolidated financial statements also generally provide more useful information than the equity method used to account for minority, active investments. The parent, because of its voting interest, can effectively control the use of the subsidiary's individual assets. Consolidation of the individual assets, liabilities, revenues, and expenses of both the parent and the subsidiary provides a more realistic picture of the operations and financial position of the single economic entity.

---

[14] *ARB No. 51* (1987). As this book goes to press, the FASB is considering replacing these standards with a new one on consolidation reporting. The new consolidation standard would retain the basic criteria for consolidation discussed in this chapter, but would require, among other changes, that (1) noncontrolling interests (minority interests) be recorded in the shareholders' equity section of the balance sheet, and (2) purchases and sales of noncontrolling interests in a subsidiary be recorded as capital transactions. However, the FASB may change its position and/or the effective date before issuing a final standard.

In a legal sense, consolidated statements merely supplement, and do not replace, the separate statements of the individual corporations, although it is common practice in the United States to present only the consolidated statements in published annual reports.

Disclosure of Consolidation Policy

The note to the financial statements that describes significant accounting policies commonly includes a statement about the consolidation policy of the parent. If a parent does not consolidate a significant majority-owned subsidiary, the notes will disclose that fact.

Example 5

Note 1 to PepsiCo's financial statements (Appendix A) states:

> Our financial statements include the consolidated accounts of PepsiCo, and the affiliates that we control. In addition, we include our share of the results of certain other affiliates based on our economic ownership interest. We do not control these other affiliates, as our ownership in these other affiliates is generally less than 50 percent. Our share of the net income of noncontrolled bottling affiliates is reported in our income statement as bottling equity income. Intercompany balances and transactions are eliminated.

Note that PepsiCo summarizes its accounting and reporting for both minority, passive (equity method) and majority, active (consolidation method) investments in this first note.

Understanding Consolidated Statements

This section discusses three concepts essential for understanding consolidated financial statements:

1. The need to eliminate intercompany balances and transactions, as PepsiCo mentions in Example 5.
2. The meaning of consolidated net income.
3. The nature of the external minority interest.

The Need to Eliminate Intercompany Activity. State corporation laws typically require each legally separate corporation to maintain its own set of books. Thus, during the accounting period, the accounting system of each corporation records transactions of that entity with all other entities (both affiliated and nonaffiliated). At the end of the period, each corporation prepares its own set of financial statements. The consolidation of these financial statements involves summing the amounts for various financial statement items across the separate company statements. The amounts resulting from the summation require adjustments, however, to eliminate the effects of *intercompany transactions.* Consolidated financial statements reflect the results of an affiliated group of companies operating as a single company. Thus, consolidated financial statements include only the transactions between the consolidated entity and others outside the group.

The eliminations to remove intercompany transactions typically appear on a *consolidation worksheet* and not on the books of any of the legal entities constituting the consolidated group. The accountant prepares the consolidated financial statements directly from the worksheet. The consolidated entity generally maintains no separate set of books.

To illustrate the need for, and the nature of, *elimination entries,* refer to the data for Company P and Company S in Exhibit 9.4. Column (1) shows the balance sheet and income statement data for Company P taken from its separate company books. Column (2) shows similar data for Company S. Column (3) sums the amounts from columns (1) and

EXHIBIT 9.4

Illustrative Data for Preparation of Consolidated Financial Statements

	Single-Company Statements		
	Company P (1)	Company S (2)	Combined (3)=(1)+(2)
Condensed Balance Sheets on December 31:			
Assets			
Accounts Receivable	$ 200,000	$ 25,000	$ 225,000
Investment in Stock of Company S (at equity)	705,000	—	705,000
Other Assets	2,150,000	975,000	3,125,000
Total Assets	$3,055,000	$1,000,000	$4,055,000
Equities			
Accounts Payable	$ 75,000	$ 15,000	$ 90,000
Other Liabilities	70,000	280,000	350,000
Common Stock	2,500,000	500,000	3,000,000
Retained Earnings	410,000	205,000	615,000
Total Equities	$3,055,000	$1,000,000	$4,055,000
Condensed Income Statement for Current Year:			
Revenues			
Sales	$ 900,000	$ 250,000	$1,150,000
Equity in Earnings of Company S	48,000	—	48,000
Total Revenues	$ 948,000	$ 250,000	$1,198,000
Expenses			
Cost of Goods Sold, excluding depreciation	$ 440,000	$ 80,000	$ 520,000
Depreciation Expense	120,000	50,000	170,000
Administrative Expenses	80,000	40,000	120,000
Income Tax Expense	104,000	32,000	136,000
Total Expenses	$ 744,000	$ 202,000	$ 946,000
Net Income	$ 204,000	$ 48,000	$ 252,000
Dividend Declarations	50,000	13,000	63,000
Increase in Retained Earnings for the Year	$ 154,000	$ 35,000	$ 189,000

(2). The amounts in column (3) include the effects of several intercompany items and therefore do not yet represent the correct amounts for consolidated assets, equities, revenues, or expenses.

Eliminating Double Counting of Intercompany Payables. Separate company records indicate that $12,000 of Company S's accounts receivable represent amounts payable by Company P. The amounts in column (3) count the current assets underlying this transaction twice: once as part of Accounts Receivable on Company S's books and a second time as Cash (or Other Assets) on Company P's books. Also, Accounts Payable in column (3) includes the liability shown on Company P's books, even though the amount is not payable to an entity external to the consolidated group. To eliminate double counting on the asset side and to report Accounts Payable at the amount payable to external entities, the elimination entry reduces the amounts for Accounts Receivable and Accounts Payable in column (3) by $12,000.

Eliminating Double Counting of Investment. Company P's balance sheet shows an asset, Investment in Stock of Company S. The subsidiary's balance sheet shows its individual assets and liabilities. The combined balance sheets in column (3) include both Company P's investment in Company S's net assets and the assets and liabilities themselves. We must eliminate Company P's account, Investment in Stock of Company S, from the sum of the balance sheets. Because the consolidated balance sheet must maintain the accounting equation, we must make corresponding eliminations on the right-hand, or equities, side as well. To understand the eliminations from the right-hand side of the balance sheet, recall that the right-hand side shows the sources of the firm's financing. Creditors (liabilities) and owners (shareholders' equity) finance Company S. Company P owns 100 percent of Company S's voting shares. Thus, the creditors of both companies and Company P's shareholders finance the assets on the consolidated balance sheet of the single economic entity. In other words, the equities of the consolidated entity are the liabilities of both companies but the shareholders' equity of Company P alone. If we added the shareholders' equity accounts of Company S to those of Company P, we would count twice the financing from Company P's shareholders (once on the parent's books and once on the subsidiary's books). Hence, when we eliminate Company P's investment account from the sum of the two companies' assets, we maintain the accounting equation by eliminating the shareholders' equity accounts of Company S.

Eliminating Double Counting of Income. Similarly, we must eliminate certain intercompany items from the sum of income statement accounts to present meaningfully the operating performance of the consolidated entity. Company P's accounts show Equity in Earnings of Company S of $48,000. Company S's records show individual revenues and expenses that net to $48,000. If we merely summed the revenues and expenses of the two companies, as column (3) of Exhibit 9.4 illustrates, we would double count the earnings of Company S. We must eliminate the account, Equity in Earnings of Company S, in preparing consolidated statements.

Eliminating Intercompany Sales. Another example of an intercompany item involves intercompany sales of inventory. Separate company records indicate that Company S sold merchandise to Company P for $40,000 during the year. None of this inventory remains in Company P's inventory on December 31. The sale of the merchandise inventory increases Sales Revenue on both Company S's books (sale to Company P for $40,000) and on Company P's books (sale to an external entity for probably a higher price). Thus, the combined amounts for Sales Revenue overstate sales from the standpoint of the consolidated entity by $40,000. Likewise, Cost of Goods Sold of both companies includes the separate company costs of the goods sold. To eliminate double counting, we must eliminate $40,000 from consolidated Cost of Goods Sold.

The Meaning of Consolidated Net Income. The amount of consolidated net income for a period exactly equals the amount that the parent shows on its separate company books from applying the equity method; that is, consolidated net income equals the following:

Parent Company's Net Income from Its Own Activities	+	Parent Company's Share of Subsidiary's Net Income	−	Profit (or + Loss) on Intercompany Transactions

A consolidated income statement differs from an equity method income statement in the *components* presented. When using the equity method for an unconsolidated subsidiary, the parent's share of the subsidiary's net income minus gain (or plus loss) on intercompany transactions appears on a single line, Equity in Earnings of Unconsolidated Subsidiary. In a consolidated income statement, we combine the individual revenues and expenses of the subsidiary (less intercompany adjustments) with those of the parent, and eliminate the account Equity in Earnings of Unconsolidated Subsidiary shown on the parent's books. Some accountants refer to the equity method as a one-line consolidation because it nets the individual revenues and expenses of the subsidiary into one account, Equity in Earnings of Unconsolidated Subsidiary.

External Minority Interest in a Consolidated Subsidiary. The parent does not always own 100 percent of the voting stock of a consolidated subsidiary. Accountants refer to the owners of the remaining shares of voting stock as the *minority interest.* These shareholders have a proportionate interest in the net assets of the subsidiary as shown on the subsidiary's separate corporate records. They also have a proportionate interest in the earnings of the subsidiary.

One issue that the accountant must confront in preparing consolidated statements is whether the statements should show only the parent's share of the assets and liabilities of the subsidiary or all of the subsidiary's assets and liabilities along with the minority interests' claim on them. GAAP requires firms to show all of the assets and liabilities of the subsidiary, because the parent, with its controlling voting interest, effectively directs the use of all the assets and liabilities, not merely an amount equal to the parent's percentage of ownership. The consolidated balance sheet and income statement in these instances, however, must disclose the interest of the minority shareholders in the consolidated subsidiary.

The amount of the minority interest appearing on the balance sheet results from multiplying the common shareholders' equity of the subsidiary by the minority's percentage of ownership. For example, if the common shareholders' equity of a consolidated subsidiary totals \$500,000 and the minority owns 20 percent of the common stock, the minority interest appears on the consolidated balance sheet at \$100,000 ($= .20 \times \$500,000$). The consolidated balance sheet shows the minority interest as part of shareholders' equity. The financial statements of PepsiCo give no indication that a minority interest exists in any of its consolidated subsidiaries.

The amount of the minority interest in the subsidiary's income results from multiplying the subsidiary's net income by the minority's percentage of ownership. The consolidated income statement shows the total consolidated income applicable to both the parent company and the consolidated subsidiary company and then adjusts net income for the amount of the subsidiary's income applicable to the minority proportionate interest. Typically, the minority interest in the subsidiary's income appears as a subtraction in calculating consolidated net income.

Limitations of Consolidated Statements

The consolidated statements do not replace those of individual corporations; rather, they supplement those statements and aid in their interpretation. Creditors must rely on the resources of one corporation and may be misled if forced to rely entirely on consolidated statements that combine the data of a company in good financial condition with one verging on insolvency. Firms can legally declare dividends only from their own retained earnings. When the parent company does not own all of the shares of the subsidiary, the outside or minority shareholders can judge the dividend constraints, both legal and financial, only by inspecting the subsidiary's statements.

Consolidation of Unconsolidated Subsidiaries and Affiliates

The analyst may wish to assess the financial position of a firm after consolidating all important majority-owned subsidiaries and minority-owned affiliates. For example, firms frequently join together in joint ventures to carry out their business activities. Chiron Corporation (Case 7.3 in Chapter 7) uses joint ventures and collaborative research agreements to develop new biotechnology-related products. Chiron does not consolidate the financial statements of the joint ventures with its financial statements, but rather uses the equity method to account for the joint ventures because they are not majority-owned by the firm.

As discussed in this chapter and Chapter 1, PepsiCo has significant investments in bottlers that are integral to its operations. As with Chiron, PepsiCo applies GAAP appropriately and does not consolidate the bottlers because they are less than majority-owned. However, consolidation of the financial statements of these affiliates with those of PepsiCo provides a glimpse of the firm from a more fully integrated, *operational*, perspective.

Exhibit 9.5 presents a consolidation worksheet for PepsiCo and its two primary bottlers, PBG and PAS. PepsiCo's balance sheet (Appendix A) provides the amounts in column (1). Note 8, "Noncontrolled Bottling Affiliates," to PepsiCo's financial statements (Appendix A) provides the amounts for columns (2) and (3). The amounts in column (4) eliminate amounts in the intercorporate investment accounts on PepsiCo's books against the shareholders' equity accounts of the affiliates. The column also shows the reclassification of a portion of the shareholders' equity accounts of the affiliates to recognize the minority interests or other external claims. The amount that Exhibit 9.5 shows for the external interest equals the total shareholders' equity of the affiliates times the external interests' ownership percentages. This percentage is 54 percent for PBG[15] and 59 percent for PAS. PepsiCo indicates in Note 8 that PBG and PAS are the firm's most significant noncontrolled bottling affiliates, but does not disclose any additional information about its other affiliates. Because of this, however, we can prepare a consolidation of PepsiCo with only PBG and PAS.

Consider now the effect of consolidating PepsiCo's bottlers on its rate of return on assets (ROA). For Year 4, Chapter 4 calculates an ROA (adjusted for the nonrecurring items discussed in that chapter) of:

$$15.4\% = \frac{\$4{,}004 + (1 - .35)(\$167) + \$0}{.5(\$25{,}327 + \$27{,}987)} = \frac{\$4{,}113}{\$26{,}657}$$

Operating income in the numerator of ROA does not change as a result of consolidation. To exclude the effect of financing from the numerator of ROA, we must add back the interest expense (net of taxes) recognized by PepsiCo's bottlers. Note 8 does not provide the amount of interest expense for those entities. We estimate the amount by assuming that the noncurrent liabilities of the bottlers represent interest-bearing debt. Based on disclosures in PepsiCo's Note 9, "Debt Obligations and Commitments" (Appendix A), we assume an average interest rate of 7.0 percent on long-term debt. The debt of PepsiCo's investees and amounts for noncurrent liabilities from Note 8 yield interest expense of

[15]Note 8 (Appendix A) indicates that PepsiCo's effective economic ownership of PBG is 46 percent when considering its 42 percent ownership of PBG's common stock, 100 percent ownership of PBG's class B common stock, and its 7 percent ownership of Bottling Group, LLC, PBG's principal operating subsidiary. Thus, the external-interests ownership percent for PBG is 54 percent (1 − .46).

EXHIBIT 9.5

PepsiCo and Equity Method Affiliates
Consolidation Worksheet
December 25, Year 4
(amounts in millions)

	PepsiCo (1)	PBG (2)	PAS (3)	Eliminations (4)	Consolidated (5)
Current Assets	$ 8,639	$ 2,039	$ 530		$11,208
Investments in Securities	3,284	—	—	(A) −1,594[a]	766
				(B) −924[a]	
Noncurrent Assets	$16,064	8,754	3,000	(A) +493[c]	$28,570
				(B) +259[e]	
Total Assets	$27,987	$10,793	$3,530		$40,544
Current Liabilities	$ 6,752	$ 1,581	$ 521		$ 8,854
Noncurrent Liabilities	7,712	6,818	1,386		15,916
Preferred Stock	(49)	—	—		(49)
External Minority Interests	—	—	—	(A) +1,293[b]	2,251
				(B) +958[d]	
Common Shareholders' Equity	13,572	2,394	1,623	(A) = −2,394[a]	13,572
				(B) = −1,623[a]	
Total Liabilities and Shareholders' Equity	$27,987	$10,793	$3,530		$40,544

[a]Information provided in PepsiCo's Note 8 (Appendix A).

[b]$1,293 = .54 × $2,394

[c]$493 = [1,594 − (.46 × $2,394)]

[d]$958 = .59 × $1,623

[e]$259 = [924 − (.41 × $1,623)]

\$575 million [= .07 × .5(\$6,818 + \$6,789 + \$1,386 + \$1,433)] for Year 4. Obviously we may inject some error into the calculation of ROA if some of the current liabilities of these entities bear interest, if some of the noncurrent liabilities do not bear interest, and if 7.0 percent is not a reasonable interest rate.

The final adjustment to the numerator of ROA to consolidate these bottlers is to add the external interest in earnings. This adjustment permits the numerator to include 100 percent of the operating income of PepsiCo and its bottlers and the denominator to include 100 percent of the assets of these entities. PepsiCo's Note 8 shows the total income for PBG and PAS bottlers for Year 4 of \$639 (\$457 + \$182), as well as PepsiCo's bottling equity income of \$380. The share of income attributable to the external interests in these two subsidiaries is therefore approximately \$259 million (= \$639 − \$380).[16] Consolidating PepsiCo's bottlers results in the following recomputed ROA for Year 4:

$$11.6\% = \frac{\$4{,}004 + (1 - .35)(\$167 + 575) + \$259}{5(\$40{,}544 + \$41{,}070)} = \frac{\$4{,}745}{\$40{,}807}$$

Thus, PepsiCo's ROA for Year 4 drops from 15.4 percent to 11.6 percent, a 25 percent decline. The capital-intensive nature of bottling reveals itself in this pro forma ratio analysis in that the asset base for PepsiCo increases dramatically when the bottling companies are consolidated. The analysis clearly points out the benefit to PepsiCo of not consolidating its financial statements with the firms that bottle its own product, and captures one of the key reasons PepsiCo divested itself of its bottlers in the 1990s.

The consolidation of majority-owned subsidiaries is a relatively recent phenomenon in some countries (such as Germany and Japan). These countries tended to follow strict legal definitions of the reporting entity. Financial reporting in these countries now generally requires the preparation of consolidated financial statements, although the requirement in Japan applies only to filings with the Ministry of Finance.

Proportionate Consolidation of Unconsolidated Subsidiaries and Affiliates

An alternative to full consolidation of PepsiCo's bottlers is proportionate consolidation. Under proportionate consolidation, the investor's share of the assets and liabilities of the affiliate appear in separate sections on the asset and liabilities sides of the balance sheet, with the equity investment account eliminated (recall that PepsiCo currently accounts for its investments using the equity method).

This alternative is especially appealing for firms that enter into joint ventures in which ownership of the venture is equally split between two firms. Chapter 7 provides several examples of these types of arrangements. Currently, firms account for investments in joint ventures using the equity method (unless FASB *Interpretation No. 46* applies) because these investments fall between minority, active investments and majority, active investments. Some accountants argue that proportionate consolidation better captures the economics of transactions in which joint control is present. The FASB has been reviewing joint venture accounting for some time, but is having difficulty identifying a standard that is operational.

---

[16]The share of the external interest is imprecise because we could not consolidate all of the noncontrolled bottling affiliates of PepsiCo. However, as stated earlier, PepsiCo discloses that PBG and PAS are PepsiCo's most significant noncontrolled bottling affiliates.

Primary Beneficiary of a Variable-Interest Entity

As discussed at the beginning of this section, firms must consider two paths for deciding the appropriate accounting for their investments. Both paths are necessary because a determination of "controlling financial interest" through levels of voting interest may not be appropriate (first path). For example, applying the majority-voting-interest rule to assess controlling financial interest will not work for investments in which control is achieved through arrangements that do *not* include voting rights, such as partnerships or trusts without governing boards. For these investments, controlling financial interest is assessed through application of *Interpretation No. 46* and a determination of the whether the investing firm is the primary beneficiary in a variable-interest entity (VIE).

As detailed shortly, if a firm's investment in another entity is classified as a VIE investment, accounting for the investment must follow the rules established in *Interpretation No. 46*. That is, the accounting based on the percentage of voting stock discussed previously is superseded by the reporting and disclosure requirements of *Interpretation No. 46*.

The FASB does not provide a precise definition of a VIE in *Interpretation No. 46*, only stating that the term refers "to an entity subject to consolidation according to the provisions of this Interpretation." VIEs can take the form of a corporation, partnership, trust, or any other legal structure used for business purposes. Examples include entities that administer real estate leases, research and development agreements, or energy-related foreign-exchange contracts. Often VIEs hold financial assets, real estate, or other property. The VIE may be passive and simply carry out a function on behalf of one or more firms (administering a commercial real estate lease, for example), or it may actively engage in some activity on behalf of one or more firms (such as conducting research and development activities). *Interpretation No. 46* uses the term "variable interest" to capture the fact that investors in VIEs have levels of interest that will vary with the success or failure of the VIE.

Although many individuals in business commonly use the term *special-purpose entities* (SPEs) instead of VIEs, the FASB purposely does not use the term because *Interpretation No. 46* applies to a larger set of entities than just SPEs. However, *Interpretation No. 46* is the direct result of the Enron debacle and the firm's abusive use of SPEs. Congress directed the FASB to swiftly address the reporting sins of Enron. The deliberative process for *Interpretation No. 46* followed a record-breaking pace, with some of its requirements taking effect almost immediately after its release by the FASB.

Application of *Interpretation No. 46*

The primary objectives of *Interpretation No. 46* are (1) to provide guidance on identifying entities for which control is achieved through means other than voting rights, and (2) to determine which firm should consolidate the VIE, labeled the primary beneficiary. The FASB concluded that consolidation by the primary beneficiary of the assets, liabilities, and results of activities of the VIE will provide the most complete information about the resources, obligations, risks, and opportunities of the consolidated company. In addition, *Interpretation No. 46* stipulates disclosures required by both the primary beneficiary and all other enterprises with a significant variable interest in a VIE.

When Is an Entity Classified as a VIE? A firm's investment in another entity is classified as a VIE investment, and thus subject to *Interpretation No. 46*, if any one of the following four conditions is met:

1. The total equity investment at risk is not sufficient to permit the VIE to finance its activities without additional subordinated financial support from other parties,

which would absorb some of the expected losses of the entity. *Interpretation No. 46* interprets this condition to be when "the equity investment at risk is not greater than the expected losses of the VIE." Also, the presumption is that an equity investment of less than 10 percent of the entity's *total assets* is not sufficient to permit the VIE to finance its activities without additional support.

2. The equity-investing firms do not have the direct or indirect ability to make decisions about the VIE's activities through voting rights or similar rights. Contractual arrangements with the subordinated providers of funds usually restrict the ability of the equity-investing firms to make decisions about the VIE's activities.
3. The equity-investing firms do not have the obligation to absorb the expected losses of the VIE if they occur. The subordinated providers of funds absorb some of the expected losses.
4. The investing firms do not have the right to receive the expected residual returns of the VIE if they occur. The subordinated providers of funds have a claim on some of the expected residual returns.

Which Entity Should Consolidate the VIE? Determining whether an investing firm should consolidate the VIE is at the heart of *Interpretation No. 46*. An investing firm consolidates the VIE if it absorbs the *majority* of the entity's expected losses if they occur, receives a *majority* of the entity's expected residual returns if they occur, or both. The consolidating firm is labeled the primary beneficiary. The firm considers the rights and obligations conveyed by its variable interests and the relationship of its variable interests to variable interests held by other firms to determine whether it will absorb a majority of expected losses, receive a majority of expected residual returns, or both. If one firm absorbs a majority of the expected losses and another firm receives a majority of the expected residual returns, the firm absorbing a majority of the losses consolidates the variable-interest entity.

Disclosure Requirements of Interpretation No. 46. Both the primary beneficiary firm and the firms holding significant variable interests in a VIE are subject to *Interpretation No. 46* disclosure rules. If material to the financial statements, the primary beneficiary must disclose (1) the nature, purpose, size, and activities of the VIE; (2) the carrying amount and classification of the consolidated assets that represent collateral for the VIE's obligations; and (3) the status of VIE creditors' recourse (if any) to the assets of the primary beneficiary. Firms holding significant variable interest in a VIE must disclose (1) the nature of its involvement with the VIE and when that involvement began; (2) the nature, purpose, size, and activities of the VIE; and (3) the investing firm's maximum exposure to loss given its involvement with the VIE.

Example 6

Univision Communications Inc. is one of the largest Spanish-language media company in the United States. Its operations include Univision Network, the most-watched Spanish-language broadcast television network in the United States, reaching 98 percent of U.S. Hispanic households; and TeleFutura Network, a general-interest Spanish-language broadcast television network, which was launched in Year 2 and currently reaches 83 percent of the Hispanic households in the United States.

Univision reported net revenues of \$433.0 million and net income of \$44.5 million for the quarter ended March 31, Year 5. The firm reported total assets of \$8.3 million at March 31, Year 5. A note to the firm's quarterly report states:

> On March 31, Year 4, the Company was required to adopt Financial Accounting Standards Board Interpretation No. 46, "Consolidation of Variable Interest Entities" ("FIN 46"). FIN 46 provides guidelines about when a company should consolidate in its financial statements the assets, liabilities and operating results of another entity (variable interest entity or "VIE"). Under the guidelines of FIN 46, the Company is required to consolidate Disa Records, a Mexico-based music recording and publishing company owned 50% by the Company and 50% by the Chavez family. The Company has a call right and the Chavez family has a put right, which requires the Company to purchase the remaining 50% of Disa Records for $75.0 million, subject to certain upward adjustments. Under the guidelines of FIN 46, the Company is also required to consolidate WLII/WSUR, Inc., which owns two television stations operating in Puerto Rico.

Disclosures vary to some degree across firms, particularly given the relative newness of *Interpretation No. 46*. Problem 9.17 provides an in-depth example of reporting and disclosures for three VIEs consolidated by the Molson Coors Brewing Company beginning in Year 4.

Identifying VIEs, determining the level of involvement (variable interests), and quantifying VIE activity is a difficult and subjective task. *Interpretation No. 46* provides only limited guidance, especially related to quantifying expected losses (condition (1) in the preceding list), which is a crucial dimension to the interpretation. Furthermore, *Interpretation No. 46* provides no guidance on how to proportion the expected losses when more than one firm has invested in the VIE. Given this, analysts should view the quality of accounting information for VIEs with skepticism, especially when the investing firm determines that consolidation of the VIE is not appropriate.

Income Tax Consequences of Investments in Securities

For income tax purposes, investments fall into two categories:

1. Investments in debt securities, in preferred stock, and in less than 80 percent of the common stock of another entity. Firms recognize interest or dividends received or receivable each period as taxable income (subject to a partial dividend exclusion), as well as gains or losses when they sell the securities.
2. Investments in 80 percent or more of the common stock of another entity. Firms can prepare consolidated tax returns for these investments.

As is evident, the methods of accounting for investments for financial and tax reporting do not overlap precisely. Thus, temporary differences will likely arise for which firms must recognize deferred taxes. PepsiCo, for example, cannot file consolidated tax returns with PBG, PAS, or other equity investments because its ownership percentage is less than 80 percent. PepsiCo reports in Note 5, "Income Taxes" (Appendix A), deferred tax liabilities of $850 million on December 25, Year 4 ($792 million on December 27, Year 3), relating to these equity investments because it includes its share of the investees' earnings each year for financial reporting but recognizes dividends received as income on its tax return.

FOREIGN CURRENCY TRANSLATION

Firms headquartered in the United States often have substantial operations outside of the country. For example, PepsiCo indicates in Note 1, "Basis of Presentation and Our Divisions" (Appendix A), that it generates approximately 37 percent of its net revenues internationally (defined as outside the United States).[17] For some firms (such as Coca-Cola), international sales dominate even though the firm is headquartered in the United States.

U.S. parent companies must translate the financial statements of foreign branches and subsidiaries into U.S. dollars before preparing consolidated financial statements for shareholders and creditors. This section describes and illustrates the translation methodology and discusses the implications of the methodology both for managing international operations and for interpreting financial statement disclosures regarding such operations.

Two general issues arise in translating the financial statements of a foreign branch or subsidiary:

1. Should the firm translate individual financial statement items using the exchange rate at the time of the transaction (referred to as the *historical exchange rate*) or the exchange rate during or at the end of the current period (referred to as the *current exchange rate*)? Financial statement items that firms translate using the historical exchange rates appear in the financial statements at the same U.S. dollar equivalent amount each period regardless of changes in the exchange rate. For example, land acquired in France for 10,000 euros when the exchange rate was $1.05 per euro appears on the balance sheet at $10,500 each period. Financial statement items that firms translate using the current exchange rate appear in the financial statements at a different U.S. dollar amount each period when exchange rates change. Thus, a change in the exchange rate to $1.10 per euro results in reporting the land at $11,000 in the balance sheet. Financial statement items for which firms use the current exchange rate give rise to a *foreign-exchange adjustment* each period.
2. Should the firm recognize the foreign-exchange adjustment as a gain or loss in measuring net income each period as it arises or should the firm defer its recognition until a future period? The foreign-exchange adjustment represents an unrealized gain or loss, much the same as changes in the market value of derivatives, marketable securities, inventories, or other assets. Should financial reporting require realization of the gain or loss through sale of the foreign operation before recognizing it, or should the unrealized gain or loss flow directly to the income statement as the exchange rate changes?

The sections that follow address these two questions.

Functional Currency Concept

Central to the translation of foreign currency items under GAAP is the *functional currency concept.*[18] Determination of the functional currency drives the accounting for translating the financial statements of foreign entities of U.S. firms into U.S. dollars.

[17]Financial reporting requires firms to disclose segment data by geographic location (foreign versus domestic) as well as by reportable operating segments and major customers (Financial Accounting Standards Board, *Statement of Financial Accounting Standards No. 131,* "Disclosures about Segments of an Enterprise and Related Information" [1997]). PepsiCo reports extensive geographic segment information in Note 1 (Appendix A). Chapter 4 provides profitability analysis of PepsiCo's geographic segment information.

[18]Financial Accounting Standards Board, *Statement of Financial Accounting Standards No. 52* (as amended by *Statement No. 130,* "Reporting Comprehensive Income"), "Foreign Currency Translation" (1981).

Foreign entities (whether branches or subsidiaries) are of two general types:

1. A foreign entity operates as a relatively self-contained and integrated unit within a particular foreign country. The functional currency for these operations is the currency of that foreign country. The rationale is that the management of the foreign unit likely makes operating, investing, and financing decisions based primarily on economic conditions within that foreign country, with minimal concern for economic conditions, exchange rates, and similar factors in other countries.
2. The operations of a foreign entity are a direct and integral component or extension of the parent company's operations. The functional currency for these operations is the U.S. dollar. The rationale is that management of the foreign unit likely makes decisions from the perspective of a U.S. manager concerned with the impact of decisions on U.S. dollar amounts.

The FASB issued *Statement No. 52* prior to the rapid growth in globalization, with firms now sourcing products, services, and capital and selling products and services and investing capital on a global basis. In these settings, no single currency may satisfactorily reflect the global activities of firms. Nonetheless, GAAP requires firms to select either the currency of the foreign unit or the U.S. dollar as the functional currency.

Statement No. 52 sets out characteristics for determining whether the currency of the foreign unit or the U.S. dollar is the functional currency. Exhibit 9.6 summarizes these

EXHIBIT 9.6

Factors for Determining Functional Currency of a Foreign Unit

	Foreign Currency Is Functional Currency	U.S. Dollar Is Functional Currency
Cash Flows of Foreign Entity	Receivables and payables denominated in foreign currency and not usually remitted to parent currently	Receivables and payables denominated in U.S. dollars and readily available for remittance to parent
Sales Prices	Influenced primarily by local competitive conditions and not responsive on a short-term basis to exchange rate changes	Influenced by worldwide competitive conditions and responsive on a short-term basis to exchange rate changes
Cost Factors	Foreign unit obtains labor, materials, and other inputs primarily from its own country	Foreign unit obtains labor, materials, and other inputs primarily from the United States
Financing	Financing denominated in currency of foreign unit or generated internally by the foreign unit	Financing denominated in U.S. dollars or ongoing fund transfers by the parent
Relations between Parent and Foreign Unit	Low volume of intercompany transactions and little operational interrelations between parent and foreign unit	High volume of intercompany transactions and extensive operational interrelations between parent and foreign unit

characteristics. The operating characteristics of a particular foreign operation may provide mixed signals regarding which currency is the functional currency. Management must exercise judgment in determining which functional currency best captures the economic effects of a foreign entity's operations and financial position. As a later section discusses, management may wish to structure certain financing or other transactions to swing the balance to favor selecting either the foreign currency or the U.S. dollar as the functional currency. Once a firm determines the functional currency of a foreign entity, it must use it consistently over time unless changes in economic circumstances clearly indicate a change in the functional currency.

Statement No. 52 provides for one exception to the guidelines in Exhibit 9.6 for determining the functional currency. If the foreign entity operates in a highly inflationary country, GAAP considers its currency too unstable to serve as the functional currency and the firm must use the U.S. dollar instead. A highly inflationary country is one that has experienced cumulative inflation of at least 100 percent over a three-year period. Some developing nations fall within this exception and pose particular problems for the U.S. parent company, as a later section discusses.

Translation Methodology—Foreign Currency Is Functional Currency

When the functional currency is the currency of the foreign unit, GAAP requires firms to use the *all-current translation method.* The left-hand column of Exhibit 9.7 summarizes the translation procedure under the all-current method.

Firms translate revenues and expenses at the average exchange rate during the period and balance sheet items at the end-of-the-period exchange rate. Net income includes only *transaction* exchange gains and losses of the foreign unit. That is, a foreign unit that has receivables and payables denominated in a currency other than its own must make a currency conversion on settlement of the account. The gain or loss from changes in the exchange rate between the time the account originated and the time of settlement is a transaction gain or loss. Firms recognize this gain or loss during the period the account is outstanding, even though it is not yet realized or settled. As Chapter 8 discusses, firms often acquire derivatives to hedge the risk of foreign currency gains and losses. Firms include the offsetting loss or gain on the derivative to the gain or loss on the item hedged in net income each period. Thus, net income increases or decreases net only to the extent that the derivative did not perfectly hedge the change in exchange rates.

When a foreign unit operates more or less independently of the U.S. parent, financial reporting assumes that only the parent's equity investment in the foreign unit is subject to exchange rate risk. The firm measures the effect of exchange rate changes on this investment each period, but includes the resulting "translation adjustment" as a component of Other Comprehensive Income, rather than net income. GAAP's rationale for this treatment is that the firm's investment in the foreign unit is for the long term; short-term changes in exchange rates therefore should not affect periodic net income. Firms recognize the cumulative amount in the translation adjustment account when measuring any gain or loss from disposing of the foreign unit.

The "translation adjustment" reported by a firm can include a second component in addition to the effect of exchange rate changes on the parent's equity investment in foreign subsidiaries or branches. Firms can hedge their investment in foreign operations using forward contracts, currency swaps, or other derivative instruments. GAAP requires firms to report the change in fair value of a derivative that qualifies as a hedge of the net investment

EXHIBIT 9.7

Summary of Translation Methodology

	Foreign Currency Is the Functional Currency (all-current method)	U.S. Dollar Is the Functional Currency (monetary/nonmonetary method)
Income Statement	Firms translate revenues and expenses as measured in foreign currency into U.S. dollars using the average exchange rate during the period. Income includes (1) realized and unrealized transaction gains and losses and (2) realized translation gains and losses when the firm sells the foreign unit.	Firms translate revenues and expenses using the exchange rate in effect when the firm made the original measurements underlying the valuations. Firms translate revenues and most operating expenses using the average exchange rate during the period. However, they translate cost of goods sold and depreciation using the historical exchange rate appropriate to the related asset (inventory, fixed assets). Net income includes (1) realized and unrealized transaction gains and losses and (2) unrealized translation gains and losses on the net monetary position of the foreign unit each period.
Balance Sheet	Firms translate assets and liabilities as measured in foreign currency into U.S. dollars using the end-of-the-period exchange rate. Use of the end-of-the-period exchange rate gives rise to unrealized transaction gains and losses on receivables and payables requiring currency conversions in the future. Firms include an unrealized translation adjustment on the net asset position of the foreign unit in a separate shareholders' equity account, not in net income, until the firm sells the foreign unit.	Firms translate monetary assets and liabilities using the end-of-the-period exchange rate. They translate nonmonetary assets and equities using the historical exchange rate.

in a foreign entity as part of the translation adjustment.[19] In this sense, the foreign currency hedge is treated similar to a cash-flow hedge (discussed and illustrated in Chapter 8) in that the change in the fair value of the hedge appears in Other Comprehensive Income. The difference is that firms do not separately disclose the change in the fair value of the hedge, but

[19]Financial Accounting Standards Board, *Statement of Financial Accounting Standards No. 133,* "Accounting for Derivative Instruments and Hedging Activities" (1998). However, if the foreign currency hedge does not qualify as a hedge of the net investment, then the criteria established in this standard for fair value and cash flow hedges are applied to determine the appropriate accounting. See Chapter 8 for a discussion of the accounting for derivatives used in fair value and cash flow hedging activities.

rather embed it in the translation adjustment, which also captures the effect of exchange rate changes on the parent's equity investment in the foreign entity.

Example 7

The functional currency for PepsiCo's foreign subsidiaries is the currency of the foreign unit. As a result, PepsiCo reports the currency translation adjustment in comprehensive income. PepsiCo's comprehensive income for Year 4 is $4,593 million. As detailed in Chapter 1, PepsiCo reports Currency Translation Adjustment of $401 million for the year as a component of comprehensive income. The Statement of Changes in Common Shareholders' Equity (Appendix A) for PepsiCo includes the $401 million currency translation adjustment in reconciling the change in Accumulated Other Comprehensive Loss for Year 4. In addition, Note 13, "Accumulated Other Comprehensive Loss" (Appendix A), reports the ending accumulated balance in Currency Translation Adjustment of –$720 million for Year 4 and –$1,121 million for Year 3. The difference between the two ending balances is $401 million, the amount reported as part of comprehensive income for Year 4.

Illustration—Foreign Currency Is Functional Currency

Exhibit 9.8 illustrates the all-current method for a foreign unit *during its first year of operations.* The exchange rate was $1:1FC on January 1, $2:1FC on December 31, and $1.5:1FC on average during the year. Thus, the foreign currency increased in value relative

EXHIBIT 9.8

Illustration of Translation Methodology When the Foreign Currency Is the Functional Currency

	Foreign Currency	U.S. Dollars	
Balance Sheet			
Assets			
Cash	FC 10	$2.0:1FC	$ 20.0
Receivables	20	$2.0:1FC	40.0
Inventories	30	$2.0:1FC	60.0
Fixed Assets, net	40	$2.0:1FC	80.0
Total	FC100		$200.0
Liabilities and Shareholders' Equity			
Accounts Payable	FC 40	$2.0:1FC	$ 80.0
Bonds Payable	20	$2.0:1FC	40.0
Total	FC 60		$120.0
Common Stock	FC 30	$1.0:1FC	$ 30.0
Retained Earnings	10		12.5[a]
Accumulated Other Comprehensive Income			
Unrealized Translation Adjustment	—		37.5[b]
Total	FC 40		$ 80.0
Total	FC100		$200.0

continued

EXHIBIT 9.8

continued

	Foreign Currency		U.S. Dollars
Income Statement			
Sales Revenue....................................	FC200	\$1.5:1FC	\$ 300.0
Realized Transaction Gain.....................	2[c]	\$1.5:1FC	3.0[c]
Unrealized Transaction Gain..................	1[d]	\$1.5:1FC	1.5[d]
Cost of Goods Sold	(120)	\$1.5:1FC	(180.0)
Selling and Administrative Expense	(40)	\$1.5:1FC	(60.0)
Depreciation Expense..........................	(10)	\$1.5:1FC	(15.0)
Interest Expense................................	(2)	\$1.5:1FC	(3.0)
Income Tax Expense	(16)	\$1.5:1FC	(24.0)
Net Income	FC 15		\$ 22.5

	Foreign Currency		U.S. Dollars
[a]Retained Earnings, Jan. 1	FC 0.0		\$ 0
Plus Net Income..	15.0		22.5
Less Dividends...	(5.0)	\$2.0:1FC	\$(10.0)
Retained Earnings, Dec. 31	FC 10.0		\$ 12.5
[b]Net Asset Position, Jan. 1	FC 30.0	\$1.0:1FC	\$ 30.0
Plus Net Income..	15.0		22.5
Less Dividends...	(5.0)	\$2.0:1FC	\$(10.0)
Net Asset Position, Dec. 31	FC 40.0		\$ 42.5
	↳	→ \$2.0:1FC	80.0
Unrealized Translation "Gain"...............................			\$ 37.5

[c]The foreign unit had receivables and payables denominated in a currency other than its own. When it settled these accounts during the period, the foreign unit made a currency conversion and realized a transaction gain of FC2.

[d]The foreign unit has receivables and payables outstanding that will require a currency conversion in a future period when the foreign unit settles the accounts. Because the exchange rate changed while the receivables/payables were outstanding, the foreign unit reports an unrealized transaction gain for financial reporting.

to the U.S. dollar during the year (that is, it takes fewer foreign currency units to acquire \$1 at the end of the year than at the beginning of the year). The firm translates all assets and liabilities on the balance sheet at the exchange rate on December 31. It translates common stock at the exchange rate on the date of issuance; the translation adjustment account includes the effects of changes in exchange rates on this investment. The translated amount of retained earnings results from translating the income statement and dividends. Note that the firm translates all revenues and expenses of the foreign unit at the average exchange rate. The foreign unit realized a transaction gain during the year and recorded it on its books. In addition, the translated amounts for the foreign unit include an unrealized transaction gain arising from exposed accounts that are not yet settled. Note (a) to Exhibit 9.8 shows the computation of translated retained earnings. The foreign unit paid the dividend on December 31.

Note (b) shows the calculation of the translation adjustment. By investing $30 in the foreign unit on January 1 and allowing the $22.5 of earnings to remain in the foreign unit throughout the year while the foreign currency was increasing in value relative to the U.S. dollar, the parent has a potential exchange "gain" of $37.5. It reports this amount as a component of comprehensive income.

Translation Methodology—U.S. Dollar Is Functional Currency

When the functional currency is the U.S. dollar, financial reporting requires firms to use the *monetary/nonmonetary translation method.* The right-hand column of Exhibit 9.7 summarizes the translation procedure under the monetary/nonmonetary method.

The underlying premise of the monetary/nonmonetary method is that the translated amounts reflect amounts that the firm would have reported if it had originally made all measurements in U.S. dollars. To implement this underlying premise, financial reporting distinguishes between monetary items and nonmonetary items.

A monetary item is an account whose nominal maturity amount does not change as the exchange rate changes. From a U.S. dollar perspective, these accounts give rise to exchange gains and losses because the number of U.S. dollars required to settle the fixed foreign currency amounts fluctuates over time with exchange rate changes. Monetary items include cash, receivables, accounts payable, and other accrued liabilities and long-term debt. Firms translate these items using the end-of-the-period exchange rate and recognize translation gains and losses. These translation gains and losses increase or decrease net income each period, whether or not the foreign unit must make an actual currency conversion to settle the monetary item. The rationale for the recognition of unrealized translation gains and losses in net income is that the foreign unit will likely make a currency conversion in the near future either to settle monetary assets and liabilities or convert foreign currency into U.S. dollars to remit a dividend to the parent, activities consistent with foreign units that operate as extensions of the U.S. parent.

A nonmonetary item is any account that is not monetary and includes inventories, fixed assets, common stock, revenues, and expenses. Firms translate these accounts using the historical exchange rate in effect when the foreign unit initially made the measurements underlying these accounts. Inventories and cost of goods sold translate at the exchange rate when the foreign unit acquired the inventory items. Fixed assets and depreciation expense translate at the exchange rate when the foreign unit acquired the fixed assets. Most revenues and operating expenses other than cost of goods sold and depreciation translate at the average exchange rate during the period. The objective is to state these accounts at their U.S. dollar-equivalent historical cost amounts. In this way, the translated amounts will reflect the U.S. dollar perspective that is appropriate when the U.S. dollar is the functional currency.

Illustration—U.S. Dollar Is Functional Currency

Exhibit 9.9 shows the application of the monetary/nonmonetary method to the data considered in Exhibit 9.8. Net income again includes both realized and unrealized transaction gains and losses. Net income under the monetary/nonmonetary translation method also includes a $22.5 translation loss.

As Note (b) to Exhibit 9.9 shows, the firm was in a net monetary liability position during a period when the U.S. dollar decreased in value relative to the foreign currency. The translation loss arises because the U.S. dollars required to settle these foreign-denominated net liabilities at the end of the year exceed the U.S. dollar amount required to settle the net liability position before the exchange rate changed.

Implications of Functional Currency Determination for Analysis

As Exhibit 9.8 and Exhibit 9.9 demonstrate, the functional currency and related translation method can significantly affect translated financial statement amounts for a foreign unit. Some summary comparisons follow:

Functional Currency Is:	Foreign Currency	U.S. Dollar
Net Income	$ 22.5	$ 5.0
Total Assets	$200.0	$145.0
Shareholders' Equity	$ 80.0	$ 25.0
Rate of Return on Assets	11.3%	3.4%
Rate of Return on Common Shareholders' Equity	28.1%	20.0%

These differences arise for two principal reasons:

1. The all-current translation method (foreign currency is the functional currency) uses current exchange rates, whereas the monetary/nonmonetary translation method (U.S. dollar is the functional currency) uses a mixture of current and historical rates. Not only are net income and total asset amounts different, but the relative proportions of receivables, inventories, and fixed assets to total assets, debt/equity ratios, and gross and net profit margins differ. When firms use the all-current translation method, the translated amounts reflect the same financial statement relationships (such as debt/equity ratios) as when measured in the foreign currency. When the U.S. dollar is the functional currency, financial statement relationships get measured in U.S. dollar-equivalent amounts and financial ratios differ from their foreign currency amounts.
2. The other major reason for differences between the two translation methods is the inclusion of unrealized translation gains and losses in net income under the monetary/nonmonetary method. Much of the debate with respect to the predecessor to *Statement No. 52*, which was *Statement No. 8*, involved the inclusion of this unrealized translation gain or loss in net income. Many companies argued that the gain or loss was a bookkeeping adjustment only and lacked economic significance, particularly when the transaction required no currency conversion to settle a monetary item. Also, its inclusion in net income often caused wide, unexpected swings in earnings, particularly in quarterly reports.

As discussed earlier, the organizational structure and operating policies of a particular foreign unit determine its functional currency. The two acceptable choices and the corresponding translation methods were designed to capture the different economic and operational relationships between a parent and its foreign affiliates. However, firms have some latitude in deciding the functional currency, and, therefore, the translation method, for each foreign unit. In many cases, the signals about the appropriate functional currency will be mixed and firms will have latitude to select between them. Some actions that management might consider to swing the balance of factors toward use of the foreign currency as the functional currency include the following:

1. *Decentralize decision making to the foreign unit.* The greater the degree of autonomy of the foreign unit, the more likely its currency will be the functional currency. The U.S. parent company can design effective control systems to monitor the activities of the foreign unit while permitting the foreign unit to operate with considerable freedom.

EXHIBIT 9.9

Illustration of Translation Methodology When the U.S. Dollar Is the Functional Currency

	Foreign Currency	U.S. Dollars	
Balance Sheet			
Assets			
Cash	FC 10	$2.0:1FC	$ 20.0
Receivables	20	$2.0:1FC	40.0
Inventories	30	$1.5:1FC	45.0
Fixed Assets, net	40	$1.0:1FC	40.0
Total	FC100		$145.0
Liabilities and Shareholders' Equity			
Accounts Payable	FC 40	$2.0:1FC	$ 80.0
Bonds Payable	20	$2.0:1FC	40.0
Total	FC 60		$120.0
Common Stock	FC 30	$1.0:1FC	$ 30.0
Retained Earnings	10		(5.0)[a]
Total	FC 40		$ 25.0
Total	FC100		$145.0
Income Statement			
Sales Revenue	FC200	$1.5:1FC	$300.0
Realized Transaction Gain	2	$1.5:1FC	3.0
Unrealized Transaction Gain	1	$1.5:1FC	1.5
Unrealized Translation Loss	—		(22.5)[b]
Cost of Goods Sold	(120)	$1.5:1FC	(180.0)
Selling and Administrative Expense	(40)	$1.5:1FC	(60.0)
Depreciation Expense	(10)	$1.0:1FC	(10.0)
Interest Expense	(2)	$1.5:1FC	(3.0)
Income Tax Expense	(16)	$1.5:1FC	(24.0)
Net Income	FC 15		$ 5.0

	Foreign Currency	U.S. Dollars	
[a]Retained Earnings, Jan. 1	FC 0	—	$ 0.0
Plus Net Income	15		5.0
Less Dividends	(5)	$2.0:1FC	(10.0)
Retained Earnings, Dec. 31	FC 10		$(5.0)

[b]Income for financial reporting includes any unrealized translation gain or loss for the period. The net monetary position of a foreign unit during the period serves as the basis for computing the translation gain or loss. The foreign unit was in a net monetary liability position during a period when the U.S. dollar decreased in value relative to the foreign currency. The translation loss arises because the U.S. dollars required to settle the net monetary liability position at the end of the year exceed the U.S. dollars required to settle the obligation at the time the firm initially recorded the transactions that give rise to change in net monetary liabilities during the period. The calculations are as follows:

continued

EXHIBIT 9.9

continued

	Foreign Currency		U.S. Dollars
Net Monetary Position, Jan. 1	FC 0.0	—	$ 0.0
Plus:			
Issue of Common Stock	30.0	$1.0:1FC	$ 30.0
Sales for Cash and on Account	200.0	$1.5:1FC	300.0
Settlement of Exposed Receivable/Payable at a Gain	2.0	$1.5:1FC	3.0
Unrealized Gain on Exposed Receivable/Payable	1.0	$1.5:1FC	1.5
Less:			
Acquisition of Fixed Assets	(50.0)	$1.0:1FC	(50.0)
Acquisition of Inventory	(150.0)	$1.5:1FC	(225.0)
Selling and Administrative Costs Incurred	(40.0)	$1.5:1FC	(60.0)
Interest Cost Incurred	(2.0)	$1.5:1FC	(3.0)
Income Taxes Paid	(16.0)	$1.5:1FC	(24.0)
Dividend Paid	(5.0)	$2.0.1FC	(10.0)
Net Monetary Liability Position, Dec. 31	(30.0)		$(37.5)
	→	$2.0.1FC	–(60.0)
Unrealized Translation Loss			$ 22.5

2. *Minimize remittances/dividends.* The greater the degree of earnings retention by the foreign unit, the more likely its currency will be the functional currency. The parent may obtain cash from a foreign unit indirectly rather than directly through remittances or dividends. For example, a foreign unit with mixed signals about its functional currency might, through loans or transfer prices for goods or services, send cash to another foreign unit whose functional currency is clearly its own currency. This second foreign unit can then remit it to the parent. Other possibilities for interunit transactions are also acceptable to ensure that *some* foreign currency rather than the U.S. dollar is the functional currency.

Research suggests that approximately 80 percent of U.S. firms with foreign operations use the foreign currency as the functional currency and the remainder use the U.S. dollar.[20] Few firms select the foreign currency for some operations and the U.S. dollar for other operations (except for operations in highly inflationary countries, where firms must use the U.S. dollar as the functional currency). Thus, it appears that firms prefer the all-current translation method, in large part because they can exclude unrealized foreign currency "gains and losses" from earnings each period and experience fewer earnings surprises. Inclusion of the change in the foreign currency translation adjustment account each period in earnings can cause large, unexpected variations in reporting earnings, a result that most managers prefer to avoid.

The question for the analyst assessing earnings quality is whether to include the change in the foreign currency translation account in earnings, or to leave it as a component of comprehensive income. The principal argument for excluding it is that the unrealized

[20]Eli Bartov and Gordon M. Bodnar, "Alternative Accounting Methods, Information Asymmetry and Liquidity: Theory and Evidence," *Accounting Review* (July 1996), pp. 397–418.

"gains or losses" may well reverse in the long term, and, in any case, will not be realized perhaps for many years. The principal arguments for including it in earnings are that (1) management has purposely chosen the foreign currency as the functional currency in order to avoid including such "gains or losses" in earnings, not because the firm allows its foreign units to operate as independent units; and (2) the change in the foreign currency translation adjustment represents the current period's portion of the eventual net gain or loss that *will* be realized. When using earnings to value a firm, Chapter 12 suggests that earnings should include all recognized value changes regardless of whether GAAP includes them in net income or other comprehensive income.

A study[21] examining the valuation relevance of the translation adjustment regressed market-adjusted returns on (1) earnings excluding exchange gains and losses, (2) transaction exchange gains and losses included in earnings, and (3) changes in the translation adjustment reported as a component of comprehensive income. The study found that the coefficient on the translation adjustment was statistically significant but smaller than that on earnings excluding all exchange gains and losses, suggesting that the market considers the translation adjustment relevant for security valuation but less persistent (as discussed in Chapter 6) than earnings excluding gains and losses. Given this finding, the FASB's decision to require firms to report the translation adjustment change as a *separate and distinct* component of comprehensive income appears on target in that it mandates the highlighting of the change.

Foreign Currency Translation and Income Taxes

Income tax laws distinguish between a foreign branch of a U.S. parent and a subsidiary of a U.S. parent. A subsidiary is a legally separate entity from the parent; a branch is not. The translation procedure of foreign branches is essentially the same as for financial reporting (except that taxable income does not include translation gains and losses until realized). That is, a firm selects a functional currency for each foreign branch and uses the all-current or monetary/nonmonetary translation method as appropriate.

For foreign subsidiaries, taxable income includes only dividends received each period (translated at the exchange rate on the date of remittance). Because parent companies typically consolidate foreign subsidiaries for financial reporting but cannot consolidate them for tax reporting, temporary differences that require the provision of deferred taxes likely arise.

Interpreting the Effects of Exchange Rate Changes on Operating Results

In addition to understanding the effects of the foreign currency translation method on a firm's financial statements, the analyst should consider how changes in exchange rates affect changes in sales levels, sales mix, and net income.

Refer to Exhibit 9.10. Assume that a firm generated sales of $10,000 within the United States and FC2,000 within a particular foreign country during Year 3. The exchange rate between the U.S. dollar and the foreign currency was $2:FC1 during Year 3. The FC2,000 of sales translates into $4,000 of foreign sales, resulting in a mix of 71.4 percent domestic sales and 28.6 percent foreign sales. For illustration, assume that domestic sales for Year 4 are $10,000 and foreign sales are FC2,000. Assume first that the U.S. dollar increases in value

[21]Billy S. Soo and Lisa Gilbert Soo, "Accounting for the Multinational Firm: Is the Translation Process Valued by the Stock Market?" *Accounting Review* (October 1995), pp. 617–637.

EXHIBIT 9.10

Illustration of the Effect of Exchange Rate Changes on Sales and Sales Mix

	Exchange Rate	Domestic Sales	Foreign Sales	Total Sales	Sales Mix	
					Domestic	Foreign
Year 3	\$2.0:FC1	\$10,000	\$4,000[a]	\$14,000	71.4%	28.6%
Year 4	\$1.8:FC1	\$10,000	\$3,600[b]	\$13,600	73.5%	26.5%
Year 4	\$2.4:FC1	\$10,000	\$4,800[c]	\$14,800	67.6%	32.4%

[a]FC2,000 × \$2:FC1 = \$4,000
[b]FC2,000 × \$1.8:FC1 = \$3,600
[c]FC2,000 × \$2.4:FC1 = \$4,800

relative to the foreign currency during Year 4, with an average exchange rate of \$1.8:FC1. The FC2,000 of foreign sales translates into \$3,600, resulting in a mix of 73.5 percent domestic sales and 26.5 percent foreign sales. Alternatively, assume that the U.S. dollar decreases in value during Year 4, with an average exchange rate of \$2.4:FC1. The FC2,000 of foreign sales translates into \$4,800, resulting in a mix of 67.6 percent domestic sales and 32.4 percent foreign sales. Without considering the effects of changes in selling price and volume, changes in exchange rates affect the level and mix of domestic versus foreign sales.

Changes in exchange rates also affect profit margins and rates of return. The profit margin for a firm is a weighted average of the profit margins of its domestic and foreign units, for which the weights are the sales mix percentages. As Exhibit 9.10 illustrates, changes in exchange rates affect the sales mix proportions (in addition to any affects on the amount for foreign-source earnings) and thereby the firm's overall profit margin.

Refer to PepsiCo's disclosures labeled "Results of Continuing Operations—Divisional Review" in its MD&A (Appendix B). PepsiCo discloses that exchange rate changes explain 2 percent of the 8 percent increase in revenues during Year 4 for the firm as a whole and 4 percent of the 14 percent increase in revenues for its PepsiCo International segment. In contrast, exchange rate changes account for only 1 percent of the increase in revenues for Year 3 for the firm as a whole and 1 percent of the increase in revenues in PepsiCo International. PepsiCo International's proportion of the revenue mix increased from 32.2 percent (= \$8,678/\$26,971) in Year 3 to 33.7 percent (= \$9,862/\$29,261) in Year 4, in part because of exchange rate changes. Exhibit 4.10 in Chapter 4 indicates that PepsiCo International is PepsiCo's least profitable segment. The increased sales mix percentage for this segment as a result of the decreasing value of the U.S. dollar during Year 4 had a dampening effect of the firm's overall profitability.

ACCOUNTING FOR STOCK-BASED COMPENSATION

Firms often give employees the right, or option, to acquire shares of common stock at a price that is less than the market price of the shares at the time they exercise the option. Use of stock options, especially as a form of employee compensation, skyrocketed in the last twenty years. Firms in the technology sector, especially since the Internet boom of the 1990s, have used options as a dominant component of their employee compensation packages.

It is especially common for firms to grant stock options to senior management each year as an element of their compensation. The stock options permit the employees to purchase shares of common stock at a price usually set equal to the market price of the stock at the time the firm grants the stock option. Employees exercise these stock options at a later time if the stock price increases above the stock option exercise price. Firms adopt stock option plans to motivate employees to take actions that will increase the market value of a firm's common shares. Unlike compensation in the form of salaries, stock options do not require firms to use cash during the period when they grant stock options to employees.

Example 8

Note 6, "Stock-Based Compensation" (Appendix A), describes the stock options PepsiCo granted to employees and members of the firm's board of directors. The PepsiCo long-term incentive plan (LTIP) is typical of plans offered by many firms. Note that PepsiCo identifies the participants as "employees at all levels" and bases the awards on such metrics as job levels and years of service with the firm. Also note that there is a vesting period (defined shortly) for the options granted to the firm's employees. At the end of Year 4, Note 6 discloses that 62 million shares were available for grants under the firm's stock-based compensation plans.

In a subsection of Note 6, "Stock-Based Compensation—Method of Accounting and Our Assumptions" (Appendix A), PepsiCo states: "We account for our employee stock options under the fair value method of accounting using a Black-Scholes model to measure stock-based compensation expense at the date of grant."

The next section describes the accounting for stock options.

Fair Value Method and Required Disclosures

An understanding of the accounting for stock-based compensation requires several definitions. Refer to Exhibit 9.11. The *grant date* is the date a firm gives a stock option to employees. The *vesting date* is the first date employees can exercise their stock options. Exercise cannot occur before the vesting date or after the end of the option's life. Firms usually structure stock option plans so that a period of time elapses between the grant date and the vesting date. Firms may either preclude employees from exercising the option for one or more years or set an exercise price sufficiently high that the employee would not desire to exercise the option until the stock price increases. Setting the vesting date later than the grant date aims to enhance employee retention and motivation. The *exercise date* is the date employees elect to exchange the option and cash for shares of common stock. The *exercise price* is the price specified in the stock option contract for purchasing the common stock. The *market price* is the price of the stock as it trades in the market.

In theory, the value of a stock option has two elements: (1) the benefit realized on the exercise date because the market price of the stock exceeds the exercise price (the *benefit element*), and (2) the length of the period during which the holder can exercise the option (the *time-value element*).

The amount of the benefit element is not known until the exercise date. In general, stock options with exercise prices less than the current market price of the stock (described as *in the money*) have a higher value than stock options with exercise prices exceeding the current market price of the stock (described as *out of the money*). The time-value element of an option's value results from the benefit it provides its holder for increases in the market price of the stock during the exercise period. An option provides the holder the right to enjoy the benefits of market price increases for the stock. This second element of an option will have

EXHIBIT 9.11

Key Stock Option Dates and Prices

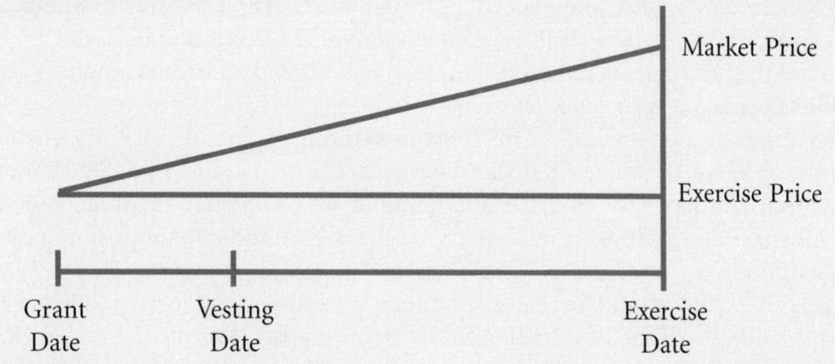

more value the longer the exercise period, the more volatile the market price of the stock, the lower the dividend yield, and the lower the discount rate. Note that a stock option may have an exercise price that exceeds the current market price (zero value for the first element) but still have a value because of the possibility that the market price will exceed the exercise price on the exercise date (positive value for the second element). As the expiration date of the option approaches, the value of the second element approaches zero.[22]

Statements No. 123 and *No. 123 (Revised 2004)* address accounting for stock options.[23] The history of these rulings is intriguing, with accounting for stock options representing one of the most controversial reporting topics in recent decades. Released in 1972, APB *Opinion No. 25* recommended but did not require firms to recognize the cost of stock options as compensation expense on the date of the grant.[24] However, very few firms followed the recommendation of *Opinion No. 25* in the ensuing years. The FASB revisited the topic in the 1990s, culminating in the board's issuing an exposure draft of a new reporting standard that would have required firms to recognize the cost of stock options as compensation expense on the date of the grant. This proposal would have superceded *Opinion No. 25,* which as stated previously recommended but did not require expensing of stock option grants. This proposal was never adopted, however, because the business community lobbied various congressional interests so vigorously that some U.S. senators pressured the FASB to withdraw its proposal. The FASB eventually issued *Statement No. 123* in 1995, which reaffirmed the conclusions of *Opinion No. 25* but required only pro forma stock option *disclosures* in the notes to the financial statements about the impact of stock option grants on earnings.

Subsequent to issuance of *Statement No. 123* in 1995, and importantly, after the reporting and accounting scandals of the early 2000s, some firms began to voluntarily treat the cost of stock options given to employees as compensation expense. These firms decided

[22]For an elaboration on the theory of option pricing, see Fischer Black and Myron Scholes, "The Pricing of Options and Corporate Liabilities," *Journal of Political Economy* (May–June 1973), pp. 637–654.

[23]Financial Accounting Standards Board, *Statement No. 123,* "Accounting for Stock-Based Compensation" (1995); Financial Accounting Standards Board, *Statement No 123 (Revised 2004),* "Accounting for Share-Based Payment" (2004).

[24]Accounting Principles Board, *Opinion No. 25,* "Accounting for Stock Issued to Employees" (1972). *Statements No. 123* and *123 (Revised 2004)* supersede *Opinion No. 25.*

either that expensing the cost of stock options is theoretically more sound, or that investors would view these firms more favorably for taking this voluntary move. Riding the growing movement of recognizing stock options as a form of compensation expense, as well as the view held by many that the accounting scandals were partially the result of poor corporate governance and reporting, including reporting for stock options, FASB again revisited the topic. The result was *Statement No. 123 (Revised 2004)*, which requires firms to use the fair value method to value stock options and report the amounts as compensation expense in the income statement.

Under the fair value method, firms must measure the value of stock options on the date of grant. Once the value of stock options is estimated using an acceptable option pricing model, firms must amortize this amount as compensation expense over the period in which an employee provides services. This is commonly the vesting period of the stock options.

Because the value of employee stock options typically cannot be measured with an observable value established by trading in an active market, *Statement No. 123 (Revised 2004)* recognizes that most firms will use an option pricing model to estimate the value of the options. *Statement No. 123 (Revised 2004)* does not require a specific option pricing model, although the Black-Scholes model[25] or a lattice model (for example, the binomial model) are most common in practice. (Note 6, "Stock-Based Compensation" (Appendix A), quoted in Example 8, discloses that PepsiCo employs the Black-Scholes model to value the firm's stock options.) A detailed discussion of option valuation models can be found in the finance literature and is beyond the scope of this text. However, any model employed must incorporate a variety of factors, including the exercise price of the option, the term of the option, the current market price of each share of underlying stock, expected stock volatility, dividends, and the risk-free interest rate.[26]

Statement No. 123 (Revised 2004) requires disclosures regarding stock option grants, their effect on total compensation expense, the methodology (model) used to value the stock options, and the key assumptions made to estimate the value of the stock options.

Example 9

In addition to Note 6 of PepsiCo's financial statements, the firm's MD&A, "Our Critical Accounting Policies—Stock-Based Compensation" (Appendix B), provides extensive stock option disclosures:

1. The firm states, "We believe that we will achieve our best results if employees act and are rewarded as business owners. Therefore, we believe stock ownership and stock-based incentive awards are the best way to align the interests of employees with those of our shareholders."
2. Grants are made at the current stock price, with three years the most common vesting period for the option grants.
3. Stock-based compensation was \$368 million for Year 4 and \$407 million for Year 3. In addition, the firm estimates that stock-based compensation will be \$320 in Year 5.
4. The Black-Scholes model is used to estimate the expected value employees will receive from stock options grants.

---

[25]See footnote 22.

[26]A critique of the reliability of various valuation models can be found in American Accounting Association Financial Accounting Standards Committee, "Response to the FASB's Exposure Draft on Share-Based Payment: An Amendment of FASB *Statements No. 123* and *No. 95*," *Accounting Horizons* (June 2005), pp. 101–114.

5. The assumptions embedded in the Black-Scholes model for Year 4 are (a) expected life over which employees are expected to hold their options (six years); (b) risk-free interest rate (3.3 percent); (c) expected volatility in PepsiCo's stock price based on historical movement in the firm's stock price (26 percent); and (d) expected dividend per year as a percent of share price (1.8 percent).

Stock-based compensation ($368 million) is relatively small for PepsiCo when compared to its total expenses for Year 4 of more than $25 billion (Appendix A). However, this is not the case for some firms, particularly technology-based firms as discussed in the beginning of this section. The analyst can use the disclosures required by *Statement No. 123 (Revised 2004)* to assess the affect on current earnings, as well as on forecasted earnings, of the stock option grants awarded by firms to their employees.

Accounting for stock options has been a controversial topic in the United States for many years. Some firms, particularly those that rely heavily on stock options for compensating employees, have argued vehemently that it is inappropriate to report stock options as a cost on the income statement. Under intense pressure, the FASB adopted *Statement No. 123 (Revised 2004)* and GAAP now requires all publicly held firms to report stock-based compensation in the income statement. We applaud the work of the Board and its ability to hold firm in its desire to require expensing this form of employee compensation.

SUMMARY

Unlike reporting topics such as revenue recognition, inventories, derivatives, leases, and deferred taxes (covered in Chapters 7 and 8), which affect one or only a few line items in the financial statements, the topics discussed in this chapter tend to affect many line items in the financial statements. The accounting for corporate acquisitions, intercorporate investments, and foreign currency translation are therefore more pervasive in their financial statement effects. This situation both increases their potential significance to the financial analyst and provides a source for concern. Full disclosure of the effects of using the purchase method or translating the financial statements of a foreign unit using the all-current method instead of the monetary/nonmonetary method is cumbersome and possibly confusing. The final topic discussed in the chapter, accounting for stock options, also suffers from extensive and sometimes confusing and contradictory disclosures. As always, the analyst must learn to work with comparability limitations and less than sufficient disclosures when interpreting financial statements affected by the topics considered in this chapter. We now move on to the valuation of firms in Chapters 10 through 14, armed with a comprehensive understanding of the reporting principles and techniques employed by firms to prepare their financial statements, and the accounting quality issues analysts tend to focus on as tools used to evaluate financial statements.

QUESTIONS, EXERCISES, PROBLEMS, AND CASES

Questions and Exercises

9.1 CORPORATE ACQUISITIONS AND GOODWILL. Not every acquisition accounted for using the purchase method results in goodwill reported in the consolidated balance sheet. Describe the valuation procedures followed by the acquiring firms to determine whether any goodwill is recorded as a result of an acquisition, and the circumstances that could lead to no recognition of goodwill in an acquisition.

9.2 CORPORATE ACQUISITIONS AND ACQUISITIONS RESERVES. Often the purchase method entails establishing one or more acquisition reserves. Define an acquisition reserve, provide several examples of such reserves, and discuss how the quality of accounting information can be diminished as a result of misusing acquisition reserves.

9.3 ACCOUNTING FOR AVAILABLE-FOR-SALE AND TRADING MARKETABLE SECURITIES. Firms invest in marketable securities for a variety of reasons. One of the most common reasons is to temporarily invest excess cash. Securities that qualify for the available-for-sale reporting classification are accounted for differently from those that qualify for the trading reporting classification. Describe (1) the similarity between the reporting for the two classifications and (2) the differences in reporting between the two classifications.

9.4 CONSOLIDATION OF VARIABLE-INTEREST ENTITIES. Some accounting theorists propose that firms should consolidate any entity in which they have a "controlling financial interest." Typically, the percentage of equity ownership that one firm has in another entity determines whether consolidation is appropriate, with greater than 50 percent ownership requiring consolidation. Why is the percentage of ownership criterion often *not* appropriate for judging whether a variable-interest entity should be consolidated, and what criterion is used to determine whether a variable-interest entity should be consolidated?

9.5 EQUITY METHOD FOR MINORITY, ACTIVE INVESTMENTS. GAAP requires firms to account for equity investments in which ownership is between 20 and 50 percent using the equity method. Ace Corporation owns 35 percent of Spear Corporation during Year 4. Spear Corporation reported net income of $100.4 million for Year 4, and declared and paid out dividends of $25 million during the year.

1. Calculate the equity income Ace Corporation reports in Year 4 related to its ownership in Spear Corporation.
2. What does Ace Corporation report in its Statement of Cash Flows for Year 4 related to its ownership in Spear Corporation?
3. Assuming that Ace Corporation's balance sheet account, Investment in Spear Corporation, is $1,100 million at the beginning of Year 4, what is the balance in the account at the end of Year 4? Support your answers with calculations.

9.6 CHOICE OF A FUNCTIONAL CURRENCY. Choosing the functional currency is a key decision for translating the financial statements of foreign entities of U.S. firms into U.S. dollars. Qing Corporation, a U.S. firm that sells car batteries, formed a wholly owned subsidiary in Mexico in order to manufacture components needed in the production of the batteries. Approximately 50 percent of the subsidiary's sales are to Qing Corporation. The subsidiary also sells the components it manufactures to independent third parties, and these sales are denominated in Mexican pesos. Financing for the manufacturing plants in Mexico is denominated in U.S. dollars, but labor contracts are denominated in both dollars and pesos. All material contracts are denominated in Mexican pesos. Senior managers of the subsidiary are employees of Qing Corporation who have been transferred to the subsidiary for a tour of international service. Is the functional currency of the subsidiary the peso or the U.S. dollar? Explain your reasoning.

9.7 FOREIGN CURRENCY AS FUNCTIONAL CURRENCY. Identify the exchange rates used to translate income statement and balance sheet items when the foreign currency is defined as the functional currency, and discuss the logic for the use of the exchange rates you identified.

9.8 ACCOUNTING FOR STOCK-BASED COMPENSATION. Historically, technology firms have been the most aggressive users of stock-based compensation in the form of stock options granted to almost all employees of the firms. What is the rationale for offering stock options as compensation, and why has this form of compensation been particularly popular with technology firms in the past?

9.9 STOCK-BASED COMPENSATION DISCLOSURES. Choose a publicly held firm of interest to you that grants stock options to its employees. Review the firm's most recent Form 10-K filing, and prepare a schedule that details the stock-based compensation disclosures provided by the firm. Use the disclosures provided by PepsiCo, as illustrated in the chapter and in Appendix A, as a template for the disclosures of the publicly held firm chosen for analysis.

Problems and Cases

9.10 EFFECT OF THE PURCHASE METHOD ON THE BALANCE SHEET. Lexington Corporation acquired all of the outstanding common stock of Chalfont, Inc. on January 1, Year 5. Lexington gave shares of its common stock with a market value of $504 million in exchange for the Chalfont common stock. Chalfont will remain a legally separate entity after the exchange, but Lexington will prepare consolidated financial statements each period with Chalfont. The transaction qualifies as a nontaxable exchange for income tax purposes. Exhibit 9.12 presents the balance sheets of Lexington and Chalfont on January 1, Year 5, just prior to the acquisition. The income tax rate is 40 percent. The following information applies to Chalfont:

1. The market value of Chalfont's fixed assets exceeds their book value by $80 million.
2. Chalfont owns a copyright with a market value of $50 million.
3. Chalfont is a defendant in a lawsuit that it expects to settle during Year 5 at a pretax cost of $30 million. The firm carries no insurance against such lawsuits. Lexington desires to establish an acquisition reserve for this lawsuit.
4. Chalfont has an unrecognized and unfunded pension benefits obligation totaling $40 million on January 1, Year 5.

Required

a. Prepare an analysis that determines the excess purchase price and shows the allocation of the excess to individual assets and liabilities under the purchase method.

b. Prepare a consolidated balance sheet for Lexington and Chalfont on January 1, Year 5, under the purchase method. Show your supporting calculations for any amount that is not simply the sum of the amounts for Lexington and Chalfont from their separate financial records.

EXHIBIT 9.12

Lexington Corporation and Chalfont, Inc.
Balance Sheets
January 1, Year 5
(amounts in millions)
(Problem 9.10)

	Lexington Corporation	Chalfont, Inc.
Cash	$ 100	$ 30
Accounts Receivable	240	90
Fixed Assets, net	1,000	360
Copyright	—	—
Deferred Tax Asset	40	—
Goodwill	—	—
Total Assets	$1,380	$480
Accounts Payable and Accruals	$ 240	$ 80
Long-Term Debt	480	100
Deferred Tax Liability	160	—
Other Noncurrent Liabilities	120	—
Common Stock	320	100
Retained Earnings	60	200
Total Equities	$1,380	$480

9.11 EFFECT OF THE PURCHASE METHOD ON THE BALANCE SHEET AND THE INCOME STATEMENT. Condensed balance sheet data for Moran Corporation and Napolitano Corporation as of January 1, Year 8, follow (amounts in millions):

	Book Values		Market Values
	Moran (1)	Napolitano (2)	Napolitano (3)
Current Assets	$1,200	$ 800	$ 900
Fixed Assets	1,800	1,200	1,500
Goodwill	—	—	
Total Assets	$ 3000	$2,000	$
Current Liabilities	$1,000	$ 600	$ 600
Noncurrent Liabilities	1,400	1,000	1,000
Shareholders' Equity	600	400	
Total Equities	$3,000	$2,000	$

The shares of Moran Corporation currently sell on the market for $40 per share. Moran Corporation wishes to acquire all of the common stock of Napolitano Corporation as of

January 1, Year 8. Moran Corporation will issue at par 10 percent, 20-year bonds for $1,200. It will use the proceeds to acquire all of the common stock of Napolitano Corporation. The firms will account for the transaction using the purchase method for financial reporting. This transaction is a taxable exchange to the shareholders of Napolitano Corporation but a nontaxable exchange for Napolitano Corporation.

Required

a. Prepare a pro forma balance sheet as of January 1, Year 8, accounting for the transaction using the purchase method of accounting. The income tax rate is 40 percent.

b. Before considering the effects of the acquisition, Moran Corporation projects net income of $300 and Napolitano Corporation projects net income of $200 for Year 8. Compute the amount of pro forma net income for Year 8 for the merged firm. Both firms use a LIFO cost-flow assumption for inventories and do not expect to liquidate a LIFO layer during Year 8. Depreciable assets have a ten-year remaining life as of January 1, Year 8. Both firms use the straight-line depreciation method. Assume that the test for goodwill impairment indicates that no impairment charge is necessary for Year 8.

9.12 ANALYSIS OF CORPORATE ACQUISITION DISCLOSURES. Northrop Grumman Corporation is a global defense company headquartered in Los Angeles, California. Northrop Grumman provides a broad array of products and services related to defense electronics, information technology, advanced aircraft, shipbuilding, and space technology. The company has more than 125,000 employees. In December, Year 2, the company purchased 100 percent of the common stock of TRW, Inc. TRW operates in the space, electronics, and automotive parts businesses. (In Year 3, Northrop Grumman spun off the automotive parts segment of TRW to a private investment firm. The investment firm, in turn, took TRW Automotive public in Year 4.) Northrop Grumman issued 69.4 million shares of its common stock at an exchange ratio of .5357 for each TRW share. These shares were valued at $107.31 per share for purchase accounting purposes. The acquisition of TRW, which was valued at approximately $12.5 billion, was accounted for using the purchase method of accounting.

Northrop Grumman stated in a recent annual report:

> Under the purchase method of accounting, the purchase price is allocated to the underlying tangible and intangible assets acquired and liabilities assumed based on their respective fair market values, with the excess recorded as goodwill. The financial statements as of December 31, Year 2, reflect preliminary estimates of the fair market value for purchased intangibles. As of December 31, Year 3, the company completed the fair market value evaluation process for TRW and recorded an aggregate increase to goodwill of $1.6 billion.

Northrop Grumman reported goodwill of $17.3 billion on its balance sheet dated December 31, Year 3. The firm's statement of cash flows, under investing activities, reported only a minor amount for businesses acquired in Year 2.

Required

a. Northrop Grumman allocated the purchase price to tangible and intangible assets acquired in the TRW acquisition before allocating an excess amount to goodwill. Describe the type of assets—both tangible and intangible—that Northrop Grumman might have acquired from TRW.

b. TRW, Inc. was valued at $12.5 billion at the time of the acquisition and yet the firms' statement of cash flows reported no significant amounts for investing activities. Explain how this is possible.

c. Northrop Grumman recorded goodwill of $1.6 billion related to the TRW acquisition, and yet the balance sheet reported an ending balance for goodwill at December 31, Year 3, of $17.3 billion. What accounts for this large difference?

d. Describe the procedures followed by Northrop Grumman to arrive at the value for goodwill of $1.6 billion.

e. *Statement No. 142* requires Northrop Grumman to assess goodwill for impairment. The firm has made many acquisitions over the years, in addition to the TRW acquisition. Review Northrop Grumman's web site (www.northropgrumman.com) and describe what disclosures the firm provides regarding its annual test of goodwill impairment.

9.13 EFFECT OF THE PURCHASE METHOD ON THE BALANCE SHEET AND INCOME STATEMENT. Ormond Co. acquired all of the outstanding common stock of Daytona Co. on January 1, Year 5. Ormond Co. gave shares of its common stock with a market value of $312 million in exchange for 100 percent of the Daytona Co. common stock. Daytona Co. will remain a legally separate entity after the exchange but Ormond Co. will prepare consolidated financial statements each period with Daytona Co. The transaction qualifies as a nontaxable exchange for income tax purposes. Exhibit 9.13 presents the balance sheets of Ormond Co. and Daytona Co.

EXHIBIT 9.13

Ormond Co. and Daytona Co.
Balance Sheets
January 1, Year 5
(amounts in millions)
(Problem 9.13)

	Ormond Co.	Daytona Co.
Cash	$ 25	$ 15
Accounts Receivable	60	40
Fixed Assets, net	250	170
Patent	—	—
Deferred Tax Asset	10	—
Goodwill	—	—
Total Assets	$345	$225
Accounts Payable and Accruals	$ 60	$ 40
Long-Term Debt	120	60
Deferred Tax Liability	40	—
Other Noncurrent Liabilities	30	—
Common Stock	80	50
Retained Earnings	15	75
Total Equities	$345	$225

on January 1, Year 5, just prior to the acquisition. The income tax rate is 40 percent. The following information applies to Daytona Co.:

1. The market value of Daytona Co.'s fixed assets exceeds their book value by $50 million.
2. Daytona Co. owns a patent with a market value of $40 million.
3. Daytona Co. is a defendant in a lawsuit that it expects to settle during Year 5 at a pretax cost of $25 million. The firm carries no insurance against such lawsuits. If permitted, Ormond Co. desires to establish an "acquisition reserve" for this lawsuit.
4. Daytona Co. has an unrecognized and unfunded retirement health care benefits obligation totaling $20 million on January 1, Year 5.

Required

a. Prepare a consolidated balance sheet for Ormond Co. and Daytona Co. on January 1, Year 5, assuming that Ormond Co. accounts for the acquisition using the purchase method.

b. Exhibit 9.14 presents income statements and balance sheets taken from the separate-company books at the end of Year 5, assuming that Ormond Co. had accounted for its acquisition of Daytona Co. using the *purchase* method. The following information applies to these companies:

1. The fixed assets of Daytona Co. had an average remaining life of five years on January 1, Year 5. The firms use the straight-line depreciation method.
2. The patent of Daytona Co. had a remaining life of ten years on January 1, Year 5.
3. Daytona Co. settled the lawsuit during Year 5 and expects no further liability.
4. Daytona Co. will amortize and fund its retirement health care benefits obligation over twenty years. It included $1 million in operating expenses during Year 5 related to amounts unrecognized and unfunded as of January 1, Year 5.
5. Assume that the test for goodwill impairment indicates that no impairment charge is necessary for Year 5.

c. Prepare a consolidated income statement for Year 5 and a consolidated balance sheet on December 31, Year 5, following the purchase method of accounting.

9.14 APPLICATION OF *STATEMENT NO. 115* FOR INVESTMENTS IN MARKETABLE EQUITY SECURITIES. Sun Trust Banks owns a large block of Coca-Cola Company (Coke) common stock that it has held for many years. SunTrust indicates in a note to its financial statements that all equity securities held by the bank, including its investment in Coke stock, are classified as available for sale. A recent annual report of SunTrust reports the following information for its Coke investment (amounts in thousands):

Coke common stock investment, market value on December 31, Year 3	$1,791,894
Coke common stock investment, market value on December 31, Year 4	$1,242,862
Net income for Year 4	$ 565,476

EXHIBIT 9.14

Ormond Co. and Daytona Co.
Consolidation Worksheet for Year 5
(amounts in millions)
(Problem 9.13)

	Ormond Co.	Daytona Co.
Income Statement for Year 5		
Sales	$ 600	$ 450
Equity in Earnings of Daytona Co.	18	—
Operating Expenses	(550)	(395)
Interest Expense	(10)	(5)
Loss on Lawsuit	—	(20)
Income Tax Expense	(23)	(12)
Net Income	$ 35	$ 18
Balance Sheet on December 31, Year 5		
Cash	$ 45	$ 25
Accounts Receivable	80	50
Investment in Daytona Co.	327[a]	—
Fixed Assets	280	195
Patent	—	—
Deferred Tax Asset	15	—
Goodwill	—	—
Total Assets	$ 747	$ 270
Accounts Payable and Accruals	$ 85	$ 55
Long-Term Debt	140	75
Deferred Tax Liability	50	—
Other Noncurrent Liabilities	40	—
Common Stock	392	50
Retained Earnings	40	90
Total Equities	$ 747	$ 270

[a]$312 initial investment + $18 equity in earnings − $3 dividend received = $327

Required

a. Calculate the effect of the change in the market value of SunTrust's investment in Coke's common stock on SunTrust's Year 4 (1) net income and (2) shareholders' equity. The income tax rate is 35 percent.

b. How does your answer to part a differ if SunTrust classified its investment in Coke's common stock as a trading security?

c. Does the value reported on SunTrust's balance sheet for the investment in Coke's stock differ depending on the firm's reason for holding the stock (that is, whether it is classified as available for sale versus trading by management)? Explain your answer.

9.15 EFFECT OF MARKET VALUE AND EQUITY METHODS ON BALANCE SHEET AND INCOME STATEMENT. Seagram acquired 11.7 percent of Time Warner on January 2, Year 3. Financial statement data for these firms at the end of Year 3 reveal the following (amounts in millions):

Seagram Assets—December 31, Year 3	
Investment in Time Warner at Market Value (11.7% ownership)	$ 1,769
All Other Assets	9,949
Total Assets	$11,718
Liabilities	$ 6,717
Shareholders' Equity	
Unrealized Appreciation in Market Value of Time Warner (pretax)	13
All Other Shareholders' Equity	4,988
Total Liabilities and Shareholders' Equity	$11,718
Income Statement for Year 3	
Dividend Revenue from Time Warner, net of taxes	$ 8
All Other Revenue and Expenses, net of taxes	371
Net Income	$ 379
Time Warner—December 31, Year 3	
Assets	$16,892
Liabilities	$15,522
Shareholders' Equity	1,370
	$16,892
Net Loss for Year 3	$ (339)

Required

a. The total common shareholders' equity of Time Warner on January 1, Year 3, was $1,810. Assume that any excess purchase price relates to goodwill. Compute the amount of goodwill related to Seagram's investment in Time Warner on the date of acquisition.

b. Assume for this part that Seagram had used the equity method instead of the market value method to account for its investment in Time Warner during Year 3. Compute the maximum amount of net income that Seagram would report for Year 3. Assume that the test for goodwill impairment indicates that no impairment charge is necessary for Year 3. The income tax rate is 35 percent.

c. Compute the total assets for Seagram on December 31, Year 3, if it had used the equity method instead of the market value method throughout Year 3.

9.16 APPLYING THE EQUITY, PROPORTIONATE CONSOLIDATION, AND FULL CONSOLIDATION METHODS. Mylan Laboratories (Mylan) is a leading firm in the generic pharmaceutical industry. Generic drugs have chemical compositions similar to ethical drugs but sell for a significantly lower price. Once the patent period ends on an ethical drug, generic drug companies break down the drug into its basic chemical elements. They then submit an application to the Food and Drug Administration (FDA) to sell a generic equivalent of the ethical drug. The ability to sell generic drugs at a lower price results from lower research and development, marketing, and other costs.

Mylan also plays a limited role in the ethical drug market with a long-term equity position in Somerset Pharmaceuticals (Somerset). The firm has held 50 percent of the common stock of Somerset for almost fifteen years. Somerset's only commercial product is the ethical drug Eldepryl, which is used for the treatment of patients with late-stage Parkinson's disease. Five years ago Somerset began the development of EMSAM (selegiline transdermal system), a product for the treatment of major depressive disorders. Unfortunately, the firm's research and development activities related to the product for Year 13 and Year 14 have been a significant drain on the firm's earnings, and to date it has not been successful in obtaining FDA approval for EMSAM.

Required

NOTE: The following additional information applies to completing parts a through i.

Exhibit 9.15 presents financial statement data for Mylan for Year 5 through Year 8. During this period, Mylan accounted for its investment in Somerset using the equity method. Equity in earnings of Somerset includes Mylan's 50 percent share of Somerset's earnings minus amortization of intangible assets resulting from the acquisition of Somerset. Such intangible assets are amortized over fifteen years. Amortization expense for intangibles totaled $924,000 in each of Years 6 through 8. Additionally, Mylan charges Somerset a management services fee each year and includes it in the Equity in Earnings of Somerset account. Somerset records this fee as an expense in measuring earnings. Exhibit 9.16 presents financial statement data for Somerset.

a. Prepare an analysis of the changes in the shareholders' equity of Somerset for each of Years 6 through 8.

b. Prepare an analysis of the changes in the Investment in and Advances to Somerset account on Mylan's books for each of Years 6 through 8. Be sure to indicate the amounts for equity in earnings of Somerset, management fee, dividend received, and other cash payments received.

c. Does the equity method, proportionate consolidation method, or full consolidation method best reflect the operating relationships between Mylan and Somerset? Explain.

d. Prepare an income statement for Mylan and Somerset for Year 6, Year 7, and Year 8 using the proportionate consolidation method.

e. Repeat part d using the full consolidation method.

f. Compute the ratio of operating income before income taxes to sales for Year 6, Year 7, and Year 8 using the equity method, proportionate consolidation method, and full consolidation method.

g. Why do the ratios computed in part f differ across the three methods of accounting for the investment in Somerset?

h. Compute the effective tax rate (that is, income tax expense divided by income before income taxes) for Year 6, Year 7, and Year 8 using the equity method, proportionate consolidation method, and full consolidation method.

i. Why do the measures of the effective tax rate computed in part h differ across the three methods of accounting for the investment in Somerset?

NOTE: The following additional information applies to completing parts j through l as related to Year 13 and Year 14.

Somerset reported a net loss of $7.1 million in Year 13 and $3.3 million in Year 14 resulting primarily from substantially higher research and development costs incurred in those

EXHIBIT 9.15

Mylan Laboratories
Financial Statement Data
(amounts in thousands)
(Problem 9.16)

	Year 5	Year 6	Year 7	Year 8
Balance Sheet				
Current Assets	$ 94,502	$120,014	$180,482	$209,572
Investment in and Advances to Somerset	18,045	13,674	14,844	17,964
Noncurrent Assets	74,408	93,032	155,779	175,789
Total Assets	$186,955	$226,720	$351,105	$403,325
Current Liabilities	$ 12,931	$ 17,909	$ 26,482	$ 17,926
Noncurrent Liabilities	6,493	5,359	7,348	5,430
Shareholders' Equity	167,531	203,452	317,275	379,969
Total Liabilities and Shareholders' Equity	$186,955	$226,720	$351,105	$403,325

	Year 6	Year 7	Year 8
Income Statement			
Sales	$131,936	$211,964	$251,773
Costs and Expenses	(100,458)	(135,759)	(188,304)
Operating Income	$ 31,478	$ 76,205	$ 63,469
Equity in Earnings of Somerset	18,664	21,136	23,596
Income before Taxes	$ 50,142	$ 97,341	$ 87,065
Income Tax Expense	(10,028)	(26,720)	(13,998)
Net Income	$ 40,114	$ 70,621	$ 73,067

	Year 6	Year 7	Year 8
Cash Flow Statement			
Net Income	$ 40,114	$ 70,621	$ 73,067
Equity in Earnings of Somerset	(18,664)	(21,136)	(23,596)
Cash Received from Somerset	23,035	19,966	20,676
Other Addbacks and Subtractions	5,962	7,959	14,690
Changes in Working Capital Accounts	(4,519)	(9,073)	(49,204)
Cash Flow from Operations	$ 45,928	$ 68,337	$ 35,633

years related to EMSAM. Based on the reported losses for Year 13 and Year 14, and an assessment by Mylan that Somerset will not return to profitability in the near future, the firm decided at the end of Year 14 to completely write off its investment in Somerset. In addition, in accordance with *APB Opinion No. 18,* Mylan stated in a recent annual report that it will temporarily cease recording the net losses of its Somerset investment in Year 15 and beyond.

j. What amounts would Mylan report as "Equity in Earnings of Somerset" on its income statement for Year 13 and Year 14? Show your calculations.

EXHIBIT 9.16

Somerset Pharmaceuticals
Financial Statement Data
(amounts in thousands)
(Problem 9.16)

	Year 5	Year 6	Year 7	Year 8
Balance Sheet				
Current Assets	$22,801	$24,597	$ 30,409	$ 27,931
Noncurrent Assets	2,802	2,791	2,670	6,043
Total Assets	$25,603	$27,388	$ 33,079	$ 33,974
Current Liabilities	$ 7,952	$15,413	$ 20,675	$ 14,918
Payable to Owners	7,274	1,490	1,796	1,002
Other Noncurrent Liabilities	3,302	975	808	642
Shareholders' Equity	7,075	9,510	9,800	17,412
Total Liabilities and Shareholders' Equity	$25,603	$27,388	$ 33,079	$ 33,974

	Year 6	Year 7	Year 8
Income Statement			
Sales	$93,513	$108,518	$111,970
Costs and Expenses	(42,041)	(49,872)	(50,465)
Income before Taxes	$51,472	$ 58,646	$ 61,505
Income Tax Expense	(18,806)	(21,789)	(19,547)
Net Income	$32,666	$ 36,857	$ 41,958

k. Assuming Somerset reports a net loss in Year 15, why does APB *Opinion No. 18* preclude Mylan from reporting its share of the loss on the firm's income statement for Year 15?

l. Mylan stated in a recent annual report: "As Somerset continues its research and development activities, including working with the FDA to obtain approval for EMSAM, its earnings may continue to be adversely affected." Given this, speculate on why Mylan continues to support the activities of Somerset.

9.17 VARIABLE-INTEREST ENTITIES. Molson Coors Brewing Company (Molson Coors) is the fifth-largest brewer in the world. It is one of the leading brewers in the United States and Canada, with the company's brands including Coors, Molson Canadian, Carling, and Killian's Irish Red. Sales exceeded 32 million barrels (1 U.S. barrel equals 31 gallons) for the year ended December 26, Year 4. The firm reported $4.3 billion of net sales for Year 4.

Molson Coors invests in various types of entities to carry out its brewing, bottling, and canning activities. The investments take the legal form of partnerships, joint ventures, and limited liability corporations, among other arrangements. The firm states in its Year 4 annual report that each of these arrangements has been tested to determine whether it qualifies as a variable-interest entity (VIE) under *Interpretation No. 46*.

The following excerpt is taken from the firm's note on variable-interest entities in its Year 4 annual report:

> Note 3. Variable Interest Entities. Once an entity is determined to be a VIE, the party with the controlling financial interest, the primary beneficiary, is required to consolidate it. We have investments in VIEs, of which we are the primary beneficiary. Accordingly, we have consolidated three joint ventures in Year 4, effective December 29, Year 3, the first day of Year 4. These include Rocky Mountain Metal Container (RMMC), Rocky Mountain Bottle Company (RMBC) and Grolsch (UK) Limited (Grolsch). The impacts to our balance sheet include the addition of net fixed assets of RMMC and RMBC totaling approximately $65 million, RMMC debt of approximately $40 million, and Grolsch net intangibles of approximately $20 million (at current exchange rates). The most significant impact to our cash flow statement for the year ended December 26, Year 4, was to increase depreciation expense by approximately $13.2 million and cash recognized on initial consolidation of the entities of $20.8 million. Our partners' share of the operating results of the ventures is eliminated in the minority interests line of the Consolidated Statements of Income.

As required under *Interpretation No. 46,* Molson Coors also provides additional information in its annual report on each of the consolidated joint ventures.

1. RMBC is a joint venture with Owens-Brockway Glass Container, Inc., in which Molson Coors holds a 50 percent interest. RMBC produces glass bottles at a glass-manufacturing facility for use at the Golden, Colorado, brewery. Under this agreement, RMBC supplies our bottle requirements, and Owens-Brockway has a contract to supply the majority of our bottle requirements not met by RMBC. In Year 3 and Year 2, the firm's share of pretax joint venture profits for the venture, totaling $7.8 million and $13.2 million, respectively, was included in cost of goods sold on the consolidated income statement.
2. RMMC, a Colorado limited liability company, is a joint venture with Ball Corporation in which Molson Coors hold a 50 percent interest. RMMC supplies the firm with substantially all the cans for its Golden, Colorado, brewery. RMMC manufactures the cans at the Molson Coors manufacturing facilities, which RMMC is operating under a use and license agreement. In Year 3 and Year 2, the firm's share of pretax joint venture profits (losses), totaling $0.1 million and ($0.6) million, respectively, was included in cost of goods sold on the consolidated income statement. As stated previously, on consolidation of RMMC, debt of approximately $40 million was added to the balance sheet. As of December 26, Year 4, Molson Coors is the guarantor of this debt.
3. Grolsch is a joint venture between CBL and Royal Grolsch N.V. in which Molson Coors holds a 49 percent interest. The Grolsch joint venture markets Grolsch branded beer in the United Kingdom and the Republic of Ireland. The majority of the Grolsch branded beer is produced by CBL under a contract brewing arrangement with the joint venture. CBL and Royal Grolsch N.V. sell beer to the joint venture, which sells the beer back to CBL (for onward sale to customers) for a price equal to what it paid, plus a marketing and overhead charge and a profit margin. In Year 3 and Year 2, the firm's share of pretax profits for this venture, totaling $3.6 million and $2.0 million, respectively, was included in cost of goods sold on the consolidated income statement. As stated previously, on consolidation, net fixed assets of approximately $4 million and net intangibles of approximately $20 million were added to the balance sheet of Molson Coors.

Required

a. Describe the operational purpose of the three VIEs consolidated by Molson Coors.

b. Molson Coors is the primary beneficiary for three investments identified as VIEs by the firm. What criteria did Molson Coors apply to determine that the firm is the primary beneficiary for these three investments?

c. For each investment, Molson Coors reports the income statement impact as a reduction of cost of goods sold on the consolidated income statement. What is the rationale for reporting the impact in this way on the income statement?

d. The firm states: "Our partners' share of the operating results of the ventures is eliminated in the minority interests line of the Consolidated Statements of Income." Define *minority interests* as it appears on the income statement and discuss why Molson Coors subtracts it to calculate consolidated net income.

e. RMBC, RMMC, and Grolsch are consolidated with the financial statements of Molson Coors because the three investments qualify as VIEs as defined in *Interpretation No. 46* and the firm determined that it is the primary beneficiary for the investments. Explain what reporting technique Molson Coors would use to account for the investments if, in fact, they did not qualify as VIEs. What would be the impact on the balance sheet? What would be the impact on the income statement? What would be the impact on the statement of cash flows?

f. The firms reports that the depreciation expense on the statement of cash flows for Year 4 increased by approximately $13.2 million as a result of consolidating the VIEs. Why is this the case?

9.18 CALCULATING THE TRANSLATION ADJUSTMENT UNDER THE ALL-CURRENT METHOD AND THE MONETARY/NONMONETARY METHOD. Foreign Sub is a wholly owned subsidiary of U.S. Domestic Corporation. U.S. Domestic Corporation acquired the subsidiary several years ago. The financial statements for Foreign Sub for Year 4 in its own currency appear in Exhibit 9.17.

The exchange rates between the U.S. dollar and the foreign currency of the subsidiary were as follows:

December 31, Year 3	$10:1FC
Average, Year 4	$8:1FC
December 31, Year 4	$6:1FC

On January 1, Year 4, Foreign Sub issued FC100 of long-term debt and FC100 of common stock in the acquisition of land costing FC200. Operating activities occurred evenly over the year.

Required

a. Assume that the currency of Foreign Sub is the functional currency. Compute the change in the cumulative translation adjustment for Year 4. Indicate whether the change increases or decreases shareholders' equity.

b. Assume that the U.S. dollar is the functional currency. Compute the amount of the translation gain or loss for Year 4. Indicate whether the amount is a gain or loss.

9.19 TRANSLATING THE FINANCIAL STATEMENTS OF A FOREIGN SUBSIDIARY; COMPARISON OF TRANSLATION METHODS. Stebbins Corporation established a wholly owned Canadian subsidiary on January 1, Year 6, by contributing US$500,000 for all of the subsidiary's common stock. The exchange rate on

EXHIBIT 9.17

Foreign Sub
Financial Statement Data
(Problem 9.18)

	December 31:	
	Year 3	**Year 4**
Cash	FC 100	FC 150
Accounts Receivable	300	350
Inventories	350	400
Land	500	700
	FC1,250	FC1,600
Accounts Payable	FC 150	FC 250
Long-Term Debt	200	300
Common Stock	500	600
Retained Earnings	400	450
	FC1,250	FC1,600

	For Year 4:
Sales	FC4,000
Cost of Goods Sold	(3,200)
Selling and Administrative	(400)
Income Taxes	(160)
Net Income	FC 240
Dividend Declared and Paid on December 31	(190)
Increase in Retained Earnings	FC 50

that date was C$1:US$.90 (that is, one Canadian dollar equaled 90 U.S. cents). The Canadian subsidiary invested C$500,000 in a building with an expected life of twenty years and rented it to various tenants for the year. The average exchange rate during Year 6 was C$1:US$.85 and the exchange rate on December 31, Year 6, was C$1:US$.80. Exhibit 9.18 shows the amounts taken from the books of the Canadian subsidiary at the end of Year 6 measured in Canadian dollars.

Required

a. Prepare a balance sheet, income statement, and retained earnings statement for the Canadian subsidiary for Year 6 in U.S. dollars, assuming that the Canadian dollar is the functional currency. Include a separate schedule showing the computation of the translation adjustment account.

b. Repeat part a but assume that the U.S. dollar is the functional currency. Include a separate schedule showing the computation of the translation gain or loss.

c. Why is the sign of the translation adjustment for Year 6 under the all-current translation method and the translation gain or loss for Year 6 under the monetary/nonmonetary translation method the same? Why do their amounts differ?

EXHIBIT 9.18

Canadian Subsidiary
Financial Statements
Year 6
(Problem 9.19)

Balance Sheet for December 31, Year 6	
Assets	
Cash	C$ 77,555
Rent Receivable	25,000
Building, net	475,000
	C$577,555
Liabilities and Equity	
Accounts Payable	6,000
Salaries Payable	4,000
Common Stock	555,555
Retained Earnings	12,000
	C$577,555
Income Statement for Year 6	
Rent Revenue	C$125,000
Operating Expenses	(28,000)
Depreciation Expense	(25,000)
Translation Exchange Loss	—
Net Income	C$ 72,000
Retained Earnings Statement for Year 6	
Balance, January 1, Year 6	C$ —
Net Income	72,000
Dividends	(60,000)
Balance, December 31, Year 6	C$ 12,000

d. Assuming that the firm could justify either translation method, which method would the management of Stebbins Corporation likely prefer for Year 6? Why?

9.20 TRANSLATING THE FINANCIAL STATEMENTS OF A FOREIGN SUBSIDIARY; SECOND YEAR OF OPERATIONS. Refer to Problem 9.19 for Stebbins Corporation for Year 6, its first year of operations. Exhibit 9.19 shows the amounts for the Canadian subsidiary for Year 7. The average exchange rate during Year 7 was C$1:US$.82 and the exchange rate on December 31, Year 7, was C$1:US$.84. The Canadian subsidiary declared and paid dividends on December 31, Year 7.

Required

a. Prepare a balance sheet, income statement, and retained earnings statement for the Canadian subsidiary for Year 7 in U.S. dollars, assuming that the Canadian dollar

EXHIBIT 9.19

Canadian Subsidiary
Financial Statements
Year 7
(Problem 9.20)

Balance Sheet	
Assets	
Cash	C$116,555
Rent Receivable	30,000
Building, net	450,000
	C$596,555
Liabilities and Equity	
Accounts Payable	7,500
Salaries Payable	5,500
Common Stock	555,555
Retained Earnings	28,000
	C$596,555
Income Statement	
Rent Revenue	C$150,000
Operating Expenses	(34,000)
Depreciation Expense	(25,000)
Translation Exchange Gain	—
Net Income	C$ 91,000
Retained Earnings Statement	
Balance, January 1, Year 7	C$ 12,000
Net Income	91,000
Dividends	(75,000)
Balance, December 31, Year 7	C$ 28,000

is the functional currency. Include a separate schedule showing the computation of the translation adjustment for Year 7 and the change in the translation adjustment account.

b. Repeat part a but assume that the U.S. dollar is the functional currency. Include a separate schedule showing the computation of the translation gain or loss.

c. Why is the sign of the translation adjustment for Year 7 under the all-current translation method and the translation gain or loss under the monetary/nonmonetary translation method the same? Why do their amounts differ?

d. Assuming that the firm could justify either translation method, which method would the management of Stebbins Corporation likely prefer for Year 7? Why?

9.21 INTERPRETING FOREIGN CURRENCY TRANSLATION DISCLOSURES. Hewlett-Packard (HP) and Sun Microsystems (Sun) derive similar proportions of their sales from the United States, Europe, Japan, and other countries. Recent annual reports of the two companies indicate that HP uses the U.S. dollar as its functional currency, whereas Sun uses the currency of each foreign operation as its functional currency. That is, Sun uses the local currencies as the functional currencies. As discussed in the chapter, choice of the functional currency impacts how the financial statements are translated into the U.S. dollar for firms headquartered in the United States, such as HP and Sun.

Required

a. The shareholders' equity section of the balance sheet of Sun and the corresponding note discussing accumulated other comprehensive income reveal the following (amounts in millions):

	June 30:	
	Year 4	Year 3
Common Stock	$ 6,607	$ 6,647
Retained Earnings	2,481	2,869
Cumulative Translation Adjustment	196	166
Treasury Stock	(2,776)	(3,169)
Other	(70)	(22)
Total	$ 6,438	$ 6,491

Did the U.S. dollar likely increase or decrease in value on average during the year ended June 30, Year 4, against the foreign currencies of the countries in which Sun conducts its operations? Explain.

b. Sun uses a FIFO cost-flow assumption for inventories and cost of goods sold. Would the gross margin in U.S. dollars (that is, sales minus cost of goods sold) of Sun likely have increased or decreased for the year ended June 30, Year 4 if it had used the U.S. dollar as its functional currency instead of the currency of its foreign operations? Explain.

c. HP also uses a FIFO cost-flow assumption for inventories and cost of goods sold. Both companies maintain net monetary asset positions in their foreign operations. HP generated a positive pretax return from foreign operations of 9.49 percent for the year ended June 30, Year 4, whereas Sun generated a negative pretax return of 0.17 percent. Would the profit margin of HP likely increase or decrease if it had used the currency of its foreign units as the functional currency? Explain.

9.22 IDENTIFYING THE FUNCTIONAL CURRENCY. Electronic Computer Systems (ECS) designs, manufactures, sells, and services networked computer systems, associated peripheral equipment, and related network, communications, and software products.

Exhibit 9.20 presents geographical segment data. ECS conducts sales and marketing operations outside the United States principally through sales subsidiaries in Canada, Europe, Central and South America, and the Far East; by direct sales from the parent corporation; and through various representative and distributorship arrangements. The company's international manufacturing operations include plants in Canada, the Far East, and Europe. These manufacturing plants sell their output to the company's sales subsidiaries, the parent corporation, or other manufacturing plants for further processing.

EXHIBIT 9.20

Electronic Computer Systems
Geographical Segment Data
(amounts in thousands)
(Problem 9.22)

	Year 3	Year 4	Year 5
Revenues			
U.S. Customers	$4,472,195	$5,016,606	$ 5,810,598
Intercompany	1,354,339	1,921,043	2,017,928
Total	$5,826,534	$6,937,649	$ 7,828,526
Europe Customers	$2,259,743	$3,252,482	$ 4,221,631
Intercompany	82,649	114,582	137,669
Total	$2,342,392	$3,367,064	$ 4,359,300
Canada, Far East, Americas Customers	$ 858,419	$1,120,356	$ 1,443,217
Intercompany	577,934	659,204	912,786
Total	$1,436,353	$1,779,560	$ 2,356,003
Eliminations	(2,014,922)	(2,694,829)	(3,068,383)
Net Revenue	$7,590,357	$9,389,444	$11,475,446
Income			
United States	$ 342,657	$ 758,795	$ 512,754
Europe	405,636	634,543	770,135
Canada, Far East, Americas	207,187	278,359	390,787
Eliminations	(126,771)	(59,690)	(38,676)
Operating Income	$ 828,709	$1,612,007	$ 1,635,000
Interest Income	116,899	122,149	143,665
Interest Expense	(88,079)	(45,203)	(37,820)
Income before Income Taxes	$ 857,529	$1,688,953	$ 1,740,845
Assets			
United States	$3,911,491	$4,627,838	$ 5,245,439
Europe	1,817,584	2,246,333	3,093,818
Canada, Far East, Americas	815,067	843,067	1,293,906
Corporate Assets (temporary cash investments)	2,035,557	1,979,470	2,057,528
Eliminations	(1,406,373)	(1,289,322)	(1,579,135)
Total Assets	$7,173,326	$8,407,386	$10,111,556

ECS accounts for intercompany transfers between geographic areas at prices representative of unaffiliated-party transactions.

Sales to unaffiliated customers outside the United States, including U.S. export sales, were $5,729,879,000 for Year 5, $4,412,527,000 for Year 4, and $3,179,143,000 for Year 3, which represented 50 percent, 47 percent, and 42 percent, respectively, of total operating revenues. The international subsidiaries have reinvested substantially all of their earnings to support operations. These accumulated retained earnings, before elimination of intercompany transactions, aggregated $2,793,239,000 at the end of Year 5, $2,070,337,000 at the end of Year 4, and $1,473,081,000 at the end of Year 3.

The company enters into forward exchange contracts to reduce the impact of foreign currency fluctuations on operations and the asset and liability positions of foreign subsidiaries. The gains and losses on these contracts increase or decrease net income in the same period as the related revenues and expenses, and for assets and liabilities, in the period in which the exchange rate changes.

Required

Discuss whether ECS should use the U.S. dollar or the currencies of its foreign subsidiaries as its functional currency.

9.23 STOCK-BASED COMPENSATION. Exhibit 9.21 includes a footnote excerpt from the annual report of the Coca-Cola Company for Year 4. The beverage company provides stock options offered to key employees under plans approved by stockholders.

Required

Review Exhibit 9.21 and answer the following questions:

a. Coke reports both pretax and after-tax stock-based compensation in its notes to the financial statements. What is the tax savings for Year 2, Year 3, and Year 4 that Coke generates for the stock-based compensation provided to its employees? Speculate what income statement line item includes this tax savings, as well as what income statement line item including the stock-based compensation expense (income statement not provided in this problem)?

b. The average option price per share and market price per share at time of grant is equal in each year ($44.69 for Year 2, $49.67 for Year 3, and $41.63 for Year 4). Discuss why Coke structured the stock option grants this way in each year.

c. What are the likely reasons that the fair value of options granted per share increased from Year 2 to Year 3, and then decreased from Year 3 to Year 4?

d. Coke does not report the market price of its stock at the time employees exercised options (3 million in Year 2, 4 million in Year 3, and 5 million in Year 4), but in each year the end-of-year market price is substantially higher than the average option exercise price reported in Exhibit 9.21 ($31.09 for Year 2, $26.96 for Year 3, and $35.54 for Year 4). Discuss why Coke is willing to sell shares of its stock to employees at a price (option exercise price) much lower than the firm could obtain for shares sold on the market (market price at time of exercise).

e. Coke employs the Black-Scholes valuation model for valuing stock option grants. Speculate on the directional effects of the key assumptions made in applying the Black-Scholes options pricing model. That is, which assumptions will result in a higher fair value for stock options and which will result in a lower fair value, and why?

9.24 STOCK-BASED COMPENSATION. Eli Lilly and Company produces pharmaceutical products for humans and animals. Exhibit 9.22 includes a footnote excerpt from the quarterly report of Lilly for the period ending March 31, Year 5. The firm first adopted *Statement No. 123 (Revised 2004)* reporting in this quarter.

EXHIBIT 9.21

Coca-Cola Company
Stock Option Disclosures
(Problem 9.23)

Note—Stock-Based Compensation (partial footnote disclosure)

Our Company currently sponsors stock option plans. Effective January 1, Year 2, our Company adopted the preferable fair value recognition provisions of Statement of Financial Accounting Standards ("SFAS") No. 123, "Accounting for Stock-Based Compensation." The fair values of the stock awards are determined using a single estimated expected life. The compensation expense is recognized on a straight-line basis over the vesting period. The total stock-based compensation expense, net of related tax effects, was $254 million in Year 4, $308 million in Year 3 and $267 million in Year 2.

	Year 4	Year 3	Year 2
Stock-Based Compensation Expense, pretax[a]	$ 345	$ 422	$ 365
Number of Options Granted[b]	31	24	29
Average Option Price per Share	$ 41.63	$ 49.67	$ 44.69
Average Market Price per Share at time of Grant	$ 41.63	$ 49.67	$ 44.69
Fair Value of Option Granted per Share	$ 8.84	$ 13.49	$ 13.10
Vesting Period of Options Granted, years	1–4	1–4	1–4
Life of Options, years	10	10	10
Option Valuation Assumptions for Black-Scholes Model[b]			
Risk-Free Interest Rate	3.8%	3.5%	3.4%
Dividend Yield	2.5%	1.9%	1.7%
Stock Volatility	23.0%	28.1%	30.2%
Expected Option Life, years	6.0	6.0	6.0
Number of Options Exercised[a]	5	4	3
Average Option Exercise Price	$ 35.54	$ 26.96	$ 31.09

[a]Amounts in millions.
[b]Weighted averages.

Required

Review Exhibit 9.22 and answer the following questions:

a. Lilly's statement of cash flows (not provided in this problem) includes an addback for stock-based compensation in calculating cash flows from operations of $108.2 million for Year 5, and $25.2 million for Year 4. Why is this the case?

b. Refer to part a. Lilly's statement of cash flows includes a cash inflow in the section on cash flows from financing activities of $12.5 million for Year 5 and $46.5 million for Year 4. The amounts are labeled "Issuance of commons stock under stock plans." Who provided these cash inflows to Lilly, and, in general terms, how are the amounts determined?

c. Lilly states in the note: "Stock options are granted to employees at exercise prices equal to the fair market value of our stock at the dates of grant." Discuss why Lilly structured the stock option grants this way.

EXHIBIT 9.22

Eli Lilly and Company
Stock Option Disclosures
(Problem 9.24)

Note—Stock-Based Compensation (partial footnote disclosure)

We adopted Statement of Financial Accounting Standards No. 123 (revised 2004), Share-Based Payment (SFAS 123R), effective January 1, Year 5. SFAS 123R requires the recognition of the fair value of stock-based compensation in net income. Stock options are granted to employees at exercise prices equal to the fair market value of our stock at the dates of grant. Generally, options fully vest three years from the grant date and have a term of 10 years. We recognize the stock-based compensation expense over the requisite service period of the individual grantees, which generally equals the vesting period.

We recognized compensation cost in the amount of $108.2 million and $25.2 million in the first quarter of Year 5 and Year 4, respectively, as well as related tax benefits of $32.8 million and $8.8 million, respectively.

Beginning with the Year 5 stock option grant, we utilized a lattice-based option valuation model for estimating the fair value of the stock options. The lattice model allows the use of a range of assumptions related to volatility, risk-free interest rate, and employee exercise behavior. Expected volatilities utilized in the lattice model are based on implied volatilities from traded options on our stock, historical volatility of our stock price, and other factors. Similarly, the dividend yield is based on historical experience and our estimate of future dividend yields. The risk-free interest rate is derived from the U.S. Treasury yield curve in effect at the time of grant. The model incorporates exercise and post-vesting forfeiture assumptions based on an analysis of historical data. The expected life of the Year 5 grants is derived from the output of the lattice model.

The weighted-average fair values of the options granted in the first quarter of Year 5 were $16.06 per option, determined using the following assumptions:

Dividend Yield	2.0%
Weighted-average Volatility	27.8%
Range of Volatilities	27.6%–30.7%
Risk-free Interest Rate	2.5%– 4.5%
Weighted-average Expected Life	7.2 years

As of March 31, Year 5, the total remaining unrecognized compensation cost related to non-vested stock options amounted to $397.5 million which will be amortized over the weighted-average remaining requisite service period of 2 years.

d. The note reports $397.5 million of remaining unrecognized compensation cost related to nonvested stock options. What portion of this amount will be reported as compensation expense in the second quarter ending June 30, Year 5, and does this amount represent total stock-based compensation expense for the quarter?

e. Prior to *Statement No. 123 (Revised 2004),* firms were required to report pro forma earnings per share, taking into consideration stock-based compensation. As discussed in the chapter, *Statement No. 123 (Revised 2004)* requires stock-based compensation to be reported in the income statement, and thus included in the calculations of reported earnings per share. Which ratio do you believe is more relevant to the analyst: (1) reported earnings per share or (2) pro forma earnings per share, taking into consideration stock-based compensation? Why?

9.25 STOCK-BASED COMPENSATION—VESTING AND VALUATION MODELS. Exhibit 9.21 and Exhibit 9.22 provide footnote excerpts to the financial reports of the Coca-Cola Company and Eli Lilly and Company that discuss the stock option grants given to the employees of the two firms. Each firm uses options extensively to reward employees for their performance.

Required

Review Exhibit 9.21 and Exhibit 9.22 and answer the following questions:

- **a.** Explain the concept of vesting and discuss why firms typically include a vesting feature in the stock-based compensation plans that they offer to their employees.
- **b.** What are the vesting characteristics of the two plans discussed in the exhibits and what effect do they have on stock-based compensation expense using the fair value method as required by *Statement No. 123 (Revised 2004)?*
- **c.** For each firm, (1) what is the life of the options granted, (2) how does option life relate to the vesting period, and (3) speculate why the weighted-average *expected* life of the options is less than the full life of the options.
- **d.** The Coca-Cola company uses the Black-Scholes valuation model for estimating the fair value of the stock options, whereas Eli Lilly and Company utilizes a lattice-based option valuation model. Both valuation techniques are permitted by GAAP. Perform an Internet search to determine which valuation model is more commonly used by the largest publicly held firms, and speculate why this is the case.

9.26 INTERPRETING STOCK OPTION DISCLOSURES. Exhibit 9.23 summarizes the information disclosed by General Electric Company (GE) regarding its stock option plans for Year 2 to Year 4. Assume an income tax rate of 35 percent.

Required

- **a.** The average option price per share and market price per share at time of grant is equal in each year ($27.37 for Year 2, $31.19 for Year 3, and $32.26 for Year 4). Speculate why GE structured the stock option grants this way in each year.
- **b.** What are the likely reasons that the fair value of options granted per share increased from Year 2 to Year 3?
- **c.** Compute the amount that GE received from the exercise of stock options each year versus the amount it would have received if it had issued the same number of shares on the market.
- **d.** Refer to your answer to part c, and discuss why GE is willing to sell shares of its stock to employees at a price (average option exercise price) much lower than the firm could obtain for shares sold on the market (average market price at time of exercise).
- **e.** Refer again to your answer to part c and compute the effect of stock-based compensation on net income for each year, assuming that stock option compensation expense equaled the difference between the market price and the exercise price of options exercised.
- **f.** Discuss the strengths and weaknesses of each of the following approaches to recognizing the cost of stock options: (1) no expense as long as the option price

EXHIBIT 9.23

General Electric Company
Stock Option Disclosures
(Problem 9.26)

	Year 4	Year 3	Year 2
Number of Options Granted[a]	27.141	8.261	46.928
Average Option Price per Share	$32.26	$31.19	$27.37
Average Market Price per Share at Time of Grant	$32.26	$31.19	$27.37
Fair Value of Option Granted per Share	$ 8.33	$ 9.44	$ 7.73
Vesting Period of Options Granted, years	1–5	1–5	1–5
Option Valuation Assumptions:			
Discount Rate	4.0%	3.5%	3.5%
Volatility	27.7%	34.7%	33.7%
Dividend Yield	2.5%	2.5%	2.7%
Expected Option Life, years	6.0	6.0	6.0
Number of Options Exercised[a]	43.110	43.829	29.146
Average Option Exercise Price	$10.54	$ 9.45	$ 9.45
Average Market Price at Time of Exercise	$32.68	$27.59	$31.86

[a]Amounts in millions.

equals the market price on the date stock options are granted, (2) expense in the year of the grant equal to value of options granted, and (3) expense in the year of exercise equal to the benefit realized by employees from purchasing shares for less than market value.

INTEGRATIVE CASE 9.1

STARBUCKS

Starbucks' company-operated retail stores generate the majority of the revenues reported by the firm on its income statement. However, the firm also generates income by licensing to others the rights to use the Starbucks name. The firm states in the MD&A section of its Year 4 Form 10-K filing:

> The Company has licensed the rights to produce and distribute Starbucks branded products to two partnerships in which the Company holds a 50 percent interest: The North American Coffee Partnership with the Pepsi-Cola Company develops and distributes bottled Frappuccino® and Starbucks DoubleShot® coffee drinks; and the Starbucks Ice Cream Partnership with Dreyer's Grand Ice Cream, Inc. develops and distributes superpremium ice creams.

Although Starbucks reports other equity investments as the end of Year 4, the firm only discusses these two in depth in its MD&A, and it appears that these two dominate the equity investments of the firm.

Starbucks provides the following information related to the firm's equity investments, which includes the pertinent data for the two partnerships discussed in the previous paragraph (amounts in millions):

	Year 4	Year 3
Income Statement		
Income from Equity Investees[a]:	$ 60.7	$ 38.4
Balance Sheet		
Equity Method Investments	$152.5	$134.3

[a]Starbucks reports two sources of income in the line item, Income from Equity Investees: (1) the firm's proportionate share of income and losses from equity investments ($23.0 million in Year 4 and $6.1 million in Year 3); and (2) gross profit on royalty and license fees earned by the firm from the equity investees ($37.7 million in Year 4 and $32.3 million in Year 3).

Required

a. The Starbucks Frappuccino and DoubleShot coffee drinks are products unique to the firm that it markets and promotes extensively throughout the United States. Given this, discuss the firm's strategic reasoning to partner with PepsiCo and Dreyer's and, as a result, forgo a portion of income generated by the sale of these products each year.

b. Starbucks does not disclose the amount of dividends it receives from equity investees, but it is reasonable to assume that the firm receives some dividends from the two partnerships. How does receipt of a cash dividend affect (1) Starbucks' net income for Year 4 and Year 3 and (2) cash flows from operations for Year 4 and Year 3?

c. For this part and part d, assume for Year 4 that income from equity investees is generated entirely from the two partnerships. Calculate the combined net income of the two partnerships for Year 4.

d. Assume that Starbucks receives dividends equal to its share of equity income from the two partnerships. What amount did Starbucks invest in other equity investments during Year 4?

e. How would Starbucks' accounting for these partnership investments differ if the firm acquired another 30 percent of the stock, resulting in an 80 percent ownership position?

CASE 9.2

FISHER CORPORATION[27]

Effective January 1, Year 12, Weston Corporation (Weston) and Fisher Corporation (Fisher) will merge their respective companies. Under the terms of the merger agreement, Weston will acquire all of the outstanding common shares of Fisher. Fisher will remain a legally separate entity. However, Weston will consolidate its financial statements with those of Fisher at the end of each accounting period. According to the

[27]The authors gratefully acknowledge the assistance of Gary M. Cypress in the preparation of this case.

merger agreement, Weston can structure the transaction under either of the following two alternatives:

Alternative A

Weston would acquire all of the outstanding common shares of Fisher for $58,500,000 in cash. To obtain the necessary cash, Weston would issue $59 million of 10 percent, twenty-year bonds on the open market. For financial reporting purposes, Weston would account for the merger using the purchase method. For tax purposes, the merger transaction is a taxable event to Fisher's shareholders. They would pay income taxes at capital gains rates on any difference between the amount received and the tax basis of their shares. The transaction would not directly involve Fisher Corporation. The tax basis of Fisher's net assets, therefore, remains the same after the acquisition as before the acquisition. The firms would choose not to do a Section 338 election to obtain a step-up in tax basis of the net assets in this case.

Alternative B

Weston would acquire all of the outstanding common shares of Fisher for the issuance of 1,800,000 shares of a new Weston preferred stock. The preferred stock would carry an annual dividend of $2 per share and would be convertible into .75 shares of Weston common stock at any time. The exchange ratio would be one share of the new preferred stock for each outstanding common share of Fisher. An independent investment banking firm has valued the preferred shares at $50 million. For financial reporting purposes, Weston would account for the merger using the purchase method. For tax purposes, the merger transaction is a nontaxable event to Fisher's shareholders. The tax basis of Fisher's net assets carry over after the acquisition. Summarizing the alternatives:

	Alternative A	**Alternative B**
Type of Consideration Given	Cash	Convertible Preferred Stock
Value of Consideration Given	$58,500,000	$50,000,000
Financial Reporting Method	Purchase	Purchase
Tax Reporting Method—Shareholders	Taxable	Nontaxable
Tax Reporting Method—Fisher	Nontaxable	Nontaxable

Financial Statements for Weston

For the five years ended December 31, Year 11 (see Exhibit 9.24), the Weston Company's revenues, net income, and earnings per share had each grown at an average compounded annual rate of 23 percent. Growth in Year 11 exceeded the average in all categories. These five-year growth rates include the recession year of Year 7, when the company's net income increased by 14 percent despite a sales decline of 5 percent. Weston accomplished this growth rate from both operations and aggressive corporate acquisitions. The company intends to continue making acquisitions in the future.

Although the company has exhibited strong financial growth, it has consistently maintained a conservative balance sheet (see Exhibit 9.25). The company's debt has steadily declined from 29 percent of long-term capital in Year 8, to 24 percent in Year 11 (see

EXHIBIT 9.24

Weston Corporation
Income Statements
For the Years Ended December 31
(amounts in thousands, except per-share amounts)
(Case 9.2)

	Year 7	Year 8	Year 9	Year 10	Year 11	Estimated Year 12[a]
Sales	$233,000	$321,300	$306,500	$361,500	$482,100	$560,000
Expenses:						
Cost of Sales	(180,700)	(251,100)	(232,800)	(273,900)	(360,600)	(415,700)
Selling and Administrative	(36,500)	(51,600)	(51,900)	(58,300)	(86,921)	(105,632)
Operating Income	$ 15,800	$ 18,600	$ 21,800	$ 29,300	$ 34,579	$ 38,668
Equity in Net Income of Nonconsolidated Entities	2,300	3,800	3,600	2,600	3,200	4,000
Other Income (expense)	(1,300)	(2,100)	(900)	(400)	(1,600)	(1,000)
Income before Taxes	$ 16,800	$ 20,300	$ 24,500	$ 31,500	$ 36,179	$ 41,668
Provision for Income Taxes	(6,800)	(7,500)	(9,900)	(14,000)	(14,179)	(14,584)
Net Income	$ 10,000	$ 12,800	$ 14,600	$ 17,500	$ 22,000	$ 27,084
Earnings per Share	$ 1.25	$ 1.60	$ 1.83	$ 2.22	$ 2.82	$ 3.47
Dividends per Share of Common Stock	$ .40	$ .40	$ .45	$ .63	$ .88	$ 1.20
Average Number of Shares of Common Stock Outstanding	8,000	8,000	8,000	7,900	7,800	7,800

[a]Before consideration of the merger with Fisher.

Exhibit 9.26). Dividends per share have ranged between 27 and 32 percent of earnings per share in each of the last five years.

The company currently projects 25 percent growth in net income and earnings per share in Year 12, with revenues increasing by 16 percent.

Financial Statements for Fisher Corporation

Exhibit 9.27 presents comparative income statements and Exhibit 9.28 presents comparative balance sheets for Fisher. Fisher's management estimates that revenues will remain approximately flat between Year 11 and Year 12, but that Fisher's net income for Year 12 will decline to $2,500,000, compared with $6,602,000 in Year 11. This decrease in net income results from a $1,000,000 increase in labor costs in Year 12, a $3,000,000 loss in the construction of a crystallization system, a $1,000,000 expenditure to meet expected OSHA requirements, and a $1,000,000 expenditure to relocate one of its product lines to a new plant facility. Fisher has 1,800,000 shares outstanding on January 1, Year 12. It currently pays a dividend of $1.22 per share.

EXHIBIT 9.25

Weston Corporation
Consolidated Balance Sheets
December 31
(amounts in thousands)
(Case 9.2)

	Year 10	Year 11	Estimated Year 12[a]
Assets			
Cash	$ 28,000	$ 28,000	$ 32,000
Accounts Receivable	84,000	90,000	100,000
Inventory	58,000	71,000	82,000
Other	4,000	13,000	13,000
Total Current Assets	$174,000	$202,000	$227,000
Property, Plant, and Equipment	$ 96,000	$116,000	$131,000
Less Accumulated Depreciation	(29,000)	(38,000)	(48,000)
Net	$ 67,000	$ 78,000	$ 83,000
Investment in Nonconsolidated Entities	42,000	45,000	47,000
Goodwill	8,400	8,000	7,800
Other Assets	6,000	7,000	7,200
Total Assets	$297,400	$340,000	$372,000
Liabilities			
Current Portion Long-Term Debt	$ 400	$ 2,000	$ —
Accounts Payable	23,000	30,000	40,000
Accrued Liabilities and Advances	67,000	78,000	91,000
Income Taxes	12,000	21,000	14,000
Total Current Liabilities	$102,400	$131,000	$145,000
Long-Term Debt	48,000	48,000	48,000
Deferred Taxes	9,000	10,000	10,000
Total Liabilities	$159,400	$189,000	$203,000
Shareholders' Equity			
Common Stock	$ 11,000	$ 11,000	$ 11,000
Capital Surplus	55,000	55,000	55,000
Retained Earnings	72,000	85,000	103,000
Total Shareholders' Equity	$138,000	$151,000	$169,000
Total Liabilities and Shareholders' Equity	$297,400	$340,000	$372,000

[a]Before consideration of the merger with Fisher.

Exhibit 9.26

Weston Corporation
Key Financial Highlights
Year 8 through Year 12
(Case 9.2)

	Year 8	Year 9	Year 10	Year 11	Estimated Year 12[a]
Earnings per Share	$ 1.60	$ 1.83	$ 2.22	$ 2.82	$ 3.53
Dividends per Share	$ .40	$ .45	$ .63	$ .88	$ 1.20
Current Ratio	1.8	2.0	1.7	1.5	1.6
Long-Term Debt as a Percentage of Long-Term Capital	28.9%	26.5%	25.8%	24.1%	22.1%
Return on Average Common Shareholders' Equity	12.4%	12.9%	13.6%	15.2%	16.9%
Book Value per Share	$ 13.50	$ 14.88	$ 17.69	$ 19.36	$ 21.68
Tangible Net Worth ($000)	$99,300	$111,600	$129,600	$143,000	$161,200
Times Interest Earned	5.7	7.8	9.8	10.9	10.0

[a]Before consideration of the merger with Fisher.

EXHIBIT 9.27

Fisher Corporation
Income Statement
(amounts in thousands)
(Case 9.2)

	Year 7	Year 8	Year 9	Year 10	Year 11	Estimated Year 12
Sales	$41,428	$ 53,541	$76,328	$109,373	$102,699	$100,000
Other Revenue and Gains	0	41	0	0	211	200
Cost of Goods Sold	(33,269)	(43,142)	(60,000)	(85,364)	(80,260)	(85,600)
Selling and Administrative Expense	(6,175)	(7,215)	(9,325)	(13,416)	(12,090)	(10,820)
Other Expenses and Losses	(2)	0	(11)	(31)	(1)	—
Earnings before Interest and Taxes	$ 1,982	$ 3,225	$ 6,992	$ 10,562	$ 10,559	$ 3,780
Interest Expense	(43)	(21)	(284)	(276)	(13)	—
Income Tax Expense	(894)	(1,471)	(2,992)	(3,703)	(3,944)	(1,323)
Net Income	$ 1,045	$ 1,733	$ 3,716	$ 6,583	$ 6,602	$ 2,457

EXHIBIT 9.28

Fisher Corporation
Balance Sheet
(amounts in thousands)
(Case 9.2)

	Year 6	Year 7	Year 8	Year 9	Year 10	Year 11
Assets						
Cash	$ 955	$ 961	$ 865	$ 1,247	$ 1,540	$ 3,100
Marketable Securities	0	0	0	0	0	2,900
Accounts/Notes Receivable	6,545	7,295	9,718	13,307	18,759	15,000
Inventories	7,298	8,686	12,797	20,426	18,559	18,000
Total Current Assets	$14,798	$16,942	$23,380	$34,980	$38,858	$39,000
Property, Plant, and Equipment	12,216	12,445	13,126	13,792	14,903	15,000
Less: Accumulated Depreciation	(7,846)	(8,236)	(8,558)	(8,988)	(9,258)	(9,000)
Other Assets	470	420	400	299	343	1,000
Total Assets	$19,638	$21,571	$28,348	$40,083	$44,846	$46,000
Liabilities						
Accounts Payable—Trade	$ 2,894	$ 4,122	$ 6,496	$ 7,889	$ 6,779	$ 7,000
Notes Payable—Non-Trade	0	0	700	3,500	0	0
Current Part Long-Term Debt	170	170	170	170	170	0
Other Current Liabilities	550	1,022	3,888	8,624	12,879	8,000
Total Current Liabilities	$ 3,614	$ 5,314	$11,254	$20,183	$19,828	$15,000
Long-term Debt	680	510	340	170	0	0
Deferred Taxes	0	0	5	228	357	1,000
Total Liabilities	$ 4,294	$ 5,824	$11,599	$20,581	$20,185	$16,000
Shareholders' Equity						
Preferred Stock	$ 0	$ 0	$ 0	$ 0	$ 0	$ 0
Common Stock	2,927	2,927	2,927	5,855	7,303	9,000
Additional Paid-In Capital	5,075	5,075	5,075	5,075	5,061	5,000
Retained Earnings	7,342	7,772	8,774	8,599	12,297	16,000
Treasury Stock	0	−27	−27	−27	0	0
Total Shareholders' Equity	$15,344	$15,747	$16,749	$19,502	$24,661	$30,000
Total Liabilities and Shareholders' Equity	$19,638	$21,571	$28,348	$40,083	$44,846	$46,000

Allocation of Purchase Price

Exhibit 9.29 shows the calculation of the purchase price and the allocation of any excess cost under each of the two alternatives for structuring the acquisition of Fisher. Notes to the calculations are as follows (amounts in thousands):

Note 1: Acquisition costs consist of printing, legal, auditing, and finder's fees, and increase the cost of the shares of Fisher acquired.

Note 2: The book value of certain long-term contracts of Fisher (relating to a crystallization system) exceeds their market value by $3,000. Fisher expects to complete these contracts during Year 12. Weston establishes a "reserve" for this loss as of the date of acquisition and includes it among current liabilities. When Fisher completes the contracts in Year 12, the consolidated entity will charge the actual loss against the "reserve" for financial reporting. It will then claim a deduction for the loss in calculating taxable income.

EXHIBIT 9.29

Fisher Corporation
Calculation of Purchase Price and Allocation of Excess Cost
(amounts in thousands)
(Case 9.2)

	Alternative A	Alternative B
Purchase Price		
Base Price	$ 58,500	$50,000
Acquisition Costs (Note 1)	500	500
Total	$ 59,000	$50,500
Book Value of Contributed Capital of Fisher	(30,000)	(30,000)
Excess of Cost over Book Value to Be Allocated to Assets and Liabilities	$ 29,000	$20,500
Allocation of Excess Cost		
Recognition of "Reserve" for Losses on Long-Term Contracts (Note 2)	3,000 Cr.	3,000 Cr.
Write-Up of Building and Equipment (Note 3)	17,000 Dr.	17,000 Dr.
Recognition of Unfunded Pension Liability (Note 4)	5,000 Cr.	5,000 Cr.
Recognition of Estimated Liability to Meet OSHA Requirements (Note 5)	1,000 Cr.	1,000 Cr.
Recognition of Estimated Costs to Relocate Facilities in Connection with Product Move (Note 6)	1,000 Cr.	1,000 Cr.
Total Allocated to Identifiable Assets and Liabilities	7,000 Dr.	7,000 Dr.
Deferred Tax Effect (Note 7)	2,450 Cr.	2,450 Cr.
Residual to Goodwill (Note 8)	24,450 Dr.	15,950 Dr.
Total Allocated	$ 29,000 Dr.	$20,500 Dr.

Note 3: The market value of Fisher's property, plant, and equipment on January 1, Year 12, is \$23,000. Their book value and tax basis is \$6,000. Thus, Weston allocates \$17,000 (= 23,000 – \$6,000) of the excess cost to property, plant, and equipment. The consolidated entity will depreciate the excess using the straight-line method over ten years for financial reporting. It cannot depreciate the excess for tax purposes.

Note 4: Fisher has an unfunded pension obligation of \$5,000 on January 1, Year 12. Fisher had planned to straight-line amortize this obligation over twenty years from January 1, Year 12. Weston allocates a portion of the purchase price to this obligation on the date of the acquisition.

Note 5: Fisher expects to incur \$1,000 of costs during Year 12 on its facilities to comply with various health and safety provisions of OSHA. Weston allocates a portion of the purchase price to recognize this expected cost.

Note 6: Weston intends to relocate the manufacture of certain product lines of Fisher to a new plant facility during Year 12. The estimated costs of relocation are \$1,000. Weston allocates a portion of the purchase price to recognize this expected cost.

Note 7: *Statement No. 109* requires firms to provide deferred taxes for differences between the book basis and tax basis of assets and liabilities. Weston allocates the \$7,000 amount of excess cost shown in Exhibit 9.29 to individual assets and liabilities for financial reporting. For tax reporting, the bases of these assets and liabilities remain the same as the amounts shown on Fisher's books before the acquisition. Thus, Weston provides deferred taxes of \$2,450 (= .35 × \$7,000). It reports \$1,750 [= .35 × (\$3,000 Cr. + \$1,000 Cr. + \$1,000 Cr.)] as a current deferred tax asset, \$1,750 (= .35 × \$5,000) as a noncurrent deferred tax asset, and \$5,950 (= .35 × \$17,000) as a noncurrent deferred tax liability. The consolidated entity eliminates these deferred taxes as it amortizes the related asset or liability.

Note 8: Weston allocates the remaining excess cost to goodwill. *Statement No. 142* does not require the firm to amortize goodwill.

Exhibits 9.30 to 9.34 present pro forma consolidated financial statements for Weston and Fisher under each of the two alternatives.

Required

a. As a shareholder of Fisher, which alternative would you choose and why? The income tax rate on capital gains is 20 percent. Would your answer differ if you were an individual investor versus a pension fund?

b. As the chief financial officer of Weston, which alternative would you choose and why?

Exhibit 9.30

Weston Corporation and Fisher Corporation
Pro Forma Consolidated Balance Sheet as of January 1, Year 12
Alternative A (Cash Exchange)
(amounts in thousands)
(Case 9.2)

	Weston (Before Acquisition)	To Record Acquisition of Fisher's Shares		Weston (After Acquisition)	Fisher (After Acquisition)	Consolidation Worksheet Entries		Pro Forma Consolidated
	(1)	(2)	(3)	(4)	(5)	(6)	(7)	(8)
Assets								
Cash	$ 28,000	(A) 59,000	(B) 59,000	$ 28,000	$ 6,000			$ 34,000
Accounts Receivable	90,000			90,000	15,000			105,000
Inventory	71,000			71,000	18,000			89,000
Other		13,000		13,000	—	(C) 1,750		14,750
Total Current Assets	$202,000			$202,000	$39,000			$242,750
Property, Plant, and Equipment	$116,000			$116,000	$15,000	(C) 8,000		$139,000
Less: Accumulated Depreciation	(38,000)			(38,000)	(9,000)	(C) 9,000		(38,000)
Net Property, Plant, and Equipment	$ 78,000			$ 78,000	$ 6,000			$101,000
Investment in Nonconsolidated Entities	45,000			$ 45,000	—			$ 45,000
Investment in Fisher	—	(B) 59,000		59,000	—	(C) 59,000		—
Goodwill	8,000			8,000	—	(C) 24,450		32,450
Other Assets	7,000			7,000	1,000	(C) 1,750		9,750
Total Assets	$340,000			$399,000	$46,000			$430,950

(A) Issue of bonds for cash and payment or acquisition costs.
(B) Purchase of Fisher's outstanding common stock.
(C) Elimination of investment in Fisher and Fisher's shareholders' equity accounts and allocation of excess purchase price (see Exhibit 9.29 for amounts).

Continued

Exhibit 9.30

continued

	Weston (Before Acquisition)	To Record Acquisition of Fisher's Shares		Weston (After Acquisition)	Fisher (After Acquisition)	Consolidation Worksheet Entries		Pro Forma Consolidated
	(1)	(2)	(3)	(4)	(5)	(6)	(7)	(8)
Liabilities								
Current Portion Long-Term Debt ..	$ 2,000			$ 2,000	$ —			$ 2,000
Accounts Payable	30,000			30,000	7,000		(C) 3,000	37,000
Accrued Liabilities and Advances ...	78,000			78,000	7,000		(C) 1,000	90,000
Income Taxes	21,000			21,000	1,000		(C) 1,000	22,000
Total Current Liabilities	$131,000			$131,000	$15,000			$151,000
Long-Term Debt	48,000		(A) 59,000	107,000	—			107,000
Other Liabilities	—			—	1,000		(C) 5,000	6,000
Deferred Taxes	10,000			10,000			(C) 5,950	15,950
Total Liabilities	$189,000			$248,000	$16,000			$279,950
Shareholders' Equity								
Preferred Stock	$ —			$ —	$ —			$ —
Common Stock	11,000			11,000	9,000	(C) 9,000		11,000
Additional Paid-In Capital	55,000			55,000	5,000	(C) 5,000		55,000
Retained Earnings	85,000			85,000	16,000	(C) 16,000		85,000
Total Shareholders' Equity	$151,000			$151,000	$30,000			$151,000
Total Liabilities and Shareholders' Equity	$340,000			$399,000	$46,000			$430,950

(A) Issue of bonds for cash and payment or acquisition costs.
(B) Purchase of Fisher's outstanding common stock.
(C) Elimination of investment in Fisher and Fisher's shareholders' equity accounts and allocation of excess purchase price (see Exhibit 9.29 for amounts).

EXHIBIT 9.31

Weston Corporation and Fisher Corporation
Pro Forma Consolidated Income Statement
For the Year Ending December 31, Year 12
Alternative A (Cash Exchange)
(amounts in thousands)
(Case 9.2)

			Consolidation Worksheet Entries		
	Weston	**Fisher**	**Dr.**	**Cr.**	**Consolidated Pro Forma**
Sales	$560,000	$100,000			$660,000
Cost of Sales	(415,700)	(85,600)	(B) 1,700	(D) 5,000	(498,000)
Selling and Administrative	(105,632)	(10,820)		(C) 250	(116,202)
Operating Income	38,668	3,580			$ 45,798
Equity in Net Income of Nonconsolidated Entities	4,000	—			4,000
Other Income (Expense)	(1,000)	200	(A) 5,900		(6,700)
Income before Taxes	41,668	3,780			$ 43,098
Provision for Income Taxes	(14,584)	(1,323)	(C) 88 (D) 1,750	(A) 2,065 (B) 595	(15,085)
Net Income	$ 27,084	$ 2,457			$ 28,013
Basic Earning per Share	$ 3.47	$ 1.37			$ 3.59
Average Number Shares of Common Stock Outstanding	7,800	1,800			7,800

(A) Interest on Debt: .10 × $59,000 = $5,900, Tax Effect: .35 × $5,900 = $2,065
(B) Depreciation Expense: $17,000 ÷ 10 = $1,700; Deferred Tax Effects = .35 × $1,700 = $595
(C) Elimination of Pension Expense: $5,000 ÷ 20 = $250, Deferred Tax Effect = .35 × $250 = $88
(D) Elimination of Contract Loss, OSHA cost, and relocation costs = $5,000; Deferred Tax Effect: .35 × $5,000 = $1,750

EXHIBIT 9.32

Weston Corporation and Fisher Corporation
Pro Forma Consolidated Balance Sheet as of January 1, Year 12
Alternative B (Preferred Stock Exchange)
(amounts in thousands)
(Case 9.2)

	Weston (Before Acquisition)	To Record Acquisition of Fisher's Shares		Weston (After Acquisition)	Fisher (After Acquisition)	Consolidation Worksheet Entries		Pro Forma Consolidated
	(1)	(2)	(3)	(4)	(5)	(6)	(7)	(8)
Assets								
Cash	$ 28,000		(A) 500	$ 27,500	$ 6,000			$ 33,500
Accounts Receivable	90,000			90,000	15,000			105,000
Inventory	71,000			71,000	18,000			89,000
Other	13,000			13,000	—	(B) 1,750		14,750
Total Current Assets	$ 202,000			$201,500	$39,000			$242,250
Property, Plant, and Equipment	$ 116,000			$116,000	$15,000	(B) 8,000		$139,000
Less: Accumulated Depreciation	(38,000)			(38,000)	(9,000)	(B) 9,000		(38,000)
Net Property, Plant, and Equipment	$ 78,000			$ 78,000	$ 6,000			$101,000
Investment in Nonconsolidated Entities	45,000			$ 45,000	—			$ 45,000
Investment in Fisher	—	(A) 50,500		50,500	—		50,500(B)	—
Goodwill	8,000			8,000	—	(B)15,950		23,950
Other Assets	7,000			7,000	1,000	(B) 1,750		9,750
Total Assets	$ 340,000			$390,000	$46,000			$421,950
Liabilities								
Current Portion Long-Term Debt	$ 2,000			$ 2,000	$ —			$ 2,000
Accounts Payable	30,000			30,000	7,000		3,000(B)	37,000
Accrued Liabilities and Advances	78,000			78,000	7,000		1,000(B)	90,000
Income Taxes	21,000			21,000	1,000		1,000(B)	22,000
Total Current Liabilities	$ 131,000			$131,000	$15,000			$151,000

EXHIBIT 9.32

continued

	Weston (Before Acquisition)	To Record Acquisition of Fisher's Shares		Weston (After Acquisition)	Fisher (After Acquisition)	Consolidation Worksheet Entries		Pro Forma Consolidated
	(1)	(2)	(3)	(4)	(5)	(6)	(7)	(8)
Long-Term Debt	48,000			48,000	—			48,000
Other Liabilities	—			—	1,000		5,000 (B)	6,000
Deferred Taxes	10,000			10,000			5,950 (B)	15,950
Total Liabilities	$189,000			$189,000	$16,000			$220,950
Shareholders' Equity								
Preferred Stock	$ —		(A) 50,000	$ 50,000	$ —			$ 50,000
Common Stock	11,000			11,000	9,000	(B) 9,000		11,000
Additional Paid-In Capital	55,000			55,000	5,000	(B) 5,000		55,000
Retained Earnings	85,000			85,000	16,000	(B) 16,000		85,000
Total Shareholders' Equity	$151,000			$201,000	$30,000			$201,000
Total Liabilities and Shareholders' Equity	$340,000			$390,000	$46,000			$421,950

(A) Issue of preferred stock for the outstanding common shares of Fisher and payment of acquisition costs.

(B) Elimination of investment in Fisher and Fisher's shareholders' equity accounts and allocation of excess purchase price (see Exhibit 9.29 for amounts).

EXHIBIT 9.33

**Weston Corporation and Fisher Corporation
Pro Forma Consolidated Income Statement
for the Year Ending December 31, Year 12
Alternative B (Preferred Stock Exchange)
(amounts in thousands)
(Case 9.2)**

	Weston	Fisher	Consolidation Worksheet Entries Dr.	Consolidation Worksheet Entries Cr.	Consolidated Pro Forma
Sales	$560,000	$100,000			$ 660,000
Cost of Sales	(415,700)	(85,600)	(A) 1,700	(C) 5,000	(498,000)
Selling and Administrative	(105,632)	(10,820)		(B) 250	(116,202)
Operating Income	38,668	3,580			$ 45,798
Equity in Net Income of Nonconsolidated Entities	4,000	—			4,000
Other Income (Expense)	(1,000)	200			(800)
Income before Taxes	$ 41,668	3,780			$ 48,998
Provision for Income Taxes	(14,584)	(1,323)	(B) 88 (C) 1,750	(A) 595	(17,150)
Net Income	$ 27,084	$ 2,457			$ 31,848
Basic Earning per Share	$ 3.47	$ 1.37			*
Average Number Shares of Common Stock Outstanding	7,800	1,800			7,800

(A) Depreciation expense = $17,000 ÷ 10 = $1,700;
Deferred tax effect = .35 × 1,700 = 595

(B) Pension expense: $5,000 ÷ 20 = $250; Deferred tax effect = .35 × $250 = $88

(C) Loss on contract, OSHA and relocation costs = $5,000;
Deferred tax effect = .35 × $5,000 = $1,750

* Basic Eps: $\frac{(\$31{,}848 - \$3{,}600)}{7{,}800} = 3.62$

Diluted Eps: $\frac{\$31{,}848}{7{,}800 + 1{,}350} = 3.48$

EXHIBIT 9.34

Weston Corporation and Fisher Corporation
Key Financial Highlights
(Case 9.2)

	Actual for Weston Corporation				Weston Corporation and Fisher Corporation Pro Forma for Year 12	
	Year 8	Year 9	Year 10	Year 11	Alternative A	Alternative B
Earnings per Common Share						
Basic	$ 1.60	$ 1.83	$ 2.22	$ 2.82	$ 3.51	$ 3.62
Diluted	—	—	—	—	—	$ 3.48
Dividends per Common Share	$ .40	$ .45	$ .63	$ .88	$ 1.20	$ 1.20
Current Ratio[a]	1.8	2.0	1.7	1.5	1.6	1.6
Long-Term Debt as Percentage of Long-Term Capital[a]	28.9%	26.5%	25.8%	24.1%	41.5%	19.3%
Return on Average Common Shareholders' Equity	12.4%	12.9%	13.6%	15.2%	17.5%	17.6%
Book Value per Common Share	$ 13.50	$ 14.88	$ 17.69	$ 19.36	$ 19.36	$ 19.36
Tangible Net Worth (000's)[a]	$99,300	$111,600	$129,600	$143,000	$118,550	$127,050
Times Interest Earned	5.7	7.8	9.8	10.9	5.1	11.3
(with preferred dividend)	—	—	—	—	—	6.4

[a]Pro forma amounts for these ratios are at date of acquisition of Fisher.

Calculation of Key Financial Ratios—Alternative A

Basic Earnings per Share: $28,013 ÷ 7,800 = $3.59

Current Ratio: $242,750 ÷ $151,000 = 1.6

Long-Term Debt to Long-Term Capital: $107,000 ÷ ($107,000 + $151,000) = 41.5%

Return on Common Equity: $28,013 ÷ .5[$151,000 + ($151,000 + $28,013 − $9,360)] = 17.5%

Common Dividend = 7,800 × $1.20 = $9,360

Book Value per Share: $151,000 ÷ 7,800 = $19.36

Tangible Net Worth: $430,950 − $32,450 − $279,950 = $118,550

Times Interest Earned: ($28,013 + $15,085 + $4,741 + $5,900) ÷ ($4,741 + $5,900) = 5.1

Interest Expense with No Merger: ($27,084 + $15,584 + X) ÷ X = 10.0; X = $4,741

continued

EXHIBIT 9.34

continued

Calculation of Key Financial Ratios—Alternative B

Basic Earnings Per Share: ($31,848 − $3,600) ÷ 7,800 = $3.62

  Preferred Dividend = 1,800 × $2.00 = $3,600

Diluted Earnings per Share: $31,848 ÷ (7,800 + 1,350) = 3.48

  Common Shares Issued on Conversion of Preferred: 1,800 × .75 = 1,350

Current Ratio: $242,250 ÷ $151,000 = 1.6

Long-Term Debt to Long-Term Capital: $48,000 ÷ ($48,000 + $201,000) = 19.3%

Return on Common Equity: ($31,848 − $3,600) ÷ .5[$151,000 + ($151,000 + $31,848 − $3,600 − $9,360)] = 17.6%

Book Value per Common Share: $151,000 ÷ 7,800 = $19.36

Tangible Net Worth: $421,950 − $23,950 − $220,950 − $50,000 = $127,050

Times Interest Earned: ($31,848 + $17,150 + $4,741) ÷ $4,741 = 11.3

  With Preferred Dividend: ($31,848 + $17,150 + $4,741) ÷ ($4,741 + $3,600) = 6.4

CASE 9.3

CLARK EQUIPMENT COMPANY: ANALYZING A JOINT PROBLEM

Clark Equipment Company, through its wholly owned subsidiaries, operates in three principal product markets:

1. Small "lift and carry" products, including excavators for digging and loaders for hauling various materials. Its Bobcat skid-steer loader maintains a 50 percent worldwide market share.
2. Axles and transmissions for use by manufacturers of cranes and large material handling machinery used in construction, mining, logging, and other industrial applications.
3. Axles and transmissions for use by manufacturers of automobiles, trucks, and tractors in the Brazilian market.

Sales for these product groups for Year 10 to Year 12 appear in the following table:

	Year 10		Year 11		Year 12	
Off-highway:						
Lift-and-carry products	$385	44%	$347	48%	$410	51%
Axles and transmissions	274	32	240	33	241	30
On-highway:						
Axles and transmissions	205	24	140	19	152	19
	$864	100%	$727	100%	$803	100%

The geographical sources of its product sales (that is, the location of its manufacturing facilities) for Year 10 to Year 12 are as follows:

	Year 10		Year 11		Year 12	
North America	$504	58%	$439	60%	$501	62%
Europe	165	19	153	21	157	20
South America	195	23	135	19	145	18
	$864	100%	$727	100%	$803	100%

Since Year 5, Clark Equipment Company has engaged in a 50-percent-owned joint venture with Volvo of Sweden. The joint venture, called VME Group, manufactures heavy earthmoving construction and mining equipment worldwide. Its principal competitors are Caterpillar, Komatsu, and, to a lesser extent, Deere & Company. Clark Equipment Company accounts for its investment in this joint venture using the equity method.

Key economic characteristics of the equipment manufacturing industry, which includes industrial, construction, and agricultural equipment, are as follows:

1. **Product lines.** Products include tractors, excavators, loaders, haulers, cranes, compactors, and similar products. Manufacturers range from worldwide, full-line producers to regional niche players. There are currently more than 700 producers in the United States, yet six companies command more than 70 percent of the

domestic market. Manufacturers compete on the basis of machine performance, price, aftermarket support, and parts availability. Approximately 20 to 30 percent of a manufacturer's sales typically come from the aftermarket. A large tractor, for example, usually consumes parts and service equal to the cost of the equipment within approximately two years of initial purchase.

2. **Production.** Equipment manufacturing is capital intensive. Manufacturers tend to centralize production around key machine components, such as engines, axles, transmissions, and hydraulics. Customizing products to particular customers' needs typically occurs at the assembly stage.
3. **Technology.** Electronic and computer-based technologies have played an increasingly important role in recent years, in both the design of the final product and its manufacturing. Robotics in particular has been applied successfully in the manufacturing process.
4. **Demand.** The relatively high cost of equipment and the cyclicality of many of the industries to which equipment manufacturers sell their products (such as construction, mining, and automotive) result in highly cyclical sales patterns. The level of interest rates, general conditions in the economy, and income tax considerations (such as depreciation rates) significantly impact sales.
5. **Marketing.** Manufacturers use a distributor network to sell their products (original equipment and parts). The distributors usually sell a single manufacturer's products, but complement the product offering with products of other manufacturers unique to the market.
6. **Financing.** The capital-intensive nature of the manufacturing process leads these firms to rely on extensive long-term debt financing. Responsibility for arranging customer financing for equipment purchases may fall on the manufacturer, the distributor, or both.

Exhibit 9.35 presents condensed balance sheets for Clark Equipment Company as of December 31, Year 9, through December 31, Year 12, and condensed income statements for Year 10 through Year 12. These financial statements report Clark Equipment Company's investment in VME Group using the equity method. Exhibit 9.36 presents similar condensed financial statement data for VME Group.

Required

a. Prepare an analysis of the changes in the Investment in VME Group account on the books of Clark for Year 9 through Year 12.

b. Exhibit 9.37 presents partial condensed balance sheets and income statements for Clark Equipment Company, assuming that it accounted for its investment in VME Group using the proportionate consolidation method (that is, Clark Equipment Company recognizes its 50 percent share of the assets, liabilities, revenues, and expenses of VME Group). Complete Exhibit 9.37 by preparing a balance sheet as of December 31, Year 12, and an income statement for Year 12 following the proportionate consolidation method.

c. Exhibit 9.38 presents partial condensed balance sheets and income statements for Clark Equipment Company, assuming that it accounted for its investment in VME Group using the full consolidation method (that is, Clark Equipment Company consolidated 100 percent of the assets, liabilities, revenues, and expenses of VME Group, and reports Volvo's share of these items as a joint owner's interest. Complete Exhibit 9.38 by preparing a balance sheet as of December 31, Year 12, and an income statement for Year 12 following the full consolidation method.

EXHIBIT 9.35

Clark Equipment Company
Condensed Financial Statement Data with VME Group Accounted for Using the Equity Method
(amounts in millions)
(Case 9.3)

	December 31:			
	Year 9	Year 10	Year 11	Year 12
Balance Sheet				
Current Assets	$ 551	$ 468	$ 520	$396
Investment in VME Group	142	168	139	125
Noncurrent Assets	319	466	465	444
Total Assets	$1,012	$1,102	$1,124	$965
Current Liabilities	$ 265	$ 282	$ 328	$187
Noncurrent Liabilities	255	238	554	519
Shareholders' Equity	492	582	242	259
Total Equities	$1,012	$1,102	$1,124	$965

	For the Year:		
	Year 10	Year 11	Year 12
Income Statement			
Sales	$ 864	$ 727	$803
Equity in Earnings of VME	26	(29)	(47)
Cost of Goods Sold	(717)	(638)[a]	(664)
Interest Expense	(22)	(26)	(26)
Other Expenses, including taxes	(109)	(85)	(92)
Net Income (Loss)	$ 42	$ (51)	$(26)

[a]Includes $20 million of charges for restructuring operations and environmental cleanup.

d. Which of the three methods of accounting for Clark's investment in VME Group (equity, proportionate consolidation, full consolidation) portrays best the economics of the relationship between the entities? Explain.

e. Exhibit 9.39 presents selected financial statement ratios for Clark Equipment Company and VME Group under each of the three methods of accounting. Calculate these ratios for Year 12. The income tax rate is 34 percent.

f. Identify the likely reasons for changes in the profitability and risk of Clark Equipment Company during the period from Year 10 to Year 12.

EXHIBIT 9.36

VME Group
Condensed Financial Statement Data
(amounts in millions)
(Case 9.3)

	December 31:			
	Year 9	Year 10	Year 11	Year 12
Balance Sheet				
Current Assets	$594	$665	$ 801	$649
Noncurrent Assets	177	231	392	321
Total Assets	$771	$896	$1,193	$970
Current Liabilities	$326	$354	$ 642	$516
Noncurrent Liabilities	187	232	299	230
Shareholders' Equity	258	310	252	224
Total Equities	$771	$896	$1,193	$970

	For the Year:		
	Year 10	Year 11	Year 12
Income Statement			
Sales	$1,325	$1,368	$1,357
Cost of Goods Sold	(1,037)	(1,110)	(1,159)
Interest Expense	(20)	(33)	(29)
Other Expenses, including taxes	(216)	(283)	(263)
Net Income (Loss)	$ 52	$ (58)	$ (94)

EXHIBIT 9.37

Clark Equipment Company
Condensed Financial Statement Data
With VME Group Accounted for Using the Proportionate Consolidation Method
(amounts in millions)
(Case 9.3)

	December 31:			
	Year 9	Year 10	Year 11	Year 12
Balance Sheet				
Current Assets	$ 848.0	$ 800.5	$ 920.5	
Noncurrent Assets	407.5	581.5	661.0	
Goodwill	13.0	13.0	13.0	
Total Assets	$1,268.5	$1,395.0	$1,594.5	
Current Liabilities	$ 428.0	$ 459.0	$649.0	
Noncurrent Liabilities	348.5	354.0	703.5	
Shareholders' Equity	492.0	582.0	242.0	
Total Equities	$1,268.5	$1,395.0	$1,594.5	

	For the Year:		
	Year 10	Year 11	Year 12
Income Statement			
Sales	$1,526.5	$1,411.0	
Cost of Goods Sold	(1,235.5)	(1,193.0)	
Interest Expense	(32.0)	(42.5)	
Other Expenses, including taxes	(217.0)	(226.5)	
Net Income (Loss)	$ 42.0	$ (51.0)	

EXHIBIT 9.38

Clark Equipment Company
Condensed Financial Statement Data
With VME Group Accounted for Using the Full Consolidation Method
(amounts in millions)
(Case 9.3)

	December 31:			
	Year 9	Year 10	Year 11	Year 12
Balance Sheet				
Current Assets	$1,145	$1,133	$1,321	
Noncurrent Assets	496	697	857	
Goodwill	13	13	13	
Total Assets	$1,654	$1,843	$2,191	
Current Liabilities	$ 591	$ 636	$ 970	
Noncurrent Liabilities	442	470	853	
Joint Owners' Interest	129	155	126	
Shareholders' Equity	492	582	242	
Total Equities	$1,654	$1,843	$2,191	

	For the Year:		
	Year 10	Year 11	Year 12
Income Statement			
Sales	$2,189	$2,095	
Cost of Goods Sold	(1,754)	(1,748)	
Interest Expense	(42)	(59)	
Other Expenses, including taxes	(325)	(368)	
Joint Owners' Interest	(26)	29	
Net Income (Loss)	$ 42	$ (51)	

EXHIBIT 9.39

Clark Equipment Company
Profitability and Risk Ratios
(Case 9.3)

	Equity Method			Proportionate Consolidation			Full Consolidation		
	Year 10	Year 11	Year 12	Year 10	Year 11	Year 12	Year 10	Year 11	Year 12
Profit Margin for ROA	6.31%	(4.93%)		4.00%	(1.77%)		4.28%	(2.06%)	
Assets Turnover	.82	.65		1.15	.95		1.25	1.04	
Return on Assets	5.16%	(3.23%)		4.59%	(1.67%)		5.36%	(2.14%)	
Profit Margin for ROCE	4.86%	(7.02%)		2.75%	(3.61%)		1.92%	(2.43%)	
Capital Structure Leverage	1.97	2.71		2.48	3.65		3.26	4.92	
Return on Common Equity	7.46%	(12.96%)		7.46%	(12.96%)		7.46%	(12.96%)	
Current Ratios (December 31)	1.66	1.59		1.74	1.42		1.78	1.36	
Fixed Asset Turnover[a]	2.20	1.56		3.09	2.27		3.67	2.70	
Long-Term Debt Ratio (December 31)[b]	29.10%	69.95%		37.90%	74.72%		39.00%	70.09%	
Cost of Goods Sold/Sales	82.99%	87.76%		80.94%	84.55%		80.13%	83.44%	

	Clark Separate Co.			VME Separate Co.		
	Year 10	Year 11	Year 12	Year 10	Year 11	Year 12
Profit Margin for ROA	3.30%	.88%		4.92%	(2.65%)	
Assets Turnover	.96	.76		1.59	1.31	
Return on Assets	3.16%	.66%		7.82%	(3.47%)	
Profit Margin for ROCE	1.85%	(3.03%)		3.92%	(4.24%)	
Capital Structure Leverage	1.68	2.35		2.94	3.72	
Return on Common Equity	2.61%	(2.64%)		18.3%	(20.64%)	
Current Ratios (December 31)	1.66	1.59		1.88	1.25	
Fixed Asset Turnover[a]	2.20	1.56		6.50	4.39	
Long-Term Debt Ratio (December 31)[b]	29.10%	69.95%		42.80%	54.57%	
Cost of Goods Sold/Sales	82.99%	87.76%		78.26%	81.14%	

[a]Assuming that noncurrent assets represent property, plant, and equipment.
[b]Assuming that noncurrent liabilities represent long term debt.

CASE 9.4

LOUCKS CORPORATION: OBTAINING SECURITY IN TRANSLATION

Loucks Corporation (Loucks), a U.S. company, manufactures and markets security alarm systems. Based on predictions of rapid economic growth in South America during the next decade, Loucks plans to establish a wholly owned subsidiary in Colombia as of January 1, Year 8, to manufacture and market security alarm systems in that country. The Colombian subsidiary will use technology developed by Loucks for the alarm systems. It will import from Loucks a portion of the electronic software needed for the systems. Assembly will take place in Colombia.

Loucks plans to contribute $100,000 to establish the subsidiary on January 1, Year 8. The exchange rate between the Colombian peso and the U.S. dollar is expected to be $.02:P1 on this date. Exhibit 9.40 presents pro forma financial statements for Year 8 for the Colombian subsidiary during its first year of operations. Exhibit 9.41 presents a partial pro forma consolidation worksheet for Loucks and its Colombian subsidiary for Year 8. The following additional information pertains to these companies during Year 8.

1. Loucks expects to sell electronic software to its Colombian subsidiary during Year 8 at a transfer (selling) price of P3,000,000. The Colombian subsidiary expects to sell all alarm systems in which this software is a component by the end of Year 8. The firms will denominate the transfers in Colombian pesos. Loucks plans to hedge its exchange exposure, including any transaction gain or loss and related loss or gain on the hedging instrument in other expenses.
2. The subsidiary expects to declare and pay a dividend to Loucks on December 31, Year 8.

Required

a. Discuss whether Loucks should use the U.S. dollar or the Colombian peso as the functional currency for its Colombian subsidiary.

b. Loucks expects the exchange rate between the U.S. dollar and the Colombian peso to change as follows during Year 8:

January 1, Year 8	$.020:P1
Average, Year 8	$.018:P1
December 31, Year 8	$.015:P1

Complete Exhibit 9.40, showing the translation of the subsidiary's accounts into U.S. dollars and assuming that the Colombian peso is the functional currency. Include a separate calculation of the translation adjustment. Using the translated amounts, complete the consolidation worksheet in Exhibit 9.41.

c. Repeat part b, assuming that the U.S. dollar is the functional currency. Include a separate calculation of the translation gain or loss. The Colombian subsidiary expects to issue bonds denominated in Colombian pesos and acquire fixed assets on January 1, Year 8.

d. Why does the sign of the translation adjustment in part b differ from the sign of the translation gain or loss in part c?

EXHIBIT 9.40

Colombian Subsidiary
Translation of Financial Statements—Year 8
(Case 9.4)

	Colombian Pesos	Exchange Rate	U.S. Dollars
Balance Sheet			
Assets			
Cash	P 700,000		
Accounts Receivable	2,000,000		
Inventories	3,500,000		
Fixed Assets, net	5,700,000		
	P 11,900,000		
Liabilities and Equity			
Accounts Payable	P 2,400,000		
Bonds Payable	4,000,000		
Common Stock	5,000,000		
Translation Adjustment	—		
Retained Earnings	500,000		
	P 11,900,000		
Income Statement			
Revenues	P 15,000,000		
Cost of Goods Sold	(10,000,000)		
Depreciation Expense	(300,000)		
Other Expenses	(2,500,000)		
Net Income	P 2,200,000		
Retained Earnings Statement			
Balance, January 1, Year 1	P —		
Plus Net Income	2,200,000		
Less Dividends	(1,700,000)		
Balance, December 31, Year 1	P 500,000		

5. Assume that actual financial statement amounts for Year 8 turn out to be exactly as projected in Exhibits 9.40 and 9.41 but that the exchange rate changes as follows:

January 1, Year 8	$.020:P1
Average, Year 8	$.022:P1
December 31, Year 8	$.025:P1

EXHIBIT 9.41

Loucks Corporation and Colombian Subsidiary
Consolidation Worksheet
(Case 9.4)

	Loucks Corp.	Colombian Subsidiary	Adjustments and Eliminations	Consolidated
Balance Sheet				
Cash	$ 48,000			
Accounts Receivable	125,000			
Inventories	260,000			
Investment in Colombian Subsidiary	?			
Fixed Assets, net	120,000			
Total Assets	$?			
Accounts Payable	$280,000			
Bonds Payable	50,000			
Common Stock	100,000			
Translation Adjustment	—			
Retained Earnings	?			
Total Equities	$?			
Income Statement				
Sales Revenue	$500,000			
Equity in Earnings of Columbian Subsidiary	?			
Cost of Goods Sold	(400,000)			
Depreciation Expense	(20,000)			
Other Expenses	(30,000)			
Net Income	$ 89,600			
Dividends	(20,000)			
Increase in Retained Earnings	$?			
Retained Earnings, January 1	167,500			
Retained Earnings, December 31	$?			

Calculate the amount of the translation adjustment under the all-current method and the translation adjustment under the monetary/nonmonetary method for Year 8. Why do the signs of the translation adjustments in part e differ from those in parts b and c?

f. Compute the net income to revenues ratio based on (1) amounts originally measured in Colombian pesos, (2) amounts measured in U.S. dollars from part b, and (3) amounts measured in U.S. dollars from part c. Why is the net income to revenues percentage the same under (1) and (2) but different under (3)?

Chapter 10

Forecasting Financial Statements

Learning Objectives

1. Develop the skills to build forecasts of future balance sheets, income statements, and statements of cash flows. The objective in building financial statement forecasts is to develop reliable and unbiased expectations for a firm's future earnings, cash flows, and dividends that the analyst can use in valuation models to estimate the firm's share value. The analyst can also use these forecasts in a wide array of decision contexts, such as strategic planning, credit analysis, corporate management, and mergers and acquisitions.

2. Understand and apply a six-step forecasting framework for building financial statement forecasts. These six steps focus on projecting (a) revenue growth, (b) operating expenses, (c) operating assets, (d) operating liabilities, financial leverage and capital structure, (e) interest, taxes, and dividends, and (f) cash flows.

3. Identify and incorporate important business and strategic factors into forecasts of future business activities, which we measure with forecasts of future accounting numbers and financial statements.

4. Understand how and when to use shortcut forecasting techniques.

5. Develop forecast models that are flexible and comprehensive, allowing the analyst to respond quickly and appropriately to important announcements by firms.

OVERVIEW

Thus far, this text has discussed the first four steps of the six-step analysis framework. Drawing on the disciplines of accounting, finance, economics, and strategy, the text has demonstrated how to apply the framework to analyze (a) the economics of a firm's industry, (b) the competitive advantages and risks of the firm's strategy, (c) the quality of the firm's accounting, and (d) the firm's performance and risk.

In the next five chapters, we take the two culminating steps of the framework: Forecasting the future operating, investing, and financing activities of the firm and then valuing the firm. The first part of this process involves forecasting value-relevant information about a firm's expected future earnings, cash flows, and dividends, and the inherent risks. The second part of the process applies valuation models to the forecasts of future earnings, cash flows, and dividends to determine the economic value of an investment, after considering its risk.

In this chapter, we shift our focus to the future. Economics teaches us that the value of an economic resource is a function of the expected future returns from the resource and the risks inherent in those expected returns. Therefore, this chapter demonstrates how to develop expectations of a firm's future operating, investing, and financing activities and capture those expectations in forecasts of future financial statements—income statements, balance sheets, and statements of cash flows. In subsequent chapters, we will use these financial statement forecasts to derive expectations of future value-relevant payoffs to the firm's common equity shareholders, including future earnings, cash flows, and dividends, and we will apply valuation models that use these expectations to determine firm value. Chapter 11 describes and implements the classical dividends-based valuation model, which is the theoretical foundation for all other approaches to firm valuation. Chapter 11 also introduces and applies models to incorporate risk into estimates of expected returns on investments and firms' costs of capital. Chapter 12 discusses and implements valuation models that assume that the value-relevant payoffs are expected future "free" cash flows that the firm that can eventually pay to shareholders as dividends. Chapter 13 discusses and implements valuation models that rely on earnings, which reflect the firm's wealth creation for shareholders. Chapter 14 discusses and applies valuation approaches that rely on comparable companies and market-based valuation multiples, such as price-earnings ratios and market-to-book ratios. Chapter 14 also discusses and illustrates some advanced valuation techniques, including reverse engineering share prices.

INTRODUCTION TO FORECASTING

Analysts build forecasts to develop a set of realistic expectations for the outcomes of future business activities. To capture these expectations, analysts develop a set of *financial statement forecasts*—expected future income statements, balance sheets, and statements of cash flows. Financial statement forecasts represent an integrated portrayal of all of the firm's future operating, investing, and financing activities. These activities will determine the firm's future profitability, growth, financial position, cash flows, and risk. Using a forecasted set of financial statements, the analyst aims to capture expectations for *all* of the factors that will determine the firm's future value-relevant payoffs to stakeholders.

Financial statement forecasts are important tools for analysts because expectations of future payoffs play a central role in equity valuation and many other financial decision contexts. A firm's share value depends on its expected future payoffs to equity stakeholders, discounted for time and risk. Using a set of financial statement forecasts, the analyst can derive reliable expectations of future value-relevant payoffs to equity shareholders—earnings, cash flows, and dividends—which are the fundamental bases for share value. Credit decisions require expectations for future cash flows available to make required future interest and principal payments. Managers' decisions about firm strategy, potential customer or supplier relationships, potential mergers or acquisitions, potential carve-outs of divisions or subsidiaries, and even whether a firm presents a good employment opportunity depend on their expectations for future payoffs from these decisions and the risks of those payoffs.

Developing forecasts of future payoffs is in many ways the most difficult step of the six-step framework of this text because it requires the analyst to estimate the effects of future activities, which involves a high degree of uncertainty. Forecast errors can prove very costly. Optimistic forecasts of future earnings and cash flows can lead the analyst to overestimate a firm's future earnings and cash flows or underestimate a firm's risk, and therefore make poor investment decisions based on an overstated value of the firm (such as paying more for a share than it is worth). Pessimistic or overly conservative forecasts can lead the analyst to understate a firm's future earnings and cash flows or overstate a firm's risk, and consequently miss valuable investment opportunities. Analysts need to develop *realistic* (unbiased and objective; not optimistic or conservative) expectations of future earnings and cash flows that will lead to well-informed investment decisions.

Superior forecasting has the potential to earn superior returns. As Chapter 1 discussed, empirical research results from the Nichols and Wahlen study suggest the potential to earn abnormal returns by correctly forecasting the *sign* of the change in annual earnings numbers.[1] Their findings indicate that if one had predicted accurately the sign of the change in earnings one year ahead for each firm in their sample during their fourteen-year study period (1988–2001), one would have earned above-market returns of roughly 19 percent per year by investing in those firms that experienced earnings increases, and one would have earned above-market returns of roughly 16 percent per year by selling short those firms that experienced earnings decreases.

The evidence in Nichols and Wahlen also suggests that the potential to earn abnormal returns increases substantially if one correctly forecasts the *sign* and *magnitude* of the change in one-year-ahead earnings.[2] Their findings imply that stock returns for the firms that experience the largest increases in earnings in a given year (that is, those firms with percentage increases in earnings that are among the top 10 percent of all sample firms that year) generate very large positive returns, beating the market by an average of nearly 50 percent per year. Their findings also indicate that stock returns for firms that experience the largest decreases in earnings in a given year (those firms with percentage decreases in earnings that fall among the bottom 10 percent of all sample firms that year) tend to earn stock returns that are on average 22 percentage points per year lower than the market as a whole.

To be sure, analysts do not have perfect foresight and cannot perfectly predict one year ahead the direction or amount of earnings increases and decreases for all firms. Nonetheless, analysts should consider the Nichols and Wahlen results encouraging because they suggest that increasing one's skills in forecasting future changes in earnings should give the analyst greater potential to earn superior returns.

Accounting researchers have also investigated whether financial statement ratios like those described throughout this text can be used to build forecast models that predict future changes in earnings with reasonable accuracy. For example, Ou and Penman built prediction models based on regressions of earnings changes on a set of financial statement ratios.[3] Their earnings-change-prediction models produce probability estimates of the

---

[1]D. Craig Nichols and James M. Wahlen, "How Do Earnings Numbers Relate to Stock Returns? A Review of Classic Accounting Research with Updated Evidence," *Accounting Horizons* 18 (December 2004), pp. 263–286. This study uses data from 1988 to 2001 to replicate the seminal findings in Ray Ball and Philip Brown, "An Evaluation of Accounting Income Numbers," *Journal of Accounting Research* (Autumn 1968), pp. 159–178; Roger Kormendi and Robert Lipe, "Earnings Innovations, Earnings Persistence, and Stock Returns," *Journal of Business* 60 (1987), pp. 323–345; and Victor Bernard and Jacob Thomas, "Post-Earnings Announcement Drift: Delayed Price Response or Risk Premium?," *Journal of Accounting Research* (1989 Supplement), pp. 1–48.

[2]See also William Beaver, Roger Clarke, and William Wright, "The Association between Unsystematic Security Returns and the Magnitude of Earnings Forecast Errors," *Journal of Accounting Research* 17 (Autumn 1979), pp. 316–341.

[3]See Jane Ou and Stephen Penman, "Financial Statement Analysis and the Prediction of Stock Returns," *Journal of Accounting and Economics* (November 1989), pp. 295–330. For examples of other studies in this area, see Baruch Lev and Ramu Thiagarajan, "Fundamental Information Analysis," *Journal of Accounting Research* (Autumn 1993), pp. 190–215; and Jeffery Abarbanell and Brian Bushee, "Abnormal Stock Returns to a Fundamental Analysis Strategy," *The Accounting Review* 73 (January 1998), pp. 19–46.

likelihood of an earnings increase. They test their earnings-change-prediction models out of sample (that is, they test the models on firms in years following the periods they use to develop the models) and they find that their probability estimates correctly predict whether one-year-ahead earnings will increase or decrease for roughly 67 percent of their firm-year observations. They also show that taking long positions in shares of firms with a high probability of an earnings increase next year, and short positions in shares of firms with a high probability of an earnings decrease next year, resulted in average market-adjusted returns of roughly 8 percent per year during their study period. This study and subsequent related studies provide encouraging results to suggest that a fundamental analysis of financial statement ratios can produce more informed forecasts of future earnings, which analysts can use to make better investment decisions.

To maximize the analyst's potential to develop reliable forecasts of financial statements and to mitigate the potential for costly forecast errors, the analyst should base forecasts on expectations that reflect the economics of the industry, the competitive advantages and risks of the firm's strategy, the quality of the firm's accounting, and the drivers of the firm's profitability and risk. The first four steps of the analytical framework of this text provide the necessary foundation for forecasting. These four steps should inform the analyst about the critical risk and success factors of the firm and the key drivers of the firm's profitability and risk. The critical factors that are the focal points for the analysis of the firm's strategy, accounting quality, profitability, and risk are the most important building blocks for forecasting the firm's future financial statements.

This chapter first outlines a six-step process for forecasting financial statements. The chapter then illustrates each of the steps by applying them to PepsiCo, developing detailed forecasts for each of the three primary financial statements for each of the next five years. The chapter then describes a set of techniques to enhance the reliability of forecasts, including sensitivity analysis, iteration, and validity checks. The chapter also describes some simplifying steps for shortcut forecasts based on time-series projections of future sales, earnings, and assets, and the conditions under which such shortcuts are more likely to be reliable and less likely to create forecast errors.

PREPARING FINANCIAL STATEMENT FORECASTS

Preparing a set of financial statement forecasts requires an analyst to consider numerous assumptions and relations. We suggest that the analyst follow the six-step forecasting process described and illustrated in this chapter to project the three principal financial statements (income statement, balance sheet, and statement of cash flows). We also suggest that the analyst implement these six steps while following several general but important principles. This section offers a set of general principles to guide the preparation of a set of financial statement forecasts, describes the six-step forecasting framework, offers several practical coaching tips on implementing the six-step sequence, and then concludes with a brief introduction of the use of FSAP for building financial statement forecasts.

General Forecasting Principles

Several key principles of forecasting deserve mention (or are worth repeating) right at the outset. **First, as noted earlier, the objective of forecasting is to produce reliable and realistic expectations of future earnings, cash flows, and dividends, which determine the value-relevant future payoffs to investment.** To maximize reliability and avoid costly forecast errors, financial statement forecasts should provide unbiased predictions of the firm's future operating, investing, and financing activities, and should not be conservative or optimistic.

Second, forecasts of financial statements should be comprehensive. The financial statement forecasts should include *all* expected future operating, investing, and financing activities to ensure complete forecasts. For example, suppose an analyst forecasts expected future sales growth and then simply projects expected future earnings assuming that the firm's profit margin on past sales will remain constant in the future. This approach fails to consider all of the elements that determine profitability from sales, and how those elements will change in the future, which can cause the earnings forecasts to be incomplete. By assuming a constant profit margin on sales, the analyst ignores whether the cost of goods sold and selling, general, and administrative expenses will increase more slowly than sales growth because of economies of scale or scope, or operating synergies.

Third, financial statement forecasts must have internally consistent assumptions and relations. Forecasts of financial statements should rely on the *additivity* within financial statements and the *articulation* across financial statements to avoid internal inconsistencies in forecasts. The analyst can rely on the internal discipline of accounting across the three primary financial statements to reduce the possibility of errors from internally inconsistent assumptions. For example, future sales growth will likely drive future growth in related elements of the financial statements, including costs of sales, inventory, accounts receivable, and property, plant, and equipment. In turn, future growth in inventory, receivables, and property, plant, and equipment will likely affect growth in related elements, including accounts payable, depreciation, short-term and long-term borrowing, interest expense, and equity capital issues. Each of these elements will, in turn, have implications for the firm's cash flows. To capture the many complex relations among operating, investing, and financing activities, financial statement forecasts should add up and should articulate with each other. The income statement should appropriately measure profit or loss for each period by including all of the revenues, expenses, gains, and losses each period. The balance sheet should capture all of the elements of financial position and should balance, and it should reflect the firm's net profit or loss. The statement of cash flows should reflect all of the cash inflows and outflows implied by the income statement and the changes in the firm's balance sheet.

Fourth, financial statement forecasts must rely on assumptions that have internal and external validity. Forecast assumptions should pass the test of common sense. The analyst should impose reality checks on the forecast assumptions. For example, do the sales growth forecast assumptions appropriately reflect the firm's strategy and the competitive conditions in the industry, including market demand and price elasticity for the firm's products, as well as the firm's productive capacity? The analyst should ensure that the assumptions in the financial statement forecasts reflect changes that management intends to make and can make in the future. The analyst should avoid building forecasts based on wishful thinking. That is, the analyst should not create forecasts based on what the analyst hopes the firm will do, or on what the analyst thinks the firm should do. Instead, the forecasts should capture what the analyst believes the firm actually can and will do in the future.

Six-Step Forecasting Game Plan

To prepare a set of financial statement forecasts, the analyst should organize and develop the numerous forecast assumptions and relations as they relate to operating, investing, and financing activities. This activity-based forecasting approach enables the analyst to identify the necessary sequence of steps to project the three principal financial statements into the future. The particular sequence of steps may vary, depending on the reason for forecasting the financial statements. We find that, for most forecasts of financial statements, this six-step sequence works well:

1. Projecting revenues from sales and other operating activities.
2. Projecting operating expenses (for example, cost of goods sold and selling, general, and administrative expenses) and deriving projected operating income (income before interest expense, interest income, and income taxes).
3. Projecting the assets (for example, cash, marketable securities, receivables, inventory, property, plant, and equipment, financial assets, and intangible assets) that will be necessary to support the level of operations projected in steps 1 and 2.
4. Projecting the operating liabilities (for example, accounts payable, accrued expenses) and the financial leverage and capital structure (for example, financial liabilities such as short-term and long-term debt, and shareholders' equity except for retained earnings) that will be necessary to finance the assets projected in step 3.
5. Determining the cost of financing the financial liabilities in the firm's capital structure projected in step 4, and any income from financial assets projected in step 2. From projected operating income from step 2, subtract interest expense on short-term and long-term debt and add interest income from investments in financial assets. Project nonrecurring or unusual gains or losses (if any), and derive projected income before tax. Subtract the projected provision for income taxes to derive projected net income. Subtract expected dividends from net income to obtain the projected change in retained earnings. At this point, check to be sure the projected balance sheet is in balance. If it is not in balance, it may indicate that the projected financial structure may need to be adjusted (for example, additional financing may be needed), and steps 4 and 5 will have to be repeated until the balance sheet is in balance.
6. Deriving the statement of cash flows from the projected income statement and the changes in the projected balance sheet amounts.

Exhibit 10.1 summarizes this procedure.

Practical Tips for Implementing the Six-Step Forecasting Game Plan

We suggest several practical coaching tips on implementing the six-step forecasting sequence. **The analyst should consider these six steps as integrated and interdependent tasks that are not necessarily sequential or linear for all firms.** The order in which an analyst implements these six steps and the amount of emphasis placed on each step will depend on the integration of the firm's operating, investing, and financing activities. For example, forecasts of revenues for a retail chain or restaurant chain may first require forecasts of the number of new stores that the chain will open. The sales forecasts for a manufacturer may depend on building a new productive plant, which may depend on obtaining long-term financing.

The amounts on the three forecasted financial statements must articulate. For example, the change in retained earnings should include net income minus dividends. The change in accumulated depreciation on the balance sheet should reflect depreciation expense on the income statement. The change in the property, plant, and equipment

EXHIBIT 10.1

A Schematic Representation of the Six-Step Process for Preparing Financial Statement Forecasts

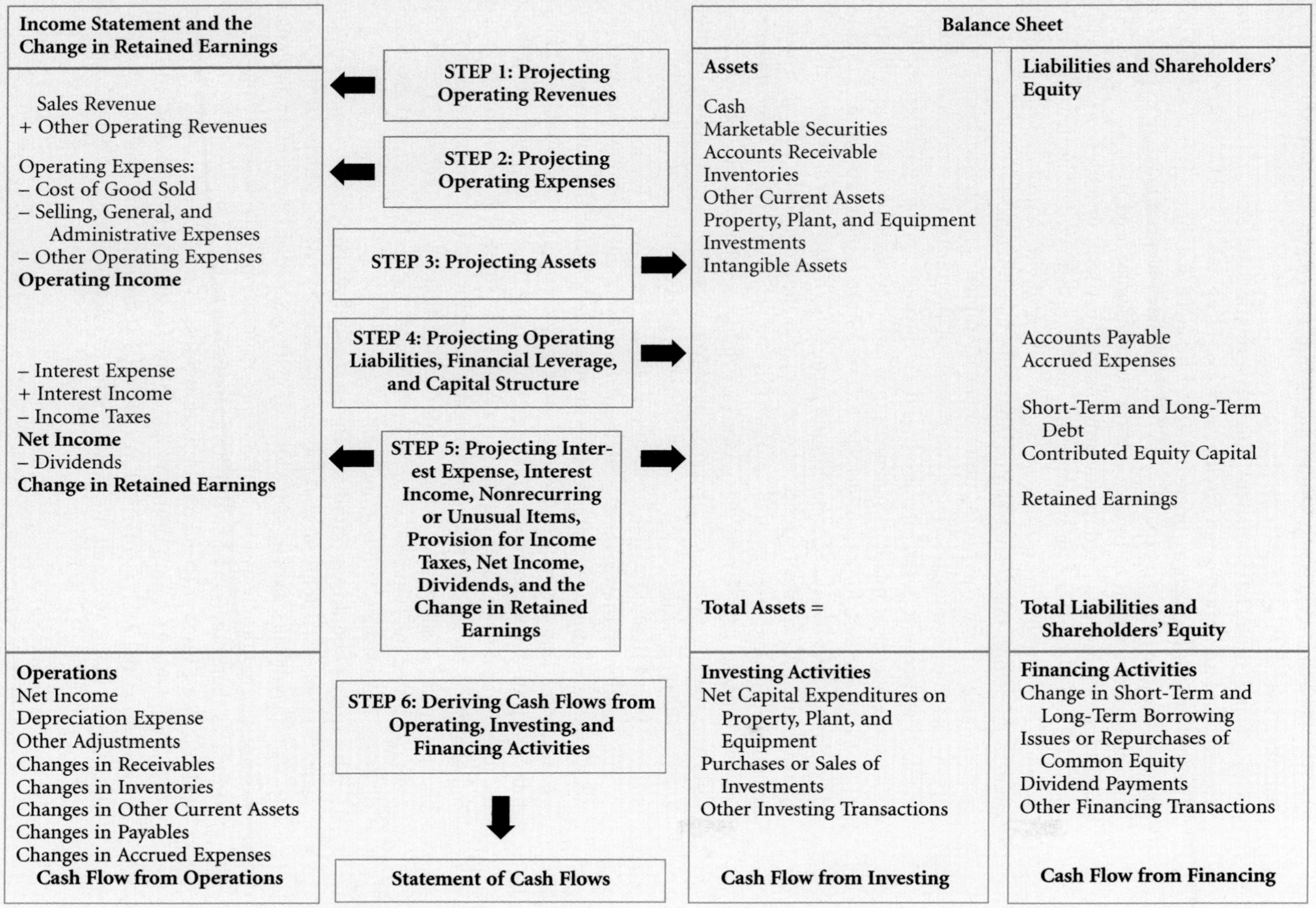
Income Statement and the Change in Retained Earnings
Sales Revenue
+ Other Operating Revenues
Operating Expenses:
– Cost of Good Sold
– Selling, General, and Administrative Expenses
– Other Operating Expenses
Operating Income
– Interest Expense
+ Interest Income
– Income Taxes
Net Income
– Dividends
Change in Retained Earnings
STEP 1: Projecting Operating Revenues
STEP 2: Projecting Operating Expenses
STEP 3: Projecting Assets
STEP 4: Projecting Operating Liabilities, Financial Leverage, and Capital Structure
STEP 5: Projecting Interest Expense, Interest Income, Nonrecurring or Unusual Items, Provision for Income Taxes, Net Income, Dividends, and the Change in Retained Earnings
Balance Sheet
Assets
Cash
Marketable Securities
Accounts Receivable
Inventories
Other Current Assets
Property, Plant, and Equipment
Investments
Intangible Assets
Total Assets =
Liabilities and Shareholders' Equity
Accounts Payable
Accrued Expenses
Short-Term and Long-Term Debt
Contributed Equity Capital
Retained Earnings
Total Liabilities and Shareholders' Equity
Operations
Net Income
Depreciation Expense
Other Adjustments
Changes in Receivables
Changes in Inventories
Changes in Other Current Assets
Changes in Payables
Changes in Accrued Expenses
Cash Flow from Operations
STEP 6: Deriving Cash Flows from Operating, Investing, and Financing Activities
Statement of Cash Flows
Investing Activities
Net Capital Expenditures on Property, Plant, and Equipment
Purchases or Sales of Investments
Other Investing Transactions
Cash Flow from Investing
Financing Activities
Change in Short-Term and Long-Term Borrowing
Issues or Repurchases of Common Equity
Dividend Payments
Other Financing Transactions
Cash Flow from Financing

amounts on the balance sheet should incorporate the effects of any capital expenditures, and the statement of cash flows should add back the amount of depreciation expense (a noncash expense) to net income and subtract capital expenditures. The net cash flow on the statement of cash flows must agree with the change in the cash balance on the balance sheet.

Preparing financial statement forecasts requires at least one flexible financial account, and an iterative and circular process. Firms rely on flexible accounts—usually financial accounts, such as financial assets, financial liabilities, equity capital, or dividends—that the firm can expand or contract to match its need for capital. For example, a firm that needs capital to finance growth in assets may need to increase short-term or long-term borrowing, or reduce investments in short-term or long-term financial assets, or issue equity shares. A firm generating excess cash may deploy that cash by paying down debt, investing it in financial assets, paying dividends, or repurchasing its own shares. Therefore, the analyst should adjust flexible financial accounts as necessary to appropriately match the firm's future financial capital structure with the firm's future operations and investments. Thus, the process of producing a set of financial statement forecasts will require several iterations and a degree of circularity. For example, the first pass through a set of financial statement forecasts may reveal to the analyst that the firm will need to increase long-term debt to finance future capital expenditures and to make the balance sheet balance. Increased long-term debt, however, will require the analyst to increase interest expense to reflect the cost of the additional debt capital, which in turn means that income taxes will fall, and net income will fall by the incremental amount of interest expense after tax savings. As a consequence, retained earnings will fall, which reveals to the analyst that the firm may have to increase long-term debt a bit more. The analyst will repeat this process until the balance sheet balances and articulates with the income statement and the statement of cash flows.[4]

The quality of the financial statement forecasts, and therefore the quality of the decisions based on those statements, will be no better than the quality of the forecast assumptions. Less technically: Garbage in, garbage out. The analyst should think carefully and justify each assumption, especially the most important assumptions that reflect the most critical risk and success factors of the firm's strategy. In addition, the analyst can impose reality checks on the assumptions by analyzing ratios, common-size, and rate-of-change financial statements using the forecasted financial statements. These analytical tools (discussed in Chapters 1, 4, and 5) may reveal that certain assumptions are unrealistic or are inconsistent with one another.

The analyst should also conduct sensitivity analysis on the financial statement forecasts. The analyst should assess, for example, the extent to which earnings will vary across different sales growth scenarios (comparing across the most likely, optimistic, and pessimistic growth rate assumptions). Some assumptions will have more significant consequences than others, and sensitivity analyses will help the analyst assess the extent to which forecast results depend on key assumptions.

The subsequent sections of this chapter illustrate the six-step procedure described previously using the analysis of PepsiCo's financial statements through Year 4 as a base. In this chapter we analyze and use PepsiCo's financial statement data from Year 0 through

[4]Most computer spreadsheet software packages facilitate iterative and circular processes. For example, in Excel, under the Tools/Options/Calculation menu, one can check the Iteration box to set the spreadsheet to automatically compute iteratively (for example, 100 times) until the computations converge to a specified maximum change.

Year 4 to carefully develop forecast assumptions and to compute financial statement forecasts for PepsiCo for Year 5 through Year 9, which we label Year +1 through Year +5 to denote that they are forecasts of activities we expect to occur one year ahead through five years ahead.[5]

Using FSAP to Prepare Forecasted Financial Statements

FSAP, the financial statement analysis package introduced in Chapter 1, contains a Forecast spreadsheet that you can use to prepare financial statement forecasts.[6] If you have not previously designed an Excel spreadsheet to prepare financial statement forecasts, you should do so *before* using the Forecast spreadsheet within FSAP. The proper design of a spreadsheet and the preparation of forecasted financial statements provide excellent learning experiences to enhance and solidify your understanding of the relationships between various financial statement items. Once you become comfortable with using spreadsheets for forecasting financial statements, then using the Forecast spreadsheet in FSAP will save time.

Note that the Forecast spreadsheet in FSAP is a general and adaptable template to use to forecast financial statements. In addition, FSAP contains a Forecast Development spreadsheet that provides a scratch pad for the analyst to derive and compute various forecast assumptions. To illustrate the use of the Forecast spreadsheet template and the Forecast Development scratch pad spreadsheet, we incorporate in FSAP the specific forecast assumptions we make for PepsiCo in this chapter. Appendix A presents the financial statements and notes from PepsiCo's Year 4 Annual Report. Appendix B presents PepsiCo's Management's Discussion and Analysis (MD&A) from the Year 4 Annual Report. Appendix C presents the output from FSAP for PepsiCo, including printouts of the Forecast spreadsheet within FSAP for PepsiCo, with explicit financial statement forecast assumptions through Year +5, as well as the Forecast Development spreadsheet with various supporting computations. The analyst will need to reprogram the assumptions made within the Forecast spreadsheet and the Forecast Development spreadsheet to capture the specific forecast assumptions for other companies. Appendix D contains a user manual for FSAP with helpful coaching tips.

All financial statement amounts throughout this chapter appear in millions. The spreadsheets take all computations to multiple decimal places. Because we express all amounts in this chapter in millions, some minor rounding differences will occasionally arise and make it appear that various subtotals and totals disagree with the sum of the individual items that make up the subtotal or total.

---

[5]Previous chapters have analyzed the most recent three years of data to evaluate PepsiCo's current profitability, risk, and accounting quality. In forecasting financial statements that extend one to five years or more into the future, it is often helpful for the analyst to draw on a longer time series of historical data to evaluate a firm's long-term trends. This is particularly helpful for stable, mature firms like PepsiCo, allowing reliable comparisons between data for Year 0 and data for Year 4. For some firms in the introduction phase of the life cycle, or firms that have recently experienced significant mergers or divestitures, a long time series of historical data may not be available or may not provide for reliable comparisons with current period data.

[6]The web site for this text (www.thomsonedu.com/accounting/stickney) contains the FSAP template for easy downloading and use.

STEP 1: PROJECTING SALES AND OTHER REVENUES

Projecting Revenues from Sales

The principal business activities of most firms involve generating revenues, which commonly involve selling products or delivering services. Analysts therefore commonly begin the process of forecasting financial statements by projecting revenues from the principal business activities of the firm. For many types of firms, analysts use the expected future level of revenues as a basis for deriving many other amounts in the financial statement forecasts.

Sales volumes and prices determine sales numbers. In the case of sales *volume*, some firms report sales volume figures (for example, automobile manufacturers report numbers of vehicles sold and beverage makers report gallons or servings sold), enabling the analyst to assess separately volume and price as drivers of historical sales growth, and to use them as a framework for predicting future sales. Other types of firms report volume-related measures of operating activities that the analyst can use to forecast sales, such as new stores for retailers and restaurant chains, and passengers and revenue-seat-miles for airlines. For a stable firm in a mature industry (for example, consumer foods), an analyst may conclude that the firm will not likely increase its market share, so the analyst might anticipate sales volume increases equal to the growth rate in the population within the firm's geographic markets. For a firm that has increased its operating capacity within a particular industry with high anticipated growth (for example, biotechnology or computer software), the analyst might consider using the industry growth rate coupled with the potential growth in the firm's operating capacity when projecting volume increases.

When projecting *prices*, the analyst should consider economy-wide factors such as the expected rate of general price inflation in the economy and the effects of changes in currency exchange rates on sales denominated in foreign currencies. When projecting prices, the analyst should also consider factors specific to the firm and its industry that might affect demand and price elasticity, such as excess or constrained capacity, raw materials surpluses or shortages, substitute products, and technological changes in products or production methods. Capital-intensive firms, such as manufacturers of paper products or computer chips, may require several years to add new capacity. If a firm competes in a capital-intensive industry that the analyst expects will operate near capacity for the next few years, then price increases will be more likely. On the other hand, if a firm competes in a capital-intensive industry in which excess capacity already exists or new capacity will become available soon, then price increases will be less likely. Further, a capital-intensive firm with excess capacity in a competitive industry may face high exit barriers, and thus may experience future price decreases. A firm in transition from the high growth to the mature phase of its life cycle, or a firm with significant technological improvements in its production processes (for example, some portions of the computer industry), might expect increases in sales volume but decreases in sales prices per unit. If a firm has established a competitive position for its brand name in its markets, or has successfully differentiated unique characteristics for its products, then that firm may have a greater potential to increase prices, or to avoid price declines, than a competitor firm with generic products.

If sales have grown at a reasonably steady rate in prior periods and nothing indicates that economic, industry, or firm-specific factors will change significantly, then the analyst can project that the historical sales growth rate will persist into the future. If the firm's historical sales growth rate is affected by a major acquisition or divestiture, then the analyst should adjust for the effects of this event when making projections (unless the firm's strategy is to make additional acquisitions or divestitures). Projecting sales for a firm with a cyclical sales pattern (for example, heavy machinery manufacturers, property-casualty insurers, and investment banks) can prove difficult. For cyclical firms, their historical growth rates for sales often reflect wide variations in both direction and amount over the business cycle. For such firms, the analyst can project a varying sales growth rate that reflects this cyclical sales pattern, as long as the analyst can identify the current point in the cycle.

Earlier chapters indicated that the consumer foods industry in the United States is mature. Industry sales have grown recently at the growth rate for the general population, approximately 2 percent per year. Consumer foods companies that have achieved growth rates higher than 2 percent have relied primarily on corporate acquisitions and expansions into international sales markets as vehicles for growth. PepsiCo has defied these industry averages, generating a compounded rate of growth in net revenues from continuing operations of 8.2 percent between Year 2 and Year 4. PepsiCo discloses in the MD&A section titled "Results of Continuing Operations—Consolidated Review" (Appendix B) information about net sales over these years, including the effects of divestitures in Years 2 and 3. Net revenue (amounts in millions) and growth rates for PepsiCo appear here:

	Year 2	Year 3	Year 4
Total Revenue Amounts	$25,112	$26,971	$29,261
Less: Divested Businesses	−134	−2	—
Net Revenue Amounts	$24,978	$26,969	$29,261
Growth Rates		+8.0%	+8.5%
Compound Growth Rate			+8.2%

In PepsiCo's Year 4 Annual Report, the MD&A section titled "Results of Continuing Operations—Division Review" (Appendix B) discloses information about sales and operating profits for each of PepsiCo's four major operating segments, grouped by product and geography: Frito-Lay North America (snack foods); PepsiCo Beverages North America (beverages); PepsiCo International (snack foods and beverages); and Quaker Foods North America (cereals and breakfast foods). For each segment, PepsiCo discloses growth rates in sales volume, which the analyst can use to evaluate the growth in demand for PepsiCo's products and to infer growth rates in average unit prices for each segment. These data on PepsiCo's sales amounts and sales volumes reveal significant differences in volume and price growth rates across their four segments. Net sales amounts from continuing operations, sales growth rates, volume growth rates, and price growth rates by segment for PepsiCo appear in Exhibit 10.2. By analyzing these volume and price growth data across different segments, an analyst can develop a more detailed and accurate understanding of the drivers of PepsiCo's sales growth, and therefore develop more reliable sales forecasts for each segment.

EXHIBIT 10.2

PepsiCo
Sales Growth Analysis by Segment

	Year 2	Year 3	Year 4
Frito-Lay North America			
Sales	$8,565	$9,091	$9,560
Percentage of total sales	34.3%	33.7%	32.7%
Growth rates		+6.1%	+5.2%
Compound annual growth rate			+5.6%
Compound annual growth in sales volume			+3.5%
Compound annual growth rate in prices			+2.0%
PepsiCo Beverages North America			
Sales	$7,200	$7,733	$8,313
Percentage of total sales	28.8%	28.7%	28.4%
Growth rates		+7.4%	+7.5%
Compound annual growth rate			+7.5%
Compound annual growth in sales volume			+3.0%
Compound annual growth rate in prices			+4.3%
PepsiCo International			
Sales	$7,749	$8,678	$9,862
Percentage of total sales	31.0%	32.2%	33.7%
Growth rates		+12.0%	+13.6%
Compound annual growth rate			+12.8%
Compound annual growth in sales volume			+8.5%
Compound annual growth rate in prices			+4.0%
Quaker Foods North America			
Sales	$1,464	$1,467	$1,526
Percentage of total sales	5.9%	5.4%	5.2%
Growth rates		+0.2%	+4.0%
Compound annual growth rate			+2.1%
Compound annual growth in sales volume			+1.5%
Compound annual growth rate in prices			+0.6%

Frito-Lay North America Sales Growth

The Frito-Lay North America segment generates PepsiCo's revenues from selling snack foods in the United States and Canada. The segment generated a compound annual sales growth rate of 5.6 percent between Years 2 and 4. PepsiCo discloses that Frito-Lay North America experienced a 3.5 percent per year compounded growth in sales volume during this period. This implies that it also experienced a 2.0 percent annual compounded growth in prices, including the effects of foreign exchange (1.056 = 1.035 × 1.020). Sales volume growth has been led by strength in its core brands, as well as new-product introductions. The modest increase in prices likely reflects the relatively price-competitive snack foods markets. An analyst might expect that sales volume growth will continue at 3.5 percent per year into the future, based on the continuing strength of Frito-Lay's core brands and its continuing ability to develop and introduce successful new products. One might also expect that future price increases will be limited to 2 percent per year, because of the competitive and mature nature of the snack foods industry in North America. These assumptions produce an annual sales growth rate of 5.6 percent (that is, 1.056 = 1.035 × 1.020).

In Year +1, PepsiCo's fiscal year (which ends on the last Saturday of December each year) will contain 53 weeks of business activity. To capture this effect in our sales forecasts for Frito-Lay North America in Year +1, we project an overall sales growth rate of 7.6 percent (that is, 1.076 = 1.035 × 1.020 × [53/52]).[7]

In Year +2, PepsiCo's fiscal year will revert to a 52-week year. Because we use the Year +1 forecast to project the Year +2 forecast, we must account for the fact that Year +2 will be one week shorter than Year +1. We therefore project a sales growth rate of 3.6 percent for Year +2 (that is, 1.036 = 1.035 × 1.020 × [52/53]). PepsiCo will not encounter another 53-week fiscal year for several years in the future, so we ignore the effects on our sales forecasts in Year +3 and beyond.

Our sales projections and growth rates for Frito-Lay North America over the first five years of the forecast horizon are as follows (allow for rounding):

Year 4 actual	$ 9,560	
Year +1 forecast	$10,287	+7.6%
Year +2 forecast	$10,655	+3.6%
Year +3 forecast	$11,248	+5.6%
Year +4 forecast	$11,875	+5.6%
Year +5 forecast	$12,536	+5.6%

PepsiCo Beverages North America Sales Growth

PepsiCo's Beverages segment in the United States and Canada experienced a compound annual sales growth rate of 7.5 percent between Years 2 and 4, which includes sales volume growth of 3.0 percent and sales price growth (including the effects of foreign exchange) of 4.3 percent. PepsiCo discloses that noncarbonated beverages (Gatorade, Aquafina, Propel) generated the strongest sales growth rates in the beverages segment, whereas carbonated soft drink and juice products generated positive but slower sales growth. The beverage segment experienced greater price growth (4.3 percent) than the snack foods segment (2.0 percent), which likely reflects a more concentrated, less price-competitive product market for beverages. An analyst might expect that PepsiCo's beverage segment will continue to sustain 3.0 percent growth in sales volume in the

[7]To further illustrate the 53rd-week effect on our sales forecasts, take Frito-Lay North America's Year 4 sales of $9,560 and assume 3.5 percent growth in sales volume compounded with 2.0 percent growth in sales prices, for a total sales growth rate of 5.6 percent. Applying that growth rate to Year 4 sales to obtain the Year +1 projection yields $9,560 × 1.056 = $10,093. If Year +1 were a 52-week year, we would expect sales to be $10,093 for the year, which implies sales of $194 per week. When we add a 53rd week to our sales projection, we end up with a sales forecast of $10,093 + $194 = $10,287 = $9,560 × 1.035 × 1.020 × (53/52), for a total sales growth rate of 7.6 percent.

future because it has a deep and broad portfolio of branded products that span the beverages market (carbonated soft drinks, sports drinks, waters, juices, coffees, teas, etc.). One may also expect that 4.3 percent price growth, which exceeded the rate of inflation in North America during that same period, is unsustainable and that PepsiCo will generate and sustain only 3.0 percent growth in prices in the future, closer to the economy-wide inflation rate. Together, these assumptions create an annual sales growth rate of 6.1 percent.

After including the 53rd-week effect, the sales growth rate in Year +1 should be 8.1 percent (that is, 1.081 = 1.03 × 1.03 × [53/52]). After reversing the 53rd-week effect on sales growth in Year +2, the sales growth rate in Year +2 should be 4.1 percent (that is, 1.041 = 1.03 × 1.03 × [52/53]). In Year +3 and thereafter, we will assume sales growth rates of 6.1 percent. Sales forecast amounts and growth rates for the PepsiCo Beverages North America segment over the first five years of the forecast horizon are as follows:

Year 4 actual	$ 8,313	
Year +1 forecast	$ 8,989	+8.1%
Year +2 forecast	$ 9,356	+4.1%
Year +3 forecast	$ 9,926	+6.1%
Year +4 forecast	$10,531	+6.1%
Year +5 forecast	$11,172	+6.1%

PepsiCo International Sales Growth

PepsiCo's International segment sells PepsiCo snack food and beverage products around the world (except in the United States and Canada, which are covered by the Frito-Lay North America and PepsiCo Beverages North America segments). The International segment is the fastest-growing segment of PepsiCo, becoming the largest revenue-producing segment in Year 4. The International segment experienced a compound annual sales growth rate of 12.8 percent between Years 2 and 4, which includes sales volume growth (including the effects of acquisitions) of 8.5 percent and sales price growth (including the effects of foreign exchange) of 4.0 percent. PepsiCo discloses that net revenue growth in the International segment was fueled by significant growth rates in sales volumes for snack foods and beverages in the Latin America, Asia Pacific, Europe, Middle East, and Africa regions. International sales growth was also fueled in part by favorable movements in the British pound and the euro relative to the U.S. dollar, partially offset by unfavorable movements in the Mexican peso relative to the dollar. In Year 4 alone, foreign currency exchange rate movements added 4.0 percent to the International segment's revenue growth.

Based on its track record of international growth, an analyst might expect PepsiCo's International segment to sustain 6.0 percent growth in sales volume in the near future. Assuming that favorable foreign currency movements will not persist into the future, an analyst might expect the International segment to sustain 3.0 percent growth in prices into the future. After including the 53rd-week effect on projected sales for Year +1, the sales growth rate forecast for the International segment in Year +1 should be 11.3 percent (that is, 1.113 = 1.06 × 1.03 × [53/52]). After reversing the 53rd-week effect on projected sales for Year +2, the sales growth rate forecast for the International segment in Year +2 should be 7.1 percent (that is, 1.071 = 1.06 × 1.03 × [52/53]). Thereafter, sales growth rates should average 9.2 percent per year. Sales amounts and growth rates for PepsiCo's International segment over the first five years of the forecast horizon are as follows:

Year 4 actual	$ 9,862	
Year +1 forecast	$10,974	+11.3%
Year +2 forecast	$11,756	+7.1%
Year +3 forecast	$12,835	+9.2%
Year +4 forecast	$14,013	+9.2%
Year +5 forecast	$15,300	+9.2%

Quaker Foods North America Sales Growth

The Quaker Foods North America segment sells cereals and breakfast foods. It is a very stable division in a mature and competitive industry. The Quaker Foods segment experienced modest sales growth over Years 2 to 4, averaging 2.1 percent per year. Quaker Foods' sales growth is the result of an average 1.5 percent growth in sales volume compounded by an average 0.6 percent increase in prices, mainly attributable to favorable effects of foreign exchange rates on prices. Looking ahead, an analyst might expect this segment to maintain 1.0 percent growth in volume and 1.0 percent price increases, leading to a steady 2.0 percent growth in net sales per year, on average. In Year +1, we expect Quaker to generate a 4.0 percent sales growth due to the effect of the 53rd week (that is, $1.040 = 1.010 \times 1.010 \times [53/52]$). In Year +2, after reversing the 53rd-week effect, we expect Quaker to experience only a 0.1 percent growth rate in sales (that is, $1.001 = 1.010 \times 1.010 \times [52/53]$). Sales forecast amounts and growth rates for the Quaker Foods North America segment over the first five years of the forecast horizon are as follows:

Year 4 actual	$1,526	
Year +1 forecast	$1,587	+4.0%
Year +2 forecast	$1,588	+0.1%
Year +3 forecast	$1,620	+2.0%
Year +4 forecast	$1,652	+2.0%
Year +5 forecast	$1,686	+2.0%

Combined Sales Growth

The following table combines the sales forecasts for each of these four segments. The table presents the projected sales amount for each segment, segment sales expressed as a percentage of total net sales (in parentheses), PepsiCo's total net sales, and annual sales growth rates for each year through forecast Year +5:

Year	Frito-Lay North America	PepsiCo Beverages North America	PepsiCo International	Quaker Foods North America	PepsiCo Total Net Sales	Sales Growth Rate
4 actual	$ 9,560 (32.7%)	$ 8,313 (28.4%)	$ 9,862 (33.7%)	$1,526 (5.2%)	$29,261 (100.0%)	
+1 forecast	$10,287 (32.3%)	$ 8,989 (28.2%)	$10,974 (34.5%)	$1,587 (5.0%)	$31,836 (100.0%)	8.8%
+2 forecast	$10,655 (31.9%)	$ 9,356 (28.1%)	$11,756 (35.2%)	$1,588 (4.8%)	$33,355 (100.0%)	4.8%
+3 forecast	$11,248 (31.6%)	$ 9,926 (27.9%)	$12,835 (36.0%)	$1,620 (4.5%)	$35,629 (100.0%)	6.8%
+4 forecast	$11,875 (31.2%)	$10,531 (27.7%)	$14,013 (36.8%)	$1,652 (4.3%)	$38,071 (100.0%)	6.9%
+5 forecast	$12,536 (30.8%)	$11,172 (27.5%)	$15,300 (37.6%)	$1,686 (4.1%)	$40,693 (100.0%)	6.9%

The Forecast spreadsheet within FSAP gives the analyst the opportunity to input specific forecast parameters (such as sales growth rates) for Year +1 through Year +5, as well as general forecast parameters for Year +6 and beyond. For Years +1 through +5, we will enter the sales growth rates and amounts shown previously. The forecast parameters for Year +6 and beyond represent general forecast assumptions over the long-run horizon. We assume PepsiCo will sustain a 3.0 percent sales growth rate in Year +6 and beyond, consistent with long-run growth in the economy and expected long-run inflation that together will average 3.0 percent per year.

The analyst can use the Forecast Development spreadsheet within FSAP to develop detailed revenues forecasts, capturing the key drivers of the firm's sales growth. We have done that here by analyzing and forecasting PepsiCo's sales volume growth and price growth separately for each of PepsiCo's four operating segments, and then combining these forecasts into an aggregate sales forecast for PepsiCo through Year +5. Appendix C provides an example of how we used the Forecast Development spreadsheet in FSAP to develop our sales forecasts for PepsiCo.

Projecting Other Revenues

Other revenues for PepsiCo primarily include income from equity investments in noncontrolled bottling operations and other affiliates. To forecast future income from equity investments in bottling affiliates, one can assume PepsiCo will earn a normal rate of return on its investments in these bottling affiliates, in which case the rate of expected return and the level of investment will drive the income amounts from unconsolidated bottling affiliates. In Year 4, PepsiCo recognized $380 million in bottling equity income on investments in noncontrolled affiliates with an average book value of $3,102 million [= ($2,920 + $3,284)/2], for a return of roughly 12 percent.[8] This rate of return seems a bit high because bottling companies are relatively low-risk, low-profit-margin businesses, and the income recognized by PepsiCo on these investments has already been adjusted for the income taxes paid by the affiliates (PepsiCo does not have to pay taxes on income from these investments until it receives dividends or sells a portion of the investment). However, in Note 8, "Noncontrolled Bottling Affiliates" (Appendix A), PepsiCo discloses that its two largest equity investments in unconsolidated bottlers have fair values that exceed their book values by a total of nearly $2 billion. Thus, the average rate of return relative to the fair value of these investments is between 7 and 8 percent, which seems reasonable relative to the risk of such investments. Therefore, assuming PepsiCo will continue to earn a similar return on these investments, an analyst can project Bottling Equity Income in future years to be 12.0 percent of the annual average book value of Investments in Noncontrolled Affiliates. We base these forecasts on future book values of these investments (rather than fair values) because the book value amounts will be necessary to forecast the balance sheet. We will describe our projections of book value amounts of Investments in Noncontrolled Affiliates when we project the assets on the balance sheet, so for now,

[8]This computation assumes that the bottling equity income account on the income statement can be compared directly to the investments in noncontrolled affiliates account on the balance sheet. This is not likely to be strictly true because PepsiCo likely aggregates other, nonbottling affiliates in the balance sheet account. In Note 8, "Noncontrolled Bottling Affiliates" (Appendix A), PepsiCo discloses that the most significant noncontrolled affiliates are bottling companies, so the computation is a reasonable estimate of PepsiCo's return on these investments.

accept the following projected investment amounts as given. The projected amounts for other revenues from Bottling Equity Income follow:

Projections of Investments in Noncontrolled Affiliates and Other Revenues from Bottling Equity Income

	Investments in Noncontrolled Affiliates				Other Revenues:
Year	Beginning Balance	Ending Balance	Average Balance	Rate of Return	Bottling Equity Income
+1	$3,284	$3,573	$3,428	12.0%	$411
+2	$3,573	$3,680	$3,626	12.0%	$435
+3	$3,680	$3,930	$3,805	12.0%	$457
+4	$3,930	$4,097	$4,013	12.0%	$482
+5	$4,097	$4,368	$4,232	12.0%	$508

STEP 2: PROJECTING OPERATING EXPENSES

The procedure for projecting operating expenses depends on the degree to which the various operating expense items have fixed or variable components. If certain operating expenses behave as variable costs that vary directly with sales, and if the analyst anticipates no changes in the relation between these expenses and sales, then the analyst can project these future operating expenses using common-size income statement percentages for such expenses relative to sales. We would multiply projected sales by the cost of goods sold percentage, by the selling and administrative expense percentage, and so on, to derive the amounts for operating expenses that vary directly with sales. Equivalently, we can project those operating expenses to grow at the same rate as sales.

More commonly, if operating expenses reflect cost structures with components of fixed costs that will not change linearly with sales (for example, the firm may experience economies of scale as sales increase or may face expenses that are fixed even if sales decrease), then using the common-size income statement approach can result in operating expense projections that are too high or too low. In this case, the analyst should attempt to estimate the variable- and fixed-cost structure of those particular operating expenses. Capital-intensive manufacturing firms often have high proportions of fixed costs in their cost structures, particularly from depreciation on property, plant, and equipment, and fixed labor charges. When the percentage change in costs of goods sold or selling, general, and administrative expenses in prior years is significantly less than the percentage change in sales, one can usually assume the presence of fixed costs. Using the historical growth rates for individual operating expense items relative to the growth rates in sales is one way to capture the effects of different mixes of variable and fixed costs. An analyst can also capture these effects by creating a separate schedule to forecast future depreciation expense amounts that tend to vary with capital spending on property, plant, and equipment rather than sales (demonstrated later in this chapter).

When projecting operating expenses as a percentage of sales, the analyst should keep in mind that an expense as a percentage of sales can change over time as follows: (a) as expenses change, holding sales constant; (b) as sales change, holding expenses constant; (c) both types of change occur simultaneously and in the same direction; or (d) both types of change occur simultaneously but in opposite directions. As an example of case (a), the analyst may expect an expense to become a smaller fraction of sales over time if the firm will create economies of scale or increased operating efficiencies. As an example of case (b), the analyst may expect that the firm will hold expenses (such as cost of goods sold) relatively steady, but will face increased competition for sales and therefore may be forced to lower sales prices, causing the expected expense-to-sales ratio to increase. In case (c), if the analyst expects both sales and operating expenses to increase (or decrease) simultaneously, the net result on the projected expense-to-sales percentage will depend on which of the two effects will be proportionally greater. In case (d), if the analyst expects sales to increase while operating expenses decrease (as might occur for a firm in transition from a start-up phase to a growth phase of its life cycle), or vice versa (sales decrease while operating expenses increase, as might occur for a firm in distress), the net result on the projected expense-to-sales percentage will depend on the direction and relative magnitudes of the two countervailing effects.

Projecting Cost of Goods Sold

The common-size income statement analysis in Chapter 4 and the common-size income statement data in the Analysis spreadsheet of FSAP (Appendix C) indicate that PepsiCo's cost of goods sold percentage has been steady, averaging 45.8 percent of sales over the five years from Year 0 to Year 4. Most recently, PepsiCo's cost of goods sold percentage ranged from 45.8 percent in Year 2 to 45.9 percent in Year 3 to 45.8 percent in Year 4. This pattern suggests that PepsiCo's cost of goods sold behaves like a variable cost. Based on the recent steady performance in controlling cost of goods sold, an analyst might be inclined to project future cost of goods sold using a similar percentage. Nothing in our analysis thus far suggests that PepsiCo's cost of goods sold percentage will rise dramatically in the future, either because PepsiCo will face future cost increases for its products or because it will face decreasing selling prices for its products. An analyst might consider whether PepsiCo will be able to improve its performance and reduce the cost of goods sold percentage over time, either by cutting costs or by increasing selling prices for its products without proportional increases in the cost of goods sold. For example, one could consider whether PepsiCo will gain further efficiencies in cost of goods sold in the future, because its main competitor in the beverage business, Coca-Cola, dropped its cost of goods sold percentage from 36.3 percent to 34.8 percent of sales over Years 2 to 4. Perhaps it is possible for PepsiCo to further reduce its cost of sales to approach Coca-Cola's cost levels. We do not make this assumption, however, because, unlike Coca-Cola, which is purely a beverage company, PepsiCo's sales include a high proportion of snack foods and breakfast foods, which likely have higher costs as a percentage of sales than beverages. Thus, we predict that PepsiCo will maintain a steady cost of goods sold at 45.8 percent of sales through Year +5 and beyond. Our cost of goods sold forecasts through Year +5 follow:

	Sales	Percentage of Sales	Cost of Goods Sold
Year +1 Projected	$31,836	45.8%	$14,581
Year +2 Projected	$33,355	45.8%	$15,276
Year +3 Projected	$35,629	45.8%	$16,318
Year +4 Projected	$38,071	45.8%	$17,436
Year +5 Projected	$40,693	45.8%	$18,638

Projecting Selling, General, and Administrative Expenses

The common-size income statement data reveal that PepsiCo's selling, general, and administrative expenses as a percentage of sales trended from 35.6 percent in Year 0 up to 36.5 percent in Year 1, and then down to 35.1 percent in Year 3 and 35.2 percent in Year 4. On this dimension, PepsiCo outperformed its rival Coca-Cola, which experienced steady selling, general, and administrative expenses of 37.6 percent of sales in Year 3 and 37.5 percent of sales in Year 4. An analyst might reasonably assume that a firm will achieve incremental efficiencies in future selling, general, and administrative expenses and reduce this percentage over time, particularly for young and growing firms with the potential to generate economies of scale or scope, or operating synergies. For a mature firm with the scale and scope of PepsiCo, it may be difficult to generate significant additional incremental efficiencies in future selling, general, and administrative expenses. We therefore project that PepsiCo will maintain selling, general, and administrative expenses equal to roughly 35.2 percent of sales in the future.

As the title of this expense account implies, selling, general, and administrative expenses encompass a wide range of operating expenses. In Note 2, "Our Significant Accounting Policies" (Appendix A), PepsiCo discloses that in Year 4, selling, general, and administrative expenses includes $1,700 million in advertising expenses, $3,300 million in shipping and handling expenses, and other amounts for expenses for compensation and employee benefits, rent, and various other expenses. If the analyst expects these individual expense items to be driven by factors other than sales growth, then the analyst may prefer to project these items individually and then sum them to obtain total selling, general, and administrative expense projections.

In the MD&A section titled "Our Critical Accounting Policies" (Appendix B), PepsiCo discusses its policies for accounting for stock-based compensation expense, which is a component of selling, general, and administrative expenses. PepsiCo discloses that it accounts for employee stock options by expensing the fair value of stock options as part of stock-based compensation expense at the date of grant, using a modified Black-Scholes valuation model. The firm discloses that stock-based compensation expense amounted to $368 million in Year 4. PepsiCo's rival Coca-Cola follows a similar accounting policy. Because PepsiCo includes the fair value of stock-based compensation as an expense in income, our projections of future selling, general, and administrative expenses implicitly include a component for stock-based compensation costs. We will project stock issues and repurchases for stock options exercises later in the chapter, when we project common shareholders' equity accounts.

The projected amounts for selling, general, and administrative expenses are as follows:

	Sales	Percentage of Sales	Selling, General, and Administrative Expenses
Year +1 Projected	$31,836	35.2%	$11,206
Year +2 Projected	$33,355	35.2%	$11,741
Year +3 Projected	$35,629	35.2%	$12,541
Year +4 Projected	$38,071	35.2%	$13,401
Year +5 Projected	$40,693	35.2%	$14,324

Projecting Other Operating Expenses

PepsiCo recognized other operating expenses that represent 0.5 percent of sales during Years 2 through 4. These expenses represent amortization of intangibles, such as brands and trademarks with limited useful lives (ranging from five to twenty years). The book value of PepsiCo's amortizable intangible assets amounts to $598 million on the Year 4 balance sheet. In Note 4, "Property, Plant, and Equipment and Intangible Assets" (Appendix A), PepsiCo discloses that it expects amortization expense for these intangible assets to amount to $141 million in Year +1, $140 million in Year +2, $24 million in Year +3, $23 million in Year +4, and $22 million in Year +5, based on Year 4 foreign-exchange rates and assuming no additional investments in amortizable intangible assets over that period. We therefore adopt these amounts as our forecasts for PepsiCo's amortization expense over this forecast horizon. We also use these amounts to reduce the net book value of the amortizable intangible asset account balance each year.

U.S. GAAP does not require amortization of goodwill or other intangible assets deemed to have indefinite useful lives. Goodwill ($3,909 million) and other nonamortizable intangible assets ($933 million) represent roughly 89 percent of PepsiCo's total intangible assets on the Year 4 balance sheet. In our forecasts we include no amortization expense for these nonamortizable intangibles.

Projecting Nonrecurring Operating Gains and Losses

PepsiCo recognized other operating losses that reflect merger-related charges for the merger with Quaker in Years 2 and 3. It also recognized impairment and restructuring charges in Year 3 in conjunction with actions taken to streamline the North American divisions and PepsiCo International and in Year 4 for consolidation of Frito-Lay North America's manufacturing network. We will accept PepsiCo's classification of these items as nonrecurring components of operations, and forecast that these amounts will be zero in the future.

Exhibit 10.3 presents forecasts of PepsiCo's income statements, as well as comprehensive income and the change in retained earnings, for Years +1 through +5. The format of this exhibit mirrors the format of the Forecast spreadsheet in FSAP (Appendix C). We discuss the projections of interest income, interest expense, income tax expense, net income, comprehensive income, and the change in retained earnings after projecting PepsiCo's balance sheet, which we discuss in the next sections.

STEP 3: PROJECTING THE ASSETS ON THE BALANCE SHEET

We prepare forecasts of the asset side of the balance sheet next. We project individual assets and then sum individual asset amounts to obtain total assets. We take this approach first to illustrate how to develop forecasts that capture different drivers of growth in different types of assets, allowing the mix of the firm's assets to change over time. Later in the chapter, we also briefly describe shortcut approaches for projecting total assets, such as using sales and total asset turnover rates to forecast total assets and then using the common-size balance sheet percentages to allocate this total among individual assets.

To develop forecasts of individual assets, the analyst must first link historical growth rates for individual assets to historical growth rates in sales or other activity-based drivers of assets. The analyst can then use those links to develop forecasts of individual assets based on sales growth forecasts, particularly for assets integrally related to operations such as accounts receivable, inventories, and fixed assets. For some types of assets, such as property, plant, and equipment and inventory, asset growth typically leads future sales growth. For other types of assets, such as accounts receivable, asset growth will lag sales growth. By using asset turnover rates to develop forecasts for individual assets, the analyst can capture the projected levels of operating activity and permit changes in the expected relations between individual assets and operating activities such as sales. Our projections of individual assets for PepsiCo illustrate the use of a combination of forecast drivers, including common-size percentages, growth rates, and asset turnovers. Exhibit 10.4 presents the projected balance sheets for PepsiCo through Year +5. The following sections discuss the projections of individual assets.

Projecting Cash

PepsiCo needs a certain amount of cash on hand to maintain sufficient liquidity for day-to-day operations. PepsiCo's cash holdings have fluctuated widely between Years 1 and 4. During Year 4, PepsiCo had an average cash balance roughly equivalent to 13 days of sales (computed as 365 days divided by the ratio of sales to the average balance in cash, or 365/[$29,261/([$820 + $1280]/2)]. By contrast, during Year 3, PepsiCo's average cash balance was roughly equivalent to 17 days of sales. PepsiCo's average cash balance varied between 13 and 17 days of sales in Years 1 and 2 as well. We assume that PepsiCo will maintain year-end cash balances equivalent to 15 days of sales, which is roughly the average number of days of sales held in cash during the period from Year 1 to Year 4.

Following this approach, we use our forecasts of sales and the number of days of sales in cash to compute the average balance in cash. For forecast Year +1, our sales forecast is $31,836 million (or an average of $87.2 million per day)[9] and we project that PepsiCo will hold an average of 15 days of sales in cash, for an average cash balance of $1,308 million. Given that the beginning balance in Year +1 is $1,280, it implies that the ending balance in cash will be $1,337 (that is, the implied ending balance equals two times the average balance minus the beginning balance). Our projected cash balances follow:

			Cash			
	Annual Sales Forecasts	Average Sales per Day	Days Sales in Cash	Average Cash Balance	Beginning Cash Balance	Ending Cash Balance
Year +1	$31,836	$ 87.2	15	$1,308	$1,280	$1,337
Year +2	$33,355	$ 91.4	15	$1,371	$1,337	$1,405
Year +3	$35,629	$ 97.6	15	$1,464	$1,405	$1,524
Year +4	$38,071	$104.3	15	$1,565	$1,523	$1,605
Year +5	$40,693	$111.5	15	$1,672	$1,605	$1,739

Forecasting Techniques. Because we rely on average cash balances to compute the number of days of sales in cash and to compute our forecasts, the preceding approach produces forecasts of the average and year-end cash balances. The analyst can use this approach for any asset and liability accounts that vary with sales, such as accounts receivable; inventories; property, plant, and equipment; and accounts payable. A desirable feature of using this approach to compute implied ending balances is that it provides a slightly greater degree of forecast precision. This approach will produce accurate forecasts of year-end account balances if the firm generates sales evenly throughout the year, and if the forecasted account varies reliably with sales. However, if the firm is likely to experience substantially different growth rates in sales and the forecasted account over the year,

[9]For greater forecast precision and internal consistency in forecast assumptions, the analyst could compute average sales per day in Year +1 using 371 days to reflect the fact that Year +1 will be a 53-week year (371 days = 53 weeks × 7 days), and using 365 days for Year +2 and beyond. For simplicity throughout this text, we use 365 days for turnover computations, which is common in practice.

EXHIBIT 10.3

PepsiCo
Actual and Forecast Statements of Net Income and Comprehensive Income and the Change in Retained Earnings
(amounts in millions; allow for rounding errors)

Actual and forecast amounts in bold; assumptions and brief explanations below forecast amounts.

	Actuals			Forecasts				
	Year 2	Year 3	Year 4	Year +1	Year +2	Year +3	Year +4	Year +5
INCOME STATEMENT								
Revenues	**$25,112**	**$26,971**	**$29,261**	**$31,836**	**$33,355**	**$35,629**	**$38,071**	**$40,693**
common size	100.0%	100.0%	100.0%	8.8%	4.8%	6.8%	6.9%	6.9%
rate of change		7.4%	8.5%	See Forecast Development worksheet for details of revenues forecasts.				
Cost of Goods Sold	**(11,497)**	**(12,379)**	**(13,406)**	**(14,581)**	**(15,276)**	**(16,318)**	**(17,436)**	**(18,638)**
common size	−45.8%	−45.9%	−45.8%	−45.8%	−45.8%	−45.8%	−45.8%	−45.8%
rate of change		7.7%	8.3%	Assume steady cost of goods sold as a percentage of sales.				
Gross Profit	**$13,615**	**$14,592**	**$15,855**	**$17,255**	**$18,078**	**$19,311**	**$20,634**	**$22,056**
common size	54.2%	54.1%	54.2%	54.2%	54.2%	54.2%	54.2%	54.2%
rate of change		7.2%	8.7%	8.8%	4.8%	6.8%	6.9%	6.9%
Selling, General, and Administrative Expense	**(8,958)**	**(9,460)**	**(10,299)**	**(11,206)**	**(11,741)**	**(12,541)**	**(13,401)**	**(14,324)**
common size	−35.7%	−35.1%	−35.2%	−35.2%	−35.2%	−35.2%	−35.2%	−35.2%
rate of change		5.6%	8.9%	Assume steady SG&A expense as a percentage of sales.				
Other Operating Expenses	**(138)**	**(145)**	**(147)**	**(141)**	**(140)**	**(24)**	**(23)**	**(22)**
common size	−0.5%	−0.5%	−0.5%	(141)	(140)	(24)	(23)	(22)
rate of change		5.1%	1.4%	Amortization expense amounts based on PepsiCo disclosures in Note 4.				
Nonrecurring Operating Losses	**(224)**	**(206)**	**(150)**	**0**	**0**	**0**	**0**	**0**
common size	−0.9%	−0.8%	−0.5%	0.0	0.0	0.0	0.0	0.0
rate of change		−8.0%	−27.2%	Assume zero.				
Operating Profit	**$ 4,295**	**$ 4,781**	**$ 5,259**	**$ 5,908**	**$ 6,197**	**$ 6,746**	**$ 7,210**	**$ 7,710**
common size	17.1%	17.7%	18.0%	18.6%	18.6%	18.9%	18.9%	18.9%
rate of change		11.3%	10.0%	12.3%	4.9%	8.8%	6.9%	6.9%

Interest Income	**36**	**51**	**74**	**91**	**97**	**101**	**107**	**113**
common size	0.1%	0.2%	0.3%	4.0%	4.0%	4.0%	4.0%	4.0%
rate of change		41.7%	45.1%	Interest rate earned on average balance in marketable securities.				
Interest Expense	**(178)**	**(163)**	**(167)**	**(204)**	**(203)**	**(220)**	**(239)**	**(243)**
common size	−0.7%	−0.6%	−0.6%	−6.0%	−6.0%	−6.0%	−6.0%	−(6.0%)
rate of change		−8.4%	2.5%	Interest rate paid on average balance in financial liabilities.				
Other Income or Gains	**280**	**323**	**380**	**411**	**435**	**457**	**482**	**508**
common size	1.1%	1.2%	1.3%	12.0%	12.0%	12.0%	12.0%	12.0%
rate of change		15.4%	17.6%	Assume normal return of 12% on bottling investments.				
Income before Tax	**$4,433**	**$4,992**	**$5,546**	**$6,207**	**$6,526**	**$7,084**	**$7,561**	**$8,088**
common size	17.7%	18.5%	19.0%	19.5%	19.6%	19.9%	19.9%	19.9%
rate of change		12.6%	11.1%	11.9%	5.2%	8.5%	6.7%	7.0%
Income Tax Expense	**(1,433)**	**(1,424)**	**(1,372)**	**(1,825)**	**(2,023)**	**(2,196)**	**(2,344)**	**(2,507)**
common size	−5.7%	−5.3%	−4.7%	−29.4%	−31.0%	−31.0%	−31.0%	−31.0%
rate of change		−0.6%	−3.7%	Effective income tax rate assumptions (negative %).				
NET INCOME	**$3,000**	**$3,568**	**$4,212**	**$4,382**	**$4,503**	**$4,888**	**$5,217**	**$5,580**
common size	11.9%	13.2%	14.4%	13.8%	13.5%	13.7%	13.7%	13.7%
rate of change		18.9%	18.0%	4.0%	2.8%	8.5%	6.7%	7.0%
Other Comprehensive Income Items	**(26)**	**405**	**381**	**0**	**0**	**0**	**0**	**0**
....	−0.1%	1.5%	1.3%	0.0	0.0	0.0	0.0	0.0
....		−1657.7%	−5.9%	Assume zero.				
COMPREHENSIVE INCOME	**$2,974**	**$3,973**	**$4,593**	**$4,382**	**$4,503**	**$4,888**	**$5,217**	**$5,580**
common size	11.8%	14.7%	15.7%	13.8%	13.5%	13.7%	13.7%	13.7%
rate of change		33.6%	15.6%	−4.6%	2.8%	8.5%	6.7%	7.0%
NET INCOME	**$3,000**	**$3,568**	**$4,212**	**$4,382**	**$4,503**	**$4,888**	**$5,217**	**$5,580**
Common Dividends	(1,042)	(1,082)	(1,438)	(1,763)	(2,404)	(2,489)	(2,644)	(2,473)
Preferred Stock Retirement	(4)	(3)	(3)	(159)	0	0	0	0
Other Adjustments	0	(11)	(2)	0	0	0	0	0
CHANGE IN RETAINED EARNINGS	**$1,954**	**$2,472**	**$2,769**	**$2,459**	**$2,099**	**$2,399**	**$2,573**	**$3,107**

EXHIBIT 10.4

PepsiCo Actual and Forecast Balance Sheets (amounts in millions; allow for rounding errors)

Actual and forecast amounts in bold; assumptions and brief explanations below forecast amounts.

	Actuals			Forecasts				
	Year 2	Year 3	Year 4	Year +1	Year +2	Year +3	Year +4	Year +5
ASSETS:								
Cash	**$ 1,638**	**$ 820**	**$ 1,280**	**$ 1,337**	**$ 1,405**	**$ 1,524**	**$ 1,605**	**$ 1,739**
common size	7.0%	3.2%	4.6%	15.0	15.0	15.0	15.0	15.0
rate of change		−49.9%	56.1%	Assume cash balances equal to 15 days of sales.				
Marketable Securities	**207**	**1,181**	**2,165**	**2,382**	**2,454**	**2,620**	**2,732**	**2,912**
common size	0.9%	4.7%	7.7%	8.0%	8.0%	8.0%	8.0%	8.0%
rate of change		470.5%	83.3%	Assume 8 percent of total assets, in line with last year.				
Accounts Receivable—Trade	**2,531**	**2,830**	**2,999**	**3,281**	**3,298**	**3,730**	**3,780**	**4,247**
common size	10.8%	11.2%	10.7%	36.0	36.0	36.0	36.0	36.0
rate of change		11.8%	6.0%	Assume 36 days to collect accounts receivable.				
Inventories	**1,342**	**1,412**	**1,541**	**1,664**	**1,694**	**1,893**	**1,940**	**2,157**
common size	5.7%	5.6%	5.5%	9.1	9.1	9.1	9.1	9.1
rate of change		5.2%	9.1%	Assume average inventory turnover 9.1 times per year.				
Other Current Assets	**695**	**687**	**654**	**596**	**613**	**655**	**683**	**728**
common size	3.0%	2.7%	2.3%	2.0%	2.0%	2.0%	2.0%	2.0%
rate of change		−1.2%	−4.8%	Assume 2.0 percent of total assets.				
CURRENT ASSETS	**$ 6,413**	**$ 6,930**	**$ 8,639**	**$ 9,259**	**$ 9,464**	**$10,421**	**$10,740**	**$11,783**
common size	27.3%	27.4%	30.9%	31.1%	30.9%	31.8%	31.5%	32.4%
rate of change		8.1%	24.7%	7.2%	2.2%	10.1%	3.1%	9.7%
Long-Term Investments	**2,611**	**2,920**	**3,284**	**3,573**	**3,680**	**3,930**	**4,097**	**4,368**
common size	11.1%	11.5%	11.7%	12%	12%	12%	12%	12%
rate of change		11.8%	12.5%	Assume 12.0 percent of total assets.				
Property, Plant, and Equipment, at cost	**13,395**	**14,755**	**15,930**	**17,522**	**19,190**	**20,971**	**22,875**	**24,909**
common size	57.1%	58.3%	56.9%	1,592	1,668	1,781	1,904	2,035
rate of change		10.2%	8.0%	PP&E assumptions—see schedule in Forecast Development spreadsheet in FSAP.				
Accumulated Depreciation	**(6,005)**	**(6,927)**	**(7,781)**	**(8,994)**	**(10,322)**	**(11,774)**	**(13,357)**	**(15,081)**
common size	−25.6%	−27.4%	−27.8%	(1,213)	(1,328)	(1,452)	(1,583)	(1,724)
rate of change		15.4%	12.3%	See depreciation schedule in Forecast Development spreadsheet in FSAP.				
Amortizable Intangible Assets, net	**801**	**718**	**598**	**457**	**317**	**293**	**270**	**248**
common size	3.4%	2.8%	2.1%	(141.0)	(140.0)	(24.0)	(23.0)	(22.0)
rate of change		−10.4%	−16.7%	Assume amortization amounts per PepsiCo disclosures; no new investments.				
Goodwill and Nonamortizable Intangibles	**4,418**	**4,665**	**4,842**	**5,268**	**5,519**	**5,896**	**6,300**	**6,734**
common size	18.8%	18.4%	17.3%	8.8%	4.8%	6.8%	6.9%	6.9%
rate of change		5.6%	3.8%	Assume growth with sales.				
Other Noncurrent Assets	**1,841**	**2,266**	**2,475**	**2,693**	**2,821**	**3,014**	**3,220**	**3,442**
common size	7.8%	8.9%	8.8%	8.8%	4.8%	6.8%	6.9%	6.9%
rate of change		23.1%	9.2%	Assume growth with sales.				
TOTAL ASSETS	**$23,474**	**$25,327**	**$27,987**	**$29,779**	**$30,670**	**$32,751**	**$34,145**	**$36,403**
common size	100.0%	100.0%	100.0%	100.0%	100.0%	100.0%	100.0%	100.0%
rate of change		7.9%	10.5%	6.4%	3.0%	6.8%	4.3%	6.6%

LIABILITIES:								
Accounts Payable—Trade	$ 1,543	$ 1,638	$ 1,731	$ 1,895	$ 1,880	$ 2,193	$ 2,118	$ 2,531
common size	6.6%	6.5%	6.2%	45.0	45.0	45.0	45.0	45.0
rate of change		6.2%	5.7%	Assume 45-day payment period.				
Notes Payable and Short-Term Debt	77	145	894	298	307	328	341	364
common size	0.3%	0.6%	3.2%	1.0%	1.0%	1.0%	1.0%	1.0%
rate of change		88.3%	516.6%	Assume 1.0 percent of total assets.				
Current Maturities of Long-Term Debt	485	446	160	361	361	631	631	413
common size	2.1%	1.8%	0.6%	361.0	361.0	631.0	631.0	413.0
rate of change		−8.0%	−64.1%	Current maturities of long-term debt per PepsiCo's long-term debt note.				
Accrued Liabilities	3,455	3,575	3,868	4,208	4,409	4,710	5,033	5,379
common size	14.7%	14.1%	13.8%	8.8%	4.8%	6.8%	6.9%	6.9%
rate of change		3.5%	8.2%	Liabilities for accrued expenses grow with SG&A expenses, which grow with sales.				
Income Taxes Payable	492	611	99	298	307	328	341	364
common size	2.1%	2.4%	0.4%	1.0%	1.0%	1.0%	1.0%	1.0%
rate of change		24.2%	−83.8%	Assume 1.0 percent of total assets.				
CURRENT LIABILITIES	$ 6,052	$ 6,415	$ 6,752	$ 7,060	$ 7,263	$ 8,189	$ 8,464	$ 9,051
common size	25.8%	25.3%	24.1%	23.7%	23.7%	25.0%	24.8%	24.9%
rate of change		6.0%	5.3%	4.6%	2.9%	12.7%	3.4%	6.9%
Long-Term Debt	2,187	1,702	2,397	2,680	2,760	2,948	3,073	3,276
common size	9.3%	6.7%	8.6%	9.0%	9.0%	9.0%	9.0%	9.0%
rate of change		−22.2%	40.8%	Assume 9.0 percent of total assets.				
Deferred Taxes	1,718	1,261	1,216	1,191	1,227	1,310	1,366	1,456
common size	7.3%	5.0%	4.3%	4.0%	4.0%	4.0%	4.0%	4.0%
rate of change		−26.6%	−3.6%	Assume 4.0 percent of total assets.				
Other Noncurrent Liabilities	4,226	4,075	4,099	4,460	4,672	4,991	5,333	5,700
common size	18.0%	16.1%	14.6%	8.8%	4.8%	6.8%	6.9%	6.9%
rate of change		−3.6%	0.6%	Liabilities for accrued expenses grow with SG&A expenses, which grow with sales.				
TOTAL LIABILITIES	$14,183	$13,453	$14,464	$15,391	$15,923	$17,437	$18,236	$19,484
common size	60.4%	53.1%	51.7%	51.7%	51.9%	53.2%	53.4%	53.5%
rate of change		−5.1%	7.5%	6.4%	3.5%	9.5%	4.6%	6.8%
SHAREHOLDERS' EQUITY								
Preferred Stock	(7)	(22)	(49)	0	0	0	0	0
common size	0.0%	−0.1%	−0.2%	0.0	0.0	0.0	0.0	0.0
rate of change		214.3%	122.7%	Assume preferred stock repurchased and retired in Year +1.				
Common Stock + Paid-In Capital	30	578	648	685	705	753	785	837
common size	0.1%	2.3%	2.3%	2.3%	2.3%	2.3%	2.3%	2.3%
rate of change		1826.7%	12.1%	Assume 2.3 percent of total assets.				
Retained Earnings	13,464	15,961	18,730	21,189	23,288	25,687	28,260	31,368
common size	57.4%	63.0%	66.9%	2,459	2,099	2,399	2,573	3,107
rate of change		18.5%	17.3%	Net changes in retained earnings (adding net income and subtracting dividends); see forecast amounts in Exhibit 10.3 on page 743.				
Accumulated Other Comprehensive Income	(1,672)	(1,267)	(886)	(886)	(886)	(886)	(886)	(886)
common size	−7.1%	−5.0%	−3.2%	0.0	0.0	0.0	0.0	0.0
rate of change		−24.2%	−30.1%	Accumulated other comprehensive income assumptions on income statement.				
Treasury Stock	(2,524)	(3,376)	(4,920)	(6,600)	(8,361)	(10,241)	(12,251)	(14,400)
common size	−10.8%	−13.3%	−17.6%	(1,680)	(1,761)	(1,880)	(2,010)	(2,149)
rate of change		33.8%	45.7%	Treasury stock repurchases, net of treasury stock reissues.				
SHAREHOLDERS' EQUITY	$ 9,291	$11,874	$13,523	$14,388	$14,747	$15,313	$15,908	$16,919
common size	39.6%	46.9%	48.3%	48.3%	48.1%	46.8%	46.6%	46.5%
rate of change		27.8%	13.9%	6.4%	2.5%	3.8%	3.9%	6.4%
TOTAL LIABILITIES AND EQUITIES	$23,474	$25,327	$27,987	$29,779	$30,670	$32,751	$34,145	$36,403
common size	100.0%	100.0%	100.0%	100.0%	100.0%	100.0%	100.0%	100.0%
rate of change		7.9%	10.5%	6.4%	3.0%	6.8%	4.3%	6.6%

or experience seasonality in sales and the forecasted account, then this approach may introduce a degree of estimation error.

A less desirable feature of this approach is that in some circumstances it can introduce artificial volatility in ending balances. To illustrate, suppose we had assumed that PepsiCo will hold only 13 days of sales in cash, consistent with the average cash balance in Year 4 (rather than 15 days of sales in cash, consistent with the average cash holdings over Years 1 to 4 calculated earlier). Notice that our computation that PepsiCo held an average of 13 days of sales in cash during Year 4 is the result of a relatively low cash balance at the start of Year 4 ($820 million) coupled with a relatively high ending cash balance ($1,280 million). Assuming PepsiCo continues to maintain cash balances equivalent to 13 days of sales would produce the following forecast amounts:

			Cash			
	Annual Sales Forecasts	Average Sales per Day	Days Sales in Cash	Average Cash Balance	Beginning Cash Balance	Ending Cash Balance
Year +1	$31,836	$ 87.2	13	$1,134	$1,280	$ 988
Year +2	$33,355	$ 91.4	13	$1,188	$ 988	$1,388
Year +3	$35,629	$ 97.6	13	$1,269	$1,388	$1,150
Year +4	$38,071	$104.3	13	$1,356	$1,150	$1,562
Year +5	$40,693	$111.5	13	$1,449	$1,562	$1,337

Because the cash balance at the beginning of Year +1 (the end of Year 4) is fairly large ($1,280), our projected ending cash balance for Year +1 ($988) is relatively low, partially to compensate for the large beginning balance in cash. The relatively low balance in cash at the end of Year +1 then triggers a relatively large balance at the end of Year +2 ($1,388) to compensate, and so on. Exhibit 10.5 depicts this type of "sawtooth" pattern of variability. In certain contexts, this type of variability is a realistic outcome of volatility in the firm's operating environment (such as seasonal or cyclical businesses).

EXHIBIT 10.5

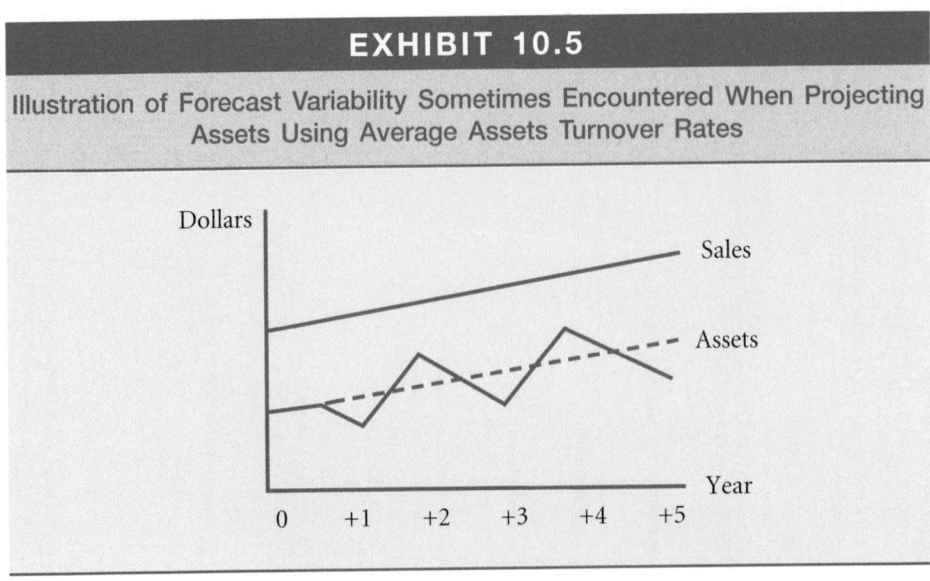

Illustration of Forecast Variability Sometimes Encountered When Projecting Assets Using Average Assets Turnover Rates

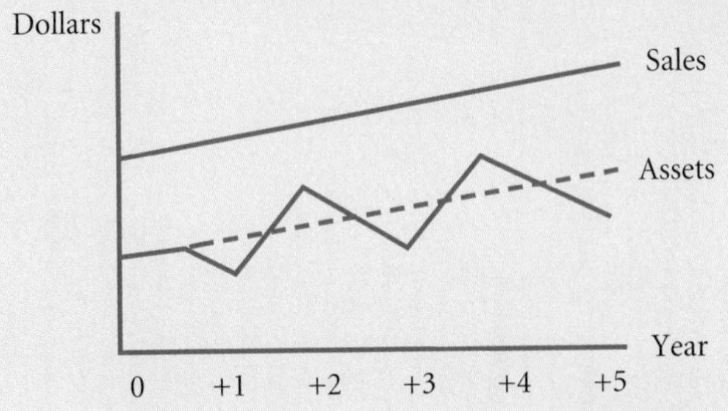

In other contexts the analyst may prefer to build forecasts that mitigate the variability in this pattern. A number of techniques exist for the analyst to produce smooth forecasts. We used one such technique earlier, when we based our forecasts on a long-run average turnover rate (in this case, we used the four-year average cash balance of 15 days of sales), rather than just the most recent turnover rate. Another technique is to project the ending balances in cash to equal the projected average balances in cash. Based on the preceding data, using average cash balances instead of implied ending cash balances would also produce smooth forecasts of growth in cash. Relative to the preceding approach, it would trigger understatements of cash in most years, but on average the amount of forecast error would not be large, as shown here:

	Average Cash Balance	Ending Cash Balance	Difference: Average Minus Ending Balance	Difference as a Percentage of Ending Cash Balance
Year +1	$1,308	$1,337	−$29	−2.2%
Year +2	$1,371	$1,405	−$34	−2.4%
Year +3	$1,464	$1,524	−$60	−3.9%
Year +4	$1,565	$1,605	−$40	−2.5%
Year +5	$1,672	$1,739	−$67	−3.9%

Another technique the analyst can use to produce smooth forecasts involves estimating the average rate of growth in cash expected over a long horizon, and then smoothing each year-end balance using this growth rate. For example, the compound growth rate in cash over the five-year forecast horizon shown previously is 6.3 percent ($=[\$1{,}739/\$1{,}280]^{(1/5)} - 1$). One could forecast cash to grow at this rate, creating a smooth growth rate in cash, and producing a cash balance forecast at the end of the forecast horizon that is equal to the forecast amount implied previously ($1,739 in Year +5).

Yet another alternative that the analyst can use to produce smooth forecasts involves basing the forecasts on asset turnover rates using year-end account balances. This approach assumes that the relation between sales and year-ending balances is stationary. Another possibility is to forecast average balances and then increase them proportionately to year-end amounts using the expected growth rate in sales from the average (or midpoint) of the year to the end of the year.

In choosing among forecasting technique alternatives, the analyst must trade off the objectives of achieving forecast precision and minimizing forecast error with avoiding unnecessary computational complexity. For our purposes, we will rely on average turnover rates to produce smooth growth rates for projecting cash, accounts receivable, inventories, and other accounts, and we will compute the implied end-of-year forecast amounts using the preceding approach.

Using the Cash Account to Balance the Balance Sheet. As we discuss in more detail later in this chapter, projecting future balance sheets requires the analyst to plug a flexible financial asset, liability, or equity account on the balance sheet to bring about an equality of assets with liabilities and shareholders' equity. For some firms, the plug may be cash. For such firms, the cash account represents the financial liquidity "safety valve." These firms often keep relatively large amounts of cash on the balance sheet for financial slack, and they use that cash when necessary to meet periodic cash requirements. For these types of firms, large inflows of cash (such as from the sale of an asset or a new debt issue) build up the cash account, and large outflows (such as for the purchase of an asset or payment of a debt) deplete the cash account. For these types of firms, analysts can forecast the cash balance as the plug needed to balance the balance sheet after all the other balance sheet amounts have been determined. If the analyst considers the projected level of cash to be too large, the analyst can then assume that the firm will invest the excess in marketable securities (if the excess is considered temporary), pay down debt, increase dividends, buy back stock, or use the excess cash in other ways. If the analyst projects the balance in cash will be too low or negative, the analyst might then assume that the firm will engage in short-term borrowing to bring cash up to a desired level.

Most firms, however, do not use cash to balance the balance sheet. Instead, most firms carefully manage cash balances to provide necessary liquidity while minimizing the amounts tied up in cash because cash accounts do not earn high rates of return. Firms typically also avoid unnecessarily large cash balances because of a concern that excess cash can lead to internal control and moral hazard problems, as well as inefficient management. For such firms, like PepsiCo, cash serves a key role in day-to-day operations, similar to other forms of working capital, such as accounts receivable and inventories. Therefore, analysts typically forecast cash by mirroring management's use of cash, and they rely on other flexible financial accounts, such as investment securities, short-term or long-term debt, or dividends, as the balance sheet plug instead of using the cash account for this purpose.

To make the three primary financial statement forecasts articulate with each other, the change in the cash balance on the projected balance sheet each year must agree with the net change in cash on the projected statement of cash flows. We will demonstrate how to compute the implied statement of cash flows later in this chapter.

Projecting Marketable Securities

During Years 0 to 3, PepsiCo's marketable securities balances (also commonly referred to as short-term investments) fluctuated inversely with the balances in cash, implying that PepsiCo managed its marketable securities and cash as complementary sources of liquidity. In years when the cash balance was relatively low, the marketable securities balance was relatively high, and vice versa. Over this period, the individual amounts of marketable securities and cash varied widely, but the common-size balance sheets indicate that the sum of these two accounts varied within a fairly narrow range. For example, in Years 2 and 3 the sum of cash and marketable securities amounted to 7.9 percent of total assets each year, even though the individual amounts of those two assets fluctuated considerably.

We could build our forecasts of marketable securities to maintain that trend, projecting marketable securities balances that, when combined with our projected cash balances, amount to 7.9 percent of total assets each year. However, PepsiCo seems to have broken away from that trend in Year 4, because marketable securities have grown to 7.7 percent of assets, and cash has grown to 4.6 percent of assets. We will assume that the marketable securities balance will continue to grow in proportion to total assets, increasing to 8.0 percent. As we describe shortly, we will forecast the specific amounts of marketable securities once we have our projections of total assets. We will also include on the forecasted income statements the interest income that we expect the marketable securities will earn.

Projecting Accounts Receivable

In Chapter 4, our analysis of PepsiCo's accounts receivable turnover ratios revealed that PepsiCo's accounts receivable collection period has grown over the last five years from an average of 33 days in Year 0 to an average of 36 days in Years 3 and 4 (in Year 4 for example, 36 days = 365/[$29,261/(.5 ×[$2,830 + $2,999])]). We project accounts receivable by assuming that PepsiCo will maintain an average 36-day collection period in the future, turning over accounts receivable approximately 10.1 times a year (= 365/36). As we demonstrated earlier for our projections of cash, we will use the average turnover rate to project PepsiCo's average accounts receivable, and then compute the implied year-ending balances. The projected amounts follow:

	Annual Sales Forecast	Average Sales per Day	Accounts Receivable			
			Days Sales in Receivables	Average Balance	Beginning Balance	Ending Balance
Year +1	$31,836	$ 87.2	36	$3,140	$2,999	$3,281
Year +2	$33,355	$ 91.4	36	$3,290	$3,281	$3,298
Year +3	$35,629	$ 97.6	36	$3,514	$3,298	$3,730
Year +4	$38,071	$104.3	36	$3,755	$3,730	$3,780
Year +5	$40,693	$111.5	36	$4,014	$3,780	$4,247

Projecting Inventories

In Chapter 4, our analysis of PepsiCo's inventory turnover ratios revealed that PepsiCo has experienced increasing inventory turnover rates during the last five years. The average number of days in inventory decreased from 42 days in Years 0 through 2, to 41 days in Year 3, to 40 days in Year 4. We project inventories using an average inventory turnover period of 40 days, or equivalently, an average turnover rate of 9.1 times per year. The projected amounts follow:

	Inventories				
	Cost of Goods Sold	Average Inventory Turnover Ratio	Average Balance	Beginning Balance	Ending Balance
Year +1	$14,581	9.1	$1,602	$1,541	$1,664
Year +2	$15,276	9.1	$1,679	$1,664	$1,694
Year +3	$16,318	9.1	$1,793	$1,694	$1,893
Year +4	$17,436	9.1	$1,916	$1,893	$1,940
Year +5	$18,638	9.1	$2,048	$1,940	$2,157

For some firms, such as retail chains, inventory is a large proportion of total assets. For such firms, the analyst should link inventory forecasts to projections of the number of stores that will be operating in future years (or even more specifically, to the number of square feet of retail space). For retail firms that operate large "big box" type stores (Wal-Mart, for example), inventory projections may grow stepwise with each new store because each new store will require millions of dollars of inventory. Retail chains with seasonal sales will strive to have new stores in place, and thus new inventory in place, before heavy selling seasons (such as the back-to-school season for casual clothing store chains or the Christmas season for toy store chains), so analysts will link inventory forecasts to forecasts of new stores in advance of these heavy selling seasons.

Projecting Other Current Assets

Other current assets usually represent items such as prepaid expenses for rent, advertising, and insurance. These items often vary in relation to the level of operating activity, such as sales, advertising, production, new stores or restaurants, and total assets. In the case of PepsiCo, other current assets have declined slowly as a percentage of total assets over the last five years, falling to roughly 2.3 percent of total assets at the end of Year 4. We will assume that other current assets will fall further to 2.0 percent of total assets in Year +1 and remain at that level of total assets in the future. As we describe shortly, we will forecast the specific amounts of other current assets once we have our projections of total assets.

Projecting Investments in Noncontrolled Affiliates

PepsiCo's long-term investments in securities represent its interests in noncontrolled affiliates, primarily bottlers. These investments grew at a compound annual rate of 2.9 percent over the last five years. From the end of Year 2 through the end of Year 4, investments in securities have increased from 11.1 percent to 11.7 percent of total assets. We assume that investments in noncontrolled affiliates will grow in proportion with total assets and remain at roughly 12.0 percent of total assets in the future.[10] Recall that we presented our forecasts of bottling equity income earlier, when we discussed projecting other revenues. Note that we based our projections of bottling equity income, which we assumed would earn a normal return of 12.0 percent, on our projections that investments in noncontrolled affiliates would amount to 12.0 percent of total assets. We will forecast the specific amounts of investments in noncontrolled affiliates once we have our projections of total assets.

Projecting Property, Plant, and Equipment

PepsiCo's fixed-assets turnover ratio remained steady at 3.5 from Year 1 to Year 3, and then increased slightly to 3.7 in Year 4 (computed as 3.7 = \$29,261/[.5 × (\$8,149 + \$7,828)]). This relatively stable fixed-assets turnover is a result of PepsiCo's steady sales growth being matched with a similar rate of steady growth in capital spending on property, plant, and equipment, which averaged roughly 5.0 percent of sales each year. In the Year 4 Annual Report, PepsiCo's MD&A section describing "Our Liquidity, Capital Resources, and Financial Position" (Appendix B) discloses that management expects capital spending to continue at a rate of approximately 5.0 percent of revenues in Year +1. Given that this expectation is consistent with PepsiCo's past capital spending, we will assume that PepsiCo's future capital spending will amount to 5.0 percent of revenues in Year +1 through Year +5. In Year +1, for example, we will project capital expenditures on property, plant, and equipment to amount to \$1,592 (= \$31,836 × 0.05). We capture these capital expenditures in our balance sheet projections by increasing property, plant, and equipment, and we capture them in our projections of the statement of cash flows by including them as cash outflows in the investing section.

PepsiCo's existing property, plant, and equipment will continue to depreciate as PepsiCo uses these assets in its operations. In addition, PepsiCo's capital expenditures on new property, plant, and equipment will trigger a new layer of depreciation expense each year. PepsiCo discloses in Note 4, "Property, Plant, and Equipment and Intangible Assets" (Appendix A), that it uses the straight-line depreciation method for financial statement purposes (it uses accelerated depreciation for tax purposes). Assuming PepsiCo depreciates all of the property, plant, and equipment to zero salvage value, we can estimate the average

[10]Consistent with continued growth in investments in noncontrolled affiliates, PepsiCo disclosed in the MD&A section titled "Our Liquidity, Capital Resources and Financial Position" (Appendix B) that early in Year +1 it completed an acquisition of a 40.5 percent interest in Snack Ventures Europe for \$750 million. PepsiCo also disclosed that it was planning to sell in Year +1 up to 7.5 million shares of PBG, its largest noncontrolled bottling affiliate, which would reduce its investments in noncontrolled affiliates by roughly \$200 million.

useful life PepsiCo uses for depreciation. To estimate the average useful life, we take the average amount in property, plant, and equipment at acquisition cost during a year and divide it by depreciation expense for that year. In Year 4, PepsiCo used an average useful life of 14.4 years for depreciation purposes (= [($15,930 + $14,755)/2]/$1,062). We will assume that PepsiCo will continue to use a 14.4-year average useful life for purposes of computing depreciation expense.[11]

To compute depreciation expense for Year +1, we need to forecast two components. The first component is depreciation on existing property, plant, and equipment, which will be $1,103 in Year +1 (= $15,930/14.4). The second component is depreciation on Year +1 capital expenditures on property, plant, and equipment, which will be $110 (= $1,592/14.4). Together, total depreciation expense in Year +1 will be $1,213 (= $1,103 + $110), and accumulated depreciation will grow to reflect this additional depreciation. Note that in Year +2, depreciation expense will consist of those two components plus a third component to reflect depreciation on Year +2 capital expenditures on property, plant, and equipment, and so on.

The projected amounts for capital expenditures; property, plant, and equipment; depreciation expense; and accumulated depreciation follow:

		Property, Plant, and Equipment				
Year	**Annual Sales Forecasts**	**Capital Expenditures (5% of Sales)**	**Ending Balance (at Cost)**	**Depreciation Expense**	**Accumulated Depreciation**	**Ending Balance (Net)**
4 actual			$15,930		($ 7,781)	$8,149
+1..........	$31,836	$1,592	$17,522	$1,213	($ 8,994)	$8,528
+2..........	$33,355	$1,668	$19,190	$1,328	($10,322)	$8,867
+3..........	$35,629	$1,781	$20,971	$1,452	($11,774)	$9,197
+4..........	$38,071	$1,904	$22,875	$1,583	($13,357)	$9,517
+5..........	$40,693	$2,035	$24,909	$1,724	($15,081)	$9,828

When forecasting fixed assets for capital-intensive firms (such as manufacturing firms or utility companies) or firms for which fixed-asset growth is a critical driver of future sales growth and earnings (for example, new stores for retail chains or restaurant chains), analysts often invest considerable time and effort in developing detailed forecasts of capital expenditures; property, plant, and equipment; and depreciation expense. For such firms, property, plant, and equipment is typically a large proportion of total assets and has a material impact on the analysts' forecasts of earnings, cash flows, and firm value. The FSAP Forecast Development spreadsheet for PepsiCo includes a model for forecasting capital expenditures; property, plant, and equipment; depreciation expense; and accumulated

[11]PepsiCo discloses that Year 4 depreciation expense equals $1.062 million in Note 4, "Property, Plant, and Equipment and Intangible Assets." In that note, PepsiCo also discloses that property, plant, and equipment includes land, which is not depreciable (although land improvements are depreciable), and construction in progress, which is not yet depreciable but will be in the future. The analyst interested in slightly greater precision could exclude these amounts from the useful-life computation and the depreciation expense projections. Also, note that on PepsiCo's Statement of Cash Flows for Year 4 (Appendix A), PepsiCo adds back $1,264 million in depreciation and amortization expense to net income, which consists of $1,062 million of depreciation expense and $202 million of amortization expense. We use the depreciation expense disclosed in Note 4 ($1,062 million) to avoid confounding our estimate of the depreciable useful life with amortization expense.

depreciation. The FSAP output (Appendix C) demonstrates the use of this model to compute the preceding data for PepsiCo.

Projecting Amortizable Intangible Assets

Amortizable intangible assets for PepsiCo primarily include brands, trademarks, and other identifiable intangible assets with limited useful lives that PepsiCo obtained through acquisitions of other companies. As discussed previously, PepsiCo amortizes these assets ratably over their estimated useful lives (ranging from five to twenty years). The book value of PepsiCo's amortizable intangible assets amounts to $598 million on the Year 4 balance sheet. Over the last three years, the balance in amortizable intangible assets has declined steadily, suggesting that PepsiCo has not made any significant investments in these types of assets during this period. In Note 4, "Property, Plant, and Equipment and Intangible Assets" (Appendix A), PepsiCo discloses the amount of amortization expense it expects on these intangible assets over the next five years, which we have included under the heading "Other Operating Expenses" on our projected income statements. We project that the amortizable intangible asset amounts will continue to decrease by the amounts of amortization expense that PepsiCo disclosed. We will also assume that PepsiCo will not make any additional investments in amortizable intangible assets, and will instead grow goodwill and nonamortizable intangible assets, which we discuss next.

Projecting Goodwill and Nonamortizable Intangible Assets

The majority of PepsiCo's intangible assets involve goodwill ($3,909 million) and brands ($928 million) with indefinite lives. These intangible assets arise when PepsiCo acquires other companies. These accounts recognize the portion of the acquisition price that PepsiCo allocates to intangible assets such as goodwill and brands. U.S. GAAP does not require firms to amortize these accounts because they have indefinite useful lives, but GAAP does require firms to test these asset values annually for impairment, and to write the carrying values down to fair value if they deem them impaired. Thus far, PepsiCo has not deemed it necessary to recognize any impairment losses on its nonamortizable intangible assets.

Acquiring other companies with valuable goodwill, brand names, and products is a key element of PepsiCo's strategy. Such acquisitions help PepsiCo create new sales growth and expand its product portfolio. It seems clear that PepsiCo will continue to pursue the strategy of making acquisitions but it is very difficult, in the absence of inside information, to forecast specific acquisitions or amounts with confidence. Thus, we assume that PepsiCo's nonamortizable intangible assets will continue to grow at the same rate as sales growth. We also assume that no future impairment charges will be necessary for these assets. The projected amounts are as follows:

	Nonamortizable Intangible Assets		
	Beginning Balance	**Sales Growth Rate**	**Ending Balance**
Year +1	$4,842	8.8%	$5,268
Year +2	$5,268	4.8%	$5,519
Year +3	$5,519	6.8%	$5,896
Year +4	$5,896	6.9%	$6,300
Year +5	$6,300	6.9%	$6,734

Projecting Other Noncurrent Assets

Other noncurrent assets for PepsiCo have grown steadily in recent years. In Years 3 and 4, they amount to just under 9.0 percent of total assets. In the absence of more information to forecast other asset amounts specifically, we will assume that other noncurrent assets will continue to grow at the same rate as sales each year. The projected amounts are as follows:

	Other Noncurrent Assets		
	Beginning Balance	**Sales Growth Rate**	**Ending Balance**
Year +1	$2,475	8.8%	$2,693
Year +2	$2,693	4.8%	$2,821
Year +3	$2,821	6.8%	$3,014
Year +4	$3,014	6.9%	$3,220
Year +5	$3,220	6.9%	$3,442

Projecting Assets That Vary as a Percentage of Total Assets

We can now project asset amounts that we expect will vary as a percentage of total assets, including marketable securities (8.0 percent), other current assets (2.0 percent), and investments in noncontrolled affiliates (12.0 percent), for a total of 22.0 percent. Projected amounts for Year +1 for all of the individual assets other than these three assets are as follows:

Cash	$ 1,337
Accounts Receivable	3,281
Inventories	1,664
Property, Plant, and Equipment, net	8,528
Amortizable Intangible Assets	457
Nonamortizable Intangible Assets	5,268
Other Noncurrent Assets	2,693
Subtotal of Assets	$23,228

The $23,228 subtotal represents 78.0 percent (= 1.00 − .08 − .02 − .12) of total assets. Projected total assets therefore equal $29,779 (= $23,228/0.78). Marketable securities equal $2,382 (= 0.08 × $29,779); other current assets equal $596 (= 0.02 × $29,779); and investments in noncontrolled affiliates equal $3,573 (= 0.12 × $29,779). The projected amounts for total assets, marketable securities, other current assets, and investments in noncontrolled affiliates in Years +1 to +5 are as follows:

Year	Total Assets	Marketable Securities (8.0%)	Other Current Assets (2.0%)	Investments (12.0%)
+1	$29,779	$2,382	$596	$3,573
+2	$30,670	$2,454	$613	$3,680
+3	$32,751	$2,620	$655	$3,930
+4	$34,145	$2,732	$683	$4,097
+5	$36,403	$2,912	$728	$4,368

STEP 4: PROJECTING LIABILITIES AND SHAREHOLDERS' EQUITY

After completing forecasts of the asset side of the balance sheet, the analyst next projects individual liability and shareholders' equity accounts. In beginning this process, the analyst already knows the total amount of liabilities and shareholders equity, which must equal the total assets in order for the balance sheet to balance.

For firms that maintain a particular capital structure over time, the analyst can use the common-size balance sheet percentages to project amounts of individual liabilities and shareholders' equities. The common-size balance sheet data for PepsiCo (Appendix C) show that the balance sheet percentages for total liabilities declined fairly dramatically over the last five years, from 63.3 percent of total assets in Year 0 to 51.7 percent in Year 4. Over the same period, shareholders' equity increased from 36.7 percent of total assets in Year 0 to 48.3 percent in Year 4. If the analyst predicts that PepsiCo's capital structure will consist of stable proportions of liabilities and equity in the future (for instance, the analyst might project that the current structure of 51.7 percent liabilities and 48.3 percent equities will continue into the future), then the analyst can use these common-size percentages and the projected amounts of total assets to project future totals of liabilities and equities. Alternatively, the analyst can project individual liabilities and shareholders' equity accounts using historical growth rates or turnover ratios. In this chapter, we illustrate forecasting individual liabilities and equities using a combination of common-size percentages, growth rates, and turnover ratios for PepsiCo, in order to develop forecasts that incorporate the projected levels of operating activities and permit changes in the expected behavior of individual liability and equity amounts over time. We consider each account next.

Projecting Accounts Payable

PepsiCo reports accounts payable and other current liabilities on a single line on its balance sheet, amounting to $5,599 million at the end of Year 4. Note 14, "Supplemental Financial Information" (Appendix A), discloses that $1,731 million of that total is attributable to accounts payable, and the remainder ($3,868 million) is attributable to accrued liabilities for selling, advertising, marketing, compensation, and other expenses. Different factors may drive the future amounts of accounts payable and accrued expenses. Future credit purchases of inventory and PepsiCo's payment policy to its suppliers will likely drive accounts payable, whereas accrued expenses will likely grow with future selling, general, and administrative expenses. Therefore, we forecast accounts payable and other current liabilities for accrued expenses separately.

PepsiCo's days payable varied around 45 days during the last five years, from a low of 41 days in Year 1 to a high of 47 days in Year 3. In the most recent year, Year 4, PepsiCo maintained an average payables period of 45 days. We assume that PepsiCo will continue to maintain an accounts payable period of 45 days in the future. To forecast future accounts payable balances, we begin by calculating forecasts of inventory purchases on account:

	Inventory Purchases				
	Year +1	Year +2	Year +3	Year +4	Year +5
Cost of Goods Sold	$14,581	$15,276	$16,318	$17,436	$18,638
Plus Ending Inventory	+1,664	+1,694	+1,893	+1,940	+2,157
Less Beginning Inventory	−1,541	−1,664	−1,694	−1,893	−1,940
Inventory Purchases	$14,704	$15,306	$16,517	$17,483	$18,855

We project accounts payable using an average 45 days payables period, or equivalently an average turnover rate of 8.1 times per year, as follows:

	Accounts Payable				
	Inventory Purchases	Payables Period	Average Balance	Beginning Balance	Ending Balance
Year +1	$14,704	45 days	$1,813	$1,731	$1,895
Year +2	$15,306	45 days	$1,887	$1,895	$1,880
Year +3	$16,517	45 days	$2,036	$1,880	$2,193
Year +4	$17,483	45 days	$2,155	$2,193	$2,118
Year +5	$18,855	45 days	$2,325	$2,118	$2,531

In this case, we rely on our prior forecasts of PepsiCo's cost of goods sold and inventory balances to compute inventory purchases, which will flow through accounts payable, and we assume that the payables period will be a constant 45 days. We then compute the average balance in accounts payable and use it to compute the implied ending balance in accounts payable. Because the accounts payable balance at the start of our forecast period was not unusually high or low relative to cost of goods sold, our forecasts project relatively smooth growth in accounts payable over time, avoiding the sawtooth pattern we discussed earlier.

Projecting Other Current Liabilities: Accrued Liabilities

As discussed in the prior section, Note 14, "Supplemental Financial Information" (Appendix A), discloses that at the end of Year 4 PepsiCo's accrued liabilities for selling, advertising, marketing, compensation, and other general and administrative expenses amount to $3,868 million. Our forecasts of income for PepsiCo assumed that selling, general, and administrative expenses would remain a steady percentage of sales, and therefore grow proportionately with sales. We therefore forecast that other current liabilities will grow with selling, general, and administrative expenses, which grow with sales.

	Other Current Liabilities		
	Beginning Balance	Sales Growth Rate	Ending Balance
Year +1	$3,868	8.8%	$4,208
Year +2	$4,208	4.8%	$4,409
Year +3	$4,409	6.8%	$4,710
Year +4	$4,710	6.9%	$5,033
Year +5	$5,033	6.9%	$5,379

Projecting Current Liabilities: Income Taxes Payable

PepsiCo's current liabilities include a separate line item for income taxes payable. Income taxes payable varies with the income tax provision on the income statement, but income taxes payable also varies with tax payments, settlements of tax disputes, mergers and acquisitions, changes in deferred tax assets and liabilities, and other elements that are difficult to predict with confidence. PepsiCo's income taxes payable have varied widely in amount over the past five years, but they have ranged within a narrow bound between

0.3 percent and 2.4 percent of total assets over that period. We will assume that PepsiCo's income taxes payable will average 1.0 percent of total assets in the future. The projected amounts are as follows:

		Income Taxes Payable	
	Total Assets	As a Percentage of Total Assets	Balance
Year +1	$29,779	1.0%	$298
Year +2	$30,670	1.0%	$307
Year +3	$32,751	1.0%	$328
Year +4	$34,145	1.0%	$341
Year +5	$36,403	1.0%	$364

Projecting Short-Term Borrowings

Note 9, "Debt Obligations and Commitments" (Appendix A), discloses that PepsiCo's short-term borrowings represent current maturities of long-term debt, short-term notes payable, and amounts borrowed under a revolving line of credit. Note 9 reveals that at the end of Year 4, total short-term borrowings were $1,054 million, which included $160 million of current maturities of long-term debt and $1,644 million of other short-term borrowings, less $750 million borrowed under the revolving line of credit, which PepsiCo reclassifies as long-term debt because of its intent and ability to refinance on a long-term basis. We forecast the amounts relating to current maturities of long-term debt and the revolving line of credit as components of PepsiCo's long-term financing strategy and we forecast separately the amounts relating to other short-term borrowings.

Note 9 implies that PepsiCo does not rely heavily on other short-term borrowings to meet temporary cash flow needs. Instead, PepsiCo relies on the revolving line of credit for those needs. PepsiCo generates substantial amounts of cash from its operations. The Statement of Cash Flows for Year 4 for PepsiCo (Appendix A) indicates that the firm generated approximately $5.1 billion of net cash flow from operating activities. Of that cash flow from operations, PepsiCo used $2.3 billion for investing activities in Year 4 and $2.3 billion for financing activities, which primarily involved paying debt, paying dividends, and repurchasing common stock. PepsiCo used the remaining $0.5 billion of cash flow from operations to increase the cash account. Given that PepsiCo generates so much cash available for financing activities, it is not surprising that short-term borrowings are a minor element of PepsiCo's financial capital structure. The common-size balance sheet data for PepsiCo indicate that short-term borrowings have ranged from 0.3 percent to 3.2 percent of total assets during the past three years. We project that short-term borrowings will be 1.0 percent of total assets in the future. We present the projected amounts for short-term borrowings in the table in the following section, which includes projected amounts for long-term debt and current maturities of long-term debt.

Projecting Long-Term Debt and Current Maturities of Long-Term Debt

Together, long-term debt plus current maturities of long-term debt have varied from a high of 13.7 percent of total assets in Year 0 to a low of 8.5 percent in Year 3, and they stand at 9.2 percent in Year 4. Note 9, "Debt Obligations and Commitments" (Appendix A), reveals that at the end of Year 4, PepsiCo has $2,397 million in long-term debt, including the $750 million under the revolving line of credit that PepsiCo classifies as long-term debt described in the previous section. We will assume that PepsiCo will maintain long-term debt equal to 9.0 percent of total assets in Year +1 and beyond.

The outstanding long-term debt is due at varying maturity dates, extending to Year +22. Note 9 also discloses information to enable the analyst to estimate the amounts due to be repaid in Year +1 ($160 million) through Year +5 and beyond ($413 million). The amount maturing in Year +2 ($361 million) will become the current maturity of long-term debt at the end of Year +1; the amount maturing in Year +3 ($361 million) will become the current maturity of long-term debt at the end of Year +2; and so on. We use these amounts and maturities to project the current maturities of long-term debt through the end of Year +5. The projected amounts for short-term borrowings, current maturities of long-term debt, and long-term debt are as follows:

		Short-Term Borrowings, Current Maturities of Long-Term Debt, and Long-Term Debt				
	Total Assets	Short-Term Borrowings (1.0%)	Current Maturities of Long-Term Debt	Long-Term Debt (9.0%)	Total Interest-Bearing Debt	As a Percentage of Total Assets
Year +1	$29,779	$298	$361	$2,680	$3,339	11.2%
Year +2	$30,670	$307	$361	$2,760	$3,428	11.2%
Year +3	$32,751	$328	$631	$2,948	$3,906	11.9%
Year +4	$34,145	$341	$631	$3,073	$4,045	11.8%
Year +5	$36,403	$364	$413	$3,276	$4,053	11.1%

In a later section of this chapter, we will use the preceding projected amounts for interest-bearing debt as a basis to project PepsiCo's future interest expense.

Projecting Other Noncurrent Liabilities

Other noncurrent liabilities are accrued liabilities for expenses that relate to pension obligations, health care obligations, long-term compensation, and other operating and administrative activities. We therefore project other noncurrent liabilities to grow with selling, general, and administrative expenses, which we project will grow with sales:

	Other Noncurrent Liabilities		
	Beginning Balance	Sales Growth Rate	Ending Balance
Year +1	$4,099	8.8%	$4,460
Year +2	$4,460	4.8%	$4,672
Year +3	$4,672	6.8%	$4,991
Year +4	$4,991	6.9%	$5,333
Year +5	$5,333	6.9%	$5,700

Projecting Deferred Income Taxes

PepsiCo's Note 5, "Income Taxes" (Appendix A), indicates that deferred taxes relate to a variety of operating items (investments in unconsolidated affiliates; property, plant, and equipment; pension benefits plans; etc.). Over the past three years, deferred income taxes have declined in amount and as a percentage of total assets, from 7.3 percent down to 4.3 percent. We project that deferred tax liabilities will decrease further to 4.0 percent of total assets, and will remain at that proportionate level of total assets in future years. The amounts are as follows:

		Deferred Income Taxes	
	Total Assets	As a Percentage of Total Assets	Ending Balance
Year +1	$29,779	4.0%	$1,191
Year +2	$30,670	4.0%	$1,227
Year +3	$32,751	4.0%	$1,310
Year +4	$34,145	4.0%	$1,366
Year +5	$36,403	4.0%	$1,456

Projecting Preferred Stock and Minority Interest

PepsiCo has a negative amount (−$49 million) in preferred stock at the end of Year 4. Note 12, "Preferred and Common Stock" (Appendix A), discloses that Quaker Foods had issued the preferred stock as part of an employee stock ownership plan, and the shares can be redeemed by plan participants or repurchased by PepsiCo at a premium. The amount of preferred stock is negative, which is unusual, because PepsiCo raised $41 million in capital by issuing the stock, and to date has paid a total of $90 million for the shares that employees have redeemed or that PepsiCo has repurchased. In Note 12, PepsiCo also discloses that the roughly 400,000 outstanding preferred shares have a fair value of $110 million at the end of Year 4. We will assume that all of these remaining shares will be either repurchased by PepsiCo or redeemed by plan participants in Year +1 at fair value. We will treat the forecast payment of $110 million as a special onetime liquidating dividend to buyback and retire these preferred shares. Because we forecast that all of the preferred shares will be retired by the end of Year +1, we will then forecast the ending balance in preferred stock to be zero at the end of Year +1. We will record the $110 million payment to retire the remaining shares and the $49 million adjustment to zero out the negative balance in the preferred-stock account by reducing retained earnings by $159 million (= $110 million + $49 million).

PepsiCo has no equity capital from minority interest shareholders. We assume that this will remain zero in the future.

Projecting Common Stock and Capital in Excess of Par Value

These paid-in common equity capital accounts increase as the firm raises capital by selling common shares to investors or to individuals exercising stock options the firm has granted, or by issuing shares in a merger or acquisition. These accounts decrease as the firm retires shares. PepsiCo's common stock and capital in excess of par value decreased from Year 0 through Year 2, but these accounts have increased in Years 3 and 4, remaining at roughly 2.3 percent of total assets. We expect PepsiCo to continue to issue stock, so we project Common Stock and Capital in Excess of Par Value to grow with total assets, remaining at 2.3 percent of total assets. The projected amounts for Common Stock and Capital in Excess of Par Value are as follows:

		Common Stock and Capital in Excess of Par Value	
	Total Assets	As a Percentage of Total Assets	Ending Balance
Year +1	$29,779	2.3%	$685
Year +2	$30,670	2.3%	$705
Year +3	$32,751	2.3%	$753
Year +4	$34,145	2.3%	$785
Year +5	$36,403	2.3%	$837

In recent years, PepsiCo has also conducted stock issue transactions for the merger with Quaker Foods and to meet stock option exercises through previously acquired treasury shares. We discuss our projections of the effects of stock issue and buyback transactions using the Treasury Stock accounts in a later section.

Projecting Accumulated Other Comprehensive Loss

According to PepsiCo's Statement of Common Shareholders' Equity at the end of Year 4 (Appendix A), Accumulated Other Comprehensive Loss is primarily attributable to the cumulative effects of losses from foreign currency translation adjustments, which were consistently large and negative through Year 1. During Years 3 and 4, these effects have begun to reverse somewhat, with PepsiCo experiencing significant positive foreign currency translation adjustments because PepsiCo has substantial international operations in countries whose currencies increased in value relative to the U.S. dollar, such as the euro and the British pound. In our previous forecasts of revenues from the PepsiCo International division, we assumed PepsiCo will continue to expand these international operations. It is difficult to forecast, however, whether the U.S. dollar will continue to decrease in value relative to the foreign currencies PepsiCo uses in its international operations. One might also expect that PepsiCo will either hedge or limit its exposure to adverse foreign currency movements. Thus, we project that PepsiCo will not experience persistent negative or positive foreign currency translation adjustments, and that Accumulated Other Comprehensive Loss will remain at its current level. This assumption is equivalent to assuming that PepsiCo's future foreign currency translation adjustments are equally likely to be positive or negative in any given year and that, on average, they will be zero over time. Accordingly, we also forecast that Other Comprehensive Income Items included in comprehensive income will also be zero in future years.

Projecting Treasury Stock

The treasury stock account decreases (that is, becomes more negative) when the firm repurchases some of its shares. The treasury stock account increases (becomes less negative) when the firm reissues treasury shares on the open market, uses them to meet stock option exercises, issues them in merger or acquisition transactions, or retires them. Over

Years 2, 3, and 4, PepsiCo has repurchased significant amounts of its common stock and used treasury shares for acquisitions and to meet stock option exercises.[12]

PepsiCo's Statement of Common Shareholders' Equity (Appendix A) reveals that it repurchased substantial amounts of treasury stock in recent years: $2,192 million in Year 2; $1,946 million in Year 3; and $2,994 million in Year 4. In PepsiCo's Year 4 Annual Report, the MD&A section titled "Our Liquidity, Capital Resources and Financial Position" (Appendix B) discloses that in 2004 the board of directors approved a plan to expand the scope of stock repurchases, so it is likely that PepsiCo will continue to make significant stock repurchases. In fact, in PepsiCo's MD&A, the firm discloses that it expects to make treasury stock purchases in the range of $2,500 million to $3,000 million in Year +1. We will assume that PepsiCo's treasury stock repurchases will grow with sales during Year +1 through Year +5 (even though this assumption will lead our initial Year +1 forecast to exceed the range of repurchases PepsiCo disclosed). We may need to revise this assumption later in our analysis if we determine that PepsiCo will not have sufficient cash flow for these repurchases, or if our equity valuation estimates indicate that the capital market has overpriced PepsiCo stock.

PepsiCo's Statement of Common Shareholders' Equity (Appendix A) also reveals that PepsiCo reissued treasury shares amounting to $936 million in Year 2, $1,094 million in Year 3, and $1,450 million in Year 4, primarily to meet stock option exercises. We assume that employees will continue to exercise stock options in future years (but we may need to revise this assumption later in our analysis if our equity valuation estimates indicate that PepsiCo's stock options are not likely to be "in the money"). We project that PepsiCo's reissues of treasury stock for stock options exercises in the future will grow with sales in Year +1 through Year +5, to reflect the incentive effects of stock options. Recall that we implicitly included in our forecast of income an expense for the fair value of stock options grants in our projections of selling, general, and administrative expenses, because PepsiCo expenses the fair value of options grants as part of stock-based compensation expense.

The projected amounts for treasury stock are as follows:

Treasury Stock

	Beginning Balance	Sales Growth Rate	Share Repurchases	Share Reissues	Ending Balance
Year 4 actual	−$3,376		−$2,994	$+1,450	−$4,920
Year +1	−$4,920	+8.8%	−$3,258	$+1,578	−$6,600
Year +2	−$6,600	+4.8%	−$3,414	$+1,653	−$8,361
Year +3	−$8,361	+6.8%	−$3,646	$+1,766	−$10,241
Year +4	−$10,241	+6.9%	−$3,898	$+1,888	−$12,251
Year +5	−$12,251	+6.9%	−$4,167	$+2,018	−$14,400

[12]The stock market often interprets share repurchase announcements as "good news," inferring that management, with its in-depth knowledge of the firm, thinks that the capital market is underpricing the firm's stock. The stock market typically reacts to this positive signal by bidding up the price of the firm's shares. Stock repurchases may also be perceived favorably by capital-markets participants because they represent a form of implicit dividend to shareholders which may be taxed at capital gains rates, which may be lower than the ordinary income tax rates on dividends (depending on the shareholders' holding period and tax status).

STEP 5: PROJECTING INTEREST EXPENSE, INTEREST INCOME, NONRECURRING OR UNUSUAL ITEMS, PROVISION FOR INCOME TAX, AND THE CHANGE IN RETAINED EARNINGS

Projecting Interest Expense

We can now project our first-iteration estimate of interest expense, based on our projected balances in interest-bearing debt, including short-term borrowing, current maturities of long-term debt, and long-term debt. Note 9, "Debt Obligations and Commitments" (Appendix A), indicates that at the end of Year 4 the interest rate on short-term borrowings was 3.2 percent and the interest rate on long-term notes (roughly half of the total long-term debt) was 4.7 percent. Note 9 also indicates that PepsiCo's zero-coupon notes carry an implicit interest rate of 13.4 percent, and other forms of long-term debt carry an average 6.2 percent interest rate. Dividing the Year 4 interest expense amount by the average amount of interest-bearing debt outstanding during Year 4 implies that PepsiCo's weighted average interest rate on debt was roughly 5.8 percent (= $167/[.5($1,054 + $2,397 + $591 + $1,702)]). We assume that interest expense will equal 6.0 percent on average interest-bearing debt (short-term borrowing, current maturities of long-term debt, and long term debt) during Year +1 through Year +5. Using the projected amounts of debt described previously, the projected interest expense amounts follow:

Interest Expense on Interest-Bearing Debt

	Short-Term Borrowings	Current Maturities of Long-Term Debt	Long-Term Debt	Total Interest-Bearing Debt	Average Interest-Bearing Debt	Interest Rate	Interest Expense
Year 4	$894	$160	$2,397	$3,451			
Year +1	$298	$361	$2,680	$3,339	$3,395	6.0%	$204
Year +2	$307	$361	$2,760	$3,428	$3,384	6.0%	$203
Year +3	$328	$631	$2,948	$3,906	$3,667	6.0%	$220
Year +4	$341	$631	$3,073	$4,045	$3,975	6.0%	$239
Year +5	$364	$413	$3,276	$4,053	$4,049	6.0%	$243

We can now enter these "first-pass" interest expense amounts in the projected income statements. If our projected balance sheets imply that PepsiCo will need larger or smaller amounts of long-term debt to finance future asset growth, then we will need to recompute the interest expense projections to reflect different amounts of debt.

Projecting Interest Income

We can also project our first-iteration estimates of PepsiCo's interest income on financial assets, such as short-term investments in marketable securities. Recall that we accounted for returns earned on long-term investments in noncontrolled bottling affiliates as part of bottling equity income, and so we do not include them here. In Year 4, PepsiCo recognized $74 million in interest income. The average amount of marketable securities during Year 4 was $1,673 million (= [$1,181 + $2,165]/2), for an average return of 4.4 percent (= $74/$1,673). This rate of return appears reasonable because it approximates the risk-free rate of return during Year 4, and it is likely that PepsiCo's marketable securities are very low-risk but highly liquid instruments. We will assume that PepsiCo will earn 4.0 percent return, which is the prevailing risk-free rate at the beginning of Year +1, on the average balance in marketable securities each year. We will also assume that PepsiCo earns no material amounts of interest income on cash and cash equivalents. This is probably not true, but cash accounts generally earn very low rates of return, so assuming no return will not introduce material forecast error. The projected amounts for interest income follow:

Interest Income

	Marketable Securities				
Year	**Beginning Balance**	**Ending Balance**	**Average Balance**	**Rate of Return**	**Interest Income**
+1	$2,165	$2,382	$2,273	4.0%	$ 91
+2	$2,382	$2,454	$2,418	4.0%	$ 97
+3	$2,454	$2,620	$2,537	4.0%	$101
+4	$2,620	$2,732	$2,676	4.0%	$107
+5	$2,732	$2,912	$2,822	4.0%	$113

If our projected balance sheets imply that PepsiCo will generate larger amounts of cash flow in future years and if we expect that they will retain larger amounts of marketable securities, then we will need to recompute the interest income projections to reflect additional interest-earning assets.

Projecting Nonrecurring or Unusual Items

As discussed in prior chapters of this text, it is not uncommon for firms' reported income statements to include other nonrecurring gains or losses that are part of operations, unusual gains or losses that are peripheral to operations, income from discontinued segments, and extraordinary gains or losses. In Year 4, for example, PepsiCo included in income a $150 million impairment and restructuring charge and a $38 million tax benefit from the settlement of a tax dispute regarding its discontinued restaurant operations. As Chapter 6 and other previous chapters discuss, the analyst must determine whether items like these are likely to persist in the future, and if so, include them in the financial statement forecasts. Given that these items are not part of PepsiCo's ongoing operations, we do not expect items like these to recur, so we project they will be zero in future years.

Projecting the Provision for Income Taxes

As Chapter 8 discusses, PepsiCo's Note 5, "Income Taxes" (Appendix A), shows the reconciliation between the statutory tax rate and PepsiCo's average, or effective, tax rate. The statutory U.S. federal income tax rate was 35.0 percent during Year 2 to Year 4. During those years PepsiCo experienced an increase in its average annual tax rate of roughly 1.0 percent from state income taxes and a decrease in its average tax rate of approximately 5.0 percent from lower tax rates in other (mainly international) tax jurisdictions, yielding an average tax rate of approximately 31.0 percent. PepsiCo realized additional temporary decreases in its average tax rates in Years 3 and 4 from the effects of the favorable settlements of audits of prior years' tax returns. As a result, in Year 4, PepsiCo enjoyed an unusually low average tax rate of 24.7 percent.

In PepsiCo's MD&A section titled "Our Critical Accounting Policies," under the heading "Income Tax Expense and Accruals" (Appendix B), PepsiCo discloses that they expect an average tax rate of 29.4 percent in Year +1. We will rely on that disclosure and assume that the average tax rate for Year +1 will be 29.4 percent. Beyond Year +1, we will assume that PepsiCo's average tax rate will revert to 31.0 percent, reflecting the combined average federal, state, and foreign tax rates.

Net Income

We have now projected all of the elements of the income statement, including first-iteration estimates of interest expense, interest income, and income taxes. Recall that Exhibit 10.3 on pages 742 and 743 presents these income statement projections. Our projected net income amounts and the implied growth rates in net income and net profit margins are as follows:

Year	Net Income	Implied Percentage Growth	Implied Net Profit Margin
4 actual	$4,212	18.0%	14.4%
+1 forecast	$4,382	4.0%	13.8%
+2 forecast	$4,503	2.8%	13.5%
+3 forecast	$4,888	8.5%	13.7%
+4 forecast	$5,217	6.7%	13.7%
+5 forecast	$5,580	7.0%	13.7%

Our forecasts of net income for PepsiCo imply more modest growth in net income and slightly lower net profit margins than PepsiCo has enjoyed in recent years. One contributing factor is the reversion of PepsiCo's effective tax rate from an unusually low level in Year 4 to higher, more normal levels in our forecast periods.

Retained Earnings

In general, the retained earnings account typically increases by the amount of net income (or decreases for net loss) and decreases for dividends. In Year 1, PepsiCo's retained earnings also decreased because PepsiCo issued treasury shares in the merger with Quaker Foods, which was accounted for as a pooling of interests (see the discussion in Chapter 9), and led to a reduction in retained earnings. During Years 2 to 4, PepsiCo's dividend payout rates varied between 36 percent and 43 percent of prior-year net income.

In the Year 4 Annual Report, PepsiCo's MD&A section titled "Our Liquidity, Capital Resources and Financial Position" (Appendix B) discloses that PepsiCo now targets an annual dividend payout policy of 45 percent of prior-year net income from continuing operations, subject to annual review by the board of directors.[13] Relying on this disclosure, we project that PepsiCo's dividend payout policy will average 45 percent of prior-year net income from continuing operations in Years +1 through +5. Therefore,

[13]The capital markets generally react positively when firms announce plans to increase dividend payouts because market participants infer that this is a signal of managers' favorable private information about expectations for future sustainable earnings and cash flows.

our forecasts of dividends to common shareholders will vary over time with lagged net income before the effects of discontinued operations. For example, our forecast of dividends to common shareholders in Year +1 is $1,878 million (= .45 × [$4,212 − $38]).

Recall that in our discussion of PepsiCo's preferred stock, we projected that PepsiCo would also reduce retained earnings by $159 million to reflect a $110 million payment in Year +1 to retire the remaining outstanding preferred shares, and to eliminate the negative $49 million balance in the preferred stock account. The implied changes in retained earnings are as follows (allow for rounding):

Retained Earnings

	Year +1	Year +2	Year +3	Year +4	Year +5
Beginning of Year	$18,730	$21,075	$23,606	$26,468	$29,486
Plus Net Income	4,382	4,503	4,888	5,217	5,580
Less Dividends to Common Shareholders	(1,878)	(1,972)	(2,026)	(2,199)	(2,348)
Less Retirement of Preferred Stock	(159)	(0)	(0)	(0)	(0)
End of Year	$21,075	$23,606	$26,468	$29,486	$32,718

Balancing the Balance Sheet

Even though we have completed first-iteration forecasts of all of the amounts on the income statement and balance sheet, our balance sheet does not balance, because we have forecast individual asset and liability accounts to capture their individual operating activities, which do not vary together perfectly. Currently, our projections of total assets minus our projections of liabilities, shareholders' equity other than retained earnings (which is a negative amount because of PepsiCo's treasury stock), and retained earnings indicate the amounts by which our balance sheets do not balance (allow for rounding):

Projections:	Year +1	Year +2	Year +3	Year +4	Year +5
Total Assets	$29,779	$30,670	$32,751	$34,145	$36,403
Liabilities	$15,391	$15,923	$17,437	$18,236	$19,484
Shareholders' Equity (other than Retained Earnings)	(6,801)	(8,542)	(10,374)	(12,352)	(14,449)
Retained Earnings	21,075	23,606	26,468	29,486	32,718
Total Liabilities and Shareholders' Equity	$29,665	$30,987	$33,531	$35,370	$37,753
Difference (= A − [L + SE])	$ 115	−$317	−$780	−$1,225	−$1,350
Change in the Difference	$ 115	−$432	−$463	−$445	−$125
Change in the Difference as a Percentage of Total Assets	0.4%	−1.4%	−1.4%	−1.3%	−0.3%

The difference between the projected totals of assets and the projected total liabilities and shareholders' equity each year represents the total amount by which we must adjust a flexible financial account to balance the balance sheet. The change in the difference represents the increment by which we must adjust the flexible financial account each year.

Thus, in Year +1, our first-iteration forecasts project that assets will exceed liabilities and equities by $115 million (about 0.4 percent of total assets). We need to adjust a flexible financial account by $115 million (by either decreasing a financial asset account or increasing a financial liability or shareholders' equity account) to balance the balance sheet. In Year +2, our first-iteration projections indicate that liabilities and equities will exceed assets by $317 million, so we will need an additional adjustment of −$432 million in Year +2 (about 1.4 percent of total assets), and so on.

We could use a number of PepsiCo's flexible financial accounts for this adjustment each year, depending on PepsiCo's strategy for investments and capital structure. We could consider the following options:

1. Adjust marketable securities or long-term investment securities if we expect that PepsiCo relies on investment securities for financial flexibility.
2. Adjust short-term or long-term debt if PepsiCo relies on debt capital for financial flexibility.
3. Adjust dividends or treasury stock repurchases if we expect that PepsiCo will adjust capital flows to common shareholders.

PepsiCo's MD&A section titled "Our Liquidity, Capital Resources and Financial Position" (Appendix B) states that PepsiCo expects to continue to return approximately all excess cash flow to shareholders through dividends and share repurchases, so we will adjust dividends as the flexible financial account. In Year +1, therefore, we must adjust our dividend forecast down by $115 million, the necessary amount to balance the balance sheet. This simply means that if PepsiCo's financial performance and position during Year +1 exactly match our forecasts, then PepsiCo will need to adjust dividend payments down slightly to keep assets in balance with liabilities and equity. In Years +2 through +5, we must adjust our dividends forecasts upward each year by the incremental amount of the necessary adjustment to balance the balance sheet (that is, $432 million in Year +2, $463 million in Year +3, and so on). This can be interpreted to mean that, if in those years PepsiCo's financial performance and position exactly match our forecasts, they will be able to pay somewhat larger dividends each year, and still have the projected assets equal the projected liabilities and equity. We refer to these adjustment amounts as *implied dividends*. The projected total amounts of dividends to common shareholders are as follows:

	Year +1	Year +2	Year +3	Year +4	Year +5
Dividends to Common Shareholders (45% of Lagged Net Income from Continuing Operations)	$1,878	$1,972	$2,026	$2,199	$2,348
Implied Dividends	−115	+432	+463	+445	+125
Total Common Dividends	$1,763	$2,404	$2,489	$2,644	$2,473

Equivalently, we could have assumed that PepsiCo will distribute the excess capital to shareholders through treasury stock repurchases rather than implied dividends. In either case, the assumption that PepsiCo will return the excess capital to shareholders through increased dividends or treasury stock repurchases will have equivalent effects on total assets, total liabilities, total shareholders' equity, and net income. After adjusting our dividends projections to include the implied dividends necessary to balance the balance sheet, the implied changes in retained earnings are as follows:

Retained Earnings	Year +1	Year +2	Year +3	Year +4	Year +5
Beginning of Year	$18,730	$21,189	$23,288	$25,687	$28,260
Plus Net Income	4,382	4,503	4,888	5,217	5,580
Less Dividends to Common Shareholders	(1,763)	(2,404)	(2,489)	(2,644)	(2,473)
Less Retirement of Preferred Stock	(159)	(0)	(0)	(0)	(0)
End of Year	$21,189	$23,288	$25,687	$28,260	$31,368

The final projections of the balance sheet total amounts, which the reader should verify by referring back to the projected balance sheets presented in Exhibit 10.4 on pages 744 and 745, are as follows (allow for rounding):

Projections:	Year +1	Year +2	Year +3	Year +4	Year +5
Total Assets	$29,779	$30,670	$32,751	$34,145	$36,403
Liabilities	$15,391	$15,923	$17,437	$18,236	$19,484
Shareholders' Equity (other than Retained Earnings)	(6,801)	(8,542)	(10,374)	(12,352)	(14,449)
Retained Earnings	21,189	23,288	25,687	28,260	31,368
Total Liabilities and Shareholders' Equity	$29,779	$30,670	$32,751	$34,145	$36,403
Difference (= A − [L + SE])	$ 0	$ 0	$ 0	$ 0	$ 0

Closing the Loop: Solving for Co-Determined Variables

If we had plugged the excess capital to interest-earning asset accounts (for example, marketable securities or long-term investment securities) or to interest-bearing liability accounts (for example, short-term or long-term debt), then we would need to adjust accordingly the projected amounts for interest income or interest expense on the income statement. This would create an additional set of co-determined variables within our financial statement forecasts. For example, assume we use long-term debt as our flexible financial account and adjust long-term debt financing by the amount PepsiCo will require to balance assets with liabilities and shareholders' equity. To determine the necessary plug to long-term debt, we need to know all of the other asset, liability, and shareholders' equity amounts, including retained earnings. To forecast retained earnings, we must know net income, which depends on interest expense on long-term debt. To determine retained earnings, we also need to know dividends, which depend on net income. Thus, we need to simultaneously solve for at least five unknown variables.

This problem might seem intractable but it is not because of the computational capabilities of computer spreadsheet programs such as Excel. To solve for multiple variables simultaneously in Excel, first click the Tools menu, and then click the Calculations menu, and then click the Iterations box, so that Excel will solve and resolve circular references up to 100 times until all the calculations fall within the specified tolerance for precision.

Then we can program each cell to calculate the variables we need, even if they are simultaneously determined. FSAP users should follow these steps to check that the Excel-based FSAP spreadsheet will compute co-determined variables simultaneously.

STEP 6: PROJECTING THE STATEMENT OF CASH FLOWS

The final step of the six-step forecasting process involves preparing a projected statement of cash flows. We prepare the statement of cash flows directly from the projected income statement and projected balance sheets. We follow the procedure described in Chapter 3 for preparing this statement. We capture all of the changes in the projected balance sheets each year and express these changes in terms of their implied effects on cash. Increases in assets imply uses of cash; decreases in assets imply sources of cash. Increases in liabilities and shareholders' equity imply sources of cash; decreases in liabilities and shareholders' equity imply uses of cash.

Exhibit 10.6 presents the projected statement of cash flows for PepsiCo for Years +1 through +5. We describe the derivation of each of the line items next.

(1) **Net Income:** We use the amounts in the forecasted income statements (Exhibit 10.3).

(2) **Depreciation Expense:** We add back the projected amount of depreciation expense we included in net income and used to compute the net change in accumulated depreciation on property, plant, and equipment. The depreciation expense forecast should reconcile with the change in accumulated depreciation on the projected balance sheet (less any decrease in accumulated depreciation from assets that were sold or retired, which we have assumed to be zero).

Amortization Expense: On line (2) we also add back amortization expense, which we projected and included in other operating expense on PepsiCo's income statement forecasts. This amortization expense reconciles with the change in amortizable intangible assets on PepsiCo's projected balance sheets because we forecast that they will make no additional investments in these types of assets. If that is not the case, then the amount of amortization expense to add back to net income should reconcile with the change in amortizable intangible asset balance, adjusted for any new investments in those assets. Note also that we do not add back any amortization expense for nonamortizable intangible assets such as goodwill and brands with indefinite lives. This is because under U.S. GAAP goodwill and other intangibles with indefinite lives are not amortized, so we included no amortization expense for these assets in our projected income statements. For some firms, if the amount of amortization expense is not large, then the analyst can ignore adding it back to net income to compute cash flow from operating activities, and simply include the net change in amortizable intangible assets in the investing section. This will understate cash inflows from operations and understate cash outflows for investing activities, but the two effects will offset so that net cash flows will not be affected.

(3), (4), (5), (6), (7), (8): Changes in operating current asset and current liability accounts other than cash appearing on the projected balance sheets.

(9), (10): Changes in deferred taxes and noncurrent liabilities for long-term accrued expenses. These items include changes in long-term accruals for expenses that are part of operations, including deferred taxes and other noncurrent liabilities that appear on the projected balance sheets.

EXHIBIT 10.6

PepsiCo
Actual and Forecast Statements of Cash Flows
(amounts in millions; allow for rounding errors)

Actual and forecast amounts in bold.

	Actuals		Forecasts				
	Year 3	Year 4	Year +1	Year +2	Year +3	Year +4	Year +5
(1) NET INCOME	$3,568	$4,212	$4,382	$4,503	$4,888	$5,217	$5,580
(2) Add back Depreciation and Amortization Expense	1,005	974	1,354	1,468	1,476	1,606	1,746
(3) (Increase) Decrease in Receivables-Trade	(299)	(169)	(282)	(17)	(431)	(50)	(467)
(4) (Increase) Decrease in Inventories	(70)	(129)	(123)	(30)	(199)	(47)	(217)
(5) (Increase) Decrease in Other Current Assets	8	33	58	(18)	(42)	(28)	(45)
(6) Increase (Decrease) in Accounts Payable—Trade	95	93	164	(15)	313	(75)	413
(7) Increase (Decrease) in Accrued Liabilities	120	293	340	201	301	323	347
(8) Increase (Decrease) in Income Taxes Payable	119	(512)	199	9	21	14	23
(9) Increase (Decrease) in Deferred Taxes	(457)	(45)	(25)	36	83	56	90
(10) Increase (Decrease) in Other Noncurrent Liabilities	(151)	24	361	213	319	342	367
NET CASH FLOWS FROM OPERATIONS	$3,938	$4,774	$6,428	$6,349	$6,728	$7,357	$7,838
(11) (Increase) Decrease in Property, Plant, and Equipment, at cost	(1,360)	(1,175)	(1,592)	(1,668)	(1,781)	(1,904)	(2,035)
(12) (Increase) Decrease in Marketable Securities	(974)	(984)	(217)	(71)	(166)	(112)	(181)
(13) (Increase) Decrease in Investment Securities	(309)	(364)	(289)	(107)	(250)	(167)	(271)
(14) (Increase) Decrease in Amortizable Intangibles	0	0	0	0	0	0	0

(15) (Increase) Decrease in Goodwill and Nonamortizable Intangibles	(247)	(177)	(426)	(251)	(376)	(404)	(434)
(16) (Increase) Decrease in Other Noncurrent Assets	(425)	(209)	(218)	(128)	(192)	(207)	(222)
NET CASH FLOWS FROM INVESTING	$(3,315)	$(2,909)	$(2,743)	$(2,226)	$(2,766)	$(2,793)	$(3,142)
(17) Increase (Decrease) in Short-Term Debt	29	463	(395)	9	291	14	(195)
(18) Increase (Decrease) in Long-Term Debt	(485)	695	283	80	187	125	203
(19) Increase (Decrease) in Preferred Stock	(15)	(27)	49	0	0	0	0
(20) Increase (Decrease) in Common Stock and Paid-In Capital	548	70	37	20	48	32	52
(21) Increase (Decrease) in Accumulated Other Comprehensive Income	405	381	0	0	0	0	0
(22) (Increase) Decrease in Treasury Stock	(852)	(1,544)	(1,680)	(1,761)	(1,880)	(2,010)	(2,149)
(23) Dividends	(1,071)	(1,443)	(1,923)	(2,404)	(2,489)	(2,644)	(2,473)
NET CASH FLOWS FROM FINANCING	$(1,441)	$(1,405)	$(3,629)	$(4,055)	$(3,843)	$(4,483)	$(4,562)
(24) **NET CHANGE IN CASH**	$ (818)	$ 460	$ 57	$ 68	$ 119	$ 82	$ 134
Check: Net change in cash—Change in cash balance	0	0	0	0	0	0	0

NOTE: We label the statements of cash flows and amounts for Year 3 and 4 as "Actuals" because we derive them from the actual balance sheet and income statement amounts in PepsiCo's financial statements, rather than from our financial statement forecasts. Appendix A presents PepsiCo's Statements of Cash Flows for Years 3 and 4, as prepared by PepsiCo according to U.S. GAAP.

(11) **Property, Plant, and Equipment:** The amount on this line captures cash outflows for the projected capital expenditures included in the change in property, plant, and equipment (at cost) on the projected balance sheet in Exhibit 10.4, less any cash inflows from sales of property, plant, and equipment. As a check, the analyst should be sure that the statement of cash flows captures all of the net cash flow implications of property, plant, and equipment. To verify this, the amount of depreciation expense added back to net income *minus* cash outflows for capital expenditures *plus* cash inflows for any asset sales or retirements should equal the change in net property, plant, and equipment on the projected balance sheet.

(12), (13) **Marketable Securities and Investment Securities (net):** The statement of cash flows classifies net purchases and sales of marketable securities (current asset) and investment securities (noncurrent asset) as investing transactions. We use the net changes in these accounts on the projected balance sheets to derive the amounts for these items on the statement of cash flows. There is likely to be some error in the implied cash flow amount from investment securities. This change should be increased (become less negative) for the excess (if any) of equity earnings over dividends received from unconsolidated affiliates (which is a noncash increase in this asset amount). Similarly, the excess of equity earnings over dividends received should also be subtracted from net income in the operating section of the statement of cash flows. Rather than making assumptions about this relatively immaterial item (the effects of which completely offset each other), we simply treat the change in investments fully as an investing transaction. This choice means that cash flows from operating activities may be slightly overstated, and cash flows from investing activities may be slightly understated by an equivalent amount, but the net change in cash each year is not affected.

(14) **Amortizable Intangible Assets:** We enter the changes in amortizable intangible assets on this line. The change in this asset account on the projected balance sheets is the net of cash outflows to acquire amortizable intangible assets plus any cash inflows from sales or retirements of such assets. As discussed in item (2), we added amortization expense and depreciation expense back to income in the operating section of the statement of cash flows. Thus, our adjustment for cash outflows or inflows for amortizable intangible assets in the investing section of the statement should not include the effects of amortization expense. Given that amortizable intangibles are commonly shown on balance sheets net of accumulated amortization, the change in the net amortizable intangible assets account balance will reflect both effects: cash flows from investing activities and amortization expense. To isolate the cash flows from investing, the analyst should add amortization expense back to the net change in this account balance.

(15) **Nonamortizable Intangible Assets:** We enter the changes in nonamortizable intangible assets on this line. Given that these assets are not amortized, the net change in the nonamortizable intangible assets balance on our projected balance sheets should reflect cash outflows to acquire new nonamortizable intangible assets less cash inflows from selling or retiring such assets. If the account balance for nonamortizable intangible assets has declined because of an impairment charge, then the analyst should add this noncash charge back to net income in the operating section of the statement of cash flows and adjust accordingly the cash flow implications from nonamortizable intangibles in the investing section of the statement of cash flows (similar to adding back amortization expense).

(16) **Other Noncurrent Assets:** We enter the changes in other noncurrent assets on this lines. The changes in the other asset accounts on the projected balance sheets are the net of cash outflows to acquire such assets plus any cash inflows from sales or retirements of such assets.

(17), (18) **Short-Term and Long-Term Debt:** Changes in interest-bearing debt (short-term notes payable, current maturities of long-term debt, and long-term debt) on the projected balance sheets are financing activities.

(19) **Preferred Stock:** The changes in minority interest and preferred stock on the projected balance sheets are financing activities. For PepsiCo in Year +1, the adjustment to zero out the negative balance in preferred stock appears as a cash inflow, but that effect is offset by an equivalent adjustment included as a cash outflow with total dividends on line 23.

(20) **Changes in Common Stock and Additional Paid-In Capital:** These amounts represent the financing cash flows from changes in the common stock and paid-in capital accounts on the projected balance sheets.

(21) **Changes in Accumulated Other Comprehensive Income:** These amounts represent the changes in the accumulated other comprehensive income account that is a component of shareholders' equity on the projected balance sheets.

(22) **Treasury Stock:** The amounts represent the net cash flow implications of treasury stock transactions, captured in the net change in the treasury stock account on the projected balance sheets.

(23) **Dividends:** The amount for common and preferred dividends equals the projected amount each year (discussed earlier in the section on Retained Earnings in the projected balance sheets). For PepsiCo in Year +1 this includes the amounts to retire outstanding preferred stock.

(24) **Net Change in Cash:** The aggregate of the amounts of cash flows from operations, investing activities, and financing activities. This total should equal the change in cash on the projected balance sheets.

Tips for Forecasting Statements of Cash Flows. The analyst should note that the statement of cash flows will not reconcile with the projected income statement and balance sheets if the balance sheets do not balance and if the income statement does not articulate with the balance sheets (that is, net income should be included in the change in retained earnings).

It is important to be aware that, unlike historical balance sheets and income statements, historical statements of cash flows commonly *do not* provide good bases for projecting future cash flows because many of the line items on the statement of cash flows are difficult to reconcile with historical changes in balance sheets. This is because, in preparing the statement of cash flows, the accountant aggregates numerous cash flows on each line item of this statement and the analyst may not be able to determine what amounts have been aggregated. For example, the accountant must report separately the net cash flow implications of a business acquisition on one line of the statement, but the business acquisition involves recognizing the acquisition of various assets and liabilities that cause changes in many asset and liability accounts. In addition, the accountant may choose to disclose details of cash flows that the analyst cannot verify. For example, the accountant might disclose separately in the statement of cash flows the amounts of marketable securities purchased and sold, but the analyst cannot verify those amounts because the analyst can only observe the net change in the marketable securities balance from the beginning to the end of the year. Thus, we recommend simply computing the implied statement of cash flows from the projected income statements and balance sheets, which the analyst can observe and verify.

SHORTCUT APPROACHES TO FORECASTING

Throughout the chapter thus far we have emphasized a methodical, detailed approach to forecasting individual accounts on the income statement and balance sheet, allowing the analyst to incorporate drivers of expected future operating, investing, and financing activities related to each account. In some circumstances, however, an analyst may find it necessary to forecast income statement and balance sheet totals directly without carefully considering each account. This shortcut approach has the potential to introduce forecasting error if the shortcut assumptions do not fit each account very well. On the other hand, if the firm is stable and mature in an industry in steady-state equilibrium, then shortcut forecasting techniques may be efficient and reliable approaches to project current steady-state conditions to the future. We next illustrate shortcut approaches for forecasting PepsiCo's income statements and balance sheets.

Projected Sales and Income Approach

We can develop shortcut projections for total sales and net income using PepsiCo's recent sales growth rates and net profit margins. Common-size and rate-of-change income statement data reveal that during Years 2 to 4 PepsiCo generated a compound growth rate in sales from continuing operations of 8.2 percent and an average net profit margin of 13.2 percent. If we simply use these ratios to forecast sales and net income over Years +1 to +5, the projected amounts would be as follows:

Year	Sales Growth Rate	Projected Sales	Net Profit Margin	Projected Net Income
4 actual		$29,261		
+1	8.2%	$31,660	13.2%	$4,179
+2	8.2%	$34,257	13.2%	$4,522
+3	8.2%	$37,066	13.2%	$4,893
+4	8.2%	$40,105	13.2%	$5,294
+5	8.2%	$43,394	13.2%	$5,728

These shortcut projections for sales are higher than the detailed sales projections we developed earlier (particularly those for Years +3 to +5), and the net income projections are lower than our detailed projections in Year +1 and become significantly higher by Year +5. By forecasting individual expense amounts, the more detailed projections capture expected changes in expenses relative to sales, whereas the shortcut approach assumes that existing relations between sales and expenses will persist indefinitely into the future.

Projected Total Assets Approach

We can project total assets using the recent historical growth rate in total assets. Between the end of Year 1 and the end of Year 4, PepsiCo's total assets grew at an annual 8.9 percent compound rate. If this growth rate continues through Year +5, total assets will increase as follows:

Year	Asset Growth Rate	Projected Total Assets
4 actual		$27,987
+1	8.9%	$30,478
+2	8.9%	$33,190
+3	8.9%	$36,144
+4	8.9%	$39,361
+5	8.9%	$42,864

Using historical growth rates to project total assets can result in erroneous projections if the analyst fails to consider the link between sales growth and asset growth. We assumed a sales growth rate for PepsiCo of 8.2 percent in the shortcut approach to sales projections, but an 8.9 percent growth in assets, which implies a slight decrease in total asset turnover from 1.1 in Years 3 and 4 to 1.05 in Year +5. An alternative shortcut approach to projecting total assets uses the total asset turnover ratio, explicitly linking sales growth and asset growth. Assume that we expect PepsiCo's total asset turnover to remain at 1.1 over the next five years. Also assume that we use the shortcut approach to estimate sales growth at 8.2 percent per year as we did previously. The calculation of projected total assets using the asset turnover ratio shortcut follows:

Year	Projected Sales	Average Asset Turnover Ratio	Projected Average Total Assets	Projected Beginning Total Assets	Projected Ending Total Assets	Implied Percent Change in Total Assets
+1	$31,660	1.1	$28,782	$27,987	$29,577	5.7%
+2	$34,257	1.1	$31,143	$29,577	$32,708	10.6%
+3	$37,066	1.1	$33,696	$32,708	$34,685	6.0%
+4	$40,105	1.1	$36,459	$34,685	$38,233	10.2%
+5	$43,394	1.1	$39,449	$38,233	$40,665	6.4%

This approach ties the projections of total assets to projections of sales. One difficulty sometimes encountered with using total assets turnover to project total assets is that it can result in unusual patterns for projected total assets. The total assets turnover uses average total assets in the denominator. If total assets changed by an unusually large (small) percentage in the most recent year preceding the projections, then the next year's assets must change by an unusually small (large) proportion to compensate. This sawtooth pattern, which we described earlier in the chapter and illustrated in Exhibit 10.5, makes little intuitive sense, given a smooth growth in sales. We encounter this problem projecting total assets for PepsiCo using its total assets turnover in the preceding data. Note that the forecasts of PepsiCo's total assets increase 5.7 percent during Year +1; 10.6 percent in Year +2; 6.0 percent in Year +3; and so on, whereas we expect PepsiCo's sales to grow smoothly at 8.2 percent per year.

The analyst can deal with that sawtooth problem by basing the asset turnover ratio on the ending balance, instead of the average balance, in total assets. As an alternative approach to deal with the sawtooth problem, the analyst can arbitrarily smooth the rate of increase in assets over a period of time. Assuming that asset turnover is stable at 1.1 and sales growth is smooth at 8.2 percent per year, the preceding data indicate that assets will increase from $27,987 million in Year 4 to $40,665 million in Year +5, which reflects a compound average annual growth rate of 7.76 percent. The following table shows the revised projected assets following this smoothed approach. Note that total assets equal $40,665 million at the end of Year +5 in both cases. We could use these smoothed total assets amounts in preparing the projected balance sheets for PepsiCo.

Year	Asset Growth Rate	Projected Total Assets
4 actual		$27,987
+1	7.76%	$30,159
+2	7.76%	$32,499
+3	7.76%	$35,021
+4	7.76%	$37,739
+5	7.76%	$40,665

Once the analyst projects total assets, common-size balance sheet percentages provide the basis for allocating this total to individual assets, as well as to liabilities and shareholders' equity. In using these common-size percentages, the analyst assumes that the firm maintains a constant mix of assets, liabilities, and equities, regardless of the level of total assets. Equivalently, the analyst assumes that each asset, liability, and equity account grows at the same growth rate as total assets. For example, the common-size balance sheet for Year 4 for PepsiCo (Appendix C) indicates that total liabilities represent 51.7 percent of total assets, and equities represent 48.3 percent of total assets. If we assume that PepsiCo will maintain exactly the same proportions of debt and equity in its capital structure in future years, and if we use these proportions and the smoothed projections of total assets, we can project total liabilities and shareholders' equity amounts for Years +1 through +5, as follows:

Year	Projected Total Assets	Projected Total Liabilities (51.7%)	Projected Shareholders' Equity (48.3%)
+1	$30,159	$15,592	$14,577
+2	$32,499	$16,802	$15,697
+3	$35,021	$18,456	$16,565
+4	$37,739	$19,511	$18,228
+5	$40,665	$21,024	$19,641

Using common-size balance sheet percentages to project individual assets, liabilities, and shareholders' equity encounters (at least) two potential shortcomings. First, the common-size percentages for individual assets, liabilities, and shareholders' equity are not independent of each other. For example, a firm such as PepsiCo that acquires and disposes of its bottlers on an ongoing basis may experience a changing proportion for investments in securities among its assets. Other asset categories may show decreasing percentages in some years even though their dollar amounts are increasing. The analyst must interpret these decreasing percentages carefully.

Second, using the common-size percentages does not permit the analyst to easily change the assumptions about the future behavior of an individual asset. For example, assume that PepsiCo intended to implement inventory control systems that should increase its inventory turnover in the future. Inventory will likely comprise a smaller percentage of total assets in the future than it has in the past. The analyst encounters difficulties adjusting the common-size balance sheet percentages to reflect the changes in inventory policies.

The following diagram summarizes the approaches to projecting assets:

	Project Individual Assets	**Project Total Assets**
Use Historical Growth Rates for Projections		
Use Asset Turnovers for Projections		

These four possible combinations yield similar projections for assets when a firm has experienced relatively stable historical growth rates for total assets and individual asset items, and relatively stable asset turnovers. If historical growth rates have varied significantly from year to year, then the analyst should use average historical growth rates to provide more reasonable projections than asset turnovers. One desirable feature of using asset turnovers, however, is that projected asset amounts incorporate projections of the level of sales. Also, management's actions to improve profitability often focus on improving asset turnovers. The analyst can incorporate the effects of these actions into the projections more easily by using the asset turnover approach than by adjusting the compound annual growth rates or common-size balance sheet percentages.

ANALYZING PROJECTED FINANCIAL STATEMENTS

As a reality check on the reasonableness of our forecast assumptions and their internal consistency, we can analyze the projected financial statements using the same ratios and other analytical tools discussed in previous chapters. Exhibit 10.7 presents a ratio analysis for PepsiCo based on the financial statement forecasts for Year +1 to Year +5. The FSAP Forecasts spreadsheet provides these ratio computations based on the financial statement forecasts.

Forecast growth rates for sales are consistent with PepsiCo's past sales growth performance. Our forecasts of net income exhibit growth rates that are much lower than those PepsiCo experienced in its recent past, driven in part by our forecast of an increase in PepsiCo's effective tax rates. The projected rate of return on assets (ROA) increases from 15.7 percent in Year +1 to 16.3 percent in Year +5, consistent with PepsiCo's recent past levels of ROA. The main driver of the increase in projected ROA is the expected slight increase in asset turnover. Similarly, the projected rate of return on common equity

EXHIBIT 10.7

PepsiCo
Financial Ratio Analysis Based on Actual and Forecast Financial Statements

	Actuals			Forecasts				
	Year 2	Year 3	Year 4	Year +1	Year +2	Year +3	Year +4	Year +5
FORECAST VALIDITY CHECK DATA:								
GROWTH								
Revenue Growth Rates	6.8%	7.4%	8.5%	8.8%	4.8%	6.8%	6.9%	6.9%
Net Income Growth Rates	25.0%	18.9%	18.0%	4.0%	2.8%	8.5%	6.7%	7.0%
Total Asset Growth Rates	8.2%	7.9%	10.5%	6.4%	3.0%	6.8%	4.3%	6.6%
RETURN ON ASSETS (based on reported amounts):								
Profit Margin for ROA	12.4%	13.6%	14.8%	14.2%	13.9%	14.1%	14.1%	14.1%
× Asset Turnover	1.1	1.1	1.1	1.1	1.1	1.1	1.1	1.2
= Return on Assets	13.8%	15.1%	16.2%	15.7%	15.4%	15.9%	16.1%	16.3%
RETURN ON ASSETS (excluding the effects of nonrecurring items):								
Profit Margin for ROA	13.2%	13.7%	14.1%	14.2%	13.9%	14.1%	14.1%	14.1%
× Asset Turnover	1.1	1.1	1.1	1.1	1.1	1.1	1.1	1.2
= Return on Assets	14.6%	15.2%	15.4%	15.7%	15.4%	15.9%	16.1%	16.3%
RETURN ON COMMON EQUITY (based on reported amounts):								
Profit Margin for ROCE	11.8%	13.2%	14.3%	13.3%	13.5%	13.7%	13.7%	13.7%
× Asset Turnover	1.1	1.1	1.1	1.1	1.1	1.1	1.1	1.2
× Capital Structure Leverage	2.5	2.3	2.1	2.1	2.1	2.1	2.1	2.1
= Return on Common Equity	32.7%	33.2%	32.9%	30.2%	30.9%	32.5%	33.4%	34.0%

RETURN ON COMMON EQUITY (excluding the effects of nonrecurring items):								
Profit Margin for ROCE	12.6%	13.3%	13.6%	13.3%	13.5%	13.7%	13.7%	13.7%
× Asset Turnover	1.1	1.1	1.1	1.1	1.1	1.1	1.1	1.2
× Capital Structure Leverage	2.5	2.3	2.1	2.1	2.1	2.1	2.1	2.1
= Return on Common Equity	34.8%	33.5%	31.2%	30.2%	30.9%	32.5%	33.4%	34.0%
OPERATING PERFORMANCE:								
Gross Profit/Revenues	54.2%	54.1%	54.2%	54.2%	54.2%	54.2%	54.2%	54.2%
Operating Profit before Taxes/Revenues	17.1%	17.7%	18.0%	18.6%	18.6%	18.9%	18.9%	18.9%
ASSET TURNOVER:								
Revenues/Average Accounts Receivable	10.7	10.1	10.0	10.1	10.1	10.1	10.1	10.1
COGS/Average Inventory	8.7	9.0	9.1	9.1	9.1	9.1	9.1	9.1
Revenues/Average Fixed Assets	3.5	3.5	3.7	3.8	3.8	3.9	4.1	4.2
LIQUIDITY:								
Current Ratio	1.1	1.1	1.3	1.3	1.3	1.3	1.3	1.3
Quick Ratio	0.7	0.8	1.0	1.0	1.0	1.0	1.0	1.0
SOLVENCY:								
Total Liabilities/Total Assets	0.6	0.5	0.5	0.5	0.5	0.5	0.5	0.5
Total Liabilities/Total Equity	1.5	1.1	1.1	1.1	1.1	1.1	1.1	1.2
Interest Coverage Ratio	25.9	31.6	34.4	31.5	33.1	33.2	32.7	34.3

(ROCE) increases from 30.2 percent in Year +1 to 34.0 percent in Year +5. This occurs because of slight projected increases in profit margin and asset turnover.

The projected capital structure leverage remains fairly stable over the forecast horizon as the result of several forecast assumptions, two of which have opposite effects on financial leverage. We assumed that PepsiCo would maintain stable proportions of interest-bearing debt to total assets through Year +5, but we also assumed that PepsiCo would continue to make significant repurchases of its common stock and increase its dividend payout policy. PepsiCo is expected to finance the treasury stock repurchases and dividends with cash flow from operations, which will reduce shareholders' equity relative to debt, thereby increasing the capital structure leverage ratio. The net effect of maintaining a steady ratio of interest-bearing debt to assets, while at the same time repurchasing shares and paying dividends, suggests that PepsiCo is expected to generate very healthy cash flows after operating and investing activities.

The operating performance ratios, liquidity ratios, asset turnover ratios, and solvency ratios remain fairly steady over time. These ratios confirm that our forecast assumptions are reasonable, are roughly in line with PepsiCo's past performance, and appear to be implemented correctly (that is, the computations appear to be working). Unfortunately, these ratios cannot confirm whether our assumptions are correct. These ratios do not tell us whether we have accurately and realistically captured PepsiCo's sales growth, profitability, cash flows, and financial position in the future. For this confirmation, only time will tell.

SENSITIVITY ANALYSIS AND REACTIONS TO ANNOUNCEMENTS

These financial statement forecasts can serve as the base case from which the analyst assesses the impact of various critical forecast assumptions for the firm, and from which the analyst reacts to new announcements from the firm. For example, with these financial statement forecasts, the analyst can assess the sensitivity of projected net income and cash flows to key assumptions about the firm's sales growth rates; gross profit margins; control over selling, general, and administrative expenses; and other assumptions. For example, using the projected financial statements (Appendix C) as the base case, the analyst can assess the impact on PepsiCo's profitability from a one-point increase or decrease in sales growth, or from a one-point increase or decrease in the gross profit margin.

The analyst can also use the projected financial statements to assess the sensitivity of the firm's liquidity and leverage to changes in key assumptions. For example, the analyst can assess the impact on PepsiCo's liquidity and solvency ratios by varying the long-term debt to assets assumptions and the interest expense assumptions. Lenders and credit analysts can use the projected financial statements to assess the conditions under which the firm's debt covenants may become binding. For example, suppose PepsiCo's long-term debt and revolving line of credit agreements require that PepsiCo maintain certain minimum liquidity and interest coverage ratios. The financial statement forecasts provide the analyst a structured approach to assess how far net income and cash flows would need to decrease, and how much long-term debt and interest expense would need to increase, before the minimum interest coverage ratio becomes binding.

The projected financial statements also enable the analyst to react quickly and efficiently to new announcements by the firm. Suppose PepsiCo announces at the beginning of Year +1 that it signed a new contract with a key distribution channel that should enable PepsiCo to increase beverage sales by an additional $1 billion by Year +3, and that this new level of sales should be sustainable into the future. The projected financial statements enable the analyst to incorporate the effects of this announcement relatively efficiently into expectations for PepsiCo's future earnings, balance sheets, and cash flows.

As an alternative example, suppose PepsiCo announces that it will discontinue purchases of treasury stock in Year +1 (but will reissue previously acquired treasury shares as needed to meet stock options exercises), and that it intends to use this cash to reduce interest-bearing debt. Our original projections included $3,258 million in treasury stock repurchases in Year +1, which will now be zero, and PepsiCo will instead use this capital to reduce debt. The analyst can efficiently incorporate the effects of this announcement into the projected financial statements. PepsiCo's original and revised projected ratios for Year +1 follow:

	Year +1 Originally Projected	Year +1 Revised Projected
Net Profit Margin for ROA	14.2%	14.2%
Return on Assets	15.7%	15.7%
Return on Common Equity	30.2%	27.5%
Capital Structure Leverage	2.1	1.9
Total Liabilities/Total Assets	51.7%	40.7%
Interest Coverage Ratio	31.5	60.5

Thus, the assumptions about the growth in treasury stock and long-term debt have significant effects on projected financial statements and ratios for PepsiCo. Various other changes in assumptions are possible. By designing a flexible computer spreadsheet for projecting financial statements, the analyst can change any one or a combination of assumptions and observe the effect on the financial statements and ratios. FSAP provides a flexible spreadsheet for forecasting.

SUMMARY

The preparation of financial statement forecasts requires numerous assumptions about the growth rate in sales, cost behavior of various expenses, levels of investments in various working capital and fixed assets, the financial capital structure of the firm, dividend payouts, and others. The analyst should carefully develop realistic expectations for these activities, and capture those expectations in financial statement forecasts that provide an objective and realistic portrait of the firm in the future. The analyst should study the sensitivity of the financial statements to the assumptions made and to the impact of different assumptions. Spreadsheet software can assist in this sensitivity analysis.

After developing careful and realistic expectations for future earnings, cash flows, and dividends using financial statement projections, the analyst can begin to make decisions with these data, including decisions about the firm as a potential equity investment or a potential credit risk. In the next four chapters, we demonstrate how to incorporate expectations for future dividends, cash flows, and earnings into estimates of firm value.

QUESTIONS, EXERCISES, PROBLEMS, AND CASES

Questions and Exercises

10.1 RELYING ON ACCOUNTING TO AVOID FORECAST ERRORS. The chapter states that forecasts of financial statements should rely on the *additivity* within financial statements and the *articulation* across financial statements to avoid internal inconsistencies in forecasts. Explain how the concepts of additivity and articulation apply to financial statement forecasts, and how these concepts can help the analyst avoid potential forecast errors.

10.2 OBJECTIVE AND REALISTIC FORECASTS. The chapter encourages analysts to develop forecasts that are realistic, objective, and unbiased. Some firms' managers tend to be optimistic. Some accounting principles tend to be conservative. Describe the differing risks and incentives managers, accountants, and analysts face, and explain how these different risks and incentives lead managers, accountants, and analysts to different biases when predicting uncertain outcomes.

10.3 PROJECTING REVENUES: THE EFFECTS OF VOLUME VERSUS PRICE. Suppose a firm has generated 10.25 percent revenue growth in the past two years, consisting of 5.0 percent growth in sales volume compounded with 5.0 percent growth in prices. Describe one firm-specific strategic factor, one industry-specific factor, and one economy-wide factor that could help this firm sustain 5.0 percent growth in sales volume next year. Describe one firm-specific strategic factor, one industry-specific factor, and one economy-wide factor that could help this firm sustain 5.0 percent growth in prices next year.

10.4 PROJECTING GROSS PROFIT: THE EFFECTS OF VOLUME VERSUS PRICE. Suppose you are analyzing a firm that is successfully executing a strategy that differentiates its products from those of its competitors. Because of this strategy, you project that next year the firm will generate 6.0 percent revenue growth from price increases and 3.0 percent revenue growth from sales volume increases. Assume that the firm's production cost structure involves strictly variable costs (that is, the cost to produce each unit of product remains the same). Should you project that the firm's gross profit will increase next year? If you project that the gross profit will increase, is the increase a result of volume growth, price growth, or both? Should you project that the firm's gross profit margin (gross profit divided by sales) will increase next year? If you project that the gross profit margin will increase, is the increase a result of volume growth, price growth, or both?

10.5 PROJECTING REVENUES, COST OF GOODS SOLD, AND INVENTORY. Walgreens is a leading chain of drugstores in the United States. Use the following data for Walgreens in Years 3 and 4 to project revenues, cost of goods sold, and inventory for Year +1. Assume that Year +1 growth in revenues and cost of goods sold will be identical to Year 4. Project the average inventory balance in Year +1 and use it to compute the implied ending inventory balance.

Walgreens (amounts in millions)	Year 3	Year 4
Sales Revenues	$32,505	$37,508
Cost of Goods Sold	$23,706	$27,310
Ending Inventory	$ 4,203	$ 4,739

10.6 THE FLEXIBLE FINANCIAL ACCOUNT. The chapter describes how firms must use flexible financial accounts to maintain equality between assets and claims on assets from liabilities and equities. Chapter 1 describes how some firms progress through different life-cycle stages, from introduction to growth to maturity to decline, and how during different stages of the life cycle firms experience very different cash flows. For each life-cycle stage, identify the different types of flexible accounts firms are more likely to use to balance the balance sheet.

10.7 DIVIDENDS AS A FLEXIBLE FINANCIAL ACCOUNT. The following data for Schwartz Company represent a summary of your first-iteration forecast amounts for Year +1. Schwartz uses dividends as a flexible financial account. Compute the amount of dividends you can assume Schwartz will pay in order to balance your projected balance sheet. Present the projected balance sheet.

	Year +1
Operating Income	$ 58
Interest Expense	−8
Income before Tax	$ 50
Tax Provision (20.0 percent effective tax rate)	−10
Net Income	$ 40
Total Assets	$200
Accrued Liabilities	$ 43
Long-Term Debt	$ 80
Common Stock, at par	$ 20
Retained Earnings (at the beginning of Year +1)	$ 34

10.8 LONG-TERM DEBT AS A FLEXIBLE FINANCIAL ACCOUNT. For this exercise, use the preceding data for Schwartz Company. Now assume that Schwartz pays common shareholders a dividend of $25 in Year +1. Assume that Schwartz uses long-term debt as a flexible financial account, increasing borrowing when it needs capital and paying down debt when it generates excess capital. For simplicity, assume that Schwartz pays 10.0 percent interest expense on the ending balance in long-term debt for the year, and that interest expense is tax deductible at Schwartz's average tax rate of 20.0 percent. Present the projected income statement and balance sheet for Year +1. (*Hint:* Because of the circularity between interest expense, net income and debt, it may require several iterations to balance the projected balance sheet and to have the projected balance sheet articulate with net income. You may find it helpful to program a spreadsheet to work the iterative computations.)

Problems and Cases

10.9 STORE-DRIVEN FORECASTS. Home Depot is a leading specialty retailer of hardware and home improvement products and is the second-largest retail store chain in the United States. It operates large, warehouse-style stores. The following table provides summary data for Home Depot in Years 4 and 5.

Home Depot (amounts in millions except number of stores)	Year 4	Year 5
Number of Stores	1,707	1,890
Sales Revenues	$64,816	$73,094
Inventory	$ 9,076	$10,076
Capital Expenditures, net	$ 3,243	$ 3,852

Required

a. Use the preceding data for Home Depot to compute average revenues per store, capital spending per new store, and ending inventory per store in Year 5.

b. Assume that Home Depot will add 200 new stores by the end of Year +1 and assume that each new store will be open for business for an average of one-half year in Year +1. For simplicity, assume that in Year +1 Home Depot's only growth will come from opening new stores. Project Year +1 sales revenues, capital spending, and ending inventory.

10.10 PROJECTING PROPERTY, PLANT, AND EQUIPMENT. Intel is a global leader in manufacturing semiconductors. Computer chip manufacturing is very capital intensive. In addition, the production processes in computer chip manufacturing require very sophisticated technology, and the technology changes rapidly, particularly with each new generation of chip. As a consequence, productive manufacturing assets in the chip industry tend to have relatively short useful lives. The following summary information relates to Intel's property, plant, and equipment for Year 3 and 4.

Intel (amounts in millions)	Year 3	Year 4
Property, Plant, and Equipment, at cost	$37,692	$39,833
Accumulated Depreciation	($22,031)	($24,065)
Property, Plant, and Equipment, net	$16,661	$15,768
Depreciation Expense		$ 4,590
Capital Expenditures, net		$ 3,843

Required

Use the following data for Intel to project property, plant, and equipment; depreciation expense; and accumulated depreciation for Year +1. Assume that Intel depreciates all property, plant, and equipment using the straight-line depreciation method and zero salvage value. Assume Intel does not sell or retire any property, plant, and equipment during Year +1.

a. Compute the average useful life Intel used in Year 4 for depreciation.

b. Project total depreciation expense for Year +1 using the following steps: (1) project depreciation expense for Year +1 on existing property, plant, and equipment at the end of Year 4; (2) project depreciation expense in Year +1 on capital expenditures in Year +1, assuming $4,000 in expenditures on depreciable assets in Year +1 and assuming that Intel takes a full year of depreciation in the first year of service; and (3) sum the results of parts (1) and (2) to obtain total depreciation expense for Year +1.

c. Project the Year +1 ending balance in property, plant, and equipment, both at cost and net of accumulated depreciation.

10.11 IDENTIFYING THE COST STRUCTURE AND PROJECTING GROSS MARGINS FOR CAPITAL-INTENSIVE, CYCLICAL BUSINESSES.

AK Steel is an integrated manufacturer of high-quality steel and steel products in capital-intensive steel mills. AK Steel produces flat-rolled carbon, stainless and electrical steel products, and carbon and stainless tubular steel products for automotive, appliance, construction, and manufacturing markets. Nucor manufactures more commodity-level steel and steel products at the lower end of the market in less capital-intensive mini-mills. The following data describe sales and cost of products sold for both firms for Years 3 and 4.

($ amounts in millions)	Year 3	Year 4
AK Steel		
Sales	$4,042	$ 5,217
Cost of Products Sold	$3,887	$ 4,554
Gross Profit	$ 155	$ 663
Gross Margin	3.8%	12.7%
Nucor		
Sales	$6,266	$11,377
Cost of Products Sold	$5,997	$ 9,129
Gross Profit	$ 269	$ 2,248
Gross Margin	4.3%	19.8%

Industry analysts anticipate the following annual changes in sales for the next five years: Year +1, 5 percent increase; Year +2, 10 percent increase; Year +3, 20 percent increase; Year +4, 10 percent decrease; Year +5, 20 percent decrease.

Required

a. The analyst can sometimes estimate the variable cost as a percentage of sales for a particular cost (for example, cost of products sold) by dividing the amount of the change in the cost item between two years by the amount of the change in sales for those two years. The analyst can then multiply the variable-cost percentage times sales to estimate the total variable cost. Subtracting the variable cost from the total cost yields an estimate of the fixed cost for that particular cost item. Follow this procedure to estimate the manufacturing cost structure (variable cost as a percentage of sales, total variable costs, and total fixed costs) for cost of products sold for both AK Steel and Nucor in Year 4.

b. Discuss the structure of manufacturing cost (that is, fixed versus variable) for each firm in light of the manufacturing process and type of steel produced.

c. Using the analysts' forecasts of sales changes, compute the projected sales, cost of products sold, gross profit, and gross margin (gross profit as a percentage of sales) of each firm for Year +1 through Year +5.

d. Why do the levels and variability of the gross margin percentages differ for these two firms over Year +1 through Year +5?

10.12 IDENTIFYING THE COST STRUCTURE. Sony Corporation manufactures and markets consumer electronics products. Selected income statement data for Year 7 and Year 8 follow (amounts in billions of yen):

	Year 7	Year 8
Sales	¥ 4,571	¥ 5,636
Cost of Goods Sold	(3,439)	(4,161)
Selling and Administrative Expenses	(918)	(1,132)
Operating Income before Income Taxes	¥ 214	¥ 343

Required

a. The analyst can sometimes estimate the variable cost as a percentage of sales for a particular cost (for example, cost of goods sold) by dividing the amount of the change in the cost item between two years by the amount of the change in sales for those two years. The analyst can then multiply the variable-cost percentage times sales to determine the total variable cost. Subtracting the variable cost from the total cost yields the fixed cost for that particular cost item. Follow this procedure to determine the cost structure (fixed cost plus variable cost as a percentage of sales) for cost of goods sold for Sony.

b. Repeat part a for selling and administrative expenses.

c. Sony Corporation projects sales to grow at the following percentages in future years: Year 9, 12 percent; Year 10, 10 percent; Year 11, 8 percent; Year 12, 6 percent. Project sales, cost of goods sold, selling and administrative expenses, and operating income before income taxes for Sony for Year 9 to Year 12, using the cost structure amounts derived in parts a and b.

d. Compute the ratio of operating income before income taxes to sales for Year 9 through Year 12.

e. Interpret the changes in the ratio computed in part d in light of the expected changes in sales.

10.13 SMOOTHING CHANGES IN ACCOUNTS RECEIVABLE. Hasbro designs, manufactures, and markets toys and games for children and adults in the United States and internationally. Hasbro's portfolio of brands and products contains some of the most well-known toys and games, under famous brands such as Playskool, Tonka Trucks, Milton Bradley, and Parker Brothers, and including such classic games as Scrabble, Monopoly, and Clue. Sales during Year 4 totaled $2,998 million. Accounts receivable totaled $608 million at the beginning of Year 4 and $579 million at the end of Year 4.

Required

a. Use the average balance to compute the accounts receivable turnover ratio for Hasbro for Year 4.

b. Hasbro has generated compounded average rate of sale growth of 3.17 percent over the past two years. Assume that Hasbro's sales will grow at that compound annual rate each year between Year 5 and Year 9 and that the accounts receivable turnover ratio each year will equal the ratio computed in part a for Year 4. Project the amount of accounts receivable at the end of Year 5 through Year 9 based on the accounts receivable turnover computed in part a. Also compute the percentage change in accounts receivable between each of the year-ends between Year 5 and Year 9.

c. Does the pattern of growth in your projections of Hasbro's accounts receivable seem reasonable, considering the assumptions of smooth growth in sales and steady turnover?

d. The changes in accounts receivable computed in part b display the "sawtooth" pattern depicted in Exhibit 10.5. Smooth the changes in accounts receivable by computing the year-end accounts receivable balances for Year 5 through Year 9 using the compound annual growth rate in accounts receivable between the end of Year 4 and the end of Year 9 from part b.

e. Smooth the changes in accounts receivable using the compound annual growth rate in accounts receivable between the end of Year 4 and the end of Year 8 from part b. Apply this growth rate to compute accounts receivable at the end of Year 5 through Year 9. Why do the amounts for ending accounts receivable using the growth rate from part d differ from those using the growth rate from this part?

f. Compute the accounts receivable turnover for Year 4 by dividing sales by the balance in accounts receivable at the end of Year 4 (instead of using average accounts receivable as in part a). Use this accounts receivable turnover ratio to compute the projected balance in accounts receivable at the end of Year 5 through Year 9. Also compute the percentage change in accounts receivable between the year-ends for Year 5 through Year 9.

10.14 SMOOTHING CHANGES IN INVENTORIES. Barnes & Noble sells books, magazines, music, and videos through retail stores and online. For a retailer like Barnes & Noble, inventory is a critical element of the business, and it is necessary to carry a wide array of titles. In Year 4, sales totaled $4,874 million and cost of sales and occupancy totaled $3,387 million. Inventories constitute the largest asset on Barnes & Noble's balance sheet, totaling $1,275 million at the end of Year 4 and $1,290 million at the end of Year 3.

Required

a. Compute the inventory turnover ratio for Barnes & Noble for Year 4.

b. Over the last two years, Barnes & Noble experienced sales growth at a compounded annual rate of 11.6 percent. Over this period the number of Barnes & Noble retail stores has remained fairly steady. Assume that sales will continue to grow at that rate each year between Year 4 and Year 9. Also assume that the cost of goods sold to sales percentage will equal that realized in Year 4 (which is very similar to the cost of goods sold percentage over the past three years). Project the amount of inventory at the end of Year 5 through Year 9 using the inventory turnover ratio computed in part a. Also compute the percentage change in inventories between each of the year-ends between Year 4 and Year 9. Does the pattern of growth in your projections of Barnes & Noble inventory seem reasonable to you, considering the assumptions of smooth growth in sales and steady cost of goods sold percentages?

EXHIBIT 10.8

Watson Corporation
Partial Income Statements
(Problem 10.15)

	Year 0 Actual	Year 1 Projected	Year 2 Projected	Year 3 Projected	Year 4 Projected
Sales	$46,000	$50,600	$56,672	$64,606	$74,943
Cost of Goods Sold	(29,900)	(32,890)	XXXX	(40,702)	(46,465)
Selling and Administrative	(10,580)	(11,638)	(12,468)	(13,567)	(14,989)
Interest Expense	(3,907)	(4,298)	d	(3,866)	(5,227)
Income Taxes	(565)	(621)	(1,372)	(2,265)	(2,892)
Net Income	$XXXX	$XXXX	$XXXX	$XXXX	$XXXX

c. The changes in inventories in part b display the "sawtooth" pattern depicted in Exhibit 10.5. Smooth the changes in the inventory forecasts between Year 4 and Year 9, using the compound annual growth rate in inventories between the end of Year 4 and the end of Year 9 implied by the projections in part b. Does this pattern of growth seem more reasonable?

d. Now suppose that, instead of following the smoothing approach in part c, you used the rate of growth in inventory during Year 4 to project future inventory balances at the end of Year 5 through Year 9. Use these projections to compute the implied inventory turnover rates. Does this pattern of growth and efficiency in inventory for Barnes & Noble seem reasonable?

10.15 IDENTIFYING FINANCIAL STATEMENT RELATIONS. Partial forecasts of financial statements for Watson Corporation appear in Exhibit 10.8 (income statement), Exhibit 10.9 (balance sheet), and Exhibit 10.10 (statement of cash flows). Selected amounts have been omitted, as well as all totals (indicated by XXXX).

Required

Determine the amount of each of the following items:

a. Dividends declared and paid during Year 1.
b. Depreciation expense for Year 1, assuming that Watson Corporation neither sold nor retired depreciable assets during Year 1.
c. Inventories at the end of Year 2.
d. Interest expense on borrowing during Year 2. The interest rate is 7 percent.
e. Other current liabilities at the end of Year 2.
f. Property, plant, and equipment at the end of Year 3, assuming that Watson Corporation neither sold nor retired depreciable assets during Year 3.
g. Retained earnings at the end of Year 3.
h. Long-term debt at the end of Year 3.
i. The income tax rate for Year 4.
j. Purchases of inventories during Year 4.

EXHIBIT 10.9

Watson Corporation
Partial Balance Sheets
(Problem 10.15)

	Year 0 Actual	Year 1 Projected	Year 2 Projected	Year 3 Projected	Year 4 Projected
Assets					
Cash	$ 1,200	$ 664	$ 206	$ 416	$ 1,262
Accounts Receivable	8,000	8,433	8,855	10,420	12,286
Inventories	7,500	8,223	c	10,711	11,333
Fixed Assets:					
Cost	110,400	120,445	126,467	f	169,895
Accumulated Depreciation	(33,100)	(36,112)	(37,917)	(45,352)	(50,938)
Total Assets	$ XXXX	$ XXXX	$ XXXX	$ XXXX	$ XXXX
Liabilities and Shareholders' Equity					
Accounts Payable	$ 2,500	$ 2,801	$ 3,107	$ 3,376	$ 3,828
Notes Payable	6,500	6,852	7,195	8,467	9,982
Other Current Liabilities	3,300	3,630	e	4,635	5,376
Long-Term Debt	45,000	49,094	51,549	h	69,251
Total Liabilities	$ XXXX	$ XXXX	$ XXXX	$ XXXX	$ XXXX
Common Stock	$ 15,000	$ 17,233	$ 17,539	$ 22,434	$ 24,319
Retained Earnings	21,700	22,043	23,700	g	31,082
Total Shareholders' Equity	$ XXXX	$ XXXX	$ XXXX	$ XXXX	$ XXXX
Total Liabilities and Shareholders' Equity	$ XXXX	$ XXXX	$ XXXX	$ XXXX	$ XXXX

10.16 PREPARING AND INTERPRETING FINANCIAL STATEMENT FORECASTS. Wal-Mart Stores (Wal-Mart) is the largest retailing firm in the world. Building on a base of discount stores, Wal-Mart has expanded into warehouse clubs and Supercenters, which sell traditional discount store items and grocery products. **FSAP**

Exhibits 10.11, 10.12, and 10.13 present the financial statements of Wal-Mart for Years 2, 3, and 4. Exhibits 4.51 to 4.53 (Case 4.2 in Chapter 4) also present summary financial statements for Wal-Mart, and Exhibit 4.54 presents selected financial statement ratios for Years 2, 3, and 4. [Note: The data presented in Chapter 4 for Wal-Mart differ slightly from the data here because the Chapter 4 data have been adjusted slightly to remove the effects of items such as discontinued operations, for purposes of computing financial analysis ratios.]

Required (additional requirements follow on page 794)

a. Design a spreadsheet and prepare a set of financial statement forecasts for Wal-Mart for Year +1 to Year +5, using the assumptions that follow. Project the amounts in the order presented (unless indicated otherwise), beginning with the income statement, then the balance sheet, and then the statement of cash flows.

EXHIBIT 10.10

Watson Corporation
Partial Statements of Cash Flows
(Problem 10.15)

	Year 0 Actual	Year 1 Projected	Year 2 Projected	Year 3 Projected	Year 4 Projected
Operations					
Net Income	$ 1,048	$ 1,153	$XXXX	$ 4,206	$ 5,370
Depreciation	2,378	b	1,805	7,435	5,586
Change in Accounts Receivable	(394)	(433)	(422)	(1,565)	(1,866)
Change in Inventories	(657)	(723)	(1,322)	(1,166)	(622)
Change in Accounts Payable	274	301	306	269	452
Change in Other Current Liabilities	300	330	436	569	741
Cash Flow from Operations	$XXXX	$ XXXX	$XXXX	$ XXXX	$ XXXX
Investing					
Acquisition of Fixed Assets	$(9,130)	$(10,045)	$(6,022)	$(24,796)	$(18,632)
Financing					
Change in Notes Payable	$ 320	$ 352	$ 343	$ 1,272	$ 1,515
Change in Long-Term Debt	3,721	4,094	2,455	10,107	7,595
Change in Common Stock	2,029	2,233	306	4,895	1,885
Dividends	(750)	a	(891)	(1,016)	(1,178)
Cash Flow from Financing	$XXXX	$ XXXX	$XXXX	$ XXXX	$ XXXX
Change in Cash	$XXXX	$ XXXX	$XXXX	$ XXXX	$ XXXX

Income Statement

Sales

Sales grew 11.6 percent in Year 3 and 11.6 percent in Year 4, primarily as a result of significant increases in same-store sales and opening new stores. The compound annual growth rate during the last five years was 12.8 percent. In the future, Wal-Mart will continue to grow internationally by opening stores and acquiring other firms, and domestically by converting discount stores to Supercenters. In addition, despite competition, Wal-Mart will likely also continue to enjoy increases in same-store sales of 5 percent to 6 percent, consistent with its experience through Year 4. Thus, assume that sales will grow 10 percent each year between Year +1 and Year +5.

Cost of Goods Sold

The cost of goods sold to sales percentage steadily decreased from 77.7 percent of sales in Year 2 to 77.1 percent in Year 4. Wal-Mart's everyday low-price strategy, its movement into grocery products, and competition will likely prevent Wal-Mart from achieving significant additional decreases in this expense percentage. Assume that the cost of goods sold to sales percentage will average 77.0 percent for Year +1 to Year +5.

EXHIBIT 10.11

Balance Sheets for Wal-Mart Stores (Problem 10.16)

	Year 2	Year 3	Year 4
Cash	$ 2,758	$ 5,199	$ 5,488
Accounts Receivable—Trade	2,108	1,254	1,715
Inventories	24,891	26,612	29,447
Other Current Assets	726	1,356	1,841
CURRENT ASSETS	**$30,483**	**$ 34,421**	**$ 38,491**
Property, Plant & Equipment—at cost	67,051	76,380	89,042
Accumulated Depreciation	(15,147)	(17,357)	(20,475)
Goodwill and Other Non-Current Assets	12,298	11,961	13,165
TOTAL ASSETS	**$94,685**	**$105,405**	**$120,223**
Accounts Payable—Trade	$17,140	$ 19,425	$ 21,671
Notes Payable and Short Term Debt	1,079	3,267	3,812
Current Maturities of Long Term Debt	4,714	3,100	3,969
Other Current Liabilities	9,684	12,048	13,436
CURRENT LIABILITIES	**$32,617**	**$ 37,840**	**$ 42,888**
Long Term Debt	19,608	20,099	23,669
Deferred Taxes and Other Non-Current Liabilities	3,123	3,843	4,270
TOTAL LIABILITIES	**$55,348**	**$ 61,782**	**$ 70,827**
Common Stock + Paid in Capital	1,922	2,566	2,848
Retained Earnings	37,924	40,206	43,854
Accumulated Other Comprehensive Income	(509)	851	2,694
SHAREHOLDERS' EQUITY	**$39,337**	**$ 43,623**	**$ 49,396**
TOTAL LIABILITIES AND EQUITIES	**$94,685**	**$105,405**	**$120,223**

Selling and Administrative Expenses

The selling and administrative expense percentage has steadily increased from 17.4 percent of sales in Year 2 to 17.9 percent of sales in Year 4. Identifying and transacting international corporate acquisitions and opening additional Supercenters will put upward pressure on this expense percentage, but the slowdown in sales growth will moderate this upper pressure. Assume that the selling and administrative expense to sales percentage will remain at 18.0 percent for Year +1 to Year +5.

Other Operating Income

Other operating income has been approximately 1 percent of revenues during the last three years. Assume that other operating income will continue at this historical pattern.

Interest Income

Wal-Mart earns a bit of interest income on its cash and cash equivalents accounts. The average interest rate earned on average cash balances was approximately 3.8 percent

EXHIBIT 10.12

Income Statements for Wal-Mart Stores (Problem 10.16)

	Year 2	Year 3	Year 4
Revenues	$229,616	$256,329	$285,222
Cost of Goods Sold	(178,299)	(198,747)	(219,793)
Gross Profit	**$ 51,317**	**$ 57,582**	**$ 65,429**
Selling, General and Administrative Expense	(39,983)	(44,909)	(51,105)
Other Operating Income	1,961	2,352	2,767
Operating Profit	**$ 13,295**	**$ 15,025**	**$ 17,091**
Interest Income	132	164	201
Interest Expense	(1,059)	(996)	(1,187)
Other Expenses or Losses	(193)	(214)	(249
Income before Tax	**$ 12,175**	**$ 13,979**	**$ 15,856**
Income Tax Expense	(4,357)	(5,118)	(5,589)
Income from Discontinued Operations	137	193	0
NET INCOME	**$ 7,955**	**$ 9,054**	**$ 10,267**
NET INCOME	**$ 7,955**	**$ 9,054**	**$ 10,267**
Other Comprehensive Income Items	759	1,360	1,843
COMPREHENSIVE INCOME	**$ 8,714**	**$ 10,414**	**$ 12,110**

during Year 4. Assume Wal-Mart will earn interest income based on a 3.8 percent interest rate on average cash balances (that is, the sum of the beginning and end of the year cash divided by 2) for Year +1 through Year +5. Note: Projecting the amount of interest income must await projection of cash on the balance sheet.

Interest Expense

Wal-Mart engages in long-term borrowing to construct new stores domestically, and in both short- and long-term borrowing to finance corporate acquisitions. The average interest rate on all interest-bearing debt was approximately 4.1 percent during Year 4. Assume a 4.1 percent interest rate for all outstanding borrowing (notes payable, long-term debt, and current portion of long-term debt) for Wal-Mart for Year +1 through Year +5. Compute interest expense on the average amount of interest-bearing debt outstanding each year (that is, the sum of the beginning and end of the year divided by 2). NOTE: Projecting the amount of interest expense must await projection of interest-bearing debt on the balance sheet.

Other Expenses

Other expenses have been approximately 0.1 percent of revenues during the last three years. Assume that other expenses will continue at this historical pattern.

EXHIBIT 10.13

Statements of Cash Flows for Wal-Mart Stores (Problem 10.16)

	Year 2	Year 3	Year 4
NET INCOME	$ 7,955	$ 9,054	$ 10,267
Add back Depreciation	3,364	3,852	4,405
Other Add backs to Net Income	474	177	263
Other Subtractions from Net Income	(55)	(143)	0
(Increase) Decrease in Accounts Receivable—Trade	(159)	373	(304)
(Increase) Decrease in Inventories	(2,219)	(1,973)	(2,635)
Increase (Decrease) in Accounts Payable—Trade	1,748	2,587	1,694
Increase (Decrease) in Other Current Liabilities	1,212	1,896	976
Other Operating Cash Flows	685	173	378
NET CASH FLOW FROM OPERATIONS	**$13,005**	**$15,996**	**$ 15,044**
Property, Plant, and Equipment Sold	311	481	953
Property, Plant, and Equipment Acquired	(9,245)	(10,308)	(12,893)
Investments Acquired	(749)	(38)	(315)
Other Investment Transactions	(156)	1,553	(96)
NET CASH FLOW FROM INVESTING ACTIVITIES	**$ (9,839)**	**$ (8,312)**	**$(12,351)**
Increase in Short-Term Borrowing	1,836	688	544
Decrease in Short-Term Borrowing	0	0	0
Increase in Long-Term Borrowing	2,044	4,099	5,832
Decrease in Long-Term Borrowing	(1,477)	(3,846)	(2,335)
Issue of Capital Stock	0	0	0
Share Repurchases—Treasury Stock	(3,383)	(5,046)	(4,549)
Dividend Payments	(1,328)	(1,569)	(2,214)
Other Financing Transactions	(62)	111	113
NET CASH FLOW FROM FINANCING ACTIVITIES	**$ (2,370)**	**$ (5,563)**	**$ (2,609)**
Effects of Exchange Rate Changes on Cash	(199)	320	205
NET CHANGE IN CASH	**$ 597**	**$ 2,441**	**$ 289**

Income Tax Expense

Wal-Mart's average income tax rate as a percentage of income before taxes has varied between 35.2 percent and 36.6 percent during the last three years. Assume an income tax rate of 36.0 percent of income before income taxes for Year +1 through Year +5. NOTE: Projecting the amount of income tax expense must await computation of income before taxes.

Balance Sheet

Cash

Cash will be the flexible financial account we will use to plug the amount necessary to equate total assets with total liabilities plus shareholders' equity. Projecting the amount of cash must await projections of all other balance sheet amounts.

Accounts Receivable

Accounts receivable will increase at the growth rate in sales.

Inventories

Wal-Mart has maintained a steady inventory turnover ratio of 7.8 times during the last two years (based on average inventory balances each year). In recent years, the expanding role of grocery products has increased Wal-Mart's inventory turnover. However, that increase has been offset by the stocking of new stores and the distribution of merchandise to stores worldwide. We will assume that inventory turnover will continue to average 7.8 times per year (every 47 days) in Years +1 to +5. Use this turnover rate to compute the average inventories each year, and then compute the implied ending inventories each year.

Prepayments

Other current assets include prepayments, which relate to ongoing operating costs, such as rent and insurance. Assume that prepayments will grow at the growth rate in sales.

Property, Plant, and Equipment—at cost

Property, plant, and equipment grew 14.4 percent annually during the most recent five years. In the most recent three years, Wal-Mart's growth in property, plant, and equipment has varied from 14.4 percent in Year 2 to 13.9 percent in Year 3 to 16.6 percent in Year 4. The construction of new Supercenters and the acquisition of established retail chains abroad will require additional investments in property, plant, and equipment. Assume that property, plant, and equipment will grow 14.4 percent each year from Year +1 through Year +5.

Accumulated Depreciation

In Years 3 and 4, the change in Wal-Mart's accumulated depreciation has averaged roughly 4.0 percent of the beginning of year balance in property, plant, and equipment — at cost. During Year +1 through Year +5 assume accumulated depreciation will increase each year by an amount equal to 4.0 percent of the beginning of year balance in property, plant and equipment — at cost.

Goodwill and Other Assets

Goodwill and other assets primarily include goodwill arising from corporate acquisitions abroad. Such acquisitions increase Wal-Mart sales. Assume that goodwill and other assets will grow at the growth rate in sales.

Accounts Payable

Wal-Mart has maintained a steady accounts payable turnover, with payment periods averaging 33 days (an average turnover ratio of roughly 11.1 times per year) during the last five years (based on average balances each year). We will assume that accounts payable turnover will continue to average 33 days in Years +1 to +5. Use this turnover rate to compute the average accounts payable each year, and then compute the implied ending accounts payable each year. Remember to add the change in inventory to the cost of goods sold to obtain the total amount of credit purchases of inventory during the year.

Short-Term Debt, Current Maturities of Long-Term Debt, and Long-Term Debt

Wal-Mart uses short-term debt, current maturities of long-term debt, and long-term debt to augment cash from operations to finance acquisitions of property, plant, and equipment, and acquisition of existing retail chains abroad. Over the past five years, the total amount of Wal-Mart's interest-bearing debt has grown at 7.3 percent compounded annually. Assume that each of three interest-bearing sources of debt capital will increase at 7.3 percent per year over Year +1 through Year +5.

Other Current Liabilities

Other current liabilities relate to accrued expenses for ongoing operating activities and are expected to grow at the growth rate in selling and administrative expenses, which are expected to grow with sales.

Other Noncurrent Liabilities

Other noncurrent liabilities include amounts related to health care benefits and deferred taxes. Assume that other noncurrent liabilities will increase at the growth rate in sales.

Common Stock

Assume that common stock and additional paid-in capital will not change.

Retained Earnings

The increase in retained earnings equals net income minus dividends. Wal-Mart paid dividends amounting to $2,214 million to common shareholders in Year 4. Over the past five years, Wal-Mart's dividends have increased at an average annual rate of 20.0 percent. Assume that dividends will grow 20.0 percent each year between Year +1 and Year +5. In addition, assume that in Year +1 through Year +5, Wal-Mart will not repurchase any treasury stock.

Accumulated Other Comprehensive Income

Assume that accumulated other comprehensive income will not change.

Cash

At this point we can now project the amount of cash on Wal-Mart's balance sheet at each year-end from Year +1 to Year +5. We assume Wal-Mart uses cash as the flexible financial account to balance the balance sheet.

Statement of Cash Flows

Depreciation Addback

Include the change in accumulated depreciation.

Other Addbacks

Assume that changes in other noncurrent liabilities on the balance sheet are operating activities.

Other Investing Transactions

Assume that changes in other noncurrent assets on the balance sheet are investing activities.

Required (continued from page 787)

b. If you have programmed your spreadsheet correctly, the projected amount of cash declines from Year +1 to Year +5, and the projected cash balance at the end of Year +5 is a negative $584 million. Given the profitability and growth projected for Wal-Mart, a negative balance in cash seems unlikely. Identify the likely reason for the negative projected amount of cash.

c. Assume now that long-term debt will grow in Year +1 to Year +5 at a growth rate of 12.0 percent, which is closer to the assumed growth rate of 14.4 percent in property, plant, and equipment—at cost. Leave the forecast assumptions for short-term debt and current maturities of long-term debt unchanged. Assess whether this growth rate in long-term debt provides more reasonable forecast amounts for cash.

d. Calculate the financial statement ratios listed in Exhibit 4.54 for Wal-Mart using the forecast amounts determined in part c for Year +1 to Year +5. Assess the projected changes in the profitability and risk of Wal-Mart for Year +1 to Year +5.

FSAP

INTEGRATIVE CASE 10.1

STARBUCKS

The Starbucks integrative case provides you with an opportunity to apply the entire six-step analysis framework of this textbook to Starbucks, an interesting, profitable, and growing company. Beginning in Chapter 1, and following each chapter of the book, we use the Starbucks Integrative Case to illustrate and apply all of the tools of financial statements analysis and valuation throughout the book. This chapter illustrates the six-step forecasting procedure by applying it to PepsiCo to develop complete financial statement forecasts through Year +5. In this portion of the integrative case, we rely on our analysis of Starbucks' financial statements through fiscal Year 4 and apply the six-step forecasting procedure of this chapter to develop complete forecasts of Starbucks' financial statements through Year +5.

Exhibits 10.14 and 10.15 provide Starbucks' financial statements for fiscal Year 2 through fiscal Year 4, in dollar amounts, common-size, and rate-of-change formats. These data report the financial performance and position of Starbucks and summarize the results of Starbucks' operating, investing, and financing activities. The common-size and rate-of-change balance sheets and income statements for Starbucks highlight relations among accounts and trends over time. Exhibit 10.16 provides store operating data through fiscal Year 4 for Starbucks, including same-store sales growth rates, new store openings, and total numbers of stores open. In addition, Exhibit 10.17 provides a detailed breakdown of Starbucks' revenues and revenue growth by segment and by store. You may wish to refer back to Exhibits 1.24 through 1.28 (Chapter 1) for additional financial statement data. You may also wish to refer back to Exhibit 4.45 (Chapter 4) for a ratio analysis of Starbucks' financial statements. All of the other chapters throughout the text have also illustrated accounting-quality issues and financial statement analysis issues for Starbucks. All of these data and analyses now come into play in this portion of the comprehensive Starbucks case, as we develop forecasts of Starbucks' future financial statements.

Required

Develop complete forecasts of Starbucks' income statements, balance sheets, and statements of cash flows for Years +1 through +5. As illustrated in this chapter, develop objective and unbiased forecast assumptions for all of Starbucks' future operating, investing, and financing activities through Year +5, and capture those expectations using financial statement forecasts.

Specifications

a. Build your own spreadsheets to develop and capture your financial statement forecast assumptions and data for Starbucks. Building your own financial statement forecast spreadsheets is an extremely valuable learning exercise in its own right. You can use the examples we developed throughout this chapter for PepsiCo as a model to follow in building your own spreadsheets. If you have already had the learning experience of building your own forecasting spreadsheets, you can build your financial statement forecasts using the FSAP template for Starbucks that accompanies this book. You can download the blank FSAP template from the book's website address: www.thomsonedu.com/accounting/stickney. Input the accounting data for Starbucks from Exhibits 1.24 to 1.26 (Chapter 1) into the Data Spreadsheet within the blank FSAP template.

b. Starbucks' operating, investing, and financing activities revolve primarily around opening and operating company-owned retail coffee shops in the United States and around the world. Starbucks' annual reports provide useful data on the number of company-operated stores Starbucks owns, the new stores it opens each year, and the same-store sales growth rates. These data reveal that Starbucks' revenues and revenue growth rates differ significantly across different segments and across U.S. versus international stores. Use these data, summarized in Exhibits 10.13 and 10.14, as a basis to forecast (a) Starbucks' future sales from existing stores, (b) the number of new company-operated stores Starbucks will open, (c) future sales from new stores, and (d) capital expenditures for new stores.

c. Starbucks' business also involves generating revenues from licensing Starbucks stores and selling Starbucks coffee and other products through foodservice accounts, grocery stores, warehouse clubs, etc. Use the data in Exhibits 10.13 and 10.14 to build forecasts of future revenues from licensing activities and foodservice and other activities.

d. Use your forecasts of capital expenditures for new stores, together with Starbucks' data on property, plant, and equipment and depreciation, to build a schedule to forecast property, plant, and equipment, and depreciation expense, as described in the chapter and illustrated in Appendix C for PepsiCo.

e. Starbucks appears to use marketable securities as the flexible financial account for balancing the balance sheet. If we follow Starbucks' practice and use marketable securities to balance the balance sheet forecasts, under reasonable forecast assumptions the forecast amounts for marketable securities will become excessively large proportions of total assets by Year +4 and +5. Therefore, build your financial statement forecasts using dividends as the flexible financial account. This assumption does not match Starbucks' policy through Year 4 of paying zero dividends. But as Starbucks matures and continues to produce excess capital, you can predict that it will initiate a dividend payment policy (or equivalently, a share repurchase policy) to begin distributing excess capital to common equity shareholders.

f. Save your forecast spreadsheets. In subsequent chapters, we will continue to use Starbucks as a comprehensive integrative case. In those chapters, we will apply the valuation models to your forecasts of Starbucks' future earnings, cash flows, and dividends to assess Starbucks' share value.

EXHIBIT 10.14

Starbucks
Income Statements in Amounts, Common-Size Percentages, and Rates of Change
Fiscal Years 2 to 4
(Integrative Case 10.1)
(amounts in millions except per-share amounts)

				Common-Size			Rates of Change		
	Year 2	Year 3	Year 4	Year 2	Year 3	Year 4	Year 3	Year 4	Compound
Company-Operated Retail Store Sales									
U.S.	$2,425.2	$2,965.6	$3,800.4	73.7%	72.8%	71.8%	22.3%	28.1%	25.2%
International	367.7	484.0	657.0	11.2%	11.9%	12.4%	31.6%	35.7%	33.7%
Total Retail Sales	$2,792.9	$3,449.6	$4,457.4	84.9%	84.6%	84.2%	23.5%	29.2%	26.3%
Specialty									
U.S. Licensing	$ 227.7	$ 301.2	$ 437.0	6.9%	7.4%	8.3%	32.3%	45.1%	38.5%
International Licensing	84.2	108.4	128.8	2.6%	2.7%	2.4%	28.7%	18.8%	23.7%
Total Licensing	$ 311.9	$ 409.6	$ 565.8	9.5%	10.1%	10.7%	31.3%	38.1%	34.7%
Foodservice and Other	184.1	216.3	271.1	5.6%	5.3%	5.1%	17.5%	25.3%	21.4%
Total Specialty	$ 496.0	$ 625.9	$ 836.9	15.1%	15.4%	15.8%	26.2%	33.7%	29.9%
Net Revenues	**$3,288.9**	**$4,075.6**	**$5,294.3**	**100.0%**	**100.0%**	**100.0%**	**23.9%**	**29.9%**	**26.9%**
Cost of Sales (including occupancy costs)	(1,347.0)	(1,681.4)	(2,191.4)	(41.0%)	(41.3%)	(41.4%)	24.8%	30.3%	27.6%
Gross Profit	**$1,941.9**	**$2,394.1**	**$3,102.8**	**59.0%**	**58.7%**	**58.6%**	**23.3%**	**29.6%**	**26.4%**
Store Operating Expenses	(1,109.8)	(1,379.6)	(1,790.2)	(33.7%)	(33.8%)	(33.8%)	24.3%	29.8%	27.0%
Other Operating Expenses	(106.1)	(141.3)	(171.6)	(3.2%)	(3.5%)	(3.2%)	33.2%	21.4%	27.2%
Depreciation and Amortization	(210.7)	(244.7)	(289.2)	(6.4%)	(6.0%)	(5.5%)	16.1%	18.2%	17.2%
General and Administrative Expenses	(234.6)	(244.6)	(304.3)	(7.1%)	(6.0%)	(5.7%)	4.2%	24.4%	13.9%
Income from Equity Investees	33.4	38.4	60.7	1.0%	0.9%	1.1%	14.8%	58.0%	34.7%
Operating Income	**$ 314.2**	**$ 422.4**	**$ 608.2**	**9.6%**	**10.4%**	**11.5%**	**34.4%**	**44.0%**	**39.1%**

Interest and Other Income, net	9.3	11.6	14.1	0.3%	0.3%	0.3%	25.0%	21.7%	23.3%
Other Gains (Losses)	13.4	0.0	0.0	0.4%	0.0%	0.0%	(100.0%)	na	(100.0%)
Income before Income Taxes	$ 336.9	$ 434.0	$ 622.3	10.2%	10.6%	11.8%	28.8%	43.4%	35.9%
Provision for Income Taxes	(125.5)	(167.1)	(231.8)	(3.8%)	(4.1%)	(4.4%)	33.2%	38.7%	35.9%
Net Income	**$ 211.4**	**$ 266.9**	**$ 390.6**	**6.4%**	**6.5%**	**7.4%**	**26.3%**	**46.3%**	**35.9%**
Net Income per Share									
Basic	$ 0.55	$ 0.68	$ 0.98						
Diluted	$ 0.53	$ 0.66	$ 0.95						

EXHIBIT 10.15

Starbucks
Balance Sheets in Amounts, Common-Size Percentages, and Rates of Change
Fiscal Years 2 to 4
(Integrative Case 10.1)
(amounts in millions)

				Common-Size			Rates of Change		
	Year 2	Year 3	Year 4	Year 2	Year 3	Year 4	Year 3	Year 4	Compound
Assets									
Current Assets									
Cash and Equivalents	$ 99.7	$ 200.9	$ 299.1	4.4%	7.2%	8.8%	101.6%	48.9%	73.2%
Short-Term Investments	227.7	149.1	353.9	10.1%	5.4%	10.4%	(34.5%)	137.3%	24.7%
Receivables	97.6	114.4	140.2	4.3%	4.1%	4.1%	17.3%	22.5%	19.9%
Inventories	263.2	342.9	422.7	11.7%	12.3%	12.5%	30.3%	23.2%	26.7%
Prepaid Expenses and Other Assets	42.4	55.2	71.3	1.9%	2.0%	2.1%	30.3%	29.3%	29.8%
Deferred Income Taxes, net	42.2	47.4	63.7	1.9%	1.7%	1.9%	12.3%	34.3%	22.8%
Total Current Assets	**$ 772.6**	**$ 910.0**	**$ 1,350.9**	**34.3%**	**32.8%**	**39.8%**	**17.8%**	**48.5%**	**32.2%**
Long-Term Investments	0.0	136.2	135.2	0.0%	4.9%	4.0%	na	(0.7%)	na
Equity and Other Investments	102.5	144.3	171.7	4.6%	5.2%	5.1%	40.7%	19.1%	29.4%
Property and Equipment, at cost	2,116.2	2,516.3	2,877.7	94.0%	90.6%	84.9%	18.9%	14.4%	16.6%
Accumulated Depreciation	(814.4)	(1,068.6)	(1,326.3)	(36.2%)	(38.5%)	(39.1%)	31.2%	24.1%	27.6%
Property and Equipment, net	$1,301.7	$ 1,447.7	$ 1,551.4	57.8%	52.1%	45.8%	11.2%	7.2%	9.2%
Other Assets	43.7	52.1	85.6	1.9%	1.9%	2.5%	19.3%	64.2%	39.9%
Other Intangible Assets	9.9	24.9	26.8	0.4%	0.9%	0.8%	152.9%	7.4%	64.8%
Goodwill	19.9	63.3	69.0	0.9%	2.3%	2.0%	218.3%	8.9%	86.1%
Total Assets	**$2,250.4**	**$ 2,778.5**	**$ 3,390.5**	**100.0%**	**100.0%**	**100.0%**	**23.5%**	**22.0%**	**22.7%**

Liabilities and Shareholders' Equity									
Current Liabilities									
Accounts Payable	$ 136.0	$ 169.0	$ 199.3	6.0%	6.1%	5.9%	24.3%	18.0%	21.1%
Accrued Compensation and Related Costs	105.9	152.6	208.9	4.7%	5.5%	6.2%	44.1%	36.9%	40.5%
Accrued Occupancy Costs	51.2	21.7	29.2	2.3%	0.8%	0.9%	(57.5%)	34.5%	(24.4%)
Accrued Taxes	54.2	54.9	63.0	2.4%	2.0%	1.9%	1.2%	14.7%	7.7%
Other Accrued Expenses	72.3	101.8	123.7	3.2%	3.7%	3.6%	40.8%	21.5%	30.8%
Deferred Revenue	42.3	73.5	121.4	1.9%	2.6%	3.6%	73.9%	65.2%	69.5%
Current Portion of Long-Term Debt	0.7	0.7	0.7	0.0%	0.0%	0.0%	1.7%	1.8%	1.7%
Total Current Liabilities	**$ 462.6**	**$ 574.2**	**$ 746.3**	**20.6%**	**20.7%**	**22.0%**	**24.1%**	**30.0%**	**27.0%**
Deferred Income Taxes, net	22.5	12.5	21.8	1.0%	0.5%	0.6%	(44.2%)	73.6%	(1.6%)
Long-Term Debt	5.1	4.4	3.6	0.2%	0.2%	0.1%	(14.2%)	(16.9%)	(15.6%)
Other Long-Term Liabilities	46.8	116.3	144.7	2.1%	4.2%	4.3%	148.5%	24.4%	75.8%
Total Liabilities	**$ 537.0**	**$ 707.4**	**$ 916.3**	**23.9%**	**25.5%**	**27.0%**	**31.7%**	**29.5%**	**30.6%**
Shareholders' Equity									
Common Stock	891.0	959.1	956.7	39.6%	34.5%	28.2%	7.6%	(0.3%)	3.6%
Additional Paid-In Capital	39.4	39.4	39.4	1.8%	1.4%	1.2%	0.0%	0.0%	0.0%
Retained Earnings	791.5	1,058.3	1,448.9	35.2%	38.1%	42.7%	33.7%	36.9%	35.3%
Accumulated Other Comprehensive Income (Loss)	(8.6)	14.3	29.2	(0.4%)	0.5%	0.9%	(266.3%)	104.9%	na
Total Shareholders' Equity	**$1,713.4**	**$ 2,071.1**	**$ 2,474.2**	**76.1%**	**74.5%**	**73.0%**	**20.9%**	**19.5%**	**20.2%**
Total Liabilities and Shareholders' Equity	**$2,250.4**	**$ 2,778.5**	**$ 3,390.5**	**100.0%**	**100.0%**	**100.0%**	**23.5%**	**22.0%**	**22.7%**

EXHIBIT 10.16

Starbucks
Store Operating Data
Fiscal Years 2 to 4
(Integrative Case 10.1)

		Year 2	Year 3	Year 4
Percentage change in comparable store sales:				
U.S.		7%	9%	11%
International		1%	7%	6%
Consolidated		6%	8%	10%
Stores Opened during the Year:				
U.S.	Company-Operated Stores	503	570	514
	Licensed Stores	264	389	417
International	Company-Operated Stores	113	99	120
	Licensed Stores	297	281	293
Totals	Company-Operated Stores	616	669	634
	Licensed Stores	561	670	710
	Grand Total Stores Opened	1,177	1,339	1,344

					Common-Size			Rates of Change		
Stores Open at Year End:		Year 2	Year 3	Year 4	Year 2	Year 3	Year 4	Year 3	Year 4	Compound
U.S.	Company-Operated Stores	3,209	3,779	4,293	54.5%	52.3%	50.1%	17.8%	13.6%	15.7%
	Licensed Stores	1,033	1,422	1,839	17.6%	19.7%	21.5%	37.7%	29.3%	33.4%
International	Company-Operated Stores	703	802	922	11.9%	11.1%	10.8%	14.1%	15.0%	14.5%
	Licensed Stores	941	1,222	1,515	16.0%	16.9%	17.7%	29.9%	24.0%	26.9%
Totals	Company-Operated Stores	3,912	4,581	5,215	66.5%	63.4%	60.9%	17.1%	13.8%	15.5%
	Licensed Stores	1,974	2,644	3,354	33.5%	36.6%	39.1%	33.9%	26.9%	30.3%
	Total Stores Open at Year End	5,886	7,225	8,569	100.0%	100.0%	100.0%	22.7%	18.6%	20.7%

EXHIBIT 10.17

Starbucks
Sales Growth Analysis by Segment
(Integrative Case 10.1)
(amounts in millions except per-store amounts)

	Year 2	Year 3	Year 4
U.S. Retail Sales	$2,425.2	$2,965.6	$3,800.4
International Retail Sales	$ 367.7	$ 484.0	$ 657.0
Total Retail Segment Sales	$2,792.9	$3,449.6	$4,457.4
Retail Segment Sales as Percentage of Total Sales	84.9%	84.6%	84.2%
Growth Rates in Retail Segment Sales		+23.5%	+29.2%
Compound Growth Rate in Retail Segment Sales			+26.3%
Total Company-Operated Stores	3,912	4,581	5,215
Net New Stores Opened during Year	616	669	634
Growth Rate in Company-Operated Stores		+17.1%	+13.8%
U.S. Company-Operated Stores	3,209	3,779	4,293
Sales per Average U.S. Store (in thousands)	$ 820.0	$ 848.8	$ 941.6
Sales Growth Rates per Average U.S. Store		+3.5%	+10.9%
International Company-Operated Stores	703	802	922
Sales per Average International Store (in thousands)	$ 568.8	$ 643.2	$ 762.2
Sales Growth Rates per Average International Store		+13.1%	+18.5%
Specialty Revenue Components:			
U.S. License Revenues	$ 227.7	$ 301.2	$ 437.0
International License Revenues	$ 84.2	$ 108.4	$ 128.8
Total License Revenues	$ 311.9	$ 409.6	$ 565.8
Foodservice and Other Revenues	$ 184.1	$ 216.3	$ 271.1
Total Specialty Segment Sales	$ 496.0	$ 625.9	$ 836.9
Specialty Segment Sales as Percentage of Total Sales	15.1%	15.4%	15.8%
Growth Rates in Specialty Segment Sales		+26.2%	+33.7%
Compound Growth Rate in Specialty Segment Sales			+29.9%
Growth Rates in License Revenues		+31.3%	+38.2%
Total Licensed Stores	1,974	2,644	3,354
Net New Licensed Stores Opened during Year	561	670	710
Growth Rates in Licensed Stores		+33.9%	+26.9%
U.S. Licensed Stores	1,033	1,422	1,839
Revenues per Average U.S. Licensed Store (in thousands)	$ 252.7	$ 245.4	$ 268.6
Revenue Growth Rates per Average U.S. Licensed Store		−2.9%	+9.2%
International Licensed Stores	941	1,222	1,515
Revenues per Average International Licensed Store (in thousands)	$ 106.2	$ 100.2	$ 94.1
Revenue Growth Rates per Average International Licensed Store		−5.7%	−6.1%

FSAP

CASE 10.2

MASSACHUSETTS STOVE COMPANY: ANALYZING STRATEGIC OPTIONS[*]

The Woodstove Market

Since the early 1990s, woodstove sales have declined from 1,200,000 units per year to approximately 100,000 units per year. The decline has occurred because of (1) stringent new federal EPA regulations, which set maximum limits on stove emissions beginning in 1992; (2) stable energy prices, which reduced the incentive to switch to woodstoves to save heating costs; and (3) changes in consumers' lifestyles, particularly the growth of two-income families.

During this period of decline in industry sales, the market was flooded with woodstoves at distressed prices as companies closed their doors or liquidated inventories made obsolete by the new EPA regulations. Downward pricing pressure forced surviving companies to cut prices, output, or both. Years of contraction and pricing pressure left many of the surviving manufacturers in a precarious position financially, with excessive inventory, high debt, little cash, uncollectible receivables, and low margins.

The shakeout and consolidation among woodstove manufacturers and, to a lesser extent, among woodstove specialty retailers, have been dramatic. The number of manufacturers selling more than 2,000 units a year (characterized within the industry as "large manufacturers") has declined from approximately 90 to 35 in the last ten years. The number of manufacturers selling less than 2,000 units per year (characterized as "small manufacturers") has declined from approximately 130 to 6. Because the current woodstove market is not large enough to support all of the surviving producers, manufacturers have attempted to diversify in order to stay in business. Seeking relief, virtually all of the survivors have turned to the manufacture of gas appliances.

The Gas Appliance Market

The gas appliance market includes three segments: (1) gas log sets, (2) gas fireplaces, and (3) gas stoves. Gas log sets are "faux fires" that can be installed in an existing fireplace. They are primarily decorative and have little heating value. Gas fireplaces are fully assembled fireboxes that can be installed in new construction or in renovated buildings and houses by a builder or contractor. They are mainly decorative and are less expensive and easier to maintain than a masonry/brick fireplace. Gas stoves are freestanding appliances with a decorative appearance and efficient heating characteristics.

The first two segments of the gas appliance market (log sets and fireplaces) are large, established, stable markets. Established manufacturers control these markets, and distribution is primarily through mass merchandisers. The third segment (gas stoves) is less than five years old. Although it is growing steadily, it has an annual volume of only about 100,000 units (almost identical to the annual volume of the woodstove market). This is the market to which woodstove manufacturers have turned for relief.

---

[*]The authors acknowledge the assistance of Tom P. Morrissey in the preparation of this case.

The gas stove market is not as heavily regulated as the woodstove market, and there are currently no EPA regulations governing the emissions of gas heating appliances. Gas stoves are perceived as more appropriate to an aging population because they provide heat and ambiance but require no effort. They can be operated with a wall switch or thermostat or by remote control. Actual fuel cost (or cost savings) is not an issue for many buyers, so a big advantage of heating with wood is no longer a consideration for many consumers. Gas stoves are sold and distributed through mass merchandisers or natural gas or propane dealers. The gas industry has the financial, promotional, organizational, and lobbying clout to support the development of the gas stove market, attributes that the tiny woodstove industry lacks.

Unfortunately, life has not been rosy for all of the woodstove companies entering this new market. Development costs and selling costs for new products using a different fuel and different distribution system have been substantial. Improvements in gas logs and gas burners have required rapid changes in product design. In contrast, woodstove designs are fairly stable and slow to change. Competition for market share has renewed pricing pressure on gas stove producers. Companies trying to maintain their woodstove sales while introducing gas products must carry large inventories to service both product lines. Failure to accurately forecast demand has left many companies with inventory shortages during the selling season, or large inventories of unsold product at the end of the season.

Many surviving manufacturers who looked to gas stoves for salvation are now quietly looking for suitors to acquire them. A combination of excessive debt and inventory levels, together with high development and distribution costs, has made financial success highly uncertain. There will be continued consolidation in this difficult market during the next five years.

Massachusetts Stove Company

Massachusetts Stove Company (MSC) is one of the six "small manufacturers" to survive the EPA regulation and industry meltdown. It has just completed its sixth consecutive year of slow but steady growth in revenue and profit since complying with the EPA regulations. Exhibits 10.18 to 10.20 present the financial statements of MSC for Year 3 to Year 7. Exhibit 10.21 presents selected financial statement ratios.

The success of MSC in recent years is a classic case of a company staying small, marketing in a specific niche, and vigorously applying a "stick to your knitting" policy. MSC is the only woodstove producer that has not developed gas products; 100 percent of its sales currently come from woodstove sales. MSC is the only woodstove producer that sells by mail order directly to consumers. The mail-order market has sheltered MSC from some of the pricing pressure that other manufacturers have had to bear. The combination of high entry costs and high risks make it unlikely that another competitor will enter the mail-order niche.

MSC's other competitive advantages are the high efficiency and unique features of its woodstoves. MSC equips its woodstoves with a catalytic combuster, which reburns gases emitted from burning wood. This reburning not only increases the heat generated by the stoves but reduces pollutants in the air. MSC offers a woodstove with inlaid soapstone. This soapstone heats up and provides warmth even after the fire has dwindled in the stove. The soapstone also adds to the attractiveness of the stove as a piece of furniture. MSC's customer base includes many middle- and upper-income individuals.

EXHIBIT 10.18

Massachusetts Stove Company
Income Statements
(Case 10.2)

	Year Ended December 31:				
	Year 3	Year 4	Year 5	Year 6	Year 7
Sales	$1,480,499	$1,637,128	$2,225,745	$2,376,673	$2,734,986
Cost of Goods Sold	(727,259)	(759,156)	(1,063,135)	(1,159,466)	(1,380,820)
Depreciation	(56,557)	(73,416)	(64,320)	(66,829)	(72,321)
Facilities Costs	(59,329)	(47,122)	(66,226)	(48,090)	(45,309)
Facilities Rental Income	25,856	37,727	38,702	42,142	41,004
Selling Expenses	(452,032)	(563,661)	(776,940)	(874,000)	(926,175)
Administrative Expenses	(36,967)	(39,057)	(46,444)	(48,046)	(111,199)
Operating Income	$ 174,211	$ 192,443	$ 247,382	$ 222,384	$ 240,166
Interest Income	712	2,242	9,541	9,209	16,665
Interest Expense	(48,437)	(44,551)	(47,535)	(52,633)	(42,108)
Net Income before Income Taxes	$ 126,486	$ 150,134	$ 209,388	$ 178,960	$ 214,723
Income Taxes Expense	(35,416)	(42,259)	(64,142)	(45,794)	(60,122)
Net Income	$ 91,070	$ 107,875	$ 145,246	$ 133,166	$ 154,601

EXHIBIT 10.19

Massachusetts Stove Company
Balance Sheets
(Case 10.2)

	December 31:					
	Year 2	Year 3	Year 4	Year 5	Year 6	Year 7
Assets						
Cash	$ 50,794	$ 19,687	$ 145,930	$ 104,383	$ 258,148	$ 351,588
Accounts Receivable	12,571	56,706	30,934	41,748	30,989	5,997
Inventories	251,112	327,627	347,883	375,258	409,673	452,709
Other Current Assets	1,368	—	—	—	—	—
Total Current Assets	$ 315,845	$ 404,020	$ 524,747	$ 521,389	$ 698,810	$ 810,294
Property, Plant, and Equipment:						
At Cost	1,056,157	1,148,806	1,164,884	1,184,132	1,234,752	1,257,673
Accumulated Depreciation	(296,683)	(353,240)	(426,656)	(490,975)	(557,804)	(630,125)
Other Assets	121,483	94,000	61,500	12,200	—	—
Total Assets	$1,196,802	$1,293,586	$1,324,475	$1,226,746	$1,375,758	$1,437,842
Liabilities and Shareholders' Equity						
Accounts Payable	$ 137,104	$ 112,815	$ 43,229	$ 60,036	$ 39,170	$ 47,809
Notes Payable	25,000	12,000	—	—	—	—
Current Portion of Long-Term Debt	27,600	29,000	21,570	113,257	115,076	27,036
Other Current Liabilities	39,530	100,088	184,194	189,732	244,241	257,252
Total Current Liabilities	$ 229,234	$ 253,903	$ 248,993	$ 363,025	$ 398,487	$ 332,097
Long-Term Debt	972,446	953,491	881,415	599,408	574,332	547,296
Deferred Income Taxes	—	—	—	—	5,460	6,369
Total Liabilities	$1,201,680	$1,207,394	$1,130,408	$ 962,433	$ 978,279	$ 885,762
Common Stock	2,000	2,000	2,000	2,000	2,000	2,000
Additional Paid-In Capital	435,630	435,630	435,630	435,630	435,630	435,630
Retained Earnings (Deficit)	(442,508)	(351,438)	(243,563)	(98,317)	34,849	189,450
Treasury Stock	—	—	—	(75,000)	(75,000)	(75,000)
Total Shareholders' Equity	$ (4,878)	$ 86,192	$ 194,067	$ 264,313	$ 397,479	$ 552,080
Total Liabilities and Shareholders' Equity	$1,196,802	$1,293,586	$1,324,475	$1,226,746	$1,375,758	$1,437,842

EXHIBIT 10.20

Massachusetts Stove Company
Statements of Cash Flows
(Case 10.2)

	Year Ended December 31:				
	Year 3	**Year 4**	**Year 5**	**Year 6**	**Year 7**
Operations					
Net Income	$ 91,070	$107,875	$ 145,246	$133,166	$ 154,601
Depreciation and Amortization	56,557	73,416	64,320	66,829	72,321
Other Addbacks	27,483	32,500	49,300	17,660	909
(Increase) Decrease in Receivables	(44,135)	25,772	(10,814)	10,759	24,992
(Increase) Decrease in Inventories	(76,515)	(20,256)	(27,375)	(34,415)	(43,036)
Decrease in Other Current Assets	1,368	—	—	—	—
Increase (Decrease) in Payables	(24,289)	(69,586)	16,807	(20,866)	8,639
Increase in Other Current Liabilities	60,558	84,106	5,538	54,509	13,011
Cash Flow from Operations	$ 92,097	$233,827	$ 243,022	$227,642	$ 231,437
Investing					
Capital Expenditures	$(92,649)	$(16,078)	$ (19,249)	$(50,620)	$ (22,921)
Cash Flow from Investing	$(92,649)	$(16,078)	$ (19,249)	$(50,620)	$ (22,921)
Financing					
Increase in Long-Term Debt	$ 10,000	$ —	$ —	$ —	$ —
Decrease in Short-Term Debt	(13,000)	(12,000)	—	—	—
Decrease in Long-Term Debt	(27,555)	(79,506)	(190,320)	(23,257)	(115,076)
Acquisition of Common Stock	—	—	(75,000)	—	—
Cash Flow from Financing	$(30,555)	$(91,506)	$(265,320)	$(23,257)	$(115,076)
Change in Cash	$(31,107)	$126,243	$ (41,547)	$153,765	$ 93,440
Cash—Beginning of Year	50,794	19,687	145,930	104,383	258,148
Cash—End of Year	$ 19,687	$145,930	$ 104,383	$258,148	$ 351,588

EXHIBIT 10.21

Massachusetts Stove Company
Financial Statement Ratios
(Case 10.2)

	Year 3	Year 4	Year 5	Year 6	Year 7
Profit Margin for ROA	8.5%	8.5%	8.1%	7.2%	6.8%
Total Assets Turnover	1.2	1.3	1.7	1.8	1.9
Rate of Return on Assets	10.1%	10.7%	14.1%	13.1%	13.1%
Profit Margin for ROCE	6.2%	6.6%	6.5%	5.6%	5.7%
Capital Structure Leverage Ratio	30.6	9.3	5.6	3.9	3.0
Rate of Return on Common Shareholders' Equity	224.0%	77.0%	63.4%	40.2%	32.6%
Cost of Goods Sold/Sales	49.1%	46.4%	47.8%	48.8%	50.5%
Depreciation Expense/Sales	3.8%	4.5%	2.9%	2.8%	2.6%
Facilities Costs Net of Rental Income/Sales	2.3%	.6%	1.2%	.3%	.2%
Selling Expense/Sales	30.5%	34.4%	34.9%	36.8%	33.9%
Administrative Expenses/Sales	2.5%	2.4%	2.1%	2.0%	4.0%
Interest Income/Sales	—	.1%	.4%	.4%	.6%
Interest Expense/Sales	3.3%	2.7%	2.1%	2.2%	1.5%
Income Tax Expense/Income before Taxes	28.0%	28.1%	30.6%	25.6%	28.0%
Accounts Receivable Turnover	42.7	37.4	61.2	65.3	147.9
Inventory Turnover	2.5	2.2	2.9	3.0	3.2
Fixed-Asset Turnover	1.9	2.1	3.1	3.5	4.2
Current Ratio	1.59	2.11	1.44	1.75	2.44
Quick Ratio	.30	.71	.40	.73	1.08
Days Accounts Receivable	9	10	6	6	3
Days Inventory Held	146	166	126	122	114
Days Accounts Payable	51	33	16	14	11
Cash Flow from Operations/Average Current Liabilities	38.1%	93.0%	79.4%	59.8%	63.4%
Long-Term Debt to Shareholders' Equity Ratio	1,106.2%	454.2%	226.8%	144.5%	99.1%
Cash Flow from Operations/Average Total Liabilities	7.6%	20.0%	23.2%	23.5%	24.8%
Interest Coverage Ratio	3.6	4.4	5.4	4.4	6.1

MSC feels that profitable growth of woodstove sales beyond gross revenues of $3 million a year in the mail-order niche is unlikely. However, no one is selling gas appliances by mail order. Many of MSC's customers and prospects have asked whether MSC plans to produce a gas stove.

The management of MSC is contemplating the development of several gas appliances to sell by mail order. There are compelling reasons for MSC to do this, as well as some good reasons to be cautious.

Availability of Space

MSC owns a 25,000-square-foot building, but occupies only 15,000 square feet. MSC leases the remaining 10,000 square feet to two tenants. The tenants pay rent plus their share of insurance, property taxes, and maintenance costs. The addition of gas appliances to its product line would require MSC to use 5,000 square feet of the space currently rented to tenants. MSC would have to give the tenant six months' notice to cancel its lease.

Availability of Capital

MSC has its own internal funds for product development and inventory, as well as an unused line of credit. But it will lose interest income (or incur interest expense) as it invests these funds in development and increased inventory.

Existing Demand

MSC receives approximately 50,000 requests for catalogs each year and has a mailing list of approximately 220,000 active prospects and 15,000 recent owners of woodstoves. There is anecdotal evidence of sufficient demand that MSC could introduce its gas stoves with little or no additional marketing expense, other than the cost of printing some catalog pages each year. MSCs management worries about the risk of the gas stove sales cannibalizing its existing woodstove sales. Also, if the current base of woodstove sales is eroded through mismanagement, inattention, or cannibalization, then attempts to grow the business through expansion into gas appliances will be self-defeating.

Vacant Market Niche

No other manufacturer is selling gas stoves by mail order. The entry costs are high and the unit volume is small, so it is unlikely that another producer will enter the niche. MSC has had the mail-order market for woodstoves to itself for approximately seven years. MSC feels that this lack of existing competition will give it additional time to develop new products. However, management also feels that a timely entry will help solidify its position in this niche.

Suppliers

MSC has existing relationships with many of the suppliers necessary to manufacture new gas products. The foundry that produces MSC's woodstove castings is one of the largest suppliers of gas heating appliances in central Europe. On the other hand, MSC will be a small, new customer for the vendors that provide the ceramic logs and gas burners. This could lead to problems with price, delivery, or service for these parts.

Synergies in Marketing and Manufacturing

MSC would sell gas appliances through its existing direct-mail marketing efforts. It will incur additional marketing expenses for photography, printing, and customer service. MSC's existing plant is capable of manufacturing the shell of the gas units. It will require additional expertise to assemble fireboxes for the gas units (valves, burners, and log sets). MSC will have to increase both its space and number of employees to process and paint the metal parts of the new gas stoves. The gross margin for the gas products should be similar to that of the woodstoves.

Lack of Management Experience

Managing new product development, larger production levels and inventories, and a more complex business will require MSC to hire more management expertise. MSC will also have to institute a new organization structure for its more complex business and define responsibilities and accountability more carefully. Up to now, MSC has operated with a fairly loose organizational philosophy.

Required (additional requirements follow on page 811)

- **a.** Identify clues from the financial statements and financial statement ratios for Year 3 to Year 7 that might suggest that Massachusetts Stove Company is in a mature business.
- **b.** Design a spreadsheet for the preparation of projected income statements, balance sheets, and statements of cash flows for MSC for Year 8 to Year 12 and prepare pro forma financial statements for each of these years under three scenarios: (1) best case, (2b) most likely, and (3) worst case. The following sections describe the assumptions to be made.

Development Costs

MSC plans to develop two gas stove models, but not concurrently. It will develop the first gas model during Year 8 and begin selling it during Year 9. It will develop the second gas model during Year 9 and begin selling it during Year 10. MSC will capitalize the development costs in the year incurred (Year 8 and Year 9) and amortize them straight line over five years, beginning with the year the particular stove is initially sold (Year 9 and Year 10). Estimated development cost for each stove are as follows:

Best Case: $100,000.
Most Likely Case: $120,000.
Worst Case: $160,000.

Capital Expenditures

Capital expenditures, other than development costs, will be as follows: Year 8, $20,000; Year 9, $30,000; Year 10, $30,000; Year 11, $25,000; Year 12, $25,000. Assume a six-year depreciable life, straight-line depreciation, and a full year of depreciation in the year of acquisition.

Sales Growth

Changes in total sales relative to total sales of the preceding year are as follows:

	Best Case			Most Likely Case			Worst Case		
Year	Wood Stoves	Gas Stoves	Total	Wood Stoves	Gas Stoves	Total	Wood Stoves	Gas Stoves	Total
8	+2%	—	+2%	−2%	—	−2%	−4%	—	−4%
9	+2%	+6%	+8%	−2%	+4%	+2%	−4%	+2%	−2%
10	+2%	+12%	+14%	−2%	+8%	+6%	−4%	+4%	+0%
11	+2%	+12%	+14%	−2%	+8%	+6%	−4%	+4%	+0%
12	+2%	+12%	+14%	−2%	+8%	+6%	−4%	+4%	+0%

Because sales of gas stoves will start at zero, the projections of sales should *use the preceding growth rates in total sales.* The growth rates shown for woodstove sales and gas stove sales simply indicate the components of the total sales increase.

Cost of Goods Sold

Manufacturing costs of the gas stoves will equal 50 percent of sales, the same as for woodstoves.

Depreciation

Depreciation will increase for the amortization of the product development costs on the gas stoves and depreciation of additional capital expenditures.

Facilities Rental Income and Facilities Costs

Facilities rental income will decrease by 50 percent beginning in Year 9 when MSC takes over 5,000 square feet of its building now rented to others and remain at that reduced level for Year 10 to Year 12. Facilities costs will increase by $30,000 beginning in Year 9 for facilities costs now paid by the tenants and for additional facilities costs required by gas stove manufacturing. These costs will remain at that increased level for Year 10 to Year 12.

Selling Expenses

Selling expenses as a percentage of sales are as follows:

Year	Best Case	Most Likely Case	Worst Case
8	34%	34.0%	34%
9	33%	33.5%	35%
10	32%	33.0%	36%
11	31%	32.5%	37%
12	30%	32.0%	38%

Administrative Expenses

Administrative expenses will increase by $30,000 in Year 8, $30,000 in Year 9, and $20,000 in Year 10, and then will remain at the Year 10 level in Years 11 and 12.

Interest Income

MSC will earn 5 percent interest on the average balance in cash each year.

Interest Expense

The interest rate on interest-bearing debt will be 6.8 percent on the average amount of debt outstanding each year.

Income Tax Expense

MSC is subject to an income tax rate of 28 percent.

Accounts Receivable and Inventories

Accounts receivable and inventories will increase at the growth rate in sales.

Property, Plant, and Equipment

Property, plant, and equipment at cost will increase each year by the amounts of capital expenditures and expenditures on development costs. Accumulated depreciation will increase each year by the amount of depreciation and amortization expense.

Accounts Payable and Other Current Liabilities

Accounts payable will increase with the growth rate in inventories. Other current liabilities primarily include advances by customers for stoves manufactured soon after the year-end. Other current liabilities will increase with the growth rate in sales.

Current Portion of Long-Term Debt

Scheduled repayments of long-term debt are as follows: Year 8, $27,036; Year 9, $29,200; Year 10, $31,400; Year 11, $33,900; Year 12, $36,600; Year 13, $39,500.

Deferred Income Taxes

Deferred income taxes relate to the use of accelerated depreciation for tax purposes and the straight-line method for financial reporting. Assume that deferred income taxes will not change.

Shareholders' Equity

Assume that there will be no changes in the contributed capital of MSC. Retained earnings will change each year in the amount of net income.

Required (continued from page 809)

c. Calculate the financial statements ratios listed in Exhibit 10.15 for MSC under each of the three scenarios for Year 8 to Year 12.

   NOTE: You should create a fourth spreadsheet as part of your preparation of the projected financial statements that will compute the financial ratios.

d. What advice would you give the management of MSC regarding its decision to enter the gas stove market? Your recommendation should consider the profitability and risks of this action as well as other factors you deem relevant.

Chapter 11

Risk-Adjusted Expected Rates of Return and the Dividends Valuation Approach

Learning Objectives

1. **Understand how to estimate risk-adjusted expected returns on equity capital, as well as weighted average costs of capital, to use to discount future payoffs to present value.**

2. **Understand how dividends valuation models work, and their conceptual and practical strengths and weaknesses.**

3. **Develop practical valuation techniques to deal with the many difficult issues involved in estimating firm value using the present value of expected future dividends:**

   a. **dividends versus cash flows versus earnings,**

   b. **cash flows to the investor versus cash flows reinvested in the firm,**

   c. **the forecast horizon, and**

   d. **continuing value.**

4. **Apply these techniques to estimate firm value using the present value of future dividends.**

5. **Develop techniques to assess the sensitivity of firm value estimates to key valuation parameters, such as discount rates and expected long-term growth rates.**

INTRODUCTION AND OVERVIEW

Economic theory teaches that the value of an investment equals the present value of the expected future payoffs from the investment discounted at a rate that reflects the risk inherent in those expected payoffs. A general model for the present value of a security (denoted as V_0 with present value denoted at time $t = 0$) with an expected life of n future periods is as follows:[1]

$$V_0 = \sum_{t=1}^{n} \frac{\text{Expected Future Payoffs}_t}{(1 + \text{Discount Rate})^t}$$

[1]Throughout this chapter, t refers to accounting periods. The valuation process determines an estimate of firm value, denoted V_0, in present value as of today, when $t = 0$. The period $t = 1$ refers to the first accounting period being discounted to present value. Period $t = n$ is the period of the expected final, or liquidating, payoff.

Even in relatively efficient securities markets, price does not necessarily equal value for every security at all times. When an investor buys a security, the investor pays the security's price and receives the security's value. When the investor sells a security, the investor receives the selling price and gives up the security's value. Price is observable, value is not; value must be estimated. Estimating the value of a security in order to make intelligent investment decisions is therefore a common objective of financial statement analysis. Investors, analysts, investment bankers, corporate managers, and others engage in financial statement analysis and valuation to determine a reliable appraisal of the value of shares of common equity. The questions they typically address include the following: What value do I think a share of common stock in a particular company is worth? Comparing my estimate of value to the current price in the market, should I make a buy, sell, or hold recommendation on a particular firm's common shares? What price should I assign to the initial public offering of a firm's common shares? What is a reasonable price to accept (or ask) as a seller or pay (or bid) as a buyer for the shares of a firm in a corporate merger or acquisition?

The six-step analysis framework that forms the structure of this book (Exhibit 1.1 in Chapter 1) is a logical sequence of steps to determine intelligent estimates of value. First, we analyze the economics and competitive conditions of the industry. Second, we analyze the particular firm's strategy in light of the competitive dynamics of the industry. Third, we assess the quality of the firm's accounting, making adjustments if necessary. Fourth, we evaluate the firm's profitability and risk with a set of financial ratios. Fifth, we use all of this information to project the firm's future financial statements. Finally, we derive from the projected financial statements our forecasts of expected future earnings, cash flows, and dividends as measures of expected future payoffs to investment. We apply valuation models to these forecasts to determine the value of the firm. Reliable forecasts of future payoffs to investment (the numerator in the general valuation model) depend on reliable forecasts of future earnings, cash flows, and dividends, which depend on an unbiased and thorough projections of the firm's future operating performance. Assessing an appropriate risk-adjusted discount rate (the denominator in the general valuation model) requires an assessment of the inherent risk in the set of expected future payoffs. Therefore, reliable estimates of firm value depend on unbiased estimates of expected future payoffs and an appropriate risk-adjusted discount rate, all of which depend on all six steps of the framework.

This chapter begins our discussion of the sixth and final step of the analytical framework of this text: valuation. The first portion of this chapter describes and demonstrates computing appropriate risk-adjusted expected rates of return on equity capital, which we will use as discount rates in all of the valuation models, and also discusses computing weighted average costs of capital. The latter portion of this chapter describes and applies the dividends-based valuation model. Throughout the chapter, we demonstrate these techniques using PepsiCo.

Looking further ahead, Chapter 12 presents and applies cash-flow-based valuation models. Chapter 13 describes and applies earnings-based valuation models. Chapters 11, 12, and 13 discuss and illustrate the important issues that determine the conceptual and practical strengths and weaknesses of each approach. In all three chapters, we illustrate the equivalence of these approaches to valuation both in the theoretical development of the dividends, cash flows, and earnings valuation models, respectively, and by applying these valuation models to the expectations of dividends, cash flows, and earnings that we derive from the financial statements forecasts we developed for PepsiCo in Chapter 10. In Chapter 14, we describe market multiples such as price-earnings ratios and market-to-book ratios that analysts use in some instances to value firms.

Equivalence among Dividends, Cash Flows, and Earnings Valuation

Equity valuation models based on dividends, cash flows, and earnings have been the topic of considerable theoretical and empirical research in recent years. These studies demonstrate that these models generally provide significant explanatory power for share prices observed in the capital markets.[2] The results indicate that share value estimates determined from dividends, cash flows, and earnings valuation models exhibit high positive correlations with the levels of stock prices observed in the capital markets across different types of firms, during different periods of time, and across different countries. In the same vein, empirical research has shown that unexpected changes in earnings, dividends, and cash flows for most firms display high positive correlations with stock returns (that is, *changes* in stock prices) observed in the capital markets. It is therefore no surprise that analysts, investors, and capital market participants commonly use dividends, cash flows, and earnings as the value-relevant attributes on which they base valuation models. When the analyst derives internally consistent forecasts of future earnings, cash flows, and dividends from a set of internally consistent financial statements, and uses the same discount rate to compute the present values of those expected earnings, cash flows, and dividends, then the valuation models yield identical estimates of value for a firm. That is, these three valuation models in their theoretical design are complementary approaches to valuation that produce equivalent value estimates.

Cash-flow-based valuation is an alternative approach that is equivalent to dividends-based valuation because the analyst can forecast and value the cash flows the firm will generate and use to pay dividends, or equivalently, forecast and value the dividends *per se.* The dividends approach focuses on wealth distribution to shareholders, while the cash-flow-based approach focuses on dividend-paying capacity. The cash-flow-based valuation approach measures and values the cash flows that are "free" to be distributed to shareholders. That is, *free cash flows* are the excess cash flows each period that are available to be distributed to shareholders, after using cash for necessary investments in operating assets and required payments to debtholders. Free cash flows can be used instead of dividends in the numerator of the general value model as the value-relevant measures of expected future payoffs to the investor. Both approaches, if implemented with consistent assumptions, will lead to identical estimates of value. This equivalence occurs because, although the cash flows into the firm will differ from the amount of the cash flows paid out of the firm in dividends in a given period, over the life of the firm the total amounts of cash flows into the firm and the total amounts of cash flows paid out of the firm in dividends will be equivalent.

The earnings-based valuation approach is another alternative equivalent to either dividends-based or free-cash-flows-based valuation. Earnings numbers measure the firm's profit (or loss) each period for common shareholders. The earnings-based valuation approach relies on earnings as measures of the capital firms create (or destroy) for common shareholders each period that will ultimately be distributed as dividends to shareholders. Thus, the earnings-based valuation approach focuses on the firm's wealth creation for shareholders, the cash-flows-based approach focuses on dividend-paying ability, and the dividends approach focuses on wealth distribution to shareholders. Exhibit 11.1 provides a conceptual illustration of these three approaches to firm valuation.

[2]For examples, see Stephen Penman and Theodore Sougiannis, "A Comparison of Dividend, Cash Flow, and Earnings Approaches to Equity Valuation," *Contemporary Accounting Research* 15, no. 3 (Fall 1998), pp. 343–383; and Jennifer Francis, Per Olsson, and Dennis Oswald, "Comparing the Accuracy and Explainability of Dividend, Free Cash Flow, and Abnormal Earnings Equity Value Estimates," *Journal of Accounting Research* 38, (Spring 2000), pp. 45–70.

EXHIBIT 11.1

Conceptual Illustration of Equivalent Approaches to Valuation Using Dividends, Cash Flows, and Earnings

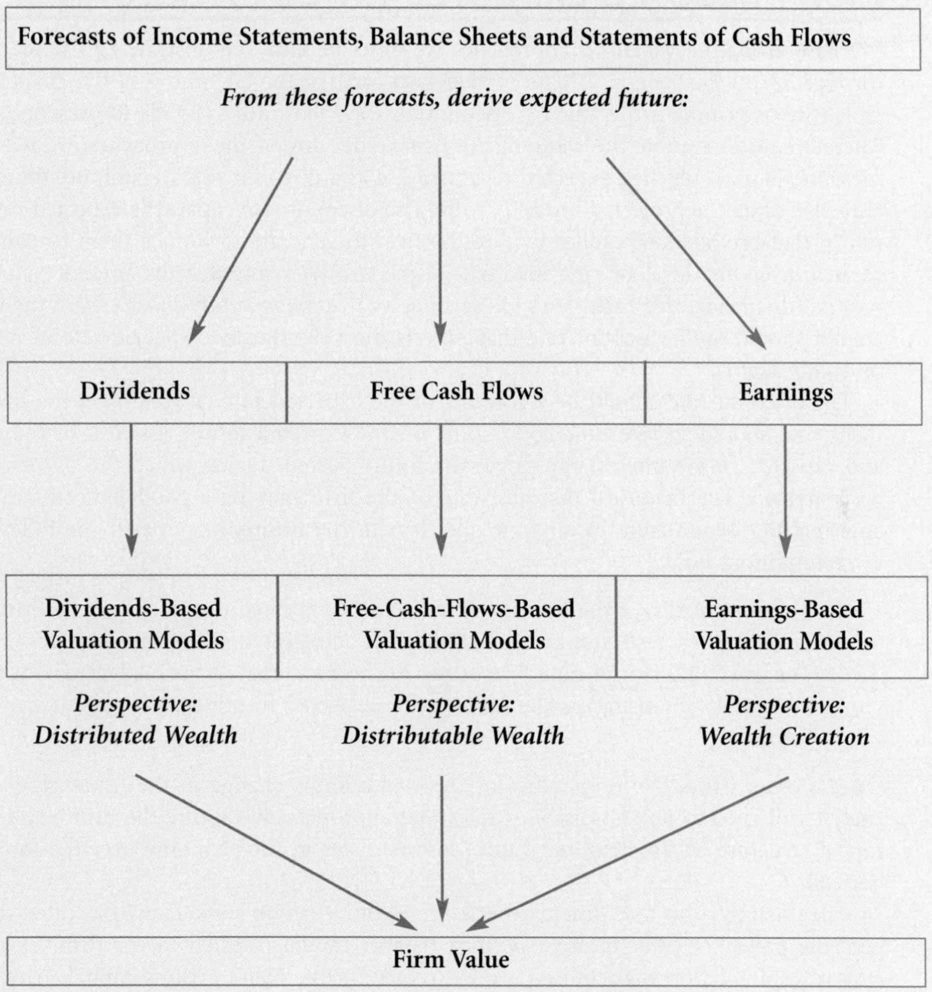

We have observed that analysts that apply these different valuation approaches gain better insights about the value of a firm than analysts that rely on only one approach in all cases. More generally, our experience suggests that analysts understand valuation more deeply and thoroughly and can apply valuation techniques across a broad array of situations when they are equipped with the ability to apply dividends, cash flows, and/or earnings valuation approaches as necessary.

All four valuation chapters—Chapters 11 through 14—emphasize that the objective of the valuation process is not a single point estimate of value *per se*, but instead the objective is to determine the reliable distribution of value estimates across the relevant ranges of critical forecast assumptions and valuation parameters. By estimating share value using cash flows, earnings, and dividends, and by assessing the sensitivity of these value estimates across a distribution of relevant forecast assumptions and valuation parameters, we seek to determine the most likely range of values for a share, which we then compare to the share's price in the capital market for an intelligent investment decision.

RISK-ADJUSTED EXPECTED RATES OF RETURN

We base all of the valuation approaches we describe and demonstrate in Chapters 11 through 14 on the general valuation model set forth at the beginning of the chapter, in which we determine firm value by discounting expected future payoffs to present value. Therefore, to determine the value of the firm under any of the approaches, we need to measure the risk-adjusted expected return to use as a discount rate to compute the present value of all the projected future payoffs. The discount rate equals the expected rate of return that providers of capital require the firm to generate to induce them to commit capital, given the level of risk involved. If the analyst computes the present value of payoffs (dividends, free cash flows, or earnings) to *common equity shareholders*, then the analyst should use a discount rate that reflects the risk-adjusted expected rate of return on *equity capital.*

The discount rate should be a forecast of the expected rate of return on the investment, and should therefore be conditional on the expected future riskiness of the firm and expected future interest rates over the future period during which the payoffs will be generated. The historical discount rate of the firm may be a good indicator of the appropriate discount rate to apply to the firm in the future, but only if the following three conditions hold:

1. The current risk of the firm is the same as the expected future risk of the firm.
2. Prevailing interest rates are good indicators of expected future interest rates.
3. The existing financial capital structure of the firm (that is, the current mix of debt and equity financing) is the same as the expected future capital structure of the firm.

On the other hand, if one or more of these conditions change in the future, then the analyst will need to project discount rates that appropriately capture the future risk and capital structure of the firm and future interest rates in the economy over the forecast horizon.

As a starting point to estimate expected rates of return on capital, analysts often compute the prevailing after-tax cost of each type of capital invested in the firm. Existing costs of capital reflect the required rates of return for the firm's existing capital structure, and they are appropriate discount rates for the firm in the future if the analyst expects the three preceding conditions to hold. Developing discount rates using costs of capital assumes that the capital markets price capital to reflect risk and, at a minimum, the firm's value is a function of its ability to generate returns that at least cover its costs of capital. We next describe and demonstrate techniques to estimate the firm's cost of equity, debt, and preferred stock capital. Following these descriptions, we describe and illustrate how to compute a weighted average cost of capital for the firm.

Cost of Common Equity Capital

Analysts commonly estimate the cost of equity capital using the theory underlying the capital asset pricing model (CAPM). The CAPM assumes that the market comprises risk-averse investors holding portfolios of assets. The CAPM assumes that, for a given level of return, risk-averse investors will seek to bear as little risk as possible, and will mitigate risk by diversifying the risks across the types of assets they hold in a portfolio. Therefore, the CAPM hypothesizes that, in equilibrium, investors should expect to earn a rate of return on a firm's common equity capital that equals the rate of return the market requires to hold the firm's stock within a diversified portfolio of stocks. In theory, the market comprises risk-averse investors who demand a rate of return that (a) compensates them for forgoing the consumption of capital and (b) compensates them with additional return (also called a risk premium) for bearing nondiversifiable risk (sometimes called systematic risk). The market's required rate of return on equity capital is therefore a function of prevailing risk-free rates of interest in the economy, plus a risk premium for bearing systematic risk, conditional on the level of nondiversifiable risk inherent in the firm's common stock.[3]

Analysts commonly measure nondiversifiable or systematic risk as the degree of covariation between a firm's stock returns and an index of stock returns for all firms in the market. Analysts often measure systematic risk using the firm's market beta, which is estimated as a regression coefficient from regressing the firm's stock returns on an index of returns reflecting a marketwide portfolio of stocks over a relevant period of time.[4] If a firm's market beta from such a regression is equal to 1, it indicates that the firm's stock returns covary identically with returns to a marketwide portfolio, indicating that the firm has the same degree of systematic risk as the average of the market as a whole. If a firm's market beta is greater than 1, it indicates that the firm has a greater degree of systematic risk than the market as a whole, whereas a firm with a market beta less than 1 has less systematic risk than the market as a whole.

The CAPM projects the expected return on common equity capital for firm j as follows:

$$E[R_{Ej}] = E[R_F] + \beta_j \times \{E[R_M] - E[R_F]\}$$

where E denotes that the related variable is an expectation; R_{Ej} denotes return on common equity in firm j; R_F denotes the risk-free rate of return; β_j denotes the market beta for firm j; and R_M denotes the return on a diversified, marketwide portfolio of stocks. According to the CAPM, a common equity security with no systematic risk (that is, a stock with $\beta_j = 0$) should be expected to earn a return equal to the expected rate of return on risk-free securities. Of course, most equity securities are not risk free. An equity security with systematic risk equal to the average amount of systematic risk of all equity securities in the market has a market beta equal to 1. The subtraction term in brackets in the preceding equation represents the average market risk premium, equal to the excess return that equity investors in the capital markets require for bearing the average amount of systematic risk in the market as a whole. Therefore, the cost of common equity capital for a firm with an average level of systematic risk should be equal to the average expected return on the market portfolio. A firm with a market beta greater than 1 has higher systematic risk than average and faces a higher cost of equity capital because the capital markets expect the firm to yield a commensurately higher return to compensate investors for bearing risk. A firm with a market beta less than 1 has lower than average systematic risk and faces a lower cost of equity capital because the capital markets expect the firm to

[3]Note that this model views nonsystematic risk as diversifiable by the investor. The market, according to CAPM, does not expect a return for a firm's nonsystematic risk because such risk can be diversified away.

[4]Researchers and analysts have developed a variety of different approaches to estimate market betas. For example, one common approach estimates a firm's market beta by regressing the firm's monthly stock returns on a marketwide index of returns (such as the S&P 500 index) over the last sixty months.

EXHIBIT 11.2

Relation between Cost of Equity Capital and Systematic Risk

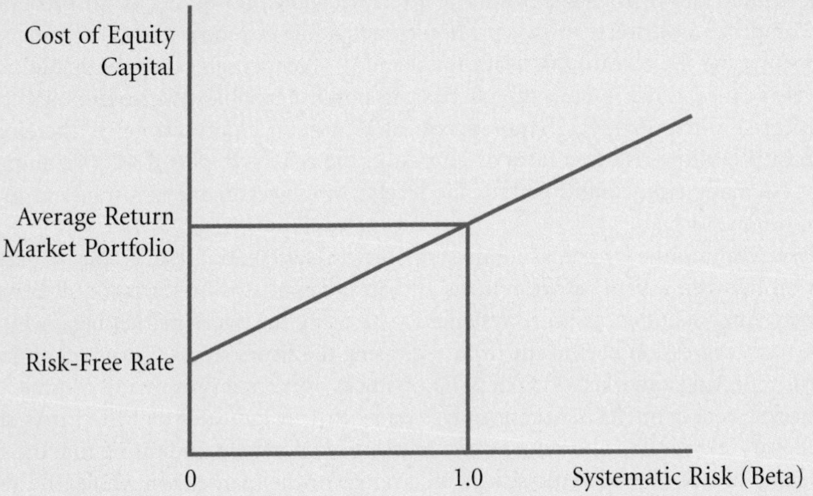

yield a commensurately lower return to investors for risk. Exhibit 11.2 depicts the relations graphically.

Exhibit 11.3 reports industry median market betas for a sample of thirty-seven industries over the years 1995–2004. These data depict wide variation in systematic risk across industries during this ten-year period, with industry median market betas ranging from a low of 0.40 (Utilities) to a high of 1.51 (Electronic and Electrical Equipment). Various financial reference sources and web sites regularly publish market betas for common equity in publicly traded firms. It is not uncommon to find considerable variation in the published amounts for market beta among the various sources. This occurs in part because of differences in the period and methodology used to calculate the betas.[5]

The analyst should use the market return on securities with zero systematic risk as the risk-free interest rate in the CAPM. Returns on such securities exhibit no correlation with returns on a diversified marketwide portfolio of stocks. Given the fact that equity securities have indefinitely long lives, it might seem appropriate to use the yield on long-term U.S. government securities. However, yields on long-term U.S. government securities tend to exhibit greater sensitivity to changes in inflation and interest rates, and therefore have a greater degree of systematic risk (although the systematic risk is still quite low), than short-term U.S. government securities. Common practice uses the yield on either short- or intermediate-term U.S. government securities as the risk-free rate. These yields have

[5]Eugene Fama and Kenneth French developed an empirical model that explains realized stock returns using three factors that they found to be correlated with returns during their study period. Their model and results indicate that, during their sample period (1963–1990), firms' stock returns were related to firms' market betas, market capitalizations (size), and market-to-book ratios (see Eugene F. Fama and Kenneth R. French, "The Cross Section of Expected Stock Returns," *Journal of Finance* (June 1992), pp. 427–465). Data to implement their model can be obtained from French's web site (mba.tuck.dartmouth.edu/pages/faculty/ken.french/data_library.html). Although the model deserves and has received a lot of attention in academics and practice, more research is necessary to determine the theoretical basis for the model, and the risk factors and risk premia that constitute the model. In addition, more research is needed to assess the empirical applicability of the model as a predictor of expected stock returns in periods following their sample period.

EXHIBIT 11.3

Relation between Industry and Systematic Risk over 1995–2004

Industry:	Median Beta during 1995–2004
Utilities	0.40
Real Estate	0.44
Tobacco	0.47
Forestry	0.48
Depository Institutions	0.49
Metal Mining	0.54
Food Processors	0.57
Grocery Stores	0.57
Insurers	0.61
Textiles	0.61
Petroleum Refining	0.66
Restaurants	0.67
Printing and Publishing	0.73
Wholesalers—Nondurables	0.73
Oil and Gas Extraction	0.75
Paper	0.76
Metal Products	0.80
Retailers—General Merchandise	0.81
Transportation Equipment	0.82
Personal Services	0.83
Hotels	0.85
Amusements and Recreation	0.86
Lumber	0.88
Health Services	0.96
Motion Pictures	0.98
Wholesalers—Durables	1.00
Retailing—Apparel	1.00
Primary Metals	1.03
Instruments and Related Products	1.04
Security and Commodity Brokers	1.13
Transportation by Air	1.14
Industrial and Commercial Machinery and Computer Equipment	1.15
Retailing—Home Furniture, Furnishings, and Equipment	1.17
Chemicals	1.18
Communications	1.25
Business Services	1.37
Electronic and Electrical Equipment	1.51

historically averaged around 6 percent over the long run, although in recent years they have averaged roughly 4 percent.

The average return on the market portfolio depends on the period studied. Historically, the realized rate of return on the market portfolio has varied between 9 and 13 percent. Thus, the excess return of the market portfolio over the risk-free rate has varied between 3 and 7 percent. Some financial economists argue that the market risk premium varies over time with investors' demand for incremental consumption. They argue that, on the margin, when the economy is healthy and growing, investors' demand for additional consumption is relatively low, and therefore they demand relatively low rates of return for postponing incremental consumption and bearing risk. Thus, risk premia tend to be lower (perhaps 3 to 4 percent) when economic conditions are strong. Conversely, when the economy is weak and investors face a higher degree of uncertainty, investors' demand for additional consumption is relatively high and therefore they demand relatively high rates of return for postponing consumption and bearing risk. Thus, risk premia tend to be higher (perhaps 6 to 7 percent) when economic conditions are weak. The theories that assert that risk premia are time-varying, and vary inversely with investors' marginal demand for consumption, seem intuitive and appear to explain risk premia observed in the capital markets quite well.

Example 1

Suppose Firm A has a market beta of 0.60 and Firm B has a market beta of 1.40. Assume that the prevailing yields on three- to five-year U.S. Treasury bonds are roughly 4.0 percent, and that the capital markets require a 5.0 percent risk premium for bearing an average amount of systematic risk. Applying the CAPM, we would compute the following expected rates of return for Firm A and Firm B:

Firm A: $E[R_A] = 4.0 + (0.60 \times 5.0) = 7.0$
Firm B: $E[R_B] = 4.0 + (1.40 \times 5.0) = 11.0$

Thus, the CAPM implies that investors should expect a 7.0 percent rate of return on capital invested in the equity of Firm A, and an 11.0 percent rate of return on capital invested in the equity of Firm B. Firm B faces a higher cost of equity capital than Firm A because it has a higher degree of systematic risk. In determining the share values of Firm A and Firm B, investors should discount to present value the expected future payoffs using a 7.0 percent discount rate for Firm A and an 11.0 percent discount rate for Firm B. If investors expect Firm A and Firm B to generate the same payoffs on average (although Firm B's payoffs will be more risky), then investors will assign a lower value to the common shares of Firm B than Firm A.

Computing the Required Rate of Return on Equity Capital for PepsiCo

At the end of Year 4 PepsiCo common stock had a market beta of roughly 0.75. At that time, U.S. Treasury bills with one to five years to maturity traded with a yield of approximately 4.0 percent, which we use as the risk-free rate. Assuming a 5.0 percent market risk premium, the CAPM indicates that PepsiCo has a cost of common equity capital of 7.75 percent [$7.75 = 4.0 + (0.75 \times 5.0)$]. At the end of Year 4, PepsiCo had 1,679 million shares outstanding and a share price of \$51.94 for a total market capital of common equity of \$87,207 million.

Adjusting Market Equity Beta to Reflect a New Capital Structure

Recall from the discussion in Chapter 5 that market equity beta reflects operating leverage, financial leverage, variability of sales, and other firm characteristics. In some settings, such as a leveraged buyout, firms plan to make significant changes in the financial capital structure. The market beta computed using historical market price data reflects the firm's existing capital structure. The analyst can adjust this beta to project what it will likely be after the firm changes the capital structure. The analyst can unlever the current beta and then relever it to reflect the new capital structure. The following formula describes an approach to estimate an unlevered market beta (sometimes referred to as an asset beta):

$$\text{Current Levered Market Beta} = \text{Unlevered Market Beta} \times \left[1 + (1 - \text{Income Tax Rate}) \times \left(\frac{\text{Current Market Value of Debt}}{\text{Current Market Value of Equity}}\right)\right]$$

To estimate the new levered beta, the analyst takes two steps. First, the analyst solves for the unlevered beta by rearranging the preceding model to divide the current levered market beta by the term in square brackets on the right-hand side of the equation, as follows:

$$\text{Unlevered Market Beta} = \text{Current Levered Market Beta} \div \left[1 + (1 - \text{Income Tax Rate}) \times \left(\frac{\text{Current Market Value of Debt}}{\text{Current Market Value of Equity}}\right)\right]$$

Second, the analyst projects the new levered beta by multiplying the unlevered beta by the term in square brackets on the right-hand side of this model after substituting the projected new ratio of the market value of debt to the market value of equity in place of the current ratio of the market value of debt to the market value of equity, as follows:[6]

$$\text{New Levered Market Beta} = \text{Unlevered Market Beta} \times \left[1 + (1 - \text{Income Tax Rate}) \times \left(\frac{\text{New Market Value of Debt}}{\text{New Market Value of Equity}}\right)\right]$$

Example 2

Suppose a firm has a market beta of 0.9, is subject to an income tax rate of 35 percent, and has a market value of debt to market value of equity ratio of 60 percent. If the risk-free rate is 6 percent and if the market risk premium is 7 percent, then according to the CAPM the market expects this firm to generate equity returns of 12.3 percent [12.3 = 6.0 + (0.9 × 7.0)]. The firm intends to adopt a new capital structure that will have a debt-to-equity ratio of 140 percent. To project the firm's levered beta under the new capital structure, we first solve for the unlevered beta, denoted X:

$$0.9 = X \times [1 + (1 - 0.35) \times (0.60/1.00)]$$

$$X = 0.9/[1 + (1 - 0.35) \times (0.60/1.00)]$$

$$X = 0.65$$

Because financial leverage is positively related to market beta, removing the effect of financial leverage reduces market beta. The unlevered beta should reflect the effects of the

[6]Note that the debt-to-equity ratios used in these computations are based on market values of debt and shareholders' equity. These market-value-based ratios will likely differ from the debt to shareholders' equity ratios discussed in Chapter 5 for assessing long-term solvency risk because the ratios in Chapter 5 are based on book values of debt and shareholders' equity.

firm's operating risk, sales volatility, and other operating factors, but not risk related to financial leverage. We relever the unlevered beta to reflect the new debt-to-equity ratio as follows:

$$Y = 0.65 \times [1 + (1 - 0.35) \times (1.40/1.00)] = 1.24$$

According to the CAPM, this firm will face an equity cost of capital of 14.68 percent [$14.68 = 6.0 + (1.24 \times 7.0)$] under the new capital structure.

Evaluating the Use of the CAPM to Measure the Cost of Equity Capital

The use of the CAPM to calculate the cost of equity capital has been subject to various criticisms:

1. Market betas for a firm should vary over time as the systematic risk of the firm changes; however, market beta estimates are quite sensitive to the time period and methodology used in their computation.
2. In theory, the CAPM measures expected returns based on the stock's risk relative to a diversified portfolio of assets across the economy, but a return index for a diversified portfolio of assets that spans the entire economy does not exist. Measuring a stock's systematic risk relative to a stock market return index such as the S&P 500 Index fails to consider covariation between the stock's returns and returns on assets outside the stock market, including other financial investments (for example, U.S. government and corporate debt securities and privately held equity), real estate, and human capital.
3. The market risk premium is not stable over time and is likewise sensitive to the time period used in its calculation. Considerable uncertainty surrounds the appropriate adjustment for the market risk premium. It is not clear whether the appropriate adjustment should be on the order of 3 percent, 7 percent, or somewhere in between.[7] As noted earlier, some financial economists now argue that the risk premium is lower in periods of economic health and growth, and higher in periods of economic weakness and uncertainty, which seems plausible and consistent with observable variation in marketwide stock returns over time. However, this approach requires more research to develop practical models for measuring firm-specific time-varying risk premia.

In light of these criticisms of the CAPM, and considering the crucial role of the risk-adjusted discount rate for common equity in valuation, our experience suggests that it is important to analyze the sensitivity of share value estimates across different discount rates for common equity. For example, the analyst should estimate values for a share of common equity in a particular firm across a relevant range of discount rates for common equity by varying the market risk premium from 3 percent to 7 percent.

---

[7]See, for example, James Claus and Jacob Thomas, "Equity Premia as Low as Three Percent? Empirical Evidence from Analysts' Earnings Forecasts for Domestic and International Stock Markets," *Journal of Finance* 56, (October 2001), pp. 1629–1666. Also see Peter Easton, Gary Taylor, Pervin Shroff, and Theodore Sougiannis, "Using Forecasts of Earnings to Simultaneously Estimate Growth and the Rate of Return on Equity Investment," *Journal of Accounting Research* 40 (June 2000), pp. 657–676.

Chapter 14 describes techniques to estimate the implicit expected rate of return on common equity securities. Chapter 14 also describes an approach to estimating the implicit discount in share price for risk by using risk-free discount rates. These techniques do not require the assumption of an asset pricing model like the CAPM.

Cost of Debt Capital

The analyst computes the after-tax cost of debt capital, including short-term and long-term notes payable, lines of credit, mortgages, bonds, and capital lease obligations, as the yield to maturity of the debt times one minus the statutory tax rate applicable to income tax deductions for interest. The yield to maturity is the rate that discounts the contractual cash flows on the debt to the debt's current fair value. If the fair value of the debt is equal to face value, then the yield to maturity equals the stated interest rate on the debt. If the fair value of the debt exceeds the face value of the debt, then yield to maturity is lower than the stated rate. This can occur after interest rates fall; previously issued fixed-rate debt will have a stated rate that exceeds current market yields for debt with comparable credit quality and terms. On the other hand, after interest rates rise, existing fixed-rate debt may have a stated rate that is lower than prevailing market rates for comparable debt, in which case the debt will have a fair value that is less than face value, and the yield to maturity will be greater than the stated rate.

Firms disclose in notes to their financial statements the stated interest rates on their existing interest-bearing debt capital. Firms also disclose in notes the estimated fair values of their interest-bearing debt, which should reflect the present value of the debt using prevailing market yields to maturity on the debt. Together, these disclosures allow the analyst to estimate prevailing market yields to maturity on the firm's outstanding debt.

In computing costs of debt capital, analysts typically exclude operating liability accounts (such as accounts payable, accrued expenses, deferred income tax liability, and retirement benefit obligations). Instead, analysts typically treat these items as part of the firm's operating activities, rather than as part of the firm's financial capital structure.

A capitalized lease obligation will generally have an implicit after-tax cost of capital equal to the after-tax yield to maturity on collateralized borrowing with equivalent risk and maturity. Firms recognize capital lease obligations on the balance sheet as financial liabilities; however, as described in Chapter 8, firms may also have significant off-balance-sheet commitments to make future payments under operating leases. If the firm has significant commitments under operating leases, then the analyst may feel it necessary to include them as a component of debt capital in the computation of the weighted average cost of capital. If the analyst elects to adjust the firm's balance sheet to capitalize operating lease commitments as obligations (as illustrated in Chapter 8), then procedurally the analyst should make three sets of adjustments to include the effects of operating leases on the weighted average cost of capital. First, the analyst should include the present value of operating lease commitments in the calculation of the weights of capital in the capital structure. Second, the analyst should include the after-tax interest rate implicit in operating lease commitments in the computation of the weighted average cost of capital. The lessor bears more risk in an operating lease than in a capital lease, so the cost of capital represented by operating leases is likely to be higher than for capital leases. Third, if the analyst treats operating leases as part of debt financing, then the cash outflow for rent payments under operating leases should be reclassified as interest and principal payments of debt when computing free cash flows. Chapter 8 discusses techniques for the required adjustments to convert operating leases to capital leases, as well as techniques to adjust for other, less common forms of off-balance-sheet financing, including contingent liabilities for receivables sold with recourse and product financing arrangements.

The income tax rate used to compute the tax effects of interest should be the firm's statutory tax rate applicable to interest expense deductions. The statutory federal tax rate applicable to interest expense deductions in the United States is 35 percent. However, state and foreign taxes may increase or decrease the combined statutory tax rate, depending on where the firm raises its debt capital. Firms do not separately disclose statutory state or foreign tax rates, but do show the effect of these taxes in the income tax reconciliation found in the income tax note. To achieve greater precision, the analyst could approximate the combined statutory tax rate applicable to interest expense deductions using information in the income tax footnote.

Cost of Preferred Equity Capital

The cost of preferred stock capital depends on the preference conditions. Preferred stock that has preference over common shares with respect to dividends and priority in liquidation generally sells near its par value. Its cost of capital is therefore the dividend rate on the preferred stock. Depending on the attributes of the preferred stock, dividends on preferred stock may give rise to a tax deduction, in which case the after-tax cost of capital will be lower than the pretax cost. Preferred stock that is convertible into common stock has both preferred and common equity attributes. Its cost is a blending of the cost of nonconvertible preferred stock and common equity.

Computing the Weighted Average Cost of Capital

In some circumstances, the analyst will need to determine the present value of payoffs to investment in all of the assets of a firm, not just the equity capital of the firm. Such circumstances might arise, for example, if the analyst is considering acquiring all of the assets of a firm, or if the analyst is considering acquiring control of a firm by acquiring all of the financial claims (common equity shares, preferred shares, and debt) on the assets of a firm. If the analyst needs to determine the present value of the payoffs from investing in the total assets of the firm, or equivalently, acquiring all of the debt, preferred and common equity claims on the firm, then the analyst should use a discount rate that reflects the weighted average required rate of return that encompasses the debt, preferred, and common equity capital used to finance the net operating assets of the firm.

A formula for the weighted average cost of capital (denoted R_A) is given here:

$$R_A = [w_D \times R_D \times (1 - \text{tax rate})] + [w_P \times R_P] + [w_E \times R_E]$$

In this formula, w denotes the weight on each type of capital, R denotes the cost of each type of capital, and *tax rate* denotes the tax rate applicable to debt capital costs. The weights used to compute the weighted average cost of capital should be the market values of each type of capital in proportion to the total market value of the financial capital structure of the firm (that is, $w_D + w_P + w_E = 1.0$). On the right-hand side of this equation, the first term in brackets measures the weighted after-tax cost of debt capital; the second term measures the weighted cost of preferred stock capital; and the third term measures the weighted cost of equity capital.

Example 3

A firm has the following capital structure on its balance sheet:

	Book Value
Long-term bonds, 10 percent annual coupon, issued at par	$20,000,000
Preferred stock, 4 percent dividend, issued at par	5,000,000
Common equity	25,000,000
Total	$50,000,000

The market values of the securities are as follows: bonds, $22,000,000; preferred equity, $5,000,000; common equity, $33,000,000. The market has priced the debt to yield 8.0 percent. The firm's income tax rate is 35 percent, so the after-tax cost of debt is 5.2 percent [= (1 − 0.35) × 8.0 percent]. Note that this rate is less than the coupon rate of 10 percent, and the market value of the debt is greater than its par value. Use of coupon rates and book values in this case would result in a higher cost of debt capital (6.5 percent = 0.65 × 10.0 percent) but a smaller weight in the weighted average. Assuming that the dividend on the preferred stock is not tax deductible, its cost is the dividend rate of 4.0 percent because it is selling for par value. The equity capital has a market beta of 0.9. Assuming a risk-free interest rate of 6.0 percent and a market premium of 7.0 percent, the cost of equity capital is 12.3 percent [= 6.0 percent + 0.9 × 7.0 percent]. The calculation of the weighted average cost of capital is as follows:

Security	Market Value	Weight	After-Tax Cost	Weighted Average
Long-Term Debt	$22,000,000	37%	5.2%	1.92%
Preferred Equity	5,000,000	8%	4.0%	0.32%
Common Equity	33,000,000	55%	12.3%	6.77%
Total	$60,000,000	100%		9.01%

Over time, the weights for debt, preferred, and equity capital may change if the analyst expects the firm's capital structure to change over the forecast horizon. In addition, the analyst may expect yields to maturity on debt capital and required rates of return on equity capital to change as interest rates in the economy change, the risk of the firm changes, or the firm's tax status changes. Thus, to capture these changes in the weighted average cost of capital, the analyst may need to compute a weighted average cost of capital for each period over the forecast horizon.

To determine the appropriate weights to use in the weighted average cost of capital, the analyst will need to determine the market values of the debt, preferred, and common equity capital. Market values for debt will be observable only for firms that have issued publicly traded debt; however, U.S. GAAP requires firms to disclose the fair value of their outstanding debt capital in notes to the financial statements each year. Fair value disclosures may not be available, however, if the firm is privately owned or is a foreign firm that is not required to follow U.S. GAAP, or if the firm is a division and does not publish its own financial statements. If market values are not observable and fair values for the firm's debt are not disclosed, then the analyst can either (a) estimate the fair value of the firm's debt if sufficient data are available about the firm's credit quality and the maturity and terms of the debt, or (b) rely on the book value of debt. The book value of debt can be a reliable estimate of fair value if the debt is recently issued, or if the debt bears a variable rate of interest, or if the debt bears a fixed rate of interest but interest rates and the firm's credit quality have been stable since the debt was issued. Because the yield to maturity on debt is inversely related to its market value, analysts sometimes approximate the cost of debt by simply using the coupon rate and the book value of debt when computing the weighted average cost of capital, particularly when interest rates are stable and the market value of debt is likely to be close to book value.

If available, market price quotations for equity securities provide the amounts for determining the market value of equity. Market prices for equity may not be available, however, if the firm is privately owned or if it is a division of a firm. The analyst can then use the book value of equity as a starting point to compute the weight of equity in the capital structure for purposes of estimating a weighted average cost of capital.

The preceding discussion reveals circular reasoning in computing weighted average costs of capital for valuation purposes. Analysts use the market values of debt and equity to compute the weighted average cost of capital, which is in turn used to compute the value of the debt and equity in the firm. This is circular reasoning because the analyst needs to know the market values to determine the weights but needs to know the weights to determine the weighted average cost of capital to use in estimating firm value. In practice, analysts can use two approaches to avoid this circularity. One approach assumes that the firm will maintain a target debt-to-equity structure in the future, based on benchmarks such as the firm's past debt-to-equity ratios, the firm's stated strategy with respect to financial leverage, or industry averages. The other approach computes iteratively the weighted average cost of capital and the value of debt and equity capital, until the weights and the values converge. Example 4 illustrates this iterative approach.

Example 4

Suppose that one wishes to compute the weighted average cost of capital and the market value of equity for a firm for which no market or fair value data are available. Also suppose that the firm has outstanding debt with a book value of \$40 million. The firm recently issued this debt and it carries a stated rate of 8.0 percent, so the analyst can assume this is a reliable measure of the cost of debt capital. The firm faces a 35 percent tax rate. The book value of equity is \$60 million. Similar firms in the same industry with comparable risks have a market beta of 1.2. Using the same risk-free rate and market risk premium as in Example 3, the cost of equity capital is 14.4 percent [= 6.0 percent + 1.2 × 7.0 percent]. The first estimate of the weighted average cost of capital is as follows:

Security	Amount	Weight	After-Tax Cost	Weighted Average
Debt	\$ 40,000,000	40%	5.2%	2.08%
Common Equity	60,000,000	60%	14.4%	8.64%
Total	\$100,000,000	100%		10.72%

After using the 10.72 percent weighted average cost of capital to discount the free cash flows to present value, the analyst determines that the firm's equity value is roughly \$120 million (calculations not shown). Therefore, the values and weights used to compute the weighted average cost of capital are inconsistent with value estimates for equity. The first-iteration estimates placed too much weight on debt and too little weight on equity. The analyst should use the revised estimate of the value of equity to recompute the weighted average cost of capital, and recompute the value of the firm. Using the revised estimates produces a weighted average cost of capital estimate as follows:

Security	Amount	Weight	After-Tax Cost	Weighted Average
Debt	$ 40,000,000	25%	5.2%	1.30%
Common Equity	120,000,000	75%	14.4%	10.80%
Total	$160,000,000	100%		12.10%

The analyst should now use the revised estimate of the weighted average cost of capital of 12.10 percent to recompute the value of equity once again, and iterate this process until the values of debt and equity converge with the weights of debt and equity.

Computing the Weighted Average Cost of Capital for PepsiCo

PepsiCo's balance sheet at the end of Year 4 shows interest-bearing debt from short-term obligations and long-term debt obligations totaling $3,451 million (= $1,054 + $2,397, as reported in Appendix A). Recall that in Chapter 10 we used information disclosed in Note 9, "Debt Obligations and Commitments" (Appendix A), to assess stated interest rates on PepsiCo's interest-bearing debt. We determined that in Year 4 PepsiCo's outstanding debt carries a weighted average interest rate of approximately 5.8 percent. In Note 10, "Risk Management" (Appendix A), PepsiCo discloses that the fair value of outstanding debt at the end of Year 4 is $3,676 million. Thus, PepsiCo has experienced an unrealized (and unrecognized) loss of $225 million (= $3,451 million − $3,676 million) on its debt capital. This unrealized loss implies that the firm's outstanding debt carries stated rates of interest that exceed prevailing market yields, which at the end of Year 4 are at relatively low levels in the U.S. economy. Expecting that prevailing yields to maturity are temporarily low, we forecast in Chapter 10 that PepsiCo's cost of debt capital will approximate 6.0 percent in Year +1 and beyond. We use the current fair value (as a proxy for market value) of PepsiCo's debt for weighting purposes. In Note 5, "Income Taxes" (Appendix A), PepsiCo discloses that the combined average federal, state, and foreign tax rate is approximately 24.7 percent in Year 4, which is unusually low for PepsiCo because of the favorable settlement of audits of prior years' tax returns. In Chapter 10, we forecast that PepsiCo will face a lower-than-normal average tax rate of roughly 29.4 percent in Year +1, and that PepsiCo's average tax rate will revert to a rate of 31.0 percent in Year +2 and beyond. Therefore, our long-run projections imply that PepsiCo faces an after-tax cost of debt capital of 4.14 percent [$4.14 = 6.0 \times (1 - 0.31)$].

PepsiCo also has −$49 million in preferred stock at book value on the Year 4 balance sheet. In Chapter 10, we forecast that PepsiCo will retire the remaining outstanding preferred stock during Year +1. We also forecast that PepsiCo will not issue any additional preferred stock capital in future years. Therefore, we do not include any preferred stock in the computation of PepsiCo's weighted average cost of capital.

Recall that earlier in this chapter we used the CAPM to determine that PepsiCo faces a 7.75 percent cost of equity capital. We also computed that at the end of Year 4 PepsiCo had 1,679 million shares outstanding and a share price of $51.94 for a total market capital of common equity of $87,207 million.

Bringing these costs of debt and equity capital together, we compute PepsiCo's weighted average cost of capital to be 7.604 percent as follows:

Capital	Value Basis	Amount	Weight	After-Tax Cost of Capital	Weighted-Average Component
Debt	Fair	$ 3,676	4.04%	4.14%	0.167%
Common	Market	$87,207	95.96%	7.75%	7.437%
Total		$90,883	100.00%		7.604%

This is just our initial estimate of PepsiCo's weighted average cost of capital. As described earlier, the weighted average cost of capital must be computed iteratively until the weights used are consistent with the present values of debt and equity capital.

RATIONALE FOR DIVIDENDS-BASED VALUATION

In theory, the value of a share of common equity is the present value of the expected future dividends.[8] Dividends are the most fundamental value-relevant measure of expected future payoffs to use to value shares because they represent the distribution of wealth to shareholders. The equity shareholder invests cash to purchase the share, and then receives cash in the form of dividends as the payoffs from holding the share, including the final "liquidating" dividend when the investor sells the share. In dividends-based valuation, we define dividends to include *all* cash flows between the firm and the common equity shareholders. Therefore, in valuation, "dividends" encompass all cash flows from the firm to shareholders through periodic dividend payments, stock buybacks, and the liquidating dividend, as well as cash flows from the shareholders to the firm when the firm issues shares (in a sense, *negative* dividends).

The rationale for using expected dividends in valuation is twofold:

1. Cash is the primary medium of exchange for consumption, which is the ultimate source of value. When individuals and firms invest in an economic resource, they forgo current consumption in favor of future consumption. Cash is the medium of exchange that will permit them to consume various goods and services in the future. An investment has value because of its ability to provide future cash flows. Dividends measure the cash that investors ultimately receive from investing in an equity share.
2. Dividends are paid in cash, and cash serves as a measurable common denominator for comparing the future benefits of alternative investment opportunities. One might compare investment opportunities involving the holding of a bond, a stock, or an office building, but comparing these alternatives requires a common measuring unit of their future benefits. The future cash flows derived from their future services serve such a function.

As a practical matter, however, quarterly or annual dividend payment amounts are arbitrary, established by a dividend policy set by the firm's managers and board of directors. Periodic dividend payments do not vary closely with firm performance from one period to the next. Some firms do not pay a regular periodic dividend, particularly young, high-growth firms. For most firms, the final liquidating dividend plays an important role, usually representing a large proportion of firm value in a dividends-based valuation.

[8]John Burr Williams, *The Theory of Investment and Value* (Cambridge, Mass.: Harvard University Press, 1938).

The final liquidating dividend arises when either the firm liquidates its assets and returns capital to shareholders, or when all of the outstanding shares of the firm are acquired by another firm in a merger or acquisition transaction, or when shareholders elect to liquidate their investment by selling shares. Therefore, to value a firm's shares using dividends, one must forecast dividends over the life of the firm (or the expected length of time the share will be held), including the final liquidating dividend (that is, the future price at which shares will be retired, acquired, or sold). Thus, the analyst faces the challenge of needing to forecast the value of shares in the future at the time of the liquidating dividend in order to value the shares today.

Dividends-Based Valuation Concepts

We describe and illustrate key concepts in dividends-based valuation methods in this section. We first present simple examples involving a single project. We then confront conceptual measurement issues regarding dividends to the investor versus cash flows to the firm, and nominal versus real dividends. Later in the chapter, we illustrate this approach with a more complex and realistic example involving the valuation of PepsiCo using dividends derived from the projected financial statements developed in Chapter 10.

Dividends Valuation for a Single-Asset Firm

Assume that a firm consists of a single asset. We expect that this asset will generate pretax net cash flows of $2,000,000 per year forever. These net cash flows can be used to satisfy the claims of all debt and equity capital stakeholders. The income tax rate is 40 percent. Assume that, after making debt service payments and paying taxes, the firm pays dividends to distribute any remaining cash flows to the equity shareholders each year. The cost of equity capital is 10 percent.

Example 5—Value of Common Equity in an All-Equity Firm

Assume that the common equity shareholders of the firm have financed the asset entirely with $10,000,000 of equity capital. We can determine the value of the common equity investment to the shareholders using the present value of dividends for common equity shareholders. The dividends to common equity shareholders each year will be as follows:

Net Pretax Cash Flow for All Debt and Equity Capital	$2,000,000
Interest Paid on Debt	(0)
Income Taxes: .40 × $2,000,000	(800,000)
Dividends for Common Equity Shareholders	$1,200,000

The value to the shareholders of the common equity in the firm is $12,000,000 (= $1,200,000/0.10). Dividing by the discount rate is appropriate because the $1,200,000 annual dividend for common equity is a perpetuity with no growth. This investment is worth $12,000,000 to those shareholders (a gain of $2,000,000 over their initial $10,000,000 investment) because of the present value of the dividends the investment will pay to the shareholders.

Example 6—Value of Common Equity in a Firm with Debt Financing

Assume the same facts as in Example 5, but now assume that the shareholders finance a portion of the investment in the asset with $6,000,000 of debt and the remainder with

$4,000,000 of equity capital. Suppose the debt is issued at par. Also assume that the debt is less risky than equity, so the debtholders demand interest of only 6 percent each year, payable at the end of each year. The income tax rate remains 40 percent and interest expense is deductible for income tax purposes. We can again determine the value of the common equity investment using the present value of dividends for common equity shareholders. The dividend to common equity each year is as follows:

Net Pretax Cash Flow for All Debt and Equity Capital	$2,000,000
Interest Paid on Debt: .06 × $6,000,000	(360,000)
Income Taxes: .40 × ($2,000,000 − $360,000)	(656,000)
Dividends for Common Equity Shareholders	$ 984,000

The value of the common equity to the shareholders in the firm is $9,840,000 (= $984,000/0.10). Dividing by the discount rate is appropriate because the $984,000 annual dividend for common equity is a perpetuity with no growth. Note that in this example, the present value of the gain to the common equity shareholders in excess of their initial investment is $5,840,000 (= $9,840,000 − $4,000,000). The gain to the shareholders is $3,840,000 (= $5,840,000 − $2,000,000) larger in this example than in the previous example because (a) the debt capital is less expensive than the equity capital, creating $2,400,000 of value for equity shareholders from capital structure leverage (= [$6,000,000 × (.10 − .06)]/.10), and (b) the net tax savings from interest expense creates $1,440,000 of value for equity shareholders (=[$800,000 − $656,000]/.10).

Dividends to the Investor versus Cash Flows to the Firm

In the beginning of this chapter, we asserted that the analyst can use dividends expected to be paid to the investor or the free cash flows expected to be generated by the firm (that will ultimately be paid to the investor) as equivalent approaches to measure value-relevant expected payoffs to shareholders. Will using net cash flows into the firm result in the same estimate of value as using dividends paid out of the firm? Cash flows paid to the investor via dividends and free cash flows to the firm that are available for common equity shareholders will differ each period to the extent that the firm reinvests a portion (or all) of the cash flows generated. However, if the firm generates a rate of return on reinvested free cash flow equal to the discount rate used by the investor (that is, the cost of equity capital), then either set of payoffs (dividends or free cash flows) will yield the same valuation of a firm's shares at a point in time. Consider the following scenarios.

Example 7—Dividend Policy Irrelevance with 100 Percent Payout

A firm expects to generate free cash flows of 15 percent annually on invested equity capital for the rest of its life, which is likely to continue for an indefinitely long period of time into the future (until say $t = n$). Equity investors in this firm require a 15 percent return each year, considering the riskiness of the firm. Assume that the firm pays out 100 percent of the free cash flows each year as a dividend. Thus, the free cash flows generated by the firm equal the cash dividends received by the investors each period. Each dollar of capital committed by the investors has a present value of future cash flows equal to one dollar. That is, over an indefinitely long period of time into the future,

$$\$1 = \sum_{t=1}^{n} \frac{\$.15}{(1.15)^t}$$

Example 8—Dividend Policy Irrelevance with Zero Payout

Assume the same facts as Example 7, except that the firm pays out none of the free cash flows as a dividend. The firm retains the \$0.15 free cash flow on each dollar of capital and reinvests it in projects expected to earn 15 percent return per year. In this case, the investor receives no periodic dividends and receives cash only when the investor sells the shares or the firm liquidates at date $t = n$. By the terminal date, n periods in the future, each dollar of capital invested in the firm today will have earned a compound rate of return of 15 percent, equal to the required rate of return. In this case also, each dollar of invested capital has a present value of future cash flows equal to one dollar. That is,

$$\$1 = \frac{(\$1.15)^n}{(1.15)^n}$$

Example 9—Dividend Policy Irrelevance with Partial Payout

Assume the same facts as Example 8, except that the firm pays out 25 percent of the free cash flow each period as a dividend and reinvests the other 75 percent in projects expected to generate a return of 15 percent. In this case also, each dollar of invested capital has a present value of future cash flows equal to one dollar. That is,

$$\$1 = \sum_{t=1}^{n} \frac{(\$.25)(.15)}{(1.15)^t} + \frac{(\$.75)(1.15)^n}{(1.15)^n}$$

These three examples illustrate the *relevance* of dividends as payoffs that are sufficient for valuation for equity shareholders, and the *irrelevance* of the firm's dividend policy in valuation.[9] The same valuation should arise whether the analyst discounts (1) the expected dividends to the investor, or (2) the expected free cash flows to the firm that are available to pay future dividends to equity shareholders. Further, the same valuation should arise whether the firm pays all of its cash flows as a dividend, or reinvests all cash flows to earn the investors' required rate of return, or pays a portion of cash flows in dividends each period and reinvests the remaining cash flows to earn the investors' required rate of return.

Nominal versus Real Dividends

Changes in general price levels (that is, inflation or deflation) cause the purchasing power of the monetary unit to change over time. Should the valuation use projected nominal dividends, which include the effects of inflation or deflation, or real dividends, which filter out the effects of changes in general purchasing power?[10] The valuation of an investment in an economic resource should be the same whether one uses nominal or real dividend amounts as long as the discount rate used is the nominal or real rate of return

---

[9]Merton Miller and Franco Modigliani, "Dividend Policy, Growth and the Valuation of Shares," *Journal of Business* (October 1961), pp. 411–433. Penman and Sougiannis test empirically the replacement property of dividends for future earnings and find support for the irrelevance of dividend policy in valuation. See Stephen H. Penman and Theodore Sougiannis, "The Dividend Displacement Property and the Substitution of Anticipated Earnings for Dividends in Equity Valuation," *The Accounting Review* (January 1997), pp. 1–21.

[10]Note that the issue here is not with specific price changes of a firm's particular assets, liabilities, revenues, and expenses. These specific price changes affect our projections of the firm's dividends, cash flows, and earnings, and should enter into the valuation of the firm. The issue is whether some portion, all, or more than all of the specific price changes represent simply an economy-wide change in the purchasing power of the monetary unit, which should not affect the value of a firm.

that is consistent with the dividend measure. That is, if projected dividends are nominal and include the effects of changes in general purchasing power of the monetary unit, then the discount rate should be nominal and include an inflation component. If projected dividends are real amounts that filter out the effects of general price changes, then the discount rate should be a real rate of return, excluding the inflation component.

Example 10—Nominal versus Real Dividends

A firm owns an asset that it expects to sell one year from today for \$115.5 million. The firm expects the general price level to increase 10 percent during this period. The real interest rate is 5 percent. The nominal discount rate should be 15.5 percent to measure the compound effects of the real rate of interest and inflation (1.155 = 1.10 × 1.05). Discounting either nominal or real dividends, the value of the asset today to the firm is \$100 million, as shown:

Nominal Dividends	×	Discount Rate Including Expected Inflation	=	Value
\$115.5 million	×	1/[(1.05) × (1.10)]	=	\$100 million

Real Dividends	×	Discount Rate Excluding Expected Inflation	=	Value
\$115.5 million/(1.10)	×	1/(1.05)	=	\$100 million

In both examples we derived the value of the equity of the firm by computing the present value of the dividends to common equity shareholders. As a practical matter, analysts usually find it more straightforward to discount nominal dividends using nominal discount rates than to first adjust nominal dividends to real dividends and then discount real dividends using real interest rates.

THE DIVIDENDS VALUATION MODEL

In this section, we present the dividends valuation model that determines the value of common shareholders' equity in the firm. In the sections following the model, we demonstrate how to implement the model using PepsiCo.

The dividends valuation model determines the value of common shareholders' equity in the firm (which we denote V_0) as the sum of the present value of all future dividends to shareholders over the life of the firm, which is indefinite and could be (in theory) infinite. In the dividends valuation model we include all-inclusive dividends (which we denote D) that encompass all of the net cash flows from the firm to shareholders through periodic dividend payments and stock buybacks, and subtract cash flows from the shareholders to the firm when the firm issues shares. In the next section, we demonstrate how to measure D. We discount the stream of future dividends to present value using the required return on common equity capital in the firm, which we denote as R_E. We express the dividends valuation approach with the following general model:

$$V_0 = \sum_{t=1}^{\infty} \frac{D_t}{(1 + R_E)^t} = \frac{D_1}{(1 + R_E)^1} + \frac{D_2}{(1 + R_E)^2} + \frac{D_3}{(1 + R_E)^3} + \cdots$$

Suppose we can reliably forecast dividend amounts through Year T. At the end of Year T, we assume that the continuing value of the common equity of the firm (which we denote V_T) will equal the present value of all expected future continuing dividends in Year T+1 and beyond, which can be expressed as:

$$V_T = \sum_{t=1}^{\infty} \frac{D_{T+1}}{(1 + R_E)^t}$$

Thus, the value of the firm today can be expressed using periodic dividends over a finite horizon to Year T plus continuing value based on dividends in Year T+1 and beyond as follows:

$$V_0 = \sum_{t=1}^{\infty} \frac{D_t}{(1 + R_E)^t} = \frac{D_1}{(1 + R_E)^1} + \frac{D_2}{(1 + R_E)^2} + \frac{D_3}{(1 + R_E)^3} + \cdots$$
$$+ \frac{D_T}{(1 + R_E)^T} + \frac{V_T}{(1 + R_E)^T}$$

This equation reveals that the estimate of value today (V_0) depends on the estimate of value in the future (V_T).

As we describe in more detail in a following section, we project the continuing dividends in the continuing value period beyond Year T using the expected, long-run steady state growth of the firm, which we specify as $(1 + g)$. Thus, we project the Year T+1 dividend by projecting each line item on the Year T income statement and balance sheet to grow at rate $(1 + g)$ and then deriving the Year T+1 dividend. As we describe in a following section, to derive dividends we first assume that accounting for the book value of the shareholders' equity (*BV*) follows the general principle of adding net income (*NI*) and subtracting dividends to common shareholders each period (that is, $BV_t = BV_{t-1} + NI_t - D_t$). We can therefore derive the Year T+1 dividend as follows:

$$D_{T+1} = NI_{T+1} + BV_T - BV_{T+1}$$

We rely on the assumption that growth in net income and book value in Year T+1 equals $(1 + g)$ to rewrite the D_{T+1} equation as follows:

$$D_{T+1} = [NI_T \times (1 + g)] + BV_T - [BV_T \times (1 + g)]$$

We assume that D_{T+1} will grow in perpetuity at rate *g*, so we can value the firm at the end of Year T using the perpetuity-with-growth model:

$$V_T = \sum_{t=1}^{\infty} \frac{D_{T+1}}{(1 + R_E)^t} = \frac{D_{T+1}}{(R_E - g)} = \frac{[NI_T \times (1 + g)] + BV_T - [BV_T \times (1 + g)]}{(R_E - g)}$$

Therefore, the present value of common equity today can be expressed using dividends as follows:

$$V_0 = \sum_{t=1}^{\infty} \frac{D_t}{(1 + R_E)^t}$$
$$= \frac{D_1}{(1 + R_E)^1} + \frac{D_2}{(1 + R_E)^2} + \frac{D_3}{(1 + R_E)^3} + \cdots + \frac{D_T}{(1 + R_E)^T} + \frac{V_T}{(1 + R_E)^T}$$

$$= \frac{D_1}{(1 + R_E)^1} + \frac{D_2}{(1 + R_E)^2} + \frac{D_3}{(1 + R_E)^3} + \cdots$$

$$+ \frac{D_T}{(1 + R_E)^T} + \frac{[NI_T \times (1 + g)] + BV_T - [BV_T \times (1 + g)]}{(R_E - g) \times (1 + R_E)^T}$$

IMPLEMENTING THE DIVIDENDS VALUATION MODEL

Implementing the dividends valuation model to determine the value of the common shareholders' equity in a firm involves measuring three elements:

1. The discount rate (denoted R_E in the preceding model) used to compute the present value of the future dividends.
2. The expected future dividends over the forecast horizon, denoted D_t in periods 1 through T in the preceding model.
3. The expected dividend at the final period of the forecast horizon, which we refer to as the *continuing dividend* (denoted D_{T+1} in the preceding model), and a forecast of the long-run growth rate (denoted g in the preceding model), in the continuing dividend beyond the forecast horizon.

We discussed computing the appropriate discount rate in the first portion of this chapter. The following sections discuss measuring the second and third of these elements.

Measuring Periodic Dividends

In this section we describe measuring value-relevant periodic dividends and illustrate this approach using PepsiCo. We also discuss the appropriate horizon for forecasting dividends.

Dividends Measurement

In dividends-based valuation, we value the common equity in a firm by measuring the present value of all net cash flows to the equity shareholders. Therefore, the objective in measuring dividends for purposes of valuing a firm for common equity shareholders is to include *all* of the cash that the shareholders will receive from holding the share.

We define total dividends as measures of all of the cash flows between the firm and the common equity shareholders each period. Total dividends encompass cash flows from the firm to common equity shareholders through periodic dividend payments, such as quarterly or annual dividends paid to shareholders each period based on the firm's dividend payout policy. We also include cash flows to common equity shareholders through stock buybacks. Further, we include cash flows from the shareholders to the firm when the firm issues shares (in a sense, *negative* dividends). Thus, to measure total value-relevant dividends that encompass all of the cash flows from the firm to common equity shareholders each period, the analyst should include the following three components:

+ Quarterly or annual dividend payments to common equity shareholders
+ Net cash flows to shareholders as a result of common equity share repurchases
− Net cash flows from shareholders through common equity issues

= Total dividends to common equity shareholders.

Alternatively, we can also rely on accounting for the shareholders' equity for a reliable framework for measuring total dividends for valuation. To begin, we assume that the accounting for shareholders' equity follows *clean surplus accounting.* Under clean surplus accounting, income must include *all* of the elements of income generated by the firm for common equity shareholders. Under U.S. GAAP, clean surplus income would encompass comprehensive income (that is, net income plus all of the unrealized gains and losses included in other comprehensive income). We also assume that the effects of all of the direct capital transactions between the firm and the common equity shareholders, such as periodic dividend payments, capital raised from issues of stock, or capital used to repurchase or retire shares, are included in the book value of common shareholders' equity.[11]

Under these simple and general principles of clean surplus accounting, we represent the accounting for common equity as follows:

$$BV_t = BV_{t-1} + I_t - D_t$$

where BV_t denotes the book value of equity at the end of year *t; I* denotes clean surplus income for year *t;* and *D* denotes direct capital transactions (dividend payments, stock issues, and stock repurchases) during year *t.* To isolate all of the cash flows between the firm and the shareholders during year *t,* simply rearrange this equation as follows:

$$D_t = I_t + BV_{t-1} - BV_t$$

Dividends used in dividends valuation, therefore, should equal clean surplus income each year, adjusted for the change in the book value of common equity as a result of direct capital transactions.

Measuring Dividends for PepsiCo

In this section, we illustrate the dividends measurement approach described previously by measuring dividends for PepsiCo. We derive our dividends expectations from our projected financial statements for PepsiCo in Chapter 10.

In developing our financial statement forecasts for PepsiCo for Year +1, for example, we projected that PepsiCo would pay common equity dividends equal to 45 percent of lagged net income from continuing operations, amounting to $1,878.3 million (= .45 × [$4,212 − $38]).[12] We also assumed that PepsiCo would use dividends as the flexible financial account to balance the balance sheet, requiring a reduction of $114.6 million in dividends to common shareholders. Therefore, we projected that net dividends would amount to $1,763.7 million (= $1,878.3 − $114.6) in Year +1.

We also projected that common stock and additional paid-in capital would remain roughly 2.3 percent of total assets. Thus, we projected that common stock and additional paid-in capital would increase from $648.0 million to $684.9 million by the end of Year +1, implying a negative dividend of −$36.9 million. Further, we projected that PepsiCo would engage in direct capital transactions with common equity shareholders through the treasury stock account. We projected that PepsiCo would pay $3,258.0 million to acquire shares, and would reissue $1,578.0 million in shares for stock options exercises. Together, these transactions would result in a net cash outflow of $1,680.0 million (= $3,258.0 − $1,578.0) from PepsiCo to common shareholders.

---

[11]We also assume that direct capital transactions between the firm and common equity shareholders are value-neutral (that is, zero net present value projects) to the existing common shareholders.

[12]In Year 4, PepsiCo generated net income from continuing operations of $4,174, based on net income of $4,212 million minus $38 million that was attributable to a tax benefit from a discontinued operation.

Bringing these components together, we projected that total value-relevant dividends to common equity shareholders in Year +1 will be (in millions):

Periodic dividend payments	$1,763.7
Net purchases of treasury stock	1,680.0
Common stock issues	−36.9
Total dividends to common equity shareholders	$3,406.8

We can reconcile this computation with the clean surplus accounting approach described earlier as follows. Our Year +1 forecast of comprehensive income is $4,381.9 million. After deducting the forecast of the liquidating dividend to retire the preferred shares, the projected amount of comprehensive income available to common shareholders is (in millions):

$$\$4,381.9 - \$159.0 = \$4,222.9$$

Total book value of common shareholders' equity is $13,572.0 million at the beginning of Year +1 and $14,388.1 million at the end of Year +1. Using the clean surplus accounting approach, dividends in Year +1 are (in millions):

$$D_t = I_t + BV_{t-1} - BV_t = \$4,222.9 + \$13,572.0 - \$14,388.1 = \$3,406.8$$

We demonstrate these computations for Years +1 through +5 in Exhibit 11.4.

Selecting a Forecast Horizon

For how many future years should the analyst project dividends? The correct answer is the expected life of the resource to be valued. This life is a finite number of years for a resource such as a machine, building, or similar resource with limits to its physical existence, or a financial instrument with a finite stated maturity (such as a bond, a mortgage, or a lease). In equity valuation contexts, however, the resource to be valued is an ownership claim on the firm, a resource that has an expected life that is indefinite, and potentially infinite. In the case of an equity security, the analyst must therefore project future dividends that, in theory, extend to infinity.

Of course, as a practical matter, the analyst cannot precisely predict a firm's dividends very many years into the future. Therefore, analysts commonly develop specific projections of all of the elements of the income statements and balance sheets for the firm and use those elements to derive forecasts of dividends over an explicit forecast horizon, say five or ten years, depending on the industry, the maturity of the firm, and the expected growth and predictability of the firm's business activities. After the explicit forecast horizon, analysts then typically use general growth assumptions to project the future income statements and balance sheets, and use them to derive the dividends that will persist each period to infinity. The analyst will therefore find it desirable to develop specific forecasts of income statements, balance sheets, and cash flows over an explicit forecast horizon that extends until the point at which a firm's growth pattern is expected to settle into steady-state equilibrium, during which dividends might be expected to grow at a steady, predictable rate.

Selecting a forecast horizon involves trade-offs. One can develop reasonably reliable projections over longer forecast horizons for stable and mature firms. Projections for such firms, as in the case of PepsiCo demonstrated in Chapter 10, capture relatively

EXHIBIT 11.4

Computation of PepsiCo's Total Dividends for the Dividends Valuation Approach

	Computing Total Dividends using Components				
	Year +1	Year +2	Year +3	Year +4	Year +5
Dividends Paid to Common Shareholders	$1,763.7	$2,404.0	$2,489.1	$2,644.0	$2,472.7
Less: Common Stock Issues	−36.9	−20.5	−47.9	−32.1	−51.9
Plus: Common Stock Repurchases	1,680.0	1,761.0	1,880.0	2,010.0	2,149.0
Total Dividends to Common Equity	$3,406.8	$4,144.5	$4,321.2	$4,622.0	$4,569.7

	Computing Total Dividends using Clean Surplus Accounting				
	Year +1	Year +2	Year +3	Year +4	Year +5
Comprehensive Income Available for Common Equity	$ 4,222.9	$ 4,503.2	$ 4,887.7	$ 5,216.8	$ 5,580.4
Plus: Beginning Book Value of Common Equity	13,572.0	14,388.1	14,746.8	15,313.3	15,908.1
Less: Ending Book Value of Common Equity	−14,388.1	−14,746.8	−15,313.3	−15,908.1	−16,918.8
Total Dividends to Common Equity	$ 3,406.8	$ 4,144.5	$ 4,321.2	$ 4,622.0	$ 4,569.7

steady-state operations. On the other hand, it is much more difficult to develop reliable projections over long forecast horizons for young, high-growth firms because their future operating performance is uncertain. In addition, a much higher proportion of the value of young growth firms will be achieved in distant future years, after they reach their potential. Thus, the analyst faces the dilemma of depending most heavily on long-run forecasts for young growth firms for which long-run projections are likely to be most uncertain. The forecasting and valuation process is particularly difficult for growth firms when the near-term dividends are projected to be zero or negative, as is common for rapidly growing firms financing growth by issuing common stock. In this case, most of the firm's value depends on dividends to be generated in years far into the future.

Unfortunately, there is no way to avoid this dilemma. The predictive accuracy of dividends forecasts many years into the future is likely to be questionable for even the most stable and predictable firms. The analyst must recognize that forecasts and value estimates for all firms, but especially growth firms, have a high degree of uncertainty and estimation risk. To mitigate this uncertainty and estimation risk, we emphasize the following points:

1. Diligently and comprehensively follow all six steps of the analysis framework. By thoroughly analyzing the firm's industry and strategy, the firm's accounting quality, and the firm's financial performance and risk ratios, the analyst will have more information to use to develop long-term forecasts that are as reliable as possible.
2. To the extent possible, confront directly the problem of long-term uncertainty by developing specific projections of dividends derived from projected income statements and balance sheets that extend five or ten years into the future, at which point the firm may be projected to reach steady-state growth.
3. Assess the sensitivity of the forecast projections and value estimates across the reasonable range of growth assumptions.

Continuing Value of Future Dividends

In the previous section, we described measuring periodic dividends over an explicit forecast horizon. In this section, we describe techniques to project dividends using a steady-state growth rate continuing beyond the explicit forecast horizon, and to measure the present value of continuing dividends beyond the explicit forecast horizon.

In some circumstances, however, the analyst may not find it necessary to forecast dividends continuing beyond the explicit forecast horizon if the analyst can reliably predict that the share will receive a future liquidating dividend. In that case, we include the liquidating dividend as a cash flow to the shareholder. The liquidating dividend might arise when the firm liquidates its assets at the end of its business life, and distributes the proceeds to shareholders to retire their shares. Alternatively, the liquidating dividend might arise when a firm's shares are acquired by another firm in a merger or acquisition transaction. The liquidating can also arise at the initiation of the shareholder when the shareholder elects to sell the share, thereby creating a liquidating cash flow from the selling price.

Projecting Continuing Dividends

In most circumstances, the analyst will not be able to reliably predict whether the share will receive a liquidating dividend. Therefore, analysts commonly find it desirable to forecast dividends over an explicit forecast horizon until the point at which the analyst expects a firm to mature into a steady-state growth pattern, during which dividends are assumed to grow at a constant rate. We refer to these dividends as "continuing" dividends, because they reflect the periodic dividends continuing into the long-run future of the firm. The long-run sustainable growth rate in future continuing dividends could be positive, negative, or zero. Sustainable growth in dividends could be driven by long-run expectations for inflation, the industry's sales, the economy in general, or the population. The analyst should select a growth rate that captures realistic expectations for the long run.

If a firm's growth pattern can be projected to settle into steady-state growth rate (denoted g in the preceding dividends valuation model) continuing after the end of the explicit forecast horizon, say after Year T, then the analyst can derive the continuing dividends from the projected income statements and balance sheets. To do so correctly, the analyst should use the expected long-run growth rate (g) to project all of the items of the Year T+1 income statement and balance sheet. That is, the analyst should project each item on the Year T+1 income statement by multiplying each item on the Year T income statement times $(1 + g)$. Likewise, the analyst should project each item on the Year T+1 balance sheet by multiplying each item on the Year T balance sheet times $(1 + g)$. The analyst can then derive Year T+1 dividends from the Year T+1 income statement and balance sheet projections. As shown previously, we can then rely on clean surplus accounting to project the Year T+1 dividend by projecting the Year T income statement and balance sheet to grow at rate $(1 + g)$ and deriving the Year T+1 dividend as follows:

$$D_{T+1} = NI_{T+1} + BV_T - BV_{T+1} = [NI_T \times (1 + g)] + BV_T - [BV_T \times (1 + g)]$$

It is necessary for the analyst to impose the long-run growth rate assumption $(1 + g)$ uniformly on the Year T+1 income statement and balance sheet projections in order to derive correctly the dividends for Year T+1. In steady state, we assume that dividends, earnings, assets, liabilities, shareholders' equity, and cash flows will grow at equivalent rates. By applying a uniform growth rate, the analyst achieves internally consistent steady-state growth across all of the projections of the firm, keeping the balance sheet in balance throughout the continuing forecast horizon, and keeping growth in dividends, cash flows, and earnings internally consistent with the assumed long-run growth rate.

In projecting continuing dividends in Year T+1 and beyond, analysts assume that the firm will settle into a long-run, sustainable growth rate. Often analysts assume that the firm's long-run sustainable growth rate will be consistent with long-run growth in the economy, on the order of 3 to 5 percent. For firms that have been growing more quickly than that (say, at 10 percent) in the years leading up to Year T+1, the long-run sustainable growth rate implies that the firm will maintain a lower growth rate in assets and equity, and thus will be able to pay out substantially larger dividends. By projecting Year T+1 net income, assets, and equity using the long-run sustainable growth rate, we can then solve for the long-run sustainable dividends the firm can pay. The continuing dividend amount we derive for Year T+1 may be significantly larger than the amounts the firm actually paid during its higher-growth-rate years. The Year T+1 dividend amount reflects the firm's transition from a high rate of reinvestment of earnings for growth in assets to reinvestment for a much lower rate of growth, thereby creating the need to solve for the long-run sustainable dividend amount.

A shortcut analysts sometimes use (in error) to compute the continuing dividends for Year T+1 is to multiply the dividends for Year T by $(1 + g)$ instead of deriving the Year T+1 dividends from changes in the income statement and balance sheet for Year T+1. If the analyst wishes to compute internally consistent and identical estimates of firm value using dividends, free cash flows, and earnings, then the analyst should *not* project dividends for Year T+1 by simply multiplying dividends for Year T by $(1 + g)$. Doing so ignores the necessary growth in all of the elements of the balance sheet and the income statement, which can introduce inconsistent forecast assumptions for dividends, cash flows, and earnings. Even if the analyst simply projects Year T+1 dividends, cash flows, and earnings to grow at an identical rate $(1 + g)$, it may impound inconsistent assumptions and lead to inconsistent value estimates if Year T dividends, cash flows, and earnings are not consistent with their long-run continuing amounts.

Example 11

Suppose the analyst develops the following forecasts for the firm in Year T−1 and Year T:

	Assets	=	Liabilities	+	Shareholders' Equity
Year T−1 Balances	$100	=	$60	+	$40
+ Net Income	+20				+20
+ New Borrowing	+6		+6		
− Dividends Paid	−10				−10
Year T Balances	$116	=	$66	+	$50

The analyst would compute Year T dividends to common equity shareholders to equal \$10. Now suppose the analyst projects that the firm will grow at a steady-state rate of 10 percent in Year T+1 and thereafter. The analyst should project Year T+1 net income, assets, liabilities, and shareholders' equity to each grow by 10 percent, and then compute Year T+1 continuing dividends, as follows:

	Assets	=	Liabilities	+	Shareholders' Equity
Year T Balances	\$116	=	\$66	+	\$50
Growth	× 1.10		× 1.10		× 1.10
Year T+1 Balances.......	\$127.6	=	\$72.6	+	\$55

The projected net income would be \$22 (= \$20 × 1.10). The Year T+1 dividends projection would be \$17 (= \$22 net income − \$5 increase in shareholders' equity). However, if the analyst had simply projected Year T dividends to grow by 10 percent, the Year T+1 projections would be only \$11 (= \$10 Year T dividends × 1.10), which is not correct. This error would reduce the estimated value of the firm using dividends, relative to the value estimate using cash flows or earnings, because of the inconsistent assumptions. Note that the correct projected Year T+1 dividend amount of \$17 is substantially larger than the \$10 dividend amount for Year T. The reason the firm can begin to pay larger dividends in Year T+1 and beyond is that the firm's long-run growth rate is 10 percent, which is lower than the Year T growth rate in assets (16 percent) and shareholders' equity (25 percent); thus this firm will not need to reinvest as much of its earnings to fund growth, and will be able to pay larger dividend amounts in Year T+1 and beyond.

Computing Continuing Value

As we demonstrated earlier in the dividends valuation model, once the analyst has computed continuing dividends for Year T+1, then the analyst can compute continuing value (sometimes called residual value or terminal value) of future dividends continuing in Years T+1 and beyond using the perpetuity-with-growth valuation model, as follows:[13]

$$V_T = \sum_{t=1}^{\infty} \frac{D_{T+1}}{(1 + R_E)^t} = \frac{D_{T+1}}{(R_E - g)} = \frac{[NI_T \times (1 + g)] + BV_T - [BV_T \times (1 + g)]}{(R_E - g)}$$

Example 12

An analyst forecasts that the dividends of a firm in Year +5 will be \$30 million, and that Year +5 earnings and cash flows will also be \$30 million. The analyst expects that the firm's income statements and balance sheets will grow uniformly over the long run, and that therefore cash flows, earnings, and dividends will all grow uniformly over the long run, but the analyst is uncertain about the steady-state long-run growth rate in Year +6 and beyond. The analyst believes the growth rate will most likely be zero but could reasonably fall in the range between +6 to −6 percent per year. Assuming a 15 percent cost of capital, the following table shows the range of possible continuing values (in millions) for the firm in present value at the beginning of the continuing value period (that is, the beginning of Year +6), and in present value as of today (that is, the continuing value is discounted to today using a factor of $1/(1.15)^5$):

[13]This formula is simply the algebraic simplification for the present value of a growing perpetuity.

Dividends in Year T	Long-Run Growth Assumption	Dividends in Year T+1	Perpetuity with Growth Factor	Continuing Value in Present Value as of: Beginning of Year T+1	Today
$30	0%	$30	$\frac{1}{(0.15 - 0.0)} = 6.67$	$200.0	$ 99.4
$30	+6%	$31.80	$\frac{1}{(0.15 - 0.06)} = 11.11$	$353.3	$175.7
$30	−6%	$28.20	$\frac{1}{(0.15 + 0.06)} = 4.76$	$134.3	$ 66.8

Analysts can also estimate continuing value using a multiple of dividends in the first year of the continuing value period. The following table shows the continuing value multiples using $1/(R - g)$ for various costs of equity capital and growth rates. The multiples increase with growth for a given cost of capital, and they decrease as the cost of capital increases for a given level of growth.

Continuing Value Multiples

Cost of Equity Capital	Growth Rates 0%	2%	4%	6%
10%	10.00	12.50	16.67	25.00
15%	6.67	7.69	9.09	11.11
18%	5.56	6.25	7.14	8.33
20%	5.00	5.56	6.25	7.14

The continuing value computation using the perpetuity-with-growth valuation model does not work when the growth rate equals or exceeds the discount rate (that is, when $g \geq R$) because the denominator in the computation is zero or negative and the resulting continuing value estimate is meaningless. In this case, the analyst cannot use the perpetuity computation illustrated here. Instead, the analyst must forecast dividend amounts for each year beyond the forecast horizon using the terminal period growth rate, and then discount each year's dividends to present value using the discount rate. The analyst should probably also reconsider whether it is realistic to expect the firm's dividends growth rate to exceed the discount rate (the expected rate of return) in perpetuity. This scenario can exist for some years, but is not likely to be sustainable indefinitely. Competition, technological change, new entrants into an industry, and similar factors eventually reduce growth rates. Thus, in applying the model, the analyst must attempt to estimate the long-term sustainable growth rate in dividends (refer to the discussion of sustainable earnings in Chapter 6).

An alternate approach for estimating the continuing value is to use the dividends multiples for comparable firms that currently trade in the market. The analyst identifies comparable companies by studying characteristics such as industry, firm size and age, past growth rates in dividends, profitability, risk, and similar factors. We discuss valuation multiples in more depth in Chapter 14.

Because of the uncertainty inherent in long-run growth rate forecasts, and because continuing value amounts are commonly large proportions of value estimates, analysts should conduct sensitivity analysis to assess how sensitive the firm value estimate is to variations in the long-run growth assumption. For example, suppose an analyst is valuing a young, high-growth company, and can reliably forecast dividends five years into the future. After that horizon, the analyst expects the firm to grow at 6 percent per year, but this is highly uncertain, and long-run growth could range from −3 percent per year to as much as 9 percent per year. The analyst should conduct sensitivity analysis on the projections and valuation, varying long-run growth across the range from −3 to 9 percent per year.

Using the Dividends Valuation Model to Value PepsiCo

At the end of Year 4, trading in PepsiCo shares on the New York Stock Exchange closed at \$51.94 per share. We therefore know the *price* at which we can buy or sell PepsiCo shares. But what is the *value* of these shares? We illustrate the valuation of PepsiCo shares using the techniques described in this chapter and the forecasts developed in Chapter 10. We develop the forecasts and valuation estimates using the Forecast and Valuation spreadsheets in FSAP.

We estimate the present value of a share of common equity in PepsiCo at the end of Year 4 (equivalently, the start of Year +1) using the risk-adjusted rate of return on PepsiCo's equity capital as the appropriate discount rate. In a prior section of this chapter we computed the PepsiCo discount rate to be 7.75 percent. Exhibit 11.4 summarizes the computations of PepsiCo's dividends in Years +1 to +5. Discounting these future dividends using PepsiCo's equity cost of capital (7.75 percent) yields a present value estimate of \$16,761.0 million. We illustrate these computations in Exhibit 11.5, and present the dividend valuation model output from FSAP in Exhibit 11.6.

To compute the continuing value of PepsiCo's dividends in Year +6 and beyond, we project that dividends will grow in perpetuity at a 3 percent growth rate, consistent with long-run average growth in the economy. We forecast Year +6 dividends as follows:

$$
\begin{aligned}
D_6 &= [NI_5 \times (1 + g)] + BV_5 - [BV_5 \times (1 + g)] \\
&= [\$5{,}580.4 \text{ million} \times 1.03] + \$16{,}918.8 \text{ million} - [\$16{,}918.8 \text{ million} \times 1.03] \\
&= \$5{,}747.8 \text{ million} + \$16{,}918.8 \text{ million} - \$17{,}426.3 \text{ million} \\
&= \$5{,}240.3 \text{ million}
\end{aligned}
$$

We use the perpetuity-with-growth model to discount dividends in the continuing value period to present value at PepsiCo's 7.75 percent cost of equity capital, as follows (allowing for rounding):

$$
\begin{aligned}
\text{Continuing Value}_0 &= [D_6 \times [1/(R_E - g)] \times [1/(1+R_E)^5] \\
&= \$5{,}240.3 \text{ million} \times [1/(0.0775 - 0.0300)] \times [1/(1+0.0775)^5] \\
&= \$5{,}240.3 \text{ million} \times 21.0526 \times 0.6885 \\
&= \$75{,}958.1 \text{ million}
\end{aligned}
$$

EXHIBIT 11.5

Valuation of PepsiCo
Present Value of Dividends to Common Equity Year +1 through Year +5 and Beyond

	Valuation of Dividends in Year +1 through Year +5				
	Year +1	**Year +2**	**Year +3**	**Year +4**	**Year +5**
Total Dividends to Common Equity (from Exhibit 11.4)	$ 3,406.8	$4,144.5	$4,321.2	$4,622.0	$4,569.7
Present Value Factors ($R_E = 7.75\%$)	0.9281	0.8613	0.7994	0.7419	0.6885
Present Value of Dividends	$ 3,161.8	$3,569.7	$3,454.2	$3,428.9	$3,146.3
Sum of Present Value Dividends, Years +1 through +5	$16,761.0				

Continuing Value based on Dividends in Year + 6 and Beyond

Project Year +6 Dividends:

$$D_6 = [NI_5 \times (1 + g)] + BV_5 - [BV_5 \times (1 + g)]$$
$$= [\$5{,}580.4 \text{ million} \times 1.03] + \$16{,}918.8 \text{ million} - [\$16{,}918.8 \text{ million} \times 1.03]$$
$$= \$5{,}747.8 \text{ million} + \$16{,}918.8 \text{ million} - \$17{,}426.3 \text{ million}$$
$$= \underline{\$5{,}240.3} \text{ million}$$

Continuing Value in Present Value ($R_E = 7.75\%$ and g = 3.0%):

$$\text{Continuing Value}_0 = D_6 \times [1/(R_E - g)] \times [1/(1+R_E)^5]$$
$$= \$5{,}240.3 \text{ million} \times [1/(0.0775 - 0.0300)] \times [1/(1+0.0775)^5]$$
$$= \$5{,}240.3 \text{ million} \times 21.0526 \times 0.6885$$
$$= \underline{\$75{,}958.1} \text{ million}$$

Total Value of PepsiCo's Dividends

Present Value of Dividends through Year +5	$16,761.0 million
+ Present Value of Continuing Value	+ 75,958.1 million
Present Value of Common Equity	$92,719.1 million
Adjust for Midyear Discounting (multiply by 1 + [R_E/2])	× 1.03875
Total Present Value of Common Equity	$96,312.0 million
Divide by Number of Shares Outstanding	÷ 1,679 million
Value per Share of PepsiCo Common Equity	= $ 57.36

EXHIBIT 11.6

Valuation of PepsiCo
Present Value of Dividends to Common Equity Year +1 through Year +5 and Beyond using the Dividends Valuation Model in FSAP

Dividends-Based Valuation	Year +1	Year +2	Year +3	Year +4	Year +5	Year +6
Dividends Paid to Common Shareholders	$ 1,763.7	$2,404.0	$2,489.1	$2,644.0	$2,472.7	
Less: Common Stock Issues	−36.9	−20.5	−47.9	−32.1	−51.9	
Plus: Common Stock Repurchases	1,680.0	1,761.0	1,880.0	2,010.0	2,149.0	
Dividends to Common Equity	$ 3,406.8	$4,144.5	$4,321.2	$4,622.0	$4,569.7	$5,240.3
Present Value Factors	0.9281	0.8613	0.7994	0.7419	0.6885	
Present Value Net Dividends	$ 3,161.8	$3,569.7	$3,454.2	$3,428.9	$3,146.3	
Sum of Present Value Net Dividends	$16,761.0					
Present Value of Continuing Value	75,958.1					
Total	$92,719.1					
Adjust to Midyear Discounting	1.03875					
Total Present Value Dividends	$96,312.0					
Shares Outstanding	1,679.0					
Estimated Value per Share	$ 57.36					
Current Share Price	$ 51.94					
Percent Difference	10%					

The total present value of PepsiCo's free cash flows to common equity shareholders is the sum of these two parts:

Present Value of Dividends through Year +5	$16,761.0 million
Present Value of Continuing Value	75,958.1 million
Present Value of Common Equity	$92,719.1 million

Midyear Discounting

Present value calculations like those illustrated earlier discount amounts for full periods. Thus, the valuation computations include Year +1 dividends discounted for a full year, Year +2 dividends discounted for two full years, and so on, which is appropriate if the dividends being discounted occur at the end of each year. Dividends often occur throughout the period. If this is the case, present value computations with full-year discounting will overdiscount these flows. To avoid overdiscounting, the analyst can compute the present value discount factors as of the midpoint of each year, thereby effectively discounting the dividends as if they occur on average in the middle of each year. Suppose the analyst uses a discount rate of 10 percent ($R = 0.10$). The Year +1 dividends would be discounted using a factor of $1/(1 + R)^{0.5} = 1/(1.10)^{0.5} = 0.9535$; the Year +2 dividends would be discounted using a factor of $1/(1 + R)^{1.5} = 1/(1.10)^{1.5} = 0.8668$; and so on. The analyst can also use a shortcut approach to this correction by adjusting the total present value to a midyear approximation by adding back one-half of a year of discounting. To make this midyear adjustment, the analyst multiplies the total present value of the discounted dividends by a factor of $1 + (R/2)$. For example, if $R = 0.10$, then the midyear adjustment is 1.05 [$= 1 + (0.10/2)$]. The Valuation spreadsheet computations in FSAP use this shortcut adjustment.[14]

Applying the midyear discounting adjustment to our computation of the present value of PepsiCo dividends results in the following:

Present Value of Common Equity.....................................	$92,719.1 million
Midyear Adjustment Factor (= 1 + [0.0775/2]):	×1.03875
Total Present Value of Common Equity	$96,312.0 million

Computing Common Equity Value per Share

Dividing by 1,679 million shares outstanding indicates that PepsiCo's common equity shares have a value of $57.36 per share. We will obtain identical value estimates for PepsiCo when we apply the free cash flows to equity valuation model in Chapter 12 and the residual income valuation model in Chapter 13. Our estimate of $57.36 value per share, as compared to the prevailing market price of $51.94 per share, indicates that PepsiCo shares at the end of Year 4 are underpriced by roughly 10 percent.

Sensitivity Analysis and Investment Decision Making

One should not place too much confidence in the *precision* of firm value estimates using these (or any) forecasts over the remaining life of any firm, even a mature firm like PepsiCo. Although we have constructed these forecasts and value estimates with care, the forecasting and valuation process has an inherently high degree of uncertainty and estimation error. Therefore, the analyst should not rely too heavily on any one point estimate of the value of a firm's shares, and instead should describe a reasonable range of values for a firm's shares.

Two critical forecasting and valuation parameters in most valuations are the long-run growth rate assumption and the cost of equity capital assumption. Analysts should conduct sensitivity analysis to test the effects of these and other key valuation parameters on the share value estimate. Sensitivity analysis tests should allow the analyst to vary these valuation parameters individually and jointly for additional insights into the correlation between share value, growth rate, and discount rate assumptions.

For PepsiCo, our base case assumptions indicate PepsiCo's share value to be roughly $57. Our base case valuation assumes a long-run growth rate of 3 percent and a cost of equity capital of 7.75 percent. We can assess the sensitivity of our estimates of PepsiCo's share value by varying these two parameters (or any other key parameters in the valuation) across reasonable ranges. Exhibit 11.7 contains the results of sensitivity analysis

[14]The valuation models described in this chapter estimate the present value of the firm as of the first day of the first year of the forecast horizon; for example, January 1 of Year +1 for a firm with an accounting period that matches the calendar year. However, analysts estimate valuations every day of the year. Suppose the analyst values a firm as of June 17, and compares the value estimate to a market price for the firm's shares on June 17. A present value calculation that determines the value of the firm as of January 1 will ignore the value accumulation between January 1 and June 17 of that year. To refine the calculation, the analyst can adjust the present value as of January 1 to a present value as of June 17 by multiplying V_0 by a future value factor that reflects value accumulation for the appropriate number of days (in this case, 168 days). For example, if the valuation date is June 17 and if $R = 0.10$, then the analyst can update the January 1 value estimate by multiplying V_0 by $(1 + R)^{(168/365)} = (1 + 0.10)^{(168/365)} = 1.0448$.

varying the long-run growth rate from 0 to 10 percent, and the cost of equity capital from 5 to 20 percent. The data in Exhibit 11.7 show that as the discount rate increases, holding growth constant, share value estimates of PepsiCo fall. Likewise, value estimates fall as growth rates decrease, holding discount rates constant. Note that we omit value estimates from this analysis when the assumed growth rate equals or exceeds the assumed discount rate, because then the continuing value computation is meaningless.

Considering the downside possibilities, we can use sensitivity analysis to consider how sensitive our share value estimate for PepsiCo is to adverse changes in long-run growth and discount rates. For example, if we reduce the long-run growth assumption to 2.0 percent, holding the discount rate constant at 7.75 percent, PepsiCo share value falls to $50.03, slightly below current market price. Similarly, if we increase the discount rate to 9.0 percent while holding constant the long-run growth assumption at 3.0 percent, PepsiCo shares have a value of $45.41, about 10 percent below current market price. If we revise both assumptions at once, and reduce the long-run growth assumption to 2.0 percent and increase the discount rate assumption to 9.0 percent, then PepsiCo's share value falls to $41.02.

On the upside, if we reduce the discount rate to 7.0 percent while holding growth constant at 3.0 percent, or if we increase the long-run growth assumption from 3.0 to 4.0 percent while holding the discount rate constant at 7.75 percent, then the value estimate jumps to more than $68 per share. If we reduce the discount rate assumption further, or increase the long-run growth rate further, our share value estimates for PepsiCo jump dramatically higher. For example, increasing the growth rate assumption to 4.0 percent and decreasing the discount rate assumption to 7.0 percent moves the share value estimate to more than $85.

These data suggest that our value estimate is sensitive to slight variations of our baseline assumptions of 3.0 percent long-run growth and a 7.75 percent discount rate, which yield a share value estimate of $57. Slight adverse variations in valuation parameters could reduce PepsiCo's share value to as low at $41, whereas slightly favorable variations could increase PepsiCo's share value to more than $85.

If our forecast and valuation assumptions are realistic, our baseline value estimate for PepsiCo is $57 per share at the end of Year 4. At that time, the market price of $51.94 per share indicates that PepsiCo shares were underpriced by about 10 percent. Under our forecast assumptions, PepsiCo's share value could vary within a range of a low of $41 per share to a high of $85 per share with only minor perturbations in our growth rate and discount rate assumptions. Given PepsiCo's $51.94 share price, these value estimates would have supported a buy recommendation at the end of Year 4, but not a strong buy.

Evaluation of the Dividends Valuation Method

The principal advantages of the dividends valuation method include the following:

1. This valuation method focuses on dividends. Economists argue that dividends provide the classical approach to valuing shares. Dividends reflect the payoffs that shareholders can consume.
2. Projected amounts of dividends result from projecting expected amounts of revenues, expenses, assets, liabilities, and shareholders' equities, therefore requiring the analyst to think through many future operating, investing, and financing decisions of a firm.

The principal disadvantages of the dividends valuation method include the following:

1. The continuing value (terminal value) tends to dominate the total value in many cases. For firms that do not pay periodic dividends, the continuing value can

EXHIBIT 11.7

Valuation of PepsiCo
Sensitivity Analysis of Value to Growth and Equity Cost of Capital

	Long-Run Growth Assumptions										
	0%	1%	2%	3%	4%	5%	6%	7%	8%	9%	10%
Discount Rates:											
5%	64.45	76.44	96.42	136.39	256.30	na	na	na	na	na	na
6%	53.44	60.92	72.16	90.87	128.31	240.63	na	na	na	na	na
7%	45.59	50.60	57.61	68.13	85.66	120.73	225.92	na	na	na	na
7.75%	41.04	44.87	50.03	57.36	68.61	88.03	129.64	282.23	na	na	na
9%	35.16	37.72	41.02	45.41	51.56	60.78	76.15	106.89	199.12	na	na
10%	31.53	33.45	35.84	38.93	43.04	48.79	57.43	71.82	100.59	186.92	na
11%	28.56	30.03	31.83	34.07	36.96	40.80	46.19	54.27	67.73	94.66	175.46
12%	26.10	27.24	28.62	30.30	32.40	35.10	38.70	43.73	51.29	63.89	89.09
13%	24.02	24.93	26.00	27.28	28.85	30.82	33.34	36.71	41.42	48.49	60.27
14%	22.25	22.97	23.82	24.82	26.02	27.49	29.33	31.69	34.83	39.24	45.85
15%	20.71	21.30	21.98	22.77	23.71	24.83	26.20	27.92	30.12	33.06	37.18
16%	19.37	19.85	20.40	21.04	21.78	22.65	23.70	24.98	26.58	28.64	31.39
17%	18.20	18.59	19.04	19.56	20.15	20.84	21.65	22.63	23.83	25.32	27.25
18%	17.16	17.48	17.85	18.27	18.75	19.30	19.95	20.71	21.62	22.74	24.13
19%	16.23	16.50	16.81	17.15	17.54	17.99	18.50	19.10	19.81	20.66	21.70
20%	15.39	15.62	15.88	16.16	16.48	16.85	17.26	17.74	18.30	18.96	19.75

comprise the total value of the firm, which requires the analyst to forecast the future value of the firm in order to compute the present value of the firm. Continuing value estimates are sensitive to assumptions made about growth rates after the forecast horizon and discount rates.

2. The projection of dividends can be time-consuming for the analyst, making it costly when the analyst follows many companies and must regularly identify under- and overvalued firms.

SUMMARY

This chapter illustrated the computation of risk-adjusted required rates of return on equity and the weighted average cost of capital, which analysts use as discount rates in valuation models. In valuation, analysts use these discount rates to compute the present value of future dividends, cash flows, or earnings. This chapter also described the dividends valuation model and applied it to value PepsiCo at the end of Year 4. As with the preparation of projected financial statements in Chapter 10, the reasonableness of the valuations depends on the reasonableness of the assumptions. The analyst should assess the sensitivity of the valuation to alternative assumptions regarding growth and discount rates, and other key drivers of value. To validate value estimates using the dividends valuation approach, the analyst should also compute the value of the firm using other approaches, such as the free-cash-flows-based approaches discussed in Chapter 12, the earnings-based approaches discussed in Chapter 13, and the valuation multiples approaches described in Chapter 14.

QUESTIONS, EXERCISES, PROBLEMS, AND CASES

Questions and Exercises

11.1 THE RISK-RETURN TRADE-OFF. Explain why analysts and investors use risk-adjusted expected rates of return as discount rates in valuation. Why do risk-adjusted expected rates of return increase with risk?

11.2 THE COMPONENTS OF THE CAPM. The CAPM computes expected rates of return using the following model (described in the chapter):

$$E[R_{Ej}] = E[R_F] + \beta_j \times \{E[R_M] - E[R_F]\}$$

Explain the role of each of the three components of this model.

11.3 NONDIVERSIFIABLE AND DIVERSIFIABLE RISK FACTORS. Identify the types of firm-specific factors that increase a firm's nondiversifiable risk (systematic risk). Identify the types of firm-specific factors that increase a firm's diversifiable risk (idiosyncratic risk or nonsystematic risk). Why do models of risk-adjusted expected returns include no expected return premia for diversifiable risk?

11.4 DEBT AND THE WEIGHTED AVERAGE COST OF CAPITAL. Why do investors typically accept a lower risk-adjusted rate of return on debt capital than equity capital? Suppose a stable, financially healthy, profitable, tax-paying firm that has been financed with all equity and no debt decides to add a reasonable amount of debt to its capital structure. What effect will that change in capital structure likely have on that firm's weighted average cost of capital?

11.5 THE DIVIDENDS VALUATION APPROACH. Explain the theory behind the dividends valuation approach. Why are dividends value-relevant to common equity shareholders?

11.6 MEASURING VALUE-RELEVANT DIVIDENDS. The chapter describes how the dividends valuation approach measures value-relevant dividends to encompass various transactions between the firm and the common shareholders. What transactions should the analyst include in value-relevant dividends for purposes of implementing the dividends valuation model, and why?

11.7 FIRMS THAT DO NOT PAY PERIODIC DIVIDENDS. Why is the dividends valuation approach applicable to firms that do not pay periodic (quarterly or annual) dividends?

11.8 VALUATION APPROACH EQUIVALENCE. Conceptually, why should an analyst expect the dividends valuation approach to yield equivalent value estimates to the valuation approach that is based on free cash flows available to be distributed to common equity shareholders?

11.9 DIVIDEND POLICY IRRELEVANCE. The chapter asserts that dividends are value-relevant even though the firm's dividend policy is irrelevant. How can that be true? What is the key assumption in the theory of dividend policy irrelevance?

Problems and Cases

11.10 CALCULATING REQUIRED RATES OF RETURN ON EQUITY CAPITAL ACROSS DIFFERENT INDUSTRIES. The data in Exhibit 11.3 on industry median betas suggest that firms in the following three sets of related industries have different degrees of systematic risk:

	Median Beta during 1995–2004
Utilities versus Petroleum Refining	0.40 versus 0.66
Grocery Stores versus Retailing—Apparel	0.57 versus 1.00
Depository Institutions (such as Banks) versus Security and Commodity Brokers	0.49 versus 1.13

Required

a. For each matched pair of industries, describe factors that characterize a typical firm's business model within each industry. Describe how such factors would contribute to differences in systematic risk.

b. For each matched pair of industries, use the CAPM to compute the required rate of return on equity capital for the median firm in each industry. Assume that the risk-free rate of return is 4.0 percent and the market risk premium is 5.0 percent.

c. For each matched pair of industries, compute the value of a $1 dividend for the median firm in each industry. Use the perpetuity-with-growth model and assume 3.0 percent long-run growth for each industry. What effect does the difference in systematic risk across industries have on the per-dollar dividend valuation of the median firm in each industry?

11.11 CALCULATING THE COST OF CAPITAL. Daimler-Chrysler AG manufactures automobiles and trucks. IBM develops and manufactures computer hardware and offers related technology services. Target Stores operates a chain of general merchandise discount retail stores. Selected data for these companies appear in the following table (amounts in millions):

	Daimler-Chrysler	IBM	Target Stores
Total Assets	$247,334	$109,183	$32,293
Interest-Bearing Debt	$103,728	$ 22,927	$ 9,538
Average Pretax Borrowing Cost	5.2%	2.5%	5.6%
Common Equity:			
Book Value	$ 45,408	$ 29,747	$13,029
Market Value	$ 51,450	$124,470	$46,520
Income Tax Rate	35.0%	35.0%	35.0%
Market Equity Beta	1.61	1.07	0.89

Required

a. The intermediate-term yields on U.S. government Treasury securities have recently been around 4.0 percent. Assume that the market risk premium is 5.0 percent. Compute the cost of equity capital for each of these three companies.

b. Compute the weighted average cost of capital for each of the three companies. For each firm, assume that the market value of the debt equals its book value.

c. Compute the unlevered market (asset) beta for each of the three companies. For each firm, assume that the market value of the debt equals its book value.

d. Assume for this part that each company is a potential leveraged buyout candidate. The buyers intend to implement a capital structure that has 75 percent debt (with a pretax borrowing cost of 8.0 percent) and 25 percent common equity. Compute the weighted average cost of capital for each company based on the new capital structure. To what extent do these revised weighted average costs of capital differ from those computed in part b?

11.12 CALCULATION OF DIVIDENDS-BASED VALUE. ExxonMobil Corporation is a petroleum and petrochemicals company. It primarily engages in the exploration, production, and sale of crude oil and natural gas and the manufacture, transportation, and sale of petroleum and petrochemical products. The company operates in approximately two hundred countries worldwide, in North America, Europe, Asia-Pacific, Africa, South America, the Middle East, and the Caspian area. During Years 2 to 4, ExxonMobil generated the following total dividends to common equity shareholders (amounts in millions):

	Year 2	Year 3	Year 4
Common Dividend Payments	$ 6,836	$ 6,945	$ 7,111
Stock Repurchases	4,660	5,694	9,206
Total Dividends	$11,496	$12,639	$16,317

Analysts project 10 percent growth in earnings over the next five years. Assuming concurrent 10 percent growth in dividends, the following table provides the amounts analysts project for total dividends for ExxonMobil for each of the next five years. In Year +6, we project total dividends for ExxonMobil assuming that ExxonMobil's income statement and balance sheet will grow at a long-term growth rate of 3 percent.

	Year +1	Year +2	Year +3	Year +4	Year +5	Year +6
Projected Growth	10%	10%	10%	10%	10%	3%
Projected Total Dividends to Common Equity	$17,949	$19,744	$21,718	$23,890	$26,279	$27,067

At the beginning of Year +1, ExxonMobil had a market beta of 0.71. At that time, intermediate term U.S. Treasuries were yielding roughly 4.0 percent. Assume that the market requires a 7.0 percent risk premium. ExxonMobil has 6,310 million shares outstanding at the beginning of Year +1 and trades at a share price of $51.

Required

a. Calculate the required rate of return on equity for ExxonMobil as of the beginning of Year +1.

b. Calculate the sum of the present value of total dividends for Year +1 through +5.

c. Calculate the continuing value of ExxonMobil at the start of Year +6 using the perpetuity-with-growth model with Year +6 total dividends. Also compute the present value as of the beginning of Year +1.

d. Compute the total present value of dividends for ExxonMobil as of the beginning of Year +1. Remember to adjust the present value for midyear discounting.

e. Compute the value per share of ExxonMobil as of the beginning of Year +1.

f. Given the share price at the start of Year +1, do ExxonMobil shares appear underpriced, overpriced, or correctly priced?

11.13 VALUING THE EQUITY OF A PRIVATELY HELD FIRM. Refer to the financial statement forecasts for Massachusetts Stove Company (MSC) prepared for Case 10.2. The management of MSC desires to know the equity valuation implications of adding gas stoves under the best, most likely, and worst scenarios. Under the three scenarios from Case 10.2, the actual amounts of net income and common shareholders' equity for Year 7 and the projected amounts for Year 8 to Year 12 are as follows:

FSAP

	Year 7	Year 8	Year 9	Year 10	Year 11	Year 12
Best-Case Scenario:						
Net Income	$154,601	$148,422	$123,226	$173,336	$ 271,725	$ 390,639
Common Equity	$552,080	$700,502	$823,728	$997,064	$1,268,789	$1,659,429
Most Likely Scenario:						
Net Income	$154,601	$135,343	$ 74,437	$ 72,899	$ 109,357	$ 149,977
Common Equity	$552,080	$687,423	$761,860	$834,759	$ 944,116	$1,094,093
Worst-Case Scenario:						
Net Income	$154,601	$128,263	$ 18,796	$(39,902)	$ (58,316)	$ (77,156)
Common Equity	$552,080	$680,343	$699,139	$659,238	$ 600,921	$ 523,766

MSC is not publicly traded and therefore does not have a market equity beta. Using the market equity beta of the one publicly traded woodstove and gas stove manufacturing firm and adjusting it for differences in the debt to equity ratio, income tax rate, and privately owned status of MSC yields a cost of equity capital for MSC of 13.55 percent.

Required

a. Use the clean surplus accounting approach to derive the projected total amount of dividends MSC pays common equity shareholders in Years 8 through 12.

b. Given that MSC is a privately held company, assume that ending book value of common equity at the end of Year 12 is a reasonable estimate of the value at which the common shareholders' equity could be liquidated. Calculate the value of the equity of MSC as of the end of Year 7 under each of the three scenarios. Ignore the midyear discounting adjustment.

c. How do these valuations affect your advice to the management of MSC regarding the addition of gas stoves to its woodstove line?

FSAP

11.14 DIVIDENDS-BASED VALUATION OF COMMON EQUITY. In Problem 10.16, we projected financial statements for Wal-Mart for Years +1 through +5. The following data include the actual amounts for Year 4 and the projected amounts for Year +1 to Year +5 for comprehensive income amounts and common shareholders' equity for Wal-Mart (amounts in millions):

	Year 4	Year +1	Year +2	Year +3	Year +4	Year +5
Comprehensive Income ...	$12,110	$11,117	$12,247	$13,473	$14,800	$16,236
Common Shareholders' Equity:						
Paid-In Capital	$ 2,848	$ 2,848	$ 2,848	$ 2,848	$ 2,848	$ 2,848
Retained Earnings	43,854	52,314	61,373	71,021	81,230	91,957
Accumulated Other Comprehensive Income	2,694	2,694	2,694	2,694	2,694	2,694
Total Common Equity	$49,396	$57,856	$66,915	$76,563	$86,772	$97,499

The market equity beta for Wal-Mart at the end of Year 4 is .80. Assume that the risk-free interest rate is 4.0 percent and the market risk premium is 5.0 percent. Wal-Mart has 4,234 million shares outstanding at the end of Year 4. At the end of Year 4, Wal-Mart's share price was $52.40.

Required

a. Use the CAPM to compute the required rate of return on common equity capital for Wal-Mart.

b. Compute the weighted average cost of capital for Wal-Mart as of the start of Year +1. At the end of Year 4, Wal-Mart had $31,450 million in outstanding interest-bearing debt on the balance sheet and no preferred stock. Assume that the balance sheet value of Wal-Mart's debt is approximately equal to the market value of the debt. During Year 4 Wal-Mart's income statement included interest expense of $1,187 million. At the beginning of Year 4, Wal-Mart had a total of $26,466 million in interest-bearing debt, so during Year 4 Wal-Mart had an average of $28,958 in interest-bearing debt. This implies that Wal-Mart faced an average interest expense during Year 4 of roughly 4.1 percent (= $1,187 million / $28,958 million). Assume that at the start of Year +1, Wal-Mart will continue to incur interest expense of 4.1 percent on debt capital, and that Wal-Mart's average tax rate is 36.0 percent.

c. Use the clean surplus accounting approach to derive the projected dividends for Wal-Mart for Years +1 through +5 based on the projected income and equity amounts.

d. Use the clean surplus accounting approach to project the continuing dividend in Year +6. Assume that the steady-state long-run growth rate will be 3 percent in Year +6 and beyond.

e. Using the required rate of return on common equity from part a as a discount rate, compute the sum of the present value of dividends for Wal-Mart for Years +1 through +5.

f. Using the required rate of return on common equity from part a as a discount rate and the long-run growth rate from part d, compute the continuing value of Wal-Mart as of the beginning of Year +5 based on Wal-Mart's continuing dividends in Years +6 and beyond. After computing continuing value, bring continuing value back to present value at the start of Year +1.

g. Compute the value of a share of Wal-Mart common stock. (1) Compute the sum of the present value of dividends including the present value of continuing value. (2) Adjust the sum of the present value using the midyear discounting adjustment factor. (3) Compute the per-share value estimate.

h. Using the same set of forecast assumptions as before, recompute the value of Wal-Mart shares under two alternative scenarios. Scenario 1: Assume that Wal-Mart's long-run growth will be 2 percent, not 3 percent as before; and assume that Wal-Mart's required rate of return on equity is 1 percentage point higher than the rate you computed using the CAPM in part a. Scenario 2: Assume that Wal-Mart's long-run growth will be 4 percent, not 3 percent as before; and assume that Wal-Mart's required rate of return on equity is 1 percentage point lower than the rate you computed using the CAPM in part a. To quantify the sensitivity of your share value estimate for Wal-Mart to these variations in growth and discount rates, compare (in percentage terms) your value estimates under these two scenarios with your value estimate from part g.

i. What reasonable range of share values would you expect for Wal-Mart common stock? Where is the current price for Wal-Mart shares relative to this range? What do you recommend?

INTEGRATIVE CASE 11.1

FSAP

STARBUCKS

Dividends-Based Valuation of Starbucks' Common Equity

In Integrative Case 10.1, we projected financial statements for Starbucks for Years +1 through +5. In this portion of the Starbucks Integrative Case, we apply the techniques in Chapter 11 to compute Starbucks' required rate of return on equity and share value based on the dividends valuation model. We also compare our value estimate to Starbucks' share price at the time of the case development to provide an investment recommendation.

The market equity beta for Starbucks at the end of Year 4 is .60. Assume that the risk-free interest rate is 4.0 percent and the market risk premium is 5.0 percent. Starbucks has 397.4 million shares outstanding at the end of Year 4. At the start of Year +1, Starbucks' share price was $47.05.

Required

a. Use the CAPM to compute the required rate of return on equity capital for Starbucks.

b. From your forecasts of Starbucks' financial statements for Years +1 through +5, derive the projected dividends using the projected amounts for the plug to dividends less the net amounts of common stock issued each year (if any). Then compute projected dividends for Starbucks for Years +1 through +5 using the clean surplus accounting approach based on projected amounts for comprehensive income and common shareholders' equity. The projected amounts of dividends under the two approaches should be identical.

c. Use the clean surplus accounting approach to project the continuing dividend in Year +6. Assume that the steady-state long-run growth rate will be 3 percent in Year +6 and beyond.

d. Using the required rate of return on common equity capital from part a as a discount rate, compute the sum of the present value of dividends for Starbucks for Years +1 through +5.

e. Using the required rate of return on common equity capital from part a as a discount rate and the long-run growth rate from part c, compute the continuing value of Starbucks as of the beginning of Year +5 based on Starbucks' continuing dividends in Years +6 and beyond. After computing continuing value, bring continuing value back to present value at the start of Year +1.

f. Compute the value of a share of Starbucks' common stock. (1) Compute the sum of the present value of dividends including the present value of continuing value. (2) Adjust the sum of the present value using the midyear discounting adjustment factor. (3) Compute the per-share value estimate.

g. Using the same set of forecast assumptions as before, recompute the value of Starbucks shares under two alternative scenarios. Scenario 1: Assume that Starbucks' long-run growth will be 2 percent, not 3 percent as before; and assume that Starbucks' required rate of return on equity is 1 percentage point higher than the rate you computed using the CAPM in part a. Scenario 2: Assume that Starbucks' long-run growth will be 4 percent, not 3 percent as before; and assume that Starbucks' required rate of return on equity is 1 percentage point lower than the rate you computed using the CAPM in part a. To quantify the sensitivity of your estimate of share value for Starbucks to variations in long-run growth and discount rates, compare (in percentage terms) your value estimates under each these two scenarios with your value estimate from part f.

h. What reasonable range of share values would you expect for Starbucks' common stock? Where is the current price for Starbucks' shares relative to this range? What do you recommend?

Chapter 12

Valuation: Cash-Flow-Based Approaches

Learning Objectives

1. Understand how cash-flow-based valuation models work, and their conceptual and practical strengths and weaknesses.
2. Apply practical valuation techniques to deal with many of the difficult issues involved in estimating firm value using the present value of expected future free cash flows:
   a. risk, discount rates, and the cost of capital;
   b. cash flows to the investor versus cash flows to the firm;
   c. nominal versus real cash flows;
   d. pretax versus after-tax cash flows;
   e. the forecast horizon;
   f. computing continuing value.
3. Understand how to measure free cash flows for all debt and equity capital stakeholders versus free cash flows for common equity shareholders, and when each measure is appropriate.
4. Understand the reasons for discounting free cash flows for common equity shareholders using a required rate of return on equity capital and discounting free cash flows for all debt and equity capital stakeholders using a weighted average cost of capital.
5. Apply all of these techniques to estimate firm value using the present value of future free cash flows for common equity shareholders and the present value of future free cash flows for all debt and equity capital stakeholders.
6. Assess the sensitivity of firm value estimates to key valuation parameters, such as discount rates and expected long-term growth rates.

INTRODUCTION AND OVERVIEW

This chapter relies heavily on the financial statement forecasts we developed for PepsiCo in Chapter 10, as well as the valuation concepts and techniques we introduced and applied in the previous chapter. In this chapter we extend valuation methodology to encompass free-cash-flows-based valuation approaches, and we apply these valuation approaches to PepsiCo.

As we introduced in Chapter 11, economic theory teaches that the value of an investment security equals the present value of the expected future payoffs from the security discounted at a rate that reflects the risk inherent in those expected payoffs. Our general model for estimating the present value of a security (denoted as V_0 with present value denoted at time $t = 0$) with an expected life of n future periods is as follows:[1]

$$V_0 = \sum_{t=1}^{n} \frac{\text{ExpectedFuturePayoffs}_t}{(1 + \text{DiscountRate})^t}$$

Valuation methods, such as the dividends-based valuation methods demonstrated in the previous chapter, the free-cash-flows-based methods demonstrated in this chapter, and the earnings-based methods demonstrated in the next chapter, are all designed to produce reliable estimates of the value of the firm's equity shares. The value estimates that these approaches produce provide the basis for intelligent investment decision making. Even in relatively efficient securities markets, price does not necessarily equal value for every security at all times. Price is observable, value is not; value must be estimated. Estimating the value of a security in order to make intelligent investment decisions is therefore a common objective of financial statement analysis. Investors, analysts, investment bankers, and managers design the financial statement analysis process to determine a reliable appraisal of the value of shares of common equity, so that the analyst can compare value to price and the comparison yields a reliable basis to assess whether a firm's equity shares are underpriced, overpriced, or fairly priced in the capital markets.

Whether an analyst will produce reliable estimates of share value as a result of the financial statement analysis and valuation process depends entirely on whether the analyst carefully and thoughtfully applies each step of the process. The six-step analysis framework that forms the structure of this book (Exhibit 1.1 in Chapter 1) is a logical set of steps that should help lead the analyst to determine reliable estimates of value. To follow these steps, the analyst should first assess the economics of the industry, the particular firm's strategy, and then carefully evaluate the quality of the firm's accounting, making adjustments if necessary. Next, the analyst should evaluate the firm's profitability and risk with a set of financial ratios. All of this information should provide the analyst with a solid foundation of information to use in projecting the firm's future financial statements. The analyst can then use those financial statement forecasts to derive expectations of future earnings, cash flows, and dividends, which are the fundamental payoff measures used in the valuation approaches. Finally, the analyst applies valuation models to these expectations to estimate the value of the firm. Forecasts of expected future payoffs (the numerator in the valuation model) depend on forecasts of future earnings, cash flows, or dividends. Assessing an appropriate risk-adjusted discount rate (the denominator in the valuation model) requires an unbiased assessment of the inherent riskiness in the set of expected future payoffs. Therefore, reliable estimates of firm value depend on unbiased expectations of future payoffs and an appropriate risk-adjusted discount rate, all of which depend on all six steps of the framework.

As we explained in the previous chapter, when the analyst derives forecasts of future earnings, cash flows, and dividends from a set of internally consistent financial statement forecasts for a firm, and uses the same discount rate within correctly specified valuation

---

[1]In this chapter, as in the previous chapter, t refers to accounting periods. The valuation process determines an estimate of firm value, denoted V_0, in present value as of today, when $t = 0$. The period $t = 1$ refers to the first accounting period being discounted to present value. Period $t = n$ is the period of the expected final payoff.

models to compute the present values of those expected earnings, cash flows, and dividends, then the valuation models will yield identical estimates of value for a firm. We applied the dividends-based valuation approach to PepsiCo and estimated that, given our forecast assumptions and valuation parameters, PepsiCo's share value should be within a fairly narrow range around $57 at the time of our analysis. In this chapter, we illustrate the equivalence of the dividends and free cash flows valuation approaches, both in the theoretical development of the models and in their application to the valuation of PepsiCo. In the next chapter, we will describe and apply the earnings-based valuation approach and demonstrate its theoretical and practical equivalence with both the dividends and free cash flows approaches.[2]

We are convinced that it is important for analysts to understand deeply the similarities and differences in the dividends, cash flows, and earnings valuation approaches, and to see their theoretical and practical equivalence. Our experience strongly suggests that applying several different valuation approaches yields better insights about the value of a firm than relying on one approach in all cases. In addition, it is our experience that an analyst is much better equipped to work successfully with clients, managers, colleagues, and subordinates in the financial statement analysis and valuation process if the analyst thoroughly understands all three valuation approaches.

Further, all four valuation chapters—Chapters 11 through 14—emphasize that the objective of the valuation process is not a single point estimate of value *per se,* but instead the objective is to determine the distribution of value estimates across the relevant ranges of critical forecast assumptions and valuation parameters. By assessing the sensitivity of these value estimates across a distribution of relevant forecast assumptions and valuation parameters, we seek to determine the most likely range of values for a share, which we then compare to the share's price for an intelligent investment decision.

RATIONALE FOR CASH-FLOW-BASED VALUATION

As we demonstrated in the previous chapter, the value of a share of common equity is the present value of the expected future dividends.[3] Dividends are fundamental expected future payoffs that analysts can use to value shares because they represent the distribution of wealth to shareholders. The equity shareholder invests cash when the share is purchased, and then receives cash through dividends as the payoffs from holding the share, including the final "liquidating" dividend when the share is sold. In dividends-based valuation, "dividends" are defined broadly to encompass all cash flows from the firm to the common equity shareholders through periodic dividend payments, stock buybacks, and the firm's liquidating dividend, as well as cash flows from the shareholders to the firm when shares are issued (negative dividends).

Cash-flow-based valuation is equivalent to dividends-based valuation. The two approaches can be considered two sides to the same coin: The analyst can value the firm based on the cash flows into the firm that will be used to pay dividends, or equivalently, value the firm using cash flows when the firm pays them out in dividends to common shareholders. In the cash flows approach, we focus on the cash that flows into the firm;

---

[2]For examples of research on the complementarity of these approaches, see Stephen Penman and Theodore Sougiannis, "A Comparison of Dividend, Cash Flow, and Earnings Approaches to Equity Valuation," *Contemporary Accounting Research* 15, no. 3 (Fall 1998), pp. 343–383, and Jennifer Francis, Per Olsson, and Dennis Oswald, "Comparing the Accuracy and Explainability of Dividend, Free Cash Flow, and Abnormal Earnings Equity Value Estimates," *Journal of Accounting Research* 38, no. 1 (Spring 2000), pp. 45–70.

[3]John Burr Williams, *The Theory of Investment and Value* (Cambridge, Mass.: Harvard University Press, 1938).

in the dividends approach we focus on the cash that flows out of the firm. Instead of focusing on wealth distribution through dividends, the cash-flow-based approach focuses on cash flows generated by the firm that create dividend-paying capacity. In any given period, the amount of cash flow into the firm and the amount of dividends paid out of the firm will likely differ; the equivalence of these two valuation approaches arises because over the lifetime of the firm the cash flows into and out of the firm will be equivalent.

The cash-flow-based valuation approach measures and values the cash flows that are "free" to be distributed to shareholders. That is, *free cash flows* are the cash flows each period that are available to be distributed to shareholders, unencumbered by necessary reinvestments in operating assets or required payments to debtholders. Free cash flows can be used instead of dividends as the value-relevant measures of expected future payoffs to the investor in the numerator of the general value model set forth at the outset of this chapter. Both approaches, if implemented with consistent assumptions, will lead to identical estimates of value.

The rationale for using expected free cash flows in valuation is twofold, and is essentially the same rationale for using dividends:

1. Cash is the ultimate source of value. When individuals and firms invest in an economic resource, they delay current consumption in favor of future consumption. Cash is the medium of exchange that will permit them to consume various goods and services in the future. A resource has value because of its ability to provide future cash flows. The free cash flows approach measures value based on the cash flows that the firm generates that can be distributed to investors.
2. Cash is a measurable common denominator for comparing the future benefits of alternative investment opportunities. One might compare investment opportunities involving the holding of a bond, a stock, or an office building, but comparing these alternatives requires a common measuring unit of their future benefits. The future cash flows derived from their future services serve such a function.

FREE-CASH-FLOWS-BASED VALUATION CONCEPTS

In the following sections, we describe and illustrate the following key concepts in free-cash-flows-based valuation methods:

- **a.** risk, discount rates, and the cost of capital;
- **b.** cash flows to the investor versus cash flows to the firm;
- **c.** nominal versus real cash flows;
- **d.** pretax versus after-tax cash flows;
- **e.** the forecast horizon;
- **f.** computing continuing value.

These concepts are the same underlying concepts we described in the previous chapter in presenting dividends-based valuation methods. Therefore, we will briefly review those concepts here and describe how they apply to free cash flows valuation. Please refer to the previous chapter for more detailed explanations of these concepts.

We first describe computing discount rates to use in free-cash-flows-based valuation, including required rates of return on equity capital and weighted average costs of capital. We then present simple examples involving a single project. Next we confront conceptual measurement issues regarding dividends to the investor versus cash flows to the firm, nominal versus real cash flows, and pretax versus after-tax cash flows. We also address forecasting horizons and computing continuing value. Later in the chapter, we illustrate the free cash flow valuation approach with a more complex and realistic example involving the valuation of PepsiCo using free cash flows derived from the projected financial statements developed in Chapter 10.

Risk, Discount Rates, and the Cost of Capital

The general valuation model is a present value model, so it requires the analyst to determine an appropriate discount rate to use to measure future payoffs in present value. In circumstances in which the analyst needs to measure and value free cash flows available to common equity shareholders, the analyst should use a discount rate that reflects the risk-adjusted required rate of return to equity capital. In other circumstances in which the analyst needs to measure and value the free cash flows available to all of the debt and equity stakeholders of the firm, the analyst should use a weighted average cost of capital that reflects the relative proportions of cash flows attributable to different sources of debt and equity capital. In this section, we briefly review the computation of the required rate of return on equity capital and the weighted average cost of capital. In a later section of this chapter we describe how to compute free cash flows to equity shareholders versus free cash flows to all debt and equity stakeholders.

Cost of Common Equity Capital

When discounting the free cash flows available to common equity shareholders, the analyst should use a risk-adjusted required rate of return on equity capital. As described in more depth in the previous chapter, analysts commonly estimate the cost of equity capital using an expected return model such as the capital asset pricing model (CAPM). The CAPM assumes that the market is composed of risk-averse investors who demand a rate of return that (a) compensates them for forgoing the consumption of capital and (b) compensates them with additional return (also called a risk premium) for bearing nondiversifiable risk (systematic risk). The market's required rate of return on equity capital is therefore a function of prevailing risk-free rates of interest in the economy, plus a risk premium for bearing nondiversifiable risk, conditional on the level of nondiversifiable risk inherent in the firm's common stock.[4]

Analysts often measure systematic risk using the firm's market beta, which is estimated as a regression coefficient from regressing the firm's stock returns on an index of returns on a marketwide portfolio of stocks over a relevant period of time.[5] Market beta is an estimate of nondiversifiable or systematic risk based on the degree of covariation between a firm's stock returns and an index of stock returns for all firms in the market. If a firm's market beta from such a regression is equal to 1, it indicates the firm's stock returns covary identically with returns to a marketwide portfolio, indicating that the firm has the same degree of systematic risk as the market as a whole. If a firm's market beta is greater than or less than 1, it indicates that the firm has a greater or lesser degree of systematic risk than the market portfolio as a whole.

---

[4]Note that this model views firm-specific nonsystematic risk as diversifiable by the investor. A competitive equilibrium capital market, according to CAPM, does not expect a return for a firm's nonsystematic risk because such risk can be diversified away.

[5]Researchers and analysts have developed a variety of different approaches to estimate market betas. For example, one common approach estimates a firm's market beta by regressing the firm's monthly stock returns on a marketwide index of returns (such as the S&P 500 index) over the last sixty months.

The CAPM computes the expected return on common equity capital for firm j as follows:

$$E[R_{Ej}] = E[R_F] + \beta_j \times \{E[R_M] - E[R_F]\}$$

where E denotes that the related variable is an expectation; R_{Ej} denotes return on common equity in firm j; R_F denotes the risk-free rate of return; β_j denotes the market beta for firm j; and R_M denotes the return on a diversified, marketwide portfolio of stocks. According to the CAPM, a common equity security with no systematic risk (that is, a stock with $\beta_j = 0$) should be expected to earn a return equal to the expected rate of return on risk-free securities. The subtraction term in brackets in the preceding equation represents the average market risk premium, equal to the excess return that equity investors in the capital markets require for bearing the average amount of systematic risk in the market portfolio. An equity security with systematic risk equal to the average amount of systematic risk of all equity securities in the market has a market beta equal to 1, and should expect to earn the same rate of return as the average stock in the market portfolio.

Computing the Weighted Average Cost of Capital

In some circumstances, the analyst will be required to value all of the assets of a firm, not just the equity capital of the firm. In such cases, the analyst should discount to present value the free cash flows available to satisfy all debt and equity claims on the firm using a weighted average cost of capital that reflects the firm's relative proportions of debt, preferred, and common equity capital, and the respective costs of each type of capital. Such circumstances might arise, for example, if the analyst is considering acquiring all of the assets of a firm, or if the analyst is considering acquiring control of a firm by acquiring all of the financial claims (common equity shares, preferred shares, and debt) on the assets of a firm. If the analyst needs to determine the present value of the payoffs from investing in the total assets of the firm, or equivalently, acquiring all of the debt, preferred and common equity claims on the firm, then the analyst should use a discount rate that reflects the weighted average required rate of return that encompasses the debt, preferred, and common equity capital used to finance the net operating assets of the firm.

A formula for the weighted average cost of capital (denoted R_A) is given here:

$$R_A = [w_D \times R_D \times (1 - \textit{tax rate})] + [w_P \times R_P] + [w_E \times R_E]$$

In this formula, the subscripts D, P, and E refer to different types of capital (debt, preferred stock, and common equity, respectively); w denotes the weight on each type of capital; R denotes the cost of each type of capital; and *tax rate* denotes the tax rate applicable to debt capital costs. The weights used to compute the weighted average cost of capital should be the market values of each type of capital in proportion to the total market value of the financial capital structure of the firm (that is, $w_D + w_P + w_E = 1.0$). On the right-hand side of this equation, the first term in brackets measures the weighted after-tax cost of debt capital; the second term measures the weighted cost of preferred stock capital; and the third term measures the weighted cost of equity capital. Refer to the previous chapter for more detailed discussions and examples of computing the cost of debt, preferred, and common equity capital.

Free Cash Flows Valuation Examples for a Single-Asset Firm

Assume that a firm consists of a single asset. We expect that this asset will generate net cash flows of $2,000,000 per year forever. The income tax rate is 40 percent. Assume that, after making debt service payments and paying taxes, the firm pays dividends to distribute any remaining free cash flows to the equity shareholders each year. The cost of equity capital is 10 percent.

Example 1—Value of Common Equity in an All-Equity Firm

Assume that the common equity shareholders of the firm have financed the asset entirely with $10,000,000 of equity capital. We can determine the value of the common equity investment to the shareholders using the present value of free cash flows for common equity shareholders. The free cash flow to common equity shareholders each year will be as follows:

Net Cash Flow	$2,000,000
Income Taxes: 0.40 × $2,000,000	(800,000)
Free Cash Flow for Common Equity Shareholders	$1,200,000

The value to the shareholders of the common equity in the firm is $12,000,000 (= $1,200,000/.10). Dividing by the discount rate is appropriate because the $1,200,000 annual free cash flow for common equity is a perpetuity with no growth. This investment is worth $12,000,000 to those shareholders (a gain of $2,000,000 over their initial investment of $10,000,000) because of the present value of the free cash flows the investment will generate and that will in turn be paid out as dividends to the shareholders.

Example 2—Value of Common Equity in a Firm with Debt Financing

Assume the same facts as before, but now assume that the shareholders finance a portion of the investment in the asset with $6,000,000 of debt, and the remainder with $4,000,000 of equity capital. For purposes of this example, assume that using this amount of debt in the firm's capital structure does not alter substantially the risk of the firm to the equity investors, so they continue to require a 10 percent rate of return on equity capital. Suppose the debt is issued at par. Also assume that the debt is less risky than equity, so the debtholders demand interest of only 6 percent each year, payable at the end of each year. The income tax rate remains 40 percent, and interest expense is deductible for income tax purposes. We can again determine the value of the common equity investment using the present value of free cash flows for common equity shareholders. The free cash flow available to common equity shareholders each year is as follows:

Net Cash Flow for All Debt and Equity Capital	$2,000,000
Interest Paid on Debt: 0.06 × $6,000,000	(360,000)
Income Taxes: 0.40 × ($2,000,000 – $360,000)	(656,000)
Free Cash Flow for Common Equity Shareholders	$ 984,000

The value of the common equity to the shareholders in the firm is $9,840,000 (= $984,000/.10). Dividing by the discount rate is appropriate because the $984,000 annual free cash flow for common equity is a perpetuity with no growth. Note that in this example, the present value of the gain to the common equity shareholders in excess of their initial investment is $5,840,000 (= $9,840,000 – $4,000,000). The gain to the shareholders is $3,840,000 (= $5,840,000 – $2,000,000) larger in this example than in the previous example because (a) the debt capital is less expensive than the equity capital, creating $2,400,000 of value for equity shareholders from capital structure leverage (= [$6,000,000 × (.10 – .06)]/.10), and (b) the net tax savings from interest expense creates $1,440,000 of value for equity shareholders (= [$800,000 – $656,000]/.10).

Now make the same assumptions as before, but instead assume that by changing the capital structure to 60 percent debt and 40 percent equity the firm becomes more risky to the equity investors, and they demand a 15 percent rate of return rather than 10 percent. Under these assumptions, the value of the common equity to the investors in the firm will be \$6,560,000 (= \$984,000/0.15). Note that in this example, the present value of the gain to the common equity investors in excess of their initial investment falls to \$2,560,000 (= \$6,560,000 – \$4,000,000). The value for equity investors from the net tax savings from interest expense falls to \$960,000 (= [\$800,000 – \$656,000]/.15) and the value for equity investors from capital structure leverage falls to \$1,600,000 (= \$2,560,000 – \$960,000).[6]

Dividends to the Investor versus Cash Flows to the Firm

The analyst can use expectations of the dividends to be paid to the investor or the free cash flows to be generated by the firm (that will ultimately be paid to the investor) as equivalent approaches to measure the value-relevant expected payoffs to shareholders. Cash flows paid to the investor via dividends and free cash flows to the firm that are available for common equity shareholders will differ each period to the extent that the firm reinvests a portion (or all) of the cash flows generated. However, if the firm generates a rate of return on reinvested free cash flow equal to the discount rate used by the investor (that is, the cost of equity capital), then either set of payoffs (dividends or free cash flows) will yield the same valuation of a firm's shares at a point in time. Consider the following scenarios.

Example 3—Free Cash Flows with 100 Percent Payout

A firm expects to generate free cash flows of 15 percent annually on invested equity capital for the rest of its life, which is an indefinitely long period of time into the future (until say $t = n$). Equity investors in this firm require a 15 percent return each year, considering the riskiness of the firm. We assume that the firm will pay out 100 percent of the free cash flows each year as a dividend. Thus, the free cash flows generated by the firm equal the cash dividends received by the investor each period. Each dollar of capital committed by the investor has a present value of future cash flows equal to one dollar. That is, over an indefinitely long period of time into the future,

$$\$1 = \sum_{t=1}^{n} \frac{\$.15}{(1.15)^t}$$

Example 4—Free Cash Flows with Zero Payout

Assume the same facts as in Example 3, except that we assume the firm will pay out none of the free cash flows as a dividend. The firm will retain the \$0.15 free cash flow on each dollar of capital and reinvest it in projects expected to earn 15 percent return per year. In this case, the investor receives no periodic dividends and receives cash only when the

---

[6]The lower value to equity investors from capital structure leverage is the net result of two effects. First, the increased risk of the firm causes the equity investors to increase the discount rate from 10 percent to 15 percent, which would (if considered in isolation) cause the value of the project to fall to \$8,000,000 (= \$1,2000,000/.15), which would imply a \$2,000,000 loss on the investors' \$10,000,000 investment. Second, the debt capital is less expensive than the equity capital, creating \$3,600,000 of value for equity investors from capital structure leverage (= [\$6,000,000 × (.15 – .06)]/.15). The net result is \$1,600,000 of value to equity investors from capital structure leverage, net of the incremental effects of risk.

investor sells the shares or the firm liquidates at date $t = n$. By the terminal date, n periods in the future, each dollar of capital invested in the firm today will have earned a compound rate of return of 15 percent, equal to the required rate of return. In this case also, each dollar of invested capital has a present value of future free cash flows equal to one dollar. That is,

$$\$1 = \frac{(\$1.15)^n}{(1.15)^n}$$

Example 5—Free Cash Flows with Partial Payout

Assume the same facts as in Example 4, except that now we assume the firm pays out 25 percent of the free cash flow each period as a dividend and reinvests the other 75 percent in projects expected to generate a return of 15 percent. In this case also, each dollar of invested capital has a present value of future cash flows equal to one dollar. That is,

$$\$1 = \sum_{t=1}^{n} \frac{(\$.25)(.15)}{(1.15)^t} + \frac{(\$.75)(1.15)^n}{(1.15)^n}$$

We used these three examples in the previous chapter to illustrate the *relevance* of dividends as payoffs that are sufficient for valuation for equity shareholders, and the *irrelevance* of the firm's dividend policy in valuation.[7] We use the same examples here to illustrate that the assumptions we make about dividend policy are the complementary assumptions we make about free cash flows reinvested in the firm. Therefore, the same valuation should arise whether the analyst discounts (1) the expected dividends to the investor, or (2) the expected free cash flows to the firm that are available to pay future dividends to equity shareholders. Further, the same valuation should arise whether the firm pays all of its free cash flows as a dividend, reinvests all free cash flows to earn the investors' required rate of return, or pays a portion of free cash flows in dividends each period and reinvests the remainder to earn the investors' required rate of return.

Nominal versus Real Cash Flows

Changes in general price levels (that is, inflation or deflation) cause the purchasing power of the monetary unit to change over time.[8] The valuation of an investment in an economic resource should be the same whether one uses nominal or real free cash flow amounts as long as the valuation uses a consistent discount rate that is the nominal or real rate of return. That is, if projected free cash flows are nominal and include the effects of changes in general purchasing power of the monetary unit, then the discount rate

---

[7]Merton Miller and Franco Modigliani, "Dividend Policy, Growth and the Valuation of Shares," *Journal of Business* (October 1961), pp. 411–433. Penman and Sougiannis test empirically the replacement property of dividends for future earnings and find support for the irrelevance of dividend policy in valuation. See Stephen H. Penman and Theodore Sougiannis, "The Dividend Displacement Property and the Substitution of Anticipated Earnings for Dividends in Equity Valuation," *The Accounting Review* (January 1997), pp. 1–21.

[8]Note that the issue here is not with specific price changes of a firm's particular assets, liabilities, revenues, and expenses. These specific price changes affect our projections of the firm's dividends, cash flows, and earnings, and should enter into the valuation of the firm. The issue is whether some portion, all, or more than all of the specific price changes represent simply an economy-wide change in the purchasing power of the monetary unit, which should not affect the value of a firm.

should be nominal and include an inflation component. If projected free cash flows are real amounts that filter out the effects of general price changes, then the discount rate should be a real rate of return, excluding the inflation component.

Example 6—Nominal versus Real Free Cash Flows

A firm owns an asset that it expects to sell one year from today for $115.5 million. The firm expects the general price level to increase 10 percent during this period. The real interest rate is 5 percent. The nominal discount rate should be 15.5 percent to measure the compound effects of the real rate of interest and inflation (1.155 = 1.10 × 1.05). Discounting either nominal or real free cash flows, the value of the asset today to the firm is $100 million, as shown:

Nominal Free Cash Flows	×	Discount Rate Including Expected Inflation	=	Value
$115.5 million	×	1/[(1.05) × (1.10)]	=	$100 million

Real Free Cash Flows	×	Discount Rate Excluding Expected Inflation	=	Value
$115.5 million/(1.10)	×	1/(1.05)	=	$100 million

In both examples we derived the value of the equity of the firm by computing the present value of the free cash flows to common equity shareholders. As a practical matter, analysts usually find it more straightforward to discount nominal free cash flows using nominal discount rates than to first adjust nominal free cash flows to real free cash flows and then discount real free cash flows using real interest rates.

Pre-Tax versus After-Tax Free Cash Flows

Will the same valuation arise if the analyst discounts pretax free cash flows at a pretax cost of capital and after-tax free cash flows at an after-tax cost of capital? The answer is no if costs of debt and equity capital receive different tax treatments. For tax purposes, firms can typically deduct the costs of debt capital but cannot deduct the costs of equity capital.

Example 7—Tax Effects on Free Cash Flows

Suppose the firm faces the following costs of capital:

	Proportion in Capital Structure	Pre-Tax Cost	Tax Effect	After-Tax Cost	Weighted Average Cost of Capital	
					Pre-Tax	After-Tax
Debt	.33	10%	.40	6%	3.33%	2.00%
Equity	.67	18%	—	18%	12.00%	12.00%
	1.00				15.33%	14.00%

Assume that this firm expects to generate $90 million of pretax free cash flows and $54 million of after-tax free cash flows [= (1 – 0.4) × $90 million] one year from today. This firm would be valued using pretax and after-tax amounts (assuming a one-year horizon) as follows:

Pre-tax:	\$90 million × 1/1.1533 = \$78.04 million
After-tax:	\$54 million × 1/1.14 = \$47.37 million

These values are not equivalent because cash inflows from assets are taxed at 40 percent and cash outflows to service debt give rise to a tax savings of 40 percent. The cost of equity capital, however, does not provide a tax benefit. The appropriate valuation in this case is \$47.37 million. Thus, the analyst should use after-tax free cash flows and the after-tax cost of capital.

Selecting a Forecast Horizon

The analyst will need to project periodic free cash flows over the remaining expected life of the resource to be valued. This life is a finite number of years for a resource with a finite physical life, such as a machine or a building, or a financial instrument with a finite stated maturity, such as a bond, a mortgage, or a lease. But an equity security is a resource that has an indefinite (and potentially infinite) life, and the analyst must therefore project future periodic free cash flows that, in theory, extend to infinity. As a practical matter, the analyst cannot precisely predict a firm's free cash flows very many years into the future. Therefore, analysts develop specific projections of the income statements and balance sheets for the firm and use those elements to derive forecasts of free cash flows over an explicit forecast horizon, say five or ten years, depending on the industry, the maturity of the firm, and the expected growth and predictability of the firm's cash flows. After the explicit forecast horizon, analysts then use general growth assumptions to project the future income statements and balance sheets, and use them to derive the free cash flows that will persist each period to infinity. The analyst will therefore find it desirable to develop specific forecasts of income statements, balance sheets, and free cash flows over an explicit forecast horizon that extends until the point at which a firm's growth pattern is expected to settle into steady-state equilibrium, during which free cash flows might be expected to grow at a steady, predictable rate.

Selecting a forecast horizon involves trade-offs. For stable and mature firms, such as PepsiCo, one can develop reasonably reliable projections over longer forecast horizons, as we demonstrated in Chapter 10. It is more difficult to develop reliable projections of free cash flows over long forecast horizons for young, high-growth firms because their future operating performance is uncertain. In addition, these firms will achieve a much higher proportion of their value in distant future years, after they reach their potential steady-state profitability. Ironically, the analyst faces the dilemma of depending most heavily on long-run forecasts for young growth firms for which long-run projections are the most uncertain. The forecasting and valuation process is particularly difficult for growth firms when the near-term free cash flows are likely to be negative, as is common for rapidly growing firms financing growth by issuing common stock. Most of the value of these firms depends on free cash flows they will generate in the long-term years.

Unfortunately, this dilemma is inevitable. The analyst must recognize that forecasts and value estimates for all firms have some degree of uncertainty and estimation risk. To mitigate this uncertainty and estimation risk, we suggest the following:

1. Apply all six steps of the analysis framework. By thoroughly analyzing the firm's industry and strategy, the firm's accounting quality, and the firm's financial performance and risk ratios, the analyst will have more information to use to develop long-term forecasts that are as reliable as possible.

2. To the extent possible, confront directly the problem of long-term uncertainty by developing specific projections of free cash flows derived from projected income statements and balance sheets that extend five or ten years into the future, at which point the firm is projected to reach steady-state growth.
3. Assess the sensitivity of the forecast projections and value estimates across the reasonable range of long-term growth parameter assumptions.

Computing Continuing Value of Future Free Cash Flows

As described in the previous section, the analyst will find it desirable to forecast free cash flows over an explicit forecast horizon, until the point at which the firm's free cash flows growth will settle into a long-run steady-state growth rate. We refer to these free cash flows as *continuing free cash flows* because they reflect the free cash flows continuing into the long-run future of the firm. The long-run steady-state growth rate in future continuing free cash flows could be positive, negative, or zero. Steady-state growth in free cash flows could be driven by long-run expectations for growth attributable to economy-wide inflation, general economic productivity, the population, or long-run growth in the industry's sales. The analyst should select a growth rate that captures realistic expectations for the long run.

If the analyst can project a firm's long-run steady-state growth rate (denoted g) continuing after the end of the explicit forecast horizon, say after Year T, then the analyst can derive the continuing free cash flows from the projected income statements and balance sheets. The same principles we demonstrated in the previous chapter for projecting continuing dividends apply here in projecting continuing free cash flows. The analyst should first use the expected long-run growth rate (g) to project all of the items of the Year T+1 income statement and balance sheet by multiplying each item on the Year T income statement and balance sheet times $(1 + g)$. The analyst can then derive the Year T+1 statement of cash flows, and thus Year T+1 free cash flows, from the Year T+1 income statement and balance sheet projections. It is necessary to impose the long-run growth rate assumption $(1 + g)$ uniformly on the Year T income statement and balance sheet projections in order to derive correctly the free cash flows for Year T+1. We assume that, in steady state, the firm's assets, liabilities, and shareholders' equity, and therefore the firm's earnings, cash flows, and dividends, will grow at equivalent rates. By applying a uniform growth rate, the analyst achieves internally consistent steady-state growth across all of the projections of the firm, keeping the balance sheet in balance throughout the continuing forecast horizon and keeping the cash flows, earnings, and dividends internally consistent with the assumed long-run growth rate.

In projecting continuing free cash flows in Year T+1 and beyond, analysts assume that the firm will settle into a long-run sustainable growth rate. Often analysts assume that the firm's long-run sustainable growth rate will be consistent with long-run growth in the economy, on the order of 3 to 5 percent. For firms that have been growing more quickly than that (say, at 10 percent) in the years leading up to Year T+1, the long-run sustainable growth rate implies that the firm will maintain a lower growth rate in assets and equity, and thus generate substantially larger amounts of free cash flow. By projecting Year T+1 net income, assets, and equity using the long-run sustainable growth rate, we can then solve for the long-run sustainable free cash flows the firm will generate. The continuing free cash flow amount we derive for Year T+1 may be significantly larger than the amounts the firm actually generated during its higher-growth-rate years. The Year T+1 free cash flow amount reflects the firm's transition from a high rate of reinvestment of cash flows for growth in assets to reinvestment for a much lower rate of growth, thereby creating the need to solve for the long-run sustainable free cash flows amount.

If the analyst wishes to compute internally consistent and identical estimates of firm value using free cash flows, earnings, and dividends, then the analyst should *not* simply project free cash flows for Year T+1 by multiplying free cash flows for Year T by $(1 + g)$. Doing so ignores the necessary growth in all of the elements of the balance sheet and the income statement, which can introduce inconsistent forecast assumptions for cash flows, earnings, and dividends. Even if the analyst simply projects Year T+1 free cash flows, earnings, and dividends to grow at an identical rate $(1 + g)$, it may impound inconsistent assumptions and lead to inconsistent value estimates if Year T cash flows, earnings, and dividends are not consistent with their long-run continuing amounts.

Example 8—Projecting Continuing Value Free Cash Flows

Suppose the analyst develops the following forecasts for the firm in Year T–1 and Year T:

	Assets	=	Liabilities	+	Shareholders' Equity
Year T−1 Balances	$100	=	$60	+	$40
+ Net Income	+20				+20
+ New Borrowing	+ 6		+6		
− Dividends Paid	−10				−10
Year T Balances	$116	=	$66	+	$50

Assume that all of the increase in assets involves growth in assets required for operations, such as inventory and equipment. The analyst would compute Year T free cash flows for common equity shareholders to equal $10 (= $20 net income – $16 increase in assets + $6 increase in liabilities). Now suppose the analyst projects that the firm will grow at a steady-state rate of 10 percent in Year T+1 and thereafter. The analyst should project Year T+1 net income, assets, liabilities, and shareholders' equity to each grow by 10 percent, and then compute Year T+1 free cash flows, as follows:

	Assets	=	Liabilities	+	Shareholders' Equity
Year T Balances	$116	=	$66	+	$50
Growth	× 1.10		× 1.10		× 1.10
Year T+1 Balances	$127.6	=	$72.6	+	$55

The projected net income would be $22 (= $20 × 1.10). The Year T+1 free cash flow projection would be $17 (= $22 net income – $11.6 increase in assets + $6.6 increase in liabilities). However, if the analyst had simply projected Year T free cash flows to grow by 10 percent, the Year T+1 projections would only be $11 (= $10 Year T free cash flow × 1.10). By making this simple projection of free cash flows, the analyst is implicitly assuming that the $16 increase in assets in Year T will grow by 10 percent in Year T+1 (= $17.6 increase in assets). This is internally inconsistent with our long-run assumption of 10 percent growth in assets, liabilities, equity, and income growth. This will understate free cash flows to equity in Year T+1 by $6 (= $11.6 increase in assets – $17.6 increase in assets). This error will understate the estimated value of the firm using free cash flows, relative to the value estimate using earnings, because of the inconsistent assumptions. Note that the correct projected Year T+1 free cash flow amount of $17 is substantially larger than the $10 free cash flow amount for Year T. The reason the firm will generate larger amounts of free cash flow in Year T+1 and beyond is that the firm's long-run growth rate is 10 percent, which is lower than the Year T growth rate in assets (16 percent) and shareholders' equity (25 percent); thus this firm will not need to reinvest as much of its cash flows to fund growth, and will generate larger free cash flow amounts in Year T+1 and beyond.

As demonstrated for dividends in the previous chapter, once the analyst has computed free cash flows for Year T+1, then the analyst can compute continuing value (sometimes called terminal value) of future free cash flows for Years T+1 and beyond using the same perpetuity-with-growth valuation model we applied to dividends.[9]

$$\begin{array}{c} \text{Continuing Value} \\ \text{at End of Forecast} \\ \text{Horizon (Year T)} \end{array} = \begin{array}{c} \text{Continuing} \\ \text{Free Cash Flow} \\ \text{Projection for T+1} \end{array} \times 1/(R-g)$$

where g denotes the projected steady-state growth rate for Years T+1 and beyond, and is applied uniformly to project the income statement and balance sheet in Year T+1, which are then used to project the continuing free cash flows in Year T+1; R denotes the appropriate risk-adjusted discount rate. Once the analyst has computed the present value of continuing value at the end of the forecast horizons (Year T), then the analyst will need to discount continuing value from that point in time to present value today, by multiplying by the present value factor of $1/(1 + R)^T$.

Example 9—Computing Continuing Value

An analyst forecasts that the free cash flow of a firm in Year +5 will be $30 million, and that Year +5 earnings and dividends will also be $30 million. The analyst expects that the firm's income statements and balance sheets will grow uniformly over the long run, and that therefore cash flows, earnings, and dividends will all grow uniformly over the long run, but the analyst is uncertain about the steady-state long-run growth rate in Year +6 and beyond. The analyst believes that the growth rate will most likely be zero but could reasonably fall between +6 and –6 percent per year. Assuming a 15 percent cost of capital, the following table shows the range of possible continuing values (in millions) for the firm in present value at the beginning of the continuing value period (that is, the beginning of Year +6, or equivalently, the end of Year +5), and in present value as of today (that is, the continuing value is discounted to today using a factor of $1/(1.15)^5$):

				Continuing Value in Present Value as of:	
Free Cash Flow in Year T	Long-Run Growth Rate	Free Cash Flow in Year T+1	Perpetuity with Growth Factor	Beginning of Year T+1	Today
$30	0%	$30	$\frac{1}{(0.15 - 0.0)} = 6.67$	$200.0	$ 99.4
$30	+6%	$31.80	$\frac{1}{(0.15 - 0.06)} = 11.11$	$353.3	$175.7
$30	−6%	$28.20	$\frac{1}{(0.15 + 0.06)} = 4.76$	$134.3	$ 66.8

[9]This formula is simply the algebraic simplification for the present value of a growing perpetuity.

Analysts can also estimate a continuing value using a multiple of free cash flow in the first year of the continuing value period to value the common stock of a firm. The following table shows the cash flow multiples using $1/(R - g)$ for various costs of equity capital and growth rates. The multiples increase with growth for a given cost of capital, and they decrease as cost of capital increases for a given level of growth.

Continuing Value Multiples

Cost of Equity Capital	Growth Rates			
	0%	2%	4%	6%
10%	10.00	12.50	16.67	25.00
12%	8.33	10.00	12.50	16.67
15%	6.67	7.69	9.09	11.11
18%	5.56	6.25	7.14	8.33
20%	5.00	5.56	6.25	7.14

The continuing value computation using the perpetuity-with-growth valuation model does not work when the growth rate equals or exceeds the discount rate (that is, when $g \geq R$) because the denominator in the computation is zero or negative and the resulting continuing value estimate is meaningless. In this case, the analyst cannot use the perpetuity computation illustrated here. Instead, the analyst must forecast free cash flow amounts for each year beyond the forecast horizon using the terminal period growth rate, and then discount each year's cash flows to present value using the discount rate. The analyst should probably also reconsider whether it is realistic to expect the firm's free cash flow growth rate to exceed the discount rate (the expected rate of return) in perpetuity. This scenario can exist for some years, but is not likely to be sustainable indefinitely. Competition, technological change, new entrants into an industry, and similar factors eventually reduce growth rates. Thus, in applying the model, the analyst must attempt to estimate the long-term sustainable growth rate in cash flows (refer to the discussion of sustainable earnings in Chapter 6).

MEASURING PERIODIC FREE CASH FLOWS

In this section, we describe and illustrate measuring value-relevant cash flows. We first present a conceptual framework for measuring free cash flows, and then describe specific practical steps to measure free cash flows from two different perspectives—free cash flows to all debt and equity stakeholders and free cash flows to common equity shareholders—and when to use each free cash flow measure.

A Framework for Free Cash Flows

A conceptual framework for free cash flows to the firm emanates from the familiar balance sheet equation, in which assets equal liabilities plus shareholders' equity:

$$A = L + SE$$

Separate all of the assets and liabilities into two categories, operating or financing:

$$OA + FA = OL + FL + SE$$

Operating assets and liabilities relate to the firm's day-to-day operations in the normal course of business. For most firms, operating assets (denoted OA) include cash and short-term investment securities necessary for operating liquidity purposes; accounts receivable; inventory; property, plant, and equipment; intangible assets (licenses, patents, trademarks, goodwill, etc.); and investments in affiliated companies. Operating liabilities (denoted OL) typically include accounts payable, accrued expenses, accrued taxes, deferred taxes, pension obligations, and other retirement benefits obligations.

Assets and liabilities related to financing activities most commonly include interest-bearing liabilities that are part of the financial capital structure of the firm, less any interest-earning assets that the firm does not use in its day-to-day management of operating liquidity and could use to retire debt or pay dividends. Financial liabilities (denoted FL) include such interest-bearing items as short-term notes payable, current maturities of long-term debt, and long-term debt in the forms of mortgages, bonds, notes, and capital lease obligations. Insofar as outstanding preferred stock contains features that indicate that it is economically similar to debt (features such as limited life, mandatory redemption, and guaranteed dividends), the analyst should include preferred stock with financial liabilities.

In some circumstances, firms may hold financial assets (denoted FA), such as excess cash and short-term or long-term investment securities, to provide the firm with liquidity to repay debt, pay dividends, and repurchase common stock. Distinguishing financial assets that the firm will use to change its financial capital structure from financial assets that the firm will use to manage liquidity for operating purposes requires a judgment call by the analyst. Analysts consider financial assets to be part of the financial structure of the firm if the firm is likely to use the financial assets to offset or retire debt, or if the financial assets could be used to pay dividends or repurchase common equity shares. For example, such financial assets may exist for a firm that is accumulating cash or investment securities for purposes of retiring debt, if the firm is required to hold certain amounts of restricted cash or investment securities under a covenant that is part of a loan agreement (such as compensating cash balances), or if the firm is maintaining and accumulating a sinking fund for bond retirement under the terms of a debentured bond. Analysts typically do not consider financial assets to be part of the financial capital structure of a firm when the financial assets are necessary to manage the liquidity needs of the firm's operating activities across different seasons or business cycles, and are held in liquid, interest-earning accounts such as cash and cash equivalents, marketable securities, and short-term investment securities. Analysts also typically do not consider financial assets to be part of the financial capital structure of the firm when the financial assets include investment securities that are part of the long-term strategy of the firm, such as investments in affiliated subsidiaries with related operating activities or strategic investments in potential acquisition targets.[10] Capital held in these types of accounts for purposes of operating liquidity or strategic investments in securities of affiliated companies or potential takeover targets should be considered operating assets and not financial assets.

---

[10]The calculation of the rate of return on assets, or ROA, in Chapter 4 assumed that all assets were operating assets and that operating income is equal to net income excluding the after-tax cost of financial liabilities. Thus, we made no adjustment to eliminate interest income on financial assets from net income in the numerator of ROA and no adjustment to eliminate financial assets in the denominator. Most manufacturing, retailing, and service firms hold only minor amounts of financial assets, so ignoring adjustments for financial assets does not usually introduce a material amount of bias to the calculation of ROA. A more precise calculation of ROA for firms with a material amount of financial assets in the capital structure adjusts the numerator to eliminate interest income and adjusts the denominator of ROA for the portions of financial assets (cash, marketable securities, and investment securities) that are part of the financial capital structure and are not directly related to operating activities.

Once the analyst has separated the balance sheet into operating and financial components, then the analyst should rearrange the balance sheet to put operating accounts on one side and financing accounts and shareholders' equity on the other:

$$\text{OA} - \text{OL} = \text{FL} - \text{FA} + \text{SE},$$

which is equivalent to

$$\text{NetOA} = \text{NetFL} + \text{SE}$$

where NetOA = OA – OL and NetFL = FL – FA. For most firms, operating assets are likely to exceed operating liabilities, and financial liabilities are likely to exceed financial assets (financial borrowing usually exceeds financial assets because the firm uses the funds obtained from borrowing to purchase operating assets).

This rearrangement of the balance sheet provides a useful basis from which to conceptualize free cash flows to the firm. If we substitute for each term the present values of the expected future net cash flows associated with operating activities, financing activities, and shareholders' equity, we can express the balance sheet in the following cash flow terms:

Present Value of Net Cash Flows from Operations
= Present Value of Net Cash Flows to Debt Financing
+ Present Value of Net Cash Flows to Shareholders' Equity

This expression indicates that the present value of the net cash flows the operations of the firm will produce determines the sum of the values of the debt and equity claims on the firm.[11] Therefore, one can estimate the value of the debt and equity capital of the firm by projecting the net cash flows from operations that are "free" to service debt and equity claims, and discounting those free cash flows to present value. We refer to this measure of free cash flows as *the free cash flows for all debt and equity capital stakeholders,* because they reflect the cash flows that are available to the debt and equity capital stakeholders in the firm as a whole.

We can rearrange the balance sheet equation slightly further:

$$\text{NetOA} - \text{NetFL} = \text{SE}$$

Using the same present value cash flow terms as before, we can express this form of the balance sheet in terms of present values of expected future cash flows as follows:

Present Value of Net Cash Flows from Operations
− Present Value of Net Cash Flows to Debt Financing
= Present Value of Net Cash Flows to Shareholders' Equity

With this expression, we can conceptualize free cash flows specifically attributable to the equity shareholders of the firm. The present value of free cash flows produced by the operations of the firm minus the present value of cash flows necessary to service claims of the net debtholders yields *the free cash flows available for equity shareholders.* We refer to this measure as the free cash flows for common equity shareholders because they capture the net free cash flows available to equity shareholders after satisfying debt claims.

[11]The next section explains how our use of Net Cash Flows from Operations in this section differs from Cash Flow from Operations reported in the Statement of Cash Flows.

Free Cash Flows Measurement

Under U.S. GAAP, firms report the statement of cash flows by decomposing the net change in cash into operating, investing, and financing activity components. These three categories do not match exactly the operating and financing classifications we need for computing free cash flows. Thus, the analyst needs to reclassify some of the components of the statement of cash flows in order to compute free cash flows for valuation purposes. In the following sections, we describe how to use the statement of cash flows to measure free cash flows from two different perspectives: *free cash flows for all debt and equity capital stakeholders* and *free cash flows for common equity shareholders,* and when to use each free cash flow measure. Exhibit 12.1 describes the computation of each of these two measures of free cash flows.

Measuring Free Cash Flows: The Statement of Cash Flows as the Starting Point

We use cash flow from operations from the projected statement of cash flows as the starting point to compute both measures of free cash flows because it is the most direct starting point, requiring the fewest adjustments. Recall from Chapter 3 that the statement of cash flows measures cash flow from operations by beginning with net income, adding back any noncash expenses or losses (such as depreciation and amortization expenses), subtracting any noncash income or gains (such as income from equity method affiliates), and then adjusting for net cash flows for operating activities (such as changes in receivables, inventory, accounts payable, and accrued expenses).

Free Cash Flows for All Debt and Equity Capital Stakeholders

Free cash flows for all debt and equity capital stakeholders are the cash flows available to make interest and principal payments to debtholders, redeem preferred shares or pay dividends to preferred shareholders, and to pay dividends and buy back shares from common equity shareholders. To measure these free cash flows, we begin with cash flow from operations from the projected statement of cash flows. To measure cash flows from operations before the effects of the firm's financial capital structure, we must add back interest expense, net of tax effects. Procedurally, the analyst adds back to cash flow from operations the interest expense on financial liabilities, net of any income tax savings from interest expense. If the analyst makes the judgment call that some or all of the firm's financial assets are savings to retire debt and pay dividends and are part of the financial capital structure of the firm (rather than part of the operating liquidity management of the firm), then the analyst subtracts from cash flow from operations the interest income on those financial assets, net of the income taxes paid on that interest income. To adjust interest expense and interest income for tax effects, the analyst typically multiplies interest expense and interest income by one minus the firm's marginal tax rate.

The analyst should also add or subtract any change in the cash balance that the firm will require for operating liquidity. Cash that the firm must maintain for operating liquidity purposes is not available to be distributed to debt or equity stakeholders, and is therefore not part of free cash flow. For example, suppose an analyst is valuing a retail store chain, and the chain must maintain the equivalent of seven days of sales in checking accounts and cash on hand at each store for purposes of conducting retail sales transactions. When the chain opens new stores it is required to hold additional cash as part of operations (just as it would need to hold additional inventory). These additional cash requirements are not available for debt and equity capital providers if the firm intends to maintain its operations. If the firm improves its cash management efficiency and reduces

EXHIBIT 12.1

Measurement of Free Cash Flows

Free Cash Flows for All Debt and Equity Stakeholders:	Free Cash Flows for Common Equity Shareholders:
Operating Activities:	**Operating Activities:**
Cash Flow from Operations Begin with cash flow from operations on the projected statement of cash flows.	**Cash Flow from Operations** Begin with cash flow from operations on the projected statement of cash flows.
Net Interest after Tax Add back interest expense and subtract interest income, net of tax effects.	
Changes in Cash Requirements for Liquidity Subtract an increase or add a decrease in cash required for purposes of liquidity for operations.	**Changes in Cash Requirements for Liquidity** Subtract an increase or add a decrease in cash required for purposes of liquidity for operations.
Equals Free Cash Flows from Operations for All Debt and Equity	***Equals Free Cash Flows from Operations for Equity***
Investing Activities:	**Investing Activities:**
Net Capital Expenditures Subtract cash outflows for capital expenditures and add cash inflows from sales of assets that comprise the productive capacity of the operations of the firm, including property, plant, and equipment; affiliated companies; and intangible assets.	**Net Capital Expenditures** Subtract cash outflows for capital expenditures and add cash inflows from sales of assets that comprise the productive capacity of the operations of the firm, including property, plant, and equipment; affiliated companies; and intangible assets.
Equals Free Cash Flows for All Debt and Equity Stakeholders	

Continued

EXHIBIT 12.1

continued

Financing Activities:

Debt Cash Flows

Add cash inflows from new borrowings or subtract cash outflows from repayments of short-term and long-term interest-bearing debt capital.

Financial Asset Cash Flows

Subtract cash outflows invested in cash, short-term or long-term investment securities (or add cash inflows from these accounts) if these financial assets are deemed to be part of the financial capital structure of the firm and are not part of the operating activities of the firm.

Preferred Stock Cash Flows

Add cash inflows from new issues of preferred stock or subtract cash outflows from preferred stock retirements and dividend payments.

Equals Free Cash Flows for Common Equity Shareholders

the amount of cash required for operating liquidity, then the firm has additional free cash flow that can be distributed to debt or equity stakeholders. Procedurally, the analyst should project the required change in cash for working capital purposes each period, and add or subtract that amount to determine free cash flow from operations.

After computing free cash flow for debt and equity stakeholders from operations, the analyst adjusts for cash flows related to capital expenditures on long-lived assets that are a part of the firm's productive capacity, such as property, plant, and equipment; affiliated companies; intangible assets; and other investing activities. The analyst should subtract cash outflows for purchases and add cash inflows from sales of assets related to the firm's long-term productive activities. The analyst can measure the cash flows for capital expenditures and other investing activities that are part of the long-term productive activities of the firm using the amounts reported in the investing activities section of the projected statement of cash flows.

As noted earlier, the analyst must make a judgment call to estimate the extent to which the capital the firm retains in financial asset accounts, such as in cash and cash equivalents, short-term securities, or long-term investment securities, is (a) necessary for the liquidity and operating capacity of the firm, or (b) a financial asset that is part of the financial capital structure of the firm and therefore distributable to debt or equity stakeholders. For example, if the analyst projects that the firm will retain financial assets by saving some portion of its cash flows each period in a securities account, and that this cash can ultimately be used to repay debt, make dividends payments, or buy back shares, then the analyst should deem these cash flows as free cash flows for debt and equity capital. In this case, the analyst should not subtract the amount of cash used to purchase the securities each period to measure free cash flows for debt and equity capital.

This adjustment requires a judgment call by the analyst because, in some circumstances, firms will retain seemingly excess cash in the cash, marketable securities, or investment securities accounts, when this cash is not in fact free for potential distribution to capital stakeholders. For example, in some cases, firms with seasonal business need to maintain large balances in cash or securities accounts in order to provide needed liquidity during particular seasons. In other cases, firms may build up large balances in investment securities accounts that represent investments in key affiliates, such as PepsiCo's and Coca-Cola's investments in bottling companies. In scenarios like these, the analyst should not assess these cash flows as "free" for potential distribution to capital stakeholders, but instead should consider these cash flows necessary investments in the liquidity and productive capacity of the firm.

Together, these computations result in free cash flows for all debt and equity capital stakeholders, which are available to service debt, pay dividends to preferred and common shareholders, buy back shares, and finance future assets. In a later section, we will describe the approach to estimate the present value of the sum of the debt and equity claims on the firm by discounting free cash flows for debt and equity capital using the weighted average cost of capital of the firm.

Free Cash Flows for Common Equity Shareholders

Free cash flows for common equity shareholders are the cash flows specifically available to the common shareholders after making all debt service payments to lenders and paying dividends to preferred shareholders. Therefore, the free cash flows for common equity shareholders amount to the free cash flows available to all debt and equity capital, less any cash flows that are attributable to debt and preferred stock claims.

To measure free cash flows for common equity shareholders, we can again begin with cash flow from operations from the projected statement of cash flows. As in the previous section, the analyst should add or subtract any change in the cash balance that the firm will require for operating liquidity, because this cash is not available to be distributed to equity shareholders, and is therefore not part of free cash flow. Procedurally, the analyst should add or subtract the projected change in cash required for liquidity purposes each period.[12]

Also as in the previous section, the analyst should adjust for cash flows for capital expenditures on long-lived assets that are a part of the firm's productive capacity, such as property, plant, and equipment; affiliated companies; intangible assets; and other investing activities. The analyst should subtract cash outflows for purchases and add cash inflows from sales of assets related to the firm's long-term productive activities.

The analyst should incorporate cash flows to debt claims by adding cash inflows from new borrowing in short- and long-term debt and subtracting cash outflows for repayments of short- and long-term debt. In calculating free cash flows to debt and equity capital, if the analyst made the judgment call that the firm saves financial capital beyond its immediate liquidity needs in a cash or investment securities account, then these cash flows reflect financing activities. Therefore, the analyst must now (1) subtract the amount of cash outflow used to purchase the securities, because this cash was obviously not paid out to equity shareholders, or (2) add the amount of cash inflow received from selling such securities, because this cash inflow is available to be distributed to equity shareholders. Finally, the analyst should also add cash inflows from new issues of preferred stock and subtract cash outflows from preferred-stock retirements and dividend payments.[13] The result of these computations is free cash flows for common equity shareholders. These cash flows are available to common equity shareholders for dividends, stock buybacks, or reinvestment in future assets. As described in a later section of this chapter, free cash flows for common equity should be discounted at the cost of equity capital to determine the present value of the common equity of the firm.

Measuring Free Cash Flows: Alternate Starting Points

In practice, different analysts use different starting points to compute free cash flows. We described both approaches previously using cash flow from operations from the projected statement of cash flows as the starting point because it is the most direct starting point, requiring the fewest adjustments. However, some analysts compute free cash flows by beginning with projected net income, some start with EBITDA (earnings before interest, taxes, depreciation, and amortization), and yet others start with NOPAT (net operating profit after tax). In Exhibit 12.2, we describe the additional steps the analyst must take to adjust each of these different starting points to determine free cash flows to all debt and equity stakeholders. In Exhibit 12.3, we describe the additional steps the analyst must take to adjust each of these different starting points to determine free cash flows to common equity shareholders.

---

[12]Note that, unlike the computation of free cash flows for all debt and equity stakeholders, we do not adjust for interest expense or interest income after tax when we compute free cash flows for equity. Our measure of free cash flow for equity already reflects net cash flows for interest payments for interest-bearing debt capital, because the statement of cash flows starts with net income to compute cash flow from operations, and because net income already reflects interest expense after tax.

[13]It might seem inappropriate to include changes in debt and preferred stock financing, which appear in the financing section of the statement of cash flows, in the valuation of a firm. Economic theory suggests that the capital structure (that is, the proportion of debt versus equity) should not affect the value. Changes in debt and preferred stock, however, affect the amount of cash available to the common shareholders. The analyst includes cash flows related to debt and preferred stock financing in free cash flows for common equity shareholders but adjusts the cost of equity capital to reflect the amounts of such senior financing in the capital structure.

EXHIBIT 12.2

Measurement of Free Cash Flows for All Debt and Equity Stakeholders from Alternate Starting Points

Starting Point:		
Net Income:	**EBITDA:**[a]	**NOPAT:**[b]
Operating Activities:	***Operating Activities:***	***Operating Activities:***
Net income	EBITDA	NOPAT
Add back all noncash expenses	Add back all noncash expenses other than depreciation and amortization	Add back all noncash expenses
Subtract all noncash income items	Subtract all noncash income items	Subtract all noncash income items
Working capital cash flows	Working capital cash flows	Working capital cash flows
Net interest after tax	Subtract cash taxes paid, net of tax savings on interest expense	
Changes in cash requirements for liquidity	Changes in cash requirements for liquidity	Changes in cash requirements for liquidity
Equals Free Cash Flows from Operations for All Debt and Equity Stakeholders	***Equals Free Cash Flows from Operations for All Debt and Equity Stakeholders***	***Equals Free Cash Flows from Operations for All Debt and Equity Stakeholders***
Investing Activities:	***Investing Activities:***	***Investing Activities:***
Net capital expenditures	Net capital expenditures	Net capital expenditures
Equals Free Cash Flows for All Debt and Equity Stakeholders	***Equals Free Cash Flows for All Debt and Equity Stakeholders***	***Equals Free Cash Flows for All Debt and Equity Stakeholders***

[a]EBITDA denotes earnings before interest, tax, depreciation, and amortization.

[b]NOPAT denotes net operating profit after tax, which equals net income adjusted for net interest expense after tax.

EXHIBIT 12.3

Measurement of Free Cash Flows for Common Equity Shareholders from Alternate Starting Points

Starting Point:		
Net Income:	**EBITDA:**[a]	**NOPAT:**[b]
Operating Activities:	***Operating Activities:***	***Operating Activities:***
Net income	EBITDA	NOPAT
Add back all noncash expenses	Add back all noncash expenses other than depreciation and amortization	Add back all noncash expenses
Subtract all noncash income items	Subtract all noncash income items	Subtract all noncash income items
Working capital cash flows	Working capital cash flows	Working capital cash flows
	Add back net interest expense	Add back net interest expense after tax
	Subtract taxes	
Changes in cash requirements for liquidity	Changes in cash requirements for liquidity	Changes in cash requirements for liquidity
Equals Free Cash Flows from Operations for Equity	***Equals Free Cash Flows from Operations for Equity***	***Equals Free Cash Flows from Operations for Equity***
Investing Activities:	***Investing Activities:***	***Investing Activities:***
Net capital expenditures	Net capital expenditures	Net capital expenditures
Financing Activities:	***Financing Activities:***	***Financing Activities:***
Debt cash flows	Debt cash flows	Debt cash flows
Financial asset cash flows	Financial asset cash flows	Financial asset cash flows
Preferred stock cash flows	Preferred stock cash flows	Preferred stock cash flows
Equals Free Cash Flows for Common Equity Shareholders	***Equals Free Cash Flows for Common Equity Shareholders***	***Equals Free Cash Flows for Common Equity Shareholders***

[a]EBITDA denotes earnings before interest, tax, depreciation, and amortization.

[b]NOPAT denotes net operating profit after tax, which equals net income adjusted for net interest expense after tax.

If the analyst starts with net income and wishes to determine free cash flows for all debt and equity stakeholders, Exhibit 12.2 indicates that the analyst must add back all noncash expense items (such as depreciation and amortization expenses), subtract all noncash income items (such as accrued income from equity method affiliates), and adjust for cash flows related to working capital. These adjustments bring the analyst up to our starting point, cash flow from operations. The analyst then incorporates the remaining steps by adjusting for net interest expense after tax, changes in cash requirements for liquidity, and capital expenditures.

Other analysts begin the computation of free cash flows for all debt and equity by starting with EBITDA (earnings before interest, taxes, depreciation, and amortization), which already includes the addback for noncash income items for depreciation and amortization, as well as an addback for interest expense (but usually not interest income) and an addback of *all* the income taxes. From this starting point, the analyst then must adjust further by adding back any other noncash expenses (apart from depreciation and amortization), adjust for noncash income items, and adjust for cash flows related to working capital activities. In addition, because EBITDA adds back all taxes, the analyst must subtract cash taxes paid, net of tax saving on interest expense. These adjustments bring the analyst up to our starting point, cash flow from operations. The analyst then incorporates the remaining steps by adjusting for changes in cash requirements for operating liquidity and capital expenditures.

Still other analysts begin the computation of free cash flows for all debt and equity stakeholders using NOPAT (net operating profit after tax), which includes net income with net interest (adjusted for tax savings) added back. From this starting point the analyst should add back all noncash expense items (such as depreciation and amortization expenses), subtract all noncash income items (such as accrued income from equity method affiliates), and adjust for cash flows related to working capital activities. The analyst then incorporates the remaining steps by adjusting for changes in cash requirements for liquidity and capital expenditures.

In practice, some analysts also use net income, EBITDA, and NOPAT as starting points to compute free cash flows for equity shareholders. We demonstrate in Exhibit 12.3 the additional steps necessary to adjust each of these starting point amounts to complete measures of free cash flows for common equity. Note that many but not all of the additional adjustments are similar to those demonstrated in Exhibit 12.2. Note also that, although it occurs in practice, it is inefficient to start with EBITDA or NOPAT to compute free cash flows for equity because it is necessary to add back interest expense after tax to both EBITDA and NOPAT.

The starting point of the computation of free cash flows is less important than the ending point. The analyst can begin the computation of free cash flows with cash from operating activities on the statement of cash flows, net income, EBITDA, or NOPAT, so long as the analyst makes all of the necessary adjustments to compute a complete measure of free cash flows as described in Exhibits 12.1, 12.2, and 12.3.

Which Free Cash Flow Measure Should Be Used?

The appropriate free cash flow measure to use—free cash flows to all debt and equity stakeholders or free cash flows to equity shareholders—depends on the resource to be valued.

1. If the objective is to value operating assets net of operating liabilities, or equivalently, the sum of the debt and equity capital of a firm, then the free cash flow for all debt and equity capital is the appropriate cash flow measure. A later section of this chapter indicates that the appropriate discount rate is the weighted average cost of capital.

2. If the objective is to value the common shareholders' equity of a firm, then the free cash flow for common equity shareholders is the appropriate cash flow measure. A later section indicates that the appropriate discount rate is the cost of equity capital.

The difference between these two valuations is the value of total interest-bearing liabilities and preferred stock. To reconcile the two valuations, one could always value interest-bearing liabilities by discounting all the future debt service cash flows (including repayments of principal) at the after-tax cost of debt capital and all the preferred-stock dividends at the cost of preferred equity. Subtracting the present value of interest-bearing liabilities and preferred stock from the present value of the sum of debt and equity capital will yield the present value of common equity. The approach followed depends on the valuation setting.

Example 10

One firm desires to acquire the net operating assets of a division of another firm. The acquiring firm will replace the financing structure of the division with a financing structure that matches its own. The relevant cash flows for valuing the division's net operating assets are the free operating cash flows those assets will generate minus the expected capital expenditures in operating assets, or equivalently, the free cash flows for all debt and equity capital. The acquiring firm would then discount these projected free cash flows for all debt and equity capital at the expected future weighted average cost of capital of the division to be acquired, which will match the weighted average cost of capital of the acquiring firm because the acquiring firm will use a similar capital structure for the division.

Example 11

An investor desires to value a potential investment in the common stock equity in a firm. The relevant cash flows are the free cash flows available to be distributed to common equity shareholders. These free cash flows measure the cash flows generated from using debt capital, minus the cash required to service the debt. Thus, free cash flows for common equity shareholders should capture any beneficial effects of financial leverage on the value of the common equity, less the cash flows required to service debt capital. The investor should discount these projected free cash flows at the required return on equity capital.

Example 12

The managers of a firm intend to acquire a firm through a leveraged buyout (LBO). The managers will offer to purchase the outstanding shares of the target firm by investing their own equity (usually 20 to 25 percent of the total) and borrowing the remainder from various lenders. The tendered shares serve as collateral for the loan (often called a *bridge loan*) during the transaction. After gaining voting control of the firm, the managers will have the firm engage in sufficient new borrowing to repay the bridge loan. Following an LBO, the firm will likely have a significantly higher debt level in the capital structure from the use of leverage to execute the takeover.

Determining the value of the common shares acquired follows the usual procedure for an equity investment (see Example 11). This value should equal the present value of free cash flows for common equity discounted at the cost of common equity capital. The valuation of the equity must reflect the new capital structure and the related increase in debt service costs. Also, the cost of equity capital will likely increase as a result of the higher level of debt in the capital structure; the common shareholders bear more risk as residual claimants on the assets of the firm. The valuation must therefore be based on the expected new cost of equity capital.

As an alternate approach that will produce the same value for the common equity, the analyst can treat an LBO as a purchase of assets (similar to Example 10). That is, compute the present value of the free cash flows for all debt and equity capital stakeholders using the expected future weighted average cost of debt and equity capital, using weights that reflect the newly leveraged capital structure of the acquired firm. This amount represents the value of net operating assets. Subtract from the present value of net operating assets the present value of debt raised to execute the LBO.[14] The result is the present value of the common equity.

CASH-FLOW-BASED VALUATION MODELS

In this chapter thus far, we have discussed all of the elements of free-cash-flow-based valuation. To bring all of the elements together, we next present equations to describe the free-cash-flow-based valuation models. In each of these equations, all of the variables used to compute firm value are *expectations* of future free cash flows, future discount rates, and future growth rates. We present the valuation equations with and without explicit terms for continuing values. Recall that Exhibit 12.1 describes the computations for free cash flows for common equity shareholders and free cash flows for all debt and equity capital stakeholders.

Valuation Models for Free Cash Flows for Common Equity Shareholders

The following equation summarizes the computation of the value of the common equity of a firm as of time $t = 0$ (denoted V_0) using the present value of free cash flows for common equity shareholders discounted at the required rate of return on equity capital (R_E):

$$V_0 = \sum_{t=1}^{\infty} [FreeCashFlowEquity_t/(1 + R_E)^t]$$

This valuation approach expresses the value of the common equity of the firm as a function of the present value of the free cash flows the firm will generate and ultimately distribute to common shareholders. Thus, the value-relevant payoff measure in this approach is the excess cash the firm will generate that is available to common equity shareholders, after meeting all other cash requirements to maintain working capital, capital expenditures, debt payments, preferred stock dividends, and so on. Given that common equity shareholders are the residual risk-bearers of the firm, this valuation approach estimates common equity value using the residual "free" cash flows available to them. It is therefore appropriate to discount these payoffs to present value using a discount rate that reflects the risk-adjusted required rate of return on common equity capital of the firm.

The following equation summarizes the computation of the value of common equity as of time $t = 0$, but in this equation, the analyst bases the valuation on the present value of the forecasts of free cash flows for common equity shareholders over a finite forecast horizon through Year T, plus the present value of continuing value of free cash flows for equity shareholders continuing in Year T+1 and beyond. The analyst computes continuing value based on the forecast assumption that the firm will grow indefinitely at rate g

[14]It is irrelevant whether any debt on the books of the target firm remains outstanding after the LBO or whether the firm engages in additional borrowing to repay existing debt, as long as the weighted average cost of capital properly includes the costs of each financing arrangement.

beginning in Year T+1 and continuing thereafter. The analyst derives free cash flows for common equity shareholders in Year T+1 from the projected income statement and balance sheet for Year T+1, in which the analyst projects all of the elements of the Year T income statement and balance sheet to grow at rate g beginning in Year T+1. The equation is as follows:

$$V_0 = \sum_{t=1}^{T} [FreeCashFlowEquity_t/(1 + R_E)^T]$$
$$+ [FreeCashFlowEquity_{T+1}] \times [1/(R_E - g)] \times [1/(1 + R_E)^T]$$

Both of these free-cash-flow-based equations represent the value of the common equity of the firm. The Valuations spreadsheet within FSAP provides a template that will calculate V_0 using the present value of free cash flows for common equity shareholders, including the continuing value computation.

Valuation Models for Free Cash Flows for All Debt and Equity Capital Stakeholders

The following equation determines the value of the net operating assets of a firm as of time $t = 0$ (denoted $VNOA_0$) by computing the present value of all future free cash flows for all debt and equity capital stakeholders (denoted *Free Cash Flow All*):

$$VNOA_0 = \sum_{t=1}^{\infty} [FreeCashFlowAll_t/(1 + R_A)^t]$$

This equation differs from the models in the previous section in three important ways. First, this valuation approach does not compute the value of common shareholders' equity (V_0); instead, it computes the value of the net operating assets of the firm, or equivalently, the value of all of the debt, preferred, and common equity claims on the net assets of the firm. Second, this model differs from the models of the previous section because it includes the analyst's forecasts (as of time $t = 0$) of all future free cash flows to all debt and equity stakeholders. The prior equation focused specifically on the value of common equity capital, measured as the present value of all future free cash flows to common equity shareholders. Third, this equation differs from the prior models because it discounts the free cash flows to present value using R_A, which denotes the expected future weighted average cost of capital (which should reflect the weighted average required rate of return on the net operating assets of the firm). The prior equations relied on a discount rate using the required rate of return to equity (R_E).

This valuation approach expresses the value of the financial claims (debt, preferred, and common equity) on the firm as a function of the present value of the free cash flows the firm's net operating assets will generate that can ultimately be distributed to debtholders, preferred stockholders, and common shareholders. Thus, the value-relevant payoff measure in this approach is the excess cash the firm's operations will generate that will be available to satisfy all capital claims. Given that these free cash flows will be distributed to debt, preferred, and common equity stakeholders, it is therefore appropriate to discount these payoffs to present value using a discount rate that reflects the weighted average cost of capital across these different capital claims.

The next equation summarizes the same computation but uses the present value of the analyst's forecasts of free cash flows for all debt and equity capital stakeholders over a finite forecast horizon through Year T (for example, T may be 5 or 10 years in the future), plus the present value of continuing value. The analyst computes continuing value based on the forecast assumption that the firm will grow indefinitely at rate g beginning in Year T+1 and continuing thereafter. The analyst derives free cash flows for all debt and equity capital stakeholders in Year T+1 from the projected income statement and balance sheet for Year T+1, in which the analyst projects all the elements of the Year T income statement and balance sheet to grow at rate g beginning in Year T+1. The equation is as follows:

$$VNOA_0 = \sum_{t=1}^{T} [FreeCashFlowAll_t/(1 + R_A)^t] + [FreeCashFlowAll_{T+1}] \times [1/(R_A - g)] \times [1/(1 + R_A)^T]$$

Both of the prior equations represent estimates of the value of the net operating assets of the firm, which is equivalent to the sum of the values of debt, preferred, and common equity capital. To isolate the value of common equity capital, the analyst must subtract the present value of all interest-bearing debt and preferred stock. The equation to compute the value of equity (denoted V_0) is as follows:

$$V_0 = VNOA_0 - VDebt_0 - VPreferred_0$$

The Valuations spreadsheet within FSAP provides a template that will calculate $VNOA_0$ and V_0 using the present value of free cash flows for all debt and equity capital stakeholders, including the continuing value computation.

In theory, the value of common equity using this valuation approach should be identical to the value of common equity using the free cash flows to equity approach, the dividends valuation approach discussed in the previous chapter, and the earnings-based approaches discussed in the following chapter. As a practical matter, however, it is sometimes difficult to get the equity value estimate from the free cash flows to all debt and equity stakeholders to match the other value estimates. The main reason is the added degrees of circularity in this valuation approach. In this approach, the market-value-based weights for debt, preferred stock, and common equity capital used in computing the weighted average cost of capital must agree with the value estimates for debt, preferred stock, and common equity. Thus, additional degrees of circularity arise because the value estimates depend on the weighted average cost of capital, and the weighted average cost of capital depends on the value estimates. To obtain an internally consistent set of value estimates for each type of capital and an internally consistent weighted average cost of capital may require a number of iterations until the weights and value estimates all agree.

FREE CASH FLOWS VALUATION OF PEPSICO

At the end of Year 4, trading in PepsiCo shares on the New York Stock Exchange closed at \$51.94 per share. We therefore know the *price* at which we can buy or sell PepsiCo shares. The free cash flows valuation methods enable us to determine the *value* of these shares. In this section, we illustrate the valuation of PepsiCo shares using the free cash flows valuation techniques described in this chapter and the forecasts developed in Chapter 10. We develop these forecast and valuation estimates using the Forecast and Valuation spreadsheets in FSAP.

In this section, we estimate the present value of a share of common equity in PepsiCo at the end of Year 4 (equivalently, the start of forecast Year +1) two ways, by estimating the present value of the following:

1. free cash flows to common equity shareholders directly, discounted at the required rate of return to common equity,
2. free cash flows to all debt and equity capital stakeholders, discounted using PepsiCo's weighted average cost of capital, and then subtracting the present value of debt claims.

To proceed with each valuation, we follow four steps:

a. estimate the appropriate discount rates for PepsiCo;
b. derive the free cash flows from the projected financial statements for PepsiCo described in Chapter 10, and make assumptions about free cash flows growth in the continuing periods beyond the forecast horizon;
c. discount the free cash flows to present value, including continuing value;
d. make the necessary adjustments to convert the present value computation to an estimate of share value for PepsiCo.

Once we have our benchmark estimate of PepsiCo's share value, we conduct sensitivity analysis to determine the reasonable range of values for PepsiCo shares. Finally, we compare this range of reasonable values to PepsiCo's share price in the market and suggest an appropriate investment decision indicated by our analysis.

Recall that in the previous chapter we used the dividends valuation approach to estimate the value of PepsiCo shares to be in a range around $57 per share. We demonstrate in this section that we obtain equivalent estimates of value using the free cash flows valuation approaches.

PepsiCo Discount Rates

To discount free cash flows to common equity shareholders, we need to compute PepsiCo's required rate of return on equity capital. To discount free cash flows to all debt and equity capital, we need to compute PepsiCo's weighted average cost of capital. In the following sections, we briefly describe the computations. Recall that we briefly explained these computations at the outset of this chapter, and we explained and described these computations in detail in the previous chapter.

Computing the Required Rate of Return on Equity Capital for PepsiCo

At the end of Year 4 PepsiCo common stock had a market beta of roughly 0.75. At that time, U.S. Treasury bills with one to five years to maturity traded with a yield of approximately 4.0 percent, which we use as the risk-free rate. Assuming a 5.0 percent market risk premium, the CAPM indicates that PepsiCo has a cost of common equity capital of 7.75 percent [$7.75 = 4.0 + (0.75 \times 5.0)$]. At the end of Year 4, PepsiCo had 1,679 million shares outstanding and a share price of $51.94 for a total market capital of common equity of $87,207 million.

Computing the Weighted Average Cost of Capital for PepsiCo

Recall that in Chapter 10 we used information disclosed in Note 9, "Debt Obligations and Commitments" (Appendix A), to assess stated interest rates on PepsiCo's interest-bearing debt. We determined that in Year 4 PepsiCo's outstanding debt carries a weighted average interest rate of approximately 5.8 percent. Expecting that prevailing yields to maturity are temporarily low, we forecast in Chapter 10 that PepsiCo's cost of debt capital will approximate 6.0 percent in Year +1 and beyond. In Note 10, "Risk Management" (Appendix A), PepsiCo discloses that the fair value of outstanding debt at the end of Year 4 is $3,676 million. We use the fair value (as a proxy for market value) of PepsiCo's debt for weighting purposes. In Note 5, "Income Taxes" (Appendix A), PepsiCo discloses that the combined average federal, state, and foreign tax rate is approximately 24.7 percent in Year 4, which is unusually low for PepsiCo because of the favorable settlement of audits of prior years' tax returns. In Chapter 10, we forecast that PepsiCo will face a lower-than-normal average tax rate of roughly 29.4 percent in Year +1, and that PepsiCo's average tax rate will revert to 31.0 percent in Year +2 and beyond. Therefore, our long-run projections imply that PepsiCo faces an after-tax cost of debt capital of 4.14 percent (4.14 = 6.0 × [1 – 0.31]).

PepsiCo also has –$49 million in preferred stock at book value on the Year 4 balance sheet. In Chapter 10, we forecast that PepsiCo will retire the remaining outstanding preferred stock during Year +1. We also forecast that PepsiCo will not issue any additional preferred stock capital in future years. Therefore, we do not include any preferred stock in the computation of PepsiCo's weighted average cost of capital.

Bringing these costs of debt and equity capital together, we compute PepsiCo's weighted average cost of capital to be 7.604 percent as follows:

Capital	Value Basis	Amount	Weight	After-Tax Cost of Capital	Weighted-Average Component
Debt	Fair	$ 3,676	4.04%	4.14%	0.167%
Common ...	Market	$87,207	95.96%	7.75%	7.437%
Total		$90,883	100.00%		7.604%

This is only our initial estimate of PepsiCo's weighted average cost of capital. As described earlier, the weighted average cost of capital must be computed iteratively until the weights used are consistent with the present values of debt and equity capital.

Computing Free Cash Flows for PepsiCo

In this section we first describe the computations for PepsiCo's free cash flows for all debt and equity stakeholders, and then we describe the computations for PepsiCo's free cash flows for common equity shareholders. Recall that we presented the steps to compute free cash flows in Exhibit 12.1.

Chapter 10 described detailed projections of PepsiCo's future statements of cash flows by making specific assumptions regarding each item in the income statement and balance sheet and then deriving the related cash flow effects using a five-year forecast horizon. We use these projections of PepsiCo's statements of cash flows to compute projected free cash flows. We present the projections of free cash flows for all debt and equity stakeholders in Exhibit 12.4 and the projections of free cash flows for common equity shareholders in Exhibit 12.5.

PepsiCo's Free Cash Flows to All Debt and Equity Capital Stakeholders

As described earlier in this chapter, we begin the computation of free cash flows with cash flows from operations from the projected statements of cash flows. In Chapter 10 we

EXHIBIT 12.4

Projected Free Cash Flows to All Debt and Equity Capital Stakeholders for PepsiCo Year +1 through Year +6

Free Cash Flows for All Debt and Equity Stakeholders	Year +1	Year +2	Year +3	Year +4	Year +5	Year +6
Net Cash Flow from Operations	$ 6,428.2	$6,349.0	$6,728.3	$7,357.4	$7,837.6	$6,441.8
Add Back: Interest Expense after Tax	143.8	140.1	151.8	164.6	167.6	172.7
Subtract: Interest Income after Tax	0.0	0.0	0.0	0.0	0.0	0.0
+ (−) Decrease (Increase) in Cash Required for Operations	−56.7	−68.1	−118.8	−81.9	−133.7	−52.2
Free Cash Flow from Operations for All Debt and Equity Stakeholders	$ 6,515.3	$6,421.0	$6,761.3	$7,440.1	$7,871.6	$6,562.3
Net Cash Flow from Investing	−2,742.6	−2,225.6	−2,766.4	−2,792.9	−3,142.1	−1,271.0
Add Back: Net Cash Flows into Financial Assets	0.0	0.0	0.0	0.0	0.0	0.0
Free Cash Flow—All Debt and Equity	$ 3,772.7	$4,195.5	$3,994.9	$4,647.2	$4,729.5	$5,291.4
Present Value Factors (R_A = 7.604%)	× 0.929	× 0.864	× 0.803	× 0.746	× 0.693	
Present Value Free Cash Flows	$ 3,506.1	$3,623.5	$3,206.4	$3,466.4	$3,278.5	
Sum of Present Value Free Cash Flows for All Debt and Equity Stakeholders for Year +1 through Year +5	$17,080.9					

EXHIBIT 12.5

Projected Free Cash Flows to Common Equity Shareholders for PepsiCo
Year +1 through Year +6

Free Cash Flows for Common Equity Shareholders	Year +1	Year +2	Year +3	Year +4	Year +5	Year +6
Net Cash Flow from Operations	$ 6,428.2	$6,349.0	$6,728.3	$7,357.4	$7,837.6	$6,441.8
+ (−) Decrease (Increase) in Cash Required for Operations	−56.7	−68.1	−118.8	−81.9	−133.7	−52.2
Net Cash Flow from Investing	−2,742.6	−2,225.6	−2,766.4	−2,792.9	−3,142.1	−1,271.0
Net Cash Flows from Debt Financing	−112.1	89.1	478.1	139.4	7.8	121.6
Net Cash Flows into Financial Assets	0.0	0.0	0.0	0.0	0.0	0.0
Net Cash Flows—Preferred Stock and Minority Interest	−110.0	0.0	0.0	0.0	0.0	0.0
Free Cash Flow for Common Equity	$ 3,406.8	$4,144.5	$4,321.2	$4,622.0	$4,569.7	$5,240.3
Present Value Factors (R_E = 7.75%)	× 0.928	× 0.861	× 0.799	× 0.742	× 0.689	
Present Value Free Cash Flows	$ 3,161.8	$3,569.7	$3,454.2	$3,428.9	$3,146.3	
Sum of Present Value Free Cash Flows for Common Equity Shareholders Year +1 through Year +5	$16,761.0					

developed our projections of PepsiCo's statements of cash flows for Year +1 through Year +5. In Year +1, for example, we project that PepsiCo's cash flows from operations will be \$6,428.2 million. We then adjust for net interest, adding back interest expense after tax. Specifically, in Year +1 we add back \$143.8 million in interest expense after tax (= \$203.7 million × [1 – 0.294]). We do not make an adjustment to subtract interest income after tax because we assume that all of PepsiCo's interest income relates to financial assets (cash and short-term investments) that are used for liquidity in operating activities and strategic investments in affiliates such as bottlers, and are not part of the capital structure. We also adjust cash flow from operations for required investments in operating cash. In Chapter 10, we projected that PepsiCo would need to maintain roughly 15 days of sales in cash for liquidity purposes; therefore PepsiCo's required cash balance grows with sales. For example, in Year +1 PepsiCo's cash balance will grow by \$56.7 million. This additional increment of cash required for liquidity is therefore not a free cash flow, so we subtract it. As a result of these adjustments, we project that PepsiCo's free cash flows for all debt and equity from operations will be \$6,515.3 million in Year +1.

We next subtract cash flows for capital expenditures using the amount of net cash flow for investing from PepsiCo's projected statements of cash flows. For example, in Year +1, we projected that net cash flows for investing activities will be \$2,742.6 million. These investing cash flows include cash outflows for purchases of marketable securities, which is appropriate because we assumed that these securities are for purposes of operating liquidity and are not financial assets that are part of the financing structure of PepsiCo. Note also that PepsiCo's investing cash flows include cash outflows for long-term investments that primarily relate to affiliated bottling companies, which we deem to be part of PepsiCo's operations and therefore not free cash flows. Therefore, we subtract the full amount of net cash flow for investing activities from the free cash flow from operations. We forecast that PepsiCo's free cash flows for all debt and equity capital stakeholders will be \$3,772.7 million (= \$6,515.3 million – \$2,742.6 million) in Year +1. We repeat these steps each year through Year +5.

To project PepsiCo's free cash flows continuing in Year +6 and beyond, we forecast that PepsiCo will sustain a long-run growth rate of 3.0 percent in free cash flows, consistent with long-term growth in the economy of 3.0 percent. To compute continuing free cash flows in Year +6, we first project each line item on PepsiCo's Year +5 income statement and balance sheet to grow at 3.0 percent per year in Year +6. We use these Year +6 projected income statement and balance sheet amounts to derive the Year +6 free cash flows for all debt and equity capital, which we project will be \$5,291.4 million. We assume that this free cash flow amount is the beginning amount of a perpetuity of continuing free cash flows that PepsiCo will generate beginning in Year +6 and growing at 3 percent each year thereafter. The computations are shown in detail in the Forecast and Valuation spreadsheets in FSAP (Appendix C), which permits specific forecast assumptions to extend as far as Year +5 into the future, with continuing value assumptions thereafter.

PepsiCo's Free Cash Flows to Common Equity

Exhibit 12.5 presents estimates of PepsiCo's free cash flows for common equity shareholders through Year +6. The computations begin with the cash flows from operations, as described earlier. As in the previous section, we adjust cash flow from operations by subtracting the additional increment of \$56.7 million of cash required for liquidity, which is not a free cash flow. Also as in the previous section, we next subtract \$2,742.6 million of projected cash outflows for capital expenditures in Year +1. Note that, unlike in the previous section, we make no adjustment for net interest expense after tax because we need to measure the free cash flows available to equity shareholders net of all debt-related cash flows. Because our starting point, cash flows from operations, is derived from net income, and because we measure net income after interest expense, our cash flows amount is therefore net of interest expense.

To further refine these cash flows to free cash flows available to common equity, we need to adjust them for other cash flows related to debt and preferred-stock financing. We first add any cash inflows from new borrowing and subtract any cash outflows for debt repayments. For example, in Year +1, we subtract $112.1 million in cash flows for our projections of PepsiCo's debt repayments. Next, we add inflows and subtract outflows related to transactions with preferred stock and minority equity shareholders (if any). In Year +1, we subtract $110.0 million for payments to retire the outstanding preferred stock. We also subtract any cash outflows and add any cash inflows related to financial asset accounts that are part of PepsiCo's capital structure (which we have deemed to be zero). The computations project $3,406.8 million in free cash flows for common equity shareholders for PepsiCo in Year +1. We repeat these steps each year through Year +5.

To project PepsiCo's free cash flows for common equity continuing in Year +6 and beyond, we again forecast that PepsiCo can sustain long-run growth of 3.0 percent. We project the Year +5 income statement and balance sheet amounts to grow at a rate of 3.0 percent in Year +6, and derive free cash flows to common equity from the projected Year +6 statements. Our computations indicate that free cash flows to common equity in Year +6 will be $5,240.3 million (shown in detail in the Forecast and Valuation spreadsheets in FSAP in Appendix C). We assume that these free cash flows will continue to grow at 3.0 percent per year thereafter.

Valuation of PepsiCo Using Free Cash Flows to Common Equity Shareholders

We estimate the present value of a share of common equity in PepsiCo at the end of Year 4 (equivalently, the start of Year +1) by discounting the free cash flows to equity using PepsiCo's 7.75 percent risk-adjusted required rate of return on equity capital as the appropriate discount rate. Exhibit 12.5 shows that PepsiCo's free cash flows for common equity through Year +5 have a present value of $16,761.0 million. We compute the present value of PepsiCo's continuing value as the present value of a growing perpetuity of free cash flows beginning in Year +6, which we project will be $5,240.3. We project these free cash flows to grow at 3.0 percent and discount them to present value using the 7.75 percent discount rate. The present value of these cash flows is $75,958.1 million. As shown in Exhibit 12.6, the present value of PepsiCo's free cash flows to common equity shareholders is the sum of these two parts:

Present Value Free Cash Flows through Year +5	$16,761.0 million
Present Value of Continuing Value in Year +6 and Beyond	75,958.1 million
Present Value of Common Equity	$92,719.1 million

As described in the previous chapter, we need to correct our present value calculations for overdiscounting. To make the correction, we multiply the present value sum by the midyear adjustment factor ($1 + [R_E/2] = 1 + [0.0775/2] = 1.03875$). The total present value of free cash flows to common equity shareholders should be $96,312.0 million (= $92,719.1 million × 1.03875).

EXHIBIT 12.6

Valuation of PepsiCo Using Free Cash Flows to Common Equity Shareholders through Year +5 and Beyond

Value of Free Cash Flows to Common Equity Shareholders in Year +1 through Year +5:

From Exhibit 12.5:	$16,761.0 million

Continuing Value of Free Cash Flows to Common Equity in Year +6 and Beyond:

Projected Year +6 Free Cash Flows to Common Equity (Exhibit 12.5): $5,240.3 million

Continuing Value in Present Value ($R_E = 7.75\%$ and $g = 3.0\%$):

$$\begin{aligned}\text{Continuing Value}_0 &= \text{FreeCashFlow}_{Year+6} \times [1/(R_E - g)] \times [1/(1 + R_E)^5]\\ &= \$5{,}240.3 \text{ million} \times [1/(0.0775 - 0.0300)] \times [1/(1 + 0.0775)^5]\\ &= \$5{,}240.3 \text{ million} \times 21.0526 \times 0.6885\\ &= \underline{\$75{,}958.1} \text{ million}\end{aligned}$$

Total Value of PepsiCo's Free Cash Flows to Common Equity Shareholders:

Present Value of Free Cash Flows through Year +5	$16,761.0 million
+ Present Value of Continuing Value	+ 75,958.1 million
Present Value of Common Equity	$92,719.1 million
Adjust for Midyear Discounting (multiply by $1 + [R_E/2]$)	× 1.03875
Total Present Value of Common Equity	$96,312.0 million
Divide by Number of Shares Outstanding	÷ 1,679 million
Value per Share of PepsiCo Common Equity	= $57.36

Dividing the total value of common equity of PepsiCo by 1,679 million shares outstanding indicates that PepsiCo's common equity shares have a value of $57.36 per share. This share value estimate is identical to the share value estimate we computed using dividends in the previous chapter. Exhibit 12.7 presents the computations to arrive at PepsiCo's common equity share value using the free cash flows to common equity shareholders approach in the Valuations spreadsheet in FSAP.

Valuation of PepsiCo Using Free Cash Flows to All Debt and Equity Capital Stakeholders

We estimate the present value of a share of common equity in PepsiCo at the end of Year 4 (equivalently, the start of Year +1) by discounting the free cash flows to all debt and equity stakeholders using PepsiCo's 7.604 percent weighted average cost of capital as the appropriate discount rate. Exhibit 12.4 shows that PepsiCo's free cash flows for all debt

EXHIBIT 12.7

FSAP Valuation of PepsiCo using Free Cash Flows to Common Equity Shareholders through Year +5 and Beyond

	1	2	3	4	5	Continuing Value
Free Cash Flows for Common Equity Shareholders	**Year +1**	**Year +2**	**Year +3**	**Year +4**	**Year +5**	**Year +6**
Net Cash Flow from Operations	$ 6,428.2	$6,349.0	$6,728.3	$7,357.4	$7,837.6	$6,441.8
+ (−) Decrease (Increase) in Cash Required for Operations	−56.7	−68.1	−118.8	−81.9	−133.7	−52.2
Net Cash Flow from Investing	−2,742.6	−2,225.6	−2,766.4	−2,792.9	−3,142.1	−1,271.0
Net Cash Flows from Debt Financing	−112.1	89.1	478.1	139.4	7.8	121.6
Net Cash Flows into Financial Assets	0.0	0.0	0.0	0.0	0.0	0.0
Net Cash Flows—Preferred Stock and Minority Interest	−110.0	0.0	0.0	0.0	0.0	0.0
Free Cash Flow for Common Equity	$ 3,406.8	$4,144.5	$4,321.2	$4,622.0	$4,569.7	$5,240.3
Present Value Factors	0.928	0.861	0.799	0.742	0.689	
Present Value Free Cash Flows	$ 3,161.8	$3,569.7	$3,454.2	$3,428.9	$3,146.3	
Sum of Present Value Free Cash Flows	$16,761.0					
Present Value of Continuing Value	$75,958.1					
Total	$92,719.1					
Adjust to midyear discounting	1.03875					
Total Present Value Free Cash Flows to Equity	$96,312.0					
Shares Outstanding	1,679.0					
Estimated Value per Share	$ 57.36					
Current share price	$ 51.94					
Percent difference	10%					
(Value/price) − 1: positive number indicates underpricing						

and equity stakeholders through Year +5 have a present value of $17,080.9 million. To compute the present value of PepsiCo's continuing value, we compute the continuing value beyond Year +5 using the perpetuity-with-growth model. First, as described earlier and shown in Exhibit 12.4, we project that PepsiCo will generate free cash flows of $5,291.4 million in Year +6, and that these free cash flows will grow at a rate of 3.0 percent indefinitely. Exhibit 12.8 demonstrates that, in present value, PepsiCo's continuing value has a present value of $79,669.3 million. The present value of PepsiCo's free cash flows to all debt and equity capital stakeholders is the sum of these two parts:

Present Value Free Cash Flows through Year +5....................	$17,080.9 million
Present Value of Continuing Value Year +6 and Beyond	79,669.3 million
Present Value of Free Cash Flows for All Debt and Equity Capital...	$96,750.2 million

Necessary Adjustments to Compute Common Equity Share Value

To narrow this computation to the present value of common equity, we need to subtract the market value of interest-bearing debt and preferred stock and add the present value of interest-earning financial assets that are part of the firm's financial capital structure. Relying on PepsiCo's fair values, we subtract $3,676 million for outstanding debt. We assumed that PepsiCo would retire the outstanding preferred stock during Year +1, so our cash outflows already account for the payment to retire that preferred stock. We assumed that PepsiCo's financial assets are not part of the financial capital structure, so we need no adjustments for them. After subtracting the value of debt, the present value of PepsiCo's common equity capital is $93,074.2 million (= $96,750.2 million – $3,676 million).

As described earlier, our present value calculations have overdiscounted these cash flows because we have discounted each year's cash flows for a full period when, in fact, PepsiCo generates cash flows throughout each period and we should discount them from the midpoint of the year to the present. Therefore, to make the correction, we multiply the present value sum by the midyear adjustment factor of 1.03802 ($= 1 + [R_A/2] = 1 + [0.07604/2]$). Therefore, the total present value of free cash flows to common equity capital stakeholders is $96,612.9 million (= $93,074.2 million × 1.03802). Dividing by 1,679 million shares outstanding indicates that PepsiCo's common equity shares have a value of $57.54 per share. Exhibit 12.8 summarizes all of these computations, and Exhibit 12.9 presents the computations to arrive at PepsiCo's common equity share value using the free cash flows to all debt and equity stakeholders approach in the Valuations spreadsheet in FSAP.

Note that our calculation of the present value of PepsiCo's common equity per share ($57.54) is slightly different from the value of $57.36 per share obtained from the free cash flows to common equity approach described previously and the dividends approach in the previous chapter. This is because we used the current market price per share of PepsiCo common stock ($51.94) in the initial weighted average cost of capital computation. As a consequence, we did not place enough weight on the market value of equity in the initial cost of capital computation. When we iterate the valuation approach and use the share value of $57.36 to determine that the value of PepsiCo common equity should be $96,612.9 million, and use this to determine the weighted average cost of equity capital, we obtain a weighted average cost of capital of 7.618 percent. After our second iteration, the valuation computations and the weights and values we use to compute the weighted average cost of capital converge. The equity value estimate of $96,612.9 million, or $57.36 per share, is the internally consistent value.

EXHIBIT 12.8

Valuation of PepsiCo Using Free Cash Flows to All Debt and Equity Stakeholders through Year +5 and Beyond

Value of Free Cash Flows to All Debt and Equity Stakeholders in Year +1 through Year +5:

From Exhibit 12.4 above: $17,080.9 million

Continuing Value of Free Cash Flows to All Debt and Equity Stakeholders in Year + 6 and Beyond:

Projected Year +6 Free Cash Flows to All Debt and Equity Stakeholders
From Exhibit 12.4: $5,291.4 million

Continuing Value in Present Value (R_A = 7.604% and g = 3.0%):

$$\text{Continuing Value}_0 = \text{FreeCashFlow}_{\text{Year}+6} \times [1/(R_A - g)] \times [1/(1 + R_A)^5]$$
$$= \$5{,}291.4 \text{ million} \times [1/(0.07604 - 0.0300)] \times [1/(1 + 0.07604)^5]$$
$$= \$5{,}291.4 \text{ million} \times 21.7202 \times 0.6932$$
$$= \$79{,}669.3 \text{ million}$$

Total Value of PepsiCo's Free Cash Flows to All Debt and Equity Stakeholders:

Present Value of Free Cash Flows through Year +5	$17,080.9 million
+ Present Value of Continuing Value	+ 79,669.3 million
Present Value of All Debt and Equity	$96,750.2 million
Subtract Market Value of Debt	−$ 3,676.0 million
Present Value of Common Equity	$93,074.2 million
Adjust for Midyear Discounting (multiply by 1 + [R_A/2])	× 1.03802
Total Present Value of Common Equity	$96,612.9 million
Divide by Number of Shares Outstanding	÷ 1,679 million
Value per Share of PepsiCo Common Equity	=$ 57.54

Sensitivity Analysis and Investment Decision Making

As we emphasized in the previous chapter, forecasts of cash flows over the remaining life of any firm, even a mature firm like PepsiCo, contain a high degree of uncertainty, so one should not place too much confidence in the *precision* of firm value estimates using these forecasts. Although we have constructed these forecasts and value estimates with care, the forecasting and valuation process has an inherently high degree of uncertainty and estimation error. Therefore, the analyst should not rely too heavily on any one point estimate of the value of a firm's shares, and instead should describe a reasonable range of values for a firm's shares.

Two critical forecasting and valuation parameters in most valuation are the long-run growth rate assumption and the cost of equity capital assumption. Analysts should conduct sensitivity analyses to test the effects of these and other key forecast assumptions

EXHIBIT 12.9

FSAP Valuation of PepsiCo Using Free Cash Flows to All Debt and Equity Stakeholders through Year +5 and Beyond

	1	2	3	4	5	Continuing Value
Free Cash Flows for All Debt and Equity Stakeholders	**Year +1**	**Year +2**	**Year +3**	**Year +4**	**Year +5**	**Year +6**
Net Cash Flow from Operations	$ 6,428.2	$6,349.0	$6,728.3	$7,357.4	$7,837.6	$6,441.8
Add Back: Interest Expense after Tax	143.8	140.1	151.8	164.6	167.6	172.7
Subtract: Interest Income after Tax	0.0	0.0	0.0	0.0	0.0	0.0
+ (−) Decrease (Increase) in Cash Required for Operations	−56.7	−68.1	−118.8	−81.9	−133.7	−52.2
Free Cash Flow from Operations	$ 6,515.3	$6,421.0	$6,761.3	$7,440.1	$7,871.6	$6,562.3
Net Cash Flow from Investing	−2,742.6	−2,225.6	−2,766.4	−2,792.9	−3,142.1	−1,271.0
Add Back: Net Cash Flows into Financial Assets	0.0	0.0	0.0	0.0	0.0	0.0
Free Cash Flow—All Debt and Equity	$ 3,772.7	$4,195.5	$3,994.9	$4,647.2	$4,729.5	$5,291.4
Present Value Factors	0.929	0.864	0.803	0.746	0.693	
Present Value Free Cash Flows	$ 3,506.1	$3,623.5	$3,206.4	$3,466.4	$3,278.5	
Sum of Present Value Free Cash Flows	$ 17,080.9					
Present Value of Continuing Value	$ 79,669.3					
Total Present Value Free Cash Flows	$ 96,750.2					
Less: Outstanding Debt (FV or BV)	$−3,676.0					
Less: Preferred Stock (FV or BV)	0.0					
Plus: Financial Assets (FV or BV)	0.0					
Present Value of Equity	$ 93,074.2					
Adjust to midyear discounting	1.0380					
Total Present Value of Equity	$ 96,612.9					
Shares Outstanding	1,679.0					
Estimated Value per Share	$ 57.54					
Current share price	$ 51.94					
Percent difference	11%					
(Value/price) − 1: positive number indicates underpricing						

and valuation parameters on the share value estimate. Sensitivity analysis tests should allow the analyst to vary these assumptions and parameters individually and jointly for additional insights into the correlation between share value, the growth rate, and the discount rate assumptions.

For PepsiCo, our base case assumptions indicate PepsiCo's share value to be roughly \$57. Our base case valuation assumptions include a long-run growth rate of 3 percent and a cost of equity capital of 7.75 percent. We can assess the sensitivity of our estimates of PepsiCo's share value by varying these two parameters (or any other key parameters in the valuation) across reasonable ranges. Exhibit 12.10 contains the results of sensitivity analysis varying the long-run growth rate from 0 to 10 percent and the cost of equity capital from 5 to 20 percent.

As we observed in our sensitivity analysis in the previous chapter, these data suggest that our value estimate is sensitive to slight variations of our baseline assumptions of 3.0 percent long-run growth and a 7.75 percent discount rate, which yield a share value estimate of \$57. Slight adverse variations in valuation parameters reduce PepsiCo's share value to as low at \$41, whereas slightly favorable variations increase PepsiCo's share value to nearly \$85. If our forecast and valuation assumptions are realistic, our baseline value estimate for PepsiCo is \$57 per share at the end of Year 4. At that time, the market price of \$51.94 per share indicates that PepsiCo shares were underpriced by about 10 percent. Under our forecast assumptions, PepsiCo's share value could vary within a range of a low of \$41 per share to a high of \$85 per share with only minor perturbations in our growth rate and discount rate assumptions. Given PepsiCo's \$51.94 share price, these value estimates would have supported a buy recommendation at the end of Year 4, but not a strong buy.

EVALUATION OF THE FREE CASH FLOWS VALUATION METHOD

The principal advantages of the present value of future free cash flows valuation method include the following:

1. This valuation method focuses on free cash flows, a base that economists would argue has more economic meaning than earnings.
2. Projected amounts of free cash flows result from projecting likely amounts of revenues, expenses, assets, liabilities, and shareholders' equities, therefore requiring the analyst to think through many future operating, investing, and financing decisions of a firm.
3. The free cash flows valuation approaches are widely used in practice.

The principal disadvantages of the present value of future free cash flows valuation method include the following:

1. The continuing value (terminal value) tends to dominate the total value in many cases. This continuing value is sensitive to assumptions made about growth rates after the forecast horizon and discount rates.
2. The projection of free cash flows can be time-consuming for the analyst, making it costly when the analyst follows many companies and must regularly identify under- and overvalued firms.

SUMMARY

This chapter illustrates valuation using the present value of future free cash flows. As with the preparation of financial statement forecasts in Chapter 10, the reasonableness of the

EXHIBIT 12.10

Valuation of PepsiCo
Sensitivity Analysis of Value to Growth and Equity Cost of Capital

	Long-Run Growth Assumptions										
	0%	1%	2%	3%	4%	5%	6%	7%	8%	9%	10%
Discount Rates:											
5%	64.45	76.44	96.42	136.39	256.30	na	na	na	na	na	na
6%	53.44	60.92	72.16	90.87	128.31	240.63	na	na	na	na	na
7%	45.59	50.60	57.61	68.13	85.66	120.73	225.92	na	na	na	na
7.75%	41.04	44.87	50.03	57.36	68.61	88.03	129.64	282.23	na	na	na
9%	35.16	37.72	41.02	45.41	51.56	60.78	76.15	106.89	199.12	na	na
10%	31.53	33.45	35.84	38.93	43.04	48.79	57.43	71.82	100.59	186.92	na
11%	28.56	30.03	31.83	34.07	36.96	40.80	46.19	54.27	67.73	94.66	175.46
12%	26.10	27.24	28.62	30.30	32.40	35.10	38.70	43.73	51.29	63.89	89.09
13%	24.02	24.93	26.00	27.28	28.85	30.82	33.34	36.71	41.42	48.49	60.27
14%	22.25	22.97	23.82	24.82	26.02	27.49	29.33	31.69	34.83	39.24	45.85
15%	20.71	21.30	21.98	22.77	23.71	24.83	26.20	27.92	30.12	33.06	37.18
16%	19.37	19.85	20.40	21.04	21.78	22.65	23.70	24.98	26.58	28.64	31.39
17%	18.20	18.59	19.04	19.56	20.15	20.84	21.65	22.63	23.83	25.32	27.25
18%	17.16	17.48	17.85	18.27	18.75	19.30	19.95	20.71	21.62	22.74	24.13
19%	16.23	16.50	16.81	17.15	17.54	17.99	18.50	19.10	19.81	20.66	21.70
20%	15.39	15.62	15.88	16.16	16.48	16.85	17.26	17.74	18.30	18.96	19.75

valuations depends on the reasonableness of the assumptions. The analyst should assess the sensitivity of the valuation to alternative assumptions regarding growth and discount rates. To validate value estimates using the free-cash-flows-based approach, the analyst should also compute the value of the firm using other approaches, such as the dividends approach described in Chapter 11, the earnings-based approach described in Chapter 13, and the valuation multiples approaches described in Chapter 14.

QUESTIONS, EXERCISES, PROBLEMS, AND CASES

Questions and Exercises

12.1 FREE CASH FLOWS. Explain free cash flows. Describe which types of cash flows are *free* and which are not. Why are free cash flows available for debt and equity stakeholders different from free cash flows that are available to common equity shareholders?

12.2 THE FREE CASH FLOWS VALUATION APPROACH. Explain the theory behind the free cash flows valuation approach. Why are free cash flows value-relevant to common equity shareholders, when they are not cash flows to those shareholders but rather are cash flows into the firm?

12.3 MEASURING VALUE-RELEVANT FREE CASH FLOWS. The chapter describes free cash flows for common equity shareholders. If the firm borrows capital in the form of debt, how does that affect free cash flows for common equity shareholders in that period? If the firm uses cash to repay debt, how does that affect free cash flows for common equity shareholders in that period?

12.4 MEASURING VALUE-RELEVANT FREE CASH FLOWS. The chapter describes free cash flows for common equity shareholders. Suppose a firm has no debt capital and uses short-term investment securities to manage operating liquidity. If the firm uses cash to purchase short-term investment securities, how does that affect free cash flows for common equity shareholders in that period? If the firm sells short-term investment securities for cash, how does that affect free cash flows for common equity shareholders in that period?

12.5 VALUATION APPROACH EQUIVALENCE. Conceptually, why should an analyst expect valuation based on dividends and valuation based on the free cash flows for common equity shareholders to yield equivalent value estimates?

12.6 FREE CASH FLOWS VALUATION WHEN FREE CASH FLOWS ARE NEGATIVE. Suppose you are valuing a healthy, growing, profitable firm and you project that the firm will generate negative free cash flows for equity shareholders in each of the next five years. Can you use the free cash flows valuation approach when cash flows are negative? If so, explain how the free cash flows approach can produce positive valuations of firms when they are expected to generate negative free cash flows over the next five years.

12.7 USING DIFFERENT FREE CASH FLOWS MEASURES. In the chapter we describe free cash flows for all debt and equity stakeholders and free cash flows for equity shareholders. Give examples of valuation settings in which one approach or the other is appropriate.

12.8 APPROPRIATE DISCOUNT RATES. Describe valuation settings in which it is appropriate to use a required rate of return on equity capital as a discount rate, and settings in which it is appropriate to use a weighted average cost of capital as a discount rate.

12.9 FREE CASH FLOWS AND DISCOUNT RATES. Describe circumstances and give an example of when free cash flows to equity shareholders and free cash flows to all debt and equity stakeholders will be identical. Under those circumstances, will the required rate of return on equity and the weighted average cost of capital be identical too? If so, why? If not, why not?

Problems and Cases

12.10 CALCULATING FREE CASH FLOWS. The 3M Company is a global diversified technology company active in the following product markets: consumer and office; display and graphics; electro and communications; health care; industrial; safety, security, and protection services; and transportation. At the consumer level 3M is probably most widely known for products such as Scotch brand transparent tape and Post-it brand notes. Exhibit 12.11 presents information from the statement of cash flows and income statement for the 3M Company for Year 2 to Year 4. During Year 2 to Year 4, 3M increased cash and cash equivalents. These increases were not required to sustain operating liquidity. The interest income reported by 3M pertains to interest earned on excess cash. 3M holds only small amounts of investments in securities, which represent strategic investments in related companies. 3M's income tax rate is 35 percent.

Required

a. Beginning with cash flows from operating activities, calculate the amount of free cash flows to all debt and equity capital stakeholders for 3M for Year 2 to Year 4.

b. Beginning with cash flows from operating activities, calculate the amount of free cash flows for common equity shareholders for 3M for Year 2 to Year 4.

c. Reconcile the amounts of free cash flows for common equity shareholders for 3M for Year 2 to Year 4 from part b with 3M's uses of cash flow for equity shareholders, including share repurchases, dividend payments, and increased holdings of cash and cash equivalents.

12.11 CALCULATING FREE CASH FLOWS. Dick's Sporting Goods is a chain of full-line sporting goods retail stores offering a broad assortment of brand name sporting goods equipment, apparel, and footwear. Dick's Sporting Goods had its initial public offering of shares in fiscal Year 3. Since then, Dick's Sporting Goods has grown its chain of retail stores rapidly, and in fiscal Year 5 acquired Galyan's, a competitor chain of retail sporting goods stores. As of the end of fiscal Year 5, Dick's Sporting Goods operated 234 stores in thirty-four states primarily throughout the eastern half of the United States. Exhibit 12.12 presents information from the statement of cash flows and income statement for Dick's Sporting Goods for Year 3 to Year 5. All of the increases in cash and cash equivalents are required to sustain operating liquidity. Dick's Sporting Goods reports no interest income on the income statement. Dick's Sporting Goods holds only small amounts of investments in securities, which represent strategic investments in related companies. Dick's Sporting Goods average income tax rate during Year 3 to Year 5 is 40 percent.

EXHIBIT 12.11

3M Company
Selected Statement of Cash Flows Information
(amounts in millions)
(Problem 12.10)

	Year 4	Year 3	Year 2
Cash Flow from Operating Activities	$ 4,378	$ 3,791	$ 2,872
Investing Activities:			
Fixed Assets Acquired	$ (868)	$ (548)	$ (680)
Acquisition of Businesses	(73)	(439)	(1,258)
(Purchase) Sale of Investments	3	18	11
Cash Flow from Investing Activities	$ (938)	$ (969)	$(1,927)
Financing Activities:			
Increase (Decrease) in Short-Term Debt	$ 399	$ (215)	$ (204)
Increase (Decrease) in Long-Term Debt	(510)	(225)	649
Increase (Decrease) in Common Stock	(1,283)	(130)	(420)
Dividends Paid	(1,125)	(1,034)	(968)
Cash Flow from Financing Activities	$(2,519)	$(1,604)	$ (943)
Increase (Decrease) in Cash	$ 921	$ 1,218	$ 2
Cash at Beginning of Year	1,836	618	616
Cash at End of Year	$ 2,757	$ 1,836	$ 618
Interest Income	$ 46	$ 28	$ 39
Interest Expense	$ 69	$ 84	$ 80

Required

a. Beginning with cash flows from operating activities, calculate free cash flows to all debt and equity capital stakeholders for Dick's Sporting Goods for Year 3 to Year 5.

b. Beginning with cash flows from operating activities, calculate free cash flows for common equity shareholders for Dick's Sporting Goods for Year 3 to Year 5.

c. Reconcile the amounts of free cash flows for common equity shareholders for Dick's Sporting Goods for Year 3 to Year 5 with Dick's Sporting Goods' sources of cash flow from equity shareholders, including the proceeds from the initial public offering of common shares and proceeds from shares issues.

d. Why do the free cash flows to all debt and equity capital stakeholders for Dick's Sporting Goods differ so much from Year 3 to Year 5? In each of these three years, why do the free cash flows to all debt and equity capital stakeholders differ so much from the free cash flows for common equity shareholders?

e. In each of these three years, Dick's Sporting Goods produces negative free cash flows for common shareholders. Does that imply that Dick's Sporting Goods is destroying the value of common equity?

EXHIBIT 12.12

Dick's Sporting Goods
Selected Statement of Cash Flows Information
(amounts in thousands)
(Problem 12.11)

	Year 5	Year 4	Year 3
CASH FLOWS FROM OPERATING ACTIVITIES:			
Net income	$ 68,905	$ 52,408	$ 38,137
Adjustments to reconcile net income to net cash from operating activities:			
Depreciation and amortization	37,621	17,554	14,420
Deferred income taxes	18,124	8,201	(5,103)
Other addbacks	7,058	28,392	3,109
Changes in current assets and liabilities:			
Accounts receivable	(3,470)	3,904	(1,984)
Inventories	(44,813)	(20,863)	(31,912)
Prepaid expenses and other assets	(2,177)	1,549	(8,218)
Accounts payable	(4,260)	(19,850)	28,122
Accrued expenses	(4,707)	12,842	12,236
Income taxes payable	0	(12,763)	7,033
Deferred revenue and other liabilities	35,560	27,840	9,845
Net cash from operating activities	**$ 107,841**	**$ 99,214**	**$ 65,685**
CASH FLOWS USED IN INVESTING ACTIVITIES:			
Capital expenditures, net	(69,257)	(52,338)	(27,131)
Payment for the purchase of Galyan's, net of $17,931 cash acquired	(351,554)	0	0
Other investing activities	6,039	6,229	0
Net cash used in investing activities	**$(414,772)**	**$(46,109)**	**$(27,131)**
CASH FLOWS FROM FINANCING ACTIVITIES:			
Proceeds from issuance of convertible notes	172,500	0	0
Revolving credit borrowings (payments), net	76,094	0	(77,073)
(Payments) borrowings on long-term debt and capital leases	(24,701)	13,364	1,303
Net proceeds from sale of common stock in initial public offering	0	183	27,936
Proceeds from sale of common stock	8,250	15,902	11,424
Net cash provided by (used in) financing activities	**$ 232,143**	**$29,449**	**$(36,410)**
NET CHANGE IN CASH	**$ (74,788)**	**$82,554**	**$2,144**
CASH, BEGINNING OF PERIOD	**93,674**	**11,120**	**8,976**
CASH, END OF PERIOD	**$ 18,886**	**$ 93,674**	**$ 11,120**
Interest Expense	$ 8,009	$ 1,831	$ 2,864
Average Tax Rate	40.0%	40.0%	40.0%

12.12 VALUING A LEVERAGED BUYOUT CANDIDATE. May Department Stores (May) operates retail department store chains throughout the United States. At the end of Year 12, May reports debt of $4,658 million and common shareholders' equity at book value of $3,923 million. The market value of its common stock is $6,705 and its market equity beta is .88.

An equity buyout group is considering a leveraged buyout of May as of the beginning of Year 13. The group intends to finance the buyout with 25 percent common equity and 75 percent debt carrying an interest rate of 10 percent. They project that the free cash flows to all debt and equity capital stakeholders of May will be as follows: Year 13, $798 million; Year 14, $861 million; Year 15, $904 million; Year 16, $850 million; Year 17, $834 million; Year 18, $884 million; Year 19, $919 million; Year 20, $947 million; Year 21, $985 million; and Year 22, $1,034 million. The group projects free cash flows to grow 3 percent annually after Year 22.

This problem sets forth the steps that the analyst might follow in deciding to acquire May and the value to place on the firm.

Required

a. Compute the unlevered market equity (asset) beta of May before consideration of the leveraged buyout. Assume that the book value of the debt equals its market value. The income tax rate is 35 percent.

b. Compute the cost of equity capital with the new capital structure that results from the leveraged buyout. Assume a risk-free rate of 4.2 percent and a market risk premium of 5.0 percent.

c. Compute the weighted average cost of capital of the new capital structure.

d. Compute the present value of the projected free cash flows to all debt and equity capital stakeholders at the weighted average cost of capital. Ignore the midyear adjustment related to the assumption that cash flows occur on average over the year. Apply the projected growth rate in free cash flows after Year 22 of 3 percent directly to the free cash flows of Year 22 in computing the continuing value.

e. Assume that the buyout group acquires May for the value determined in part d. Will May generate sufficient cash flow each year to service the interest on the debt, assuming that the realized free cash flows coincide with projections?

12.13 VALUING A LEVERAGED BUYOUT CANDIDATE. Experian Information Systems (Experian) is a wholly owned subsidiary of TRW, a publicly traded company. The subsidiary has total assets of $555,443 thousand, long-term debt of $1,839 thousand, and common equity at book value of $402,759 thousand.

An equity buyout group is planning to acquire Experian from TRW in a leveraged buyout as of the beginning of Year 6. The group plans to finance the buyout with 60 percent debt that has an interest cost of 10 percent per year and 40 percent common equity. Analysts for the buyout group project free cash flows to all debt and equity capital stakeholders as follows (in thousands): Year 6, $52,300; Year 7, $54,915; Year 8, $57,112; Year 9, $59,396; Year 10, $62,366. Because Experian is not a publicly traded firm, it does not have a market equity beta. The company most comparable to Experian is Equifax. Equifax has an equity beta of .86. The market value of Equifax's debt is $366.5 thousand and its common equity is $4,436.8 thousand. Assume an income tax rate of 35 percent throughout this problem.

This problem sets forth the steps that the analyst might follow in valuing a leveraged buyout candidate.

Required

a. Compute the unlevered market equity (asset) beta of Equifax.

b. Assuming that the unlevered market equity beta of Equifax is appropriate for Experian, compute the equity beta of Experian after the buyout with its new capital structure.

c. Compute the weighted average cost of capital of Experian after the buyout. Assume a risk-free interest rate of 4.2 percent and a market risk premium of 5.0 percent.

d. The analysts at the buyout firm project that free cash flows for all debt and equity capital stakeholders of Experian will increase 5.0 percent each year after Year 10. Compute the present value of the free cash flows at the weighted average cost of capital. Ignore the midyear adjustment related to the assumption that cash flows occur on average over the year. Apply the projected growth rate in free cash flows after Year 10 of 5.0 percent directly to the free cash flows of Year 10 in computing the continuing value.

e. Assume that the buyout group acquires Experian for the value determined in part d. Will Experian generate sufficient cash flow each year to service the debt, assuming that actual free cash flows to all debt and equity capital stakeholders coincide with projections?

12.14 APPLYING VARIOUS PRESENT VALUE APPROACHES TO VALUATION. An equity buyout group intends to acquire Wedgewood Products (Wedgewood) as of the beginning of Year 8. The buyout group intends to finance 40 percent of the acquisition price with 10 percent annual coupon debt, and 60 percent with common equity. The income tax rate is 40 percent. The cost of equity capital is 14 percent. Analysts at the buyout firm project the following free cash flows for all debt and equity capital stakeholders for Wedgewood (in millions): Year 8, $2,100; Year 9, $2,268; Year 10, $2,449; Year 11, $2,645; and Year 12, $2,857. The analysts project that free cash flows for all debt and equity capital stakeholders will increase 8 percent each year after Year 12.

Required

a. Compute the weighted average cost of capital for Wedgewood based on the proposed capital structure.

b. Compute the total purchase price of Wedgewood (debt plus common equity). To do this, discount the free cash flows for all debt and equity capital stakeholders at the weighted average cost of capital. Ignore the midyear adjustment related to the assumption that cash flows occur on average over the year. Apply the projected growth rate in free cash flows after Year 12 of 8 percent directly to the free cash flows of Year 12 in computing the continuing value.

c. Given the purchase price determined in part b, compute the total amount of debt, the annual interest cost, and the free cash flows to common equity shareholders for Year 8 to Year 12.

d. The present value of the free cash flows for common equity shareholders when discounted at the 14 percent cost of equity capital should equal the common equity portion of the total purchase price computed in part b. Determine the growth rate in free cash flows for common equity shareholders after Year 12 that will result in a present value of free cash flows for common equity shareholders equal to 60 percent of the purchase price computed in part b.

e. Why does the implied growth rate in free cash flows to common equity shareholders determined in part d differ from the 8 percent assumed growth rate in free cash flows for all debt and equity capital stakeholders?

f. The adjusted present value valuation approach separates the total value of the firm into the value of an all-equity firm and the value of the tax savings from interest deductions. Assume that the cost of unlevered equity is 11.33 percent. Compute the present value of the free cash flows to all debt and equity capital stakeholders at this unlevered equity cost. Compute the present value of the tax savings from interest expense deductions using the pretax cost of debt as the discount rate. Compare the total of these two present values to the purchase price determined in part b.

12.15 VALUING THE EQUITY OF A PRIVATELY HELD FIRM. Refer to the projected financial statements for Massachusetts Stove Company (MSC) prepared for Case 10.2. The management of MSC desires to know the equity valuation implications of not adding gas stoves versus adding gas stoves under the best, most likely, and worst scenarios. Under the three scenarios from Case 10.2 and a fourth scenario involving not adding gas stoves, the projected free cash flows to common equity shareholders for Year 8 to Year 12, and assumed growth rates thereafter, are as follows:

FSAP

Year	Best	Most Likely	Worst	No Gas
8	$ 73,967	$ 47,034	$ 3,027	$162,455
9	$ 52,143	$ (3,120)	$(84,800)	$132,708
10	$213,895	$135,939	$ 48,353	$106,021
11	$315,633	$178,510	$ 36,605	$ 81,840
12	$432,232	$220,010	$ 10,232	$ 60,007
13–17	20% Growth	10% Growth	Zero Growth	Zero Growth
After Year 17	10% Growth	5% Growth	Zero Growth	Zero Growth

MSC is not publicly traded and therefore does not have a market equity beta. Using the market equity beta of the one publicly traded woodstove and gas stove manufacturing firm and adjusting it for differences in the debt to equity ratio, income tax rate, and privately owned status of MSC yields a cost of equity capital for MSC of 13.55 percent.

Required

a. Calculate the value of the equity of MSC as of the end of Year 7 under each of the four scenarios. Ignore the midyear adjustment related to the assumption that cash flows occur on average over the year. Apply the growth rates in free cash flows to common equity shareholders after Year 12 directly to the free cash flow of the preceding year (that is, Year 13 free cash flow equals the free cash flow for Year 12 times the given growth rate; Year 18 free cash flow equals the free cash flow for Year 17 times the given growth rate).

b. How do these valuations affect your advice to the management of MSC regarding the addition of gas stoves to its woodstove line?

FSAP

12.16 FREE-CASH-FLOWS-BASED VALUATION. The Coca-Cola Company is a global soft drink beverage company (ticker symbol = KO) that is a primary and direct competitor with PepsiCo. The data in Exhibits 12.13, 12.14, and 12.15 include the actual amounts for Year 4 and projected amounts for Year +1 to Year +5 for the income statements, balance sheets, and statements of cash flows for Coca-Cola (in millions).

The market equity beta for Coca-Cola at the end of Year 4 is .76. Assume that the risk-free interest rate is 4.0 percent and the market risk premium is 5.0 percent. Coca-Cola has 2,409 million shares outstanding at the end of Year 4. At the end of Year 4, Coca-Cola's share price was $41.64.

Required

Part I—Computing Coca-Cola's Share Value Using Free Cash Flows to Common Equity Shareholders

a. Use the CAPM to compute the required rate of return on common equity capital for Coca-Cola.

b. Derive the projected free cash flows for common equity shareholders for Coca-Cola for Years +1 through +6 based on the projected financial statements. Assume that Coca-Cola's changes in cash each year are necessary for operating liquidity purposes. The financial statement forecasts for Year +6 assume that Coca-Cola will experience a steady-state long-run growth rate of 3 percent in Year +6 and beyond.

c. Using the required rate of return on common equity from part a as a discount rate, compute the sum of the present value of free cash flows for common equity shareholders for Coca-Cola for Years +1 through +5.

d. Using the required rate of return on common equity from part a as a discount rate, and the long-run growth rate from part b, compute the continuing value of Coca-Cola as of the start of Year +6 based on Coca-Cola's continuing free cash flows for common equity shareholders in Year +6 and beyond. After computing continuing value as of the start of Year +6, discount it to present value at the start of Year +1.

e. Compute the value of a share of Coca-Cola common stock. (1) Compute the total sum of the present value of all future free cash flows for equity shareholders (from parts c and d). (2) Adjust the total sum of the present value using the midyear discounting adjustment factor. (3) Compute the per-share value estimate.

Part II—Computing Coca-Cola's Share Value Using Free Cash Flows to All Debt and Equity Stakeholders

f. At the end of Year 4, Coca-Cola had $7,178 million in outstanding interest-bearing short-term and long-term debt on the balance sheet and no preferred stock. Assume that the balance sheet value of Coca-Cola's debt is approximately equal to the market value of the debt. These forecasts assume that Coca-Cola will face an interest rate of 4.4 percent on debt capital, and that Coca-Cola's average tax rate

EXHIBIT 12.13

The Coca-Cola Company
Income Statements for Year 4 (Actual) and Year +1 through +6 (Projected)
(amounts in millions)
(Problem 12.16)

	Actual	Projected					
	Year 4	Year +1	Year +2	Year +3	Year +4	Year +5	Year +6
Revenues	$21,962	$23,060	$24,213	$25,424	$26,695	$28,030	$28,871
Cost of Goods Sold	(7,638)	(8,302)	(8,717)	(9,153)	(9,610)	(10,091)	(10,393)
Gross Profit	$14,324	$14,758	$15,496	$16,271	$17,085	$17,939	$18,477
Selling, General, and Administrative Expense	(8,146)	(8,763)	(9,201)	(9,661)	(10,144)	(10,651)	(10,971)
Other Operating Income	645	612	578	604	630	656	676
Other Operating Expenses	(480)	0	0	0	0	0	0
Operating Profit	$ 6,343	$ 6,608	$ 6,873	$ 7,214	$ 7,571	$ 7,944	$ 8,182
Interest Income	157	189	112	117	123	129	133
Interest Expense	(196)	(249)	(238)	(300)	(322)	(343)	(354)
Other Expenses or Losses	(82)	0	0	0	0	0	0
Income before Tax	$ 6,222	$ 6,547	$ 6,746	$ 7,031	$ 7,372	$ 7,730	$ 7,962
Income Tax Expense	(1,375)	(2,292)	(2,361)	(2,461)	(2,580)	(2,705)	(2,787)
Net Income	$ 4,847	$ 4,256	$ 4,385	$ 4,570	$ 4,792	$ 5,024	$ 5,175

EXHIBIT 12.14

The Coca-Cola Company
Balance Sheets for Year 4 (Actual) and Year +1 through +6 (Projected)
(amounts in millions)
(Problem 12.16)

	Actual	Projected					
	Year 4	Year +1	Year +2	Year +3	Year +4	Year +5	Year +6
Assets							
Cash	$ 6,707	$ 2,527	$ 2,780	$ 2,792	$ 3,058	$ 3,085	$ 3,178
Marketable Securities	61	132	139	145	151	157	162
Accounts Receivable—Trade	2,171	2,378	2,398	2,617	2,649	2,880	2,966
Inventories	1,420	1,493	1,566	1,646	1,726	1,814	1,869
Other Current Assets	1,735	1,589	1,666	1,738	1,814	1,884	1,940
Current Assets	$12,094	$ 8,119	$ 8,549	$ 8,937	$ 9,399	$ 9,820	$10,115
Long-Term Investments in Bottlers	9,306	7,945	8,331	8,689	9,068	9,418	9,701
Property, Plant, and Equipment, at cost	10,149	11,302	12,513	13,784	15,119	16,520	17,016
Accumulated Depreciation	(4,058)	(4,875)	(5,780)	(6,777)	(7,871)	(9,066)	(9,338)
Goodwill and Other Assets	3,836	3,993	4,157	4,330	4,511	4,702	4,843
Total Assets	$31,327	$26,484	$27,769	$28,963	$30,225	$31,394	$32,336

	Actual	Projected					
	Year 4	Year +1	Year +2	Year +3	Year +4	Year +5	Year +6
Liabilities:							
Accounts Payable—Trade	$ 2,238	$ 2,351	$ 2,465	$ 2,594	$ 2,716	$ 2,861	$ 2,947
Notes Payable and Short-Term Debt	4,531	1,723	4,165	4,344	4,534	4,709	4,850
Current Maturities of Long-Term Debt	1,490	43	21	7	406	406	418
Other Current Liabilities	2,712	2,942	3,088	3,236	3,392	3,552	3,658
Current Liabilities	$10,971	$ 7,058	$ 9,739	$10,181	$11,049	$11,528	$11,874
Long-Term Debt	1,157	2,384	2,499	2,607	2,720	2,826	2,910
Deferred Taxes	450	530	555	579	605	628	647
Other Noncurrent Liabilities	2,814	2,955	3,102	3,258	3,420	3,591	3,699
Total Liabilities	$15,392	$12,926	$15,896	$16,625	$17,794	$18,573	$19,130
Shareholders' Equity:							
Common Stock + Paid-In Capital	5,803	5,803	5,803	5,803	5,803	5,803	5,977
Retained Earnings	29,105	28,728	29,043	31,508	33,601	35,992	37,071
Accumulated Other Comprehensive Income	(1,348)	(1,348)	(1,348)	(1,348)	(1,348)	(1,348)	(1,388)
Treasury Stock	(17,625	(19,625	(21,625	(23,625	(25,625	(27,625	(28,454)
Shareholders' Equity	$15,935	$13,558	$11,873	$12,338	$12,431	$12,822	$13,206
Total Liabilities and Shareholders' Equity	$31,327	$26,484	$27,769	$28,963	$30,225	$31,394	$32,336

EXHIBIT 12.15

The Coca-Cola Company
Projected Statements of Cash Flows for Year +1 through +6
(amounts in millions)
(Problem 12.16)

	Projected					
	Year +1	Year +2	Year +3	Year +4	Year +5	Year +6
Statement of Cash Flows						
Net Income	$ 4,256	$ 4,385	$ 4,570	$ 4,792	$ 5,024	$ 5,175
Add Back Depreciation	817	905	997	1,094	1,195	251
(Increase) Decrease in Receivables	(207)	(21)	(218)	(33)	(231)	(86)
(Increase) Decrease in Inventories	(73)	(73)	(80)	(80)	(88)	(54)
(Increase) Decrease in Other Current Assets	146	(77)	(72)	(76)	(70)	(57)
(Increase) Decrease in Accounts Payable	113	115	128	123	145	86
Increase (Decrease) in Other Current Liabilities	230	146	149	156	159	107
Increase (Decrease) in Deferred Taxes	80	26	24	25	23	19
Increase (Decrease) in Other Noncurrent Liabilities	141	148	155	163	171	108
Net Cash Flows from Operations	**$ 5,502**	**$ 5,554**	**$ 5,653**	**$ 6,164**	**$ 6,329**	**$ 5,548**
(Increase) Decrease in Property, Plant, and Equipment, at cost	(1,153)	(1,211)	(1,271)	(1,335)	(1,401)	(496)
(Increase) Decrease in Marketable Securities	(71)	(6)	(6)	(6)	(6)	(5)
(Increase) Decrease in Investments in Bottlers	1,361	(386)	(358)	(379)	(351)	(283)
(Increase) Decrease in Other Assets	(157)	(165)	(173)	(181)	(190)	(120)
Net Cash Flows from Investing	**$ (20)**	**$(1,767)**	**$(1,808)**	**$(1,901)**	**$(1,949)**	**$ (903)**
Increase (Decrease) in Short-Term Debt	(4,255)	2,421	165	588	175	153
Increase (Decrease) in Long-Term Debt	1,227	116	107	114	105	85
Increase (Decrease) in Common Stock and Paid-In Capital	0	0	0	0	0	174
Dividends	(4,633)	(4,070)	(2,105)	(2,699)	(2,634)	(4,095)
Treasury Stock	(2,000)	(2,000)	(2,000)	(2,000)	(2,000)	(829)
Other Equity Adjustments	0	0	0	0	0	(40)
Net Cash Flow from Financing	**$(9,662)**	**$(3,534)**	**$(3,832)**	**$(3,997)**	**$(4,354)**	**$(4,552)**
Net Change in Cash	**$(4,180)**	**$ 253**	**$ 13**	**$ 266**	**$ 27**	**$ 93**

will be 35.0 percent. Compute the weighted average cost of capital for Coca-Cola as of the start of Year +1.

g. Beginning with projected net cash flows from operations, derive the projected free cash flows for all debt and equity stakeholders for Coca-Cola for Years +1 through +6 based on the projected financial statements. Assume that the change in cash each year is related to operating liquidity needs.

h. Using the weighted average cost of capital from part f as a discount rate, compute the sum of the present value of free cash flows for all debt and equity stakeholders for Coca-Cola for Years +1 through +5.

i. Using the weighted average cost of capital from part f as a discount rate, and the long-run growth rate from part b, compute the continuing value of Coca-Cola as of the start of Year +6 based on Coca-Cola's continuing free cash flows for all debt and equity stakeholders in Year +6 and beyond. After computing continuing value as of the start of Year +6, discount it to present value as of the start of Year +1.

j. Compute the value of a share of Coca-Cola common stock. (1) Compute the total value of Coca-Cola's net operating assets using the total sum of the present value of free cash flows for all debt and equity stakeholders (from parts h and i). (2) Subtract the value of outstanding debt to obtain the value of equity. (3) Adjust the present value of equity using the midyear discounting adjustment factor. (4) Compute the per-share value estimate of Coca-Cola's common equity shares.

NOTE: Do not be alarmed if your share value estimate from part e is slightly different from your share value estimate from part j. The weighted average cost of capital computation in part f used the weight of equity based on the market price of Coca-Cola's stock at the end of Year 4. The share value estimates from parts e and j likely differ from the market price, so the weights used to compute the weighted average cost of capital are not internally consistent with the estimated share values.

Part III—Sensitivity Analysis and Recommendation

k. Using the free cash flows to common equity shareholders, recompute the value of Coca-Cola shares under two alternative scenarios. Scenario 1: Assume that Coca-Cola's long-run growth will be 2 percent, not 3 percent as before; and assume that Coca-Cola's required rate of return on equity is 9 percent. Scenario 2: Assume that Coca-Cola's long-run growth will be 4 percent, not 3 percent as before; and assume that Coca-Cola's required rate of return on equity is 7 percent. To quantify the sensitivity of your share value estimate for Coca-Cola to these variations in growth and discount rates, compare (in percentage terms) your value estimates under these two scenarios with your value estimate from part e.

l. Using these data at the end of Year 4, what reasonable range of share values would you have expected for Coca-Cola common stock? At that time, what was the market price for Coca-Cola shares relative to this range? What would you have recommended?

12.17 FREE-CASH-FLOWS-BASED VALUATION. In Problem 10.16, we projected financial statements for Wal-Mart Stores for Years +1 through +5. The data in Exhibits 12.16, 12.17, and 12.18 include the actual amounts for Year 4 and the projected amounts for Year +1 to Year +5 for the income statements, balance sheets, and statements of cash flows for Wal-Mart (in millions).

FSAP

EXHIBIT 12.16

Wal-Mart Stores
Income Statements for Year 4 (Actual) and Year +1 through +5 (Projected)
(amounts in millions)
(Problem 12.17)

	Actual	Projected				
	Year 4	Year +1	Year +2	Year +3	Year +4	Year +5
Revenues	$285,222	$313,744	$345,119	$379,630	$417,594	$459,353
Cost of Goods Sold	(219,793)	(241,583)	(265,742)	(292,315)	(321,547)	(353,702)
Gross Profit	$ 65,429	$ 72,161	$ 79,377	$ 87,315	$ 96,047	$105,651
Selling, General, and Administrative Expense	(51,354)	(56,474)	(62,121)	(68,333)	(75,167)	(82,684)
Other Operating Income	2,968	3,137	3,451	3,796	4,176	4,594
Operating Profit	$ 17,091	$ 18,824	$ 20,707	$ 22,778	$ 25,056	$ 27,561
Interest Income	201	219	281	325	341	324
Interest Expense	(1,187)	(1,359)	(1,507)	(1,671)	(1,854)	(2,057)
Other Expenses	(249)	(314)	(345)	(380)	(418)	(459)
Income before Tax	$ 15,856	$ 17,370	$ 19,136	$ 21,052	$ 23,125	$ 25,369
Income Tax Expense	(5,589)	(6,253)	(6,889)	(7,579)	(8,325)	(9,133)
Net Income	$ 10,267	$ 11,117	$ 12,247	$ 13,473	$ 14,800	$ 16,236

EXHIBIT 12.17

Wal-Mart Stores
Balance Sheets for Year 4 (Actual) and Year +1 through +5 (Projected)
(amounts in millions)
(Problem 12.17)

	Actual	Projected				
	Year 4	Year +1	Year +2	Year +3	Year +4	Year +5
Assets						
Cash	$ 5,488	$ 6,038	$ 8,750	$ 8,352	$ 9,600	$ 7,429
Accounts Receivable—Trade	1,715	1,887	2,075	2,283	2,511	2,762
Inventories	29,447	32,497	35,641	39,311	43,137	47,556
Other Current Assets	1,841	2,025	2,228	2,450	2,695	2,965
Current Assets	$ 38,491	$ 42,446	$ 48,694	$ 52,396	$ 57,943	$ 60,712
Property, Plant, and Equipment, at cost	89,042	101,864	116,532	133,313	152,510	174,472
Accumulated Depreciation	(20,475)	(24,037)	(28,111)	(32,773)	(38,105)	(44,205)
Goodwill and Other Assets	13,165	14,482	15,930	17,523	19,275	21,202
Total Assets	$120,223	$134,755	$153,045	$170,460	$191,623	$212,180
Liabilities:						
Accounts Payable—Trade	$ 21,671	$ 22,564	$ 26,056	$ 27,464	$ 31,370	$ 33,386
Notes Payable and Short-Term Debt	3,812	4,090	4,389	4,709	5,053	5,422
Current Maturities of Long-Term Debt	3,969	4,259	4,570	4,903	5,261	5,645
Other Current Liabilities	13,436	14,780	16,258	17,883	19,672	21,639
Current Liabilities	$ 42,888	$ 45,693	$ 51,272	$ 54,960	$ 61,356	$ 66,092
Long-Term Debt	23,669	26,509	29,690	33,253	37,244	41,713
Other Noncurrent Liabilities	4,270	4,697	5,167	5,683	6,252	6,877
Total Liabilities	$ 70,827	$ 76,899	$ 86,129	$ 93,897	$104,851	$114,682
Shareholders' Equity:						
Common Stock + Paid-In Capital	2,848	2,848	2,848	2,848	2,848	2,848
Retained Earnings	43,854	52,314	61,373	71,021	81,230	91,957
Accumulated Other Comprehensive Income	2,694	2,694	2,694	2,694	2,694	2,694
Shareholders' Equity	$ 49,396	$ 57,856	$ 66,915	$ 76,563	$ 86,772	$ 97,499
Total Liabilities and Shareholders' Equity	$120,223	$134,755	$153,045	$170,460	$191,623	$212,180

EXHIBIT 12.18

Wal-Mart Stores
Projected Statements of Cash Flows for Year +1 through +5
(amounts in millions)
(Problem 12.17)

	Year +1	Year +2	Year +3	Year +4	Year +5
Statement of Cash Flows					
Net Income	$ 11,117	$ 12,247	$ 13,473	$ 14,800	$ 16,236
Add Back Depreciation	3,562	4,075	4,661	5,333	6,100
(Increase) Decrease in Receivables	(172)	(189)	(208)	(228)	(251)
(Increase) Decrease in Inventories	(3,050)	(3,144)	(3,670)	(3,825)	(4,419)
(Increase) Decrease in Other Current Assets	(184)	(203)	(223)	(245)	(270)
(Increase) Decrease in Accounts Payable	893	3,492	1,408	3,906	2,016
Increase (Decrease) in Other Current Liabilities	1,344	1,478	1,626	1,788	1,967
Increase (Decrease) in Other Noncurrent Liabilities	427	470	517	568	625
Net Cash Flows from Operations	**$ 13,937**	**$ 18,226**	**$ 17,585**	**$ 22,097**	**$ 22,004**
(Increase) Decrease in Property, Plant and Equipment, at cost	(12,822)	(14,668)	(16,781)	(19,197)	(21,961)
(Increase) Decrease in Other Assets	(1,317)	(1,448)	(1,593)	(1,752)	(1,927)
Net Cash Flows from Investing	**$(14,139)**	**$(16,117)**	**$(18,374)**	**$(20,949)**	**$(23,889)**
Increase (Decrease) in Short-Term Debt	568	609	654	702	753
Increase (Decrease) in Long-Term Debt	2,840	3,181	3,563	3,990	4,469
Increase (Decrease) in Common Stock + Paid-In Capital	0	0	0	0	0
Dividends	(2,657)	(3,188)	(3,826)	(4,591)	(5,509)
Net Cash Flow from Financing	**$ 751**	**$ 602**	**$ 391**	**$ 101**	**$ (287)**
Net Change in Cash	**$ 550**	**$ 2,712**	**$ (398)**	**$ 1,248**	**$ (2,171)**

The market equity beta for Wal-Mart at the end of Year 4 is .80. Assume that the risk-free interest rate is 4.0 percent and the market risk premium is 5.0 percent. Wal-Mart has 4,234 million shares outstanding at the end of Year 4. At the end of Year 4, Wal-Mart's share price was $52.40.

Required

Part I—Computing Wal-Mart's Share Value Using Free Cash Flows to Common Equity Shareholders

a. Use the CAPM to compute the required rate of return on common equity capital for Wal-Mart.

b. Beginning with projected net cash flows from operations, derive the projected free cash flows for common equity shareholders for Wal-Mart for Years +1 through +5 based on the projected financial statements. Assume that any change in cash each year is used for operating liquidity purposes.

c. Project the continuing free cash flow for common equity shareholders in Year +6. Assume that the steady-state long-run growth rate will be 3 percent in Year +6 and beyond. Project that the Year +5 income statement and balance sheet amounts will grow by 3 percent in Year +6, and then derive the projected statement of cash flows for Year +6. Derive the projected free cash flow for common equity shareholders in Year +6 from the projected statement of cash flows for Year +6.

d. Using the required rate of return on common equity from part a as a discount rate, compute the sum of the present value of free cash flows for common equity shareholders for Wal-Mart for Years +1 through +5.

e. Using the required rate of return on common equity from part a as a discount rate, and the long-run growth rate from part c, compute the continuing value of Wal-Mart as of the start of Year +6 based on Wal-Mart's continuing free cash flows for common equity shareholders in Year +6 and beyond. After computing continuing value as of the start of Year +6, discount it to present value at the start of Year +1.

f. Compute the value of a share of Wal-Mart common stock. (1) Compute the total sum of the present value of all future free cash flows for equity shareholders (from parts d and e). (2) Adjust the total sum of the present value using the midyear discounting adjustment factor. (3) Compute the per share value estimate.

NOTE: If you worked Problem 11.14 from Chapter 11 and computed Wal-Mart's share value using the dividends valuation approach, compare your value estimate from that problem with the value estimate you obtain here. They should be the same.

Part II—Computing Wal-Mart's Share Value Using Free Cash Flows to All Debt and Equity Stakeholders

g. At the end of Year 4, Wal-Mart had $31,450 million in outstanding interest-bearing short-term and long-term debt on the balance sheet and no preferred stock. Assume that the balance sheet value of Wal-Mart's debt is approximately equal to the market value of the debt. During Year 4 Wal-Mart's income statement included interest expense of $1,187 million. At the beginning of Year 4, Wal-Mart had a total of $26,466 million in interest-bearing debt, so during Year 4 Wal-Mart had an average of $28,958 in interest-bearing debt. This implies that Wal-Mart faced an average interest expense during Year 4 of roughly 4.1 percent (= $1,187 million/

$28,958 million). Assume that at the start of Year +1, Wal-Mart will continue to incur interest expense of 4.1 percent on debt capital, and that Wal-Mart's average tax rate will be 36.0 percent. Compute the weighted average cost of capital for Wal-Mart as of the start of Year +1.

h. Beginning with projected net cash flows from operations, derive the projected free cash flows for all debt and equity stakeholders for Wal-Mart for Years +1 through +5 based on the projected financial statements.

i. Project the continuing free cash flows for all debt and equity stakeholders in Year +6. Use the projected financial statements for Year +6 from part c to derive the projected free cash flow for all debt and equity stakeholders in Year +6.

j. Using the weighted average cost of capital from part g as a discount rate, compute the sum of the present value of free cash flows for all debt and equity stakeholders for Wal-Mart for Years +1 through +5.

k. Using the weighted average cost of capital from part g as a discount rate, and the long-run growth rate from part c, compute the continuing value of Wal-Mart as of the start of Year +6 based on Wal-Mart's continuing free cash flows for all debt and equity stakeholders in Year +6 and beyond. After computing continuing value as of the start of Year +6, discount it to present value as of the start of Year +1.

l. Compute the value of a share of Wal-Mart common stock. (1) Compute the total value of Wal-Mart's net operating assets using the total sum of the present value of free cash flows for all debt and equity stakeholders (from parts j and k). (2) Subtract the value of outstanding debt to obtain the value of equity. (3) Adjust the present value of equity using the midyear discounting adjustment factor. (4) Compute the per-share value estimate of Wal-Mart's common equity shares.

NOTE: Do not be alarmed if your share value estimate from part f is slightly different from your share value estimate from part l. The weighted average cost of capital computation in part g used the weight of equity based on the market price of Wal-Mart's stock at the end of Year 4. The share value estimates from parts f and l likely differ from the market price, so the weights used to compute the weighted average cost of capital are not internally consistent with the estimated share values.

Part III—Sensitivity Analysis and Recommendation

m. Using the free cash flows to common equity shareholders, recompute the value of Wal-Mart shares under two alternative scenarios. Scenario 1: Assume that Wal-Mart's long-run growth will be 2 percent, not 3 percent as before; and assume that Wal-Mart's required rate of return on equity is 1 percentage point higher than the rate you computed using the CAPM in part a. Scenario 2: Assume that Wal-Mart's long-run growth will be 4 percent, not 3 percent as before; and assume that Wal-Mart's required rate of return on equity is 1 percentage point lower than the rate you computed using the CAPM in part a. To quantify the sensitivity of your share value estimate for Wal-Mart to these variations in growth and discount rates, compare (in percentage terms) your value estimates under these two scenarios with your value estimate from part f.

n. Using these data at the end of Year 4, what reasonable range of share values would you have expected for Wal-Mart common stock? At that time, what was the market price for Wal-Mart shares relative to this range? What would you have recommended?

INTEGRATIVE CASE 12.1

FSAP

STARBUCKS

Free Cash Flows Valuation of Starbucks' Common Equity

In Integrative Case 10.1, we projected financial statements for Starbucks for Years +1 through +5. In this portion of the Starbucks Integrative Case, we use the projected financial statements from Integrative Case 10.1 and apply the techniques in Chapter 12 to compute Starbucks' required rate of return on equity and share value based on the free cash flows valuation model. We also compare our value estimate to Starbucks' share price at the time of the case development to provide an investment recommendation.

The market equity beta for Starbucks at the end of Year 4 is .60. Assume that the risk-free interest rate is 4.0 percent and the market risk premium is 5.0 percent. Starbucks has 397.4 million shares outstanding at the end of Year 4. At the start of Year +1, Starbucks' share price was $47.05.

Required

Part I—Computing Starbucks' Share Value Using Free Cash Flows to Common Equity Shareholders

a. Use the CAPM to compute the required rate of return on common equity capital for Starbucks.

b. Using your projected financial statements from Integrative Case 10.1 for Starbucks, begin with projected net cash flows from operations and derive the projected free cash flows for common equity shareholders for Starbucks for Years +1 through +5. You will need to determine whether your projected changes in cash are necessary for operating liquidity purposes.

c. Project the continuing free cash flow for common equity shareholders in Year +6. Assume that the steady-state long-run growth rate will be 3 percent in Year +6 and beyond. Project that the Year +5 income statement and balance sheet amounts will grow by 3 percent in Year +6, and then derive the projected statement of cash flows for Year +6. Derive the projected free cash flow for common equity shareholders in Year +6 from the projected statement of cash flows for Year +6.

d. Using the required rate of return on common equity from part a as a discount rate, compute the sum of the present value of free cash flows for common equity shareholders for Starbucks for Years +1 through +5.

e. Using the required rate of return on common equity from part a as a discount rate, and the long-run growth rate from part c, compute the continuing value of Starbucks as of the start of Year +6 based on Starbucks' continuing free cash flows for common equity shareholders in Year +6 and beyond. After computing continuing value as of the start of Year +6, discount it to present value at the start of Year +1.

f. Compute the value of a share of Starbucks common stock. (1) Compute the total sum of the present value of free cash flows for equity shareholders (from parts d and e). (2) Adjust the total sum of the present value using the midyear discounting adjustment factor. (3) Compute the per-share value estimate.

NOTE: If you worked Integrative Case 11.1 from Chapter 11 and computed Starbucks' share value using the dividends valuation approach, compare your value estimate from that case with the value estimate you obtain here. They should be the same.

Part II—Computing Starbucks' Share Value Using Free Cash Flows to All Debt and Equity Stakeholders

g. At the end of Year 4, Starbucks only had $4.4 million in outstanding interest-bearing short-term and long-term debt on the balance sheet and no preferred stock. Starbucks is repaying this debt in annual installments of roughly $0.8 million per year, and will fully retire the remaining debt over the next five years. Assume that the balance sheet value of Starbucks' debt equals the market value of the debt. Starbucks faced an interest rate of roughly 1 percent on its outstanding debt during Year 4. Assume that Starbucks will continue to face the same interest rate on this outstanding debt capital over the remaining life of the debt. Using the amounts on the Starbucks' Year 4 income statement in Exhibit 1.25 for Integrative Case 1.1 in Chapter 1, compute Starbucks' average tax rate in Year 4. Assume that Starbucks will continue to face the same income tax rate over the forecast horizon. Compute the weighted average cost of capital for Starbucks as of the start of Year +1. Compare your computation of Starbucks' weighted average cost of capital with your estimate of Starbucks' required return on equity from part a. The two amounts should be virtually identical. Why?

h. Based on your projections of Starbucks' financial statements, begin with projected net cash flows from operations and derive the projected free cash flows for all debt and equity stakeholders Starbucks for Years +1 through +5. Compare your forecasts of Starbucks' free cash flows for all debt and equity stakeholders Years +1 through +5 with your forecast of Starbucks' free cash flows for equity shareholders in part b. The two projected sets of free cash flows under the two approaches should be very similar but not identical. Why are the amounts so similar? Why are they not identical—what causes the difference each year?

i. Project the continuing free cash flows for all debt and equity stakeholders in Year +6. Use the projected financial statements for Year +6 from part c to derive the projected free cash flow for all debt and equity stakeholders in Year +6.

j. Using the weighted average cost of capital from part g as a discount rate, compute the sum of the present value of free cash flows for all debt and equity stakeholders for Starbucks for Years +1 through +5.

k. Using the weighted average cost of capital from part g as a discount rate, and the long-run growth rate from part c, compute the continuing value of Starbucks as of the start of Year +6 based on Starbucks' continuing free cash flows for all debt and equity stakeholders in Year +6 and beyond. After computing continuing value as of the start of Year +6, discount it to present value at the start of Year +1.

l. Compute the value of a share of Starbucks common stock. (1) Compute the value of Starbucks' net operating assets using the total sum of the present value of free cash flows for all debt and equity stakeholders (from parts j and k). (2) Subtract the value of outstanding debt to obtain the value of equity. (3) Adjust the present value of equity using the midyear discounting adjustment factor. (4) Compute the per-share value estimate.

m. Compare your share value estimate from part f with your share value estimate from part l. These values should be nearly identical because Starbucks has very little debt.

Part III—Sensitivity Analysis and Recommendation

n. Using the free cash flows to common equity shareholders, recompute the value of Starbucks shares under two alternative scenarios. Scenario 1: Assume that Starbucks' long-run growth will be 2 percent, not 3 percent as before; and assume that Starbucks' required rate of return on equity is 1 percentage point higher than the rate you computed using the CAPM in part a. Scenario 2: Assume that Starbucks' long-run growth will be 4 percent, not 3 percent as before; and assume that Starbucks' required rate of return on equity is 1 percentage point lower than the rate you computed using the CAPM in part a. To quantify the sensitivity of your share value estimate for Starbucks to these variations in growth and discount rates, compare (in percentage terms) your value estimates under these two scenarios with your value estimate from part f.

o. At the end of Year 4, what reasonable range of share values would you have expected for Starbucks common stock? At that time, where was the market price for Starbucks shares relative to this range? What would you have recommended?

p. If you computed Starbucks' common equity share value using the dividends valuation approach in Integrative Case 11.1, compare the value estimate you obtained in that case with the estimate you obtained in this case. They should be identical.

CASE 12.2

FSAP

HOLMES CORPORATION: LBO VALUATION

Holmes Corporation is a leading designer and manufacturer of material handling and process equipment for heavy industry in the United States and abroad. Its sales have more than doubled and its earnings increased more than sixfold in the past five years. In material handling, Holmes is a major producer of electric overhead and gantry cranes, ranging from 5 tons in capacity to 600-ton giants, the latter used primarily in nuclear and conventional power-generating plants. It also builds underhung cranes and monorail systems for general industrial use carrying loads up to 40 tons, railcar movers, railroad and mass transit shop maintenance equipment, and a broad line of advanced package conveyors. Holmes is a world leader in evaporation and crystallization systems and also furnishes dryers, heat exchangers, and filters to complete its line of chemical processing equipment sold internationally to the chemical, fertilizer, food, drug, and paper industries. For the metallurgical industry, it designs and manufactures electric arc and induction furnaces, cupolas, ladles, and hot metal distribution equipment.

The information on the following pages appears in the Year 15 annual report of Holmes Corporation.

Highlights

	Year 15	Year 14
Net Sales	$102,698,836	$109,372,718
Net Earnings	6,601,908	6,583,360
Net Earnings per Share	3.62*	3.61*
Cash Dividends Paid	2,241,892	1,426,502
Cash Dividends per Share	1.22*	.78*
Shareholders' Equity	29,333,803	24,659,214
Shareholders' Equity per Share	16.07*	13.51*
Working Capital	23,100,863	19,029,626
Orders Received	95,436,103	80,707,576
Unfilled Orders at End of Period	77,455,900	84,718,633
Average Number of Common Shares Outstanding during Period	1,824,853*	1,824,754*

*Adjusted for June, Year 15, and June, Year 14, 5-for-4 stock distributions.

Net Sales, Net Earnings, and Net Earnings per Share by Quarter

(adjusted for 5-for-4 stock distribution in June, Year 15, and June, Year 14)

	Year 15			Year 14		
	Net Sales	Net Earnings	Per Share	Net Sales	Net Earnings	Per Share
First Quarter	$ 25,931,457	$1,602,837	$ .88	$ 21,768,077	$1,126,470	$ .62
Second Quarter	24,390,079	1,727,112	.95	28,514,298	1,716,910	.94
Third Quarter	25,327,226	1,505,118	.82	28,798,564	1,510,958	.82
Fourth Quarter	27,050,074	1,766,841	.97	30,291,779	2,229,022	1.23
	$102,698,836	$6,601,908	$3.62	$109,372,718	$6,583,360	$3.61

Common Stock Prices and Cash Dividends Paid per Common Share by Quarter

(adjusted for 5-for-4 stock distribution in June, Year 15, and June, Year 14)

	Year 15			Year 14		
	Stock Prices		Cash Dividends	Stock Prices		Cash Dividends
	High	Low	per Share	High	Low	per Share
First Quarter	$22 1/2	$18 1/2	$ .26	$11 1/4	$ 9 1/2	$.16
Second Quarter	25 1/4	19 1/2	.26	12 3/8	8 7/8	.16
Third Quarter	26 1/4	19 3/4	.325	15 7/8	11 5/8	.20
Fourth Quarter	28 1/8	23 1/4	.375	20 7/8	15 7/8	.26
			$1.22			$.78

Management's Report to Shareholders

Year 15 was a pleasant surprise for all of us at Holmes Corporation. When the year started, it looked as though Year 15 would be a good year but not up to the record performance of Year 14. However, due to the excellent performance of our employees and the benefit of a favorable acquisition, Year 15 produced both record earnings and the largest cash dividend outlay in the company's 93-year history.

There is no doubt that some of the attractive orders received in late Year 12 and early Year 13 contributed to Year 15 profit. But of major significance was our organization's favorable response to several new management policies instituted to emphasize higher corporate profitability. Year 15 showed a net profit on net sales of 6.4 percent, which not only exceeded the 6.0 percent of last year but represents the highest net margin in several decades.

Net sales for the year were $102,698,836, down 6 percent from the $109,372,718 of a year ago but still the second largest volume in our history. Net earnings, however, set a new record at $6,601,908, or $3.62 per common share, which slightly exceeded the $6,583,360, or $3.61 per common share earned last year.

Cash dividends of $2,241,892 paid in Year 15 were 57 percent above the $1,426,502 paid a year ago. The record total resulted from your Board's approval of two increases during the year. When we implemented the 5-for-4 stock distribution in June, Year 15, we maintained the quarterly dividend rate of $.325 on the increased number of shares for the January payment. Then, in December, Year 15, we increased the quarterly rate to $.375 per share.

Year 15 certainly was not the most exuberant year in the capital equipment markets. Fortunately, our heavy involvement in ecology improvement, power generation, and international markets continued to serve us well, with the result that new orders of $95,436,103 were 18 percent over the $80,707,576 of Year 14.

Economists have predicted a substantial capital spending upturn for well over a year, but, so far, our customers have displayed stubborn reluctance to place new orders amid the uncertainty concerning the economy. Confidence is the answer. As soon as potential buyers can see clearly the future direction of the economy, we expect the unleashing of a large latent demand for capital goods, producing a much-expanded market for Holmes' products.

Fortunately, the accelerating pace of international markets continues to yield new business. Year 15 was an excellent year on the international front as our foreign customers continue to recognize our technological leadership in several product lines. Net sales of Holmes products shipped overseas and fees from foreign licensees amounted to $30,495,041, which represents a 31 percent increase over the $23,351,980 of a year ago.

Management fully recognizes and intends to take maximum advantage of our technological leadership in foreign lands. The latest manifestation of this policy was the acquisition of a controlling interest in Societé Francaise Holmes Fermont, our Swenson process equipment licensee located in Paris. Holmes and a partner started this firm 14 years ago as a sales and engineering organization to function in the Common Market. The company currently operates in the same mode. It owns no physical manufacturing assets, subcontracting all production. Its markets have expanded to include Spain and the East European countries.

Holmes Fermont is experiencing strong demand in Europe. For example, in early May, a $5.5 million order for a large potash crystallization system was received from a French engineering company representing a Russian client. Management estimates that Holmes Fermont will contribute approximately $6 to $8 million of net sales in Year 16.

Holmes' other wholly owned subsidiaries—Holmes Equipment Limited in Canada, Ermanco Incorporated in Michigan, and Holmes International, Inc., our FSC (Foreign Sales Corporation)—again contributed substantially to the success of Year 15. Holmes Equipment Limited registered its second best year. However, capital equipment markets in Canada have virtually come to a standstill in the past two quarters. Ermanco achieved the best year in its history, while Holmes International, Inc. had a truly exceptional year because of the very high level of activity in our international markets.

The financial condition of the company showed further improvement and is now unusually strong as a result of very stringent financial controls. Working capital increased to $23,100,863 from $19,029,626, a 21 percent improvement. Inventories decreased 6 percent from $18,559,231 to $17,491,741. The company currently has no long-term or short-term debt, and has considerable cash in short-term instruments. Much of our cash position, however, results from customers' advance payments which we will absorb as we make shipments on the contracts. Shareholders' equity increased 19 percent to $29,393,803 from $24,690,214 a year ago.

Plant equipment expenditures for the year were $1,172,057, down 18 percent from $1,426,347 of Year 14. Several appropriations approved during the year did not require expenditures because of delayed deliveries beyond Year 15. The major emphasis again was on our continuing program of improving capacity and efficiency through the purchase of numerically controlled machine tools. We expanded the Ermanco plant by 50 percent, but since this is a leasehold arrangement, we made only minor direct investment. We also improved the Canadian operation by adding more manufacturing space and installing energy-saving insulation.

Labor relations were excellent throughout the year. The Harvey plant continues to be nonunion. We negotiated a new labor contract at the Canadian plant, which extends to March 1, Year 17. The Pioneer Division in Alabama has a labor contract that does not expire until April, Year 16. While the union contract at Ermanco expired June 1, Year 15, work continues while negotiation proceeds on a new contract. We anticipate no difficulty in reaching a new agreement.

We exerted considerable effort during the year to improve Holmes' image in the investment community. Management held several informative meetings with security analyst groups to enhance the awareness of our activities and corporate performance.

The outlook for Year 16, while generally favorable, depends in part on the course of capital spending over the next several months. If the spending rate accelerates, the quickening pace of new orders, coupled with present backlogs, will provide the conditions for another fine year. On the other hand, if general industry continues the reluctant spending pattern of the last two years, Year 16 could be a year of maintaining market positions while awaiting better market conditions. Management takes an optimistic view and thus looks for a successful Year 16.

The achievement of record earnings and the highest profit margin in decades demonstrates the capability and the dedication of our employees. Management is most grateful for their efforts throughout the excellent year.

T. R. Varnum	T. L. Fuller
President	Chairman
March 15, Year 16	

Review of Operations

Year 15 was a very active year although the pace was not at the hectic tempo of Year 14. It was a year that showed continued strong demand in some product areas but a dampened rate in others. The product areas that had some special economic circumstances enhancing demand fared well. For example, the continuing effort toward ecological improvement fostered excellent activity in Swenson process equipment. Likewise, the energy concern and the need for more electrical power generation capacity boded well for large overhead cranes. On the other hand, Holmes' products that relate to general industry and depend on the overall capital spending rate for new equipment experienced lesser demand, resulting in lower new orders and reduced backlogs. The affected products were small cranes, underhung cranes, railcar movers, and metallurgical equipment.

Year 15 was the first full year of operations under some major policy changes instituted to improve Holmes' profitability. The two primary revisions were the restructuring of our marketing effort along product division lines, and the conversion of the product division incentive plans to a profit-based formula. The corporate organization adapted extremely well to the new policies. The improved profit margin in Year 15, in substantial part, was a result of the changes.

International activity increased markedly during the year. Surging foreign business and the expressed objective to capitalize on Holmes' technological leadership overseas resulted in the elevation of Mr. R. E. Foster to officer status as Vice President-International. The year involved heavy commitments of the product division staffs, engineering groups, and manufacturing organization to such important contracts as the $14 million Swenson order for Poland, the $8 million Swenson project for Mexico, the $2 million crane order for Venezuela, and several millions of dollars of railcar movers for all areas of the world.

The acquisition of control and commencement of operating responsibility of Societé Francaise Holmes Fermont, the Swenson licensee in Paris, was a major milestone in our international strategy. This organization has the potential of becoming a very substantial contributor in the years immediately ahead. Its long-range market opportunities in Europe and Asia are excellent.

Material Handling Products

Material handling equipment activities portrayed conflicting trends. During the year, when total backlog decreased, the crane division backlog increased. This was a result of several multimillion dollar contracts for power plant cranes. The small crane market, on the other hand, experienced depressed conditions during most of the year as general industry withheld appropriations for new plant and equipment. The underhung crane market experienced similar conditions. However, as Congressional attitudes and policies on investment unfold, we expect capital spending to show a substantial upturn.

The Transportation Equipment Division secured the second order for orbital service bridges, a new product for the containment vessels of nuclear power plants. This design is unique and allows considerable cost savings in erecting and maintaining containment shells.

The Ermanco Conveyor Division completed its best year with the growing acceptance of the unique XenoROL design. We expanded the Grand Haven plant by 50 percent to effect further cost reduction and new concepts of marketing.

The railcar moving line continued to produce more business from international markets. We installed the new 11TM unit in six domestic locations, a product showing signs of exceptional performance. We shipped the first foreign 11TM machine to Sweden.

Process Equipment Products

Process equipment again accounted for slightly more than half of the year's business.

Swenson activity reached an all-time high level with much of the division's effort going into international projects. The large foreign orders required considerable additional work to cover the necessary documentation, metrification when required, and general liaison.

We engaged in considerably more subcontracting during the year to accommodate one-piece shipment of the huge vessels pioneered by Swenson to effect greater equipment economies. The division continued to expand the use of computerization for design work and contract administration. We developed more capability during the year to handle the many additional tasks associated with turnkey projects. Swenson research and development efforts accelerated in search of better technology and new products. We conducted pilot plant test work at our facilities and in the field to convert several sales prospects into new contracts.

The metallurgical business proceeded at a slower pace in Year 15. However, with construction activity showing early signs of improvement, and automotive and farm machinery manufacturers increasing their operating rates, we see intensified interest in metallurgical equipment.

Financial Statements

The financial statements of Holmes Corporation and related notes appear in Exhibits 12.19 through 12.21. Exhibit 12.22 presents five-year summary operating information for Holmes.

Notes to Consolidated Financial Statements Year 15 and Year 14

Note A—Summary of Significant Accounting Policies

Significant accounting policies consistently applied appear below to assist the reader in reviewing the company's consolidated financial statements contained in this report.

EXHIBIT 12.19

Holmes Corporation
Balance Sheet
(amounts in thousands)
(Case 12.2)

	Year 10	Year 11	Year 12	Year 13	Year 14	Year 15
Cash	$ 955	$ 962	$ 865	$ 1,247	$ 1,540	$ 3,857
Marketable Securities	0	0	0	0	0	2,990
Accounts/Notes Receivable	6,545	7,295	9,718	13,307	18,759	14,303
Inventories	7,298	8,685	12,797	20,426	18,559	17,492
Current Assets	$14,798	$16,942	$23,380	$34,980	$38,858	$38,642
Investments	0	0	0	0	0	422
Property, Plant, and Equipment	12,216	12,445	13,126	13,792	14,903	15,876
Less: Accumulated Depreciation	(7,846)	(8,236)	(8,558)	(8,988)	(9,258)	(9,703)
Other Assets	470	420	400	299	343	276
Total Assets	$19,638	$21,571	$28,348	$40,083	$44,846	$45,513
Accounts Payable—Trade	$ 2,894	$ 4,122	$ 6,496	$ 7,889	$ 6,779	$ 4,400
Notes Payable—Nontrade	0	0	700	3,500	0	0
Current Portion Long-Term Debt	170	170	170	170	170	0
Other Current Liabilities	550	1,022	3,888	8,624	12,879	11,142
Current Liabilities	$ 3,614	$ 5,314	$11,254	$20,183	$19,828	$15,542
Long-Term Debt	680	510	340	170	0	0
Deferred Tax (NCL)	0	0	0	216	328	577
Other Noncurrent Liabilities	0	0	0	0	0	0
Total Liabilities	$ 4,294	$ 5,824	$11,594	$20,569	$20,156	$16,119
Common Stock	$ 2,927	$ 2,927	$ 2,927	$ 5,855	$ 7,303	$ 9,214
Additional Paid-In Capital	5,075	5,075	5,075	5,075	5,061	5,286
Retained Earnings	7,342	7,772	8,774	8,599	12,297	14,834
Accumulated Other Comprehensive Income	0	0	5	12	29	60
Treasury Stock	0	(27	(27	(27	0	0
Total Shareholders' Equity	$15,344	$15,747	$16,754	$19,514	$24,690	$29,394
Total Liabilities and Shareholders' Equity	$19,638	$21,571	$28,348	$40,083	$44,846	$45,513

EXHIBIT 12.20

Holmes Corporation
Income Statement
(amounts in thousands)
(Case 12.2)

	Year 11	Year 12	Year 13	Year 14	Year 15
Sales	$41,428	$53,541	$76,328	$109,373	$102,699
Other Revenues and Gains	0	41	0	0	211
Cost of Goods Sold	(33,269)	(43,142)	(60,000)	(85,364)	(80,260)
Selling and Administrative Expense	(6,175)	(7,215)	(9,325)	(13,416)	(12,090)
Other Expenses and Losses	(2)	0	(11)	(31)	(1)
Operating Income	$ 1,982	$ 3,225	$ 6,992	$ 10,562	$ 10,559
Interest Expense	(43)	(21)	(284)	(276)	(13)
Income Tax Expense	(894)	(1,471)	(2,992)	(3,703)	(3,944)
Net Income	$ 1,045	$ 1,733	$ 3,716	$ 6,583	$ 6,602

Consolidation—The consolidated financial statements include the accounts of the company and its subsidiaries after eliminating all intercompany transactions and balances.

Inventories—Inventories generally appear at the lower of cost or market, with cost determined principally on a first-in, first-out method.

Property, plant, and equipment—Property, plant, and equipment appear at acquisition cost less accumulated depreciation. When the company retires or disposes of properties, it removes the related costs and accumulated depreciation from the respective accounts and credits, or charges any gain or loss to earnings. The company expenses maintenance and repairs as incurred. It capitalizes major betterments and renewals. Depreciation results from applying the straight-line method over the estimated useful lives of the assets as follows:

Buildings	30 to 45 years
Machinery and equipment	4 to 20 years
Furniture and fixtures	10 years

Intangible assets—The company has amortized the unallocated excess of cost of a subsidiary over net assets acquired (that is, goodwill) over a 17-year period. Beginning in Year 16, GAAP no longer requires amortization of goodwill.

Research and development costs—The company charges research and development costs to operations as incurred ($479,410 in Year 15, and $467,733 in Year 14).

Pension plans—The company and its subsidiaries have noncontributory pension plans covering substantially all of their employees. The company's policy is to fund accrued pension costs as determined by independent actuaries. Pension costs amounted to $471,826 in Year 15, and $366,802 in Year 14.

EXHIBIT 12.21

Holmes Corporation
Statement of Cash Flows
(amounts in thousands)
(Case 12.2)

	Year 11	Year 12	Year 13	Year 14	Year 15
Operations					
Net Income	$1,045	$1,733	$3,716	$ 6,583	$ 6,602
Depreciation and Amortization	491	490	513	586	643
Other Addbacks	20	25	243	151	299
Other Subtractions	0	0	0	0	(97)
(Increase) Decrease in Receivables	(750)	(2,424)	(3,589)	(5,452)	4,456
(Increase) Decrease in Inventories	(1,387)	(4,111)	(7,629)	1,867	1,068
Increase (Decrease) Accounts Payable—Trade	1,228	2,374	1,393	1,496	(2,608)
Increase (Decrease) in Other Current Liabilities	473	2,865	4,737	1,649	(1,509)
Cash from Operations	$1,120	$ 952	$ (616)	$ 6,880	$ 8,854
Investing					
Fixed Assets Acquired, net	$ (347)	$ (849)	$ (749)	$(1,426)	$(1,172)
Investments Acquired	0	0	0	0	(3,306)
Other Investing Transactions	45	0	81	(64)	39
Cash Flow from Investing	$ (302)	$ (849)	$ (668)	$(1,490)	$(4,439)
Financing					
Increase in Short-Term Borrowing	$ 0	$ 700	$2,800	$ 0	$ 0
Decrease in Short-Term Borrowing	0	0	0	(3,500)	0
Increase in Long-Term Borrowing	0	0	0	0	0
Decrease in Long-Term Borrowing	(170)	(170)	(170)	(170)	(170)
Issue of Capital Stock	0	0	0	0	315
Acquisition of Capital Stock	(27)	0	0	0	0
Dividends	(614)	(730)	(964)	(1,427)	(2,243)
Other Financing Transactions	0	0	0	0	0
Cash Flow from Financing	$ (811)	$ (200)	$1,666	$(5,097)	$(2,098)
Net Change in Cash	$ 7	$ (97)	$ 382	$ 293	$ 2,317
Cash, Beginning of Year	955	962	865	1,247	1,540
Cash, End of Year	$ 962	$ 865	$1,247	$ 1,540	$ 3,857

Revenue recognition—The company generally recognizes income on a percentage-of-completion basis. It records advance payments as received and reports them as a deduction from billings when earned. The company recognizes royalties, included in net sales, as income when received. Royalties total $656,043 in Year 15, and $723,930 in Year 14.

EXHIBIT 12.22

Holmes Corporation
Five-Year Summary of Operations
(Case 12.2)

	Year 15	Year 14	Year 13	Year 12	Year 11
Orders Received	**$ 95,436,103**	$ 80,707,576	**$121,445,731**	$89,466,793	**$55,454,188**
Net Sales	**102,698,836**	109,372,718	**76,327,664**	53,540,699	**41,427,702**
Backlog of Unfilled Orders	**77,455,900**	84,718,633	**113,383,775**	68,265,708	**32,339,614**
Earnings before Taxes on Income	**$ 10,546,213**	$ 10,285,943	**$ 6,708,072**	$ 3,203,835	**$ 1,939,414**
Taxes on Income	**3,944,305**	3,702,583	**2,991,947**	1,470,489	**894,257**
Net Earnings	**6,601,908**	6,583,360	**3,716,125**	1,733,346	**1,045,157**
Net Property, Plant, and Equipment	**$ 6,173,416**	$ 5,644,590	**$ 4,803,978**	$ 4,568,372	**$ 4,209,396**
Net Additions to Property	**1,172,057**	1,426,347	**748,791**	848,685	**346,549**
Depreciation and Amortization	**643,231**	585,735	**513,402**	490,133	**491,217**
Cash Dividends Paid	**$ 2,242,892**	$ 1,426,502	**$ 963,935**	$ 730,254	**$ 614,378**
Working Capital	**23,100,463**	19,029,626	**14,796,931**	12,126,491	**11,627,875**
Shareholders' Equity	**29,393,803**	24,690,214	**19,514,358**	15,754,166	**15,747,116**
Earnings per Common Share (1)	**$ 3.62**	$ 3.61	**$ 2.03**	$ .96	**$ .57**
Dividends per Common Share (1)	**1.22**	.78	**.53**	.40	**.34**
Book Value per Common Share (1)	**16.07**	13.51	**10.68**	9.18	**8.62**
Number of Shareholders, December 31	**2,157**	2,024	**1,834**	1,792	**1,787**
Number of Employees, December 31	**1,549**	1,550	**1,551**	1,425	**1,303**
Shares of Common Outstanding, December 31 (1)	**1,824,853**	1,824,754	**1,824,754**	1,824,941	**1,827,515**
% Net Sales by Product Line					
Material Handling Equipment	**46.1%**	43.6%	**51.3%**	54.4%	**63.0%**
Processing Equipment	**53.9%**	56.4%	**48.7%**	45.6%	**37.0%**

Note: (1) Based on number of shares outstanding on December 31 adjusted for the 5-for-4 stock distributions in June, Year 13, Year 14, and Year 15.

Income taxes—The company provides no income taxes on unremitted earnings of foreign subsidiaries since it anticipates no significant tax liabilities should foreign units remit such earnings. The company makes provision for deferred income taxes applicable to timing differences between financial statement and income tax accounting, principally on the earnings of a foreign sales subsidiary which existing statutes defer in part from current taxation.

Note B—Foreign Operations

The consolidated financial statements in Year 15 include net assets of $2,120,648 ($1,847,534 in Year 14), undistributed earnings of $2,061,441 ($1,808,752 in Year 14), sales of $7,287,566 ($8,603,225 in Year 14), and net income of $454,999 ($641,454 in Year 14) applicable to the Canadian subsidiary.

The company translates balance sheet accounts of the Canadian subsidiary into U.S. dollars at the exchange rates at the end of the year, and operating results at the average of exchange rates for the year.

Note C—Inventories

Inventories used in determining cost of sales appear below:

	Year 15	Year 14	Year 13
Raw materials and supplies	$ 8,889,147	$ 9,720,581	$ 8,900,911
Work in process	8,602,594	8,838,650	11,524,805
Total inventories	$17,491,741	$18,559,231	$20,425,716

Note D—Short-Term Borrowing

The company has short-term credit agreements which principally provide for loans of 90-day periods at varying interest rates. There were no borrowings in Year 15. In Year 14, the maximum borrowing at the end of any calendar month was $4,500,000 and the approximate average loan balance and weighted average interest rate, computed by using the days outstanding method, was $3,435,000 and 7.6 percent. There were no restrictions upon the company during the period of the loans and no compensating bank balance arrangements required by the lending institutions.

Note E—Income Taxes

Provision for income taxes consists of:

	Year 15	Year 14
Current		
Federal	$2,931,152	$2,633,663
State	466,113	483,240
Canadian	260,306	472,450
Total current provision	$3,657,571	$3,589,353
Deferred		
Federal	$ 263,797	$ 91,524
Canadian	22,937	21,706
Total deferred	$ 286,734	$ 113,230
Total provision for income taxes	$3,944,305	$3,702,583

Reconciliation of the total provision for income taxes to the current federal statutory rate of 35 percent is as follows:

	Year 15		Year 14	
	Amount	**%**	**Amount**	**%**
Tax at statutory rate	$3,691,000	35.0%	$3,600,100	35.0%
State taxes, net of U.S. tax credit	302,973	2.9	314,106	3.1
All other items	(49,668)	(.5)	(211,623)	(2.1)
Total provision for income taxes	$3,944,305	37.4%	$3,702,583	36.0%

Note F—Pensions

The components of pension expense appear below:

	Year 15	Year 14
Service Cost	$476,490	$429,700
Interest Cost	567,159	446,605
Expected Return on Pension Investments	(558,373)	(494,083)
Amortization of Actuarial Gains and Losses	(13,450)	(15,420)
Pension Expense	$471,826	$366,802

The funded status of the pension plan appears below.

	December 31:	
	Year 15	**Year 14**
Accumulated Benefit Obligation	$5,763,450	$5,325,291
Effect of Salary Increases	1,031,970	976,480
Projected Benefit Obligation	$6,795,420	$6,301,771
Pension Fund Assets	6,247,940	5,583,730
Excess Pension Obligation	$ 547,480	$ 718,041

Assumptions used in accounting for pensions appear below:

	Year 15	Year 14
Expected Return on Pension Assets	10%	10%
Discount Rate for Projected Benefit Obligation	9%	8%
Salary Increases	5%	5%

Note G—Common Stock

As of March 20, Year 15, the company increased the authorized number of shares of common stock from 1,800,000 shares to 5,000,000 shares.

On December 29, Year 15, the company increased its equity interest (from 45 percent to 85 percent) in Societé Francaise Holmes Fermont, a French affiliate, in exchange for 18,040 of its common shares in a transaction accounted for as a purchase. The company credited the excess of the fair value ($224,373) of the company's shares issued over their par value ($90,200) to additional contributed capital. The excess of the purchase cost over the underlying value of the assets acquired was insignificant.

The company made a 25 percent common stock distribution on June 15, Year 14, and on June 19, Year 15, resulting in increases of 291,915 shares in 1994 and 364,433 shares in Year 15, respectively. We capitalized the par value of these additional shares by a transfer of $1,457,575 in Year 14 and $1,822,165 in Year 15 from retained earnings to the common stock account. In Year 14 and Year 15, we paid cash of $2,611 and $15,340, respectively, in lieu of fractional share interests.

In addition, the company retired 2,570 shares of treasury stock in June, Year 14. The earnings and dividends per share for Year 14 and Year 15 in the accompanying consolidated financial statements reflect the 25 percent stock distributions.

Note H—Contingent Liabilities

The company has certain contingent liabilities with respect to litigation and claims arising in the ordinary course of business. The company cannot determine the ultimate disposition of these contingent liabilities but, in the opinion of management, they will not result in any material effect upon the company's consolidated financial position or results of operations.

Note I—Quarterly Data (unaudited)

Quarterly sales, gross profit, net earnings, and earnings per share for Year 15 appear below:

	Net Sales	Gross Profit	Net Earnings	Earnings per Share
First	$ 25,931,457	$ 5,606,013	$1,602,837	$ .88
Second	24,390,079	6,148,725	1,727,112	.95
Third	25,327,226	5,706,407	1,505,118	.82
Fourth	27,050,074	4,977,774	1,766,841	.97
Year	$102,698,836	$22,438,919	$6,601,908	$3.62

The first quarterly results are restated for the 25 percent stock distribution on June 19, Year 15.

Auditors' Report

Board of Directors and Stockholders

Holmes Corporation

We have examined the consolidated balance sheets of Holmes Corporation and Subsidiaries as of December 31, Year 15 and Year 14, and the related consolidated statements of earnings and cash flows for the years then ended. Our examination was made in accordance with generally accepted auditing standards, and accordingly included such tests of the accounting records and such other auditing procedures as we considered necessary in the circumstances.

In our opinion, the financial statements referred to above present fairly the consolidated financial position of Holmes Corporation and Subsidiaries at December 31, Year 15 and Year 14, and the consolidated results of their operations and changes in cash flows for the years then ended, in conformity with generally accepted accounting principles applied on a consistent basis.

SBW, LLP
Chicago, Illinois
March 15, Year 16

Required

A group of Holmes' top management is interested in acquiring Holmes in a leveraged buyout.

a. Describe briefly the factors that make Holmes an attractive and, conversely, an unattractive leveraged buyout candidate.

b. (This question requires coverage of Chapter 10.) Prepare projected financial statements for Holmes Corporation for Year 16 through Year 20 excluding all financing (that is, project the amount of operating income after taxes, assets, and cash flows from operating and investing activities). State the underlying assumptions made.

c. Ascertain the value of Holmes' common shareholders' equity using the present value of its future cash flows valuation approach. Assume a risk-free interest rate of 4.2 percent and a market premium of 5.0 percent. Note that information in part e may be helpful in this valuation. Assume the following financing structure for the leveraged buyout:

Type	Proportion	Interest Rate	Term
Term Debt	50%	8%	7-Year Amortization[a]
Subordinated Debt	25	12%	10-Year Amortization[a]
Shareholders' Equity	25		
	100%		

[a]Holmes must repay principal and interest in equal annual payments.

d. (This question requires coverage of Chapter 13.) Ascertain the value of Holmes' common shareholders' equity using the residual income approach.

e. (This question requires coverage of Chapter 14.) Ascertain the value of Holmes' common shareholders' equity using the residual ROCE model, and the price-to-earnings ratio and the market value to book value of comparable companies' approaches. Selected data for similar companies for Year 15 appear in the following table (amounts in millions):

	Agee Robotics	**GI Handling Systems**	**LJG Industries**	**Gelas Corp.**
Industry:	**Conveyor Systems**	**Conveyor Systems**	**Cranes**	**Industrial Furnaces**
Sales	$4,214	$28,998	$123,034	$75,830
Net Income	$ 309	$ 2,020	$ 9,872	$ 5,117
Assets	$2,634	$15,197	$ 72,518	$41,665
Long-Term Debt	$ 736	$ 5,098	$ 23,745	$ 8,869
Common Shareholders' Equity	$1,551	$ 7,473	$ 38,939	$26,884
Market Value of Common Equity	$6,915	$20,000	$102,667	$41,962
Market Beta	1.12	.88	.99	.93

f. Would you attempt to acquire Holmes Corporation after completing the analyses in parts a through e? If not, how would you change the analyses to make this an attractive leveraged buyout?

Chapter 13

Valuation: Earnings-Based Approaches

Learning Objectives

1. **Understand earnings-based valuation, particularly the value relevance of earnings versus dividends versus cash flows.**

2. **Understand the conceptual and practical strengths and weaknesses of the earnings-based valuation method, also known as the residual income valuation method.**

3. **Develop conceptual understanding and practical techniques to deal with the important issues involved in earnings-based valuation:**

   a. **the role of book values of common shareholders' equity, earnings, dividends, and clean surplus accounting;**

   b. **measuring required (or "normal") income by multiplying beginning-of-period book value of equity by the risk-adjusted required rate of return on equity capital;**

   c. **measuring residual (or "abnormal") income each period by subtracting required income from expected future income;**

   d. **determining the value of common equity as the sum of book value of common shareholders' equity plus the present value of expected future residual income over the forecast horizon plus the present value of residual income continuing beyond the forecast horizon.**

4. **Apply the residual income valuation method to estimate common shareholders' equity value. Demonstrate the residual income valuation approach by valuing the common shareholders' equity of PepsiCo.**

5. **Assess the sensitivity of firm value estimates to key valuation parameters, such as discount rates and expected long-term growth rates.**

6. **Identify potential causes of errors if the residual income, free cash flows, and dividends valuations do not determine identical value estimates.**

INTRODUCTION AND OVERVIEW

The earnings number is the single most widely followed measure of firm performance. The accounting profession and firms themselves have designed the accrual accounting process to measure earnings as the bottom line of the firm's profitability each period. As a result, firms' earnings numbers play central roles as the primary measures of performance used in the capital markets for capital allocation.

Because of the demand in the capital markets for earnings numbers, firms usually release quarterly and annual income numbers to the public as soon as the accountants have prepared and verified them, often weeks *before* the firms release their detailed quarterly and annual income statements, balance sheets, statements of cash flows, and notes. Firms commonly announce earnings numbers during conference calls and press conferences attended by investors, analysts, managers, board members, and the financial press. Analysts often spend enormous amounts of time and effort building (and when new information arrives, revising) forecasts of firms' upcoming quarterly and annual earnings numbers. Sell-side analysts sell their earnings forecasts to interested investors, brokers, and fund managers. Commercial firms such as I/B/E/S and First Call have built businesses on compiling and distributing daily data on analysts' earnings forecasts. The financial media provide daily coverage of firms' earnings announcements. For example, the *Wall Street Journal* provides a summary report of firms' earnings announcements each day in its Earnings Digest section. The *Wall Street Journal* also reports daily data on each firm's stock trading activity, including a daily price-earnings ratio. In fact, because of the demand for and attention devoted to earnings numbers among capital markets participants, U.S. GAAP also requires firms to report earnings numbers scaled on a *per-share* basis within the financial statements (see related discussion in Chapter 4).[1]

Firms' share prices usually react quickly to earnings announcements, and the direction and magnitude of the market's reaction depends on the direction and magnitude of the earnings news relative to the market's expectations. Firms that announce earnings that exceed the market's expectations ("good news") often experience significant jumps in share price during the day of and the days immediately following the announcement. Likewise, firms that announce earnings that fall short of the market's expectations ("bad news") usually experience a decline in share price, and, in some circumstances, severe drops, during the day of and the days immediately following the announcement. As we have noted in several prior chapters, the seminal Ball and Brown (1968) study and many other research studies, including the Nichols and Wahlen (2004) study described in Chapter 1 and Exhibit 1.14, have shown that firms' stock returns are highly positively correlated with changes in earnings numbers.[2]

Because earnings numbers provide such important information to external stakeholders such as investors and others, earnings numbers also play key roles in capital allocation within firms. New project proposals within firms are often evaluated based on the effects the new projects will have on reported earnings. In addition, corporate governance processes commonly reward and punish managers based on whether firm performance meets certain earnings targets. Managers who meet or exceed specified earnings targets are usually rewarded with substantial bonuses. Managers who consistently fall short of earnings targets typically need to explain why they failed to meet the targets, and if the explanations are not satisfactory, they may find themselves fired and replaced.

---

[1]Financial Accounting Standards Board, Statement of *Financial Accounting Standard* No. 128, "Earnings per Share" (1997).

[2]Ray Ball and Philip Brown, "An Evaluation of Accounting Income Numbers," *Journal of Accounting Research* (Autumn 1968), pp. 159–178. D. Craig Nichols and James Wahlen, "How Do Earnings Numbers Relate to Stock Returns? A Review of Classic Accounting Research with Updated Evidence," *Accounting Horizons*, December 2004, pp. 263–286.

In light of all of these observations, it is logical that accounting earnings numbers provide a basis for valuation because earnings are the primary measures of firm performance produced by the accrual accounting system, because earnings numbers play such a critical role in the capital markets and the pricing of shares, and because earnings numbers are used in corporate management for internal capital allocation and for aligning the incentives of managers with shareholders. This chapter describes the conceptual and practical strengths and weaknesses of the earnings-based valuation model known as the residual income valuation model. The residual income valuation model uses expected future net income and the book value of common shareholders' equity as the basis for valuation.

To describe and explain the residual income valuation model, and to demonstrate the practical application of the model, this chapter takes four important steps. Exhibit 13.1 illustrates these steps and some of the key questions we address in this chapter. First, we describe the rationale behind earnings-based valuation. Second, we describe and explain the theoretical and conceptual foundation for residual income valuation, with a number of illustrations and examples. Third, we demonstrate the practical application of the residual income model by applying it to value the common shareholders' equity of PepsiCo. As we apply the model to PepsiCo, we describe the key measurement and implementation issues. Fourth, we come full circle in valuation by demonstrating the internal consistency in dividends, free cash flows, and residual income valuation. We demonstrate that these three valuation approaches yield identical valuations if applied properly. We also help the analyst understand how to identify and correct valuation errors if the three valuation models do not agree.

The residual income valuation model in this chapter provides a powerful approach that is a complementary equivalent to the classical dividends-based valuation approach presented in Chapter 11 and to the free-cash-flow-based valuation approach presented in Chapter 12. The residual income valuation model in this chapter forms the basis for the market-based multiples described in Chapter 14, including the market-to-book ratio and the price-earnings ratio.

RATIONALE FOR EARNINGS-BASED VALUATION

As Exhibit 13.1 illustrates, the first step we take to understand residual income valuation is to understand how accrual accounting earnings can be a valid foundation for value. As Chapter 11 and 12 discuss, economic theory teaches that the value of any resource equals the present value of the expected future payoffs from the resource discounted at a rate that reflects the risk inherent in those expected future payoffs. As we began Chapters 11 and 12, we again start with the same general model for the present value of a security (denoted V_0, with present value denoted as of time $t = 0$) with an expected life of n future periods, as follows:[3]

$$V_0 = \sum_{t=1}^{n} \frac{\text{ExpectedFuturePayoffs}_t}{(1 + \text{DiscountRate})^t}$$

As Chapter 11 describes, in theory, the value of a share of common equity should equal the present value of the *expected future dividends* the shareholder will receive.[4]

---

[3]In this chapter, we use the same notation as in prior chapters, where t refers to accounting periods. The valuation process determines an estimate of firm value, denoted V_0, in present value as of today, when $t = 0$. The period $t = 1$ refers to the first accounting period being discounted to present value. Period $t = n$ is the period of the expected final, or liquidating, return.

[4]John Burr Williams, *The Theory of Investment and Value* (Cambridge, Mass.: Harvard University Press, 1938).

EXHIBIT 13.1

Steps to Understanding Residual Income Valuation

1. Rationale

- What is the rationale for using earnings as a basis for valuation?
- What are the practical advantages and concerns associated with using earnings to determine common shareholders' equity value?

2. Theoretical and Conceptual Foundations for Residual Income Valuation

- What theories and concepts support residual income valuation?
- How do we measure residual income? What does it represent?

3. Practical Application

- What steps do we take to determine value using the residual income valuation method?
- What value estimate do we get from this approach for the common shareholders' equity of PepsiCo?
- What implementation issues do we need to understand in order to use the residual income model?

4. Linking Residual Income Valuation to Dividends Valuation and Free Cash Flow Valuation

- Conceptually, why is the residual income valuation approach consistent with the dividends valuation approach and with the free cash flows to equity valuation approach?
- Practically, does the value estimate we obtain for PepsiCo using the residual income valuation approach agree with the estimate from Chapter 11 using the dividends valuation approach and Chapter 12 using the free cash flows to equity valuation approach?
- What if the value estimates do not agree across these three models? How do we find and correct possible valuation errors?

Dividends are the fundamental, value-relevant attribute of expected future returns because they represent the distribution of wealth from the firm to the shareholders. The equity shareholder receives dividends as the payoffs from holding a share, including the final "liquidating" dividend when the firm liquidates the share or the investor sells the share. Thus, to value a firm's shares using dividends, one can discount to present value the expected future dividends over the life of the firm (or the expected length of time the share will be held), including the final liquidating dividend.

The residual income valuation approach presented in this chapter parallels the dividends-based valuation approach and the cash-flow-based valuation approach, except that it uses a different measure of payoffs. The residual income valuation approach uses expected future earnings and book value of common shareholders' equity to determine the value-relevant expected future payoffs to the investor (that is, the numerator of the preceding general value model), in place of future dividends or future free cash flows.

The rationale for using expected earnings as a basis for valuation is straightforward: Earnings provide the ultimate measure of profitability. Earnings numbers measure the net profits or losses of the firm for the shareholders, the ultimate residual claimants of the performance and risk of the firm. Over the life of the firm, earnings measure the total wealth created by the firm for the shareholders. Instead of focusing valuation on wealth distribution through dividends payments, and instead of focusing valuation on dividend-paying capacity in free cash flows, residual income valuation focuses on *earnings as a periodic measure of shareholder wealth creation.* We described in Exhibit 11.1 in Chapter 11 the differences in valuation approach perspectives between dividends as measures of distributed wealth, free cash flows as measures of distributable wealth, and earnings as value-relevant measures of wealth creation.

Instead of focusing valuation on wealth distributed through expected future payoffs of dividends to shareholders, the valuation process can instead focus on expected future payoffs by measuring expected future wealth creation—the capital the firm creates for the shareholders. To measure wealth creation, the accrual accounting process produces periodic performance statements—income statements that measure and report income—that estimate the net amount of economic resources earned and consumed by the firm each period. Accrual accounting also produces periodic statements of financial position—balance sheets that measure assets, liabilities, and shareholders' equity—that report the economic resources that the firm can control and use to produce expected future economic benefits and the claims on those resources. To produce informative measures of financial performance and position that are relevant and reliable, the accounting profession develops and implements accounting standards through which the accrual accounting process measures income, assets, liabilities, and shareholders' equity using estimates of economic resources earned and consumed each period, rather than just relying on simplistic measures of cash inflows and cash outflows, which often do not reflect economic value received and consumed each period. For some examples, consider that to measure a firm's economic performance and position in a given period, it makes sense to measure the following:

- revenues *earned* from operating performance during that period, not just the amounts of cash collected from customers that period;
- expenses incurred for resources that were *consumed* in that period, not just the amounts of cash paid out of the firm that period;
- the portion of the long-lived resources consumed during that period, such as periodic depreciation of a building each year of its useful life, rather than recognizing the full cost of the building in the year the firm pays for it and ignoring the consumption of the building in all the other years that the firm uses it;
- the cost of commitments made during that period to pay retirement benefits to employees in future periods, rather than ignoring those commitments and measuring their effects only when the firm pays cash.

Accrual accounting earnings are far from perfect performance measures, but, by virtue of accounting standards, they will more closely match the firm's underlying economic performance in a given period than will the net cash inflows or outflows of that period.

Over the life of a firm, the capital invested in the firm by the shareholders plus the income of the firm (the wealth created by the firm for the shareholders) will reflect the value of the firm to the shareholders. Cash is the ultimate medium of exchange; therefore, over the life of the firm, the cash flows that are distributable to shareholders will equal the shareholders' capital investments in the firm plus the lifetime earnings of the firm. Thus, valuation of shareholders' equity in a firm using the capital invested in the firm plus earnings over the life of the firm is equivalent to valuation using distributable cash flows over the life of the firm, and both are equivalent to valuation using dividends over the life of the firm.[5]

EARNINGS-BASED VALUATION: PRACTICAL ADVANTAGES AND CONCERNS

Although earnings, cash flows, and dividends are equally valid bases for valuation, the emphasis placed on earnings by firms and the capital markets makes it a natural starting point for valuation. Earnings numbers provide a measure of performance each period that can be used more directly and efficiently in valuation than cash flows or dividends. Earnings numbers align with the focus of the capital markets and corporate managers and boards of directors on periodic performance measurement, whereas dividends and cash flows do not. Analysts, investors, the capital markets, managers, boards, and the financial press focus on earnings forecasts and earnings reports, rather than free cash flow forecasts and free cash flow amounts. Firms usually don't hold press conferences to announce free cash flows. Analysts rarely publish free cash flow forecasts. The *Wall Street Journal* does not publish a "free cash flow digest" every day. Boards of directors and compensation committees typically do not establish managers' bonus plans based on achieving free cash flow targets. As a practical matter, it is therefore more direct for the analyst to go straight from earnings into valuation, rather than taking a detour to free cash flows.[6]

As Exhibit 13.2 depicts, estimating firm value using free cash flows adds an intermediary step to the valuation process. As we demonstrate in Chapter 12, our approach to valuing a firm using free cash flows requires that we initially forecast future income statements and balance sheets. Then we derive the implied forecasts of cash flows from these income statements and balance sheets by making adjustments for the accruals in earnings, for the cash flows invested in working capital, and for capital expenditures. We use these cash flows to determine free cash flows, which we then use to compute value. Under our residual income approach, we begin valuation immediately after we forecast future income statements and balance sheets. The two valuations should ultimately be the same, but the free cash flows approach requires more computations, which increases the potential for error.

Economists sometimes argue that earnings are not a value-relevant attribute on which to base valuation. They assert that earnings are not as reliable or as meaningful as cash or dividends for valuing investments. When considering earnings, economists sometimes point out that firms pay dividends in cash, not earnings; investors can spend cash but cannot spend earnings for future consumption. This concern is alleviated in valuation, however, by the fact that the differences between earnings, cash flows, and dividends are

[5]Over sufficiently long time periods, net income equals free cash flows to common equity. The effect of year-end accruals to convert cash flows to net income lessens as the measurement period lengthens. The correlation between firms' earnings and stock returns increases as the earnings measurement interval increases. The values of R^2 for various intervals are: one year, 5 percent; two years, 15 percent; five years, 33 percent; ten years, 63 percent. See Peter D. Easton, Trevor S. Harris, and James A. Ohlson, "Aggregate Accounting Earnings Can Explain Most of Security Returns," *Journal of Accounting and Economics* (1992), pp. 119–142.

[6]Researchers have directed considerable attention to the question of whether cash flows or earnings associate more closely with stock returns. This research indicates that earnings and cash flows cumulated over long periods of time are highly positively correlated with stock returns over long periods (for example, five-year periods), but that for shorter periods, earnings show a stronger association with stock returns than cash flows. See Patricia M. Dechow, "Accounting Earnings and Cash Flows as Measures of Firm Performance: The Role of Accounting Accruals," *Journal of Accounting and Economics* (1994), pp. 3–42; C. S. Cheng, Chao-Shin Liu, and Thomas F. Schaefer, "Earnings Permanence and the Incremental Information Content of Cash Flow from Operations," *Journal of Accounting Research* (Spring 1996), pp. 173–181; and Richard G. Sloan, "Do Stock Prices Fully Reflect Information in Accruals and Cash Flows about Future Earnings," *Accounting Review* (July 1996), pp. 289–315.

EXHIBIT 13.2

Residual Income Valuation Requires Fewer Steps Than Free Cash Flows Valuation

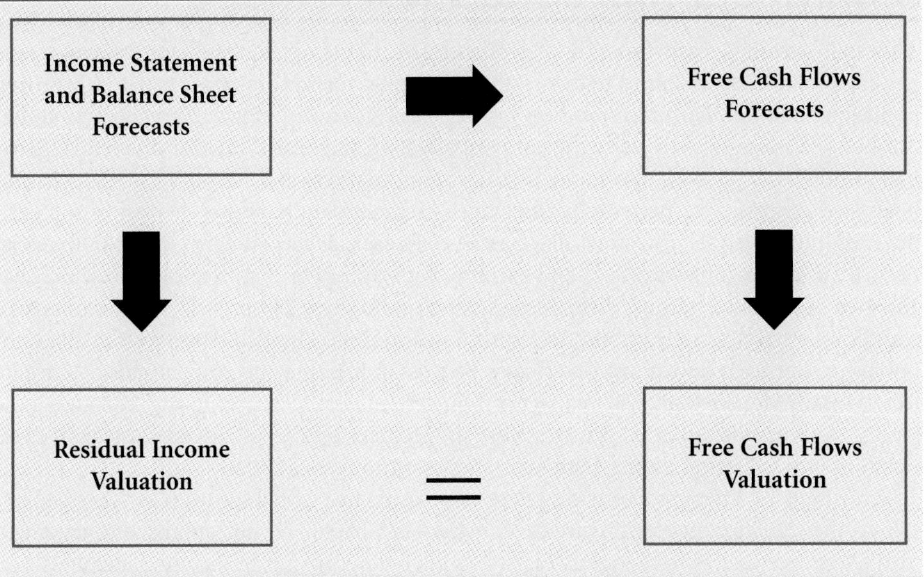

timing differences: earnings numbers measure when the firm creates wealth, whereas free cash flows measure when the firm realizes wealth in cash, and dividends measure when the firm distributes wealth shareholders. Over the life of the firm the present values of future earnings, cash flows, and dividends will be equal.

Some economists worry that accrual accounting earnings numbers reflect accounting methods that no longer reflect underlying economic values—for example, depreciation or amortization expenses based on outdated acquisition cost valuations of assets; expenses for research and development that have turned out to be successful; or advertising expenses that have created economically valuable brand equity. Value measurement based on expected earnings over the remaining life of the firm alleviates this concern. Over time, the accrual accounting process will ultimately self-correct measurement errors in accounting numbers. For example, if fixed asset book values are "too high" or "too low" for a company, over time (and it usually does not take long) accrual accounting will correct itself because the subsequent depreciation expenses will be "too high" or "too low," accordingly. If the current balance sheet does not recognize intellectual capital value created by successful research and development, or brand value created by successful marketing, accrual accounting will correct itself over time as the firm earns returns on this intangible capital.[7]

Some economists voice concerns that earnings can be subject to purposeful management or manipulation by a firm. To be sure, analysts should always be alert to the possibility

[7]Indeed, when an analyst asserts that a firm's current balance sheet accounting numbers do not reflect underlying economic values, how does the analyst know that? When an analyst asserts that a firm's balance sheet omits a valuable intangible asset in the form of intellectual property or brand equity, how has the analyst assessed the amount of the omission? Usually, analysts base assertions like these on their assessments that the firm will generate future profits from operations that utilize these economic assets. Earnings-based valuation captures exactly the same idea. Firm value depends on expected future earnings over the remaining life of the firm.

that some firms may engage in earnings management (or worse, earnings manipulation and fraudulent reporting) in some periods, and we spend considerable attention in earlier chapters to help analysts understand how to assess firms' accounting quality. But this is more of a concern about earnings as a measure of current-period performance than about a firm's lifetime expected earnings for valuation purposes. In addition, this concern is not really an issue for valuation because residual income valuation relies on the analyst's forecasts of expected future earnings, not on past earnings reports that the firm may have managed (unless, of course, the analyst's forecasts naively project that the past managed earnings numbers will persist in future years). Ironically, firms can explicitly manage cash flows each period. Free cash flows each period depend on cash inflows and outflows, which the firm can control by accelerating or delaying certain cash payments or cash collections in that particular period. Over the remaining lifetime of the firm, which is the focus of the analyst's forecasting and valuation, the firm's earnings and cash flows will be determined ultimately by the success of the firm's operating, investing, and financing activities, not by the manipulation of past earnings or cash flows.

THEORETICAL AND CONCEPTUAL FOUNDATIONS FOR RESIDUAL INCOME VALUATION[8]

As Exhibit 13.1 illustrates, the second step toward understanding residual income valuation is to establish the theoretical and conceptual foundation for the residual income valuation approach. The foundation for residual income valuation is the classical dividends-based valuation model from Chapter 11, in which the value of common shareholders' equity is the present value of all future dividends to shareholders over the remaining life of the firm. As described in Chapter 11, in dividends-based valuation we define dividends to be all-inclusive measures of the cash flows between the firm and the common equity shareholders, encompassing cash flows from the firm to shareholders through periodic dividend payments, stock buybacks, and the firm's liquidating dividend, as well as cash flows from the shareholders to the firm when the firm issues shares (which we measure as negative dividends).

As Chapter 11 discusses, we assume that we can estimate (using the CAPM or some other risk-based asset-pricing model) an appropriate rate of return (which we denote R_E) that the capital markets expect for the risk associated with common equity capital in the firm. The dividends-based valuation approach expresses the value of common shareholders' equity (denoted V_0) as the present value of all expected future dividends (which we denote D) with the following general model:

$$V_0 = \sum_{t=1}^{\infty} \frac{D_t}{(1 + R_E)^t} = \frac{D_1}{(1 + R_E)^1} + \frac{D_2}{(1 + R_E)^2} + \frac{D_3}{(1 + R_E)^3} + \cdots$$

Analysts and investors commonly find it desirable to identify and forecast economic variables that determine the firm's future dividends and that can therefore substitute for dividends to yield a valuation that is equivalent to the value estimate one would obtain

[8]Credit for the rigorous development of the residual income valuation model goes to James Ohlson in J. A. Ohlson, "A Synthesis of Security Valuation Theory and the Role of Dividends, Cash Flows, and Earnings," *Contemporary Accounting Research* (Spring 1990), pp. 648–676; J. A. Ohlson, "Earnings, Book Values, and Dividends in Equity Valuation," *Contemporary Accounting Research* (Spring 1995), pp. 661–687; and G. A. Feltham and J. A. Ohlson, "Valuation and Clean Surplus Accounting for Operating and Financial Activities," *Contemporary Accounting Research* (Spring 1995), pp. 216–230. The ideas underlying the earnings-based valuation approach trace to early work by G. A. D. Preinreich, "Annual Survey of Economic Theory: The Theory of Depreciation," *Econometrica* (1938), pp. 219–241; and E. Edwards and P. W. Bell, *The Theory and Measurement of Business Income* (Berkeley: University of California Press, 1961).

using dividends. Accounting numbers provide a solution. Accounting for the book value of common shareholders' equity (denoted *BV*) in a firm can be expressed as follows:

$$BV_t = BV_{t-1} + NI_t - D_t$$

In this expression, book value of common shareholders' equity at the end of Year t (BV_t) is equal to book value at the end of Year $t-1$ (BV_{t-1}) plus net income for Year t (NI_t) minus the all-inclusive dividends during Year t (D_t). As in the dividends valuation approach described in Chapter 11, we assume that accounting for net income and book value of shareholders' equity follows *clean surplus accounting.* Clean surplus accounting simply means that net income includes all of the recognized elements of income of the firm for common equity shareholders (that is, all of the amounts in the income statement and all of the other comprehensive income items) and dividends include all direct capital transactions between the firm and the common equity shareholders (that is, periodic dividend payments, share repurchases, and share issues). We can rearrange the accounting equation for the book value of common shareholders' equity to isolate dividends, as follows:

$$D_t = NI_t + BV_{t-1} - BV_t$$

In this expression, dividends equal net income plus the change in book value from direct capital transactions with common shareholders.

Example 1

Suppose the firm had shareholders' equity on the balance sheet at a book value of \$5,000 at the end of Year $t-1$. Suppose during Year t, the firm earns net income of \$600, pays dividends to shareholders of \$360, issues new stock to raise \$250 of capital, and uses \$50 to repurchase common shares. The book value of shareholders' equity at the end of Year t is as follows:

$$\begin{aligned} BV_t = BV_{t-1} + NI_t - D_t &= \$5{,}000 + \$600 - \$360 + \$250 - \$50 \\ &= \$5{,}000 + \$240 + \$200 = \$5{,}440 \end{aligned}$$

In this example, all-inclusive dividends (D_t) in year t amount to \$160. Using the expression for dividends shows the following:

$$D_t = NI_t + BV_{t-1} - BV_t = \$600 + \$5{,}000 - \$5{,}440 = \$160$$

One can verify this amount of all-inclusive dividends in this example by recognizing that the dividends paid minus the cash received from issuing shares plus the cash paid through share repurchases equals the total amount of all-inclusive dividends of \$160 (= \$360 − \$250 + \$50).

Because dividends equal net income plus the change in book value of common shareholders' equity, we can substitute net income plus the change in the book value of common shareholders' equity into the classical dividends valuation model, as follows:

$$\begin{aligned} V_0 &= \sum_{t=1}^{\infty} \frac{D_t}{(1+R_E)^t} = \sum_{t=1}^{\infty} \frac{NI_t + BV_{t-1} - BV_t}{(1+R_E)^t} \\ &= \frac{NI_1 + BV_0 - BV_1}{(1+R_E)^1} + \frac{NI_2 + BV_1 - BV_2}{(1+R_E)^2} + \frac{NI_3 + BV_2 - BV_3}{(1+R_E)^3} + \cdots \end{aligned}$$

Algebraically,

$$\frac{BV_{t-1}}{(1 + R_E)^t} = \frac{BV_{t-1}}{(1 + R_E)^{t-1}} - \frac{R_E \times BV_{t-1}}{(1 + R_E)^t}$$

We substitute the right-hand side expression for the present value of BV_{t-1} into the equation for V_0, rearrange terms, and simplify to obtain the following expression for the *residual income valuation model*—a valuation model for common shareholders' equity that is consistent with dividends-based valuation, yet relies on earnings and book values:

$$V_0 = BV_0 + \sum_{t=1}^{\infty} \frac{NI_t - (R_E \times BV_{t-1})}{(1 + R_E)^t}$$

$$= BV_0 + \frac{NI_1 - (R_E \times BV_0)}{(1 + R_E)^1} + \frac{NI_2 - (R_E \times BV_1)}{(1 + R_E)^2} + \frac{NI_3 - (R_E \times BV_2)}{(1 + R_E)^3} + \cdots$$

The intuition for the residual income valuation model is straightforward. The value of common shareholders' equity is equal to the book value of common equity, plus the present value of all expected future *residual income,* which is the amount by which expected future earnings exceed the required earnings, for the remaining life of the firm. The *required earnings* (also known as *normal earnings*) of the firm equals the product of the required rate of return on common equity capital times the book value of common equity capital at the beginning of each period. We compute required earnings for period t as $R_E \times BV_{t-1}$. Required earnings reflect the earnings the firm must earn in period t simply to provide a return to common equity that is equal to the cost of common equity capital.

We measure *residual income* (sometimes called *abnormal earnings*) by the subtraction term $NI_t - (R_E \times BV_{t-1})$. Residual income is the difference between the net income the analyst expects the firm to generate and the required earnings of the firm. Residual income in period t measures the amount of wealth that the analyst expects the firm to earn in period t for common equity shareholders above (or below) the earnings required to cover the cost of equity capital. If the analyst expects that the firm will generate net income each period in the future that is exactly equal to required earnings (that is, $NI_t - (R_E \times BV_{t-1}) = 0$ for all future periods), then the analyst expects the firm to exactly cover the cost of equity capital, no more, no less. In that case, the value of the firm is exactly equal to the book value of common shareholders' equity. On the other hand, if the analyst expects that the firm will earn positive amounts of residual income, then the value of the firm is equal to book value of common shareholders' equity plus the present value of all expected future residual income.[9]

Illustrations of Residual Income Measurement and Valuation

The following examples illustrate residual income measurement and the residual income valuation model under various assumptions.

[9]Applications of the concept of residual income in valuation and corporate governance practices can be found in G. B. Stewart, *The Quest for Value* (New York: Harper Collins, 1991), and in the expanding literature on Economic Value Added. As noted earlier, the concept of residual income in the economics literature and the accounting literature predates the commercialization of Economic Value Added by decades.

Example 2

Suppose investors have invested \$10,000 in common equity in a company. Given the risk of the company, the investors expect to earn a 12 percent return, and they expect the company to pay out 100 percent of income in dividends each year. The required earnings of the company each period are as follows:

$$R_E \times BV_{t-1} = 0.12 \times \$10{,}000 = \$1{,}200$$

Suppose the investors forecast that the company will generate exactly \$1,200 in net income each year. The investors should compute the residual income of the firm as follows:

$$NI_t - (R_E \times BV_{t-1}) = \$1{,}200 - (0.12 \times \$10{,}000) = \$0$$

Using the residual income approach, investors would value this firm based on book value plus expected future residual income as follows:

$$\begin{aligned} V_0 &= BV_0 + \sum_{t=1}^{\infty} \frac{NI_t - (R_E \times BV_{t-1})}{(1 + R_E)^t} \\ &= \$10{,}000 + \sum_{t=1}^{\infty} \frac{\$1{,}200_t - (0.12 \times \$10{,}000_{t-1})}{(1 + 0.12)^t} \\ &= \$10{,}000 + \sum_{t=1}^{\infty} \frac{\$0_t}{(1 + 0.12)^t} = \$10{,}000 \end{aligned}$$

In this case, the firm's expected future income exactly equals the required level of earnings necessary to cover the cost of equity capital, so residual income is zero, and the value of the firm is equal to the book value of common equity invested in the firm. The value of the firm under the residual income model is identical to the value determined using the dividends valuation model, which would value the company as a stream of dividends in perpetuity with no growth:

$$V_0 = \frac{\$1{,}200}{.12} = \$10{,}000$$

Example 3

Now assume the same facts as in Example 2, but suppose investors expect the company to pay out no dividends each year, and all the earnings will be reinvested in projects that will generate the investors' required 12 percent rate of return. The required earnings of the firm in period 1 will be as follows:

$$R_E \times BV_0 = 0.12 \times \$10{,}000 = \$1{,}200$$

After adding retained earnings of \$1,200 to book value of equity at the end of period 1, the required earnings of the company in period 2 will be:

$$R_E \times BV_1 = 0.12 \times \$11{,}200 = \$1{,}344$$

After adding retained earnings of \$1,344 to book value of equity at the end of period 2 the required earnings of the company in period 3 will be:

$$R_E \times BV_2 = 0.12 \times \$12{,}544 = \$1{,}505$$

These computations show that the required earnings of the firm will grow as the firm retains and reinvests earnings, on which the investors expect the firm to earn the required rate of return.

Suppose the investors expect that the firm will generate future earnings each period that will exactly match required earnings each period, so earnings in period 1 will be \$1,200, earnings in period 2 will be \$1,344, and earnings in period 3 will be \$1,505. Also suppose the investors expect that the firm will continue to reinvest all of its earnings and will continue to generate the required level of earnings each year over the remaining life of the firm (that is, continuing in period 4 and beyond). We can determine the value of equity capital in the firm using the residual income model as follows:

$$
\begin{aligned}
V_0 &= BV_0 + \sum_{t=1}^{\infty} \frac{NI_t - (R_E \times BV_{t-1})}{(1 + R_E)^t} \\
&= \$10{,}000 + \frac{\$1{,}200 - (0.12 \times \$10{,}000)}{(1.12)^1} + \frac{\$1{,}344 - (0.12 \times \$11{,}200)}{(1.12)^2} \\
&\quad + \frac{\$1{,}505 - (0.12 \times \$13{,}544)}{(1.12)^3} + \sum_{t=4}^{\infty} \frac{NI_t - (0.12 \times BV_{t-1})}{(1 + 0.12)^t} \\
&= \$10{,}000 + \frac{\$0}{(1.12)^1} + \frac{\$0}{(1.12)^2} + \frac{\$0}{(1.12)^3} + \sum_{t=4}^{\infty} \frac{\$0_t}{(1 + 0.12)^t} \\
&= \$10{,}000
\end{aligned}
$$

Example 4

Now assume the same facts as in Example 3, but suppose investors expect that the firm will simply reinvest the earnings in cash or other types of assets that will earn no additional return for each of the next three periods. The investors expect that the firm will continue to earn \$1,200 per period on the original investment of \$10,000, but they expect that the reinvestment of earnings in the first three periods will produce no incremental return. Also assume for simplicity that in period 4 and beyond, the firm will invest in projects that will earn a total of 12 percent return for equity shareholders.

The required earnings of the firm in period 1 will be as follows:

$$R_E \times BV_0 = 0.12 \times \$10{,}000 = \$1{,}200$$

After adding retained earnings of \$1,200 to book value of equity at the end of period 1, the required earnings of the company in period 2 will be:

$$R_E \times BV_1 = 0.12 \times \$11{,}200 = \$1{,}344$$

After adding retained earnings of \$1,200 to book value of equity at the end of period 2, the required earnings of the company in period 3 will be:

$$R_E \times BV_2 = 0.12 \times \$12{,}400 = \$1{,}488$$

We can determine the value of equity capital in the firm using the residual income model as follows:

$$V_0 = BV_0 + \sum_{t=1}^{\infty} \frac{NI_t - (R_E \times BV_{t-1})}{(1 + R_E)^t}$$

$$= \$10{,}000 + \frac{\$1{,}200 - (0.12 \times \$10{,}000)}{(1.12)^1} + \frac{\$1{,}200 - (0.12 \times \$11{,}200)}{(1.12)^2}$$

$$+ \frac{\$1{,}200 - (0.12 \times \$12{,}400)}{(1.12)^3} + \sum_{t=4}^{\infty} \frac{NI_t - (0.12 \times BV_{t-1})}{(1 + 0.12)^t}$$

$$= \$10{,}000 + \frac{\$0}{(1.12)^1} + \frac{\$1{,}200 - \$1{,}344}{(1.12)^2} + \frac{\$1{,}200 - \$1{,}488}{(1.12)^3} + \sum_{t=4}^{\infty} \frac{\$0_t}{(1 + 0.12)^t}$$

$$= \$10{,}000 + \$0 - \$115 - \$205 + \$0$$

$$= \$9{,}680$$

This example shows that by reinvesting earnings to earn zero return rather than the required 12 percent return, the firm's earnings will be \$144 less than required earnings in period 2, and \$288 less than required earnings in period 3. In present value terms, the firm will destroy \$115 of shareholder value in period 2 and \$205 of shareholder value in period 3.

Example 5

Now assume the same facts as in Example 2, in which investors have invested \$10,000 in common equity in a firm, expect to earn a 12 percent return, and expect the company to pay out 100 percent of income in dividends each year. Now suppose investors expect that the firm will earn net income of \$1,000 in Year +1, \$2,000 in Year +2, \$1,500 in Year +3, and \$1,200 each year thereafter. Investors should compute the residual income valuation as follows:

$$V_0 = BV_0 + \sum_{t=1}^{\infty} \frac{NI_t - (R_E \times BV_{t-1})}{(1 + R_E)^t}$$

$$= \$10{,}000 + \frac{\$1{,}000 - (0.12 \times \$10{,}000)}{(1.12)^1} + \frac{\$2{,}000 - (0.12 \times \$10{,}000)}{(1.12)^2}$$

$$+ \frac{\$1{,}500 - (0.12 \times \$10{,}000)}{(1.12)^3} + \sum_{t=4}^{\infty} \frac{\$1{,}200 - (0.12 \times \$10{,}000)}{(1 + 0.12)^t}$$

$$= \$10{,}000 + \frac{-\$200}{(1.12)^1} + \frac{\$800}{(1.12)^2} + \frac{\$300}{(1.12)^3} + \sum_{t=4}^{\infty} \frac{\$0}{(1 + 0.12)^t}$$

$$= \$10{,}000 - \$178 + \$638 + \$214 + \$0$$

$$= \$10{,}674$$

In this example, the firm will generate residual income amounts of −\$200 in Year +1, \$800 in Year +2, \$300 in Year +3, and \$0 each year thereafter. The firm destroys shareholder wealth in Year +1 by failing to earn sufficient income to cover the cost of equity capital, but the firm generates increasing shareholder wealth in Years +2 and +3, and exactly covers the cost of equity capital each year thereafter. Given these assumptions, the present value of the firm under the residual income model is \$10,674.

RESIDUAL INCOME VALUATION MODEL WITH FINITE HORIZON EARNINGS FORECASTS AND CONTINUING VALUE COMPUTATION

Analysts cannot precisely forecast income statements and balance sheets of firms for many years into the future. Therefore, analysts commonly forecast income statements and balance sheets over a foreseeable, finite horizon and then make simplifying growth rate assumptions for the years continuing after the forecast horizon. We can modify the residual income valuation model to include explicit forecasts of net income and book value of common equity through Year T (where T is a finite horizon, say five or ten years in the future) and then apply a constant growth rate assumption (denoted g) to project residual income for Year T+1 and all years thereafter. We used similar approaches to forecast and value dividends in Chapter 11 and free cash flows in Chapter 12.

To deal with the uncertainty in long-run forecasts, the analyst will find it desirable to forecast net income, book value of shareholders' equity, and residual income over an explicit forecast horizon, until the point at which the analyst expects the firm's growth pattern to settle into steady-state growth, during which earnings, dividends, and cash flows will grow at a steady, predictable rate. We refer to residual income in this long-run steady-state growth period as *continuing* residual income, because it reflects residual income earned by the firm continuing into the long-run future. The long-run steady-state growth rate in future continuing residual income could be positive, negative, or zero. Steady-state growth in residual income could be driven by long-run expectations for inflation, the industry's sales, the economy in general, or the population. In some industries, competitive dynamics eventually drive long-run projections of the future returns earned by the firm (for example, the future ROCE) to an equilibrium level equal to the long-run expected cost of equity capital in the firm. Once a firm reaches that point, the firm can be expected to earn zero residual income in the future. The analyst should select a continuing growth rate in residual income that captures realistic long-run expectations for the firm.

To compute residual income in Year T+1, the analyst should first project Year T+1 net income by multiplying Year T net income by the growth factor $(1 + g)$. Year T+1 residual income (denoted RI_{T+1}) can then be computed as follows:

$$RI_{T+1} = [NI_T \times (1 + g)] - [R_E \times BV_T]$$

By estimating RI_{T+1} this way, the analyst will also be able to apply the same uniform long-run growth factor $(1 + g)$ to estimate Year T+1 income statement and balance sheet amounts, and compute internally consistent projections for Year T+1 free cash flows and dividends, which the analyst can then use in free cash flow value models and dividends value models to determine internally consistent value estimates. We demonstrated these approaches in Chapters 11 and 12.

In addition, by computing RI_{T+1} this way, the analyst will avoid a potential mistake in forecasting RI_{T+1} by simply projecting $RI_{T+1} = RI_T \times (1 + g)$. This shortcut projection implicitly assumes the following:

$$RI_T \times (1 + g) = [NI_T - (R_E \times BV_{T-1})] \times (1 + g) = NI_T \times (1 + g) - R_E \times BV_{T-1} \times (1 + g)$$

This assumption requires $BV_T = BV_{T-1} \times (1 + g)$, which is not necessarily true. In words, residual income in Year T+1 depends on book value at the end of Year T. We assume constant growth at rate $(1 + g)$ in residual income beginning in Year T+1. Thus, the only way residual income in Year T+1 will equal residual income in Year T times (1 + g) is if book value in Year T happened to grow at the same rate (1 + g). This will not necessarily be the case. The analyst can easily avoid this forecast error for RI_{T+1} by correctly computing $RI_{T+1} = [NI_T \times (1 + g)] - [R_E \times BV_T]$.

After computing RI_{T+1}, the analyst can treat RI_{T+1} as a growing perpetuity of residual income beginning in Year T+1. The analyst can discount the perpetuity of residual income to present value using the perpetuity-with-growth value model described in Chapters 11 and 12. We include the continuing value computation into the finite-horizon residual income model as follows:

$$V_0 = BV_0 + \sum_{t=1}^{\infty} \frac{NI_t - (R_E \times BV_{t-1})}{(1 + R_E)^t}$$

$$= \underset{(1)}{BV_0} + \underset{(2)}{\sum_{t=1}^{T} \frac{NI_t - (R_E \times BV_{t-1})}{(1 + R_E)^t}}$$

$$+ \underset{(3)}{\left[((NI_T \times (1 + g)) - (R_E \times BV_T)) \times \frac{1}{(R_E - g)} \times \frac{1}{(1 + R_E)^T}\right]}$$

This model computes the value of common equity based on three parts: (1) book value of shareholders' equity at time $t = 0$ (the BV_0 term); (2) the present value of residual income over the explicit forecast horizon through Year T (the summation term); and (3) continuing value based on the present value of residual income as a perpetuity with growth beginning in Year T+1 (the term in brackets). To compute continuing value, we first compute residual income in Year T+1 (the term $NI_T \times (1 + g) - (R_E \times BV_T)$). We assume that residual income in Year T+1 will grow at constant rate g in perpetuity, beginning in Year T+1, so we compute continuing value as of the start of Year T+1 using the perpetuity-with-growth valuation factor (the term $1/(R_E - g)$). Finally, we discount continuing value to present value at time $t = 0$ using the present value factor (the term $1/(1 + R_E)^T$).

VALUATION OF PEPSICO USING THE RESIDUAL INCOME MODEL

Step 3 toward understanding residual income valuation, as Exhibit 13.1 illustrates, is the practical application step. In this step, we apply the residual income valuation approach to value the common shareholders' equity in PepsiCo. As Chapters 11 and 12 describe, PepsiCo shares closed trading at \$51.94 on the New York Stock Exchange at the end of Year 4. In Chapter 11, we determined our central estimate of the value of PepsiCo shares at the end of Year 4 to be roughly \$57.36 using the projected financial statement forecasts developed in Chapter 10 and applying the dividends-based valuation approach. We obtained the same value estimate for PepsiCo shares in Chapter 12, using the same projected financial statement forecasts developed in Chapter 10 and the free cash flow valuation approaches. We next illustrate the valuation of PepsiCo shares using the residual income valuation model techniques described in this chapter and the forecasts developed in Chapter 10. The Forecast and Valuation spreadsheets of FSAP (Appendix C) also demonstrate the forecasts and valuation estimates.

We value PepsiCo with the residual income approach, following these five steps:

1. Estimate the appropriate discount rate using the risk-adjusted required rate of return on equity capital.
2. Determine the book value of common shareholders' equity on PepsiCo's Year 4 balance sheet, project expected future residual income from the financial statement forecasts for PepsiCo described in Chapter 10, and project long-run growth in residual income in the continuing periods beyond the forecast horizon.
3. Discount the expected future residual income to present value, including continuing value.
4. Add the book value of equity and the present value of expected future residual income to determine the total value of common shareholders' equity, correct for midyear discounting, and then divide by the number of shares outstanding to convert this total to an estimate of share value for PepsiCo.
5. Examine sensitivity analysis for the estimate of PepsiCo's share value to determine the reasonable range of values for PepsiCo shares.

After illustrating this five-step valuation process, we will compare the range of reasonable values to PepsiCo's share price in the market and suggest an appropriate investment decision indicated by our analysis.

Discount Rates for Residual Income

To compute the appropriate discount rate for residual income, we again use the CAPM to estimate the market's required rate of return on PepsiCo's common stock, as demonstrated in Chapters 11 and 12. At the end of Year 4, PepsiCo's common stock had a market beta of roughly 0.75. At the same time, U.S. Treasury bills with one to five years to maturity traded with a yield of approximately 4.0 percent, which we use as the risk-free rate. Assuming a 5.0 percent market risk premium, the CAPM indicates that PepsiCo had a cost of common equity capital of 7.75 percent $[R_E = 7.75 = 4.0 + (0.75 \times 5.0)]$ at the end of Year 4, the beginning of the valuation period. We used this same cost of common equity capital to value PepsiCo shares in Chapter 11 using the present value of future dividends and in Chapter 12 using the free cash flows to common equity shareholders' valuation model.

Using the residual income valuation model, we do not need to compute the weighted average cost of capital. This does not mean that we ignore debt capital or the costs related to debt capital. Instead, we rely on accounting to capture the effects of debt. We project book value of shareholders' equity after subtracting debt from total assets, and we project net income after subtracting interest expense net of tax effects.

PepsiCo's Book Value of Equity and Residual Income

According to PepsiCo's balance sheet (Appendix A), book value of common shareholders' equity is $13,572.0 million at the end of Year 4. This amount is the starting point for the residual income valuation model, the term denoted BV_0 in the valuation equations.

We project residual income each period in the finite forecast horizon in four steps. First, we compute forecasts of expected future net income for each period. Second, we compute forecasts of expected future book value of common shareholders' equity at the beginning of each period. Third, we compute expected future required income, which is the product of the cost of equity capital times the book value of common shareholders' equity at the beginning of each period (that is, we compute required income as $R_E \times BV_{t-1}$). Fourth, we determine expected future residual income by subtracting expected future required income from expected future net income [$= NI_t - (R_E \times BV_{t-1})$].

We completed the first and second steps in Chapter 10. Chapter 10 developed our projections of PepsiCo's future net income by making specific assumptions regarding each line item in the income statement. Chapter 10 also developed specific forecasts of common shareholders' equity on the balance sheet by making specific assumptions about PepsiCo's assets, liabilities, and common equity, including specific forecasts of dividends, stock issues, and stock buybacks. Exhibit 13.3 presents projections of PepsiCo's net income, book value of shareholders' equity, required income, and residual income through Year +5 using the forecasts discussed in Chapter 10 and a 7.75 percent cost of equity capital.

In Year +1, for example, we projected PepsiCo's net income to be $4,381.9 million. We forecasted other comprehensive income items to be zero, so projected comprehensive income and net income are equal. (Recall from our earlier discussion that the residual income model requires that we measure income for common equity shareholders comprehensively, using clean surplus accounting.) We projected that preferred stock outstanding would be liquidated, requiring liquidating dividends of $159.0 million in Year +1, so net income available to common shareholders is $4,222.9 million (= $4,381.9 million − $159.0 million). Given that PepsiCo's book value of common shareholders' equity at the beginning of Year +1 is $13,572.0 million and PepsiCo's cost of equity capital is 7.75 percent, we project Year +1 required earnings to be $1,051.8 million (= 0.0775 × $13,572.0 million). Therefore, we project that Year +1 residual income will be $3,171.1 million (= $4,222.9 million − $1,051.8 million).

To project PepsiCo's residual income continuing in Year +6 and beyond, we forecast that PepsiCo can sustain long-run growth in net income and book value of equity of 3.0 percent per year, consistent with long-run average growth in the economy of 3.0 percent. It is the same assumption we made in forecasting long-run growth in Year +6 and beyond for dividends in Chapter 11 and for free cash flows in Chapter 12. We project that

EXHIBIT 13.3

Valuation of PepsiCo
Present Value of Residual Income Year +1 through Year +5

	Year +1	Year +2	Year +3	Year +4	Year +5
Common Shareholders' Equity (at beginning of year; denoted BV_{t-1})	$13,572.0	$14,388.1	$14,746.8	$15,313.3	$15,908.1
Comprehensive Income Available for Common Shareholders	$ 4,222.9	$ 4,503.2	$ 4,887.7	$ 5,216.8	$ 5,580.4
Required Income ($R_E \times BV_{t-1}$)	$ 1,051.8	$ 1,115.1	$ 1,142.9	$ 1,186.8	$ 1,232.9
Residual Income [$NI_t - (R_E \times BV_{t-1})$]	$ 3,171.0	$ 3,388.1	$ 3,744.8	$ 4,030.0	$ 4,347.6
Present Value Factors (R_E = 7.75 percent)	0.928	0.861	0.799	0.742	0.689
Present Value Residual Income	$ 2,943.0	$ 2,918.2	$ 2,993.5	$ 2,989.8	$ 2,993.4
Sum of Present Value Residual Income, Year +1 through Year +5	$14,837.8				

Year +6 residual income will be \$4,436.6 million, computed by projecting Year +5 net income to grow by 3.0 percent and subtracting required earnings, measured as the equity cost of capital times book value at the end of Year +5, as follows:

$$
\begin{aligned}
RI_6 &= [NI_5 \times (1 + g)] - [R_E \times BV_5] \\
&= (\$5{,}580.4 \text{ million} \times 1.03) - (0.0775 \times \$16{,}918.8 \text{ million}) \\
&= \$5{,}747.8 \text{ million} - \$1{,}311.2 \text{ million} = \$4{,}436.6 \text{ million}
\end{aligned}
$$

Discounting PepsiCo's Residual Income to Present Value

We discount residual income to present value using PepsiCo's 7.75 percent cost of equity capital. Exhibit 13.3 shows that the sum of the present value of PepsiCo's residual income from Year +1 through Year +5 is \$14,837.8 million.

We compute the present value of PepsiCo's continuing value of residual income as a perpetuity beginning in Year +6 with growth at a 3.0 percent rate. To compute the continuing value estimate, we use the perpetuity-with-growth valuation model, which determines the present value of the growing perpetuity at the start of the perpetuity period. We then discount that value back to present value at time $t = 0$. We compute the present value of the continuing value of PepsiCo's residual income as follows (allowing for rounding):

$$
\begin{aligned}
\text{Continuing Value}_0 &= [NI_5 \times (1 + g) - (R_E \times BV_5)] \times [1/(R_E - g)] \times [1/(1 + R_E)^5] \\
&= [(\$5{,}580.4 \text{ million} \times 1.03) - (0.0775 \times \$16{,}918.8 \text{ million})] \\
&\quad \times [1/(0.0775 - 0.03)] \times [1/(1 + 0.0775)^5] \\
&= [\$5{,}747.8 \text{ million} - \$1{,}311.2 \text{ million}] \times 21.0526 \times 0.6885 \\
&= \$4{,}436.6 \text{ million} \times 21.0526 \times 0.6885 \\
&= \$64{,}309.3 \text{ million}
\end{aligned}
$$

The total present value of PepsiCo's residual income is the sum of these two parts:

Present Value Residual Income Year +1 through Year +5 (Exhibit 13.3)	\$14,837.8 million
Present Value of Continuing Value in Year +6 and Beyond	\$64,309.3 million
Present Value of Residual Income	\$79,147.1 million

Necessary Adjustments to Compute Common Equity Share Value

To compute the total value of common equity, we add PepsiCo's book value of common equity to the present value of residual income. The total value of common equity of PepsiCo as of the beginning of Year +1 is \$92,719.1 million (= \$13,572.0 million + \$79,147.1 million).

As Chapter 11 and 12 describe, our present value calculations overdiscount because they discount each year's residual income for full periods when, in fact, income is generated throughout each period and should be discounted from the midpoint of each year to the present. Therefore, to make the correction we multiply the total by the midyear discounting adjustment factor $[1 + (R_E/2) = 1 + (0.0775/2) = 1.03875]$. Therefore, the total present value of common shareholders' equity should be $96,312.0 million (= $92,719.1 million × 1.03875).

Dividing by 1,679 million shares outstanding indicates that PepsiCo's common equity shares have a value of $57.36 per share. This value estimate is identical to the value estimate based on dividends in Chapter 11 and free cash flows to common equity shareholders in Chapter 12. Exhibit 13.4 summarizes the computations to arrive at PepsiCo's common equity share value. Exhibit 13.5 presents the residual income model valuation for PepsiCo from FSAP.

Sensitivity Analysis and Investment Decision Making

We cautioned in Chapters 11 and 12 and we reiterate here that one should not place too much confidence in the precision of firm value estimates using these (or any) forecasts for residual income over the remaining life of any firm, even a mature firm like PepsiCo. Although we have constructed these forecasts and value estimates with care, the forecasting and valuation process has an inherently high degree of uncertainty and estimation error. Therefore, the analyst should not rely too heavily on any one point estimate of the value of a firm's shares, and instead should describe a reasonable range of values for a firm's shares.

Two critical forecasting and valuation parameters are the long-run growth assumption, which we forecast to be 3.0 percent, and the cost of equity capital, which we forecast

EXHIBIT 13.4

Valuation of PepsiCo Using the Residual Income Valuation Model

Valuation Steps	Computations	Amounts
Sum of Present Value Residual Income Year +1 through Year +5	See Exhibit 13.3	+$14,837.8
Add Present Value of Continuing Value	Year +6 residual income assumed to grow at 3.0%; discounted at 7.75%	+ 64,309.3
Total Present Value Residual Income		=$79,147.1
Add Beginning Book Value of Equity	Book Value of Equity from Year 4 Balance Sheet	+ 13,572.0
Total		=$92,719.1
Adjust to Midyear Discounting	Multiply by $1 + (R_E / 2)$	× 1.03875
Total Present Value of Common Equity		=$96,312.0
Divide by Shares Outstanding	1,679 million shares outstanding	÷ 1,679.0
Estimated Value per Share		=$ 57.36
Current Price per Share		$ 51.94
Percent Difference	Positive number indicates underpricing	10%

EXHIBIT 13.5

Valuation of PepsiCo
Residual Income Valuation Approach

Residual Income Valuation	Year +1	Year +2	Year +3	Year +4	Year +5	Year +6
Comprehensive Income Available for Common Shareholders	$ 4,222.9	$ 4,503.2	$ 4,887.7	$ 5,216.8	$ 5,580.4	$ 5,747.8
Lagged Book Value of Common Shareholders' Equity (at t − 1)	$13,572.0	$14,388.1	$14,746.8	$15,313.3	$15,908.1	$16,918.8
Required Earnings	$ 1,051.8	$ 1,115.1	$ 1,142.9	$ 1,186.8	$ 1,232.9	$ 1,311.2
Residual Income	$ 3,171.0	$ 3,388.1	$ 3,744.8	$ 4,030.0	$ 4,347.6	$ 4,436.6
Present Value Factors	0.928	0.861	0.799	0.742	0.689	
Present Value Residual Income	$ 2,943.0	$ 2,918.2	$ 2,993.5	$ 2,989.8	$ 2,993.4	
Sum of Present Value Residual Income	$14,837.8					
Present Value of Continuing Value	$64,309.3					
Total	$79,147.1					
Add Beginning Book Value of Equity	$13,572.0					
Present Value of Equity	$92,719.1					
Adjust to Midyear Discounting	1.03875					
Total Present Value of Equity	$96,312.0					
Shares Outstanding	1,679.0					
Estimated Value per Share	$ 57.36					
Current Share Price	$ 51.94					
Percent Difference	10%					
(Value/price) − 1: positive number indicates underpricing						

to be 7.75 percent. With these assumptions, our base case estimate is that PepsiCo common shares should be valued at roughly $57 per share. As in Chapters 11 and 12, we assess the sensitivity of our estimate of PepsiCo's share value by varying these two parameters across reasonable ranges. Exhibit 13.6 contains the results of sensitivity analysis varying the long-run growth assumption from 0 to 10 percent and the cost of equity capital from 5 to 20 percent. The data in Exhibit 13.6 show that share value estimates of PepsiCo are inversely related to discount rates, holding growth constant. In contrast, share value estimates are positively related to growth rates, holding discount rates constant. We omit share value estimates from this analysis when the growth rate equals or exceeds the discount rate, because then the continuing value computation is meaningless.

As we observed in our sensitivity analyses in Chapters 11 and 12, these data suggest that our value estimate is sensitive to slight variations of our baseline assumptions of 3.0 percent long-run growth and a 7.75 percent discount rate. Slight adverse variations in valuation parameters reduce PepsiCo's share value to as low as $41, whereas slightly favorable variations increase PepsiCo's share value to nearly $85. If our forecast and valuation assumptions are realistic, our baseline value estimate for PepsiCo is $57 per share at the end of Year 4. At that time, the market price of $51.94 per share indicates that PepsiCo shares were underpriced by about 10 percent. Under our forecast assumptions, PepsiCo's share value could vary within a range of a low of $41 per share to a high of $85 per share with only minor perturbations in our growth rate and discount rate assumptions. Given PepsiCo's $51.94 share price, these value estimates would have supported a buy recommendation at the end of Year 4, but not a strong buy.

RESIDUAL INCOME MODEL IMPLEMENTATION ISSUES

The residual income valuation model is a rigorous and straightforward valuation approach, but the analyst should be aware of three important implementation issues: (1) "dirty surplus" accounting items, (2) common stock transactions, and (3) portions of net income attributable to equity claimants other than common shareholders. The next three sections describe these three issues.

Dirty Surplus Accounting

The first implementation issue arises because the residual income model requires that the analyst follow clean surplus accounting in developing expectations for future earnings, dividends, and book values. This means that the expected future income amounts should include all of the income recognized by the firm for the common equity shareholders, and all-inclusive dividends should include all capital transactions with common equity shareholders. Currently, U.S. GAAP does not follow clean surplus accounting. U.S. GAAP admits four *dirty surplus* items. These items are the other comprehensive income amounts that firms recognize directly in shareholders' equity. The four dirty surplus items are unrealized fair value gains and losses on available-for-sale investment securities; foreign currency translation gains and losses; minimum pension liability adjustments; and the effects of cash flow hedges. U.S. GAAP requires that firms recognize these items in *comprehensive income* but does not require that firms recognize them in net income until they are realized (for example, when the firm realizes gains or losses by selling an available-for-sale investment security). Firms usually report comprehensive income in the Statement of Common Shareholders' Equity or in a note to the financial statements.

For example, PepsiCo reported in the Consolidated Statement of Common Shareholders' Equity and again in Note 13, "Accumulated Other Comprehensive Loss" (Appendix A),

EXHIBIT 13.6

Valuation of PepsiCo
Sensitivity Analysis of Share Value Estimates to Growth and Equity Cost of Capital

Residual Income Valuation Sensitivity Analysis:

	Long-Run Growth Assumptions										
	0%	**1%**	**2%**	**3%**	**4%**	**5%**	**6%**	**7%**	**8%**	**9%**	**10%**
Discount Rates											
5%	64.45	76.44	96.42	136.39	256.30	na	na	na	na	na	na
6%	53.44	60.92	72.16	90.87	128.31	240.63	na	na	na	na	na
7%	45.59	50.60	57.61	68.13	85.66	120.73	225.92	na	na	na	na
7.75%	41.04	44.87	50.03	57.36	68.61	88.03	129.64	282.23	na	na	na
9%	35.16	37.72	41.02	45.41	51.56	60.78	76.15	106.89	199.12	na	na
10%	31.53	33.45	35.84	38.93	43.04	48.79	57.43	71.82	100.59	186.92	na
11%	28.56	30.03	31.83	34.07	36.96	40.80	46.19	54.27	67.73	94.66	175.46
12%	26.10	27.24	28.62	30.30	32.40	35.10	38.70	43.73	51.29	63.89	89.09
13%	24.02	24.93	26.00	27.28	28.85	30.82	33.34	36.71	41.42	48.49	60.27
14%	22.25	22.97	23.82	24.82	26.02	27.49	29.33	31.69	34.83	39.24	45.85
15%	20.71	21.30	21.98	22.77	23.71	24.83	26.20	27.92	30.12	33.06	37.18
16%	19.37	19.85	20.40	21.04	21.78	22.65	23.70	24.98	26.58	28.64	31.39
17%	18.20	18.59	19.04	19.56	20.15	20.84	21.65	22.63	23.83	25.32	27.25
18%	17.16	17.48	17.85	18.27	18.75	19.30	19.95	20.71	21.62	22.74	24.13
19%	16.23	16.50	16.81	17.15	17.54	17.99	18.50	19.10	19.81	20.66	21.70
20%	15.39	15.62	15.88	16.16	16.48	16.85	17.26	17.74	18.30	18.96	19.75

that in Year 4 other comprehensive income items totaled \$381 million. As a result of these adjustments in Year 4, PepsiCo's comprehensive income was \$4,593 million (= net income of \$4,212 million plus comprehensive income items totaling \$381 million). By the end of Year 4, total accumulated other comprehensive loss (which measures total accumulated comprehensive income adjustments over the life of PepsiCo and is included as a component of shareholders' equity) declined from −\$1,267 million to −\$886 million. As Chapters 9 and 10 describe, the main culprit driving other comprehensive income for PepsiCo has been foreign currency translation adjustments, amounting to \$401 million in Year 4, and a cumulative total of −\$720 million.

The four dirty surplus items in U.S. GAAP typically arise because of unrealized gains and losses attributable to changes in market prices, such as changes in investment security fair values, foreign currency exchange rates, or interest rates. Thus, in expectation, the analyst may determine that such gains and losses are certain to occur, but that it is impossible to predict with precision either the sign or amount of the future unrealized gains and losses. In that case, the analyst would likely forecast the expected future dirty surplus items to be zero, on average, and therefore forecast net income and comprehensive income to be equal. We used this assumption in building forecasts for PepsiCo in Chapter 10.

On the other hand, if the analyst can project the amounts and timing of future unrealized gains and losses from available-for-sale investment securities, foreign currency translations, minimum pension liability adjustments, or cash flow hedges, then the analyst should incorporate these unrealized gains and losses in comprehensive income forecasts, and base the residual income valuation on comprehensive income rather than net income. To allow for either possibility (expectations of zero or nonzero comprehensive income adjustments in the future), the residual income model in the Valuation spreadsheet in FSAP begins with forecasts of future comprehensive income.

Common Stock Transactions

Common stock transactions that change the intrinsic value of existing common shareholders' equity can also cause violations of the clean surplus accounting relation and hinder the ability of the residual income model to measure firm value. To illustrate, consider that when the firm sells common shares or repurchases common shares at transaction prices that exactly reflect the intrinsic value of the shares (that is, share sales or repurchases that are zero net present value projects for existing shareholders), then these transactions leave the existing shareholders' value unchanged, and clean surplus accounting holds for these transactions. On the other hand, suppose the firm issues common shares at a price that is lower than their intrinsic value. This transaction has a dilutive effect on (that is, reduces the value of) all of the existing common shares. Net income and the all-inclusive dividend do not reflect this loss in value to existing shareholders, so it violates clean surplus accounting.

It is reasonable to assume that clean surplus accounting for most common stock transactions holds, in expectation, because most issues and repurchases of common shares are accounted for at market value. Most of these capital transactions will likely have zero net present value effects on existing shareholders and will conform to clean surplus accounting.

The most prominent exception, however, is the issuance of common equity shares for employee stock options exercises. As Chapter 9 discusses, the exercise of stock options by employees at strike prices below the prevailing market price dilutes the existing shareholders' equity value. If the firm estimates the fair value of the employee stock options at the time it grants them, and recognizes the estimated value of the grants as an expense in measuring net income, then it mitigates the violation of clean surplus accounting. In this case, the analyst should forecast the fair value of expected future options grants and subtract these estimated expenses in forecasting expected future net income. We followed this approach in Chapter 10 in building our forecasts of net income for PepsiCo, because PepsiCo expenses the fair value of stock options at the date of grant. Under *Statement No. 123 (Revised 2004),* all firms following U.S. GAAP will expense the fair value of stock options at the date of grant beginning with fiscal years beginning after June 2005. Prior to the implementation of this statement, however, some firms will elect not to recognize the fair value of stock options grants as an expense in income. Under U.S. GAAP, these firms must disclose an estimate of the expense in the notes to the annual financial statements. The analyst can use these disclosures to estimate future expenses for stock options grants.

It is not uncommon for firms to repurchase common equity shares in the market and then use these shares to fulfill stock option exercises. In that case, the accounting for the stock repurchase at market value and the issue of the treasury share at the option strike price captures the dilutive effect of the option exercise on shareholders' equity. For example, if the firm repurchases a share in the market for $60 and issues it to an employee exercising an option with a strike price of $40, then the net effect of the accounting will capture the $20 decrease in shareholders' equity. On the other hand, if the firm fulfills stock option exercises by issuing new shares (or treasury shares repurchased in prior periods at prices that do not reflect the current-period market value), then the accounting will reflect the issue of the shares at the option's strike price, and the dilutive effect on existing shareholders will violate clean surplus accounting.

In Year 4, for example, PepsiCo reports in the Consolidated Statement of Common Shareholders' Equity (Appendix A) that it repurchased a total of 58 million shares for $2,994 million, implying an average cost of $51.62 per share. PepsiCo also discloses in that statement that it issued 32 million treasury shares for options exercises, thereby increasing equity capital by $1,136 million ($1,434 million in the Repurchased Common Stock account less $298 million in the Capital in Excess of Par Value account), for an average book value of $35.50 per share issued. The difference between the average cost of $51.62 per share and average book value of $35.50 per share indicates an average dilution of $16.12 per share issued. Given that PepsiCo issued 32 million shares, the total dilution is $516 million. With 1,679 shares outstanding, that amounts to $0.307 dilution per outstanding share, which is roughly 0.6 percent of the year-end share price of $51.94.

If the analyst is valuing a firm with substantial amounts of options outstanding that the analyst expects will be exercised (options that the analyst expects will ultimately expire or be forfeited pose no problems for valuation), or a firm that is likely to grant large numbers of options in the future that are likely to be exercised, then the analyst should explicitly forecast future stock-based compensation expenses that include the fair values of future options grants, and forecast the future dilutive effects of options exercises on the book value of common equity, and include these effects in valuation.[10]

Portions of Net Income Attributable to Equity Claimants Other Than Common Shareholders

In some circumstances, a portion of net income is attributable to equity claimants other than common shareholders. For example, preferred stockholders may be entitled to preference in dividends over common shareholders. Also, minority shareholders have a claim on the portion of net income that is attributable to their share of the equity in the

[10]For an illustration of stock options and valuation, see Leonard Soffer, "SFAS No. 123 Disclosures and Discounted Cash Flow Valuation," *Accounting Horizons* 14, no. 2 (June 2000), pp. 169–189.

subsidiary they own. For purposes of residual income measurement and valuation, these portions of net income do not represent net income available to the common equity shareholders and should be excluded from residual income. Residual income valuation should be based on the net income available for common equity shareholders. In the case of PepsiCo in Year +1, for example, we forecast that PepsiCo will pay a $159 million liquidating dividend to retire outstanding preferred stock, so we measure residual income after subtracting this dividend to determine net income available to common equity shareholders. PepsiCo did not have any minority-equity shareholders at the end of Year 4.

CONSISTENCY IN RESIDUAL INCOME, DIVIDENDS, AND FREE CASH FLOW VALUE ESTIMATES

As Exhibit 13.1 illustrates, the fourth and final step toward understanding residual income valuation, and valuation in general, is to understand the internal consistency between the dividends valuation approach, the free cash flows valuation approach, and the earnings-based valuation approach. Throughout Chapters 11, 12, and 13, we have anchored the discussions of each of the valuation approaches on the common, general valuation model, and we have conceptually and theoretically linked each valuation approach to that general model. Along the way, we have demonstrated the internal consistency of these approaches through our analysis and valuation of PepsiCo, and we have demonstrated the equivalence of value estimates based on residual income, free cash flows, and dividends.

The former baseball player and coach Yogi Berra is reported to have said, "In theory, practice and theory are the same. In practice, they're not." In theory, all three valuation models, when correctly implemented with internally consistent assumptions, will produce the same estimates of value. In practice, the analyst may discover that the three models yield different value estimates. If so, the analyst should check the analysis for one or more of the following three common errors (errors that we have experienced ourselves):[11]

1. *Incomplete or inconsistent earnings and cash flow forecasts.* The analyst should be sure that projected earnings, cash flows, and dividends are complete and based on assumptions that are consistent with one another. As Chapter 10 emphasizes, the analyst can reduce the chance of incomplete or inconsistent forecasts by forecasting complete financial statements in which the balance sheets balance, the income statements add up, and the statements of cash flows articulate with the income statements and the changes in the balance sheets. The analyst should also ensure that projected shareholders' equity reflects clean surplus accounting. As suggested in Chapter 10, relying on the additivity and articulation of financial statements will help the analyst avoid inconsistent forecasts.
2. *Inconsistent estimates of weighted average costs of capital.* Suppose the analyst computes the present value of free cash flows to all debt and equity capital using the weighted average cost of capital as a discount rate, and then subtracts the present value of debt and preferred stock to determine the present value of common equity value (as shown in Chapter 12). The only way the value estimates from this approach will be identical with value estimates from the residual income approach or the dividends approach is if the weighted average cost of capital uses weights

[11]For a more complete description of diagnosing errors that can cause differences in the three value model estimates, see Russell Lundholm and Terry O'Keefe, "Reconciling Value Estimates from the Discounted Cash Flow Model and the Residual Income Model," *Contemporary Accounting Research* 2001 (Summer), pp. 1–26.

that are perfectly internally consistent with the present values of debt, preferred stock, and common equity. Thus, the analyst may have to iterate the computation of the weighted average cost of capital a number of times until the weights and present values are all internally consistent.

3. *Incorrect continuing value computations.* In Chapters 11, 12, and 13, we have emphasized that the analyst must take care to estimate the continuing value estimate, particularly the Year T+1 amount for residual income, free cash flow, and dividends. If the analyst uses inconsistent assumptions to project the beginning amounts used to compute continuing value, then the value estimates will not agree. To avoid this problem, the analyst should first project the Year T+1 income statement and balance sheet amounts assuming a uniform rate of growth $(1 + g)$, and then use these projections to derive the Year T+1 amounts for residual income, free cash flow, and dividends. The derived amounts for Year T+1 can then be used as the starting values of the perpetuity to calculate continuing value. A common error analysts make is to simply assume that residual income, free cash flows, and dividends in Year T will all grow at the same rate g. This shortcut will *not* ensure consistent assumptions and valuation. As described in the past three chapters, that shortcut may impound inconsistent assumptions in the Year T+1 amounts, and therefore inconsistent value estimates.

SUMMARY

Chapters 11, 12, and 13 have described and applied multiple approaches to valuation, using the present value of projected dividends, the present value of projected free cash flows, and the present value of projected residual income. Together, these approaches provide theoretically sound and practically applicable approaches to convert forecasts of future cash flows, earnings, and dividends into estimates of firm value. In Chapter 14, we examine a variety of additional valuation techniques, including the use of valuation multiples. Our experience with valuation suggests that using multiple valuation approaches yields more useful insights than using just one method in all circumstances.

QUESTIONS, EXERCISES, PROBLEMS, AND CASES

Questions and Exercises

13.1 REQUIRED INCOME. Explain required income. What does required income represent? How is required income conceptually analogous to interest expense?

13.2 RESIDUAL INCOME. Explain residual income. What does residual income represent? What does residual income measure?

13.3 INTERPRETING RESIDUAL INCOME. If a firm's residual income for a particular year is positive, does that mean the firm was profitable? If a firm's residual income for a particular year is negative, does that mean the firm necessarily reported a loss on the income statement? What does it mean if a firm's residual income is zero?

13.4 THE EFFECTS OF INVESTMENTS ON RESIDUAL INCOME. Assume that the firm's cost of equity capital is 10 percent and the firm's existing assets and operations generate a 10 percent return on common equity. If the firm raises additional equity capital and invests in assets that will generate a return less than 10 percent, what effect will that investment have on the firm's residual income? If the firm raises additional equity capital and invests in assets that will generate a rate of return that exceeds 10 percent, what effect will that investment have on the firm's residual income?

13.5 THE EFFECTS OF BORROWING ON RESIDUAL INCOME. If the firm borrows capital from a bank and invests it in assets that earn a return greater than the interest rate charged by the bank, what effect will that have on residual income for the firm? How does that effect compare with the effects of capital structure leverage described in Chapter 4?

13.6 THE EFFECTS OF COMPETITION ON RESIDUAL INCOME. If the firm competes in a very competitive, mature industry, what effect will competitive conditions have on residual income for the firm and others in the industry? Now suppose the firm holds a competitive advantage in an industry, but the advantage is not likely to be sustainable for more than a few years because of the potential for entry in the industry. As the firm's competitive advantage diminishes, what effect will that have on that firm's residual income?

13.7 THE RESIDUAL INCOME VALUATION APPROACH. Explain the theory behind the residual income valuation approach. Why is residual income value-relevant to common equity shareholders, when it does not represent reported earnings?

13.8 THE RESIDUAL INCOME VALUATION APPROACH. Explain the two roles of book value of common shareholders' equity in the residual income valuation approach.

13.9 VALUATION APPROACH EQUIVALENCE. Conceptually, why should an analyst expect valuation based on dividends, valuation based on the free cash flows for common equity shareholders, and valuation based on the residual income approach to yield equivalent value estimates?

13.10 APPROPRIATE DISCOUNT RATES. Why is it appropriate to use the required rate of return on equity capital (rather than the weighted average cost of capital) as the discount rate in the residual income valuation approach?

13.11 THE EFFECTS OF CONSERVATIVE ACCOUNTING ON RESIDUAL INCOME VALUATION. Suppose you are applying the residual income valuation model to value a firm with extremely conservative accounting. Suppose, for example, the firm is following GAAP but the firm does not recognize a substantial intangible asset on the balance sheet (perhaps the firm has expensed substantial amounts of research and development expenditures that have lead to valuable intellectual property, or expensed substantial amounts of advertising that have created a valuable brand name). As a consequence of this extremely conservative accounting, the firm reports assets and equity at book values that are much lower than their respective economic values. Explain why the residual income value estimates will not be distorted by conservative accounting. How does the residual income valuation model correct for the effects of conservative accounting and understated book values of equity?

13.12 THE EFFECTS OF AGGRESSIVE ACCOUNTING ON RESIDUAL INCOME VALUATION. Suppose you are applying the residual income valuation model to value a firm with extremely aggressive accounting. Suppose, for example, the firm has a substantially overvalued asset on the balance sheet (perhaps the firm has a large amount of goodwill on the balance sheet from a prior acquisition, and it has delayed recording a necessary impairment charge that would write off the value of the goodwill). As a consequence of this extremely aggressive accounting, the firm reports assets and equity at book values that are much higher than their respective economic values. Explain why the residual income value estimates will not be distorted by aggressive accounting. How does the residual income valuation model correct for the effects of aggressive accounting and overstated book values of equity?

Problems and Cases

13.13 COMPUTING RESIDUAL INCOME. The following data represent total assets, book value, and market value of common shareholders' equity (dollar amounts in millions) for Daimler-Chrysler AG, IBM, and Target Stores. Daimler-Chrysler AG manufactures automobiles and trucks. IBM develops and manufactures computer hardware and offers related technology services. Target Stores operates a chain of general merchandise discount retail stores. In addition, these data include existing market betas for these three firms and analysts' consensus forecasts of net income for Year +1 (in millions). Assume for each firm that analysts expect Year +1 net income and comprehensive income to be identical. Assume that the risk-free rate of return in the economy is 4.0 percent and the market risk premium is 5.0 percent.

	Daimler-Chrysler	IBM	Target Stores
Total Assets	$247,334	$109,183	$32,293
Common Equity:			
Book Value	$ 45,408	$ 29,747	$13,029
Market Value	$ 51,450	$124,470	$46,520
Market Equity Beta	1.61	1.07	0.89
Analysts' Consensus Forecasts of Net Income for Year +1	$ 3,284	$ 8,137	$ 2,371

Required

a. Using the CAPM, compute the required rate of return on equity capital for each firm.
b. Project required income for Year +1 for each firm.
c. Project residual income for Year +1 for each firm.
d. What do the different amounts of residual income imply about each firm?

13.14 COMPUTING RESIDUAL INCOME. The following data represent total assets, book value, and market value of common shareholders' equity (dollar amounts in millions) for Microsoft, Intel, and Dell, three firms involved in different aspects of the computer technology industry. Microsoft develops, manufactures, licenses, and supports software products. Intel develops and manufactures semiconductor chips and microprocessors for the computing and communications industries. Dell designs and manufactures a range of computer hardware systems, such as laptops, desktops, and servers. These data also include existing market betas for these three firms and analysts' consensus forecasts of net income for Year +1 (in millions). Assume for each firm that analysts expect Year +1 net income and comprehensive income to be identical. Assume that the risk-free rate of return in the economy is 4.0 percent and the market risk premium is 5.0 percent.

	Microsoft	Intel	Dell
Total Assets	$ 70,815	$ 48,413	$23,215
Common Equity:			
Book Value	$ 48,115	$ 38,579	$ 6,485
Market Value	$283,790	$146,170	$71,350
Market Equity Beta	0.88	1.17	0.91
Analysts' Consensus Forecasts of Net Income for Year +1	$ 12,874	$ 8,709	$ 3,816

Required

a. Using the CAPM, compute the required rate of return on equity capital for each firm.
b. Project required income for Year +1 for each firm.
c. Project residual income for Year +1 for each firm.
d. What do the different amounts of residual income imply about each firm?

13.15 COMPUTING RESIDUAL INCOME. The following data represent total assets, book value, and market value of common shareholders' equity (dollar amounts in millions) for three firms that are roughly the same size in terms of market capitalization and have roughly equivalent levels of systematic risk. Each of these firms—Southwest Airlines, Kroger, and Yum! Brands—operates in a different industry, but they all operate in very competitive industries. Southwest Airlines is a domestic U.S. airline providing low-cost, point-to-point air transportation services. Kroger operates retail supermarkets across the United States. Yum! Brands operates and franchises quick-service restaurants, including KFC, Pizza Hut, Taco Bell, Long John Silver's, and A&W All-American Food Restaurants. These data also include existing market betas for these three firms and analysts' consensus forecasts of net income for Year +1 (in millions). Assume for each firm that analysts expect Year +1 net income and comprehensive income to be identical. Assume that the risk-free rate of return in the economy is 4.0 percent and the market risk premium is 5.0 percent.

	Southwest Airlines	Kroger	Yum! Brands
Total Assets	$11,337	$20,491	$ 5,696
Common Equity:			
Book Value	$ 5,524	$ 3,540	$ 1,595
Market Value	$12,920	$14,000	$14,770
Market Equity Beta	1.23	1.25	1.12
Analysts' Consensus Forecasts of Net Income for Year +1	$ 475	$ 932	$ 747

Required

a. Using the CAPM, compute the required rate of return on equity capital for each firm.
b. Project required income for Year +1 for each firm.
c. Project residual income for Year +1 for each firm.
d. What do the different amounts of residual income imply about each firm?

13.16 EQUITY VALUATION USING THE RESIDUAL INCOME MODEL. Morrissey Tool Company manufactures machine tools for various other manufacturing firms. The firm is wholly owned by Kelsey Morrissey. The firm's accountant developed the following long-term forecasts of net income:

Year +1: $213,948
Year +2: $192,008
Year +3: $187,444
Year +4: $196,442
Year +5: $206,667

The accountant expects net income to grow 5 percent annually after Year +5. Kelsey withdraws 30 percent of net income each year as a dividend. Total common shareholder's equity on January 1, Year +1, is $1,111,141. Kelsey expects to earn a rate of return on her invested equity capital of 12 percent each year.

Required

a. Using the residual income valuation model, compute the value of Morrissey Tool Company as of January 1, Year +1.
b. What advice would you give Kelsey regarding her ownership of the firm?

13.17 EQUITY VALUATION USING THE RESIDUAL INCOME AND DIVIDEND DISCOUNT MODELS. Priority Contractors provides maintenance and cleaning services to various corporate clients in New York City. The firm has provided you with the following forecasts of net income for Year +1 to Year +5:

Year +1: $478,246
Year +2: $491,882
Year +3: $485,568
Year +4: $515,533
Year +5: $554,198

Total common shareholders' equity was $2,224,401 on January 1, Year +1. The firm does not expect to pay a dividend during the period of Year +1 to Year +5. The cost of equity capital is 12 percent.

Required

a. Compute the value of Priority Contractors on January 1, Year +1, using the residual income valuation model. The firm expects net income to grow 5 percent annually after Year +5.
b. Compute the value of Priority Contractors on January 1, Year +1, using the dividend discount model.

13.18 EQUITY VALUATION USING THE RESIDUAL INCOME, FREE CASH FLOW, AND DIVIDEND DISCOUNT MODELS. Exhibit 13.7 presents selected data from projected financial statements for Steak n Shake for Year +1 to

FSAP

EXHIBIT 13.7

Steak n Shake
Selected Financial Information
(amounts in millions)
(Problem 13.18)

	Year +1	Year +2	Year +3	Year +4	Year +5	Year +6	Year +7	Year +8	Year +9	Year +10	Year +11[a]
Common Equity, Beginning of Year	$165.8	$177.6	$192.0	$206.0	$216.6	$227.7	$234.2	$238.1	$239.4	$255.8	$269.5
Net Income	24.5	25.8	27.6	29.6	31.8	34.2	36.8	39.5	53.9	57.0	58.7
Dividends	(12.7)	(11.4)	(13.6)	(19.0)	(20.8)	(27.7)	(32.9)	(38.2)	(37.4)	(43.3)	(50.6)
Common Equity, End of Year[b]	$177.6	$192.0	$206.0	$216.6	$227.7	$234.2	$238.1	$239.4	$255.8	$269.5	$277.6
Cash Flow from Operations	$ 45.4	$ 51.2	$ 56.3	$ 61.5	$ 67.1	$ 72.9	$ 78.9	$ 85.2	$ 85.6	$ 92.4	$ 73.2
Cash Flow for Investing	(35.2)	(41.1)	(41.9)	(42.7)	(43.5)	(44.4)	(45.2)	(46.0)	(47.3)	(48.1)	(22.1)
Cash Flow for Long-Term Debt	(.5)	2.0	—	1.0	(2.0)	—	—	—	—	—	—
Cash Flow for Dividends	(12.7)	(11.4)	(13.6)	(19.0)	(20.8)	(27.7)	(32.9)	(38.2)	(37.4)	(43.3)	(50.6)
Net Change in Cash	$ (3.0)	$ 0.7	$ 0.8	$ 0.8	$ 0.8	$ 0.8	$ 0.8	$ 1.0	$ 0.9	$ 1.0	$ 0.5

[a]The amounts for Year +11 result from increasing each income statement and balance sheet amount by the expected long-term growth rate of 3 percent and then deriving the amounts for the statement of cash flows.

[b]Amounts on this line may differ from the amounts above due to rounding of intermediate computations.

Year +11. The amounts for Year +11 reflect a long-term growth assumption of 3 percent. The cost of equity capital is 9.34 percent.

Required

a. Compute the value of Steak n Shake as of January 1, Year +1, using the residual income model.

b. Repeat part a using the present value of expected free cash flows to the common equity shareholders.

c. Repeat part a using the dividend discount model.

d. Identify the reasons for any differences in the valuations in parts a, b, and c.

e. The market value of Steak n Shake on January 1, Year +1, is $309.98 million. Based on your valuations in parts a, b, and c, what is your assessment of the market value of this firm?

13.19 RESIDUAL INCOME VALUATION. The Coca-Cola Company is a global soft drink beverage company (ticker symbol = KO) that is a primary and direct competitor with PepsiCo. The data in Exhibits 12.13, 12.14, and 12.15 in Chapter 12 include the actual amounts for Year 4 and projected amounts for Year +1 to Year +6 for the income statements, balance sheets, and statements of cash flows for Coca-Cola (in millions). FSAP

The market equity beta for Coca-Cola at the end of Year 4 is .76. Assume that the risk-free interest rate is 4.0 percent and the market risk premium is 5.0 percent. Coca-Cola has 2,409 million shares outstanding at the end of Year 4. At the end of Year 4, Coca-Cola's share price was $41.64.

Required

Part I—Computing Coca-Cola's Share Value Using the Residual Income Valuation Approach

a. Use the CAPM to compute the required rate of return on common equity capital for Coca-Cola.

b. Derive the projected residual income for Coca-Cola for Years +1 through +6 based on the projected financial statements. The financial statement forecasts for Year +6 assume that Coca-Cola will experience a steady-state long-run growth rate of 3 percent in Year +6 and beyond.

c. Using the required rate of return on common equity from part a as a discount rate, compute the sum of the present value of residual income for Coca-Cola for Years +1 through +5.

d. Using the required rate of return on common equity from part a as a discount rate, and the long-run growth rate from part b, compute the continuing value of Coca-Cola as of the start of Year +6 based on Coca-Cola's continuing residual income in Year +6 and beyond. After computing continuing value as of the start of Year +6, discount it to present value at the start of Year +1.

e. Compute the value of a share of Coca-Cola common stock. (1) Compute the total sum of the present value of all residual income (from parts c and d). (2) Add the book value of equity as of the beginning of the valuation (that is, as of the end of Year 4, or the start of Year +1). (3) Adjust the total sum of the present value of residual income plus book value of common equity using the midyear discounting adjustment factor. (4) Compute the per-share value estimate.

Part II—Sensitivity Analysis and Recommendation

f. Using the residual income valuation approach, recompute the value of Coca-Cola shares under two alternative scenarios. Scenario 1: Assume that Coca-Cola's long-run growth will be 2 percent, not 3 percent as before; and assume that Coca-Cola's required rate of return on equity is 9 percent. Scenario 2: Assume that Coca-Cola's long-run growth will be 4 percent, not 3 percent as before; and assume that Coca-Cola's required rate of return on equity is 7 percent. To quantify the sensitivity of your share value estimate for Coca-Cola to these variations in growth and discount rates, compare (in percentage terms) your value estimates under these two scenarios with your value estimate from part e.

g. Using these data at the end of Year 4, what reasonable range of share values would you have expected for Coca-Cola common stock? At that time, what was the market price for Coca-Cola shares relative to this range? What would you have recommended?

h. If you completed Problem 12.16 in Chapter 12, compare the value estimate you obtained in part e of that problem (using the free cash flows to common equity shareholders valuation approach) with the value estimate you obtain here using the residual income valuation approach. The value estimates should be the same. If you have not completed Problem 12.16, it would be valuable to do so now.

FSAP

13.20 RESIDUAL INCOME VALUATION. In Problem 10.16, we projected financial statements for Wal-Mart Stores for Years +1 through +5. The data in Exhibits 12.16, 12.17, and 12.18 in Chapter 12 include the actual amounts for Year 4 and the projected amounts for Year +1 to Year +5 for the income statements, balance sheets, and statements of cash flows for Wal-Mart (in millions).

The market equity beta for Wal-Mart at the end of Year 4 is .80. Assume that the risk-free interest rate is 4.0 percent and the market risk premium is 5.0 percent. Wal-Mart has 4,234 million shares outstanding at the end of Year 4. At the end of Year 4, Wal-Mart's share price was $52.40.

Required

Part I—Computing Wal-Mart's Share Value Using the Residual Income Valuation Approach

a. Use the CAPM to compute the required rate of return on common equity capital for Wal-Mart.

b. Derive the projected residual income for Wal-Mart for Years +1 through +5 based on the projected financial statements.

c. Project the continuing residual income in Year +6. Assume that the steady-state long-run growth rate will be 3 percent in Year +6 and beyond. Project that the Year +5 income statement and balance sheet amounts will grow by 3 percent in Year +6, and then derive the projected amount of residual income for Year +6.

d. Using the required rate of return on common equity from part a as a discount rate, compute the sum of the present value of residual income for Wal-Mart for Years +1 through +5.

e. Using the required rate of return on common equity from part a as a discount rate, and the long-run growth rate from part c, compute the continuing value of Wal-Mart as of the start of Year +6 based on Wal-Mart's continuing residual income in Year +6 and beyond. After computing continuing value as of the start of Year +6, discount it to present value at the start of Year +1.

f. Compute the value of a share of Wal-Mart common stock. (1) Compute the total sum of the present value of all future residual income (from parts d and e). (2) Add the book value of equity as of the beginning of the valuation (that is, as of the end of Year 4, or the start of Year +1). (3) Adjust the total sum of the present value of residual income plus book value of common equity using the midyear discounting adjustment factor. (4) Compute the per-share value estimate.

Part II—Sensitivity Analysis and Recommendation

g. Using the residual income valuation method, recompute the value of Wal-Mart shares under two alternative scenarios. Scenario 1: Assume that Wal-Mart's long-run growth will be 2 percent, not 3 percent as before; and assume that Wal-Mart's required rate of return on equity is 1 percentage point higher than the rate you computed using the CAPM in part a. Scenario 2: Assume that Wal-Mart's long-run growth will be 4 percent, not 3 percent as before; and assume that Wal-Mart's required rate of return on equity is 1 percentage point lower than the rate you computed using the CAPM in part a. To quantify the sensitivity of your share value estimate for Wal-Mart to these variations in growth and discount rates, compare (in percentage terms) your value estimates under these two scenarios with your value estimate from part f.

h. Using these data at the end of Year 4, what reasonable range of share values would you have expected for Wal-Mart common stock? At that time, what was the market price for Wal-Mart shares relative to this range? What would you have recommended?

i. If you worked Problem 11.14 from Chapter 11 and computed Wal-Mart's share value using the dividends valuation approach, compare your value estimate from part g of that problem with the value estimate you obtained here. Similarly, if you worked Problem 12.17 from Chapter 12 and computed Wal-Mart's share value using the free cash flows to common equity shareholders, compare your value estimate from part f of that problem with the value estimate you obtained here. You should obtain the same value estimates for Wal-Mart shares under all three approaches. If you have not yet worked both of those problems, it would be valuable to do so now.

INTEGRATIVE CASE 13.1

FSAP

STARBUCKS

Residual Income Valuation of Starbucks' Common Equity

In Integrative Case 10.1, we projected financial statements for Starbucks for Years +1 through +5. In this portion of the Starbucks Integrative Case, we use the projected financial statements from Integrative Case 10.1 and apply the techniques in Chapter 13 to compute Starbucks' required rate of return on equity and share value based on the residual income valuation model. We also compare our value estimate to Starbucks' share price at the time of the case development to provide an investment recommendation.

The market equity beta for Starbucks at the end of Year 4 is .60. Assume that the risk-free interest rate is 4.0 percent and the market risk premium is 5.0 percent. Starbucks has 397.4 million shares outstanding at the end of Year 4. At the start of Year +1, Starbucks' share price was $47.05.

Required

Part I—Computing Starbucks' Share Value Using the Residual Income Valuation Approach

a. Use the CAPM to compute the required rate of return on common equity capital for Starbucks.

b. Using your projected financial statements from Integrative Case 10.1 for Starbucks, derive the projected residual income for Starbucks for Years +1 through +5.

c. Project the continuing residual income in Year +6. Assume that the steady-state long-run growth rate will be 3 percent in Year +6 and beyond. Project that the Year +5 income statement and balance sheet amounts will grow by 3 percent in Year +6, and then derive the projected residual income for Year +6.

d. Using the required rate of return on common equity from part a as a discount rate, compute the sum of the present value of residual income for Starbucks for Years +1 through +5.

e. Using the required rate of return on common equity from part a as a discount rate, and the long-run growth rate from part c, compute the continuing value of Starbucks as of the start of Year +6 based on Starbucks' continuing residual income in Year +6 and beyond. After computing continuing value as of the start of Year +6, discount it to present value at the start of Year +1.

f. Compute the value of a share of Starbucks common stock. (1) Compute the total sum of the present value of all future residual income (from parts d and e). (2) Add the book value of equity as of the beginning of the valuation (that is, as of the end of Year 4, or the start of Year +1). (3) Adjust the total sum of the present value of residual income plus book value of common equity using the midyear discounting adjustment factor. (4) Compute the per-share value estimate.

Part II—Sensitivity Analysis and Recommendation

g. Using the residual income valuation approach, recompute the value of Starbucks shares under two alternative scenarios. Scenario 1: Assume that Starbucks' long-run growth will be 2 percent, not 3 percent as before; and assume that Starbucks' required rate of return on equity is 1 percentage point higher than the rate you computed using the CAPM in part a. Scenario 2: Assume that Starbucks' long-run growth will be 4 percent, not 3 percent as before; and assume that Starbucks' required rate of return on equity is 1 percentage point lower than the rate you computed using the CAPM in part a. To quantify the sensitivity of your share value estimate for Starbucks to these variations in growth and discount rates, compare (in percentage terms) your value estimates under these two scenarios with your value estimate from part f.

h. At the end of Year 4, what reasonable range of share values would you have expected for Starbucks common stock? At that time, where was the market price for Starbucks shares relative to this range? What would you have recommended?

i. If you computed Starbucks' common equity share value using the dividends valuation approach in Integrative Case 11.1 in Chapter 11, compare the value estimate you obtained in that case with the estimate you obtained in this case. Similarly, if you computed Starbucks' common equity share value using the free cash flows to common equity shareholders valuation approach in Integrative Case 12.1 in Chapter 12, compare the value estimate you obtained in that case with the estimate you obtained in this case. You should obtain the same value estimates under all three approaches. If you have not yet worked both of those cases, it would be valuable to do so now.

Chapter 14

Valuation: Market-Based Approaches

Learning Objectives

1. Understand the practical advantages and disadvantages of using market multiples in valuation.

2. Apply a version of the residual income valuation model to compute the value-to-book (VB) ratio as a theoretically correct valuation multiple. The value-to-book ratio is a ratio of the intrinsic value of shareholders' equity (as we would compute it using the residual income, free cash flows, or dividends valuation approaches of the previous chapters) over the book value of shareholders' equity. Understand how to make investment decisions by comparing the value-to-book ratio to the market-to-book (MB) ratio, which is the ratio of market value to book value of shareholders' equity. Also understand how to compare VB ratios and MB ratios to analyze values of firms over time and to compare values across firms.

3. Understand and compute the firm's value-earnings ratio (VE) as a theoretically correct earnings-valuation multiple. Understand how to incorporate growth into the VE ratio to compute the value-earnings-growth ratio (VEG). Understand how to make investment decisions by comparing the VE and VEG ratios to the price-earnings ratio (PE) and the price-earnings-growth ratio (PEG), respectively. Use VE and VEG ratios and PE and PEG ratios to analyze values of firms over time and compare values across firms.

4. Understand the role of the following factors on market multiples: (a) risk and the cost of equity capital, (b) growth, (c) differences between current and expected future earnings, and (d) alternative accounting methods and principles. Use these factors to explain how VB, VE, and VEG ratios should differ across firms, and why MB, PE, and PEG ratios actually do differ across firms.

5. Estimate the price differential—the difference between market price and "risk-neutral value," which we compute using the residual income model and the risk-free rate of return as the discount rate.

6. Use the residual income model to reverse engineer a firm's stock price to determine either the implicit expected return or the implicit expected long-run growth rate.

7. Understand the role of capital market efficiency in valuation and the academic evidence on the degree to which the capital market efficiently impounds earnings information into share prices.

8. Understand how to exploit the information in earnings for investment decisions by accurately forecasting future earnings, appropriately reacting when firms announce earnings numbers each quarter and each year, and effectively incorporating earnings into valuation.

INTRODUCTION AND OVERVIEW

Chapters 1 to 13 have focused on using the information in accounting numbers, financial statements, and related notes to analyze firms' fundamental characteristics of profitability, risk, growth, and value. These prior chapters have established a coherent framework to attack a difficult but interesting problem—how to analyze and value a business. Using this framework to analyze and value a business, we must first understand the firm's industry and business strategy, and then we use that understanding to assess the quality of the firm's accounting, making adjustments as necessary. We then evaluate the firm's profitability, risk, growth, efficiency, liquidity, and leverage, using a set of financial ratios. On the foundation of these steps, we construct forecasts of future financial statements, from which we derive the expected future earnings, cash flows, and dividends that form the bases for valuation. We apply the dividends model, the free cash flows model, and the residual income model to value the firm, and we use these models to assess the sensitivity of firm value to key valuation parameters, such as costs of capital and expected growth rates. To culminate this process, we compute the realistic range of firm value estimates and compare this range of values to the firm's share price in the capital market in order to make an intelligent investment decision.

Exhibit 14.1 provides a summary representation of the fundamentals-driven valuation process. The top of the exhibit depicts the firm's value drivers, such as expected future earnings, cash flows, growth, and risk, which constitute the economic foundations of valuation. We capture these value drivers in forecasts of future financial statements, and then convert these forecasts into value estimates using valuation models, such as the residual income model, the free cash flows model, and the dividends model.

In this chapter, we continue our focus on fundamental characteristics of profitability, risk, growth, and value, but now we augment that analytical approach with techniques that allow us to exploit the information in *market value* and *share price*. We describe and apply a variety of techniques that compare the firm's market value or share price to the

EXHIBIT 14.1

Fundamentals of Valuation

Fundamental Value Drivers over the Remaining Life of the Firm:
Expected Future Earnings, Cash Flows, Growth, Risk

↓

Financial Statement Forecasts

↓

Compute:
Book Value of Common Equity plus Present Value of Expected Future Residual Income
= Present Value of Expected Future Free Cash Flows to Common Equity Shareholders
= Present Value of Expected Future Dividends

↓

Firm Value

EXHIBIT 14.2

Market Multiples

Fundamental Value Drivers over the Remaining Life of the Firm:
Expected Future Earnings, Cash Flows, Growth, Risk

↓

Summary Accounting Numbers:
Book Value of Common Shareholders' Equity; Earnings; Long-Run Growth

↓

Market Multiples:
Market-to-Book Ratios; Price-Earnings Ratios; Price-Earnings-Growth Ratios

↓

Firm Value

firm's fundamentals. The techniques we describe in this chapter include commonly used market multiples—market-to-book ratios, price-earnings ratios, and price-earnings-growth ratios—which provide efficient shortcuts to the valuation process. As Exhibit 14.2 depicts, market multiples rely on the same set of value drivers in the valuation process as the valuation models discussed in Chapters 11, 12, and 13—earnings, cash flows, growth, and risk—but market multiples collapse the valuation process in two important ways:

1. Instead of developing financial statement forecasts, market multiples use just one or two reported accounting numbers to represent the value drivers.
2. Instead of using extensive present value computations, market multiples summarize value using relatively simple ratios of market value of common equity to summary reported accounting numbers.

In this chapter, we also introduce techniques to infer and exploit the information in share prices, including computing price differentials and reverse engineering share prices. In the last section of the chapter, we summarize several fundamental insights from accounting and finance research on how efficiently the market uses accounting earnings to price stocks. The research findings are very encouraging for those interested in using earnings numbers and accounting information for fundamental analysis and valuation of stocks and for developing trading strategies.

MARKET MULTIPLES OF ACCOUNTING NUMBERS

Throughout this text we have described how to analyze and exploit the information in a wide array of numbers—accounting amounts, footnote data, management's disclosures, financial ratios, growth rates, and others—but thus far we have not analyzed and exploited the information in one very important number: share price. The market price for a share of common equity is a very special and informative number because it reflects the aggregate expectations of all of the market participants following that particular stock. The market price reflects the result of the market's trading activity in that stock. It summarizes the aggregate information the market participants have about the firm, and the aggregate expectations for the firm's future profitability, growth, and risk. The market price of a share does not mean that all market participants agree that the price is the correct value for the share; indeed, the market price simply indicates the equilibrium point at which the forces of supply (market participants potentially willing to sell the stock—the "ask" side of trading) and the forces of demand (market participants potentially willing to buy the stock—the "bid" side of trading) are momentarily in balance. Stock prices are dynamic, constantly changing with the arrival of new information that changes investors' expectations about share value and triggers trading in the firm's shares in the market. We can analyze share price to obtain a wealth of value-relevant information.

Market participants commonly calibrate firm valuation using market value or share price expressed as a multiple of a fundamental summary accounting number, such as the market-to-book ratio or the price-earnings ratio. Thus, market multiples capture *relative* valuation per dollar of book value or per dollar of earnings. In this way, market multiples measure value relative to a key accounting number as a common denominator, thereby enabling analysts to draw inferences about a particular firm's relative market capitalization, to assess changes in a firm's relative valuation over time, to compare valuation across firms, and to project comparable firms' values. For example, price-earnings ratios allow an analyst to quickly gauge and compare the multiples at which the market is capitalizing different firms' annual earnings.

Market multiples can provide useful and efficient fundamental valuation ratios but they must be applied and interpreted carefully, after considering the firm's expected future profitability, growth, and risk. Multiples like market-to-book ratios and price-earnings ratios are relative value metrics and therefore are not meaningful by themselves. For example, an analyst cannot determine whether a particular firm's price-earnings ratio should be 10, 20, 50, or some other number unless the analyst knows the firm's fundamental characteristics—expected future profitability, growth, and risk. Similarly, an analyst cannot determine whether a particular firm's price-earnings ratio should be higher or lower than some other firm's price-earnings ratio (or an industry average price-earnings ratio) unless the analyst knows how the firm's expected future profitability, growth, and risk characteristics compare to those characteristics of the other firm or the industry as a whole.

Analysts sometimes apply market multiples to estimate value in ad hoc ways. Valuation using market multiples may be efficient (sometimes called the "quick and dirty" approach) but may also be misleading. An analyst might be tempted to value a firm using that firm's historical average or the industry average market multiple. The firm's historical average market-to-book ratio, for example, may be an appropriate fit for the valuation of the firm today, but only if the firm's fundamental characteristics today match those of the firm's past. In the same vein, an industry average price-earnings multiple may be an appropriate yardstick for valuing a particular firm, but only if that firm's fundamental characteristics match the industry averages. If the firm's fundamentals are different today than they were in the past, or if the firm's fundamentals do not match the industry averages, then market multiples must be adjusted to reflect the firm's fundamental characteristics.

This chapter continues to emphasize the distinction between *value* and *price*, focusing on how to compute *value*-based multiples that reflect the firm's fundamentals and that can be compared to market *price*-based multiples. This focus also directs our attention to the factors that drive multiples, so that the analyst can avoid being ad hoc and can correctly adjust historical or industry average multiples to reflect appropriately the firm's expected profitability, growth, and risk.

MARKET-TO-BOOK AND VALUE-TO-BOOK RATIOS[1]

The market-to-book (MB) ratio can be computed by dividing the firm's market value of common equity at a point in time by the book value of common shareholders' equity from the firm's most recent balance sheet. For example, at the end of Year 4, PepsiCo's market value was \$87,207.3 million (= \$51.94 per share × 1,679 million shares), and PepsiCo's Year 4 book value of common shareholders' equity was \$13,572.0 million (see PepsiCo's consolidated balance sheet or statement of common shareholders' equity in Appendix A). Thus, PepsiCo was trading at an MB ratio equal to 6.426 (= \$87,207.3 million/ \$13,572.0 million). The MB ratio measures market value as a multiple of accounting book value at a point in time. The MB ratio reflects what the market value *is* but it does not tell us what the ratio *should be*, given our estimate of intrinsic value.

A Theoretical Model of the Value-to-Book Ratio

To compute a ratio that reflects our expectation of the firm's intrinsic value to book value, we need to compute the value-to-book (VB) ratio—the intrinsic value of common shareholders' equity divided by the book value of common shareholders' equity. The VB ratio can be computed directly using the residual income model developed in Chapter 13. In fact, the VB ratio model is a version of the residual income model that is scaled by book value of common shareholders' equity. The numerator of the VB ratio is the estimated value of common equity, which takes into account the book value of common shareholders' equity, expected future profitability, growth, risk, and the time value of money. The analyst can compare the VB ratio to the MB ratio to evaluate share price and make an investment decision, in exactly the same manner as we compared intrinsic value to share price in previous chapters. The analyst can also use the VB ratio of one firm to estimate the value of a comparable firm, provided the analyst makes the appropriate and necessary adjustments to the VB ratio so that it matches the comparable firm's fundamental characteristics. This section demonstrates the theoretical and empirical relation between intrinsic value, book value, and market value.

Using the same notation from prior chapters, we compute the VB ratio with the following model:

$$\frac{V_0}{BV_0} = 1 + \sum_{t=1}^{\infty} \frac{[ROCE_t - R_E] \times \dfrac{BV_{t-1}}{BV_0}}{(1 + R_E)^t}$$

In short, the VB ratio should be equal to one plus the present value of expected future residual return on common equity (the $[ROCE_t - R_E]$ term in the equation) times cumulative growth in book value (the BV_{t-1}/BV_0 term). The growth in book value indicates the

[1]As we noted in Chapter 13, credit for the rigorous development of the residual income model, and its extension to the value-to-book ratio model, goes to James Ohlson in J. A. Ohlson, "A Synthesis of Security Valuation Theory and the Role of Dividends, Cash Flows, and Earnings," *Contemporary Accounting Research* (Spring 1990), pp. 648–676; J. A. Ohlson, "Earnings, Book Values, and Dividends in Equity Valuation," *Contemporary Accounting Research* (Spring 1995), pp. 661–687; and G. A. Feltham and J. A. Ohlson, "Valuation and Clean Surplus Accounting for Operating and Financial Activities," *Contemporary Accounting Research* (Spring 1995), pp. 216–230. The ideas underlying the value-to-book ratio also trace to early work by G. A. D. Preinreich, "Annual Survey of Economic Theory: The Theory of Depreciation," *Econometrica* (1938), pp. 219–241; and E. Edwards and P. W. Bell, *The Theory and Measurement of Business Income* (Berkeley: University of California Press), 1961.

increase in net assets on which firms can earn residual income. The growth in book value depends on ROCE, dividend payout, and changes in common stock outstanding.

To derive this model, recall from Chapter 13 the following expression for the residual income valuation model:

$$V_0 = BV_0 + \sum_{t=1}^{\infty} \frac{NI_t - (R_E \times BV_{t-1})}{(1 + R_E)^t}$$

Under the residual income valuation model, the value of common shareholders' equity is equal to the book value of common equity plus the present value of all expected future residual income, which is the amount by which expected future earnings exceed required earnings, for the remaining life of the firm.[2] We compute the required earnings (or "normal" earnings) of the firm in year t as the product of the required rate of return on common equity capital times the book value of common equity at the beginning of year t ($R_E \times BV_{t-1}$). Required earnings captures the amount of net income the firm must generate in order to provide a return to common equity capital that is equal to the cost of common equity capital. We measure *residual income* (sometimes referred to as "abnormal earnings") by the subtraction term, $NI_t - (R_E \times BV_{t-1})$. Residual income is the difference between expected net income in year t and required earnings of the firm in year t. Residual income measures the amount of wealth that the analyst expects the firm to create (or destroy) in year t for common equity shareholders above (or below) the required return to equity capital.

To convert the residual income model into a model for the VB ratio, we scale both sides of the equation by BV_0, which produces the following equation:

$$\frac{V_0}{BV_0} = \frac{BV_0}{BV_0} + \sum_{t=1}^{\infty} \frac{\frac{NI_t}{BV_0} - \left(R_E \times \frac{BV_{t-1}}{BV_0}\right)}{(1 + R_E)^t}$$

We rewrite BV_0 divided by BV_0 as equal to 1. We rewrite the NI_t/BV_0 term as follows:

$$\frac{NI_t}{BV_0} = \frac{NI_t}{BV_{t-1}} \times \frac{BV_{t-1}}{BV_0} = ROCE_t \times \frac{BV_{t-1}}{BV_0}$$

To rewrite NI_t/BV_0 this way, we state $ROCE_t = NI_t/BV_{t-1}$. Note that this computation of $ROCE_t$ divides net income in period t by book value of common equity at the beginning of period t. This ROCE computation differs slightly from the approach in Chapter 4 in which we compute ROCE as net income divided by the average book value of equity during period t.[3]

---

[2]Chapter 13 explains that the residual income valuation model depends on clean surplus accounting for book value of common shareholders' equity, which requires that expected future earnings forecasts are comprehensive measures of income for the firm's common equity shareholders, and that expected future dividends reflect all capital transactions between the firm and common equity shareholders. Throughout this chapter, when we refer to expected future "earnings" or "net income" in the context of residual income valuation, we mean expected future comprehensive income available for common shareholders under clean surplus accounting.

[3]Theoretical and empirical research on the VB ratio defines ROCE as net income to common shareholders for a year divided by common shareholders' equity at the *beginning* of the year. In contrast, in prior chapters (particularly Chapter 4) in which we have used ROCE to assess profitability, we have used *average* common shareholders' equity in the denominator of ROCE. The theoretical development and application of the VB model in this section uses shareholders' equity at the beginning of the year, although the bias in using average shareholders' equity should not be particularly significant for most firms.

Note also that BV_{t-1}/BV_0 is the cumulative growth factor in book value of common equity between year 0 (the date of the valuation) and period $t - 1$. As indicated previously, growth in book value is a function of the earnings generated each period plus additional capital contributions by shareholders, less equity capital paid out to shareholders through dividends and stock buybacks. The growth in book value indicates growth in net assets invested, on which a firm can earn abnormal returns.

By decomposing the term NI_t/BV_0 into these two parts, we can restate NI_t/BV_0 as the product of profitability times growth: ROCE in year t times the cumulative growth in book value from year 0 to the start of year t. Return on common equity is a function of profitability relative to beginning-of-year common equity; beginning-of-year common equity is a function of cumulative growth. We can substitute these two components of NI_t/BV_0 into the VB equation, as follows:

$$\frac{V_0}{BV_0} = 1 + \sum_{t=1}^{\infty} \frac{\left(ROCE_t \times \frac{BV_{t-1}}{BV_0}\right) - \left(R_E \times \frac{BV_{t-1}}{BV_0}\right)}{(1 + R_E)^t}$$

Now both terms in the numerator of the summation term are multiplied by the same cumulative book value growth factor. We rearrange that equation as follows:

$$\frac{V_0}{BV_0} = 1 + \sum_{t=1}^{\infty} \frac{[ROCE_t - R_E] \times \frac{BV_{t-1}}{BV_0}}{(1 + R_E)^t}$$

We now have a useful model for the value-to-book ratio. Next we consider each term.

First, as a starting point, the VB ratio will equal one, to reflect the book value of common equity invested in the firm. The summation term indicates how the VB ratio should differ from one as a function of the firm's expected future abnormal profitability (the $ROCE_t - R_E$ term) times the firm's cumulative growth in book value (the BV_{t-1}/BV_0 term), all of which is discounted to present value, reflecting the firm's cost of equity capital (R_E) and the time value of money. Thus, the residual income model specifies the firm's VB ratio as a function of the firm's value drivers: capital in place, profitability, cost of equity capital, growth, risk, and time value of money. The VB model provides a valuation approach in which all of the inputs to valuation can be expressed as forecasts of rates—expected future ROCE, R_E, and growth. The only dollar amount the analyst needs in order to use the VB ratio to compute the dollar value of common shareholders' equity is the book value of common shareholders' equity, which is observable from the shareholders' equity section of the balance sheet.

The expression for the VB ratio provides some insights into valuation:

- Economics teaches that, in equilibrium, firms will earn a return equal to the cost of capital (that is, ROCE $= R_E$). The VB model indicates that a firm in steady-state equilibrium earning ROCE $= R_E$ will maintain (not create or destroy) shareholder wealth and will be valued at book value (that is, VB $= 1$).
- A firm's value should be greater than its book value of common equity insofar as the firm will generate wealth for common equity shareholders by earning a return (ROCE) that exceeds the cost of capital (R_E). That is, VB > 1 if ROCE $> R_E$. Firms that earn a return that is less than the cost of equity capital (that is, ROCE $< R_E$) will destroy shareholder wealth and will be valued below book value (that is, VB < 1).
- By itself, growth does not add value. Growth adds value to shareholders only if the growth creates additional residual income for common equity shareholders. If

expected ROCE equals R_E on new projects (that is, zero NPV projects), then these new projects will not create (or destroy) common shareholders' equity value. New projects will be abnormally profitable and create new wealth for equity shareholders (that is, be positive NPV projects) only when expected ROCE exceeds R_E.

- The risk of the firm increases the equity cost of capital. Increasing the equity cost of capital reduces firm value in two ways: (1) by increasing the required ROCE the firm must earn to cover the increased cost of capital R_E (that is, the "hurdle rate" goes up); and (2) by increasing the discount rate used to compute the present value of residual income.
- If a firm's VB ratio differs from the industry average VB ratio, it should be because the firm's expected future ROCE, R_E, and/or book value growth differ from the industry averages.
- If a firm's VB ratio changes over time, it should be because current expectations for the firm's future ROCE, R_E, and/or book value growth differ from the past expectations for the firm's future ROCE, R_E, and/or book value growth, respectively.

Example 1

Suppose an analyst is evaluating a firm with $1,000 of book value of common equity and a cost of equity capital equal to 10 percent. Assume that the analyst forecasts that the firm will earn ROCE of 15 percent from Year +1 through Year +3, but then after Year +3 the firm will earn ROCE equal to 10 percent. The analyst also expects that the firm will reinvest all net income (that is, pay zero dividends), and it will not issue or repurchase stock. Using the VB ratio approach, the analyst should assign the firm a VB ratio equal to one plus the present value of future residual ROCE times growth. The present value of future residual ROCE times growth is determined as follows:

Year	Expected ROCE	Residual ROCE = ROCE − R_E	Cumulative Book Value Growth Factor to Year $t-1$	Residual ROCE Times Cumulative Growth	Present Value Factor	Present Value of Residual ROCE Times Cumulative Growth
+1	0.15	0.05	$1.00 = (1.15)^0$	0.05000	0.9091	0.04545
+2	0.15	0.05	$1.15 = (1.15)^1$	0.05750	0.8264	0.04752
+3	0.15	0.05	$1.3225 = (1.15)^2$	0.06613	0.7513	0.04968
+4	0.10	0.00	$1.52088 = (1.15)^3$	0.00000	0.6830	0.00000

The sum of the present values of residual ROCE times cumulative growth through Year +3 equals 0.14265, and the sum in all years after Year +3 is zero. The VB ratio of this firm is therefore 1.14265. Note that we have determined this VB ratio with all of the inputs expressed in rates. We can multiply the VB ratio by book value of equity to determine that firm value is $1,142.65 (= 1.14265 VB ratio × $1,000 book value of equity). We can confirm this value using dollar amounts and the residual income model approach from Chapter 13, as follows:

Year	Expected ROCE	Expected Earnings	Cumulative Book Value at the end of Year $t-1$ (BV_{t-1})	Required Income $= BV_{t-1} \times R_E$	Required Income	Present Value Factor	Present Value of Residual Income
+1	0.15	\$150.00 = 0.15 × 1,000	\$1,000	\$100 = 1,000 × 0.10	\$50.00 = 150 − 100	0.9091	\$45.45
+2	0.15	\$172.50 = 0.15 × 1,150	\$1,150 = 1,000 + 150	\$115 = 1,150 × 0.10	\$57.50 = 172.50 − 115	0.8264	\$47.52
+3	0.15	\$198.38 = 0.15 × 1,322.5	\$1,322.5 = 1,150 + 172.50	\$132.25 = 1,322.5 × 0.10	\$66.13 = 198.38 − 132.25	0.7513	\$49.68
+4	0.10	\$152.09 = 0.10 × 1,520.88	\$1,520.88 = 1,322.50 + 198.38	\$ 152.09 = 1,520.88 × 0.10	\$0.00 = 152.09 − 152.09	0.6830	\$ 0.00

The sum of the present values of residual income through Year +3 equals \$142.65, the sum in all years after Year +3 is zero, and book value of equity is \$1,000, so the residual income model confirms that firm value is \$1,142.65.

APPLICATION OF THE VALUE-TO-BOOK MODEL TO PEPSICO

In Chapter 13, we determined that PepsiCo's share value at the end of Year 4 should be within a fairly narrow range centered on \$57.36. We determined this amount using the financial statement forecasts developed in Chapter 10 and the residual income valuation model. We next illustrate the valuation of PepsiCo shares using the value-to-book model. We rely on the same financial statement forecasts developed in Chapter 10, the same equity cost of capital (7.75 percent), and the same long-run growth rate (3.0 percent). We also demonstrate the forecasts and valuation models in the FSAP Forecasts and Valuation spreadsheets in Appendix C.

To compute the VB model for PepsiCo and to use it to make an investment decision with regard to PepsiCo shares, we follow these eight steps:

1. For each forecast year we project the expected ROCE, computed as NI_t/BV_{t-1}.
2. We compute expected residual ROCE each forecast year by subtracting the equity cost of capital from expected ROCE.
3. We determine the cumulative growth factor in book value of common shareholders' equity to the beginning of each forecast year (computed as BV_{t-1}/BV_0).
4. We multiply the expected residual ROCE by the cumulative growth factor.
5. We discount to present value the expected residual ROCE times growth, including continuing value.
6. We compute the implied VB ratio by summing one (the ratio of book value over book value) plus the present value of all expected future residual ROCE times growth, including continuing value.
7. We multiply the implied VB ratio by the midyear discounting adjustment factor $[1 + (R_E/2)]$, as described in prior chapters.

8. We compare the implied VB ratio to the MB ratio to determine whether market price is greater than, equal to, or less than our estimate of value. Equivalently, we can multiply the implied VB ratio by book value of equity to determine the value of common shareholders' equity, and then divide by the number of shares outstanding to convert this total to an estimate of value per share, which we then compare directly to market share price.

We next illustrate each of these eight steps with PepsiCo. The Year +1 projected ROCE is 31.1 percent, computed as projected comprehensive income available for common shareholders in Year +1 divided by book value of common equity at the start of Year +1 (= \$4,222.9 million/\$13,572.0 million). The residual ROCE is 23.4 percent after subtracting 7.75 percent for the cost of equity capital. The cumulative growth factor in book value (BV_{t-1}/BV_0) in Year +1 is 1.0, because Year +1 is the first year of the valuation horizon.[4] The product of Year +1 residual ROCE and the cumulative growth factor is therefore 23.4 percent, which we discount to present value using a 7.75 percent cost of equity capital. Exhibit 14.3 presents these computations for PepsiCo for Year +1 through Year +5. The sum of the present value of residual ROCE times growth in Year +1 through Year +5 is 1.093.[5]

We use the same steps to compute the Year +6 residual ROCE for purposes of computing continuing value. As described in the previous chapter, we project comprehensive income in Year +6 to grow by the 3.0 percent long-run growth rate. We compute book value as of the start of Year +6 (the end of Year +5), compute implied residual ROCE, and multiply by the cumulative growth factor in book value up to the beginning of Year +6. The projected ROCE in Year +6 is 34.0 percent [= $(NI_5 \times [1 + g])/BV_5$ = (\$5,580.4 million × 1.03)/\$16,918.8 million = \$5,747.8 million/\$16,918.8 million]. After subtracting the 7.75 percent cost of equity capital, the projected residual ROCE in Year +6 is 26.2 percent. Cumulative growth in book value from Year 0 to the beginning of Year +6 (the end of Year +5) is 1.247 (= BV_5/BV_0 = \$16,918.8 million/\$13,572.0 million). We therefore project that in Year +6 the product of residual ROCE times cumulative growth is 32.7 percent (= 26.2 percent × 1.247).

We use the Year +6 residual ROCE times growth (32.7 percent) in the continuing value computation, as follows (allowing for rounding):

$$\begin{aligned}
\text{Continuing Value}_0 &= [(NI_5 \times (1+g)/BV_5) - R_E] \times [BV_5/BV_0] \times [1/(R_E - g)] \times [1/(1+R_E)^5] \\
&= [(\$5{,}580.4 \times 1.03/\$16{,}918.8) - 0.0775] \times [\$16{,}918.8/\$13{,}572.0] \\
&\quad \times [1/(0.0775 - 0.03)] \times [1/(1 + 0.0775)^5] \\
&= 0.262 \times 1.247 \times 21.053 \times 0.689 \\
&= 4.738
\end{aligned}$$

The total present value of PepsiCo's expected residual ROCE with growth, expressed as components of the VB ratio, is the sum of these two parts (allow for rounding):

---

[4]We project that PepsiCo's book value of common equity will grow to \$14,388.1 million during Year +1. Therefore the cumulative growth factor in book value of common equity as of the start of Year +2 will be 1.060 (= \$14,388.1 million/\$13,572.0 million).

[5]This amount should be interpreted as a component of the VB ratio because all of the computations in the model are scaled by BV_0. Thus, the amount 1.093 should be interpreted as an estimate of the amount of residual income PepsiCo will create in Years +1 through +5 that, in present value, is equal to 1.093 times the book value of common equity. To reconcile this computation with the residual income model computations in Chapter 13, recognize that 1.093 times book value of \$13,572.0 million equals \$14,837.8 (allow for rounding), which is the sum of the present value of residual income through Year +5 computed in Exhibit 13.2.

EXHIBIT 14.3

Valuation of PepsiCo
Present Value of Residual ROCE in Year +1 through Year +5
(amounts in millions)

	Year +1	Year +2	Year +3	Year +4	Year +5
Comprehensive Income Available for Common Shareholders	$ 4,222.9	$ 4,503.2	$ 4,887.7	$ 5,216.8	$ 5,580.4
Divide by book value of common shareholders' equity (at $t-1$)	$13,572.0	$14,388.1	$14,746.8	$15,313.3	$15,908.1
Equals Implied ROCE	0.311	0.313	0.331	0.341	0.351
Residual ROCE (after subtracting 0.0775 percent required return on common equity)	0.234	0.235	0.254	0.263	0.273
Cumulative Growth Factor as of $t-1$	× 1.000	× 1.060	× 1.087	× 1.128	× 1.172
Residual ROCE Times Growth	0.234	0.250	0.276	0.297	0.320
Present Value Factors	× 0.928	× 0.861	× 0.799	× 0.742	× 0.689
Present Value Residual ROCE Times Growth	0.217	0.215	0.221	0.220	0.221
Sum of Present Value Residual ROCE Times Growth	1.093				

Present Value of Residual ROCE in Year +1 through Year +5	1.093
Present Value of Continuing Value of ROCE in Year +6 and Beyond	4.738
Present Value of All Future Residual ROCE	5.832

To compute the VB ratio for common equity, we need to add PepsiCo's beginning book value of common equity expressed as a ratio of beginning book value of equity, which is, of course, equal to one. Also, as described in prior chapters, our present value calculations overdiscount because they discount each year's residual ROCE for full periods when, in fact, the firm generates residual ROCE throughout each period and we should discount from the midpoint of each year to the present. Therefore, to make the correction, we multiply the present value sum by the midyear discounting adjustment factor $[1 + (R_E/2) = 1 + (0.0775/2) = 1.03875]$. Making these two adjustments produces the implied VB ratio as follows:

Present Value of All Future Residual ROCE	5.832
Add Beginning Book Value	+1.000
Total	6.832
Multiply by the Midyear Correction Factor	×1.03875
Implied VB Ratio	7.096

These computations suggest that PepsiCo common equity should be valued at 7.096 times the book value of equity at the start of the valuation horizon, which is the end of Year 4. At the end of Year 4, PepsiCo's market value was $87,207.3 million (= $51.94 per share × 1,679 million shares), and PepsiCo's Year 4 book value of common shareholders' equity was $13,572.0 million (Appendix A). Thus, PepsiCo was trading at an MB ratio equal to 6.426 (= $87,207.3 million/$13,572.0 million). The VB ratio of 7.096 is 10 percent greater than the MB ratio, implying that PepsiCo shares were underpriced by 10 percent at that time.

Equivalently, we can convert the VB ratio into a share value estimate for purposes of comparing to market price per share. If we multiply book value equity by the VB ratio, we obtain the value estimate of PepsiCo common equity of $96,312.0 million (= $13,572.0 million × 7.096 VB ratio; allow for rounding). Dividing by 1,679 million shares outstanding indicates that PepsiCo's common equity shares have a value of $57.36 per share, which is identical to the value estimates we obtained from the residual income model in Chapter 13, the free cash flows to common equity shareholders model in Chapter 12, and the dividend models in Chapter 11. We summarize the computations to arrive at PepsiCo's common equity share value using the value-to-book approach in Exhibit 14.4, where we present the value-to-book model application for PepsiCo from FSAP.

We can conduct a sensitivity analysis for the estimate of PepsiCo's VB ratio to assess a reasonable range of VB ratios for PepsiCo. We will find that the sensitivity of the VB ratio estimate is identical to the sensitivity of the residual income model value estimates demonstrated in Chapter 13. This is to be expected because both models use the same forecasts and valuation assumptions, and the VB model is a scaled version of the residual income model.

Reasons Why VB Ratios and MB Ratios May Differ from One

We described earlier a number of *economic* reasons why VB and MB ratios may differ from one. For example, the firm may have competitive advantages that enable it to earn an ROCE that is greater than R_E. To the extent that the firm can create and sustain these competitive advantages, the firm will increase the magnitude and persistence over time of the degree to which ROCE exceeds R_E, thereby increasing the VB and MB ratios. In addition, to the extent the firm will generate future growth by investing in abnormally profitable projects, the VB and MB ratios will differ from one.

A firm's VB and MB ratio may differ from one for *financial reporting* reasons in addition to economic reasons.[6] The firm may have investments in projects for which reporting methods and principles cause ROCE to differ from R_E. For example, firms may make substantial investments in successful research and development projects, brand equity, human capital, or other intangible resources. If these investments are internally generated through research and development activities, marketing and advertising activities, or human capital recruiting and training activities, then firms are typically required to expense investments in these activities according to conservative accounting principles (as is common under GAAP in the United States and most countries, as we discuss in

[6]Ryan found that book value changes lag market value changes in part because U.S. GAAP uses historical cost valuations for assets. The lag varies in part based on the degree of capital intensity of firms. See Stephen Ryan, "A Model of Accrual Measurement and Implications for the Evolution of the Book-to-Market Ratio," *Journal of Accounting Research* (Spring 1995), pp. 95–112.

EXHIBIT 14.4

Valuation of PepsiCo
Value-to-Book Approach
(amounts in millions)

RESIDUAL INCOME VALUATION **Value-to-Book Approach**	**Year +1**	**Year +2**	**Year +3**	**Year +4**	**Year +5**	**Continuing Value** **Year +6**
Comprehensive Income Available for Common Shareholders	$ 4,222.9	$ 4,503.2	$ 4,887.7	$ 5,216.8	$ 5,580.4	$ 5,747.8
Book Value of Common Shareholders' Equity (at $t - 1$)	$13,572.0	$14,388.1	$14,746.8	$15,313.3	$15,908.1	$16,918.8
Implied ROCE	0.311	0.313	0.331	0.341	0.351	0.340
Residual ROCE	0.234	0.235	0.254	0.263	0.273	0.262
Cumulative Growth Factor as of $t - 1$	1.000	1.060	1.087	1.128	1.172	1.247
Residual ROCE Times Growth	0.234	0.250	0.276	0.297	0.320	0.327
Present Value Factors	0.928	0.861	0.799	0.742	0.689	
Present Value Residual ROCE Times Growth	0.217	0.215	0.221	0.220	0.221	
Sum of Present Value Residual ROCE Times Growth	1.093					
Present Value of Continuing Value	4.738					
Total Present Value Residual ROCE	5.832					
Add one for book value of equity at $t - 1$	1.00					
Sum	6.832					
Adjust to midyear discounting	1.03875					
Implied Value-to-Book Ratio	7.096					
Times Beginning Book Value of Equity	$13,572.0					
Total Present Value of Equity	$96,312.0					
Shares Outstanding	1,679.0					
Estimated Value per Share	$ 57.36					
Current Share Price	$ 51.94					
Percent Difference	10%					

Chapters 7 and 8).[7] If these investments subsequently develop into successful and profitable resources, then the firm will have substantial off-balance-sheet assets and off-balance-sheet common shareholders' equity. These off-balance-sheet assets generate net income, but by being off balance sheet they cause common shareholders' equity to be understated, so ROCE is relatively high. These effects can be observed among certain firms in many different industries, such as pharmaceuticals, biotechnology, software, and consumer goods.

PepsiCo and Coca-Cola, for example, have created substantial off-balance-sheet brand equity over many years of successful product development, advertising, and brand-building activities. Following U.S. GAAP, these firms have expensed their investments in these activities. Thus, for these firms, the book value of common shareholders' equity does not recognize the off-balance-sheet value of brand equity. Relative to R_E, ROCE for PepsiCo and Coca-Cola is very high and likely will continue to be very high for many years in the future.

Over a sufficiently long period of time, however, the impact of accounting principles on the VB and MB ratio will diminish because economics teaches us to expect that competitive equilibrium forces will drive ROCE to converge to R_E in the long run. Also, the self-correcting nature of accounting will eventually eliminate biases in ROCE and book value of equity. For example, consider a biotechnology company that invests for several years in research and development to develop a particular drug. During the initial years of research, the firm incurs research costs that the firm is required to expense under U.S. GAAP. Its ROCE and book value of equity will be "low" during these years. After successfully developing and then marketing the drug, ROCE will be "high" because the firm generates revenues without matching expenses for research costs. The "high" ROCE will increase retained earnings, and, over time, the initial conservative biases in ROCE and book value will be corrected.

Empirical Data on MB Ratios

Exhibit 14.5 presents descriptive statistics for MB ratios across thirty-seven industries during the decade from 1995 to 2004 (the same industries and years for which we provided data on median market betas in Exhibit 11.3 in Chapter 11).[8] The descriptive statistics include the 25th percentile, median, and 75th percentile MB ratios for the sample as a whole and for each industry, listed in ascending order of the median MB ratio. The median MB ratio for this sample is 1.83, but these data reveal substantial variation in MB ratios across industries and within industries during this ten-year period.

The differences in industry median MB ratios in Exhibit 14.5 relate in part to differences in competitive conditions driving differences in growth and ROCE relative to R_E, as well as differences in alternative accounting principles. For example, in an industry that can be characterized as mature and competitive, the median firm will likely generate ROCE that is close to R_E and will not likely generate unusually high rates of growth. Such firms tend to have median MB ratios closer to one. Firms in mature and competitive

[7]GAAP in the United States and other countries, and the IFRS developed by the IASB, typically require expensing expenditures on internally generated intangible resources, such as research and development and advertising, because it is inherently difficult to reliably measure the value of these resources because the future cash flows associated with them are highly uncertain.

[8]To compute these descriptive statistics on market-to-book value ratios, we deleted firm-years with negative book value of equity. We also deleted firm-year observations in the top 1 percent of the distribution as potential outliers with undue influence on the descriptive statistics.

EXHIBIT 14.5

Descriptive Statistics on Market-to-Book Ratios, 1995–2004

Industry:	25th Percentile	Median	75th Percentile
Full Sample* on Compustat (N = 49,670 firm-years)	1.15	1.83	2.84
Textiles	0.80	1.27	1.96
Insurers	0.99	1.35	1.86
Real Estate	0.85	1.38	2.44
Primary Metals	0.94	1.45	2.20
Hotels	0.89	1.45	2.26
Wholesalers—Durables	0.91	1.47	2.35
Metal Products	1.01	1.55	2.30
Depository Institutions	1.15	1.55	2.09
Paper	1.17	1.58	2.53
Transportation by Air	1.11	1.62	3.00
Utilities	1.36	1.69	2.10
Lumber and Wood Products	1.20	1.77	2.70
Forestry	0.84	1.80	2.69
Restaurants	1.11	1.81	2.86
Grocery Stores	1.15	1.88	3.13
Wholesalers—Nondurables	1.16	1.88	3.07
Retailers—General Merchandise	0.96	1.89	3.65
Transportation Equipment	1.28	1.90	3.01
Motion Pictures	1.06	1.92	3.20
Oil and Gas Extraction	1.38	2.00	2.87
Amusements and Recreation	1.23	2.02	3.16
Retailers—Home Furniture, Furnishings and Equipment	1.09	2.03	3.87
Security and Commodity Brokers	1.32	2.10	3.94
Food Processors	1.30	2.13	3.67
Industrial and Commercial Machinery and Computer Equipment	1.39	2.14	3.47
Retailers—Apparel	1.32	2.16	3.64
Metal Mining	1.36	2.18	3.20
Petroleum Refining	1.54	2.24	2.81
Personal Services	1.17	2.24	3.36
Electronic and Electrical Equipment	1.39	2.31	3.84
Printing and Publishing	1.47	2.35	3.79
Health Services	1.47	2.37	3.83
Instruments and Related Products	1.50	2.38	3.94
Communications	1.64	2.64	4.44
Chemicals	1.73	2.75	4.91
Business Services	1.85	3.17	5.72
Tobacco	2.69	5.16	11.63

*To compute these descriptive statistics on market-to-book value ratios, we deleted firm-years with negative book value of equity. We also deleted firm-year observations in the top 1 percent of the distribution as potential outliers with undue influence on the descriptive statistics.

industries such as textiles, insurance, real estate, primary metals, metal products, and banking tend to have MB ratios that are lower than the sample average. With respect to accounting, the assets of firms in some of these industries—particularly banks and insurers—are primarily investments in financial assets, some of which appear on the balance sheet at fair value, and thus MB ratios are closer to one.

In contrast, some of the industries with relatively high MB ratios are more likely to have off-balance-sheet assets and shareholders' equity. For example, the chemical industry includes pharmaceutical firms, which expense research and development expenditures in the year incurred. The health services, personal services, and business services industries expense compensation costs in the year incurred and do not capitalize the value of their employees on the balance sheet. The balance sheet understates the economic value of key resources in each of these industries. These industries have MB ratios considerably in excess of one.

Empirical Research Results on the Predictive Power of MB Ratios

Several empirical studies have found that MB ratios are fairly stable, mean reverting slowly over time, and that MB ratios are reliable predictors of future growth in book value and expected future ROCE (implying that ROCE also mean reverts slowly).[9] For example, Bernard grouped roughly 1,900 firms into ten portfolios each year between 1972 and 1981 based on their MB ratios. He then computed the mean ROCE for each portfolio in the formation year and for each of the ten subsequent years. Exhibit 14.6 summarizes a portion of Bernard's results, grouping firms in the lowest three MB portfolios, middle four MB portfolios, and highest three MB portfolios.[10]

The data in Exhibit 14.6 indicate that firms with the highest MB ratios tend to have the highest ROCEs through Year +10, and firms with the lowest MB ratios tend to have the lowest ROCEs through Year +10. The results from the Bernard study also indicate that firms with the highest MB ratios have the highest growth rates in book value of equity through Year +10, and firms with the lowest MB ratios have the lowest growth rates through Year +10. The results in the Bernard study also indicate (although it is not apparent from the summary of results in Exhibit 14.6) that the predictive power of MB ratios for future ROCEs tends to diminish as the horizon lengthens. In Year +10, for example, there is relatively little difference in ROCEs across firms in the third through ninth MB portfolios, as these firms experience ROCEs that tend to converge to 14 percent. These results are consistent with the steady mean reversion in ROCEs over time, consistent with movement toward competitive equilibrium.

---

[9]Victor L. Bernard, "Accounting-Based Valuation Methods, Determinants of Market-to-Book Ratios and Implications for Financial Statement Analysis," working paper, University of Michigan, 1993; Jane A. Ou and Stephen H. Penman, "Financial Statement Analysis and the Evaluation of Market-to-Book Ratios," working paper, Columbia University, 1995; Stephen H. Penman, "The Articulation of Price-Earnings Ratios and Market-to-Book Ratios and the Evaluation of Growth" *Journal of Accounting Research* 34, no. 2 (Autumn 1996), pp. 235–259; William H. Beaver and Stephen G. Ryan, "Biases and Lags in Book Value and Their Effects on the Ability of the Book-to-Market Ratio to Predict Book Return on Equity," *Journal of Accounting Research* 38, no. 1 (Spring 2000), pp. 127–149.

[10]To reduce the effects of survivorship bias, Bernard included firms that did not survive the entire ten-year future horizon, and included any gain or loss on the cessation of the firm (from bankruptcy, takeover, or liquidation) in the final year ROCE.

EXHIBIT 14.6

The Relation between MB Ratios, Future ROCE, and Future Book Value Growth

		Median ROCE for Year:			
MB Portfolio	**Mean MB Ratio**	**0**	**+1**	**+5**	**+10**
Low	0.67	0.11	0.09	0.12	0.12
Medium	1.15	0.11	0.13	0.14	0.14
High	2.65	0.10	0.17	0.16	0.20
		Cumulative Percent Increase in Book Value through Year:			
		0	**+1**	**+5**	**+10**
Low	0.67	0%	15%	54%	190%
Medium	1.15	0%	15%	69%	204%
High	2.65	0%	21%	139%	394%

PRICE-EARNINGS AND VALUE-EARNINGS RATIOS

As we noted in Chapter 13, many capital markets participants devote enormous amounts of time and energy to forecasting and analyzing firms' earnings numbers. It is therefore no surprise that the market multiple that receives the most frequent use and attention is the price-earnings (PE) ratio. Analysts' reports and the financial press make frequent references to PE ratios. *The Wall Street Journal* reports PE ratios as part of the daily coverage of stock prices and trading activity. Investors and analysts increasingly evaluate ratios that integrate the PE ratio with expected future earnings growth to capture explicitly the links between price, earnings, and growth.

This section relies on data for PepsiCo first to demonstrate the theoretical model for computing value-earnings (VE) ratios and then to describe computing and using PE ratios from a practical perspective. We then discuss the strict assumptions implied by PE ratios and describe the conditions in which PE ratios may not capture appropriately the theoretical relation between value and earnings and the difficulties one encounters in reconciling actual PE ratios with those indicated by the theoretical value-earnings model. In this section, we also incorporate the role of earnings growth and examine price-earnings-growth (PEG) ratios. We conclude the section by describing empirical data on PE ratios, the predictive power of PE ratios, and the empirical evidence on the articulation between PE ratios and MB ratios.

A Model for the Value-Earnings Ratio

The value-earnings (VE) ratio is the value of common shareholders' equity divided by earnings for a single period. The previous chapter described how to determine common equity value as a function of present value of expected *future* earnings and the residual income model. In the residual income model, we use clean surplus accounting and measure future earnings as expected future comprehensive income available for common shareholders. Thus, in theory, the analyst should measure the VE ratio as the value of common equity divided by next period's expected comprehensive income. This way, the VE ratio achieves consistent alignment of *perspective* (numerator and denominator both forward-looking) and *measurement* (numerator and denominator both based on income measurement that is comprehensive for equity shareholders).

If one has already computed firm value using the forecasting and valuation models developed in the last four chapters, then computing the VE ratio is a simple matter of division. For example, in prior chapters we estimated PepsiCo's common shareholders' equity value to be \$96,312.0 million at the end of Year 4. We also projected that Year +1 comprehensive income will equal net income available for common shareholders, which will equal \$4,222.9 million. Thus, we can compute the VE ratio for PepsiCo at the end of Year 4 as follows:

$$V_0/E_1 = \$96{,}312.0 \text{ million}/\$4{,}222.9 \text{ million} = 22.8,$$

or equivalently, on a per-share basis, as follows:

$$\begin{aligned} Vps_0/Eps_1 = {} & (\$96{,}312.0 \text{ million}/1{,}679 \text{ million shares})/(\$4{,}222.9 \text{ million}/ \\ & 1{,}679 \text{ million shares}) = \$57.36/\$2.52 = 22.8 \end{aligned}$$

We can also derive the VE ratio from the VB ratio determined using the residual income model in the previous section. For this derivation, we employ an algebraic step to derive the firm's VE ratio from the firm's VB ratio, as follows:

$$V_0/E_1 = V_0/BV_0 \times BV_0/E_1 = V_0/BV_0 \times (1/ROCE_1)$$

Using this approach, we can derive PepsiCo's VE ratio from the VB ratio we computed in the previous section, as follows:

$$\begin{aligned} V_0/E_1 &= V_0/BV_0 \times BV_0/E_1 = V_0/BV_0 \times (1/ROCE_1) \\ &= (\$96{,}312.0 \text{ million}/\$13{,}572.0 \text{ million}) \times (\$13{,}572.0 \text{ million}/\$4{,}222.9 \text{ million}) \\ &= 7.096 \times 3.214 \\ &= 7.096 \times (1/0.311) \\ &= 22.8 \end{aligned}$$

Thus, we compute that PepsiCo's VE ratio should equal 22.8. We convert PepsiCo's VB ratio of 7.096 into the VE ratio by multiplying by $1/ROCE_1$, which we project will be the inverse of 31.1 percent.

Notice that we simply derived the VE ratio from the computation that PepsiCo's value is equal to \$96,312.0 million, which is based on specific forecasts of PepsiCo's future earnings. Obviously, using value to compute a VE ratio will not provide any new information about PepsiCo's value. So what is the point of computing a VE ratio?

The VE ratio provides the analyst a theoretically correct benchmark to evaluate the firm's PE ratio. We can compare PepsiCo's VE ratio of 22.8 to PepsiCo's PE ratio to assess the market value of PepsiCo shares. This comparison is equivalent to comparing V to P (that is, value to price). With the theoretically correct VE ratio, we can also project VE ratios for other firms, after making adjustments as necessary to capture the other firms' fundamental characteristics of profitability, growth, and risk. In addition, with the theoretically correct VE ratio, we have a benchmark to gauge other firms' PE ratios in order to assess whether the market is underpricing or overpricing their shares. In the next section, we discuss the practical advantages and disadvantages in using PE ratios as shortcut valuation metrics.

Price-Earnings Ratios

As a practical matter, analysts, the financial press, and financial databases commonly measure PE ratios as current-period share price divided by reported earnings per share for either the most recent prior fiscal year or the most recent four quarters (sometimes referred to as the trailing-twelve-months earnings per share).[11] *The Wall Street Journal* and financial data web sites such as Yahoo! Finance commonly compute PE ratios this way. With this approach, we compute the PE ratio for PepsiCo as of the end of Year 4 as follows: Price per share_4/Earnings per share_4 = \$51.94/\$2.45 = 21.2. Thus, at the end of Year 4, PepsiCo shares traded at a multiple of 21.2 times Year 4 earnings per share.[12]

The common approach to compute the PE ratio by dividing market price by earnings per share for the most recent year is practical because analysts can readily observe price per share and historical earnings per share for most firms. This approach is efficient because it does not require the analyst to produce a computation of value or a forecast of earnings. However, this common approach creates a logical misalignment for valuation purposes because it divides *historical* earnings into share price that reflects the present value of *future* earnings. If historical earnings contain unusual or nonrecurring gains or losses that are not expected to persist in future earnings, then the analyst should cleanse the reported historical earnings of these effects in order to compute a PE ratio that reflects earnings that are likely to persist in the future. Chapter 6 describes techniques to identify elements of income that are unusual and nonrecurring, adjust reported earnings to eliminate their effects, and thereby measure recurring, persistent earnings.

As an alternative approach to create a more logical alignment of price and earnings, the analyst can compute the PE ratio by dividing share price by the analyst's forecast of future earnings per share—for example, expected earnings per share one year ahead. A PE ratio based on expected future earnings, however, requires the analyst to forecast future earnings (or have access to another analyst's forecast). The reliability of a forward-looking PE ratio then depends on the reliability of the earnings forecast. Earnings forecast errors will distort forward-looking PE ratios.

---

[11]In theory, to be consistent with clean surplus accounting and residual income valuation, the denominator should be based on comprehensive income per share. However, analysts, the financial press, and financial databases rarely compute PE ratios based on comprehensive income per share, in part because (a) U.S. GAAP does not yet require reporting comprehensive income on a per-share basis, and (b) the other comprehensive income items are usually unrealized gains and losses that are not likely to be permanent components of income each period. We follow traditional practice in this chapter and compute PE ratios using reported earnings figures.

[12]The common approach to computing PE ratios can also be slightly distorted by differences in the numbers of shares outstanding at year-end used by the market to compute share price versus the weighted average numbers of shares outstanding used to compute earnings per share under U.S. GAAP. If we compute PepsiCo's PE ratio using amounts in millions rather than per-share amounts, we obtain a PE ratio of 20.8 [= \$87,207 million/(net income of \$4,212 million − \$3 million preferred dividends − \$22 million preferred-stock redemption premium)]. This PE ratio is slightly lower than the PE ratio of 21.2 based on per-share amounts because PepsiCo reports earnings per share based on the weighted average number of common shares outstanding during the year (consistent with U.S. GAAP) rather than the number of shares outstanding at year-end.

We compute the forward-looking PE ratio for PepsiCo as of the end of Year 4 using our forecast that Year +1 earnings (comprehensive income available to common shareholders) will be \$4,222.9 million as follows: Price per share_0/Earnings per share_{+1} = \$51.94 per share/(\$4,222.9 million/1,679 million shares) = \$51.94/\$2.52 = 20.6. Thus, at the end of Year 4, PepsiCo shares traded at a multiple of 20.6 times the Year +1 earnings forecast. PepsiCo's VE ratio of 22.8 is 10 percent greater than PepsiCo's PE ratio of 20.6 at the end of Year 4, consistent with our prior estimates of PepsiCo's value.[13]

Notice that we simply derived the PE ratio by dividing PepsiCo's market share price by either earnings per share of the past year or by our forecasts of PepsiCo's future earnings per share. Obviously, using price to compute a PE ratio will not provide any new information about PepsiCo's share *value.* So what is the point of computing a PE ratio?

PE ratios are practical tools used by analysts interested in valuation shortcuts. In some circumstances, analysts need to react with timely ballpark estimates of valuation, and PE ratios provide a quick way to estimate firm value as a multiple of earnings. Analysts commonly assess benchmark PE ratios that they expect a firm to have based on past PE ratios for that firm, or industry-average PE ratios, or comparable firms' PE ratios. Analysts use benchmarks like these to project a firm's PE ratio quickly, using one-period earnings as a common denominator for relative valuations, rather than engaging in the extensive computations necessary to determine the correct value-earnings ratio to assess whether the market has priced the firm's shares appropriately.

Analysts also use PE ratios as potentially informative benchmarks to project earnings-based valuation multiples that they use to compare valuations across companies or to project the valuations of other companies. For example, we could compare PepsiCo's PE ratio to the PE ratios of Coca-Cola, Cadbury-Schweppes, or other beverage companies. We might also use PepsiCo's PE ratio to project valuations for these beverage companies, or to project valuations for privately held firms or divisions of companies. Investment bankers use comparable companies' PE ratios, for example, to benchmark reasonable ranges of share prices for initial public offerings.

PE ratios have the advantage of speed and efficiency, but they are not necessarily precise valuation estimates. When using PE ratios, therefore, the analyst must be careful to adjust them to match the fundamental characteristics of different companies. For example, PepsiCo's PE ratio should differ from Coca-Cola's insofar as the fundamental characteristics of profitability, growth, and risk differ across these two firms. Such differences might arise, for example, because PepsiCo derives a major portion of earnings from the snack food business, which Coca-Cola does not have. Similarly, Coca-Cola derives more of its earnings from international beverage sales than does PepsiCo. These and other factors cause the profitability, growth, and risk of PepsiCo and Coca-Cola to differ, and therefore cause their PE ratios to differ. We will describe PE ratio differences in more detail after we first describe the conceptual basis for PE ratios.

PE Ratios Project Firm Value from Permanent Earnings

What should a firm's PE ratio be? What is an appropriate valuation multiple for a firm's earnings? We have seen that, in theory, the firm's PE ratio should equal the firm's VE ratio. However, if the analyst has not computed value in order to determine the VE ratio and wishes to use a shortcut PE ratio instead, what is the correct PE ratio to use?

---

[13]In this case, our forecasts of net income and comprehensive income for PepsiCo in Year +1 are the same, so the PE ratio using earnings per share is equal to that using comprehensive income per share.

In projecting firm value using a simple PE ratio (that is, one that uses only one period of earnings and ignores earnings growth), the analyst imposes a strong assumption on the earnings number for a single period: The analyst treats this earnings number (whether it is a trailing earnings number or a one-period-ahead forecast) as the beginning amount of a permanent stream of earnings, valued as a perpetuity. Conceptually, suppose that the firm's common shareholders' equity value equals its market value, that the firm's earnings will be constant in the future, and that the firm's investors expect a rate of return R_E. Under these conditions, we can value the firm's common equity using the perpetuity model based on one-year-ahead earnings (denoted E_1), as follows:

$$V_0 = P_0 = E_1/R_E$$

Rearranging slightly, under these assumptions the firm's VE and PE ratios are as follows:

$$V_0/E_1 = P_0/E_1 = 1/R_E$$

Thus, strictly speaking, the PE multiple assumes that firm value is the present value of a constant stream of expected future earnings, discounted at a constant expected future discount rate. Under these conditions, the analyst can value the firm simply using a multiple of one-period-ahead earnings, and the PE ratio of the firm is simply the inverse of the discount rate.

To illustrate this model with an example, assume that the market expects the firm to generate earnings of $700 next period and requires a 14 percent return on equity capital. The market value of the firm at the beginning of the next period should be $5,000 (= $700/0.14). Note that the inverse of the 14 percent discount rate translates into a PE ratio of 7.14 (= 1/0.14). Thus, $700 times 7.14 equals $5,000.

The simple PE ratio assumes that future earnings will be permanent, which is not realistic for most firms. Most firms' earnings are not expected to remain constant; most firms' earnings grow. Not surprisingly, such strict assumptions match the fundamental characteristics of very few firms. We have already seen that such strict assumptions do not fit PepsiCo. Under the assumptions that PepsiCo's earnings will be constant in the future, and that PepsiCo's constant future ROCE will equal the 7.75 percent cost of equity capital, then PepsiCo's PE ratio should be 12.9 (= 1/0.0775). This PE ratio is far below the theoretically derived VE ratio of 22.8 for PepsiCo.

Descriptive Data on PE Ratios

The following table includes descriptive statistics of price-earnings ratios (share price to one-year-ahead earnings: P_t/E_{t+1}, as well as share price to trailing earnings: P_t/E_t) during the years 1995–2004. These data represent a broad cross-sectional sample drawn from the Compustat database, excluding all firm-years with negative earnings.[14]

Price-Earnings Ratio	25th Percentile	Median	75th Percentile
P_t/E_{t+1}	9.99	13.86	21.31
P_t/E_t	10.97	16.35	26.09

[14]It does not make sense to compute PE ratios on the basis of negative earnings. PE ratios assume that earnings are permanent; negative earnings are not likely to be permanent.

Exhibit 14.7 includes descriptive statistics on forward-looking PE ratios (share price to one-year-ahead earnings: P_t/E_{t+1}) for the same thirty-seven industries described in Exhibit 14.3 (MB ratios) and Exhibit 11.3 (market betas) during the years 1995–2004. Exhibit 14.7 lists the industries in ascending order of the median PE ratios. To describe the industry-wide variation in PE ratios, Exhibit 14.7 also includes the 25th percentile PE ratio and the 75th percentile PE ratio for each industry.

These descriptive data indicate substantial differences in median PE ratios across industries during 1995–2004. The firms in the insurance, transportation by air, and transportation equipment industries experienced the lowest median PE ratios during that period, whereas firms in the communications, metal mining, and business services industries experienced the highest median PE ratios. These data also depict wide variation in PE ratios across firms within each industry. For example, most of these thirty-seven industries experienced wide differences between the 25th percentile and the 75th percentile PE ratio during 1995–2004. With only a few exceptions, within most industries the 75th percentile PE ratio was more than double the 25th percentile PE ratio.[15]

What Factors Cause PE Ratios to Differ across Firms?

The same set of economic factors that may cause firms' MB ratios to differ also cause PE ratios to differ across firms. The primary drivers of differences in PE ratios across firms are the fundamental drivers of value: risk, profitability, and growth. In addition to economic factors, differences across firms in accounting methods and accounting principles, and differences across time in accounting earnings, can also drive differences in PE ratios. We describe the effects of each of these determinants of PE ratios in the sections that follow, saving growth for last because we will expand on the role of growth in determining PE ratios.

Risk and the Cost of Capital. As the previous discussion points out, firms with equivalent amounts of earnings but different levels of risk and therefore different costs of equity capital will experience different PE ratios (and different VE ratios). All else equal, a more risky firm will experience a lower market value and PE ratio. However, only firms facing rare circumstances experience PE ratios that equal the inverse of the equity cost of capital, so a variety of other forces also cause PE ratios to differ.

Profitability. A firm with competitive advantages will be able to earn ROCE that exceeds R_E. To the extent that the firm can sustain these competitive advantages, the persistence over time of the degree to which ROCE exceeds R_E will increase, thereby increasing the PE ratio relative to similar firms that do not have sustainable competitive advantages. Thus, both the magnitude and the persistence of the difference between ROCE and R_E will increase PE ratios across firms.

Accounting Differences. In addition to economic factors, firms' PE ratios may differ for accounting reasons—especially differences in accounting methods, principles, and the periodic nature of earnings measurement. Some firms select accounting methods that are conservative with respect to income recognition and asset measurement (for example, LIFO for inventories during periods of rising input prices and accelerated depreciation of fixed assets). Some firms invest in projects for which accounting principles are conservative. For example, firms may make substantial investments in intangible activities that must be expensed under conservative accounting principles, leading to economic assets

[15]The analyst must be careful with PE ratios because they are sensitive to earnings numbers that are near zero. Firms with earnings that are positive but temporarily very low will experience PE ratios that are temporarily very high.

EXHIBIT 14.7

Descriptive Statistics on Ratios of Share Price to One-Year-Ahead Earnings (P_t/E_{t+1}), 1995–2004

Industry:	25th Percentile	Median	75th Percentile
Insurance	8.32	11.44	16.95
Transportation by Air	7.86	11.96	22.33
Transportation Equipment	8.99	12.08	18.38
Tobacco	11.01	12.45	16.94
Metal Products	8.74	12.47	19.39
Textiles	9.99	12.67	19.80
Depository Institutions	10.09	12.82	16.88
Wholesalers—Durables	8.40	12.92	20.83
Forestry	5.37	12.95	25.76
Real Estate	8.03	13.04	24.60
Lumber and Wood Products	9.94	13.05	19.07
Petroleum Refining	8.77	13.16	18.85
Security and Commodity Brokers	8.01	13.50	20.30
Metals	8.46	13.51	20.57
Utilities	11.12	13.59	17.22
Retailers—Apparel	9.52	13.66	18.62
Wholesalers—Nondurables	9.17	13.85	21.31
Oil and Gas Extraction	7.77	13.88	24.25
Restaurants	10.58	14.79	22.84
Industrial and Commercial Machinery and Computer Equipment	10.44	15.79	28.09
Retailers—Home Furniture, Furnishings and Equipment	10.54	15.86	25.49
Amusements and Recreation	10.09	16.11	25.04
Retailers—General Merchandise	11.81	16.20	23.79
Health Services	11.00	16.34	25.23
Paper	10.98	16.39	23.86
Printing and Publishing	11.32	16.55	24.08
Grocery Stores	12.43	16.93	25.46
Hotels	9.98	16.97	25.20
Food Processors	11.36	17.00	26.27
Motion Pictures	9.70	17.36	33.98
Electronic and Electrical Equipment	10.80	17.83	31.13
Personal Services	12.39	18.07	26.29
Chemicals	12.74	18.25	28.68
Instruments and Related Products	11.78	18.46	30.62
Communications	12.59	19.28	36.01
Metal Mining	12.79	20.68	39.27
Business Services	13.36	22.16	38.51

To compute these descriptive statistics on price-earnings ratios, we divided firm value (computed as year-end closing price times number of shares outstanding) by one-year-ahead net income. We deleted firm-years with negative one-year-ahead net income.

that are off balance sheet, such as successful research and development, brand equity, and human capital. The effects of accounting methods and principles on reported earnings and PE ratios will likely change over the firm's lifetime. All else held equal, conservative accounting will reduce reported earnings early in the life of the firm (for example, when accelerated depreciation charges are high or research and development is being expensed), thereby increasing the PE ratio. Ironically, later in the life of the firm, after the investments have been completely expensed, reported earnings will be higher, and PE ratios will be lower.

Accounting measures earnings in annual periods. Firms' PE ratios will be significantly different when one-period earnings are unusually high or low and therefore not representative of earnings in perpetuity. For example, if earnings include an unusual loss (or gain) that will not persist, then the firm's PE ratio will be unusually high (or low) that period. Transitory gains and losses that affect a single period of accounting earnings can cause PE ratios to be more volatile than the long-run expectations of earnings warrant. In particular, if the analyst uses PE ratios based on trailing-twelve-months earnings that include nonrecurring gains or losses that are not expected to persist, the PE ratios will be artificially volatile.

Continuing the simple example introduced earlier, assume that the analyst expects the firm to generate earnings next period of $600 instead of $700 because the firm will recognize a $100 restructuring charge. If the market views this charge as nonrecurring (that is, not a permanent change in earnings), then the market price should fall to roughly $4,900 (= $5,000 − $100) in the no-growth scenario, and the PE ratio for the period will be 8.17 (= $4,900/$600), instead of 7.14 (= $5,000/$700). Conversely, if the current period's earnings exceed their expected permanent level, then the PE ratio will be less than normal.

The analyst must assess whether the lower or higher level of earnings for the period (and therefore higher or lower PE ratio) represents a transitory phenomenon or a change to a new lower or higher level of permanent earnings. If the analyst expects that the decrease in earnings from $700 to $600 will be permanent, then the market price (assuming no change in risk or growth) should decrease to $4,286 (= $600/.14). Thus, the PE ratio remains the same at 7.14 (= 1/.14).

To illustrate the effects of accounting differences on PE ratios across firms, consider the historical data in the following table, which includes PE ratios (computed as year-end share price over trailing earnings per share) for PepsiCo and Coca-Cola for the Years 0 and 1.

		PE Ratio	Price per Share	Earnings per Share
Year 0:	PepsiCo	31.9	$46.25	$1.45
	Coca-Cola	69.3	$60.94	$0.88
Year 1:	PepsiCo	34.2	$46.18	$1.35
	Coca-Cola	29.5	$47.15	$1.60

Considered at face value, the PE ratios for PepsiCo and Coca-Cola in Year 0 indicate that the market valued Coca-Cola's earnings at a multiple of 69.3, more than twice PepsiCo's earnings multiple of 31.9, implying that Coca-Cola had lower cost of capital, higher growth, and/or greater profitability than PepsiCo. To the contrary, however, Coca-Cola recognized a large restructuring charge in income in Year 0, driving EPS down to only $0.88, thereby temporarily inflating Coca-Cola's PE ratio. Thus, the big jump in Coca-Cola's PE ratio occurred largely because earnings temporarily declined that year, and did not reflect the market's expectations for Coca-Cola's long-term earnings. In Year 1, both firms reported earnings closer to normal levels and their PE ratios were quite similar.

Growth. Holding all else equal, PE ratios will be greater for firms that the market expects will generate greater earnings growth with future investments in abnormally profitable projects. In the next section, we discuss techniques analysts use to incorporate earnings growth into PE ratios.

Incorporating Earnings Growth into Price-Earnings Ratios

Analysts commonly modify the PE ratio to incorporate expected future earnings growth. In this section, we describe and apply two related approaches to include expected future earnings growth in the computation of the PE ratio: (1) the perpetuity-with-growth approach and (2) the price-earnings-growth approach.[16]

The Perpetuity-with-Growth Approach

The perpetuity-with-growth approach assumes that the firm can be valued as the present value of a permanent stream of future earnings that will grow at constant rate g. In this case, we can express VE and PE ratios as perpetuity-with-growth models, as follows:

$$V_0 = P_0 = E_1 \times 1/(R_E - g), \text{ so } V_0/E_1 = P_0/E_1 = 1/(R_E - g)$$

To continue the illustration, assume that the market expects that the firm's earnings will be \$700 next year and will grow 5 percent each year thereafter. The model suggests that the PE ratio should be 11.11 [= 1.0/(0.14 − 0.05)] and market value should be \$7,778 (= \$700 × 11.11). The present value of the expected future growth in earnings adds \$2,778 (= \$7,778 − \$5,000) to the value of the firm.

PE ratios are particularly sensitive to the growth rate. If the growth rate is 6 percent instead of 5 percent, the ratio becomes 12.50 [= 1.0/(0.14 − 0.06)] and the market value becomes \$8,750 (= \$700 × 12.50). The sensitivity occurs because the model assumes that the firm will grow at the specified growth rate in perpetuity. Competition, new discoveries or technologies, or other factors eventually erode rapid growth rates in an industry. In using the constant growth version of the PE ratio, the analyst should select a long-run equilibrium growth rate in earnings.

This expression for the VE and PE ratio underscores the joint importance of risk and growth in valuation. Given the relation between expected return (R_E) and risk, the VE and PE ratio should be inversely related to risk. Holding current period earnings and growth constant, higher risk levels should translate into lower PE and VE ratios, and vice versa. Risk-averse investors will not pay as much for a higher-risk security as for a lower-risk security with identical expected earnings and growth. In contrast, VE and PE should relate positively to growth. Holding current period earnings and R_E constant, firms with higher expected long-run growth rates in earnings should experience higher VE and PE ratios.

With respect to our valuation of PepsiCo at the end of Year 4, we assumed that PepsiCo would experience a long-run growth rate of 3.0 percent beginning in Year +6 and beyond. If we assume that PepsiCo will experience a 3.0 percent constant growth rate

[16]In recent research, James Ohlson and Beate Juettner-Nauroth develop a theoretical model for the price-earnings ratio that incorporates short-term and long-term earnings per share growth. The model is a promising addition to the earnings-based valuation literature, providing new insights into the relation between value, earnings, and growth. See James Ohlson and Beate Juettner-Nauroth, "Expected EPS and EPS Growth as Determinants of Value," *Review of Accounting Studies* (June–September 2005), pp. 349–365.

in earnings beginning in Year +1, then using the perpetuity-with-growth approach we calculate the PE ratio for PepsiCo as follows:

$$P_0/E_1 = 1/(R_E - g) = 1/(0.0775 - 0.030) = 21.05$$

Clearly, incorporating growth makes a big difference in PepsiCo's PE ratio (as compared to the PE ratio of 12.9 that ignores growth). Assuming PepsiCo's earnings grow at 3.0 percent per year beginning in Year +1, this PE with growth ratio would value PepsiCo shares at a multiple of 21.05 times the Year +1 earnings forecast. This PE ratio is still less than the theoretically correct VE ratio of 22.8, however, because it does not take into account our forecasts that project that PepsiCo earnings will grow at an average rate of 5.8 percent from Year +1 to Year +5. Thus, this PE ratio understates the value of PepsiCo's expected earnings growth during those years.

The Price-Earnings-Growth Approach

An alternative ad hoc approach to incorporate growth into PE ratios has emerged from practice in recent years, in which analysts divide the price-earnings ratio by the expected medium-term earnings growth rate (expressed as a percentage; some analysts use the expected earnings growth rate over a three- to five-year horizon). This approach produces the so-called PEG ratio seen with increasing frequency in practice. Analysts compute the PEG ratio as follows:

$$PEG_0 = (\text{Price per share}_0/\text{Earnings per share}_1)/(g \times 100)$$

Analysts and the financial press use the PEG ratio as a rule of thumb to assess share price relative to earnings and expected future earnings growth. Although there is little theoretical foundation for this rule of thumb (which tends to vary across analysts), proponents of PEG ratios generally assert that firms normally have PEG ratios near 1.0, indicating that market price fairly reflects expected earnings growth. This rule of thumb arises under the following set of assumptions: (a) The firm's earnings behave as a perpetuity with growth; (b) the firm's earnings generate an ROCE equivalent to R_E; (c) all of the firm's growth arises from reinvesting all of its earnings; and (d) all of the reinvested earnings generate an ROCE equivalent to R_E, so the firm's earnings growth rate is equivalent to R_E. Under this set of assumptions, the PEG ratio rule of thumb follows (for notation, assume $(g \times 100) = G = R_E$):

$$\begin{aligned} PEG_0 &= (\text{Price per share}_0/\text{Earnings per share}_1)/(g \times 100) \\ &= P_0/E_1/G = 1/R_E/R_E = 1 \end{aligned}$$

Using this rule of thumb, proponents assert that market prices for firms with PEG ratios less than one are low relative to growth, and market prices for firms with PEG ratios greater than one are high relative to growth. Proponents of PEG ratios argue that this heuristic provides a convenient means to rank stocks, taking into account one-year-ahead earnings and expected earnings growth.[17]

In Chapter 10, we assumed that PepsiCo would experience earnings growth of roughly 5.8 percent per year through Year +5. Using this growth rate assumption and our Year +1

[17]Mark Bradshaw demonstrates an empirical link between PEG ratios and sell-side analysts' target price recommendations in "The Use of Target Prices to Justify Sell-Side Analysts' Stock Recommendations," *Accounting Horizons* 16, no. 1 (March 2002), pp. 27–41.

earnings per share forecast, we compute PepsiCo's PEG ratio at the end of Year 4 as follows:

$$\begin{aligned} PEG_4 &= (\text{Price per share}_4/\text{Earnings per share}_{+1})/(g \times 100) \\ &= (\$51.94/(\$4{,}222.9 \text{ million}/1{,}679 \text{ million shares}))/(0.058 \times 100) \\ &\quad (\$51.94/\$2.52)/(0.058 \times 100) \\ &= 20.6/5.8 = 3.55 \end{aligned}$$

Thus, PepsiCo shares traded at the end of Year 4 at a PEG ratio of 3.55. Based on the PEG heuristic, PepsiCo's PEG ratio of 3.55 suggests that the market price for PepsiCo shares reflects substantial overpricing of PepsiCo's earnings growth.

The PEG ratio heuristic does not take into account, however, differences in risk and costs of equity capital across firms. For example, PepsiCo's PEG ratio seems high because it does not account for the fact that PepsiCo's expected future ROCE is significantly greater than PepsiCo's R_E because of PepsiCo's substantial off-balance-sheet brand equity. In addition, this heuristic does not take into account the fact that PepsiCo is likely to achieve this future earnings growth with relatively low risk (PepsiCo's beta is 0.75). The PEG ratio deserves considerable attention from researchers and practitioners so that its uses and limitations can be tested and understood.

PE Ratio Measurement Issues

Thus far, we have discussed a variety of different measurement issues for PE ratios. Forward-looking PE ratios divide share price by one-year-ahead earnings forecasts, which is theoretically more correct; however, such forecasts are not readily available for all firms, and they depend on analysts' forecast assumptions, which can differ widely. Therefore, as noted earlier, in practice the analyst is most likely to encounter PE ratios in *The Wall Street Journal* or on financial data web sites that are most commonly measured as share price divided by earnings per share for either the most recent prior fiscal year or the most recent four quarters. This is a sensible approach because historical earnings are observable and unique; however, computation of PE ratios using historic earnings introduces the potential for bias. To recap, the analyst should be aware of (at least) the following two types of measurement error:

1. *Growth.* Simple ratios of price over earnings do not explicitly consider firm-specific differences in long-term earnings growth. The price-earnings ratios described in the prior sections provide mechanisms that incorporate growth into price-earnings multiples.
2. *Transitory earnings.* Past earnings are historical and may not be indicative of expected future "permanent" earnings levels. Insofar as historic earnings contain transitory gains or losses, or other components of income that are not expected to recur, they can cause the PE ratio to vary wildly.

In addition, the analyst must also be aware of the potential bias in PE ratios because of differences in firms' dividend payouts. Dividends displace future earnings. A dividend paid in year t reduces market price by the amount of the dividend, but the dividend is not subtracted from earnings. The dividend paid will cause future earnings to decline because the firm has paid out a portion of its resources to shareholders. Price should therefore decline by the present value of the firm's forgone amount of expected future return on assets distributed as dividends. Thus, for dividend-paying firms, dividends cause a mismatch between current-period price and lagged earnings. To eliminate this mismatch, the analyst should compute a PE ratio with growth for a dividend-paying firm as follows: $(P_t + D_t)/E_t = 1/(R_E - g)$.

Empirical Properties of PE Ratios

The theoretical models indicate that the PE ratio is related to R_E, the cost of equity capital, and g, the growth rate in future earnings. Several empirical studies have examined the relation between PE ratios, risk (measured using market beta), and growth (measured using realized prior growth rates or analysts' forecasts of future growth). These studies have found that approximately 50 to 70 percent of the variability in PE ratios across firms relates to risk and growth.[18]

PE Ratios as Predictors of Future Earnings Growth. Penman studied the relation between PE ratios and changes in earnings per share for all firms on the Compustat database for the years 1968–1985.[19] For each year, Penman grouped firms into twenty portfolios based on the level of their PE ratios. He then computed the percentage change in earnings per share for the formation year, and for each of the nine subsequent years. Penman then aggregated the results across years. The following table presents a subset of the aggregate results.

	Median Percentage Change in Earnings per Share in:				
PE Portfolio:	**Year 0**	**Year +1**	**Year +2**	**Year +3**	**Year +4**
High	3.9%	52.2%	17.5%	17.8%	15.0%
Medium	14.0%	11.8%	11.6%	13.7%	15.8%
Low	18.4%	4.8%	10.2%	12.3%	13.1%

The results for the portfolio formation year are consistent with transitory components in earnings. Firms with high PE ratios experienced low percentage changes in earnings during the formation year relative to the preceding year. Firms with low PE ratios experienced high percentage changes in earnings during the formation year. The results for Year +1 after the formation year suggest a counterbalancing effect of the earnings change in the formation year. A low-percentage increase in earnings is followed by a high-percentage earnings increase for the high PE portfolios, and vice versa for the low PE portfolios.

The results for subsequent years reflect the tendency toward mean reversion in percentage earnings changes to a level in the mid-teens. This result is consistent with the data presented in Exhibit 14.6 for ROCE, in which Bernard observed a mean reversion in ROCE toward the mid-teens. The mean reversion suggests systematic directional changes in earnings growth over time (that is, serial autocorrelation), but the reversion takes several years to occur.

Articulation of MB and PE Ratios. In the same research study, Penman also used the residual income valuation model and empirical data to examine the articulation between firms' PE and MB ratios.[20] Penman predicts that MB should be "normal" (that is, roughly equal to one) when the market expects the firm to earn zero residual income in the future. The MB ratio will be high (greater than one) or low (less than one) if the market expects the firm to earn positive or negative future residual income. At the same

[18]See William Beaver and Dale Morse, "What Determines Price-Earnings Ratios?," *Financial Analysts Journal* (July–August 1978), pp. 65–76; and Paul Zarowin, "What Determines Earnings-Price Ratios: Revisited," *Journal of Accounting, Auditing and Finance* (Summer 1990), pp. 439–454.

[19]Stephen H. Penman, "The Articulation of Price-Earnings Ratios and Market-to-Book Ratios and the Evaluation of Growth," *Journal of Accounting Research* 34, no. 2 (Autumn 1996), pp. 235–259.

[20]*Ibid.*

time, Penman predicts that PE ratios will be normal (that is, roughly equal to the inverse of R_E) when the firm earns current-period residual income that is equal to expected future residual income (that is, a firm with current ROCE equal to long-run expected ROCE, which should equal long-run expected R_E). In contrast, PE ratios should be high when the firm earns current residual income less than long-run expected residual income (that is, current ROCE is unusually low, causing PE to be high). PE ratios should be low when the firm earns current residual income that is greater than long-run expected residual income (that is, current ROCE is temporarily high, causing PE to be low.) Thus, MB ratios will be determined primarily by expected future residual income, whereas PE ratios will be a function of the difference between current and expected future residual income.

To study the articulation of PE and MB ratios, Penman collected data from the CRSP and Compustat databases on roughly 2,574 firms during the years 1968–1985. Each sample year, Penman ranked and grouped these firms into twenty portfolios based on PE ratios. He also ranked and grouped the same firms each year into three MB ratio portfolios, classifying MB ratios less than 0.90 as low, MB ratios greater than 1.10 as high, and MB ratios in between as normal.

Exhibit 14.8 presents a matrix summarizing a portion of the results from Penman's study. Exhibit 14.8 presents residual income figures after assuming a 10.0 percent cost of capital for all firm-years, and after scaling by beginning-of-period book value of common equity (so they are essentially residual ROCE figures). We denote current-period residual income as CRI, and future residual income one year ahead and six years ahead as FRI_1 and FRI_6, respectively.

EXHIBIT 14.8

The Articulation of Market-to-Book (MB) and Price-Earnings (PE) Ratios

	MB Ratio Portfolios:		
PE Ratio Portfolios:	**High**	**Normal**	**Low**
High (Portfolios 15–20)	CRI < FRI > 0 CRI: −0.50 to 0.07 FRI_1: −0.07 to 0.08 FRI_6: 0.01 to 0.11	CRI < FRI = 0 CRI: −0.36 to −0.04 FRI_1: −0.13 to −0.03 FRI_6: −0.06 to 0.07	CRI < FRI < 0 CRI: −0.24 to −0.06 FRI_1: −0.13 to −0.06 FRI_6: −0.01 to 0.02
Normal (Portfolios 7–14)	CRI = FRI > 0 CRI: 0.07 to 0.10 FRI_1: 0.08 to 0.10 FRI_6: 0.11 to 0.14	CRI = FRI = 0 CRI: −0.02 to 0.04 FRI_1: −0.02 to 0.04 FRI_6: 0.01 to 0.06	CRI = FRI < 0 CRI: −0.05 to 0.00 FRI_1: −0.04 to 0.00 FRI_6: −0.02 to 0.03
Low (Portfolios 1–6)	CRI > FRI > 0 CRI: 0.12 to 0.41 FRI_1: 0.12 to 0.25 FRI_6: 0.11 to 0.24	CRI > FRI = 0 CRI: 0.05 to 0.22 FRI_1: 0.05 to 0.15 FRI_6: 0.07 to 0.12	CRI > FRI < 0 CRI: 0.00 to 0.06 FRI_1: −0.01 to 0.04 FRI_6: 0.03 to 0.05

Source: We obtained these data from Table 4 in Stephen H. Penman, "The Articulation of Price-Earnings Ratios and Market-to-Book Ratios and the Evaluation of Growth," *Journal of Accounting Research* 34, no. 2 (Autumn 1996), pp. 235–259.

Penman's research results generally support his predictions and shed light on the residual income conditions that cause MB ratios and PE ratios to covary. Examining future residual income across columns of the matrix, Penman's results suggest that MB ratios correlate positively with future residual income, consistent with the results from Bernard in Exhibit 14.6. Future residual income is substantially higher for high-MB firms than for low-MB firms. Examining the results across rows, high-PE-ratio firms tend to have current-period residual income that is much lower than future residual income, suggesting that PE ratios for these firms are temporarily high because residual income is temporarily low. In contrast, firms with low PE ratios tend to have current residual income that is greater than the future residual income, suggesting that these firms are experiencing low PE ratios because residual income is temporarily high. Penman's results provide intuition about when MB ratios should be high, low, or normal, and concurrently, when PE ratios should be high, low, or normal.

Summary of VE and PE Ratios

Summarizing, the VE and PE ratios are determined by the following:

1. Risk.
2. Growth.
3. Differences between current and expected future (permanent) earnings.
4. Alternative accounting methods and principles.

The analyst must assess each of these elements when estimating VE and PE ratios, particularly when evaluating PE ratios based on reported earnings and when projecting PE ratios to value nontraded firms. The theoretical model indicates the factors affecting the PE ratio but does not provide an unambiguous signal of the "correct" PE ratio for a particular firm. The analyst should be aware of the following considerations when using PE ratios:

1. The PE ratio is particularly sensitive to the cost of equity capital and to the earnings growth rate because it assumes that a firm can increase earnings at that rate forever. The analyst should select a sustainable long-term growth rate when applying the PE model.
2. The theoretical PE model does not work when the growth rate in earnings exceeds the cost of equity capital. Firms are unlikely to increase earnings at rates exceeding the cost of equity capital forever. Competition will eventually force growth rates to decrease.
3. The theoretical PE model does not work when the cost of equity capital and the growth rate in earnings are similar in amount. The denominator of the theoretical model approaches zero and the theoretical PE ratio becomes exceeding large.
4. The PE model does not work when earnings are negative because the PE ratio assumes that earnings are permanent and negative earnings cannot persist in perpetuity.
5. Before concluding that the market is undervaluing or overvaluing a firm because the actual PE ratio differs from the theoretically correct VE ratio, the analyst should assess whether earnings of the period include transitory elements. The analyst should cleanse the current period's earnings for unusual, nonrecurring income items before measuring the PE ratio for the period.
6. When comparing actual PE ratios of firms, the analyst should consider the impact of their use of different accounting methods and principles.

Using Market Multiples of Comparable Firms

The analyst can use the PE and MB ratios of comparable firms to assess the corresponding ratios of publicly traded firms. The analyst can also value firms whose common shares are not publicly traded by using PE ratios and MB ratios of comparable firms that are publicly traded. The theoretical models assist in this valuation task by identifying the variables that the analyst should use in selecting comparable firms. Bhojraj and Lee demonstrate a technique for selecting comparable firms in multiples-based valuation by computing "warranted multiples" based on factors that drive cross-sectional differences in multiples, such as expected profitability, growth, and cost of capital.[21] Alford examined the accuracy of the PE valuation models using industry, risk, ROCE, and earnings growth as the bases for selecting comparable firms.[22] The results indicate that industry membership, particularly at a three-digit SIC code level, provides a useful basis for comparisons if firms in the same industry experience similar profitability, face similar risks, and grow at similar rates. Thus, in some circumstances, industry membership serves as an effective proxy for the variables in the PE valuation model. However, as the data in Exhibit 14.7 reveal, substantial differences commonly exist in PE ratios of firms within the same industry. The warranted-multiples approach of Bhojraj and Lee provides a mechanism to determine comparable companies within industries and across different industries.

PRICE DIFFERENTIALS[23]

To what extent has the market discounted the value of a firm's common equity for risk? On a per-share level, what is the per-share price impact of risk? Is the discount for risk that the market has impounded in a firm's share price sufficient to compensate for risk? Or is the discount too large or too small relative to risk? We rely on an adaptation of the residual income model to address these questions. We use the residual income model and risk-free rates of return to estimate *risk-neutral value*. We then subtract market price from risk-neutral value to assess the *price differential*—the amount the market has discounted share price for risk.

As we described in detail in the previous chapter, the residual income model determines the present value of common shareholders' equity as follows:

$$V_0 = BV_0 + \sum_{t=1}^{\infty} \frac{NI_t - (R_E \times BV_{t-1})}{(1 + R_E)^t}$$

To implement this model, the analyst must estimate the cost of equity capital (R_E) for purposes of computing residual income $[NI_t - (R_E \times BV_{t-1})]$ and for discounting residual income to present value at $1/(1 + R_E)^t$. But the state of the art in financial economics does not provide a clear picture of how R_E should be determined. Substantial controversy surrounds expected returns models like the CAPM. What is the appropriate measure for market beta? In addition to market betas, do other risk factors belong in the expected

[21]Sanjeev Bhojraj and Charles M. C. Lee, "Who Is My Peer? A Valuation-Based Approach to the Selection of Comparable Firms," *Journal of Accounting Research* 40, no. 2 (May 2002), pp. 407–439.

[22]Andrew W. Alford, "The Effect of the Set of Comparable Firms on the Accuracy of the Price-Earnings Valuation Method," *Journal of Accounting Research* (Spring 1992), pp. 94–108.

[23]This section relies heavily on Stephen Baginski and James Wahlen, "Residual Income Risk, Intrinsic Values, and Share Prices," *Accounting Review* 78, no. 1 (January 2003), pp. 327–351.

returns model, such as firm size, market-to-book ratios, or some other set of risk factors? Assuming one can identify the appropriate risk factors that are priced in the market, what are the appropriate risk premia to use to determine expected returns for each of these factors? At an even more fundamental level, questions arise about whether risk and expected returns should be measured based on covariation between a firm's returns and a market index of returns. These questions arise in part because market-based models like the CAPM are essentially circular—should stock prices and realized returns be used to estimate risk to determine expected returns to evaluate stock prices? Or should risk and expected returns be based on covariation between a firm's returns and an economy-wide measure of consumption, on the theory that investors' risk aversion is driven by the need to diversify volatility in expected future consumption?

In light of the critical role of risk and expected returns in valuation, and in light of the uncertainty surrounding how to measure risk and expected returns, the analyst needs a variety of tools to assess the impact of risk on share prices and firm values. One such tool involves computing price differentials. If the analyst substitutes the prevailing risk-free rate of interest (denoted R_F; for example, the yield on one- to five-year U.S. Treasury securities) for the cost of equity capital, the residual income model can be used to determine risk-neutral value (denoted RNV_0), which is an estimate of the value of the firm in a risk-neutral market:

$$RNV_0 = BV_0 + \sum_{t=1}^{\infty} \frac{NI_t - (R_F \times BV_{t-1})}{(1 + R_F)^t}$$

Risk-neutral value represents the value of the firm, based on book value of equity and forecasts of expected future earnings, in the absence of discounting for risk. Dividing risk-neutral value by the number of shares outstanding gives risk-neutral value per share, which represents the hypothetical value at which shares would trade in a risk-neutral market. Market price per share of common equity reflects the risk-discounted value in a market that is risk averse. Therefore, market price per share can be subtracted from risk-neutral value per share to determine the total discount in share price for risk. We refer to this difference as the *price differential* (denoted *PDIFF*), computed as follows:

$$PDIFF_0 = RNV \text{ per share}_0 - \text{Price per share}_0$$

The analyst can evaluate the price differential to assess whether the market discount for risk is sufficient to compensate the investor to hold the firm's shares and bear risk. If the analyst assesses that $PDIFF_0$ is large relative to the risk of the firm, then perhaps the firm's shares may be overdiscounted for risk (undervalued). On the other hand, if the analyst assesses that $PDIFF_0$ is small relative to firm risk, then perhaps the firm's shares are underdiscounted for risk (overvalued). In the next section, we illustrate how to compute the PDIFF for PepsiCo. In the following section that discusses reverse engineering, we describe and apply more formal methods to gauge the magnitude of PDIFF.

Computing PDIFF for PepsiCo

To compute the price differential of PepsiCo as of the end of Year 4, we rely on the forecast assumptions developed in Chapter 10 and the residual income model developed in the previous chapter. However, instead of using a 7.75 percent cost of equity capital for PepsiCo for purposes of computing residual income and discounting it to present value,

EXHIBIT 14.9

Price Differential of PepsiCo
Present Value of Residual Income in Year +1 through Year +5 after Discounting at the Risk-Free Rate of Interest (4.0 percent)
(amounts in millions)

	Year +1	Year +2	Year +3	Year +4	Year +5
Lagged Book Value of Common Shareholders' Equity (at $t - 1$)	$13,572.0	$14,388.1	$14,746.8	$15,313.3	$15,908.1
Comprehensive Income Available for Common Shareholders	$ 4,222.9	$ 4,503.2	$ 4,887.7	$ 5,216.8	$ 5,580.4
Required Earnings	$ 542.9	$ 575.5	$ 589.9	$ 612.5	$ 636.3
Residual Income	$ 3,680.0	$ 3,927.7	$ 4,297.8	$ 4,604.3	$ 4,944.1
Present Value Factors	× 0.962	× 0.925	× 0.889	× 0.855	× 0.822
Present Value Residual Income...	$ 3,538.5	$ 3,631.3	$ 3,820.7	$ 3,935.8	$ 4,063.7
Sum of Present Value Residual Income	$18,990.0				

we instead use the risk-free interest rate at the time of the valuation. At the end of Year 4, U.S. Treasury bills with one to five years to maturity yielded roughly 4.0 percent. Exhibit 14.9 reports that the present value of PepsiCo's expected future residual income in Year +1 through Year +5 amounts to $18,990.0 million, computed using the 4.0 percent risk-free discount rate.

To compute continuing value, we use the now-familiar perpetuity-with-growth model [$= 1/(R_F - g)$], assuming that long-term growth for PepsiCo will be 3.0 percent and the risk-free discount rate is 4.0 percent. The present value of continuing value under this approach is $416,806.6 million. After adding book value of common equity at the end of Year 4, adjusting for midyear discounting, and dividing by the number of shares outstanding, we estimate that the PepsiCo shares have a risk-neutral value of $272.99. Subtracting the market price at Year 4 of $51.94 per share, we estimate the price-differential to be $221.05. These computations suggest that PepsiCo shares have been discounted by the risk-averse market by roughly $221.05 per share below the value at which they would trade in a hypothetical risk-neutral market, conditional on the forecast assumptions in Chapter 10. These computations indicate that PepsiCo shares traded at the end of Year 4 at a price equal to roughly 19 percent of risk-neutral value (= $51.94/$272.99). Exhibit 14.10 presents these computations.

In Chapters 11 through 13, we estimated that PepsiCo shares may have been underpriced at the end of Year 4 by roughly 10 percent, conditional on our forecast assumptions and valuation models. The price differential computation indicates that the market imposed a substantial discount to PepsiCo's expected future residual income, relative to the risk of PepsiCo. To more formally evaluate the relative magnitude of the price differential, we next turn to the method of reverse engineering market values.

EXHIBIT 14.10

Price Differential of PepsiCo
(amounts in millions)

Valuation Steps:	Computations:	Amounts:
Sum of Present Value Residual Income in Year +1 through Year +5	Discounted at the risk-free rate of interest of 4.0 percent. See Exhibit 14.9.	$ 18,990.0
Add Continuing Value in Present Value	Year +6 residual income assumed to grow at 3.0% in perpetuity; discounted at 4.0%. Computations not shown.	+$416,806.6
Total Present Value Residual Income		$435,796.6
Add Beginning Book Value of Equity	Book value of equity from Year 4 balance sheet.	+$ 13,572.0
		$449,368.6
Adjust for Midyear Discounting	Multiply by $1 + (R_F/2)$.	× 1.020
Present Value of Common Equity		$458,356.0
Shares Outstanding		÷ 1,679.0
Risk-Neutral Value per Share		$ 272.99
Current Price per Share		−$ 51.94
Price Differential		$ 221.05
Price Differential as a Percent of Risk-Neutral Value		19.0%

REVERSE ENGINEERING

In this text we have described the process of using a firm's fundamental characteristics to estimate firm value. This process can be characterized essentially as a puzzle with four pieces, or as an equation with four variables: value, expected future profitability, expected long-run future growth, and expected risk-adjusted discount rates. As we have described the valuation process thus far, we have developed forecasts and expectations about three of the variables—expected future profitability, long-run growth, and risk-adjusted discount rates—and we have used them to determine the fourth variable, firm value. In fact, we can make assumptions about any three of the four variables and then determine the fourth variable.

We can, for example, treat the market value of common equity as one of the "known" variables. We can assume that V_0 equals market value (that is, we can assume that intrinsic value equals price). We can then develop forecast assumptions for any two other variables, and solve for the missing fourth variable. We refer to this process as *reverse engineering* stock prices because it reverses the valuation process; the analyst assumes that intrinsic value equals market price, and then solves for the assumptions the market appears to be making in order to value the firm's shares at market price. For example, if we assume that the intrinsic value of a firm's shares equals the market's share price, and if we use the consensus analysts' forecasts for future earnings and growth as reasonable proxies for the market's expectations, then we can solve for the implied expected risk-adjusted rate of return on common equity that is consistent with the observed market price, conditional on the analysts' assumptions about earnings and growth. This is essentially equivalent to solving for the internal rate of return on the stock.

As another example, suppose we assume that the intrinsic value of a firm's shares equals the market's share price, and we assume that the market's risk-adjusted expected return on a stock can be determined by an asset pricing model such as the CAPM, and we assume analysts' consensus earnings forecasts through Year +5 are reasonable proxies for the market's earnings expectations. We can then solve for the long-run growth rate implicit in the firm's stock price, conditional on the other assumptions.

The process of reverse engineering stock prices allows the analyst to infer a set of assumptions that appear to be impounded into the firm's share price. The analyst can then assess whether the assumptions the market appears to be making are realistic, optimistic, or pessimistic. If the analyst determines that the market's assumptions seem optimistic, this suggests that the market has overpriced the stock (or perhaps the analyst is just too pessimistic). Alternatively, if the analyst determines that the market's assumptions are pessimistic, this suggests that the market has underpriced the stock (or again, the analyst may be wrong). Reverse engineering is an analytical approach through which the analyst can infer and judge the assumptions implicit in a stock price.

Reverse Engineering PepsiCo's Stock Price

To illustrate the process of reverse engineering, we apply the approach to PepsiCo, using the end of Year 4 market price of $51.94 per share. To reverse engineer PepsiCo's $51.94 share price, we will again rely on the residual income model in the previous chapter and the forecasts developed in Chapter 10.

Assume we want to solve for the expected rate of return (that is, the risk-adjusted discount rate) implied by PepsiCo's Year 4 share price of $51.94. Assume also that we believe our forecasts of earnings and book value of common equity for PepsiCo through Year +5 and our forecast of 3.0 percent long-run growth are realistic proxies for the market's expectations. Armed with share price, profitability and growth forecasts through Year +5, and a constant long-run growth assumption beyond Year +5, we can use the residual income value model to solve for the discount rate that reduces future earnings and book value to a present value equal to $51.94 per share.

Procedurally, one way to solve for the implied expected return on PepsiCo stock, conditional on the price, earnings, and growth assumptions, is to begin by estimating the value of common equity using the risk-free discount rate, as in the preceding price differential illustration. The initial value will likely far exceed the market price because the future residual income has not been discounted for risk. In applying the price differential model to PepsiCo in the previous section, we determined that PepsiCo's risk-free value was $272.99 per share. We then steadily increase the discount rate as necessary until the residual income model value exactly agrees with the market price of $51.94 per share. Following this approach, the implied expected rate of return on PepsiCo stock is 8.246 percent. At this discount rate, conditional on the residual income and growth assumptions, the present value of PepsiCo shares is $51.94 per share, exactly equal to market price. Recall that we assumed PepsiCo common equity had a required rate of return of 7.75 percent based on the CAPM. However, this reverse engineering approach indicates that if we buy a share of PepsiCo stock at the market price of $51.94, it will yield an 8.246 percent rate of return, conditional on our other assumptions. The Valuation spreadsheet in FSAP allows the analyst to make these iterative computations easily by simply varying the discount rate for equity capital.

To demonstrate another example, we can also reverse engineer PepsiCo's Year 4 stock price to solve for the implicit long-run growth assumption. To illustrate, we again assume that the market price of $51.94 per share reflects intrinsic value, and we assume that our earnings and book value forecasts through Year +5 are reasonable proxies for the market's expectations. We now return to our original assumption that the risk-adjusted discount rate for PepsiCo stock is 7.75 percent, based on the CAPM. With this, we have established three assumptions—value, earnings through Year +5, and the risk-adjusted discount rate—and we can solve for the missing piece of the puzzle: long-run implied growth. We begin with the long-run growth assumption set at zero. We compute our first estimate of share value using the zero growth assumption, and we compare that estimate to market price. The first estimate will likely be substantially lower than market price because market price probably includes the present value of the market's expectations for long-run growth. For PepsiCo, the initial value estimate assuming zero growth is $41.04 per share. We steadily increase the long-run growth parameter assumption as necessary until the present value from the residual income model equals market price. In the case of PepsiCo at the end of Year 4, market price of $51.94 only reflects long-run growth of 2.299 percent (significantly lower than our expectation of 3.0 percent long-run growth). That is, conditional on our assumptions for residual income through Year +5 and on our assumption that PepsiCo's cost of equity capital is 7.75 percent, if the market expects that long-run growth will be 2.299 percent, then the present value of PepsiCo shares exactly agrees with the market price of $51.94.[24]

THE RELEVANCE OF ACADEMIC RESEARCH FOR THE WORK OF THE SECURITY ANALYST[25]

Academic accounting researchers develop and test models to explain the observed relation between accounting information and stock prices. The research usually proposes theories and models for this relation analytically and then tests the models empirically on large data sets involving many firms for many years. The results of this research have provided many insights into multifaceted dimensions of the relations between accounting numbers and a wide variety of capital market variables such as stock prices, stock returns reactions around earnings announcements, stock returns cumulated over long periods of time, trading volume, analysts' and managers' earnings forecasts, equity costs of capital, implied market risk premia, market betas and other risk factors, bankruptcy, earnings management, and many others. Throughout this text, we have referred to relevant examples of empirical accounting research, including the classic study by Ball and Brown that helped set the stage for future research by being the first to show that changes in earnings correlate with unexpected changes in stock prices.[26] As we demonstrated in Exhibit 1.14 in Chapter 1, the Nichols and Wahlen replication of the Ball and Brown results indicate that, in their sample over the period 1988–2002, merely the difference in the sign of the change in annual earnings (whether positive or negative) was associated with nearly a

---

[24]Again, note that the Valuation spreadsheet in FSAP is a useful tool that allows the analyst to establish assumptions for earnings and the cost of capital, and then vary the long-run growth assumption to reverse engineer share price.

[25]This section draws heavily from Clyde P. Stickney, "The Academic's Approach to Securities Research: Is It Relevant to the Analyst?" *Journal of Financial Statement Analysis* (Summer 1997), pp. 52–60.

[26]Ray Ball and Philip Brown, "An Empirical Evaluation of Accounting Income Numbers," *Journal of Accounting Research* (Autumn 1968), pp. 159–178.

35 percent difference in annual market-adjusted stock returns.[27] The average sample firm that reported an earnings increase in a given year experienced stock returns that on average "beat" the market average by 19 percent, while the average sample firm that reported an earnings decrease in a given year experienced stock returns that on average fell 16 percent short of the market average.

Accounting academics and the research process itself provide important elements that should lead to reliable insights into the relation between accounting numbers and stock market variables. For example, academic researchers are trained to base their predictions and hypotheses as much as possible on formal theory integrating economics, finance, and accounting (rather than ad hoc or ex post reasoning). Academics commonly test these predictions with rigorous quasi-scientific methods on large empirical samples of real data. Academics usually have no commercial interest in the results, so the findings should not be biased by the need to obtain a particular conclusion, or the need to sell. Furthermore, academic research is not published in a leading scholarly research journal unless it survives the stringent peer review process. Few research studies pass the "publish" test; most "perish."

Despite these strong advantages leading the academic accounting research process toward reliable conclusions and insights about the relation between accounting numbers and market variables, the natural question for the security analyst is: Are the academic research models and empirical findings relevant to my task of making buy, sell, or hold recommendations on individual firms? This concluding section offers some thoughts on this important question. This section also summarizes the role of market efficiency and describes some of the empirical evidence to date on the relative degree of market efficiency with respect to earnings numbers. We consider the results to date to be very encouraging for analysts.

Level-of-Aggregation Issue

Both the academic and professional analyst communities must recognize that their interests involve different levels of aggregation. The academic is interested primarily in "big picture" explanations—conclusions and results that predict and explain the relation between accounting information and stock market variables in general. The analyst is concerned with specific assessments of the value of individual firms. The academic might seek to answer the question: What is the sign and significance of the relation between investments in research and development and stock market returns? Does this relation differ across industries? The analyst is more concerned with whether specific investments in research and development by a particular firm, such as Eli Lilly or Intel, are likely to enhance profitability and stock returns within the next three years. Academic research describes general tendencies that provide a basis for the analyst to assess the link between accounting numbers and a firm's value, and to identify deviations from the average for individual firms. Professional analysts create value by acting on the deviations (that is, taking positions in underpriced or overpriced stocks). Academics should not expect immediate application of their research findings to the work of the professional analyst. Professional analysts should not expect to apply the results of academic research immediately and specifically to their day-to-day responsibilities.

[27]D. Craig Nichols and James Wahlen, "How Do Earnings Numbers Relate to Stock Returns? A Review of Classic Accounting Research with Updated Evidence," *Accounting Horizons* 15, no. 4 (December 2004), pp. 263–286.

Theory Development and Practice Feed Each Other

The previous section identifies the common ground shared by the academic and professional analyst communities. Both communities share the desire to better understand how accounting information relates to stock prices. The activities of each community influence the other. Academics are keenly interested in predicting and explaining analysts' earnings forecasts and price targets, and, more generally, in explaining the actions of market participants on the whole. Analysts, directly or indirectly, rely on theories and results from academic research to inform their analysis. Much of what analysts learn in their academic training (such as in undergraduate and MBA programs) and in professional development training is developed and validated by academic work (including textbooks like this one that seek to link practice, theory, and research). Consider, for example, the impact that academic research relating to earnings forecasts, market reactions to earnings, risk and expected returns, and bankruptcy prediction have had on the work of the securities analyst during the last several decades. Consider the success of the academic community in identifying and explaining market pricing "anomalies," such as why the market does not fully incorporate information about past earnings changes when making earnings predictions, and the numerous portfolios and trading strategies that have emerged to exploit these anomalies.

Has the Theory of Capital Market Efficiency Gotten in the Way?

For most of the last several decades, academic research has presumed that the capital markets exhibit a relatively high degree of efficiency with respect to accounting information. In contrast, many analysts view their task as the constant pursuit of market inefficiencies—temporarily mispriced securities. Academics generally perceive market efficiency from the perspective of the big picture, with a view of large samples and market movements in general, whereas analysts see market efficiency from the front lines, experiencing daily swings in market prices that are sometimes hard to explain in the context of an efficient market. Thus, it is not surprising that at times the differences in perspective on the degree of market efficiency may create more of a wall, rather than a bridge, between academics and professional analysts. This section seeks to reach a common understanding, and the next section provides some striking evidence on the degree of market efficiency with respect to earnings.

Capital markets may be described as "efficient" with regard to accounting information if market prices react *completely* and *quickly* to available accounting information. Notice that efficiency should be described as a matter of degree, not as an absolute. The issue is not whether the capital markets are efficient. Rather, the issue is the degree to which the capital markets impound in prices all the available value-relevant information.

The term *completely* in this description implies the degree to which market participants identify the value-relevant implications of all available accounting information so that market prices reflect economic values without systematic bias. For example, a market that reflects a relatively high degree of information efficiency would impound in prices the value-relevant information in the persistence of earnings over time, and accounting information disclosed in footnotes as well as in the financial statements. A market that is relatively efficient will impound in stock prices the economic implications of all value-relevant accounting information, even including items that may be disclosed in the notes.

The term *quickly* in this description suggests that market participants cannot consistently earn abnormal returns using accounting information for a long period of time after the information has been made public. If capital markets exhibit a high degree of efficiency, market prices should react quickly (within a matter of days) to capture any value-relevant signals in the accounting information.

The degree of efficiency with respect to complete and quick reactions in an information-efficient capital market depends on analysts and financial statement analysis. Analysts study accounting information to assess appropriate values for stocks and to take positions in underpriced or overpriced securities, thereby driving stock market prices to efficient levels. The speed with which analysts can forecast, anticipate, analyze, and react to accounting information causes prices to move before accounting information is released, and to react quickly to surprises in the information when it is released.

Also consider what a high degree of market efficiency does not imply. A capital market with a high degree of information efficiency does not necessarily price all stocks correctly every day. As a practical matter, relatively efficient markets experience valuation errors at the level of the individual firm; but these random inefficiencies cancel out at an aggregated market level and do not tend to persist for long periods of time.[28] Analysts are driving forces involved in identifying and correcting security mispricings. A capital market with a high degree of information efficiency does not necessarily have perfect foresight—surprises happen. Firms frequently surprise the market by announcing earnings numbers that are higher or lower than the market's expectations. Again, analysts drive market prices to react quickly and completely to new information.

Striking Evidence on the Degree of Market Efficiency and Inefficiency with Respect to Earnings

Two studies by Bernard and Thomas provide the most striking evidence to date on the degree of market efficiency and inefficiency with respect to accounting earnings.[29] The Bernard and Thomas results during the post-earnings-announcement period suggest that the market's reaction to quarterly earnings news is highly, but not completely, efficient. Nichols and Wahlen (2004) used data from 1988 to 2002 to replicate the seminal results in Bernard and Thomas (which were based on data from the years 1974–1986). Nichols and Wahlen collected a sample of 90,470 quarterly earnings announcements for firms on the CRSP and Compustat databases. They ranked all sample firms each quarter into ten portfolios on the basis of each firm's unexpected earnings (unexpected earnings equals actual earnings per share minus analysts' consensus forecast of earnings per share, scaled by price per share as of sixty trading days prior to the earnings announcement for cross-sectional comparability). They studied the average abnormal (market-adjusted) stock returns to each portfolio over the sixty trading days leading up to the quarterly earnings announcement, and over the sixty trading days following the announcement. Exhibit 14.11 depicts a portion of the Nichols and Wahlen results, which mirror the Bernard and Thomas results.

The results in Exhibit 14.11 during the preannouncement period indicate that the market is highly efficient in anticipating and reacting to quarterly earnings surprises. Firms with quarterly earnings surprises in the "good news" portfolios—portfolios 7 through

---

[28]For a discussion of these issues, see Ray Ball, "The Earnings-Price Anomaly," *Journal of Accounting and Economics* (1992), pp. 319–345.

[29]Victor Bernard and Jacob Thomas, "Post-Earnings Announcement Drift: Delayed Price Response or Risk Premium?" *Journal of Accounting Research* 27 (Supplement, 1989), pp. 1–36; and "Evidence That Stock Prices Do Not Fully Reflect the Implications of Current Earnings for Future Earnings," *Journal of Accounting and Economics* 13, no. 4 (1990), pp. 305–340.

EXHIBIT 14.11

Evidence from Nichols and Wahlen (2004) Replication of Bernard and Thomas (1989) on Market Efficiency with Respect to Quarterly Earnings

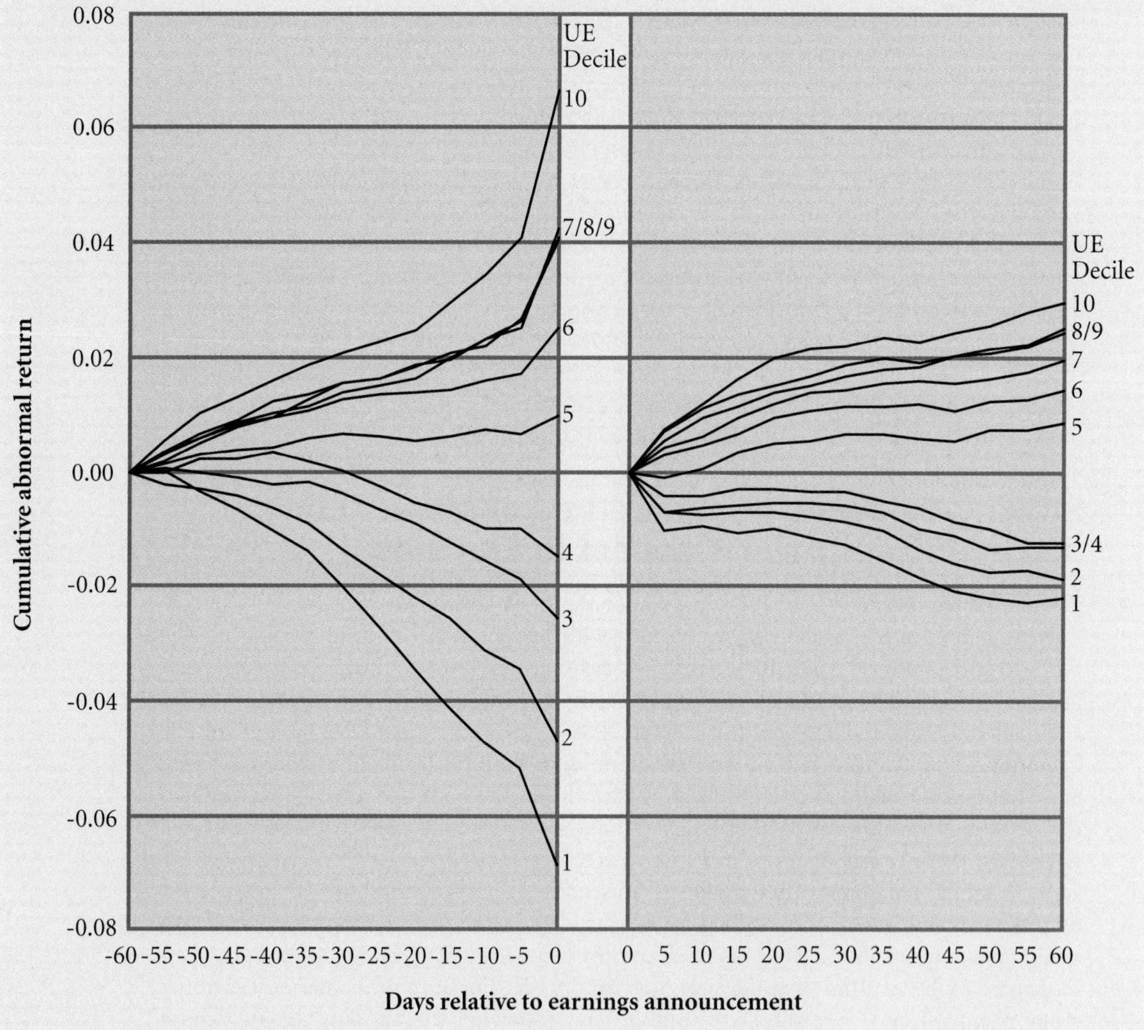

We form portfolios each quarter based on the magnitude of unexpected earnings per share scaled by price per share as of 60 trading days before the earnings announcement. The sample includes 90,470 firm-quarter observations.

10—experience positive cumulative abnormal returns during the sixty days prior to and including the release of earnings. Firms with quarterly earnings surprises in the "bad news" portfolios—portfolios 1 through 4—experience negative cumulative abnormal returns during the sixty days prior to and including the release of earnings. The average difference in cumulative abnormal returns between portfolio 10 (roughly +6.7 percent) and portfolio 1 (roughly −6.8 percent) was roughly 13.5 percent *per quarter.* These results suggest that the market anticipates and reacts quickly to quarterly earnings information.

The results in Exhibit 14.11 during the postannouncement period suggest that the market's reaction to quarterly earnings news is highly, but not completely, efficient. In the postannouncement period, Nichols and Wahlen measured the cumulative abnormal returns to the exact same portfolios over the sixty trading days after the earnings announcements. If the market's reactions to quarterly earnings were on average quick and complete, these portfolios should exhibit no systematic abnormal returns in the postannouncement period. Upon the announcement of earnings, market prices should adjust efficiently within a few days of the announcement. Postannouncement abnormal returns should arise only from new information that arrives during those sixty days, and the postannouncement abnormal returns should not be associated with the prior quarter's earnings news.

The results for the postannouncement period clearly indicate significant cumulative abnormal returns for the firms in portfolio 10 (best news) and portfolio 1 (worst news). Mean cumulative abnormal returns amount to roughly +3.0 percent and −2.2 percent for the best and worst news portfolios, respectively. In a follow up study, Bernard and Thomas (1990) show that, in part, the market seems to underreact to the persistence in current-period earnings for future-period earnings, failing to fully anticipate the momentum in quarterly earnings changes.

Taken together, the Bernard and Thomas studies reveal that the market is highly but not completely efficient with respect to quarterly earnings. The results from the Nichols and Wahlen study using current data suggest that the Bernard and Thomas findings still hold. We consider these results to be very encouraging for analysts. We interpret the results to suggest that analysts who can sharpen their ability to forecast future earnings and take long positions in (buy) shares of firms experiencing earnings increases and short positions in (sell) shares of firms experiencing earnings decreases during the sixty-day preannouncement period have the potential to earn some portion of the preannouncement abnormal returns. Similarly, analysts who can sharpen their ability to react appropriately once earnings are announced have some potential to earn a portion of the postannouncement abnormal returns. These findings suggest that there are returns to be earned by being good at forecasting and reacting to earnings.

We believe that the state-of-the-art of market efficiency is exactly where analysts would like it to be. The market is very efficient with respect to accounting information, but not perfectly efficient. Some stocks are temporarily mispriced, but the market tends to correct mispricings in a relatively short period of time. Financial statement analysis, particularly focusing on earnings, can help the analyst identify stocks whose prices may be temporarily out of equilibrium. Insightful financial statement analysis can lead to intelligent investment decisions and better-than-average returns.

SUMMARY

This chapter examines the use of market multiples in valuation by relying on the residual income model to develop the theoretical rationale relating market prices to economic drivers of value and to accounting fundamentals. This chapter describes the conceptual basis and practical application of market multiples such as the market-to-book value ratio, the price-earnings ratio, and the price-earnings-growth ratio. The chapter focuses on four variables, or factors, that affect these market multiples: (1) risk and the cost of equity capital, (2) the expected future growth rate in earnings, (3) the presence of permanent and transitory components in the earnings of a particular year, and (4) the effects of accounting methods and principles on reported earnings and the book value of common shareholders' equity. For decades, analysts have relied heavily on price-earnings ratios to relate market prices to earnings. However, in recent years, analysts and academics alike increasingly recognize that transitory elements in earnings and earnings growth can cloud the interpretation of the price-earnings ratio as an indicator of value. Analysts and academics are shifting emphasis to the price-earnings-growth ratio and to the market-to-book ratio. Transitory earnings elements of a particular period have less effect on the market-to-book ratio. This chapter also demonstrates techniques to exploit the information in market value by calculating price differentials and by reverse engineering stock prices to infer the assumptions the market must be making. The chapter concludes by describing the relevance of academic research for the professional analyst, including highlighting key research results that appear to be very encouraging for the analyst interested in using earnings and financial statement data to analyze and value firms.

QUESTIONS, EXERCISES, PROBLEMS, AND CASES

Questions and Exercises

14.1 RESIDUAL ROCE. Explain residual ROCE (return on common shareholders' equity). What does residual ROCE represent? What does residual ROCE measure?

14.2 THE VALUE-TO-BOOK VALUATION APPROACH. In conceptual terms, explain the value-to-book valuation approach. Explain how the value-to-book approach described and demonstrated in Chapter 14 relates to the residual income valuation approach described and demonstrated in Chapter 13.

14.3 INTERPRETING VALUE-TO-BOOK RATIOS. Explain the implications of a value-to-book ratio that is exactly equal to one. Explain the implications of a value-to-book ratio that is greater than one. Explain the implications of a value-to-book ratio that is less than one.

14.4 INTERPRETING VALUE-TO-BOOK RATIOS. Explain the implications of a value-to-book ratio that is greater than the market-to-book ratio. Explain the implications of a value-to-book ratio that is less than the market-to-book ratio.

14.5 VALUE-TO-BOOK RATIO DRIVERS. Identify three economic factors that will drive one firm's value-to-book ratio higher than those of other firms in the same industry. Identify three accounting factors that will drive one firm's value-to-book ratio higher than those of other firms in the same industry.

14.6 VALUE-TO-BOOK RATIO DRIVERS. Identify three economic factors that will drive a firm's value-to-book ratio to decrease over time. Identify three accounting factors that will drive a firm's value-to-book ratio to decrease over time.

14.7 THE VALUE-EARNINGS RATIO. In conceptual terms, explain the value-earnings ratio. Explain the difference between the value-earnings ratio and the price-earnings ratio. What is the critical assumption about future earnings in both the value-earnings and price-earnings ratios?

14.8 THE PRICE-EARNINGS RATIO. In practice, it is common to observe price-earnings ratios measured as current-period price divided by trailing-twelve-months (or most recent annual) earnings per share. Identify and explain three potential flaws inherent in this measurement of the price-earnings ratio as a valuation multiple.

14.9 PRICE-EARNINGS RATIO DRIVERS. Identify three economic factors that will drive one firm's price-earnings ratio higher than those of other firms in the same industry. Identify three accounting factors that will drive one firm's price-earnings ratio in a given period higher than those of other firms in the same industry.

14.10 PRICE-EARNINGS RATIO DRIVERS. Identify three economic factors that will drive a firm's price-earnings ratio to decrease over time. Identify three accounting factors that will drive a firm's price-earnings ratio down in a given period.

14.11 MARKET-TO-BOOK VERSUS PRICE-EARNINGS RATIOS. Explain why market-to-book multiples demonstrate less variance over time and across firms than do price-earnings multiples.

14.12 PRICE DIFFERENTIALS. Explain price differentials in conceptual terms. What does a price differential measure? How does a price differential relate to risk?

14.13 REVERSE ENGINEERING SHARE PRICES. Explain reverse engineering of share prices in conceptual terms. How does reverse engineering of share prices enable an analyst to infer (or deduce) the assumptions that the capital markets appear to impound in share price?

14.14 MARKET EFFICIENCY. What does market efficiency mean? What does market efficiency *not* mean? Explain how market efficiency relates to the *amount* of information that affects share prices and the *speed* with which information affects share prices.

14.15 ANALYSTS' ROLE IN MARKET EFFICIENCY. Explain the analysts' role in making the capital markets efficient.

14.16 MARKET EFFICIENCY WITH RESPECT TO QUARTERLY EARNINGS SURPRISES. Using the evidence presented in Exhibit 14.11, describe the extent to which the market is efficient with respect to quarterly earnings surprises during the sixty trading days prior to quarterly earnings announcements. Using the evidence presented in Exhibit 14.11, describe the extent to which the market is efficient with respect to quarterly earnings surprises during the sixty trading days following quarterly earnings announcements.

Problems and Cases

14.17 USING MARKET MULTIPLES TO ASSESS VALUES AND MARKET PRICES. Problem 13.18 and Exhibit 13.7 in Chapter 13 present selected data from projected financial statements for Steak n Shake for Year +1 to Year +11. The amounts for Year +11 reflect a long-term growth assumption of 3 percent. The cost of equity capital is 9.34 percent. The market value of common shareholders' equity in Steak n Shake on January 1, Year +1, is $309.98 million.

FSAP

Required

a. Compute the value-to-book ratio as of January 1, Year +1, using the residual ROCE valuation method.

b. Using the analyses developed in part a, prepare an exhibit summarizing the following ratios for Steak n Shake as of January 1, Year +1:

1. Value-to-book ratio (use the amounts from part a).
2. Market-to-book ratio.
3. Value-earnings ratio, using reported earnings for Year 0 of $21.8 million.
4. Price-earnings ratio, using reported earnings for Year 0 of $21.8 million.
5. Value-earnings ratio, using projected earnings for Year +1 of $24.5 million.
6. Price-earnings ratio, using projected earnings for Year +1 of $24.5 million.

c. Compute the risk-neutral value of Steak n Shake as of January 1, Year +1, using a risk-free rate of 4.2 percent. Use the projected earnings for Year +1 to Year +10, and the projected earnings for Year +11 given in Exhibit 13.7. Maintain the continuing value growth assumption of 3 percent. Compute the price differential for Steak n Shake as of January 1, Year +1. Compute the ratio of market value to risk-neutral value for Steak n Shake as of January 1, Year +1.

d. Use reverse engineering to solve for the long-run growth rate in continuing residual income in Year +11 and beyond that is implicitly impounded in the market value of Steak n Shake on January 1, Year +1. Use the 9.34 percent cost of equity capital and the projected earnings amounts for Year +1 to Year +10 in Exhibit 13.7 before solving for the long-run growth rate in continuing residual income.

e. Using the analyses in parts a to d, evaluate the extent of mispricing (if any) of Steak n Shake by the market.

14.18 INTERPRETING MARKET-TO-BOOK RATIOS. Exhibit 14.12 presents data from a recent year on market-to-book ratios, ROCE, the cost of equity capital, and price-earnings ratios for seven pharmaceutical companies. (Note that price-earnings ratios for these firms typically fall in the 30–35 range.) Exhibit 14.12 also provides historical data on the five-year average rate of growth in earnings and dividend payout ratios for each firm. The data on excess earnings years represent the number of years that each firm would need to earn a rate of return on common shareholders' equity (ROCE) equal to that in Exhibit 14.12 in order to produce value-to-book ratios that equal the market-to-book ratios shown. For example, Bristol-Myers Squibb would need to earn an ROCE of 48.9 percent for 58.3 years in order for the present value of the excess earnings over the cost of equity capital to produce a value-to-book ratio that matches the market-to-book ratio of 13.9.

Required

Assume that market share prices for each firm are reasonably efficient (that is, do not simply assume that the market has overvalued or undervalued these firms). Considering the theoretical determinants of the market-to-book ratio, discuss the likely reasons for the relative ordering of these seven companies on their market-to-book ratios.

14.19 SENSITIVITY OF THE THEORETICAL MODELS OF VALUE-EARNINGS AND VALUE-TO-BOOK TO CHANGES IN ASSUMPTIONS. This problem explores the sensitivity of the value-earnings and value-to-book models to changes in underlying assumptions. We recommend that you design a computer spreadsheet to perform the calculations, particularly for the value-to-book ratio.

EXHIBIT 14.12

Selected Data for Pharmaceutical Companies
(Problem 14.18)

Company	MB	ROCE	Cost of Equity	Dividend Payout Ratio	PE	Growth in Earnings	Excess Earnings Years
Bristol-Myers Squibb	13.9	.489	.134	.77	32.4	.068	58.3
Warner Lambert	13.0	.350	.133	.48	42.7	.051	32.2
Eli Lilly	12.4	.281	.155	.42	49.3	.110	89.8
Pfizer	11.2	.350	.143	.43	40.4	.152	27.8
Abbott Laboratories	10.4	.428	.113	.39	26.9	.116	13.5
Merck	10.3	.331	.154	.46	31.8	.130	41.9
Wyeth	6.9	.340	.138	.51	25.0	.065	24.6

Required

a. Compute the value-earnings ratio under each of the following sets of assumptions:

Scenario	Cost of Equity Capital	Growth Rate in Earnings
A	.15	.06
B	.15	.08
C	.15	.10
D	.13	.06
E	.13	.08
F	.13	.10
G	.11	.06
H	.11	.08
I	.11	.10

b. Assess the sensitivity of the value-earnings ratio to changes in the cost of equity capital and changes in the growth rate.

c. Compute the value-to-book ratio under each of the following sets of assumptions:

Scenario	ROCE	Cost of Equity Capital	Dividend Payout Percentage	Years of Excess Earnings
A	.20	.13	.30	10
B	.18	.13	.30	10
C	.14	.13	.30	10
D	.18	.15	.30	10
E	.18	.11	.30	10
F	.18	.13	.40	10
G	.18	.13	.20	10
H	.18	.13	.30	15
I	.18	.13	.30	20

d. Assess the sensitivity of the value-to-book ratio to changes in the assumptions made about the various underlying variables.

14.20 MARKET MULTIPLES AND REVERSE ENGINEERING SHARE PRICES. In 2000, Enron enjoyed remarkable success in the capital markets. During that year, Enron's shares increased in value by 89 percent, while the S&P 500 Index fell by 9 percent. At the end of 2000, Enron's shares were trading at roughly $83 per share, and all of the sell-side analysts following Enron recommended the shares as either a "buy" or a "strong buy." With 752.2 million shares outstanding, Enron had a market capitalization of $62,530 million and was one of the largest firms (in terms of market value) in the United States. At year-end 2000, Enron's book value of common shareholders equity was $11,470 million.

At year-end 2000, Enron posted earnings per share of $1.19. Among sell-side analysts following Enron, the consensus forecast for earnings per share was $1.31 per share for 2001 and $1.44 per share for 2002, with 10 percent earnings growth expected from 2003 to 2005. At the time, Enron was paying dividends equivalent to roughly 40 percent of earnings and it was expected to maintain that payout policy.

At year-end 2000, Enron had a market beta of 1.7. The risk-free rate of return was 4.3 percent, and the market risk premium was 5.0 percent.

Required

a. Use the CAPM to compute the required rate of return on common equity capital for Enron.

b. Use year-end 2000 data to compute the following ratios for Enron:

i. Market-to-book.

ii. Price-earnings (using 2000 earnings per share).

iii. Price-earnings (using consensus forecast earnings per share for 2001).

c. Assume that at year-end 2000, Enron's market price equals value, that the consensus analysts' earnings per share forecasts through 2005 are reliable proxies for market expectations, that Enron will maintain a 40 percent dividend payout rate, and that beyond 2005 Enron's long-run earnings growth rate will be 3.0 percent. Reverse engineer Enron's $83 share price to solve for the implied expected return on Enron shares.

d. What do these analyses suggest about investing in Enron's shares at a price of $83?

NOTE: The data provided in this problem, and the inferences you draw from them, do not depend on foresight of Enron declaring bankruptcy by the end of 2001.

14.21 VALUATION OF COCA-COLA USING MARKET MULTIPLES. FSAP
The Coca-Cola Company is a global soft drink beverage company (KO ticker symbol) that is a primary and direct competitor with PepsiCo. The data in Exhibits 12.13, 12.14, and 12.15 in Chapter 12 include the actual amounts for Year 4 and projected amounts for Year +1 to Year +6 for the income statements, balance sheets, and statements of cash flows for Coca-Cola (amounts in millions).

The market equity beta for Coca-Cola at the end of Year 4 is .76. Assume that the risk-free interest rate is 4.0 percent and the market risk premium is 5.0 percent. Coca-Cola has 2,409 million shares outstanding at the end of Year 4. At the end of Year 4, Coca-Cola's share price was $41.64.

In this problem, we use these actual and projected financial statement data to apply the techniques in Chapter 14 to compute Coca-Cola's required rate of return on equity and share value based on the value-to-book valuation model. We also compare our value-to-book ratio estimate to Coca-Cola's market-to-book ratio at the end of Year 4 to determine an investment recommendation. In addition, we compute the value-earnings and price-earnings ratios, compute the price differential, and reverse engineer Coca-Cola's share price as of the end of Year 4.

Required

Part I—Computing Coca-Cola's Value-to-Book Ratio Using the Value-to-Book Valuation Approach

a. Use the CAPM to compute the required rate of return on common equity capital for Coca-Cola.

b. Using the projected financial statements in Chapter 12, Exhibits 12.13 to 12.15, derive the projected residual ROCE (return on common shareholders' equity) for Coca-Cola for Years +1 through +5.

c. Assume that the steady-state long-run growth rate will be 3 percent in Year +6 and beyond. Project that the Year +5 income statement and balance sheet amounts will grow by 3 percent in Year +6, and then derive the projected residual ROCE for Year +6 for Coca-Cola.

d. Using the required rate of return on common equity from part a as a discount rate, compute the sum of the present value of residual ROCE for Coca-Cola for Years +1 through +5.

e. Using the required rate of return on common equity from part a as a discount rate, and the long run growth rate from part c, compute the continuing value of Coca-Cola as of the start of Year +6 based on Coca-Cola's continuing residual ROCE in Year +6 and beyond. After computing continuing value as of the start of Year +6, discount it to present value at the start of Year +1.

f. Compute Coca-Cola's value-to-book ratio as of the end of Year 4 with the following three steps. (1) Compute the total sum of the present value of all future residual ROCE (from parts d and e). (2) To the total from item (1), add one (representing the book value of equity as of the beginning of the valuation as of the end of Year 4). (3) Adjust the total sum from item (2) using the midyear discounting adjustment factor.

g. Compute Coca-Cola's market-to-book ratio as of the end of Year 4. Compare the value-to-book ratio to the market-to-book ratio. What investment decision does the comparison suggest? What does the comparison suggest regarding the pricing of Coca-Cola shares in the market: underpriced, overpriced, or fairly priced?

h. Use the value-to-book ratio to project the value of a share of common equity in Coca-Cola.

i. If you computed Coca-Cola's common equity share value using the free cash flows to common equity valuation approach in Problem 12.16 in Chapter 12 and/or the residual income valuation approach in Problem 13.19 in Chapter 13, compare the value estimate you obtained in those problems with the estimate you obtained in this case. You should obtain the same value estimates under all three approaches. If you have not yet worked those prior problems, it would be valuable to do so now.

Part II—Analyzing Coca-Cola's Share Price Using the Value-Earnings Ratio, the Price-Earnings Ratio, Price Differentials, and Reverse Engineering

j. Use the forecast data for Year +1 to project Year +1 earnings per share. To do so, divide the projection of Coca-Cola's comprehensive income available for common shareholders in Year +1 by the number of common shares outstanding at the end of Year 4. Using this Year +1 earnings per share forecast, and using the share value computed in part h, compute Coca-Cola's value-earnings ratio.

k. Using the Year +1 earnings per share forecast from part j, and using the share price at the end of Year 4, compute Coca-Cola's price-earnings ratio. Compare Coca-Cola's value-earnings ratio with its price-earnings ratio. What investment decision does the comparison suggest? What does the comparison suggest regarding the pricing of Coca-Cola shares in the market: underpriced, overpriced, or fairly priced? Does this comparison lead to the same conclusions that you reached by comparing value-to-book ratios with market-to-book ratios in part g?

l. Compute Coca-Cola's price differential at the end of Year 4. Compute Coca-Cola's price differential as a percentage of Coca-Cola's risk-neutral value. What dollar amount and what percentage amount has the market discounted Coca-Cola shares for risk?

m. Reverse engineer Coca-Cola's share price at the end of Year 4 to solve for the implied expected rate of return. First, assume that value equals price, and assume that the earnings and growth forecasts through Year +6 and beyond are reliable proxies for the market's expectations for Coca-Cola. Then solve for the implied expected rate of return (the discount rate) the market has impounded in Coca-Cola's share price. *(Hint: Begin with the forecast and valuation spreadsheet you developed to value Coca-Cola shares. Vary the discount rate until you solve for the discount rate that makes your value estimate exactly equal the end of Year 4 market price of $41.64 per share.)*

n. Reverse engineer Coca-Cola's share price at the end of Year 4 to solve for the implied expected long-run growth. First, assume that value equals price, and assume that the earnings forecasts through Year +5 are reliable proxies for the market's expectations for Coca-Cola. Also assume that the discount rate implied by the CAPM (computed in part a) is a reliable proxy for the market's expected rate of return. Then solve for the implied expected long-run growth rate the market has impounded in Coca-Cola's share price. *(Hint: Begin with the forecast and valuation spreadsheet you developed to value Coca-Cola shares, and use the CAPM discount rate. Set the long-run growth parameter initially to zero. Increase the long-run growth rate until you solve for the growth rate that makes your value estimate exactly equal the end of Year 4 market price of $41.64 per share.)*

14.22 ANALYSIS OF COMPARABLE COMPANIES USING MARKET MULTIPLES. In this chapter, we evaluated shares of common equity in PepsiCo using the value-to-book approach, market multiples, price differentials, and reverse engineering. The Coca-Cola Company is a direct competitor with PepsiCo. The data in Exhibits 12.13, 12.14, and 12.15 in Chapter 12 include the actual amounts for Year 4 and projected amounts for Year +1 to Year +6 for the income statements, balance sheets, and statements of cash flows for Coca-Cola (amounts in millions). In the previous problem, Problem 14.21, we evaluated shares of common equity in Coca-Cola using the value-to-book approach, market multiples, price differentials, and reverse engineering.

FSAP

Required

a. Prepare an exhibit using the data and analyses for PepsiCo from this chapter and the data and analyses for Coca-Cola from the previous problem that will allow you to compare these two competitors on the following dimensions:

1. Cost of equity capital (R_E).
2. ROCE for Year 4.
3. Projected ROCE for Year +1.
4. Book value of common shareholders' equity.
5. Market value of common shareholders' equity.
6. Intrinsic value of common shareholders' equity.
7. Value-to-book ratio.
8. Market-to-book ratio.
9. Value-earnings ratio (using Year +1 projected comprehensive income).
10. Price-earnings ratio (using Year +1 projected comprehensive income).
11. Value-earnings ratio (using Year 4 reported earnings per share).
12. Price-earnings ratio (using Year 4 reported earnings per share).
13. Price differential (on a per-share basis).
14. Price as a percentage of risk-neutral value.

15. Reverse engineer to solve for implied expected rate of return (assuming 3 percent long-run growth).
16. Reverse engineer to solve for implied long-run growth (assuming the cost of equity capital as the discount rate).

b. What inferences can you draw from these comparisons about the valuation of PepsiCo versus Coca-Cola? In the chapter, we concluded that PepsiCo shares were slightly underpriced in the market at the end of Year 4, whereas in the previous problem we concluded that Coca-Cola shares were slightly overpriced in the market at the end of Year 4. How are these comparisons consistent with these conclusions?

FSAP

14.23 VALUATION OF WAL-MART USING MARKET MULTIPLES. Problem 10.16 projects financial statements for Wal-Mart Stores for Years +1 through +5. The data in Exhibits 12.16, 12.17, and 12.18 in Chapter 12 include the actual amounts for Year 4 and the projected amounts for Year +1 to Year +5 for the income statements, balance sheets, and statements of cash flows for Wal-Mart (amounts in millions).

The market equity beta for Wal-Mart at the end of Year 4 is .80. Assume that the risk-free interest rate is 4.0 percent and the market risk premium is 5.0 percent. Wal-Mart has 4,234 million shares outstanding at the end of Year 4. At the end of Year 4, Wal-Mart's share price was $52.40.

In this problem, we use these actual and projected financial statement data to apply the techniques in Chapter 14 to compute Wal-Mart's required rate of return on equity and share value based on the value-to-book valuation model. We also compare our value-to-book ratio estimate to Wal-Mart's market-to-book ratio at the end of Year 4 to determine an investment recommendation. In addition, we compute the value-earnings and price-earnings ratios, compute the price differential, and reverse engineer Wal-Mart's share price as of the end of Year 4.

Required

Part I—Computing Wal-Mart's Value-to-Book Ratio Using the Value-to-Book Valuation Approach

a. Use the CAPM to compute the required rate of return on common equity capital for Wal-Mart.

b. Using the projected financial statements in Chapter 12, Exhibits 12.16 to 12.18, derive the projected residual ROCE (return on common shareholders' equity) for Wal-Mart for Years +1 through +5.

c. Assume that the steady-state long-run growth rate will be 3 percent in Year +6 and beyond. Project that the Year +5 income statement and balance sheet amounts will grow by 3 percent in Year +6, and then derive the projected residual ROCE for Year +6 for Wal-Mart.

d. Using the required rate of return on common equity from part a as a discount rate, compute the sum of the present value of residual ROCE for Wal-Mart for Years +1 through +5.

e. Using the required rate of return on common equity from part a as a discount rate, and the long-run growth rate from part c, compute the continuing value of Wal-Mart as of the start of Year +6 based on Wal-Mart's continuing residual ROCE in Year +6 and beyond. After computing continuing value as of the start of Year +6, discount it to present value at the start of Year +1.

f. Compute Wal-Mart's value-to-book ratio as of the end of Year 4 with the following three steps. (1) Compute the total sum of the present value of all future residual ROCE (from parts d and e). (2) To the total from item (1), add one (representing the book value of equity as of the beginning of the valuation as of the end of Year 4). (3) Adjust the total sum from item (2) using the midyear discounting adjustment factor.

g. Compute Wal-Mart's market-to-book ratio as of the end of Year 4. Compare the value-to-book ratio to the market-to-book ratio. What investment decision does the comparison suggest? What does the comparison suggest regarding the pricing of Wal-Mart shares in the market: underpriced, overpriced, or fairly priced?

h. Use the value-to-book ratio to project the value of a share of common equity in Wal-Mart.

i. If you computed Wal-Mart's common equity share value using the dividends valuation approach in Problem 11.14 in Chapter 11, and/or the free cash flows to common equity valuation approach in Problem 12.17 in Chapter 12, and/or the residual income valuation approach in Problem 13.20 in Chapter 13, compare the value estimate you obtained in those problems with the estimate you obtained in this case. You should obtain the same value estimates under all four approaches. If you have not yet worked those prior problems, it would be valuable to do so now.

Part II—Analyzing Wal-Mart's Share Price Using the Value-Earnings Ratio, the Price-Earnings Ratio, Price Differentials, and Reverse Engineering

j. Use the forecast data for Year +1 to project Year +1 earnings per share. To do so, divide the projection of Wal-Mart's comprehensive income available for common shareholders in Year +1 by the number of common shares outstanding at the end of Year 4. Using this Year +1 earnings per share forecast, and using the share value computed in part h, compute Wal-Mart's value-earnings ratio.

k. Using the Year +1 earnings per share forecast from part j, and using the share price at the end of Year 4, compute Wal-Mart's price-earnings ratio. Compare Wal-Mart's value-earnings ratio with its price-earnings ratio. What investment decision does the comparison suggest? What does the comparison suggest regarding the pricing of Wal-Mart shares in the market: underpriced, overpriced, or fairly priced? Does this comparison lead to the same conclusions that you reached by comparing value-to-book ratios with market-to-book ratios in part g?

l. Compute Wal-Mart's price differential at the end of Year 4. Compute Wal-Mart's price differential as a percentage of Wal-Mart's risk-neutral value. What dollar amount and what percentage amount has the market discounted Wal-Mart shares for risk?

m. Reverse engineer Wal-Mart's share price at the end of Year 4 to solve for the implied expected rate of return. First, assume that value equals price, and assume that the earnings and growth forecasts through Year +6 and beyond are reliable proxies for the market's expectations for Wal-Mart. Then solve for the implied expected rate of return (the discount rate) the market has impounded in Wal-Mart's share price. *(Hint: Begin with the forecast and valuation spreadsheet you developed to value Wal-Mart shares. Vary the discount rate until you solve for the discount rate that makes your value estimate exactly equal the end of Year 4 market price of $52.40 per share.)*

n. Reverse engineer Wal-Mart's share price at the end of Year 4 to solve for the implied expected long-run growth. First, assume that value equals price, and assume that the earnings forecasts through Year +5 are reliable proxies for the market's expectations for Wal-Mart. Also assume that the discount rate implied by the CAPM (computed in part a) is a reliable proxy for the market's expected rate of return. Then solve for the implied expected long-run growth rate the market has impounded in Wal-Mart's share price. *(Hint: Begin with the forecast and valuation spreadsheet you developed to value Wal-Mart shares, and use the CAPM discount rate. Set the long-run growth parameter initially to zero. Increase the long-run growth rate until you solve for the growth rate that makes your value estimate exactly equal the end of Year 4 market price of $52.40 per share.)*

FSAP

INTEGRATIVE CASE 14.1

STARBUCKS

Valuation of Starbucks' Common Equity Using Market Multiples

Integrative Case 10.1 projects financial statements for Starbucks for Years +1 through +5. In this portion of the Starbucks Integrative Case, we use the projected financial statements from Integrative Case 10.1 and apply the techniques in Chapter 14 to compute Starbucks' required rate of return on equity and share value based on the value-to-book valuation model. We will also compare our value-to-book ratio estimate to Starbucks' market-to-book ratio at the time of the case to determine an investment recommendation. In addition, we will compute the value-earnings and price-earnings ratios, compute the price differential, and reverse engineer Starbucks' share price as of the end of Year 4.

The market equity beta for Starbucks at the end of Year 4 is .60. Assume that the risk-free interest rate is 4.0 percent and the market risk premium is 5.0 percent. Starbucks has 397.4 million shares outstanding at the end of Year 4. At the start of Year +1, Starbucks' share price was $47.05.

Required

Part I—Computing Starbucks' Value-to-Book Ratio Using the Value-to-Book Valuation Approach

a. Use the CAPM to compute the required rate of return on common equity capital for Starbucks.

b. Using your projected financial statements from Integrative Case 10.1 for Starbucks, derive the projected residual ROCE (return on common shareholders' equity) for Starbucks for Years +1 through +5.

c. Assume that the steady-state long-run growth rate will be 3 percent in Year +6 and beyond. Project that the Year +5 income statement and balance sheet amounts will grow by 3 percent in Year +6, and then derive the projected residual ROCE for Year +6.

d. Using the required rate of return on common equity from part a as a discount rate, compute the sum of the present value of residual ROCE for Starbucks for Years +1 through +5.

e. Using the required rate of return on common equity from part a as a discount rate, and the long-run growth rate from part c, compute the continuing value of

Starbucks as of the start of Year +6 based on Starbucks' continuing residual ROCE in Year +6 and beyond. After computing continuing value as of the start of Year +6, discount it to present value at the start of Year +1.

f. Compute Starbucks' value-to-book ratio as of the end of Year 4 with the following three steps. (1) Compute the total sum of the present value of all future residual ROCE (from parts d and e). (2) To the total from item (1), add one (representing the book value of equity as of the beginning of the valuation as of the end of Year 4). (3) Adjust the total sum from item (2) using the midyear discounting adjustment factor.

g. Compute Starbucks' market-to-book ratio as of the end of Year 4. Compare the value-to-book ratio to the market-to-book ratio. What investment decision does the comparison suggest? What does the comparison suggest regarding the pricing of Starbucks' shares in the market: underpriced, overpriced, or fairly priced?

h. Use the value-to-book ratio to project the value of a share of common equity in Starbucks.

i. If you computed Starbucks' common equity share value using the dividends valuation approach in Integrative Case 11.1 in Chapter 11, and/or the free cash flows to common equity valuation approach in Integrative Case 12.1 in Chapter 12, and/or the residual income valuation approach in Integrative Case 13.1 in Chapter 13, compare the value estimate you obtained in those cases with the estimate you obtained in this case. You should obtain the same value estimates under all four approaches. If you have not yet worked those prior cases, it would be valuable to do so now.

Part II—Analyzing Starbucks' Share Price Using the Value-Earnings Ratio, the Price-Earnings Ratio, Price Differentials, and Reverse Engineering

j. Use your forecast data for Year +1 to project Year +1 earnings per share. To do so, divide your projection of Starbucks' comprehensive income available for common shareholders in Year +1 by the number of common shares outstanding at the end of Year 4. Using this Year +1 earnings per share forecast, and using the share value computed in part h, compute Starbucks' value-earnings ratio.

k. Using the Year +1 earnings per share forecast from part j, and using the share price at the end of Year 4, compute Starbucks' price-earnings ratio. Compare Starbucks' value-earnings ratio with its price-earnings ratio. What investment decision does the comparison suggest? What does the comparison suggest regarding the pricing of Starbucks' shares in the market: underpriced, overpriced, or fairly priced? Does this comparison lead to the same conclusions that you reached by comparing value-to-book ratios with market-to-book ratios in part g?

l. Compute Starbucks' price differential at the end of Year 4. Compute Starbucks' price differential as a percentage of Starbucks' risk-neutral value. What dollar amount and what percentage amount has the market discounted Starbucks' shares for risk?

m. Reverse engineer Starbucks' share price at the end of Year 4 to solve for the implied expected rate of return. First, assume that value equals price, and assume that your earnings and growth forecasts through Year +6 and beyond are reliable proxies for the market's expectations for Starbucks. Then solve for the implied expected rate of return (the discount rate) the market has impounded in Starbucks' share price. *(Hint: Begin with the forecast and valuation spreadsheet you have developed to value Starbucks' shares. Vary the discount rate until you solve for the discount rate that makes your value estimate exactly equal the end of Year 4 market price of $47.05 per share.)*

n. Reverse engineer Starbucks' share price at the end of Year 4 to solve for the implied expected long-run growth. First, assume that value equals price, and assume that your earnings forecasts through Year +5 are reliable proxies for the market's expectations for Starbucks. Also assume that the discount rate implied by the CAPM (computed in part a) is a reliable proxy for the market's expected rate of return. Then solve for the implied expected long-run growth rate the market has impounded in Starbucks' share price. *(Hint: Begin with the forecast and valuation spreadsheet you have developed to value Starbucks' shares, and use the CAPM discount rate. Set the long-run growth parameter initially to zero. Increase the long-run growth rate until you solve for the growth rate that makes your value estimate exactly equal the end of Year 4 market price of $47.05 per share.)*

Appendix **A**

Financial Statements and Notes for PepsiCo, Inc. and Subsidiaries

Consolidated Statement of Income

PepsiCo, Inc. and Subsidiaries
Fiscal years ended December 25, Year 4, December 27, Year 3 and December 28, Year 2

(in millions except per share amounts)	Year 4	Year 3	Year 2
Net Revenue	**$29,261**	$26,971	$25,112
Cost of sales	**13,406**	12,379	11,497
Selling, general and administrative expenses	**10,299**	9,460	8,958
Amortization of intangible assets	**147**	145	138
Impairment and restructuring charges	**150**	147	–
Merger-related costs	–	59	224
Operating Profit	**5,259**	4,781	4,295
Bottling equity income	**380**	323	280
Interest expense	**(167)**	(163)	(178)
Interest income	**74**	51	36
Income from Continuing Operations before Income Taxes	**5,546**	4,992	4,433
Provision for Income Taxes	**1,372**	1,424	1,433
Income from Continuing Operations	**4,174**	3,568	3,000
Tax Benefit from Discontinued Operations	**38**	–	–
Net Income	**$ 4,212**	$ 3,568	$ 3,000
Net Income per Common Share — Basic			
Continuing operations	**$2.45**	$2.07	$1.69
Discontinued operations	**0.02**	–	–
Total	**$2.47**	$2.07	$1.69
Net Income per Common Share — Diluted			
Continuing operations	**$2.41**	$2.05	$1.68
Discontinued operations	**0.02**	–	–
Total	**$2.44***	$2.05	$1.68

*Based on unrounded amounts.
See accompanying notes to consolidated financial statements.

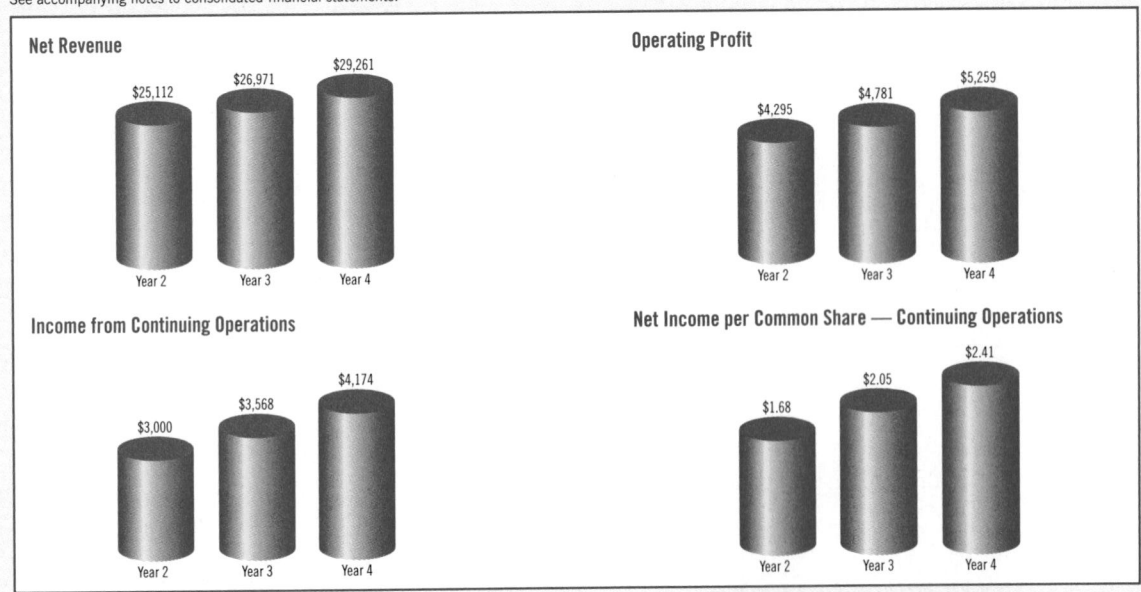

Net Revenue

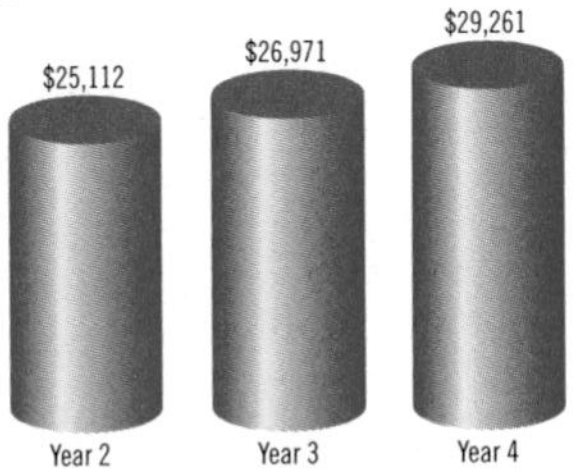

Operating Profit

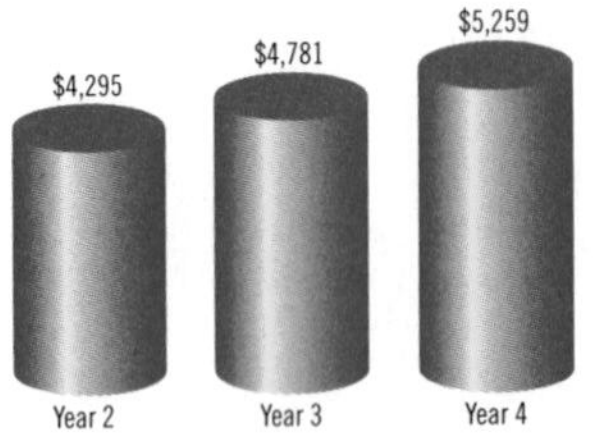

Income from Continuing Operations

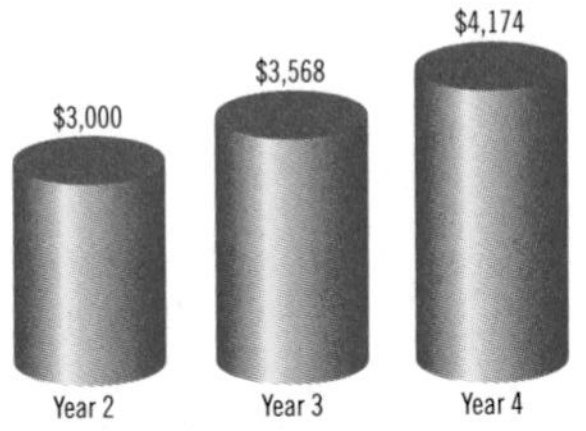

Net Income per Common Share — Continuing Operations

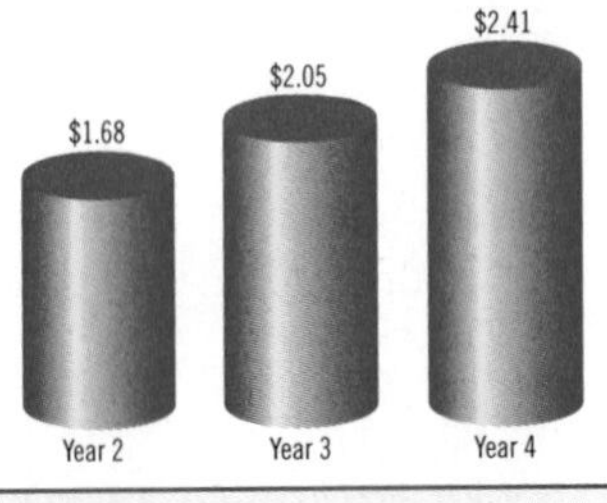

Consolidated Statement of Cash Flows

PepsiCo, Inc. and Subsidiaries
Fiscal years ended December 25, Year 4, December 27, Year 3 and December 28, Year 2

(in millions)	Year 4	Year 3	Year 2
Operating Activities			
Net income	$ 4,212	$ 3,568	$ 3,000
Adjustments to reconcile net income to net cash provided by operating activities			
Depreciation and amortization	1,264	1,221	1,112
Stock-based compensation expense	368	407	435
Merger-related costs	–	59	224
Impairment and restructuring charges	150	147	–
Cash payments for merger-related costs and restructuring charges	(92)	(109)	(123)
Tax benefit from discontinued operations	(38)	–	–
Pension plan contributions	(458)	(535)	(820)
Bottling equity income, net of dividends	(297)	(276)	(222)
Deferred income taxes	17	(323)	174
Other non-cash charges and credits, net	341	415	263
Changes in operating working capital, excluding effects of acquisitions and dispositions			
Accounts and notes receivable	(130)	(220)	(260)
Inventories	(100)	(49)	(53)
Prepaid expenses and other current assets	(31)	23	(78)
Accounts payable and other current liabilities	216	(11)	426
Income taxes payable	(268)	182	270
Net change in operating working capital	(313)	(75)	305
Other	(100)	(171)	279
Net Cash Provided by Operating Activities	5,054	4,328	4,627
Investing Activities			
Capital spending	(1,387)	(1,345)	(1,437)
Sales of property, plant and equipment	38	49	89
Acquisitions and investments in noncontrolled affiliates	(64)	(71)	(351)
Divestitures	52	46	376
Short-term investments, by original maturity			
More than three months — purchases	(44)	(38)	(62)
More than three months — maturities	38	28	122
Three months or less, net	(963)	(940)	697
Snack Ventures Europe consolidation	–	–	39
Net Cash Used for Investing Activities	(2,330)	(2,271)	(527)
Financing Activities			
Proceeds from issuances of long-term debt	504	52	11
Payments of long-term debt	(512)	(641)	(353)
Short-term borrowings, by original maturity			
More than three months — proceeds	153	88	707
More than three months — payments	(160)	(115)	(809)
Three months or less, net	1,119	40	40
Cash dividends paid	(1,329)	(1,070)	(1,041)
Share repurchases — common	(3,028)	(1,929)	(2,158)
Share repurchases — preferred	(27)	(16)	(32)
Proceeds from exercises of stock options	965	689	456
Net Cash Used for Financing Activities	(2,315)	(2,902)	(3,179)
Effect of exchange rate changes on cash and cash equivalents	51	27	34
Net Increase/(Decrease) in Cash and Cash Equivalents	460	(818)	955
Cash and Cash Equivalents, Beginning of Year	820	1,638	683
Cash and Cash Equivalents, End of Year	$ 1,280	$ 820	$ 1,638

See accompanying notes to consolidated financial statements.

Consolidated Balance Sheet

PepsiCo, Inc. and Subsidiaries
December 25, Year 4 and December 27, Year 3

(in millions except per share amounts)	Year 4	Year 3
ASSETS		
Current Assets		
Cash and cash equivalents	$ 1,280	$ 820
Short-term investments	2,165	1,181
	3,445	2,001
Accounts and notes receivable, net	2,999	2,830
Inventories	1,541	1,412
Prepaid expenses and other current assets	654	687
Total Current Assets	8,639	6,930
Property, Plant and Equipment, net	8,149	7,828
Amortizable Intangible Assets, net	598	718
Goodwill	3,909	3,796
Other nonamortizable intangible assets	933	869
Nonamortizable Intangible Assets	4,842	4,665
Investments in Noncontrolled Affiliates	3,284	2,920
Other Assets	2,475	2,266
Total Assets	$27,987	$25,327
LIABILITIES AND SHAREHOLDERS' EQUITY		
Current Liabilities		
Short-term obligations	$ 1,054	$ 591
Accounts payable and other current liabilities	5,599	5,213
Income taxes payable	99	611
Total Current Liabilities	6,752	6,415
Long-Term Debt Obligations	2,397	1,702
Other Liabilities	4,099	4,075
Deferred Income Taxes	1,216	1,261
Total Liabilities	14,464	13,453
Preferred Stock, no par value	41	41
Repurchased Preferred Stock	(90)	(63)
Common Shareholders' Equity		
Common stock, par value 1⅔¢ per share (issued 1,782 shares)	30	30
Capital in excess of par value	618	548
Retained earnings	18,730	15,961
Accumulated other comprehensive loss	(886)	(1,267)
	18,492	15,272
Less: repurchased common stock, at cost (103 and 77 shares, respectively)	(4,920)	(3,376)
Total Common Shareholders' Equity	13,572	11,896
Total Liabilities and Shareholders' Equity	$27,987	$25,327

See accompanying notes to consolidated financial statements.

Consolidated Statement of Common Shareholders' Equity

PepsiCo, Inc. and Subsidiaries
Fiscal years ended December 25, Year 4, December 27, Year 3 and December 28, Year 2

	Year 4		Year 3		Year 2	
(in millions)	Shares	Amount	Shares	Amount	Shares	Amount
Common Stock	1,782	$ 30	1,782	$ 30	1,782	$ 30
Capital in Excess of Par Value						
Balance, beginning of year		548		207		115
Stock-based compensation expense		368		407		435
Stock option exercises[a]		(298)		(66)		(339)
Other		–		–		(4)
Balance, end of year		618		548		207
Retained Earnings						
Balance, beginning of year		15,961		13,489		11,535
Net income[b]		4,212		3,568		3,000
Cash dividends declared — common		(1,438)		(1,082)		(1,042)
Cash dividends declared — preferred		(3)		(3)		(4)
Cash dividends declared — RSUs		(2)		–		–
Other		–		(11)		–
Balance, end of year		18,730		15,961		13,489
Accumulated Other Comprehensive Loss						
Balance, beginning of year		(1,267)		(1,672)		(1,646)
Currency translation adjustment[b]		401		410		56
Cash flow hedges, net of tax[b]		(7)		(12)		18
Minimum pension liability adjustment, net of tax[b]		(19)		7		(99)
Other[b]		6		–		(1)
Balance, end of year		(886)		(1,267)		(1,672)
Repurchased Common Stock						
Balance, beginning of year	(77)	(3,376)	(60)	(2,524)	(26)	(1,268)
Share repurchases	(58)	(2,994)	(43)	(1,946)	(53)	(2,192)
Stock option exercises	32	1,434	26	1,096	19	931
Other	–	16	–	(2)	–	5
Balance, end of year	(103)	(4,920)	(77)	(3,376)	(60)	(2,524)
Total Common Shareholders' Equity		$13,572		$11,896		$ 9,530

(a) Includes total tax benefit of $183 million in Year 4, $340 million in Year 3 and $136 million in Year 2.
(b) Combined, these amounts represent total comprehensive income of $4,593 million in Year 4, $3,973 million in Year 3 and $2,974 million in Year 2.
See accompanying notes to consolidated financial statements.

Notes to Consolidated Financial Statements

Note 1 — Basis of Presentation and Our Divisions

Basis of Presentation

Our financial statements include the consolidated accounts of PepsiCo, Inc. and the affiliates that we control. In addition, we include our share of the results of certain other affiliates based on our economic ownership interest. We do not control these other affiliates, as our ownership in these other affiliates is generally less than 50%. Our share of the net income of noncontrolled bottling affiliates is reported in our income statement as bottling equity income. See Note 8 for additional information on our noncontrolled bottling affiliates. Our share of other noncontrolled affiliates is included in division operating profit. Intercompany balances and transactions are eliminated.

The preparation of our consolidated financial statements in conformity with generally accepted accounting principles requires us to make estimates and assumptions that affect reported amounts of assets, liabilities, revenues, expenses and disclosure of contingent assets and liabilities. Actual results could differ from these estimates.

Impairment and restructuring charges and merger-related costs (described in Note 3) and net tax benefits from continuing and discontinued operations (described in Note 5) affect the comparability of our consolidated results. See "Our Divisions" below and for additional unaudited information on these items, see "Items Affecting Comparability" in Management's Discussion and Analysis.

Tabular dollars are in millions, except per share amounts. All per share amounts reflect common per share amounts, assume dilution unless noted, and are based on unrounded amounts. Certain reclassifications were made to prior year amounts to conform to the Year 4 presentation.

Our Divisions

We manufacture or use contract manufacturers, market and sell a variety of salty, sweet and grain-based snacks, carbonated and non-carbonated beverages, and foods through our North American and international business divisions. Our North American divisions include the United States and Canada. The accounting policies for the divisions are the same as those described in Note 2, except for certain allocation methodologies for stock-based compensation expense and pension and retiree medical expense as described in the unaudited information in "Our Critical Accounting Policies."

Division results are based on how our Chairman and Chief Executive Officer manages our divisions. Division results exclude significant restructuring and impairment charges, merger-related costs and divested businesses. For additional unaudited information on our divisions, see "Our Operations" in Management's Discussion and Analysis.

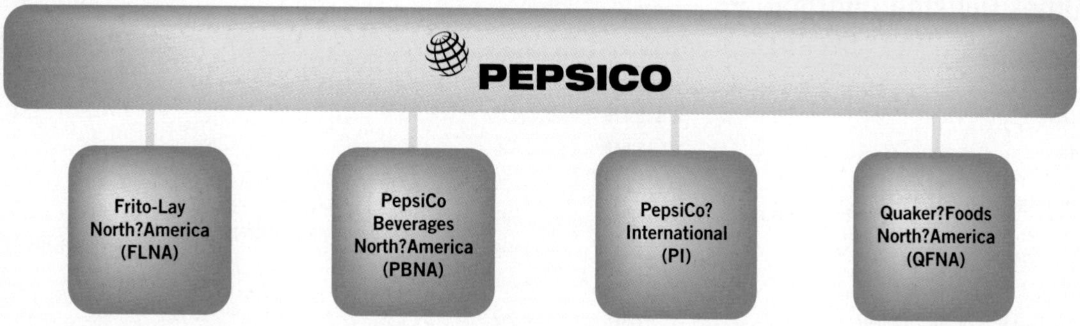

	Year 4	Year 3	Year 2	Year 4	Year 3	Year 2
	Net Revenue			Operating Profit		
FLNA	$ 9,560	$ 9,091	$ 8,565	$2,389	$2,242	$2,081
PBNA	8,313	7,733	7,200	1,911	1,690	1,485
PI	9,862	8,678	7,749	1,323	1,061	910
QFNA	1,526	1,467	1,464	475	470	458
Total division	29,261	26,969	24,978	6,098	5,463	4,934
Divested businesses	–	2	134	–	26	23
Corporate	–	–	–	(689)	(502)	(438)
	29,261	26,971	25,112	5,409	4,987	4,519
Impairment and restructuring charges	–	–	–	(150)	(147)	–
Merger-related costs	–	–	–	–	(59)	(224)
Total	$29,261	$26,971	$25,112	$5,259	$4,781	$4,295

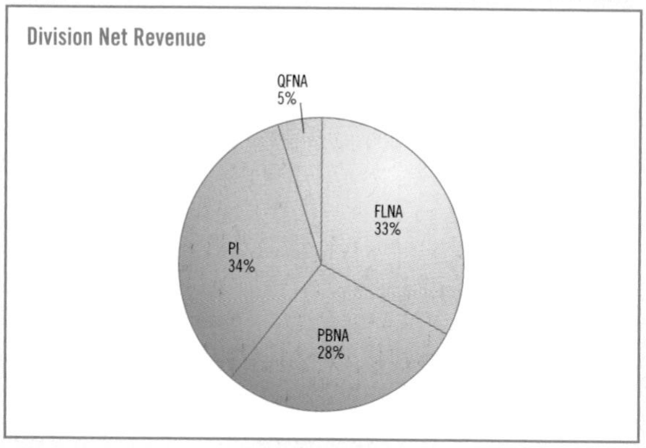

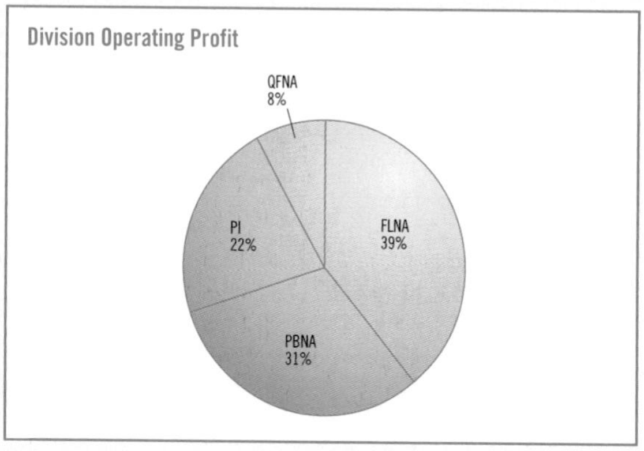

Divested Businesses
During Year 3, we sold our Quaker Foods North America Mission pasta business. During Year 2, we sold our Quaker Foods North America bagged cereal business and our PepsiCo International food businesses in Colombia and Venezuela. The results of these businesses are reported as divested businesses.

Corporate
Corporate includes costs of our corporate headquarters, centrally managed initiatives, such as our BPT initiative, unallocated insurance and benefit programs, foreign exchange transaction gains and losses, profit-in-inventory elimination adjustments for our noncontrolled bottling affiliates and certain other items.

Impairment and Restructuring Charges and Merger-Related Costs — See Note 3.

Other Division Information

	Year 4	Year 3	Year 2	Year 4	Year 3	Year 2
	Total Assets			Capital Spending		
FLNA	**$ 5,476**	$ 5,332	$ 5,099	**$ 469**	$ 426	$ 523
PBNA	**6,048**	5,856	5,691	**265**	332	367
PI	**8,921**	8,109	7,275	**537**	521	473
QFNA	**978**	995	1,001	**33**	32	50
Total division	**21,423**	20,292	19,066	**1,304**	1,311	1,413
Corporate(a)	**3,569**	2,384	2,072	**83**	34	24
Investments in bottling affiliates	**2,995**	2,651	2,336	**–**	–	–
	$27,987	$25,327	$23,474	**$1,387**	$1,345	$1,437

Total Assets

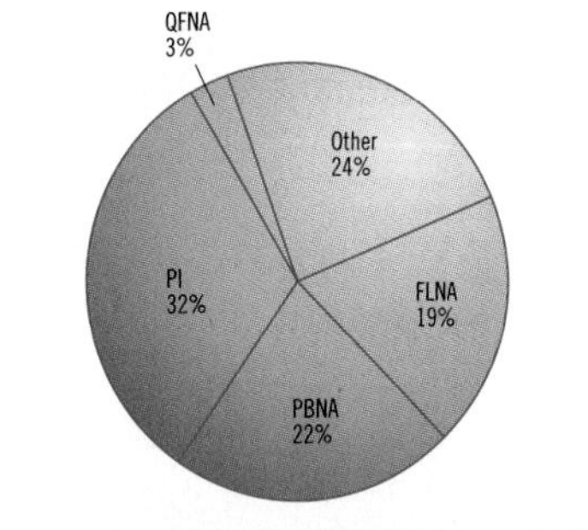

Capital Spending

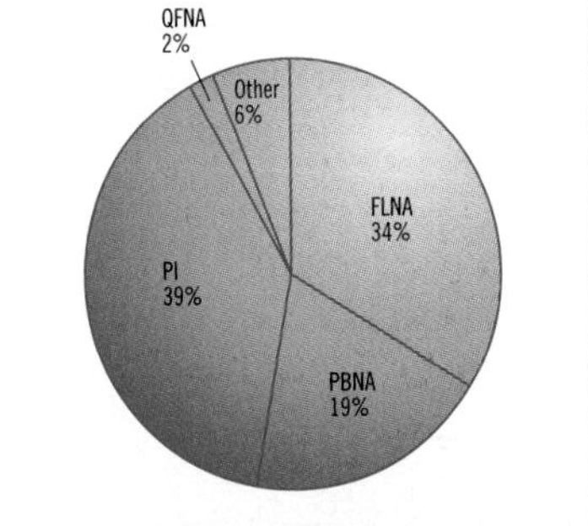

Net Revenue

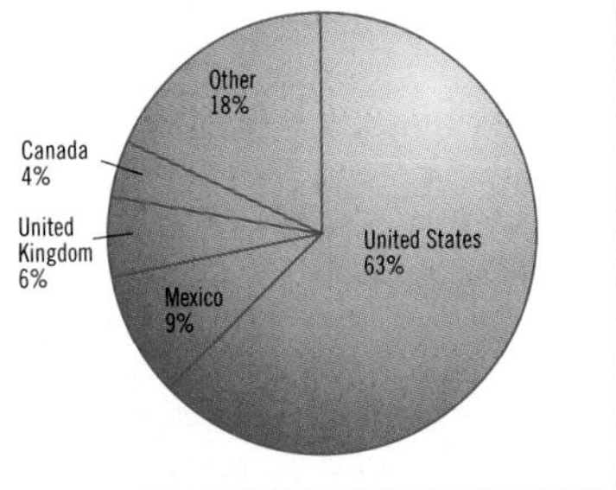

	Year 4	Year 3	Year 2	Year 4	Year 3	Year 2
	Amortization of Intangible Assets			Depreciation and Other Amortization		
FLNA	**$ 3**	$ 3	$ 3	**$ 420**	$ 416	$399
PBNA	**75**	75	70	**258**	245	206
PI	**68**	66	64	**382**	350	300
QFNA	**1**	1	1	**36**	36	37
Total division	**147**	145	138	**1,096**	1,047	942
Divested businesses	**–**	–	–	**–**	–	3
Corporate	**–**	–	–	**21**	29	29
	$147	$145	$138	**$1,117**	$1,076	$974

Long-Lived Assets

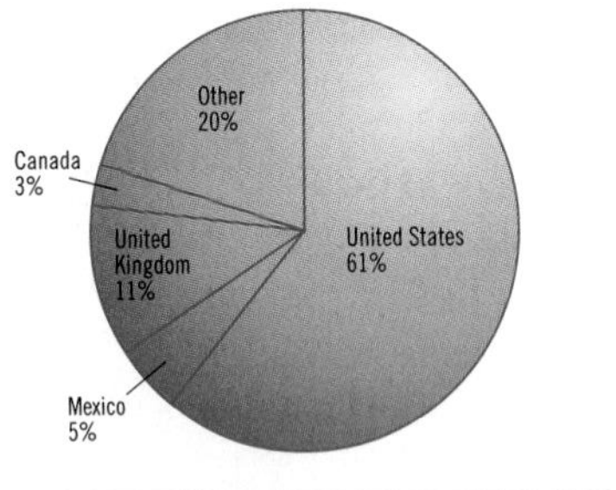

	Year 4	Year 3	Year 2	Year 4	Year 3	Year 2
	Net Revenue(b)			Long-Lived Assets(c)		
U.S.	**$18,329**	$17,377	$16,588	**$10,212**	$ 9,907	$ 9,767
Mexico	**2,724**	2,642	2,686	**878**	869	764
United Kingdom	**1,692**	1,510	1,106	**1,896**	1,724	1,529
Canada	**1,309**	1,147	967	**548**	508	410
All other countries	**5,207**	4,295	3,765	**3,339**	3,123	2,750
	$29,261	$26,971	$25,112	**$16,873**	$16,131	$15,220

(a) Corporate assets consist principally of cash, cash equivalents and short-term investments, primarily held outside the U.S., and property, plant and equipment.

(b) Represents net revenue from businesses operating in these countries.

(c) Long-lived assets represent net property, plant and equipment, nonamortizable and net amortizable intangible assets and investments in noncontrolled affiliates. These assets are reported in the country where they are primarily used.

Note 2 — Our Significant Accounting Policies

Revenue Recognition

We recognize revenue upon shipment or delivery to our customers in accordance with written sales terms that do not allow for a right of return. However, our policy for direct-store-delivery (DSD) and chilled products is to remove and replace damaged and out-of-date products from store shelves to ensure that our consumers receive the product quality and freshness that they expect. Similarly, our policy for warehouse distributed products is to replace damaged and out-of-date products. Based on our historical experience with this practice, we have reserved for anticipated damaged and out-of-date products. For additional unaudited information on our revenue recognition and related policies, including our policy on bad debts, see "Our Critical Accounting Policies" in Management's Discussion and Analysis. We are exposed to concentration of credit risk by our customers, Wal-Mart and PBG. Wal-Mart represents approximately 11% of our net revenue and PBG represents approximately 10%. We have not experienced credit issues with these customers.

Sales Incentives and Other Marketplace Spending

We offer sales incentives through various programs to our customers and consumers. Sales incentives are accounted for as a reduction of revenue and totaled $6.6 billion in Year 4, $6.0 billion in Year 3 and $5.5 billion in Year 2. Most of these incentive arrangements have terms of no more than one year. However, we have arrangements, such as fountain pouring rights, which may extend up to 15 years. Costs incurred to obtain these arrangements are expensed over the contract period and the remaining balance of $337 million at December 25, Year 4 and $359 million at December 27, Year 3 is included in other assets in our Consolidated Balance Sheet. For additional unaudited information on our sales incentives, see "Our Critical Accounting Policies" in Management's Discussion and Analysis.

Other marketplace spending includes the costs of advertising and other marketing activities and is reported as selling, general and administrative expenses. Advertising expenses were $1.7 billion in Year 4, $1.6 billion in Year 3 and $1.5 billion in Year 2. Deferred advertising costs are not expensed until the year first used and consist of:

- media and personal service prepayments,
- promotional materials in inventory, and
- production costs of future media advertising.

Deferred advertising costs of $137 million at year-end Year 4 and Year 3 are classified as prepaid expenses in the Consolidated Balance Sheet.

Distribution Costs

Distribution costs, including the costs of shipping and handling activities, are reported as selling, general and administrative expenses for DSD distribution systems. For our other distribution systems, these costs are reported in cost of sales. Shipping and handling expenses classified as selling, general and administrative expenses were $3.3 billion in Year 4, $3.0 billion in Year 3 and $2.8 billion in Year 2.

Cash Equivalents

Cash equivalents are investments with original maturities of three months or less.

Commitments and Contingencies

We are subject to various claims and contingencies related to lawsuits, taxes and environmental matters, as well as commitments under contractual and other commercial obligations. We recognize liabilities for contingencies and commitments when a loss is probable and estimable. For additional information on our commitments, see Note 9.

Other Significant Accounting Policies

Our other significant accounting policies are disclosed as follows:

- *Property, Plant and Equipment and Intangible Assets* — Note 4 and, for additional unaudited information on brands and goodwill, see "Our Critical Accounting Policies" in Management's Discussion and Analysis.
- *Income Taxes* — Note 5 and, for additional unaudited information, see "Our Critical Accounting Policies" in Management's Discussion and Analysis.
- *Stock-Based Compensation Expense* — Note 6 and, for additional unaudited information, see "Our Critical Accounting Policies" in Management's Discussion and Analysis.
- *Pension, Retiree Medical and Savings Plans* — Note 7 and, for additional unaudited information, see "Our Critical Accounting Policies" in Management's Discussion and Analysis.
- *Risk Management* — Note 10 and, for additional unaudited information, see "Our Business Risks" in Management's Discussion and Analysis.

Note 3 — Impairment and Restructuring Charges and Merger-Related Costs

Impairment and Restructuring Charges

In the fourth quarter of Year 4, we incurred a charge of $150 million ($96 million after-tax or $0.06 per share) in conjunction with the consolidation of FLNA's manufacturing network as part of its ongoing productivity program. Of this charge, $93 million relates to asset impairment, primarily reflecting the closure of four U.S. plants. Production from these plants has been redeployed to other FLNA facilities in the U.S. The remaining $57 million includes employee-related costs of $29 million, contract termination costs of $8 million and other exit costs of $20 million. Employee-related costs primarily reflect the termination costs for approximately 700 employees. As of December 25, Year 4, substantially all terminations have occurred. Through December 25, Year 4, we have paid $27 million, incurred non-cash charges of $8 million, leaving a remaining accrual of $22 million. This accrual is included in other current liabilities and payments are expected through mid-year Year 6.

In the fourth quarter of Year 3, we incurred a charge of $147 million ($100 million after-tax or $0.06 per share) in conjunction with actions taken to streamline our North American divisions and PepsiCo International. These actions were taken to increase focus and eliminate redundancies at PBNA and PI, and to improve the efficiency of the supply chain at FLNA. Of this charge, $81 million related to asset impairment, reflecting $57 million for the closure of a snack plant in Kentucky, the retirement of snack manufacturing lines in Maryland and Arkansas and $24 million for the closure of a PBNA office building in Florida. The remaining $66 million included employee-related costs of $54 million and facility and other exit costs of $12 million. Employee-related costs primarily reflect the termination costs for approximately 850 sales, distribution, manufacturing, research and marketing employees. As of December 25, Year 4, all terminations have occurred and substantially no accrual remains.

Merger-Related Costs

In connection with the Quaker merger in Year 1, we recognized merger-related costs of $59 million ($42 million after-tax or $0.02 per share) and $224 million ($190 million after-tax or $0.11 per share) in Year 3 and Year 2, respectively. At December 25, Year 4, we had related accruals of $34 million (primarily employee-related) which are included within other current liabilities in the Consolidated Balance Sheet.

Note 4 — Property, Plant and Equipment and Intangible Assets

	Useful Life	Year 4	Year 3	Year 2
Property, plant and equipment, net				
Land and improvements	10 – 30 yrs.	$ 646	$ 591	
Buildings and improvements	20 – 44	3,605	3,415	
Machinery and equipment, including fleet	5 – 15	10,950	10,170	
Construction in progress		729	579	
		15,930	14,755	
Accumulated depreciation		(7,781)	(6,927)	
		$ 8,149	$ 7,828	
Depreciation expense		$1,062	$1,020	$929
Amortizable intangible assets, net				
Brands	5 – 40	$1,008	$ 985	
Other identifiable intangibles	3 – 15	225	212	
		1,233	1,197	
Accumulated amortization		(635)	(479)	
		$ 598	$ 718	
Amortization expense		$147	$145	$138

Depreciation and amortization are recognized on a straight-line basis over an asset's estimated useful life. Land is not depreciated and construction in progress is not depreciated until ready for service. Amortization of intangible assets for each of the next five years, based on Year 4 foreign exchange rates, is expected to be $141 million in Year 5, $140 million in Year 6, $24 million in Year 7, $23 million in Year 8 and $22 million in Year 9.

Depreciable and amortizable assets are only evaluated for impairment upon a significant change in the operating or macroeconomic environment. In these circumstances, if an evaluation of the undiscounted cash flows indicates impairment, the asset is written down to its estimated fair value, which is generally based on discounted future cash flows. Useful lives are periodically evaluated to determine whether events or circumstances have occurred which indicate the need for revision. For additional unaudited information on our amortizable brand policies, see "Our Critical Accounting Policies" in Management's Discussion and Analysis.

Nonamortizable Intangible Assets

Perpetual brands and goodwill are assessed for impairment at least annually to ensure that discounted future cash flows continue to exceed the related book value. A perpetual brand is impaired if its book value exceeds its fair value. Goodwill is evaluated for impairment if the book value of its reporting unit exceeds its fair value. A reporting unit can be a division or business within a division. If the fair value of an evaluated asset is less than its book value, the asset is written down based on its discounted future cash flows to fair value. No impairment charges resulted from the required impairment evaluations. The change in the book value of nonamortizable intangible assets during Year 4 is as follows:

	Balance, Beginning of Year	Acquisitions	Translation and Other	Balance, End of Year
Frito-Lay North America				
Goodwill	$ 130	$ –	$ 8	**$ 138**
PepsiCo Beverages North America				
Goodwill	2,157	–	4	**2,161**
Brands	59	–	–	**59**
	2,216	–	4	**2,220**
PepsiCo International				
Goodwill	1,334	29	72	**1,435**
Brands	808	–	61	**869**
	2,142	29	133	**2,304**
Quaker Foods North America				
Goodwill	175	–	–	**175**
Corporate				
Pension intangible	2	–	3	**5**
Total goodwill	3,796	29	84	**3,909**
Total brands	867	–	61	**928**
Total pension intangible	2	–	3	**5**
	$4,665	$29	$148	**$4,842**

Note 5 — Income Taxes

	Year 4	Year 3	Year 2
Income before income taxes — continuing operations			
U.S.	$2,946	$3,267	$3,178
Foreign	2,600	1,725	1,255
	$5,546	$4,992	$4,433
Provision for income taxes — continuing operations			
Current: U.S. Federal	$1,030	$1,326	$ 948
Foreign	256	341	256
State	69	80	55
	1,355	1,747	1,259
Deferred: U.S. Federal	11	(274)	146
Foreign	5	(47)	11
State	1	(2)	17
	17	(323)	174
	$1,372	$1,424	$1,433
Tax rate reconciliation — continuing operations			
U.S. Federal statutory tax rate	35.0%	35.0%	35.0%
State income tax, net of U.S. Federal tax benefit	0.8	1.0	1.0
Lower taxes on foreign results	(5.4)	(5.5)	(3.5)
Settlement of prior years audit	(4.8)	(2.2)	–
Merger-related costs and impairment and restructuring charges	–	0.1	1.0
Other, net	(0.9)	0.1	(1.2)
Annual tax rate	24.7%	28.5%	32.3%
Deferred tax liabilities			
Investments in noncontrolled affiliates	$ 850	$ 792	
Property, plant and equipment	857	806	
Pension benefits	669	563	
Intangible assets other than nondeductible goodwill	153	146	
Safe harbor leases	13	33	
Zero coupon notes	46	53	
Other	144	199	
Gross deferred tax liabilities	2,732	2,592	
Deferred tax assets			
Net carryforwards	666	535	
Stock-based compensation	402	332	
Retiree medical benefits	402	343	
Other employee-related benefits	379	384	
Various current and noncurrent liabilities	460	482	
Gross deferred tax assets	2,309	2,076	
Valuation allowances	(564)	(438)	
Deferred tax assets, net	1,745	1,638	
Net deferred tax liabilities	$ 987	$ 954	
Deferred taxes included within:			
Prepaid expenses and other current assets	$229	$307	
Deferred income taxes	$1,216	$1,261	
Analysis of valuation allowances			
Balance, beginning of year	$438	$487	$511
Provision/(benefit)	118	(52)	(22)
Other additions/(deductions)	8	3	(2)
Balance, end of year	$564	$438	$487

For additional unaudited information on our income tax policies, including our reserves for income taxes, see "Our Critical Accounting Policies" in Management's Discussion and Analysis.

Carryforwards, Credits and Allowances

Operating loss carryforwards totaling $4.3 billion at year-end Year 4 are being carried forward in a number of foreign and state jurisdictions where we are permitted to use tax operating losses from prior periods to reduce future taxable income. These operating losses will expire as follows: $0.1 billion in Year 5, $3.1 billion between Year 6 and Year 24 and $1.1 billion may be carried forward indefinitely. In addition, certain tax credits generated in prior periods of approximately $49.3 million are available to reduce certain foreign tax liabilities through Year 11. We establish valuation allowances for our deferred tax assets when the amount of expected future taxable income is not likely to support the use of the deduction or credit.

Tax Benefit from Discontinued Operations

In the fourth quarter of Year 4, we reached agreement with the taxing authorities for an open issue related to our discontinued restaurant operations which resulted in a tax benefit of $38 million or $0.02 per share.

Undistributed International Earnings

At December 25, Year 4, we had approximately $11.9 billion of undistributed international earnings. We have not recognized any U.S. tax expense on these earnings, since we intend to reinvest the earnings outside the U.S. for the foreseeable future, subject to the opportunity afforded us as a result of the American Jobs Creation Act of 2004 (AJCA), which was signed by the President on October 22, 2004. The AJCA creates a temporary incentive for U.S. corporations to repatriate undistributed international earnings by providing an 85% dividends received deduction. The deduction is subject to a number of limitations and uncertainty remains as to how to interpret certain provisions in the AJCA. Therefore, we have not decided on whether, or to what extent, we might repatriate undistributed foreign earnings to the U.S. Until further guidance is available from the Treasury Department, or possibly from Congress, it is difficult to fully quantify the impact of the AJCA if we were to take advantage of that legislation. Based on our analysis to date, however, the maximum amount that we can repatriate under the AJCA is $7.5 billion, which would result in a tax liability of approximately $475 million based on our expectation of how the AJCA will be interpreted. We expect to finalize our assessment of the opportunity presented by the AJCA as soon as further guidance is available, which could be as early as the first or second quarter of Year 5.

Note 6 — Stock-Based Compensation

Our stock-based compensation program is a broad-based program designed to attract and retain employees while also aligning employees' interests with the interests of our shareholders. Employees at all levels participate in our stock-based compensation program. In addition, members of our Board of Directors participate in our stock-based compensation program in connection with their service on our Board. Stock options and restricted stock units (RSUs) are granted to employees under the Year 3 Long-Term Incentive Plan (LTIP), our only active stock-based plan. At year-end Year 4, 62 million shares were available for future executive and SharePower grants. For additional unaudited information on our stock-based compensation program, see "Our Critical Accounting Policies" in Management's Discussion and Analysis.

SharePower Grants

SharePower options are awarded under our Year 3 LTIP to all eligible employees, based on job level or classification, and in the case of international employees, tenure as well. Options become exercisable after three years and have a 10-year term. In Year 4, SharePower grants represented approximately 38% of our annual employee option grants.

Executive Grants

All senior management and certain middle management are eligible for LTIP grants. All stock option grants have an exercise price equal to the fair market value of our common stock on the day of grant and generally have a 10-year term with vesting after three years. There have been no reductions to the exercise price of previously issued awards, and any repricing of awards would require approval of our shareholders.

Beginning in Year 4, executives who are awarded long-term incentives based on their performance are offered the choice of stock options or RSUs. RSUs also generally vest after three years of service and each restricted stock unit can be settled in a share of our stock after the vesting period. Senior officers do not have a choice and are granted 50% stock options and 50% RSUs. Executives who elect RSUs receive one RSU for every four stock options that would have otherwise been granted. Vesting of RSU awards for senior officers is contingent upon the achievement of pre-established performance targets. In Year 4, we granted three million RSUs with a weighted-average fair value of $47.28.

Method of Accounting and Our Assumptions

We account for our employee stock options under the fair value method of accounting using a Black-Scholes model to measure stock-based compensation expense at the date of grant. Two of our anchor bottlers, PBG and PAS, will be adopting SFAS 123R in Year 5. They are currently evaluating the impact of SFAS 123R on their respective financial statements, which will impact our bottling equity income.

Our weighted-average Black-Scholes fair value assumptions include:

	Year 4	Year 3	Year 2
Expected life	6 yrs.	6 yrs.	6 yrs.
Risk free interest rate	3.3%	3.1%	4.4%
Expected volatility	26%	27%	27%
Expected dividend yield	1.8%	1.15%	1.14%

Our Stock Option Activity(a)

	Year 4		Year 3		Year 2	
	Options	Average Price(b)	Options	Average Price(b)	Options	Average Price(b)
Outstanding at beginning of year	198,173	$38.12	190,432	$36.45	176,922	$32.35
Granted	14,137	47.47	41,630	39.89	37,376	48.75
Exercised	(31,614)	30.57	(25,833)	26.74	(19,558)	23.32
Forfeited/expired	(6,435)	43.82	(8,056)	43.56	(4,308)	39.01
Outstanding at end of year	174,261	40.05	198,173	38.12	190,432	36.45
Exercisable at end of year	94,643	$36.41	97,663	$32.56	82,620	$30.14
Weighted average fair value of options granted		$12.04		$11.21		$15.20

Stock options outstanding and exercisable at December 25, Year 4(a)

	Options Outstanding			Options Exercisable	
Range of Exercise Price	Options	Average Life(c)	Average Price(b)	Options	Average Price(b)
$14.40 to $21.54	4,209	1.75 yrs.	$20.69	4,209	$20.69
$23.00 to $33.75	24,291	3.49	29.97	24,129	29.98
$34.00 to $43.50	98,348	6.17	39.34	59,580	38.97
$43.75 to $54.25	47,413	7.76	48.56	6,725	47.44
	174,261	6.04	40.05	94,643	36.41

(a) Options are in thousands and include options previously granted under Quaker plans. No additional options or shares may be granted under the Quaker plans.

(b) Weighted-average exercise price.

(c) Weighted-average contractual life remaining in years.

Note 7 — Pension, Retiree Medical and Savings Plans

Our pension plans cover full-time employees in the U.S. and certain international employees. Benefits are determined based on either years of service or a combination of years of service and earnings. U.S. retirees are also eligible for medical and life insurance benefits (retiree medical) if they meet age and service requirements. Generally, our share of retiree medical costs is capped at specified dollar amounts, which vary based upon years of service, with retirees contributing the remainder up to the total cost. We use a September 30 measurement date and all plan assets and liabilities are reported as of that date. The cost or benefit of plan changes which increase or decrease benefits for prior employee service (prior service cost) is included in expense on a straight-line basis over the average remaining service period of employees expected to receive benefits.

The Medicare Act was signed into law in December 2003 and we applied the provisions of the Medicare Act to our plans in Year 4. The Medicare Act provides a subsidy for sponsors of retiree medical plans who offer drug benefits equivalent to those provided under Medicare. Our Year 4 retiree medical costs were $7 million lower as a result of the Medicare Act and our Year 4 liability was reduced by $80 million. We expect our Year 5 retiree medical costs to be approximately $10 million lower as a result of the Medicare Act. Further guidance on the Medicare Act is pending which could impact our previously recognized amounts.

For additional unaudited information on our pension and retiree medical plans and related accounting policies and assumptions, see "Our Critical Accounting Policies" in Management's Discussion and Analysis.

	Year 4	Year 3	Year 2
Weighted average pension assumptions			
Liability discount rate	6.1%	6.1%	6.7%
Expense discount rate	6.1%	6.7%	7.4%
Expected return on plan assets	7.8%	8.2%	9.1%
Rate of salary increases	4.4%	4.4%	4.4%
Components of pension expense			
Service cost	$ 220	$ 178	$ 156
Interest cost	318	284	265
Expected return on plan assets	(390)	(359)	(329)
Amortization of prior service cost	7	6	6
Amortization of experience loss	90	48	4
Pension expense	245	157	102
Settlement/curtailment loss	5	–	–
Special termination benefits	20	4	9
Total	$ 270	$ 161	$ 111
Weighted average retiree medical assumptions			
Liability discount rate	6.1%	6.1%	6.7%
Expense discount rate	6.1%	6.7%	7.5%
Components of retiree medical expense			
Service cost	$ 38	$ 33	$ 25
Interest cost	72	73	66
Amortization of prior service benefit	(8)	(3)	(7)
Amortization of experience loss	19	13	3
Retiree medical expense	121	116	87
Special termination benefits	4	–	1
Total	$ 125	$ 116	$ 88

	Year 4	Year 3	Year 4	Year 3
	Pension		Retiree Medical	
Change in projected benefit liability				
Liability at beginning of year	$5,214	$4,324	$1,264	$1,120
Service cost	220	178	38	33
Interest cost	318	284	72	73
Plan amendments	(16)	5	(41)	(63)
Participant contributions	9	6	–	–
Experience loss	334	541	58	171
Benefit payments	(234)	(208)	(76)	(70)
Settlement/curtailment loss	(11)	–	–	–
Special termination benefits	19	4	4	–
Foreign currency adjustment	67	80	–	–
Liability at end of year	$5,920	$5,214	$1,319	$1,264
Liability at end of year for service to date	$4,943	$4,350		

	Year 4	Year 3	Year 4	Year 3
	Pension		Retiree Medical	
Change in fair value of plan assets				
Fair value at beginning of year	$4,245	$3,537	$ –	$ –
Actual return on plan assets	469	281	–	–
Employer contributions/ funding	453	552	76	70
Participant contributions	9	6	–	–
Benefit payments	(234)	(208)	(76)	(70)
Settlement/curtailment loss	(11)	–	–	–
Foreign currency adjustment	59	77	–	–
Fair value at end of year	$4,990	$4,245	$ –	$ –
Funded status as recognized in the Consolidated Balance Sheet				
Funded status at end of year	$ (930)	$ (969)	$(1,319)	$(1,264)
Unrecognized prior service cost/(benefit)	22	44	(116)	(83)
Unrecognized experience loss	2,393	2,207	473	434
Fourth quarter benefit payments	12	6	19	19
Net amounts recognized	$1,497	$1,288	$ (943)	$ (894)
Net amounts as recognized in the Consolidated Balance Sheet				
Other assets	$1,866	$1,581	$ –	$ –
Intangible assets	5	2	–	–
Other liabilities	(424)	(334)	(943)	(894)
Accumulated other comprehensive loss	50	39	–	–
Net amounts recognized	$1,497	$1,288	$(943)	$(894)
Components of increase in unrecognized experience loss				
Decrease in discount rate	$ 4	$446	$ –	$ 60
Employee-related assumption changes	261	(6)	109	80
Liability-related experience different from assumptions	69	100	31	32
Actual asset return different from expected return	(79)	78	–	–
Amortization of losses	(90)	(48)	(19)	(13)
Other, including foreign currency adjustments and 2003 Medicare Act	21	30	(82)	–
Total	$186	$600	$ 39	$159
Selected information for plans with liability for service to date in excess of plan assets				
Liability for service to date	$(511)	$(383)	$(1,319)	$(1,264)
Projected benefit liability	$(912)	$(727)	$(1,319)	$(1,264)
Fair value of plan assets	$ 172	$123	–	–

Of the total projected pension benefit liability at year-end Year 4, $637 million relates to plans that we do not fund because of unfavorable tax treatment.

Future Benefit Payments

Our estimated future benefit payments to beneficiaries are as follows:

	Year 5	Year 6	Year 7	Year 8	Year 9	Years 10-14
Pension	$215	$220	$235	$255	$280	$1,855
Retiree medical	$85	$80	$85	$90	$95	$515

These benefit payments to beneficiaries include payments made from both funded and unfunded pension plans. The above payments exclude any discretionary contributions we may make. We expect such contributions to be approximately $400 million in Year 5.

Pension Assets

The expected return on pension plan assets is based on our historical experience, our pension plan investment guidelines, and our expectations for long-term rates of return. Our pension plan investment guidelines are established based upon an evaluation of market conditions, tolerance for risk and cash requirements for benefit payments. Our target allocation for Year 5 and actual pension plan asset allocation are as follows:

	Target Allocation	Actual Allocation	
Asset Category	Year 5	Year 4	Year 3
Equity securities	60%	60%	57%
Debt securities	40%	39%	34%
Other, primarily cash	–	1%	9%
Total	100%	100%	100%

Pension assets include approximately 5.5 million shares of PepsiCo common stock with a market value of $267 million in Year 4, and 5.5 million shares with a market value of $251 million in Year 3. Our investment policy limits the investment in PepsiCo stock at the time of investment to 10% of the fair value of plan assets.

Retiree Medical Cost Trend Rates

An average increase of 11% in the cost of covered retiree medical benefits is assumed for Year 5. This average increase is then projected to decline gradually to 5% in Year 10 and thereafter. These assumed health care cost trend rates have an impact on the retiree medical plan expense and liability. However, the cap on our share of retiree medical costs limits the impact. A 1 percentage point change in the assumed health care trend rate would have the following effects:

	1% Increase	1% Decrease
Year 4 service and interest cost components	$4	$(3)
Year 4 benefit liability	$46	$(41)

Savings Plan

Our U.S. employees are eligible to participate in 401(k) savings plans, which are voluntary defined contribution plans. The plans are designed to provide employees with retirement savings and strengthen their incentive to build shareholder value. We make matching contributions on a portion of eligible pay based on years of service. In Year 4, our contribution was $35 million.

Note 8 — Noncontrolled Bottling Affiliates

Our most significant noncontrolled bottling affiliates are The Pepsi Bottling Group (PBG) and PepsiAmericas (PAS). Approximately 10% of our net revenue reflects sales to PBG.

The Pepsi Bottling Group

In addition to approximately 42% of PBG's outstanding common stock that we own at year-end Year 4, we own 100% of PBG's class B common stock and approximately 7% of the equity of Bottling Group, LLC, PBG's principal operating subsidiary. This gives us economic ownership of approximately 46% of PBG's combined operations. PBG's summarized financial information is as follows:

	Year 4	Year 3	Year 2
Current assets	$ 2,039	$ 3,039	
Noncurrent assets	8,754	8,505	
Total assets	$10,793	$11,544	
Current liabilities	$1,581	$2,478	
Noncurrent liabilities	6,818	6,789	
Minority interest	445	396	
Total liabilities	$8,844	$9,663	
Our investment	$1,594	$1,353	
Net revenue	$10,906	$10,265	$9,216
Gross profit	$5,250	$5,050	$4,215
Operating profit	$976	$956	$898
Net income	$457	$416	$428

In December Year 2, PBG acquired Pepsi-Gemex, a franchise bottler in Mexico, in which we previously held a 34% ownership interest. The table above includes the results of Pepsi-Gemex from the transaction date forward.

Our investment in PBG, which includes the related goodwill, was $320 million higher than our ownership interest in their net assets at year-end Year 4. Based upon the quoted closing price of PBG shares at year-end Year 4, the calculated market value of our shares in PBG, excluding our investment in Bottling Group, LLC, exceeded our investment balance by approximately $1.7 billion.

PepsiAmericas

At year-end Year 4, we owned approximately 41% of PepsiAmericas and their summarized financial information is as follows:

	Year 4	Year 3	Year 2
Current assets	$ 530	$ 576	
Noncurrent assets	3,000	3,021	
Total assets	$3,530	$3,597	
Current liabilities	$ 521	$ 599	
Noncurrent liabilities	1,386	1,433	
Total liabilities	$1,907	$2,032	
Our investment	$924	$847	
Net revenue	$3,345	$3,237	$3,240
Gross profit	$1,423	$1,360	$1,272
Operating profit	$340	$316	$301
Income from continuing operations	$182	$158	$136
Net income	$182	$158	$130

Our investment in PAS, which includes the related goodwill, was $253 million higher than our ownership interest in their net assets at year-end Year 4. Based upon the quoted closing price of PAS shares at year-end Year 4, the calculated market value of our shares in PepsiAmericas exceeded our investment balance by approximately $277 million.

In December Year 4, PAS announced their acquisition of a regional bottler, Central Investment Corporation, for $340 million.

Related Party Transactions

Our significant related party transactions involve our noncontrolled bottling affiliates. We sell concentrate to these affiliates that is used in the production of carbonated soft drinks and non-carbonated beverages. We also sell certain finished goods to these affiliates and we receive royalties for the use of our trademarks for certain products. Sales of concentrate and finished goods are reported net of bottler funding. For further unaudited information on these bottlers, see "Our Customers" in Management's Discussion and Analysis. These transactions with our bottling affiliates are reflected in our consolidated financial statements as follows:

	Year 4	Year 3	Year 2
Net revenue	$4,170	$3,699	$3,455
Selling, general and administrative expenses	$114	$128	$105
Accounts and notes receivable	$157	$158	
Accounts payable and other current liabilities	$95	$138	

Such amounts are settled on terms consistent with other trade receivables and payables. See Note 9 regarding our guarantee of certain PBG debt.

In addition, we coordinate, on an aggregate basis, the negotiation and purchase of sweeteners and other raw materials requirements for certain of our bottlers with suppliers. Once we have negotiated the contracts, the bottlers order and take delivery directly from the supplier and pay the suppliers directly. Consequently, these transactions are not reflected in our consolidated financial statements. As the contracting party, we could be liable to these suppliers in the event of any nonpayment by our bottlers, but we consider this exposure to be remote.

Note 9 — Debt Obligations and Commitments

	Year 4	Year 3
Short-term debt obligations		
Current maturities of long-term debt	$ 160	$ 446
Other borrowings (3.2% and 5.1%)	1,644	520
Amounts reclassified to long-term debt	(750)	(375)
	$1,054	$ 591
Long-term debt obligations		
Short-term borrowings, reclassified	$ 750	$ 375
Notes due Years 5-26 (4.7% and 5.7%)	1,274	1,186
Zero coupon notes, $575 million due Years 5-12 (13.4%)	321	330
Other, due Years 5-14 (6.2% and 6.4%)	212	257
	2,557	2,148
Less: current maturities of long-term debt obligations	(160)	(446)
	$2,397	$1,702

The interest rates in the above table reflect weighted-average rates as of year-end.

Short-term borrowings are reclassified to long-term when we have the intent and ability, through the existence of the unused lines of credit, to refinance these borrowings on a long-term basis. At year-end Year 4, we maintained $1.5 billion in corporate lines of credit subject to normal banking terms and conditions. These credit facilities support short-term debt issuances and remained unused as of December 25, Year 4. Of the $1.5 billion, $750 million expires in June Year 5 with the remaining $750 million expiring in June Year 9. Upon consent of PepsiCo and the lenders, these facilities can be extended an additional year. In addition, $267 million of our debt was outstanding on various lines of credit maintained for our international divisions. These lines of credit are subject to normal banking terms and conditions and are committed to the extent of our borrowings.

Interest Rate Swaps

We entered into interest rate swaps in Year 4 to effectively change the interest rate of a specific debt issuance from a fixed rate to a variable rate. The notional amount of the interest rate swaps outstanding at December 25, Year 4 was $500 million. The interest rate received was 3.2% and the weighted-average interest rate paid was 1.7%. The variable weighted-average interest rate that we pay is linked to LIBOR and is subject to change. The terms of the interest rate swaps match the terms of the debt they modify. The swaps terminate in Year 7.

At December 25, Year 4, approximately 67% of total debt, after the impact of the associated interest rate swaps, was exposed to variable interest rates, compared to 43% at December 27, Year 3. In addition to variable rate long-term debt, all debt with maturities of less than one year is categorized as variable for purposes of this measure.

Cross Currency Interest Rate Swaps

In Year 4, we entered into a cross currency interest rate swap to hedge the currency exposure on U.S. dollar denominated debt of $50 million held by a foreign affiliate. The terms of this swap match the terms of the debt it modifies. The swap terminates in Year 8. The unrealized loss related to this swap was $3 million at December 25, Year 4, resulting in a U.S. dollar liability of $53 million.

Long-Term Contractual Commitments

Payments Due by Period	Total	Year 5	Year 6–7	Year 8–9	Year 10 & beyond
Long-term debt obligations[(a)]	$2,397	$ –	$ 722	$1,262	$ 413
Non-cancelable operating leases	666	155	193	120	198
Purchasing commitments[(b)]	4,386	1,225	1,243	792	1,126
Marketing commitments	1,413	440	422	262	289
Other commitments	136	104	25	6	1
	$8,998	$1,924	$2,605	$2,442	$2,027

(a) Excludes current maturities of long-term debt of $160 million which are classified within current liabilities.

(b) Includes approximately $30 million of long-term commitments which are reflected in other liabilities in our Consolidated Balance Sheet.

The above table reflects non-cancelable commitments as of December 25, Year 4 based on year-end foreign exchange rates.

Most long-term contractual commitments, except for our long-term debt obligations, are not recorded in our Consolidated Balance Sheet. Non-cancelable operating leases primarily represent building leases. Non-cancelable purchasing commitments are primarily for oranges and orange juices to be used for our Tropicana brand beverages. Non-cancelable marketing commitments primarily are for sports marketing and with our fountain customers. Bottler funding is not reflected in our long-term contractual commitments as it is negotiated on an annual basis. See Note 7 regarding our pension and retiree medical obligations and discussion below regarding our commitments to noncontrolled bottling affiliates and former restaurant operations.

Off-Balance Sheet Arrangements

It is not our business practice to enter into off-balance sheet arrangements, other than in the normal course of business, nor is it our policy to issue guarantees to our bottlers, noncontrolled affiliates or third parties. However, certain guarantees were necessary to facilitate the separation of our bottling and restaurant operations from us. In connection with these transactions, we have guaranteed $2.3 billion of Bottling Group, LLC's long-term debt through Year 12 and $39 million of YUM! Brands, Inc. (YUM) outstanding obligations, primarily property leases. The terms of our Bottling Group, LLC debt guarantee are intended to preserve the structure of PBG's separation from us and our payment obligation would be triggered if Bottling Group, LLC failed to perform under these debt obligations or the structure significantly changed. Our guarantees of certain obligations ensured YUM's continued use of certain properties. These guarantees would require our cash payment if YUM failed to perform under these lease obligations.

See "Our Liquidity, Capital Resources and Financial Position" in Management's Discussion and Analysis for further unaudited information on our borrowings.

Note 10 — Risk Management

We are exposed to the risk of loss arising from adverse changes in:

- commodity prices, affecting the cost of our raw materials and energy;
- foreign exchange risks;
- interest rates;
- stock prices; and
- discount rates, affecting the measurement of our pension and retiree medical liabilities.

In the normal course of business, we manage these risks through a variety of strategies, including the use of derivative instruments designated as cash flow and fair value hedges. See "Our Business Risks" in Management's Discussion and Analysis for further unaudited information on our business risks.

For cash flow hedges, changes in fair value are generally deferred in accumulated other comprehensive loss within shareholders' equity until the underlying hedged item is recognized in net income. For fair value hedges, changes in fair value are recognized immediately in earnings, consistent with the underlying hedged item. Hedging transactions are limited to an underlying exposure. As a result, any change in the value of our derivative instruments would be substantially offset by an opposite change in the value of the underlying hedged items. Hedging ineffectiveness and a net earnings impact occur when the change in the value of the hedge does not offset the change in the value of the underlying hedged item. If the derivative instrument is terminated, we continue to defer the related gain or loss and include it as a component of the cost of the underlying hedged item. Upon determination that the underlying hedged item will not be part of an actual transaction, we recognize the related gain or loss in net income in that period. We do not use derivative instruments for trading or speculative purposes and we limit our exposure to individual counterparties to manage credit risk.

Commodity Prices

We are subject to commodity price risk because our ability to recover increased costs through higher pricing may be limited in the competitive environment in which we operate. This risk is managed through the use of fixed-price purchase orders, pricing agreements, geographic diversity and cash flow hedges. We use cash flow hedges, with terms of no more than two years, to hedge price fluctuations related to a portion of our anticipated commodity purchases, primarily for corn, heating oil and natural gas. Any ineffectiveness is recorded immediately. However, our commodity hedges have not had any significant ineffectiveness. We classify both the earnings and cash flow impact from these hedges consistent with the underlying hedged item. During the next 12 months, we expect to reclassify gains of less than $1 million from accumulated other comprehensive loss into net income.

Foreign Exchange

Our operations outside of the U.S. generate over a third of our net revenue of which Mexico, the United Kingdom and Canada comprise nearly 20%. As a result, we are exposed to foreign currency risks from unforeseen economic changes and political unrest. On occasion, we enter into hedges, primarily forward contracts with terms of no more than two years, to reduce the effect of foreign exchange rates. Ineffectiveness on these hedges has not been material.

Interest Rates

We centrally manage our debt and investment portfolios considering investment opportunities and risks, tax consequences and overall financing strategies. We may use interest rate and cross currency interest rate swaps to manage our overall interest expense and foreign exchange risk. These instruments effectively change the interest rate and currency of specific debt issuances. These swaps are entered into concurrently with the issuance of the debt that they are intended to modify. The notional amount, interest payment and maturity date of the swaps match the principal, interest payment and maturity date of the related debt. These swaps are entered into only with strong creditworthy counterparties, are settled on a net basis and are of relatively short duration.

Stock Prices

The portion of our deferred compensation liability that is based on certain market indices and on our stock price is subject to market risk. We hold mutual fund investments and prepaid forward contracts to manage this risk. Changes in the fair value of these investments and contracts are recognized immediately in earnings and are offset by changes in the related compensation liability.

Fair Value

All derivative instruments are recognized in our Consolidated Balance Sheet at fair value. The fair value of our derivative instruments is generally based on quoted market prices. Book and fair values of our derivative and financial instruments are as follows:

	Year 4		Year 3	
	Book Value	Fair Value	Book Value	Fair Value
Assets				
Cash and cash equivalents[a]	$1,280	$1,280	$820	$820
Short-term investments[b]	$2,165	$2,165	$1,181	$1,181
Forward exchange contracts[c]	$8	$8	$3	$3
Commodity contracts[c]	$11	$11	$4	$4
Prepaid forward contracts[c]	$120	$120	$107	$107
Liabilities				
Forward exchange contracts[d]	$35	$35	$33	$33
Commodity contracts[d]	$8	$8	–	–
Debt obligations	$3,451	$3,676	$2,293	$2,569
Interest rate swaps[d]	$1	$1	–	–
Cross currency interest rate swaps[e]	$3	$3	–	–

Included in the Consolidated Balance Sheet under the captions noted above or as indicated below.

(a) Book value approximates fair value due to the short maturity.

(b) Principally short-term time deposits and includes $118 million at December 25, Year 4 and $103 million at December 27, Year 3 of mutual fund investments used to manage a portion of market risk arising from our deferred compensation liability.

(c) Includes contracts not designated as hedges and reported within current assets and other assets.

(d) Includes contracts not designated as hedges and reported within current liabilities and other liabilities.

(e) Included within long-term debt.

This table excludes guarantees, including our guarantee of $2.3 billion of Bottling Group, LLC's long-term debt. The guarantee had a fair value of $46 million at December 25, Year 4 and $35 million at December 27, Year 3 based on an external estimate of the cost to us of transferring the liability to an independent financial institution. See Note 9 for additional information on our guarantees.

Note 11 — Net Income per Common Share from Continuing Operations

Basic net income per common share is net income available to common shareholders divided by the weighted average of common shares outstanding during the period. Diluted net income per common share is calculated using the weighted average of common shares outstanding adjusted to include the effect that would occur if in-the-money employee stock options were exercised and RSUs and preferred shares were converted into common shares. Options to purchase 7.0 million shares in Year 4, 49.0 million shares in Year 3 and 37.9 million shares in Year 2 were not included in the calculation of diluted earnings per common share because these options were out-of-the-money. Out-of-the-money options had average exercise prices of $52.88 in Year 4, $48.27 in Year 3 and $48.29 in Year 2.

The computations of basic and diluted net income per common share from continuing operations are as follows:

	Year 4		Year 3		Year 2	
	Income	Shares[(a)]	Income	Shares[(a)]	Income	Shares[(a)]
Net income	$4,174		$3,568		$3,000	
Preferred shares:						
Dividends	(3)		(3)		(4)	
Redemption premium	(22)		(12)		(25)	
Net income available for common shareholders	$4,149	1,696	$3,553	1,718	$2,971	1,753
Basic net income per common share	$2.45		$2.07		$1.69	
Net income available for common shareholders	$4,149	1,696	$3,553	1,718	$2,971	1,753
Dilutive securities:						
Stock options and RSUs	–	31	–	17	–	25
ESOP convertible preferred stock	24	2	15	3	28	3
Unvested stock awards	–	–	–	1	–	1
Diluted	$4,173	1,729	$3,568	1,739	$2,999	1,782
Diluted net income per common share	$2.41		$2.05		$1.68	

(a) Weighted average common shares outstanding.

Note 12 — Preferred and Common Stock

As of December 25, Year 4, there were 3.6 billion shares of common stock and three million shares of convertible preferred stock authorized. The preferred stock was issued only for an employee stock ownership plan (ESOP) established by Quaker and these shares are redeemable by the ESOP participants. The preferred stock accrues dividends at an annual rate of $5.46 per share. At year-end Year 4, there were 803,953 preferred shares issued and 424,853 shares outstanding. Each share is convertible at the option of the holder into 4.9625 shares of common stock. The preferred shares may be called by us upon written notice at $78 per share plus accrued and unpaid dividends.

As of December 25, Year 4, 0.4 million outstanding shares of preferred stock with a fair value of $110 million and 18 million shares of common stock were held in the accounts of ESOP participants. Quaker made the final award to its ESOP plan in June Year 1.

	Year 4		Year 3		Year 2	
	Shares	Amount	Shares	Amount	Shares	Amount
Preferred stock	0.8	$41	0.8	$41	0.8	$41
Repurchased preferred stock						
Balance, beginning of year	0.3	$63	0.2	$48	0.1	$15
Redemptions	0.1	27	0.1	15	0.1	33
Balance, end of year	0.4	$90	0.3	$63	0.2	$48

Note 13 — Accumulated Other Comprehensive Loss

Comprehensive income is a measure of income which includes both net income and other comprehensive income or loss. Other comprehensive loss results from items deferred on the balance sheet in shareholders' equity. Other comprehensive income was $381 million in Year 4, $405 million in Year 3, and other comprehensive loss was $26 million in Year 2. The accumulated balances for each component of other comprehensive loss were as follows:

	Year 4	Year 3	Year 2
Currency translation adjustment	$(720)	$(1,121)	$(1,531)
Cash flow hedges, net of tax(a)	(19)	(12)	–
Minimum pension liability adjustment(b)	(154)	(135)	(142)
Other	7	1	1
Accumulated other comprehensive loss	$(886)	$(1,267)	$(1,672)

(a) Includes $6 million gain in Year 4, $8 million gain in Year 3 and $4 million loss in Year 2 for our share of our equity investees' accumulated derivative activity. Deferred losses reclassified into earnings were $10 million in Year 4, no impact in Year 3, and $2 million in Year 2.

(b) Net of taxes of $77 million in Year 4, $67 million in Year 3 and $72 million in Year 2. Also, includes $121 million in Year 4, $110 million in Year 3 and $99 million in Year 2 for our share of our equity investees' minimum pension liability adjustments.

Note 14 — Supplemental Financial Information

	Year 4	Year 3	Year 2
Accounts receivable			
Trade receivables	$2,505	$2,309	
Other receivables	591	626	
	3,096	2,935	
Allowance, beginning of year	105	116	$121
Charged to expense	18	32	38
Deductions(a)	(25)	(43)	(46)
Other(b)	(1)	–	3
Allowance, end of year	97	105	$116
Net receivables	$2,999	$2,830	
Inventory(c)			
Raw materials	$ 665	$ 618	
Work-in-process	156	160	
Finished goods	720	634	
	$1,541	$1,412	
Accounts payable and other liabilities			
Accounts payable	$1,731	$1,638	
Accrued marketplace spending	1,285	1,243	
Accrued compensation and benefits	961	851	
Dividends payable	387	274	
Insurance accruals	131	151	
Other current liabilities	1,104	1,056	
	$5,599	$5,213	
Other liabilities			
Reserves for income taxes	$1,567	$1,775	
Other	2,532	2,300	
	$4,099	$4,075	
Other supplemental information			
Rent expense	$245	$231	$194
Interest paid	$137	$147	$119
Income taxes paid, net of refunds	$1,833	$1,530	$700
Acquisitions(d)			
Fair value of assets acquired	$ 78	$178	$ 626
Cash paid and debt issued	(64)	(71)	(351)
Liabilities assumed	$ 14	$107	$ 275

(a) Includes accounts written off.

(b) Includes collections of previously written off accounts and currency translation effects.

(c) Inventories are valued at the lower of cost or market. Cost is determined using the average, first-in, first-out (FIFO) or last-in, first-out (LIFO) methods. Approximately 16% in Year 4 and 10% in Year 3 of the inventory cost was computed using the LIFO method. The differences between LIFO and FIFO methods of valuing these inventories are not material.

(d) Includes our acquisition of the Wotsits brand in the United Kingdom for $228 million in Year 2.

Management's Responsibility for Financial Reporting

To Our Shareholders:

At PepsiCo, our actions — the actions of all our associates — are governed by our Worldwide Code of Conduct. This code is clearly aligned with our stated values — a commitment to sustained growth, through empowered people, operating with responsibility and building trust. Both the code and our core values enable us to operate with integrity — both within the letter and the spirit of the law. Our code of conduct is reinforced consistently at all levels and in all countries. We have maintained strong governance policies and practices for many years.

The management of PepsiCo is responsible for the objectivity and integrity of our consolidated financial statements. The Audit Committee of the Board of Directors has engaged independent registered public accounting firm, KPMG LLP, to audit our consolidated financial statements and they have expressed an unqualified opinion.

We are committed to providing timely, accurate and understandable information to investors. This encompasses the following.

Maintaining strong controls over financial reporting. Our system of internal control is based on the control criteria framework of the Committee of Sponsoring Organizations of the Treadway Commission published in their report titled, *Internal Control — Integrated Framework.* The system is designed to provide reasonable assurance that transactions are executed as authorized and accurately recorded; that assets are safeguarded; and that accounting records are sufficiently reliable to permit the preparation of financial statements that conform in all material respects with accounting principles generally accepted in the U.S. We maintain disclosure controls and procedures designed to ensure that information required to be disclosed in reports under the Securities Exchange Act of 1934 is recorded, processed, summarized and reported within the specified time periods. We monitor these internal controls through self-assessments and an ongoing program of internal audits. Our internal controls are reinforced through our Worldwide Code of Conduct, which sets forth our commitment to conduct business with integrity, and within both the letter and the spirit of the law.

Exerting rigorous oversight of the business. We continuously review our business results and strategies. This encompasses financial discipline in our strategic and daily business decisions. Our Executive Committee is actively involved — from understanding strategies and alternatives to reviewing key initiatives and financial performance. The intent is to ensure we remain objective in our assessments, constructively challenge our approach to potential business opportunities and issues, and monitor results and controls.

Engaging strong and effective Corporate Governance from our Board of Directors. We have an active, capable and diligent Board that meets the required standards for independence, and we welcome the Board's oversight as a representative of our shareholders. Our Audit Committee comprises independent directors with the financial literacy, knowledge and experience to provide appropriate oversight. We review our critical accounting policies, financial reporting and internal control matters with them and encourage their direct communication with KPMG LLP, with our General Auditor, and with our General Counsel. We have recently named a senior compliance officer to lead and coordinate our compliance policies and practices.

Providing investors with financial results that are complete, transparent and understandable. The consolidated financial statements and financial information included in this report are the responsibility of management. This includes preparing the financial statements in accordance with accounting principles generally accepted in the U.S., which require estimates based on management's best judgment.

PepsiCo has a strong history of doing what's right. We realize that great companies are built on trust, strong ethical standards and principles. Our financial results are delivered from that culture of accountability, and we take responsibility for the quality and accuracy of our financial reporting.

Peter Bridgman

Peter A. Bridgman
Senior Vice President and Controller

Indra K. Nooyi

Indra K. Nooyi
President and Chief Financial Officer

Steven S Reinemund

Steven S Reinemund
Chairman of the Board and Chief Executive Officer

Management's Report on Internal Control over Financial Reporting

To Our Shareholders:

Our management is responsible for establishing and maintaining adequate internal control over financial reporting, as such term is defined in Rule 13a-15(f) of the Exchange Act. Under the supervision and with the participation of our management, including our Chief Executive Officer and Chief Financial Officer, we conducted an evaluation of the effectiveness of our internal control over financial reporting based upon the framework in Internal Control — Integrated Framework issued by the Committee of Sponsoring Organizations of the Treadway Commission. Based on that evaluation, our management concluded that our internal control over financial reporting is effective as of December 25, Year 4.

KPMG LLP, an independent registered public accounting firm, has audited the consolidated financial statements included in this Annual Report and, as part of their audit, has issued their report, included herein, (1) on our management's assessment of the effectiveness of our internal controls over financial reporting and (2) on the effectiveness of our internal control over financial reporting.

Peter A. Bridgman
Senior Vice President and Controller

Indra K. Nooyi
President and Chief Financial Officer

Steven S Reinemund
Chairman of the Board and Chief Executive Officer

Report of Independent Registered Public Accounting Firm

Board of Directors and Shareholders
PepsiCo, Inc.:

We have audited the accompanying Consolidated Balance Sheet of PepsiCo, Inc. and Subsidiaries as of December 25, Year 4 and December 27, Year 3 and the related Consolidated Statements of Income, Cash Flows and Common Shareholders' Equity for each of the years in the three-year period ended December 25, Year 4. We have also audited management's assessment, included in the accompanying Management's Report on Internal Control over Financial Reporting, that PepsiCo, Inc. and Subsidiaries maintained effective internal control over financial reporting as of December 25, Year 4, based on criteria established in Internal Control — Integrated Framework issued by the Committee of Sponsoring Organizations of the Treadway Commission (COSO). PepsiCo, Inc.'s management is responsible for these consolidated financial statements, for maintaining effective internal control over financial reporting, and for its assessment of the effectiveness of internal control over financial reporting. Our responsibility is to express an opinion on these consolidated financial statements, an opinion on management's assessment, and an opinion on the effectiveness of PepsiCo, Inc.'s internal control over financial reporting based on our audits.

We conducted our audits in accordance with the standards of the Public Company Accounting Oversight Board (United States). Those standards require that we plan and perform the audits to obtain reasonable assurance about whether the financial statements are free of material misstatement and whether effective internal control over financial reporting was maintained in all material respects. Our audit of financial statements included examining, on a test basis, evidence supporting the amounts and disclosures in the financial statements, assessing the accounting principles used and significant estimates made by management, and evaluating the overall financial statement presentation. Our audit of internal control over financial reporting included obtaining an understanding of internal control over financial reporting, evaluating management's assessment, testing and evaluating the design and operating effectiveness of internal control, and performing such other procedures as we considered necessary in the circumstances. We believe that our audits provide a reasonable basis for our opinions.

A company's internal control over financial reporting is a process designed to provide reasonable assurance regarding the reliability of financial reporting and the preparation of financial statements for external purposes in accordance with generally accepted accounting principles. A company's internal control over financial reporting includes those policies and procedures that (1) pertain to the maintenance of records that, in reasonable detail, accurately and fairly reflect the transactions and dispositions of the assets of the company; (2) provide reasonable assurance that transactions are recorded as necessary to permit preparation of financial statements in accordance with generally accepted accounting principles, and that receipts and expenditures of the company are being made only in accordance with authorizations of management and directors of the company; and (3) provide reasonable assurance regarding prevention or timely detection of unauthorized acquisition, use, or disposition of the company's assets that could have a material effect on the financial statements.

Because of its inherent limitations, internal control over financial reporting may not prevent or detect misstatements. Also, projections of any evaluation of effectiveness to future periods are subject to the risk that controls may become inadequate because of changes in conditions, or that the degree of compliance with the policies or procedures may deteriorate.

In our opinion, the consolidated financial statements referred to above present fairly, in all material respects, the financial position of PepsiCo, Inc. and Subsidiaries as of December 25, Year 4 and December 27, Year 3, and the results of their operations and their cash flows for each of the years in the three-year period ended December 25, Year 4, in conformity with United States generally accepted accounting principles. Also, in our opinion, management's assessment that PepsiCo, Inc. maintained effective internal control over financial reporting as of December 25, Year 4, is fairly stated, in all material respects, based on criteria established in Internal Control — Integrated Framework issued by COSO. Furthermore, in our opinion, PepsiCo, Inc. maintained, in all material respects, effective internal control over financial reporting as of December 25, Year 4, based on criteria established in Internal Control — Integrated Framework issued by COSO.

KPMG LLP
New York, New York
February 24, Year 5

Selected Financial Data (in millions except per share amounts, unaudited)

Quarterly	First Quarter	Second Quarter	Third Quarter	Fourth Quarter
Net revenue				
Year 4	$6,131	$7,070	$7,257	$8,803
Year 3	$5,530	$6,538	$6,830	$8,073
Gross profit				
Year 4	$3,320	$3,857	$3,957	$4,721
Year 3	$2,996	$3,546	$3,714	$4,336
Impairment and restructuring charges[(a)]				
Year 4	–	–	–	$150
Year 3	–	–	–	$147
Merger-related costs[(b)]				
Year 3	$11	$11	$9	$28
Net income — continuing operations				
Year 4	$804	$1,059	$1,364	$947
Year 3	$698	$944	$1,012	$914
Tax benefit from discontinued operations[(c)]				
Year 4	–	–	–	$38
Net income per common share — basic, continuing operations				
Year 4	$0.47	$0.62	$0.80	$0.56
Year 3	$0.40	$0.55	$0.59	$0.53
Net income per common share — diluted, continuing operations				
Year 4	$0.46	$0.61	$0.79	$0.55
Year 3	$0.40	$0.54	$0.58	$0.52
Cash dividends declared per common share				
Year 4	$0.16	$0.23	$0.23	$0.23
Year 3	$0.15	$0.16	$0.16	$0.16
Year 4 stock price per share[(d)]				
High	$53.00	$55.48	$55.71	$53.00
Low	$45.30	$50.28	$48.41	$47.37
Close	$50.93	$54.95	$50.84	$51.94
Year 3 stock price per share[(d)]				
High	$44.06	$45.11	$47.98	$48.88
Low	$36.24	$38.06	$43.10	$44.11
Close	$41.50	$44.74	$44.33	$46.47

The first, second, and third quarters consist of 12 weeks and the fourth quarter consists of 16 weeks.

(a) Impairment and restructuring charges were $150 million ($96 million or $0.06 per share after-tax) in Year 4 and $147 million ($100 million or $0.06 after-tax) in Year 3 (see Note 3).

(b) Merger-related costs (see Note 3):

Year 3	1Q	2Q	3Q	4Q
Pre-tax	$11	$11	$9	$28
After-tax	$10	$9	$6	$17
Per share	–	–	–	$0.01

(c) Fourth quarter Year 4 net income was $985 million or $0.58 per share, reflecting a tax benefit from discontinued operations of $38 million or $0.02 per share. See Note 5.

(d) Represents the composite high and low sales price and quarterly closing prices for one share of PepsiCo common stock.

Five-Year Summary	Year 4	Year 3	Year 2
Net revenue	$29,261	$26,971	$25,112
Income from continuing operations	$4,174	$3,568	$3,000
Net income	$4,212	$3,568	$3,000
Income per common share — basic, continuing operations	$2.45	$2.07	$1.69
Income per common share — diluted, continuing operations	$2.41	$2.05	$1.68
Cash dividends declared per common share	$0.850	$0.630	$0.595
Total assets	$27,987	$25,327	$23,474
Long-term debt	$2,397	$1,702	$2,187

Five-Year Summary (cont.)	Year 1	Year 0
Net revenue	$23,512	$22,337
Net income	$2,400	$2,543
Income per common share — basic	$1.35	$1.45
Income per common share — diluted	$1.33	$1.42
Cash dividends declared per common share	$0.575	$0.555
Total assets	$21,695	$20,757
Long-term debt	$2,651	$3,009

- As a result of the adoption of SFAS 142 and the consolidation of SVE in Year 2, the data provided above is not comparable.
- Includes restructuring and impairment charges of:

	Year 4	Year 3	Year 1	Year 0
Pre-tax	$150	$147	$31	$184
After-tax	$96	$100	$19	$111
Per share	$0.06	$0.06	$0.01	$0.06

- In Year 3, we voluntarily adopted the fair value method of accounting for stock options. We selected the retroactive restatement method as described in SFAS 148, *Accounting for Stock-Based Compensation — Transition and Disclosure,* to adopt this accounting. Under this method, we restated our Year 3, Year 2 and Year 1 results to recognize stock-based compensation expense as follows:

	Year 3	Year 2	Year 1
Pre-tax	$407	$435	$385
After-tax	$293	$313	$262
Per share	$0.16	$0.17	$0.14

- Fiscal year Year 0 was not restated for this adoption.
- Includes Quaker merger-related costs of:

	Year 3	Year 2	Year 1
Pre-tax	$59	$224	$356
After-tax	$42	$190	$322
Per share	$0.02	$0.11	$0.18

- The Year 0 fiscal year consisted of fifty-three weeks compared to fifty-two weeks in our normal fiscal year. The 53rd week increased Year 0 net revenue by an estimated $294 million and net income by an estimated $44 million (or $0.02 per share).
- Cash dividends per common share are those of pre-merger PepsiCo prior to the effective date of the merger.
- In the fourth quarter of Year 4, we reached agreement with the IRS for an open issue related to our discontinued restaurant operations which resulted in a tax benefit of $38 million or $0.02 per share.

Reconciliation of GAAP and Non-GAAP Information

We recognized certain tax benefits in the third and fourth quarters of Year 4. In addition, we incurred restructuring and impairment charges in the fourth quarter of Year 4 related to Frito-Lay's manufacturing consolidation, as well as restructuring charges in the fourth quarter of Year 3 in conjunction with the streamlining of our North American divisions and PepsiCo International.

Net income and earnings per share excluding the impact of these tax benefits and the restructuring and impairment charges are not measures defined by generally accepted accounting principles (GAAP). We believe investors should consider our net income and earnings per share without the impact of these tax benefits and the restructuring and impairment charges as these measures are more indicative of our ongoing performance.

Net Income Reconciliation

	Year 4	Year 3	Growth
Reported net income	$4,212	$3,568	18%
Tax benefits	(304)	(109)	
Restructuring and impairment charges	96	100	
Net income excluding tax benefits and restructuring and impairment charges	$4,004	$3,560*	12%

*Based on unrounded amounts.

Diluted EPS Reconciliation

	Year 4	Year 3	Growth
Reported diluted EPS	$2.44	$2.05	19%
Impact of tax benefits	(0.18)	(0.06)	
Restructuring and impairment charges	0.06	0.06	
Diluted EPS excluding tax benefits and restructuring and impairment charges	$2.32	$2.05	13%

GLOSSARY

Anchor bottlers: The Pepsi Bottling Group (PBG), PepsiAmericas, Inc. (PAS) and Pepsi Bottling Ventures (PBV).

Bottler: customers who we have granted exclusive contracts to sell and manufacture certain beverage products bearing our trademarks within a specific geographical area.

Bottler Case Sales (BCS): measure of physical 8 oz. case volume of beverages bearing our trademarks that bottlers have sold to independent distributors and retailers. BCS is reported on a monthly basis.

Bottler funding: financial incentives we give to our bottlers to assist in the distribution and promotion of our beverage products.

Business Process Transformation (BPT): our comprehensive multi-year effort to drive efficiencies. It includes efforts to physically consolidate, or hardwire, key business functions to take advantage of our scale. It also includes moving to a common set of processes that underlie our key activities, and supporting them with common technology application. And finally, it includes our SAP installation, the computer system that will link all of our systems and processes.

Concentrate Shipments and Equivalents (CSE): measure of our physical beverage volume to our customers. This measure is reported on our fiscal year basis.

Consumers: people who eat and drink our products.

Customers: franchise bottlers and independent distributors and retailers.

CSD: carbonated soft drinks.

Derivatives: financial instruments, such as Chicago Board of Trade commodity futures and options, that we use to manage our risk arising from changes in commodity prices, interest rates, foreign exchange rates and stock prices.

Direct-Store-Delivery (DSD): delivery system used by us and our bottlers to deliver snacks and beverages directly to retail stores where our products are merchandised.

Effective net pricing: reflects the year-over-year impact of discrete pricing actions, sales incentive activities and mix resulting from selling varying products in different package sizes and in different countries.

Management operating cash flow: net cash provided by operating activities less capital spending plus sales of property, plant and equipment. It is our primary measure used to monitor cash flow performance.

Marketplace spending: sales incentives offered through various programs to our customers and consumers, as well as advertising and other marketing activities.

Power of One: our initiative that enables us to leverage all of our products, services and talents for the advantage of our retail partners.

Servings: common metric reflecting our consolidated physical unit volume. Our divisions' physical unit measures are converted into servings based on U.S. Food and Drug Administration guidelines for single-serving sizes of our products.

Smart Spot: our initiative that helps consumers find our products that can contribute to healthier lifestyles.

Transaction gains and losses: the impact on our consolidated financial statements of exchange rate changes arising from specific transactions.

Translation adjustments: the impact of the conversion of our foreign affiliates' financial statements to U.S. dollars for the purpose of consolidating our financial statements.

Appendix B

Management's Discussion and Analysis for PepsiCo, Inc. and Subsidiaries

Management's Discussion and Analysis and Consolidated Financial Statements

Our Business

Our discussion and analysis is an integral part of understanding our financial results. Definitions of key terms can be found in the glossary on page 1046. Tabular dollars are presented in millions, except per share amounts. All per share amounts reflect common per share amounts, assume dilution unless noted, and are based on unrounded amounts. Percentage changes are based on unrounded amounts.

Our Operations

We are a leading, global snack and beverage company. We manufacture, market and sell a variety of salty, convenient, sweet and grain-based snacks, carbonated and non-carbonated beverages and foods. We are organized in four divisions:

- Frito-Lay North America,
- PepsiCo Beverages North America,
- PepsiCo International, and
- Quaker Foods North America.

Our North American divisions operate in the United States (U.S.) and Canada. Our international divisions operate in over 200 countries, with our largest operations in Mexico and the United Kingdom. Additional information concerning our divisions and geographic areas is presented in Note 1.

Frito-Lay North America

Frito-Lay North America (FLNA) manufactures or uses contract manufacturers, markets, sells and distributes branded snacks. These snacks include Lay's potato chips, Doritos flavored tortilla chips, Tostitos tortilla chips, Cheetos cheese flavored snacks, Fritos corn chips, Ruffles potato chips, branded dips, Rold Gold pretzels, Quaker Chewy granola bars, Sun Chips multigrain snacks, Munchies snack mix, Grandma's cookies, Lay's Stax potato crisps, Quaker Fruit & Oatmeal bars, Quaker Quakes corn and rice snacks, Cracker Jack candy coated popcorn, and Go Snacks. FLNA branded products are sold to independent distributors and retailers.

PepsiCo Beverages North America

PepsiCo Beverages North America (PBNA) manufactures or uses contract manufacturers, markets and sells beverage concentrates, fountain syrups and finished goods, under various beverage brands including Pepsi, Mountain Dew, Gatorade, Tropicana Pure Premium, Sierra Mist, Mug, Tropicana juice drinks, Propel, SoBe, Slice, Dole, Tropicana Twister and Tropicana Season's Best. PBNA also manufactures, markets and sells ready-to-drink tea and coffee products through joint ventures with Lipton and Starbucks. In addition, PBNA licenses the Aquafina water brand to its bottlers and markets this brand. PBNA sells concentrate and finished goods for some of these brands to bottlers licensed by us, and some of these branded products are sold directly by us to independent distributors and retailers. The franchise bottlers sell our brands as finished goods to independent distributors and retailers. PBNA's volume reflects sales to its independent distributors and retailers, and the sales of beverages bearing our trademarks that franchise bottlers have reported as sold to independent distributors and retailers.

All of our divisions positively contributed to net revenue and operating profit growth in Year 4.

PepsiCo International

PepsiCo International (PI) manufactures through consolidated businesses as well as through noncontrolled affiliates, a number of leading salty and sweet snack brands including Gamesa and Sabritas in Mexico, Walkers in the United Kingdom, and Smith's in Australia. Further, PI manufactures or

Net Revenue Contribution to Growth

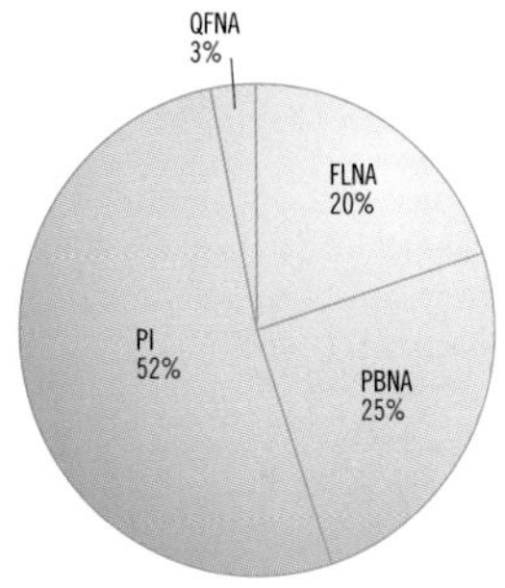

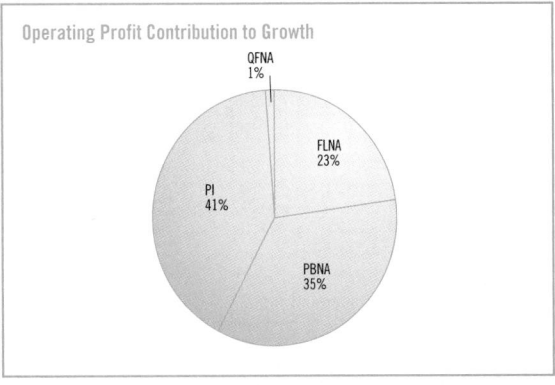

Operating Profit Contribution to Growth

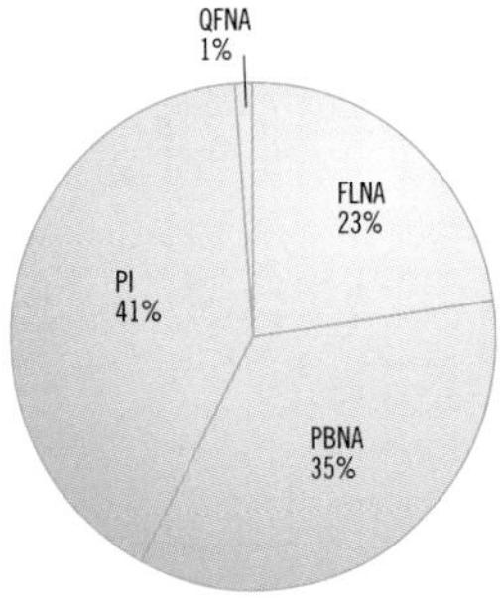

uses contract manufacturers, markets and sells many Quaker brand snacks. PI also manufactures, markets and sells beverage concentrates, fountain syrups and finished goods under the brands Pepsi, 7UP, Mirinda, Gatorade, Mountain Dew and Tropicana. These brands are sold to franchise bottlers, independent distributors and retailers. However, in certain markets, PI operates its own bottling plants and distribution facilities. PI also licenses the Aquafina water brand to certain of its franchise bottlers. PI reports two measures of volume. Snack volume is reported on a system-wide basis, which includes our own volume and the volume sold by our noncontrolled affiliates. Beverage volume reflects company-owned and franchise bottler sales of beverages bearing our trademarks to independent distributors and retailers.

Quaker Foods North America

Quaker Foods North America (QFNA) manufactures or uses contract manufacturers, markets and sells cereals, rice, pasta and other branded products. QFNA's products include Quaker oatmeal, Aunt Jemima mixes and syrups, Quaker grits, Cap'n Crunch and Life ready-to-eat cereals, Rice-A-Roni, Pasta Roni and Near East side dishes. These branded products are sold to independent distributors and retailers.

Our Customers

Our customers include franchise bottlers and independent distributors and retailers. We grant our bottlers exclusive contracts to sell and manufacture certain beverage products bearing our trademarks within a specific geographic area. These arrangements specify the amount to be paid by our bottlers for concentrate and full goods and for Aquafina royalties, as well as the manufacturing process required for product quality.

Since we do not sell directly to the consumer, we rely on and provide financial incentives to our customers to assist in the distribution and promotion of our products. For our independent distributors and retailers, these incentives include volume-based rebates, product placement fees, promotions and displays. For our bottlers, these incentives are referred to as bottler funding and are negotiated annually with each bottler to support a variety of trade and consumer programs, such as consumer incentives, advertising support, new product support, and vending and cooler equipment placement. Consumer incentives include coupons, pricing discounts and promotions, such as sweepstakes and other promotional offers. Advertising support is directed at advertising programs and supporting bottler media. New product support includes targeted consumer and retailer incentives and direct marketplace support, such as point-of-purchase materials, product placement fees, media and advertising. Vending and cooler equipment placement programs support the acquisition and placement of vending machines and cooler equipment. The nature and type of programs vary annually. The level of bottler funding is at our discretion because these incentives are not required by the terms of our bottling contracts.

Retail consolidation has increased the importance of major customers and further consolidation is expected.

Sales to Wal-Mart Stores, Inc. represent approximately 11% of our total net revenue. Retail consolidation has increased the importance of major customers and further consolidation is expected. Our top five retail customers currently represent approximately 27% of our Year 4 North American net revenue, with Wal-Mart representing approximately 14%. In addition, sales to The Pepsi Bottling Group (PBG) represent approximately 10% of our total net revenue. See "Our Related Party Bottlers" and Note 8 for more information on our anchor bottlers.

Our Related Party Bottlers

We have ownership interests in certain of our bottlers. Our ownership is less than 50% and since we do not control these bottlers, we do not consolidate their results. We include our share of their net income based on our percentage of economic ownership in our income statement as bottling equity income. We have designated three related party bottlers, PBG, PepsiAmericas, Inc. (PAS) and Pepsi Bottling Ventures LLC (PBV), as our anchor bottlers. Our anchor bottlers distribute approximately 65% of our North American beverage volume and approximately 20% of our international beverage volume. Our anchor bottlers participate in the bottler funding programs described above. Approximately 12% of our total Year 4 sales incentives related to these bottlers. See Note 8 for additional information on these related parties and related party commitments and guarantees.

Our Distribution Network

Our products are brought to market through direct-store-delivery, broker-warehouse and foodservice and vending distribution networks. The distribution system used depends on customer needs, product characteristics, and local trade practices.

Direct-Store-Delivery

We and our bottlers operate direct-store-delivery systems that deliver snacks and beverages directly to retail stores where the products are merchandised by our employees or our bottlers. Direct-store-delivery enables us to merchandise with maximum visibility and appeal. Direct-store-delivery is especially well-suited to products that are restocked often and respond to in-store promotion and merchandising.

Our products are brought to market through direct-store-delivery, broker-warehouse and foodservice and vending distribution networks.

Broker-Warehouse

Some of our products are delivered from our warehouses to customer warehouses and retail stores. These less costly systems generally work best for products that are less fragile and perishable, have lower turnover, and are less likely to be impulse purchases.

Foodservice and Vending

Our foodservice and vending sales force distributes snacks, foods and beverages to third-party foodservice and vending distributors and operators, and for certain beverages, distributes through our bottlers. This distribution system supplies our products to schools, businesses, stadiums, restaurants and similar locations.

Our Competition

Our businesses operate in highly competitive markets. We compete against global, regional and private label manufacturers on the basis of price, quality, product variety and effective distribution. Our chief beverage competitor, The Coca-Cola Company, has a slightly larger share of CSD consumption in the United States, while we have a larger share of chilled juices and isotonics. In addition, The Coca-Cola Company maintains a significant CSD share advantage in many markets outside North America. Further, our snack brands hold significant leadership positions in the snack industry worldwide and face local and regional competitors, as well as national and global snack competitors, on issues related to price, quality, variety and distribution. Success in this competitive environment is dependent on effective promotion of existing products and the introduction of new products. We believe that the strength of our brands, innovation and marketing, coupled with the quality of our products and flexibility of our distribution network, allow us to compete effectively.

Other Relationships

Certain members of our Board of Directors also serve on the boards of certain vendors and customers. Those Board members do not participate in our vendor selection and negotiations nor in our customer negotiations. Our transactions with these vendors and customers are in the normal course of business and are consistent with terms negotiated with other vendors and customers. In addition, certain of our employees serve on the boards of our anchor bottlers and other affiliated companies and do not receive incremental compensation for their Board services.

Our Business Risks

We are subject to risks in the normal course of business due to adverse developments affecting:
- **our reputation;**
- **information technology;**
- **product demand and retail consolidation;**
- **global economic and environmental conditions;**
- **regulatory environment;**
- **workforce retention; and**
- **market risks.**

Our Approach to Managing Risks

We manage our risks through an integrated risk management framework.

This framework includes:

- the PepsiCo Executive Risk Council (PERC), comprised of a cross-functional, geographically diverse, senior management group which meets periodically to identify, assess, prioritize and address primarily strategic and reputational risks;
- Division Risk Committees (DRC), comprised of cross-functional senior management teams which meet regularly each year to identify, assess, prioritize and address division-specific operating risks;
- PepsiCo's Risk Management Office, which manages the overall process, provides ongoing guidance, tools and analytical support to the PERC and DRC, identifies and assesses potential risks, and facilitates ongoing communication between the parties, as well as to PepsiCo's Audit Committee; and
- PepsiCo Corporate Audit, which confirms the ongoing effectiveness of the risk management framework through periodic audit and review procedures.

Also see "Market Risks" below for a discussion on how we manage specific market risks.

Our Reputation

We have a longstanding history of maintaining a good reputation globally which is critical to selling our branded products. If we fail to maintain high standards for product quality and integrity, our reputation could be jeopardized. In addition, we must protect our reputation by maintaining high ethical, social and environmental standards for all of our operations and activities. Damage to our reputation might result in rejection of our products by consumers and a loss of brand equity, as well as require additional resources to rebuild our reputation.

We have a longstanding history of maintaining a good reputation globally which is critical to selling our branded products.

Information Technology

Information technology is becoming increasingly important as an enabler to operating efficiently and interfacing with customers, as well as maintaining financial accuracy and efficiency. If we do not allocate, and effectively manage, the resources necessary to build and sustain the proper technology infrastructure, we could be subject to transaction errors, processing inefficiencies, the loss of customers, business disruptions, or the loss of or damage to intellectual property through security breach.

As discussed by our chairman, we have embarked on our multiyear BPT initiative that includes the delivery of an SAP enterprise resource planning application, as well as the migration to common business processes across our North American operations. The inability to deliver our goals may impact our ability to (1) process transactions accurately and efficiently, and (2) remain in step with the changing needs of the trade, which could result in the loss of customers. In addition, the failure to either deliver the application on time, or anticipate the necessary readiness and training needs, could lead to business disruption.

Information technology is becoming increasingly important as an enabler to operating efficiently and interfacing with customers.

Product Demand and Retail Consolidation

We are a consumer products company operating in highly competitive markets and rely on continued demand for our products. To generate revenues and profits, we must sell products that appeal to our customers and to consumers. As our chairman notes, our continued success is dependent on our product innovation, including maintaining a strong pipeline of new products, effective sales incentives, appropriate advertising campaigns and marketing programs, and the ability to secure adequate shelf space at our retailers. In addition, our success depends on our responses to consumer trends, such as low carbohydrate diets, consumer health concerns, including obesity and the consumption of certain ingredients, and changes in product category consumption and consumer demographics, including the aging of the general population. Seasonal weather conditions, particularly for sports drinks and hot cereals, can also impact demand. Our top five retail customers now represent approximately 27% of our North American net revenue reflecting the continuing consolidation of the retail trade. In this environment, there continue to be competitive product and pricing pressures, as well as challenges in maintaining profit margins. We must maintain mutually beneficial relationships with our key customers, including our retailers and anchor bottlers, to effectively compete.

Global Economic and Environmental Conditions

Unforeseen global economic and environmental changes and political unrest may result in business interruption, supply constraints, foreign currency devaluation, inflation, deflation or decreased demand. Economic conditions in North America could also adversely impact growth. For example, rising fuel costs may impact the sales of our products in convenience stores where our products are generally sold in higher margin single serve packages.

Our continued growth requires us to develop our leadership bench and to implement programs, such as our long-term incentive program, designed to retain talent.

Regulatory Environment

Changes in laws, regulations and the related interpretations may alter the environment in which we do business and, therefore, impact our results or increase our liabilities. Such regulatory environment changes include changes in food and drug laws, laws related to advertising and deceptive marketing practices, accounting standards, taxation requirements, competition laws and environmental laws, including the regulation of water consumption and treatment.

Workforce Retention

Our continued growth requires us to develop our leadership bench and to implement programs, such as our long-term incentive program, designed to retain talent. We also compete to hire new employees, and then must train them and develop their skills and competencies. We have in place human resource programs, including our diversity and inclusion focus mentioned by our chairman, aimed at hiring, developing and retaining our talented and motivated workforce which provides us with competitive advantage. However, unplanned turnover could deplete our institutional knowledge base and erode our competitive advantage.

Market Risks

We are exposed to the market risks arising from adverse changes in:

- **commodity prices, affecting the cost of our raw materials and energy;**
- **foreign exchange rates;**
- **interest rates;**
- **stock prices; and**
- **discount rates, affecting the measurement of our pension and retiree medical liabilities.**

In the normal course of business, we manage these risks through a variety of strategies, including productivity initiatives, global purchasing programs and hedging strategies. Ongoing productivity initiatives involve the identification of meaningful cost saving opportunities or efficiencies and effective implementation. Our global purchasing programs include fixed-price purchase orders and pricing agreements. Our hedging strategies involve the use of derivatives designated as cash flow and fair value hedges. The fair value of our hedges fluctuates based on market rates and prices. The sensitivity of our hedges to these market fluctuations is discussed below. See Note 10 for further discussion of these hedges and our hedging policies. See "Our Critical Accounting Policies" for a discussion of the exposure of our pension plan assets and pension and retiree medical liabilities to risks related to stock prices and discount rates.

Inflationary, deflationary and recessionary conditions impacting these market risks also impact the demand for and pricing of our products. See "Product Demand and Retail Consolidation" and "Global Economic and Enviromental Conditions" above for further discussion.

Commodity Prices

Our open commodity derivative contracts designated as hedges had a face value of $155 million at December 25, Year 4 and $43 million at December 27, Year 3. These derivatives resulted in a net unrealized loss of $1 million at December 25, Year 4 and $4 million at December 27, Year 3. We estimate that a 10% decline in commodity prices would have resulted in an unrealized loss of $16 million in Year 4 and $1 million in Year 3.

Foreign Exchange

Financial statements of foreign subsidiaries are translated into U.S. dollars using period-end exchange rates for assets and liabilities and weighted-average exchange rates for revenues and expenses. Adjustments resulting from translating net assets are reported as a separate component of accumulated other comprehensive loss within shareholders' equity, called currency translation adjustment.

Our operations outside of the U.S. generate over a third of our net revenue of which Mexico, the United Kingdom and Canada comprise nearly 20%. As a result, we are exposed to foreign currency risks, including unforeseen economic changes and political unrest. During Year 4, the impact of the favorable euro and British pound was partially offset by the unfavorable Mexican peso resulting in a contribution of almost 2 percentage points to revenue growth. If declines in the Mexican peso continue and are not offset, our future results will be adversely impacted.

Exchange rate gains or losses related to foreign currency transactions are recognized as transaction gains or losses in the income statement as incurred. We may enter into derivatives to manage our exposure to foreign currency transaction risk. Our foreign currency derivatives had a total face value of $908 million at December 25, Year 4 and $484 million at December 27, Year 3. These contracts had net unrealized losses of $27 million at December 25, Year 4 and $30 million at December 27, Year 3, respectively. We estimate that an unfavorable 10% change in the exchange rates would have resulted in an unrealized loss of $123 million in Year 4 and $50 million in Year 3, respectively.

Interest Rates

We centrally manage our debt and investment portfolios considering investment opportunities and risks, tax consequences and overall financing strategies. We may use interest rate and cross currency interest rate swaps to manage our overall interest expense and foreign exchange risk. These instruments effectively change the interest rate and currency of specific debt issuances. These swaps are entered into concurrently with the issuance of the debt that they are intended to modify. The notional amount, interest payment and maturity date of the swaps match the principal, interest payment and maturity date of the related debt. Our counterparty credit risk is considered low because these swaps are entered into only with strong creditworthy counterparties, are generally settled on a net basis and are of relatively short duration.

Our operations outside of the U.S. generate over a third of our net revenue of which Mexico, the United Kingdom and Canada comprise nearly 20%.

Assuming year-end Year 4 and Year 3 variable rate debt and investment levels, a one point increase in interest rates would have decreased net interest expense by $11 million in Year 4 and $10 million in Year 3.

Stock Prices

A portion of our deferred compensation liability is tied to certain market indices and our stock price. We manage these market risks with mutual fund investments and prepaid forward contracts for the purchase of our stock. The combined gains or losses on these investments are offset by changes in our deferred compensation liability, which are included in corporate selling, general and administrative expenses.

We discuss expectations regarding our future performance, such as our business outlook, in our annual and quarterly reports, press releases, and other written and oral statements. These "forward-looking statements" are based on currently available competitive, financial and economic data and our operating plans. They are inherently uncertain, and investors must recognize that events could turn out to be significantly different from our expectations. The preceding discussion of risks is by no means all inclusive but is designed to highlight what we believe are important factors to consider when evaluating our trends and future results.

Our Critical Accounting Policies

An appreciation of our critical accounting policies is necessary to understand our financial results. These policies may require management to make difficult and subjective judgments regarding uncertainties, and as a result, such estimates may significantly impact our financial results. The precision of these estimates and the likelihood of future changes depend on a number of underlying variables and a range of possible outcomes. Other than our accounting for stock-based compensation and certain allocation methodologies for pension and retiree medical, our critical accounting policies do not involve the choice between alternative methods of accounting. We applied our critical accounting policies and estimation methods consistently in all periods presented and have discussed these policies with our Audit Committee.

Our critical accounting policies arise in conjunction with the following:
- **revenue recognition,**
- **brand and goodwill valuations,**
- **income tax expense and accruals,**
- **stock-based compensation expense, and**
- **pension and retiree medical plans.**

Revenue Recognition

Our products are sold for cash or on credit terms. Our credit terms, which are established in accordance with local and industry practices, typically require payment within 30 days of delivery and may allow discounts for early payment. We recognize revenue upon shipment or delivery to our customers in accordance with written sales terms that do not allow for a right of return. However, our policy for DSD and chilled products is to remove and replace damaged and out-of-date products from store shelves to ensure that consumers receive the product quality and freshness they expect. Similarly, our policy for warehouse distributed products is to replace damaged and out-of-date products. Based on our historical experience with this practice, we have reserved for anticipated damaged and out-of-date products. Our bottlers have a similar replacement policy and are responsible for the products they distribute.

Our commitment to freshness and product dating serves to regulate the quantity of product shipped or delivered.

Our policy is to provide customers with product when needed. In fact, our commitment to freshness and product dating serves to regulate the quantity of product shipped or delivered. In addition, DSD products are placed on the shelf by our employees with customer shelf space limiting the quantity of product. For product delivered through our other distribution networks, customer inventory levels are monitored.

As discussed in "Our Customers," we offer sales incentives through various programs to customers and consumers. Sales incentives are accounted for as a reduction of sales and totaled $6.6 billion in Year 4, $6.0 billion in Year 3 and $5.5 billion in Year 2. Sales incentives include payments to customers for performing merchandising activities on our behalf, such as payments for in-store displays, payments to gain distribution of new products, payments for shelf space, and discounts to promote lower retail prices. A number of our sales incentives, such as bottler funding and customer volume rebates, are based on annual targets, and accruals are established during the year for the expected payout. These accruals are based on our historical experience with similar programs and require management judgment with respect to estimating customer participation and performance levels. The terms of most of our incentive arrangements do not exceed a year, and therefore do not require highly uncertain long-term estimates. For interim reporting, we estimate total annual sales incentives and record a pro rata share in proportion to revenue. Certain arrangements, including fountain pouring rights, may extend up to 15 years. The costs incurred to obtain these arrangements are recognized over the life of the contract as a reduction of revenue, and the outstanding balances of $337 million at year-end Year 4 and $359 million at year-end Year 3 are included in other assets in our Consolidated Balance Sheet.

We estimate and reserve for our bad debt exposure based on our experience with past due accounts. Our method of determining the reserves has been consistent during the years presented in the consolidated financial statements. Bad debt expense is classified within selling, general and administrative expenses in our Consolidated Statement of Income.

Brand and Goodwill Valuations

We sell products under a number of brand names, many of which were developed by us. The brand development costs are expensed as incurred. We also purchase brands and goodwill in acquisitions. Upon acquisition, the purchase price is first allocated to identifiable assets and liabilities, including brands, based on estimated fair value, with any remaining purchase price recorded as goodwill.

We believe that a brand has an indefinite life if it has significant market share in a stable macroeconomic environment, and a history of strong revenue and cash flow performance that we expect to continue for the foreseeable future. If these perpetual brand criteria are not met, brands are amortized over their expected useful lives, which generally range from five to 20 years. Determining the expected life of a brand requires considerable management judgment and is based on an evaluation of a number of factors, including the competitive environment, market share, brand history and the macroeconomic environment of the countries in which the brand is sold.

Goodwill, including the goodwill that is part of our noncontrolled bottling investment balances, and perpetual brands are not amortized. Perpetual brands and goodwill are assessed for impairment at least annually to ensure that discounted future cash flows continue to exceed the related book value. A perpetual brand is impaired if its book value exceeds its fair value. Goodwill is evaluated for impairment if the book value of its reporting unit exceeds its fair value. A reporting unit can be a division or business within a division. If the fair value of an evaluated asset is less than its book value, the asset is written down to fair value based on its discounted future cash flows.

We did not recognize any impairment charges for perpetual brands or goodwill during the years presented.

Amortizable brands are only evaluated for impairment upon a significant change in the operating or macroeconomic environment. If an evaluation of the undiscounted cash flows indicates impairment, the asset is written down to its estimated fair value, which is based on its discounted future cash flows.

Considerable management judgment is necessary to evaluate the impact of operating and macroeconomic changes and to estimate future cash flows. Assumptions used in our impairment evaluations, such as forecasted growth rates and our cost of capital, are consistent with our internal forecasts and operating plans. These assumptions could be adversely impacted by certain of the risks discussed in the "Our Business Risks" section, including, but not limited to, operating risks, product demand and the competitive landscape.

We did not recognize any impairment charges for perpetual brands or goodwill during the years presented. As of December 25, Year 4, we had $4.8 billion of perpetual brands and goodwill, of which nearly 75% related to Tropicana and Walkers. In our most recent impairment evaluations for Tropicana and Walkers, no impairment charges would have resulted even if the fair market values resulting from our discounted cash flow analyses were assumed to be 5% lower.

Income Tax Expense and Accruals

In Year 4, our annual tax rate for continuing operations was 24.7% compared to 28.5% in Year 3 as discussed in "Other Consolidated Results." The tax rate in Year 4 decreased 3.8 percentage points primarily as a result of the favorable resolution of certain open tax issues. For Year 5, our annual tax rate is expected to be 29.4%, reflecting the absence of the favorable Year 4 resolutions, and excluding any impact of the potential repatriation of certain undistributed international earnings discussed below and in Note 5.

Our annual tax rate is based on our income, statutory tax rates and tax planning opportunities available to us in the various jurisdictions in which we operate. Significant judgment is required in determining our annual tax rate and in evaluating our tax positions. We establish reserves when, despite our belief that our tax return positions are fully supportable, we believe that certain positions are subject to challenge and that we may not succeed. We adjust these reserves, as well as the related interest, in light of changing facts and circumstances, such as the progress of a tax audit. An estimated effective tax rate for a year is applied to our quarterly operating results. In the event there is a significant or unusual item recognized in our quarterly operating results, the tax attributable to that item is separately calculated and recorded at the same time as that item. We consider the tax benefits from the resolution of prior year tax matters to be such items.

Our annual tax rate for continuing operations was 24.7% in Year 4 compared to 28.5% in Year 3.

Tax law requires items to be included in the tax return at different times than the items are reflected in the financial statements. As a result, our annual tax rate reflected in our financial statements is different than that reported in our tax return (our cash tax rate). Some of these differences are permanent, such as expenses that are not deductible in our tax return, and some differences reverse over time, such as depreciation expense. These temporary differences create deferred tax assets and liabilities. Deferred tax assets generally represent items that can be used as a tax deduction or credit in our tax return in future years for which we have already recorded the tax benefit in our income statement. We establish valuation allowances for our deferred tax assets when we believe expected future taxable income is not likely to support the use of a deduction or credit in that tax jurisdiction. Deferred tax liabilities generally represent tax expense recognized in our financial statements for which payment has been deferred, or expense for which we have already taken a deduction in our tax return but we have not yet recognized as expense in our financial statements.

We have not recognized any U.S. tax expense on undistributed international earnings since we intend to reinvest the earnings outside the U.S. for the foreseeable future, subject to the opportunity afforded us as a result of the American Jobs Creation Act of 2004 (AJCA). Our undistributed earnings are approximately $11.9 billion at December 25, Year 4, and $8.8 billion at December 27, Year 3. We are currently contemplating taking advantage of the AJCA for up to $7.5 billion of our undistributed foreign earnings. See Note 5 for further discussion on the AJCA and its potential impact on our Year 5 results.

A number of years may elapse before a particular matter, for which we have established a reserve, is audited and finally resolved. The number of years with open tax audits varies depending on the tax jurisdiction. During Year 4, we recognized $266 million of tax benefits related to the favorable resolution of certain open tax issues. In addition, in Year 4, we recognized a benefit of $38 million upon agreement with the U.S. Internal Revenue Service (IRS) on an open issue related to our discontinued restaurant operations. At the end of Year 3, we entered into agreements with the IRS for open years through Year –3. These agreements resulted in a tax benefit of $109 million in the fourth quarter of Year 3. As part of these agreements, we also resolved the treatment of certain other issues related to future tax years.

The IRS has initiated their audits of our tax returns for the years Year –2 through Year 2. Our tax returns subsequent to Year 2 have not yet been examined. While it is often difficult to predict the final outcome or the timing of resolution of any particular tax matter, we believe that our reserves reflect the probable outcome of known tax contingencies. Settlement of any particular issue would usually require the use of cash. Favorable resolution would be recognized as a reduction to our annual tax rate in the year of resolution. Our tax reserves, covering all federal, state and foreign jurisdictions, are presented in the balance sheet within other liabilities (see Note 14), except for any amounts relating to items we expect to pay in the coming year which are included in current income taxes payable. For more information on the impact of the resolution of open tax issues, see "Other Consolidated Results" and "Our Liquidity, Capital Resources and Financial Position."

Stock-Based Compensation Expense

We believe that we will achieve our best results if our employees act and are rewarded as business owners. Therefore, we believe stock ownership and stock-based incentive awards are the best way to align the interests of employees with those of our shareholders. Historically, following competitive market practices, we have used stock option grants as our primary form of long-term incentive compensation. These grants are made at the current stock price, meaning each employee's exercise price is equivalent to our stock price on the date of grant. Employees must generally provide three additional years of service to earn the grant, referred to as the vesting period. Our options generally have a 10-year term, which means our employees would have up to seven years after the vesting period to elect to pay the exercise price to purchase one share of our stock for each option exercised. Employees benefit from stock options to the extent our stock price appreciates above the exercise price after vesting and during the term of the grant. There have been no reductions to the exercise price of previously issued awards, and any repricing of awards would require approval of our shareholders.

Our new executive compensation program, effective for Year 4, strengthens the relationship between pay and individual performance.

Our new executive compensation program, effective for Year 4, strengthens the relationship between pay and individual performance through greater differentiation in the amount of base pay, bonus and stock-based compensation based on an employee's responsibility and performance. The new program results in a shift of both cash and stock-based compensation to our top performing executives. In addition, our new program provides executives, who are awarded long-term incentives based on their performance, with a choice of stock options or restricted stock units (RSUs). RSUs generally vest after three years of service and each restricted stock unit can be settled in a share of our stock after the vesting period. Executives who elect RSUs receive one RSU for every four stock options that would have otherwise been granted. Senior officers do not have a choice and are granted 50% stock options and 50% RSUs. Vesting of RSU awards for senior officers is contingent upon the achievement of pre-established performance targets.

We also continued, as we have since Year –1, to grant an annual award of stock options to all eligible employees, based on job level or classification under our broad-based stock option program, SharePower. As part of the new compensation program in Year 4, the SharePower program grant was reduced by approximately 50% for employees in the U.S. and replaced with matching contributions of PepsiCo stock to our 401(k) savings plans. We did not reduce the SharePower award for international employees and continued using tenure as a base for delivering the award in addition to job level and classification. For additional information on our 401(k) savings plans, see Note 7.

Method of Accounting
We account for our employee stock options under the fair value method of accounting using a Black-Scholes valuation model to measure stock-based compensation expense at the date of grant. We do not expect Statement of Financial Accounting Standards (SFAS) 123R, *Share-Based Payment*, to materially impact our financial statements upon adoption no later than in the fourth quarter of Year 5. Two of our anchor bottlers, PBG and PAS, will be adopting SFAS 123R in Year 5. They are currently evaluating the impact of SFAS 123R which will consequently impact our bottling equity income.

Beginning in Year 4, our divisions were held accountable for stock-based compensation expense and, therefore, this expense is allocated to our divisions as an incremental employee compensation cost. Prior year division results have been adjusted for comparability. The allocation of compensation expense is approximately 28% FLNA, 19% PBNA, 32% PI, 4% QFNA and 17% corporate unallocated. The expense allocated to our divisions excludes any impact of changes in our Black-Scholes assumptions which reflect market conditions over which division management has no control. Therefore, any variances between allocated expense and our actual expense are recognized in corporate unallocated expenses.

Our Assumptions

	Year 5	Year 4	Year 3	Year 2
Expected life	6 yrs.	6 yrs.	6 yrs.	6 yrs.
Risk free interest rate	3.8%	3.3%	3.1%	4.4%
Expected volatility	22%	26%	27%	27%
Expected dividend yield	1.8%	1.8%	1.15%	1.14%

Our Black-Scholes model estimates the expected value our employees will receive from the options based on a number of assumptions, such as interest rates, employee exercises, our stock price and dividend yield. The table above includes our weighted-average fair value assumptions.

The expected life is a significant assumption as it determines the period for which the risk free interest rate, volatility and dividend yield must be applied. The expected life is the period over which our employee groups are expected to hold their options. It is based on our historical experience with similar grants. The risk free interest rate is based on the expected U.S. Treasury rate over the expected life. Volatility reflects movements in our stock price over the most recent historical period equivalent to the expected life. Dividend yield is estimated over the expected life based on our stated dividend policy and forecasts of net income, share repurchases and stock price.

Year 5 Estimated Expense and Sensitivity of Assumptions
Our stock-based compensation expense, including RSUs, is as follows:

	Estimated Year 5	Year 4	Year 3
Stock-based compensation expense	$320	$368	$407

If we assumed a 100 basis point change in the following assumptions, our estimated Year 5 stock-based compensation expense would increase/(decrease) as follows:

	100 Basis Point Increase	100 Basis Point Decrease
Risk free interest rate	$ 4	$(4)
Expected volatility	$ 1	$(1)
Expected dividend yield	$(6)	$ 7

If the expected life were assumed to be one year longer, our estimated Year 5 stock-based compensation expense would increase by $9 million. If the expected life were assumed to be one year shorter, our estimated Year 5 stock-based compensation expense would decrease by $6 million. As noted, changing the assumed expected life impacts all of the Black-Scholes valuation assumptions as the risk free interest rate, expected volatility and expected dividend yield are estimated over the expected life.

Pension and Retiree Medical Plans

Our pension plans cover full-time employees in the U.S. and certain international employees. Benefits are determined based on either years of service or a combination of years of service and earnings. U.S. retirees are also eligible for medical and life insurance benefits (retiree medical) if they meet age and service requirements. Generally, our share of retiree medical costs is capped at specified dollar amounts, which vary based upon years of service, with retirees contributing the remainder up to the total cost.

Our Assumptions

The pension or retiree medical benefits expected to be paid are expensed over the employees' expected service. We must make many assumptions to measure our annual pension and retiree medical expense, including:

- the interest rate used to determine the present value of liabilities (discount rate);
- the expected return on assets in our funded plans;
- the rate of salary increases for plans where benefits are based on earnings;
- certain employee-related factors, such as turnover, retirement age and mortality; and
- for retiree medical benefits, health care cost trend rates.

The assumptions, assets and liabilities used to measure our annual pension and retiree medical expense are determined as of September 30 (measurement date) and all plan assets and liabilities are reported as of that date. Our assumptions reflect our historical experience and management's best judgment regarding future expectations. Some of these assumptions require significant management judgment and could have a material impact on the measurement of our pension and retiree medical benefit expense and obligation. However, any impact from the changes in retiree medical assumptions would be mitigated by the cap on these benefits.

Our Year 5 pension expense is estimated to be approximately $310 million and retiree medical expense is estimated to be approximately $135 million.

Since pension and retiree medical liabilities are measured on a discounted basis, the discount rate is a significant assumption. At each measurement date, the discount rate is based on interest rates for high-quality, long-term corporate debt securities with maturities comparable to our liabilities. The expected return on pension plan assets is based on our historical experience, our pension plan investment strategy, and our expectations for long-term rates of return. Our pension plan investment strategy is reviewed annually and is based upon plan liabilities, an evaluation of market conditions, tolerance for risk and cash requirements for benefit payments. We use a third-party consultant to assist us in determining our investment allocation and modeling our long-term rate assumptions. Our current investment allocation target for our U.S. plans is 60% equity securities, with the balance in fixed income securities. Our current assumed rate of return on plan assets is 7.8%, reflecting an estimated long-term return of 9.3% from equity securities and an estimated 5.8% from fixed income securities. As permitted by U.S. generally accepted accounting principles, plan assets used in determining the expected return component of annual pension expense reflect the difference between the actual and the expected return in any one year over five years. Therefore, it takes five years for the gain or loss from any one year to be fully included in the measurement of plan assets.

Other gains and losses resulting from actual experience differing from our assumptions are also determined at each measurement date. If this net accumulated gain or loss exceeds 10% of the greater of plan assets or liabilities, a portion of the net gain or loss is included in expense for the following year. The cost or benefit of plan changes, such as increasing or decreasing benefits for prior employee service, is included in expense on a straight-line basis over the average remaining service period of the employees expected to receive benefits.

Weighted-average assumptions for pension and retiree medical expense are the following:

	Year 5	Year 4	Year 3
Pension			
Expense discount rate	6.1%	6.1%	6.7%
Expected rate of return on plan assets	7.8%	7.8%	8.2%
Expected rate of salary increases	4.3%	4.4%	4.4%
Retiree medical			
Expense discount rate	6.1%	6.1%	6.7%
Current health care cost trend rate	11.0%	12.0%	10.0%

Future Expense

Our Year 5 pension expense is estimated to be approximately $310 million and retiree medical expense is estimated to be approximately $135 million. These estimates incorporate the Year 5 assumptions, as well as the impact of the increased pension plan assets resulting from our discretionary contributions of $400 million in Year 4, and the impact of the Medicare Prescription Drug, Improvement and Modernization Act of 2003 (Medicare Act) as discussed in Note 7. Changes in our Year 5 assumptions include updates to our mortality tables, employee turnover assumptions, and retirement age assumptions. These changes result in an increase in our pension experience loss amortization for Year 5 of $45 million. In addition, the increase in amortization for Year 5 pension expense reflects the absence of asset gain amortization of approximately $50 million in Year 4 in accordance with our methodology discussed above. An analysis of the estimated change in pension and retiree medical expense follows:

- **In Year 5, we expect contributions to be about the same as Year 4 with approximately $400 million expected to be discretionary.**
- **Our cash payments for retiree medical are estimated to be $85 million in Year 5.**

	Pension	Retiree Medical
Year 4 expense	$245	$121
Increase in experience loss amortization	100	21
Impact of funding	(36)	–
Increase in prior service benefit amortization	(3)	(4)
Other, including impact of 2003 Medicare Act	4	(3)
Year 5 estimated expense	$310	$135

Pension service costs, including the impact of demographic assumption changes on service costs, are reflected in division results, with the impact of changes in discount and asset return rates, gains and losses, and the impact of funding reflected in corporate unallocated. Under this policy, approximately $20 million of the increased pension and retiree medical expense in Year 5 will be reflected in corporate unallocated expense.

Based on our current assumptions, which reflect our prior experience and current plan provisions, and assuming we are allowed to make annual discretionary contributions of approximately $400 million, we expect our pension expense to increase by approximately $15 million in Year 6. In Year 7, our pension expense would begin to decrease, with the expense dropping to approximately $220 million by Year 10 as unrecognized asset losses are fully amortized. If our assumptions and our plan provisions for retiree medical remain unchanged and our experience mirrors these assumptions, we expect our annual retiree medical expense beyond Year 5 to approximate $140 million.

Sensitivity of Assumptions

A decrease in the discount rate or a decrease in the expected rate of return on assets would increase pension expense. The estimated impact of a 25 basis point change in the discount rate on Year 5 pension expense is a change of approximately $32 million. The estimated impact on Year 5 pension expense of a 25 basis point change in the expected rate of return on assets is a change of approximately $13 million. See Note 7 regarding the sensitivity of our retiree medical cost assumptions.

Future Funding

We make contributions to pension trusts maintained to provide plan benefits for certain pension plans. These contributions are made in accordance with applicable tax regulations that provide for current tax deductions for our contributions, and taxation to the employee only upon receipt of plan benefits. Generally, we do not fund our pension plans when our contributions would not be currently deductible or when the employee would be taxed prior to receipt of benefit.

Our pension contributions for Year 4 were $458 million of which $400 million was discretionary. In Year 5, we expect contributions to be about the same with approximately $400 million expected to be discretionary and the remainder satisfying minimum requirements. Our cash payments for retiree medical are estimated to be $85 million in Year 5. As our retiree medical plans are not subject to regulatory funding requirements, we fund these plans on a pay-as-you-go basis. For estimated future benefit payments, including our pay-as-you-go payments as well as those from trusts, see Note 7.

Our Financial Results

Items Affecting Comparability

The year-over-year comparisons of our financial results are affected by the following items:

	Year 4	Year 3
Operating profit		
Impairment and restructuring charges	$(150)	$(147)
Merger-related costs	–	$(59)
Net income		
Impairment and restructuring charges	$(96)	$(100)
Merger-related costs	–	$(42)
Net tax benefits — continuing operations	$266	$109
Tax benefit from discontinued operations	$38	–
Net income per common share — diluted		
Impairment and restructuring charges	$(0.06)	$(0.06)
Merger-related costs	–	$(0.02)
Net tax benefits — continuing operations	$0.15	$0.06
Tax benefit from discontinued operations	$0.02	–

For the items and accounting changes affecting our Year 2 results, see Note 1 and our Year 2 Annual Report.

Impairment and Restructuring Charges and Merger-Related Costs

In the fourth quarter of Year 4, we incurred restructuring and impairment charges of $150 million in conjunction with the consolidation of FLNA's manufacturing network in connection with its ongoing productivity program. Savings from this productivity program have been and are expected to be used to offset increased marketplace spending.

In the fourth quarter of Year 3, we incurred a restructuring charge of $147 million in conjunction with the streamlining of our North American divisions and PepsiCo International. Also, during Year 3 and in Year 2, we incurred costs associated with our merger with The Quaker Oats Company (Quaker).

For additional information, see Note 3.

Net Tax Benefits — Continuing Operations

In the fourth quarter of Year 4, we recognized $45 million of tax benefits related to the completion of the IRS audit for pre-merger Quaker open tax years. In the third quarter of Year 4, we recognized $221 million of tax benefits related to a reduction in foreign tax accruals following the resolution of certain open tax issues with foreign tax authorities, and a refund claim related to prior U.S. tax settlements.

At the end of Year 3, we entered into agreements with the IRS for open tax years through Year –3. These agreements resulted in a tax benefit of $109 million. As part of these agreements, we also resolved the treatment of certain other issues related to future tax years.

For additional information, see "Our Critical Accounting Policies."

Tax Benefit from Discontinued Operations

In the fourth quarter of Year 4, we reached agreement with the IRS for an open issue related to our discontinued restaurant operations which resulted in a tax benefit of $38 million.

Results of Continuing Operations — Consolidated Review

In the discussions of net revenue and operating profit below, effective net pricing reflects the year-over-year impact of discrete pricing actions, sales incentive activities and mix resulting from selling varying products in different package sizes and in different countries.

Servings

Since our divisions each use different measures of physical unit volume (i.e., kilos, pounds and case sales), a common servings metric is necessary to reflect our consolidated physical unit volume. Our divisions' physical volume measures are converted into servings based on U.S. Food and Drug Administration guidelines for single-serving sizes of our products.

Total servings increased 6% in Year 4 compared to Year 3 as servings for beverages worldwide grew 7% and servings for snacks worldwide grew over 5%. All of our divisions positively contributed to the total servings growth. Total servings increased 5% in Year 3 compared to Year 2 primarily due to contributions from PI, PBNA and FLNA.

Net Revenue and Operating Profit

				Change	
	Year 4	Year 3	Year 2	**Year 4**	Year 3
Division net revenues	**$29,261**	$26,969	$24,978	**8%**	8%
Divested businesses	**–**	2	134		
Total net revenue	**$29,261**	$26,971	$25,112	**8%**	7%
Division operating profit	**$6,098**	$5,463	$4,934	**12%**	11%
Corporate unallocated	**(689)**	(502)	(438)	**38%**	14%
Merger-related costs	**–**	(59)	(224)		
Impairment & restructuring charges	**(150)**	(147)	–		
Divested businesses	**–**	26	23		
Total operating profit	**$5,259**	$4,781	$4,295	**10%**	11%
Division operating profit margin	**20.8%**	20.3%	19.8%	**0.5**	0.5
Total operating profit margin	**18.0%**	17.7%	17.1%	**0.3**	0.6

Year 4

Division net revenue increased 8%, primarily due to strong volume gains across all divisions, favorable product mix, primarily at PBNA and PI, and net favorable foreign currency movements. The volume gains contributed over 4 percentage points, the favorable mix contributed almost 2 percentage points, and the net favorable foreign currency contributed almost 2 percentage points to division net revenue growth.

Total operating profit increased 10% and margin increased 0.3 percentage points. Division operating profit increased 12% and division margin increased 0.5 percentage points. These gains reflect leverage from the revenue growth, partially offset by increased selling, general and administrative expenses, primarily corporate unallocated expenses. In addition, total operating profit growth reflects the absence of merger-related costs in Year 4.

Year 3

Net revenue increased 7%. Division net revenue increased 8%, primarily due to the strong volume which contributed 4 percentage points of growth. Favorable product and country mix, as well as North American snack and concentrate price increases, contributed over 2 percentage points to the growth. Favorable foreign currency movements contributed nearly 1 percentage point to the net revenue growth.

Total operating profit increased 11% and margin increased 0.6 percentage points. Division operating profit increased 11% and division margin increased 0.5 percentage points. These gains were driven by the strong volume and higher effective net pricing. Cost of sales increased 8%, reflecting increased commodity costs, particularly corn oil and natural gas. Selling, general and administrative expenses increased 6% driven by higher selling costs primarily reflecting the increased volume and increased fuel costs. Unfavorable foreign currency reduced operating profit growth by nearly 1 percentage point. In addition, total operating profit reflects the benefit from lower merger-related costs, offset by the Year 3 impairment and restructuring charges of $147 million.

Corporate Unallocated Expenses
Corporate unallocated expenses include the costs of our corporate headquarters, centrally managed initiatives such as our BPT initiative, unallocated insurance and benefit programs, foreign exchange transaction gains and losses, profit-in-inventory elimination adjustments for our noncontrolled bottling affiliates, and certain other items.

In Year 4, corporate unallocated expenses increased 38%. Higher employee-related costs contributed 18 percentage points of the increase, an accrual recognized in the fourth quarter for the settlement of a contractual dispute with a former business partner represented 10 percentage points of the increase, and higher costs related to our BPT initiative contributed 4 percentage points of the increase. Corporate departmental expenses increased 2% compared to prior year.

In Year 3, corporate unallocated expenses increased 14% primarily reflecting our Year 3 investment in our BPT initiative. Higher employee-related costs, including deferred compensation, and corporate departmental costs also contributed to the increase. The increase in the deferred compensation costs is partially offset by the decrease in net interest expense. Corporate departmental expenses increased 3% reflecting staffing and other costs related to our health and wellness initiatives.

Other Consolidated Results

				Change	
	Year 4	Year 3	Year 2	**Year 4**	Year 3
Bottling equity income	**$380**	$323	$280	**18%**	16%
Interest expense, net	**$(93)**	$(112)	$(142)	**(17)%**	(21)%
Annual tax rate	**24.7%**	28.5%	32.3%		
Net income — continuing operations	**$4,174**	$3,568	$3,000	**17%**	19%
Net income per common share — continuing operations — diluted	**$2.41**	$2.05	$1.68	**18%**	22%

Bottling equity income includes our share of the net income or loss of our noncontrolled bottling affiliates as described in "Our Customers." Our interest in these bottling investments may change from time to time. Any gains or losses from these changes, as well as other transactions related to our bottling investments, are also included on a pre-tax basis. Over time, we expect to be selling shares of PBG stock to trim our ownership to the level at the time of PBG's initial public offering. Our ownership has increased as a result of PBG's share repurchase program. During Year 5, we intend to sell up to 7.5 million shares of PBG stock. The resulting lower ownership percentage will reduce the equity income from PBG that we recognize.

Year 4
Bottling equity income increased 18%, primarily reflecting increased earnings from our anchor bottlers and favorable comparisons from international bottling investments, primarily as a result of the nationwide strike in Venezuela in early Year 3.

Net interest expense declined 17% primarily due to favorable interest rates and higher average cash balances, partially offset by higher average debt balances and lower gains in the market value of investments used to economically hedge a portion of our deferred compensation liability. The offsetting increase in deferred compensation costs is reported in corporate unallocated expenses within selling, general and administrative expenses.

The annual tax rate decreased 3.8 percentage points compared to the prior year, primarily as a result of tax benefits from the resolution of open items with tax authorities in both years, as discussed in "Items Affecting Comparability." The tax benefits reduced our tax rate by 2.6 percentage points. Increased benefit from concentrate operations and favorable changes arising from agreements with the Internal Revenue Service in the fourth quarter of Year 3 also contributed to the decline in rate.

Net income from continuing operations increased 17% and the related net income per common share from continuing operations increased 18%. These increases primarily reflect the solid operating profit growth and our lower annual tax rate. The absence of merger-related costs in Year 4 and increased bottling equity income also contributed to the growth.

Year 3
Bottling equity income increased 16%. This increase primarily reflects a favorable comparison to the impairment charge taken in Year 2 on a Latin American bottling investment, and increased earnings from PBG and PAS in Year 3.

Net interest expense declined 21% primarily due to a gain of $22 million on investments used to economically hedge a portion of our deferred compensation liability versus losses of $18 million in the prior year. This net gain was partially offset by lower investment rates.

The annual tax rate decreased 3.8 percentage points compared to the prior year. At the end of Year 3, we entered into agreements with the IRS. These agreements resulted in a tax benefit of $109 million, reducing our tax rate by over 2 percentage points. Lower taxes on foreign results, including the impact of our new concentrate operations, also reduced our tax rate by nearly 2 percentage points. The impact of lower nondeductible merger-related costs contributed 0.9 percentage points to the decrease.

Net income increased 19% and the related net income per common share increased 22%. These increases primarily reflect the solid operating profit growth, our lower annual tax rate and increased bottling equity income. The benefit of lower merger-related costs was largely offset by the impairment and restructuring charges. Net income per common share also reflects the benefit of a reduction in average shares outstanding primarily as a result of share repurchase activity.

Results of Continuing Operations — Division Review

The results and discussions below are based on how our Chief Executive Officer monitors the performance of our divisions. Prior year amounts exclude the results of divested businesses. For additional information on these items and our divisions, see Note 1.

	FLNA	PBNA	PI	QFNA	Divested Businesses	Total
Net Revenue, Year 4	**$9,560**	**$8,313**	**$9,862**	**$1,526**	**–**	**$29,261**
Net Revenue, Year 3	$9,091	$7,733	$8,678	$1,467	$2	$26,971
% Impact of:						
Volume	3%	3%	7%	3%	–	4%
Effective net pricing	2	4	2	–	–	2
Foreign exchange	–	–	4	1	–	2
Acquisition/divestitures	–	–	1	–	–	–
% Change	*5%*	*7%*	*14%*	*4%*	*N/A*	*8%*

	FLNA	PBNA	PI	QFNA	Divested Businesses	Total
Net Revenue, Year 3	$9,091	$7,733	$8,678	$1,467	$2	$26,971
Net Revenue, Year 2	$8,565	$7,200	$7,749	$1,464	$134	$25,112
% Impact of:						
Volume	4%	3%	7%	–	–	4%
Effective net pricing	2	4	2	–	–	2
Foreign exchange	1	1	1	1	–	1
Acquisition/divestitures	–	–	2	–	–	–
% Change	*6%*	*7%*	*12%*	–	*N/A*	*7%*

Frito-Lay North America

	Year 4	Year 3	Year 2	% Change Year 4	% Change Year 3
Net revenue	**$9,560**	$9,091	$8,565	5	6
Operating profit	**$2,389**	$2,242	$2,081	7	8

Year 4

Net revenue grew 5% reflecting volume growth of 3% and positive effective net pricing due to salty snack pricing actions and favorable mix. Pound volume grew primarily due to new products, single-digit growth in Lay's Classic potato chips, strong double-digit growth in Variety Pack, and mid single-digit growth in Tostitos and Fried Cheetos. Lay's Stax and Doritos Rollitos led the new product growth. These gains were partially offset by single-digit declines in Doritos and Fritos, and double-digit declines in Rold Gold and Quaker Toastables.

Operating profit grew nearly 7% reflecting the positive pricing actions and volume growth. Higher commodity costs, driven by corn oil and energy costs were largely offset by cost leverage generated from ongoing productivity initiatives.

On September 1, Year 4, we introduced our new "Smart Spot" program which helps consumers identify products in our portfolio that can contribute to a healthier lifestyle. Products qualifying for our new Smart Spot program represented approximately 10% of Year 4 FLNA net revenue. These products experienced high single-digit revenue growth and the balance of the portfolio had mid single-digit revenue growth. See our website at www.smartspot.com for additional information on our new Smart Spot program.

FLNA volume grew 3% and 4% in Year 4 and Year 3, respectively.

Year 3

Net revenue growth of 6% reflects volume growth of 4% and positive effective net pricing. Pound volume grew primarily due to new products, double-digit growth in Cheetos, Munchies snack mix and Quaker Chewy Granola bars, and single-digit growth in branded dips and Doritos. Quaker Toastables, Lay's Stax and the Natural snack line led the new product growth. These gains were partially offset by double-digit declines in Rold Gold, Lay's Bistro, and Go Snacks. Modest pricing actions on certain salty snacks and favorable mix led the positive effective net pricing. These gains were partially offset by higher trade spending on product innovation.

Operating profit growth of 8% reflects the volume growth and positive effective net pricing. These gains were partially offset by increased commodity costs, particularly corn oil and natural gas. Increased commodity costs reduced operating profit growth by 3 percentage points, more than offsetting the cost leverage generated from productivity initiatives.

PepsiCo Beverages North America

	Year 4	Year 3	Year 2	% Change Year 4	% Change Year 3
Net revenue	$8,313	$7,733	$7,200	7	7
Operating profit	$1,911	$1,690	$1,485	13	14

Year 4

Net revenue increased 7% and volume increased 3%. The volume increase reflects non-carbonated beverage growth of 10% and a slight increase in carbonated soft drinks (CSDs). The non-carbonated beverage growth was fueled by double-digit growth in Gatorade, Aquafina and Propel, as well as the introduction of bottler-distributed Tropicana juice drinks.

Beverage volume increased 3% in Year 4 driven by non-carbonated beverage growth of 10%.

Tropicana Pure Premium increased slightly for the year. The carbonated soft drink performance reflects a low single-digit increase in Trademark Mountain Dew and a slight increase in Trademark Sierra Mist, offset by a slight decline in Trademark Pepsi. Across the trademarks, high single-digit diet CSD growth was substantially offset by a low single-digit decline in regular CSDs. The increase in Trademark Mountain Dew reflects growth in both Diet and regular Mountain Dew and the limited time only offering of Mountain Dew Pitch Black, substantially offset by declines in both Mountain Dew Code Red and LiveWire. The performance of Trademark Pepsi reflects declines in regular Pepsi, Pepsi Twist and Pepsi Blue, mostly offset by increases in Diet Pepsi and the introduction of Pepsi Edge. Favorable product mix contributed 3 percentage points to net revenue growth, primarily reflecting a migration to non-carbonated beverages. Additionally, concentrate and fountain price increases taken in the first quarter contributed 1 percentage point to net revenue growth.

Operating profit increased 13% reflecting the net revenue growth, partially offset by higher selling, general and administrative costs, as well as costs related to marketplace initiatives.

Products qualifying for our new Smart Spot program represented over 60% of net revenue. These products experienced high single-digit revenue growth, and the balance of the portfolio had mid single-digit revenue growth.

Year 3

Net revenue increased 7% on volume growth of 3%. The volume growth reflects non-carbonated growth of 8% and carbonated beverage growth of 1.5%. Double-digit growth in Gatorade, Aquafina and Propel drove the non-carbonated portfolio. Tropicana chilled products growth was low single-digit. The carbonated beverage performance reflects the national launch of Sierra Mist and high single-digit growth in diet carbonated beverages, primarily Diet Pepsi. Declines in trademark Pepsi, excluding diet, partially offset this carbonated beverage growth. Higher effective net pricing contributed 4 percentage points to the net revenue growth. The higher effective net pricing reflects a favorable product mix shift to the higher priced non-carbonated beverages, and fountain and concentrate price increases, partially offset by increased promotional spending. The price increases contributed 1 percentage point to the net revenue growth.

Operating profit increased 14 percentage points reflecting the higher effective net pricing, volume gains and purchasing efficiencies. These gains were partially offset by increased advertising and marketing expenses. The higher effective net pricing contributed 9 percentage points to the operating profit growth with product mix contributing 7 percentage points.

PepsiCo International

				% Change	
	Year 4	Year 3	Year 2	Year 4	Year 3
Net revenue	$9,862	$8,678	$7,749	14	12
Operating profit	$1,323	$1,061	$910	25	17

Year 4

International snacks volume grew 8%, comprised of 7% in our Latin America region, 8% in our Europe, Middle East & Africa region and 14% in our Asia Pacific region. These gains were driven by high single-digit growth at Sabritas in Mexico, strong double-digit growth in India, low single-digit growth at Gamesa in Mexico coupled with double-digit growth in Egypt, Venezuela, Turkey and Brazil.

Beverage volume grew 12%, comprised of 14% in our Europe, Middle East & Africa region, 15% in our Asia Pacific region and 8% in our Latin America region. Broad-based increases were led by double-digit growth in the Middle East and China, high single-digit growth in Mexico and double-digit growth in India, Germany, Russia and Venezuela. Favorable comparisons as a result of the Year 3 national strike in Venezuela and the German deposit law impact contributed to the growth in Venezuela and Germany. Both carbonated soft drinks and non-carbonated beverages grew at double-digit rates.

Net revenue grew 14% driven by the broad-based volume growth and favorable mix. Foreign currency impact contributed 4 percentage points of growth driven by the favorable British pound and euro, partially offset by the unfavorable Mexican peso. Acquisitions contributed less than 1 percentage point.

Operating profit grew 25% driven largely by the volume and favorable mix. The favorable comparison of certain reserve actions taken in Year 3 on potentially unrecoverable beverage assets contributed 2 percentage points of growth. Foreign currency impact contributed almost 3 percentage points of growth driven by the favorable British pound and euro, partially offset by the unfavorable Mexican peso.

In Year 4, PI revenue grew 14% making it our largest division.

Year 3

International snacks volume grew 6%, comprised of 3% in our Latin America region, 10% in our Europe, Middle East and Africa region and 16% in our Asia Pacific region. These gains were driven by double-digit growth from Walkers in the United Kingdom, India, Turkey and Russia, and low single-digit growth at Sabritas in Mexico. Mid single-digit sweet growth was led by Gamesa in Mexico.

Beverage volume grew 8%, comprised of 8% in our Latin America region, 6% in our Europe, Middle East and Africa region and 11% in our Asia Pacific region. Broad-based increases were led by double-digit growth in the Middle East, China, Brazil, India, Russia and Thailand and mid single-digit growth in Mexico. Volume gains in India driven by competitive pricing actions were offset by double-digit declines in Germany due to the new one-way bottle deposit requirement imposed by the government.

Net revenue grew 12% driven by higher volume across most markets. Acquisitions contributed nearly 2 percentage points of growth and favorable foreign currency contributed 1 percentage point as the favorable euro and British pound substantially offset the unfavorable Mexican peso. These gains were partially offset by the impact of the German one-way beverage deposits and competitive beverage pricing actions in India.

Operating profit grew 17% largely due to the drivers of net revenue growth. Acquisitions contributed 2 percentage points of growth. Unfavorable foreign currency reduced operating profit by 6 percentage points due to the impact of the peso on our Mexican snack businesses. In addition, operating profits were reduced by 2 percentage points due to reserve actions taken on potentially unrecoverable beverage assets.

Quaker Foods North America

	Year 4	Year 3	Year 2	% Change Year 4	% Change Year 3
Net revenue	$1,526	$1,467	$1,464	4	–
Operating profit	$475	$470	$458	1	3

Year 4

Net revenue increased 4% and volume increased 3%. The volume increase reflects high single-digit growth in Oatmeal and double-digit growth in Life cereal, partially offset by a mid single-digit decline in Cap'n Crunch cereal. The Life cereal growth was led by the introduction of Honey Graham Life. Favorable product mix, reflecting growth in higher revenue per pound brands, was offset by promotional spending behind new products. Favorable Canadian exchange rates contributed 1 percentage point to net revenue growth.

Operating profit increased 1% reflecting the net revenue growth, substantially offset by an unfavorable cost of sales comparison and higher advertising and marketing costs. Products qualifying for our new Smart Spot program represented approximately half of net revenue and had high single-digit revenue growth. The balance of the portfolio was flat.

In Year 4, QFNA volume grew 3% driven by strong performance in oatmeal and Life cereal.

Year 3

Net revenue and volume were flat compared to prior year as the national launch of Breakfast Squares and Canadian Oatmeal to Go growth were offset by declines in Rice and Pasta Roni side dishes and in our hot cereal business. A favorable Canadian exchange rate, which contributed 1 percentage point to net revenue growth, and ready-to-eat cereal price increases, were offset by unfavorable product mix and increased promotional spending related to the Breakfast Squares launch.

Operating profit grew 3% compared to prior year. Lower advertising and marketing spending contributed over 4 percentage points to operating profit growth, while favorable cost of sales contributed almost 5 percentage points. These gains were partially offset by an unfavorable product mix, which reduced operating profit growth by 7 percentage points. The unfavorable product mix reflects declines in higher margin products.

Our Liquidity, Capital Resources and Financial Position

Our strong cash-generating capability and financial condition give us ready access to capital markets throughout the world. Our principal source of liquidity is our operating cash flow. This cash-generating capability is one of our fundamental strengths and provides us with substantial financial flexibility in meeting operating, investing and financing needs. In addition, we have revolving credit facilities that are further discussed in Note 9. Our cash provided from operating activities is somewhat impacted by seasonality. Working capital needs are impacted by weekly sales, which are generally highest in the third quarter due to seasonal and holiday-related sales patterns, and generally lowest in the first quarter.

Year 4 Cash Utilization

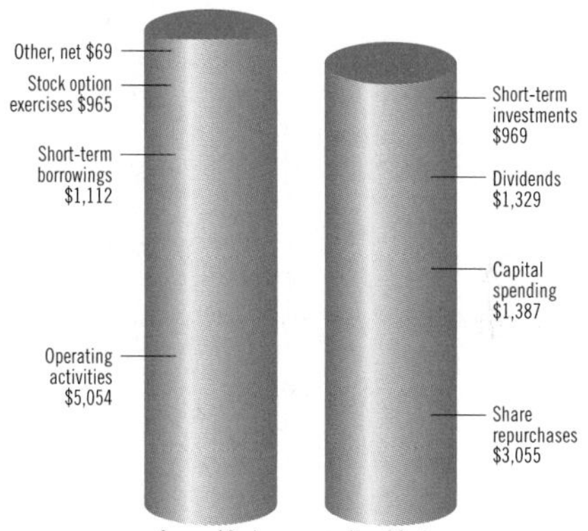

Operating Activities
In Year 4, our operations provided $5.1 billion of cash, primarily reflecting our solid business results, partially offset by net tax payments of $1.8 billion and pension plan contributions of $458 million of which $400 million was discretionary. In Year 3, our operations provided $4.3 billion of cash reflecting our solid business results, partially offset by net tax payments of $1.5 billion and pension plan contributions of $535 million of which $500 million was discretionary. The year-over-year increase in cash flows from operations is primarily attributable to our solid business results and effective working capital management, partially offset by the higher tax payments in Year 4.

Investing Activities
In Year 4, we used $2.3 billion for investing, primarily reflecting capital spending of $1.4 billion and short-term investments of almost $1.0 billion. In Year 3, we used $2.3 billion for investing, primarily reflecting capital spending of $1.3 billion and short-term investments of nearly $1.0 billion.

We expect capital spending to continue at a rate of approximately 5% of net revenue in Year 5. In December Year 4, we announced that we would acquire General Mills, Inc.'s 40.5% ownership interest in Snack Ventures Europe (SVE) for $750 million. The transaction was completed in February Year 5 and funded with existing international cash. In addition, in Year 5, we will generate cash from the expected sale of up to 7.5 million shares of PBG stock.

Financing Activities
In Year 4, we used $2.3 billion for financing, primarily reflecting share repurchases at a cost of $3.0 billion and dividend payments of $1.3 billion, partially offset by net issuances of short-term borrowings of $1.1 billion and proceeds from exercises of stock options of nearly $1.0 billion. This compares to $2.9 billion used for financing in Year 3, primarily reflecting share repurchases at a cost of $1.9 billion and dividend payments of $1.1 billion.

In the second quarter of Year 4, our Board of Directors authorized a new $7.0 billion share repurchase program. Since inception of the new program, we have repurchased $2.1 billion of shares, leaving $4.9 billion of remaining authorization. We target an annual dividend payout of approximately 45% of prior year's net income from continuing operations. Each spring we review our capital structure with our Board, including our dividend policy and share repurchase activity.

Management Operating Cash Flow
We focus on management operating cash flow as a key element in achieving maximum shareholder value, and it is the primary measure we use to monitor cash flow performance. However, it is not a measure provided by accounting principles generally accepted in the U.S. Since net capital spending is essential to our product innovation initiatives and maintaining our operational capabilities, we believe that it is a recurring and necessary use of cash. As such, we believe investors should also consider net capital spending when evaluating our cash from operating activities. The table to the left reconciles the net cash provided by operating activities as reflected in our Consolidated Statement of Cash Flows to our management operating cash flow.

	Year 4	Year 3	Year 2
Net cash provided by operating activities	$ 5,054	$ 4,328	$ 4,627
Capital spending	(1,387)	(1,345)	(1,437)
Sales of property, plant and equipment	38	49	89
Management operating cash flow	$ 3,705	$ 3,032	$ 3,279

Year 3 Cash Utilization

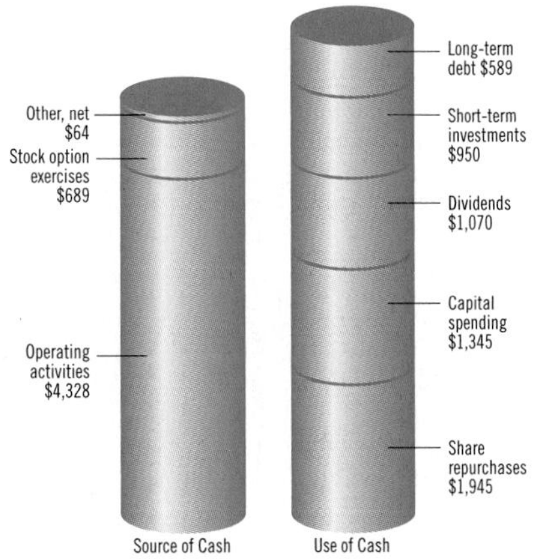

Year 2 Cash Utilization

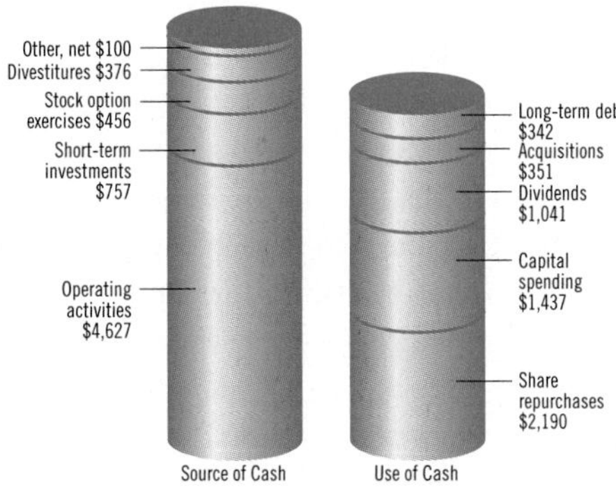

Management operating cash flow was used primarily to repurchase shares and pay dividends. We expect management operating cash flow in Year 5 to exceed $4.1 billion reflecting our underlying business growth. We expect to continue to return approximately all of our management operating cash flow to our shareholders through dividends and share repurchases, and expect our share repurchases to range from $2.5 billion to $3.0 billion in Year 5. However, see "Our Business Risks" for certain factors that may impact our operating cash flows.

Credit Ratings

Our debt ratings of Aa3 from Moody's and A+ from Standard & Poor's contribute to our ability to access global capital markets. We have maintained strong investment grade ratings for over a decade. Moody's rating reflects an upgrade from A1 to Aa3 in Year 4 due to the strength of our balance sheet and cash flows. Each rating is considered strong investment grade and is in the first quartile of their respective ranking systems. These ratings also reflect the impact of our anchor bottlers' cash flows and debt.

As discussed in Note 5, we are evaluating our options with respect to repatriating undistributed international earnings under the AJCA. If we decide to repatriate funds in excess of available international cash, we would be required to borrow funds. We would not expect this activity to adversely impact our credit ratings.

Credit Facilities and Long-Term Contractual Commitments

See Note 9 for a description of our credit facilities and long-term contractual commitments.

Off-Balance Sheet Arrangements

It is not our business practice to enter into off-balance sheet arrangements, other than in the normal course of business, nor is it our policy to issue guarantees to our bottlers, noncontrolled affiliates or third parties. However, certain guarantees were necessary to facilitate the separation of our bottling and restaurant operations from us. As of year-end Year 4, we believe it is remote that these guarantees would require any cash payment. See Note 9 for a description of our off-balance sheet arrangements.

Financial Position

Significant changes in our consolidated balance sheet from December 27, Year 3 to December 25, Year 4 not discussed above were as follows:

- Investments in noncontrolled affiliates increased $364 million primarily due to higher equity income, partially offset by dividends received.
- Income taxes payable decreased $512 million primarily reflecting net tax payments of $1.8 billion, partially offset by our current provision. The payments include $760 million paid in the second quarter as a result of our Year 3 settlement with the IRS.

Future Outlook

Our long-term financial targets are mid single-digit volume and net revenue growth, and low double-digit EPS growth. The results of any one year may differ from our long-term targets. Our Year 5 results will include the results of a 53rd week.

Appendix C

Financial Statement Analysis Package (FSAP)

Output from FSAP for PepsiCo Inc. and Subsidiaries

FSAP

The Financial Statement Analysis Package (**FSAP**) that accompanies this text is a user-friendly, adaptable series of Excel®-based spreadsheet templates. FSAP enables the user to manually input financial statement data for a firm and then perform financial statement analysis, forecasting, and valuation. FSAP contains five spreadsheets: Data, Analysis, Forecasts, Forecast Development, and Valuation.

Appendix C presents the output of these spreadsheets within FSAP using the data for PepsiCo. The output includes the profitability and risk ratios for PepsiCo for recent years, financial statement forecasts, and a variety of valuation models applied to the forecasted data for PepsiCo.

Appendix D (p. 1114) presents a user manual for FSAP. The web site for this book (www.thomsonedu.com/accounting/stickney) contains the FSAP template, including the FSAP output using PepsiCo, which users can download.

Data Spreadsheet

Analyst Name: **Stickney, Brown & Wahlen**
Company Name: **PepsiCo**

Year (Most recent in far right column.)	**9**	**0**	**1**	**2**	**3**	**4**
BALANCE SHEET DATA						
Cash	1,246	1,038	683	1,638	820	1,280
Marketable Securities	93	467	966	207	1,181	2,165
Accounts Receivable—Trade	1,958	2,129	2,142	2,531	2,830	2,999
Inventories	1,165	1,192	1,310	1,342	1,412	1,541
Other Current Assets (1)	708	791	752	695	687	654
Other Current Assets (2)	0	0	0	0	0	0
CURRENT ASSETS	5,170	5,617	5,853	6,413	6,930	8,639
Long Term Investments in Securities	2,846	2,979	2,871	2,611	2,920	3,284
Property, Plant & Equipment—at cost	10,216	11,466	12,180	13,395	14,755	15,930
Accumulated Depreciation	−3,550	−4,908	−5,304	−6,005	−6,927	−7,781
Amortizable Intangible Assets (net)	4,735	4,714	875	801	718	598
Goodwill and Nonamortizable Intangibles	0	0	3,966	4,418	4,665	4,842
Other Non-Current Assets (1)	531	889	1,254	1,841	2,266	2,475
Other Non-Current Assets (2)	0	0	0	0	0	0
TOTAL ASSETS	19,948	20,757	21,695	23,474	25,327	27,987
Accounts Payable—Trade	1,335	1,212	1,238	1,543	1,638	1,731
Notes Payable and Short Term Debt	388	202	35	77	145	894
Current Maturities of Long Term Debt	0	0	319	485	446	160
Other Current Liabilities (1)	3,004	3,317	3,223	3,455	3,575	3,868
Other Current Liabilities (2)	0	64	183	492	611	99
CURRENT LIABILITIES	4,727	4,795	4,998	6,052	6,415	6,752
Long Term Debt	3,527	3,009	2,651	2,187	1,702	2,397
Deferred Taxes	1,209	1,367	1,496	1,486	1,261	1,216
Other Non-Current Liabilities (1)	3,384	3,960	3,876	4,226	4,075	4,099
Other Non-Current Liabilities (2)	0	0	0	0	0	0
TOTAL LIABILITIES	12,847	13,131	13,021	13,951	13,453	14,464
Minority Interest in Subsidiaries	0	0	0	0	0	0
Preferred Stock	23	22	26	−7	−22	−49
Common Stock + Paid in Capital	593	409	43	237	578	648
Retained Earnings	14,921	16,510	11,519	13,489	15,961	18,730
Accumulated Other Comprehensive Income	−1,085	−1,374	−1,646	−1,672	−1,267	−886
Other Equity Adjustments	−45	−21	0	0	0	0
Treasury Stock	−7,306	−7,920	−1,268	−2,524	−3,376	−4,920
SHAREHOLDERS' EQUITY	7,101	7,626	8,674	9,523	11,874	13,523
TOTAL LIABILITIES AND EQUITIES	19,948	20,757	21,695	23,474	25,327	27,987

Continued

Data Spreadsheet (continued)

Year (Most recent in far right column.)	9	0	1	2	3	4
INCOME STATEMENT DATA						
Revenues	25,093	22,337	23,512	25,112	26,971	29,261
Cost of Goods Sold	−10,326	−10,226	−10,750	−11,497	−12,379	−13,406
Gross Profit	14,767	12,111	12,762	13,615	14,592	15,855
Selling, General and Administrative Expense	−11,018	−7,962	−8,574	−8,958	−9,460	−10,299
Other Operating Expenses (1)	−193	−147	−165	−138	−145	−147
Other Operating Expenses (2)	0	0	0	0	0	0
Other Operating Expenses (3)	0	0	0	0	0	0
Other Operating Income	0	0	0	0	0	0
Non-Recurring Operating Gains	0	0	0	0	0	0
Non-Recurring Operating Losses	−73	−184	−387	−224	−206	−150
Operating Profit	3,483	3,818	3,636	4,295	4,781	5,259
Interest Income	130	85	67	36	51	74
Interest Expense	−421	−272	−219	−178	−163	−167
Other Income or Gains	83	130	160	280	323	380
Unusual Income or Gains	1,000	0	0	0	0	0
Other Expenses or Losses	0	0	0	0	0	0
Unusual Expenses or Losses	0	0	0	0	0	0
Income before Tax	4,275	3,761	3,644	4,433	4,992	5,546
Income Tax Expense	−1,770	−1,218	−1,244	−1,433	−1,424	−1,372
Minority Interest in Earnings	0	0	0	0	0	0
Income from Discontinued Operations	0	0	0	0	0	38
Extraordinary Gains (Losses)	0	0	0	0	0	0
Changes in Accounting Principles	0	0	0	0	0	0
NET INCOME (computed)	2,505	2,543	2,400	3,000	3,568	4,212
Net Income (enter reported amount as a check)	2,505	2,543	2,400	3,000	3,568	4,212
Other Comprehensive Income Items	54	−289	−272	−26	405	381
COMPREHENSIVE INCOME	2,559	2,254	2,128	2,974	3,973	4,593

Continued

Data Spreadsheet (continued)

Year (Most recent in far right column.)	9	0	1	2	3	4
STATEMENT OF CASH FLOWS DATA						
NET INCOME	2,505	2,543	2,400	3,000	3,568	4,212
Add back Depreciation and Amortization Expenses	1,156	1,093	1,082	1,112	1,221	1,264
Other Addbacks to Net Income	1,046	556	1,074	1,096	1,028	876
Other Subtractions from Net Income	−1,181	−215	−822	−1,165	−1,243	−885
(Increase) Decrease in Accounts Receivable—Trade	−141	−52	7	−260	−220	−130
(Increase) Decrease in Inventories	−202	−51	−75	−53	−49	−100
(Increase) Decrease in Other Current Assets (1)	−209	−35	−6	−78	23	−31
(Increase) Decrease in Other Curr. Assets (2)	0	0	0	0	0	0
Increase (Decrease) in Acct. Payable—Trade	357	219	−236	426	−11	216
Increase (Decrease) in Other Current Liabilities (1)	0	0	0	0	0	0
Increase (Decrease) in Other Current Liabilities (2)	0	0	0	0	0	0
Increase (Decrease) in Other Non-Current Liabilities (1)	274	335	389	270	182	−268
Increase (Decrease) in Other Non-Current Liabilities (2)	0	−215	7	279	−171	−100
Other Operating Cash Flows	0	0	0	0	0	0
NET CASH FLOW FROM OPERATIONS	3,605	4,178	3,820	4,627	4,328	5,054
Property, Plant, and Equipment Sold	130	57	0	89	49	38
Property, Plant, and Equipment Acquired	−1,341	−1,352	−1,324	−1,437	−1,345	−1,387
(Increase) Decrease in Marketable Securities	23	−374	−500	757	−950	−969
Investments Sold	513	33	0	376	46	52
Investments Acquired	−430	−98	−432	−351	−71	−64
Other Investment Transactions (1)	0	0	0	0	−67	39
Other Investment Transactions (2)	0	0	0	0	0	0
NET CASH FLOW FROM INVESTING ACTIVITIES	−1,172	−1,734	−2,256	−527	−2,271	−2,330
Increase in Short Term Borrowing	3,699	199	788	747	128	1,272
Decrease in Short Term Borrowing	−5,572	−155	−880	−809	−115	−160
Increase in Long Term Borrowing	3,480	130	324	11	52	504
Decrease in Long Term Borrowing	−1,216	−879	−573	−353	−641	−512
Issue of Capital Stock	383	690	1,147	456	689	965
Share repurchases—Treasury Stock	−1,285	−1,430	−1,726	−2,190	−1,945	−3,055
Dividend Payments	−935	−949	−994	−1,041	−1,070	−1,329
Other Financing Transactions (1)	−382	−254	−5	0	0	0
Other Financing Transactions (2)	0	0	0	0	0	0
NET CASH FLOW FROM FINANCING ACTIVITIES	−1,828	−2,648	−1,919	−3,179	−2,902	−2,315
Effects of exchange rate changes on cash	3	−4	0	34	27	51
NET CHANGE IN CASH	608	−208	−355	955	−818	460

Continued

Data Spreadsheet (continued)

Year (Most recent in far right column.)	9	0	1	2	3	4
SUPPLEMENTAL DATA						
Statutory Tax Rate	0.350	0.350	0.350	0.350	0.350	0.350
Average Tax Rate	0.414	0.324	0.341	0.323	0.285	0.247
After-tax Effects of Nonrecurring and Unusual Items on Net Income	225	−111	−218	−190	−33	208
Preferred Stock Dividends (total, if any)	4	4	5	29	15	25
Common Shares Outstanding	1,759	1,749	1,756	1,722	1,705	1,679
Earnings per Share (basic)	1.41	1.45	1.35	1.69	2.07	2.45
Common Dividends per Share	0.53	0.54	0.57	0.60	0.63	0.79
Market Price per Share	33.65	46.25	46.18	40.41	46.47	51.94
FINANCIAL DATA CHECKS						
Assets − Liabilities − Equities	0	0	0	0	0	0
Net Income (computed) − Net Income (reported)	0	0	0	0	0	0
Cash Changes	0	0	0	0	0	0

Analysis Spreadsheet

Analyst Name: **Stickney, Brown & Wahlen**
Company Name: **PepsiCo**

DATA CHECKS

Assets − Liabilities − Equities	0	0	0	0	0
Net Income (computed) − Net Income (reported)	0	0	0	0	0
Cash Changes		0	0	0	0

In the computations below, a #DIV/0! message indicates that a ratio denominator is zero.

PROFITABILITY FACTORS:

Year	**0**	**1**	**2**	**3**	**4**
RETURN ON ASSETS (based on reported amounts):					
Profit Margin for ROA	12.2%	10.8%	12.4%	13.6%	14.8%
× Asset Turnover	1.1	1.1	1.1	1.1	1.1
= Return on Assets	13.4%	12.0%	13.8%	15.1%	16.2%
RETURN ON ASSETS (excluding the effects of nonrecurring items):					
Profit Margin for ROA	12.7%	11.7%	13.2%	13.7%	14.1%
× Asset Turnover	1.1	1.1	1.1	1.1	1.1
= Return on Assets	13.9%	13.0%	14.6%	15.2%	15.4%
RETURN ON COMMON EQUITY (based on reported amounts):					
Profit Margin for ROCE	11.4%	10.2%	11.8%	13.2%	14.3%
× Asset Turnover	1.1	1.1	1.1	1.1	1.1
× Capital Structure Leverage	2.8	2.6	2.5	2.3	2.1
= Return on Common Equity	34.6%	29.5%	32.7%	33.2%	32.9%
RETURN ON COMMON EQUITY (excluding the effects of nonrecurring items):					
Profit Margin for ROCE	11.9%	11.1%	12.6%	13.3%	13.6%
× Asset Turnover	1.1	1.1	1.1	1.1	1.1
× Capital Structure Leverage	2.8	2.6	2.5	2.3	2.1
= Return on Common Equity	36.1%	32.2%	34.8%	33.5%	31.2%
OPERATING PERFORMANCE:					
Gross Profit/Revenues	54.2%	54.3%	54.2%	54.1%	54.2%
Operating Profit/Revenues	17.1%	15.5%	17.1%	17.7%	18.0%
Net Income/Revenues	11.4%	10.2%	11.9%	13.2%	14.4%
Comprehensive Income/Revenues	10.1%	9.1%	11.8%	14.7%	15.7%
Gross Profit Control Index	92.1%	100.1%	99.9%	99.8%	100.2%
Operating Profit Control Index	123.1%	90.5%	110.6%	103.6%	101.4%
PERSISTENT OPERATING PERFORMANCE (excluding the effects of nonrecurring items):					
Gross Profit/Revenues	54.2%	54.3%	54.2%	54.1%	54.2%
Persistent Operating Profit/Revenues	17.9%	17.1%	18.0%	18.5%	18.5%
Persistent Net Income/Revenues	11.9%	11.1%	12.7%	13.4%	13.7%
GROWTH:					
Revenue Growth	−11.0%	5.3%	6.8%	7.4%	8.5%
Net Income Growth	1.5%	−5.6%	25.0%	18.9%	18.0%
Persistent Net Income Growth	16.4%	−1.4%	21.8%	12.9%	11.2%

Continued

Analysis Spreadsheet (continued)

RISK FACTORS:

Year	0	1	2	3	4
LIQUIDITY:					
Current Ratio	1.17	1.17	1.06	1.08	1.28
Quick Ratio	0.76	0.76	0.72	0.75	0.95
Operating Cash Flow to Current Liabilities	87.8%	78.0%	83.7%	69.4%	76.8%
ASSET TURNOVER:					
Accounts Receivable Turnover	10.9	11.0	10.7	10.1	10.0
Days Receivables Held	33	33	34	36	36
Inventory Turnover	8.7	8.6	8.7	9.0	9.1
Days Inventory Held	42	42	42	41	40
Accounts Payable Turnover	8.1	8.9	8.3	7.8	8.0
Days Payables Held	45	41	44	47	45
Net Working Capital Days	30	34	32	30	31
Revenues/Average Net Fixed Assets	3.4	3.5	3.5	3.5	3.7
Revenues/Average Cash	19.6	27.3	21.6	21.9	27.9
Days Sales Held in Cash	18.7	13.4	16.9	16.6	13.1
SOLVENCY:					
Total Liabilities/Total Assets	63.3%	60.0%	59.4%	53.1%	51.7%
Total Liabilities/Shareholders' Equity	172.2%	150.1%	146.5%	113.3%	107.0%
Long Term Debt/Long Term Capital	28.3%	23.4%	18.7%	12.5%	15.1%
Long Term Debt/Shareholders' Equity	39.5%	30.6%	23.0%	14.3%	17.7%
Operating Cash Flow to Total Liabilities	32.2%	29.2%	34.3%	31.6%	36.2%
Interest Coverage Ratio (reported amounts)	14.83	17.64	25.90	31.63	34.44
Interest Coverage ratio (recurring amounts)	15.50	19.41	27.16	32.89	35.11
RISK FACTORS:					
Bankruptcy Predictors:					
Altman Z Score	6.57	6.20	5.53	6.18	6.35
Bankruptcy Probability	0.00%	0.00%	0.00%	0.00%	0.00%
Earnings Manipulation Predictors:					
Beneish Earnings Manipulation Score	−2.62	−2.74	−2.61	−2.49	−2.61
Earnings Manipulation Probability	0.44%	0.31%	0.46%	0.65%	0.46%
STOCK MARKET-BASED RATIOS:					
Stock Returns	39.1%	1.1%	−11.2%	16.5%	13.5%
Price-Earnings Ratio (reported amounts)	31.90	34.21	23.91	22.45	21.20
Price-Earnings Ratio (recurring amounts)	30.48	30.97	21.81	22.00	21.78
Market Value to Book Value Ratio	10.6	9.4	7.3	6.7	6.4

Continued

Analysis Spreadsheet (continued)

INCOME STATEMENT ITEMS AS A PERCENT OF REVENUES:

Year	**0**	**1**	**2**	**3**	**4**
Revenues	100.0%	100.0%	100.0%	100.0%	100.0%
Cost of Goods Sold	−45.8%	−45.7%	−45.8%	−45.9%	−45.8%
Gross Profit	**54.2%**	**54.3%**	**54.2%**	**54.1%**	**54.2%**
Selling, General and Administrative Expense	−35.6%	−36.5%	−35.7%	−35.1%	−35.2%
Other Operating Expenses (1)	−0.7%	−0.7%	−0.5%	−0.5%	−0.5%
Other Operating Expenses (2)	0.0%	0.0%	0.0%	0.0%	0.0%
Other Operating Expenses (3)	0.0%	0.0%	0.0%	0.0%	0.0%
Other Operating Income	0.0%	0.0%	0.0%	0.0%	0.0%
Non-Recurring Operating Gains	0.0%	0.0%	0.0%	0.0%	0.0%
Non-Recurring Operating Losses	−0.8%	−1.6%	−0.9%	−0.8%	−0.5%
Operating Profit	**17.1%**	**15.5%**	**17.1%**	**17.7%**	**18.0%**
Interest Income	0.4%	0.3%	0.1%	0.2%	0.3%
Interest Expense	−1.2%	−0.9%	−0.7%	−0.6%	−0.6%
Other Income or Gains	0.6%	0.7%	1.1%	1.2%	1.3%
Unusual Income or Gains	0.0%	0.0%	0.0%	0.0%	0.0%
Other Expenses or Losses	0.0%	0.0%	0.0%	0.0%	0.0%
Unusual Expenses or Losses	0.0%	0.0%	0.0%	0.0%	0.0%
Income before Tax	**16.8%**	**15.5%**	**17.7%**	**18.5%**	**19.0%**
Income Tax Expense	−5.5%	−5.3%	−5.7%	−5.3%	−4.7%
Minority Interest in Earnings	0.0%	0.0%	0.0%	0.0%	0.0%
Income from Discontinued Operations	0.0%	0.0%	0.0%	0.0%	0.1%
Extraordinary Gains (Losses)	0.0%	0.0%	0.0%	0.0%	0.0%
Changes in Accounting Principles	0.0%	0.0%	0.0%	0.0%	0.0%
NET INCOME (computed)	11.4%	10.2%	11.9%	13.2%	14.4%
Other Comprehensive Income Items	−1.3%	−1.2%	−0.1%	1.5%	1.3%
COMPREHENSIVE INCOME	10.1%	9.1%	11.8%	14.7%	15.7%

Continued

Analysis Spreadsheet (continued)

In the computations below, a #DIV/0! message indicates that a ratio denominator is zero.

INCOME STATEMENT ITEMS: GROWTH RATES

Year	0	1	2	3	4	
	YEAR TO YEAR CHANGES IN PERCENT					COMPOUND GROWTH RATE
Revenues	−11.0%	5.3%	6.8%	7.4%	8.5%	3.1%
Cost of Goods Sold	−1.0%	5.1%	6.9%	7.7%	8.3%	5.4%
Gross Profit	**−18.0%**	**5.4%**	**6.7%**	**7.2%**	**8.7%**	**1.4%**
Selling, General and Administrative Expenses	−27.7%	7.7%	4.5%	5.6%	8.9%	−1.3%
Other Operating Expenses (1)	−23.8%	12.2%	−16.4%	5.1%	1.4%	−5.3%
Other Operating Expenses (2)	#DIV/0!	#DIV/0!	#DIV/0!	#DIV/0!	#DIV/0!	#DIV/0!
Other Operating Expenses (3)	#DIV/0!	#DIV/0!	#DIV/0!	#DIV/0!	#DIV/0!	#DIV/0!
Other Operating Income	#DIV/0!	#DIV/0!	#DIV/0!	#DIV/0!	#DIV/0!	#DIV/0!
Non-Recurring Operating Gains	#DIV/0!	#DIV/0!	#DIV/0!	#DIV/0!	#DIV/0!	#DIV/0!
Non-Recurring Operating Losses	152.1%	110.3%	−42.1%	−8.0%	−27.2%	15.5%
Operating Profit	**9.6%**	**−4.8%**	**18.1%**	**11.3%**	**10.0%**	**8.6%**
Interest Income	−34.6%	−21.2%	−46.3%	41.7%	45.1%	−10.7%
Interest Expense	−35.4%	−19.5%	−18.7%	−8.4%	2.5%	−16.9%
Other Income or Gains	56.6%	23.1%	75.0%	15.4%	17.6%	35.6%
Unusual Income or Gains	−100.0%	#DIV/0!	#DIV/0!	#DIV/0!	#DIV/0!	−100.0%
Other Expenses or Losses	#DIV/0!	#DIV/0!	#DIV/0!	#DIV/0!	#DIV/0!	#DIV/0!
Unusual Expenses or Losses	#DIV/0!	#DIV/0!	#DIV/0!	#DIV/0!	#DIV/0!	#DIV/0!
Income before Tax	**−12.0%**	**−3.1%**	**21.7%**	**12.6%**	**11.1%**	**5.3%**
Income Tax Expense	−31.2%	2.1%	15.2%	−0.6%	−3.7%	−5.0%
Minority Interest in Earnings	#DIV/0!	#DIV/0!	#DIV/0!	#DIV/0!	#DIV/0!	#DIV/0!
Income from Discontinued Operations	#DIV/0!	#DIV/0!	#DIV/0!	#DIV/0!	#DIV/0!	#DIV/0!
Extraordinary Gains (Losses)	#DIV/0!	#DIV/0!	#DIV/0!	#DIV/0!	#DIV/0!	#DIV/0!
Changes in Accounting Principles	#DIV/0!	#DIV/0!	#DIV/0!	#DIV/0!	#DIV/0!	#DIV/0!
NET INCOME (computed)	**1.5%**	**−5.6%**	**25.0%**	**18.9%**	**18.0%**	**11.0%**
Other Comprehensive Income Items	−635.2%	−5.9%	−90.4%	−1657.7%	−5.9%	47.8%
COMPREHENSIVE INCOME	**−11.9%**	**−5.6%**	**39.8%**	**33.6%**	**15.6%**	**12.4%**

Continued

Analysis Spreadsheet (continued)

COMMON SIZE BALANCE SHEET—AS A PERCENT OF TOTAL ASSETS

Year	0	1	2	3	4
ASSETS:					
Cash	5.0%	3.1%	7.0%	3.2%	4.6%
Marketable Securities	2.2%	4.5%	0.9%	4.7%	7.7%
Accounts Receivable—Trade	10.3%	9.9%	10.8%	11.2%	10.7%
Inventories	5.7%	6.0%	5.7%	5.6%	5.5%
Other Current Assets (1)	3.8%	3.5%	3.0%	2.7%	2.3%
Other Current Assets (2)	0.0%	0.0%	0.0%	0.0%	0.0%
CURRENT ASSETS	**27.1%**	**27.0%**	**27.3%**	**27.4%**	**30.9%**
Long Term Investments in Securities	14.4%	13.2%	11.1%	11.5%	11.7%
Property, Plant & Equipment—at cost	55.2%	56.1%	57.1%	58.3%	56.9%
Accumulated Depreciation	−23.6%	−24.4%	−25.6%	−27.4%	−27.8%
Amortizable Intangible Assets (net)	22.7%	4.0%	3.4%	2.8%	2.1%
Goodwill and Nonamortizable Intangibles	0.0%	18.3%	18.8%	18.4%	17.3%
Other Non-Current Assets (1)	4.3%	5.8%	7.8%	8.9%	8.8%
Other Non-Current Assets (2)	0.0%	0.0%	0.0%	0.0%	0.0%
TOTAL ASSETS	**100.0%**	**100.0%**	**100.0%**	**100.0%**	**100.0%**
LIABILITIES:					
Accounts Payable—Trade	5.8%	5.7%	6.6%	6.5%	6.2%
Notes Payable and Short Term Debt	1.0%	0.2%	0.3%	0.6%	3.2%
Current Maturities of Long Term Debt	0.0%	1.5%	2.1%	1.8%	0.6%
Other Current Liabilities (1)	16.0%	14.9%	14.7%	14.1%	13.8%
Other Current Liabilities (2)	0.3%	0.8%	2.1%	2.4%	0.4%
CURRENT LIABILITIES	**23.1%**	**23.0%**	**25.8%**	**25.3%**	**24.1%**
Long Term Debt	14.5%	12.2%	9.3%	6.7%	8.6%
Deferred Taxes	6.6%	6.9%	6.3%	5.0%	4.3%
Other Non-Current Liabilities (1)	19.1%	17.9%	18.0%	16.1%	14.6%
Other Non-Current Liabilities (2)	0.0%	0.0%	0.0%	0.0%	0.0%
TOTAL LIABILITIES	**63.3%**	**60.0%**	**59.4%**	**53.1%**	**51.7%**
Minority Interest in Subsidiaries	0.0%	0.0%	0.0%	0.0%	0.0%
Preferred Stock	0.1%	0.1%	0.0%	−0.1%	−0.2%
Common Stock + Paid in Capital	2.0%	0.2%	1.0%	2.3%	2.3%
Retained Earnings	79.5%	53.1%	57.5%	63.0%	66.9%
Accumulated Other Comprehensive Income	−6.6%	−7.6%	−7.1%	−5.0%	−3.2%
Other Equity Adjustments	−0.1%	0.0%	0.0%	0.0%	0.0%
Treasury Stock	−38.2%	−5.8%	−10.8%	−13.3%	−17.6%
SHAREHOLDERS' EQUITY	**36.7%**	**40.0%**	**40.6%**	**46.9%**	**48.3%**
TOTAL LIABILITIES AND EQUITIES	**100.0%**	**100.0%**	**100.0%**	**100.0%**	**100.0%**

Continued

Analysis Spreadsheet (continued)

In the computations below, a #DIV/0! message indicates that a ratio denominator is zero.

BALANCE SHEET ITEMS: GROWTH RATES

Year	0	1	2	3	4	
	YEAR TO YEAR CHANGES IN PERCENT					COMPOUND GROWTH RATE
ASSETS:						
Cash	−16.7%	−34.2%	139.8%	−49.9%	56.1%	0.5%
Marketable Securities	402.2%	106.9%	−78.6%	470.5%	83.3%	87.7%
Accounts Receivable—Trade	8.7%	0.6%	18.2%	11.8%	6.0%	8.9%
Inventories	2.3%	9.9%	2.4%	5.2%	9.1%	5.8%
Other Current Assets (1)	11.7%	−4.9%	−7.6%	−1.2%	−4.8%	−1.6%
Other Current Assets (2)	#DIV/0!	#DIV/0!	#DIV/0!	#DIV/0!	#DIV/0!	#DIV/0!
CURRENT ASSETS	**8.6%**	**4.2%**	**9.6%**	**8.1%**	**24.7%**	**10.8%**
Long Term Investments in Securities	4.7%	−3.6%	−9.1%	11.8%	12.5%	2.9%
Property, Plant & Equipment—at cost	12.2%	6.2%	10.0%	10.2%	8.0%	9.3%
Accumulated Depreciation	38.3%	8.1%	13.2%	15.4%	12.3%	17.0%
Amortizable Intangible Assets (net)	−0.4%	−81.4%	−8.5%	−10.4%	−16.7%	−33.9%
Goodwill and Nonamortizable Intangibles	#DIV/0!	#DIV/0!	11.4%	5.6%	3.8%	#DIV/0!
Other Non-Current Assets (1)	67.4%	41.1%	46.8%	23.1%	9.2%	36.0%
Other Non-Current Assets (2)	#DIV/0!	#DIV/0!	#DIV/0!	#DIV/0!	#DIV/0!	#DIV/0!
TOTAL ASSETS	**4.1%**	**4.5%**	**8.2%**	**7.9%**	**10.5%**	**7.0%**
Accounts Payable—Trade	−9.2%	2.1%	24.6%	6.2%	5.7%	5.3%
Notes Payable and Short Term Debt	−47.9%	−82.7%	120.0%	88.3%	516.6%	18.2%
Current Maturities of Long Term Debt	#DIV/0!	#DIV/0!	52.0%	−8.0%	−64.1%	#DIV/0!
Other Current Liabilities (1)	10.4%	−2.8%	7.2%	3.5%	8.2%	5.2%
Other Current Liabilities (2)	#DIV/0!	185.9%	168.9%	24.2%	−83.8%	#DIV/0!
CURRENT LIABILITIES	**1.4%**	**4.2%**	**21.1%**	**6.0%**	**5.3%**	**7.4%**
Long Term Debt	−14.7%	−11.9%	−17.5%	−22.2%	40.8%	−7.4%
Deferred Taxes	13.1%	9.4%	−0.7%	−15.1%	−3.6%	0.1%
Other Non-Current Liabilities (1)	17.0%	−2.1%	9.0%	−3.6%	0.6%	3.9%
Other Non-Current Liabilities (2)	#DIV/0!	#DIV/0!	#DIV/0!	#DIV/0!	#DIV/0!	#DIV/0!
TOTAL LIABILITIES	**2.2%**	**−0.8%**	**7.1%**	**−3.6%**	**7.5%**	**2.4%**
Minority Interest in Subsidiaries	#DIV/0!	#DIV/0!	#DIV/0!	#DIV/0!	#DIV/0!	#DIV/0!
Preferred Stock	−4.3%	18.2%	−126.9%	214.3%	122.7%	−216.3%
Common Stock + Paid in Capital	−31.0%	−89.5%	451.2%	143.9%	12.1%	1.8%
Retained Earnings	10.6%	−30.2%	17.1%	18.3%	17.3%	4.7%
Accumulated Other Comprehensive Income	26.6%	19.8%	1.6%	−24.2%	−30.1%	−4.0%
Other Equity Adjustments	−53.3%	−100.0%	#DIV/0!	#DIV/0!	#DIV/0!	−100.0%
Treasury Stock	8.4%	−84.0%	99.1%	33.8%	45.7%	−7.6%
SHAREHOLDERS' EQUITY	**7.4%**	**13.7%**	**9.8%**	**24.7%**	**13.9%**	**13.7%**
TOTAL LIABILITIES AND EQUITIES	**4.1%**	**4.5%**	**8.2%**	**7.9%**	**10.5%**	**7.0%**

Continued

Analysis Spreadsheet (continued)

RETURN ON ASSETS ANALYSIS (excluding the effects of non-recurring items)

Level 1		**RETURN ON ASSETS**					
		2	**3**	**4**			
		14.6%	15.2%	15.4%			

Level 2	**PROFIT MARGIN FOR ROA**			**ASSET TURNOVER**			
	2	**3**	**4**	**2**	**3**	**4**	
	13.2%	13.7%	14.1%	1.1	1.1	1.1	
Level 3	**2**	**3**	**4**	**2**	**3**	**4**	
Revenues	100.0%	100.0%	100.0%	10.7	10.1	10.0	**Receivables**
Cost of Goods Sold	−45.8%	−45.9%	−45.8%	8.7	9.0	9.1	**Inventory**
Selling, Gen., & Admin. Expense	−35.7%	−35.1%	−35.2%	3.5	3.5	3.7	**Fixed Assets**
Other Operating Expenses (1)	−0.5%	−0.5%	−0.5%				
Other Operating Expenses (2)	0.0%	0.0%	0.0%				
Other Operating Expenses (3)	0.0%	0.0%	0.0%				
Operating Profit	18.0%	18.5%	18.5%				
Interest Income	0.1%	0.2%	0.3%				
Other Income, Gains, Expenses and Losses	1.1%	1.2%	1.3%				
Income before Tax	19.3%	19.9%	20.0%				
Income Tax Expense	−6.1%	−6.1%	−6.0%				
Profit Margin for ROA*	13.2%	13.7%	14.1%				

*Amounts may not sum due to rounding.

Continued

Analysis Spreadsheet (continued)

RETURN ON COMMON SHAREHOLDERS' EQUITY ANALYSIS
(excluding the effects of non-recurring items)

	RETURN ON COMMON SHAREHOLDERS' EQUITY		
	2	**3**	**4**
	34.8%	33.5%	31.2%
	2	**3**	**4**
PROFIT MARGIN FOR ROCE	12.6%	13.3%	13.6%
ASSET TURNOVER	1.1	1.1	1.1
CAPITAL STRUCTURE LEVERAGE	2.5	2.3	2.1

Forecasts Spreadsheet

FSAP OUTPUT: FINANCIAL STATEMENT FORECASTS

Analyst Name: Stickney, Brown & Wahlen
Company Name: PepsiCo

Format:
Actual Amounts
Common Size Percentage
Rate of Change Percentage

Format:
Forecast Amounts
Forecast assumption
Forecast assumption explanation

Year +6 and beyond:
Long-Run Growth Rate: 3.0%
Long-Run Growth Factor: 103.0%

	Actuals			Forecasts					
Year	**2**	**3**	**4**	**Year +1**	**Year +2**	**Year +3**	**Year +4**	**Year +5**	**Year +6**
INCOME STATEMENT									
Revenues	**25,112**	**26,971**	**29,261**	**31,836**	**33,355**	**35,629**	**38,071**	**40,693**	**41,914**
common size	100.0%	100.0%	100.0%	8.8%	4.8%	6.8%	6.9%	6.9%	
rate of change		7.4%	8.5%	See Forecast Development worksheet for details of revenues forecasts.					
Cost of Goods Sold	**−11,497**	**−12,379**	**−13,406**	**−14,581**	**−15,276**	**−16,318**	**−17,436**	**−18,638**	**−19,197**
common size	−45.8%	−45.9%	−45.8%	−45.8%	−45.8%	−45.8%	−45.8%	−45.8%	
rate of change		7.7%	8.3%	Assume steady cost of goods sold as a percent of sales.					
Gross Profit	**13,615**	**14,592**	**15,855**	**17,255**	**18,078**	**19,311**	**20,634**	**22,056**	**22,717**
common size	54.2%	54.1%	54.2%	54.2%	54.2%	54.2%	54.2%	54.2%	54.2%
rate of change		7.2%	8.7%	8.8%	4.8%	6.8%	6.9%	6.9%	3.0%
Selling, General and Administrative Expense	**−8,958**	**−9,460**	**−10,299**	**−11,206**	**−11,741**	**−12,541**	**−13,401**	**−14,324**	**−14,754**
common size	−35.7%	−35.1%	−35.2%	−35.2%	−35.2%	−35.2%	−35.2%	−35.2%	
rate of change		5.6%	8.9%	Assume steady SG&A expense as a percent of sales.					

Continued

Forecasts Spreadsheet (continued)

Other Operating Expenses (1)	**−138**	**−145**	**−147**	**−141**	**−140**	**−24**	**−23**	**−22**	**−23**
common size	−0.5%	−0.5%	−0.5%	−141	−140	−24	−23	−22	
rate of change		5.1%	1.4%	Amounts based on PepsiCo disclosures in Note 4.					
Other Operating Expenses (2)	**0**	**0**	**0**	**0**	**0**	**0**	**0**	**0**	**0**
common size	0.0%	0.0%	0.0%	0.0%	0.0%	0.0%	0.0%	0.0%	
rate of change		#DIV/0!	#DIV/0!	Explain other operating expense assumptions (negative % of sales).					
Other Operating Expenses (3)	**0**	**0**	**0**	**0**	**0**	**0**	**0**	**0**	**0**
common size	0.0%	0.0%	0.0%	0.0%	0.0%	0.0%	0.0%	0.0%	
rate of change		#DIV/0!	#DIV/0!	Explain other operating expense assumptions (negative % of sales).					
Other Operating Income	**0**	**0**	**0**	**0**	**0**	**0**	**0**	**0**	**0**
common size	0.0%	0.0%	0.0%	0.0	0.0	0.0	0.0	0.0	
rate of change		#DIV/0!	#DIV/0!	Explain assumptions.					
Non-Recurring Operating Gains	**0**	**0**	**0**	**0**	**0**	**0**	**0**	**0**	**0**
common size	0.0%	0.0%	0.0%	0.0	0.0	0.0	0.0	0.0	
rate of change		#DIV/0!	#DIV/0!	Explain assumptions.					
Non-Recurring Operating Losses	**−224**	**−206**	**−150**	**0**	**0**	**0**	**0**	**0**	**0**
common size	−0.9%	−0.8%	−0.5%	0.0	0.0	0.0	0.0	0.0	
rate of change		−8.0%	−27.2%	Explain assumptions.					
Operating Profit	**4,295**	**4,781**	**5,259**	**5,908**	**6,197**	**6,746**	**7,210**	**7,710**	**7,941**
common size	17.1%	17.7%	18.0%	18.6%	18.6%	18.9%	18.9%	18.9%	18.9%
rate of change		11.3%	10.0%	12.3%	4.9%	8.8%	6.9%	6.9%	3.0%

Continued

Forecasts Spreadsheet (continued)

	Actuals			Forecasts					
Year	**2**	**3**	**4**	**Year +1**	**Year +2**	**Year +3**	**Year +4**	**Year +5**	**Year +6**
Interest Income	**36**	**51**	**74**	**91**	**97**	**101**	**107**	**113**	**116**
common size	0.1%	0.2%	0.3%	4.0%	4.0%	4.0%	4.0%	4.0%	
rate of change		41.7%	45.1%	Interest rate earned on average balance in marketable securities.					
Interest Expense	**−178**	**−163**	**−167**	**−204**	**−203**	**−220**	**−239**	**−243**	**−250**
common size	−0.7%	−0.6%	−0.6%	−6.0%	−6.0%	−6.0%	−6.0%	−6.0%	
rate of change		−8.4%	2.5%	Interest rate paid on average balance in financial liabilities.					
Other Income or Gains	**280**	**323**	**380**	**411**	**435**	**457**	**482**	**508**	**523**
common size	1.1%	1.2%	1.3%	12.0%	12.0%	12.0%	12.0%	12.0%	
rate of change		15.4%	17.6%	Assume normal return of 12% on bottling investments.					
Unusual Income or Gains	**0**	**0**	**0**	**0**	**0**	**0**	**0**	**0**	**0**
common size	0.0%	0.0%	0.0%	0.0	0.0	0.0	0.0	0.0	
rate of change		#DIV/0!	#DIV/0!	Explain assumptions.					
Other Expenses or Losses	**0**	**0**	**0**	**0**	**0**	**0**	**0**	**0**	**0**
common size	0.0%	0.0%	0.0%	0.0	0.0	0.0	0.0	0.0	
rate of change		#DIV/0!	#DIV/0!	Explain assumptions.					
Unusual Expenses or Losses	**0**	**0**	**0**	**0**	**0**	**0**	**0**	**0**	**0**
common size	0.0%	0.0%	0.0%	0.0	0.0	0.0	0.0	0.0	
rate of change		#DIV/0!	#DIV/0!	Explain assumptions.					
Income before Tax	**4,433**	**4,992**	**5,546**	**6,207**	**6,526**	**7,084**	**7,561**	**8,088**	**8,330**
common size	17.7%	18.5%	19.0%	19.5%	19.6%	19.9%	19.9%	19.9%	19.9%
rate of change		12.6%	11.1%	11.9%	5.2%	8.5%	6.7%	7.0%	3.0%
Income Tax Expense	**−1,433**	**−1,424**	**−1,372**	**−1,825**	**−2,023**	**−2,196**	**−2,344**	**−2,507**	**−2,582**
common size	−5.7%	−5.3%	−4.7%	29.4%	31.0%	31.0%	31.0%	31.0%	
rate of change		−0.6%	−3.7%	Effective income tax rate assumptions.					

Continued

Forecasts Spreadsheet (continued)

Minority Interest in Earnings	**0**	**0**	**0**	**0**	**0**	**0**	**0**	**0**	**0**
common size	0.0%	0.0%	0.0%	0.0	0.0	0.0	0.0	0.0	
rate of change		#DIV/0!	#DIV/0!	Explain assumptions.					
Income from Discontinued Operations	**0**	**0**	**38**	**0**	**0**	**0**	**0**	**0**	**0**
common size	0.0%	0.0%	0.1%	0.0	0.0	0.0	0.0	0.0	
rate of change		#DIV/0!	#DIV/0!	Explain assumptions.					
Extraordinary Gains (Losses)	**0**	**0**	**0**	**0**	**0**	**0**	**0**	**0**	**0**
common size	0.0%	0.0%	0.0%	0.0	0.0	0.0	0.0	0.0	
rate of change		#DIV/0!	#DIV/0!	Explain assumptions.					
Changes in Accounting Principles	**0**	**0**	**0**	**0**	**0**	**0**	**0**	**0**	**0**
common size	0.0%	0.0%	0.0%	0.0	0.0	0.0	0.0	0.0	
rate of change		#DIV/0!	#DIV/0!	Explain assumptions.					
NET INCOME	**3,000**	**3,568**	**4,212**	**4,382**	**4,503**	**4,888**	**5,217**	**5,580**	**5,748**
common size	11.9%	13.2%	14.4%	13.8%	13.5%	13.7%	13.7%	13.7%	13.7%
rate of change		18.9%	18.0%	4.0%	2.8%	8.5%	6.7%	7.0%	3.0%
Other Comprehensive Income Items	**−26**	**405**	**381**	**0**	**0**	**0**	**0**	**0**	**0**
common size	−0.1%	1.5%	1.3%	0.0	0.0	0.0	0.0	0.0	
rate of change		−1657.7%	−5.9%	Explain assumptions.					
COMPREHENSIVE INCOME	**2,974**	**3,973**	**4,593**	**4,382**	**4,503**	**4,888**	**5,217**	**5,580**	**5,748**
common size	11.8%	14.7%	15.7%	13.8%	13.5%	13.7%	13.7%	13.7%	13.7%
rate of change		33.6%	15.6%	−4.6%	2.8%	8.5%	6.7%	7.0%	3.0%

Forecasts Spreadsheet (continued)

FSAP OUTPUT: FINANCIAL STATEMENT FORECASTS

Analyst Name: **Stickney, Brown & Wahlen**
Company Name: **PepsiCo**

	Format:	Format:	Year +6 and beyond:
	Actual Amounts	**Forecast Amounts**	
	Common Size Percentage	Forecast assumption	Long-Run Growth Rate: 3.0%
	Rate of Change Percentage	Forecast assumption explanation	Long-Run Growth Factor: 103.0%

	Actuals			**Forecasts**					
Year	**2**	**3**	**4**	**Year +1**	**Year +2**	**Year +3**	**Year +4**	**Year +5**	**Year +6**
BALANCE SHEET									
ASSETS:									
Cash	**1,638**	**820**	**1,280**	**1,337**	**1,405**	**1,524**	**1,605**	**1,739**	**1,791**
common size	7.0%	3.2%	4.6%	15.0	15.0	15.0	15.0	15.0	
rate of change		−49.9%	56.1%	Assume cash balances equal to 15 days sales.					
Marketable Securities	**207**	**1,181**	**2,165**	**2,382**	**2,454**	**2,620**	**2,732**	**2,912**	**3,000**
common size	0.9%	4.7%	7.7%	8.0%	8.0%	8.0%	8.0%	8.0%	
rate of change		470.5%	83.3%	Assume eight percent of total assets, up slightly from last year.					
Accounts Receivable—Trade	**2,531**	**2,830**	**2,999**	**3,281**	**3,298**	**3,730**	**3,780**	**4,247**	**4,374**
common size	10.8%	11.2%	10.7%	36.0	36.0	36.0	36.0	36.0	
rate of change		11.8%	6.0%	Assume 36 days to collect sales in accounts receivable.					
Inventories	**1,342**	**1,412**	**1,541**	**1,664**	**1,694**	**1,893**	**1,940**	**2,157**	**2,221**
common size	5.7%	5.6%	5.5%	9.1	9.1	9.1	9.1	9.1	
rate of change		5.2%	9.1%	Assume average inventory turnover of roughly 9.1 times per year.					
Other Current Assets (1)	**695**	**687**	**654**	**596**	**613**	**655**	**683**	**728**	**750**
common size	3.0%	2.7%	2.3%	2.0%	2.0%	2.0%	2.0%	2.0%	
rate of change		−1.2%	−4.8%	Assume 2.0 percent of total assets.					
Other Current Assets (2)	**0**	**0**	**0**	**0**	**0**	**0**	**0**	**0**	**0**
common size	0.0%	0.0%	0.0%	0.0	0.0	0.0	0.0	0.0	
rate of change		#DIV/0!	#DIV/0!	Other current assets assumptions.					
CURRENT ASSETS	**6,413**	**6,930**	**8,639**	**9,259**	**9,464**	**10,421**	**10,740**	**11,783**	**12,136**
common size	27.3%	27.4%	30.9%	31.1%	30.9%	31.8%	31.5%	32.4%	32.4%
rate of change		8.1%	24.7%	7.2%	2.2%	10.1%	3.1%	9.7%	3.0%

Continued

Forecasts Spreadsheet (continued)

Long Term Investments in Securities	**2,611**	**2,920**	**3,284**	**3,573**	**3,680**	**3,930**	**4,097**	**4,368**	**4,499**
common size	11.5%	11.7%	12%	12%	12%	12%	12%		
rate of change		11.8%	12.5%	Assume 12.0 percent of total assets.					
Property, Plant & Equipment—at cost	**13,395**	**14,755**	**15,930**	**17,522**	**19,190**	**20,971**	**22,875**	**24,909**	**25,657**
common size	57.1%	58.3%	56.9%	1,592	1,668	1,781	1,904	2,035	
rate of change		10.2%	8.0%	PP&E assumptions—see schedule in forecast development.					
Accumulated Depreciation	**−6,005**	**−6,927**	**−7,781**	**−8,994**	**−10,322**	**−11,774**	**−13,357**	**−15,081**	**−15,534**
common size	−25.6%	−27.4%	−27.8%	(1,213)	(1,328)	(1,452)	(1,583)	(1,724)	
rate of change		15.4%	12.3%	See depreciation schedule in forecast development worksheet.					
Amortizable Intangible Assets (net)	**801**	**718**	**598**	**457**	**317**	**293**	**270**	**248**	**255**
common size	3.4%	2.8%	2.1%	−141.0	−140.0	−24.0	−23.0	−22.0	
rate of change		−10.4%	−16.7%	Assume amortization per PepsiCo disclosures; assume no new .investments.					
Goodwill and Nonamortizable Intangibles	**4,418**	**4,665**	**4,842**	**5,268**	**5,519**	**5,896**	**6,300**	**6,734**	**6,936**
common size	18.8%	18.4%	17.3%	8.8%	4.8%	6.8%	6.9%	6.9%	
rate of change		5.6%	3.8%	Assume growth with sales.					
Other Non-Current Assets (1)	**1,841**	**2,266**	**2,475**	**2,693**	**2,821**	**3,014**	**3,220**	**3,442**	**3,545**
common size	7.8%	8.9%	8.8%	8.8%	4.8%	6.8%	6.9%	6.9%	
rate of change		23.1%	9.2%	Assume growth with sales.					
Other Non-Current Assets (2)	**0**	**0**	**0**	**0**	**0**	**0**	**0**	**0**	**0**
common size	0.0%	0.0%	0.0%	0.0	0.0	0.0	0.0	0.0	
rate of change		#DIV/0!	#DIV/0!	Other non-current assets assumptions.					
TOTAL ASSETS	**23,474**	**25,327**	**27,987**	**29,779**	**30,670**	**32,751**	**34,145**	**36,403**	**37,495**
common size	100.0%	100.0%	100.0%	100.0%	100.0%	100.0%	100.0%	100.0%	100.0%
rate of change		7.9%	10.5%	6.4%	3.0%	6.8%	4.3%	6.6%	3.0%

Continued

Forecasts Spreadsheet (continued)

	Actuals			Forecasts					
Year	**2**	**3**	**4**	**Year +1**	**Year +2**	**Year +3**	**Year +4**	**Year +5**	**Year +6**
LIABILITIES:									
Accounts Payable—Trade	**1,543**	**1,638**	**1,731**	**1,895**	**1,880**	**2,193**	**2,118**	**2,531**	**2,607**
common size	6.6%	6.5%	6.2%	45.0	45.0	45.0	45.0	45.0	
rate of change		6.2%	5.7%	Assume 45 day payment period.					
Notes Payable and Short Term Debt	**77**	**145**	**894**	**298**	**307**	**328**	**341**	**364**	**375**
common size	0.3%	0.6%	3.2%	1.0%	1.0%	1.0%	1.0%	1.0%	
rate of change		88.3%	516.6%	Assume 1.0 percent of total assets.					
Current Maturities of Long Term Debt	**485**	**446**	**160**	**361**	**361**	**631**	**631**	**413**	**425**
common size	2.1%	1.8%	0.6%	361.0	361.0	631.0	631.0	413.0	
rate of change		−8.0%	−64.1%	Current maturities of long-term debt per long-term debt note.					
Other Current Liabilities (1)	**3,455**	**3,575**	**3,868**	**4,208**	**4,409**	**4,710**	**5,033**	**5,379**	**5,541**
common size	14.7%	14.1%	13.8%	8.8%	4.8%	6.8%	6.9%	6.9%	
rate of change		3.5%	8.2%	Liabilities for accrued expenses grow with SG&A expenses, which grow with sales.					
Other Current Liabilities (2)	**492**	**611**	**99**	**298**	**307**	**328**	**341**	**364**	**375**
common size	2.1%	2.4%	0.4%	1.0%	1.0%	1.0%	1.0%	1.0%	
rate of change		24.2%	−83.8%	Assume 1.0 percent of total assets.					
CURRENT LIABILITIES	**6,052**	**6,415**	**6,752**	**7,060**	**7,263**	**8,189**	**8,464**	**9,051**	**9,323**
common size	25.8%	25.3%	24.1%	23.7%	23.7%	25.0%	24.8%	24.9%	24.9%
rate of change		6.0%	5.3%	4.6%	2.9%	12.7%	3.4%	6.9%	3.0%

Continued

Forecasts Spreadsheet (continued)

Long Term Debt	**2,187**	**1,702**	**2,397**	**2,680**	**2,760**	**2,948**	**3,073**	**3,276**	**3,375**
common size	9.3%	6.7%	8.6%	9.0%	9.0%	9.0%	9.0%	9.0%	
rate of change		−22.2%	40.8%	Assume 9.0 percent of total assets.					
Deferred Taxes	**1,486**	**1,261**	**1,216**	**1,191**	**1,227**	**1,310**	**1,366**	**1,456**	**1,500**
common size	6.3%	5.0%	4.3%	4.0%	4.0%	4.0%	4.0%	4.0%	
rate of change		−15.1%	−3.6%	Assume 4.0 percent of total assets.					
Other Non-Current Liabilities (1)	**4,226**	**4,075**	**4,099**	**4,460**	**4,672**	**4,991**	**5,333**	**5,700**	**5,871**
common size	18.0%	16.1%	14.6%	8.8%	4.8%	6.8%	6.9%	6.9%	
rate of change		−3.6%	0.6%	Liabilities for accrued expenses grow with SG&A expenses, which grow with sales.					
Other Non-Current Liabilities (2)	**0**	**0**	**0**	**0**	**0**	**0**	**0**	**0**	**0**
common size	0.0%	0.0%	0.0%	0.0	0.0	0.0	0.0	0.0	
rate of change		#DIV/0!	#DIV/0!	Other non-current liabilities assumptions.					
TOTAL LIABILITIES	**13,951**	**13,453**	**14,464**	**15,391**	**15,923**	**17,437**	**18,236**	**19,484**	**20,069**
common size	59.4%	53.1%	51.7%	51.7%	51.9%	53.2%	53.4%	53.5%	53.5%
rate of change		−3.6%	7.5%	6.4%	3.5%	9.5%	4.6%	6.8%	3.0%

Continued

Forecasts Spreadsheet (continued)

	Actuals			Forecasts					
Year	**2**	**3**	**4**	**Year +1**	**Year +2**	**Year +3**	**Year +4**	**Year +5**	**Year +6**
SHAREHOLDERS' EQUITY									
Minority Interest in Subsidiaries	**0**	**0**	**0**	**0**	**0**	**0**	**0**	**0**	**0**
common size	0.0%	0.0%	0.0%	0.0	0.0	0.0	0.0	0.0	
rate of change		#DIV/0!	#DIV/0!	Minority interest assumptions.					
Preferred Stock	**−7**	**−22**	**−49**	**0**	**0**	**0**	**0**	**0**	**0**
common size	0.0%	−0.1%	−0.2%	0.0	0.0	0.0	0.0	0.0	
rate of change		214.3%	122.7%	Preferred stock assumptions.					
Common Stock + Paid in Capital	**237**	**578**	**648**	**685**	**705**	**753**	**785**	**837**	**862**
common size	1.0%	2.3%	2.3%	2.3%	2.3%	2.3%	2.3%	2.3%	
rate of change		143.9%	12.1%	Assume 2.3 percent of total assets.					
Retained Earnings	**13,489**	**15,961**	**18,730**	**21,189**	**23,288**	**25,687**	**28,260**	**31,368**	**32,282**
common size	57.5%	63.0%	66.9%						
rate of change		18.3%	17.3%	Add net income and subtract dividends; see dividends forecast box below.					
Accumulated Other Comprehensive Income	**−1,672**	**−1,267**	**−886**	**−886**	**−886**	**−886**	**−886**	**−886**	**−886**
common size	−7.1%	−5.0%	−3.2%	0.0	0.0	0.0	0.0	0.0	
rate of change		−24.2%	−30.1%	Accumulated other comprehensive income assumptions on income statement.					
Other Equity Adjustments	**0**	**0**	**0**	**0**	**0**	**0**	**0**	**0**	**0**
common size	0.0%	0.0%	0.0%	0.0	0.0	0.0	0.0	0.0	
rate of change		#DIV/0!	#DIV/0!	Other equity adjustments assumptions.					
Treasury Stock	**−2,524**	**−3,376**	**−4,920**	**−6,600**	**−8,361**	**−10,241**	**−12,251**	**−14,400**	**−14,832**
common size	−10.8%	−13.3%	−17.6%	−1680	−1761	−1880	−2010	−2149	
rate of change		33.8%	45.7%	Treasury stock repurchases, net of treasury stock reissues.					
SHAREHOLDERS' EQUITY	**9,523**	**11,874**	**13,523.0**	**14,388.1**	**14,747**	**15,313**	**15,908**	**16,919**	**17,426**
common size	40.6%	46.9%	48.3%	48.3%	48.1%	46.8%	46.6%	46.5%	46.5%
rate of change		24.7%	13.9%	6.4%	2.5%	3.8%	3.9%	6.4%	3.0%

Continued

Forecasts Spreadsheet (continued)

TOTAL LIABILITIES AND EQUITIES	**23,474**	**25,327**	**27,987**	**29,779**	**30,670**	**32,751**	**34,145**	**36,403**	**37,495**
common size	100.0%	100.0%	100.0%	100.0%	100.0%	100.0%	100.0%	100.0%	100.0%
rate of change		7.9%	10.5%	6.4%	3.0%	6.8%	4.3%	6.6%	3.0%
Check figures: Balance Sheet A=L+OE?	0	0	0	0	0	0	0	0	0
				Initial adjustment needed to balance the balance sheet:					
				115	**−432**	**−463**	**−445**	**−125**	**−2,415**
				Account adjusted:	**Dividends**				
				Dividends forecasts:					
Common Dividends:				**1,878**	**1,972**	**2,026**	**2,199**	**2,348**	**2,418**
				45.0%	45.0%	45.0%	45.0%	45.0%	
				Assume 45% dividend payout of lagged net income from continuing operations.					
Preferred Dividends:				**159**	**0**	**0**	**0**	**0**	**0**
				159.0	0.0	0.0	0.0	0.0	
				Enter preferred stock dividend payments, if any.					
Implied Dividends:				**−115**	**432**	**463**	**445**	**125**	**2,415**
				Implied dividend amount to balance the balance sheet.					
Total Dividends:				**1,923**	**2,404**	**2,489**	**2,644**	**2,473**	**4,833**
				Total dividend forecast amounts.					

Forecasts Spreadsheet (continued)

FSAP OUTPUT: FINANCIAL STATEMENT FORECASTS

Analyst Name: Stickney, Brown & Wahlen
Company Name: PepsiCo

	Actuals		Forecasts					
Year	**3**	**4**	**Year +1**	**Year +2**	**Year +3**	**Year +4**	**Year +5**	**Year +6**
IMPLIED STATEMENT OF CASH FLOWS								
NET INCOME	3,568	4,212	4,382	4,503	4,888	5,217	5,580	5,748
Add back Depreciation Expense	1,005	974	1,354	1,468	1,476	1,606	1,746	445
(Increase) Decrease in Receivables—Trade	−299	−169	−282	−17	−431	−50	−467	−127
(Increase) Decrease in Inventories	−70	−129	−123	−30	−199	−47	−217	−65
(Increase) Decrease in Other Current Assets (1)	8	33	58	−18	−42	−28	−45	−22
(Increase) Decrease in Other Current Assets (2)	0	0	0	0	0	0	0	0
Increase (Decrease) in Accounts Payable—Trade	95	93	164	−15	313	−75	413	76
Increase (Decrease) in Other Current Liabilities (1)	120	293	340	201	301	323	347	161
Increase (Decrease) in Other Current Liabilities (2)	119	−512	199	9	21	14	23	11
Increase (Decrease) in Deferred Taxes	−225	−45	−25	36	83	56	90	44
Increase (Decrease) in Other Non-Current Liabilities (1)	−151	24	361	213	319	342	367	171
Increase (Decrease) in Other Non-Current Liabilities (2)	0	0	0	0	0	0	0	0
NET CASH FLOW FROM OPERATIONS	**4,170**	**4,774**	**6,428**	**6,349**	**6,728**	**7,357**	**7,838**	**6,442**

Continued

Forecasts Spreadsheet (continued)

(Increase) Decrease in Prop., Plant, & Equipment at cost	−1,360	−1,175	−1,592	−1,668	−1,781	−1,904	−2,035	−747
(Increase) Decrease in Marketable Securities	−974	−984	−217	−71	−166	−112	−181	−87
(Increase) Decrease in Investment Securities	−309	−364	−289	−107	−250	−167	−271	−131
(Increase) Decrease in Amortizable Intangibles	0	0	0	0	0	0	0	0
(Increase) Decrease in Goodwill and Nonamortizable Intangibles	−247	−177	−426	−251	−376	−404	−434	−202
(Increase) Decrease in Other Non-Current Assets (1)	−425	−209	−218	−128	−192	−207	−222	−103
(Increase) Decrease in Other Non-Current Assets (2)	0	0	0	0	0	0	0	0
NET CASH FLOW FROM INVESTING	**−3,315**	**−2,909**	**−2,743**	**−2,226**	**−2,766**	**−2,793**	**−3,142**	**−1,271**
Increase (Decrease) in Short Term Debt	29	463	−395	9	291	14	−195	23
Increase (Decrease) in Long Term Debt	−485	695	283	80	187	125	203	98
Increase (Decrease) in Minority Interest and Preferred Stock	−15	−27	49	0	0	0	0	0
Increase (Decrease) in Common Stock + Paid in Capital	341	70	37	20	48	32	52	25
Increase (Decrease) in Accumulated OCI and Oth. Eq. Adjs.	405	381	0	0	0	0	0	0
Increase (Decrease) in Treasury Stock	−852	−1,544	−1,680	−1,761	−1,880	−2,010	−2,149	−432
Dividends	−1,096	−1,443	−1,923	−2,404	−2,489	−2,644	−2,473	−4,833
NET CASH FLOW FROM FINANCING	**−1,673**	**−1,405**	**−3,629**	**−4,055**	**−3,843**	**−4,483**	**−4,562**	**−5,119**
NET CHANGE IN CASH	**−818**	**460**	**57**	**68**	**119**	**82**	**134**	**52**
Check Figure:								
Net change in cash—Change in cash balance	0	0	0	0	0	0	0	0

Continued

Forecasts Spreadsheet (continued)

FSAP OUTPUT: FINANCIAL STATEMENT FORECASTS

Analyst Name: Stickney, Brown & Wahlen
Company Name: PepsiCo

	Actuals			Forecasts					
Year	**2**	**3**	**4**	**Year +1**	**Year +2**	**Year +3**	**Year +4**	**Year +5**	**Year +6**
FORECAST VALIDITY CHECK DATA:									
GROWTH									
Revenue Growth Rates:	6.8%	7.4%	8.5%	8.8%	4.8%	6.8%	6.9%	6.9%	3.0%
Net Income Growth Rates:	25.0%	18.9%	18.0%	4.0%	2.8%	8.5%	6.7%	7.0%	3.0%
Total Asset Growth Rates	8.2%	7.9%	10.5%	6.4%	3.0%	6.8%	4.3%	6.6%	3.0%
RETURN ON ASSETS (based on reported amounts):									
Profit Margin for ROA	12.4%	13.6%	14.8%	14.2%	13.9%	14.1%	14.1%	14.1%	14.1%
× Asset Turnover	1.1	1.1	1.1	1.1	1.1	1.1	1.1	1.2	1.1
= Return on Assets	13.8%	15.1%	16.2%	15.7%	15.4%	15.9%	16.1%	16.3%	16.0%
RETURN ON ASSETS (excluding the effects of nonrecurring items):									
Profit Margin for ROA	13.2%	13.7%	14.1%	14.2%	13.9%	14.1%	14.1%	14.1%	14.1%
× Asset Turnover	1.1	1.1	1.1	1.1	1.1	1.1	1.1	1.2	1.1
= Return on Assets	14.6%	15.2%	15.4%	15.7%	15.4%	15.9%	16.1%	16.3%	16.0%
RETURN ON COMMON EQUITY (based on reported amounts):									
Profit Margin for ROCE	11.8%	13.2%	14.3%	13.3%	13.5%	13.7%	13.7%	13.7%	13.7%
× Asset Turnover	1.1	1.1	1.1	1.1	1.1	1.1	1.1	1.2	1.1
× Capital Structure Leverage	2.5	2.3	2.1	2.1	2.1	2.1	2.1	2.1	2.2
= Return on Common Equity	32.7%	33.2%	32.9%	30.2%	30.9%	32.5%	33.4%	34.0%	33.5%
RETURN ON COMMON EQUITY (excluding the effects of nonrecurring items):									
Profit Margin for ROCE	12.6%	13.3%	13.6%	13.3%	13.5%	13.7%	13.7%	13.7%	13.7%
× Asset Turnover	1.1	1.1	1.1	1.1	1.1	1.1	1.1	1.2	1.1
× Capital Structure Leverage	2.5	2.3	2.1	2.1	2.1	2.1	2.1	2.1	2.2
= Return on Common Equity	34.8%	33.5%	31.2%	30.2%	30.9%	32.5%	33.4%	34.0%	33.5%

Continued

Forecasts Spreadsheet (continued)

OPERATING PERFORMANCE:									
Gross Profit/Revenues	54.2%	54.1%	54.2%	54.2%	54.2%	54.2%	54.2%	54.2%	54.2%
Operating Profit Before Taxes/Revenues	17.1%	17.7%	18.0%	18.6%	18.6%	18.9%	18.9%	18.9%	18.9%
ASSET TURNOVER:									
Revenues/Average Accounts Receivable	10.7	10.1	10.0	10.1	10.1	10.1	10.1	10.1	9.7
COGS/Average Inventory	8.7	9.0	9.1	9.1	9.1	9.1	9.1	9.1	8.8
Revenues/Average Fixed Assets	3.5	3.5	3.7	3.8	3.8	3.9	4.1	4.2	4.2
LIQUIDITY:									
Current Ratio	1.1	1.1	1.3	1.3	1.3	1.3	1.3	1.3	1.3
Quick Ratio	0.7	0.8	1.0	1.0	1.0	1.0	1.0	1.0	1.0
SOLVENCY:									
Total Liabilities/Total Assets	0.6	0.5	0.5	0.5	0.5	0.5	0.5	0.5	0.5
Total Liabilities/Total Equity	1.5	1.1	1.1	1.1	1.1	1.1	1.1	1.2	1.2
Interest Coverage Ratio	25.9	31.6	34.4	31.5	33.1	33.2	32.7	34.3	34.3

Forecast Development Spreadsheet

This Forecast Development spreadsheet provides work space in which the analyst can:

—build detailed sales revenue forecasts
—build forecasts of capital expenditures, depreciation expense, PP&E, and accumulated depreciation.
—build detailed forecasts of other financial statement amounts.

It is not necessary to use this spreadsheet to build financial statement forecasts in the FSAP Forecasts spreadsheet. If you use this spreadsheet to build more detailed forecasts, the you will need to link these forecast amounts to the appropriate cells in the financial statements in the FSAP Forecasts spreadsheet.

Analyst Name: **Stickney, Brown & Wahlen**
Company Name: **PepsiCo**

SALES REVENUE FORECAST DEVELOPMENT

	Actuals			Forecasts				
Year	**2**	**3**	**4**	**Year +1**	**Year +2**	**Year +3**	**Year +4**	**Year +5**
Revenues	**25,112**	**26,971**	**29,261**	**31,836**	**33,355**	**35,629**	**38,071**	**40,693**
rate of change		7.4%	8.5%	8.8%	4.8%	6.8%	6.9%	6.9%
				Enter sales growth rate assumptions.				

Sales Forecasts for PepsiCo:

Year	**2**	**3**	**4**	**Year +1**	**Year +2**	**Year +3**	**Year +4**	**Year +5**
Sales Forecasts Combined by Segments:								
Frito-Lay North America	8,565	9,091	9,560	**10,287**	**10,655**	**11,248**	**11,875**	**12,536**
PepsiCo Beverages North America	7,200	7,733	8,313	**8,989**	**9,356**	**9,926**	**10,531**	**11,172**
PepsiCo International	7,749	8,678	9,862	**10,974**	**11,756**	**12,835**	**14,013**	**15,300**
Quaker Foods North America	1,464	1,467	1,526	**1,587**	**1,588**	**1,620**	**1,652**	**1,686**
Discontinued Operations	134	2	0					
PepsiCo Total	25,112	26,969	29,261	**31,836**	**33,355**	**35,629**	**38,071**	**40,693**
Growth rates		7.4%	8.5%	8.8%	4.8%	6.8%	6.9%	6.9%

Continued

Forecast Development Spreadsheet (continued)

Frito-Lay North America	8,565	9,091	9,560	**10,287**	**10,655**	**11,248**	**11,875**	**12,536**
growth rates		6.1%	5.2%	7.6%	3.6%	5.6%	5.6%	5.6%
compound growth			5.6%					
compound growth in volume			3.5%	3.5%	3.5%	3.5%	3.5%	3.5%
compound growth in prices			2.1%	2.0%	2.0%	2.0%	2.0%	2.0%
53rd week effect				1.019	0.981			
PepsiCo Beverages North America	7,200	7,733	8,313	**8,989**	**9,356**	**9,926**	**10,531**	**11,172**
growth rates		7.4%	7.5%	8.1%	4.1%	6.1%	6.1%	6.1%
compound growth			7.5%					
compound growth in volume			3.0%	3.0%	3.0%	3.0%	3.0%	3.0%
compound growth in prices			4.3%	3.0%	3.0%	3.0%	3.0%	3.0%
53rd week effect				1.019	0.981			
PepsiCo International	7,749	8,678	9,862	**10,974**	**11,756**	**12,835**	**14,013**	**15,300**
growth rates		12.0%	13.6%	11.3%	7.1%	9.2%	9.2%	9.2%
compound growth			12.8%					
compound growth in volume			8.5%	6.0%	6.0%	6.0%	6.0%	6.0%
compound growth in prices			4.0%	3.0%	3.0%	3.0%	3.0%	3.0%
53rd week effect				1.019	0.981			
Quaker Foods North America	1,464	1,467	1,526	**1,587**	**1,588**	**1,620**	**1,652**	**1,686**
growth rates		0.2%	4.0%	4.0%	0.1%	2.0%	2.0%	2.0%
compound growth			2.1%					
compound growth in volume			1.5%	1.0%	1.0%	1.0%	1.0%	1.0%
compound growth in prices			0.6%	1.0%	1.0%	1.0%	1.0%	1.0%
53rd week effect				1.019	0.981			

Continued

Forecast Development Spreadsheet (continued)

FORECAST DEVELOPMENT: CAPITAL EXPENDITURES, PROPERTY, PLANT AND EQUIPMENT, AND DEPRECIATION

Capital Expenditures:				**CAPEX Forecasts**				
Year	2	3	4	Year +1	Year +2	Year +3	Year +4	Year +5
CAPEX:								
PP&E Acquired	1,437	1,345	1,387					
PP&E Sold	−89	−49	−38					
Net CAPEX	1,348	1,296	1,349	**1,592**	**1,668**	**1,781**	**1,904**	**2,035**
Net CAPEX as a percent of:								
Gross PP&E	10.1%	8.8%	8.5%					
Revenues	5.4%	4.8%	4.6%	**5.0%**	**5.0%**	**5.0%**	**5.0%**	**5.0%**

Property, Plant and Equipment and Depreciation				**Property, Plant and Equipment and Depreciation Forecasts:**				
Year	2	3	4	Year +1	Year +2	Year +3	Year +4	Year +5
PP&E at cost:								
Beginning balance at cost:				**15,930**	**17,522**	**19,190**	**20,971**	**22,875**
Add: CAPEX forecasts from above:				**1,592**	**1,668**	**1,781**	**1,904**	**2,035**
Ending balance at cost:	13,395	14,755	15,930	**17,522**	**19,190**	**20,971**	**22,875**	**24,909**
Accumulated Depreciation:								
Beginning Balance:				**−7,781**	**−8,994**	**−10,322**	**−11,774**	**−13,357**
Subtract: Depreciation expense forecasts from below:				**−1,213**	**−1,328**	**−1,452**	**−1,583**	**−1,724**
Ending Balance:	−6,005	−6,927	−7,781	**−8,994**	**−10,322**	**−11,774**	**−13,357**	**−15,081**
PP&E—net	7,390	7,828	8,149	**8,528**	**8,867**	**9,197**	**9,517**	**9,828**

Continued

Forecast Development Spreadsheet (continued)

Depreciation Expense Forecast Development:		Depreciation expense forecast on existing PP&E:				
Existing PP&E at cost:	15,930	1,103	1,103	1,103	1,103	1,103
Remaining balance to be depreciated.	8,149					
PP&E Purchases:		**Depreciation expense forecasts on new PP&E:**				
Capex Year +1	1,592	110	110	110	110	110
Capex Year +2	1,668		115	115	115	115
Capex Year +3	1,781			123	123	123
Capex Year +4	1,904				132	132
Capex Year +5	2,035					141
Total Depreciation Expense		1,213	1,328	1,452	1,583	1,724

Depreciation methods:	2	3	4
PPE at Cost	13,395	14,755	15,930
Average Depreciable PPE		14,075	15,343
Depreciation Expense	929	1,020	1,062
Implied Average Useful Life in Years		13.8	14.4
Useful Life Forecast Assumption:			14.4
			(in years)

Valuation Spreadsheet

FSAP OUTPUT: **FINANCIAL STATEMENT FORECASTS**
Analyst Name: **Stickney, Brown & Wahlen**
Company Name: **PepsiCo**

VALUATION PARAMETER ASSUMPTIONS

COST OF EQUITY CAPITAL:	
Equity risk factor (market beta)	0.75
Risk free rate	4.0%
Market risk premium	5.0%
Required rate of return on common equity:	7.75%
Current share price	$ 51.94
Number of shares outstanding	1,679.0
Current market value	$ 87,207
Implied value of equity	$ 96,312
Long-run growth assumption used in forecasts	3.0%
Long-run growth assumption used in valuation	3.0%
(Both long-run growth assumptions should be the same.)	

COST OF DEBT CAPITAL	
Debt capital	$3,676
Cost of debt capital, before tax	6.0%
Effective tax rate	31.0%
COST OF PREFERRED STOCK	
Preferred stock capital	$ —
Preferred dividends	$ —
Implied yield	0.0%
WEIGHTED AVERAGE COST OF CAPITAL	
Weight of equity in capital structure	0.96
Weight of debt in capital structure	0.04
Weight of preferred in capital structure	0.00
Weighted average cost of capital	7.604%

Valuation Spreadsheet (continued)

FSAP OUTPUT: **FINANCIAL STATEMENT FORECASTS**
Analyst Name: **Stickney, Brown & Wahlen**
Company Name: **PepsiCo**

	1	2	3	4	5	Continuing Value
DIVIDENDS BASED VALUATION	**Year +1**	**Year +2**	**Year +3**	**Year +4**	**Year +5**	**Year +6**
Dividends Paid to						
Common Shareholders	1,763.7	2,404.0	2,489.1	2,644.0	2,472.7	
Less: Common Stock Issues	−36.9	−20.5	−47.9	−32.1	−51.9	
Plus: Common Stock Repurchases	1,680.0	1,761.0	1,880.0	2,010.0	2,149.0	
Dividends to Common Equity	3,406.8	4,144.5	4,321.2	4,622.0	4,569.7	5,240.3
Present Value Factors	0.928	0.861	0.799	0.742	0.689	
Present Value Net Dividends	3,161.8	3,569.7	3,454.2	3,428.9	3,146.3	
Sum of Present Value Net Dividends ...	16,761.0					
Present Value of Continuing Value	75,958.1					
Total	92,719.1					
Adjust to midyear discounting	1.03875					
Total Present Value Dividends	96,312.0					
Shares Outstanding	1,679.0					
Estimated Value per Share	$ 57.36					
Current share price	$ 51.94					
Percent difference	10%					
(Value/price) − 1: positive number indicates underpricing.						

Valuation Spreadsheet (continued)

FSAP OUTPUT: **FINANCIAL STATEMENT FORECASTS**
Analyst Name: **Stickney, Brown & Wahlen**
Company Name: **PepsiCo**

FREE CASH FLOWS FOR COMMON EQUITY SHAREHOLDERS	1 Year +1	2 Year +2	3 Year +3	4 Year +4	5 Year +5	Continuing Value Year +6
Net Cash Flow from Operations	6,428.2	6,349.0	6,728.3	7,357.4	7,837.6	6,441.8
+(−) Decrease (Increase) in Cash Required for Operations	−56.7	−68.1	−118.8	−81.9	−133.7	−52.2
Net Cash Flow from Investing	−2,742.6	−2,225.6	−2,766.4	−2,792.9	−3,142.1	−1,271.0
Net Cash Flows from Debt Financing	−112.1	89.1	478.1	139.4	7.8	121.6
Net Cash Flows into Financial Assets	0.0	0.0	0.0	0.0	0.0	0.0
Net Cash Flows—Preferred Stock and Minority Interest	−110.0	0.0	0.0	0.0	0.0	0.0
Free Cash Flow for Common Equity	3,406.8	4,144.5	4,321.2	4,622.0	4,569.7	5,240.3
Present Value Factors	0.928	0.861	0.799	0.742	0.689	
Present Value Free Cash Flows	3,161.8	3,569.7	3,454.2	3,428.9	3,146.3	
Sum of Present Value Free Cash Flows	16,761.0					
Present Value of Continuing Value	75,958.1					
Total	92,719.1					
Adjust to midyear discounting	1.03875					
Total Present Value Free Cash Flows to Equity	96,312.0					
Shares Outstanding	1,679.0					
Estimated Value per Share	$ 57.36					
Current share price	$ 51.94					
Percent difference	10%					

(Value/price) −1: positive number indicates underpricing.

Valuation Spreadsheet (continued)

FSAP OUTPUT: **FINANCIAL STATEMENT FORECASTS**
Analyst Name: **Stickney, Brown & Wahlen**
Company Name: **PepsiCo**

FREE CASH FLOW VALUATION SENSITIVITY ANALYSIS:

		Long-Run Growth Assumptions:										
		0%	1%	2%	3%	4%	5%	6%	7%	8%	9%	10%
Discount	5%	64.45	76.44	96.42	136.39	256.30	na	na	na	na	na	na
Rates:	6%	53.44	60.92	72.16	90.87	128.31	240.63	na	na	na	na	na
	7%	45.59	50.60	57.61	68.13	85.66	120.73	225.92	na	na	na	na
	7.75%	41.04	44.87	50.03	57.36	68.61	88.03	129.64	282.23	na	na	na
	9%	35.16	37.72	41.02	45.41	51.56	60.78	76.15	106.89	199.12	na	na
	10%	31.53	33.45	35.84	38.93	43.04	48.79	57.43	71.82	100.59	186.92	na
	11%	28.56	30.03	31.83	34.07	36.96	40.80	46.19	54.27	67.73	94.66	175.46
	12%	26.10	27.24	28.62	30.30	32.40	35.10	38.70	43.73	51.29	63.89	89.09
	13%	24.02	24.93	26.00	27.28	28.85	30.82	33.34	36.71	41.42	48.49	60.27
	14%	22.25	22.97	23.82	24.82	26.02	27.49	29.33	31.69	34.83	39.24	45.85
	15%	20.71	21.30	21.98	22.77	23.71	24.83	26.20	27.92	30.12	33.06	37.18
	16%	19.37	19.85	20.40	21.04	21.78	22.65	23.70	24.98	26.58	28.64	31.39
	17%	18.20	18.59	19.04	19.56	20.15	20.84	21.65	22.63	23.83	25.32	27.25
	18%	17.16	17.48	17.85	18.27	18.75	19.30	19.95	20.71	21.62	22.74	24.13
	19%	16.23	16.50	16.81	17.15	17.54	17.99	18.50	19.10	19.81	20.66	21.70
	20%	15.39	15.62	15.88	16.16	16.48	16.85	17.26	17.74	18.30	18.96	19.75

Valuation Spreadsheet (continued)

FSAP OUTPUT: **FINANCIAL STATEMENT FORECASTS**
Analyst Name: **Stickney, Brown & Wahlen**
Company Name: **PepsiCo**

FREE CASH FLOWS FOR ALL DEBT AND EQUITY STAKEHOLDERS	**1** **Year +1**	**2** **Year +2**	**3** **Year +3**	**4** **Year +4**	**5** **Year +5**	**Continuing Value** **Year +6**
Net Cash Flow from Operations	6,428.2	6,349.0	6,728.3	7,357.4	7,837.6	6,441.8
Add back: Interest Expense after tax	143.8	140.1	151.8	164.6	167.6	172.7
Subtract: Interest Income after tax	0.0	0.0	0.0	0.0	0.0	0.0
+(−) Decrease (Increase) in Cash Required for Operations	−56.7	−68.1	−118.8	−81.9	−133.7	−52.2
Free Cash Flow from Operations	6,515.3	6,421.0	6,761.3	7,440.1	7,871.6	6,562.3
Net Cash Flow from Investing	−2,742.6	−2,225.6	−2,766.4	−2,792.9	−3,142.1	−1,271.0
Add back: Net Cash Flows into Financial Assets	0.0	0.0	0.0	0.0	0.0	0.0
Free Cash Flow—All Debt and Equity	3,772.7	4,195.5	3,994.9	4,647.2	4,729.5	5,291.4
Present Value Factors	0.929	0.864	0.803	0.746	0.693	
Present Value Free Cash Flows	3,506.1	3,623.5	3,206.4	3,466.4	3,278.5	
Sum of Present Value Free Cash Flows	17,080.9					
Present Value of Continuing Value	79,669.3					
Total Present Value Free Cash Flows	96,750.2					
Less: Outstanding Debt (FV or BV)	−3,676.0					
Less: Preferred Stock (FV or BV)	0.0					
Plus: Financial Assets (FV or BV)	0.0					
Present Value of Equity	93,074.2					
Adjust to midyear discounting	1.03802					
Total Present Value of Equity	96,612.9					
Shares Outstanding	1,679.0					
Estimated Value per Share	$ 57.54					
Current share price	$ 51.94					
Percent difference	11%					

(Value/price) − 1: positive number indicates underpricing.

Valuation Spreadsheet (continued)

FSAP OUTPUT:	**FINANCIAL STATEMENT FORECASTS**
Analyst Name:	**Stickney, Brown & Wahlen**
Company Name:	**PepsiCo**

	1	2	3	4	5	Continuing Value
RESIDUAL INCOME VALUATION	**Year +1**	**Year +2**	**Year +3**	**Year +4**	**Year +5**	**Year +6**
Comprehensive Income Available for Common Shareholders	4,222.9	4,503.2	4,887.7	5,216.8	5,580.4	5,747.8
Lagged Book Value of Common Shareholders' Equity (at $t-1$)	13,572.0	14,388.1	14,746.8	15,313.3	15,908.1	16,918.8
Required Earnings	1,051.8	1,115.1	1,142.9	1,186.8	1,232.9	1,311.2
Residual Income	3,171.0	3,388.1	3,744.8	4,030.0	4,347.6	4,436.6
Present Value Factors	0.928	0.861	0.799	0.742	0.689	
Present Value Residual Income	2,943.0	2,918.2	2,993.5	2,989.8	2,993.4	
Sum of Present Value Residual Income	14,837.8					
Present Value of Continuing Value	64,309.3					
Total	79,147.1					
Add: Beginning Book Value of Equity	13,572.0					
Present Value of Equity	92,719.1					
Adjust to midyear discounting	1.03875					
Total Present Value of Equity	96,312.0					
Shares Outstanding	1,679.0					
Estimated Value per Share	$ 57.36					
Current share price	$ 51.94					
Percent difference	10%					

(Value/price) − 1: positive number indicates underpricing.

Valuation Spreadsheet (continued)

FSAP OUTPUT: **FINANCIAL STATEMENT FORECASTS**
Analyst Name: **Stickney, Brown & Wahlen**
Company Name: **PepsiCo**

RESIDUAL INCOME VALUATION SENSITIVITY ANALYSIS:

	Long-Run Growth Assumption:										
	0%	1%	2%	3%	4%	5%	6%	7%	8%	9%	10%
Discount 5%	64.45	76.44	96.42	136.39	256.30	na	na	na	na	na	na
Rates: 6%	53.44	60.92	72.16	90.87	128.31	240.63	na	na	na	na	na
7%	45.59	50.60	57.61	68.13	85.66	120.73	225.92	na	na	na	na
7.75%	41.04	44.87	50.03	**57.36**	68.61	88.03	129.64	282.23	na	na	na
9%	35.16	37.72	41.02	45.41	51.56	60.78	76.15	106.89	199.12	na	na
10%	31.53	33.45	35.84	38.93	43.04	48.79	57.43	71.82	100.59	186.92	na
11%	28.56	30.03	31.83	34.07	36.96	40.80	46.19	54.27	67.73	94.66	175.46
12%	26.10	27.24	28.62	30.30	32.40	35.10	38.70	43.73	51.29	63.89	89.09
13%	24.02	24.93	26.00	27.28	28.85	30.82	33.34	36.71	41.42	48.49	60.27
14%	22.25	22.97	23.82	24.82	26.02	27.49	29.33	31.69	34.83	39.24	45.85
15%	20.71	21.30	21.98	22.77	23.71	24.83	26.20	27.92	30.12	33.06	37.18
16%	19.37	19.85	20.40	21.04	21.78	22.65	23.70	24.98	26.58	28.64	31.39
17%	18.20	18.59	19.04	19.56	20.15	20.84	21.65	22.63	23.83	25.32	27.25
18%	17.16	17.48	17.85	18.27	18.75	19.30	19.95	20.71	21.62	22.74	24.13
19%	16.23	16.50	16.81	17.15	17.54	17.99	18.50	19.10	19.81	20.66	21.70
20%	15.39	15.62	15.88	16.16	16.48	16.85	17.26	17.74	18.30	18.96	19.75

Valuation Spreadsheet (continued)

FSAP OUTPUT: **FINANCIAL STATEMENT FORECASTS**
Analyst Name: **Stickney, Brown & Wahlen**
Company Name: **PepsiCo**

	1	2	3	4	5	Continuing Value
RESIDUAL INCOME VALUATION Market-to-Book Approach	**Year +1**	**Year +2**	**Year +3**	**Year +4**	**Year +5**	**Year +6**
Comprehensive Income Available for Common Shareholders	4,222.9	4,503.2	4,887.7	5,216.8	5,580.4	5,747.8
Book Value of Common Shareholders' Equity (at $t-1$)	13,572.0	14,388.1	14,746.8	15,313.3	15,908.1	16,918.8
Implied ROCE	31.1%	31.3%	33.1%	34.1%	35.1%	34.0%
Residual ROCE	23.4%	23.5%	25.4%	26.3%	27.3%	26.2%
Cumulative growth factor as of $t-1$	100.0%	106.0%	108.7%	112.8%	117.2%	124.7%
Residual ROCE times growth	23.4%	25.0%	27.6%	29.7%	32.0%	32.7%
Present Value Factors	0.928	0.861	0.799	0.742	0.689	
Present Value Residual ROCE times growth	0.217	0.215	0.221	0.220	0.221	
Sum of Present Value Residual ROCE times growth	1.09					
Present Value of Continuing Value	4.74					
Total Present Value Residual ROCE	5.83					
Add one for book value of equity at $t-1$	1.00					
Sum	6.83					
Adjust to midyear discounting	1.03875					
Implied Market-to-Book Ratio	7.096					
Times Beginning Book Value of Equity	13,572.0					
Total Present Value of Equity	96,312.0					
Shares Outstanding	1,679.0					
Estimated Value per Share	$ 57.36					
Current share price	$ 51.94					
Percent difference	10%					

(Value/price) −1: positive number indicates underpricing.

Sensitivity analysis for the market-to-book approach should be identical to that of the residual income approach.

Appendix D

User Manual for Financial Statement Analysis Package (FSAP)

INTRODUCTION TO FSAP

FSAP is a user-friendly, adaptable Excel spreadsheet template. FSAP enables the user to manually input financial statement data for a firm and then perform financial statement analysis, forecasting, and valuation. The objective of FSAP is simply to provide users with a usable template for these computations. The objective of FSAP is *not* to provide the critical analytical judgments that are required of the user. The user of FSAP must provide the careful analysis of whether a firm's financial statement ratios are improving or deteriorating, and must think carefully through what the most appropriate forecast and valuation assumptions should be. FSAP simply provides financial statement analysis and valuation calculators for the careful analyst to use.

Selected problems and cases in chapters throughout the text may be worked using FSAP. For a list of these problems and cases, see the text web site (www.thomsonedu.com/accounting/stickney). The text highlights these FSAP-enabled problems and cases with an FSAP icon in the margin beside the problem. Specific cells within each spreadsheet within FSAP contain red triangular tags that link to comments with instructions and suggestions that provide a great deal of help for users. To get started using FSAP, first download the FSAP template from the text's web site, read this User Guide for an overview of the program and its five spreadsheets, and review the completed output from FSAP for PepsiCo in Appendix C. As you use and become familiar with FSAP, refer back to this User Guide and the output in Appendix C and review the information in the red comment tags within FSAP for help as needed.

FSAP STRUCTURE

FSAP is an Excel-based financial statement analysis program that contains five spreadsheets:

1. Data Spreadsheet: Contains balance sheet, income statement, statement of cash flows, and other data for a particular company.
2. Analysis Spreadsheet: Computes various financial statement ratios, common-size financial statements, and percentage change financial statements using the financial statement data in the Data Spreadsheet.
3. Forecasts Spreadsheet: Permits the user to program the spreadsheet to prepare forecasted income statements, balance sheets, and statements of cash flows.
4. Forecast Development Spreadsheet: Provides the user with space to develop other supporting computations for the Forecasts Spreadsheet, such as detailed forecasts of sales. Also provides the user with a template for forecasting capital expenditures; property, plant, and equipment; depreciation expense; and accumulated depreciation.
5. Valuation Spreadsheet: After the user inputs valuation parameters, the Valuation Spreadsheet computes common equity share value using the five different valuation models demonstrated in the text, including two free-cash-flows valuation models, two residual income valuation models, and the dividends valuation model. The Valuation Spreadsheet also compares the share value estimate to market price and analyzes the sensitivity of the share value estimate to different valuation parameter assumptions, varying the discount rate and the long-term growth rate assumptions.

The web site for this book (www.thomsonedu.com/accounting/stickney) contains the FSAP template, which users should download to their computer. Each spreadsheet within

FSAP contains red triangular tags that provide information for inputting items in a particular row of the spreadsheets. These spreadsheets follow the usual procedures for inserting data into cells; adjusting cell, column, and row size; and printing within Excel. Specific comments on each spreadsheet follow.

DATA SPREADSHEET

The Data Spreadsheet is designed to contain six years of financial statement data. However, the user can input fewer years of data as well. It is important that the user input the most recent year of financial statement data in column G, regardless of the number of years of financial statement inputted. A user inputting four years of financial statement data, for example, would use columns D, E, F, and G and columns B and C would remain empty. Several financial ratios use average amounts of assets, liabilities, and shareholders' equity for the year. For this reason, the user should input one more year of balance sheet data than the number of years of data for the income statement and statement of cash flows. Otherwise, ratios using average amounts of assets for the year will be inaccurate for the earliest year of data.

Although the user can download financial statement data from other sources and paste them into the Data Spreadsheet, we find it more efficient to input the financial statement data manually. Online sources of financial statement data often use different titles and sequencing of accounts from those in FSAP. The user must conform data from other sources to the FSAP template because the spreadsheets within FSAP use the Data Spreadsheet as their base. Thus, the user should not change, add, or delete rows or columns within FSAP because doing so may compromise computations throughout FSAP that rely on the Data Spreadsheet. The user can, however, change account titles in the Data Spreadsheet as necessary to match the account titles of the particular firm. The Data Spreadsheet contains a number of generic account titles that can be changed to fit the particular firm (such as Other Current Assets (1) and (2), Other Noncurrent Assets (1) and (2), Other Current Liabilities (1) and (2), and Other Noncurrent Liabilities (1) and (2)).

Particular attention should be paid to inputting income statement data items in rows 57 to 62 and rows 66 to 69. The red triangular tags describe the amounts that should appear on each line. When inputting data in these rows, the user must assess whether the income items are usual and recurring or unusual and nonrecurring for a particular firm. As Chapter 6 discusses more fully, distinguishing between these two categories of income items is important for both assessing the past operating performance of a firm and forecasting its likely future performance. The Analysis Spreadsheet computes certain financial ratios both including and excluding unusual and nonrecurring items.

Amounts entered in row 73 (discontinued operations), row 74 (extraordinary gains and losses), and row 75 (changes in accounting principles) should be consistent with the reporting of these three items in the firm's income statement. These categories should not be used for unusual or nonrecurring items reported by a firm in the continuing operations section of the income statement. The user should input the latter items in rows 61 and 62 for operating items and rows 67 and 69 for non-operating items.

FSAP automatically computes the amounts of various subtotals and totals within the Data Spreadsheet. These items are shaded in gray in the Data Spreadsheet and serve in checking the mathematical accuracy of inputted amounts. FSAP checks to ensure that total assets equal total liabilities and shareholders' equity; that total revenues and gains minus total expenses and losses equal reported net income; and that cash flows from operating, investing, and financing activities equal the change in cash on the balance sheet. These financial data checks appear in rows 132 to 134 of the Data Spreadsheet. Any material nonzero amounts (that are not due to rounding) in these rows require the user to recheck amounts inputted to identify and correct the error.

In addition to basic financial statement data, the Data Spreadsheet requires the inputting of other data in rows 122 to 129. Particular care should be exercised in inputting amounts in row 124, After-tax Effects on Nonrecurring and Unusual Items on Net Income. Recall that the user inputs the *pretax* effects of unusual and nonrecurring income items in rows 61, 62, 67, and 69. Row 124 requires the user to determine or estimate the tax effect of items in these four rows and enter their *after-tax* amounts in this row. This is an important step because it affects the computation of financial ratios in the Analysis Spreadsheet that distinguish between reported amounts and amounts that exclude the effect of nonrecurring items.

ANALYSIS SPREADSHEET

The Analysis Spreadsheet begins by repeating the Data Checks section of the Data Spreadsheet to remind the user that this section should contain all zeros. If not, the user should return to the Data Spreadsheet and correct any errors before using the financial ratios and other analyses in the Analysis Spreadsheet.

The Analysis Spreadsheet relies entirely on data entered into the Data Spreadsheet and does not require any inputs from the user. The Analysis Spreadsheet shows the amounts for the profitability and risk ratios discussed in Chapters 4 and 5 using both reported amounts and amounts excluding nonrecurring income items. The Analysis Spreadsheet also presents common-size and percentage change income statements and balance sheets, as discussed in Chapter 1. Note that the compound growth rates in column G for rows 145 to 174 are based on six years of income statement data. These compound growth rates are not accurate if the user has inputted less than six years of income statement data. If the latter is the case, the user needs to program the compound annual growth rate formula in column G to reflect the number of years of income statement data inputted. For example, if the user has inputted four years of data, the user should reprogram the compound growth rates to divide the Data Spreadsheet amounts in column G by the amounts in column D instead of those in Column B, and then raise the result to the 1/3 power instead of to the 1/5 power.

FORECASTS SPREADSHEET

FSAP provides the user with a template to build financial statement forecasts extending to Year +6 in the future. The user can program the Forecasts Spreadsheet to accommodate a wide array of forecast assumptions, capturing those assumptions in projected income statements, balance sheets, and statements of cash flows. For the financial statement projections to work properly, FSAP must be programmed for circular references and calculations. The user should make sure that this is the case as follows: Click on the Tools menu, then click on the Options menu, then click on the Calculation tab, and then make sure that a check mark appears in the Iterations box (if the box is blank, click on it, and a check mark should appear).

The first three columns of the Forecasts Spreadsheet contain actual balance sheet and income statement amounts for the company from the Data Spreadsheet and various financial ratios from the Analysis Spreadsheet to aid in developing forecasts. The amounts shown for the statement of cash flows in the Forecasts Spreadsheet contain the implied amounts that result from changes in balance sheet accounts and will not likely equal the reported cash flows amounts from the company data file. The Forecasts Spreadsheet permits the user to build forecasts for each element of the income statement and balance sheet from Year +1 to Year +6. Forecasts for each financial statement item can be developed using three rows of the spreadsheet. In the first row, using Revenues for example, the analyst should program the computations for the Revenues forecast amounts. In FSAP, the amounts in the first row for each account are highlighted and boldfaced. The analyst can use the row immediately below the forecast amounts to input specific forecast assumptions, such as the revenue growth rates used to compute the revenue forecast amounts. The analyst should use the second row below the forecast amounts to input brief descriptions and explanations of the forecast assumptions.

The Forecasts Spreadsheet automatically computes the statements of cash flows implied by the income statement and balance sheet forecasts. The Forecasts Spreadsheet also computes whether the statement of cash flows reconciles with the change in cash on the balance sheet as a quick check of whether the statements agree with one another.

The Forecasts and Valuation Spreadsheets require an assumption about the long-run growth rate in financial statement amounts. The Forecasts Spreadsheet allows the user to input the long-run growth rate assumption for Year +6 and beyond in cell J20. To compute financial statement forecasts for Year +6, the analyst should *only* enter the long-run growth rate assumption in cell J20. The Forecast Spreadsheet automatically applies that growth rate to each account in the financial statements to compute constant growth rate financial statements for Year +6. Assuming the user has forecasted income statement and balance sheet amounts for Year +1 to Year +5, and that the user has entered a long-run growth rate for Year +6 and beyond in cell J20, then the Valuation Spreadsheet computes valuation estimates using the forecast amounts through Year +6 and assuming that the firm will grow at this long-term growth rate. For the forecasts and valuation estimates to be consistent, the analyst must be sure to input the same rate of long-term growth in cell J20 in the Forecasts Spreadsheet and in cell E27 in the Valuation Spreadsheet.

The Forecasts Spreadsheet requires the user to plug a flexible financial account to balance the balance sheet. The default plug account on the balance sheet in FSAP is dividends, but the user can easily change the plug account to an account such as cash, notes payable, or any other flexible financial account on the balance sheet. The user should initially forecast the amounts in the row for the balance sheet account that will be plugged. After programming all of the income statement and balance sheet accounts (including the account to be plugged), the user should scroll to rows 233 and 235 of the Forecasts Spreadsheet. These rows indicate the initial amount of the plug needed to balance the balance sheet. Row 237 asks the user to name the account to be plugged. The computations below row 237 assume that dividends will be the default plug and allow the analyst to compute the ordinary amount of dividends (for both common and preferred stock) and then adjust that amount by the amount of the plug needed to balance the balance sheet (initially, this amount will equal the amount in row 235). FSAP then subtracts the amount of the implied dividends, including the plug amount, from retained earnings. After the plug, the balance sheet check figures in row 233 should then be zero.

The Forecasts Spreadsheet plug account can be changed from dividends (the default plug) to any other account on the balance sheet. To change the plug account from dividends to cash, for example, the user should first program the expected amounts of cash balances (before the effects of the plug) in row 124, and forecast all of the other balance sheet and income statement amounts. Then the analyst should program the common and preferred dividend amounts in rows 239 and 242 to equal the normal dividend forecasts. The analyst should also input the implied dividend amounts in row 245 to be zero. In row 235, the user should program the computation for the necessary plug to cash by subtracting from total liabilities and shareholders' equity (row 230) the amounts for asset account other than cash. To be specific, the amount in cell E235 should be set as follows: (= E230 − E127 − E130 − E133 − E136 − E139 − E145 − E148 − E151 − E154 − E157 − E160 − E163). The user should then program the forecast for cash on cell E124 to equal the plug amount in cell E235. After doing so for each of the forecast years, the amounts in the check figures row 233 should then be zero, indicating that the balance sheet is in balance.

FORECAST DEVELOPMENT SPREADSHEET

The FSAP user does not need to use the Forecast Development Spreadsheet. It is an optional spreadsheet that provides the user with space to develop other supporting computations for the Forecasts Spreadsheet, such as detailed forecasts of sales. The Forecast Development Spreadsheet provides the user with a template for forecasting capital expenditures; property, plant, and equipment; depreciation expense; and accumulated depreciation.

VALUATION SPREADSHEET

FSAP provides valuation estimates using the forecasts developed in the Forecast Spreadsheet and the following five valuation models:

- Dividends
- Free Cash Flows for Common Equity Shareholders
- Free Cash Flows for All Debt and Equity Shareholders
- Residual Income
- Residual Income—The Market-to-Book Value Approach

In order for the Valuation Spreadsheet to compute the value of a firm using these valuation models, the user must input the appropriate valuation parameters, such as the parameters needed to compute the equity cost of capital using the CAPM, the inputs necessary to compute the weighted average cost of capital, the number of shares outstanding, the long-run expected growth rate, and the current share price. The analyst must input these assumptions in the valuation parameter cells that are highlighted in bold blue font at the top of the Valuation Spreadsheet. The Valuation Spreadsheet automatically provides the analyst with a comparison of the value estimate with current share price. The Valuation Spreadsheet also automatically provides sensitivity analysis for the free-cash-flows-based valuation models and the residual income–based models by varying the assumptions for the equity cost of capital and the long-run growth rate across wide ranges.

Index

D

E

F

G

H

I

J

K

L

P

Q

R

SUMMARY OF KEY FINANCIAL STATEMENT RATIOS

(Indicates Page in Text Where Ratio is Initially Discussed)

PROFITABILITY RATIOS

Profit Margin for ROA (Page 205) $= \dfrac{\text{[Net Income + (1 – Tax Rate)(Interest Expense) + Minority Interest in Earnings]}}{\text{Sales}}$

Total Assets Turnover (Page 205) $= \dfrac{\text{Sales}}{\text{Average Total Assets}}$

Return on Assets (ROA) (Page 200) $= \dfrac{\text{[Net Income + (1 – Tax Rate)(Interest Expense) + Minority Interest in Earnings]}}{\text{Average Total Assets}}$

Profit Margin for ROCE (Page 233) $= \dfrac{\text{(Net Income – Preferred Dividends)}}{\text{Sales}}$

Capital Structure Leverage Ratio (Page 233) $= \dfrac{\text{Average Total Assets}}{\text{Average Common Shareholders' Equity}}$

Return on Common Equity (ROCE) (Page 230) $= \dfrac{\text{(Net Income – Preferred Dividends)}}{\text{Average Common Shareholders' Equity}}$

Cost of Goods Sold Percentage (Page 217) $= \dfrac{\text{Cost of Goods Sold}}{\text{Sales}}$

Selling and Administrative Expense Percentage (Page 217) $= \dfrac{\text{Selling and Administrative Expense}}{\text{Sales}}$

Income Tax Expense Percentage (on operating income) (Page 220) $= \dfrac{\text{[Income Tax Expense + (Tax Rate)(Interest Expense)]}}{\text{Sales}}$

Accounts Receivable Turnover (Page 222) $= \dfrac{\text{Sales}}{\text{Average Accounts Receivable}}$

Inventory Turnover (Page 223) $= \dfrac{\text{Cost of Goods Sold}}{\text{Average Inventories}}$

Fixed Asset Turnover (Page 224) $= \dfrac{\text{Sales}}{\text{Average Fixed Assets}}$